MINITAB INC ®
Making Data Analysis Easier

A student version of MINITAB is also available
This CD-ROM contains the student version of
Release 12 (for Windows® 95 or 98), and the
necessary documentation and data files.

Please use ISBN 0-13-026082-7 to order this special package.

Integration Is the Key!

■ Use of Microsoft Excel and MINITAB

We believe that the use of computer software—be it a spreadsheet application such as Microsoft Excel or a statistical package such as MINITAB—is an integral part of learning statistics. Rather than focusing on computations, we place the emphasis on analyzing data and interpreting the output. This means that the text includes a vast amount of computer output from Microsoft Excel and MINITAB—all fully integrated into the fabric of the text and the students' learning process.

■ Detailed Appendices

Included at the end of each chapter, these comprehensive appendices explain how to use MINITAB and Microsoft Excel—providing guidance to the student every step of the way. In addition, an appendix is provided after Chapter 1 that explains the basics of the Windows operating environment.

■ PHStat and Data Files

As noted on the facing page, students receive a free CD-ROM with every Levine, Ramsey, and Smidt text purchased from Prentice Hall. This CD-ROM comes complete with PHStat and the text's data files—providing students with another handy resource for analysis and mastery of the text material.

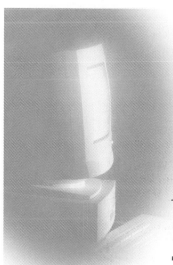

APPLIED STATISTICS
for Engineers and Scientists

Using Microsoft Excel® and MINITAB®

David M. Levine
Baruch College (CUNY)

Patricia P. Ramsey
Fordham University

Robert K. Smidt
California Polytechnic State University, San Luis Obispo

PRENTICE HALL, Upper Saddle River, New Jersey 07458

Library of Congress Cataloging-in-Publication Data

Levine, David M.,
    Applied statistics for engineers and scientists: using Microsoft Excel and MINITAB /
  David M. Levine, Patricia P. Ramsey, Robert K. Smidt.
      p. cm.
    ISBN 0-13-488801-4
    1. Engineering—Statistical methods—Data processing. 2. Microsoft Excel (Computer
file) 3. MINITAB. 4. Electronic spreadsheets. I. Ramsey, Patricia P. II. Smidt, Robert K.
III. Title.
TA340.L49 2001
519.5′024′62—dc21   00-039992

Acquisitions Editor: *Kathleen Boothby Sestak*
Assistant Vice President of Production and Manufacturing: *David W. Riccardi*
Executive Managing Editor: *Kathleen Schiaparelli*
Senior Managing Editor: *Linda Mihatov Behrens*
Production Editor: *Bob Walters*
Manufacturing Buyer: *Alan Fischer*
Manufacturing Manager: *Trudy Pisciotti*
Marketing Manager: *Angela Battle*
Marketing Assistant: *Vince Jansen*
Director of Marketing: *John Tweeddale*
Associate Editor, Mathematics/Statistics Media: *Audra J. Walsh*
Editorial Assistant/Supplements Editor: *Joanne Wendelken*
Art Director: *Maureen Eide*
Assistant to the Art Director: *John Christiana*
Interior Design: *Jayne Conte*
Art Editor: *Grace Hazeldine*
Art Manager: *Gus Vibal*
Director of Creative Services: *Paul Belfanti*
Cover Design: *Joseph Sengotta*
Cover Photo: *George B. Diebold/The Stock Market*
Compositor: *Interactive Composition Corporation*
Art Studio: *Network Graphics, Inc.*

© 2001 by Prentice-Hall, Inc.
Upper Saddle River, New Jersey 07458

Printed in the United States of America
10 9 8 7 6 5 4 3 2

ISBN 0-13-488801-4

Prentice-Hall International (UK) Limited, *London*
Prentice-Hall of Australia Pty. Limited, *Sydney*
Prentice-Hall of Canada Inc., *Toronto*
Prentice-Hall Hispanoamericana, S.A., *Mexico*
Prentice-Hall of India Private Limited, *New Delhi*
Prentice-Hall of Japan, Inc., *Tokyo*
Pearson Education Asia Pte. Ltd.
Editora Prentice-Hall to Brasil, Ltda., *Rio de Janeiro*

This Book is Dedicated to Our Spouses
Marilyn, Philip, and Lygia
and to Our Children
Sharyn, Catherine, Robert, Jesse, and Luke

Contents

Appendices

Preface

Introduction

The primary questions that must be answered when a new statistics text for engineers and scientists is written relate to the issue of the contribution of the textbook to the pedagogy of teaching statistics to this audience of students and to how the text will differ from the many texts that are already available. These questions can be answered for the proposed text only in the context of recommendations that have been made as the result of a 1984 conference on the statistical education of engineers [Hogg(1985)] and a 1993 Quality Engineering Workshop [Hogg(1994)]. Among the recommendations made was that engineers need to appreciate the following statistical concepts:

1. omnipresence of variability;
2. the use of simple graphical tools such as run charts, histograms, scatter plots, probability plots, residual plots, and control charts;
3. basic concepts of statistical inference;
4. the importance and essentials of carefully planned design of experiments;
5. the philosophies of Shewhart, Deming, and other practitioners concerning the quality of products and services.

The Hogg(1994) article proposed a core course of topics for engineering students. This proposed text is based on the curriculum model presented in that article.

Educational Philosophy

In our many years of teaching introductory statistics courses to students majoring in a wide variety of disciplines, we have continually searched for ways to improve the teaching of these courses. Over the years, our vision has come to include the following:

1. Students need a frame of reference when learning a subject, especially one that is not their major. This frame of reference for engineering and science students should be applications to the various areas of engineering and the sciences. The discussion of each statistical topic should include references to at least one of these areas of application.
2. Virtually all the students taking introductory statistics courses for engineers and scientists are majoring in areas other than statistics. Introductory courses should, therefore, focus on the underlying principles that are important for nonstatistics majors.
3. The use of spreadsheet and/or statistical software should be integrated into all aspects of the introductory statistics course. The reality that exists in the workplace is that spreadsheet software (and sometimes statistical software)

is typically available on one's computer desktop. Our teaching approach needs to recognize this reality and make our courses more consistent with the workplace environment.

4. Textbooks that use software must provide detailed instructions that maximizes the student's ability to use the software with a minimum risk of failure.

5. Instruction for each topic should focus on (1) the application of the topic to an area of engineering or the sciences, (2) the interpretation of results, (3) the presentation of assumptions, (4) the evaluation of the assumptions, and (5) the discussion of what should be done if the assumptions are violated. These points are particularly important in regression, forecasting and in hypothesis testing. Although the illustration of some computations is inevitable, the focus on computations should be minimized.

6. Both classroom examples and homework exercises should relate to actual or realistic data as much as possible. Introductory courses should avoid an over-concentration on one topic area and instead provide breadth of coverage of a variety of statistical topics. This will help students avoid the "I can't see the forest for the trees" syndrome.

The main features of this proposed text are summarized in the following sections.

Main Feature: Emphasis on Data Analysis and Interpretation of Computer Output

The personal computer revolution has dramatically changed how information is analyzed in the workplace and how statistics should be taught in the classroom. In this text, we take the position that the use of computer software in the form of a spreadsheet application such as Microsoft Excel or a statistical package such as MINITAB is an integral part of learning statistics. We emphasize analyzing data, interpreting the output from Microsoft Excel and MINITAB, and explaining how to use this software while reducing the emphasis on computation. In order to carry out our approach, we have integrated this output into the fabric of the text. For example, our coverage of tables and charts in Chapter 2 focuses on the interpretation of various charts, not on their construction by hand. In Chapter 9 on hypothesis testing, we have made sure to include extensive computer output so that the p-value approach can be used. The presentation of simple linear regression in Chapter 12, assumes that software such as Microsoft Excel or MINITAB will be used, and thus our focus is on the interpretation of the output, not on hand calculations (which have been placed in a separate section of the chapter).

Main Feature: Problems, Case Studies, and Team Projects

"Learning" results from "doing." This text provides the student with the opportunity to select from many problems (most with multiple parts) presented at the ends of sections as well as at the ends of chapters. Most of these problems use real data and apply to realistic situations in various fields of engineering and the sciences. Students can aid their comprehension by engaging in multiple hands-on exercises as detailed below.

- The end-of-section problems give the students the opportunity to reinforce what they have just learned.
- The chapter review problems included at the end of each chapter are based on the concepts and methods learned throughout the chapter.

- Answers to Selected Odd-Numbered Problems appear at the end of the text.
- Detailed Case Studies are included at the end of several chapters.
- The *Whitney Gourmet Cat Food Company* case study is included at the end of most chapters, as an integrating theme.

Main Feature: Appendices on Using Microsoft Excel and MINITAB

Rather than rely on the supplementary manuals, that accompany statistical software packages, it is a much better pedagogical approach to provide an explanation of how the software is used in the text while employing the in-chapter examples. Detailed appendices are included at the end of all chapters that explain how to use MINITAB, the most popular statistical software for introductory business statistics, and Microsoft Excel, the dominant spreadsheet package. In addition, an appendix is provided after Chapter 1 that explains the basics of the Windows operating environment.

Main Feature: Statistics Add-In for Microsoft Excel — PHStat

The CD-ROM that accompanies the text includes the PHStat Statistics add-in for Microsoft Excel that facilitates its use in introductory statistics courses. Although Microsoft Excel is a spreadsheet package, it contains features that enable it to perform statistical analysis for many of the topics in this text. In some cases, however, such analyses are cumbersome in the off-the-shelf version of Microsoft Excel. The PHStat statistics add-in provides a custom menu of choices that leads to dialog boxes which enable users to make entries and selections to perform specific analyses. PHStat minimizes the work associated with setting up statistical solutions in Microsoft Excel by automating the creation of spreadsheets and charts. PHStat, along with Microsoft Excel's Data Analysis tool, now allows users to perform statistical analyses on virtually all topics covered in this text.

Main Feature: Pedagogical Aids

Numerous features designed to create a more stimulating learning environment throughout the text include:

- conversational writing style;
- a *Using Statistics* example that illustrates the application of at least one of the statistical methods covered in each chapter in engineering and the sciences;
- real data for many of the examples and problems;
- exhibit boxes that highlight important concepts;
- comment boxes that focus on assumptions of statistical methods;
- problem sets with varied levels of difficulty and complexity;
- key terms;
- chapter opening quotes from a philosopher, historical figure, well-known statistician or from literature;
- chapter ending problems that begin with *Checking Your Understanding* problems that require students to demonstrate their understanding of concepts;
- explanation and illustration of statistical tables;
- side notes in which additional material appears adjacent to where it is referenced.

Main Feature: Statistical Topics Covered

The text focuses on such topics as tables and charts (Chapter 2), descriptive statistics (Chapter 3), control charts (Chapters 6 and 7), experimental design (Chapters 10 and 11), regression (Chapters 12 and 13), and statistical inference (Chapters 8 and 9). This emphasis is consistent with the recommendations presented by Hogg(1994).

Perhaps the important statistical method used by engineers in industry is experimental design. Simply stated, engineers need to know how to conduct experiments where multiple factors are varied. Thus, in addition to coverage of one- and two-factor designs, this text discusses the concept of interaction in depth. Further, it provides coverage of factorial and fractional-factorial designs, using both a graphical approach and a confirmatory hypothesis-testing approach. In addition, the contributions of the Japanese engineer Genichi Taguchi are introduced.

By providing this comprehensive coverage of quality and experimental design, the text provides an orientation that allows the presentation of statistical tools in an organizational context, instead of in isolation. The goal is for students to learn not just how to use the tools but why and how statistical methods are useful in a wide variety of industrial settings. A portion of Chapter 1 is devoted to quality management, including both key themes and the contribution of individuals such as W. Edwards Deming, Joseph Juran, and Walter Shewhart.

Main Feature: Full Supplement Package

The supplement package that accompanies this text includes:

- **Instructor's Solution Manual**—written by M&N Toscano. This solutions manual is enriched with extra detail in the problem solutions and many Excel solutions. ISBN 0-13-027423-2.
- **Student Solutions Manual**—written by M&N Toscano. To order this supplement for your students, use ISBN 0-13-028681-8.

About the *World Wide Web*

The text has a home page on the World Wide Web with an address of **http://www.prenhall.com/levine**. There is a separate home page on the World Wide Web for the PHStat add-in, **http://www.prenhall.com/phstat** that provides user assistance and periodic updates.

Acknowledgements

We are extremely grateful to the many organizations and companies that allowed us to use their data in developing problems and examples throughout the text. We would like to thank American Cyanamid Company, American Society for Testing and Materials, Biometrika, Environmental Progress, Graphics Press, Journal of Energy Resources Technology, Journal of Engineering for Industry, Journal of Structural Engineering, Journal of the Minerals, Metals and Materials Society, Journal of Water Resources Planning and Management, New England Journal of Medicine, Newsday, Noise Control Engineering Journal, Philosophical Transactions of the Royal Society,

Quality and Reliability Engineering International, Quality Engineering, Quality Progress, Technometrics, The American Statistician, and The Free Press.

We would also like to express our gratitude to David Cresap, University of Portland, Dr. C. H. Aikens, The University of Tennesee—Knoxville, and Dr. Robert L. Armacost, University of Central Florida for their constructive comments during the writing of this text.

We offer special thanks to Kathy Boothby Sestak, Joanne Wendelken, Ann Heath, and Gina Huck of the editing team at Prentice Hall, and to Bob Walters our Production Editor. Thanks also to Brian Baker for his copyediting and M&N Toscano for their accuracy checking.

References

1. Hogg, R. V.; "A Core in Statistics for Engineering Students," *The American Statistician,* 48 (1994), 285–287
2. Hogg, R. V. et al.; "Statistical Education for Engineers: An Initial Task Force Report," *The American Statistician,* 39 (1985), 168–175

Concluding Remarks

We have gone to great lengths to make this text both pedagogically sound and error-free. If you have any suggestions, note material requiring clarification, or find potential errors, please contact us at **David_Levine@BARUCH.CUNY.EDU** or **DavidMLevine@MSN.COM**

David M. Levine
Patricia P. Ramsey
Robert K. Smidt

Introduction to Statistics and Quality Improvement

"Statistical thinking will one day be as necessary for efficient citizenship as the ability to read and write."

H.G. WELLS

 ## 1.1 WHAT IS STATISTICS?

The term *statistics* can have many meanings. It is sometimes used as a synonym for numerical information. Such numerical values are often referred to as data or statistics. Examples of such statistics are grades on student exams, measures on a Richter scale, the diameter of a ball bearing, the amount of reactant in a chemical experiment, and the temperature increases in a supercomputer. When used in this context, the term statistics is a plural noun. The term statistics can also be used as a singular noun and, as such, represents a body of knowledge that enables one to do the following:

1. draw useful conclusions from numerical information;
2. make decisions in a rational and objective way;
3. predict and control events;
4. strive for excellence and increase quality and productivity.

The field of statistics is sometimes categorized into two areas. The first area is referred to as *descriptive statistics*.

Descriptive statistics consists of methods dealing with the collection, tabulation, summarization, and presentation of data.

These methods describe the various aspects of a data set. Descriptive statistical methods have their beginnings in the inventories kept by early civilizations, such as the Babylonians, Egyptians, and Chinese. For example, the Old Testament of the Bible refers to the numbering or counting of the people of Israel and to the casting of lots for selection by chance, and the Romans kept careful counts of people, possessions, and wealth in the territories they conquered. Similarly, the Domesday Book of the late eleventh century enumerated the lands and wealth of England. The Middle Ages also saw the growth of governments and religious institutions and their recording of births, deaths, and marriages. These early methods were primarily lists and counts kept for purposes of taxation and military conscription.

Although statistical methods developed throughout history in many different cultures, modern statistical concepts are considered to have developed in Europe in the late seventeenth century with the growth of mathematics and probability theory. (See Reference 10.) Theories of probability or chance have their historical roots in games of chance. By the seventeenth century, interest in gambling and the development of mathematical methods combined and resulted in early rules of probability. The development of theories of probability led to the inception of the second major field of statistics, called *inferential statistics,* in the beginning of the twentieth century. Statisticians such as Pearson, Fisher, Neyman, Wald, and Tukey pioneered in the development of the methods of inferential statistics, which are widely applied in so many fields today.

> **Inferential statistics** consists of methods that permit one to reach conclusions and make estimates about populations based upon information from a sample.

Populations and samples are defined as follows:

> A **population** or **universe** consists of all members of a class or category of interest. Its size is usually denoted by "N."
>
> A **sample** is some portion or subset of a population. Its size is usually denoted by "n."

If every member of a population is evaluated, a **census** has been performed, and any summary value of all of the individual measurements is called a **parameter.** If only a subset or a sample of a population has been evaluated, any summary value of such measurements is called a **statistic.** Inferential statistics, therefore, involves using sample statistics to estimate population parameters.

> A **census** is an enumeration or evaluation of every member of a population.
>
> A **parameter** is a summary measure of the individual observations made in a census of an entire population.
>
> A **statistic** is a summary measure of the individual observations made by evaluation of a sample.

1.2 WHY STUDY STATISTICS?

More than a half-century ago, Walter Shewhart, the father of statistical quality control, said that

> "The long range contribution of statistics depends not so much upon getting a lot of highly trained statisticians into industry as it does in creating a statistically minded generation of physicists, chemists, engineers and others who will in any way have a hand in developing and directing the production processes of tomorrow."

Engineers and scientists, as individuals who are continually applying the scientific method to their field of endeavor, are also constantly dealing with numerical information that needs to be analyzed. It is from this perspective that we should consider why engineers and scientists need to know about statistics. Among the reasons for learning statistics are:

1. to know how to present and describe numerical information properly;
2. to know how to draw conclusions about large populations from sample information only;
3. to know how to improve processes and how to engineer quality into a product;
4. to design experiments to learn more about the natural world and to model physical relationships;
5. to know how to obtain reliable forecasts or predictions of real-world responses.

A road map of this text from the perspective of these five reasons for learning statistics is presented in Figure 1.1. From this road map, we observe that the first three chapters include coverage of methods involved in the collection, presentation, and description of information. Chapters 4 and 5 provide thorough coverage of the concepts of probability, probability distributions, and sampling distributions, so that subsequently the reader will learn how to draw conclusions about large populations based only upon information obtained from samples (which are taught in Chapters 8 and 9). Chapters 6 and 7 contain coverage of statistical applications in quality and productivity that are essential for process improvement. Chapters 10 and 11 discuss the fundamental principles of experimental design, which are critical to the proper use of the scientific method. The text concludes with Chapters 12 and 13, which focus

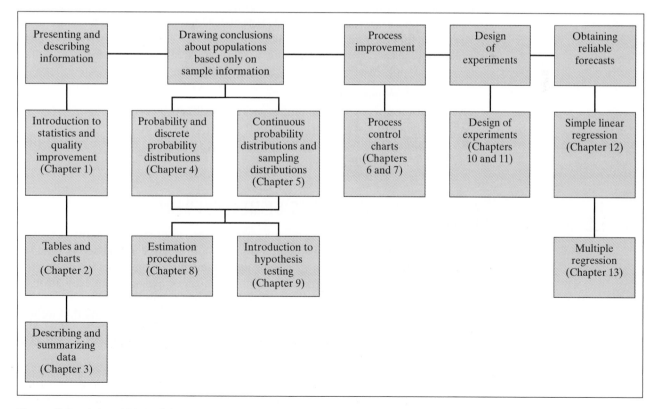

Figure 1.1   A Road Map of the Text

on regression and multiple-regression analysis that provides methods for obtaining forecasts.

1.3 STATISTICAL THINKING: UNDERSTANDING AND MANAGING VARIABILITY

Statistical thinking starts with an awareness and understanding that no two things are exactly alike and that variability is inherent in all things. Statistical thinking is the ability to identify, quantify, reduce, and control the kinds of variability that reduce the quality of our performance, of the objects we make, and of our actions as individuals, groups, and societies. Variability is not inherently undesirable. It is essential to variety and creativity and often enriches our lives. Ours would be a much poorer world if all people were identical and every artist painted exactly the same picture; however, in areas where uniformity, consistency, and dependability are essential or desirable, we must recognize that variability reduces quality and hampers excellence.

To function in the technological world, consistency is essential. Without consistency and predictability, interacting with people and objects would result in chaos. Research has shown that consumers value consistency in products and services and associate dependability and reliability with quality. Recent experience has shown that brands of automobiles perceived to be dependable and reliable have captured an ever-increasing share of the world market. Industry standards calling for uniformity of design and manufacture of various parts and products, such as light bulbs, automobile tires, screw threads, and computer disks, not only make high-volume production and distribution possible but also permit interchangeability of parts and simplify daily life and business.

The philosophy and work of W. Edwards Deming, considered by many to be one of the founding fathers of the global quality movement, are based on the principles that reduction in variation leads to increased quality and that increased quality results in increased productivity. **Statistical thinking** is, therefore, the following:

1. an understanding of variation;
2. an awareness of when and how variability affects quality;
3. an ability to identify variability that can be controlled;
4. a commitment to controlling and reducing variability in a never-ending striving for quality improvement.

1.4 VARIABLES, TYPES OF DATA, AND LEVELS OF MEASUREMENT

Data can be in the form either of categories, counts, or of measurements. A collection of related categorical or numeric information is called a **data set**. A data set can represent the evaluation of numerous objects on a single characteristic, the evaluation of many characteristics of a single object or event, or the evaluation of many characteristics on a large number of objects or events.

In this section, we define and distinguish among the types of data that we will be using throughout this text.

Variables and Constants

A **variable** can be defined as a characteristic that can take different values.

Examples of variables are measures of temperature, height, weight, cost, and gender.

Constants are characteristics that have values that do not change.

Examples of constants are pi (π), the ratio of the circumference of a circle to its diameter ($\pi = 3.14159...$), and e, the base of the natural (or *Napierian*) logarithms ($e = 2.71828...$).

Types of Variables

Different types of variables produce different types of data. **Categorical variables** yield values that can be placed only into categories or classes. Examples are gender, species, causes of a shutdown of a nuclear plant, type of cancer, and brand of computer owned. **Numerical variables** yield numerical values. One way of categorizing numerical variables is to consider them to be either *discrete* or *continuous*.

Discrete variables are *countable,* in that there is a gap between each possible value. Most often, these variables result from a process of counting and are thus restricted to whole numbers or integer values.

Discrete variables measure countable whole units, such as the number of defective welds in a length of pipe, the number of logic errors in a computer program, or the number of vehicles crossing a bridge in a 24-hour period. Because they are numerical counts of things, discrete variables usually answer the question, how many? Such counts are reported in whole numbers and, as such, represent discrete data.

Continuous variables represent numerical measurements on a *continuous* dimension or scale and can take any numerical value within a continuum or interval.

Examples of continuous variables are length, weight, age, or the diameter of a steel cable. For example, length can be measured to the nearest meter, decimeter, centimeter, millimeter, or even fractions of a millimeter. Continuous variables theoretically take any of an infinite number of values between the lower and upper limits of an interval. In practice, the number of values obtained is not infinite since the exactness of such measurements is limited by the precision of the measuring instruments used or conventions such as rounding monetary amounts to the nearest cent, age to the nearest year, or weight to the nearest pound.

Levels of Measurement and Types of Measurement Scales

In addition to considering variables as either categorical or numerical, data can be classified with respect to the degree to which it possesses the four properties of identity, order, distance, and an absolute zero point. These properties result in four widely recognized types of scales of measurement. They can be ordered in terms of power from weakest to strongest, so they are often referred to as **levels of measurement.** These levels of measurement are represented by the *nominal, ordinal, interval,* and *ratio* scales.

Nominal Scales

> **Nominal scales** identify, name, classify, or categorize objects or events with no natural ordering of categories.

In a nominal scale objects or events are evaluated on a characteristic and classified into a category. Variables such as gender, type of computer, blood type, and species are examples of categorical variables. Each of these identifies a category into which individuals fall, so they are nominal variables. Additional examples of nominal variables are type of transmission in an automobile (automatic or manual), type of fuel used for heating a home, or type of electric wire used. The categories used when evaluating an individual or object on a nominal scale should be *mutually exclusive* and *collectively exhaustive*.

> **Mutually exclusive** means that each item classified falls into one and only one category.
>
> **Collectively exhaustive** means that there is a complete set of categories available, so that all items can be classified.

Nominally scaled variables are the weakest kind of data because they identify only the category into which the item being classified belongs. Because there is no logical or inherent order to the categories, the only analyses possible with this type of scale involves counts or proportions of items that fall into the various categories.

Ordinal Scales

> **Ordinal scales,** like nominal scales, identify, name, classify, or categorize objects or events, but they have the additional property of a logical or natural order to the categories or values.

Examples of ordinal scales are tire rating, college class (freshman, sophomore, junior, and senior), or automobile size (subcompact, compact, intermediate, full-size). Any time that individuals or objects are *ranked* on some dimension, an ordinal scale of measurement is being used. Although ordinal scales are more powerful than nominal scales, because they have the properties of both identity and order, they are still a fairly weak form of measurement, because the distances between ordered categories do not represent equal intervals. Ordinal scales permit comparison of scores or categories in terms of smaller and larger, higher and lower, or from best to worst. They do not permit comparisons in terms of how much larger, lower, or better.

Interval Scales

> **Interval scales** identify, have ordered values, and have the additional property of equal distances or intervals between scale values.

Interval scales identify, name, classify, or categorize as do nominal and ordinal scales and have ordered categories or values like ordinal scales. They have an important additional property: *equal distances* or *intervals* between scores or scale values. For example, temperature measured on either the Celsius or Fahrenheit scales represents interval-scaled data. A one-degree difference on the Celsius scale represents the same quantity any place on the scale. A ten-degree increase in temperature from 20°C to 30°C represents the same temperature change as a ten-degree increase from 80°C to 90°C. Because intervals between scores are equal, scores can be compared based on the size of the differences between them. They can be added to and subtracted from one another and, in this manner, new variables can be created.

It is interesting to note that scores on classroom exams and standardized achievement tests such as the SAT, GRE, and GMAT are, at best, interval-scale measurements. A score of zero on an exam does not mean that a student knows nothing or has a complete absence of knowledge. It is, therefore, not reasonable to claim that one student is twice as knowledgeable as another is because he or she happened to earn an exam grade twice as high as the other does.

Ratio Scales

Ratio scales identify, order, represent equal distances between score values, and have an absolute zero point.

Ratio scales have all of the properties of nominal, ordinal, and interval scales, and they have an additional property: an absolute zero point. Sometimes this is referred to as a real zero point. This means that a scale value or score of zero represents a complete absence of the characteristic being measured. If temperature is measured on the Kelvin scale, a value of zero indicates a complete absence of temperature and a situation in which it would be impossible to become colder. Anyone who has spent time outdoors in winter in northern latitudes can attest to the fact that if the temperature is 0° as measured by either the Fahrenheit or Celsius scales, it can still become a good deal colder. This is why these scales are considered interval scales; they do not possess a real zero point.

Other examples of ratio scales are time, voltage, speed, electrical resistance, and diameter. Ratio scales have equal intervals between scale values like interval scales, so all the arithmetic operations that can be performed on interval data can be used with ratio data. In addition, the property of absolute zero permits one to make ratios of values. For example, a rod that is 3 feet long can be compared to a rod that is 6 feet long by making a ratio of their measurements. We could say that the 3-foot rod is half ($3/6 = 1/2$) the length of the 6-foot rod, or that the 6-foot rod is twice ($6/3 = 2$) the length of the 3-foot rod. This ability to make ratios of scores to compare measurements permits even more sophisticated forms of analysis. Ratio data are, therefore, considered to be the highest form of data available.

It is possible to transform data from a higher-level scale of measurement into a measure on a lower-level scale. For example, we could take a ratio scale such as length and collapse it into an ordinal scale by transforming the numerical measurements of length into ranks from longest to shortest, or we could collapse it further by classifying the individual lengths as short, medium, or long. Transformations in the opposite direction from a weak level of measurement to a higher level of measurement are not possible.

Attribute Measures and Variables Measures

Engineers and managers working in the area of quality improvement (discussed in Chapters 6 and 7) often use the terminology *attribute measures* and *variables measures* to represent two classes of measurement. **Attribute measures** either are nominal variables based on counts or involve proportions calculated from discrete data. Examples of attribute measures are the number of defective or nonconforming items, the proportion of defective items, or the number or proportion of times an event occurs. **Variables measures** are continuous variables such as time measured in minutes, height or length measured in inches or centimeters, weight measured in pounds or kilograms, temperature measured in degrees Celsius or Fahrenheit, tensile strength measured in pounds per square inch, or any other variables measured on an interval or ratio scale.

PROBLEMS

1.1 For each of the following, indicate whether it is a discrete or a continuous variable.
- **(a)** The number of minutes it takes to read a page in this text.
- **(b)** The number of chapters in the text.
- **(c)** The weight of the text.
- **(d)** The number of problems in the text.
- **(e)** The number of times the letter *e* appears on a page.
- **(f)** The length of a page in inches.

1.2 From weakest to strongest, what is the correct order of ordinal, ratio, nominal, and interval levels of measurement? For each of these levels of measurement, provide two examples of variables that can be used to describe a student.

1.3 Suppose that the following information is obtained from Cathy Theo on her application for a home mortgage loan at the North Jersey State Bank. For each of the following responses, indicate whether it is a continuous variable and which type of measurement scale it represents.
- **(a)** Place of Residence: Morristown, New Jersey
- **(b)** Type of Residence: Single family home
- **(c)** Date of Birth: August 13, 1966
- **(d)** Projected Monthly Payments: $2,479
- **(e)** Occupation: Director of Food Chemistry
- **(f)** Employer: Venus Candy Company
- **(g)** Number of Years at Job: 10
- **(h)** Annual Income: $140,000
- **(i)** Amount of Mortgage Requested: $220,000
- **(j)** Term of Mortgage: 15 years

1.4 A team of ornithologists is doing field research by using a mist net to capture migrating birds. They collect the following information:
- **(a)** Species
- **(b)** Weight
- **(c)** Wing span
- **(d)** Condition, either poor, fair, good, or excellent
- **(e)** Band ID number
- **(f)** Approximate age

Indicate whether each of these is an attribute measure or a variables measure.

1.5 The management of a company manufacturing gourmet cat food would like to improve its process of packaging its food in plastic containers. Among the measures to be collected are the following:
- **(a)** weight of the filled container;
- **(b)** weight of the unfilled container;
- **(c)** whether an individual filled container conforms to specifications;
- **(d)** number of containers produced without dents;
- **(e)** time needed to fill a batch of containers;
- **(f)** number of conforming containers filled per day.

Indicate whether each of these is an attribute measure or a variables measure.

1.5 OPERATIONAL DEFINITIONS

Operational definitions have long been one of the essential elements of *the scientific method*. The Scientific Method is the basis for all scientific exploration and discovery. Once a problem is identified, hypotheses are empirically tested by experimentation or observation. Such experimentation and observation require careful collection and analysis of data that will refute or support the hypotheses. It is only recently that operational definitions have been recognized as essential to communication in organizations, whether the organization is manufacturing a product or providing a service.

> The purpose of an **operational definition** is to convey meaning that will be precisely the same to different individuals and will remain stable over time.

An operational definition defines a characteristic of an object or event, not just by descriptive adjectives such as red, hard, safe, defective, or sufficiently large, but by the active process or set of operations by which the characteristic is evaluated. Operational definitions are characterized by the following:

1. specific criterion or criteria to be applied to an object or event;
2. a specific test or measurement of the object or event—the particular operations or procedures used to test or measure must be specified and agreed to;
3. a decision as to whether the object or event has met the criterion or criteria—all objects or events that meet the criteria fit the definition, all others do not.

We can illustrate the concept of an operational definition as follows. Suppose that the manager of an office with 20 workers was continually mediating disputes between workers about the level of air conditioning in the office. The workers were constantly adjusting the thermostat up and down and arguing about the comfort level of the work area. The group finally agreed to stop fooling around with the thermostat and to adjust it downward only if it was "too hot." Each of the 21 people involved knew what "too hot" meant. For each of them, "too hot" was when he or she was personally uncomfortable. Individuals differ in their perception of and sensitivity to heat, however, so there were 21 separate definitions of "too hot." This group agreement to "adjust the thermostat only when it was too hot" did nothing to solve the problem because they lacked an operational definition. Another meeting was called and the 21 people agreed that it was too hot when the thermometer on the wall on the sunny side of the office registered 80°F. They now had an operational definition on which they could base their actions and the decision as to whether they should turn down the thermostat.

Note that the operational definition of "too hot" contained a specific criterion (80°F), a specific test or measurement of the criterion (temperature to be measured by the thermometer on the wall on the sunny side of the office), and a decision as to whether the temperature met the criterion (all readings of 80°F or higher constituted a "too hot" situation). Now they only had to come to agreement as to which wall the sun was shining on. This was an easier problem to solve, because they agreed that it was unnecessary to measure the amount of light falling on wall surfaces on a daily basis and reached a consensus that the sunny side was the left side of the room before noon and the right side after noon. For an operational definition to be useful, individuals or groups not only must be able to understand and agree upon the criteria and terms used in the definition but also must have the means and ability to evaluate objects and events relative to the criteria.

PROBLEMS

1.6 Provide an operational definition for each of the following:
  (a) a good student;
  (b) a good teacher;
  (c) an outstanding employee;
  (d) a round ball.

1.7 Provide an operational definition for each of the following:
  (a) being on time for a meeting;
  (b) fast service;
  (c) soup that is too hot;
  (d) commuting time to school or work.

1.6 SAMPLING

Most research techniques and many statistical process-control techniques involve the use of sampling. A sample is selected, evaluated, and studied in an effort to gain information about the larger population from which the sample was drawn. In Section 1.1, we learned that a sample is defined as a subset or part of a population. Although, by definition, samples will be smaller than the populations from which they are drawn, samples can be very small or very large. A single student can be considered a sample of all students at a given university, while a very large sample consisting of millions of households is selected to respond to a lengthy questionnaire that is part of the decennial census in the United States.

A sample represents a population, and information obtained from a sample is generalized to be true for the entire population from which it was drawn. The validity or accuracy of generalizations from samples to populations depends on how well a sample represents its population. A well-selected sample can provide information comparable to that obtained by a census.

Advantages of Sampling

Studying a sample instead of a population can have several advantages.

1. **Cost**—Samples can be studied at much lower cost. The smaller number of units or individuals involved in a sample requires less time and money to evaluate. Samples can provide affordable, accurate, and useful information in cases where a census would cost more than the value of the information obtained.
2. **Time**—Samples can be evaluated more quickly than populations. If a decision had to wait for the results of a census, a critical advantage might be missed, or the information might be made obsolete by events or changes that took place while the data were being collected and analyzed.
3. **Accuracy**—Any time data are collected, there is a chance for errors to occur. Errors of measurement, incorrect recording of data, transposition of digits, recording of information in the wrong area of a form, and errors in entering data into a computer can all influence the accuracy of results. In general, the larger the data set, the more opportunity there is for errors to occur. A sample can provide a data set that is small enough to monitor carefully and can permit careful training and supervision of data gatherers and handlers.

4. **Feasibility**—In some research situations, the population of interest is not available for study. A substantial portion of the population might not yet exist or might no longer be available for evaluation. In other cases, evaluation of an item requires its destruction. For example, a manufacturer interested in how much pressure could be applied to a part before it cracked could not perform a census without destroying the entire production run.

5. **Scope of Information**—When evaluating a smaller group, it is sometimes possible to gather more extensive information on each unit evaluated.

The validity and, therefore, the usefulness of information obtained from a sample depends on how closely sample values or statistics estimate population values or parameters. If a sample is to accurately represent a population, it must be unbiased. Biased samples will contain systematic error caused by overrepresentation of some types of individuals or units, while other types are underrepresented. Data obtained from severely biased samples can be worse than no data at all, because they can lead to erroneous conclusions.

Types of Samples

Samples are considered to be either probability or nonprobability samples.

Probability Samples

A **probability sample** is one in which the probability or chance of selecting an element from a population for inclusion in the sample is known.

Knowing the probability of an element's being selected is based on the fact that elements are selected by chance, and knowledge of both the size of the population and the method of selection allows one to calculate the probability of selection. There are many types of probability samples. The simplest probability sample and one of the most widely used is the **simple random sample.** A simple random sample is one in which

1. all elements of a population have an equal chance of being selected for inclusion in the sample;
2. all possible samples of a given size have an equal probability of being selected.

Selection of a simple random sample often involves the use of a table of random numbers or random digits, such as the one provided in Appendix A, Table A.1. Tables of random numbers are constructed so that each of the digits from 0 through 9 has an equal probability of appearing in each position. Tables and lists of random numbers can be generated by computer and are tested statistically to insure that the requirements of independence and equal probability are satisfied. A portion of the larger table in Appendix A is reproduced in Table 1.1 on page 12, to illustrate how such tables can be used to select a simple random sample from lists of the population.

Suppose that a company manufacturing an "ice melt" product that was expected to melt snow and ice at temperatures as low as 15 degrees Fahrenheit was interested in testing the product's ability to perform as expected. A recently manufactured batch of the product consisted of 5,000 ten-pound bags. Here, the advantages of sampling should be self-evident. Not only would it be very time consuming to actually test every bag of the product, but also, because the test involves the use of the product in a destructive manner, if all 5,000 bags were tested, there

TABLE 1.1

USING A TABLE OF RANDOM NUMBERS

ROW	00000 12345	00001 67890	11111 12345	Column 11112 67890	22222 12345	22223 67890	33333 12345	33334 67890
01	49280	88924	35779	00283	81163	07275	89863	02348
02	61870	41657	07468	08612	98083	97349	20775	45091
03	43898	65923	25078	86129	78496	97653	01550	08078
04	62993	93912	30454	84598	56095	20664	12872	64647
05	33850	58555	51438	85507	71865	79488	76783	31708
06	97340	03364	88472	04334	63919	36394	11095	92470
07	70543	29776	10087	10072	55980	64688	68239	20461
08	89382	93809	00796	95945	34101	81277	66090	88872
09	37818	72142	67140	50785	22380	16703	53362	44940
10	60430	22834	14130	96593	23298	56203	92671	15925
11	82975	66158	84731	19436	55790	69229	28661	13675
12	39087	71938	40355	54324	08401	26299	49420	59208
13	55700	24586	93247	32596	11865	63397	44251	43189
14	14756	23997	78643	75912	83832	32768	18928	57070
15	32166	53251	70654	92827	63491	04233	33825	69662
16	23236	73751	31888	81718	06546	83246	47651	04877
17	45794	26926	15130	82455	78305	55058	52551	47182
18	09893	20505	14225	68514	46427	56788	96297	78822
19	54382	74598	91499	14523	68479	27686	46162	83554
20	94750	89923	37089	20048	80336	94598	26940	36858
21	70297	34135	53140	33340	42050	82341	44104	82949
22	85157	47954	32979	26575	57600	40881	12250	73742
23	11100	02340	12860	74697	96644	89439	28707	25815
24	36871	50775	30592	57143	17381	68856	25853	35041
25	23913	48357	63308	16090	51690	54607	72407	55538

Source: Partially extracted from The Rand Corporation, *A Million Random Digits with 100,000 Normal Deviates* (Glencoe, Ill.: The Free Press, 1955).

would be no product remaining to sell. Thus, we can begin by defining a labeling scheme for the 5,000 bags so that each will have a unique identification. The identified bags will serve as our sampling frame. Once the frame is assembled, we can assign a unique number to each of the members of the frame. Because we have 5,000 bags, we will need a four-digit number to identify each member of the frame uniquely. We can use numbers starting at 0001 and ending at 5000. We would then enter the random number table at some random starting point. Closing one's eyes and marking a spot on the table with a pencil is one method that can be used to locate our random starting point. Suppose we mark row 6, column 2. Once we have our starting point, we can move in any direction, up or down columns, across rows, or even diagonally. For this example, we will go across rows. Each member of our frame is identified with a four-digit number, so we will need to select four-digit numbers from the table. The first four-digit number starting at row 6, column 2 is 7340. Whenever we reach a number that is outside the range of the numbers we have assigned to our frame, we disregard it and continue on to the next random number in the table. Because 7340 is outside the range of our frame, the highest value of which is 5000, we discard or ignore this number and continue reading across rows until we find a number that is represented in our frame. The next four-digit number, 0336, is in our frame, and bag number 336 is selected for inclusion in our sample. The next number, 4884, is also represented in our frame, so bag number 4884 is the second bag selected. Continuing across the row, we find the next number is outside the range of our frame, so it is disregarded. We continue to row 6, columns 18 to 21 and select bag 3346 for inclusion in the sample. This procedure continues until the number of bags selected is 50, which is the number we had decided is necessary to make up an adequate sample for our purposes.

It is often easier to select numbers by reading down columns in a systematic way. For example, if we randomly select row 16, column 11 as our starting point, we could use the digits in columns 11 to 14 in row 16 and select bag number 3188 for inclusion in the sample. We could then continue down to row 17 and, using the same columns of digits, select bag number 1513. Row 18 provides number 1422. The number provided by row 19 is disregarded because it is outside the scope of the frame. We could continue selecting bags in this manner until 50 have been selected.

Sampling With and Without Replacement

In selecting four-digit numbers from the table, it is possible to obtain a specific number more than once. When this happens, the action we take depends on whether we are sampling with or without replacement. If we are **sampling with replacement,** a member of the population can be represented more than once in a sample. In such cases, any member of the frame whose number occurs twice is selected and is evaluated a second time. If we are **sampling without replacement,** we disregard any numbers that have already been selected for inclusion in the sample.

Sometimes the elements of a frame are prenumbered or have a unique number, such as a serial, invoice, or other identification number assigned for another purpose. As long as such numbers are unique, in that no two elements share the same number and no element has more than one number assigned to it, these numbers can be used as a basis for selection.

Systematic Random Samples

Another type of probability sample that is widely used is a systematic random sample.

> A **systematic random sample** is one in which, starting from an element selected at random, every kth element in the frame is selected for inclusion in the sample.

If the frame contains N elements and the researcher needs a sample of size n, k can be determined by dividing the size of the frame by the desired sample size (that is, $k = N/n$) and rounding to the nearest integer.

Systematic random samples are often easier to select and can be just as representative of a population as a simple random sample. It would be easier to select every 20th bag in a stack of bags than the 9th, 42d, 91st, 214th, and so on. Similarly, it would be easier to instruct a clerk or computer to select every kth unit of output than to use a table of random numbers.

Another way of selecting a systematic random sample is to make k some standard time interval instead of a fixed number of elements. This method is often used when the flow of elements past the sampling and inspection point is rapid; that often occurs in high-volume production processes.

Although a random starting point in the frame is desirable, one is possible only when the frame is such that the researcher can go back to the beginning of the list. Sometimes this is not possible, as when sampling fish passing through a fish ladder on a dam, or when parts reach the end of a line and are ready to be packed and shipped. In such cases, one can start at the beginning of the element flow, provided that the sampling continues long enough to give each element in the frame a chance of being selected.

Systematic random samples can be biased if the elements in the sampling frame are arranged in a pattern characterized by k or if there is a periodicity to the frame or flow of elements past the inspection point. Periodicity in the frame can be a serious problem when k is a time interval instead of a fixed number. For example, if a service organization chose to sample all customers requesting information every seventh day, a biased sample could result, because customers who call on weekends or on Mondays may not be representative of the total population of customers.

Nonprobability Samples

Nonprobability samples are not as scientifically rigorous as probability samples and should be used only when it is impossible to perform a probability sample or when a probability sample would not be cost effective. Among the types of nonprobability samples are convenience samples, judgment samples, and quota samples.

Convenience samples, as their name implies, are based on easy availability for evaluation of members of a population. It is based on the principle of "taking what you can get" quickly and easily. For example, the dean of a school who was interested in student attitudes toward a proposed curriculum change might distribute a short questionnaire to students who happen to be gathered in a lounge area. Such a sample may not be truly representative of all students attending the school, because students who frequent the student lounge may be different from those who do not, but such a sample would be easier to obtain than a random sample of students.

Judgment samples rely on the opinion or judgment of some expert. Members of the population are selected for inclusion in the sample because they are judged to be typical or representative of the population by an individual with some expertise or experience with the population.

When **quota samples** are used, members of the population are selected based on characteristics judged to be important to the study. Individuals are selected so that the proportions falling into each of the categories of the characteristics are equal to the proportions found in the population.

Nonprobability samples can have the advantages of convenience, speed, and lower cost. The disadvantages are lack of accuracy due to bias and limited generalizability of results. Probability samples should be used whenever possible, and nonprobability samples should be used only in situations where one wants rough approximations at low cost or in initial or pilot investigations that will later be followed up by more rigorous research.

PROBLEMS

1.8 Suppose that a soft drink bottling company wanted to take a sample of the 20,000 filled bottles that are stored in inventory at a bottling plant. Each bottle is identified by a five-digit identification number and by a code that indicates which of the 20 types of soft drink is contained in the bottle. For each of the following, indicate the type of sample being employed:

  (a) a sample of every fiftieth bottle at the bottling plant;

  (b) a sample of the first fifty bottles filled on a given day at the bottling plant;

  (c) a random sample of bottles taken from all 20,000 bottles in inventory.

1.9 Given a population with $N = 97$ numbered from 01 to 97, draw a sample of $n = 10$ starting in column 1, row 12 of the table of random numbers (Table A.1) and reading across rows.

  (a) Sample without replacement. List the ten random numbers selected.

  (b) Sample with replacement. List the ten random numbers selected.

  (c) Are there any differences between the results in (a) and (b)? Explain your answer.

1.10 Given a population with $N = 5,000$, numbered from 0001 to 5000, draw a sample of $n = 15$ starting in column 1, row 5 of the table of random numbers (Table A.1) and reading down columns.

  (a) Sample without replacement. List the 15 random numbers selected.

  (b) Sample with replacement. List the 15 random numbers selected.

  (c) Are there any differences between the results in (a) and (b)? Explain your answer.

1.7 STATISTICAL AND SPREADSHEET SOFTWARE

The availability of computer technology has profoundly changed the field of statistics in the last 30 years. Mainframe packages, such as SAS and SPSS, became popular during the 1960s and 1970s. During the 1980s, the field of statistical software experienced a vast technological revolution. In addition to the usual improvements manifested in periodic updates, the availability of personal computers led to the development of many new packages that used a menu-driven interface, and personal-computer versions of existing packages such as SAS, SPSS, and MINITAB quickly became available. The late 1980s and the 1990s represented a continuing period of technological advances. Rapid advances in computer hardware meant that larger amounts of computer memory were available at lower cost. This capacity enabled package developers to include additional, more sophisticated statistical procedures in each subsequent version of their packages. In addition, the advent of desktop productivity tools, such as the Microsoft Excel spreadsheet application, has altered the decision-making processes of many engineers and scientists. Today, an ever-increasing number of engineers and scientists use spreadsheet applications as the means to directly retrieve and analyze data. Because the use of these software packages is now so commonplace throughout the business, academic, and research communities, in this text we will illustrate output from a statistical package, MINITAB, and also from a spreadsheet package, Microsoft Excel. In addition, appendices that follow chapters of this text will contain explanations of how to use MINITAB and Microsoft Excel for the topics that have been discussed in the chapter. Although statistical and spreadsheet software has made even the most sophisticated analyses feasible, problems arise when statistically unsophisticated users who do not understand the assumptions behind procedures or the limitations of results are misled by computer-generated statistical output. For pedagogical reasons, we believe that it is important that the applications of the methods covered in the text be illustrated through the use of worked-out examples.

 ## 1.8 INTRODUCTION TO QUALITY

As economies and markets have become more interdependent, industrial sectors that have scientific and industrial components have had to look beyond their traditional local competitors and realize that they must compete on a global basis. This need applies to individual manufacturing, research, or service businesses as well as to regional and national economies. Quality and productivity and the relationship between them become essential for survival and growth in this environment. Productivity is fundamental to economic survival, and an increasing body of evidence supports the fact that the key to productivity is quality. In the remainder of this chapter, we will explain both the relationship between quality and productivity and how global competitiveness requires new ways of thinking and new approaches to management and to problem solving. We will also show how statistics has played a historical role in quality and is essential to the understanding and practice of quality-improvement philosophies.

> **Quality** is defined by the individual needs, expectations, perceptions, and experience of the customer. An overall definition of quality is fitness for use.

For a product or service to have value, it must be useful in the sense that it fills a customer's need and that it functions as the customer expects it to function. Customers have traditionally been thought of as the end users or purchasers of a product or service. In a quality environment, it is important to broaden this definition of customers to include all persons within an organization who receive or are affected by the output of your work. Three broad types of quality can be considered: quality of design, quality of conformance, and quality of performance.

> **Quality of design** refers to intentional differences between products or services that are designed by an engineer or planner.

Products or services can have a variety of intentional grades, levels, or styles and come with or without a variety of special or additional features. Differences in quality of design can be based, for example, on the type of material that is used in the manufacture of a product. An inexpensive plastic pen and a gold or gold-plated pen perform the same function and may perform equally well in most circumstances, but they differ in quality of design. The gold pen will be more valuable because of its gold content, attractiveness, durability or style, and it will be considered by many to be of higher quality.

Good quality of design starts with consumer research to assess the needs and expectations of customers and involves close communication between customers, management, designers, and suppliers. The research methods involved in obtaining good quality of design depend on an understanding of statistical methods such as sampling, analysis, summarization, and presentation of data. Communication and feedback from the customer should continue on an ongoing basis in an effort to improve quality and customer satisfaction continually.

Quality of conformance refers to the degree to which a product or service conforms to, meets, and exceeds the standards set forth in the design specifications.

The more consistently and uniformly the standards are met, the higher the quality of conformance. The relationship between uniformity (consistency) and quality may not be as obvious as the relationship between intentional design and quality, but, in many ways, it is more important. A product could be designed to meet functional requirements, have a variety of options, be made of luxurious material, and be the height of current style. Although consumers often prefer to have several choices and options when selecting a product or service, they do not want variability in outcomes once they have made their selection. No matter how excellent in terms of quality of design, if the manufactured products or their component parts are highly variable, even within technical specification limits set out in the design, the product may not function consistently and reliably (or at all). It will be perceived to be (and, in fact, will be) low in quality. The level of quality of conformance is determined by the variability of the manufactured product and its constituent components.

The greater the variability, the lower the quality. To increase quality of conformance, we must decrease variability. Variability can be controlled and reduced if the process by which the product is manufactured or the service provided is continually monitored and analyzed by using statistical methods. Quality of conformance is the responsibility of everyone involved: managers, scientists, engineers, and so on. If statistical monitoring of a process indicates that an unacceptable amount of variability is being produced, the only way to reduce variability is to change the process. Most substantive changes in a process can be made only by management, so reduction of variability is the responsibility of management. The statistical tools that enable managers and engineers to monitor, control, and ultimately reduce variability, thereby improving quality of conformance, will be discussed in Chapters 6 and 7.

Quality of performance refers to the long-term consistent functioning of the product and the related product characteristics of reliability, safety, serviceability, and maintainability.

The degree of quality of performance is closely related to and limited by quality of conformance. It is also affected by the behavior of the manufacturer and the customer after the product has been produced. Failure of the manufacturer to meet responsibilities for such things as delivery, installation, service, parts, and warranty will reduce the quality of performance. Failure of the customer to adequately meet periodic service and maintenance requirements or misuse of the product will also result in a decrease in the quality of performance. If the owner of an automobile with excellent quality of design and quality of conformance fails to regularly change the oil, check the transmission fluid, check the air in the tires, or meet other maintenance requirements set forth by the manufacturer, the automobile will not function optimally and will eventually not function at all. Quality of performance is the responsibility of both management and customers.

It is the responsibility of management to assess quality of performance over time by monitoring such areas as after-sales service calls, maintenance records, and feedback on customer satisfaction. Management's responsibility for quality does not end with the sale of a product or service. Assessment of quality of performance should continue throughout the life of the product and requires ongoing communication between management and the customer. Survey research techniques and statistical methods are widely used to facilitate this communication and to provide the information that management requires for strategic planning, new-product development, redesign of products and services, and increased quality of performance.

PROBLEMS

1.11 For each of the following, indicate the type or types of quality involved:

(a) a "luxury" car comes with manual locks and windows;

(b) a cook bakes a cake using a prepared mix that specifies that the cake should be baked at 350° but sets the oven at 375°;

(c) An automobile manufacturer produces its new line of cars only in two-door models, while consumer research indicates that families with young children prefer four-door models;

(d) a case of ball bearings designed to be 10 mm in diameter contains bearings as small as 8 mm and as large as 12 mm in diameter;

(e) a mail-order birthday gift arrives two days late;

(f) a child's bicycle comes unassembled, and the instructions for assembly are unclear or missing;

(g) a manufacturer produces ski jackets that are the same in terms of basic style but come in a choice of down, wool, or Thinsulate™ insulation.

1.9 A HISTORY OF QUALITY AND PRODUCTIVITY

Although there is no written record, a need for leadership and some notion of quality must have existed among tribal bands of early men and women. The earliest economies of these hunting and gathering groups required ever-increasing communication and coordination between members. Even in a gathering economy, we can imagine quality playing a role, as members, through experience, consider some sticks, stones, or other materials to be better and more fit for use than others. As economies developed from finding tools or products to making them, concepts of quality must have developed and become more important. Once tools that had multiple parts requiring assembly were developed, such as a stone ax head inserted into a wooden handle or a spear point joined to a shaft, the idea of quality must have developed to include the concept of a primitive or rough design standard or specification. Although individuals made their own tools to meet their individual needs, parts had to be made to fit together. If one component broke, wore out, or was lost, a suitable replacement had to be found or made. Although design specifications in terms of quantifiable measurement had not yet developed, rough concepts of standardization, interchangeability of parts, and tolerance limits in terms of fit must have begun to develop.

In craftsman or cottage-industry economies, artisans and farmers who produced products lived in close proximity and communication with their customers and were well aware of their customers' needs and expectations. Fitness for use and a perception of good workmanship on the part of the artisan defined quality. Although one-of-a-kind products were produced, many everyday utilitarian products made by the same person followed the same design or model and were very similar. This early specialization of individuals who concentrated on making one class of products was an early form of division of labor and increased the productivity of the overall economy. These artisans and farmers were self-managing and were responsible for providing the quality that their market demanded.

As the capacity to produce goods grew so great that more than local needs could be met, trade developed, inventories were kept, and customers were billed. These activities all required record-keeping. Early examples of the technology of writing are frequently lists and inventories kept for trade or tax purposes. Historical endeavors on a large scale, such as the building of pyramids or temples by the Egyptians, by the Aztecs in Central America, and by the Greeks, and the network of Roman roads all required planning and coordination. Work was supervised by managers and careful measurements were made. These formal measurements are an early example of monitoring work to ensure adherence to specifications and ensure quality.

During the Middle Ages, the growth of guilds occurred, and the apprenticeship system developed. Master craftsmen supervised and directed the training and the quality of work of apprentices and journeymen. Guilds not only managed the training of members in a craft but kept track of the needs of their customers and determined standards of quality and workmanship for the products made. The reputation of the guild rested on the quality of the work of its members. Responsibility for standards and quality rested not just with the individual craftsperson—it was also monitored by the guild.

The industrial revolution and the beginnings of the factory system increased the need for standardization of products and separated owner-managers from workers. As early as 1776, Adam Smith in *The Wealth of Nations* (Reference 19) pointed out the increases in productivity and quantity of work that would result from the division of labor. He attributed this increased productivity to the increase in dexterity of the workers performing one task, to the time saved when workers did not have to switch from one task to another, and to the invention and use of machines that facilitated labor. Factories required ever-increasing amounts of raw materials. Monitoring of the quality, consistency, and supply of raw materials became more important. This emphasis increased the need for data gathering and increased the responsibility and role of managers beyond the supervision of workers. Initially, the factory system was limited. Even in industries such as textile manufacture, it coexisted with individual craftspeople. It wasn't until the late nineteenth and early twentieth centuries that the modern industrial system developed and that manufacturing of products was taken out of the hands of the individual worker or artisan. As the size of an enterprise increased, departmental specialization developed, and management of the enterprise grew beyond the ability of individual owner-managers to control. New levels and methods of management were required.

Frederick W. Taylor tried to address some of the problems created by the factory system and the need to manage large numbers of uneducated and unskilled workers. He is credited with developing the school of Scientific Management in the United States. Scientific Management attempted to increase productivity while benefiting workers, by making it easier for them to perform their job. It required studying the work to be done in detail, determining the optimal methods for performing a job, and carefully training workers to perform each of the steps required. Taylor was concerned that workers were learning their jobs by watching others work and imitating them, rather than by standardized training. This method of learning by watching was traditional and predated the Middle Ages. Inherent in this system was the problem of worker training worker, which is still an issue today. Although effective in a craft or guild economy, workers trained this way can learn only as much as the worker who trained them, and unfortunately will usually learn all the things the other worker does idiosyncratically or incorrectly. The factory system required large numbers of workers and standardization of work to be effective. Taylor saw that the old methods were no longer effective and that it was management's responsibility to specify the best way to do a job and to train and supervise workers.

Unfortunately, as it developed, Scientific Management had the effect of further separating management from workers. It took responsibility for quality out of the hands of the individual worker and put it into the hands of inspectors, supervisors, foremen, and industrial engineers. The research necessary to analyze a job required a great deal of observing, recording, and analyzing of data. The method of controlling and assuring quality was mass inspection of items produced.

The development of the moving assembly line by Henry Ford further increased the division of labor by breaking down complex jobs into ever more limited and simple tasks that could be performed by unskilled labor. Although this change greatly increased productivity, workers became even less responsible for the quality of the product. Thus, the need for inspection grew. In such circumstances, quality was maintained by weeding out defective or unacceptable items. The underlying or real causes of defects were not sought out and identified. Defects were usually blamed on the worker, and punitive action was taken.

By the 1920s, alternatives to 100-percent inspection began to be considered. At Bell Telephone Laboratories, Walter A. Shewhart, Harold F. Dodge, and Harold G. Romig developed statistically based methods of quality control. Shewhart understood the effects of uncontrolled variability and the losses it caused. In 1924, he introduced the concept of statistical quality control and developed the statistical control chart that, as we will see later in Chapters 6 and 7, became the key to reduction of variability. In 1929, Dodge and Romig developed procedures for statistically based acceptance sampling that eliminated the need for 100-percent inspection.

World War II demanded increased productivity from American technology, industry, and agriculture. Productivity and quality became more important, and statistical methods for the control of quality were widely employed in a variety of industries. Some of the statistical techniques developed during the war were considered so essential to the war effort that they were classified *top secret* by the United States government.

The year 1946 saw the formation of the American Society for Quality Control. The end of the war also found much of the industrial base devastated in Europe and, especially, in Japan. The United States was the only industrial economy not damaged by the war, and, consequently, demand for its products was high. In a competitive free market or consumers' market, quality level tends to be set by the customer; in a producers' market, quality tends to be set by the manufacturer. Many American industries at the time, realizing they could sell just about anything, regardless of quality, abandoned their commitment to quality and the use of the quality-assurance and quality-control methods that had helped win the war. Emphasis shifted from quality to marketing, advertising, and creating demand in order to "push products out the door." The practice was to meet demand with little regard for quality.

In 1950, the Union of Japanese Scientists and Engineers (JUSE) invited W. Edwards Deming to come to Japan to help them rebuild their industrial base and improve the quality image of Japanese products. At the time, the phrase "Made in Japan" had become synonymous with inferior workmanship and poor quality. Deming showed the Japanese that, by proper use of statistical quality-control techniques and a commitment to quality, they would not only recover but become the best in the world. The work of Deming and of others, such as Armand Feigenbaum, Kaoru Ishikawa, Joseph Juran, and Homer Sarasohn, with their emphasis on quality, is the basis for the rise of Japan to an economic power.

Interest in quality was dormant in the United States until the late 1970s. By that time, many large American companies, such as Motorola, Ford, and Xerox, found themselves under severe competitive pressure from Japanese companies who were able to manufacture higher quality products at lower prices than their American competitors. In 1980, NBC-TV produced a documentary titled "If Japan Can—Why Can't We?" that included an interview with W. Edwards Deming, who was virtually unknown in his home country. This program sparked a reemergence of interest in quality by American companies, first in the manufacturing sector, then in the service industries. To encourage quality improvement in the United States, the Malcolm Baldrige National Quality Award was approved in 1987, to recognize American companies that excel in quality management. This award is based on seven categories: leadership, strategic planning, customer and market focus, information and analysis, human resource development and management, process management, and business results. Among the companies that have won this award are Motorola, Xerox, Federal Express, Cadillac Motor Company, Ritz-Carlton Hotels, AT&T Universal Card Services, and Eastman Chemical Company. Quality improvement is now considered to be an integral part of the strategy of any company that seriously wants to compete in the global economy. In the next section, we will discuss the basic themes of this approach.

1.10 THEMES OF QUALITY MANAGEMENT

Introduction

Quality management views the meeting of customer needs as a primary goal and focuses on quality to increase productivity, reduce costs, increase profit, and compete effectively in a global market. It is based on the work of Deming and of others who have contributed to the quality movement, such as Armand Feigenbaum, Joseph Juran, Homer Sarasohn, Genichi Taguchi, Kaoru Ishikawa, and Myron Tribus, and it integrates the practices of statistical quality control and participative management. The themes displayed in Exhibit 1.1 are fundamental to quality management:

EXHIBIT 1.1 Themes of Quality Management

1. The primary focus is on process improvement.

2. Most of the variation in a process is due to the system and not to the individual.

3. Teamwork is an integral part of a quality-management organization.

4. Customer satisfaction is a primary organizational goal.

5. Organizational transformation needs to occur to implement quality management.

6. Fear must be removed from organizations.

7. Higher quality costs less, not more, but it requires an investment in training.

Theme 1—The Primary Focus Is on Process Improvement

Management's role is no longer viewed as the managing and controlling of people by motivating, disciplining, and rewarding them. Management's role is managing the process. By process, we mean the following.

A **process** is a sequence of steps that describe an activity from beginning to end.

Managers, engineers, scientists, and workers must work together to improve the process, reduce variability, and improve quality and productivity. This approach focuses on problem prevention and views problems as opportunities to improve the process, not as embarrassments to be covered up.

One well known approach for accomplishing this is the **Shewhart–Deming cycle** presented in Figure 1.2, also known as the Plan-Do-Study-Act cycle or PDSA cycle. It shows the four steps required to improve a process and illustrates that management's efforts are continuous and never-ending.

The first step is *planning*. Planning is based on data collected to determine customer needs and the quality characteristics customers consider important. If data to answer these questions are not available, they must be collected. Previous data on quality of conformance and quality of performance should also be considered. Such tools as cause-and-effect diagrams, flow charts, Pareto charts, histograms, run charts, control charts, and scatter diagrams, which will be presented in later chapters, can facilitate planning. The planning step involves teamwork between managers and individuals from such areas within the organization as research and development, design, engineering, marketing, operations, purchasing, sales, and customer service. It also can be helpful to include other members of the process from outside the organization, such as suppliers and customers. Once the best plan based on the data at hand is formulated, we can proceed to the second step.

Doing involves implementing the plan agreed to in Step 1. During implementation, careful attention must be given to the operational definitions and specifications set forth in the plan. If we are introducing a new product or service or have made major changes in the process, we might want to do a pilot run and implement the plan on a small scale or a trial basis.

Step 3, *studying,* involves evaluating the process and the output of the process. Statistical process-control charts (discussed in Chapters 6 and 7) can be used at this step to monitor quality characteristics and the variability of the process. It is important to monitor the process at many stages. Checking only final products is not sufficient. Variability introduced into the product or service at an early stage will combine with variability from later stages and in the end will be greater than the sum of its parts. Evaluation only at the end of the process will not indicate where in the process variability was caused, nor will it provide information on what caused it and how we might reduce it. Checking must take place over time, at as many stages of the process as possible. Checking and studying the process never end.

In Step 4, *acting,* examination of the data collected and control charts produced in the studying step will tell us whether or not the process is in a state of statistical control, (see Chapter 6) with only chance or common causes of variability operating. If the process is not in a state of statistical control, special causes are operating. We must work to identify these special causes and eliminate them. It is

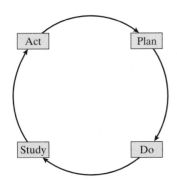

Figure 1.2   The Shewhart–Deming cycle

only when the process is in a state of control that we can consider modifications to the process and attempt to reduce variation and improve quality. In either case, the data will suggest some action to be taken.

From Step 4, we proceed back to Step 1. We now can use what we have learned in previous steps and in the actions suggested by the data to formulate a plan. We continue planning, doing, studying, and acting, indefinitely. The circle that surrounds the steps in Figure 1.2 indicates that the steps are not really separate but flow into one another to form an integrated system of process management. The arrows indicate the direction of the flow, and the fact that there is no break in the circle indicates that the need for process management never ends.

Organizations need to innovate as well as continually improve existing processes. We may have heard how the new technology of the automobile put buggy-whip manufacturers out of business. In fact, not all of them failed. Those that saw the future innovated and, with very little retraining and retooling, made a fortune producing fan belts. Meeting and planning for the future require research on customer needs. Staying in business requires the development of new or higher-quality products and services that will better fill current and future needs. Innovation also requires that resources be put into the maintenance and acquisition of plant and equipment and into a search for new types, sources, and availability of materials.

Theme 2—Most of the Variation in a Process Is Due to the System and Not to the Individual

Both Deming and Juran (References 2, 3, 7, 9, and 23) have pointed out that the causes of most problems and errors (believed to be 85–90%) lie in the system or process and are not under the control of the employee. In such situations, no amount of monitoring of employees' errors and no rewards or punishments based on these counts can improve the system. No employee can do better than the system permits. Analysis of differences in performance ratings in such systems could well say nothing about the true quality of the work of employees or about how skilled or dedicated they are.

Many traditional management theories stress the importance of managers' motivating employees; they assume that motivation is the primary determinant of productivity. If most of the variation is due to the system, however, motivation is of limited value. Workers must know what their jobs are, must have the skills, ability, tools, and resources to do their jobs, and must work with managers and engineers to improve and change the system of operation.

Theme 3—Teamwork Is an Integral Part of a Quality-Management Organization

Division of labor, specialization, and the size of modern enterprises all interacted to fragment organizations into divisions, departments, units, and sub-units. Within these groupings, further separation by functional area and sub-specialization occurred. Work units were separated by floors within buildings, by buildings within a complex, or by geographical distances ranging from across town to hundreds or thousands of miles. Elaborate organizational charts were required just to keep track of what was happening. Very few individuals, if any, understood all the parts or how they functioned and interacted. The management of each unit, either unaware or unconcerned about the problems of other units, worked to fulfill the goals of its unit, interacting with other units only when necessary—often, that was when problems had occurred.

Under such a system, the work of one area usually got done at the expense of another area. Units naturally (or sometimes by design of top management) were encouraged to compete with one another. Competition was considered to be healthy. Unfortunately, such fragmentation of the process—such physical isolation, competition, and lack of communication—became a barrier between units.

Process management views the satisfying of the customer and the meeting of customer needs as the major goal of an enterprise. *Customers* comprise all the individuals or groups working within the process, as well as vendors, suppliers, and final end users of the product or service that the enterprise provides. When this view is taken, all units and functional areas within the enterprise become customers of one another. They must stay as close to their internal customers as to their external customers. Top management should foster communication and cooperation between staff areas. Managers of staff areas should work together and ensure that their staffs communicate with each other on an ongoing basis.

Teamwork should replace competition at all levels and across all areas. The basic philosophy becomes "none of us is as smart as all of us." Problem-solving teams whose members come from a variety of management levels and functional areas are an effective means of removing barriers and of encouraging individuals to work together. Managers and their staffs might need training in how to work as teams. Management should see that the resources required for such training are available. Teamwork helps to create trust and remove barriers and creates a sense of long-term commitment to overriding goals.

Theme 4—Customer Satisfaction Is a Primary Organizational Goal

The primary goal of an organization needs to be customer satisfaction. As quality of both manufactured products and services has improved, customers are increasingly unwilling to accept mistakes, poor service, and unreliable products and will simply shift their business to a company that provides reliable products and good service.

Management must be committed to constant improvement in quality of products and services and to improving long-term competitive position. Their goal should be to stay in business, grow, and provide jobs. The long-term benefit must be considered to be not only to the board of directors and the shareholders but to all stakeholders or members of the extended process, such as workers, suppliers, and customers. It is easy to become involved with day-to-day current problems and crises and how to solve them, but, if one is to stay in business, the long-range view and attention to the problems of tomorrow must be considered.

Many organizations that have adopted the philosophy and practice of quality management find that an organizational mission and goals statement that clearly sets out the never-ceasing commitment to constant improvement, reduction of variation, and increased quality insures that all stakeholders understand the constancy of purpose everyone must have in working together for the future.

Theme 5—Organizational Transformation Needs to Occur to Implement Quality Management

The quality-management philosophy is based on continuous quality improvement. Managers and engineers must realize that we have entered a new economic era. If we do not make a commitment to ever-increasing quality and to the increase in productivity that goes with it, we will not be competitive in a global free market. Such changes mean that the organizational culture might need to be altered drastically. Everyone must have the courage to continually examine the way things are done and to be willing to break with tradition and institute new structures and procedures and accept new responsibilities. This is not an easy thing to do, particularly in a period in which a company is enjoying short-term prosperity. It is often the case that it takes a calamity to get organizations and people to change, but it is better to change before the calamity occurs, rather than wait to act while in a weakened position after some negative experiences.

Theme 6—Fear Must Be Removed from Organizations

In the past, management has often used fear as a motivational tool and has ignored, or was unaware of, its economic consequences. There are many kinds of fear that operate in a business environment. There is fear of learning something new. Some managers and engineers are afraid they will not be able to learn new ways. Others are afraid that learning something new means that, all along, they had been wrong. Top management is afraid of looking bad to their board of directors. Middle managers and workers are afraid of speaking out when something is wrong, asking for clarification, or admitting mistakes. These fears help perpetuate the current system and make it impossible for either the company or individual employees to improve. Another type of fear relates to the fear that sharing information may lead to someone else's getting a better rating.

Such fears prevent people from thinking and destroy intrinsic motivation. Often, what will happen in such an environment is that people will not initiate action, because they do not really know what will be viewed positively and what will be viewed negatively. Such fears need to be removed from the workplace in order to achieve quality improvement.

Theme 7—Higher Quality Costs Less, Not More, But It Requires an Investment in Training

Organizations practicing process management must invest resources in education and training. All members of the organization must learn what their jobs are and what is expected of them. They must then be trained to do those jobs. Management's job is managing the process. Although many managers will specialize in one functional area, if they are to be effective they must be familiar with all aspects of the organization and the extended process. At one time, managers worked their way up from entry-level positions within a company. Over the course of their careers, they held a variety of positions in different areas. They knew their organization and how it functioned, and they understood the problems faced by workers at different levels and with a variety of jobs.

Two things occurred to change this practice. One was the increasing specialization within an organization. Division of labor had an effect on managers as well as workers. As companies organized into more specialized functional areas, managers found that their jobs became narrower. They became specialists in the management of specific limited areas, in a manner similar to the way in which division of labor changed the worker's job from the manufacturing of an entire product to the performing of simple limited tasks. Division of labor took responsibility for the quality of work away from artisans and craftsmen. Specialist management took responsibility for the quality of the entire process away from individual managers.

In addition to managers, workers have a right to know what their jobs are and to receive the training necessary for them to do their jobs well. Their job and the steps necessary to do it should be carefully set forth by using operational definitions. Workers should feel that they are part of an extended process and should understand their role in it. Individuals differ in the style of learning best suited to them and the time necessary for them to learn. Some skills require different methods of training from others. Using experts, management must research the most effective methods to teach a variety of skills to a variety of individuals. Training programs should be innovative and flexible. No one method of teaching or learning will work effectively for all individuals and all jobs.

All members of an organization should be trained in the basic statistical methods required to manage a process. They do not have to become statisticians or experts, but they should be trained to the degree required by their job and their role in the management and improvement of the process. Everyone should understand variability and be able to use basic statistical tools. Organizations that take a long-term view and have a commitment to quality will find that investing in the education and training of all members of the process pays rich dividends.

1.11   THE CONNECTION BETWEEN QUALITY AND STATISTICS

In the preceding three sections of this chapter, we have provided a discussion of the different types of quality, along with the history of quality and the themes of quality management. Awareness and understanding of the statistical concepts and tools of greatest importance to an engineer or scientist will be the subject of the remainder of the text. Familiarity with these statistical tools will enable them to function in organizations that are committed to achieving process improvement and to competing successfully in the global economy.

KEY TERMS

Attribute measures 8	Judgment sample 14
Categorical variables 5	Levels of measurement 5
Census 2	Mutually exclusive 6
Collectively exhaustive 6	Nominal scales 6
Constants 5	Nonprobability samples 11
Continuous variable 5	Numerical variables 5
Convenience sample 14	Operational definitions 9
Data 4	Ordinal scales 6
Data set 4	Parameter 2
Descriptive statistics 1	Population 2
Discrete variable 5	Probability samples 11
Inferential statistics 2	Process 22
Interval scales 6	Quality 16

CHAPTER REVIEW *Checking Your Understanding*

1.12 What is the difference between descriptive and inferential statistics?

1.13 How does a population differ from a sample?

1.14 What is the difference between a parameter and a statistic?

1.15 What is the difference between discrete variables and continuous variables?

1.16 What are the various levels of measurement?

1.17 What is the difference between attribute measures and variables measures?

1.18 What is an operational definition, and why is it so important?

1.19 What is the difference between probability and nonprobability sampling?

1.20 What are the differences between quality of design, quality of conformance, and quality of performance?

1.21 How does quality management differ from more traditional managerial approaches?

1.22 Describe the four steps in the Shewhart–Deming cycle.

Problems

1.23 For each of the following, indicate which type of measurement scale it represents. Provide an operational definition for each.

(a) The distances in feet between the desks in an office.

(b) The sizes of the desks in an office.

(c) The gender of the workers in an office.

(d) The commuting time of the workers in an office.

(e) The job classification of the workers in an office.

(f) The temperature in the copier room.

1.24 For each of the following, indicate which type of measurement scale it represents. Provide an operational definition for each.

(a) Weight of an automobile.

(b) Exterior color of an automobile.

(c) Size classification of an automobile.

(d) Original cost of an automobile.

(e) Rankings of automobile models by a consumer organization.

(f) Trunk size of an automobile.

1.25 Suppose that the following information is obtained from each student exiting from the campus bookstore during the first week of classes:

(a) Amount of time spent in the bookstore.

(b) Gender.

(c) Academic major.

(d) Class status.

(e) Grade-point average.

(f) Method of payment.

(g) Number of textbooks purchased.

For each of the these, indicate which type of measurement scale it represents. Provide an operational definition for each.

1.26 The Data and Story Library (DASL), **http://lib.stat.cmu.edu/DASL**, is an on-line library of data files and stories that illustrate the use of basic statistical methods. Each data set has one or more associated stories. The stories are classified by method and by subject. Access this World Wide Web site and, after reading a story, summarize how statistics has been used in one of the subject areas.

1.27 Access the following World Wide Web site provided by Microsoft Corp. for Microsoft Excel (**http://www.microsoft.com/office/excel**). Explain how you think Microsoft Excel could be useful to an engineer or scientist.

1.28 Access the World Wide Web site for MINITAB (**http://www.MINITAB.com**). Explain how the use of a statistical software package such as MINITAB might be useful to an engineer or scientist.

WHITNEY GOURMET CAT FOOD COMPANY CASE

Background

It has been estimated by research organizations that there are more than seventy million cats kept as pets in homes in the United States. The market for cat food is an extremely large and lucrative one that has attracted corporations such as Heinz, Nestle, Mars, and Ralston Purina, along with a multitude of small companies that attempt to occupy a market niche with specialty products. Often, these specialty products are sold only in pet-food stores and in veterinarian's offices, not in supermarkets. In recent years, changing lifestyles and attitudes have led to an increasing demand for a higher-quality food product that will be eaten with greater regularity and enthusiasm by the family cat, which is often the only companion for the individual with whom it lives.

Several years ago, the founder of the Whitney Gourmet Cat Food Company, Marilyn Cone, began experimenting with the preparation of home-made cat food for her cat Whitney (for whom the company is named). Her idea was based on the belief that alternate types of meat and seafood, along with a chunkier formulation with less fillers, would lead to higher level of satisfaction (and less finicky behavior) by cats, without the sacrifice of nutritional standards. Within a short period of time, her cottage industry was ready to become commercial, and a processing plant was obtained and developed for producing canned cat food. Currently, two types of food are made, one based on kidney parts, the other formulated with pieces of shrimp. In the five years that the company has been operating commercially, sales have risen rapidly, particularly in the past three years, during which the number of sales outlets has been greatly expanded. The rapid expansion of the company has, however, led to the realization that it was too large to be managed as a cottage industry any longer. Senior management of the company, under the leadership of Ms. Cone, is increasingly conscious of the need to increase the efficiency of operations and strive for ever-improving quality levels.

Phase 1

A task force consisting of corporate-level officers, engineers, and department heads was formed to consider how to go about the quality-improvement effort. There was agreement that the first step was the development of a mission statement for the company that could succinctly communicate its mission to both customers and employees.

Once the mission statement was developed, the task force turned to a discussion of which areas of operations should be examined for improvement opportunities. After much brainstorming and discussion, the task force decided that one critical area for improvement was the number of cans that were deemed to be nonconforming (for any one of a variety of reasons).

As Al Brenner, the production manager, and a team of other managers and engineers brainstormed about how to go about the quality-improvement process, the group realized that, in the rapid expansion that had taken place in the past three years, perhaps not enough attention had been paid to training workers properly for their jobs. The company had been running two shifts of workers for the past year, in an effort to keep up with demand for the product, and it had several hundred people working on various aspects of the production and canning process. One of the aspects that concerned the group was whether the three inspectors who worked on each shift were applying the current definition for what was to be considered a nonconforming can of cat food consistently. The team decided that an evaluation of the final process, inspection of cans, needed to be carried out.

TABLE WG1.1

INSPECTION TEST RESULTS OF TWELVE CANS OF CAT FOOD

| | Inspector | | | | | |
| | Shift 1 | | | Shift 2 | | |
CLASSIFICATION	1	2	3	4	5	6
Nonconforming	4	4	4	4	4	4
Conforming	8	8	8	8	8	8

Al Brenner, the production manager, selected twelve cans that ranged in his opinion from clearly conforming, to marginal, to nonconforming for one of several reasons. The cans were tagged with an identification number and placed on tables set up in a conference room. The six inspectors, three from each of the two shifts, independently were instructed to evaluate the cans in the same way that they did on their job every day. Inspection test results are summarized in Table WG1.1.

Exercises

WG1.1 What conclusions about the consistency of the inspectors can you draw?

WG1.2 What other information concerning the inspection test results would be useful to obtain?

STOP

Do Not Read Below until the Phase-1 Exercises have been completed.

Phase 2

The team realized that, in order to study the consistency among the inspectors completely, a tally of the results for each individual can by each inspector had to be available. Table WG1.2 represents a summary of the inspection decisions made by each of the six inspectors for the twelve cans.

Exercises

WG1.3 What conclusions about the inspection process can you now reach after examining Table WG1.2?

WG1.4 Set up a table that would help you to analyze the disagreements between the inspectors.

TABLE WG1.2

INSPECTION TEST RESULTS OF 12 CANS OF CAT FOOD, TALLIED BY INSPECTOR

Can	Inspector	Conforming	Nonconforming	Reason
1	1	×		
	2	×		
	3	×		
	4		×	Blemish on top of can
	5		×	Blemish on top of can
	6	×		
2	Accepted by all			
3*	1		×	Pull tab missing
	2		×	Pull tab missing
	3		×	Pull tab missing
	4		×	Pull tab missing
	5		×	Pull tab missing
	6		×	Pull tab missing

(Continued)

TABLE WG1.2 (Continued)

INSPECTION TEST RESULTS OF 12 CANS OF CAT FOOD, TALLIED BY INSPECTOR

Can	Inspector	Conforming	Nonconforming	Reason
4*	Accepted by all			
5*	1	×		
	2		×	Crack in top of can
	3		×	Crack in top of can
	4	×		
	5	×		
	6		×	Improper pull-tab location
6*	1		×	Surface defect on side of can
	2	×		
	3		×	Surface defect on side of can
	4		×	Surface defect on side of can
	5	×		
	6	×		
7	Accepted by all			
8	Accepted by all			
9*	1		×	Crack in side of can
	2		×	Crack in side of can
	3	×		
	4	×		
	5	×		
	6		×	Crack in side of can
10	1	×		
	2		×	Improper location of pull tab
	3	×		
	4	×		
	5		×	Surface defect on side of can
	6	×		
11*	1		×	Crack in top of can
	2	×		
	3		×	Crack in top of can
	4		×	Blemish on top of can
	5		×	Crack in top of can
	6		×	Crack in top of can
12	Accepted by all			

*Classified as nonconforming by production manager

REFERENCES

1. Cochran, W. G.; *Sampling Techniques,* 3d ed.; New York: Wiley, 1977
2. Deming, W. E.; *Out of the Crisis;* Cambridge, MA: Massachusetts Institute of Technology, Center for Advanced Engineering Study, 1986
3. Deming, W. E.; *The New Economics for Industry, Government, and Education;* Cambridge, MA: Massachusetts Institute of Technology, Center for Advanced Engineering Study, 1993

4. Dobyns, L. and C. Crawford-Mason; *Quality or Else;* PBS Video Series, Silver Spring, MD: CC-M Productions, 1991

5. Dobyns, L. and C. Crawford-Mason; *Quality or Else*; Boston, MA: Houghton-Mifflin, 1991

6. Feigenbaum, A. V.; *Total Quality Control,* 3d ed.; New York: McGraw-Hill, 1983

7. Gabor, A.; *The Man Who Discovered Quality;* New York: Time Books, 1990

8. Halberstam, D.; *The Reckoning;* New York: Avon Books, 1986

9. Juran, J. M.; *Juran on Leadership for Quality;* New York: The Free Press, 1989

10. Kendall, M. G. and R. L. Plackett, eds.; *Studies in the History of Statistics and Probability, vol. II;* London: Charles W. Griffin, 1977

11. *Microsoft Excel 2000 for Windows;* Redmond, WA: Microsoft Corp., 1999

12. *MINITAB Version 12;* State College, PA: MINITAB, Inc., 1998

13. Pearson, E. S., ed.; *The History of Statistics in the Seventeenth and Eighteenth Centuries;* New York: Macmillan, 1978

14. Pearson, E. S. and M. G. Kendall, eds.; *Studies in the History of Statistics and Probability;* Darien, CT: Hafner, 1970

15. Rand Corporation; *A Million Random Digits with 100,000 Normal Deviates;* New York: Free Press, 1955

16. Shewhart, W. A.; *Economic Control of Quality of Manufactured Product;* New York: Van Nostrand–Reinhard, 1931, reprinted by the American Society for Quality Control, Milwaukee, WI, 1980

17. Shewhart, W. A.; *Statistical Methods from the Viewpoint of Quality Control,* edited by W. E. Deming; Washington, D.C.: Graduate School, Department of Agriculture, 1939; Dover Press, 1986

18. Skrebec, Q. R.; "Ancient process control and its modern implications," *Quality Progress,* 25 (1990), 49–52

19. Smith, A.; *The Wealth of Nations* (1776); New York: Modern Library, 1937

20. Snee, R. D.; "Statistical thinking and its contribution to total quality," *American Statistician,* 44 (1990), 116–121

21. Taylor, F. W.; "The Principles of Scientific Management," *Bulletin of the Taylor Society,* (December 1916); Reprinted in *Classics of Organizational Theory,* J. Shafritz and P. Whitlock, eds.; New York: Moore Publishing Co., 1978

22. Walton, M.; *Deming Management at Work;* New York: G. P. Putnam and Sons, 1990

23. Walton, M.; *Deming Management Method;* New York: Perigee Books, Putnam Publishing Group, 1986

APPENDIX 1.1 *Basics of the Windows User Interface*

In this appendix, we first provide an orientation to the basic concepts necessary to operate any program, such as Microsoft Excel or MINITAB, that runs in a Windows user interface in which windows or frames are used as containers to subdivide the screen. In this user interface, although communication can be done with some combination of keystrokes, many pointing or choosing tasks are more easily done by using a pointer device such as a mouse, trackball, or touchpad. Moving a pointer device moves a **mouse pointer,** an on-screen graphic that in its most common form takes the shape of an arrow. Moving a mouse pointer over another object and pressing one of the buttons on the pointer device defines a mouse operation. Four types of mouse operations used in Microsoft Excel or MINITAB are defined in Exhibit A1.1.1 on page 32.

In a windowing environment, mouse operations are applied to a variety of on-screen objects. First and foremost among these objects are **windows,** frames that serve as containers for other windows or for the objects described in this appendix. Many windows can be selected and dragged from one position on the screen to another, and

---

EXHIBIT A1.1.1 Types of Mouse Operations

1. To **select** an on screen object, move the mouse pointer (by moving the mouse) directly over an object and then press the left mouse button (or click the single button, if your mouse contains only one button). If the on-screen object being selected is a button, **click** is often used as an alternative to the verb *select,* as in the phrase "click the OK button."

2. To **drag** or move an object, first move the mouse pointer over an object and then, while holding down the left (or single) mouse button, move the mouse. After the object has been dragged, release the mouse button.

3. To **double-click** an object, move the mouse pointer directly over an object and press the left (or single) mouse button twice in rapid succession.

4. To **right-click** an object, move the mouse pointer directly over an object and press the right mouse button. If your mouse contains only one mouse button, right-clicking is the same as simultaneously holding down the control key and pressing the mouse button.

---

sometimes they are capable of being **resized** (having their length and width dimensions changed).

Other common objects in a windowing environment are free-floating icons, menu bars, task or tool bars, and dialog boxes.

Free-Floating Icons

Free-floating **icons,** graphics that represent a specific application or document, can be selected and dragged from one position to another. Activating an icon representing Microsoft Excel would be a typical way of starting the Excel program.

Menu Bars

Menu bars are the horizontal lists of words that represent a set of choices. Selection of one of the choices results in the display of a **pull-down menu,** a list of more word choices.

Task or Tool Bars

Task or **tool bars** are groups of fixed-position icons or **buttons,** clickable graphics that simulate the operation of a mechanical push button. Tool bars can be either free-floating or fixed ("snapped" into an on-screen position). In applications such as Microsoft Excel, there are tool bars that represent different categories of user actions, such as formatting, editing, or drawing.

Dialog Boxes

Making a certain selection on a menu or tool bar often results in a special type of window called a **dialog box.** Dialog boxes are used to display status messages or to prompt you to make choices or supply additional information. Common to many dialog boxes are the objects listed in Exhibit A1.1.2.

EXHIBIT A1.1.2 Objects Common to Dialog Boxes

- **Drop-down list** boxes allow selection from a nonscrollable list that appears when the drop-down button, located on the right edge of the box, is clicked.

- **Scrollable list** boxes display a list of items, in this case, files or folders, for selection. When the list is too long to be seen in its entirety in the box, clicking the right scroll button or dragging the slider on the scroll bar at the bottom of the list box reveals the rest of the choices.

- **Edit** boxes provide an area into which a value can be edited or typed. Edit boxes are often combined with either a scroll-down list box or spinner buttons, to provide an alternative to the typing of a value.

- **Option** buttons represent a set of mutually exclusive choices. Selecting an option button (also known as a radio button) always deselects, or clears, the other option buttons in the set, thereby allowing only one choice at a time.

- **Check** boxes allow the selection of optional actions. Unlike option buttons, more than one check box in a set can be selected at a given time.

- Clicking the **Open** or **OK** buttons causes an application to execute an operation with the current values and choices as shown in the dialog box.

- Clicking the **Cancel** button closes a dialog box and cancels the operation.

COMMENT: ABBREVIATED NOTATION FOR MENU SELECTION

In this text, the authors will abbreviate menu selections by using the vertical slash character | to separate menu choices. For example, **File | Open** will be used instead of the longer "select the File menu and then select the Open choice." In addition, as was done with **File | Open,** the actual selections will be in **bold-faced** type.

APPENDIX 1.2 *Introduction to Microsoft Excel*

Microsoft Excel and This Text

Microsoft Excel is an example of a spreadsheet application program, the type of personal productivity program best suited for the interactive manipulation of numeric data. Spreadsheet applications allow users to make entries onto electronic versions of paper **worksheets,** rectangular arrays of (horizontal) rows and (vertical) columns into which entries are made. They were first used in business, but today the flexibility of modern spreadsheets makes them an everyday problem-solving tool for many, including students learning statistical problem-solving in a course for engineers and scientists.

Of the many spreadsheet programs available, the authors have chosen to use Microsoft Excel in this text, and not just for the obvious reasons that the program is widely available and incorporates the commonly used Microsoft Office user interface. Microsoft Excel also contains special statistical functions and procedures that aid in the analysis of data and can accept add-ins, preprogrammed procedures that extend the functionality of Excel. These features help construct statistical solutions in Excel and simplify its use. (On many occasions, the Excel appendices use the Prentice Hall PHStat add-in supplied on the CD-ROM that accompanies this text, to further streamline the use of Excel, as explained in the Add-ins section of this appendix.)

Microsoft Excel also allows users to create workbooks, collections of electronic worksheets and other information, which are combined into a single disk file. Worksheets facilitate the development of solutions that are consistent with the rules of good application design. In this text, the solutions generated follow the predictable pattern of placing the problem's data, calculations, and graphical objects on separate sheets. These separate-sheet designs, in turn, enhance the reusability of the workbooks, provide easier opportunities for modifying the workbooks, and generally aid in the clarity of the presentation of the results.

Although it is useful as a tool for learning statistics, readers should be aware that using Microsoft Excel is not an all-purpose substitute for using a standard statistical package. Very large data sets, or data sets with unusual statistical properties, can cause Excel, as well as any add-in code being used, to produce invalid results.

Getting Familiar with the Microsoft Excel Application Window

When Microsoft Excel program or workbook icons are double-clicked, Windows loads Excel, and an Excel application window similar to the one shown in Figure A1.2.1 appears.

Users can configure the exact combination and placement of objects that appear in this window. In Figure A1.2.1, as in all illustrations of the Excel application in this text, the standard and formatting toolbars have been configured to appear below the menu bar. The worksheet displayed in the workspace area has been maximized (opened to cover the entire workspace area). Sets of resizing and closing buttons appear on the title bar and the menu bar. Scroll bars, both horizontal and vertical, allow for the display of parts of the worksheet currently off-screen. Sheet tabs identifying the names of the individual sheets provide a means of "turning" to another sheet in the workbook. A status bar displays information about the current operation and the state of certain keyboard toggles.

Specifying Worksheet Locations

Part of the design process when using a spreadsheet application involves placing the data, calculations, and results required, along with such titles and labels as column headings, into a grid formed by individual worksheets. Using a standard notation for worksheets, we refer to the columns of a worksheet by letters and to the rows by numbers, to identify into which cells (intersections of the columns and rows) entries should be placed. Under this system, the cell reference A1 refers to the cell in the first column and the first row (the upper-left-corner cell); cell reference B4 refers to the cell in the second column and the fourth row.

Because a Microsoft Excel workbook can contain multiple worksheets, this column letter and row number format is, in certain contexts, insufficient to specify the particular cell of interest. When a worksheet design calls for cell entries on one worksheet to refer to cells on another worksheet, the cell reference must be written in the form:

Sheetname!ColumnRow

Using this notation, one can distinguish between two similarly located cells of two different sheets in the workbook. For example, Data!A1 and Calculations!A1 refer to the upper-

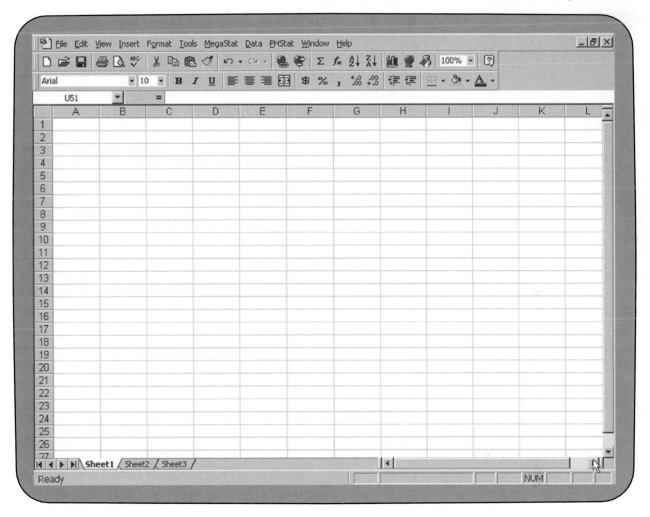

Figure A1.2.1   The Excel application window

left corner cell of the data and calculations sheets, respectively. This extended notation is necessary only when the cell reference is to a worksheet other than the current one, into which entries are being made.

Beside individual cells, references can be made to cell ranges that are rectangular groups of adjacent cells. Cell ranges are written using the cell references to the upper-left-most and lower-right-most cells in the block. The cell range form is

UpperLeft:LowerRight

For example, the cell range A1:B3 refers to the six-cell worksheet block containing the cells A1, B1, A2, B2, A3, and B3; the range A1:A8 refers to the first eight cells in the first column of the worksheet. Ranges in the form

Sheetname! UpperLeft:LowerRight

are allowed and refer to ranges not on the current sheet.

Sometimes, there is a need to distinguish between two similarly located cells on two similarly named worksheets in two different workbooks located in the same folder or directory. In such cases, cell references are written in the form

'[Workbookname]Sheetname'!ColumnRow

—as in '[FISH]Data'!A1, referring to the upper-left-corner cell on the Data worksheet in the FISH workbook.

Configuring Microsoft Excel

Microsoft Excel allows for a custom configuration of the Excel application window. Readers of this text may want to make their Excel windows appear as similar as possible to Figure A1.2.1 and other illustrations of the application window that appear in the text. To configure Microsoft Excel so that the application window matches the illustrations in the text, load and run Excel, and then follow the steps in Exhibit A1.2.1.

Renaming Worksheets

Giving self-descriptive names to individual workbook objects can make using the workbook easier. By default, Microsoft Excel names worksheets serially in the form *Sheet1, Sheet2,* and so on. Better names are ones that reflect the content of the sheets, such as "data" for a sheet that contains the data to be analyzed and "calculations" for a sheet that holds the necessary calculations for an analysis. To give sheets a descriptive name, double-click the sheet tab of the sheet to be renamed, type a new sheet name, and press the enter key.

Entering Data in Excel Workbooks

Now that we have provided a basic orientation to Microsoft Excel and its user interface, we are ready to use Excel in an illustrative example. Suppose that data are available concerning the pulse rate (in beats per minute) of five patients undergoing an annual physical examination. The results are illustrated in Table A1.2.1.

TABLE A1.2.1

PULSE RATE (IN BEATS PER MINUTE) OF FIVE PATIENTS UNDERGOING AN ANNUAL PHYSICAL EXAMINATION

Name	Pulse Rate (in beats per minute)
Allen	62
Barry	70
Diane	72
Kim	58
Susan	52

We are now ready to use Microsoft Excel to perform statistical analysis on these data. For our data of Table A1.2.1, we decide that the first column heading (Name) should appear in cell A1. Using the same reasoning, we determine that the Pulse Rate heading should appear in cell B1 and that the values of each variable for the five patients should appear in the next five rows (2 through 6). Having specified cell addresses for the various parts of the worksheet, we are now ready to enter values into the cells of a sheet that we will name Data. To do this, activate the Microsoft Excel application, and select **File | New** to create a new, blank worksheet window. Rename Sheet1 as **Data.**

Select cell **A1** by clicking its interior. A special border, the **cell highlight,** appears around the cell. This highlight indicates that cell A1 is now the **active cell,** the cell into which the next value to be typed will be entered. (Also note that A1, the address of the active cell, appears in the cell reference box.) Type the column heading Name. As you type, notice that your keystrokes appear both in the edit box of the formula bar and in cell A1 itself. Press

---

EXHIBIT A1.2.1 Configuring Microsoft Excel

---

1. To display the formula and status bars and the standard and formatting toolbars:

   - Select **View.** If the **Formula** bar is not checked, select it. If the **Status** bar is not checked, select it.
   - Select **View | Toolbars.** If the **Standard** choice is not checked, select it. If the **Formatting** choice is not checked, select it.

   To standardize the display of the worksheet area:

   - Select **Tools | Options.** In the Options dialog box, in the Window options group select the **View** tab (if another tab's options are visible). Select the **Gridlines, Zero Values, Row & Column Headers, Horizontal Scroll Bar, Vertical Scroll Bar,** and **Sheet Tabs** check boxes. Deselect (uncheck) the **Formulas** check box if it has been selected. Click the **OK** button.

2. To verify calculation, edit, and general display options that are used in the text:

   - Select **Tools | Options.** In the Options dialog box, select the **Calculations** tab, and verify that the **Automatic** option button of the Calculations group has been selected. Select the **Edit** tab, and verify that all check boxes except the Fixed Decimal check box have been selected. Select the **General** tab. Verify that the **R1C1 Reference Style** box is deselected (unchecked). Change the value in the **Sheets in New Workbook** edit box to 3 (if it is some other value). Select **Arial** (or a similar font) from the **Standard Font** list box. Select **10** from the **Size** drop-down list box.

3. To verify the installation of the Data Analysis ToolPak add-in:

   - Select **Tools.** Select **Data Analysis** if it appears on the Tools menu choice, and verify that the dialog box that appears contains an Analysis Tools scrollable list box. Click the **Cancel** button. This verifies the installation of the tools.
   - If Data Analysis does not appear on the Tools menu, select **Add-Ins** from the menu. In the Add-Ins dialog box, select the **Analysis ToolPak** and the **Analysis ToolPak-VBA** check boxes—if these check boxes appear—from the **Add-Ins Available:** list. Click the **OK** button. Exit Excel (Select **File | Exit.**). Rerun Excel, and follow the instructions in the previous paragraph to verify installation.
   - If you cannot find the Analysis ToolPak or the Analysis ToolPak-VBA check boxes in the Add-Ins Available: list, most likely these special add-in files were not selected during the Microsoft Excel setup process. For example, if you used the "Typical " option of the Microsoft Excel/Office setup program, the (Data) Analysis Toolpak add-ins used in this text were not selected, and you would need to run the Microsoft Excel/Office setup program a second time to include them. (See the "install and use the Analysis ToolPak" on-line help topic for further information.)

the **Enter** key (or click the check button to the left of the edit box) to complete the entry. (Users of keyboards that do not contain an Enter key should press the Return key when instructions in this text call for pressing the Enter key.) Continue by selecting cell B1 and entering the column heading Pulse Rate.

Now that the column headings have been entered, we can begin to enter the values that will appear underneath them. We will type in values by columns, using the feature of the Enter (Return) key to automatically advance the cell highlight down one row after each entry. (If we wished to enter values by rows, we would end each entry by pressing the Tab key, which would advance the cell highlight one column to the right.)

Select cell A2, type the name Allen, and press the Enter (Return) key. Then type the remainder of the names in cells A3–A6, being sure to press the Enter key after each name. Select cell B2, and enter the pulse rate of 62 from Table A1.2.1 into cell B2. Then continue by entering the corresponding amounts of 70, 72, 58, and 52 into cells B3 through B6. Having now entered all the data from our source table into the Data worksheet, we should save a copy of our work on disk, by using **File | Save** or **File | Save As,** before continuing.

COMMENT: CORRECTING ERRORS

As you make entries into a worksheet, at some point you will probably make a typing error. To correct typing errors, you can do one of the following:

- To cancel the current entry while typing it, press the **Escape** key, or click the "X" button on the formula bar.

- To erase characters to the left of the cursor one character at a time, press the **Backspace** key.

- To erase characters to the right of the cursor one character at a time, press the **Delete** key.

- To replace an in-text error: first, click at the start of the error; next, drag the mouse pointer over the rest of the error; finally, type the replacement text. If you change your mind, you can undo your last edit by selecting the command **Edit | Undo.** If you change your mind again and wish to keep the edit after all, select **Edit | Redo.**

Developing Formulas to Perform Calculations

Now that we have saved our work, we are ready to compute a simple statistic, the total pulse rate of the five patients. One way to generate the total pulse rate value would be to just manually sum the values, adding 62, 70, 72, 58, and 52 to get 314 as the total pulse rate.

Although it might be argued that for this very small and very simple problem, manual calculation would be the best method to obtain the total amount, more generally it is wiser to have Microsoft Excel generate the calculation than to do it yourself. To have Excel generate these calculations, we will need to develop and enter formulas, or instructions to perform a calculation or some other task, in the appropriate cells of our Data worksheet (cell B7 in this example).

To distinguish them from other types of cell entries, all formulas always begin with the = (equal sign) symbol. Creating formulas requires knowledge of the **operators,** or special symbols, used to express arithmetic operations. Operators used in formulas in this text include addition ($+$), subtraction ($-$), multiplication ($*$), division ($/$), and exponentiation [a number raised to a power] ($\wedge$).

Because our definition of the total of the pulse rates calls for the addition of five quantities, we will use the $+$ (plus sign) in our *total pulse rate* formula, combining it with the cell addresses containing the values we wish to add. In the case of calculating the total pulse rate for the five patients, cells B2, B3, B4, B5, and B6 on the Data sheet are added together.

By assembling these pieces, we could form the formula

$$=\text{Data!B2} + \text{Data!B3} + \text{Data!B4} + \text{Data!B5} + \text{Data!B6}$$

and enter it into cell B7. Because we are entering a formula in the same sheet as the sheet to which it refers, we can instead write the formula by using the shorthand notation

$$=\text{B2} + \text{B3} + \text{B4} + \text{B5} + \text{B6}$$

and Microsoft Excel will correctly interpret the addresses as referring to the current (Data) sheet.

Using Functions in Formulas

In our discussion of formulas, we used the plus sign arithmetic operator to construct our formula. We could just as easily have used the sum function, one of many such preprogrammed instructions that can be used when solving a variety of common arithmetic, business, engineering, and statistical problems.

To use the Sum function, we type the formula =SUM(B2:B6) into cell B7 instead of the formula =B2 + B3 + B4 + B5 + B6. In the formula =SUM(B2:B6), the word SUM identifies the sum function, the pair of parentheses ( ) bracket the cells of interest, and B2:B6 is the address of the cell range of interest, the cells whose values will be used by the function.

COMMENT: COPYING OBJECTS IN MICROSOFT EXCEL

Objects ranging from a single cell to an entire worksheet can be copied, to simplify or speed implementation of a worksheet design. Generally, copying involves first selecting the object and then selecting the appropriate copy and paste commands.

- To copy a single cell entry or a range of entries, select the cell containing the entries to be copied (or the cell range) by dragging the mouse pointer through all the cells of the range. Select **Edit | Copy.** Select the cell (or select the first cell of the range) to receive the copy. Select **Edit | Paste.** (Note: Copying entries that contain formulas might not result in duplicate entries. See Appendix 3.1 for an explanation of absolute addresses.)

- To copy an entire worksheet, select the worksheet to be copied by clicking on its sheet tab. Select **Edit | Move or Copy Sheet.** In the Move or Copy dialog box, select the **Create a Copy** check box. Select **New Book** from the To book: drop-down list box, if the copy of the worksheet is to be placed in a new workbook. Select the workbook position for the copy by selecting the appropriate choice from the Before sheet: list box. Click the **OK** button.

Wizards

Wizards are sets of linked dialog boxes that guide the user through the task of creating certain workbook objects. Users enter information and make selections in the linked boxes and advance through the set by clicking a Next button (and, ultimately, a Finish button to create the object—clicking a Cancel button cancels the task.) As an example, consider the Microsoft Excel **Text Import Wizard** that assists in the importing, or transferring, of data from a text file into a worksheet. (A text file contains unlabeled and unformatted values that are separated by *delimiters,* such as spaces, commas, or tab characters.).

To demonstrate this wizard, assume that a set of fish weights have been stored in the text file FISH.TXT—such a file is supplied on the CD-ROM that accompanies this book. To import the data from this file into an Excel worksheet, select **File | Open.** In the Open dialog box, select the folder that contains the FISH.TXT file from the Look in: drop-down list. Select the **Text Files** (*.prn; *.txt; *.csv) choice from the Files of type: drop-down list. The All Files (*.*) choice can also be selected. Enter the name **FISH.TXT** in the File name: edit box, or select it from the file list box. (If the file does not appear in the file list box, verify that the previous two steps were done correctly.) Click the **OK** button.

This sequence launches the three-step *Text Import Wizard.* In the Text Import Wizard Step 1 dialog box, select the **Delimited** option button (because the data values for the variables in this file have been placed in fixed-width columns). Note that what this book calls variables are called fields in the dialog box. Click the **Next** button. In the Text Import Wizard Step 2 dialog box, in the Delimiters group, select the space edit box if the variables have been separated with spaces or the Tab edit box if the variables have been separated with a Tab. Click the **Next** button to accept the placement of the data from each line in the text file into columns. (Dragging the vertical column separator line would alter the placement, if necessary.) In the Text Import Wizard Step 3 dialog box, select the **General** option button under the Column data format heading. Click the **Finish** button. The data of the text file is transferred to a new worksheet, named after the text file name (FISH in this example), in a new workbook. Saving the data as a Microsoft Excel workbook by selecting **File | Save As,** save as type **Microsoft Excel Workbook.** Click the **Save** button.

Objects created by wizards should be reviewed for errors. Objects containing errors can be either edited (typically by right-clicking the object and selecting the appropriate choice from the shortcut menu) or else deleted and then recreated by the wizard. (In this example, a good procedure would be to review the data just transferred and, perhaps, insert column headings, too, by first selecting any cell in row 1, then selecting **Insert | Rows,** and finally entering the actual column headings.)

Add-Ins

Add-ins are optional preprogrammed procedures that extend the functionality of Microsoft Excel. Some add-ins, such as the Data Analysis ToolPak previously mentioned, are supplied with the Microsoft Excel program files and can be installed (made permanently available to users) by running the Microsoft Excel setup program. Other, so-called "third party" add-ins, such as the Prentice Hall PHStat add-in that is supplied on the CD-ROM that accompanies this text, are loaded or installed separately.

Add-ins typically modify the menu bar of Microsoft Excel, either by inserting a new menu choice into a pre-existing menu or by inserting a new menu of choices. Once selected, some add-in choices lead to dialog boxes that ask the user to enter information and make selections; others generate new objects or results directly.

For example, the Data Analysis ToolPak add-in inserts the choice Data Analysis into the preexisting Tools menu; the PHStat add-in inserts the PHStat pull-down menu into the menu bar. (See Figure A1.2.2) Selecting Tools | Data Analysis causes the ToolPak add-in to display the Data Analysis dialog box, in which the statistical analysis of interest can be selected. Selecting PHStat from the menu bar pulls down a menu of choices (as in Figure A1.2.2) from which the operation of interest can be selected. These selections then lead to one or more dialog boxes or to the generation of some workbook object.

Many separately obtained add-ins, including PHStat, can also be loaded temporarily by double-clicking the **PHStat for Excel 97/2000** or the **PHStat for Excel 95** icons on the Desktop (per the Installation instructions for PHStat in Appendix D) or by using the procedure to open an Excel workbook file. (Selecting PHStat from the Prentice Hall Add-Ins Start menu loads the add-in under this latter method). When loaded temporarily, add-ins can trigger the Microsoft macro virus dialog box that warns of the possibility of viruses. Should this dialog box appear, click the **Enable Macros** button to allow a virus-free add-in (such as PHStat) to be loaded. Care should be taken never to load an add-in temporarily that is already permanently installed, because unpredictable results can occur.

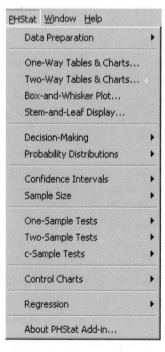

Figure A1.2.2   PHStat menu

An important reminder: to make use of Microsoft Excel and the PHStat add-in in this text, you will need to install the Analysis ToolPak and Analysis ToolPak-VBA add-ins that are supplied with Microsoft Excel and set up and install (or temporarily load) the Prentice Hall PHStat add-in included on the CD-ROM that accompanies the text. You must install the ToolPak add-ins to use PHStat; PHStat will refuse to run if it detects that the ToolPak add-ins were not previously installed.

The World Wide Web address **http://www.prenhall.com/phstat** contains answers to frequently asked questions about PHStat. It also enables users to update to the latest version of PHStat.

Summary

In this appendix, we have provided an introduction to the basic features of the Microsoft Excel application. In the remainder of the Excel appendices in this text, we will be learning about many additional aspects of Microsoft Excel in the context of specific statistical analyses.

APPENDIX 1.3 *Introduction to MINITAB*

What Are Statistical Software Application Programs?

In Section 1.7, when we discussed how software could help the engineer and scientist use data to make decisions, we stated that a statistical software package named MINITAB would be illustrated in this book. Statistical software application programs contain a collection of statistical methods that help provide solutions to engineering or scientific problems. These programs allow users who are relatively unskilled in statistics to access a wide variety of statistical methods for their data sets of interest. In this book, we will be illustrating and explaining the use of the MINITAB statistical software in appendices at the ends of the chapters. The latest version of MINITAB operates in a windowing environment. Readers who are not familiar with such an operating environment should read Appendix 1.1, which explains the basic features of this environment.

Entering Data using MINITAB

There are two fundamental methods for obtaining data for use with MINITAB: entering data at a keyboard, and importing data from a file. To begin, open MINITAB to obtain a window that should look similar to Figure A1.3.1.

This window contains several features that need to be discussed. At the top of the window is a Menu bar from which you make selections that allow you to obtain statistics, display graphs, store and save data, and perform many other operations. Below the Menu bar is a Session window, which displays text output (such as tables of statistics). Below the

TABLE A1.3.1

PULSE RATE (IN BEATS PER MINUTE) OF FIVE PATIENTS UNDERGOING AN ANNUAL PHYSICAL EXAMINATION

Name	Pulse Rate (in beats per minute)
Allen	62
Barry	70
Diane	72
Kim	58
Susan	52

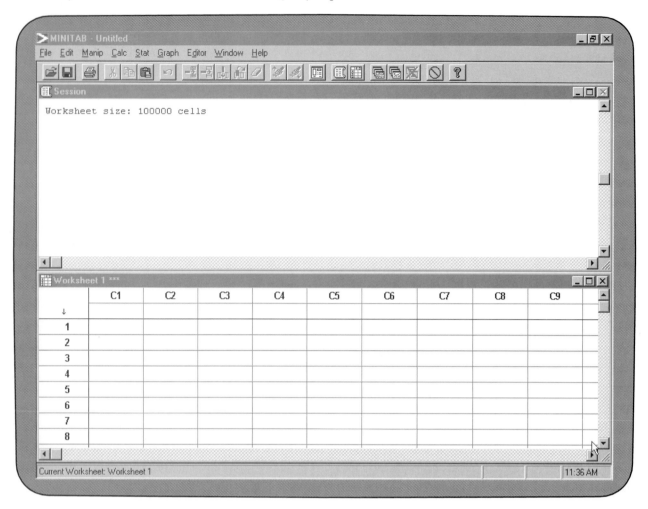

Figure A1.3.1   The MINITAB Worksheet and Session Window

Session window is the Data window, a rectangular array of rows and columns where you enter, edit, and view data. Note that the first row in the Data window lists the columns, which are generically labeled C1, C2, and so on. The following row contains an arrow in the first column and then a set of blank columns. This row serves as a place holder in which labels for variable names are entered.

Data may be entered via the keyboard in the cells in the Data window. If the arrow points down, pressing Enter moves the active cell (into which numbers are entered) down; if the arrow points right, pressing Enter moves the active cell to the right. Clicking the arrow will change the direction of the data entry.

As an illustrative example, suppose that data are available concerning the pulse rate (in beats per minute) of five patients undergoing an annual physical examination. The results are illustrated in Table A1.3.1.

Begin in the row above the horizontal line containing the numbered rows. This row is used to provide labels for each variable. In the first column (labeled C1), enter the label of the first variable (Name) and press the **Enter** key. This moves the cursor to the first row of this column. Enter Allen in row 1, Barry in row 2, Diane in row 3, Kim in row 4, and Susan in row 5. Move the cursor to the heading area at the top of column 2 (under C2), and enter Pulse as the label for this column. After pressing enter to move to row 1 in column C2, we enter 62, the pulse rate for Allen. Continuing, enter the pulse rates for the other four patients in rows 2 to 5, respectively.

When performing statistical analyses throughout this book, we often encounter data sets with a large number of observations. When such sets have been previously entered and stored in a data file, it makes sense to try to import the contents of the file into a Data sheet, to avoid having to reenter each observation one at a time. Each data set in this text has been stored on the CD-ROM in several different formats, including the MINITAB format (.MTW). To import the contents of a MINITAB worksheet, open the MINITAB file of interest located in the appropriate directory, by selecting **File | Open Worksheet** on the menu bar and then selecting the appropriate file from the directory.

Although MINITAB can import data that have been stored in any one of various special file types (such as Microsoft Excel), it is possible that in other situations you will find data stored as text files, files that contain unlabeled and unformatted values that are separated by such delimiters as spaces, commas, or tab characters. To open data from a file, we need to use the command **File | Open Worksheet.** This will provide us with the Open Worksheet dialog box. Many different files, including MINITAB files (.MTW), Microsoft Excel (.XLS), data (.DAT), and text (.TXT), can be opened from this dialog box. Making sure that the proper file type appears in the List of Files of Type Box, select the file that you wish to open. To see how the file will look on the worksheet, click the Preview option.

If the first row of the file begins with data and does not contain the variable names (as is the case with the files ending in .TXT that are contained on the CD-ROM that accompanies this book), click the **Options** box. In the Variable Names group, select the **None** option button. In the Field Definitions group, select the **Free Format** options button. Click the **OK** button. When you are ready to open the selected file, click **Open** to open the selected file, so that it will appear in the Data window. Enter labels for each variable as appropriate, and save the file as a MINITAB worksheet by selecting **File | Save Worksheet As.**

2

Tables and Charts

"A picture is worth a thousand words."

CONFUCIUS

USING STATISTICS

Dover sole are a species of flatfish commercially harvested from Morro Bay and Port San Luis in California. Fishermen believe that there are two different stocks of Dover sole in the area, separated by the depth at which they are caught, and they argue that the quotas for the fish (which are regulated by federal and state laws) should reflect the presence of the two stocks. Toward this end, a study was conducted in which 50 Dover sole taken from shallow water (1,200 to 1,800 feet) and 50 Dover sole taken from deep water (2,700 to 3,300 feet) were examined in terms of their body length, body depth, body width, body weight, and gender. The objective was to determine whether any differences existed between the body structures of the two groups.

2.1 INTRODUCTION AND THE HISTORY OF GRAPHICS

The use of graphics is an activity that has undergone development throughout recorded history. In early civilizations (per References 1 and 7), graphics were used for mapping areas of land. In more recent civilizations, evidence is available that by the tenth or eleventh century, planetary movements were depicted as cyclic lines and that by the thirteenth century, musical notation was shown as a series over time.

Perhaps the first intensive development of graphical tools occurred during the seventeenth and eighteenth centuries, out of the need to obtain a spatial organization of multiple measurements. Two-dimensional plots were used by Halley in 1686 to analyze barometric readings against elevation above sea level. Bar charts were developed by Playfair near the end of the eighteenth century (1786), and two-dimensional graph paper was available by 1794. It is interesting to note that, in the years prior to the nineteenth century, scientists exhibited a clear preference for tables over graphical forms.

Some of the real advantages of graphs were, however, expressed two centuries ago by Playfair (per Reference 1), who said in 1801:

> "I have succeeded in proposing and putting into practice a new and useful mode of stating accounts, . . . as much information may be obtained in five minutes as would require whole days to imprint on the memory, in a lasting manner, by a table of figures."

The development of modern statistics in the United States and Europe led to the invention of numerous new graphical tools, including the pie chart (1801), the cumulative frequency curve (1821), the histogram (1833), polar area charts (used by Florence Nightingale to improve sanitary conditions for the British army in 1857), and graphs using logarithmic grids.

The first half of the twentieth century saw the diffusion of statistical graphs both into the mass media and into the educational curriculum (in the form of college courses and textbooks). Interestingly, after World War II, research in statistical graphics appeared to decline in the statistical community, as emphasis shifted to the development of new statistical theories and methods. Ironically, it was the invention of the digital computer and the development of statistical and spreadsheet software, first for mainframe computers and subsequently for personal computers (see Section 1.7), that led to a resurrection of interest in statistical graphics.

The reemergence of interest in graphics had as its impetus two different developments. The first related to the speed with which the computer could process large amounts of data, enabling new graphical representations to be formulated to picture data that had a multidimensional structure. Second, graphical representations that are conceptually simple but computationally complex, such as residual plots in regression (as in Section 12.6), could be made readily available as part of statistical software and spreadsheet packages.

In this section, we have briefly presented a history of statistical graphics up to our present information age. In the remainder of this chapter, we will discuss a variety of important graphical tools that are helpful in understanding a process, analyzing the results obtained from studying a process, and presenting such results in a form that is easily understandable.

2.2 SOME TOOLS FOR STUDYING A PROCESS: PROCESS FLOW DIAGRAMS AND CAUSE-AND-EFFECT DIAGRAMS

In Chapter 1, we examined the fundamental ideas of the Quality or Process Management approach, and we discussed seven themes for the improvement of any manufacturing or service process. In order to help us understand any process of interest to us, we need to examine two extremely useful process-understanding tools. These two graphical tools are the process flow diagram and the cause-and-effect (or Ishikawa) diagram.

One of the most important stages in research design is deciding which variables to monitor and how much data to collect. Having a clear understanding of a problem or process before collecting data can lead to the selection of the most appropriate variables to study. As this is the primary purpose of both diagrams, either or both of these tools should be used before any data have been collected and before we begin to develop the many tables and charts that are available to help analyze a process.

Process Flow Diagrams

The first process-understanding tool is a **process flow diagram.** This diagram, which is also used extensively in information systems, serves as a pictorial representation of a system and allows one to see the flow of steps in a process from its beginning to its termination. Such a diagram is invaluable in understanding a process and serves as a road map for locating and solving problems and improving quality. The symbols commonly used in a process flow diagram are depicted in Figure 2.1.

The oval **terminal symbol** is used at the beginning and end of the process as a start/stop symbol. The rectangular **process symbol** is used to indicate that a step of the process is to be performed. The diamond-shaped **decision symbol** provides only one way in, but two ways out, so that alternative paths may be taken based on the answer to a question or a decision made in the course of the process. The small circle serves as an **on-page connector,** which can be used to avoid crossing flow lines on a page. In extensive or complex processes, more than one page may be necessary to complete the diagram; in such cases, the **off-page connector** symbol is used to indicate the page and location on which the flow continues. If more information than can be written inside a symbol is required for clarity, an **annotation symbol** or open-sided rectangle connected to the body of the main chart can be used. Finally, **flow arrows** and lines are used to indicate unambiguously the direction of the flow. Exhibit 2.1 presents guidelines for constructing process flow diagrams.

Now that we have defined some of the symbols used in the process flow diagram, we illustrate the process flow diagram with two examples.

The first example involves using a combination toaster–broiler oven. Figure 2.2 presents the process flow diagram for using a certain model of this appliance. We observe that this process flow diagram indicates an immediate decision that needs to be made: whether the toast or broil component is to be used; then it

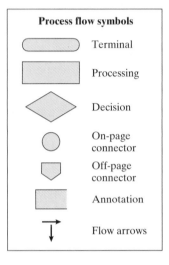

Figure 2.1 Process flow symbols

EXHIBIT 2.1 Guidelines for Constructing Process Flow Diagrams

1. The flow direction should be from left to right and from top to bottom.
2. Use the simplest symbols possible.
3. Flow lines with arrows should connect all symbols, so that there is no ambiguity about direction of the flow.
4. All symbols have only one outflow arrow, except the decision diamond.
5. Make sure that each feedback loop has an escape.
6. Make sure that all steps are included.
7. Words and labels are written only *inside* the symbols, except the words that indicate the alternatives for a decision diamond.
8. Use an annotation symbol for additional information.
9. Symbols may be numbered sequentially for easy reference.
10. Avoid crossing flow lines. Use on-page connector symbols.
11. If more than one page is necessary, use off-page connector symbols.

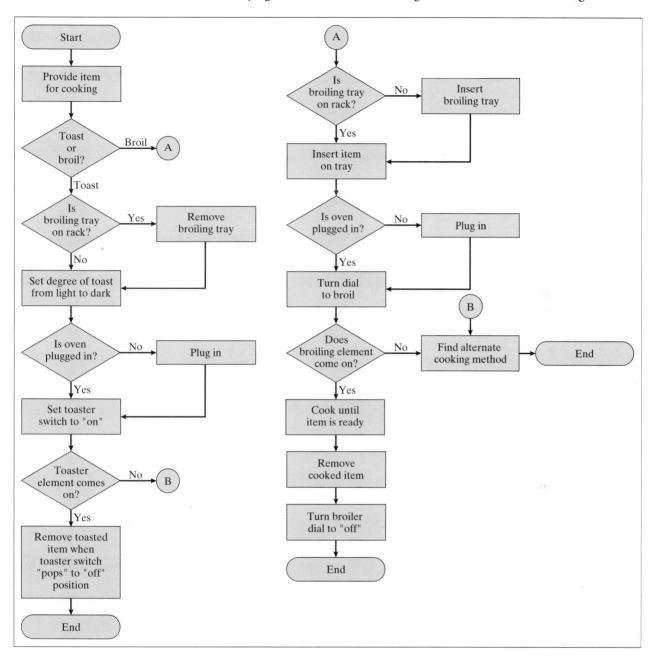

Figure 2.2   Process flow diagram for using a toaster–broiler oven

proceeds with further decisions concerning the presence of the broiling tray and whether the appliance is plugged in. In addition, there are various process steps that deal with inserting the cooking item, setting the broiling dial or toasting level, and cooking the item. In summary, the process flow diagram provides us with a more thorough understanding of how to use the appliance and, furthermore, could serve as a useful tool for explaining the operation of the appliance to another person.

A second example of a process flow diagram is presented in Figure 2.3, which shows the process used to manufacture therapeutic transdermal systems or skin

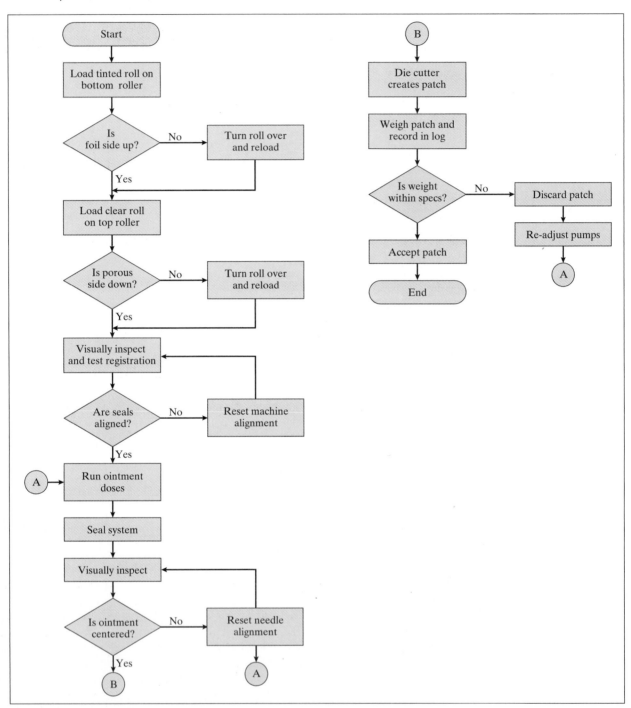

Figure 2.3   Process flow diagram for the manufacture of therapeutic transdermal systems

patches used to deliver fixed dosages of a drug over time. Figure 2.3 shows that the first step involves loading a roll of plastic film onto the machine. This roll is two-ply film, with one side skin tone and the other side nonporous foil on which the ointment will be deposited. The next step is a decision diamond that asks whether the foil side is facing up. If the answer is no, the roll must be repositioned. If the answer is yes, one proceeds to the next step and loads the top roll that is also a two-ply film. One ply is a clear porous thin film coated with adhesive that will adhere to human skin without interfering with the porosity of the film. The second ply is a thicker nonporous clear plastic film that seals the ointment into the patch and is removed before the patch is applied. The next steps involve testing registration of the rolls, visually inspecting alignment of seals, and resetting machine timing when they are not aligned properly. Once aligned properly, the *run ointment doses* step deposits ointment on the foil side of the bottom roll of film, which is then sealed to the top roll. Visual inspection determines whether the ointment dose is centered. If it is centered, a die cutter creates a patch that is weighed. If the patch weight is not within specifications, the patch is discarded and the ointment pumps are readjusted. If patch weight is within specifications, the patch is accepted and the process ends.

The Cause-and-Effect Diagram

The **cause-and-effect diagram** was developed by Kaoru Ishikawa to illustrate the relationship between an effect and a set of possible causes that produces the effect. (See Reference 10.) For this reason, it is also known as an **Ishikawa diagram.** This diagram can help to organize ideas and identify cause-and-effect relationships, thereby helping to identify factors that might be causing variability in process output. The name **fishbone diagram** (see Figure 2.4) comes from the way that the various causes and effects are arranged on the diagram. Typically, the *effect,* be it a problem, a goal, or an outcome, is shown on the right-hand side of the diagram, and the major *causes* are listed on the left-hand side of the diagram. Although effects in specific processes can have any number of major causes, many effects can be represented by one or more of the following five generic *major cause* categories:

1. people or personnel;
2. material or supplies;
3. equipment or machines;
4. procedures or methods;
5. environment.

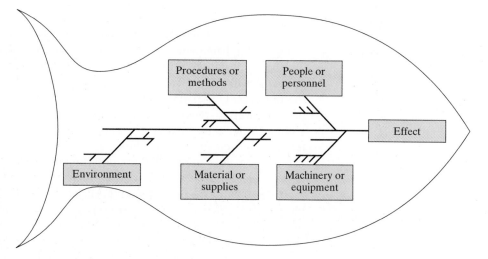

Figure 2.4   The Fishbone Diagram

Within each of these major categories, specific causes are listed as branches and sub-branches of the major category *tree*. Thus, the overall impression of the cause-and-effect diagram is that of a fish skeleton, inspiring the name *fishbone*.

Once the causes have been organized and the diagram constructed, one can attempt to identify the most likely causes or those that have the most impact on the effect. Relationships between the individual causes and the effect should be verified and quantified when possible.

The cause-and-effect diagram can be useful in helping one to understand a process either in a scientific setting, in a service or manufacturing industry, or in one's daily life. Before a fishbone diagram can be constructed, one needs to define clearly the problem to be solved or the goal to be reached. The result will serve as the effect and will be placed on the right-hand side of the diagram. Next, we need to develop a list of as many causes as possible. An individual can generate such a list, but, for most processes, it is preferable for a group to generate the list in one or more brainstorming sessions. A structured method of brainstorming called the **Nominal Group Technique** can be helpful at this stage of analyzing a process. (See Reference 15.) Once the list of causes has been generated, it is examined to see whether major categories of causes are apparent. A major category might either be specific to the process being analyzed or be one of the five generic categories.

In order to demonstrate the construction of a fishbone diagram, we will look at two specific examples. Figure 2.5 represents a fishbone diagram for the difficulties that are encountered by users of a computer system within a company. When difficulties occur, calls are made to a help line that is maintained by the computer systems department. In Figure 2.5, we can observe that categories related to causes of the specific effect of time delay in solving computer problems have been indicated. These categories are methods, machinery, people, and materials. Under *Materials* are branches such as wiring, ribbons, and manuals. Some branches, such as manuals, have sub-branches such as systems hardware, printers, systems software, and PC software (some of which have further sub-branches). Under *People* are branches such as time availability, knowledgeable assistance, and the availability of outside assistance. Similar listings are shown for *Machinery* and *Methods*.

As a second example of a cause-and-effect diagram, Figure 2.6 on page 52 represents a fishbone diagram constructed to study the causes of weight variation in transdermal therapeutic systems or skin patches used to deliver fixed dosages of a drug over time. Drug dosage is partly determined by the amount of ointment contained in the patch, so consistency of patch weights is essential to proper dosage. The effect *variation in patch weights* appears on the right side of the diagram. Under the category of *People,* among the possible sub-causes are training, weight recording error, fatigue, operator experience, and time availability. Under the category *Methods,* such things as calibration schedules, maintenance and cleaning procedures, and manufacturing specifications are listed. Problems such as pump seizures, equipment fatigue, and air in lines are listed as part of the *Equipment* category. Sub-causes can be further broken down and their causes may be indicated by branches from the sub-causes lines. For example, the sub-cause *ointment consistency* under the main category *Material* has two sub-branches, one representing the age of ointment and another the presence of air bubbles.

Process flow diagrams and Ishikawa or fishbone diagrams can help us to focus on the factors that affect a process and therefore should be monitored by

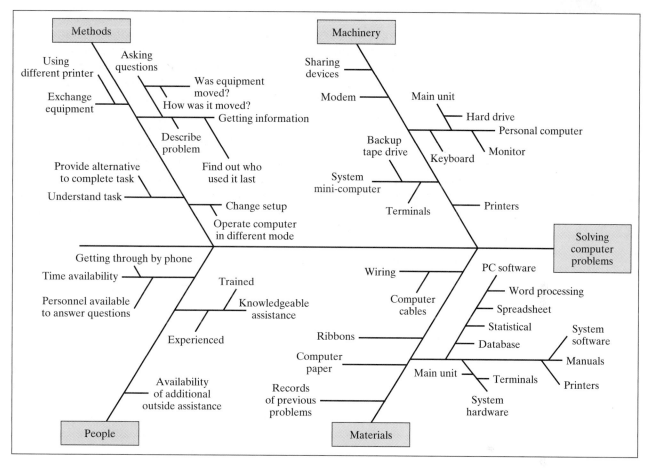

Figure 2.5   Fishbone diagram for solving computer problems by phone

evaluation and data collection. Such monitoring can help us verify and modify our view of the process, evaluate the strength of the effects the factors have on the process, and improve the process itself.

PROBLEMS

2.1 Compare and contrast the process-flow and fishbone diagrams.

2.2 Set up process-flow and fishbone diagrams for your own personal process of getting ready to go to work or school in the morning.

2.3 Set up process-flow and fishbone diagrams for the process of making a long-distance phone call from a pay phone.

2.4 Set up process-flow and fishbone diagrams for the process of changing a flat tire.

2.5 **(a)** Set up process-flow and fishbone diagrams for the registration process at your school.
(b) On the basis of the diagrams developed in (a), what improvements can you suggest in the registration process?

2.6 Set up process-flow and fishbone diagrams for the process of taping a TV program on your VCR.

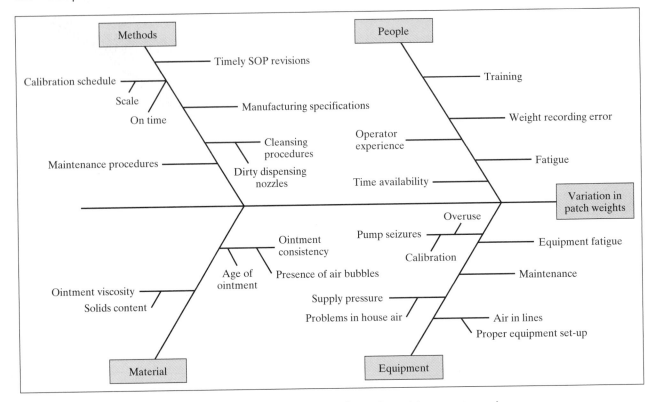

Figure 2.6   Cause-and-effect diagram for variation in weights of transdermal therapeutic patches

2.3 THE IMPORTANCE OF THE TIME-ORDER PLOT

In some situations, data will be obtained from a cross-section of observations collected at the same point in time. In other situations, however, data will be collected serially over many periods of time. It is the latter situation that will be the focus of this section.

When data are collected over time, and before any tables, charts, and descriptive summary measures are developed, it is crucial that the variable (or variables) of interest be plotted in time order. *Until one can be reasonably certain that no patterns in the data exist over time, the use of any other methods of analysis is premature and conclusions drawn from them may be misleading.* Once there is reason to believe that the data are stable over the time periods involved, other more appropriate methods of analysis can be employed. The reason for this emphatic statement is that, when a variable changes over time, time is a *lurking* variable, one that has an important effect on the original variable of interest yet has not been included among those under consideration. (See Reference 11.)

One chart that is helpful in studying this issue is called the **run chart**. It is a simple plot of the variable of interest on the vertical Y axis and the time period on the horizontal X axis. This chart can be illustrated by referring to an example concerning the daily low temperature (F°) recorded at the Westchester County, New York Airport during the month of January in a recent year. These data are presented in Table 2.1.

Figure 2.7 is a run chart for the data of Table 2.1.

From Figure 2.7, we can observe that the data appear to be relatively stable, with no evidence of a pattern over time. Thus, for these data, it would be appropriate

TABLE 2.1

DAILY LOW TEMPERATURE (F°) DURING JANUARY

Day	Temperature	Day	Temperature	Day	Temperature
1	22	11	20	21	19
2	22	12	29	22	38
3	19	13	33	23	30
4	40	14	26	24	29
5	37	15	27	25	28
6	30	16	22	26	23
7	30	17	25	27	27
8	33	18	21	28	24
9	22	19	17	29	19
10	18	20	22	30	18
JANTEMP				31	26

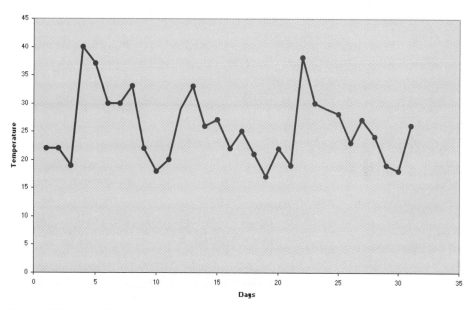

Figure 2.7   Run chart obtained from Microsoft Excel for the daily low Temperature (F°) during January

to proceed with the development of other tables, charts, and descriptive summary measures. These will be the topic of the remainder of this chapter and the next chapter.

Unfortunately, in some instances it will not be the case that the data will be stable over time. For instance, we can examine the data presented in Table 2.2 on page 54 concerning the viscosity of ink that is used on lithographic printing presses. For these types of printing presses, ink is applied to paper to form an image. For ink to flow through the press to be applied to the paper, it must have a certain viscosity (or resistance to flow). Viscosity that is too high can cause the ink to flow onto the paper too slowly; viscosity that is too low can cause too much ink to flow onto the paper. A viscosity measurement is taken at the end of a production batch and represents the entire batch. Table 2.2 presents the viscosity of 25 successive batches of ink produced by a paste-ink manufacturer on a particular day.

Figure 2.8 is a run chart for the data of Table 2.2.

From Figure 2.8, we observe that a downward trend appears evident in the viscosity of the ink over the 25 batches produced during the day. Thus, it would be *inappropriate* to merely combine all 25 batches for summary purposes, because something has occurred during the day to change the viscosity over time. This should be investigated before any additional analyses are performed.

TABLE 2.2

INK VISCOSITY OF 25 CONSECUTIVE BATCHES OF PASTE INK

Batch	Viscosity	Batch	Viscosity	Batch	Viscosity
1	305	9	306	17	273
2	294	10	300	18	282
3	309	11	310	19	287
4	314	12	307	20	276
5	311	13	299	21	275
6	315	14	284	22	285
7	301	15	290	23	274
8	298	16	280	24	270
VISCOS				25	263

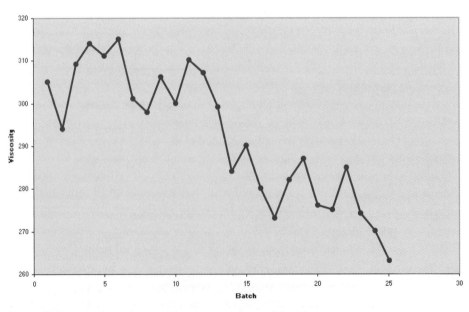

Figure 2.8   Run chart obtained from Microsoft Excel for ink viscosity

PROBLEMS

2.7 An environmental engineer monitored sound level in a building every 15 seconds, to determine whether noise levels were within EPA standards. The table below presents the noise levels recorded in dBA units for 45 15-second intervals.

Interval	dBA	Interval	dBA	Interval	dBA
1	66	16	66	31	85
2	56	17	70	32	70
3	70	18	72	33	76
4	72	19	72	34	70
5	67	20	65	35	74
6	68	21	70	36	72
7	70	22	70	37	70
8	71	23	72	38	70
9	74	24	64	39	75
10	69	25	68	40	70
11	72	26	71	41	70
12	70	27	70	42	68
13	70	28	70	43	70
14	70	29	78	44	69
15	72	30	86	45	73

NOISE

(a) Construct a time-order plot of these data.
(b) Do you find any trends or patterns in these data?

2.8 Every 30 minutes during the production process, a therapeutic transdermal system or skin patch is sampled and weighed as part of the quality-control program. The following table presents the weights in milligrams of 30 sequentially sampled patches.

Sample	Weight	Sample	Weight	Sample	Weight
1	1908	11	1916	21	1980
2	1972	12	1900	22	1916
3	1908	13	1892	23	1924
4	1900	14	1884	24	1972
5	1956	15	1972	25	1916
6	1916	16	1956	26	1908
7	1892	17	1916	27	1988
8	1940	18	1884	28	1844
9	1956	19	1924	29	1948
10	1924	20	1940	30	1836

TRANSDRM

(a) Construct a time-order plot of these data.
(b) Do you find any trends or patterns in these data?

2.9 The following table presents the monthly mean reclaimed water discharge, in cubic feet per second, from a water reclamation facility.

YEAR

Month	1990	1991	1992	1993
January	6.8	7.2	5.8	8.0
February	7.7	10.7	7.8	8.6
March	6.0	5.5	5.2	6.7
April	6.0	5.5	5.8	6.0
May	5.6	5.3	5.1	5.2
June	5.4	5.1	4.7	4.7
July	4.6	4.4	4.2	4.4
August	4.8	4.7	4.4	4.5
September	5.6	4.8	4.7	3.6
October	5.2	5.1	4.3	5.1
November	4.4	5.1	4.8	5.0
December	4.4	5.1	4.8	5.0

RECWATER

Source: City of San Luis Obispo

(a) Construct a time-order plot of these data.
(b) Do you find any trends or patterns in these data?

2.10 A transportation engineer monitored the number of automobiles that traveled through an intersection. The table below presents the data for a 24-hour period during a weekday.

Hour	Hourly Total	Hour	Hourly Total
0:00	52	12:00	625
1:00	31	13:00	620
2:00	15	14:00	537
3:00	8	15:00	637
4:00	8	16:00	665
5:00	13	17:00	625
6:00	58	18:00	484
7:00	210	19:00	361
8:00	473	20:00	273
9:00	461	21:00	222
10:00	472	22:00	195
11:00	524	23:00	114

TRAFFIC

(a) Construct a time-order plot of these data.
(b) Do you find any trends or patterns in these data?
(c) Do you find a problem with using this data set to make decisions about traffic patterns?

2.4 TABLES AND CHARTS FOR NUMERICAL DATA

Now that we have discussed these two process-understanding tools, as well as the run chart, we can turn to a variety of tables, charts, and graphs that can be developed once the appropriate data have been collected. These graphs will be the subject of the remainder of this chapter.

Stem-and-Leaf Displays

The **stem-and-leaf display** is a valuable and versatile tool for organizing a set of data and for understanding how the values distribute and cluster over the range of the observations in the data. A stem-and-leaf display separates data entries into leading digits or stems and trailing digits or leaves. To illustrate this tool, we return to our *Using Statistics* example introduced on page 44. First, we will examine the length in millimeters of 58 male Dover sole randomly sampled from catches landed at Morro Bay and Port San Luis in California. These data are presented in Table 2.3.

TABLE 2.3

LENGTH IN MILLIMETERS OF 58 MALE DOVER SOLE

386 358 370 381 398 341 339 347 397 387 340 427 381 394 384 331 415 420 395 366
371 364 408 398 389 405 339 390 414 410 436 439 419 423 421 388 403 411 392 419
398 409 371 371 373 420 387 410 417 451 346 393 439 374 412 404 425 413

FISH

In this example, the body lengths of the male Dover sole all have three-digit integer numbers, so the hundreds and tens columns are the leading digits and the remaining column (the units column) is the trailing digit. Thus, an entry of 373 (corresponding to a body length of 373 mm) has a stem of 37 and a trailing digit or leaf of 3.

Figure 2.9 depicts the stem-and-leaf display (obtained from MINITAB) of the body lengths achieved by the 58 male Dover sole. The second column of numbers are the stems or leading digits of the data, while the leaves or *trailing digits* branch out to the right of these numbers. The first column of numbers represents the cumulative number of values less than or equal to the stem that contains the middle ranked value, or for stems greater than the middle ranked value, the cumulative number of values equal to or greater than a particular stem. Thus, a value of 8 next to a stem of 35 means that there are 8 values at or less than a stem of 35.

An examination of Figure 2.9 allows us to begin drawing conclusions about the body lengths achieved by the male Dover sole. Among the conclusions we can reach from the stem-and-leaf display are the following:

1. The smallest body length is 331 millimeters.
2. The largest body length is 451 millimeters.
3. The body lengths of the 58 male Dover sole are spread out between the smallest and largest body lengths, with some concentration between 370 and 420 millimeters.
4. There seem to be more body lengths smaller than 370 mm than larger than 440 mm.

```
Stem-and-leaf of Length-M   N   = 58
Leaf Unit = 1.0


      3    33 199
      7    34 0167
      8    35 8
     10    36 46
     16    37 011134
     24    38 11467789
     (9)   39 023457888
     25    40 34589
     20    41 0012245799
     10    42 001357
      4    43 699
      1    44
      1    45 1
```

Figure 2.9   *Stem-and-leaf display (obtained from MINITAB) of the body lengths (in millimeters) achieved by the 58 male Dover sole*
Source: Data are taken from Table 2.1 on page 46.

5. Some male Dover sole have the same body length—for example, there are two with body lengths of 339, 381, 387, 410, 420, and 439 and three with body lengths of 371 and 398.

The Frequency Distribution

As the number of observations obtained gets large, it becomes necessary to condense the data further into appropriate summary tables, in order to present, analyze, and interpret the findings properly. Thus, we can arrange the data into **class groupings** (i.e., categories) according to conveniently established divisions of the range of the observations. Such an arrangement of data in tabular form is called a frequency distribution.

> A **frequency distribution** is a summary table in which the data are arranged into conveniently established, numerically ordered class groupings or categories.

When the observations are grouped or condensed into frequency distribution tables, the process of data analysis and interpretation is made much more manageable and meaningful, because the major data characteristics can be approximated. In constructing the frequency distribution table, attention must be given to selecting the appropriate *number* of class groupings for the table, obtaining a suitable *class interval* or *width* of each class grouping, and establishing the *boundaries* of each class grouping so as to avoid overlapping.

Selecting the Number of Classes

The number of class groupings to be used is dependent primarily on the number of observations in the data. Larger numbers of observations allow for a larger number of class groups. In general, however, the frequency distribution should have at least five class groupings, but no more than 15. If there are not enough class groupings, or if there are too many, little new information is learned.

Obtaining the Class Intervals

When we are developing the frequency distribution table, it is desirable that each class grouping have the same width. To determine the width of each **class interval,** the *range* of the data is divided by the number of class groupings desired:

DETERMINING THE WIDTH OF A CLASS INTERVAL

$$\text{Width of interval} \cong \frac{\text{range}}{\text{number of desired class groupings}} \qquad (2.1)$$

To illustrate the construction of a frequency distribution, we will use the data on lengths of male Dover sole presented in Table 2.3 on page 56.

Since there were only 58 male Dover sole sampled, six class groupings are sufficient. From the data in Table 2.3, the range is computed as $451 - 331 = 120$. By using Equation (2.1), the width of the class interval is approximated as

$$\text{Width of interval} \cong \frac{120}{6} = 20.$$

Establishing the Boundaries of the Classes

To construct the frequency distribution table, it is necessary to establish clearly defined **class boundaries** for each class grouping, so that the observations can be properly tallied into the classes. Overlapping of classes must be avoided.

The width of each class interval for the body length data has been set at 20 millimeters; the boundaries of the various class groupings must now be established so as to include the entire range of observations. Whenever possible, these boundaries should be chosen to facilitate the reading and interpreting of data. Thus, the first class interval ranges from 330 to 349.99 millimeters, the second from 350 to 369.99 millimeters, and so on, until they have been tallied into seven classes, each having an interval width of 20 millimeters, without overlapping. By establishing these boundaries, all 58 observations can be tallied into seven classes, as shown in Table 2.4.

The main advantage of using this summary table is that the major data characteristics should immediately become clear to the reader. For example, we see from Table 2.4 that the *approximate range* in the body lengths achieved by these 58 male Dover sole is from 330 to 470 millimeters and, typically, the body lengths tend to cluster between 370 and 430 millimeters.

On the other hand, the major disadvantage of this summary table is that we cannot know how the individual values are distributed within a particular class interval without access to the original data. Thus, for the three male Dover sole whose body length is between 350 and 370 millimeters, it is not clear from Table 2.4 whether the values are distributed throughout the interval, cluster near 350 millimeters, or cluster near 370 millimeters. The *class midpoint* (360 millimeters), however, is the value used to represent the body lengths for all three male Dover sole contained in this particular interval, when the original data are no longer available.

TABLE 2.4

FREQUENCY DISTRIBUTION OF LENGTH IN MILLIMETERS OF 58 MALE DOVER SOLE

Length in mm	Number of Fish
330 to 349.99	7
350 to 369.99	3
370 to 389.99	14
390 to 409.99	14
410 to 429.99	16
430 to 449.99	3
450 to 469.99	1

Source: Data are taken from Table 2.3 on page 56.

The **class midpoint** is the point halfway between the boundaries of a class and is representative of the data within that class.

The class midpoint for the interval "330 to 349.99" is 340. (The other class midpoints are, respectively, 360, 380, 400, 420, 440, and 460 millimeters.)

Subjectivity in Selecting Class Boundaries

The selection of class boundaries for frequency distribution tables is highly subjective. For data sets that do not contain many observations, the choice of a particular set of class boundaries over another might yield a different picture to the reader. For example, for the male Dover sole data, using a class-interval width of 10 instead of 20 (as is used in Table 2.4) may cause shifts in the way in which the observations distribute among the classes. This is particularly true if the number of observations in the data set is not very large.

Such shifts in data concentration do not occur only because the width of the class interval is altered. We might keep the interval width at 20 millimeters but choose different lower and upper class boundaries. Such manipulation can also cause shifts in the way in which the data distribute—especially if the size of the data set is not very large. Fortunately, as the number of observations in a data set increases, alterations in the selection of class boundaries affect the concentration of data less and less.

The Relative Frequency Distribution and the Percentage Distribution

The frequency distribution is a summary table into which the original data are grouped to facilitate data analysis. To enhance the analysis, however, it is almost always desirable to form either the relative frequency distribution or the percentage distribution, depending on whether we prefer proportions or percentages. These two equivalent distributions are shown in Table 2.5 on page 60.

The **relative frequency distribution** is formed by dividing the frequencies in each class of the frequency distribution (Table 2.4) by the total number of observations. A **percentage distribution** can then be formed by multiplying each relative frequency or proportion by 100.0. Thus, the proportion of male Dover sole that achieved a body length of 430 to under 450 is 0.0517, while the percentage is 5.17%.

TABLE 2.5

RELATIVE FREQUENCY DISTRIBUTION OF LENGTHS OF 58 MALE DOVER SOLE

Length in millimeters	Proportion	Percentage
330 to 349.99	0.1207	12.07
350 to 369.99	0.0517	5.17
370 to 389.99	0.2414	24.14
390 to 409.99	0.2414	24.14
410 to 429.99	0.2758	27.58
430 to 449.99	0.0517	5.17
450 to 469.99	0.0172	1.72

Source: Data are taken from Table 2.4.

Working with a base of 1 for proportions or 100.0 for percentages is usually more meaningful than using the frequencies themselves. In fact, the use of the relative frequency distribution or percentage distribution becomes essential whenever one set of data is being compared with other sets of data, especially if the numbers of observations in each set differ. To illustrate, recall that in the *Using Statistics* example introduced on page 44, we indicated a need to compare the male and female Dover sole. The lengths of 42 female fish are presented in Table 2.6.

TABLE 2.6

LENGTH IN MILLIMETERS OF 42 FEMALE DOVER SOLE

363 345 361 337 442 351 341 357 292 373 360 380 375 357 388 384 349 350 386 394 334
379 355 376 382 327 393 366 316 389 390 405 356 342 400 366 385 362 369 412 364 457

FISH

To compare the lengths for the two types of fish, male and female, we need to develop a percentage distribution for the female fish. Table 2.7 depicts both a frequency and percentage distribution for the lengths of the sample of 42 female Dover sole.

Note that the class groupings selected in Table 2.7 match, where possible, those selected in Table 2.5 for the male Dover sole. In order to make comparisons, the boundaries of the classes should match (or at least be multiples of each other).

Now that separate percentage distributions are available for the male Dover sole in Table 2.5 and the female Dover sole in Table 2.7, a combined percentage distribution table that contains both groups can be developed, as in Table 2.8. Using the percentage distributions of the two groups, we can now make comparisons between the lengths of male and female fish. The male fish are concentrated in the range from 370 mm to 430 mm; the female fish are concentrated in the range from 350 mm to 390 mm. There are no male fish less than 330 mm, but 3 of the 42 female fish (or 7.14 percent) are below 330 mm in length. Further comparison can be based upon graphs of these percentage distributions.

TABLE 2.7

FREQUENCY DISTRIBUTION AND PERCENTAGE DISTRIBUTION OF LENGTHS OF 42 FEMALE DOVER SOLE

Length in mm	Frequency	Percentage of Fish
290 to 309.99	1	2.38
310 to 329.99	2	4.76
330 to 349.99	6	14.28
350 to 369.99	14	33.34
370 to 389.99	11	26.19
390 to 409.99	5	11.90
410 to 429.99	1	2.38
430 to 449.99	1	2.38
450 to 469.99	1	2.38

TABLE 2.8

PERCENTAGE DISTRIBUTIONS OF LENGTHS OF MALE AND FEMALE DOVER SOLE

Length in mm	Male Percentage	Female Percentage
290 to 309.99	0.00	2.38
310 to 329.99	0.00	4.76
330 to 349.99	12.07	14.29
350 to 369.99	5.17	33.34
370 to 389.99	24.14	26.19
390 to 409.99	24.14	11.90
410 to 429.99	27.58	2.38
430 to 449.99	5.17	2.38
450 to 469.99	1.72	2.38

Cumulative Distributions

Another way to look at data is to obtain the cumulative percentages. The cumulative distribution and its associated cumulative polygon provide information about sets of data that cannot be obtained from the frequency distribution itself.

The Cumulative Percentage Distribution

The cumulative percentage distributions of Tables 2.9 and 2.10 can be derived from the percentage distribution, such as in Table 2.8.

A **cumulative percentage distribution** table is constructed by first recording the lower boundaries of each class of the distribution and then adding an additional boundary at the end. The cumulative percentages in the "less than" column are obtained by determining the percentage of observations that are less than each of these lower boundary values. Cumulative percentage distributions can be used to determine the proportion or percent of cases falling above or below specified

TABLE 2.9

CUMULATIVE PERCENTAGE DISTRIBUTION OF LENGTHS OF 58 MALE DOVER SOLE

Length in mm	Percentage Less Than Indicated Value
330	0.00
350	12.07
370	17.24
390	41.37
410	65.51
430	93.09
450	98.26
470	99.99

TABLE 2.10

CUMULATIVE PERCENTAGE DISTRIBUTION OF LENGTHS OF 42 FEMALE DOVER SOLE

Length in mm	Percentage Less Than Indicated Value
290	0.00
310	2.38
330	7.14
350	21.42
370	54.76
390	80.95
410	92.85
430	95.23
450	97.61
470	100.00

values of interest. Thus, from Table 2.10, we observe that 0.00 percent are less than 290 mm, 2.38 percent are less than 310 mm, 7.14 percent are less than 330 mm, and so on, until all values (i.e., 100 percent) are less than 470 mm. This cumulation process is shown in detail in Table 2.11.

The Histogram

Although it is attributed to Confucius, it is still often said that "one picture is worth a thousand words." Indeed, statisticians often employ graphic techniques to describe sets of data more vividly. In particular, a histogram is used to describe numerical data that have been grouped into frequency, relative frequency, or percentage distributions.

A **histogram** is a vertical bar chart in which the rectangular bars are constructed at the boundaries of each class.

TABLE 2.11

FORMING THE CUMULATIVE PERCENTAGE DISTRIBUTION FOR THE 42 FEMALE DOVER SOLE

Length in mm	Percentage In Class Interval	Percentage Less Than Lower Boundary of Class
290 to 309.99	2.38	0.00
310 to 329.99	4.76	2.38
330 to 349.99	14.28	7.14 = 2.38 + 4.76
350 to 369.99	33.34	21.42 = 2.38 + 4.76 + 14.28
370 to 389.99	26.19	54.76 = 2.38 + 4.76 + 14.28 + 33.34
390 to 409.99	11.90	80.95 = 2.38 + 4.76 + 14.28 + 33.34 + 26.19
410 to 429.99	2.38	92.85 = 2.38 + 4.76 + 14.28 + 33.34 + 26.19 + 11.90
430 to 449.99	2.38	95.23 = 2.38 + 4.76 + 14.28 + 33.34 + 26.19 + 11.90 + 2.38
450 to 469.99	2.38	97.61 = 2.38 + 4.76 + 14.28 + 33.34 + 26.19 + 11.90 + 2.38 + 2.38
470 to 489.99	0.00	99.99 = 2.38 + 4.76 + 14.28 + 33.34 + 26.19 + 11.90 + 2.38 + 2.38 + 2.38

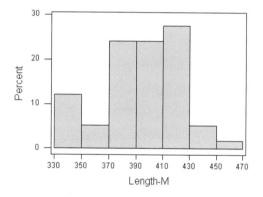

Figure 2.10   Percentage histogram, obtained from MINITAB, of the body lengths of the 58 male Dover sole

When plotting a histogram, the variable of interest is displayed along the horizontal axis; the vertical axis represents the number, proportion, or percentage of observations per class interval.

A percentage histogram of the body lengths of the 58 male Dover sole is presented in Figure 2.10, which has been obtained from MINITAB.

As can be seen from Figure 2.10, although some male Dover sole fall into the lower and upper intervals, most are concentrated in the intervals from 370 mm to 430 mm. This is the same conclusion we reached in examining the percentage distribution presented in Table 2.8.

When comparing two or more sets of data, neither the stem-and-leaf displays nor the histograms can be constructed on the same graph. For example, superimposing the vertical bars of one histogram on another would cause difficulty in interpretation. For such cases, it is necessary to construct relative frequency or percentage polygons.

The Polygon

As with histograms, when plotting polygons the variable of interest is also displayed along the horizontal axis, and the vertical axis represents the number, proportion, or percentage of observations per class interval. In this book, we will concern ourselves with the latter.

> The **percentage polygon** is formed by having a value in each class represent the data in that class and then connecting the sequence of points at their respective class percentages.

Because consecutive midpoints are connected by a series of straight lines, the polygon is sometimes jagged in appearance. When dealing with a very large set of data, if we were to make the boundaries of the classes in its frequency distribution closer together (and thereby increase the number of classes in that distribution), the jagged lines of the polygon would "smooth out."

Figure 2.11 shows the percentage polygon obtained from Microsoft Excel for the body lengths of 58 male Dover sole and 42 female Dover sole. The differences in the structure of the two distributions, previously discussed when comparing the male and female distributions presented in Table 2.8, are clearly displayed here. As

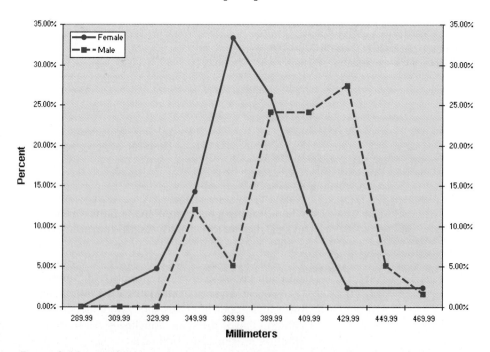

Figure 2.11   Percentage polygons obtained from Microsoft Excel of the body lengths of male and female Dover sole

with Table 2.8, we conclude that the female Dover sole are concentrated in the intervals from 350 mm to 390 mm. It is now clearer that the high points of the female distribution occur in lower intervals than those for the male distribution. If we examine the extremes of the distributions, we see that both the male and female samples had observations that fell into the higher intervals, but only the female sample had lengths in the intervals below 330 mm. It seems that the lengths of female Dover sole are more variable (or spread out) over the range of observed values.

Polygon Construction

Notice that the polygon in Figure 2.11, by Microsoft Excel, has points whose values on the X axis represent the upper limit of the class interval. For example, observe the points plotted on the X axis at 409.99. The value for the male Dover sole (the higher value) represents the fact that 24.14% of these fish have body lengths of between 390 and 409.99. The value for the female Dover sole (the lower value) represents the fact that 11.90% of these fish have body lengths of between 390 and 409.99. Notice, too, that, when polygons or histograms are constructed, the vertical axis should show the true zero or "origin," so as not to distort or otherwise misrepresent the character of the data. The horizontal axis, however, does not need to specify the zero point for the phenomenon of interest. For aesthetic reasons, the range of the variable should constitute the major portion of the chart.

The Cumulative Polygon (Ogive)

The **cumulative polygon** or **ogive** is a graphic representation of a cumulative distribution table. As with histograms and polygons, when plotting cumulative polygons the phenomenon of interest is also displayed along the horizontal axis, and the vertical axis represents the number, proportion, or percentage of cumulated observations. Again, we will concern ourselves here with the latter.

To construct a cumulative percentage polygon (also known as an ogive), we note that our variable of interest—body length—is again plotted on the horizontal axis, while the cumulative percentages (from the "less than" column) are plotted on the vertical axis.

Figure 2.12 on page 66 illustrates the cumulative percentage polygons (obtained from Microsoft Excel) of the body lengths (in millimeters) of the 58 male Dover sole and the 42 female Dover sole. As was the case with the percentage polygons obtained from Excel, the upper limits of the classes are noted on the X axis. For example, for the male Dover sole, 65.51% had a body length less than or equal to 409.99; for the female Dover sole, the percentage was 92.85.

From Figure 2.12, we note that, in general, the female Dover sole ogive is drawn to the left of the male Dover sole ogive. For example, 25% of all male Dover sole have body lengths below about 380 millimeters, while 25% of all female Dover sole have body lengths below about 350 millimeters. In addition, 50% of all male Dover sole have body lengths below about 400 millimeters, while 50% of all female Dover sole have body lengths below about 370 millimeters. Furthermore, 75% of all male Dover sole have body lengths below about 415 millimeters, while 75% of all female Dover sole have body lengths below about 385 millimeters. These comparisons enable us to confirm our earlier impression that the body lengths tend to be higher for the males than for the female Dover sole.

Body Length of Dover Sole

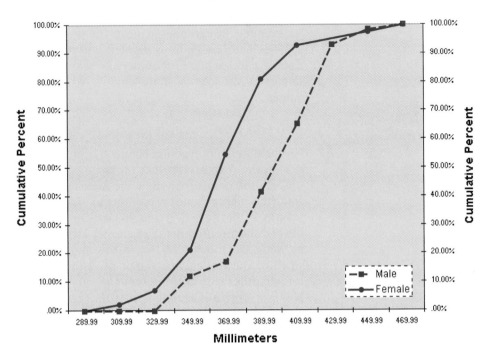

Figure 2.12   Cumulative percentage polygons (obtained from Microsoft Excel) of the body lengths of male and female Dover sole

PROBLEMS

2.11 Form the stem-and-leaf display, given the following raw data from a sample of $n = 7$ midterm exam scores in calculus:

80 54 69 98 93 53 74

2.12 We are given the following stem-and-leaf display representing the amount of gasoline purchased in gallons (with leaves in tenths of gallons) for a sample of 25 cars that use a particular service station on the New Jersey Turnpike.

```
 9 | 714
10 | 82230
11 | 561776735
12 | 394282
13 | 20
```

(a) Place the data in order from lowest to highest.
(b) What amount of gasoline (in gallons) is the most likely to be purchased?
(c) Construct a frequency distribution and a percentage distribution.
(d) Form the cumulative frequency distribution and the cumulative percentage distribution.
(e) Plot the percentage histogram.
(f) Plot the percentage polygon.
(g) Plot the ogive (cumulative percentage polygon).
(h) Is there a concentration of the purchase amounts in the center of the distribution?

2.13 We are given the ordered arrays in the accompanying table dealing with the lengths of life (in hours) of a sample of forty 100-watt light bulbs produced by Manufacturer A and a sample of forty 100-watt light bulbs produced by Manufacturer B.

Manufacturer A				
684	697	720	773	821
831	835	848	852	852
859	860	868	870	876
893	899	905	909	911
922	924	926	926	938
939	943	946	954	971
972	977	984	1,005	1,014
1,016	1,041	1,052	1,080	1,093

Manufacturer B				
819	836	888	897	903
907	912	918	942	943
952	959	962	986	992
994	1,004	1,005	1,007	1,015
1,016	1,018	1,020	1,022	1,034
1,038	1,072	1,077	1,077	1,082
1,096	1,100	1,113	1,113	1,116
1,153	1,154	1,174	1,188	1,230

BULBS

(a) Form the frequency distribution for each brand. (Hint: For purposes of comparison, choose class-interval widths of 100 hours for each distribution.)

(b) For purposes of answering part (d), form the frequency distribution for each brand according to the following schema (if you have not already done so in part (a) of this problem):

   Manufacturer A: 650 but less than 750, 750 but less than 850, and so on

   Manufacturer B: 750 but less than 850, 850 but less than 950, and so on

(c) Change the class-interval width in (b) to 50, so that you have intervals from 650 to under 700, 700 to under 750, 750 to under 800, and so on. Comment on the results of these changes.

(d) Form the percentage distributions from the frequency distributions developed in (b).

(e) Plot the percentage histograms on separate graphs.

(f) Plot the percentage polygons on one graph.

(g) Form the cumulative frequency distributions.

(h) Form the cumulative percentage distributions.

(i) Plot the ogives (cumulative percentage polygons) on one graph.

(j) Which manufacturer has bulbs that have a longer life, Manufacturer A or Manufacturer B? Explain.

2.14 An airflow experiment compared two different terminal devices that are used to diffuse air throughout a space, thereby providing heating and/or cooling. Fifty diffusers of each type were randomly selected in a building that contained 1100 diffusers per floor. The table following presents the airflow measurements in cubic feet per minute obtained in this experiment.

Carnes 3-Way Diffusers									
245	230	180	200	180	255	195	220	195	200
225	240	300	240	285	250	295	295	270	285
225	255	190	275	280	205	215	270	265	290
310	250	215	270	295	210	235	160	235	280
250	240	295	285	190	250	310	290	250	300

Krueger 4-Way Diffusers									
275	225	230	240	205	225	265	225	190	275
240	205	250	265	230	300	275	240	245	250
200	270	245	230	225	285	275	250	200	255
265	230	250	195	240	225	230	290	230	250
225	275	205	245	250	300	275	260	255	230

AIRFLOW

(a) Construct a stem-and-leaf display for the Carnes 3-Way airflow data and for the Krueger 4-Way airflow data.

(b) Construct a frequency distribution for the Carnes 3-Way airflow data and for the Krueger 4-Way airflow data.

(c) Construct a relative frequency or percentage distribution for the Carnes 3-Way airflow data and for the Krueger 4-Way airflow data.

(d) Construct cumulative percentage distributions for the Carnes and Krueger diffusers.

(e) Construct a histogram for the Carnes 3-Way airflow data and for the Krueger 4-Way airflow data.

(f) Construct a percentage polygon for the Carnes 3-Way airflow data and for the Krueger 4-Way airflow data.

(g) Construct a cumulative percentage polygon for the Carnes 3-Way airflow data and for the Krueger 4-Way airflow data.

(h) Based on the results of (a)–(g), what conclusions can you reach concerning differences between Carnes and Krueger diffusers?

2.15 As part of a study of the effect of noise barriers on traffic noise abatement, microphones were placed at 40 reference locations. The table below presents sound levels measured in dB.

Measured Levels (dB)								
77.5	75.8	76.2	74.4	74.7	71.8	72.2	66.5	74.2
73.7	74.0	78.0	78.2	74.8	66.5	72.8	72.8	74.4
77.8	77.2	76.3	82.3	81.0	74.7	76.7	78.4	81.8
80.9	78.8	76.9	76.8	75.8	79.0	78.3	78.1	76.5
78.4	77.5	80.0	75.9					

NOISE2

Source: Noise Control Engineering Journal, 45, 1, 1997, p. 54

(a) Construct a frequency distribution for the noise-level data.

(b) Construct a relative frequency or percentage distribution for the noise-level data.

(c) Construct a cumulative percentage distribution for the noise-level data.

(d) Construct a histogram for the noise-level data.

(e) Construct a frequency polygon and a percentage polygon for the noise-level data.

(f) Construct a cumulative percentage polygon for these data.

(g) What conclusions can you make about noise levels from the results of (a)–(f)?

2.16 Forty hospitalized psychiatric patients participated in a study of blood cholesterol levels. The table below presents gender and the cholesterol levels of these patients.

Males Cholesterol									
226	152	345	204	257	166	136	186	147	187
252	178	365	218	291	284				

Females Cholesterol									
219	210	179	186	179	207	154	130	177	173
241	202	164	221	171	144	119	125	251	146
192	198	142	191						

CHOLEST

(a) Construct a frequency distribution for cholesterol levels of male patients and for those of female patients.

(b) Construct a relative frequency or percentage distribution for the cholesterol levels of male patients and for those of female patients.

(c) Construct cumulative percentage distributions for the male and female patients.

(d) Construct a histogram for the cholesterol levels of male patients and for those of female patients.

(e) Construct a percentage polygon for the cholesterol levels of male patients and for those of female patients.

(f) Construct a cumulative percentage polygon for the cholesterol levels of male patients and for those of female patients.

(g) Based on the results of (a)–(f), what conclusions can you reach concerning differences between male and female patients?

2.17 The following data represent the number of daily calls received at a toll-free telephone number of a large European airline over a period of 30 consecutive non-holiday workdays (Monday to Friday):

Day	Number of Calls	Day	Number of Calls
1	3,060	16	3,004
2	3,370	17	2,685
3	3,087	18	3,618
4	3,135	19	3,369
5	3,805	20	3,353
6	3,234	21	3,277
7	3,105	22	3,066
8	3,168	23	3,341
9	3,235	24	3,181
10	3,174	25	3,252
11	3,603	26	3,161
12	3,256	27	3,186
13	3,075	28	3,347
14	3,187	29	3,275
15	3,060	30	3,129

CALLSDLY

(a) Set up a run chart of the number of daily calls. Is the number of daily calls stable over the 30 days?

(b) Construct a stem-and-leaf display.

(c) Construct the frequency distribution and the percentage distribution.

(d) Plot the frequency histogram.

(e) Plot the frequency polygon.

(f) Form the cumulative percentage distribution.

(g) Plot the cumulative percentage polygon.

(h) What conclusions can the operations manager in charge of customer service for the airline reach concerning traffic on the toll-free number?

2.18 Engineers monitored emissions of hydrocarbons and carbon monoxide from a sample of 46 automobiles. Their data in g/m is presented in the table below.

Vehicle	HC	CO	Vehicle	HC	CO	Vehicle	HC	CO
1	0.50	5.01	16	0.73	14.97	31	0.47	4.74
2	0.65	14.67	17	0.83	15.13	32	0.52	4.29
3	0.46	8.60	18	0.57	5.04	33	0.56	5.36
4	0.41	4.42	19	0.34	3.95	34	0.70	14.83
5	0.41	4.95	20	0.41	3.38	35	0.51	5.69
6	0.39	7.24	21	0.37	4.12	36	0.52	6.35
7	0.44	7.51	22	1.02	23.53	37	0.57	6.02
8	0.55	12.30	23	0.87	19.00	38	0.51	5.79
9	0.72	14.97	24	1.10	22.92	39	0.36	2.03
10	0.64	7.98	25	0.65	11.20	40	0.48	4.62
11	0.83	11.53	26	0.43	3.81	41	0.52	6.78
12	0.38	4.10	27	0.48	3.45	42	0.61	8.43
13	0.38	5.21	28	0.41	1.85	43	0.58	6.02
14	0.50	12.10	29	0.51	4.10	44	0.46	3.99
15	0.60	9.62	30	0.41	2.26	45	0.47	5.22
						46	0.55	7.47

EMISSION

Source: Technometrics Vol. 22, 4, p. 487.

For the data relating to hydrocarbons and carbon monoxide:
(a) Construct a stem-and-leaf display.
(b) Construct a histogram
(c) Construct a percentage polygon.
(d) Construct a cumulative percentage polygon.
(e) On the results of (a)–(d), what conclusions can you reach concerning carbon monoxide and hydrocarbon emissions?

2.19 The table below presents data on dry matter yield (DMY) and nitrogen concentration (NC) for sorghum grown on the Lincoln, Nebraska, municipal water biosolids use site in 1990 and 1991.

Observation	DMY mg/ha	NC g/kg	Observation	DMY mh/ha	NC g/kg
1	12.7	15.1	7	11.9	13.6
2	13.0	16.0	8	20.7	13.4
3	18.6	12.8	9	14.6	13.1
4	14.6	13.6	10	21.1	13.3
5	20.7	12.9	11	22.2	12.7
6	17.2	13.1	12	18.2	14.1

(*Continued*)

Observation	DMY mg/ha	NC g/kg	Observation	DMY mg/ha	NC g/kg
13	14.8	14.8	19	18.8	14.8
14	13.5	15.3	20	17.1	14.0
15	13.7	13.7	21	11.6	11.8
16	15.6	13.4	22	15.8	12.7
17	20.6	12.2	23	17.9	14.7
18	19.5	12.7			

SORGHUM

For the data relating to dry-matter yield and nitrogen concentration
(a) Construct a stem-and-leaf display.
(b) Construct a histogram.
(c) Construct a percentage polygon.
(d) Construct a cumulative percentage polygon.
(e) On the results of (a)–(d), what conclusions can you reach concerning nitrogen concentration and dry-matter yield?

2.5 CHECKSHEETS AND SUMMARY TABLES

When dealing with categorical phenomena, the responses can be tallied into checksheets and summary tables or categorical frequency distributions and then graphically displayed as bar charts, pie charts, or Pareto diagrams. The **checksheet** consists of a tally of the number of occurrences in each category of the variable studied. The **summary table** represents a tally of the frequency of occurrence in each category and the corresponding percentage in the category.

To illustrate the development of the checksheet and summary table, we can refer to data obtained from a large injection-molding company that manufactures plastic molded components used in computer keyboards, washing machines, automobiles, and television sets. The data presented in Table 2.12 on page 70 corresponds to all computer keyboards produced during a 3-month period.

From Table 2.12, we conclude that, although no one category accounts for a majority of the corrections, the most frequently occurring defects are due to warpage (31.42 percent), damage (16.43 percent), pin marks (13.19 percent), and scratches (6.99 percent). These four categories account for 68.03 percent of the causes of defects. It is apparent that the injection-molding company would benefit most by focusing on reduction of these types of errors when changing the process of manufacturing injection-molding components. Locating the most frequently occurring problems allows us to identify the areas of opportunity that can result in the most improvement. For this reason, in Section 2.7 we will study different graphic displays for categorical variables.

TABLE 2.12

SUMMARY TABLE OF CAUSES OF DEFECTS IN COMPUTER
KEYBOARDS IN A 3-MONTH PERIOD

Cause	Frequency	Percentage
Black spot	413	6.53
Damage	1039	16.43
Jetting	258	4.08
Pin mark	834	13.19
Scratches	442	6.99
Shot mold	275	4.35
Silver streak	413	6.53
Sink mark	371	5.87
Spray mark	292	4.62
Warpage	1987	31.42
Total	6324	100.00

TABLE 2-12.XLS

Source: U. H. Acharya and C. Mahesh, "Winning back the customer's confidence: A case study on the application of design of experiments to an injection-molding process," *Quality Engineering,* 11, 1999, 357–363.

PROBLEMS

2.20 You have been asked to perform a traffic study in which you will observe and record the vehicle traffic entering an intersection where two roads cross.
  (a) Design a checksheet to record the number of vehicles traveling through the intersection going north, going south, going east, and going west.
  (b) Design a checksheet for monitoring the number of vehicles that do not pass through the intersection but make a turn into a cross street.
  (c) Select an intersection and record data for 100 vehicles.
  (d) Construct a summary table for your data.

2.21 **(a)** Construct a checksheet for recording the number of times you encounter traffic-control devices, such as stop signs, yield signs, and signal lights, when traveling by motor vehicle.
  (b) Collect data when traveling to or from school or work or when taking an extended trip.
  (c) Construct a summary table for your data.

2.22 You are interested in the number of people who communicate with you by various means, such as telephone, e-mail, fax, pager, mail, and notes.
  (a) Construct a checksheet to record the number of times you are reached by each method.
  (b) Collect data for a one-week period and construct a summary table.

2.6 CONCENTRATION DIAGRAMS

Concentration diagrams are a type of spatial checksheet in which the location of nonconformances is tallied on a schematic diagram or picture of the item to be studied. Two well-known examples of the use of concentration diagrams for manufactured products relate to automobile painting and to combat aircraft. A concentration diagram of an automobile indicates the places on the automobile in which imperfections in the painting process have been discovered. A tally of these imperfections by location highlights those locations where imperfections are more likely to occur. In terms of combat aircraft that return to base after having been hit by enemy fire, a concentration diagram serves to highlight areas of the plane that, when hit, did not result in the destruction of the aircraft. The *absence* of tallies in particular areas of damaged planes indicates that hits in those surface areas may result in the destruction of the aircraft.

The construction of a concentration diagram usually involves the following steps:

1. A schematic diagram or picture of the object or process of interest is obtained by making a drawing of, taking a picture of, or using a copy of the object to be studied.
2. Data are collected, and the diagram or picture is marked in the appropriate location with a symbol or tally mark.
3. The diagram or picture then serves as the basis for identifying or locating areas for improvement.

A recent example, presented by Bisgaard (Reference 2), illustrates the application of the concentration diagram in the manufacturing of die-cast V-6 cylinder blocks. Figure 2.13 is a concentration diagram of a V-6 cylinder block. A schematic drawing of the block was used to record defects such as inclusions and small porosities. Examination of this concentration diagram or defect map shows that defects tend to concentrate on the upper half of the cylinder bores and on cylinder bores 5 and 6 on the right of the diagram. When approached by the quality team, the engineers in the casting division explained that the hot metal enters the mold from the left side, which is physically the lower end of the mold. Because of gravity and the metal flow pattern, the right side and top of each cylinder bore fill last. Molten metal carries a layer of slack, carbon, or other impurities on its upper surface as it flows, and these impurities can become trapped at the top of the mold, causing

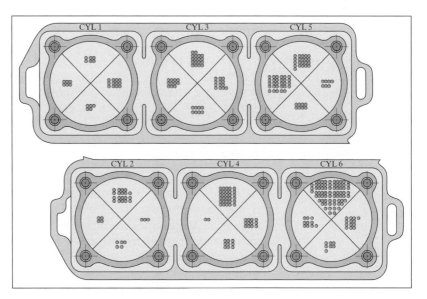

Figure 2.13   Concentration diagram of a V-6 cylinder block
Source: Bisgaard, S. "Quality Quandaries: The importance of graphics in problem solving and detective work," *Quality Engineering,* Vol. 9, (1996), 157–162.

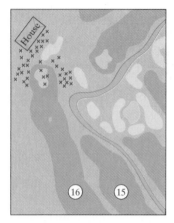

Figure 2.14 Concentration diagram for locating a house near a golf course

porosities and inclusions in the final product. After studying the diagram, the casting engineers realized that the risers that permit trapped air and impurities to escape from the mold needed to be repositioned. After this was done, the number of defects was dramatically reduced.

A second application of the concentration diagram (per Reference 14) relates to the proper placement of a house to be built on a location that was close to a golf course. The site needed to be selected so as to minimize the chance that the house (or an individual) would be struck by an errant golf ball. Data were collected by having a *statistics graduate student* sit at the location for a week and plot where the golf balls landed. A concentration diagram of these data is presented in Figure 2.14. After viewing the concentration diagram, the developer decided to build the house on the spot indicated by the rectangle in Figure 2.14. The use of such methods as concentration diagrams in this instance does not serve to eliminate all risk of damage. The author of the article reported that, upon visiting the house, he found a broken window with a golf ball inside the house!

PROBLEMS

2.23 Create a concentration diagram for a room or other area of your campus. Record the number of pieces of litter and other debris found in the area at the end of a day. Based on your diagram, where would you suggest relocating or placing additional trash containers?

2.24 Create a concentration diagram for a shirt or top. Record the number of stains or dirt spots accumulated at the end of each day for a week. You may use yourself or a friend as a subject in this exercise.

2.25 Create a concentration diagram for an automobile. Collect data on dents and scrapes by examining cars in a parking lot.

 ## 2.7 GRAPHING CATEGORICAL DATA

When dealing with categorical phenomena, once the observations are tallied into summary tables, they can then be graphically displayed as either bar charts, pie charts, or Pareto diagrams.

The Bar Chart

In Table 2.12 on page 70, the numbers of defects in computer keyboards were tallied in various categories. To express the information provided in Table 2.12 graphically, a percentage bar chart can be displayed. Figure 2.15 depicts a percentage bar chart obtained from Microsoft Excel. In **bar charts**, each category is depicted by a bar, the length of which represents the frequency or percentage of observations falling into a category.

From Figure 2.15, we observe that the bar chart allows us to directly compare the percentage of defects in terms of causes. More than 30 percent of the defects are due to warpage; more than 16 percent of the defects are due to damage. Very few of the defects are due to jetting, shot mold, or spraying.

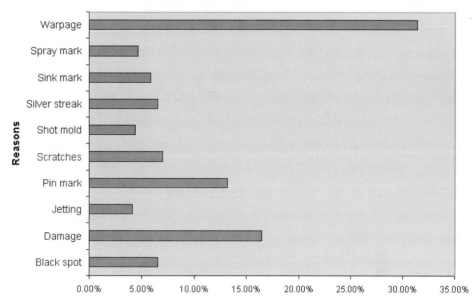

Figure 2.15   Percentage bar chart obtained from Microsoft Excel for defects in computer keyboards

Source: Data are taken from Table 2.12 on page 70.

The Pie Chart

Another widely used graphical display to visually express categorical data from a summary table is the pie chart. Figure 2.16 on page 74 depicts a percentage pie chart for the defects data presented in Table 2.12.

The pie chart is based on the fact that the circle has 360°. The pie is divided into slices according to the percentage in each category. As an example: In Table 2.12, 31.42% of the defects are classified as due to warpage. Thus, in constructing the pie chart, 360 degrees is multiplied by 0.3142, resulting in a slice that takes up 113° of the 360° of the circle. From Figure 2.16, we observe that the pie chart lets us visualize the portion of the entire pie that is in each category. We can see that warpage takes up almost a third of the pie, and defects due to damage comprise about one-sixth of the pie.

The purpose of graphical presentation is to display data accurately and clearly. Figures 2.15 and 2.16 attempt to convey the same information with respect to defects in computer keyboards. Whether these charts succeed, however, has been a matter of much concern. (See References 3 and 4.) In particular, some research in the human perception of graphs (Reference 5) concludes that the pie chart presents the weaker display. The bar chart is preferred to the pie chart, because it has been observed that the human eye can more accurately judge length comparisons against a fixed scale (as in a bar chart) than angular measures (as in a pie chart). In addition, the bar chart allows comparison of categories.

On the other hand, the pie chart clearly shows that the total for all categories adds to 100%. Thus, the selection of a particular chart is still highly subjective and

Defects in Computer Keyboards

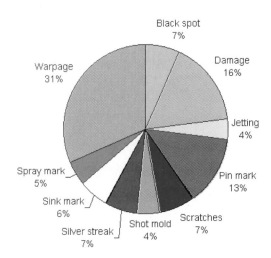

Figure 2.16   Pie chart obtained from Microsoft
Excel for defects in computer keyboards
Source: Data are taken from Table 2.12 on page 70.

is often dependent on the intention of the user. If a comparison of categories is most important, use a bar chart. If observing the portion of the whole that is in a particular category is most important, use a pie chart.

The Pareto Diagram

A graphical device for portraying categorical data that often provides more visual information than either the bar chart or the pie chart is the Pareto diagram. This is particularly true as the number of categories or groups for the categorical variable of interest increases. The **Pareto diagram** is a special type of vertical bar chart in which the categorized responses are plotted in the descending rank order of their frequencies and combined with a cumulative polygon on the same scale. The main principle behind this graphical device is its ability to separate the "vital few" from the "trivial many," enabling us to focus on the important categories. Hence, the chart achieves its greatest utility when the categorical variable of interest contains many categories. The Pareto diagram is widely used in conjunction with fishbone and process-flow diagrams (as in Section 2.2) and in the statistical control of process and product quality (as in Chapters 6 and 7).

In order to obtain a Pareto diagram, we first develop a summary table in which the categories are ordered based on the percentage of defects present (rather than in alphabetical order). Table 2.13 presents such a table for the computer keyboard defects data. The percentages for the ordered categories can also be cumulated as part of the table. Thus, from Table 2.13, we observe that warpage is the first category listed (with 31.42 percent of the defects), followed by damage (with 16.43 percent), followed by pin mark (with 13.19 percent). The two most frequently occurring categories, warpage and damage, account for 47.85 percent of the defects; the three most frequently occurring categories, warpage, damage, and

TABLE 2.13

ORDERED SUMMARY TABLE OF CAUSES OF DEFECTS IN COMPUTER KEYBOARDS IN A 3-MONTH PERIOD

Cause	Frequency	Percentage	Cumulative Percentage
Warpage	1987	31.42	31.42
Damage	1039	16.43	47.85
Pin mark	834	13.19	61.04
Scratches	442	6.99	68.03
Black spot	413	6.53	74.56
Silver streak	413	6.53	81.09
Sink mark	371	5.87	86.96
Spray mark	292	4.62	91.58
Shot mold	275	4.35	95.93
Jetting	258	4.08	100.00
Total	6324	100.00	

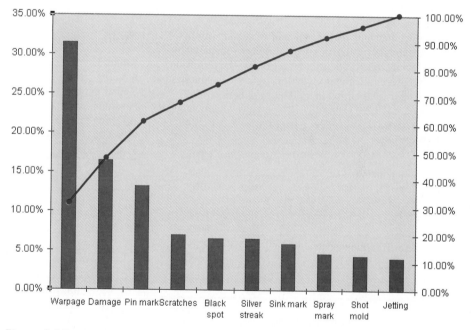

Figure 2.17   Pareto diagram obtained from Microsoft Excel for defects in computer keyboards
Source: Data are taken from Table 2.12 on page 70.

pin mark, account for 61.04 percent of the corrections, and so on. The results displayed in tabular form in Table 2.13 are plotted in the Pareto diagram obtained from Microsoft Excel, illustrated in Figure 2.17.

In Figure 2.17, the bars are presented vertically, for viewing clarity, along with a cumulative percentage line. If we follow the cumulative line, which is plotted at the category midpoint at a height equal to the total cumulative percentage, we note that these first three categories account for about 61 percent of the corrections.

In constructing the Pareto diagram, the vertical axis on the left side of the chart represents percentage of occurrence; the vertical axis on the right side of the chart contains the cumulative percentages (from 100 on top to 0 on the bottom), and the horizontal axis is labeled by the categories of interest. When studying a Pareto diagram, one's focus should be on the magnitude of the differences in the adjacent categories and the cumulative percentages of these categories. Because the Pareto diagram has ordered the categories by frequency or percentage of occurrences, we can see that concentrating our efforts on the reduction of defects due to warpage, damage, and pin marks would result in the greatest payoff in reduction of defects, followed by scratches and black spots.

In order to have the categories collectively exhaustive, in some situations it will be necessary to use a category labeled *Other* or *Miscellaneous*. In these situations, the bar representing these categories is placed to the right of the other bars, which are ordered by frequency.

PROBLEMS

2.26 Surface finishing technology is of increasing importance in many industries, such as motor vehicle manufacturing, construction, and electronics. The following table presents different types of engineering coatings and their total output in millions of dollars.

Type of Coating	Total Output
Organic	1450
Hot Dip Galvanizing	355
Vitreous Enamel	40
Electroplating	705
PVD & CVD	24
Hard Facing	100
Surface Heat Treatment	325
Anodizing	65
Tin Plate	40
Other	250

    (a) Construct a pie chart for these data.
    (b) Construct a bar chart for these data.
    (c) Construct a Pareto chart for these data.
    (d) Based on the results of (a)–(c), what conclusions can you reach concerning the types of engineering coatings used in surface finishing technology?

2.27 A pharmaceutical manufacturing process uses a high-speed compressing machine as part of the process of tablet production. The table below presents the percent of time the compression machine spent on each of several activities, both before a quality improvement study and after the study on how to reduce set-up time for the machine.

Activity	Before	After
Running	36.5	56.7
Set-up	27.9	7.5
Repair in progress	6.5	5.6
Awaiting repair	5.7	2.0
Awaiting granule	5.6	8.6
Awaiting operator/setter	15.7	8.6
Miscellaneous	2.0	11.3

Source: Gilmore, M. and Smith, D.J. (1996), Set-up reduction in pharmaceutical manufacturing: an action research study. *International Journal of Operations and Production Management*, 16, 3, 4–17.

    (a) Construct a pie chart for the *before* data.
    (b) Construct a pie chart for the *after* data.
    (c) Compare the pie charts for the *before* and the *after* data. What conclusions can you draw?
    (d) Construct a bar chart for the *before* data.
    (e) Construct a bar chart for the *after* data.
    (f) Compare the bar charts for the *before* and the *after* data. What conclusions can you draw?
    (g) Construct a Pareto chart for the *before* data.
    (h) Construct a Pareto chart for the *after* data.
    (i) Compare the Pareto charts for the *before* and the *after* data. What conclusions can you draw? Do the Pareto charts offer any additional insight on these data?

2.28 The following data refer to the major error categories encountered during debugging and code changes in computer programs. It was collected by a software development firm.

Type of Corrections	Number of Corrections	Percentage of Corrections
Computational	65	9.0
Configuration	22	3.1
Data Base Interface	6	0.8
Data Handling	131	18.2
Documentation	6	0.8
I/O	118	16.4
Logic	187	25.9
Preset Data Base	30	4.2
Questions	8	1.1
Recurrent	9	1.3
Routine/Routine Interface	59	8.2
Software Interface	8	1.1
User Requested Change	48	6.7
Unidentified	7	1.0

(a) Construct a pie chart for these data.
(b) Construct a bar chart for these data.
(c) Construct a Pareto chart for these data.
(d) Based on the results of (a)–(c), if the software development company wants to reduce errors encountered during debugging and code changes in computer programs, what categories should it focus on? Explain.

2.29 The operations manager at a cereal packaging plant said that, in her experience, typically there are nine reasons that result in the production of unacceptable cereal cartons at the end of the packaging process: broken carton (R), bulging carton (G), cracked carton (C), dirty carton (D), hole in carton (H), improper package weight (I), printing error (P), unreadable label (U), and unsealed box top (S).

The raw data below represent a sample of 50 unacceptable cereal cartons taken from the past week's production, and the reasons for nonconformance are indicated:

U G U S H D D R I U S U S U G C S U D R S U D U S

S D P R S I S U D G S S U S D G S C U D D S S S U

(a) Construct a summary table for these data.
(b) Construct a bar chart for these data.
(c) Construct a pie chart for these data.
(d) Construct a Pareto chart for these data.
(e) Based on the results of (a)–(d), if the operations manager wants to reduce nonconforming cereal cartons, what categories should she focus on? Explain.

2.30 As part of a study of turbine airfoil degradation in the Persian Gulf War, chemical analysis of Saudi Arabian sands were performed. The table below presents the chemical analysis of dune sand and river-bed sand. Data represent percent of sand sample represented by each component.

Component	Dune Sand	River-Bed Sand
SO_2	90.8	12.3
CaO	1.5	25.9
Al_2O_3	2.5	5.2
Fe_2O_3	0.8	0.9
MgO	0.5	15.6
NiO	1.0	0.2
TiO	0.2	0.2
Na_2O	0.2	0.2
K_2O	0.5	0.1
CO_2	5.6	39.4
SO_2	1.3	8.5

Source: Journal of the Minerals, Metals and Materials Society, (1994) 46, 12, 39.

(a) Construct a pie chart for the dune sand data.
(b) Construct a pie chart for the river-bed sand data.
(c) Compare the pie charts for the dune and the river-bed sand. What conclusions can you draw?
(d) Construct a bar chart for the dune sand data.
(e) Construct a bar chart for the river-bed sand data.
(f) Compare the bar charts for the dune and the river-bed sand. What conclusions can you draw?
(g) Construct a Pareto chart for the dune sand data.
(h) Construct a Pareto chart for the river-bed sand data.
(i) Compare the Pareto charts for the dune and the river-bed sand. What conclusions can you draw? Do the Pareto charts offer any additional insight on these data?

2.31 A quality study was performed on the manufacture of Application Specific Integrated Circuits (ASIC). The following table presents the number of rejects, by reject category, for nonconforming units, out of a total output quantity of 1126 units.

Type of Nonconformance	Number Rejected
Foreign Material Debris	45
Bond Misalignment	11
Die Residual Metal	7
Abnormal Thermode	5
Burnt Lead	5
Tape Skewed	4
No Bond	4
Tape Bent Lead	4
Correlation Unit	3
Scratches on Die	2
Wrong Orientation	2
Lost/Missing Units	2
Other	17

(a) Construct a pie chart for these data.
(b) Construct a bar chart for these data.
(c) Construct a Pareto chart for these data.
(d) Compare the pie chart, the bar chart, and the Pareto chart for these data. What conclusions can you draw? Do the Pareto charts offer any additional insight on these data?

2.8 TABLES AND CHARTS FOR BIVARIATE CATEGORICAL DATA

Often, we need to examine simultaneously the responses to two categorical variables. In this section, we will examine some tabular and graphical methods of cross-classifying and presenting such data. In particular, we will develop the contingency table and the side-by-side bar chart.

The Contingency Table

In order to study the responses to two categorical variables simultaneously, we first form a two-way table of cross-classification, known as a **contingency** or **cross-classification table**. As an illustration, we return to the *Using Statistics* example on page 44, concerning Dover sole. Recall that one of the questions of interest relates to the location of fish in shallow and deep water for each gender. Table 2.14 represents a cross-classification table of these two categorical variables for the 100 Dover sole sampled.

TABLE 2.14

CONTINGENCY TABLE DISPLAYING GENDER AND DEPTH AT WHICH THE FISH WAS CAUGHT

	Depth		
Gender	Shallow	Deep	Totals
Male	9	49	58
Female	41	1	42
Totals	50	50	100

To construct this contingency table, the joint responses for each of the 100 Dover sole (see the FISH data file), with respect to gender and to depth at which the fish was caught, are tallied into one of the four possible "cells" of the table. Thus, the first fish listed is classified as a female caught at a shallow depth. These joint responses are tallied into the cell composed of the second row and first column. The remaining 99 joint responses are recorded in a similar manner.

In order to explore any possible pattern or relationship between gender and the depth at which the fish were caught, it is useful to first convert these results into percentages based on the following three totals:

1. the overall total (i.e., the 100 sampled Dover sole);
2. the row totals (i.e., the genders of the Dover sole);
3. the column totals (i.e., the depth at which the fish were caught).

This is accomplished in Tables 2.15, 2.16, and 2.17, respectively.

Let us examine some of the many findings present in these tables. Among the findings in Table 2.15, we note that 58% of the Dover sole sampled are male, 50% were caught in shallow water, and 41% are female who were caught in shallow water.

From Table 2.16, we note that 84.48% of the males were caught in deep water, and 97.62% of the females were caught in shallow water. From Table 2.17, we note that 82% of the Dover sole caught in shallow water were female and that 98% of

TABLE 2.15

CONTINGENCY TABLE DISPLAYING GENDER AND DEPTH AT WHICH
THE FISH WAS CAUGHT (BASED ON TOTAL PERCENTAGES)

	Depth		
Gender	Shallow	Deep	Totals
Male	9	49	58
Female	41	1	42
Totals	50	50	100

TABLE 2.16

CONTINGENCY TABLE DISPLAYING GENDER AND DEPTH AT WHICH
THE FISH WAS CAUGHT (BASED ON ROW PERCENTAGES)

	Depth		
Gender	Shallow	Deep	Totals
Male	15.52	84.48	100
Female	97.62	2.38	100
Totals	50	50	100

TABLE 2.17

CONTINGENCY TABLE DISPLAYING GENDER AND DEPTH AT WHICH
THE FISH WAS CAUGHT (BASED ON COLUMN PERCENTAGES)

	Depth		
Gender	Shallow	Deep	Totals
Male	18	98	58
Female	82	2	42
Totals	100	100	100

the Dover sole caught in deep water are male. The tables, therefore, reveal an obvious pattern: males are found in deep water, females are found in shallow water.

The Side-by-Side Bar Chart

A useful way to display bivariate categorical data visually, when looking for patterns or relationships, is by constructing a **side-by-side bar chart**. Thus, for example, using the data from Table 2.14, Figure 2.18 on page 80 is a side-by-side bar chart, obtained from the PHStat add-in for Excel, that enables a comparison of male and females based on the depth at which the fish were caught.

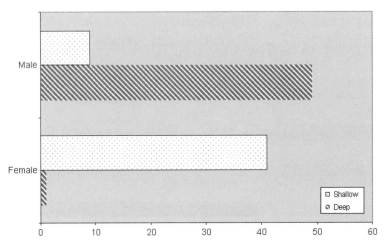

Figure 2.18   A side-by-side bar chart obtained from the PHStat add-in for Microsoft Excel of gender, based on the depth at which the fish were caught

PROBLEMS

2.32 The following data represent the bivariate responses to two questions asked in a survey of 40 college students majoring in engineering—Gender (Male = M; Female = F) and Major (Computer Science = C; Electrical = E; Other = O) :

Gender: M M M F M F F M F M F M M M M F F M
Major: E C C O E C E E C C E E E O C O E E
Gender: F F M M M F M F F M M F M M M M F
Major: E C C C E E O O C E E E C C E E E
Gender: M F M M
Major: C C E C

    (a) Tally the data into a 2 × 3 contingency table, where the two rows represent the gender categories and the three columns represent the student major categories.

    (b) Form a contingency table based on percentages of all 40 student responses.

    (c) Form a contingency table based on row percentages.

    (d) Form a contingency table based on column percentages.

    (e) Using the results from (a), construct a side-by-side bar chart of gender based on student major.

2.33 As part of a study of lifestyle and women's health, it was found that, out of 32 women who smoked, 22 showed signs of osteoporosis, and 10 did not. Out of a sample of 44 women who did not smoke, 16 showed signs of osteoporosis, and 28 did not.

    (a) Construct a cross-tabulation table for these data.

    (b) Construct a table of percentages based on the table total.

    (c) Construct a table of percentages based on the row totals.

    (d) Construct a table of percentages based on the column totals.

    (e) Using the results from (a), construct a side-by-side bar chart of smoking status based on signs of osteoporosis.

    (f) What conclusions do you draw from these analyses?

2.34 The results of a study made as part of a yield improvement effort at a semiconductor manufacturing facility provided defect data for a sample of 450 wafers. The following table presents a summary of the responses to two questions: "Was a particle found on the die that produced the wafer?" and "Is the wafer good or bad?"

CROSS-CLASSIFICATION OF CONDITION OF DIE AND WAFER QUALITY

Quality of Wafer	Condition of Die		Totals
	No Particles	Particles	
Good	320	14	334
Bad	80	36	116
Totals	400	50	450

Source: Hall, S. W., Analysis of Defectivity of Semiconductor Wafers by Contingency Table. *Proceedings Institute of Environmental Sciences*, Vol. 1, (1994), 177–183.

(a) Construct a table of percentages based on the table total.

(b) Construct a table of percentages based on the row totals.

(c) Construct a table of percentages based on the column totals.

(d) Using these data, construct a side-by-side bar chart of quality of wafer based on condition of die.

(e) What conclusions do you draw from these analyses?

2.35 Sea Otter (*Enhydra lutris*) skulls were studied for asymmetry. Each skull was categorized by age: pup, juvenile, or adult, and by sagittal crest asymmetry. Out of 15 pup skulls studied, 11 had sagittal crests deflected to the left side, 3 were deflected to the right side, and 1 was symmetrical. Of 96 juvenile skulls, 61 had sagittal crests deflected to the left side, 14 were deflected to the right side, and 21 were symmetrical. Of 276 adult skulls studied, 86 had sagittal crests deflected to the left side, 82 were deflected to the right side, and 108 were symmetrical.

(a) Construct a cross-tabulation table for these data.

(b) Construct a table of percentages based on the table total.

(c) Construct a table of percentages based on the row totals.

(d) Construct a table of percentages based on the column totals.

(e) Using the results from (a), construct a side-by-side bar chart of age based on sagittal crest asymmetry.

(f) What conclusions do you draw from these analyses?

2.36 A computer engineer studied the differences between an unoptimized and an optimized program and found that, of the 319 references in the unoptimized program, 186 were register references, 45 were immediate references, and 88 were indirect references. For the optimized program, there were 164 references, of which 88 were register references, 29 were immediate references, and 47 were indirect references.

(a) Construct a cross-tabulation table for these data.

(b) Construct a table of percentages based on the table total.

(c) Construct a table of percentages based on the row totals.

(d) Construct a table of percentages based on the column totals.

(e) Using the results from (a), construct a side-by-side bar chart of type of program based on type of reference.

(f) What conclusions do you draw from these analyses?

2.37 Each day, at a large hospital, several hundred laboratory tests are performed. The rate at which these tests are improperly done, for a variety of reasons, and thereby need to be redone, seems steady at about 4 percent. In an effort to get to the root cause of these nonconformances (tests that need to be redone), the director of the lab decides to keep records for a period of one week of the nonconformances, subdivided by the shift of workers who performed the lab tests. The results were as follows:

	Shift		
Lab Tests Performed	Day	Evening	Totals
Nonconforming	16	24	40
Conforming	654	306	960
Totals	670	330	1000

(a) Construct a table of row percentages.

(b) Construct a table of column percentages.

(c) Construct a table of total percentages.

(d) Which type of percentage, row, column, or total, do you think is most informative for these data? Explain.

(e) Using these data construct a side-by-side bar chart of nonconformances by shift.

(f) What conclusions concerning the pattern of nonconforming laboratory tests can the laboratory director reach?

2.9 GRAPHICAL EXCELLENCE

To this point, we have studied how a collected set of data is presented in tabular and chart form. Among the methods for describing and communicating statistical information, well-designed graphical displays are usually the simplest and the most powerful. Good graphical displays permit understanding and insights into what the data mean. If our analysis is to be enhanced by visual displays of data, it is essential that the tables and charts be presented clearly and carefully. Tabular frills and other **"chartjunk"** must be eliminated, so as not to cloud the message given by the data with unnecessary adornments (References 8, 16, 17, and 18).

The widespread use of spreadsheet applications and graphics software has led to a proliferation of graphics in recent years. Much of the graphics presented have served as useful presentations of the data involved, but, unfortunately, the inappropriate and improper nature of many presentations has only compounded the impression that the only purpose of statistics is to use numbers to mislead.

Principles of Graphical Excellence

Perhaps the best-known proponent of the proper presentation of data in graphs is Professor Edward R. Tufte, who has written a series of books that are devoted to proper methods of graphical design (References 16, 17, and 18). It is the work of Tufte that we will focus on in this section. Exhibit 2.2 lists the essential features of graphical data.

In *The Visual Display of Quantitative Information* (Reference 16), Tufte suggested five principles of graphical excellence. These are listed in Exhibit 2.3. There are several ways in which the excellence of a graph can be evaluated. One important measure is the **data-ink ratio,** presented in Equation (2.2).

EXHIBIT 2.2 Features of Graphical Data

The basic features of a proper graph include the following:

1. showing the data;
2. getting the viewer to focus on the substance of the graph, not on how the graph was developed;
3. avoiding distortion;
4. encouraging comparisons of data;
5. serving a clear purpose;
6. being integrated with the statistical and verbal descriptions of the graph.

EXHIBIT 2.3 Principles of Graphical Excellence

1. Graphical excellence is a well-designed presentation of data that provides substance, statistics, and design.
2. Graphical excellence communicates complex ideas with clarity, precision, and efficiency.
3. Graphical excellence gives the viewer the largest number of ideas, in the shortest time, with the least ink.
4. Graphical excellence almost always involves several dimensions.
5. Graphical excellence requires telling the truth about the data.

DATA-INK RATIO

The data-ink ratio is the proportion of the graphic's ink that is devoted to nonredundant display of data information.

$$\text{Data-ink ratio} = \frac{\text{Data-ink}}{\text{Total ink used to print the graphic}} \tag{2.2}$$

The objective is to maximize the proportion of the ink used in the graph that is devoted to the data. Within reasonable limits, non-data-ink and redundant-data-ink should be eliminated. Non-data-ink includes aspects of the graph that do not relate to the substantive features of the data, as well as grid lines that may be imposed on the graph. Chartjunk can be defined as follows

Chartjunk is decoration that is non-data-ink or redundant-data-ink.

In its extreme form, chartjunk represents self-promoting graphics that focuses the viewer on the style of the graph, not on the data presented in the graph. Tufte has referred to this type of graph as "The Duck".

A central feature of graphical excellence is the importance of not using a graph to distort the data that it represents. A graph does not distort if its visual representation is consistent with its numerical representation. The amount of distortion can be measured by the **lie factor.**

LIE FACTOR

$$\text{Lie factor} = \frac{\text{Size of the effect shown in the graph}}{\text{Size of the effect shown in the data}} \tag{2.3}$$

One principle involved here is that any variation in the design of a graph must be consistent with the variation that exists in the data. Often, changes in the graph are not consistent with variations in the data, so they produce a distortion between what the data represents and what the graph is showing.

In order to understand these principles better, it would be useful to study several examples of graphs that are deficient in graphical excellence.

Figure 2.19 represents a graph printed in the *New York Times* of the annual oyster catch in Chesapeake Bay, in millions of bushels, for a time period that stretches more than a century, from the 1890s until 1992.

In Figure 2.19, the icon representing the estimated 20 million bushels of oysters caught in the 1890s does not appear to be five times the size of the icon representing the estimated 4 million bushels caught in 1962. Such an illustration might catch the eye, but it usually doesn't show anything that could not be presented better in a summary table or a plot of the data over time. (See Section 2.3.)

Exaggerated icons and symbols are chartjunk. They result in a distortion of the visual impact. Let's examine Figure 2.20 on page 84. Note that, in this chart, the magnitude of the 10.8 million transportation, trade, and retail jobs is underrepresented by a truck icon that is smaller than the icon representing the 5.6 million jobs for farm family members. Also, the can icon representing the 1.3 million food-processing jobs is far too large compared to the icons representing the 2.1 million farm worker jobs, the 2.6 million manufacturing jobs, and the 4.1 million jobs in

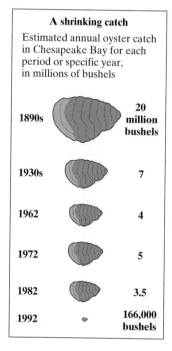

Figure 2.19 "Improper" display of estimated oyster catch (in millions of bushels) in Chesapeake Bay over various time periods

Source: Adapted from *The New York Times*, October 17, 1993, p. 26.

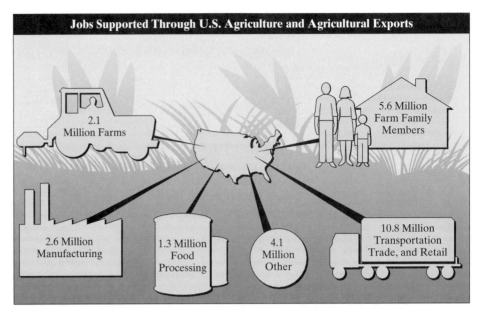

Figure 2.20 "Improper" display of jobs supported through United States agriculture and agricultural exports.
Source: Adapted from *The New York Times,* October 19, 1993, Advertising Supplement, p. D18.

Figure 2.21 Plot of New York City milk prices
Source: "Pricing Milk," by Steve Madden, *Newsday,* Feb. 8, 1998.
Reprinted with permission © Newsday, Inc., 1998.

other areas of agriculture and exporting. A simple summary table, a bar chart, a pie chart, or a Pareto diagram would have been more effective at portraying the data accurately.

Other types of eye-catching displays that we typically see in magazines and newspapers often include information that is not necessary and just adds excessive nondata-ink. Figure 2.21 is an example of one such display.

The graph in Figure 2.21 shows the trend in milk prices in New York City from 1987 to 1997. The prices shown are the price per gallon that farmers received and the metro-area supermarket price. Although the point of the graph is to show the differences in these two sets of prices, the graph suffers from excessive chartjunk. The amount of ink used to display the cow is much too large relative to the data-ink.

In summation, we are active consumers of information that we hear or see daily through the various media. Because much of what we hear or read is junk, we must learn to evaluate critically and to discard that which has no real value. We must also keep in mind that the junk we are provided with is sometimes based on ignorance; at other times, as we shall discuss next, it is planned and malicious. The bottom line—*be critical* and *be skeptical* of information provided.

According to Tufte (Reference 16), for many people, the first word that comes to mind when they think about statistical charts is "lie." Too many graphics distort the underlying data, making it hard for the reader to learn the truth. Ethical considerations arise when we are deciding what data to present in tabular and chart format and what not to present. It is vitally important, when presenting data, to document both good and bad results. When making oral presentations and presenting written reports, it is essential that the results be given in a fair, objective, and neutral manner. Thus, we must try to distinguish between poor data presentation and unethical presentation. Again, the key is *intent*. Often, when fancy tables and chartjunk are presented or pertinent information is omitted, it is done simply out of ignorance; however, unethical behavior occurs when an individual willfully hides the facts by distorting a table or chart or by failing to report pertinent findings.

PROBLEMS

2.38 (Student Project) Bring to class a chart from a newspaper or magazine that you believe to be a poorly drawn representation of a continuous variable. Be prepared to submit the chart to the instructor with comments about why you feel that it is inappropriate. Also, be prepared to present and comment on this in class.

2.39 (Student Project) Bring to class a chart from a newspaper or magazine that you believe to be a poorly drawn representation of some categorical variable. Be prepared to submit the chart to the instructor with comments about why you feel that it is inappropriate.

Also, be prepared to present this and to comment on it in class.

2.40 (Student Project) Bring to class a chart from a newspaper or magazine that you believe to contain too much "chartjunk" that clouds the message given by the data. Be prepared to submit the chart to the instructor with comments about why you feel that it is inappropriate. Also, be prepared to present and comment on this in class. Using the data presented, prepare a graphical presentation that you feel presents the data in a clear, a fair, or more efficient manner.

KEY TERMS

annotation symbol   46
bar charts   72
cause-and-effect diagram   49
chartjunk   82
checksheets   69
class boundaries   58
class groupings   57
class intervals   58
class midpoints   59

concentration diagram   70
contingency table   78
cross-tabulation table   78
cumulative percentage distribution   61
cumulative percentage polygon   65
data-ink ratio   83
decision symbol   46
fishbone diagram   49
flow arrows   46

CHAPTER REVIEW *Checking Your Understanding*

2.41 Why is the process-flow diagram useful in understanding a process?

2.42 Why is the fishbone diagram useful in process improvement?

2.43 When data have been collected over time, why is it important to first create a time-order plot?

2.44 Under what circumstances would you prefer to use a Pareto diagram as opposed to a pie chart? When might the pie chart be preferable?

2.45 How do histograms and polygons differ with respect to their construction and use?

2.46 Why is a concentration diagram useful as a type of spatial checksheet?

2.47 Under what circumstances should you use a bar chart?

2.48 Under what circumstances should you use a pie chart?

2.49 Under what circumstances should you use a Pareto diagram?

2.50 What types of percentage breakdowns are useful when examining a cross-classification table?

2.51 How does the bar chart differ from the side-by-side bar chart?

Chapter Review Problems

2.52 An experiment was conducted to assess the effect of using magnets at the filler point in the manufacture of coffee filter packs. The table below presents the weights of filter packs in grams. Thirty packs produced with magnets are to be compared to 45 packs produced without magnets.

With Magnets

| 20.1 | 20.1 | 19.6 | 19.5 | 19.4 | 20.4 | 19.6 | 13.5 | 19.7 | 20.6 | 20.2 | 20.4 | 19.9 | 20.4 | 20.1 |
| 19.7 | 19.2 | 19.3 | 19.5 | 19.1 | 20.4 | 20.6 | 20.6 | 20.1 | 20.2 | 20.0 | 19.8 | 20.8 | 19.6 | 19.3 |

Without Magnets

21.4	20.5	20.2	20.6	21.4	20.1	19.9	19.7	21.2	20.7	20.9	20.2	20.1	20.7	20.4
21.0	20.5	20.0	20.6	20.8	19.5	19.7	20.0	20.4	20.2	20.5	20.4	21.3	20.4	20.2
20.5	20.7	19.8	20.7	20.2	20.0	20.5	20.6	20.6	19.9	20.0	20.2	20.6	19.9	20.4

MAGNETS

(a) Construct a frequency distribution and a relative frequency distribution (or a percentage distribution) for weights of coffee filter packs in the *with magnets* group and in the *without magnets* group.

(b) Compare the frequency distributions and relative frequency distributions obtained for the *with magnets* group and for the *without magnets* group. What conclusions do you draw from these analyses?

(c) Compare the relative frequency distributions with the corresponding percentage distributions for these groups. Do you have a preference as to the type of distribution that is best for these data?

(d) Construct a histogram for the *with magnets* group, and for the *without magnets* group.

(e) Compare the results you obtained in (d) for the two groups. What conclusions can you draw from these analyses?

(f) Plot cumulative percentage polygons for the two groups. What conclusions can you draw from these analyses?

2.53 The following data represent the amount of soft drink filled in a subgroup of 50 consecutive two-liter bottles. The results (in liters), listed horizontally in the order of being filled, were as follows:

2.109	2.086	2.066	2.075	2.065
2.057	2.052	2.044	2.036	2.038
2.031	2.029	2.025	2.029	2.023
2.020	2.015	2.014	2.013	2.014
2.012	2.012	2.012	2.010	2.005
2.003	1.999	1.996	1.997	1.992
1.994	1.986	1.984	1.981	1.973
1.975	1.971	1.969	1.966	1.967
1.963	1.957	1.951	1.951	1.947
1.941	1.941	1.938	1.908	1.894

DRINK

(a) Construct a frequency distribution and a percentage distribution.

(b) Plot a frequency histogram.

(c) Set up a run chart of the amount of fill.

(d) From the chart developed in (c), what conclusions can you reach about the process of filling two-liter bottles of soft drink?

(e) In light of the conclusions reached in (d), what can you state about the use of the histogram developed in (b)?

2.54 The following data indicate fat and cholesterol information concerning popular protein foods (fresh red meats, poultry, and fish).

Food	Calories	Protein (g)	Fat (g)	% Calories from Saturated Fat	Cholesterol (mg)
Beef, ground, extra lean	250	25	58	23	82
Beef, ground, regular	287	23	66	26	87
Beef, round	184	28	24	12	82
Brisket	263	28	54	21	91
Flank steak	244	28	51	22	71
Lamb leg roast	191	28	38	16	89
Lamb loin chop, broiled	215	30	42	17	94
Liver, fried	217	27	36	12	482
Pork loin roast	240	27	52	18	90
Sirloin	208	30	37	15	89
Spareribs	397	29	67	27	121
Veal cutlet, fried	183	33	42	20	127
Veal rib roast	175	26	37	15	131
Chicken, with skin, roasted	239	27	51	14	88

(Continued)

Food	Calories	Protein (g)	Fat (g)	% Calories from Saturated Fat	Cholesterol (mg)
Chicken, no skin, roast	190	29	37	10	89
Turkey, light meat, no skin	157	30	18	6	69
Clams	98	16	6	0	39
Cod	98	22	8	1	74
Flounder	99	21	12	2	54
Mackerel	199	27	77	20	100
Ocean perch	110	23	13	3	53
Salmon	182	27	24	5	93
Scallops	112	23	8	1	56
Shrimp	116	24	15	2	156
Tuna	181	32	41	10	48

PROTEIN

Source: United States Department of Agriculture.

For the data relating to the number of calories and the cholesterol for the popular protein foods,

(a) construct the stem-and-leaf display;
(b) construct the frequency distribution and the percentage distribution;
(c) plot the percentage histogram;
(d) plot the percentage polygon;
(e) form the cumulative percentage distribution;
(f) plot the cumulative percentage polygon.
(g) What conclusions can you draw from these analyses?

2.55 A bottling company maintains records concerning the number of unacceptable bottles of soft drink obtained from the filling and capping machines. Data for one week are available that indicate the reasons for the nonconformances. The results are as follows:

Reason for Nonconformance	Frequency
Broken bottle	47
Cracked bottles	29
Dirty bottles	84
Foreign matter in bottles	32
Improper filling height	146
Missing caps	17
Unsealed caps	105

(a) Construct a bar chart of the reasons for nonconforming bottles.
(b) Construct a Pareto diagram of the reasons for nonconforming bottles.
(c) Construct a pie chart of the reasons for nonconforming bottles.
(d) Explain how a concentration diagram might be useful in reducing the number of nonconforming bottles.
(e) Explain why you might prefer to use a Pareto diagram rather than a pie chart for these data.

2.56 A consultant for a water district studied daily water usage in a sample of single-family homes in a suburban area for a one-week period during a recent summer. Average daily water usage for various purposes was as follows:

Reason for Water Usage	Gallons per Day
Bathing/showering	117.3
Car washing	10.6
Cooking	3.8
Dish washing	14.8
Drinking	8.7
Laundering	26.1
Lawn watering	123.4
Shrub watering	36.9
Swimming pool usage	27.4

(a) Construct a bar chart for water usage.
(b) Construct a Pareto diagram for water usage.
(c) Construct a pie chart for water usage.
(d) Explain why you might prefer to use a Pareto diagram rather than a pie chart for these data.
(e) What other information about lawn watering (the largest usage category) would be useful in developing a strategy for water conservation?
(f) If the water district wanted to develop a water reduction plan, which reasons for water usage should be focused on?

2.57 In a recent year, municipal sewage treatment plants in the United States discharged nearly 33 billion gallons of effluent (liquids) and sludge (semisolids) each day. The percentage of waste treated by each of several methods was as follows:

Type of Sewage Treatment	Percentage
Cleaned and recycled for agricultural and ground water recharge	1.5
Primary Treatment: removes 30% of oxygen-demanding organisms and 60% of solids	19.2
Secondary Treatment: removes 85% of contaminants and solids	40.5
Tertiary Treatment: removes over 95% of contaminants and solids	38.7

(a) Construct a bar chart of the type of sewage treatment received.
(b) Construct a Pareto diagram of the type of sewage treatment received.
(c) Construct a pie chart of the type of sewage treatment received.
(d) Which chart can you interpret most quickly and accurately? Why?
(e) What conclusions can you reach concerning the type of sewage treatment received?

2.58 The following table represents the sources of toxic materials released into the air, and percentage emitted by each source, in the United States in a recent year.

Source of Toxic Material	Percentage
Asbestos demolition	4
Gases given off during manufacture of formaldehyde	5

(Continued)

Source of Toxic Material	Percentage
Gasoline marketing	3
Hazardous waste treatment, storage, and disposal	5
Motor vehicles	58
Solvent use/degreasing	1
Wood smoke	4
Other due to cars, homes, and businesses	2
Large industrial sources:	
Chemical users/producers	2
Coal and oil combustion	1
Electroplating	6
Gases given off during manufacture of formaldehyde	2
Heating/refrigeration systems	3
Iron and steel	1
Other from large industrial sources	6

Note: Percentage might not add to 100, because of rounding.

(a) Construct a bar chart of the sources of toxic material released into the air.
(b) Construct a Pareto diagram of the sources of toxic material released into the air.
(c) Construct a pie chart of the sources of toxic material released into the air.
(d) Which chart can you interpret most quickly and accurately? Why?
(e) What conclusions can you reach about the release of toxic material into the air?

2.59 The table below presents the waste profile in percentages, for Los Angeles, California in a recent year.

Sorting Category	Percentage
Newspaper	7.8
Corrugated	7.8
Mixed Paper	3.6
Plastic	4.6
Yard Waste	24.3
Glass	6.5
Ferrous	5.9
Nonferrous	1.9
Textiles	4.1
Organic	5.7
Inorganic	11.4
Wood	14.6
Leather and Rubber	1.8

(a) Construct a bar chart of the sources of municipal waste.
(b) Construct a Pareto diagram of the sources of municipal waste.
(c) Construct a pie chart of the sources of municipal waste.
(d) Which chart can you interpret most quickly and accurately? Why?
(e) What conclusions can you reach about the waste profile of Los Angeles?

2.60 Polyester mortar uses unsaturated polyester resins based on recycled polyethylene terephthalate (PET) plastic waste and sand and fly-ash fillers. The table on page 91 presents unsaturated polyester resin formulation.

Components	Percent by Weight
Recycled PET	22.0
Diethylene glycol	19.0
Maleic anhydride	17.0
Phthalic anhydride	9.0
Styrene	33.0

(a) Construct a bar chart of the components of unsaturated polyester resin formulation.
(b) Construct a Pareto diagram of the components of unsaturated polyester resin formulation.
(c) Construct a pie chart of the components of unsaturated polyester resin formulation.
(d) Which chart can you interpret most quickly and accurately? Why?
    The table below presents the major trace components of fly ash and the concentration of each component, reported in mg/L.

Components	Concentration
Sulfate	330.00
Calcium	197.00
Aluminum	13.10
Sodium	7.30
Boron	6.73
Potassium	4.80
Strontium	2.51
Chloride	2.00
Fluoride	2.00
Barium	0.30
Molybdenum	0.30
Lithium	0.23
Vanadium	0.21
Chromium	0.13

Source: Rebeiz, K. S., J. W. Rosett, and A. P. Craft; Strength Properties of Polyester Mortar Using PET and Fly Ash Wastes; *Journal of Energy Engineering,* April 1996, 10–19.

(e) Construct a bar chart of the major trace components of fly ash.
(f) Construct a Pareto diagram of the major trace components of fly ash.
(g) Construct a pie chart of the major trace components of fly ash.
(h) Which chart can you interpret most quickly and accurately? Why?

2.61 A utility company that provides natural gas to consumers in four counties in a state in the northeastern United States monitors the number of leak repairs in their gas distribution system. The tables below present the number of leaks caused by broken cast-iron pipes, cast-iron-pipe joint leaks, leaks due to corroded steel pipes, and other causes, for the month of December in three years, for each of the areas served.

	County A			
Year	Cast-Iron Pipe Break	Cast-Iron Joint Break	Corroded Steel	Other
1	1	44	146	21
2	2	42	120	23
3	5	139	133	43

(*Continued*)

Year	Cast-Iron Pipe Break	Cast-Iron Joint Break	Corroded Steel	Other
1	0	172	0	50
2	4	257	6	55
3	9	696	25	89

County B

Year	Cast-Iron Pipe Break	Cast-Iron Joint Break	Corroded Steel	Other
1	7	190	9	39
2	5	230	13	17
3	20	169	19	25

County C

Year	Cast-Iron Pipe Break	Cast-Iron Joint Break	Corroded Steel	Other
1	2	59	77	56
2	1	31	71	35
3	3	60	102	36

County D

For each of the four counties,
(a) construct a table of row percentages;
(b) construct a table of column percentages;
(c) construct a table of total percentages.
(d) Which type of percentage (row, column, or total) do you think is most informative for these data? Explain.
(e) What conclusions concerning the pattern of leaks in each county can you draw?

2.62 A study of superemitting vehicles (defined as vehicles whose emissions are several times California certification standards) reports the distribution of smog check failure type of 296 superemitters detected during confirmatory smog check inspections at baseline at the California Air Resources Board. The table below presents these results.

Failure Type	Percent of Vehicles
Visual, Functional, & Emissions	36
Visual & Emissions	10
Functional & Emissions	20
Emissions	13
Visual & Functional	13
Visual	2
Functional	6

Source: Rajan, S. C.; Diagnosis and Repair of Excessively Emitting Vehicles; *Journal of Air & Waste Management Association,* 46, October, 1996, 940–951.

(a) Construct a bar chart of the types of failures.
(b) Construct a Pareto diagram of the types of failures.
(c) Construct a pie chart of the types of failures.
(d) Which chart can you interpret most quickly and accurately? Why?
(e) What conclusions can you reach about the types of failures?

2.63 Suppose that you wish to study characteristics of 1996 automobiles in terms of the following variables: miles per gallon, fuel tank capacity, length, width, weight, wheel base, turning circle requirement, luggage capacity, height, front leg room, and front head room. For each of these variables, **AUTO96**

(a) construct the stem-and-leaf display;

(b) construct the frequency distribution and the percentage distribution;

(c) plot the percentage histogram;

(d) plot the percentage polygon;

(e) form the cumulative percentage distribution;

(f) plot the cumulative percentage polygon.

(g) What conclusions can you draw concerning the 1996 automobiles?

(h) Suppose that you wanted to compare front-wheel-drive cars with rear-wheel-drive cars. Do (a)–(g) for each of these groups. What conclusions can you reach concerning differences between front-wheel-drive cars and rear-wheel-drive cars?

(i) Form a contingency table cross-classifying type of drive (front versus rear) with type of gasoline.

(j) Plot a side-by-side bar chart of type of drive (front versus rear) with type of gasoline.

(k) Based on the results of (i) and (j), does there appear to be a relationship between type of drive (front versus rear) and type of gasoline?

2.64 In the *Using Statistics* example discussed in this chapter, the length of male Dover sole was compared to the length of female Dover sole. That analysis is to be extended by comparing these two groups in terms of body depth, body width, and body weight. For each group, **FISH**

(a) construct the stem-and-leaf display;

(b) construct the frequency distribution and the percentage distribution;

(c) plot the percentage histogram;

(d) plot the percentage polygon;

(e) form the cumulative percentage distribution;

(f) plot the cumulative percentage polygon.

(g) What conclusions can you draw concerning the differences between male and female Dover sole?

(h) Suppose that you wanted to compare Dover sole caught in shallow water and in deep water. Do (a)–(g) for each of these groups. What conclusions can you reach concerning differences between Dover sole caught in shallow water and in deep water?

WHITNEY GOURMET CAT FOOD COMPANY CASE

Phase 1

One of the concerns of the production team relates to the weight of the cans of cat food. Research indicates that there will be increasing competition in the gourmet cat food market as larger companies begin to attack the segment of the market that smaller companies, such as Whitney, have gained in the past several years. There is also evidence that consumers seem to make purchasing decisions on the basis of price, quality, and consistency of the product. One of the aspects of consistency appears to be the perception of the fill level of the can when it is opened. This is primarily a function of the amount of food that the extruding machine places in the can, and it is measured by the weight of the filled can. Legal requirements for a can labeled as 3 ounces allow for a fill of no less than 2.95 ounces, and a fill of more than 3.10 ounces can result in overpacking of the can and in spillage when the can is opened.

Each week, 100 cans of each of the two products, kidney and shrimp, are randomly selected for evaluation by the State Department of Weights and Measures. The company traditionally has selected 50 cans of each type from each of the two shifts of workers. The results for the latest week are summarized in Table WG2.1 on page 94.

TABLE WG2.1

WEIGHTS OF A SAMPLE OF CANS OF CAT FOOD
(IN OUNCES)

Kidney

Shift 1

3.0298	2.9912	2.9867	3.0558	3.0220	2.9708	2.9989	3.0120	3.0147	3.0057
3.0064	3.0118	3.0022	2.9882	3.0230	3.0159	3.0259	3.0054	3.0108	2.9930
3.0418	3.0353	3.0099	3.0398	3.0193	3.0094	3.0019	3.0322	3.0277	2.9953
3.0199	3.0256	2.9956	2.9940	2.9929	3.0127	3.0197	2.9911	2.9974	3.0196
3.0057	3.0514	3.0233	3.0262	3.0264	2.9920	3.0393	3.0075	2.9968	2.9914

Shift 2

3.0457	3.0620	2.9888	3.0665	3.0156	3.0385	3.0458	3.0778	3.0652	3.0038
3.0160	3.0175	3.1002	3.0335	3.0535	3.0469	3.0586	3.0380	3.0378	3.0328
2.9792	3.0468	3.0396	3.0460	3.0590	3.0608	3.0180	3.0174	3.0231	3.0399
3.0428	3.0556	3.0045	3.0475	3.0280	3.0667	3.0308	3.0732	3.0497	3.0121
3.0690	3.0175	3.0353	3.0176	3.0530	3.0641	3.0628	3.0431	3.0283	3.0412

Shrimp

Shift 1

3.0189	2.9663	3.0120	2.9931	3.0394	3.0268	2.9932	2.9608	3.0258	3.0409
2.9900	3.0189	3.0282	3.0369	2.9816	3.0395	2.9723	2.9970	3.0826	3.0070
2.9571	2.9745	3.0167	3.0099	3.0386	2.9338	3.0053	3.0359	2.9682	3.0023
3.0447	3.0799	2.9774	2.9998	3.0147	3.0430	2.9918	3.0057	2.9861	2.9851
2.9970	2.9645	3.0336	3.0221	2.9234	3.0345	3.0509	2.9809	3.0345	2.9641

Shift 2

2.9800	3.0092	2.9781	3.0547	3.0384	3.0193	3.0718	2.9220	3.0487	3.0228
2.9999	3.0438	3.0122	3.0934	2.9865	3.0171	3.0315	3.0086	2.9743	3.0403
3.0186	2.9799	3.0264	3.0129	3.0060	3.0075	2.9357	3.0260	3.0409	2.9782
3.0207	3.0204	3.0119	3.0495	3.0624	3.0333	3.0329	3.0212	2.9497	2.9710
3.0743	3.0474	3.0878	3.0346	2.9864	2.9916	3.0696	2.9933	3.0224	2.9840

 WG21

Exercises

WG2.1 (a) Set up all appropriate tables and charts for the weight of canned kidney and canned shrimp.

(b) Write a report to management that summarizes the results obtained from the tables and charts developed in (a).

Phase 2

Once the team focusing on the nonconforming cans of cat food realized that different inspectors were operationally defining nonconformance in ways that were not consistent with each other or with the criteria used by the production manager, additional training had to be provided to develop operational definitions that were understood, and could be followed, by all the inspectors. Data collected for the first month after the training was conducted indicated the percentages of the nonconformances that were due to the various reasons. The results are summarized in Table WG2.2.

Exercises

WG2.2 (a) Construct the graphical presentation that you feel is the most useful in gaining insights from the data of Table WG2.2.

TABLE WG2.2	

SUMMARY TABLE OF REASONS FOR NONCONFORMANCE IN CANNED CAT FOOD

Reason	Percentage of Nonconformances
Blemish on top of can	16
Crack in side of can	9
Crack in top of can	35
Improper pull tab location	14
Pull tab missing	15
Surface defect on side of can	8
Others	3

(b) Based on the graph that was constructed in (a), write a report to management concerning the percentage of different types of nonconformances in canned cat food.

WG2.3 At this stage of the analysis, what other information concerning the different types of nonconformances would be useful to obtain?

STOP

Do Not Continue Until the Phase 2 Exercises Have Been Completed

Phase 3

As the team studying the nonconforming cans examined the data of Table WG2.2, they realized that the data did not allow them to compare the types of nonconformances pro-duced by each of the two shifts. The group decided that it would be useful to obtain separate data concerning nonconformances for each of the two shifts. These data are summarized in Table WG2.3.

Exercises

WG2.4 (a) Construct the graphical presentation that you feel is the most useful in gaining insights from the data of Table WG2.3.

(b) Based on the graph that was constructed in (a), write a report to management concerning the percentages of different types of nonconformances in canned cat food for the two shifts.

WG2.5 At this stage of the analysis, what other information concerning the different types of nonconformances for the two shifts would be useful to obtain?

TABLE WG2.3		

SUMMARY TABLE OF REASONS FOR NONCONFORMANCE IN CANNED CAT FOOD FOR THE TWO SHIFTS

Reason	Shift 1 Percentage of Nonconformances	Shift 2 Percentage of Nonconformances
Blemish on top of can	14	18
Crack in side of can	11	6
Crack in top of can	42	30
Improper pull tab location	10	16
Pull tab missing	8	20
Surface defect on side of can	10	7
Others	5	3

REFERENCES

1. Beniger, J. M. and D. L. Robyn; "Quantitative Graphics in Statistics," *The American Statistician,* 32, (1978), 1–11
2. Bisgaard, S.; "Quality Quandaries: The Importance of Graphics in Problem Solving and Detective Work," *Quality Engineering,* Vol. 9, (1996), 157–162
3. Chambers, J. M., W. S. Cleveland, B. Kleiner, and P. Tukey; *Graphical Methods for Data Analysis;* Boston: Duxbury Press, 1983
4. Cleveland, W. S.; "Graphs in Scientific Publications," *The American Statistician,* 38, (1984), 261–269
5. Cleveland, W. S. and R. McGill; "Graphical Perception: Theory, Experimentation, and Application to the Development of Graphical Methods," *Journal of the American Statistical Association,* 79 (1984), 531–554
6. Croxton, F., D. Cowden, and S. Klein; *Applied General Statistics*, 3d ed.; Englewood Cliffs, NJ: Prentice–Hall, 1967
7. Feinberg, S. E.; "Graphical Methods in Statistics," *The American Statistician,* 33 (1979), 165–178
8. Gunter, B.; "Good Graphs, Bad Graphs, and Ducks," *Quality Progress,* July 1988, 86–87
9. Huff, D.; *How to Lie With Statistics;* New York: W. W. Norton, 1954
10. Ishikawa, K.; *What Is Total Quality Control? The Japanese Way* (trans. by D. J. Lu); Englewood Cliffs, NJ: Prentice–Hall, 1985
11. Joiner, B. J.; "Lurking variables," *The American Statistician,* 35 (1981), 227–233
12. *Microsoft Excel 2000;* Redmond, WA: Microsoft Press, 1999
13. MINITAB *For Windows Version 12;* State College, PA: MINITAB, Inc., 1998
14. Schleusener, R.; "Concentration Diagrams," *American Society for Quality Control Statistics Division Newsletter*, 13 (Winter 1993), 5–6
15. Sink, D. S.; "Using the Nominal Group Technique Effectively," *National Productivity Review*, Spring 1983, 174–184
16. Tufte, E. R.; *The Visual Display of Quantitative Information;* Cheshire, CT: Graphics Press, 1983
17. Tufte, E. R.; *Envisioning Information;* Cheshire, CT: Graphics Press, 1990
18. Tufte, E. R.; *Visual Explanations;* Cheshire, CT: Graphics Press, 1997
19. Tukey, J.; *Exploratory Data Analysis;* Reading, MA: Addison–Wesley, 1977

APPENDIX 2.1   *Using Microsoft Excel for Tables and Charts*

In this chapter, we have developed numerous tables and charts. Each of these tables and charts can be obtained by using Microsoft Excel.

Ordering a Set of Data

The Data | Sort command is used in Microsoft Excel to place a set of data in order from lowest to highest (or vice-versa). For example, to order the Dover sole from lowest body length to highest body length, open the **FISH.XLS** workbook. Select **Data | Sort.** In the Sort By list box, select **Length.** Select the **Ascending** button to obtain data ordered from lowest to highest. Select the **Header Row** option button. Click the **OK** button. You will observe that the body lengths are sorted in ascending order.

Obtaining a Stem-and-Leaf Display

The PHStat add-in should be used for a stem-and-leaf display. To obtain the stem-and-leaf display of the body length of the male Dover sole, sort the data by gender, so that the females are in rows 2–43, and the males are in rows 44–101. Select **PHStat | Stem-and-Leaf**

Display. Enter **A44:A101** in the cell range edit box, enter **10** in the set stem unit as edit box, and click the **OK** button.

Using the Data Analysis Tool to Obtain Frequency Distributions, Cumulative Frequency Distributions, and Histograms

The Data Analysis tool is an add-in supplied by Microsoft Excel that is used to perform many of the statistical procedures that we will discuss in the text. The Histogram option of the Data Analysis tool is used to obtain both a frequency distribution and charts such as a histogram and cumulative percentage polygon. To use the Histogram option of the Data Analysis tool, the upper class boundaries of the class intervals must be entered on the sheet that contains the data to be analyzed. Open the **FISH.XLS** workbook, and make the Data Sheet active by clicking on the Data Sheet tab. If you have not already done so, sort the data so that the 42 female Dover sole are in rows 2–43 and the 58 male Dover sole are in rows 44–101. Enter the specified upper class limits of 289.99, 309.99, 329.99, 349.99, 369.99, 389.99, 409.99, 429.99, 449.99, and 469.99 in cells G2:G11.

To create the histogram and cumulative percentage polygon for the body length of the 58 male Dover sole, select **Tools | Data Analysis.** Select **Histogram** from the Analysis Tools list box that appears. Click the **OK** button to display the Histogram dialog box. If Data Analysis is not a choice on your Tools menu, the Data Analysis component of Excel has not been installed. Review Appendix A1.2 before continuing. In the Input Range edit box, enter **Data!A44:A101.** Enter **Data! G2:G11** in the Bin Range edit box. Select the **New Worksheet Ply** button and enter **Histogram** as the name of the new sheet. Select the **Cumulative Percentages** and **Chart Output** check boxes. Leave the Pareto check box unselected. Click the **OK** button.

Excel will generate both a frequency distribution and a cumulative percentage distribution and will superimpose the cumulative percentage polygon onto the histogram. Observe that the frequencies and cumulative percentages provided refer to the upper boundaries of the class. This means that 12.07% of the male Dover sole have body lengths less than 350 millimeters, 17.14% have body lengths less than 370, and so on. Observe also that a different vertical axis is included for each chart, because the two graphs are superimposed. The vertical axis on the left side of the chart provides frequencies for the histogram, while the vertical axis on the right provides percentages for the cumulative percentage polygon.

Observe that this chart contains four mistakes: the X axis labels cannot be seen clearly; there are gaps between the bars that correspond to the class intervals; there is an additional class, labeled *More* by Excel, that has been incorrectly plotted; and the secondary Y axis scale exceeds 100%.

To expand the chart to display the X axis labels clearly, select a cell in the Histogram sheet that is outside the chart box. Then click in the white area inside the chart box. Move the mouse pointer directly over the lower left corner of the chart box until the mouse pointer changes to a small double-sided arrow. With the pointer still a double-sided arrow, drag the mouse pointer toward cell D15. As you drag the mouse pointer it changes to a simple plus sign and the area of the chart expands. When the mouse pointer is over cell D15, release the mouse button. The chart is now enlarged, and X axis labels appear.

To delete the additional class, click the Histogram sheet tab. Select the cell range **A12:C12** (containing the *More* row of the frequency distribution table). Select **Edit | Delete**. In the Delete dialog box, select the **Shift Cells up** option button. Click the **OK** button.

To eliminate the gaps between bars, right-click inside one of the bars to select the plotted frequencies. Right-click over the bar to display a shortcut menu. Select **Format Data Series** from this menu. In the Format Data Series dialog box, click the **Options** tab. Change the value in the Gap Width edit box to **0**. Click the **OK** button. The bars are now plotted without gaps.

To correct the secondary Y-axis scale, right-click the secondary axis on the right side of the chart. Select **Format Axis** from the shortcut menu that appears. In the Format Axis dialog box, click the **Scale** tab. Change the value in the Maximum edit box to **1**. Click the **OK** button. Further refinement of the chart is possible by selecting and then editing the title and axis labels.

Using the Chart Wizard to Obtain Polygons and Histograms

The Microsoft Excel Chart Wizard is a series of four dialog boxes, displayed one at a time, that allow you to create a variety of charts for both numerical and categorical variables. The first dialog box asks you to select the type of chart desired. The second dialog box asks you to specify the orientation of your data and the cell ranges containing the data and data labels for the chart. The third dialog box gives you control over most of the formatting options, including the content and placement of titles and a legend. The fourth dialog box allows you to choose between placing a chart on its own (new) chart sheet or in a pre-existing worksheet. (Charts created in this text are always placed on new sheets.) Charts created by the Chart Wizard can be refined by further editing.

To use the Chart Wizard to generate a frequency polygon for the body length of 58 male Dover sole, open the **FISH.XLS** workbook that was used to generate the histogram by using the Data Analysis Tool. Click the **Histogram** sheet tab, because we need to use the bins, and put either the frequency or cumulative percentage in each of the bins, as follows:

To obtain the frequency polygon from the Chart Wizard, start the Chart Wizard by selecting the command **Insert | Chart**. In the first dialog box, select the **Standard Types** tab and then select **Line** from the Chart type: list box. Note that the choices under the Chart sub type: heading change as a selection from the Chart type: list is made and that a description of the currently selected sub-type appears below the choices. Select the first choice in the second row of sub-types, the choice described as "Line with markers displayed at each data value." Click the **Next** button to continue to the second dialog box.

In the second dialog box, select the **Data Range** tab, enter **Histogram!B2:B11** in the Data range: edit box, and select the **Columns** option button in the Series in: group. Select the **Series** tab. In the Category (X) axis labels: edit box enter = **Histogram!A2:A11**. Note that this entry must include the equals sign (=). Click the **Next** button.

In the third dialog box, select the **Titles** tab. Enter Body Length of Male Dover Sole in the Chart Title: edit box, enter Millimeters in the Category (X) axis: edit box, and enter **Frequency** in the Value (Y) axis: edit box. Select the **Axes** tab. Select both the (X) axis and the (Y) axis check boxes. Select the Automatic option under the (X) axis check box. Select the **Gridlines** tab. Deselect all gridlines. Select the **Legend** tab. Deselect the **Show Legend** check box. Select the **Data Labels** tab. Select the **None** option button under the Data labels heading. Select the **Data Table** tab. Deselect the **Show data table** check box. Click the **Next** button.

In the fourth dialog box, select the **As new sheet**: option button and enter **Frequency** Polygon in the edit box to the right of the option button. Click the **Finish** button to create the chart. If we examine this frequency polygon, we see that the category markings on the X-axis refer to the upper limits of the classes, not the class midpoints.

In addition, if we wanted to obtain a percentage polygon or a cumulative percentage polygon, we would use the column of percentages or cumulative percentages instead of the column of frequencies when we define the range for the data. To obtain a percentage polygon, we need to calculate percentages. On the Histogram sheet, with the cursor in column C, select **Insert | Column** to insert a new column. In cell B13, enter the formula **=SUM(B2:B11)** to obtain the total frequency. To calculate the percentages, first enter **=B2/$B$13** in cell C2. In this formula, note that the address in the denominator has been entered as an *absolute address*. This is an address that will not be adjusted by Excel during the copying operation. We use this here because we want to divide each frequency by the same total frequency. Copy cell C2 down the column through cell C11. Change the values in column C to percentage by clicking the % button. Click the **Increase decimal** button twice to obtain two-decimal-place accuracy.

The Chart Wizard can also be used to superimpose two polygons on the same graph, as was done in Figure 2.11 on page 64 for the percentage polygons and in Figure 2.12 on page 66 for the cumulative percentage polygons for the male and female Dover sole. To do so, first we must use the Data Analysis Tool for the 42 female Dover sole in a manner similar to how the histogram, frequency distribution, and cumulative frequencies were obtained on the Histogram sheet for the male Dover sole. On the Data sheet, the body lengths for the females should already be sorted in cells A2:A43. Use the bin values 289.99, 309.99, 329.99, 349.99, 369.99, 389.99, 409.99, 429.99, 449.99, and 469.99 in cells G2:G11. Follow the same instructions for these female Dover sole as were used for the males, naming the New Worksheet Ply HistogramF.

On the HistogramF sheet, obtain percentages for the female Dover sole in a manner similar to that which was used for the male Dover sole on the Histogram sheet. Copy the percentages and cumulative percentages to columns D and E of the Histogram sheet.

To obtain the two percentage polygons from the Chart Wizard, start the Chart Wizard by selecting the command **Insert | Chart.** In the first dialog box, select the **Custom Types** tab and then select **Line on Two Axes** from the Chart type: list box. Click the **Next** button to continue to the second dialog box.

In the second dialog box, select the **Data Range** tab and enter **Histogram!C2:C11, Histogram!E2:E11** in the Data range: edit box. Note that, because the ranges were not located in adjacent columns, *their cell ranges are separated by a comma.* Select the **Columns** option button in the Series in: group. Continue by selecting the **Series** tab. In the Category (X) axis labels: edit box, enter **=Histogram!A2:A11**. Note that this entry must include the equals sign (=).Click on **Series 1** in the Series edit box, and enter **Female** in the Name: edit box. Click on **Series 2** in the Series edit box, and enter **Male** in the Name: edit box. Click the **Next** button.

In the third dialog box, select the **Titles** tab. Enter **Body Length of Dover Sole** in the Chart Title: edit box, enter **Millimeters** in the Category (X) axis: edit box, and enter **Percent** in the Value (Y) axis: edit box. Select the **Axes** tab. Select the (X) axis and (Y) axis check boxes for Primary axis, but deselect the secondary X axis. Select the **Gridlines** tab. Deselect all the choices. Select the **Legend** tab. Select the **Show legend** check box. Select the **Data labels** tab. Select the **None** option button under the Data labels heading. Select the **Data Table** tab. Deselect the Show data table check box. Click the **Next** button.

In the fourth dialog box, select the **As new sheet:** option button, and enter **Percentage Polygons** in the edit box to the right of the option button. Click the **Finish** button to create the chart. A chart similar to Figure 2.12 can be obtained by using the two sets of cumulative percentages. If the scale for the vertical axis on the right side of the graph has a different maximum value, right-click on this vertical axis. Select **Format Axis.** Select the **Scale** tab and change the maximum value to the same maximum value as the vertical axis on the left side of the graph.

Using the Chart Wizard to Obtain a Run Chart

To use the Chart Wizard to generate a run chart of January temperatures, open the **JANTEMP.XLS** workbook. Click the **Data** sheet tab.

To obtain the run chart from the Chart Wizard, start the Chart Wizard by selecting the command **Insert | Chart.** In the first dialog box, select the **Standard Types** tab and then select **XY (Scatter)** from the Chart type: list box. Select the first choice in the third row of subtypes, the one described as **"Scatter with data points connected by lines."** Click the **Next** button to continue to the second dialog box.

In the second dialog box, select the **Data Range** tab, enter **Data!B1:B32** in the Data range: edit box, and select the **Columns** option button in the Series in: group. Click the **Next** button. (Note: Excel assumes that the first variable in the cell range is to appear on the horizontal axis and the second variable is to appear on the vertical axis, as is the case for the JANTEMP.XLS workbook. To switch this designation, click the Series tab and enter the proper cell ranges in the X-value and Y-value edit boxes.)

In the third dialog box, select the **Titles** tab. Enter **January Temperature** in the Chart Title: edit box, enter day in the Category (X) axis: edit box, and enter **Temperature** in the Value (Y) axis: edit box. Select the **Axes** tab. Select both the (X) axis and (Y) axis check boxes. Select the **Gridlines** tab. Deselect check boxes. Select the **Legend** tab. Deselect the Show legend check box. Select the **Data labels** tab. Select the **None** option button under the Data labels heading. Click the **Next** button.

In the fourth dialog box, select the **As new sheet**: option button, and enter **Run Chart** in the edit box to the right of the option button. Click the **Finish** button to create the chart.

Using the PHStat Add-In to Obtain a One-Way Summary Table, a Bar Chart, a Pie Chart, and a Pareto Diagram

If raw data are available, the PHStat add-in can be used to obtain a summary table, a bar chart, a pie chart, and a Pareto diagram. For example, to obtain these for the male and female Dover sole, open the **FISH.XLS** workbook. Select **PHStat | One-way tables & Charts**. Enter **E1:E101** in the Variable cell range edit box. Select the **First cell contains Label** check box. Select the **Bar Chart**, **Pie chart**, and **Pareto Diagram** check boxes. Click the **OK** button. On separate sheets, the add-in produces a frequency table, a bar chart, a pie chart, and a Pareto diagram.

Using the Chart Wizard to Obtain Bar Charts, Pie Charts, and Pareto Diagrams

If a summary table is already available, such as Table 2.12 on page 70, the Chart Wizard can be used to generate a bar chart, a pie chart, or a Pareto Diagram. To obtain these charts for the data of Table 2.12, open the **TABLE2-12.XLS** workbook, and click on the **Data** sheet tab.

To obtain the bar chart generated in Figure 2.15 on page 73, start the Chart Wizard by selecting the command **Insert | Chart.** In the first dialog box, select the **Standard Types** tab, and then select **Bar** from the Chart type: list box. Select the first choice in the top row of subtypes, the choice described as **"Clustered Bar"**; click the **Next** button to continue to the second dialog box.

In the second dialog box, select the **Data Range** tab, enter **Data!C2:C11** in the Data range: edit box, and select the **Columns** option button in the Series in: group. Continue by selecting the **Series** tab. In the Category (X) axis labels: edit box, enter = **Data!A2:A11**. Note that this entry must include the equals sign (=). Click the **Next** button.

In the third dialog box, select the Titles tab. Enter **Defects in Computer Keyboards** in the Chart Title: edit box, enter **Percentage** in the Category (X) axis: edit box, and enter **Reasons** in the Value (Y) axis: edit box. Select the **Axes** tab. Select both the (X) axis and (Y) axis check boxes. Deselect the **Gridlines** tab. Select the **Legend** tab. Deselect the Show legend check box. Select the **Data labels** tab. Select the **None** option button under the Data labels heading. Select the **Data Table** tab. Deselect the Show data table check box. Click the **Next** button.

In the fourth dialog box, select the **As new sheet:** option button, and enter **Bar** in the edit box to the right of the option button. Click the **Finish** button to create the chart.

To obtain the pie chart generated in Figure 2.16 on page 74, start the Chart Wizard by selecting the command **Insert | Chart.** In the first dialog box, select the **Standard Types** tab, and then select **Pie** from the Chart type: list box. Select the first choice in the top row of subtypes, the choice described as **"Pie"**; click the **Next** button to continue to the second dialog box.

In the second dialog box, select the **Data Range** tab, enter **Data!C2:C11** in the Data range: edit box, and select the **Columns** option button in the Series in: group. Continue by selecting the **Series** tab. In the Category (X) axis labels: edit box, enter = **Data!A2:A11**. Note that this entry must include the equals sign (=). Click the **Next** button.

In the third dialog box, select the **Titles** tab. Enter **Defects in Computer Keyboards** in the Chart Title: edit box. Select the **Legend** tab. Deselect the Show legend check box. Select the **Data labels** tab. Select the **Show labels and percent** option button. Click the **Next** button.

In the fourth dialog box, select the **As new sheet**: option button, and enter **Pie** in the edit box to the right of the option button. Click the **Finish button** to create the chart.

To obtain a Pareto diagram, we need to sort the categories in descending order according to the percentage in each category. Select the range **A2:C11.** Select **Data | Sort.** In the Sort by drop-down list box, select %. Select the **Descending** option botton. Click the **OK** button.

To obtain cumulative frequencies, first enter the label **Cumulative %** in cell D1. Enter **=C2** in cell D2. Enter **= D2 + C3** in cell D3 and copy this down to cell D11.

To use the Chart Wizard, select **Insert | Chart.** In the first dialog box, select the **Custom Types** tab and then select **Line - Column on Two Axes** from the Chart type: list box. Click the **Next** button to continue to the second dialog box.

In the second dialog box, select the **Data Range** tab, and enter **Data! C2:D11** in the Data range: edit box. Select the **Columns** option button in the Series in: group. Continue by selecting the **Series** tab. In the Category (X) axis labels: edit box, enter = **Data!A2:A11.** Click the **Next** button.

In the third dialog box, select the **Titles** tab. Enter **Pareto Diagram** in the Chart Title: edit box, and enter Group in the Category (X) axis: edit box. Select the **Axes** tab. Select the Primary axis Category (X) axis and both of the Value (Y) axis check boxes. Select the **Gridlines** tab. Deselect all the choices. Select the **Legend** tab. Deselect the Show Legend check box. Select the **Data labels** tab. Select the **None** option button under the Data labels heading. Select the **Data Table** tab. Deselect the Show data table check box. Click the **Next** button.

In the fourth dialog box, select the **As new sheet:** option button, and enter **Pareto** in the edit box to the right of the option button. Click the **Finish** button to create the chart. To correct the secondary Y axis scale, right-click the secondary axis on the right side of the chart. Select **Format Axis** from the shortcut menu that appears. In the Format Axis dialog box, click the **Scale** tab. Change the value in the Maximum edit box to **1.**

Using PHStat to Obtain a Two-Way Summary Table and Side-by-Side Bar Chart

If raw data are available, the PHStat add-in can be used to obtain a two-way contingency table and a side-by-side bar chart. For example, to obtain these for the gender and depth at which the fish was caught for the Dover sole, open the **FISH.XLS** workbook. Select **PHStat | Two-Way Tables & Charts.** Enter **E1:E101** in the Row Variable cell range edit box. Enter **F1:F101** in the Column Variable cell range edit box. Select the **First cell in both Ranges contains Label** check box. Select the **Side-by-Side Bar Chart** check box. Click the **OK** button. On separate sheets, the add-in produces a contingency table and a side-by-side bar chart.

APPENDIX 2.2 *Using MINITAB for Tables and Charts*

In this chapter, we have developed a variety of tables and charts for the body length of Dover sole. Many of these tables and charts can be obtained by accessing MINITAB.

Obtaining a Stem-and-Leaf Display

To obtain the stem-and-leaf display of Figure 2.9 on page 57, we need to unstack the data to separate the body length of the 58 males from those of the 42 females. To unstack the Dover sole data, open the **FISH.MTW** file and select **MANIP | Stack | Unstack | Unstack.** In the Unstack dialog box, enter **C1** or **'Length'** in the Unstack the data in edit box. Enter **C7 C8** in the Store Unstacked data in edit box. Enter **C5** or **'Gender'** in the Using Subscripts in: edit box. Click the **OK** button.

The body lengths are now stored in columns C7 (females) and C8 (males). After providing labels for these variables, select **Stat | EDA | Stem-and-Leaf.** In the Stem-and-Leaf dialog box, enter **C8** or **'Length-M'** in the Variables edit box and **10** in the Increment edit box (to have the stems equal to multiples of 10). Click the **OK** button.

Obtaining a Histogram

With the data unstacked (as was the case with the stem-and-leaf display), to obtain the histogram depicted in Figure 2.10 on page 63, select **Graph | Histogram.** In the Graph variables edit box, enter C8 or **'Length-M'.** Click the **Options** button. Under Type of Histogram, click the **Percent** button. Under Type of Interval, click the **Cutpoint** button. Under Definition of Interval, click **Midpoint/cutpoint** positions and enter the values **330 350 370 390 410 430 450 470.** Click the **OK** button to return to the Histogram dialog box. Click the **OK** button to obtain the histogram.

Obtaining a Run Chart

To obtain a run chart as illustrated in Figure 2.7 on page 53, open the file **JANTEMP.MTW.** Select **Graph | Plot.** In the Graph variables edit box, in row 1, enter **C2 Temp** in the Y column and **C1 Day** in the X column. Click the **OK** button.

Obtaining a Bar Chart

To obtain a bar chart for a categorical variable, open the file **FISH.MTW.** Select **Graph | Chart.** In the Graph Variables edit box, select **C5** or **'Gender',** and enter this variable in row 1 in the X column. Click the **OK** button.

Obtaining a Pie Chart

To obtain a pie chart for a categorical variable, open the file **FISH.MTW.** Select **Graph | Pie Chart.** In the Chart data in edit box, select **C5** or **'Gender'.** Enter a title in the Title edit box. Click the **OK** button.

Obtaining a Pareto Diagram

To obtain a Pareto diagram for a categorical variable, open the file **FISH.MTW.** Select **Stat | Quality Tools | Pareto Chart.** In the Chart Defects data in edit box, select **C5** or **'Gender'.** Click the **OK** button.

Obtaining a Contingency Table

To obtain a two-way contingency table, open the **FISH.MTW** file. Select **Stat | Tables | cross Tabulation.** In the Classification Variables edit box, select **C5** or **'Gender'** and **C6** or **'Level'.** In the Display check box, you can select Counts, Row percents, Column percents, and Total percents. Click the **OK** button.

Obtaining a Side-by Side Bar Chart

To obtain a side-by-side bar chart, open the **FISH.MTW** file. Select **Graph | Chart.** Enter **C5** or **'Gender'** in the Graph Variables edit box in row 1 in the X column. In the Data display edit box, be sure that, in row 1, the Display column indicates Bar and the For each column indicates Graph. In the Group variables column, select **C6** or **'Level'.** Click the **Options** button. In the Groups within X edit box, select Cluster and enter **C6** or **'Level'.** Under Order Groups Based on, select the **Total Y to 100% within each X category** check box to obtain percentages for each group. Click the **OK** button to return to the Chart dialog box. Click the **OK** button again to obtain the side-by-side bar chart.

chapter

3

Describing and Summarizing Data

"In God we trust. All others must use data."

W. EDWARDS DEMING

USING STATISTICS

A medical-device manufacturing facility needs to use large amounts of purified water in its production process. Management wishes to compare two water-purification systems with respect to pH, conductivity, total aerobic microbial population, total organic carbon, bacterial endotoxin, and coliform population. The first water-purification system is an ultra-pure water system that uses triple-pass reverse osmosis, a CDI electric deionizer unit, and a heated distribution system. The second water-purification system uses two mixed-bed (cation and anion beds together) deionizers and 0.2-micron filtration.

3.1 INTRODUCTION: WHAT'S AHEAD

In Chapter 2 we focused on data presentation. Although its techniques are extremely useful for providing an overall picture of one or more sets of data, there remains the need for providing concise statistical summary measures for various characteristics of the data being analyzed. In this chapter, therefore, a variety of descriptive summary measures will be developed.

By more formally examining some general properties of data, we will see how we can better summarize, understand, and convey the information contained in a data set. There are four major properties that describe a set of numerical data:

1. central tendency;
2. variability;
3. skewness;
4. kurtosis.

In any analysis and/or interpretation, a variety of descriptive measures representing the properties of central tendency, variability, skewness, and kurtosis can be used to extract and summarize the major features of the set of data. If these

103

measures are computed from a sample of data, they are called **statistics;** if they are computed from an entire population of data, they are called **parameters.** (In an attempt to make clear the distinction between sample statistics and population parameters, we will generally use Roman letters to indicate sample statistics and Greek letters to indicate population parameters.)

In order to introduce the relevant ideas in this chapter, we refer to a set of data presented in Table 3.1. Table 3.1 presents the pH values obtained from samples drawn from the two water-purification systems described in the Using Statistics example.

TABLE 3.1

pH VALUES OF WATER SAMPLED FROM ULTRA-PURE AND DEIONIZING SYSTEMS

Water Sample											
1	2	3	4	5	6	7	8	9	10	11	12
Ultra-Pure											
5.04	5.18	5.32	5.33	5.39	5.09	5.41	5.20	5.31	5.46	4.31	5.40
Deionizing											
5.18	5.49	5.34	5.34	5.19	5.29	5.33	5.45	5.42	5.63	5.55	4.39

 WATER

3.2 MEASURES OF CENTRAL TENDENCY, VARIATION, AND SHAPE

Most sets of data show a distinct tendency to group or cluster about a central point. Thus, for any particular set of data, it is possible to select some typical value or **average** to represent or describe the entire set. Such a descriptive value is referred to as a measure of **central tendency** or **location.**

Five measures of central tendency are described in this section. They are the arithmetic mean, the median, the mode, the midrange, and the midhinge.

The Arithmetic Mean

The **arithmetic mean** (also called the *mean*) is the most commonly used measure of central tendency. It is calculated by summing the observed numerical values of a variable in a set of data and then dividing the total by the number of observations involved.

For a population containing a set of N observations, $X_1, X_2, \ldots, X_N$, the arithmetic mean (represented by the symbol μ, the Greek letter mu) can be written as

$$\mu = \frac{X_1 + X_2 + \cdots + X_N}{N}.$$

To simplify the notation, the term

$$\sum_{i=1}^{N} X_i$$

(meaning the summation of all the X_i values) is used whenever we wish to add together a series of observations—that is,

$$\sum_{i=1}^{N} X_i = X_1 + X_2 + \cdots + X_N.$$

Using this summation notation, the arithmetic mean of the population is more simply expressed as follows:

$$\mu = \frac{\sum\limits_{i=1}^{N} X_i}{N} \tag{3.1}$$

where

μ = population arithmetic mean

N = number of observations or population size

X_i = ith observation of the variable X

$\sum\limits_{i=1}^{N} X_i$ = summation of all X_i values in the population

For a sample containing a set of n observations $X_1, X_2, \ldots, X_n$, the arithmetic mean of a sample (represented by the symbol $\overline{X}$, called X bar) is written as

$$\overline{X} = \frac{X_1 + X_2 + \cdots + X_n}{n}.$$

Using this summation notation, the arithmetic mean of the sample can be more simply expressed as follows:

$$\overline{X} = \frac{\sum\limits_{i=1}^{n} X_i}{n} \tag{3.2}$$

where

$\overline{X}$ = sample arithmetic mean

n = number of observations or sample size

X_i = ith observation of the variable X

$\sum\limits_{i=1}^{n} X_i$ = summation of all X_i values in the sample

For our pH data for the ultra-pure system in Table 3.1,

$$X_1 = 5.04$$
$$X_2 = 5.18$$
$$X_3 = 5.32$$

$$\cdot$$
$$\cdot$$
$$\cdot$$

$$X_{12} = 5.40$$

The arithmetic mean for this data is calculated as

$$\overline{X} = \frac{\sum_{i=1}^{n} X_i}{n} = \frac{5.04 + 5.18 + 5.32 + \cdots + 5.40}{12}$$

$$\overline{X} = \frac{62.44}{12} = 5.2033$$

Note that the mean is computed as 5.20. Although 5.20 is close to one of the observations in this data set, we will frequently find that computed mean values are not equal to any of the original observations. We can observe from the **dot scale** of Figure 3.1 that, for this set of data, five observations are smaller than the mean and seven are greater. In fact, the mean acts as a *balancing point* or fulcrum. The distance between the dot and the mean represents the deviation of an observation from the mean. The sum of the negative deviations from the mean is counterbalanced by the sum of the positive deviations from the mean (see Derivation 3.1).

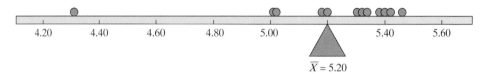

$$\overline{X} = 5.20$$

Figure 3.1   Dot scale representing the pH value of 12 water samples from the ultra-pure system

We can also see that the calculation of the mean is based on all the observations $(X_1, X_2, \ldots, X_n)$ in the set of data. No other commonly used measure of central tendency possesses this characteristic. Because all observations contribute to its computation, the arithmetic mean makes use of all the information available.

COMMENT: WHEN TO USE THE ARITHMETIC MEAN

Because its computation is based on every observation, the arithmetic mean is greatly affected by an extreme value or values, particularly if a small set of data is involved. In such cases, the arithmetic mean may present a distorted representation of what the data are conveying; hence, in some situations, the mean may not be the best measure of location for data sets that contain one or more atypical or extreme observations. For example, if the most alkaline samples of water in our data set had a pH of 13 instead of 5.46, the mean would be 5.83. This measure would not adequately represent the center of the data set.

To further demonstrate the characteristics of the mean, we will consider the data for the deionized system displayed in Table 3.1 on page 104.

The dot scale for the deoinized system is displayed in Figure 3.2.

For the water from the deionizing system,

$$\sum_{i=1}^{n} X_i = 63.60, \text{ and } n = 12;$$

as a result,

$$\overline{X} = \frac{63.60}{12} = 5.3000$$

DERIVATION 3.1   (Optional)

To show that $\sum_{i=1}^{n} (X_i - \overline{X}) = 0$, we have

$$\sum_{i=1}^{n} (X_i - \overline{X}) = \sum_{i=1}^{n} X_i - \sum_{i=1}^{n} \overline{X}$$

Because, for any fixed set of data, $\overline{X}$ can be considered a constant,

$$\sum_{i=1}^{n} \overline{X} = n\overline{X}$$

Therefore,

$$\sum_{i=1}^{n} (X_i - \overline{X}) = \sum_{i=1}^{n} X_i - n\overline{X}$$

However, from Equation (3.2),

$$n\overline{X} = \sum_{i=1}^{n} X_i$$

Therefore,

$$\sum_{i=1}^{n} (X_i - \overline{X}) = \sum_{i=1}^{n} X_i - \sum_{i=1}^{n} X_i$$

so that

$$\sum_{i=1}^{n} (X_i - \overline{X}) = 0$$

$\overline{X} = 5.30$

Figure 3.2   Dot scale representing the pH value of 12 water samples from the deionized system

We see that the mean for deionized water is above the mean for the water from the ultra-pure system. Examination of Figure 3.2 shows that four values are below the mean for the deionized water. This information will be useful to us when we examine the property of symmetry.

The Median

The **median** is the middle value in an ordered sequence of data. If there are no ties, half of the observations will be smaller than the median, and half of the observations will be larger than the median. In addition, the median is *unaffected* by extreme values in a set of data. Thus, whenever an extreme observation is present, it may be more appropriate to use the median rather than the mean to describe a set of data.

To calculate the median from a set of data collected in its raw form, we must first place the data in numerical order. Such an arrangement is called an **ordered array.** We then use the *positioning-point formula*

$$\frac{n + 1}{2}$$

to find the place in the ordered array that corresponds to the median value.

Rule 1   If there are an *odd* number of observations in the data set, the median is represented by the numerical value corresponding to the positioning point, the $(n + 1)/2$ ordered observation.

Rule 2   If there are an *even* number of observations in the data set, then the positioning point lies between the two observations in the middle of the data set. The median is then the *average* of the numerical values corresponding to these two middle observations.

Even-Sized Sample

For the ultra-pure water samples, the raw data were

5.04 5.18 5.32 5.33 5.39 5.09 5.41 5.20 5.31 5.46 4.31 5.40

The ordered array becomes

4.31 5.04 5.09 5.18 5.20 | 5.31 5.32 | 5.33 5.39 5.40 5.41 5.46

Ordered

Observation   1   2   3   4   5 | 6   7 | 8   9   10   11   12

Median = 5.315

For these data, the positioning point is $(n + 1)/2 = (12 + 1)/2 = 6.5$. Therefore, the median is obtained by averaging the sixth and seventh ordered observations:

$$\frac{5.31 + 5.32}{2} = 5.315$$

As can be seen from the ordered array, the median is unaffected by the magnitude of the extreme observations. Regardless of whether the largest pH value is 5.46, 8.00, or 13.00, the median will still be 5.315.

Odd-Sized Sample

Had the number of observations been an odd number, the median would have been represented by the numerical value of the $(n + 1)/2$ observation in the ordered array. Thus, if there were an additional value of 6.00 for the ultra-pure water samples, the ordered array would be

4.31 5.04 5.09 5.18 5.20 5.31 | 5.32 | 5.33 5.39 5.40 5.41 5.46 6.00

Ordered   Median

Observation   1   2   3   4   5   6 | 7 | 8   9   10   11   12   13

Median = 5.32

The median-positioning point is the $(n + 1)/2 = 7$, so the median is the seventh ordered observation. Thus, the median is 5.32, the middle value in the ordered sequence.

Ties in the Data

When computing the median, we ignore the fact that tied values may be present in the data. For example, in the data set for deionized water, we have the following ordered array of pH values:

4.39 5.18 5.19 5.29 5.33 | 5.34 5.34 | 5.42 5.45 5.49 5.55 5.63

Ordered

Observation   1   2   3   4   5   6   7   8   9   10   11   12

Median = 5.34

For this even-sized data set, the median positioning point is the $(n + 1)/2 = 6.5$ ordered observation. The sixth ordered observation is 5.34, and the seventh ordered observation is also 5.34, so the average of 5.34 and 5.34 is equal to 5.34.

The Mode

Occasionally, when describing a set of data, the mode is used as a measure of central tendency. The **mode** is the most frequently occurring value in a data set. The mode can often be identified by referring to a histogram or polygon. It can also be directly obtained from the ordered array.

When using the ordered array of the pH values of the deionized water,

4.39 5.18 5.19 5.29 5.33 5.34 5.34 5.42 5.45 5.49 5.55 5.63,

we see that the mode is equal to 5.34.

Unfortunately, for several reasons, the mode is often not a particularly useful statistic. In some circumstances, if each value occurs only once, there will be no unique mode. For example, for the ultra-pure water, no unique mode occurs, because each value has appeared only once. In other circumstances, there will be several widely differing modes in the same set of data. In addition, the mode may be greatly affected by the change of a single value. These last two circumstances can be illustrated by the data set for deionized water. If the first value were 5.19 instead of 5.18, there would be two modes, one equal to 5.19, and the other equal to 5.34. In very large data sets, this problem will not usually occur if the population from which the sample was drawn is truly unimodal. Distributions with a single mode are referred to as **unimodal.** Distributions with two modes are referred to as **bimodal.**

Distributions may have several modes in which case they are referred to as multimodal. In such situations, it is sometimes the case that two or more different populations have been mixed together. For example, if we were studying the heights of students, we would almost certainly have a bimodal distribution if we combined the heights of males with the heights of females. If the output from more than two processes, such as machines, workers or suppliers, were combined, it is possible that there could be even more than two modes.

The Midrange

Another measure of central tendency that is commonly used to report daily atmospheric temperature is the midrange. The **midrange** is the average of the *smallest* and *largest* observations in a set of data. This can be written as

$$\text{Midrange} = \frac{X_{\text{smallest}} + X_{\text{largest}}}{2} \qquad (3.3)$$

When using the ordered array of pH values for the ultra-pure water,

$\boxed{4.31}$ 5.04 5.09 5.18 5.20 5.31 5.32 5.33 5.39 5.40 5.41 $\boxed{5.46}$,

the midrange is computed from Equation (3.3) as

$$\text{Midrange} = \frac{X_{\text{smallest}} + X_{\text{largest}}}{2}$$

$$= \frac{4.31 + 5.46}{2} = 4.885$$

Despite its simplicity, the midrange must be used cautiously. Because it involves only the smallest and largest observations in a data set, it becomes distorted as a measure of central tendency if an outlier or extreme value is present. If we compare the mean, median, and midrange of the pH values of the ultra-pure water samples, we find that the mean = 5.2033, the median = 5.315, and the midrange = 4.885. The midrange is considerably lower than either the mean or median, because its value has been pulled down by the extreme low value of 4.31.

The Midhinge: A Measure of Central Tendency Based on the Quartiles

Obtaining the Quartiles

In addition to the median, which divides a distribution into two equal parts, it is often useful to obtain measures that divide a distribution or data set into several equal parts. In general, these measures are called **quantiles.** In fields of application such as psychology and education, special quantiles such as the **deciles** (which split the ordered data into *tenths*) and the **percentiles** (which split the ordered data into *hundredths*) play an important role. In this chapter, our concern will be the **quartiles,** the values that split the ordered array into *quarters* (four equal parts).

The median is the value that splits the ordered array in half (50.0 percent of the observations are smaller and 50.0 percent of the observations are larger); the quartiles are descriptive measures that split the ordered data into four quarters.

The **first quartile, Q_1,** is the value such that 25.0 percent of the observations are smaller and 75.0 percent are larger.

The **second quartile Q_2,** is the value such that 50.0 percent of the observations are smaller and 50.0 percent are larger. It is the median.

The **third quartile, Q_3,** is the value such that 75.0 percent of the observations are smaller and 25.0 percent are larger.

The first step in identifying the quartile values for a data set is to obtain an ordered array of the n observations in the set. We can then approximate the quartiles from the set of n observations by using the following *positioning-point formulas.*[1]

[1] When dealing with a population, we replace n, the sample size, by N, the size of the population, in the positioning-point formula

$$Q_1 = \text{value corresponding to the } \frac{n+1}{4} \text{ ordered observation.}$$

$$Q_2 = \text{median, the value corresponding to the } \frac{2(n+1)}{4} = \frac{n+1}{2}$$
ordered observation.

$$Q_3 = \text{value corresponding to the } \frac{3(n+1)}{4} \text{ ordered observation.}$$

The following rules are used for obtaining the quartile values:

1. If the resulting positioning point is an integer, the particular numerical observation corresponding to that positioning point is chosen for the quartile.
2. If the resulting positioning point is halfway between two integers, the average of their corresponding observations is selected.
3. If the resulting positioning point is neither an integer nor a value halfway between two integers, a simple rule is to round off to the nearest integer and select the numerical value of the corresponding observation.

Thus, for the pH values of the 12 ultra-pure water samples, referring to the ordered array on page 108, we have

$$Q_1 = \frac{n+1}{4} \text{ ordered observation}$$

$$= \frac{12+1}{4} = 3.25 \text{ ordered observation}$$

Because 3.25 is neither an integer nor halfway between two integers, we follow Rule 3 and round to the nearest integer value. The positioning point for Q_1 is 3; the third ordered observation, 5.09, represents Q_1.

$$\text{Median} = \frac{n+1}{2} \text{ ordered observation}$$

$$= \frac{12+1}{2} = 6.5 \text{ ordered observation.}$$

Because 6.5 is halfway between two integers (6 and 7), we use Rule 2, average the sixth and seventh ordered observations $(5.31 + 5.32)/2 = 5.315$, and obtain the value of 5.315 for Q_2, the median.

$$Q_3 = \frac{3(n+1)}{4} \text{ ordered observation}$$

$$= \frac{3(12+1)}{4} = 9.75 \text{ ordered observation}$$

Because 9.75 is neither an integer nor halfway between two integers, we follow Rule 3 and round to the nearest integer value. The positioning point for Q_3 is 10; the tenth ordered observation, 5.40, represents Q_3.

Obtaining the Midhinge

[2]The hinges are measures of non-central location developed by Tukey (see Reference 4) that are similar to the quartiles.

Quartiles are useful in the development of a measure of location that is called the **midhinge**.[2] The midhinge is the mean of the first and third quartiles in a set of data.

$$\text{Midhinge} = \frac{Q_1 + Q_3}{2} \qquad (3.4)$$

The midhinge is composed only of the first and third quartiles, so it is not affected by extreme values in the data, as the midrange is. In Section 3.3, we will see how a comparison of the midhinge and the median will provide additional information concerning the symmetry of a set of data.

For the pH values of the ultra-pure water, we have

$$\text{Midhinge} = \frac{5.09 + 5.40}{2} = 5.245$$

Measures of Variation

A second important property that describes a set of data is variability. **Variability** or **dispersion** is the amount of variation or spread in the data. Four measures of variability are the range, the interquartile range, the variance, and the standard deviation.

The Range

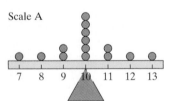

The **range** is the difference between the largest and smallest observations in a set of data—that is,

$$\text{Range} = X_{\text{largest}} - X_{\text{smallest}} \qquad (3.5)$$

For the ordered array of the pH values of the 12 ultra-pure water samples,

4.31 5.04 5.09 5.18 5.20 5.31 5.32 5.33 5.39 5.40 5.41 5.46 ,

the range is $5.46 - 4.31 = 1.15$.

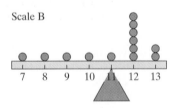

Thus, we can say that the largest difference in pH between any two ultra-pure water samples is 1.15.

The range measures the total spread in a set of data. Although the range is a simple, easily computed measure of dispersion, its main weakness is that it takes into account only the largest and smallest values and fails to account for how the values are distributed between these two extremes. This can be observed in Figure 3.3. Thus, as evidenced by Scale C, it would be misleading, and therefore improper, to use the range as a measure of dispersion when extreme observations are present.

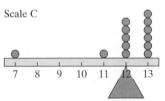

The Interquartile Range

Figure 3.3   Comparing three data sets with the same range

In contrast to the range, which measures only differences between the extremes, the **interquartile range** (also called **midspread**) is the difference between the third quartile and the first quartile. Thus, it measures the variation in the middle 50 percent of the data, and, unlike the range, is not affected by extreme values.

$$\text{Interquartile range} = Q_3 - Q_1 \tag{3.6}$$

For the data concerning the pH values of the ultra-pure water samples, we have

$$\text{Interquartile range} = 5.40 - 5.09 = 0.31$$

Thus, we can say that the range of the "middle half" of the water samples is 0.31.

The Variance and the Standard Deviation

Neither the range nor the interquartile range takes into account how all of the values in the set of data are distributed. Two commonly used measures of dispersion that do take into account each of the values are the **variance** and its square root, the **standard deviation.** These measures evaluate how values spread out or disperse around the mean.

Both the variance and the standard deviation are based on how much each observation deviates from a central point represented by the mean. In general, the greater the distances between the individual observations and the mean, the greater the variability of the data set. Because the mean acts as a balancing point for observations larger and smaller than it, the sum of the deviations around the mean is always zero. (See Derivation 3.1 on page 107 for the proof.)

$$\sum_{i=1}^{n} (X_i - \bar{X}) = 0$$

Thus, the variance and standard deviation could not merely use $\sum_{i=1}^{n} (X_i - \bar{X})$ as a factor. If, however, we square the difference between each value and the mean, to obtain $\sum_{i=1}^{n} (X_i - \bar{X})^2$, this resulting quantity, called a **sum of squares (SS),** could serve as the basis for a measure of variability. Because all observations contribute to the sum of squares, the magnitude of the sum of squares is affected by the number of observations in the data set. Therefore, it makes sense to divide the sum of squares by the number of observations, to take this factor into account. In populations, this is what is defined as the **population variance, σ^2.** Thus, for a set containing N observations $X_1, X_2, \ldots, X_N$, the population variance (given by the symbol σ^2) is written as:

$$\sigma^2 = \frac{(X_1 - \mu)^2 + (X_2 - \mu)^2 + \cdots + (X_N - \mu)^2}{N}$$

By using summation notation, the preceding formula can be more simply expressed as

$$\sigma^2 = \frac{\sum_{i=1}^{N} (X_i - \mu)^2}{N} \tag{3.7}$$

where

μ = population arithmetic mean

N = population size

X_i = ith value of the variable X

$\sum_{i=1}^{N} (X_i - \mu)^2$ = sum of all the squared differences between the X_i values and μ

The **sample variance, s^2,** is calculated by:

$$s^2 = \frac{\sum_{i=1}^{n} (X_i - \overline{X})^2}{n-1} \tag{3.8}$$

where

$\overline{X}$ = sample arithmetic mean

n = sample size

X_i = ith value of the variable X

$\sum_{i=1}^{n} (X_i - \overline{X})^2$ = sum of all the squared differences between the X values and $\overline{X}$

The denominator $n - 1$ is used for the sample variance, because the sample variance calculated this way is a better estimate of the population variance σ^2 than if n were used as the denominator. If the sample size n is large, it does not make much difference whether we divide by n or by $n - 1$.

Defining the Standard Deviation

The variance is defined in squared units such as ft^2 or sec^2. By taking the square root of the variance, we obtain a measure in the same units as the original data. This is called the standard deviation. For the **population standard deviation, σ,** we have

$$\sigma = \sqrt{\sigma^2} = \sqrt{\frac{\sum_{i=1}^{N} (X_i - \mu)^2}{N}} \tag{3.9}$$

while for the **sample standard deviation, s,** we have

$$s = \sqrt{s^2} = \sqrt{\frac{\sum_{i=1}^{n} (X_i - \overline{X})^2}{n-1}} \tag{3.10}$$

Calculating s^2 and s

To compute the sample variance, we do the following:

1. Obtain the difference between each observation and the mean.
2. Square each difference.
3. Add the squared results together.
4. Divide this sum of the squared differences by $n - 1$.

To obtain the sample standard deviation, we take the square root of the variance. Table 3.2 summarizes the computations necessary for the group of 12 ultra-pure water samples.

TABLE 3.2

SUMMARY CALCULATIONS FOR THE VARIANCE AND STANDARD DEVIATION FOR THE 12 WATER SAMPLES DRAWN FROM THE ULTRA-PURE SYSTEM

Water Sample	pH Value X_i	Deviations from Mean $(X_i - \bar{X})$	Squared Deviations from Mean $(X_i - \bar{X})^2$
1	5.04	−0.1633	0.0267
2	5.18	−0.0233	0.0005
3	5.32	+0.1167	0.0136
4	5.33	+0.1267	0.0161
5	5.39	+0.1867	0.0349
6	5.09	−0.1133	0.0128
7	5.41	+0.2067	0.0427
8	5.20	0.0000	0.0000
9	5.31	+0.1067	0.0114
10	5.46	+0.2567	0.0659
11	4.31	−0.8933	0.7980
12	5.40	+0.1967	0.0387
		0.0037*	1.0613

*Rounding error.

By using Equation (3.8), along with the results displayed in Table 3.4, we calculate as follows:

$$s^2 = \frac{\sum_{i=1}^{n} (X_i - \bar{X})^2}{n - 1}$$

$$= \frac{(5.04 - 5.2033)^2 + (5.18 - 5.2033)^2 + \cdots + (5.40 - 5.2033)^2}{12 - 1}$$

$$= \frac{1.0613}{11}$$

$$= 0.0965 \text{ (in squared units)}$$

and so the sample standard deviation is computed as

$$s = \sqrt{s^2} = \sqrt{\dfrac{\sum\limits_{i=1}^{n}(X_i - \overline{X})^2}{n-1}} = \sqrt{0.0965} = 0.3106$$

Thus, the standard deviation, s, is 0.3106.

Note that the third column of Table 3.4 contains the $(X_i - \overline{X})$ values, and $\sum\limits_{i=1}^{n}(X_i - \overline{X})$ is indicated at the bottom of this column. For this example, this value is approximately zero (the only reason it is not exactly zero is rounding error). In the squaring process, observations that are farther from the mean get more weight than observations closer to the mean. Thus, the value 4.31, which is 0.8933 below the mean, contributes substantially more to the magnitude of s^2 and s than the value 5.18, which is only 0.0233 below the mean.

To understand the characteristics of a data set completely, we need to study not only measures of central tendency but also measures of variability. The differences between the individual values and the mean are squared in computing the variance and standard deviation, so *neither of these measures can ever be negative.* In fact, s^2 and s can be zero only when there is no variation at all in the data. This can only occur if each and every value is exactly the same. Clearly, we recognize that data are inherently variable and that all items or people will virtually never be exactly the same.

What the Variance and the Standard Deviation Indicate

The variance and the standard deviation are measuring the scatter around the mean—that is, how larger observations are spread out above it and how smaller observations distribute below it.

The variance possesses certain useful mathematical properties; however, its computation results in squared units, such as squared milligrams, squared inches, and so on. Thus, our primary measure of dispersion will be the standard deviation, whose value (because it is the square root of the variance) is in the original units of the data, such as milligrams, inches, and so on.

Therefore, we generalize as in Exhibit 3.1:

EXHIBIT 3.1 Understanding Variation in Data

1. The more spread out or dispersed the data are, the larger will be the range, variance, and standard deviation.

2. The more concentrated or homogeneous the data are, the smaller will be the range, variance, and standard deviation.

3. If all the observations are the same (so that there is no variation in the data), the range, variance, and standard deviation will all be zero.

4. The range, variance, and standard deviation cannot *ever* be negative.

Shapes of Distributions

A third important property of a set of data is the shape of its distribution. We can evaluate the shape of a distribution by considering two characteristics of data sets: **symmetry** and **kurtosis.** Both symmetry and kurtosis evaluate the manner in which the data are distributed around their mean.

Symmetry

A **symmetric** distribution can be defined as one in which the upper half is a mirror image of the lower half of the distribution. If a vertical line is drawn through the mean of the distribution depicted by a histogram or a polygon, the lower half could be "folded over" and would coincide with the upper half of the distribution.

Either the distribution of the data is **symmetrical** or it is not. If the distribution of the data is not symmetrical, it is called asymmetric or **skewed.** Data sets that are asymmetric can be either positively or negatively skewed. Positive skewness arises when the mean is pulled upward in the direction of high or positive values by the presence of one or more unusually high values. Negative skewness occurs when the mean is pulled downward toward low or negative values by the presence of one or more unusually low values.

One way to identify symmetry simply involves the comparison of the mean and the median. If these two measures are equal, we may generally consider the data to be symmetrical. If the mean is greater than the median, the data may be described as *positive* or **right-skewed.** If the mean is less than the median, the data are considered to be *negative* or **left-skewed.** In summary:

Mean > median: positive or right-skewed

Mean = median: symmetry

Mean < median: negative or left-skewed

Figure 3.4 on page 118 illustrates the relationship between the mean and median in these three types of distributions.

For our group of 12 ultra-pure water samples, the pH values were displayed along the dot scale in Figure 3.1 (on page 106). The mean equals 5.20 and the median equals 5.315, so we conclude that the data may be slightly left-skewed.

Determining Symmetry by Using the Five-Number Summary

In this section, we studied a variety of measures of central tendency and noncentral location. A **five-number summary** consists of

$$X_{\text{smallest}} \quad Q_1 \quad \text{Median} \quad Q_3 \quad X_{\text{largest}}$$

For our data concerning the pH values of the ultra-pure water, the five-number summary is

$$4.31 \quad 5.09 \quad 5.315 \quad 5.40 \quad 5.46$$

The five-number summary is used to study the shape of the distribution. If the data were perfectly symmetrical, the following would usually be true:

1. The distance from Q_1 to the median would equal the distance from the median to Q_3.
2. The distance from X_{smallest} to Q_1 would equal the distance from Q_3 to X_{largest}.
3. The median, the midhinge, and the midrange would all be equal; these measures would also be equal to the mean.

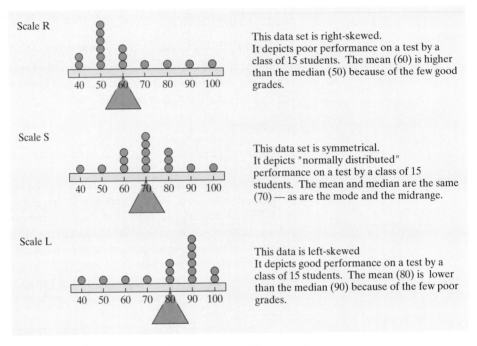

Scale R

This data set is right-skewed. It depicts poor performance on a test by a class of 15 students. The mean (60) is higher than the median (50) because of the few good grades.

Scale S

This data set is symmetrical. It depicts "normally distributed" performance on a test by a class of 15 students. The mean and median are the same (70) — as are the mode and the midrange.

Scale L

This data is left-skewed It depicts good performance on a test by a class of 15 students. The mean (80) is lower than the median (90) because of the few poor grades.

Figure 3.4 A comparison of three data sets differing in shape

For asymmetric distributions, however, the following will usually be true:

1. In right-skewed distributions, the distance from Q_3 to $X_{largest}$ greatly exceeds the distance from $X_{smallest}$ to Q_1.
2. In right-skewed distributions, midrange > midhinge > median
3. In left-skewed distributions, the distance from $X_{smallest}$ to Q_1 greatly exceeds the distance from Q_3 to $X_{largest}$.
4. In left-skewed distributions, median > midhinge > midrange.

From the results obtained on pages 108, 111, and 112, we know that

1. Median = 5.315 > midhinge = 5.245 > midrange = 4.8850.
2. The distance from $X_{smallest}$ to Q_1 is 0.78, while the distance from Q_3 to $X_{largest}$ is 0.06.

Therefore, we conclude that the distribution of pH values is left-skewed.

Comparing the mean and median and using the five-number summary are useful ways of obtaining rough estimates of symmetry or skewness. If it is important to obtain a more precise determination of whether a distribution of data is symmetrical, relatively simple and more exact tests are available. (See Reference 3.)

Kurtosis

Kurtosis concerns the relative concentration of values in the center of the distribution as compared to the tails. In terms of this property, we can define three types of distributions: *leptokurtic, mesokurtic,* and *platykurtic.* These three types of distributions are depicted in Figure 3.5. A **leptokurtic** distribution is characterized by a prominent peak and by a relatively large proportion of values falling in the tails. The prefix *lepto* means thin and refers to the taller, thinner peak of the distribution. A **mesokurtic** distribution is one in which the values are predominantly located in

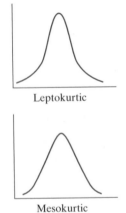

Leptokurtic

Mesokurtic

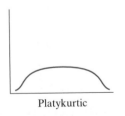

Platykurtic

Figure 3.5 Three types of kurtosis

the center of the distribution, with relatively few values falling in the tails. The normal or bell-shaped curve, which will be discussed in Section 5.3, is an example of a mesokurtic distribution. A **platykurtic** distribution is one in which the values are relatively spread out through the range of the distribution, so that the peak is relatively flat and very few values appear in the tails. The prefix *platy* means flat and refers to the relatively flattened peak or central portion of the distribution.

Unlike with symmetry, where we could either compare the relative positions of the mean and the median or use the five-number summary, there is no similar comparison that can be made to assess the kurtosis of a distribution. For a study of measures of kurtosis, see Reference 3.

Interpreting Microsoft Excel and MINITAB Descriptive Statistics Output

Now that we have discussed the characteristics of central tendency, variation, and shape, we can examine descriptive statistics output obtained from Microsoft Excel and from MINITAB about the pH of the 12 samples from the ultra-pure system and the 12 samples from the deionizing system.

Figure 3.6 represents output obtained from the Descriptive Statistics option of the Data Analysis tool of Microsoft Excel.

We note that Excel has provided the (arithmetic) mean, median, mode, standard deviation, variance, range, minimum, maximum, and count (sample size), all of which have been discussed in this section. In addition, Excel has computed the Standard Error, along with statistics for Kurtosis and Skewness. The *standard error* is the standard deviation divided by the square root of the sample size; it will be discussed in Chapter 5. *Skewness* is a measure of lack of symmetry in the data and is based on a statistic that is a function of the cubed differences around the arithmetic mean. *Kurtosis* is a measure of the relative concentration of values in the center of

	A	B	C	D
1	Ultra-Pure		Deionizing	
2				
3	Mean	5.203333	Mean	5.3
4	Standard Error	0.089665	Standard Error	0.09142
5	Median	5.315	Median	5.34
6	Mode	#N/A	Mode	5.34
7	Standard Deviation	0.31061	Standard Deviation	0.316687
8	Sample Variance	0.096479	Sample Variance	0.100291
9	Kurtosis	6.922946	Kurtosis	6.994039
10	Skewness	-2.45382	Skewness	-2.38012
11	Range	1.15	Range	1.24
12	Minimum	4.31	Minimum	4.39
13	Maximum	5.46	Maximum	5.63
14	Sum	62.44	Sum	63.6
15	Count	12	Count	12
16	Largest(1)	5.46	Largest(1)	5.63
17	Smallest(1)	4.31	Smallest(1)	4.39
18				

Figure 3.6   Descriptive statistics obtained from Microsoft Excel about the pH of 12 samples from the ultra-pure system and 12 samples from the deionizing system

Descriptive Statistics

Variable	Type	N	Mean	Median	TrMean	StDev
pH	Ultra-Pure	12	5.2033	5.3150	5.2670	0.3106
	Deionizing	12	5.3000	5.3400	5.3580	0.3167

Variable	Type	SE Mean	Minimum	Maximum	Q1	Q3
pH	Ultra-Pure	0.0897	4.3100	5.4600	5.1125	5.3975
	Deionizing	0.0914	4.3900	5.6300	5.2150	5.4800

Figure 3.7   Descriptive statistics, obtained from MINITAB, about the pH of 12 samples from the ultra-pure system and 12 samples from the deionizing system

the distribution as compared to the tails; it is based on the differences around the arithmetic mean raised to the fourth power. This measure is not discussed in this text. (See Reference 1.)

Figure 3.7 represents descriptive statistics output, obtained from MINITAB, about the pH of 12 samples from the ultra-pure system and 12 samples from the deionizing system.

We observe that, for each of these two water purification systems, MINITAB has computed the sample size n, (arithmetic) mean, median, standard deviation (labeled StDev), minimum, maximum, and first and third quartile, all of which have been discussed in this section. In addition, MINITAB has computed the *trimmed mean* (labeled as Tr Mean), which trims possible outliers by removing the smallest and largest five percent of the observations and averaging the remaining values. In addition, MINITAB computes the *standard error of the mean* (labeled as SE Mean), which is equal to the standard deviation divided by the square root of the sample size. It will be discussed in Chapter 5.

From Figures 3.6 and 3.7, there appears to be very little difference between the mean, the median, and the standard deviation of the pH. The first quartile and third quartiles are slightly lower for the ultra-pure system than for the deionizing system.

PROBLEMS

3.1 The operations manager of a plant that manufactures tires wishes to compare the actual inner diameter of two grades of tires, each of which is expected to be 575 mm. A sample of five tires of each grade was selected, and the results representing the inner diameters of the tires, ordered from smallest to highest, were as follows:

Grade X	Grade Y
568 570 575 578 584	573 574 575 577 578

(a) For each of the two groups, compute the
   (1) arithmetic mean,
   (2) median,
   (3) standard deviation.

(b) Which grade of tire is providing better quality? Explain.
(c) What would be the effect on your answers in (a) and (b) if the last value for grade Y had been 588 instead of 578? Explain.

3.2 In a study to determine their tensile strength, bolts were tested until failure in an impact environment. The amount of energy absorbed by each of 18 bolts is presented in ft/lb, as follows:

35.32 33.34 31.56 36.24 35.69 29.63 33.46 36.91 33.03
31.04 33.05 34.04 33.25 34.88 31.24 37.23 36.26 36.14

BOLTS

(a) Calculate the
- (1) arithmetic mean,
- (2) median,
- (3) mode,
- (4) midrange,
- (5) quartiles,
- (6) midhinge,
- (7) range,
- (8) interquartile range,
- (9) variance,
- (10) standard deviation.

(b) Compare the mean and median values. Do you think the distribution is skewed? If so, in what direction? Explain.

(c) Use the five-number summary to evaluate the distribution. What conclusions do you reach about the shape of the distribution? Why?

3.3 The daily low temperature (°F) was recorded at the Westchester County, New York Airport during the month of January in a recent year. These data are as follows:

22 22 19 40 37 30 30 33 22 18 20 29 33 26 27 22
25 21 17 22 19 38 30 29 28 23 27 24 19 18 26

JANTEMP

(a) Calculate the
- (1) arithmetic mean,
- (2) median,
- (3) mode,
- (4) midrange,
- (5) quartiles,
- (6) midhinge,
- (7) range,
- (8) interquartile range,
- (9) variance,
- (10) standard deviation.

(b) Compare the mean and median values. Do you think the distribution is skewed? If so, in what direction? Explain.

(c) Use the five-number summary to evaluate the distribution. What conclusions do you reach about the shape of the distribution?

3.4 An engineering student measured voltage output in 24 brand-new 1.5-volt (AA) batteries. The student's data are as follows:

1.577 1.588 1.576 1.570 1.586 1.582 1.580 1.585
1.587 1.580 1.579 1.580 1.584 1.593 1.585 1.581
1.577 1.585 1.583 1.585 1.577 1.587 1.582 1.587

VOLTAGE

(a) Calculate the
- (1) arithmetic mean,
- (2) median,
- (3) mode,
- (4) midrange,
- (5) quartiles,
- (6) midhinge,
- (7) range,
- (8) interquartile range,
- (9) variance,
- (10) standard deviation.

(b) Compare the mean and median values. Do you think the distribution is skewed? If so, in what direction? Explain.

(c) Use the five-number summary to evaluate the distribution. What conclusions do you reach about the shape of the distribution?

3.5 An environmental engineer monitored sound level in a building every 15 seconds to determine whether noise levels were within EPA standards. The values below presents the noise levels, recorded in dBA units, for 45 15-second intervals.

66 56 70 72 67 68 70 71 74 69 72 70 70 70 70 72
66 70 72 72 65 70 70 72 64 68 71 70 70 70 78 86
85 70 76 70 74 72 70 70 75 70 70 68 70 69 73

NOISE

(a) Calculate the
- (1) arithmetic mean,
- (2) median,
- (3) mode,
- (4) midrange,
- (5) quartiles,
- (6) midhinge,
- (7) range,
- (8) interquartile range,
- (9) variance,
- (10) standard deviation.

(b) Compare the mean and median values. Do you think the distribution is skewed? If so, in what direction? Explain.

(c) Use the five-number summary to evaluate the distribution. What conclusions do you reach about the shape of the distribution?

3.6 A problem with a telephone line, which prevents a customer from receiving or making calls, is disconcerting both to the customer and the telephone company. These problems can be of two types: those that are located inside a central office, and those that are located on lines between the central office and the customer's equipment. The following data represent samples of 20 problems reported to two different offices of a telephone company and the time taken to clear these problems from the customers' lines (in minutes).

Central Office I—Time to Clear Problems

1.48 1.75 0.78 2.85 0.52 1.60 4.15
3.97 1.48 3.10 1.02 0.53 0.93 1.60
0.80 1.05 6.32 3.93 5.45 0.97

Central Office II—Time to Clear Problems

7.55 3.75 0.10 1.10 0.60 0.52 3.30
2.10 0.58 4.02 3.75 0.65 1.92 0.60
1.53 4.23 0.08 1.48 1.65 0.72

PHONE

For each of the two central office locations, do all of the following:

(a) Compute the
- (1) arithmetic mean,
- (2) median,
- (3) midrange,
- (4) first quartile,
- (5) third quartile,
- (6) midhinge,
- (7) range,
- (8) interquartile range,
- (9) variance,
- (10) standard deviation.

(b) List the five-number summary.
(c) Tell whether the data are skewed. (If so, how?) Explain.
(d) Compare your analyses of the clearing times in the two central offices. Do you find similarities or differences in their distributions? Explain.
(e) What would be the effect on the results, and on your conclusions, if the first value for Central Office II had incorrectly been recorded as 27.55 instead of 7.55?

3.7 In many manufacturing processes, there is a term called *work in process,* often abbreviated as WIP. In a book-manufacturing plant, this represents the time it takes for sheets from a press to be folded, gathered, sewn, tipped on endsheets, and bound. The following data represent samples of 20 books at each of two production plants and the processing time (operationally defined as the time in days from when the books came off the press to when they were packed in cartons) for these jobs.

Plant A

```
5.62    5.29   16.25   10.92   11.46   21.62   8.45    8.58
5.41   11.42   11.62    7.29    7.50    7.96   4.42   10.50
7.58    9.29    7.54    8.92
```

Plant B

```
 9.54   11.46   16.62   12.62   25.75   15.41   14.29
13.13   13.71   10.04    5.75   12.46    9.17   13.21
 6.00    2.33   14.25    5.37    6.25    9.71
```

WIP

For each of the two plants, do all of the following:
(a) Compute the
　(1) arithmetic mean,　(6) midhinge,
　(2) median,　(7) range,
　(3) midrange,　(8) interquartile range,
　(4) first quartile,　(9) variance,
　(5) third quartile,　(10) standard deviation.
(b) List the five-number summary.
(c) Tell whether the data are skewed. (If so, how?) Explain.
(d) Compare your analyses of the processing times in the two plants. Do you find similarities or differences in their distributions? Explain.

3.8 A company that sells automotive replacement parts wishes to study its process of developing parts for this market. In particular, it wishes to evaluate the development time for its products. This time is operationally defined as beginning at the time that the company president signs off on the document and procurement procedure and ending at the time that the product actually arrives in inventory. For a given quarterly time period, a sample of 20 replacement parts developed

was selected. The results in terms of development time in days were as follows:

```
38.2  29.7  33.4  74.1  34.4  32.5  35.4
30.4  58.5  51.8  22.3  24.1  31.5  32.8
37.3  36.4  32.2  32.2  46.2  35.4
```

PARTS

(a) Compute the
　(1) arithmetic mean,　(6) midhinge,
　(2) median,　(7) range,
　(3) midrange,　(8) interquartile range,
　(4) first quartile,　(9) variance,
　(5) third quartile,　(10) standard deviation.
(b) List the five-number summary.
(c) Tell whether the data are skewed? (If so, how?) Explain.

3.9 An airflow experiment compared two different terminal devices that are used to diffuse air throughout a space and thereby provide heating and/or cooling. Fifty diffusers of each type were randomly selected in a building that contained 1100 diffusers per floor. The data below presents the airflow measurements, in cubic feet per minute, obtained in this experiment.

Carnes 3-Way Diffusers

```
245 230 180 200 180 255 195 220 195 200 225 240
300 240 285 250 295 295 270 285 225 255 190 275
280 205 215 270 265 290 310 250 215 270 295 210
235 160 235 280 250 240 295 285 190 250 310 290
250 300
```

Krueger 4-Way Diffusers

```
275 225 230 240 205 225 265 225 190 275 240 205
250 265 230 300 275 240 245 250 200 270 245 230
225 285 275 250 200 255 265 230 250 195 240 225
230 290 230 250 225 275 205 245 250 300 275 260
255 230
```

AIRFLOW

For each of the two diffusers, do all of the following:
(a) Compute the
　(1) arithmetic mean,　(6) midhinge,
　(2) median,　(7) range,
　(3) midrange,　(8) interquartile range,
　(4) first quartile,　(9) variance,
　(5) third quartile,　(10) standard deviation.
(b) List the five-number summary for each diffuser.
(c) Tell whether the data are skewed for either diffuser. (If so, how?) Explain.
(d) Compare your analyses for the Carnes and Krueger diffusers. Do you find similarities or differences in their distributions?

3.3 THE BOX-AND-WHISKER PLOT

In its simplest form, a **box-and-whisker-plot** provides a graphical representation of the data through the five-number summary. Such a plot is depicted in Figure 3.8 for the pH values of the ultra-pure water samples.

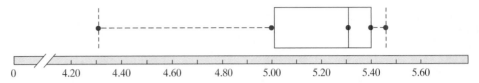

Figure 3.8   Box-and-whisker plot for the pH of 12 samples obtained from the ultra-pure system

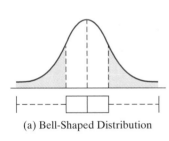

(a) Bell-Shaped Distribution

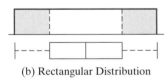

(b) Rectangular Distribution

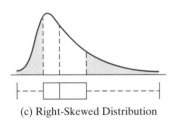

(c) Right-Skewed Distribution

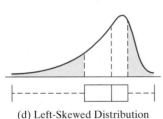

(d) Left-Skewed Distribution

Figure 3.9   Box-and-whisker plots for four hypothetical distributions

The vertical line drawn within the box represents the location of the median value in the data. The vertical line at the left side of the box represents the location of Q_1, and the vertical line at the right side of the box represents the location of Q_3. Therefore, the box contains the middle 50 percent of the values in a distribution. The lower 25 percent of the data are represented by a dashed line (a whisker) connecting the left side of the box to the location of the smallest value, $X_{smallest}$. In a similar manner, the upper 25 percent of the data are represented by a dashed line connecting the right side of the box to the largest value, $X_{largest}$.

In order to illustrate how the shape of a distribution affects the box-and-whisker plot, Figure 3.9 depicts four such plots: one each for a bell-shaped curve, a rectangular curve, a right-skewed curve, and a left-skewed curve. In Panel A, a bell-shaped curve, we observe that, because most of the data are located near the center of the distribution, the quartiles are located closer to the median than to the extremes of the distribution. We also note that, because the bell-shaped curve is symmetric, the median is equidistant from the quartiles, and the distance from $X_{smallest}$ to Q_1 is the same as from Q_3 to $X_{largest}$. Panel B depicts a rectangular or uniform distribution in which all values are equally likely to occur. Therefore, the quartiles are located equidistant between the extremes and the median in this distribution. The rectangular distribution is symmetric, so again the median is equidistant from the quartiles, and the distance from $X_{smallest}$ to Q_1 is the same as from Q_3 to $X_{largest}$. In Panel C, the positive or right-skewed distribution, we note that there is a long tail on the right side of the distribution. The distance between Q_1 and the median is less than the distance between the median and Q_3, while the distance between the smallest value and Q_1 is less than the distance between Q_3 and the largest value. In Panel D, the negative or left-skewed distribution, we note that there is a long tail on the left side of the distribution. The distance between Q_1 and the median is greater than the distance between the median and Q_3, while the distance between the smallest value and Q_1 is greater than the distance between Q_3 and the largest value.

Now that we have examined the box-and-whisker plots for these different types of distributions, we return to Figure 3.8 to evaluate the box-and-whisker plot for the pH values of the ultra-pure water samples. By visually representing the five-number summary, we can not only study the various measures of location and dispersion but also roughly evaluate the symmetry of the distribution. From Figure 3.8, we observe that the center of the distribution is asymmetric, with the median located much closer to Q_3 than it is to Q_1. (Remember that the median = 5.315 and

PH of Water Purification Systems

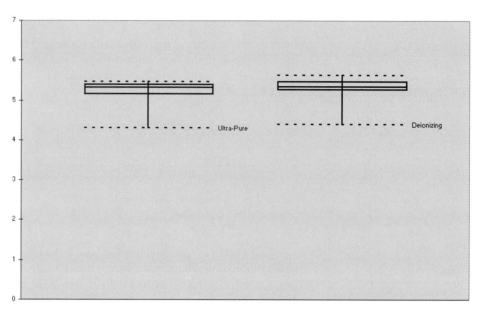

Figure 3.10   Side-by-side box-and-whisker plots, obtained from the PHStat add-in for Microsoft Excel, of the pH values of 12 samples from the ultra-pure system and 12 samples from the deionizing system

the midhinge = 5.245.) In addition, the lower tail appears to be substantially longer than the upper tail, giving us reason to believe that the distribution of pH values is left-skewed. (Remember that the midrange here is 4.885.) In summary, it is clear that the examination of the box-and-whisker plot provides a much more thorough understanding of the distribution of a set of data than would have been obtained if we would have merely studied the mean, median, and standard deviation.

The box-and-whisker plot is also useful as a tool for graphically comparing two or more groups. In such situations, we can set up side-by-side plots of the groups. Figure 3.10 represents side-by-side box-and-whisker plots of the pH values of the ultra-pure water (see Figure 3.8) and the deionized water, obtained from the PHStat add-in for Microsoft Excel. Figure 3.11 represents the box-and-whisker plots obtained from MINITAB. Note that the PHStat add-in for Microsoft Excel and MINITAB both provide vertical box-and-whisker plots. In addition, the asterisks on the MINITAB plot indicate outlier values.

Side-by-side box-and-whisker plots enable us to evaluate the similarities and differences in the various descriptive characteristics of the data clearly. From Figures 3.10 and 3.11, in terms of location, we can observe that, although the median pH of the two types of purified water is about the same, the third quartile and the minimum and maximum pH values are slightly larger for deionized water than for ultra-pure water.

In terms of dispersion, although the ranges for these groups are about the same, the interquartile range is slightly smaller for the deionized water than for the ultra-pure water.

In terms of symmetry, both groups appear to be left-skewed, because each has a much longer tail on the lower (left in a horizontal plot) side of the box;

Boxplots of pH by Type

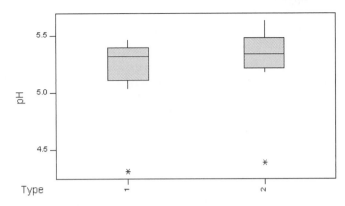

Figure 3.11   Side-by-side box-and-whisker plots, obtained from MINITAB, of the pH values of 12 samples from the ultra-pure system and 12 samples from the deionizing system

however, if we consider the symmetry of the middle 50% of each distribution (represented by the box), we find that the median for the deionized water samples is centered in the box and is equidistant from Q_1 and Q_3, indicating that the middle 50% of this distribution is symmetrical. On the other hand, as we observed previously, the median for the ultra-pure water samples is much closer to Q_3 than to Q_1, indicating that the middle 50% of this distribution is left-skewed. In summary, then, the use of side-by-side box-and-whisker plots enable us through its concise pictorial format, to compare several groups.

www.prenhall.com

PROBLEMS

3.10 Use the data from Problem 3.2 on page 120, concerning the study to determine the tensile strength of bolts.
   (a) Construct a box-and-whisker plot for the tensile-strength data.
   (b) What conclusions do you reach about the way the data is distributed? Explain.

3.11 Use the daily low temperature (°F) which was recorded at the Westchester County, New York Airport during the month of January in 1993, presented in Problem 3.3 on page 121.
   (a) Construct a box-and-whisker plot for the temperature data.
   (b) What conclusions do you reach about the shape of the distribution?

3.12 Use the voltage output data for 24 brand-new 1.5-volt (AA) batteries, presented in Problem 3.4 on page 121.
   (a) Construct a box-and-whisker plot for the voltage data.

   (b) What conclusions do you reach about the way the data is distributed?

3.13 Use the data collected by an environmental engineer who monitored sound level in a building every 15 seconds to determine whether noise levels were within EPA standards, presented in Problem 3.5 on page 121.
   (a) Construct a box-and-whisker plot for the sound-level data.
   (b) What conclusions do you reach about the way the data is distributed?

3.14 Use the data of Problem 3.6 on page 121, concerning time to clear problems in telephone lines.
   (a) For the two offices, construct a side-by-side box-and-whisker plot.
   (b) What conclusions do you reach about the way the data is distributed in each office? What recommendations would you make to the supervisors of each office?

3.15 Use the data of Problem 3.7 on page 122, concerning the processing time of book production.
  (a) Construct a side-by-side box-and-whisker plot.
  (b) What conclusions do you reach about the way the data is distributed in each plant?

3.16 Use the data of Problem 3.9 on page 122, from the air-flow experiment that compared two different terminal devices which are used to diffuse air throughout a space (thereby providing heating and/or cooling).

  (a) Construct a side-by-side box-and-whisker plot.
  (b) What conclusions do you reach about the way the data is distributed?
  (c) Compare your box-and-whisker plots for the Carnes 3-Way and the Krueger 4-Way diffusers. Do you find similarities or differences in the shapes of their distributions?

KEY TERMS

CHAPTER REVIEW *Checking Your Understanding*

3.17 What characteristics are useful in describing a set of numerical data?

3.18 What do we mean by a measure of location?

3.19 What are the differences between the various measures of location, and what are their advantages and disadvantages?

3.20 What do we mean by a measure of variation?

3.21 What are the differences between the various measures of variation, and what are their advantages and disadvantages?

3.22 What is meant by the property of shape?

3.23 How does skewness differ from kurtosis?

3.24 How does variation differ from kurtosis?

3.25 What are the advantages of using the box-and-whisker plot?

Chapter Review Problems

3.26 In addition to measuring pH values of water samples, the study of water purification systems described in this chapter measured the conductivity (in μSiemens/cm); the total aerobic microbial population (TAMP), in terms of the number of colony-forming units (CFU), where one CFU is equivalent to one original bacterium or fungus, measured in CFU/100 ml; and total organic carbon (TOC), measured in ppb.

  The table on page 127 presents these measurements for the ultra-pure and the deionizing systems.

ULTRA-PURE SYSTEM

Sample	Conductivity	TAMP	TOC
1	0.958	0	240
2	0.737	6	260
3	0.736	2	170
4	0.538	0	140
5	0.652	44	160
6	0.616	11	167
7	0.668	0	221
8	0.645	0	340
9	0.517	4	210
10	0.877	0	62
11	1.365	1	107
12	1.306	0	19

DEIONIZING SYSTEM

Sample	Conductivity	TAMP	TOC
1	0.631	1	170
2	0.547	0	45
3	0.488	1	210
4	0.452	26	330
5	0.872	1	290
6	0.565	0	250
7	0.472	2	190
8	0.763	9	160
9	0.476	0	250
10	0.636	0	157
11	0.732	0	6
12	0.520	0	24 **WATER**

For conductivity, TAMP, and TOC for each system, calculate the following:

(a) the mean,
(b) the median,
(c) the mode,
(d) the midrange,
(e) the quartiles,
(f) the midhinge,
(g) Which measure of central tendency do you feel is most useful for each of the variables and why?
(h) the range,
(i) the interquartile range,
(j) the variance and standard deviation.
(k) Use the five-number summary to evaluate the distribution. What conclusions do you reach about the shape of the distribution?
(l) Construct a box-and-whisker plot for each of the three variables for the ultra-pure system and for the deionizing system.
(m) Compare your results for conductivity, TOC, and TAMP for the ultra-pure system with those for the deionizing system. How do the systems differ in regard to these variables?

3.27 A hydrologic study of rainfall and water discharge through wadis in Saudi Arabia collected data on rainfall depth and runoff depth during and after storms. The table at the top of page 128 presents rainfall depth in mm and runoff depth in mm for 16 storms.

Storm Number	Rainfall Depth	Runoff Depth
1	25.5	2.18
2	14.5	1.67
3	39.0	4.05
4	11.5	1.12
5	13.4	1.66
6	27.3	2.49
7	41.2	1.96
8	13.8	1.18
9	7.6	0.50
10	14.6	0.76
11	27.5	0.87
12	13.2	3.66
13	7.2	0.07
14	17.0	2.82
15	9.2	1.00
16	15.0	1.37 **RAINFALL**

Source: Sorman, A. U. Estimation of Peak Discharge Using GIUH Model in Saudi Arabia. *Journal of Water Resources Planning and Management,* July/August 1995, pp. 287–293.

For rainfall depth and runoff depth, do the following:

(a) Calculate the

(1) arithmetic mean,	(6) midhinge,
(2) median,	(7) range,
(3) mode,	(8) interquartile range,
(4) midrange,	(9) variance,
(5) quartiles,	(10) standard deviation.

(b) Compare the mean and median values for rainfall depth and runoff depth. Do you think the distributions may be skewed? If so, in what direction? Explain.

(c) Use the five-number summary to evaluate the distributions. What conclusions do you reach about the shape of the distributions? Are the variables *rainfall depth* and *runoff depth* distributed differently? Explain.

(d) Construct a box-and-whisker plot for the rainfall-depth and the runoff depth data. What conclusions do you reach about the way the data is distributed? Explain.

(e) Based on the results of (d), are the variables *rainfall depth* and *runoff depth* distributed differently? Explain.

3.28 Engineers monitored emissions of hydrocarbons, carbon monoxide, and nitrogen oxide from a sample of 46 automobiles, in *g/m.* Their data are presented in the table below.

Vehicle	HC	CO	NO	Vehicle	HC	CO	NO
1	0.50	5.01	1.28	11	0.83	11.53	1.32
2	0.65	14.67	0.72	12	0.38	4.10	1.47
3	0.46	8.60	1.17	13	0.38	5.21	1.24
4	0.41	4.42	1.31	14	0.50	12.10	1.44
5	0.41	4.95	1.16	15	0.60	9.62	0.71
6	0.39	7.24	1.45	16	0.73	14.97	0.51
7	0.44	7.51	1.08	17	0.83	15.13	0.49
8	0.55	12.30	1.22	18	0.57	5.04	1.49
9	0.72	14.97	0.60	19	0.34	3.95	1.38
10	0.64	7.98	1.32	20	0.41	3.38	1.33

(Continued)

Vehicle	HC	CO	NO	Vehicle	HC	CO	NO
21	0.37	4.12	1.20	34	0.70	14.83	1.16
22	1.02	25.53	0.86	35	0.51	5.69	1.73
23	0.87	19.00	0.78	36	0.52	6.35	1.45
24	1.10	22.92	0.57	37	0.57	6.02	1.31
25	0.65	11.20	0.95	38	0.51	5.79	1.51
26	0.43	3.81	1.79	39	0.36	2.03	1.80
27	0.48	3.45	2.20	40	0.48	4.62	1.47
28	0.41	1.85	2.27	41	0.52	6.78	1.15
29	0.51	4.10	1.78	42	0.61	8.43	1.06
30	0.41	2.26	1.87	43	0.58	6.02	0.97
31	0.47	4.74	1.83	44	0.46	3.99	2.01
32	0.52	4.29	2.94	45	0.47	5.22	1.12
33	0.56	5.36	1.26	46	0.55	7.47	1.39

EMISSION

Source: Technometrics, Vol. 22, 4, 1987, p. 487

For hydrocarbons, carbon monoxide, and nitrogen oxide, do the following:

(a) Calculate the

    (1) arithmetic mean,   (6) midhinge,
    (2) median,   (7) range,
    (3) mode,   (8) interquartile range,
    (4) midrange,   (9) variance,
    (5) quartiles,   (10) standard deviation.

(b) Compare the mean and median values for hydrocarbons, carbon monoxide, and nitrogen oxide. Do you think the distributions may be skewed and, if so, in what direction? Explain.

(c) Use the five-number summary to evaluate the distributions. What conclusions do you reach about the shape of the distributions? Are the variables *hydrocarbons*, *carbon monoxide*, and *nitrogen oxide* distributed differently? Explain.

(d) Construct a box-and-whisker plot for the *hydrocarbons, carbon monoxide*, and *nitrogen oxide* data. What conclusions do you reach about the way the data is distributed? Explain.

(e) Are the variables *hydrocarbons, carbon monoxide*, and *nitrogen oxide* distributed differently? Explain.

3.29 The table below presents data on dry-matter yield (DMY) and nitrogen concentration (NC) for sorghum grown on the Lincoln, Nebraska, municipal water bio-solids use site in 1990 and 1991.

Observation	DMY mg/ha	NC g/kg	Observation	DMY mg/ha	NC g/kg
1	12.7	15.1	13	14.8	14.8
2	13.0	16.0	14	13.5	15.3
3	18.6	12.8	15	13.7	13.7
4	14.6	13.6	16	15.6	13.4
5	20.7	12.9	17	20.6	12.2
6	17.2	13.1	18	19.5	12.7
7	11.9	13.6	19	18.8	14.8
8	20.7	13.4	20	17.1	14.0
9	14.6	13.1	21	11.6	11.8
10	21.1	13.3	22	15.8	12.7
11	22.2	12.7	23	17.9	14.7
12	18.2	14.1			

SORGHUM

(a) For dry-matter yield (DMY) and nitrogen concentration (NC), calculate the following:
(1) arithmetic mean, (6) midhinge,
(2) median, (7) range,
(3) mode, (8) interquartile range,
(4) midrange, (9) variance,
(5) quartiles, (10) standard deviation.

(b) Compare the mean and median obtained for the dry-matter yield and the nitrogen concentration. Do you think the distributions may be skewed and, if so, in what direction?

(c) Use the five-number summary to evaluate the distribution of the dry-matter yield and the nitrogen concentration. What conclusions do you reach about the shape of the distribution?

(d) Compare your analyses of dry-matter yield and nitrogen concentration. Do you find similarities or differences in the shapes of their distributions? Explain.

(e) Construct a box-and-whisker plot for the dry-matter yield and the nitrogen concentration. What conclusions do you reach about the way the data is distributed? Explain?

(f) Compare your box-and-whisker plots for dry-matter yield and nitrogen concentration. Do you find similarities or differences in the shapes of their distributions? Explain.

3.30 The following table presents the monthly mean reclaimed-water discharge, in cubic feet per second, from a water-reclamation facility.

YEAR

Month	1	2	3	4
January	6.8	7.2	5.8	8.0
February	7.7	10.7	7.8	8.6
March	6.0	5.5	5.2	6.7
April	6.0	5.5	5.8	6.0
May	5.6	5.3	5.1	5.2
June	5.4	5.1	4.7	4.7
July	4.6	4.4	4.2	4.4
August	4.8	4.7	4.4	4.5
September	5.6	4.8	4.7	3.6
October	5.2	5.1	4.3	5.1
November	4.4	5.1	4.8	5.0
December	4.4	5.1	4.8	5.0

RECLAIM

(a) For each year, calculate the
(1) arithmetic mean, (6) midhinge,
(2) median, (7) range,
(3) mode, (8) interquartile range,
(4) midrange, (9) variance,
(5) quartiles, (10) standard deviation.

(b) Compare the mean and median values for the reclaimed-water discharge data for each year. Do you think the distributions may be skewed and, if so, in what direction?

(c) Use the five-number summary to evaluate the distribution of the reclaimed-water discharge data for each year. What conclusions do you reach about the shape of the distributions?

(d) Compare your analyses for the years. Do you find similarities or differences in the shapes of their distributions?

(e) Construct side-by-side box-and-whisker plots for the reclaimed-water discharge data for the four years. Do you think the distributions may be skewed and, if so, in what direction? What other conclusions do you reach about the way the data is distributed?

(f) Compare your box-and-whisker plots for the four years. Do you find similarities or differences in the way data is distributed?

3.31 A study of municipal solid waste (MSW) collected from an industrial park recorded the cubic yards per day collected each day for a 92-day period. The data file **WASTE** includes the day of the week (Monday =1, Tuesday =2, and so on) and the number of cubic yards of waste collected each day.

    For the 92 days of municipal solid waste data, do the following:

(a) Set up a run chart. Are there any trends or patterns in the data?

(b) Calculate the
    (1) arithmetic mean,   (6) midhinge,
    (2) median,   (7) range,
    (3) mode,   (8) interquartile range,
    (4) midrange,   (9) variance,
    (5) quartiles,   (10) standard deviation.

(c) List the five-number summary.

(d) Construct the box-and-whisker plot.

(e) Are the data skewed? If so, how?

(f) Do (a)–(e) for the municipal solid waste data, collected on weekdays (days 1, 2, 3, 4, and 5)

(g) Do (a)–(e) for the municipal solid waste data collected on weekends (days 6 and 7).

(h) Compare the analysis for weekday collections with the analysis for weekend collections. How are they different or similar?

3.32 A study of single-event shocks experienced in mobile machinery measured unweighted peak-to-peak shock values, weighted peak-to-peak shock values, and operators' subjective ratings of severity of shocks. These data are included in the data file **SHOCK**. (*Source:* Spang, K.; Assessment of whole-body vibration containing single event shocks; *Noise Control Engineering Journal,* 45, 1, 1997, 19–25).

    For each of the variables, (unweighted peak-to-peak, weighted peak-to-peak, and subjective rating), do the following:

(a) Calculate the
    (1) arithmetic mean,   (6) midhinge,
    (2) median,   (7) range,
    (3) mode,   (8) interquartile range,
    (4) midrange,   (9) variance,
    (5) quartiles,   (10) standard deviation.

(b) List the five-number summary.

(c) Construct the box-and-whisker plot.

(d) Are the data skewed? If so, how? Explain.

3.33 One of the functions of the computer systems department of a newspaper relates to the reporting of the activities of the mainframe computer system. Typically, in any given day, more than 100 different jobs need to be processed on the system. These jobs vary in requirements, from very small jobs (which require a minimum of access to data-cartridge storage devices) to large, complex jobs that need to access in excess of 200 different data cartridges. The data presented on the top of page 132 consist of an ordered array of the number of data cartridges that needed to be accessed by 111 jobs on a recent day.

Ordered Array of Number of Data Cartridges Accessed Per Job on a Recent Day

1 1 1 1 1 1 2 2 2 2 2 2 3 3 3 3 4 4 4 4 4 4 5 5 5 5 5 5 5 6 6 6 7 7 7 7 8 8
8 8 9 10 10 10 10 10 11 12 12 13 14 14 15 17 18 18 18 18 19 20 20 20 20 21
22 23 24 28 28 29 30 30 30 30 31 32 33 35 37 40 40 42 43 50 52 55 56 59 60
60 67 74 80 86 91 94 96 100 111 126 127 131 137 140 144 147 164 166 170 182
212 237
NEWSPAPER

(a) Set up all appropriate tables and charts for the number of data cartridges accessed by jobs on a recent day.

(b) Compute all descriptive summary measures, a stem-and-leaf display, and a box-and-whisker plot relating to the number of data cartridges accessed for jobs that you believe would be useful in preparing a report to management.

(c) What conclusions can you draw from (a) and (b)?

3.34 An experiment was conducted to assess the effect of using magnets at the filler point in the manufacture of coffee filter packs. The table below presents the weights of filter packs in grams. Thirty packs produced with magnets are to be compared to 45 packs produced without magnets.

With Magnets

20.1 20.1 19.6 19.5 19.4 20.4 19.6 13.5 19.7 20.6 20.2 20.4 19.9 20.4 20.1
19.7 19.2 19.3 19.5 19.1 20.4 20.6 20.6 20.1 20.2 20.0 19.8 20.8 19.6 19.3

Without Magnets

21.4 20.5 20.2 20.6 21.4 20.1 19.9 19.7 21.2 20.7 20.9 20.2 20.1 20.7 20.4
21.0 20.5 20.0 20.6 20.8 19.5 19.7 20.0 20.4 20.2 20.5 20.4 21.3 20.4 20.2
20.5 20.7 19.8 20.7 20.2 20.0 20.5 20.6 20.6 19.9 20.0 20.2 20.6 19.9 20.4

MAGNETS

For each of the methods (with magnets, and without magnets), do the following:

(a) Calculate the

    (1) arithmetic mean,   (6) midhinge,
    (2) median,   (7) range,
    (3) mode,   (8) interquartile range,
    (4) midrange,   (9) variance,
    (5) quartiles,   (10) standard deviation.

(b) List the five-number summary.

(c) Construct the box-and-whisker plot.

(d) Are the data skewed? If so, how?

(e) Compare the results you obtained for the *with-magnets* group with the results you obtained for the *without-magnets* group. Does the use of magnets have an effect on the weight of the filter packs produced?

3.35 For the 1996 automobiles (see the data file **AUTO96**), for each of the following variables—highway miles per gallon, fuel tank capacity, length, width, weight, wheel base, turning circle capacity, luggage capacity, front leg room, and front head room—do the following:

(a) Calculate the

    (1) arithmetic mean,   (6) midhinge,
    (2) median,   (7) range,
    (3) mode,   (8) interquartile range,
    (4) midrange,   (9) variance,
    (5) quartiles,   (10) standard deviation.

(b) List the five-number summary.

(c) Construct the box-and-whisker plot.

(d) Are the data skewed? If so, how?

WHITNEY GOURMET CAT FOOD COMPANY CASE

The team that was involved in selecting the weekly samples of kidney and shrimp cans realized that, in addition to the numerous tables and charts that had been prepared (based on Table WG2.1 (page 94), relating to the weights of the cans), various descriptive summary measures relating to location, variation, and skewness should be obtained to make any report provided to management more useful.

Exercises

WG3.1 (a) Compute all descriptive summary measures, stem-and-leaf displays, and box-and-whisker

plots relating to the weight of the cat food cans that you believe would be useful in preparing a report to management.

(b) Write a report to the plant manager that summarizes the results obtained from the descriptive summary measures, stem-and-leaf displays, and box-and-whisker plots developed in (a).

REFERENCES

1. *Microsoft Excel 2000;* Redmond, WA: Microsoft Press, 1999
2. *MINITAB for Windows Version 12;* State College, PA: MINITAB, Inc., 1998
3. Ramsey, P. P. and P. H. Ramsey; "Simple Tests of Normality in Small Samples," *Journal of Quality Technology,* 22, (1990), 299–309
4. Tukey, J.; *Exploratory Data Analysis;* Reading, MA: Addison–Wesley, 1977

APPENDIX 3.1   *Using Microsoft Excel for Descriptive Statistics*

Using the Data Analysis Tool

Although various Microsoft Excel functions, such as AVERAGE, MEDIAN, and STDEV, can be used to compute individual statistics, the Data Analysis tool can simultaneously obtain a set of descriptive statistics, as displayed in Figure 3.6 on page 119. The Data Analysis tool can be accessed from the Tools menu by selecting Tools | Data Analysis, and then Descriptive Statistics can be chosen from the Analysis Tools list box.

To obtain the descriptive statistics for the pH of the 12 ultra-pure samples and the 12 deionizing samples, open the **WATER.XLS** workbook. Select **Tools | Data Analysis.** Then choose **Descriptive Statistics** from the Analysis Tools list box and click the **OK** button. In the Input Range edit box, enter **B1:B13,** because the pH values for the ultra-pure system are in rows 2–13 and the variable label is in row 1. Select the **Grouped By Columns** option button. Select the **Labels in First Row** check box. Leave the Confidence Levels for Mean check box unchecked—it will be discussed in Chapter 8. To obtain the minimum and maximum values, select the Kth Largest and the Kth Smallest check boxes, and enter 1 in their edit boxes. Select the New Worksheet Ply option button, and enter the name **Descriptive** in its edit box. Select the **Summary Statistics** check box. Click the **OK** button. To obtain descriptive statistics for the deionizing samples, repeat the instructions for ultra-pure, but change the Input Range box to B14:B25, and leave the labels in First Row check box unchecked.

Using the PHStat Add-In to Obtain a Box-and-Whisker Plot

To obtain the box-and-whisker plot using PHStat, with the WATER.XLS workbook open, select **PHStat | Box-and-Whisker Plot.** In the Data Variable Cell Range edit box, enter **B1:B25**. Select the **First cell contains label** check box. There are multiple groups which are stacked (all the pH values for the two groups are in a single column), so select the **Multiple Groups—Stacked** button, and enter **A1:A25** in its edit box. Select the five-number summary check box. Click the **OK** button. If a box-and-whisker plot for a single group is desired, the single-group variable input option would be selected.

APPENDIX 3.2   *Using MINITAB for Descriptive Statistics*

Obtaining Descriptive Statistics and a Box-and-Whisker Plot

To obtain the descriptive statistics for the pH of the 12 ultra-pure samples and the 12 deionizing samples, open the **WATER.MTW** file. Select **STAT | Basic Statistics | Display Descriptive Statistics.** In the Descriptive Statistics dialog box, in the Variables List box, enter the **'pH' or C2.** Select the **By Variable** check box and enter **'Type' or C1.** Select **Graphs.** Select the **Boxplot of data** check box. Click the **OK** button. Click the **OK** button again.

chapter

4

Probability and Discrete Probability Distributions

"The theory of probabilities is nothing more than good sense confirmed by calculations."

PIERRE SIMON, MARQUIS DE LAPLACE

USING STATISTICS

In the creation of the supports for a retaining wall for a county highway, a certain number of welds are required. The welds need to be inspected by a representative of the county to insure that they were done properly; however, in many cases, a large number of welds is involved, so a sample of welds is selected. Among the information that needs to be determined is the probability that, in a given sample taken from a population of welds, all the welds will be found to be done properly. In addition, to evaluate the quality of all welds, it is helpful to determine the probability that the first weld that was not done properly will be found on a certain sample selected.

4.1 INTRODUCTION

The word *probability* is often thought of as synonymous with *chance, likelihood,* or *possibility*—words that we hear with respect to the behavior of the stock market, weather forecasting, quality control or health issues. Put in its simplest terms, a **probability** is the numeric value representing the chance, likelihood, or possibility that a particular event will occur, be it an economic recession, a rainy day, a non-conforming unit of production, or the outcome *red* in one spin of a roulette wheel. In all these instances, the probability attached is a proportion or fraction whose values range *between 0 and 1, inclusive.*

The basic elements of probability theory are the individual outcomes of a particular process, be it an experimental trial or a natural phenomenon. Each possible type of occurrence is referred to as an **event.** Each individual or distinct outcome is referred to as an **elementary event.** For example, when tossing a coin, the two possible outcomes are heads and tails. Each of these represents an elementary event. An event is a set of elementary events. When rolling a standard six-sided die (see Figure 4.1), in which the six faces of the die contain either one, two, three, four, five, or six dots, there are six possible elementary events. An event can be any one

Figure 4.1   The six sides of a pair of dice

135

of these elementary events, or a subset of all of them. For example, the event of an *even number of dots* is represented by three elementary events (i.e., two, four, or six dots).

There are three distinct approaches that can be taken with respect to the assignment of a probability to an event's occurring: the *classical* or *theoretical* approach; the *empirical* approach; and the *subjective* approach.

The **classical or theoretical approach** for assigning probability is based on prior knowledge of the process involved. Classical probability always assumes that all elementary events are equally likely to occur. When this is true, then $P(A)$, the probability that a particular event A will occur, is defined as follows:

$$P(A) = \frac{X_A}{T} \tag{4.1}$$

where

X_A = number of ways A can occur

T = total number of elementary events

We can illustrate classical probability by referring again to a standard six-sided die. If this die is rolled a single time, the probability of obtaining the face with two dots is $1/6$, because there is only one face that contains exactly two dots, out of a total of six possible faces (i.e., elementary events). The assumption made by the classical (theoretical) approach is that the rolling process is totally random and has no memory, so that each of the six faces is equally likely to occur on each and every roll of the die. Thus, on any roll, the probability of obtaining the face with two dots remains $1/6$. In the long run, assuming the process is working properly, we theoretically expect 1,000 out of 6,000 rolls to result in a face with two dots.

The **empirical approach** to assigning probability does not assume that all elementary events are equally likely. Although the probability of event A occurring is still defined as the ratio of the number of ways that A can occur to the total number of elementary events, as in Equation (4.1), the number of ways that event A could occur is based on relative frequencies obtained from empirically observed data, not on theoretical reasoning or assumed knowledge of a process.

The empirical approach can be illustrated by referring to an example concerning errors encountered during debugging and code changes (see Problem 2.28 on page 77). If an error was randomly selected from all the errors listed, the probability that an error was a logic error is determined as a relative frequency. The relative frequency of logic errors is obtained by dividing the number of logic errors, 187 in this example, by the total number of errors, 722 in this example. Using Equation (4.1), we have

$$P \text{ (Logic error)} = \frac{\text{Number of logic errors}}{\text{Total number of errors}}$$

$$= \frac{187}{722}$$

$$= 0.259$$

We can illustrate this empirical probability with a second example. Each year, ratings are compiled concerning the performance of new cars during the first 90 days

TABLE 4.1

CROSS-CLASSIFICATION TABLE OF COUNTRY IN WHICH THE
MANUFACTURER IS BASED AND WHETHER THE NEW CAR NEEDS
A REPAIR IN THE FIRST 90 DAYS OF USE

Country of Manufacture	Needs a Repair in the First 90 Days of Use		Totals
	Yes	No	
United States	7	293	300
Not United States	13	187	200
Totals	20	480	500

of use. Suppose that the cars have been categorized according to two attributes: whether the car needs a warranty-related repair (yes or no), and the country in which the manufacturer is based (United States or not United States). Based on a sample of 500 cars, 20 new cars needed a warranty repair, 300 of the cars were manufactured by an American-based company, and 7 of the new cars need a warranty repair and were manufactured by a United States based company. Table 4.1 summarizes these results.

If a single new car were randomly selected from the 500 new cars, the probability that it would need a repair during the first 90 days of use would be determined by a relative frequency. The relative frequency of new cars needing repairs is obtained by dividing the number of new cars needing repairs, 20, by the total number of new cars, 500. Using Equation (4.1), we have

$$P \text{ (Needs repair)} = \frac{\text{Number that need repair}}{\text{Total number of new cars}}$$

$$= \frac{20}{500}$$

$$= 0.04$$

The first example, concerning logic errors, and this example, concerning warranty repairs, both illustrated a single event, because we were interested only in whether a logic error occurred or the new car needed a repair during the first 90 days of use. In the second example, we were not concerned with the country of manufacture of the automobile. If, however, we are interested in evaluating not only whether the new car needed a repair during the first 90 days of use but *also* whether the car was manufactured in the United States, we would have a joint event.

A **joint event** is one defined by two or more characteristics.

The probability of a joint event is still defined as in Equation (4.1), but the number of ways that the event could occur refers to the joint event, not to the elementary event.

For example (referring again to the data of Table 4.1), if we wanted to find the probability of selecting an automobile that needed a repair *and* was manufactured by a United States-based company, we would determine the number of new cars that had both these characteristics (7) and divide by the total number of new cars (500). Thus, we have

$$P \text{ (Needs repair } and \text{ is U.S. based)} = \frac{\text{Number that need repair and are U.S. based}}{\text{Total number of new cars}}$$

$$\frac{7}{500} = 0.014$$

It is not always possible to use either the classical approach or the empirical approach when assigning probabilities. In such circumstances, where either the number of elementary events is unknown or data are not available for the calculation of relative frequencies, the **subjective approach** is often used. Subjective probabilities can be based on expert opinion or even gut feelings or hunches. Whereas the process-knowledge-based classical approach and the observed-data-based empirical approach to probability assignment are considered *objective,* a subjective approach to probability assessment is taken by individuals who employ various modes of intuition to judge the likely outcome of an event. Different individuals would provide differing assessments as to what future traffic patterns will be, what the weather will be like tomorrow, or what future economic conditions will be.

PROBLEMS

4.1 For each of the following, indicate whether it is an example of the classical, empirical, or subjective approach to probability:
  (a) that the next toss of a fair coin will result in a head;
  (b) that the next tire manufactured will last more than 25,000 miles;
  (c) that the next child born in a certain hospital will be a girl;
  (d) that three cars will drive through a certain intersection within the next minute.

4.2 SOME RULES OF PROBABILITY

There are several basic rules that govern the theory of probability.

Rule 1   A probability is a number between 0 and 1 that is assigned to an event or outcome of some process or experiment.

The smallest possible probability value is 0. An event or outcome that has a probability of 0 is called a *null event* and has no chance of occurring. When rolling a single die, the event of obtaining a face with seven dots has a probability of 0, because such an event cannot occur. In addition, no event can possibly have a probability that is below 0.

    The largest possible probability value is 1.0. An event or outcome that has a probability of 1.0 is called a *certain event* and must occur. When rolling a single die, the event of obtaining a face with fewer than seven dots has a probability of 1.0, because it is certain that one of the elementary events of one, two, three, four, five, or six dots must occur. This set of elementary events is also considered to be

collectively exhaustive, because one of them must occur. In addition, no event can have a probability that is above 1.0.

Rule 2   The event that A does not occur is called "A **complement**" or simply "not-A" and is given the symbol A'. If $P(A)$ represents the probability of event A's occurring, then $1 - P(A)$ represents the probability that event A will not occur.

For example, in the case of the die, the complement of obtaining the face that contains two dots is *not* obtaining the face that contains two dots. The probability of obtaining the face containing two dots is $1/6$, so the probability of not obtaining the face that contains two dots is $1 - 1/6 = 5/6$;

$$P \text{ (Not face 2)} = 1 - P \text{ (Face 2)}$$
$$= 1 - 1/6$$
$$= 5/6$$
$$= 0.833$$

In the case of the new cars, the complement of needing a warranty repair is *not* needing a warranty repair. The probability of needing a warranty repair is $20/500 = 0.04$, so the probability of not needing a warranty repair is $1 - 0.04 = 0.96$.

Rule 3   If two events A and B are *mutually exclusive,* then the probability that *both* event A and event B will occur is 0 [that is, $P(A \text{ and } B) = 0$].

If two events are **mutually exclusive,** they *cannot* occur at the same time. On one roll of a single die, we cannot obtain both the face with two dots *and* the face with four dots. Similarly, in the case of the new cars, if a new car is manufactured by a United States-based company, it cannot simultaneously be manufactured by a company that is not based in the United States.

Rule 4   If two events A and B are *mutually exclusive,* then the probability that *either* event A or event B will occur is the sum of their separate probabilities.

$$P(A \text{ or } B) = P(A) + P(B) \tag{4.2}$$

In the example concerning the single die, if we wanted to know the probability of obtaining the face that has two dots *or* the face that has three dots, we would have:

$$P \text{ (Face 2 or Face 3)} = P \text{ (Face 2)} + P \text{ (Face 3)}$$
$$= \frac{1}{6} + \frac{1}{6}$$
$$P \text{ (Face 2 or Face 3)} = \frac{2}{6} = \frac{1}{3} = 0.333$$

This addition rule for mutually exclusive events can be extended to consider cases in which there are more than two events. In the case of the die, suppose we want to know the probability of obtaining an even-numbered outcome (i.e., two, four, or six). Extending Equation (4.2), we have the following:

$$P\,(\text{Even}) = P\,(\text{Face } 2 \text{ or } 4 \text{ or } 6) = P\,(\text{Face } 2) + P\,(\text{Face } 4) + P\,(\text{Face } 6)$$

$$= \frac{1}{6} + \frac{1}{6} + \frac{1}{6}$$

$$= \frac{3}{6} = \frac{1}{2}$$

$$P\,(\text{Even}) = P\,(\text{Face } 2 \text{ or } 4 \text{ or } 6) = 0.50$$

Rule 5   If events in a set are mutually exclusive and collectively exhaustive, the sum of their probabilities must add to 1.0.

In the example of the single die, the events of a face with an even number of dots and a face with an odd number of dots are mutually exclusive and collectively exhaustive. They are mutually exclusive because even and odd *cannot* occur simultaneously on the roll of a single die; they are collectively exhaustive because either even or odd *must* occur on a particular roll. Therefore, the probability of a face with an even *or* odd number of dots is:

$$P\,(\text{Even or odd}) = P\,(2 \text{ or } 4 \text{ or } 6) + P\,(1 \text{ or } 3 \text{ or } 5)$$

$$= \frac{3}{6} + \frac{3}{6}$$

$$P\,(\text{Even or odd}) = \frac{6}{6} = 1.0$$

In the case of the new cars, if we wanted to know the probability that a new car needed a repair or did not need a repair, we would have:

$$P\,(\text{needs a repair or does not need a repair}) = P\,(\text{needs a repair})$$

$$+ P\,(\text{does not need a repair})$$

$$= \frac{20}{500} + \frac{480}{500}$$

$$= \frac{500}{500} = 1.0$$

Rule 6   If two events A and B are *not* mutually exclusive, then the probability of either event A *or* event B (or both) will occur is the sum of their separate probabilities *minus* the joint probability of their simultaneous occurrence.

$$P(A \text{ or } B) = P(A) + P(B) - P(A \text{ and } B) \qquad (4.3)$$

where

$P\,(A \text{ and } B)$ is the joint probability of events A *and* B occurring simultaneously.

We can illustrate this situation by referring again to the example concerning the repairs needed on new cars. In the results presented in Table 4.1 on page 137, we can observe that the events of a car's needing a repair and a car's being manufactured by a U.S.-based company are not mutually exclusive, because 7 new cars both needed a repair and were manufactured by a U.S.-based company. Thus, to determine the probability of needing a repair or being manufactured by a U.S.-based company, we add the probability of needing a repair to the probability of being manufactured by a U.S.-based company and then subtract the *joint* probability of simultaneously needing a repair and being manufactured by a U.S.-based company. The reason that this joint probability must be subtracted is that *it has already been included twice:* in computing the probability of needing a repair, and in computing the probability of being manufactured by a U.S.-based company. Therefore, it has been "double counted," so it must be subtracted to provide the correct result. Thus, we have the following:

P (needing a repair *or* being manufactured by a U.S.-based company)

$$= P \text{ (needing a repair)} + P \text{ (manufactured by a U.S.-based company)}$$

$$- P \text{ (needing a repair } and \text{ being manufactured by a U.S.-based company)}$$

$$= \frac{20}{500} + \frac{300}{500} - \frac{7}{500}$$

$$= \frac{313}{500}$$

$$= 0.626$$

Rule 7   In some situations, the *occurrence* of one event affects the *probability of occurrence* of another event. The conditional probability of B occurring given that A has occurred is equal to the joint probability that both *A and B* will occur divided by the probability of A occurring.

$$P\,(B|A) = \frac{P(A \text{ and } B)}{P(A)} \tag{4.4}$$

We can illustrate the concept of *conditional probability* by referring to the survey displayed in Table 4.1 on page 137. Suppose that we wanted to find the probability that a new car needs a repair given that the car was manufactured by a U.S.-based company. In other words, *for those cars manufactured by a U.S.-based company,* we want to find the probability that a new car needs a repair. From Table 4.1, we note that there are 300 cars manufactured by a U.S.-based company. Of these 300 cars, 7 needed repairs. Therefore, from Equation (4.4), the probability that a car needs a repair given that the car was manufactured by a U.S.-based company is computed as follows:

P (needs a repair | manufactured by a U.S.-based company)

$$= \frac{P \text{ (needs a repair and manufactured by U.S.-based company)}}{P \text{ (manufactured by U.S.-based company)}}$$

$$= \frac{7/500}{300/500} = \frac{7}{300}$$

$$= 0.0233$$

We could calculate the probability by working with the first row of Table 4.1 by dividing the number of U.S. cars needing repair, 7, by the total number of U.S. cars,

300. This makes us realize that the conditional probability is just a probability obtained for only part of all the possible events. However, often a table such as Table 4.1 is not available, so we would need to use Equation (4.4) in such situations to calculate conditional probabilities.

Rule 8   If two events *A and B* are *independent,* then the probability that *both* event *A and* event *B* will occur is equal to the product of their respective probabilities.

$$P(A \text{ and } B) = P(A) \times P(B) \qquad (4.5a)$$

Two events are **independent** if the occurrence of one event in no way affects the probability of the second event. That is, *A* and *B* are independent if and only if $P(A) = P(A \mid B)$ and $P(B) = P(B \mid A)$.

In the case of rolling a single die twice, it is reasonable to assume that the result of the second roll is independent of the result of the first roll. Thus, to determine the probability that we would obtain the face that contains five dots on *each* of two rolls, we would have:

$$P(5 \text{ dots on roll } 1 \text{ and } 5 \text{ dots on roll } 2) = P(5 \text{ dots on roll } 1) \times P(5 \text{ dots on roll } 2)$$

$$= \frac{1}{6} \times \frac{1}{6}$$

$$= \frac{1}{36}$$

Rule 9   If two events *A and B* are *not* independent, then the probability that both *A and B* will occur is the product of the probability of event *A* times the conditional probability of event *B* occurring given that event *A* has occurred.

$$P(A \text{ and } B) = P(A) \times P(B \mid A) \qquad (4.5b)$$

where

$P(B \mid A)$ is the **conditional probability** of event *B* occurring given that event *A* has occurred.

To show an example of Equation (4.5b), let us return to the *Using Statistics* example on page 135. Suppose that, in creating supports for a retaining wall, 8 welds are required, of which six were done properly. If a county inspector randomly selects two welds, what is the probability that both welds were done properly? Here Equation (4.5b) could be used in the following way:

If

$$A = \text{first weld is done properly}$$

and

$$B = \text{second weld is done properly}$$

we have

$$P(A \text{ and } B) = P(A) \times P(B \mid A)$$

The probability that the first weld is done properly is 6/8 or 3/4, because six of the eight welds were done properly. Now, we are selecting the second weld without giving the first weld any chance of being selected again (sampling without replacement), so the number of welds remaining after the first selection will be 7. If the first weld was done properly, the probability that the second was done properly is 5/7, because five welds done properly remain. Therefore, by using Equation (4.5b), we have the following:

$$P(A \text{ and } B) = \left(\frac{6}{8}\right)\left(\frac{5}{7}\right)$$

$$= \frac{30}{56}$$

$$= 0.5357$$

Thus, there is a 53.57% chance that, if the inspector evaluates two welds, then he will not detect any weld(s) done improperly.

PROBLEMS

4.2 As part of the yield-improvement effort at a semiconductor-manufacturing facility, a patterned wafer inspection system was used to provide defect data for a sample of 450 wafers. The results were cross-classified according to two characteristics: "Was a particle found on the die that produced the wafer?", and "Is the wafer good or bad?"

CONDITION OF DIE

Quality of Wafer	No Particles	Particles	Total
Good	320	14	334
Bad	80	36	116
Total	400	50	500

(a) Give an example of a simple event.
(b) Give an example of a joint event.
(c) What is the complement of the event *a good wafer?*
(d) Why is a good wafer with no particles a joint event?
(e) Suppose that a wafer is selected at random. What is the probability that the wafer
   (1) is good?
   (2) has no particles?
   (3) is good *or* has no particles?
   (4) is good *and* has no particles?
(f) Suppose that the wafer selected has no particles. What then is the probability that it is good?

(g) Suppose that the wafer selected has particles. What then is the probability that it is good?
(h) Explain the difference between your answers to (f) and (g).
(i) Suppose that the wafer selected is good. What then is the probability that it has no particles?
(j) Explain the difference between your answers to (f) and (i).

4.3 Diagnostic tests are available for a variety of medical conditions. Although these tests are extremely reliable, they sometimes provide incorrect results. Suppose that the probability that the test will give a positive diagnosis (indicating that the disease is present) is 0.04. Given that the test diagnosis is positive, the probability that the person *has* the disease is 0.95. Given that the test diagnosis is negative, the probability that the person does *not* have the disease is 0.99.
(a) Give an example of a simple event.
(b) Give an example of a joint event.
(c) If a diagnostic test result is selected at random, what is the probability that
   (1) the test diagnosis is negative?
   (2) the test diagnosis is negative *and* the patient does not have the disease?
   (3) the test diagnosis is positive *and* the patient has the disease?

(4) the disease is present?

(5) the test diagnosis is positive *or* the patient has the disease?

(d) Suppose that we know that the disease is present in a particular individual. What then is the probability that the test diagnosis for this individual will be positive?

(e) Suppose that we know the probability that the test diagnosis for an individual is positive. What then is the probability that the disease is present in this particular individual?

(f) Explain why the answers in (d) and (e) are not the same.

Hint: Set up a 2 × 2 cross-classification table to evaluate the probabilities.

4.4 A soft-drink bottling company maintains records concerning the number of unacceptable bottles of soft drink obtained from the filling and capping machines. The probability, based on past data, that a bottle came from machine 1 and was nonconforming is 0.01 and that a bottle came from machine 2 and was nonconforming is 0.025. Half the bottles are filled on machine 1 and the other half are filled on machine 2.

(a) Give an example of a simple event.

(b) Give an example of a joint event.

(c) If a filled bottle of soft drink is selected at random, what is the probability that

(1) it is a nonconforming bottle?

(2) it is filled on machine 2?

(3) it is filled on machine 1 *and* is a conforming bottle?

(4) it is filled on machine 2 *and* is a conforming bottle?

(5) it is filled on machine 1 *or* is a conforming bottle?

(d) Suppose that we know that a bottle is filled on machine 1. What is the probability that it is nonconforming?

(e) Suppose that we know that the bottle is nonconforming. What is the probability that it was filled on machine 1?

(f) Explain the difference between the answers to (d) and (e).

Hint: Set up a 2 × 2 cross-classification table to evaluate the probabilities.

4.5 Suppose that two cards are to be randomly selected from a standard deck of 52 playing cards, *without* replacement.

(a) What is the probability that both cards are red?

(b) What is the probability that the first card is an ace *and* the second card is either a ten, jack, queen, or king?

(c) If you were returning the card to the deck before selecting the second card, what would be your answers in (a) and in (b)?

4.6 Suppose that you believe that the probability that you will get a grade of B or above in Statistics is 0.6 and that the probability that you will get a grade of B or above in Calculus is 0.5. If these events are independent, what is the probability that you will get grades of B or above in both Statistics and Calculus? Give some plausible reasons why these events might not be independent.

4.7 A shipment of 50 personal computers has 40 intact, eight damaged but operative, and two inoperative. If two personal computers are randomly selected *without* replacement from the shipment,

(a) what is the probability that both are intact?

(b) what is the probability that both are damaged but operative?

(c) If you were returning the first personal computer to the shipment before selecting the second, what would be your answers in (a) and in (b)?

(d) If three personal computers were to be selected without replacement, what is the probability that all three are damaged but operative?

(e) What would be your answer to (d) if you sampled *with* replacement?

 ## 4.3 THE PROBABILITY DISTRIBUTION

Development

Now that we have defined the concept of probability and illustrated the application of some of the rules of probability, we can extend our discussion to situations in which there are many different possible outcomes to a variable of interest. In order to do so, let us first consider an electrical circuit that consists of three relays, each of which, independently, can remain open or closed when its switch is thrown.

Suppose that the probability that a relay remains open is 0.5. The possible outcomes that can occur in terms of the number of relays that remain open are listed as follows:

Outcomes	First Relay	Second Relay	Third Relay
1	Open	Open	Open
2	Open	Open	Closed
3	Open	Closed	Open
4	Open	Closed	Closed
5	Closed	Open	Open
6	Closed	Open	Closed
7	Closed	Closed	Open
8	Closed	Closed	Closed

We obtain the probability of occurrence of a particular outcome [for example, first relay open (O_1), second relay open (O_2), and third relay open (O_3)] by extending Equation (4.5a) to the case of three events (i.e., relays). Thus, we compute:

$$P(O_1 \text{ and } O_2 \text{ and } O_3) = P(O_1) \times P(O_2) \times P(O_3)$$

Since each relay has a probability of being open of 0.5, we have,

$$P(O_1 \text{ and } O_2 \text{ and } O_3) = (0.5)(0.5)(0.5)$$
$$P(O_1 \text{ and } O_2 \text{ and } O_3) = 0.125$$

Another way of looking at this example in this special case where $p = 0.5$ is to consider each of the rows as a distinct outcome or elementary event. The event O_1 and O_2 and O_3 can only occur one way, and there are eight elementary events, so, from Equation (4.1), we have

$$P(A) = \frac{X_A}{T}$$
$$P(O_1 \text{ and } O_2 \text{ and } O_3) = 1/8 = 0.125$$

Similar calculations can be done for each of the other seven possible outcomes. (In this instance, the probability that the relay is open is 0.5, and therefore the probability of being open is the same as the probability of being closed.) We can then organize the results in terms of the probability of obtaining a particular number of open relays in three independent relays. When we do so, we find that there is one outcome in which there are zero open relays, three outcomes in which there is one open relay, three outcomes in which there are two open relays, and one outcome in which there are three open relays.[1] These results are summarized in Table 4.2 on page 146.

Table 4.2 is an example of a probability distribution for a discrete random variable.

A **probability distribution** for a discrete random variable is a complete set of all possible distinct outcomes and their probabilities of occurring. Because all possible outcomes are listed, the sum of the probabilities must add to 1.0.

Table 4.2 satisfies this definition of the probability distribution, because all outcomes (0, 1, 2, and 3 relays open) are listed, and because the sum of the probabilities is 1.0.

[1] This is actually an example of a process that follows the binomial distribution, which will be covered in Section 4.4.

TABLE 4.2

DISTRIBUTION OF THE EXPECTED RESULTS OF THE NUMBER OF RELAYS THAT REMAIN OPEN AMONG THREE RELAY SWITCHES

Number of Relays Open	Frequency	Probability
0	1	0.125
1	3	0.375
2	3	0.375
3	1	0.125
	8	1.000

As a second example of a probability distribution, suppose that the number of defective welds in a length of pipe has the probability distribution illustrated in Table 4.3.

TABLE 4.3

NUMBER OF DEFECTIVE WELDS IN A LENGTH OF PIPE

Number of Defective Welds	Probability
0	0.60
1	0.20
2	0.10
3	0.05
4	0.03
5	0.01
6	0.01

Table 4.3 also satisfies the definition of the probability distribution, because all outcomes (0, 1, 2, 3, 4, 5, and 6 defective welds) are listed, and because the sum of the probabilities is 1.0.

The Expected Value or Average of a Discrete Random Variable

The mean (μ_x) of a probability distribution is called the *expected value* of the random variable x.

The **expected value** of a discrete random variable is defined as its weighted average over all possible outcomes, with the weight for each outcome being the relative frequency or probability associated with that outcome.

This summary measure is obtained by multiplying each possible outcome X_i by its corresponding probability $P(X_i)$ and then summing the resulting products. Thus, the expected value of the discrete random variable X, symbolized as $E(X)$, is expressed as follows:

$$\mu_x = E(X) = \sum_{\text{all } X_i} X_i P(X_i) \tag{4.6}$$

where

$$X = \text{discrete random variable of interest}$$

$$X_i = i\text{th outcome of } X$$

$$P(X_i) = \text{probability of occurrence of the } i\text{th outcome of } X$$

$$i = 1, 2, \ldots$$

For our example concerning the three relay switches (Table 4.2), the expected value of the number of open relays is computed as:

$$\mu_x = E(X) = \sum_{\text{all } X_i} X_i P(X_i) = (0)(0.125) + (1)(0.375) + (2)(0.375) + (3)(0.125)$$

$$= 0 + 0.375 + 0.750 + 0.375$$

$$\mu_x = E(X) = 1.50$$

Notice that, in this example, the average or expected value of the number of open relays is a value that cannot itself occur. That the average is 1.5 open relays tells us that, in the long run, if we perform this circuit-opening experiment many times, the average number of open relays we can expect will be 1.5.

In the second example, concerning the number of defective welds in a length of pipe, the expected value of the number of defective welds is computed as follows:

$$\mu_x = E(X) = \sum_{\text{all } X_i} X_i P(X_i) = (0)(0.60) + (1)(0.20) + (2)(0.10) + 3(0.05)$$

$$+ (3)(0.125) + (5)(0.01) + (6)(0.01)$$

$$= 0 + 0.20 + 0.20 + 0.15 + 0.12 + 0.05 + 0.06$$

$$\mu_x = E(X) = 0.78$$

This means that (given the probabilities for each number of defective welds) the average number of defective welds is expected to be 0.78.

Variance and Standard Deviation of a Discrete Random Variable

The **variance (σ_x^2) of a discrete random variable** is defined as the weighted average of the squared differences between each possible outcome and the average value of the outcomes, with the weights being the probabilities associated with each of the outcomes.

This summary measure is obtained by multiplying each squared difference $(X_i - \mu_x)^2$ by its corresponding probability $P(X_i)$ and then summing the resulting products. Thus, the variance of the discrete random variable X is expressed as follows:

$$\sigma_x^2 = \sum_{\text{all } X_i} (X_i - \mu_x)^2 P(X_i) \tag{4.7}$$

where

X = discrete random variable of interest

X_i = ith outcome of X

$P(X_i)$ = probability of occurrence of the ith outcome of X

$i = 1, 2, \ldots$

In addition, the standard deviation, σ_x, of the probability distribution of a discrete random variable is the square root of the variance and is given by

$$\sigma_x = \sqrt{\sum_{\text{all } X_i} (X_i - \mu_x)^2 P(X_i)} \qquad (4.8)$$

For our example concerning the three relay switches (Table 4.2 on page 146), the variance and standard deviation of the number of open relays are computed as follows:

$$\sigma_x^2 = \sum_{i=1}^{N} (X_i - \mu_x)^2 P(X_i) = (0 - 1.5)^2(0.125) + (1 - 1.5)^2(0.375)$$

$$+ (2 - 1.5)^2(0.375) + (3 - 1.5)^2(0.125)$$

$$= 2.25(0.125) + 0.25(0.375) + 0.25(0.375) + 2.25(0.125)$$

$$= 0.75$$

and

$$\sigma_x = \sqrt{0.75}$$

$$\sigma_x = 0.866$$

For our example concerning the number of defective welds (Table 4.3), the variance and standard deviation of the number of defective welds is computed as:

$$\sigma_x^2 = \sum_{i=1}^{N} (X_i - \mu_x)^2 P(X_i) = (0 - 0.78)^2(0.60) + (1 - 0.78)^2(0.20)$$

$$+ (2 - 0.78)^2(0.10) + (3 - 0.78)^2(0.05) + (4 - 0.78)^2(0.03)$$

$$+ (5 - 0.78)^2(0.01) + (6 - 0.78)^2(0.01)$$

$$= 0.6084(0.60) + 0.0484(0.20) + 1.4884(0.10) + 4.9284(0.05) + 10.3684(0.03)$$

$$+ 17.8084(0.01) + 27.2484(0.01)$$

$$= 0.36504 + 0.00968 + 0.14884 + 0.24642 + 0.311052 + 0.178084 + 0.272484$$

$$= 1.5316$$

and

$$\sigma_x = \sqrt{1.5316}$$

$$\sigma_x = 1.2376$$

In this section, we have developed the concept of a probability distribution and have defined the expected value (or average), the standard deviation, and the variance of a discrete probability distribution. In the remainder of the chapter, we will focus on specific discrete probability distributions that are important in statistics.

PROBLEMS

4.8 You are given the following discrete probability distributions:

Distribution A		Distribution B	
X	$P(X)$	X	$P(X)$
0	0.40	0	0.10
1	0.30	1	0.20
2	0.20	2	0.30
3	0.10	3	0.40

(a) Compute the mean (expected value) for each distribution.
(b) Compute the variance and standard deviation for each distribution.
(c) Compare the results for both (a) and (b) for the two distributions.

4.9 You are given the following discrete probability distributions:

Distribution A		Distribution B	
X	$P(X)$	X	$P(X)$
0	0.25	0	0.20
1	0.25	1	0.40
2	0.25	2	0.20
3	0.25	3	0.20

(a) Compute the mean (expected value) for each distribution.
(b) Compute the variance and standard deviation for each distribution.
(c) Compare the results for both (a) and (b) for the two distributions.

4.10 The following table contains the probability distribution for the number of retransmissions necessary to successfully transmit a 1024K data package through a double-satellite hookup:

X	$P(X)$
0	0.35
1	0.35
2	0.25
3	0.05

(a) Compute the mean (expected value).
(b) Compute the variance and standard deviation.
(c) From the results of (a) and (b), what conclusions can you reach about retransmissions?

4.11 The following table contains the probability distribution of the number of traffic accidents daily in a small city.

X	$P(X)$
0	0.10
1	0.20
2	0.45
3	0.15
4	0.05
5	0.05

(a) Compute the mean (expected value).
(b) Compute the variance and standard deviation.
(c) From the results of (a) and (b), what conclusions can you reach about traffic accidents in this small city?

4.12 A manufacturer of designer jeans must decide whether to build a large factory or a small factory in a particular location. The profit per pair of jeans manufactured is estimated as $10. A small factory will have an annual cost of $200,000 and provide a production capacity of 50,000 jeans per year. A large factory will have an amortized annual cost of $400,000 and provide a production capacity of 100,000 jeans per year. Four levels of product demand are possible. They are 10,000 (probability of 0.1), 20,000 (probability of 0.4), 50,000 (probability of 0.2), and 100,000 (probability of 0.3) pairs of jeans per year.
(a) Compute the expected profit (in thousands of dollars) for each of the two factory sizes.
(b) Compute the standard deviation (in thousands of dollars) for each of the two factory sizes.
(c) On the basis of the results of (a) and (b), what size factory would you choose to build? Explain.

4.4 THE BINOMIAL DISTRIBUTION

Many investigations involving probability distributions are based on attribute measures that result from the tallies or counts of one of two outcomes of a categorical variable having only two classifications, arbitrarily called success or failure. When classifying each event studied as either a success or a failure, it is not important which outcome is classified as a success and which one is classified as a failure. For example, in the context of statistical process control (which will be studied in Chapters 6 and 7), an item that has failed inspection could be classified as a success, since our goal may be to study nonconformances. In such circumstances, we can apply the binomial probability distribution to analyze the number of nonconforming items in a sample of n units.

Developing the Mathematical Model

The **binomial distribution** possesses three essential properties:

1. Each elementary event is classified into one of two mutually exclusive and collectively exhaustive categories, such as success or failure.
2. The probability of an outcome being classified as success, p, is constant from trial to trial and the probability of an outcome being classified as failure, $1 - p$, is constant from trial to trial.
3. The outcome (success or failure) on a particular trial is independent of the outcome on any other trial.

The random variable X representing the binomial distribution is the number of successes in a sample of n trials. Thus, the random variable X takes on any value from 0 through n. The binomial distribution has two parameters: n, the number of trials, and p, the probability of obtaining a success, which remains constant from trial to trial. The following mathematical model represents the binomial probability distribution for obtaining a certain number ($X = x$) of successes, given a knowledge of the parameters n and p:

$$P(X = x \mid n, p) = \frac{n!}{x!(n - x)!} p^x (1 - p)^{n-x} \qquad (4.9)$$

where

$$P(X = x \mid n, p) = \text{the probability that } X = x, \text{ given a knowledge of } n \text{ and } p$$

$$n = \text{sample size}$$

$$p = \text{probability of success}$$

$$1 - p = \text{probability of failure}$$

$$x = \text{number of successes in the sample } (X = 0, 1, 2, \ldots, n)$$

In Equation (4.9), the product

$$p^x (1 - p)^{n-x}$$

indicates the probability of obtaining exactly x successes from a sample of n trials in a *particular* sequence or arrangement, while the term

$$\frac{n!}{x!(n-x)!}$$

indicates *how many* such sequences or arrangements of the x successes are possible. The term $n!$ is called n *factorial* and is defined for integers greater than one as $(n)(n-1)(n-2)\cdots(1)$. Thus, $5! = (5)(4)(3)(2)(1) = 120$. In addition, by definition, $1! = 1$ and $0! = 1$.

This $\dfrac{n!}{x!(n-x)!}$ term is often written in an alternative manner, by using $\dbinom{n}{x}$ or the notation $C_{n,x}$

$$\binom{n}{x} = C_{n,x} = \frac{n!}{x!(n-x)!}$$

To demonstrate an application of the binomial probability distribution, let us refer again to our example on page 146 concerning the probability distribution of the number of open relay switches. In fact, this relay switching process fits the properties of the binomial distribution: for each relay switch, only two outcomes are possible (i.e., open and closed). The probability of obtaining an open switch is assumed to remain constant from switch to switch, because the outcome of each switch is considered to be independent of the outcome of all other switches.

Thus, with three switches considered, and a probability of a switch being opened of 0.5, we have $n = 3$, and $p = 0.5$. If we wanted to find the probability of obtaining two open switches out of three switches by using Equation (4.9), we have the following:

$$P(X = 2 \mid n = 3, p = 0.5) = \frac{n!}{x!(n-x)!}p^x(1-p)^{n-x}$$

$$= \frac{3!}{2!(3-2)!}(0.5)^2(1-0.05)^{3-2}$$

$$= \frac{3!}{2!1!}(0.5)^2(1-0.5)^1$$

$$= \frac{3!}{2!1!}(0.5)(0.5)(0.5)$$

$$= (3)(0.125) = 0.375$$

Note, in this computation, that 0.125 is the probability of obtaining a particular sequence of two open switches out of three switches. As we observed in Section 4.3, however, three such sequences of two open switches out of three switches exist—*open open closed, open closed open,* and *closed open open.* Therefore, the probability of obtaining exactly two open switches out of three switches (regardless of the order of the open and closed switches) is $(3)(0.125) = 0.375$.

If we were interested in finding the probability that all three switches will be open, we have

$$P(X = 3 \mid n = 3, p = 0.5) = \frac{n!}{x!(n-x)!} p^x (1-p)^{n-x}$$

$$= \frac{3!}{3!(3-3)!} (0.5)^3 (1-0.5)^{3-3}$$

$$= \frac{3!}{3!0!} (0.5)^3 (1-0.5)^0$$

$$= \frac{3!}{3!0!} (0.5)(0.5)(0.5)$$

$$= (1)(0.125) = 0.125$$

Note, in this computation, that 0.125 is the probability of obtaining a sequence of three consecutive open switches. Only one such sequence exists—*open open open*—so the probability of obtaining exactly three open switches in a sample of three switches is 0.125.

To find the probability that we will obtain *at least* two open switches out of three switches (the probability of obtaining two or three open switches), we calculate as follows:

$$P(X \geq 2 \mid n = 3, p = 0.5) = P(X = 2 \mid n = 3, p = 0.5) + P(X = 3 \mid n = 3, p = 0.5)$$

$$= 0.375 + 0.125$$

$$= 0.50$$

If we already know the probability of two or more open switches, and we want to find the probability that *fewer* than two open switches will occur, we subtract its complement (the probability of at least two open switches) from 1.0. Therefore,

$$P(X < 2) = 1 - P(X \geq 2)$$

$$= 1 - 0.50$$

$$= 0.50$$

As a second example of the binomial distribution, suppose that there are five switches, but the probability that each switch is open is only .16. What would be the chance of obtaining at least four open switches out of five switches? By using Equation (4.9) with $n = 5$, $p = 0.16$, for $X = 4$ or $X = 5$, we obtain the following:

$$P(X \geq 4 \mid n = 5, p = 0.16) = P(X = 4 \mid n = 5, p = 0.16) + P(X = 5 \mid n = 5, p = 0.16)$$

Thus,

$$P(X = 4 \mid n = 5, p = 0.16) = \frac{n!}{x!(n-x)!} p^x (1-p)^{n-x}$$

$$= \frac{5!}{4!(5-4)!} (0.16)^4 (1-0.16)^{5-4}$$

$$= \frac{5!}{4!1!} (0.16)^4 (1-0.16)^1$$

$$= \frac{5!}{4!1!} (0.16)(0.16)(0.16)(0.16)(0.84)$$

$$= (5)(0.00055) = 0.00275$$

and

$$P(X = 5 \mid n = 5, p = 0.16) = \frac{n!}{x!(n - x)!}p^x(1 - p)^{n-x}$$

$$= \frac{5!}{5!(5 - 5)!}(0.16)^5(1 - 0.16)^{5-5}$$

$$= \frac{5!}{5!0!}(0.16)^5(1 - 0.16)^0$$

$$= \frac{5!}{5!0!}(0.16)(0.16)(0.16)(0.16)(0.16)(1)$$

$$= (1)(0.00010) = 0.00010$$

Therefore,

$$P(X \geq 4 \mid n = 5, p = 0.16) = P(X = 4 \mid n = 5, p = 0.16) + P(X = 5 \mid n = 5, p = 0.16)$$

$$= 0.00275 + 0.00010$$

$$= 0.00285$$

Computations such as the ones we have done in these examples become quite tedious, especially as n gets large. Fortunately, it is not necessary to use Equation (4.9) to calculate the probabilities. We can obtain the probabilities from Microsoft Excel or MINITAB. (See Appendices 4.1 and 4.2.) Figure 4.2 represents output from the PHStat add-in for Microsoft Excel, and Figure 4.3 on page 154 represents output from MINITAB for the binomial distribution with parameters $n = 5$ and $p = 0.16$.

	A	B	C	D	E	F	G
1	Binomial Probabilities for Open Relay Switches						
2							
3	Sample size	5					
4	Probability of success	0.16					
5	Mean	0.8					
6	Variance	0.672					
7	Standard deviation	0.819756					
8							
9	Binomial Probabilities Table						
10		X	P(X)	P(<=X)	P(<X)	P(>X)	P(>=X)
11		0	0.418212	0.418212	0	0.581788	1
12		1	0.398297	0.816509	0.418212	0.183491	0.581788
13		2	0.151732	0.968241	0.816509	0.031759	0.183491
14		3	0.028901	0.997143	0.968241	0.002857	0.031759
15		4	0.002753	0.999895	0.997143	0.000105	0.002857
16		5	0.000105	1	0.999895	0	0.000105

Figure 4.2 Binomial distribution calculations for $n = 5$ and $p = 0.16$ obtained from the PHStat add-in for Microsoft Excel

Characteristics of Binomial Distributions

Each time a set of parameters n and p is specified, a particular binomial probability distribution can be generated.

```
Binomial with n = 5 and p = 0.160000

        x          P( X = x)
     0.00            0.4182
     1.00            0.3983
     2.00            0.1517
     3.00            0.0289
     4.00            0.0028
     5.00            0.0001
```

Figure 4.3   Binomial distribution calculations for $n = 5$ and $p = 0.16$ obtained from MINITAB

Shape of Binomial Distributions

Binomial distributions can be symmetrical or skewed. Whenever $p = 0.5$, the binomial distribution will be symmetrical regardless of how large or small the value of n. When $p \neq 0.5$, however, the distribution will be skewed. If $p < 0.5$, the distribution will be positive or right-skewed; if $p > 0.5$, the distribution will be negative or left-skewed. The closer p is to 0.5 and the larger the number of observations in the sample, n, the more nearly symmetrical the distribution will be. This can be illustrated in Figure 4.4. Panel A represents the probability distribution of obtaining the face five on three rolls of a die; Panel B represents the probability distribution of obtaining heads on three tosses of a fair coin; Panel C represents the probability distribution of obtaining heads on four tosses of a fair coin. A comparison of Panels A and B shows the effect of differing values of p on the shape of the distribution. A value of p below 0.5 results in a right-skewed distribution. A comparison of Panels B and C shows the effect on shape when the probabilities for success are the same, but the sample sizes differ. Although both distributions are symmetric, Panel C has a smaller probability of having values at either extreme.

The Mean

The mean of a binomial distribution is the product of its two parameters, n and p (see Derivation 4.1 on page 156). That is,

$$\mu_x = np \tag{4.10}$$

The mean is the expected or average value of the random variable X.

For example, when dealing with three switches and $p = 0.5$, we observed that the expected value or mean was 1.5, the product of the sample size ($n = 3$) and the probability of an open switch ($p = 0.5$).

We can examine what the mean of a binomial probability distribution would be in other circumstances. If there are 100 switches and the probability that each switch is open is 0.5, how many open switches would we expect to obtain?

We should expect 50 open switches, because n (the sample size) is 100 and p (the probability of an open switch on any selection) is 0.5. Thus, in this situation,

$$\mu_x = np = (100)(0.5) = 50.$$

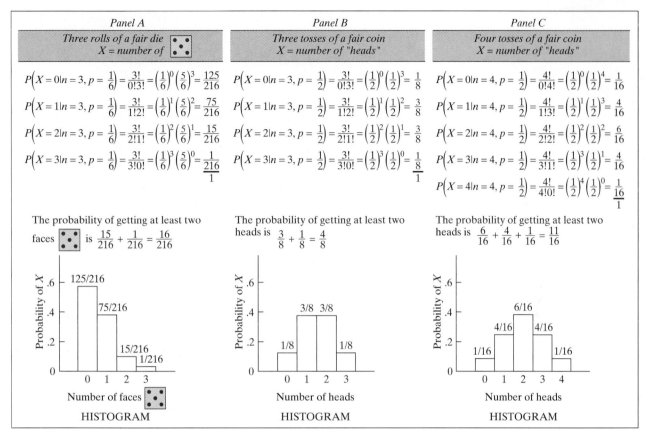

Figure 4.4   Characteristics of three binomial distributions

Suppose further that items produced by a stable process were inspected and classified as conforming or nonconforming, and that the probability of an item's being nonconforming was $p = 0.02$. How many items in a sample of $n = 50$ would we expect to be nonconforming?

From Equation (4.10), we have $\mu_x = np = (50)(0.02) = 1$. Thus, we would expect that there would be one nonconforming item in a sample of 50.

The Standard Deviation

The standard deviation of a binomial distribution is obtained as follows:

$$\sigma_x = \sqrt{np(1 - p)} \qquad (4.11)$$

Thus, in our example involving 100 switches with $p = 0.5$, the standard deviation of the number of open switches is computed to be $\sigma_x = \sqrt{np(1 - p)} = \sqrt{(100)(0.5)(0.5)} = 5$.

We can also compute the standard deviation in our example in which items produced by a stable process were inspected and classified as conforming or nonconforming, where the probability of an item's being nonconforming was

$p = 0.02$. For this example, the standard deviation of the number of noncon-forming items is

$$\sigma_x = \sqrt{np(1-p)} = \sqrt{50(0.02)(0.98)}$$
$$\sigma_x = 0.99$$

DERIVATION 4.1 (OPTIONAL)   The Expected Value of the Binomial Distribution

By using equations (4.6) and (4.9), we can reason as follows:

$$E(X) = \sum_{x=1}^{n} x \binom{n}{x} p^x (1-p)^{n-x}$$

$$E(X) = \sum_{x=1}^{n} x \frac{n!}{x!(n-x)!} p^x (1-p)^{n-x}$$

$$E(X) = \sum_{x=1}^{n} \frac{n!}{(x-1)!(n-x)!} p^x (1-p)^{n-x}$$

$$E(X) = \sum_{x=1}^{n} \frac{n(n-1)!}{(x-1)!(n-x)!} p \cdot p^{x-1} (1-p)^{n-x}$$

$$E(X) = np \sum_{x=1}^{n} \frac{(n-1)!}{(x-1)!(n-x)!} p^{x-1} (1-p)^{n-x}$$

let $y = x - 1$. Then, when $x = 1, y = 0$ and when $x = n, y = (n-1)$.

$$E(X) = np \sum_{y=0}^{n-1} \frac{(n-1)!}{(y)![(n-1)-y)]!} p^y (1-p)^{(n-1)-y}$$

The quantity inside the summation sign is $P(y)$, where y is a binomial random variable based on $n - 1$ trials. Therefore,

$$\sum_{y=0}^{n-1} \frac{(n-1)!}{y![(n-1)! - y!]} p^y \cdot p^{(n-1)-y} = 1$$

and

$$E(X) = np$$

PROBLEMS

4.13 Using the binomial distribution, determine the following:
(a) If $n = 4$ and $p = 0.20$, then $P(X = 1) = ?$
(b) If $n = 4$ and $p = 0.80$, then $P(X = 3) = ?$
(c) If $n = 5$ and $p = 0.30$, then $P(X \leq 1) = ?$
(d) If $n = 6$ and $p = 0.40$, then $P(X > 1) = ?$
(e) If $n = 3$ and $p = 0.10$, then $P(X < 2) = ?$

4.14 Using the binomial distribution, determine the following:
(a) If $n = 5$ and $p = 0.10$, then $P(X = 2) = ?$
(b) If $n = 5$ and $p = 0.10$, then $P(X < 3) = ?$
(c) If $n = 6$ and $p = 0.30$, then $P(X \leq 1) = ?$
(d) If $n = 6$ and $p = 0.30$, then $P(X > 1) = ?$
(e) If $n = 3$ and $p = 0.15$, then $P(X < 3) = ?$

4.15 Suppose that a student is taking a multiple-choice exam in which each question has four choices. Assuming that she has no knowledge of the correct answers to any of these questions, she has decided on a strategy in which she places four balls (marked A, B, C, and D) into a box. She randomly selects one ball for each question and replaces the ball in the box after its marking is noted. The marking on the ball will determine her answer to the question.

   (a) If there are five multiple-choice questions on the exam, what is the probability that she will get
      (1) five questions correct?
      (2) at least four questions correct?
      (3) no questions correct?
      (4) no more than two questions correct?
   (b) What assumptions are necessary in (a)?
   (c) What are the mean and standard deviation of the probability distribution in (a)?

4.16 An important part of the customer-service responsibilities of a telephone company relates to the speed with which troubles in residential service can be repaired. Suppose that past data indicate that the likelihood is 0.70 that troubles in residential service can be repaired on the same day.

   (a) For the first five troubles reported on a given day, what is the probability that
      (1) all five will be repaired on the same day?
      (2) at least three will be repaired on the same day?
      (3) fewer than two will be repaired on the same day?
   (b) What assumptions are necessary in (a)?
   (c) What are the mean and standard deviation of the probability distribution in (a)?
   (d) What would be your answers in (a) if the likelihood is 0.80 that troubles in residential service can be repaired on the same day?
   (e) Compare the results of (a) and (d).

4.17 A paper by D. Butler and N.J.D. Graham, "Modeling Dry Weather Wastewater Flow in Sewer Networks," *Journal of Environmental Engineering,* 1995, describes a use of the binomial distribution. Domestic appliances (baths, showers, toilets and the like) are connected to an outfall or sewage treatment that works through a series of pipes. The authors propose a model in which each appliance has a probability p of discharging in a brief time interval.

   (a) If 6 appliances in a single-family house each have a probability of discharge of $p = 0.05$, what is the probability that, in a brief time interval,
      (1) none of the appliances is discharging?
      (2) fewer than two of the appliances are discharging?
      (3) at least one appliance is discharging?
   (b) What assumptions are necessary in (a)?
   (c) What are the mean and standard deviation of the probability distribution in (a)?

4.18 In a paper by Eng, Karol, and Yeh, "A Growable Packet (ATM) Switch Architecture: Design Principles and Applications," *IEEE Transactions on*

Communications, 1992, the authors describe a data packet switch that uses the statistical behavior of packet arrivals to reduce interconnection complexity. The binomial distribution is used to model the number of packets, out of n, that arrive at any output of the system. Suppose that 16 packets are in the system and the probability of any one packet's arriving an output X is $p = 0.15$.

   (a) What is the probability that exactly 2 of the packets arrive at an output?
   (b) What is the probability that at least 2 of the packets arrive at an output?
   (c) What is the probability that no more than 1 packet arrives at an output?
   (d) What is the expected number of packets arriving at an output?
   (e) What is the standard deviation of the number of packets arriving at an output?
   (f) What would be your answers to (a)–(e) if the probability of any one packet arriving at an output is 0.10?

4.19 A manufacturer of compact-disk players subjects the equipment to a comprehensive testing process for all mechanical and electrical functions before the equipment leaves the factory. Ideally, the hope is that each compact-disk player passes on the first test. Suppose that past data indicate that the probability that a compact-disk player passes the first test is 0.90.

   (a) If four compact-disk players are randomly selected, what is the probability that
      (1) all four pass the first test?
      (2) none passes the first test?
      (3) at least three pass the first test?
      (4) fewer than two pass the first test?
   (b) What assumptions are necessary in (a)?
   (c) What are the mean and standard deviation of the probability distribution in (a)?
   (d) What would be your answers in (a) if the probability that a compact-disk player passes the first test is 0.99?

4.20 Suppose that past experience has shown that the likelihood that a personal computer is upgraded within one year of purchase is 0.25.

   (a) If four personal computers are randomly selected, what is the probability that
      (1) all four are upgraded?
      (2) none is upgraded?
      (3) at least three are upgraded?
      (4) fewer than two are upgraded?
   (b) What assumptions are necessary in (a)?
   (c) What are the mean and standard deviation of the probability distribution in (a)?
   (d) What would be your answers in (a) if the likelihood that a personal computer is upgraded is 0.15?
   (e) Compare your answers in (a) and (d).

4.21 Suppose that 10% of Monarch butterflies have damaged wings. If a random sample of ten Monarch butterflies is selected, what is the probability that
(a) more than four have damaged wings?

(b) between two and five (inclusive) have damaged wings?
(c) What would be your answers to (a) and (b) if the sample size selected had been eight Monarch butterflies?

4.5 THE HYPERGEOMETRIC DISTRIBUTION

In Section 4.4, we developed the binomial probability distribution to determine the probability of x successes in n trials when the probability of a success on any trial remained constant from trial to trial. In many circumstances, the probability of a success on the outcome of a particular trial is not the same as on a different trial because the data have been selected *without* replacement from a finite population.

To illustrate a situation in which the hypergeometric distribution should be used instead of the binomial distribution, let us return to the example on page 135, in which the inspection of welds was considered. In this example, there were 8 welds done, of which six were done properly. We found that the probability of having both welds done properly in a sample of two welds inspected was equal to 0.5357. In this example, each weld can be selected for inspection only once, so we are sampling without replacement. Previously, in this example, we observed that the probability of finding a properly done weld changed on the second selection as compared to the first weld selected, because sampling without replacement was involved. Suppose that, instead of selecting a sample of two welds out of the eight welds done, we decided to select a sample of three welds and wanted to determine the probability that exactly two of the three welds were done properly. In this case, two welds out of three selected could be done properly in the following three ways:

WELD SELECTED

1	2	3
Done properly	Done properly	Not done properly
Done properly	Not done properly	Done properly
Not done properly	Done properly	Done properly

If we define

p_1 = probability of a properly done weld on the first selection,

p_2 = probability of a properly done weld on the second selection, given a properly done weld on the first selection,

$(1 - p_3)$ = probability of an improperly done weld on the third selection, given a properly done weld on the first selection and a properly done weld on the second selection,

then to find the probability of two properly done welds in three selections *in the specific order* of done properly, done properly, and not done properly, we have

$$(p_1)(p_2)(1 - p_3) = (6/8)(5/7)(2/6)$$
$$= 60/336$$
$$= 0.17857$$

There are 3 possible arrangements for two welds done properly out of three selected, each of which has the probability of $60/336 = 0.17857$, so the probability that exactly two welds out of three are done properly *irrespective of the order selected* is

$$(3)(0.17857) = 0.53571$$

As the sample size n increases, using this intuitive approach becomes computationally unwieldy; another approach involving the hypergeometric distribution is needed.

In general, the mathematical expression of the **hypergeometric distribution** for obtaining X successes, given a knowledge of the sample size n, the population size N, and the number of successes in the population A, is written as follows:

$$P(X = x \mid n, N, A) = \frac{\binom{A}{x}\binom{N-A}{n-x}}{\binom{N}{n}}$$

$$= \frac{\frac{A!}{x!(n-x)!} \times \frac{(N-A)!}{(n-x)!(\{N-A\}-\{n-x\})!}}{\frac{N!}{n!(N-n)!}}$$

(4.12)

where

$P(X = x \mid n, N, A)$ = the probability that $X = x$, given knowledge of n, N, and A

n = sample size

N = population size

A = number of successes in the population

$N - A$ = number of failures in the population

x = number of successes in the sample

Using Equation (4.12) to determine the probability that exactly two welds are done properly out of three selected when there are six welds done properly in a population of eight welds, we obtain

$$P(X = 2 \mid n = 3, N = 8, A = 6) = \frac{\binom{6}{2}\binom{8-6}{3-2}}{\binom{8}{3}}$$

$$= \frac{\frac{6!}{2!4!} \times \frac{2!}{1!1!}}{\frac{8!}{3!5!}}$$

$$= 0.53571$$

Computations such as the ones we have done in this example can become quite tedious, especially as n gets large. We can obtain the probabilities by using

Microsoft Excel. (See Appendix 4.1.) Figure 4.5 represents output from the PHStat add-in for Microsoft Excel for the hypergeometric distribution for the example concerning the probability that exactly two welds are done properly out of three selected when there are six welds done properly in a population of eight welds.

	A	B	C	D	E	F	G
1	Weld Inspection Probabilities						
2				PHStat User Note:			
3	Sample size	3		If the #NUM! Message appears in the			
4	No. of successes in population	6		Probabilities Table, the number of			
5	Population size	8		successes is larger than the sample			
6				size--an impossibility.			
7	Hypergeometric Probabilities Table						
8		X	P(x)				
9		0	#NUM!				
10		1	0.107143				
11		2	0.535714				
12		3	0.357143				
13		4	#NUM!				
14		5	#NUM!				
15		6	#NUM!				
16							

Figure 4.5   Hypergeometric distribution calculations obtained from the PHStat add-in for Microsoft Excel for the welding example

Characteristics of Hypergeometric Distributions

Each time a set of parameters n, A, and N is specified, a particular hypergeometric probability distribution can be generated. The mean of the hypergeometric distribution is computed as in Equation (4.13).

$$\mu = E(X) = \frac{nA}{N} \tag{4.13}$$

In our example concerning the three welds selected without replacement, $n = 3$, $A = 6$, and $N = 8$, so

$$\mu = E(X) = \frac{(3)(6)}{8} = 2.25$$

The standard deviation of the hypergeometric distribution is obtained from

$$\sigma_x = \sqrt{\frac{nA(N - A)}{N^2}} \cdot \sqrt{\frac{N - n}{N - 1}} \tag{4.14}$$

where the expression $\sqrt{\frac{N - n}{N - 1}}$ is a finite population correction factor that results from sampling without replacement from a finite population.

Referring to our example concerning the three welds selected without replacement, where $n = 3, A = 6$, and $N = 8$, we have

$$\sigma_x = \sqrt{\frac{3(6)(8-6)}{8^2}}\sqrt{\frac{8-3}{8-1}}$$

$$= \sqrt{0.5625}\sqrt{\frac{5}{7}}$$

$$= 0.6339$$

Using the Binomial Distribution to Approximate the Hypergeometric Distribution

Under certain circumstances, the binomial distribution provides an excellent approximation to the hypergeometric distribution. As a general rule, when sampling without replacement from a finite population, if the sample size n is less than 5% of the population size N, the binomial distribution usually provides an excellent approximation.

Suppose that, in our example concerning the three welds selected without replacement, there were a total of 30 welds in the population, of which 24 were done properly. Find the probability that, if a sample of 3 welds is selected without replacement, exactly two of the welds were done properly.

By using the hypergeometric distribution with $n = 3, N = 30$, and $A = 24$, we obtain

$$P(X = 2 \mid n = 3, N = 30, A = 24) = \frac{\binom{24}{2}\binom{30-24}{3-2}}{\binom{30}{3}}$$

$$= \frac{\dfrac{24!}{2!22!} \times \dfrac{6!}{1!5!}}{\dfrac{30!}{3!27!}}$$

$$= 0.40788$$

By using the binomial distribution with $n = 3$ and $p = 24/30 = 0.8$, we have

$$P(X = 2 \mid n = 3, p = 0.8) = \frac{3!}{2!1!}(0.8)^2(0.2)^{3-2}$$

$$= 0.3840$$

Even though the sample size in this example was 10% of the population size (3/30), the result obtained from the binomial distribution is close to that from the hypergeometric distribution.

PROBLEMS

4.22 Determine the following:
 (a) If $n = 4, N = 10$, and $A = 5$, then
  $P(X = 3 \mid n, N, A) = ?$
 (b) If $n = 4, N = 10$, and $A = 5$, then
  $P(X < 3 \mid n, N, A) = ?$
 (c) If $n = 3, N = 20$, and $A = 2$, then
  $P(X = 1 \mid n, N, A) = ?$
 (d) If $n = 5, N = 15$, and $A = 5$, then
  $P(X = 3 \mid n, N, A) = ?$

4.23 Suppose that a standard deck of playing cards is shuffled and five cards are to be selected without replacement. What is the probability that
(a) four of the cards will be red?
(b) two of the cards will be sevens?
(c) none of the cards will be a heart?
(d) all five of the cards will be aces?

4.24 Suppose that a new car dealer has 30 cars available for immediate sale, of which 10 are classified as compact cars. What is the probability that, of the next five purchases from these cars available for immediate sale,
(a) one will be a compact car?
(b) at least one will be a compact car?
(c) three will be compact cars?
(d) all five will be compact cars?
(e) What assumptions are necessary in (a)–(d)?

4.25 In a shipment of 15 hard disks, five are defective. If four of the disks in the shipment are randomly selected for inspection, what is the probability that
(a) exactly one is defective?
(b) at least one is defective?
(c) no more than two are defective?
(d) What is the average number of defective hard disks that you would expect to obtain in the sample of four hard disk drives?

4.26 Suppose that you are trying to send three different FAX messages to a particular FAX machine. Unknown to you, someone else is sending seven different messages to the same FAX machine. A short time after all these messages have been sent, the receiving FAX machine displays the message "seven messages received." If the messages that are lost are independent of the sender, what is the probability that
(a) none of your messages was lost?
(b) exactly one of your messages was lost?
(c) all three of your messages were lost?

4.27 A state lottery is conducted in which six winning numbers are randomly selected from a total of 54 numbers. If you select six numbers, what is the probability that you will select
(a) all six winning numbers?
(b) five winning numbers?
(c) four winning numbers?
(d) none of the winning numbers?
(e) What is the average number of winning numbers that you would expect to select?
(f) What would be your answers to (a)–(e) if the six winning numbers were randomly selected from a total of 40 numbers?

4.6 THE NEGATIVE BINOMIAL AND GEOMETRIC DISTRIBUTIONS

In Sections 4.4 and 4.5, we discussed the binomial and hypergeometric distributions. Each of these distributions is used in situations in which there are only two possible outcomes (or elementary events) on each trial, and the probability of a certain number of successes in a certain number of trials is to be determined. The binomial distribution is used in situations in which the probability of success remains constant from trial to trial; the hypergeometric distribution is used when sampling without replacement from a finite population.

In this section, we consider the situation in which we want to find the probability that the xth success occurs on the nth trial, given a constant probability of success p. The distribution that we will develop is the negative binomial distribution. For the special case in which we are determining the probability that the first success occurs on the nth trial, we will use the geometric distribution.

The Negative Binomial Distribution

The **negative binomial distribution** is used to determine the probability that the xth success occurs on the nth trial, there is a constant probability of success p. The mathematical expression for this distribution is

$$P(n) = p(n|x, p) = \binom{n-1}{x-1} p^x (1-p)^{n-x} \quad X = 1, 2, \ldots \quad (4.15)$$

where

p = probability of success on any trial

n = number of trials until the xth success is observed

Notice that this notation is the reverse of the binomial distribution. Here the random variable is n not x. To illustrate the application of the negative binomial distribution, we can examine the following example. In a contention system for data transmission lines, suppose that the probability of successfully capturing a line on any attempt is 0.40 and that this probability stays constant over all attempts. What is the probability that the third data transmission line is captured in the fifth attempt? Using the negative binomial distribution with $n = 5$, $X = 3$, and $p = 0.4$, we have

$$P(n = 5) = \binom{5 - 1}{3 - 1}(.4)^3(1 - .4)^{5-3}$$

$$= 0.13824$$

Computations such as the ones we have done in this example can become quite tedious, especially as n gets large. Fortunately, it is not necessary to use Equation (4.15) to calculate the probabilities. We can obtain the probabilities by accessing Microsoft Excel. (See Appendix 4.1.) Figure 4.6 represents output from Microsoft Excel for the negative binomial distribution and the geometric distribution for the data-transmission example.

	A	B	C	D	E
1		Negative Binomial and Geometric Probabilities			
2					
3	Number of successes	3	1	1	1
4	Number of trials	5	3	6	2
5	p	0.4	0.05	0.05	0.05
6	Number of failures	2	2	5	1
7	Probability	0.13824	0.045125	0.038689	0.0475

Figure 4.6   Negative binomial distribution calculations obtained from Microsoft Excel for the data-transmission example

Characteristics of the Negative Binomial Distribution

The mean of the negative binomial distribution is

$$\mu_n = \frac{x}{p} \tag{4.16}$$

and the standard deviation is equal to

$$\sigma_n = \sqrt{\frac{x(1 - p)}{p^2}} \tag{4.17}$$

For our data-transmission example, from Equations (4.16) and (4.17) the mean number of trials until the third success is

$$\mu_n = \frac{3}{0.4} = 7.5$$

and the standard deviation is

$$\sigma_n = \sqrt{\frac{3(1 - 0.4)}{0.4^2}} = 3.354$$

The Geometric Distribution

In many applications of the negative binomial distribution, we are interested in the special case of determining the probability that the first success ($x = 1$) occurs on the nth trial. For this special case, the **geometric distribution** can be used. From Equation (4.15), with $x = 1$, we have

$$P(n) = \binom{n - 1}{x - 1} p^x (1 - p)^{n - x}$$

and so the equation for the geometric distribution, representing the probability that the first success occurs on the nth trial, is

$$P(n) = P(n|p) = p(1 - p)^{n-1} \quad X = 1, 2, \ldots \qquad (4.18)$$

To illustrate the use of the geometric distribution, let us study the following example.

Suppose that an engineer is creating supports by using a combination of concrete and waste materials. According to her calculations, only 5% of all such supports should fail to meet standards. She decides that she will test a sequence of these supports until she finds one that does not meet standards. Assuming that her calculations are correct, she would like to find the probability that she finds a support that does not meet standards (a) on the third attempt, (b) on the sixth attempt, and (c) at some time after her second attempt.

To find the probability that a nonconforming support is found on the third attempt, with $n = 3$ and $p = 0.05$, by using Equation (4.18) we obtain

$$P(n = 3) = (0.05)(1 - 0.05)^{3-1}$$
$$= 0.04513$$

To find the probability that a nonconforming support is found on the sixth attempt, with $n = 6$ and $p = 0.05$, by using Equation (4.18) we obtain

$$P(n = 6) = (0.05)(1 - 0.05)^{6-1}$$
$$= 0.03869$$

To find the probability that a nonconforming support is found sometime after the second attempt, we need to find the complement of finding the nonconforming support on the first or second attempt. Thus,

$$P(n > 2) = 1 - [P(n = 1) + P(n = 2)]$$

so that

$$P(n = 1) = (0.05)(1 - 0.05)^{1-1}$$
$$= 0.05$$
$$P(n = 2) = (0.05)(1 - 0.05)^{2-1}$$
$$= 0.0475$$

and therefore

$$P(n > 2) = 1 - [P(n = 1) + P(n = 2)] = 1 - [0.05 + 0.0475] = 0.9025$$

Suppose that 10% of the supports fail to meet standard. Then $p = 0.10$, and the respective results are

$$P(n = 3) = (0.10)(1 - 0.10)^{3-1}$$
$$= 0.081$$
$$P(n = 6) = (0.10)(1 - 0.10)^{6-1}$$
$$= 0.059049$$
$$P(n = 1) = (0.10)(1 - 0.10)^{1-1}$$
$$= 0.10$$
$$P(n = 2) = (0.10)(1 - 0.10)^{2-1}$$
$$= 0.09$$

and therefore

$$P(n > 2) = 1 - [P(n = 1) + P(n = 2)] = 1 - [0.10 + 0.09] = 0.81$$

Therefore, as would be expected, as the probability of a success (in this case a nonconforming support) increases, the probability of finding an occurrence of the success by the nth trial also increases.

Characteristics of the Geometric Distribution

The geometric distribution represents the special case of the negative binomial distribution with $x = 1$, so the mean of the geometric distribution is

$$\mu_n = \frac{1}{p} \tag{4.19}$$

and the standard deviation is equal to

$$\sigma_n = \sqrt{\frac{(1 - p)}{p^2}} \tag{4.20}$$

Refer to the concrete supports example on page 164; by using Equations (4.19) and (4.20), the mean number of trials until the first successes can be calculated as follows:

$$\mu_n = \frac{1}{0.05} = 20$$

and the standard deviation is

$$\sigma_n = \sqrt{\frac{(1 - 0.05)}{0.05^2}} = 19.494$$

PROBLEMS

4.28 For a negative binomial distribution, determine the following:
(a) If $p = 0.5$, and $x = 2$, $P(n = 5) = ?$
(b) If $p = 0.3$, and $x = 2$, $P(n = 5) = ?$
(c) If $p = 0.5$, and $x = 4$, $P(n = 10) = ?$
(d) If $p = 0.2$, and $x = 1$, $P(n = 6) = ?$
(e) If $p = 0.3$, and $x = 1$, $P(n = 6) = ?$
(f) If $p = 0.3$, and $x = 1$, $P(n = 3) = ?$
(g) Find the mean and the standard deviation in parts (a)–(f).

4.29 Suppose that 35% of all computer scientists have worked on a neural-net program. A representative for a company who is seeking computer scientists who have worked on a neural-net program will continue to interview computer scientists until she finds two who have worked on a neural-net program.
(a) What is the probability that the interviewing process will end with the
(1) second interview?
(2) fifth interview?
(3) tenth interview?
(b) What is the average and the standard deviation of the number of interviews that need to be done until she finds two computer scientists who have worked on a neural-net program?

4.30 A quality-control inspector will sample products obtained from a manufacturing process until two nonconforming products are found. Suppose that the process produces nonconforming products 10% of the time.
(a) What is the probability that the inspector will find the second nonconforming product in the
(1) third inspection?
(2) fifth inspection?
(3) tenth inspection?
(b) What is the average and the standard deviation of the number of inspections that need to be done before the second nonconforming product is found?
(c) What would be your answers to (a) and (b) if the process produces nonconforming products 8% of the time?

4.31 One in twenty children is born with overlapping toes (usually with no harmful effect). If a doctor searches the records of births at a particular hospital,
(a) what is the probability that the first record showing a child born with overlapping toes occurs in the
(1) first record searched?

(2) fifth record searched?
(3) tenth record searched?
(b) What are the average and the standard deviation of the number of records that need to be searched before the second child with overlapping toes is found?
(c) What would be your answers to (a) and (b) if 20% of the children had overlapping toes?

4.32 One test that people who wish to donate blood must undergo is a test of iron level. Individuals with insufficient iron levels are not permitted to donate blood. A preliminary inexpensive screening test is initially performed for iron level. If an individual fails this test, he or she is given a more expensive second test of iron level. Suppose that 30% of the people who fail the first test pass the second test and are allowed to donate blood. A doctor is searching for a blood donor among those who failed the first test. She randomly selects individuals from those who failed the first test.
(a) What is the probability that the doctor will find a suitable donor on the
(1) second selection?
(2) fourth selection?
(3) tenth selection?
(b) What would be your answers in (a) if the doctor were searching for two suitable donors who failed the first test but passed the second test?

4.33 Suppose that the proportion of fatal single-car accidents that involve alcohol consumption on the part of the driver is 60%. If the records of fatal single-car accidents in a geographical area are examined,
(a) what is the probability that the third accident involving alcohol consumption on the part of the driver is found in the
(1) third record examined?
(2) fifth record examined?
(3) tenth record examined?
(b) In part (a), what are the average and standard deviation of the number of records that need to be examined until the third involving alcohol consumption on the part of the driver is found?
(c) What is the probability that the first accident involving alcohol consumption on the part of the driver is found in the
(1) third record examined?
(2) fifth record examined?
(3) tenth record examined?
(d) In part (c), what are the average and standard deviation of the number of records that need to be

examined until the first involving alcohol consumption on the part of the driver is found?

4.34 An assembly line at a manufacturing plant that produces computer disks currently produces 8% of its disks with bad sectors.
  (a) If disks are randomly selected, what is the probability that the first disk found to have a bad sector is the
    (1) third disk selected?
    (2) fifth disk selected?
    (3) tenth disk selected?

  (b) What are the average and standard deviation of the number of disks that need to be inspected until the first disk with a bad sector is found?
  (c) What would be your answers in (a) and (b) if 4% of the disks have bad sectors?
  (d) What would be your answers in (a) and (b) if the inspector were looking for the third disk with a bad sector?

4.7 THE POISSON DISTRIBUTION

Many investigations, including those dealing with the quality of products or services, are based on counts of the number of nonconformities or defects per sampled continuum or *area of opportunity*. An **area of opportunity** is a continuous unit or interval of time, volume, or such area in which more than one occurrence of an event may occur. Examples are the number of pits in a square meter of metal or the number of fleas on the body of a dog. In such circumstances, the **Poisson probability distribution** provides the underlying basis for calculating these types of probabilities. This includes applications to the theory of area of opportunity control charts that will be discussed in Section 6.5.

A Poisson process is said to exist if we can observe discrete events in an area of opportunity—some continuous interval of time, space, or area—in such a manner that if we subdivide the area of opportunity into very small, equal-sized subareas of opportunity so that

1. the probability of observing exactly one success in any subarea of opportunity is stable.
2. the probability of observing two or more successes in any subarea of opportunity is zero.
3. the occurrence of a success in any one subarea of opportunity is statistically independent of that in any other.

The following are some examples of Poisson-distributed phenomena:

- number of calls *per hour* coming into the switchboard of a police station;
- number of claims for missing baggage *per day* at a particular airport;
- number of power surges *per day* in a nuclear power plant;
- number of falls *per month* in a hospital's AIDS unit;
- number of defective welds in 10 meters of pipe;
- number of cars entering an intersection in a 24-hour period;
- number of chips *per cookie* in a pack of Marilyn's chocolate-chip cookies.

In each of the preceding cases, the discrete random variable X, the number of successes *per area of opportunity,* is representative of a Poisson process regardless of whether the interval represents time, length, surface area, and so on.

A *Poisson distribution* is characterized by only one parameter, λ. While the Poisson random variable X refers to the number of successes per area of opportunity, the parameter λ refers to the expected or average number of successes per area of opportunity. In theory, the Poisson random variable X takes on all integer values from 0 through ∞. From a practical viewpoint, however, there are few cases in which the probability of observing a very large value for X is non-negligible.

The following mathematical model represents the Poisson probability distribution for obtaining $X = x$ successes per area of opportunity, given a knowledge of the parameter λ:

$$P(X = x \mid \lambda) = \frac{e^{-\lambda}\lambda^x}{x!} \quad X = 0, 1, \dots \tag{4.21}$$

where

$P(X = x \mid \lambda) =$ the probability that $X = x$, given a knowledge of λ

$\lambda =$ expected number of nonconformities per area of opportunity

$e =$ mathematical constant approximated by 2.71828

$x =$ number of successes per area of opportunity in the sample $(X = 0, 1, 2, \dots, \infty)$

To demonstrate an application of the Poisson probability distribution, let us consider a food processing plant that bakes *Marilyn's* chocolate-chip cookies. Once the chocolate chips are placed into the vats of cookie dough and mixed, the dough is sent to extruders which shape the cookies. Even though the dough is thoroughly mixed, random factors or chance affect the process, and as a result, not all cookies produced have exactly the same number of chips. If the design specifications for the cookies call for an average of 4.5 chips per cookie, what is the probability that a cookie has no more than (i.e., at most) two chocolate chips?

To solve this, we use Equation (4.21) as follows. The probability that exactly two chocolate chips are in the next cookie is

$$P(X = 2 \mid \lambda = 4.5) = \frac{e^{-\lambda}\lambda^x}{x!}$$

$$= \frac{e^{-4.5}(4.5)^2}{2!} = \frac{(2.71828)^{-4.5}(4.5)^2}{2!}$$

$$= \frac{20.25}{(2.71828)^{4.5}(2)}$$

$$= 0.1125$$

The probability that the next cookie has exactly one chocolate chip is

$$P(X = 1 \mid \lambda = 4.5) = \frac{e^{-\lambda}\lambda^x}{x!}$$

$$= \frac{e^{-4.5}(4.5)^1}{1!} = \frac{(2.71828)^{-4.5}(4.5)^1}{1!}$$

$$= \frac{4.5}{(2.71828)^{4.5}(1)}$$

$$= 0.0500$$

The probability that zero chocolate chips are in the next cookie is

$$P(X = 0 \mid \lambda = 4.5) = \frac{e^{-\lambda}\lambda^x}{x!}$$

$$= \frac{e^{-4.5}(4.5)^0}{0!} = \frac{(2.71828)^{-4.5}(4.5)^0}{0!}$$

$$= \frac{1}{(2.71828)^{4.5}(1)}$$

$$= 0.0111$$

Thus, the probability that *no more than* two chocolate chips are in the next cookie is

$$P(X \leq 2 \mid \lambda = 4.5) = P(X = 0 \mid \lambda = 4.5) + P(X = 1 \mid \lambda = 4.5)$$

$$+ P(X = 2 \mid \lambda = 4.5)$$

$$= .0111 + 0.0500 + 0.1125$$

$$= 0.1736$$

Marilyn, the founder and CEO, suspected that her customers' judgment of cookie quality was influenced by the number of chocolate chips they found in cookies. After consumer research confirmed this, she became concerned that, if up to 17% of her cookies could contain two or fewer chips, customers would be dissatisfied. She asked a quality team from the production department to study the problem and suggest methods of reducing the probability of cookies with only two or fewer chips. The team suggested that the target value of 4.5 chocolate chips per cookie be increased to 6.0. For $\lambda = 6.0$, using Equation (4.21), we have:

$$P(X \leq 2 \mid \lambda = 6.0) = P(X = 0 \mid \lambda = 6.0) + P(X = 1 \mid \lambda = 6.0)$$

$$+ P(X = 2 \mid \lambda = 6.0)$$

$$= 0.0025 + 0.0149 + 0.0446$$

$$= 0.0620$$

Thus, increasing the average number of chocolate chips to 6.0 reduces the probability of having two or fewer chips to 6.2%.

Computations such as the ones we have done become quite tedious, especially as λ gets large. Fortunately, it is not necessary to use Equation (4.21) to calculate the probabilities. We can obtain the probabilities from Microsoft Excel or MINITAB. (See Appendices 4.1 and 4.2.) Figure 4.7 on page 170 represents output from the PHStat add-in Microsoft Excel, Figure 4.8 on page 171 represents output from MINITAB, both for the Poisson distribution with parameter $\lambda = 4.5$.

Characteristics of the Poisson Distribution

Each time the parameter λ is specified, a particular Poisson probability distribution can be generated. Attention must be given to the shape, the mean, and the standard

	A	B	C	D	E	F	G
1	Poisson Probabilities for Chocolate Chips						
2							
3	Average/Expected number of successes:			4.5			
4							
5	Poisson Probabilities Table						
6		X	P(X)	P(<=X)	P(<X)	P(>X)	P(>=X)
7		0	0.011109	0.011109	0.000000	0.988891	1.000000
8		1	0.049990	0.061099	0.011109	0.938901	0.988891
9		2	0.112479	0.173578	0.061099	0.826422	0.938901
10		3	0.168718	0.342296	0.173578	0.657704	0.826422
11		4	0.189808	0.532104	0.342296	0.467896	0.657704
12		5	0.170827	0.702930	0.532104	0.297070	0.467896
13		6	0.128120	0.831051	0.702930	0.168949	0.297070
14		7	0.082363	0.913414	0.831051	0.086586	0.168949
15		8	0.046329	0.959743	0.913414	0.040257	0.086586
16		9	0.023165	0.982907	0.959743	0.017093	0.040257
17		10	0.010424	0.993331	0.982907	0.006669	0.017093
18		11	0.004264	0.997596	0.993331	0.002404	0.006669
19		12	0.001599	0.999195	0.997596	0.000805	0.002404
20		13	0.000554	0.999748	0.999195	0.000252	0.000805
21		14	0.000178	0.999926	0.999748	0.000074	0.000252
22		15	0.000053	0.999980	0.999926	0.000020	0.000074
23		16	0.000015	0.999995	0.999980	0.000005	0.000020
24		17	0.000004	0.999999	0.999995	0.000001	0.000005
25		18	0.000001	1.000000	0.999999	0.000000	0.000001
26		19	0.000000	1.000000	1.000000	0.000000	0.000000
27		20	0.000000	1.000000	1.000000	0.000000	0.000000

Figure 4.7   Poisson distribution calculations for $\lambda = 4.5$ obtained from the PHStat add-in for Microsoft Excel

deviation of the Poisson distribution. A Poisson distribution will be right-skewed, but will approach symmetry with a peak in the center as λ gets large.

The Mean and the Standard Deviation

An important property of the Poisson distribution is that the mean μ_x and the variance σ_x^2 are each equal to the parameter λ. Thus, the mean or expected value of the random variable X is given by (see Derivation 4.2)

$$\mu_x = \lambda \tag{4.22}$$

and the standard deviation is given by

$$\sigma_x = \sqrt{\lambda} \tag{4.23}$$

In our example concerning the chocolate-chip cookies, $\lambda = 4.5$, so the mean or expected number of chocolate chips is 4.5 per cookie and the standard deviation is the square root of 4.5, which is 2.1 chocolate chips per cookie.

```
Poisson with mu = 4.50000

        x           P( X = x)
     0.00             0.0111
     1.00             0.0500
     2.00             0.1125
     3.00             0.1687
     4.00             0.1898
     5.00             0.1708
     6.00             0.1281
     7.00             0.0824
     8.00             0.0463
     9.00             0.0232
    10.00             0.0104
    11.00             0.0043
    12.00             0.0016
    13.00             0.0006
    14.00             0.0002
    15.00             0.0001
    16.00             0.0000
    17.00             0.0000
    18.00             0.0000
    19.00             0.0000
    20.00             0.0000
```

Figure 4.8   Poisson distribution calculations
for $\lambda = 4.5$ obtained from MINITAB

DERIVATION 4.2 (OPTIONAL)   The Mean of the Poisson Distribution

From Equations (4.6) and (4.21),

$$E(x) = \sum_{x=1}^{\infty} x \frac{\lambda^x e^{-\lambda}}{x!}$$

$$E(x) = \sum_{x=1}^{\infty} \frac{\lambda^x e^{-\lambda}}{(x-1)!}$$

$$E(x) = \sum_{x=1}^{\infty} \frac{\lambda \cdot \lambda^{x-1} e^{-\lambda}}{(x-1)!}$$

$$E(x) = \lambda \sum_{x=1}^{\infty} \frac{\lambda^{x-1} e^{-\lambda}}{(x-1)!}$$

Letting $y = (x - 1)$, we obtain

$$E(X) = \lambda \sum_{y=0}^{\infty} \frac{\lambda^y e^{-\lambda}}{y!}$$

Since $\sum_{y=0}^{\infty} \frac{\lambda^y e^{-\lambda}}{y!} = 1$

$$E(X) = \lambda$$

PROBLEMS

4.35 Using Equation (4.21) or Microsoft Excel or MINITAB, determine the following:
   (a) If $\lambda = 3.5$, then $P(X = 0) = ?$
   (b) If $\lambda = 5.0$, then $P(X = 3) = ?$
   (c) If $\lambda = 0.5$, then $P(X \geq 2) = ?$
   (d) If $\lambda = 10$, then $P(X < 5) = ?$
   (e) If $\lambda = 15$, then $P(X = 12 \ or \ 13 \ or \ 14) = ?$

4.36 T. Shibata ("Statistical and Stochastic Approaches to Localized Corrosion," *Corrosion Science,* 1996) reports the use of the Poisson distribution to describe the number of pits on the surface of a material. Suppose the mean rate of pitting on a surface is 5 per square foot. What is the probability of
   (a) two pits appearing in a square foot?
   (b) no pits appearing in a square foot?
   (c) no more than three pits appearing in a square foot?
   (d) fewer than two pits appearing in a square foot?

4.37 Leung and Kit-Leung ("Using delay-time analysis to study the maintenance problem of gearboxes," *International Journal of Operations & Production Management,* 1996) use the Poisson distribution to model the number of faults that arise in the gearboxes of buses. Suppose the faults occur at an average rate of 2.5 per month. Find the probability that
   (a) no faults are found in a month;
   (b) two faults are found in a month;
   (c) at least one fault is found in a month;
   (d) no more than one fault is found in a month.

4.38 Everett and Applegate ("Solid Waste Transfer Station Design," *Journal of Environmental Engineering,* 1995) use the Poisson distribution to model the number of collection vehicles arriving at a station per hour. Suppose the collection vehicles arrive at an average rate of 6 per hour. Find the probability that
   (a) no collection vehicles arrive in an hour;
   (b) five collection vehicles arrive in an hour;
   (c) at least two collection vehicles arrive in an hour;
   (d) no more than three collection vehicles arrive in an hour.

4.39 Barbour and Kafetzaki ("A host-parasite model yielding heterogeneous parasite loads," *Journal of Mathematical Biology,* 1993) comment that many models of parasitic infections use the Poisson distribution. Suppose the number of parasites on a host has a Poisson distribution with a mean of 10. Find the probability that
   (a) there are 8 parasites on a host;
   (b) there are 8 or 9 parasites on a host;
   (c) there are no parasites on a host.

4.40 The number of power surges at a nuclear plant follows a Poisson distribution with an average of 0.5 power surges per day.
   (a) What is the probability that on a given day
      (1) there will be zero power surges?
      (2) there will be at least one power surge?
      (3) there will be between 3 and 5 power surges (inclusive)?
   (b) What is the probability that there will be between 3 and 5 power surges (inclusive) in a ten-day period?
   (c) What is the standard deviation of the number of power surges in a day?

4.41 Based on past experience, it is assumed that the number of flaws in rolls of grade 2 paper follows a Poisson distribution with an average of one flaw per five feet of paper.
   (a) What is the probability that there will be at least one flaw in a 12-foot length of paper?
   (b) What is the probability that there will be between five and fifteen flaws (inclusive) in a 50-foot length of paper?

4.8 SUMMARY AND OVERVIEW

In this chapter, we have discussed various rules of probability, so that the probability distribution and its characteristics could be defined. The development of the probability distribution led us to consider the binomial, hypergeometric, negative binomial, geometric, and Poisson distributions. These distributions serve as the foundation of the control charts that we will discuss in Chapter 6. In the next chapter we will continue our development of probability distributions with a discussion of several important continuous distributions.

KEY TERMS

area of opportunity 167
binomial distribution 150
classical approach 136
collectively exhaustive 139
complement 139
conditional probability 142
elementary event 135
empirical approach 136
event 135
expected value 146
geometric distribution 164

hypergeometric distribution 159
independence 142
joint event 137
mutually exclusive 139
negative binomial distribution 162
Poisson distribution 167
probability 135
probability distribution 145
subjective approach 138
variance of a discrete random variable 147

CHAPTER REVIEW *Checking Your Understanding*

To check your understanding of the key concepts discussed in this chapter, you should be able to answer each of the following questions:

4.42 What are the differences between classical probability, empirical probability, and subjective probability?

4.43 What is the difference between a simple event and a joint event?

4.44 How can the addition rule be used to find the probability of occurrence of event *A or B*?

4.45 What is the difference between mutually exclusive events and collectively exhaustive events?

4.46 How does conditional probability relate to the concept of statistical independence?

4.47 How does the multiplication rule differ for events that are and are not independent?

4.48 What is the meaning of the expected value of a probability distribution?

4.49 What are the assumptions of the binomial distribution?

4.50 What are the assumptions of the hypergeometric distribution?

4.51 What is the difference between the assumptions of the binomial and of the hypergeometric distributions?

4.52 How does the binomial distribution differ from the negative binomial distribution?

4.53 How does the geometric distribution differ from the negative binomial distribution?

4.54 What are the assumptions of the Poisson distribution?

4.55 What are the major differences between the assumptions of the binomial and of the Poisson distributions?

Chapter Review Problems

4.56 In the carnival game of Chuck-a-Luck, three fair dice are rolled. The player may place a bet on any of the six numbers 1, 2, 3, 4, 5, or 6. For each $1 bet on a particular number, the player will lose $1 if none of the three dice show the number selected, will win $1 if one of the three dice show the number selected, will win $2 if two of the three dice show the number selected, or will win $3 if all three dice show the number selected. For a given number selected (i.e., the number two),

    (a) form the probability distribution representing the different monetary outcomes for placing a $1 bet on it;

    (b) compute the expected value for the distribution developed in (a) and interpret its meaning.

    (c) Would you play the game of Chuck-a-Luck? Discuss.

4.57 In a paper, "Repeated Mapping of Environmental Particles on Surfaces to Evaluate Location Precision and Detection Efficiency," published in the *Proceedings of the Institute of Environmental Sciences* in 1992, Cooper, Haller, and Batchelder looked at the performance of instruments designed to measure and record apparent sizes of particles on a surface. They hypothesized that the number of particles detected would follow a binomial distribution. Suppose that the probability that a particle is detected is 0.60.

(a) If there are five particles on the surface, what is the probability that
    (1) three will be detected?
    (2) at least three will be detected?
    (3) all five will be detected?
    (4) none will be detected?

(b) What are the mean and standard deviation of the probability distribution in (a)?

(c) What would be your answers in (a) and (b) if there were 10 particles on the surface?

(d) What would be your answers in (a) and (b) if the probability that a particle is detected were 0.70?

4.58 Suppose that an organization was trying to create a team of eight people from different departments who had knowledge of a particular manufacturing process. A total of 30 people within the organization have knowledge of the process, of which 10 are from the design department. If members of the team were to be selected at random

(a) What is the probability that the team will contain
    (1) no members from the design department?
    (2) at least one member from the design department?
    (3) all its eight members from the design department?

(b) How many members of the design department would be expected to be on the team?

Suppose that, in this large organization, it actually turns out that 20% of all the employees have knowledge of the process. What then is the probability that

(c) the first member of the team is selected at the third employee interview?

(d) the first member of the team is selected at the fifth employee interview?

(e) the third member of the team is selected at the eighth employee interview?

(f) the team is completed at the twentieth employee interview?

(g) What is the expected number of employees that would need to be interviewed before the team is completed?

4.59 Suppose that the probability that an experimental Local Area Network sends a corrupted data packet is 2 in ten thousand (0.0002).

(a) If a random sample of 5 data packets is selected,
    (1) what is the average number of packets you would expect to be corrupted?
    (2) what is the probability that at least one of them is corrupted?

(b) If a random sample of 10,000 data packets is selected,
    (1) what is the probability that at least one of them is corrupted?
    (2) what is the average number of packets you would expect to be corrupted?

Hint for (b): Think of the entire set of 10,000 packets as an area of opportunity.

4.60 A quality-control inspector is randomly selecting batteries manufactured on an assembly line to determine whether they meet company specifications. Past experience indicates that 95% of the batteries meet specifications.

(a) If a sample of 4 batteries is selected, what is the probability that
    (1) exactly three of them meet the specifications?
    (2) at least three of them meet specifications?

(b) If a sample of 20 batteries is selected,
    (1) what is the probability that exactly 18 of them meet specifications?
    (2) what is the probability that at least 18 of them meet specifications?
    (3) what are the average and standard deviation of the number that would be expected to meet specifications?

(c) What is the probability that the first one that meets specifications occurs on the second battery tested?

(d) What is the probability that the fourth one that meets specifications occurs on the fifth battery tested?

(e) What is the average number of batteries that would need to be tested until two batteries that did not meet specifications were found?

4.61 Near a water-intake port of an ocean-side nuclear power plant, there are 20 quadrats that are routinely inspected. This inspection involves determining the types of marine life that are being pulled into the plant. Regularly, 5 of the 20 quadrats are randomly selected to be inspected by divers. Suppose that, at one particular time, 8 of the 20 quadrats contain a certain protected species.

(a) What is the probability that of the 5 quadrats inspected

(1) none contains the protected species?

(2) at least one contains the protected species?

(3) all five contain the protected species?

(b) What are the average and standard deviation of the number of inspected quadrats that you would expect to contain the protected species?

Suppose that there were a very large number of quadrats near the plant and that 40% of the quadrats contain the protected species. If a sample of 5 quadrats were inspected,

(c) what is the probability that of the 5 quadrats inspected,

(1) none contains the protected species?

(2) at least one contains the protected species?

(3) all five contain the protected species?

(d) What are the average and standard deviation of the number of quadrats that you would expect to contain the protected species?

(e) Compare your answers to (a) and (b) with those of (c) and (d). Explain the differences.

4.62 Both male and female parrotfish can reach maturity and become supermale parrotfish. Suppose that the proportion of supermale parrotfish that were originally female is 0.40.

(a) If the director of an aquarium receives eight supermale parrotfish, what is the probability that

(1) three were originally female?

(2) at least three were originally female?

(b) Suppose that the director has an unlimited supply of supermale parrotfish and is interested in sampling these until she finds three that were originally female. What is the probability that she will find her third such parrotfish

(1) on her eighth attempt?

(2) on her tenth attempt?

4.63 Lilienfeld ("Rapid Determination of Particle Concentration Bounds From Zero or Low Counts," *Proceedings—Institute of Environmental Sciences*, 1992) discusses the number of particles in such areas as clean rooms, work environments, fabrication processes, and so on. The number of particles is characterized by a Poisson model. Suppose that the number of particles present in a "clean room" of a fabrication process is Poisson-distributed, with an average of 4 particles. What is the probability that the number of particles present in the room is

(a) zero?

(b) at least one?

(c) more than 4?

4.64 McNamara and Houston ("Risk-Sensitive Foraging: A Review of the Theory," *Bulletin of Mathematical Biology*, 1993) examine the effects of the energy gained by an animal during foraging on its future reproductive success. One part includes a Poisson model for the number of food items of a type found during foraging. Suppose that the number of certain food items found during foraging has a Poisson distribution with a mean of 1.0. Find the probability that

(a) none of these food items is found;
(b) two of these food items are found;
(c) at least one of these food items is found;
(d) no more than one of these food items is found.
(e) What would be your answers to (a)–(d) if the number of certain food items found during foraging has a Poisson distribution with a mean of 2.0?

4.65 Suppose that the number of flaws in sheets of anodized steel follows a Poisson distribution with an average of one flaw in a 20 square foot area. What is the probability that there will be

(a) exactly one flaw in a 20 square foot area;
(b) at least one flaw in a 20 square foot area;
(c) exactly five flaws in a 100 square foot area;
(d) at least five flaws in a 100 square foot area;
(e) explain the difference in the results of (a) and (b) as compared to those of (c) and (d).

REFERENCES

1. Hogg, R. V. and A. T. Craig; *Introduction to Mathematical Statistics,* 5th ed.; Upper Saddle River, N.J.: Prentice-Hall, 1995
2. Larsen, R. L. and M. L. Marx; *An Introduction to Mathematical Statistics and Its Applications,* 3d ed.; Upper Saddle River, NJ: Prentice-Hall, 2000
3. *Microsoft Excel 2000;* Redmond, WA: Microsoft Corp., 1999
4. *MINITAB Reference Manual Release 12;* State College, PA: MINITAB, Inc., 1998

APPENDIX 4.1   *Using Microsoft Excel for Probability and Probability Distributions*

In this chapter, we studied basic probability, the probability distribution in general, and such particular probability distributions as the binomial, the hypergeometric, the negative binomial, the geometric, and the Poisson distributions. The PHStat add-in for Microsoft Excel can be used to obtain results for each of these topics.

Using PHStat for Basic Probability

To calculate the simple and joint probabilities, use the **Data Preparation | Probabilities** choice of the PHStat add-in. As an example, consider the *performance of new cars* outcomes of Table 4.1, on page 137. Here is what to do to calculate probabilities based on these data. If the PHStat add-in has not been previously loaded, load the add-in using the instructions of Appendix 1.2. Select **File | New** to open a new workbook (or open the existing workbook into which the probabilities worksheet is to be inserted). Select **PHStat | Data Preparation | Probabilities.** The add-in inserts a worksheet containing calculations for simple and joint probabilities. In the newly inserted worksheet, enter **"United States"** (event A) in cell B5, **"Not United States"** (event A') in cell B6, **"Yes"** (event B) in cell C4, and **"No"** (event B') in cell D4 for the Sample Space events. In the same worksheet, enter **7** (the event A *and B* value) in cell C5, **13** (the event A' *and B* value) in cell C6, **293** (the event A *and B'* value) in cell D5, and **187** (the event A' *and B'* value) in cell D6. The inserted worksheet calculates and presents the probabilities in a table similar to the one shown in Table 4.1.

Using PHStat for the Expected Value and Standard Deviation of a Probability Distribution

To calculate expected values and measures of variation from a probability distribution, use the **Decision-Making | Expected Monetary Value** choice of the PHStat add-in. As an example, consider the number of defective welds problem discussed in Table 4.3 on page 146. To calculate expected values and related measures for this problem, if the PHStat add-in has not been previously loaded, load the add-in using the instructions of Appendix 1.2. Select **File | New** to open a new workbook (or open the existing workbook into which the criteria for the decision-making worksheet are to be inserted). Select **PHStat | Decision-Making | Expected Monetary Value.** In the Expected Monetary Value dialog box, enter **7** in the Number of Events: edit box. Enter **1** in the Number of Alternative Actions: edit box. Enter **Defective Welds Analysis** in the Output Title: edit box. Select the **Measures of Variation** check box. Click the **OK** button.

The add-in inserts a worksheet that contains areas for a payoff table, statistics, and intermediate calculations. Enter the probabilities for the events in the cell range B5:B11. Enter **.6** in cell B5, **.2** in cell B6, **.1** in cell B7, **.05** in cell B8, **.03** in cell B9, **.01** in cell B10, and **.01** in cell B11. Enter the payoffs (number of defective welds) in the cell range C5:C11. Enter **0** in cell C5, **1** in cell C6, **2** in cell C7, **3** in cell C8, **4** in cell C9, **5** in cell C10, and **6** in cell C11. The completed worksheet will contain the computations for the expected value (labeled as expected monetary value), variance, and standard deviation, for the number of defective welds.

Using PHStat to Obtain Binomial Probabilities

To calculate binomial probabilities, use the **Probability Distributions | Binomial** choice of the PHStat add-in. As an example, consider the relay switching problem discussed in section 4.4. To calculate the binomial probabilities for this problem, do the following. If the PHStat add-in has not been previously loaded, load the add-in using the instructions of Appendix 1.2. Select **File | New** to open a new workbook (or open the existing workbook into which the binomial probabilities worksheet is to be inserted). Select **PHStat | Probability Distributions | Binomial.** In the Binomial Probability Distribution dialog box, enter **5** in the Sample Size: edit box. Enter **.16** in the Probability of Success: edit box. Enter **0** (zero) in the Outcomes From: edit box and enter **5** in the Outcomes To: edit box. Enter **Binomial Probabilities for Open Relay Switches** in the Output Title: edit box. Select the **Cumulative Probabilities** and **Histogram** check boxes. Click the **OK** button. On separate sheets, the add-in produces a table of binomial probabilities (similar to those shown in Figure 4.2, on page 153) and a histogram.

The PHStat add-in for the binomial distribution is based on the BINOMDIST function of Microsoft Excel. The format of this function is:

$$\text{BINOMDIST}(X, n, p, cumulative)$$

where

X = the number of successes

n = the sample size

p = the probability of success

cumulative = a True or False value that determines whether the function computes the probability of X of fewer successes (True) or computes the probability of exactly X successes (False)

For example, BINOMDIST(3, 5, .16, False) would calculate the probability of obtaining exactly three open relay switches from a sample of five relay switches. Changing the False value to True would calculate the probability of 3 or fewer open relay switches.

Using PHStat to Obtain Hypergeometric Probabilities

To calculate hypergeometric probabilities, use the **Probability Distributions | Hypergeometric** choice of the PHStat add-in. As an example, consider the weld inspection problem discussed in section 4.5. To calculate the hypergeometric probabilities for this problem, follow these steps: If the PHStat add-in has not been previously loaded, load the add-in using the instructions of Appendix 1.2. Select **File | New** to open a new workbook (or open the existing workbook into which the hypergeometric probabilities worksheet is to be inserted). Select **PHStat | Probability Distributions | Hypergeometric.** In the Hypergeometric Probability Distribution dialog box, enter **3** in the Sample Size: edit box. Enter **6** in the No. of Successes in Population: edit box. Enter **8** in the Population Size: edit box. Enter **Hypergeometric Probabilities for Weld Inspection** in the Output Title: edit box. Select the **Histogram** check box. Click the **OK** button. On separate sheets, the add-in produces a table of hypergeometric probabilities and a histogram, similar to those shown in Figure 4.5 on page 160.

The PHStat add-in for the hypergeometric distribution is based on the HYPGEOMDIST function of Microsoft Excel. The format of this function is:

$$HYPGEOMDIST(X, n, A, N)$$

where

X = number of successes

n = the sample size

A = the number of successes in the population

N = the population size

Using Microsoft Excel to Obtain Negative Binomial Probabilities

The NEGBINOMDIST function of Microsoft Excel can be used to obtain probabilities from the negative binomial distribution. The format of this function is:

$$NEGBINOMDIST(n - X, X, p)$$

$n - X$ = the number of failures

X = the number of successes

p = the probability of success

To illustrate the negative binomial distribution, we return to the example on page 163, concerning data transmission lines. We computed the probability that the third data transmission line is captured in the fifth attempt as 0.13824. To obtain this result, we would enter the formula =NEGBINOMDIST(*2, 3, .4*) in a cell (B7 in Figure 4.6 on page 163). To obtain a geometric probability, the number of successes is one, so that to find the probability that a nonconforming support is found on the third attempt, with p = 0.05, we would enter the formula =NEGBINOMDIST(*2, 1, .05*) in a cell (C7 in Figure 4.6).

Using PHStat to Obtain Poisson Probabilities

To calculate Poisson probabilities, use the **Probability Distributions | Poisson** choice of the PHStat add-in. As an example, consider the food-processing problem discussed in section 4.7. To calculate the Poisson probabilities for this problem, follow these steps: If the PHStat add-in has not been previously loaded, load the add-in using the instructions of Appendix 1.2. Select **File | New** to open a new workbook (or open the existing workbook into which the Poisson probabilities worksheet is to be inserted). Select **PHStat | Probability Distributions | Poisson.** In the Poisson Probability Distribution dialog box, enter **4.5** in the Average/Expected No. of Successes: edit box. Enter **Poisson Probabilities for Chocolate Chips** in the Output Title: edit box. Select the **Cumulative Probabilities** and **Histogram** check boxes. Click the **OK** button.

On separate sheets, the add-in produces a table of Poisson probabilities (similar to the one shown in Figure 4.7, on page 170) and a histogram.

The PHStat add-in for the Poisson distribution is based on the POISSON function of Microsoft Excel. The format of this function is:

$$\text{POISSON}(X, lambda, cumulative)$$

where

X = number of successes

lambda = the average or expected number of successes

cumulative = a True or False value that determines whether the function computes the probability of X of fewer successes (True) or computes the probability of exactly X successes (False)

For example, POISSON(3, 4.5, False) would calculate the probability of obtaining exactly three chocolate chips in a cookie when the average number of chocolate chips was 4.5. Changing the False value to True would calculate the probability of 3 or more chocolate chips.

APPENDIX 4.2   *Using MINITAB for Probability and Probability Distributions*

In this chapter, we studied basic probability, the probability distribution in general, and such particular probability distributions as the binomial, the hypergeometric, the negative binomial, the geometric, and the Poisson. MINITAB can be used to obtain results for some of these topics.

Using MINITAB to Obtain Binomial Probabilities

To illustrate the use of MINITAB, consider the relay switching problem discussed in section 4.4. To obtain this result using MINITAB, enter the values **0, 1, 2, 3, 4, and 5** in rows 1–6 of column C1. Select **Calc | Probability Distributions | Binomial** to compute binomial probabilities. In the Binomial Distribution dialog box, select **Probability option** to obtain the exact probabilities of X successes for all values of X. In the Number of trials: edit box, enter the sample size of **5.** In the Probability of success: edit box, enter **.16.** Select the Input column option button and enter **C1** in the edit box. Click the **OK** button. A table of binomial probabilities similar to those shown in Figure 4.3 on page 154 is obtained.

Using MINITAB to Obtain Poisson Probabilities

To illustrate how to obtain Poisson probabilities using MINITAB, suppose we return to the food-processing problem of section 4.7. We computed the probability that there would be two chocolate chips in the next cookie baked, if the average number of chocolate chips were 4.5 per cookie, as 0.1125. To obtain this result using MINITAB, enter the values 0 through 20 in rows 1–21 of column C1. Select **Calc | Probability Distributions | Poisson** to compute Poisson probabilities. In the Poisson Distribution dialog box, select **Probability option** to obtain the exact probabilities of X successes for all values of X. In the Mean edit box, enter the λ value of 3. Select the **Input column** option button and enter **C1** in the edit box. Click the **OK** button. You will obtain the output displayed in Figure 4.8 on page 171.

chapter 5

Continuous Probability Distributions and Sampling Distributions

"The 'Law of Frequency of Error' (the normal distribution) reigns with serenity and in complete self-effacement amidst the wildest confusion. The huger the mob the more perfect is its sway. It is the supreme law of Unreason. Whenever a large sample of chaotic elements are taken in hand an unsuspected and most beautiful form of regularity proves to have been latent all along."

FRANCIS GALTON

USING STATISTICS

An industrial sewing machine uses ball bearings that are targeted to have a specific diameter. Because of variation in the manufacturing process, some of the ball bearings have diameters that are outside the limits (called specification limits) under which the ball bearing can operate properly within the machine. How can we determine what percentage of the ball bearings will have diameters that fall outside the specification limits and what can we do to ensure that as many ball bearings as possible have diameters that fall within the specification limits?

5.1 INTRODUCTION TO CONTINUOUS PROBABILITY DISTRIBUTIONS

In Chapter 4, we defined the probability distribution for a discrete random variable and determined how to obtain the mean (expected value), the variance, and the standard deviation for any discrete variable. In addition, we studied the binomial, hypergeometric, negative binomial, geometric, and Poisson distributions, specific discrete probability distributions that are commonly applied in engineering and the sciences.

In this chapter, we will focus on continuous variables, those variables for which *any* value within a range of values can occur. These distributions differ from discrete variables in the following ways:

1. *Any* value within the range of the variable can occur, rather than just specific values.
2. The probability of occurrence of a specific value X is zero.
3. Probabilities can be obtained by cumulating an area under a curve.

In order to find the probability within an interval from a to b, we need to find the **probability density function** $f(X)$ for the variable X. This density function is a non-negative function represented by the particular curve defined. In general, for a continuous variable, the probability of falling between a and b can be defined as

$$P(a \le X \le b) = \int_a^b f(x)\,dx \qquad -\infty < X < \infty \qquad (5.1)$$

When the integral over the entire range of the variable equals 1, Equation (5.1) represents a probability distribution.

As was the case with discrete variables, it is often useful to obtain the cumulative distribution function, the area between the lowest possible value of x and a given value of x. This is expressed in Equation (5.2).

$$P(X \le b) = \int_{-\infty}^b f(x)\,dx \qquad (5.2)$$

For continuous variables, the rules of probability and expected values are the same as for discrete variables, except that the integral sign replaces the summation sign used for discrete variables.

The mean or expected value for a continuous variable is equal to

$$\mu = E(X) = \int_{-\infty}^{\infty} xf(x)\,dx \qquad (5.3)$$

and the variance is equal to

$$\sigma^2 = \int_{-\infty}^{\infty} (X - \mu)^2 f(x)\,dx \qquad (5.4)$$

Now that we have defined the probability density function and expected value and variance for a continuous variable in general, we will turn our discussion to specific continuous distributions. We will begin with, the uniform (or rectangular) distribution, that is widely used in practice.

5.2 THE UNIFORM DISTRIBUTION

The **uniform distribution** is one in which a value is equally likely to occur anywhere in the range between the smallest value a and the largest value b. The probability density function for the uniform distribution is

$$f(x) = \begin{cases} \dfrac{1}{b-a} & \text{if } a \le x \le b \\[2mm] 0 & \text{elsewhere} \end{cases} \qquad (5.5)$$

where

   a is the minimum value of x and

   b is the maximum value of x.

The expected value and variance of the uniform distribution are

$$\mu = \frac{a + b}{2} \qquad (5.6)$$

and

$$\sigma^2 = \frac{(b - a)^2}{12} \qquad (5.7)$$

One of the most common uses of the uniform distribution is in the selection of random numbers. When simple random sampling is conducted (as in Section 1.7), each value is assumed to come from a distribution that is uniformly distributed between a minimum value 0 and a maximum value 1. What would be the probability of obtaining a random number between 0.10 and 0.30?

   For a uniform distribution in which $a = 0$ and $b = 1$, from Equation (5.5)

$$f(x) = \frac{1}{1 - 0} = 1$$

and so the uniform distribution is plotted as in Figure 5.1.

DERIVATION 5.1 (OPTIONAL) The Mean of a Uniform Distribution

$$\mu = E(X) = \int_{-\infty}^{\infty} x f(x)\,dx$$

$$f(x) = \frac{1}{b - a} \text{ if } a \leq x \leq b$$

Thus,

$$\mu = \int_{a}^{b} x \frac{1}{b - a}\,dx$$

$$\mu = \left. \frac{0.5x^2}{b - a} \right|_{a}^{b}$$

$$\mu = \frac{b^2 - a^2}{2(b - a)}$$

$$\mu = \frac{(b - a)(a + b)}{2(b - a)}$$

$$\mu = \frac{a + b}{2}$$

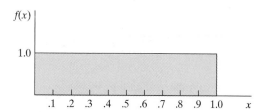

Figure 5.1   Probability density function for a uniform distribution with $a = 0$ and $b = 1$

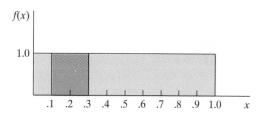

Figure 5.2   Finding $P(0.10 < x < 0.30)$ for a uniform distribution with $a = 0$ and $b = 1$

The total area under the rectangle is its base (1.0) times its height ($f(x) = 1.0$); the resulting area, 1.0, satisfies the requirement that the area under any probability density function equals 1.0. Thus, the area between 0.10 and 0.30, depicted in Figure 5.2, is equal to the base (which is $0.30 - 0.10 = 0.20$) times the height (1.0). Therefore, we have

$$P(0.10 < x < 0.30) = (\text{Base})(\text{Height}) = (0.20)(1.0) = 0.20$$

From Equations (5.6) and (5.7), the expected value and standard deviation of the distribution are computed as follows:

For $a = 0$ and $b = 1$, we have

$$\mu = \frac{a + b}{2}$$

$$\mu = \frac{0 + 1}{2} = 0.5$$

and

$$\sigma^2 = \frac{(1 - 0)^2}{12}$$

$$\sigma^2 = \frac{1}{12} = 0.0833$$

$$\sigma = \sqrt{0.0833} = 0.2887$$

Thus, the expected value is 0.5 and the standard deviation is 0.2887.

PROBLEMS

5.1 Suppose we sample from a uniform distribution with $a = 0$ and $b = 10$.
  (a) What is the probability of obtaining a value
    (1) between 5 and 7?
    (2) between 2 and 3?
  (b) What is the expected value?
  (c) What is the standard deviation?

5.2 A token ring local area network provides an inter-token time having a uniform distribution between 0 and 2 seconds.
  (a) What is the probability that the time will be
    (1) less than 0.6 seconds?
    (2) between 0.4 and 1.6 seconds?
    (3) greater than 1.8 seconds?
    (4) greater than 2 seconds?
  (b) What is the expected value of the inter-token time?
  (c) What is the standard deviation of the inter-token time?

5.3 At an ocean-side nuclear power plant, sea water is used as part of the cooling system. This use raises the temperature of the water that is discharged back into the ocean. The amount that the water temperature is raised has a uniform distribution over the interval from 10 to 25°C.
  (a) What is the probability that the temperature increase will be
    (1) less than 20°C?
    (2) between 20 and 22°C?
  (b) Suppose that a temperature increase of more than 18°C is considered to be potentially harmful to the environment. What is the probability, at any point of time, that the temperature increase is potentially dangerous?
  (c) What is the expected value of the temperature increase?

  (d) What is the standard deviation of the temperature increase?

5.4 The interarrival time of nuclear particles in a Monte Carlo simulation of a reaction is designed to have a uniform distribution over an interval from 0 to 0.5 milliseconds.
  (a) What is the probability that the interarrival time between two particles will be
    (1) less than 0.2 milliseconds?
    (2) between 0.1 and 0.3 milliseconds?
    (3) more than 0.35 milliseconds?
  (b) What is the expected value of the interarrival time?
  (c) What is the standard deviation of the interarrival time?

5.5 The time of possible failure for a continuous-operation device monitoring air quality has a uniform distribution over a 24-hour day.
  (a) If, based on the time of year, daylight is between 5:55 a.m. and 7:38 p.m., what is the probability that failure will occur during daylight hours?
  (b) If the device is in secondary mode from 10 p.m. to 5 a.m., what is the probability that failure will occur during secondary hours?
  (c) If the device has a self-checking computer chip that determines whether the device is operational every hour on the hour, what is the probability that failure will be detected within ten minutes of its occurrence?
  (d) If the device has a self-checking computer chip that determines whether the device is operational every hour on the hour, what is the probability that it will take at least 40 minutes to detect that a failure has occurred?

5.3 THE NORMAL DISTRIBUTION

Now that we have studied the uniform distribution as well as the discrete probability distributions in Chapter 4, we turn our attention to a particular distribution that is undoubtedly the most widely used distribution in statistics, the bell-shaped curve or **normal distribution.** It is a statistical distribution that is used to represent a wide variety of variables that are measured on a continuous scale. Many natural phenomena have been found to follow a normal distribution. For example, physical characteristics such as height and weight tend to be

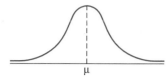

Figure 5.3   The normal distribution

normally distributed. Other examples of normally distributed variables are the time to accomplish an activity, measurement errors, the dimension of industrial parts, and voltage output. An example of a normal distribution is depicted in Figure 5.3.

The normal distribution is important in statistics for four main reasons:

1. Numerous phenomena measured on continuous scales have been shown to follow (or can be approximated by) the normal distribution.
2. We can use the normal distribution to approximate various discrete probability distributions, such as the binomial and the Poisson.
3. It provides the basis for the statistical process-control charts to be discussed in Chapters 6 and 7.
4. It provides the basis for classical statistical inference. (See Chapters 8–11.)

The normal distribution has several important theoretical properties, illustrated in Exhibit 5.1.

EXHIBIT 5.1 Properties of the Normal Distribution

1. It is bell-shaped and symmetrical in appearance.

2. Its measures of central tendency (mean, median, mode, midrange, and midhinge) are all identical.

3. Its probabilities are determined by two characteristics: its mean, μ_x, and its standard deviation, σ_x.

4. Its associated variable has a theoretically infinite range $(-\infty < X < \infty)$.

In practice, some of the variables we observe only approximate these theoretical properties. This approximation occurs for several reasons, including the following: (1) the underlying distribution might be only approximately normal; and (2) the practical range is not infinite but lies primarily between 3 standard deviations above and 3 standard deviations below the mean. In addition, we must realize that some continuous variables are not normally distributed and cannot be approximated by a normal distribution. Whether a variable can be approximated by a normal distribution can be determined in several ways, including by the use of such charts as normal probability plots (as in Section 5.5), box-and-whisker plots (per Section 3.3), histograms and polygons (per Section 2.4), and tests of normality. (See Reference 8.)

The Mathematical Expression for the Normal Distribution

The mathematical expression or model representing the normal distribution is denoted by the symbol $f(X)$. For the normal distribution, the model used to obtain the desired probabilities is

$$f(X) = \frac{1}{\sqrt{2\pi}\sigma_X} e^{-(1/2)[(X-\mu_x)/\sigma_X]^2} \tag{5.8}$$

where

e is the mathematical constant approximated by 2.71828

π is the mathematical constant approximated by 3.14159

μ_X is the population mean

σ_X is the population standard deviation

X is any value of the continuous variable, where $(-\infty < X < \infty)$.

Although this mathematical expression might look complex and imposing, we need to examine it further to see its features from a more simplified perspective. Since e and π are mathematical constants, the probabilities of the variable X depend on only two characteristics of the normal distribution: the population mean, μ_X, and the population standard deviation, σ_X. Every time we specify a *particular combination* of μ_X and σ_X, a *different* normal probability distribution will be generated. We illustrate this in Figure 5.4, where three different normal distributions are depicted. Distributions A and B have the same mean (μ_X) but have different standard deviations. Distributions A and C have the same standard deviation (σ_X) but have different means. Finally, distributions B and C depict two normal distributions which differ with respect to both μ_X and σ_X.

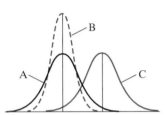

Figure 5.4   Three normal distributions having differing parameters μ_x and σ_x

The Standard Normal Distribution

The mathematical expression in Equation (5.8) is computationally complex, so it would be useful to have a set of tables that provides the desired probabilities. An infinite number of combinations of μ_X and σ_X exists, however, so an infinite number of tables would be required. Fortunately, there is a better way. By *standardizing* a normally distributed random variable, we will need only one table. (See Table A.2.) By using the transformation formula for **Z,** the **standard normal score,**

$$Z = \frac{X - \mu_x}{\sigma_x} \qquad (5.9)$$

any normally distributed variable X can be converted to a *standardized normal variable Z.* The mean of a set of Z scores is equal to zero, and its standard deviation is equal to 1. As can be seen from Equation (5.9), standard normal scores represent the deviations of raw scores from their mean (that is, $X - \mu_X$), expressed in standard deviation units. Positive values of Z represent original values that were above the mean; negative values of Z represent original values that were below the mean. We can always convert any set of normally distributed data to its standardized form and determine any desired probabilities from the table of the standard normal distribution (Appendix A, Table A.2).

To see how the transformation formula [Equation (5.9)] can be applied, let us return to the *Using Statistics* example presented on page 180. Suppose that an industrial sewing machine uses ball bearings that are targeted to have a diameter of 0.50 inch. The limits (called specification limits) under which the ball bearing can operate are 0.49 inch (lower) and 0.51 inch (upper). Past experience has indicated that the actual diameter is approximately normally distributed, with a mean $\mu_X = 0.503$ in. and a standard deviation $\sigma_X = 0.004$ in.

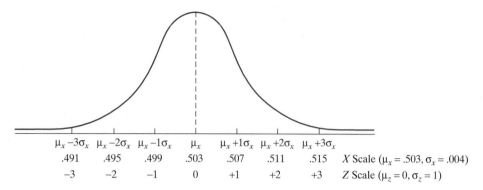

$\mu_x-3\sigma_x$	$\mu_x-2\sigma_x$	$\mu_x-1\sigma_x$	μ_x	$\mu_x+1\sigma_x$	$\mu_x+2\sigma_x$	$\mu_x+3\sigma_x$	
.491	.495	.499	.503	.507	.511	.515	X Scale ($\mu_x=.503$, $\sigma_x=.004$)
−3	−2	−1	0	+1	+2	+3	Z Scale ($\mu_z=0$, $\sigma_z=1$)

Figure 5.5   Transformation of Scales

We see from Figure 5.5 that every measurement X has a corresponding standardized measurement Z obtained from the transformation formula [Equation (5.9)]. Thus, from Figure 5.5, we observe that a diameter of 0.507 inch is equivalent to 1 standardized unit (that is, 1 *standard deviation unit*) above the mean, because

$$Z = \frac{0.507 - 0.503}{0.004} = +1.0$$

and that a diameter of 0.491 inch is equivalent to 3 standardized units (3 *standard deviation units*) below the mean, because

$$Z = \frac{0.491 - 0.503}{0.004} = -3.0$$

Thus, the standard deviation has become the unit of measurement. In other words, 0.507 inch is 0.004 inch (1 standard deviation) higher than the average of 0.503 inch, while 0.491 inch is 0.012 inch (3 standard deviations) lower than the average amount.

Using the Normal Probability Tables

Because the normal distribution is a continuous probability distribution, we need to focus on finding the area between two different X values. The total area under the curve adds to one, so the proportion of the area under the curve within an interval between two values represents the probability of obtaining a value within that interval.

Now, suppose that we would like to determine the proportion of all ball bearings that have a diameter between 0.503 and 0.507 inch. (For our purposes, this is the same as determining the probability that a single ball bearing will have a diameter between 0.503 and 0.507 inch.) The answer is found by using Table A.2, the table of the probabilities of the standard normal distribution.

Table A.2 presents the probabilities or areas under the standard normal curve, calculated from the mean, $\mu_Z = 0$, to the particular transformed value of interest, Z. Using Equation (5.9), we can calculate Z for the value of X under consideration. We can then use this table to determine the probability: the area under the standard normal curve from the mean ($\mu_Z = 0$) to the transformed value of interest, Z. Only positive entries for Z are listed in the table, because we are dealing with a symmetric distribution with a mean of zero. Therefore, the area from the mean to $+Z$ (Z standard deviations above the mean) must be identical to the area from the mean to $-Z$ (Z standard deviations below the mean).

To use Table A.2, we calculate Z values to two decimal places. Thus the Z value corresponding to $X = 0.507$ inch is $(0.507 - 0.503)/0.004 = +1.00$. To read the probability or the area under the curve from the mean, $Z = 0.0$, to $Z = +1.00$, we scan down the Z column from Table A.2 until we locate the appropriate row (in this case, $Z = 1.0$). Next, we read across this row until we intersect the column that contains the hundredths place of our desired Z value (in this case, .00).

This process is illustrated in Table 5.1 (which is a replica of Table A.2). The value in the body of the standard normal distribution table represents the area of the curve falling between the mean and the Z value of interest. For $Z = +1.00$, this probability is 0.3413. As depicted in Figure 5.6, 34.13 percent of all the ball bearings will have a diameter between 0.503 and 0.507 inch. Alternatively, we can state that there is a 34.13 percent chance that a single ball bearing will have a diameter between 0.503 and 0.507 inch.

TABLE 5.1

OBTAINING AN AREA UNDER THE NORMAL CURVE

Z	.00	.01	.02	.03	.04	.05	.06	.07	.08	.09
0.0	.0000	.0040	.0080	.0120	.0160	.0199	.0239	.0279	.0310	.0359
0.1	.0398	.0438	.0478	.0517	.0557	.0596	.0636	.0675	.0714	.0753
0.2	.0793	.0832	.0871	.0910	.0948	.0987	.1026	.1064	.1103	.1141
0.3	.1179	.1217	.1255	.1293	.1331	.1368	.1406	.1443	.1480	.1517
0.4	.1554	.1591	.1628	.1664	.1700	.1736	.1772	.1808	.1844	.1879
0.5	.1915	.1950	.1985	.2019	.2054	.2088	.2123	.2157	.2190	.2224
0.6	.2257	.2291	.2324	.2357	.2389	.2422	.2454	.2486	.2518	.2549
0.7	.2580	.2612	.2642	.2673	.2704	.2734	.2764	.2794	.2823	.2852
0.8	.2881	.2910	.2939	.2967	.2995	.3023	.3051	.3078	.3106	.3133
0.9	.3159	.3186	.3212	.3238	.3264	.3289	.3315	.3340	.3365	.3389
1.0	.3413	.3438	.3461	.3485	.3508	.3531	.3554	.3577	.3599	.3621

Source: Extracted from Table A.2.

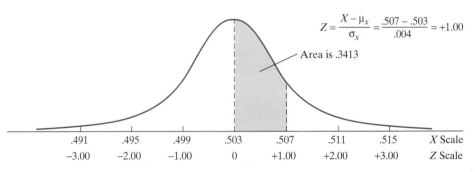

$$Z = \frac{X - \mu_x}{\sigma_x} = \frac{.507 - .503}{.004} = +1.00$$

Area is .3413

	.491	.495	.499	.503	.507	.511	.515	X Scale
	−3.00	−2.00	−1.00	0	+1.00	+2.00	+3.00	Z Scale

Figure 5.6   Determining the area between the mean and Z from the standard normal distribution

Suppose that we wanted to determine the proportion of all ball bearings that have a diameter between 0.491 and 0.503 inch. For this example, we would use Equation (5.9), with $X = 0.491$, as follows:

$$Z = \frac{0.491 - 0.503}{0.004} = -3.0$$

This result means that a diameter of 0.491 inch is 3 standard deviations (or Z units) below the mean of 0.493 inch. From Table A.2, we note that only positive Z values are shown in the table; however, we can work with negative Z values if we remember that, because the normal distribution is a symmetric distribution, the area between the mean and $+Z$ is equal to the area between the mean and $-Z$. Thus, the area between the mean and $Z = -3.0$ is the same as the area between the mean and $Z = +3.0$.

Using Table A.2, we find that the area between the mean and $Z = 3.0$ is 0.49865. We display this in Figure 5.7.

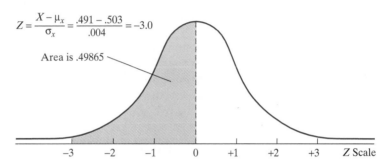

Figure 5.7   Finding the area between the mean and $Z = -3.0$

Now that we have learned to use Table A.2 in conjunction with Equation (5.9), we can evaluate many different types of probability applications having to do with the normal distribution. In doing so, we will use our information about the diameter of the ball bearings that assumes a population mean $\mu_X = 0.503$ inch and a population standard deviation $\sigma_X = 0.004$ inch.

Finding the Probabilities Corresponding to Known Values

As an example, suppose that we wish to find the probability that a randomly selected ball bearing will be between the target and the actual mean. First, it is helpful to set up Figure 5.8. In this figure, we indicate the value of the target, equal to 0.50 inch, and the mean, equal to 0.503 inch. Then we find the Z value (that represents the distance in standard deviation units) between the target, 0.50, and the mean, 0.503. By using Equation (5.9), we have

$$Z = \frac{0.50 - 0.503}{0.004} = -0.75$$

By using Table A.2, we find that the area between the mean and $Z = 0.75$ (which is the same as between the mean and $Z = -0.75$) is 0.2734. Thus, we state that the probability of obtaining a diameter between the target of 0.50 and the mean of 0.503 is 0.2734 or 27.34%.

Now that we have found an area between an individual value X and the mean, how can we determine the probability that a randomly selected ball bearing

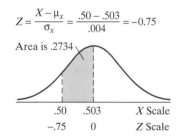

Figure 5.8   Finding the area between the mean and 0.50 inch

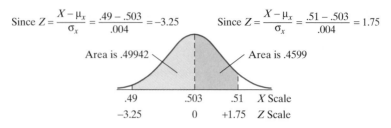

Since $Z = \dfrac{X - \mu_x}{\sigma_x} = \dfrac{.49 - .503}{.004} = -3.25$ Since $Z = \dfrac{X - \mu_x}{\sigma_x} = \dfrac{.51 - .503}{.004} = 1.75$

Area is .49942   Area is .4599

.49   .503   .51   X Scale
−3.25   0   +1.75   Z Scale

Figure 5.9   Finding the area between 0.49 and 0.51 inch

will have a diameter between the lower specification limit, 0.49 inch, and the upper specification limit, 0.51 inch?

From Figure 5.9, we can observe that one of the values of interest is above the mean of 0.503 inch, while the other value is below it. Table A.2 permits us only to find probabilities from a *particular value of interest to the mean,* but we can obtain our desired probability in three steps:

1.   Determine the probability represented by the area from the mean to the upper specification limit, 0.51 inch.
2.   Determine the probability represented by the area from the mean to the lower specification limit, 0.49 inch.
3.   Add the two results.

To find the area from the mean to 0.51 inch (step 1), we have

$$Z = \frac{0.51 - 0.503}{0.004} = 1.75$$

Looking up a Z value in Table A.2, we find that the area between the mean and a Z value of 1.75 is 0.4599. Thus, the probability that a ball bearing has a diameter between the mean of 0.503 and the upper specification limit of 0.51 is 0.4599.

In a similar manner, we can find the area between the mean, 0.503, and the lower specification limit, 0.49, as follows:

$$Z = \frac{0.490 - 0.503}{0.004} = -3.25$$

Looking up a Z value in Table A.2, we find that the area between the mean and a Z value of 3.25 is 0.49942. Thus, the probability that a ball bearing has a diameter between the mean, 0.503, and the lower specification limit, 0.49, is 0.49942.

If we add 0.4599 (the area between the mean, 0.503, and the upper specification limit, 0.51) and 0.49942 (the area between the mean and the lower specification limit), we obtain 0.95932. Thus, the probability that the diameter of the ball bearing will be between the lower and upper specification limits is 0.95932 or 95.932%.

Now that we have found the probabilities in these two examples, how can we determine the probability that a randomly selected ball bearing will have a diameter between the lower specification limit of 0.49 inch and the target of 0.50 inch?

Both values of interest are below the mean; we observe from Figure 5.10 that the desired probability (or area under the curve between our two desired values) is less than 0.5000. Our transformation formula [Equation (5.9)] permits us only to

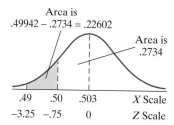

Area is
.49942 − .2734 = .22602

Area is
.2734

| .49 | .50 | .503 | X Scale |

| −3.25 | −.75 | 0 | Z Scale |

Figure 5.10   Finding the area between 0.49 and 0.50 inch

find probabilities from a *particular value of interest to the mean,* but we can obtain the desired probability in three steps:

1. Determine the probability or area under the curve from the mean to the lower specification limit, 0.49 inch.
2. Determine the probability or area under the curve from the mean to the target, 0.50 inch.
3. Subtract the area between the mean and 0.50 inch from the area between the mean and 0.49 inch.

For this example, we have already completed steps 1 and 2 in answering our two previous examples. (See Figures 5.8 and 5.9.) We know that the area from the mean to 0.49 inch is 0.49942 and that the area from the mean to 0.50 inch is 0.2734. Therefore, we have 0.49932 − 0.2734 = 0.22602. Thus, there is a 22.602 percent chance that we will obtain a diameter between the lower specification limit of 0.49 inch and the target of 0.50 inch.

Now, how can we find the probability that a randomly selected ball bearing will have a diameter above the upper specification limit?

We need to examine the shaded area of Figure 5.11.

Table A.2 permits us only to find areas under the standard normal distribution from the mean to Z, not from Z to ∞. Thus, we must find the probability from the mean to Z and subtract this result from the area from the mean to ∞, which is 0.5000, to obtain the desired answer.

To determine the area under the curve from the mean to 0.51 inch, we have

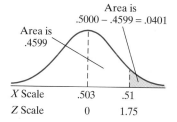

Area is
.4599

Area is
.5000 − .4599 = .0401

| X Scale | .503 | .51 |

| Z Scale | 0 | 1.75 |

Figure 5.11   Finding the area above 0.51 inch

$$Z = \frac{0.51 - 0.503}{0.004} = 1.75$$

In Figure 5.9 on page 190, we computed the probability between the mean and 0.51 as 0.4599. Using this information, the area from $Z = 1.75$ to $Z = \infty$ (where ∞ is the theoretical upper limit of the right tail) must be 0.5000 − 0.4599 = 0.0401. This is indicated in Figure 5.11. We state that there is a 4.01 percent chance of obtaining a ball bearing that has a diameter greater than the upper specification limit, 0.51 inch.

Finding the Values Corresponding to Known Probabilities

In our previous applications regarding the normal distribution, we determined the probabilities when given information about X values. Now, however, we wish to determine the particular values of the X variable that correspond to known probabilities. In order to illustrate how such values of X are obtained, we turn to a different question: we want to know the diameter that will be exceeded by 93 percent of the ball bearings.

To answer this question, we need to examine Figure 5.12. What we must first realize is that the unknown here is X, *not* the area under the curve. Our objective now is to find the value of X that is exceeded by 93 percent of the values. The next issue deals with the question of the position of the X value in relation to the mean. 93 percent of the values *exceed* X, so 7 percent are less than X. Thus, as displayed in Figure 5.12, X is below the mean. The fact that 7 percent of the values are below X (the lower tail area in this example) also tells us that 43 percent of all the values fall between X and the mean; thus, the area between X and the mean is 0.4300. We know that the area above the mean is 0.5000, and so we can confirm that the area above X is 0.9300.

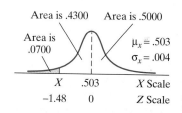

Area is .4300   Area is .5000

Area is
.0700

$\mu_x = .503$
$\sigma_x = .004$

| X | .503 | X Scale |

| −1.48 | 0 | Z Scale |

Figure 5.12   Finding Z to determine X

TABLE 5.2

OBTAINING AN AREA UNDER THE NORMAL CURVE

Entry represents area under the standardized normal distribution from the mean to Z

Z	.00	.01	.02	.03	.04	.05	.06	.07	.08	.09
0.0	.0000	.0040	.0080	.0120	.0160	.0199	.0239	.0279	.0319	.0359
0.1	.0398	.0438	.0478	.0517	.0557	.0596	.0636	.0675	.0714	.0753
0.2	.0793	.0832	.0871	.0910	.0948	.0987	.1026	.1064	.1103	.1141
⋮	⋮	⋮	⋮	⋮	⋮	⋮	⋮	⋮	⋮	⋮
1.3	.4032	.4049	.4066	.4082	.4099	.4115	.4131	.4147	.4162	.4177
1.4	.4192	.4207	.4222	.4236	.4251	.4265	.4279	.4292	.4306	.4319
1.5	.4332	.4345	.4357	.4370	.4382	.4394	.4406	.4418	.4429	.4441

Source: Extracted from Table A.2.

Having this information answers our question of interest only partially. We need to determine the distance between X and the mean in Z (or standard deviation) units, so that we can solve for X by using our transformation formula [Equation (5.9)]. The area between X and the mean is 0.4300; we can use Table A.2 to determine the corresponding Z value. (This is the opposite of what we have done previously when we used the Z value to find the appropriate area). Using the body of Table A.2, we search for an area of 0.4300. The closest result is 0.4306, as shown in Table 5.2 (a replica of Table A.2).

Working from this area value to the margins of the table, we see that the Z value corresponding to the particular Z row (1.4) and Z column (0.08) is 1.48. When we recall that our X value is below the mean, we know that Z must be negative, and, therefore, $Z = -1.48$.

Once Z is obtained, we can use the transformation formula [Equation (5.9)] to determine the value of interest, X. Now,

$$Z = \frac{X - \mu_x}{\sigma_x}$$

so

$$X = \mu_x + Z\sigma_x \qquad (5.10)$$

By substituting, we compute

$$X = 0.503 + (-1.48)(.004) = 0.49708 \text{ inch}$$

Thus, we would expect 93 percent of the ball bearings to have a diameter that is more than 0.49708 inch. Conversely, 7 percent of the ball bearings will have a diameter that is less than 0.49708 inch.

As a review, to find a *particular* value associated with a known probability, we need to take the steps displayed in Exhibit 5.2.

We illustrate these steps in the following example. Suppose that we wanted to determine the values between which 95% of all the ball bearing diameters will fall. If we assume that the 95% is symmetrically distributed around the mean, then, as displayed in Figure 5.13, the area between the mean and the upper value of $X(X_U)$ is 0.475 as is the area between the mean and the lower value of $X(X_L)$.

EXHIBIT 5.2 Finding the Particular Value Associated with a Known Probability

1. Sketch the normal curve, and then place the values for the means (μ_x and μ_z) on the respective X and Z scales.

2. Determine whether X is above the mean or below the mean.

3. Split the appropriate half of the normal curve into two parts—the portion from the desired X to the mean, and the portion from the desired X to the tail.

4. Shade the area of interest.

5. By using Table A.2, determine the appropriate Z value corresponding to the area under the normal curve from the desired X to the mean μ_x.

6. By using Equation (5.10), solve for X.

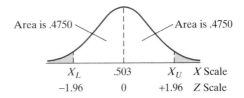

Area is .4750   Area is .4750

| | X_L | .503 | X_U | X Scale |
| | −1.96 | 0 | +1.96 | Z Scale |

Figure 5.13   Finding X_L and X_U for an area of 0.95

TABLE 5.3

OBTAINING AN AREA UNDER THE NORMAL CURVE

Z	.00	.01	.02	.03	.04	.05	.06	.07	.08	.09
0.0	.0000	.0040	.0080	.0120	.0160	.0199	.0239	.0279	.0319	.0359
0.1	.0398	.0438	.0478	.0517	.0557	.0596	.0636	.0675	.0714	.0753
0.2	.0793	.0832	.0871	.0910	.0948	.0987	.1026	.1064	.1103	.1141
:	:	:	:	:	:	:	:	:	:	:
.8	.4641	.4649	.4656	.4664	.4671	.4678	.4686	.4693	.4699	.4706
1.9	.4713	.4719	.4726	.4732	.4738	.4744	.4750	.4756	.4761	.4767

Source: Extracted from Table A.2.

From Figure 5.13, and because the area between X and the mean is 0.4750, we can use Table A.2 to determine the corresponding Z value. Using the body of Table A.2, we search for an area of 0.4750 (as in Table 5.3), and we determine that the corresponding Z value is exactly 1.96. Therefore, the upper value of Z is $+1.96$, and the lower value of Z is -1.96. By using Equation (5.10), we can compute the values of X_U and X_L as follows:

$$X = \mu_x + Z\sigma_x$$
$$X_U = 0.503 + 1.96(0.004) = 0.51084 \text{ inch}$$

and

$$X_L = 0.503 - 1.96(0.004) = 0.49516 \text{ inch}$$

Thus, we can conclude that 95% of the ball bearings will have diameters between 0.49516 inch and 0.51084 inch.

Now that we have used Table A.2 to obtain normal probabilities, we will illustrate how to do so with Microsoft Excel and MINITAB. Figure 5.14 illustrates output obtained from the PHStat add-in for Microsoft Excel. (See Appendix 5.1.) Figure 5.15 illustrates MINITAB output. (See Appendix 5.2)

	A	B	C	D
1	Diameters of Ball Bearings			
2				
3	Mean	0.503		
4	Standard Deviation	0.004		
5				
6	Probability for X<=	0.491		
7	Z Value	-3		
8	P(X<=0.491)	0.001349967		
9				
10	Probability for X>	0.51		
11	Z Value	1.75		
12	P(X>0.51)	0.040059114		
13				
14	Probability for X<0.491 or X >0.51	0.041409081		
15				
16	Probability for range	0.49	<= X <=	0.51
17	Z Value for 0.49	-3.25		
18	Z Value for 0.51	1.75		
19	P(X<=0.49)	0.000577086		
20	P(X<=0.51)	0.959940886		
21	P(0.49<=X<=0.51)	0.9593638		
22				
23	Find X and Z			
24	Cumulative Percentage:	7.00%		
25	Z Value	-1.475791578		
26	X Value	0.497096834		

Figure 5.14   Obtaining normal probabilities from the PHStat add-in for Microsoft Excel

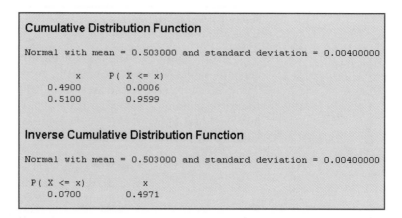

Cumulative Distribution Function

Normal with mean = 0.503000 and standard deviation = 0.00400000

```
        x        P( X <= x)
   0.4900         0.0006
   0.5100         0.9599
```

Inverse Cumulative Distribution Function

Normal with mean = 0.503000 and standard deviation = 0.00400000

```
P( X <= x)            x
   0.0700         0.4971
```

Figure 5.15   Obtaining normal probabilities from MINITAB

PROBLEMS

5.6 You are given a standard normal distribution having a mean of 0 and standard deviation of 1 (Table A.2).
   (a) What is the probability that
   - (1) Z is between 0 and $+1$?
   - (2) Z is between 1.25 and 1.75?
   - (3) Z is between -1.55 and $+1.55$?
   - (4) Z is less than -2.0?
   - (5) Z is greater than -1.0?
   - (6) Z is less than -2.0 or greater than $+1.0$?
   (b) What is the value of Z if 80 percent of the possible Z values are larger?
   (c) What is the value of Z if 5 percent of the possible Z values are larger?
   (d) Between what two values of Z (symmetrically distributed around the mean) will 90 percent of all possible Z values be contained?

5.7 You are given a standard normal distribution having a mean of 0 and standard deviation of 1 (Table A.2).
   (a) What is the probability that
   - (1) Z is between 0 and -2?
   - (2) Z is between -1.25 and 2.25?
   - (3) Z is between -1.75 and $+1.75$?
   - (4) Z is less than -1.50?
   - (5) Z is greater than -1.50?
   - (6) Z is less than -1.0 or greater than $+1.50$?
   - (7) Z is less than -3.0 or greater than $+3.0$?
   (b) What is the value of Z if 90 percent of the possible Z values are larger?
   (c) What is the value of Z if 1 percent of the possible Z values are larger?
   (d) Between what two values of Z (symmetrically distributed around the mean) will 99 percent of all possible Z values be contained?

5.8 Verify the following:
   (a) The area under the normal curve between 2 standard deviations above and below the mean is 0.9544.
   (b) The area under the normal curve between 3 standard deviations above and below the mean is 0.9973.

5.9 A machine used to extract juice from oranges obtains an amount from each orange that is approximately normally distributed, with a mean of 4.70 ounces and a standard deviation of 0.40 ounces.
   (a) What is the probability that a randomly selected orange will contain
   - (1) between 4.70 and 5.00 ounces?
   - (2) between 5.00 and 5.50 ounces?
   - (3) between 4.00 and 5.00 ounces?
   - (4) more than 4.00 ounces?
   - (5) more than 5.00 ounces?
   (b) Seventy-seven percent of the oranges will contain at least how many ounces of juice?
   (c) Ninety percent of the oranges will contain an amount that is between what two values (symmetrically distributed around the mean)?

5.10 A process used in filling bottles with soft drink results in net weights that are normally distributed, with a mean of 2 liters and a standard deviation of 0.05 liter. Bottles filled to less than 95 percent of the listed net weight (1.90 liters in this case) can make the manufacturer subject to penalty by the state office of consumer affairs; bottles filled above 2.10 liters may cause excess spillage upon opening.
   (a) What proportion of the bottles will contain
   - (1) Between 1.90 and 2.0 liters?
   - (2) Between 1.90 and 2.10 liters?
   - (3) Below 1.90 liters?
   - (4) Below 1.90 liters or above 2.10 liters?
   - (5) Above 2.10 liters?
   - (6) Between 2.05 and 2.10 liters?
   (b) Ninety-nine percent of the bottles would be expected to contain at least how much soft drink?
   (c) Ninety-nine percent of the bottles would be expected to contain an amount that is between which two values (symmetrically distributed around the mean)?
   (d) Explain the difference between the results in (b) and those in (c).
   (e) Suppose that, in an effort to reduce the number of bottles that are less than 1.90 liters, the bottler sets the filling machine so that the mean is 2.02 liters. Under these circumstances, what would be your answers for (a), (b), and (c)?

5.11 The diameter of an automobile tire is normally distributed, with a mean of 575 mm and a standard deviation of 5 mm.
   (a) What is the probability that a randomly selected tire has a diameter
   - (1) between 575 and 579 mm?
   - (2) 572 and 580 mm?
   - (3) above 570 mm?
   - (4) below 580 mm?
   (b) 80% of the tires will have diameters above what value?
   (c) 80% of the tires will have diameters between what two values (symmetrically distributed around the mean)?

(d) Explain the difference between your answers to (b) and (c).

(e) Suppose that the standard deviation of the diameter could be reduced to 0.04 mm. What would be your answers to (a)–(d)?

5.12 A paper by X.D. Fand and Y. Zhang, "Assuring the Matchable Degree in Selective Assembly via a Predictive Model Based on Set Theory and Probability Method," *Transactions of the ASME,* 1996, discusses the manufacturing problem of accurately machining matching parts such as shafts that fit into a valve hole. They describe the sizes of both the shaft and the valve hole as having a normal distribution. Suppose a particular design requires a shaft with a diameter of 22.000 mm., but shafts with diameters between 21.900 and 22.010 are acceptable. Also suppose that the manufacturing process yields shafts with diameters normally distributed with a mean of 22.002 mm. and a standard deviation of 0.005 mm. For this process, what is

(a) the proportion of shafts with diameters between 21.90 and 22.00?

(b) the probability of an acceptable shaft?

(c) the diameter which will be exceeded by only 2% of the shafts?

(d) What would be your answers in (a)–(c) if the standard deviation of the shaft diameter was 0.004?

5.13 Kyser and Collins ("Reliability Enhancement of a New Computer," *ESS* PROCEEDINGS—Institute of Environmental Sciences, 1995) describe a program to enhance the reliability of the CPU board in a massively parallel RISC processor system. A part of the paper concentrates on a parity problem labeled a Comm Logic failure. The errors seem to occur as a function of temperature and have a normal distribution with a mean of 80°C and a standard deviation of 20°C.

(a) What is the probability that an error occurs at lower than 77 degrees?

(b) What is the probability that an error occurs at between 74 and 84 degrees?

(c) Above what temperature will 25% of the errors occur?

5.14 A 1996 paper by Daniel Gibbons, "An Examination of the Factor of Safety as it Relates to the Design of the Compressive Strength of Concrete," *Civil Engineering,* 1996, describes the compressive strength of concrete for freshwater exhibition tanks as having a mean of 6,000 psi and a standard deviation of 240 psi. Assuming that the compressive strength is normally distributed, answer the following questions.

(a) What is the probability that the compressive strength of a sample of concrete is between 5,500 and 6,500 psi?

(b) What is the probability that the compressive strength of a sample of concrete is between 5,000 and 5,900 psi?

(c) What is the probability that the compressive strength of a sample of concrete is less than 6,750 psi?

(d) What is the probability that the compressive strength of a sample of concrete is less than 5,800 psi?

(e) Below what psi will 20% of the compressive strengths of samples of concrete be?

(f) Above what psi will 70% of the compressive strengths of samples of concrete be?

(g) Above what psi will 15% of the compressive strengths of samples of concrete be?

5.4 THE STANDARD NORMAL DISTRIBUTION AS AN APPROXIMATION TO THE BINOMIAL AND POISSON DISTRIBUTIONS

Now that we have discussed the standard normal distribution, we can turn in this section to one of its very important properties, the fact that, under certain conditions, it can be used to approximate various other probability distributions, such as the binomial and the Poisson. The motivation for employing the normal approximation to these discrete probability distributions is that, if the sample size is sufficiently large, the normal distribution serves as a good approximation to these two probability distributions. Such approximations are used in statistical process control (as in Chapters 6 and 7) and in statistical inference (as in Chapters 8–9).

Approximating the Binomial Distribution

As a general rule (per Reference 9), the normal distribution can be used to approximate the binomial distribution when the variance, $np(1 - p)$, is at least 10.

We recall from Section 4.4 that the mean of the binomial distribution is

$$\mu_X = np$$

and that the standard deviation of the binomial distribution is obtained from

$$\sigma_X = \sqrt{np(1-p)}$$

Substituting into the transformation formula Equation (5.9),

$$Z = \frac{X - \mu_x}{\sigma_x}$$

we have

$$Z = \frac{X - np}{\sqrt{np(1-p)}} \tag{5.11}$$

where

$\mu_X = np$, the mean of the binomial distribution

$\sigma_X = \sqrt{np(1-p)}$, the standard deviation of the binomial distribution

X = number of successes

To illustrate this, let us return to the example on page 144 that related to the probability that a switch was opened. Suppose that instead of examining a sample of three switches, as was done previously, we wish to consider a sample of 100 switches and want to determine the probability that more than 60 switches will be open.

Assuming that a sample of 100 switches is used, the average number of switches opened $\mu_x = np = 100(0.50) = 50$, and the variance $np(1-p) = 100(0.5)(1-0.5) = 25$. The variance is greater than 10, so we can use the normal distribution to approximate the binomial distribution. To find the area between 50 and 60 switches opened, we have

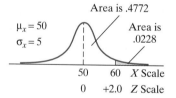

Area is .4772
$\mu_x = 50$
$\sigma_x = 5$
Area is .0228
50   60 X Scale
0   +2.0 Z Scale

Figure 5.16   Finding $P(X > 60)$

$$Z = \frac{X - np}{\sqrt{np(1-p)}} = \frac{60 - 50}{\sqrt{100(.5)(1-.5)}} = \frac{10}{5} = +2.00$$

Here, the number of successes (defined as a open switch) is 60. Hence, the approximate probability that X does not exceed this value corresponds to a value of $+2.00$ on the standardized Z scale. This is depicted in Figure 5.16.

Using Table A.2, we find that the area under the curve between the mean and $Z = +2.0$ is 0.4772. Thus, the desired area above $X = 60$ (or $Z = +2.0$) is $0.5000 - 0.4772 = 0.0228$. Therefore, there is a 0.0228 probability or a 2.28 percent chance that more than 60 of the switches would be opened.

Approximating the Poisson Distribution

As a general rule, the normal distribution can be used to approximate the Poisson distribution whenever the parameter λ is at least 5.

We recall from Section 4.7 on page 170 that the mean of the Poisson distribution is

$$\mu_x = \lambda$$

and that the standard deviation of the Poisson distribution is

$$\sigma_x = \sqrt{\lambda}$$

Substituting into the transformation formula Equation (5.9),

$$Z = \frac{X - \mu_x}{\sigma_x}$$

we have

$$Z = \frac{X - \lambda}{\sqrt{\lambda}} \qquad\qquad (5.12)$$

where

$\mu_x = \lambda$, the mean of the Poisson distribution

$\sigma_x = \lambda$, the standard deviation of the Poisson distribution

X = number of successes

To illustrate this, let us return to our example on page 168 that related to the food-processing plant that baked Marilyn's chocolate chip cookies. Suppose that we were now concerned with the number of chocolate chips in the super-size cookie, whose design specification calls for an average of 15 chips per cookie. We wish to determine the approximate probability that a cookie contains fewer than ten chocolate chips.

From Equation (5.12), and using the normal approximation to the Poisson distribution (because $\mu_x = \lambda = 15$), we have

$$Z = \frac{X - \lambda}{\sqrt{\lambda}} = \frac{10 - 15}{\sqrt{15}} = \frac{-5}{3.873} = -1.29$$

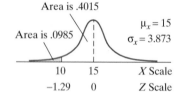

Figure 5.17   Finding $P(X < 10)$

Here the number of successes (in this case, chocolate chips) is ten. Hence, the approximate probability that X is between this value and the mean corresponds to the area between a value of -1.29 and the mean on the standard normal distribution or Z scale. This is depicted in Figure 5.17.

Using Table A.2, we find the area under the curve between the mean and $Z = -1.29$ is 0.4015. Thus the desired area below $X = 10$ ($Z = -1.29$) is $0.5000 - 0.4015 = 0.0985$. Therefore, there is a 0.0985 probability or a 9.85 percent chance that the number of chocolate chips in the super-sized cookie is less than ten.

PROBLEMS

5.15 Suppose that past records indicate that the probability is 0.04 that a new car will need a warranty repair in the first 90 days of use. What is the approximate probability that, for the next 500 cars sold,
(a) fewer than ten need a warranty repair?
(b) between 15 and 25 need a warranty repair?
(c) more than 15 need a warranty repair?

5.16 Suppose that a student is taking a multiple-choice exam in which each question has four choices. Believing that she has no knowledge of the correct answers to any of these questions, she has decided on a strategy in which she will place four balls (marked A, B, C, and D) into a box. For each question, she will randomly select one ball and then replace the ball in the box. The marking on the ball will determine her answer to the question.

Suppose that the exam consists of 100 multiple-choice questions and that a passing grade is 60 questions correct. What is the approximate probability that on this exam she will get
(a) at least 30 questions correct?
(b) fewer than 20 questions correct?
(c) between 15 and 35 questions correct?
(d) a passing grade?

5.17 An important part of the customer-service responsibilities of a telephone company relate to the speed with which troubles in residential service can be repaired. Suppose that past data indicate that the likelihood is 0.70 that troubles in a residential service can be repaired on the same day. Of 50 troubles reported in a given day, what is the approximate probability that
(a) at least 25 will be repaired by the end of the day?
(b) at least 40 will be repaired by the end of the day?
(c) fewer than 30 will be repaired by the end of the day?

5.18 A manufacturer of compact-disk players subjects the equipment to a comprehensive testing process for all mechanical and electrical functions before the equipment leaves the factory. Ideally, the hope is that each compact-disk player passes on the first test. Suppose that past data indicate that the probability that a compact-disk player passes the first test is 0.90.

If 200 players are randomly selected, what is the approximate probability that
(a) at least 190 pass the first test?

(b) between 175 and 190 pass the first test?
(c) fewer than 185 pass the first test?

5.19 Suppose that the number of undeliverable e-mail messages per day for a certain system follows a Poisson distribution with an average of 50. What is the approximate probability that, on a given day,
(a) there will be at least 35 undeliverable email messages?
(b) there will be at least 50 undeliverable email messages?
(c) there will be between 40 and 60 undeliverable email messages?

5.20 The number of power surges at a nuclear plant follows a Poisson distribution with an average of 15 power surges per month.
(a) What is approximate probability that, in a given month,
   (1) there will be fewer than 5 power surges?
   (2) there will be at least 10 power surges?
   (3) there will be between 10 and 20 power surges?
(b) What is the standard deviation of the number of power surges in a month?

5.21 From past experience, it is assumed that the number of flaws in rolls of grade-2 paper follows a Poisson distribution with an average of one flaw per five linear feet of paper.
(a) What is the approximate probability that there will be at least five flaws in a 50-foot length of paper?
(b) What is the approximate probability that there will be between five and fifteen flaws in a 50-foot length of paper?

5.5 THE NORMAL PROBABILITY PLOT

Now that we have discussed the normal distribution and its properties, it would be useful to be able to evaluate whether a particular variable is approximately normally distributed. A graphical method for accomplishing this is the **normal probability plot.**

Using a Normally Transformed Scale

There are several approaches to obtaining a normal probability plot. One approach (used by MINITAB) involves the transformation of the vertical scale of cumulative probabilities in a special way. The use of this transformation is illustrated by first referring to the cumulative probability distribution of a set of normally distributed values contained in Table 5.4 on page 200.

The cumulative percentage polygon (see Section 2.4) for the data of Table 5.4 is plotted in Figure 5.18.

TABLE 5.4

CUMULATIVE PROBABILITIES FOR SELECTED VALUES FROM THE NORMAL DISTRIBUTION

Z	Cumulative % (Percent of Values Less Than Z)	Z	Cumulative % (Percent of Values Less Than Z)
−3.0	0.135	+0.5	69.150
−2.5	0.620	+1.0	84.130
−2.0	2.280	+1.5	93.320
−1.5	6.680	+2.0	97.720
−1.0	15.870	+2.5	99.380
−0.5	30.850	+3.0	99.865
−0.0	50.000		

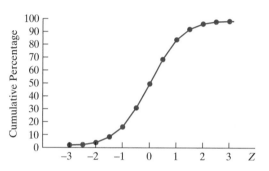

Figure 5.18   Cumulative percentage polygon for the data presented in Table 5.4

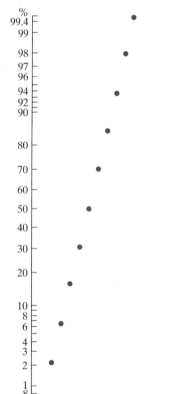

Figure 5.19   Normal probability plot for the data presented in Table 5.4

In Figure 5.18, we observe the S-shaped cumulative percentage polygon typical of a normal distribution. The transformation of the vertical Y-axis scale, as in the normal probability scale shown in Figure 5.19, results in the set of data points that plot approximately along a straight line if the variable (X) is normally distributed.

To illustrate this phenomenon, Figure 5.19 depicts the same set of Z values presented in Table 5.4 plotted on this transformed vertical scale. We see that this set of Z values (which is from a normal distribution) plots along a straight line on this transformed vertical scale.

However, Figure 5.20 represents a different picture. In Panel A, which shows a left-skewed distribution, the curve rises more rapidly at first, and then the rate of increase declines. In contrast to this, for the right-skewed distribution illustrated in Figure 5.20 (b), the curve rises more slowly at first, and then the rate of increase rapidly increases. Thus, by examining the normal probability plot, we can determine whether a set of data is approximately normally distributed. As a general rule, this graphical approach is considered appropriate only when the set of data contains at least 20 observations.

In order to illustrate the use of this transformed scale, let us return to our data concerning the length of the male Dover sole, discussed in Chapter 2, and plot these data on normal probability paper. In using **normal probability paper,** the

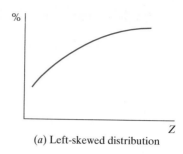

(a) Left-skewed distribution

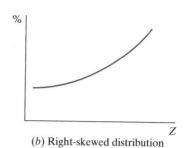

(b) Right-skewed distribution

Figure 5.20   Normal probability plots for a left-skewed distribution and a right-skewed distribution

vertical plotting position (the cumulative percentage p_i for the ith observation in an ordered array) is usually defined (per Reference 1) as follows:

$$p_i = \frac{(i - 0.5)}{n} \cdot 100\% \qquad (5.13)$$

where

p_i = cumulative percentage for value i

i = the specific ordered observation $i = 1, \ldots, n$

n = the number of observations

Because $n = 58$ for the fish length data, we have

$$p_1 = \frac{(1 - 0.5)}{58} \cdot 100\% = 0.86\%,$$

$$p_2 = \frac{(2 - 0.5)}{58} \cdot 100\% = 2.59\%,$$

$$\cdots,$$

$$p_{58} = \frac{(58 - 0.5)}{58} \cdot 100\% = 99.14\%$$

Table 5.5 represents the length (arranged in ascending order) and cumulative percentage (p_i) values for the length of male Dover sole originally presented in Table 2.3 on page 56.

TABLE 5.5

RANKS, CUMULATIVE PERCENTAGE, AND LENGTH OF 58 MALE FISH

Rank	Cumulative Percentage (p_i)	Length	Rank	Cumulative Percentage (p_i)	Length
1	0.86	331	30	50.86	397
2	2.59	339	31	52.59	398
3	4.31	339	32	54.31	398
4	6.03	340	33	56.03	398
5	7.76	341	34	57.76	4.03
6	9.48	346	35	59.48	404
7	11.21	347	36	61.21	405
8	12.93	358	37	62.93	408
9	14.66	364	38	64.66	409
10	16.38	366	39	66.38	410
11	18.10	370	40	68.10	410
12	19.83	371	41	69.83	411
13	21.55	371	42	71.55	412
14	23.28	371	43	73.28	413
15	25.00	373	44	75.00	414
16	26.72	374	45	76.72	415
17	28.45	381	46	78.45	417
18	30.17	381	47	80.17	419
19	31.90	384	48	81.90	419
20	33.62	386	49	83.62	420
21	35.34	387	50	85.34	420
22	37.07	387	51	87.07	421
23	38.79	388	52	88.79	423
24	40.52	389	53	90.52	425
25	42.24	390	54	92.24	427
26	43.97	392	55	93.97	436
27	45.69	393	56	95.69	439
28	47.41	394	57	97.41	439
29	49.14	395	58	99.14	451

[1]For those who do not have access to MINITAB, a special type of graph paper with the vertical scale transformed to allow the study of probabilities is included in Appendix B.1.

Figure 5.21 represents the plot of the data of Table 5.5 obtained from MINITAB[1] when using this transformed vertical scale.

Our initial impression from this figure plotted on normal probability paper is that, except for several points at the lower end of the scale, the plot of the ordered values seems to approximately follow a straight line. Thus, from an exploratory perspective, it appears reasonable to conclude that the lengths of the male fish are approximately normally distributed. If we desire to confirm this, we would need to evaluate the normality assumption more formally. (See Reference 8.)

Using the Quantile—Quantile Plot

[2]For a review of quantiles, see Section 3.2.

Another graphical technique, which can be used as an alternative to transforming the vertical axis to evaluate whether a set of data is normally distributed, is the **Quantile–Quantile plot** or *Q–Q* **plot.** In this method, each quantile[2] value is

Normal Probability of the Length of Male Dover Sole

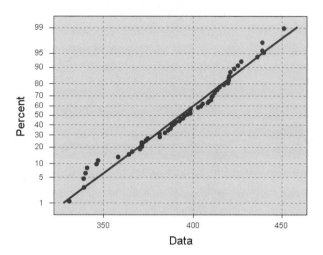

Figure 5.21   Normal probability plot obtained from
MINITAB for the length of male Dover sole

transformed to a Z score and the *ordered array* of observed scores and the Z scores
are plotted. A normally distributed set of data yields a straight line.

In Section 5.3, we determined the probabilities corresponding to known
values of normally distributed variables. For example, we found that 93% of the
values are greater than $Z = -1.48$ (and 7% are less than -1.48). Thus, the **standard normal quantile value** corresponding to the 7th percentile is -1.48. Any
desired quantile value can be obtained in a similar manner. The process that
allows us to obtain the corresponding Z value is called the **inverse normal scores
transformation.**

Using the symbol O to represent a quantile point, in general, we can define
the standard normal quantiles as follows:

> The **first standard normal quantile, O_1,** is the Z value on a standard normal
> distribution below which the proportion $1/(n + 1)$ of the area under the
> curve is contained.

> The ***i*th standard normal quantile, O_i,** is the Z value on a standard normal
> distribution below which the proportion $i/(n + 1)$ of the area under the curve
> is contained.

> The ***n*th (and largest) standard normal quantile, O_n,** is the Z value on a standard normal distribution below which the proportion $n/(n + 1)$ of the area
> under the curve is contained.

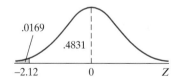

Figure 5.22   Finding the first
standard normal observed
value O_1 from a data set with
58 observations

For the length of the sample of 58 male Dover sole, the first ordered quantile value
represents the Z value *below which* $1/(58 + 1) = 1/59 = 0.0169$ of the area under
the normal curve is located. From Figure 5.22, we see that the area from O_1 to the
mean is $0.5000 - 0.0169 = 0.4831$. From Table A.2, the normal distribution table,
we observe that the corresponding Z value is -2.12.

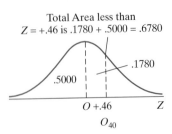

Total Area less than
Z = +.46 is .1780 + .5000 = .6780

.5000

.1780

O +.46   Z

O_{40}

Figure 5.23   Finding the 40th standard normal observed value O_{40} from a data set with 58 observations

To obtain a different standard normal ordered value (that is, quantile), such as the 40th standard normal ordered value, O_{40}, we need to find the Z value *below which* $40/(58 + 1) = 40/59 = 0.6780$ of the area under the normal curve is located. From Figure 5.23, we observe that the corresponding Z value is +0.46.

This process of obtaining Z values corresponding to the standard ordered values is carried out for all ordered values from $i = 1$ to n. Because the sample size n for the male Dover sole data is 58, we calculate Z values from 1 to 58. Table 5.6 summarizes the ranks, the ordered values [equal to $i/(n - 1)$], the corresponding Z values, and the corresponding lengths for the sample of 58 male Dover sole.

TABLE 5.6

RANKS, ORDERED VALUES, Z VALUES, AND LENGTHS OF 58 MALE FISH

Rank	Ordered Value	Z Value	Length	Rank	Ordered Value	Z Value	Length
1	0.0169	−2.12	331	30	0.5085	+0.02	397
2	0.0339	−1.83	339	31	0.5254	+0.06	398
3	0.0508	−1.64	339	32	0.5424	+0.11	398
4	0.0678	−1.49	340	33	0.5593	+0.15	398
5	0.0847	−1.37	341	34	0.5594	+0.19	403
6	0.1017	−1.27	346	35	0.5932	+0.24	404
7	0.1186	−1.18	347	36	0.6102	+0.28	405
8	0.1356	−1.10	358	37	0.6271	+0.32	408
9	0.1525	−1.03	364	38	0.6441	+0.37	409
10	0.1695	−0.96	366	39	0.6610	+0.42	410
11	0.1864	−0.89	370	40	0.6780	+0.46	410
12	0.2034	−0.83	371	41	0.6949	+0.51	411
13	0.2203	−0.77	371	42	0.7119	+0.56	412
14	0.2373	−0.72	371	43	0.7288	+0.61	413
15	0.2542	−0.66	373	44	0.7458	+0.66	414
16	0.2712	−0.61	374	45	0.7627	+0.72	415
17	0.2881	−0.56	381	46	0.7797	+0.77	417
18	0.3051	−0.51	381	47	0.7966	+0.83	419
19	0.3220	−0.46	384	48	0.8136	+0.89	419
20	0.3390	−0.42	386	49	0.8305	+0.96	420
21	0.3559	−0.37	387	50	0.8475	+1.03	420
22	0.3729	−0.32	387	51	0.8644	+1.10	421
23	0.3898	−0.28	388	52	0.8814	+1.18	423
24	0.4068	−0.24	389	53	0.8983	+1.27	425
25	0.4237	−0.19	390	54	0.9153	+1.37	427
26	0.4407	−0.15	392	55	0.9322	+1.49	436
27	0.4576	−0.11	393	56	0.9492	+1.64	439
28	0.4746	−0.06	394	57	0.9661	+1.83	439
29	0.4915	−0.02	395	58	0.9831	+2.12	451

Figure 5.24 represents the Quantile–Quantile plot (with the Z value on the X axis and the length of the fish on the Y axis) obtained from the PHStat add-in for Microsoft Excel for these data.

From Figure 5.24, we observe that the plot appears to be approximately a straight line, indicating that the lengths of the male Dover sole are approximately normally distributed.

Length of Male Dover Sole

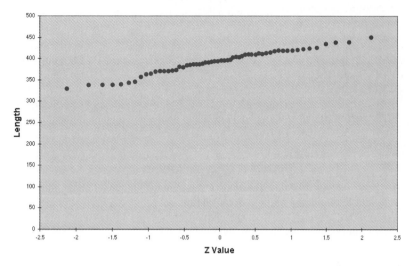

Figure 5.24   Quantile-Quantile plot, obtained from the PHStat add-in for Microsoft Excel, of the length of male Dover sole

PROBLEMS

5.22 The following data represent an ordered array of test scores for 20 students in a section of a statistics course.

40 43 46 49 52 55 58 61 64 67 70 73 76 79 82
85 88 91 94 96

TEST

(a) Construct a normal probability or a Quantile-Quantile plot of the test scores.
(b) From the results of (a), do you conclude that the test scores appear to be normally distributed? Explain.

5.23 The following data represent the mean tensile strength (in pounds) of 32 small sections of wire removed from cables at random spots on the Williamsburg Bridge in New York City, which was built in 1903.

5,421 5,631 5,833 6,024 6,130 6,167 6,514 6,435
6,399 6,232 6,730 6,444 6,607 6,432 6,569 6,346
5,949 6,262 6,515 6,628 6,358 6,778 5,758 5,773
6,373 6,751 6,475 6,078 5,929 6,539 5,948 6,556

BRIDGE

Source: Matteo, J., G. Deodatis, and D. P. Billington, "Safety Analysis of Suspension-Bridge Cables: Williamsburg Bridge," *Journal of Structural Engineering,* Vol. 120, Nov. 1994, pp. 3197–3199.

(a) Construct a normal probability or a Quantile-Quantile plot of the mean tensile strength.
(b) From the results of (a), does the mean tensile strength appear to be normally distributed? Explain.

5.24 The following data represent an ordered array of the daily amount of municipal solid waste (in cubic yards) collected from an industrial park over a period of 68 weekdays.

414 471 583 596 600 642 644 666 672
676 681 686 706 712 712 720 726 730
736 760 762 764 781 794 795 798 818
832 836 837 842 859 859 860 872 874
877 882 883 886 889 895 906 910 913
928 928 944 948 970 972 975 978 985
988 1010 1036 1050 1056 1062 1080 1084 1092
1110 1128 1334

SWASTE

(a) Construct a normal probability or a Quantile-Quantile plot of the amount of municipal solid waste.
(b) From the results of (a), does the amount of municipal solid waste appear to be normally distributed? Explain.

5.25 The following data represent the level of chromium (μg/g) found in household dust in windowsill concentrations on forty consecutive days in an urban environment.

315.98	102.48	34.53	124.67	158.07	9.29	108.00
221.10	45.61	167.15	57.31	31.58	85.89	135.58
69.55	11.56	45.35	170.83	27.64	9.62	19.18
97.84	27.26	67.27	27.83	20.36	52.96	244.64
31.75	89.69	203.41	4.71	81.72	195.27	40.53
67.69	23.50	57.96	74.19	15.37		

DUST

(a) Construct a normal probability or a Quantile-Quantile plot of the amount of chromium.
(b) From the results of (a), does the amount of chromium appear to be normally distributed? Explain.

5.26 The following data represent the measured voltage output of 24 new 1.5 volt (AA) batteries.

1.577	1.584	1.588	1.593	1.576	1.585	1.570	1.581
1.586	1.577	1.582	1.585	1.580	1.583	1.585	1.585
1.587	1.577	1.580	1.587	1.579	1.582	1.580	1.587

VOLTAGE

(a) Construct a normal probability or a Quantile-Quantile plot of the measured voltage output.

(b) From the results of (a), does the measured voltage output appear to be normally distributed? Explain.

5.27 In a rubber-edge manufacturing factory, the raw rubber is compounded through a kneading machine and then cut into thin ribbon strips. The strips are loaded onto mold machines and thermocast into the desired shapes of rubber edges. The weights (in grams) of a sample of rubber edges were as follows:

8.63	8.59	8.63	8.67	8.64	8.57	8.53	8.59	8.66	8.54
8.65	8.61	8.67	8.65	8.64	8.64	8.51	8.61	8.65	8.62
8.57	8.60	8.54	8.69	8.52	8.63	8.72	8.58	8.66	8.66
8.57	8.66	8.62	8.66	8.69	8.57	8.58	8.65	8.68	8.56
8.54	8.65	8.65	8.62	8.66	8.61	8.64	8.73	8.62	8.60
8.69	8.50	8.58	8.63	8.66	8.59	8.69	8.70	8.54	8.62
8.63	8.61	8.65	8.59	8.61	8.56	8.64	8.65	8.67	8.61
8.64	8.61	8.67	8.65	8.55	8.71	8.75	8.56	8.62	8.66

RUBBER

(a) Construct a normal probability or a Quantile-Quantile plot of the weight of rubber edges.
(b) From the results of (a), does the weight of rubber edges appear to be normally distributed? Explain.

Source: W. L. Pearn and K. S. Chen, "A practical implementation of the process capability index Cpk," *Quality Engineering*, 1997, 9, 721–737.

5.6 THE LOGNORMAL DISTRIBUTION

Now that we have discussed the normal distribution and the normal probability plot, we will study a distribution that is obtained when a right-skewed variable is transformed using natural logarithms and the transformed values are normally distributed. This distribution is called the **lognormal distribution.**

The probability density function for a nonnegative random variable X that follows a lognormal distribution is:

$$f(X) = \frac{1}{\sqrt{2\pi}\sigma_{\ln(X)}} e^{-(1/2)[(\ln(X)-\mu_{\ln(x)})/\sigma_{\ln(x)}]^2} \quad X > 0 \tag{5.14}$$

where

e is the mathematical constant approximated by 2.71828

π is the mathematical constant approximated by 3.14159

$\mu_{\ln(x)}$ is the population mean of the $\ln(x)$

$\sigma_{\ln(x)}$ is the population standard deviation of the $\ln(x)$

X is any value of the continuous variable, where $(0 < X < \infty)$

The mean of a variable X that follows a lognormal distribution is equal to

$$E(X) = \mu_{(x)} = e^{\mu_{\ln(x)} + \sigma^2_{\ln(x)}/2} \tag{5.15}$$

and the standard deviation of a variable X that follows a lognormal distribution is equal to

$$\sigma_x = \sqrt{e^{2\mu_{\ln(x)} + \sigma^2_{\ln(x)}} \cdot \left(e^{\sigma^2_{\ln(x)}} - 1\right)} \tag{5.16}$$

Because the natural logarithm of X is normally distributed, we find the areas under the normal curve by using Equation (5.9) for the standard normal distribution, and substituting $\ln(X)$ for X.

$$Z = \frac{\ln(X) - \mu_{\ln(x)}}{\sigma_{\ln(x)}} \tag{5.17}$$

To illustrate the lognormal distribution, we will suppose that a set of silicon wafers was inspected and that the numbers of particles present were recorded. These wafers were then left exposed in a clean room for a period of one week, and the numbers of particles were then recounted. If the increase in the number of particles can be approximated by a lognormal distribution, with the natural logarithm of the increase having a mean of 4 and a standard deviation of 1.5, find the mean and standard deviation of the increase and determine the probability that the increase in particles is less than 100.

For these data, using Equations (5.15) and (5.16), we have

$$E(X) = \mu_{(x)} = e^{4 + (1.5)^2/2} = e^{4 + (2.25)/2}$$

$$= e^{5.125} = 168.17$$

and

$$\sigma_x = \sqrt{e^{2(4) + (1.5)^2} \cdot \left(e^{(1.5)^2} - 1\right)}$$

$$\sigma_x = \sqrt{e^{10.25} \cdot \left(e^{2.25} - 1\right)}$$

$$\sigma_x = \sqrt{28282.542(8.488)}$$

$$\sigma_x = 489.96$$

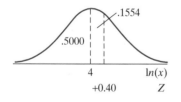

Figure 5.25 Finding the area below $Z = +0.40$

The probability that the increase in particles is less than 100 can be found by using Equation (5.17) and is illustrated in Figure 5.25.

$$Z = \frac{\ln(X) - \mu_{\ln(x)}}{\sigma_{\ln(x)}}$$

$$Z = \frac{\ln(100) - 4}{1.5}$$

$$Z = \frac{4.605 - 4}{1.5} = +0.40$$

Thus, from Table A.2, the area between the mean and a Z value of $+0.40$ is .1554, and the area below $Z = +0.40$ is $0.1554 + 0.5000 = 0.6554$. We may conclude then, that there is a 65.54% chance that the increase in the number of particles on a silicon wafer will be less than 100.

In order to illustrate the right-skew characteristic of the original variable, the number of particles, suppose we determine the probability that the increase in the number of particles is less than the mean number of particles (which is 168.17). From Equation (5.17), we have

$$Z = \frac{\ln(168.17) - 4}{1.5}$$

$$Z = \frac{5.125 - 4}{1.5} = +0.75$$

From Table A.2, the area between the mean and a Z value of $+0.75$ is 0.2734, and the area below $Z = +0.75$ is $0.2734 + 0.5000 = 0.7734$. We conclude that there is a 77.34% chance that the increase in the number of particles on a silicon wafer will be less than 168.17. Note that the probability of obtaining a value below the mean number of particles is 0.7734, not the 0.50 value which would occur if the distribution of the increase in particles were normally distributed instead of being lognormally distributed.

Now that we have used equation (5.17) to obtain lognormal probabilities, we will illustrate how Microsoft Excel and MINITAB can be used instead (see Appendices 5.1 and 5.2). Figure 5.26 illustrates output obtained from Microsoft Excel; Figure 5.27 illustrates MINITAB output.

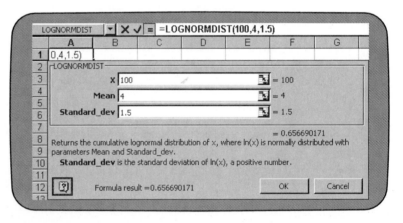

Figure 5.26   Obtaining lognormal probabilities from Microsoft Excel

Cumulative Distribution Function

Lognormal with location = 4.00000 and scale = 1.50000

x	P(X <= x)
100.0000	0.6567

Figure 5.27   Obtaining lognormal probabilities from MINITAB

PROBLEMS

5.28 Suppose that the variable X is lognormally distributed with $\mu_{\ln(x)} = 5$ and $\sigma_{\ln(x)} = 2$.
  (a) Find $\mu(x)$.
  (b) Find $\sigma(x)$.
  (c) What is the probability that X is
      (1) below 50?
      (2) above 30?
      (3) between 30 and 70?

5.29 The distribution of the grain size of dolomite along a minor thrust fault is lognormally distributed, with the natural logarithm of the grain size having a mean of 3.1 microns and a standard deviation of 1.2 microns.
  (a) What is the average grain size?
  (b) What is the standard deviation of the grain size?
  (c) What is the probability of finding a grain size
      (1) below 5 microns?
      (2) above 10 microns?
      (3) between 5 and 15 microns?

5.30 Suppose that the annual rainfall in a particular county is lognormally distributed, with the natural logarithm of the amount of rainfall having a mean of 1.5 meters per year and a standard deviation of 0.1 meters per year.

(a) What is the average amount of rainfall per year?
(b) What is the standard deviation of the amount of rainfall per year?
(c) What is the probability that, in the next year, the rainfall will be
      (1) below 1 meter?
      (2) above 2 meters?
      (3) between 1 and 2 meters?

5.31 Suppose that the time to install an internal fax/modem in a laptop computer follows a lognormal distribution, with the natural logarithm of the installation time having a mean of 2.5 minutes and a standard deviation of 0.5 minutes.
  (a) Find the average installation time.
  (b) Find the standard deviation of the installation time.
  (c) What is the probability that an installation will be completed in
      (1) less than 15 minutes?
      (2) more than 20 minutes?
      (3) between 15 and 30 minutes?

5.7 THE EXPONENTIAL DISTRIBUTION

The **exponential distribution** is widely used in *waiting time* (or *queuing*) theory to model the length of time between arrivals at a service facility such as a bridge toll plaza, a banking ATM machine, or a hospital emergency room. This distribution is defined by a single parameter, λ, the average number of arrivals per unit of time.

The probability density function for the length of time between arrivals is given by

$$f(X) = \lambda e^{-\lambda x} \text{ for } X > 0 \qquad (5.18)$$

The average time between arrivals μ is given by

$$\mu = \frac{1}{\lambda} \qquad (5.19)$$

and the standard deviation of the time between arrivals σ is given by

$$\sigma = \frac{1}{\lambda} \qquad (5.20)$$

The cumulative distribution for the probability that the length of time before the next arrival is less than X is given by:

$$P(\text{arrival time} \le X) = 1 - e^{-\lambda x} \qquad (5.21)$$

where e is the mathematical constant approximated by 2.71828.

To illustrate an application of the exponential distribution, suppose that customers arrive at an automatic teller machine of a bank at the rate of 20 per hour. What is the probability that the next customer arrives within 6 minutes (0.1 hour)?

For this example, $\lambda = 20$, because the arrival rate is 20 per hour, and $X = 0.1$ hour. From Equation (5.21), we have

$$P(\text{arrival time} \le 0.1) = 1 - e^{-20(.1)}$$
$$P(\text{arrival time} \le 0.1) = 1 - e^{-2}$$
$$= 1 - (2.71828)^{-2}$$
$$P(\text{arrival time} \le 0.1) = 1 - 0.1353$$
$$= 0.8647$$

Thus, the probability that a customer will arrive within six minutes is 0.8647 or 86.47%. Using Equations (5.19) and (5.20), we find that the average and standard deviation of the time between arrivals μ and σ are

$$\mu = \sigma = \frac{1}{20} = 0.05 \text{ hour or 3 minutes}$$

Note that in this example we have provided the value for λ, the average number of arrivals per unit of time. If μ, the average time between arrivals, was specified, then in Equation (5.21) μ would have to be converted to λ. Thus, if μ were equal to one arrival every 3 minutes (or 0.05 hour), then λ would be equal to 20 arrivals per hour.

Now that we have used equation (5.21) to obtain exponential probabilities, we will illustrate how Microsoft Excel and MINITAB can be used instead. (See Appendices 5.1 and 5.2.) Figure 5.28 illustrates output obtained from the PHStat add-in for Microsoft Excel; Figure 5.29 illustrates MINITAB output.

	A	B	C	D	E
1	Exponential Probability for Customer Arrivals				
2					
3	Mean	20			
4	X Value	0.1			
5	P(<=X)	0.864665			

Figure 5.28   Obtaining exponential probabilities from the PHStat add-in for Microsoft Excel

```
Cumulative Distribution Function

Exponential with mean = 0.0500000

        x        P( X <= x)
     0.1000         0.8647
```

Figure 5.29   Obtaining exponential probabilities from MINITAB: Note: The mean assigned using MINITAB is $1/\lambda$.

PROBLEMS

5.32 Suppose that X is exponentially distributed with $\lambda = 5$.
    (a) Find $\mu(x)$.
    (b) Find $\sigma(x)$.
    (c) What is the probability that:
        (1) $X < 1$?   (2) $X > 3$?   (3) $3 < X < 5$?

5.33 Suppose that autos arrive at a group of toll booths located at the entrance to a bridge at the rate of 50 per minute during the 5–6 p.m. hour. If an auto has just arrived,
    (a) What is the probability that the next auto arrives within 3 seconds (0.05 minute)?
    (b) What is the probability that the next auto arrives within 1 second (0.0167 minute)?
    (c) What is the average time between arrivals?
    (d) What is the standard deviation of the time between arrivals?
    (e) What would be your answers to (a)–(d) if the rate of arrival of autos were 60 per minute?
    (f) What would be your answers to (a)–(d) if the rate of arrival of autos were 30 per minute?

5.34 Telephone calls arrive at the help desk of a large computer software company at the rate of 15 per hour.
    (a) What is the probability that the next call arrives within 3 minutes (0.05 hours)?

    (b) What is the probability that the next call arrives within 15 minutes (0.25 hours)?
    (c) What is the average time between arrivals?
    (d) What is the standard deviation of the time between arrivals?

5.35 Suppose golfers arrive at the starter's booth of a public golf course at the rate of 8 per hour during the Monday–Friday midweek period. If a golfer has just arrived, what is the probability that the next golfer arrives within
    (a) 15 minutes (0.25 hour)?
    (b) 3 minutes (0.05 hour)?
    (c) Suppose that the actual arrival rate on Fridays is 15 per hour. What would be your answers to (a) and (b) on Fridays?

5.36 Suppose that the time between injury accidents in an automobile factory has an exponential distribution with a mean of 10 days.
    (a) What is the probability that the time between two consecutive injuries is less than 5 days?
    (b) What is the probability that the time between two consecutive injuries is less than 10 days?
    (c) What is the average time between injuries?
    (d) What is the standard deviation of the time between injuries?

5.8 THE WEIBULL DISTRIBUTION

Another continuous distribution that is general enough to model many phenomena, including the time until failure of industrial products, is the **Weibull distribution.** This distribution is defined by two parameters, usually denoted by α and β. The α parameter represents a shape factor. Changing its value for a given β changes the shape of the distribution. The β parameter is a scale factor that represents the size of the units in which X is measured. The exponential distribution is a special case of the Weibull distribution for which α equals 1 and $\beta = 1/\lambda$.

The probability distribution for a variable X that is Weibull distributed is

$$f(X) = \frac{\alpha}{\beta^\alpha} X^{\alpha-1} e^{-(x/\beta)^\alpha} \quad x \geq 0 \tag{5.22}$$

The cumulative distribution function of X can be expressed as follows:

$$P(X \leq x) = 1 - e^{-(x/\beta)^\alpha} \quad X \geq 0 \tag{5.23}$$

To illustrate the application of the Weibull distribution, suppose that, at various stages in the preparation of silicon wafers used as material for computer chips, the wafers need to be smoothed. The time necessary to smooth a silicon wafer to within 100 microns of specifications has a Weibull distribution with $\alpha = 2$ seconds and $\beta = 50$ seconds. What is the probability that the time required to smooth a wafer is less than 10 seconds? From Equation (5.23), with $\alpha = 2$ and $\beta = 50$, we have

$$P(X \leq 10) = 1 - e^{-(10/50)^2}$$
$$P(X \leq 10) = 1 - e^{-(.2)^2}$$
$$P(X \leq 10) = 1 - 0.9608 = 0.0392$$

Thus, the probability that the time required to smooth a wafer will be less than 10 seconds is 0.0392.

Now that we have used equation (5.23) to obtain exponential probabilities, we will illustrate how Microsoft Excel and MINITAB can be used instead. (See Appendices 5.1 and 5.2.) Figure 5.30 illustrates output obtained from Microsoft Excel; Figure 5.31 illustrates MINITAB output.

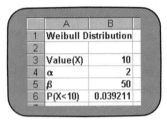

	A	B
1	Weibull Distribution	
2		
3	Value(X)	10
4	α	2
5	ß	50
6	P(X<10)	0.039211

Figure 5.30   Obtaining Weibull probabilities from Microsoft Excel

Cumulative Distribution Function

Weibull with first shape parameter = 2.00000 and second = 50.0000

          x   P(X <= x)
  10.0000   0.0392

Figure 5.31   Obtaining Weibull probabilities from MINITAB

DERIVATION 5.2 (OPTIONAL)   Obtaining the Exponential Distribution as a Special Case of the Weibull Distribution

When $\alpha = 1$, the Weibull distribution reduces to

$$f(X) = \frac{1}{\beta} e^{-(x/\beta)} X \geq 0$$

Because β is the mean of the exponential distribution and is equal to $1/\lambda$, we obtain Equation (5.18) on page 209:

$$f(X) = \lambda e^{-\lambda x} \text{ for } X > 0$$

PROBLEMS

5.37 Suppose that X follows a Weibull distribution with $\alpha = 2.5$ and $\beta = 10$. Find the probability that
  (a) $X < 5$
  (b) $X < 10$
  (c) $X < 20$

5.38 The distribution of the forecasted flood crest of a local flood-warning system follows a Weibull distribution with $\alpha = 2$ feet and $\beta = 6$ feet. Find the probability that the flood crest will be forecast as
  (a) less than 5 feet.
  (b) less than 10 feet.
  (c) less than 15 feet.

5.39 An important characteristic in reliability is the time between failures of a process. Suppose that the process in question, the robotic welding of bicycles, has a Weibull distribution for the time between failures (in hours), with $\alpha = 3$ and $\beta = 10$. Find the probability that the time between failures will be
  (a) less than 5 hours;
  (b) at least two hours;
  (c) between 6 and 15 hours.
  (d) What would be your answers to (a)–(c) if $\alpha = 5$?

5.40 The design of ocean-based structures, such as oil platforms and remote sensing devices, is affected by various weather conditions. Suppose that, in one offshore location being considered for an oil platform, the wind velocity (in mph) has a Weibull distribution with $\alpha = 4$ and $\beta = 40$, while the wave height (in feet) has a Weibull distribution with $\alpha = 4$ and $\beta = 8$. Find the probability that the
  (a) wind velocity will be less than 20 mph.
  (b) wind velocity will be more than 50 mph.
  (c) wave height will be between 5 and 10 feet.
  (d) wave height will be greater than 8 feet.
  (e) Suppose that we want to find the probability that the wind velocity will be more than 50 mph at the same time that the wave height is greater than 8 feet. Can we just multiply the probabilities that we calculated in (b) and (d)? Why, or why not?

5.41 Suppose that the life of a roller bearing (in thousands of hours) follows a Weibull distribution with $\alpha = 1.5$ and $\beta = 10$. Find the probability that the life of the roller bearing will be
  (a) less than 10,000 hours;
  (b) at least 5,000 hours;
  (c) between 5,000 and 10,000 hours.
  (d) What would be your answers in (a)–(c) if $\alpha = 1.0$?

5.9 SAMPLING DISTRIBUTION OF THE MEAN

In Section 1.1, we defined inferential statistics as methods which permit one to make inferences and estimates about population parameters that are based on statistics calculated from sample data. The major goal of most studies is to use sample information to draw conclusions about a population, *not* about the obtained sample. As one example, a computer engineer, in selecting a sample of silicon wafers, is interested only in using the sample mean for estimating the population average thickness. Likewise, a fisheries biologist is interested in the sample results only as a way of estimating the length or the proportion of males in the population of fish located in a specific body of water. Thus, in such situations, summary statistics such as the sample mean or the sample proportion are used for drawing conclusions about the corresponding population parameters.

In practice, a single sample of predetermined size is randomly selected (see Section 1.6) from a fixed population. Hypothetically, in order to be able to use the sample statistic to estimate the exact value of the population parameter, we should examine every possible sample of a given size n that *could* occur. (This is *hypothetical;* it would *never* be practical, and is usually impossible, to actually draw all possible samples of a given size.) If this selection of all possible samples of the same size actually were to be drawn, and if a particular statistic of interest, such as the mean or proportion, were to be computed for each sample, the distribution of these sample statistics would be referred to as a **sampling distribution** of the statistic. The sample mean and the sample proportion are two statistics that are of major importance in most studies, and we will be concerned with their respective sampling distributions in this section.

Sampling Distribution of the Mean

In Section 5.3, we studied the properties of populations that were normally distributed. Such population distributions are symmetric and bell-shaped in form and are characterized by their two parameters, the mean, μ_x, and the standard deviation, σ_x. Given such a population of size N and a continuous variable X that is normally distributed with mean μ_x and standard deviation σ_x, the **sampling distribution of the mean** formed by taking all possible samples of *a given size n* will also be normally distributed and will have a mean

$$\mu_{\bar{x}} = \mu_x$$

and a standard deviation

$$\sigma_{\bar{x}} = \sigma_x/\sqrt{n}$$

This standard deviation of the sampling distribution of the mean is also referred to as the **standard error of the mean.**

However, there are many situations in which we will know that a particular population is not normally distributed or for which we believe it would be unrealistic to assume a normal distribution. In many of these instances, the **central limit theorem** will enable us to develop the sampling distribution of the mean.

> **Central Limit Theorem.** Regardless of the shape of the underlying population of the continuous variable X having mean μ_x and standard deviation σ_x, the sampling distribution of the mean formed by taking all possible samples of a given size n will more and more closely approximate a normal distribution with mean $\mu_{\bar{x}} = \mu_x$ and standard error of the mean $\sigma_{\bar{x}} = \sigma_x/\sqrt{n}$ as the sample size n increases.

The effect of the central limit theorem is illustrated in Figure 5.32, which shows the sampling distribution of the mean for samples drawn from three parent populations that differ in shape. As can be seen from Panel (a), if a population is normally distributed, the sampling distribution of the mean will always be normally distributed regardless of the sample size. In Panel (b), the parent population is uniformly distributed or rectangular in shape. Although it is symmetrical, it does not have the characteristic bell-shape of the normal distribution. We observe, however, that even for samples as small as $n = 2$, the sampling distribution of the mean is triangular in shape and closer to a bell-shape than the original population. When $n = 5$, the sampling distribution of the mean is more nearly bell-shaped; by the case with $n = 30$, it is approximately normally distributed. In Panel (c), the population represents a positive or right-skewed distribution. The sampling distribution of the mean for samples with $n = 2$ and for samples with $n = 5$ still appear to be somewhat skewed to the right, but not as skewed as the parent population. When $n = 30$, the sampling distribution of the mean is approximately normally distributed. Therefore, our conclusions can be presented as in Exhibit 5.3 on page 216.

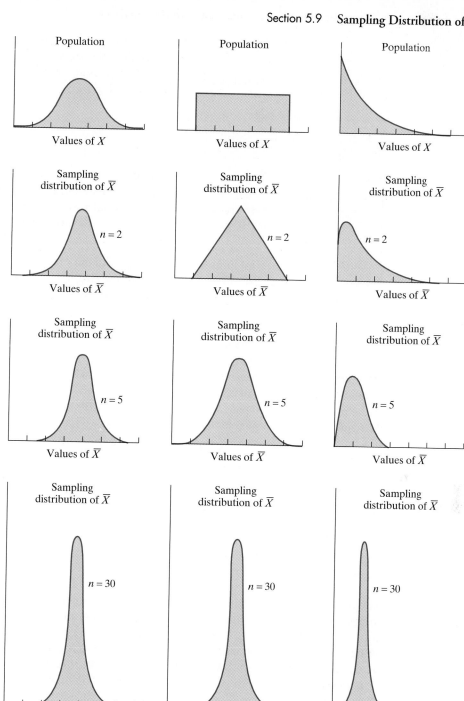

Figure 5.32   Sampling distribution of the mean for different populations for samples of n = 2, 5, and 30

EXHIBIT 5.3 Normality and the Sampling Distribution of the Mean

1. For most population distributions, regardless of shape, the sampling distribution of the mean is approximately normally distributed if samples of at least 30 observations are selected.

2. If the population distribution is fairly symmetrical, the sampling distribution of the mean is approximately normal if samples of at least 15 observations are selected.

3. If the population distribution is normally distributed, the sampling distribution of the mean is normally distributed regardless of the sample size.

To summarize, the central limit theorem is of crucial importance in many statistical applications. If we are given a large enough sample size, it enables us to make inferences about the population mean in cases where we do not know the specific shape of the population distribution and even in cases where we know that the population is *not* normally distributed.

Now that we have discussed the standard error of the mean and the central limit theorem, we return to the *Using Statistics* example on page 180 concerning the diameter of ball bearings. Recall that the diameter of the ball bearings was normally distributed with a mean μ_x of 0.503 inch and a standard deviation σ_x of 0.004 inch. When using Equation (5.9) on page 186, recall that the probability of obtaining a *particular ball bearing* having a diameter between 0.503 and 0.507 inch is computed as follows:

$$Z = \frac{X - \mu_x}{\sigma_x} = \frac{0.507 - 0.503}{0.004} = 1.00$$

and, from Table A.2, the area under the standard normal distribution from the mean ($Z = 0.0$) to a standard Z value of -1.00 is 0.3413. Thus, the probability or chance that a *particular ball bearing* will have a diameter between 0.503 and 0.507 inch is 0.3413 (see Figure 5.6 on page 188). That is, 34.13 percent of the ball bearings from this population of ball bearings can be expected to have a diameter between 0.503 and 0.507 inch.

Now, however, the question concerns the probability of selecting a *particular sample* of four ball bearings whose average diameter (i.e., the sample mean) is between 0.503 and 0.507 inch. By analogy to Equation (5.9) which compared how a *specific individual value*, X, differed from its mean μ_x in terms of standardized Z units, we now study how the mean of a *particular sample* $\overline{X}$ differs from $\mu_{\bar{x}}$, the mean of all possible sample means in the sampling distribution, in terms of standard Z units. Substituting $\overline{X}$ for X, $\mu_{\bar{x}}$ for μ_x, and $\sigma_{\bar{x}}$ for σ_x in our equation for Z, we have

$$Z = \frac{\overline{X} - \mu_{\bar{x}}}{\sigma_{\bar{x}}} \tag{5.24a}$$

or

$$Z = \frac{\overline{X} - \mu_{\bar{x}}}{\dfrac{\sigma_x}{\sqrt{n}}} \tag{5.24b}$$

For $n = 4$, using Equation (5.24b), we have

$$Z = \frac{0.507 - 0.503}{\dfrac{0.004}{\sqrt{4}}} = +2.00$$

From Table A.2, we find the area under the normal curve from the mean to $Z = 2.00$ to be 0.4772. Therefore, the probability that a particular sample of 4 ball bearings will have a mean diameter between 0.503 and 0.507 inch is 0.4772. Thus, we note that 47.72 percent of all possible samples of four ball bearings from this population are expected to have an average between 0.503 and 0.507 inch.

Comparing the two results, we observe that a much greater percentage of sample means than of individual ball bearings will be close to 0.503, the true population or process mean. This is because the sampling distribution of the mean is less variable than the distribution of individual values. Sample means will cluster closer to the population mean $\mu_{\bar{x}}$ of all possible sample means in the sampling distribution than the individual values cluster around μ_x. Similarly, there is a much greater likelihood of randomly selecting a particular ball bearing X with a diameter far below the true mean than there is of randomly selecting a particular sample of 4 ball bearings whose average diameter $\overline{X}$ is that far below the true mean.

Instead of determining the proportion of sample means that is expected to fall within a certain interval, we might be more interested in finding the interval within which a fixed proportion of sample means would fall. To illustrate this, suppose we wanted to find an interval around the population mean that would include the middle 95 percent of the sample means based on samples of $n = 25$ ball bearings. The 95 percent is divided into two equal parts, half (or 47.5 percent) below the mean and half (or 47.5 percent) above the mean. (See Figure 5.13 on page 193.)

Analogously to the procedures used in Section 5.3, we are determining a distance below and above the population mean containing a specific area of the normal curve. From Equation (5.24b), we have

$$Z_L = \frac{\overline{X}_L - \mu_{\bar{x}}}{\dfrac{\sigma_x}{\sqrt{n}}}$$

where Z_L = the lower value, or $-Z$, and

$$Z_U = \frac{\overline{X}_U - \mu_{\bar{x}}}{\dfrac{\sigma_x}{\sqrt{n}}}$$

where Z_U = the upper value or, $+Z$. Therefore, $\overline{X}_L$, the lower value of $\overline{X}$, is

$$\overline{X}_L = \mu_x - Z\frac{\sigma_x}{\sqrt{n}} \tag{5.25a}$$

and $\overline{X}_U$, the upper value of $\overline{X}$, is

$$\overline{X}_U = \mu_x + Z\frac{\sigma_x}{\sqrt{n}} \tag{5.25b}$$

Since $\sigma_x = 0.004$ inch, $n = 25$ ball bearings, and the value of Z corresponding to an area of 0.475 from the center of the normal curve is 1.96, the lower and upper values of $\overline{X}$ can be found as follows:

$$\overline{X}_L = 0.503 - (1.96)\frac{0.004}{\sqrt{25}} = 0.503 - 0.001568 = 0.501432$$

$$\overline{X}_U = 0.503 + (1.96)\frac{0.004}{\sqrt{25}} = 0.503 + 0.001568 = 0.504568$$

Our conclusion is that 95 percent of all sample means based on samples of 25 ball bearings should fall between 0.501432 and 0.504568 inch.

PROBLEMS

5.42 Suppose that X is normally distributed with $\mu_x = 10$ and $\sigma_x = 2$. If $n = 16$,
(a) what is the probability that the sample mean will be above 9.5?
(b) what is the probability that the sample mean will be between 9 and 10.5?
(c) there is a 80 percent chance that the sample mean will be above what value?

5.43 Suppose that a machine filling mini-boxes of raisins fills the boxes so that the weight of the boxes has a population mean $\mu_x = 14.1$ grams and a population standard deviation $\sigma_x = 1.4$ grams. If a random sample of 49 boxes is selected,
(a) what is the probability that the sample mean will be above 14 grams?
(b) there is a 99 percent chance that the sample mean will be above what value?
(c) What assumptions are necessary in order to answer (a) and (b)?
(d) If a random sample of 64 boxes is selected, what would be your answers for (a) and (b)?

5.44 Repair time for an oil change at a car dealership has a population mean $\mu_x = 40$ minutes and a population standard deviation $\sigma_x = 5$ minutes. If a random sample of 100 oil changes is selected,
(a) what is the probability that the sample mean is above 38.5 minutes?
(b) there is a 95 percent chance that the sample mean is above which value?

(c) What assumptions are necessary in order to answer (a) and (b)?
(d) If a random sample of 50 oil changes is selected, what would be your answers for (a) and (b)?

5.45 A machine used to extract juice from oranges obtains an amount from each orange that is approximately normally distributed, with a mean of 4.70 ounces and a standard deviation of 0.40 ounces. Suppose that a sample of 25 oranges is selected.
(a) What is the probability that the sample mean will be at least 4.60 ounces?
(b) There is a 70 percent chance that the sample average will fall between what two values symmetrically distributed around the population mean?
(c) There is a 77 percent chance that the sample average will be above which value?
(d) Compare the results of (b) against those of Problem 5.9(b) on page 195. Explain any differences.

5.46 A process used in filling bottles with soft drink results in net weights that are normally distributed, with a mean of 2 liters and a standard deviation of .05 liter. Suppose that a sample of 100 bottles is selected.
(a) What is the probability that the average is at least 1.99 liters?
(b) There is a 99 percent probability that the sample average will be above which value?
(c) Compare the results of (b) against those of Problem 5.10(b) on page 195. Explain any differences.

5.10 SAMPLING DISTRIBUTION OF THE PROPORTION

In the case of a categorical variable where each individual or item in the population can be classified as either possessing or not possessing a particular characteristic or attribute, such as a switch that is opened or closed, an individual who is healthy or ill, or an item that conforms or does not conform to design specifications, the two possible outcomes can be called a success (given a value of 1) and a failure (given a value of 0) to represent respectively the presence or absence of the attribute. In such situations, the sample mean $\overline{X}$ of these zeros and ones is the sample proportion p possessing the attribute. The sample mean $\overline{X}$ is an estimator of the underlying population mean μ_x for continuously scaled variables; analogously, the sample statistic p is an estimator of the true population proportion π for categorical or attribute data.

By analogy to the previous section, the **sampling distribution of the proportion** formed by computing the statistic p from all possible samples of size n from a population of size N with replacement will tend to be approximately normally distributed, with the mean being π, the true population proportion, and with the **standard error of the proportion** being

$$\sigma_p = \sqrt{\frac{\pi(1-\pi)}{n}}$$

[3] In Section 5.4, we stated that the normal distribution could be used to approximate the binomial distribution when the variance, $n\pi(1-\pi)$ was at least 10.

provided that the constant sample size n used for drawing all possible samples is "large enough[3]." Therefore, when we view things in this manner, we use the normal distribution to evaluate the sampling distribution of the proportion. Thus, we transform Equation (5.24) on page 216 to a form suitable for sample proportions, as follows:

using

$$Z = \frac{\overline{X} - \mu_{\bar{x}}}{\sigma_{\bar{x}}}$$

with $\overline{X} = p$, $\mu_x = \pi$ and $\sigma_p = \sqrt{\frac{\pi(1-\pi)}{n}}$, we have

$$Z = \frac{p - \pi}{\sqrt{\dfrac{\pi(1-\pi)}{n}}} \qquad (5.26)$$

In order to demonstrate this, suppose that one in every ten compact-disk players manufactured fails to pass an initial inspection test. If a sample of 400 is selected, what is the probability that the sample proportion p of disk players that fail that test is between 0.10 and 0.12?

From Equation (5.26),

$$Z = \frac{p - \pi}{\sqrt{\dfrac{\pi(1-\pi)}{n}}}$$

we have

$$Z = \frac{0.12 - 0.10}{\sqrt{\dfrac{(0.10)(0.90)}{400}}} = \frac{0.02}{\sqrt{\dfrac{0.09}{400}}}$$

$$Z = \frac{0.02}{0.015} = 1.33$$

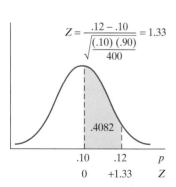

$$Z = \frac{.12 - .10}{\sqrt{\dfrac{(.10)(.90)}{400}}} = 1.33$$

.4082

| .10 | .12 | p |
| 0 | +1.33 | Z |

Figure 5.33 Finding the area between 0.10 and 0.12

From Table A.2, the area under the normal curve from $Z = 0$ to $Z = 1.33$ is 0.4082. Therefore, the probability of obtaining a sample with a proportion between 0.10 and 0.12 is 0.4082. This means that if the true proportion of compact disk players that fail the first inspection test is 0.10, then 40.82 percent of all samples of size 400 would be expected to have sample proportions between 0.10 and 0.12. (See Figure 5.33.)

PROBLEMS

5.47 Suppose that $\pi = 0.20$ and $n = 100$. What is the probability that p will be
   (a) between 0.20 and 0.25?
   (b) between 0.25 and 0.30?
   (c) below 0.25?
   (d) What would be your answer to (a)–(c) if $n = 25$?

5.48 Suppose that past records indicate that the probability that a new car will need a warranty repair in the first 90 days of use is 0.04. If a random sample of 400 new cars is selected, what is the probability that the proportion of new cars needing a warranty repair in the first 90 days will be
   (a) between 0.04 and 0.06?
   (b) above 0.05?
   (c) If a sample size of 300 is selected, what would be your answers in (a) and (b)?

5.49 A political pollster is conducting an analysis of sample results in order to make predictions on election night for a two-candidate election. If a specific candidate receives at least 56 percent of the votes in the sample, then the candidate should be forecast as the winner of the election. If a random sample of 100 voters is selected, what is the probability that a candidate will be forecast to be the winner when
   (a) the true percentage of the candidate's vote is 50.5 percent?
   (b) the true percentage of the candidate's vote is 60 percent?
   (c) the true percentage of the candidate's vote is 49 percent?

(d) If the sample size had been increased to 400, what would be your answers to (a), (b), and (c)? Discuss.

5.50 An important part of the customer-service responsibilities of a telephone company relate to the speed with which troubles in residential service can be repaired. Suppose that past data indicate that the likelihood is 0.70 that troubles in residential service can be repaired on the same day. If a sample of 100 troubles is selected, what is the probability that the proportion repaired on the same day is
   (a) between 0.70 and 0.75?
   (b) at least 0.70?
   (c) between 0.60 and 0.80?
   (d) What would be your answers to (a)–(c) if $n = 50$?

5.51 A manufacturer of disk drives subjects the equipment to a comprehensive testing process for all mechanical and electrical functions before the equipment leaves the factory. Ideally, the hope is that each disk drive passes on the first test. Suppose that past data indicate that the probability that a disk drive passes on the first test is 0.95. If 1000 players are randomly selected, what is the probability that the proportion that pass on the first test is
   (a) between 0.95 and 0.96?
   (b) between 0.94 and 0.97?
   (c) at least 0.93?
   (d) What would be your answers to (a)–(c) if $n = 500$?

 ## 5.12 SUMMARY

In this chapter, we developed several continuous distributions that are extensively used in engineering and the sciences. The normal distribution serves as the foundation of the control charts that we shall discuss in Chapters 6 and 7; the concept of the sampling distribution is central to the development of statistical inference that will be the subject of Chapters 8–11.

KEY TERMS

CHAPTER REVIEW *Checking Your Understanding*

To check your understanding of the key concepts discussed in this chapter, you should be able to answer each of the following questions:

5.52 What shape will the uniform distribution have regardless of its range?

5.53 Why is it that only one table of the normal distribution is needed to find any probability under the normal curve?

5.54 How would you find the area between two values under the normal curve when both values are on the same side of the mean?

5.55 How would you find the X value that corresponds to a given percentile of the normal distribution?

5.56 Under what circumstances can the normal distribution be used to approximate the binomial and Poisson distributions?

5.57 Why do the individual observations have to be converted to standard normal ordered values in order to develop a normal probability plot?

5.58 How does the lognormal distribution differ from the normal distribution?

5.59 In the exponential distribution, what is the relationship between the average time between arrivals and the average number of arrivals per unit of time?

5.60 In the Weibull distribution, what factors affect the cumulative distribution function of X?

5.61 Why does the standard error of the mean decrease as the sample size increases?

5.62 Why does the sampling distribution of the mean follow a normal distribution for a large enough sample even though the population may not be normally distributed?

Problems

5.63 Suppose the time to transmit an e-mail message is normally distributed with a mean of 0.72 seconds and a standard deviation of 0.10 seconds.
  (a) What is the probability that an e-mail message will require
    (1) more than one second to transmit?
    (2) between 0.70 and 0.80 second to transmit?
  (b) What is the 70th percentile of the transmission time?
  (c) 90% of the messages will take at least how many seconds to be transmitted?
  Suppose that a sample of 16 e-mail messages is selected.
  (d) What is the probability that the average time for an e-mail message to be transmitted is
    (1) more than 0.70 second?
    (2) between 0.70 and 0.80 second?
  (e) 90% of the average transmission times will be between what two values?
  (f) Explain the difference between the results of (a)(2) and those of (d)(2).

5.64 Suppose that the volume of sound generated by heavy machinery in a factory is normally distributed, with a mean of 50 dB and a standard deviation of 10 dB.
  (a) What is the probability that the volume of sound measurement at a particular time is
    (1) between 45 and 55 dB?
    (2) between 40 and 60 dB?
    (3) above 80 dB?

(b) 20% of the sound volumes will be below what value?

(c) There is a 99% chance that the sound volume will be below what value?

If measurements are taken twice an hour during an eight hour period,

(d) what is the probability that the average volume of sound measurement for that day is
  (1) between 45 and 55 dB?
  (2) above 55 dB?

(e) There is a 98% chance that the average volume of sound measurement for that day will be below what value?

(f) Explain the difference between the results of (a)(1) and those of (d)(1).

5.65 Marine biologists scuba dive to collect marine samples near a seaside construction site. The time that they are able to stay underwater has a normal distribution with a mean of 70 minutes and a standard deviation of 5 minutes.

(a) What is the probability that a randomly selected scuba diver can stay underwater
  (1) between 60 and 80 minutes?
  (2) more than 85 minutes?
  (3) at least 60 minutes?

(b) 0.1% of the scuba divers will be unable to stay underwater more than how many minutes?

(c) 95% of the scuba divers will be able to stay under water more than how many minutes?

Suppose that a sample of four scuba divers is selected.

(d) What is the probability that the average amount of time the scuba divers can stay under water is
  (1) greater than 65 minutes?
  (2) between 65 and 75 minutes?

(e) There is a 90% chance that the average amount of time will be between what two values?

5.66 The production department of a newspaper has embarked upon a quality-improvement effort. After several brainstorming sessions, the team has chosen as its first project an issue that relates to the blackness of the newspaper print. Each day a determination needs to be made concerning how "black" the newspaper is printed. This is measured with a densitometer that records the results on a standard scale. The target value for blackness on the scale is 1.0. Data collected over the past year indicate that the blackness is approximately normally distributed with an average of 1.005 and a standard deviation of 0.10.

Each day, one spot on the first newspaper printed is chosen and the blackness of the spot is measured. Suppose that the blackness of the newspaper is considered acceptable if the blackness of the spot is between 0.95 and 1.05. Assuming that the distribution has not changed from what it was in the past year, what is the probability that the blackness of the spot is

(a) less than 1.0?

(b) between 0.95 and 1.0?

(c) between 1.0 and 1.05?

(d) less than 0.95 or greater than 1.05?

(e) If the objective of the production team is to reduce the probability that the blackness is below 0.95 or above 1.05, would it be better off focusing on process improvement that lowered the blackness to the target value of 1.0 or on process improvement that reduced the standard deviation to 0.075? Explain.

Suppose that, on each day, 20 spots on the first newspaper printed are chosen and the blackness of each spot is measured. Suppose that the blackness of the newspaper is considered acceptable if the average blackness of these 20 spots is between 0.95 and 1.05. Assuming that the distribution of blackness has not changed from what it has been in the past year, what is the probability that the average blackness of the twenty spots is

    (f) less than 1.0?

    (g) between 0.95 and 1.0?

    (h) between 1.0 and 1.05?

    (i) Unacceptable, that is, less than 0.95 or greater than 1.05?

5.67 An article published in 1993 by McCarron and Jones, "Achieving full capability from situ particle monitoring" in the *Proceedings of the Institute of Environmental Sciences* (pp. 99–106), discussed the results of experiments run to determine the optimal location of an in-situ particle monitor in a high-current ion implanter. Part of the experimentation included a particle count of a typical production run, which was found to have approximately a lognormal distribution. Suppose that the natural logarithm of the particle count has a mean of 4.5 and a standard deviation of 1.3.

    (a) What is the expected value of the particle count?

    (b) What is the standard deviation of the particle count?

    (c) What is the probability that the particle count will be

        (1) below 100?

        (2) below 200?

        (3) between 100 and 200?

    (d) What would be your answers to (a)–(c) if the natural logarithm of the particle count has a mean of 5?

    (e) What would be your answers to (a)–(c) if the natural logarithm of the particle count has a standard deviation of 1.5?

5.68 The time between unplanned shutdowns of a power plant has an exponential distribution with a mean of 20 days. Find the probability that the time between two unplanned shutdowns is

    (a) less than 14 days;

    (b) more than 21 days;

    (c) less than 7 days.

    (d) Suppose that the time between unplanned shutdowns of a power plant has a Weibull distribution with $\alpha = 1.5$ and $\beta = 20$. Recalculate the results of (a)–(c) using this distribution, and compare the results.

5.69 The acidification of lakes in parts of the United States is a problem of great concern. A survey of characteristics of lakes in the midwestern and eastern United States was carried out to study acidification. One of the variables measured was acid-neutralizing capacity (ANC). This variable describes the capability of a lake to neutralize acid; low values can lead to a loss of biological resources. The data file LAKES contains the acid neutralizing capacity of two types of lakes, seepage lakes and drainage lakes.

LAKES

    (a) Construct a normal probability plot of the acid-neutralizing capacities of all the lakes.

    (b) Based on the results of (a), do the acid-neutralizing capacities of all the lakes appear to be normally distributed? Explain.

    (c) Construct a normal probability plot of the acid-neutralizing capacities of the seepage lakes.

    (d) From the results of (c), do the acid-neutralizing capacities of the seepage lakes appear to be normally distributed? Explain.

    (e) Construct a normal probability plot of the acid-neutralizing capacities of the drainage lakes.

    (f) From the results of (e), do the acid-neutralizing capacities of the drainage lakes appear to be normally distributed? Explain.

    (g) Create a new variable that consists of the natural logarithm of the acid-neutralizing capacity of each lake. Do (a)–(f) using the natural logarithm of the acid-neutralizing capacity.

    (h) What differences are there between the results of (a)–(f) and those of (g) Explain any differences.

5.70 The following data represents the parts per million (ppm) of impurities present in 80 samples of a chemical.

```
29 20 22 11 16 14 19 14 16 15 13 20 17 18 17 16 19 24 20 25 16 21  0
26 10 23 14 14 13 17 10 12 12 22 18 19  0 18 13 18 17 11 14 13  0 14
 0 16 15 19 21 15 19 15 12 17 14 15 15 11 20 23 14 12 28 16 11 10  0
12 14 15 16 13 15 18 13 17 13 21
```

IMPURITIES

Source: Schneider, H., W. J. Kasperski, T. Ledford, and W. Kraushaar, "Control charts for skewed and censored data," *Quality Engineering,* 5, 1995, 263–274

(a) Construct a normal probability plot of the parts per million of impurities of a chemical.

(b) Based on the results of (a), does the parts per million of impurities of a chemical appear to be normally distributed. Explain.

WHITNEY GOURMET CAT FOOD COMPANY CASE

Phase 1

The team involved with studying the filling process of the canned cat food decided that they needed to obtain additional insight into the process before determining actions that could be taken to improve the output in terms of the consistency of the weight of the filled cans. After several brainstorming sessions involving individuals whose jobs represented each aspect of the filling process, the team realized that different processes might be involved, depending on whether kidney or shrimp cat food was being canned. A decision is made at the beginning of the week by the production manager, in consultation with the marketing department, that reflects the forecast demand for each of the two types of cat food produced. Generally, the objective is to maximize the length of the time period during which a single type of food is canned, so as to minimize the time involved in setting up and cleaning the extruding machines in preparation for a new type of food.

The team needs to be concerned with two aspects of the weight of the canned cat food. The first consideration is that the legal limit for a canned product that is marked as 3 ounces is 2.95 ounces. Instances that result in the discovery of more than a specified number of sampled cans that are below this limit by the State Weights and Measures Department can result in substantial fines, along with adverse publicity that can erode public confidence in the company. The second consideration relates to the opposite problem: trying to make sure that the can does not contain too much food. The reasons for this are twofold. First, if more than 3.10 ounces is placed in the sealed can, there will be a strong possibility that some of the food will be spilled when the tab for the can is opened. Second, exceeding the labeled amount on the can can have financial repercussions, because providing more of the product than is indicated on the label will reduce the number of cans that can be filled from a batch of prepared product.

Exercises

WG5.1 What probabilities concerning the weight of the canned cat food do you think the team should be most concerned with? Explain.

WG5.2 What probability distribution do you think might be useful in helping to find the probabilities stated in Exercise WG5.1? Explain why you chose this distribution.

STOP

Do Not Continue Until the Phase 1 Exercises Have Been Completed.

Phase 2

As the team began to discuss the problem of estimating the probability of filling cans with a weight below 2.95 ounces or above 3.10 ounces, it needed to develop an approach that would allow the estimation of the probabilities under a reasonable set of assumptions. Rick Reed, a member of the team, suggested that the team begin by assuming that the canned weight could be approximated by a normal distribution. He further suggested that the team determine the probability of obtaining cans with a weight below 2.95 ounces or above 3.10 ounces under different scenarios, in terms of the average filled amount and the standard deviation of the filled amount.

Exercises

WG5.3 Assuming a normal distribution for the filled-can weight, find the probability of obtaining cans with a weight below 2.95 ounces or above 3.10 ounces for each of the following combinations of population mean μ and standard deviation σ:

(a) $\mu = 3.00$ and $\sigma = .05$;
(b) $\mu = 3.02$ and $\sigma = .03$;
(c) $\mu = 2.99$ and $\sigma = .02$;
(d) $\mu = 3.03$ and $\sigma = .04$;
(e) $\mu = 3.01$ and $\sigma = .025$.

WG5.4 Base your answers on the results of Exercise WG 5.3:

(a) If we wish to minimize the probability of obtaining cans with a weight below 2.95 ounces or above 3.10 ounces, which of the five combinations of μ and σ would you recommend?

(b) If we wish to minimize the probability of obtaining cans with a weight below 2.95 ounces, which of the five combinations of μ and σ would you recommend?

(c) If we wish to minimize the probability of obtaining cans with a weight above 3.10 ounces, which of the five combinations of μ and σ would you recommend?

STOP

Do Not Continue Until the Phase 2 Exercises Have Been Completed.

Phase 3

After evaluating the effects of changes in the average and the standard deviation of the weight on the probability of obtaining cans that weighed less than 2.95 ounces or more than 3.10 ounces, the team realized that it needed to answer three questions: (1) Is it reasonable to assume that the weight of the filled cans follows a normal distribution? (2) What is the average weight of the filled cans? (3) What is the standard deviation of the filled cans? In seeking answers to these questions, a consultant to the team, Nancy Livingston, suggested that data already available for the previous month (Table WG2.1 on page 94) be analyzed to obtain answers to these three questions.

Exercises

WG5.5 Consider the data of Table WG2.1 on page 94.

(a) Is the weight of the canned cat food normally distributed? Explain.

(b) If the process is not changed, what proportion of the filled cans will weigh less than 2.95 ounces? Explain.

(c) If the process is not changed, what proportion of the filled cans will weigh more than 3.10 ounces? Explain.

REFERENCES

1. Box, G. E. P., W. Hunter, and S. Hunter; *Statistics for Experimenters;* New York: John Wiley, 1978
2. Gunter, B.; "Q–Q Plots," *Quality Progress,* February 1994, pp. 81–86
3. Hogg, R. V. and Craig, A. T.; *Introduction to Mathematical Statistics,* 5th ed.; Upper Saddle River, NJ: Prentice-Hall, 1995
4. Larsen, R. L. and M. L. Marx; *Mathematical Statistics and its Applications,* 3rd ed.; Upper Saddle River, NJ: Prentice-Hall, 2000
5. *Microsoft Excel 2000;* Redmond, WA: Microsoft Corp., 1999
6. *MINITAB Reference Manual Release 12;* State College, PA.: MINITAB, Inc., 1998
7. Nelson, L. S.; " Constructing Normal Probability Paper," *Journal of Quality Technology,* 8, (1976), 56–57
8. Ramsey, P. P. and P. H. Ramsey; "Simple tests of normality in small samples," *Journal of Quality Technology,* 22, (1990), 299–309
9. Ramsey, P. P. and P. H. Ramsey, "Evaluating the normal approximation to the binomial test," *Journal of Educational Statistics,* 13, (1988), 173–182

APPENDIX 5.1 *Using Microsoft Excel for Continuous Probability Distributions and Sampling Distributions*

In this chapter, we studied such probability distributions as the normal, lognormal, exponential, and Weibull, along with the normal probability plot and sampling distributions. Microsoft Excel and/or the PHStat add-in for Microsoft Excel can be used to obtain results for each of these topics.

Using PHStat to Obtain Normal Probabilities

To answer probability questions pertaining to the normal distribution, use the **Probability Distributions | Normal** choice of the PHStat add-in. As an example, consider the following questions posed in Section 5.3 for the ball-bearing production process that has a mean of 0.503 inch and a standard deviation of 0.004 inch.

1. What is the probability that a ball bearing will have a diameter less than 0.491 inch?
2. What is the probability that a ball bearing will have a diameter greater than 0.491 inch?
3. What is the probability that a ball bearing will have a diameter between 0.49 and 0.51 inch?
4. 7% of the ball bearings will have diameters less than how many inches?

To answer these questions, if the PHStat add-in has not been previously loaded, load the add-in using the instructions of Appendix 1.2. Select **File | New** to open a new workbook (or open the existing workbook into which the probabilities worksheet is to be inserted). Select **PHStat | Probability Distributions | Normal.** In the Normal Probability Distribution dialog box, enter **.503** in the Mean: edit box. Enter **.004** in the Standard Deviation: edit box. Select the **Probability for: X <=** check box, and enter **.491** in its edit box (for question 1). Select the **Probability for: X >** check box, and enter **.51** in its edit box (for question 2). Select the **Probability for range:** check box, and enter **.49** and **.51**, respectively, in the two edit boxes for this selection (for question 3). Select the **X for Cumulative Percentage:** check box, and enter **7** in its edit box (for question 4). Enter **Normal Probabilities** in the Output Title: edit box. Click the **OK** button. The add-in inserts a worksheet that reports the probabilities (and the X and Z values) for these questions, as shown in Figure 5.14 on page 194.

Using PHStat to Obtain a Normal Probability Plot

To generate a normal probability plot from a set of data, use the **Probability Distributions | Normal Probability Plot** choice of the PHStat add-in. As an example, consider the sample of 58 male Dover sole first used in Section 2.4. To generate a normal probability plot from the length values in this example, if the PHStat add-in has not been previously loaded, load the add-in using the instructions of Appendix 1.2. Open the **FISH.XLS** workbook, and click the **Data** sheet tab. Verify that the lengths appear in column A, sorted with the females preceding the males. Select **PHStat | Probability Distributions | Normal Probability Plot.** In the Normal Probability Plot dialog box, enter **A44:A101** in the Variable Cell Range: edit box. Enter **Normal Probability Plot for length of Male Dover Sole** in the Output Title: edit box. Click the **OK** button. On separate sheets, the add-in inserts a table of ranks, cumulative proportions, Z-values, and lengths and a chart containing the normal probability plot for the net asset value data (see Figure 5.24 on page 205).

Using Microsoft Excel for the Lognormal Distribution

We can use the LOGNORMDIST function as the basis for computing lognormal probabilities in an Excel worksheet. The format of this function is:

$$\text{LOGNORMDIST}(X, \text{mean}, \text{standard deviation})$$

where

$$X = \text{the } X\text{-value of interest}$$

$$\text{Mean} = \text{the mean of the lognormal distribution}$$

$$\text{Standard deviation} = \text{the standard deviation of the lognormal distribution}$$

The function returns the cumulative probability of obtaining a value less than or equal to X. As an example, consider the example in Section 5.6 in which the number of particles follows a lognormal distribution with a mean of 4 and a standard deviation of 1.5. To obtain the probability of obtaining a value of less than or equal to 100, select **File | New** to open a new workbook, or open an existing workbook, to a new sheet. Select the **Function Wizard.** In the Function Wizard dialog box, select **Statistical** and **LOGNORMDIST.** Click the **OK** button. Enter **100** in the X edit box, **4** in the Mean edit box, and **1.5** in the Standard_Dev edit box. The dialog box will appear as in Figure 5.26 on page 208. Alternatively, enter **=LOGNOR-MDIST(100,4,1.5)** in a selected cell, and press **Enter.** The computed value of 0.65069 will be returned in that cell.

Using PHStat to Obtain Exponential Probabilities

To answer probability questions pertaining to the exponential distribution, use the **Probability Distributions | Exponential** choice of the PHStat add-in. As an example, consider the bank-customer arrival times example in Section 5.7, which has a λ value of 20 per hour. To find the probability that the next customer arrives within 6 minutes (0.1 hour), if the PHStat add-in has not been previously loaded, load the add-in using the instructions of Appendix 1.2. Select **File | New** to open a new workbook (or open the existing workbook into which the probabilities worksheet is to be inserted). Select **PHStat | Probability Distributions | Exponential.** In the Exponential Probability Distribution dialog box, enter **20** in the Mean per unit(Lambda): edit box (for the value of λ). Enter **0.1** in the X Value: edit box. Enter **Exponential Probabilities for Customer Arrivals** in the Output Title: edit box. Click the **OK** button. The add-in inserts a worksheet containing the exponential probability similar to the one shown in Figure 5.28 on page 210.

Using Microsoft Excel to Obtain Weibull Probabilities

We can use the Weibull function as the basis for computing Weibull probabilities in an Excel worksheet. The format of this function is:

$$\text{WEIBULL}(X, \alpha, \beta, \text{True})$$

where

$X = $ the X-value of interest

$\alpha = $ the α parameter

$\beta = $ the β parameter

The function returns the cumulative probability of obtaining a value less than or equal to X when the fourth argument is entered as true. To illustrate this function consider the example in Section 5.8, in which the time necessary for smoothing a silicon wafer follows a Weibull distribution with $\alpha = 2$ and $\beta = 50$. To obtain the probability of obtaining a value of less than or equal to 10, select **File | New** to open a new workbook, or open an existing workbook to a new sheet. Enter **Weibull Distribution** as a title in cell A1. Enter labels for value(X), α, β, and ="P(X<"&B3&")" in cells A3–A6 respectively. Enter **10** in cell B3, **2** in cell B4, **50** in cell B5. Enter **=WEIBULL(B3, B4, B5, True)** in cell B6. The results obtained will be similar to Figure 5.30 on page 212.

Generating Sampling Distributions using the PHStatAdd-in for Microsoft Excel

To generate simulated sampling distributions from a uniformly distributed or a standardized normally distributed population, use the **Probability Distributions | Sampling Distributions Simulation** choice of the PHStat add-in. For example, to generate a simulated sampling distribution from a uniform or standardized normal population, using 100 samples of sample size 30, select **File | New** to open a new workbook (or open the existing workbook into which the simulated distribution worksheet is to be inserted). Select **PHStat | Probability Distributions | Sampling Distributions Simulation.** In the Sampling Distributions Simulation dialog box, enter **100** in the Number of Samples: edit box. Enter **30** in the Sample Size: edit box.

Select either the Uniform or Standardized Normal option button, depending on the type of simulation desired. Enter Simulated Sampling Distribution in the Output Title: edit box. Select the **Histogram** check box. Click the **OK** button.

APPENDIX 5.2 *Using MINITAB for Continuous Probability Distributions and Sampling Distributions*

Using MINITAB to Obtain Normal Probabilities

In Section 5.3, we studied the bell-shaped normal distribution and examined numerous applications in which we computed the probability or area under the normal curve. Rather than using Equations (5.9) and (5.10) and Table A.2 to compute these probabilities, we can use MINITAB. Refer to the example in Section 5.3 in which $\mu = 0.503$ and $\sigma = 0.004$. To find the area between 0.49 and 0.51, we separately find the area below an X value of 0.51 and the one below an X value of 0.49. To do so, first enter **.49** and **.51** in the first two rows in column C1. Select **Calc | Probability Distributions | Normal.** Select the **Cumulative probability** option button. Enter **.503** in the Mean edit box and **.004** in the Standard Deviation edit box. Enter **C1** in the Input column edit box. Click the **OK** button. You will obtain the output displayed in the first panel of Figure 5.15 on page 194.

To obtain the Z value corresponding to a cumulative area of 0.07, enter **.07** in row 1 of column C2. Select **Calc | Probability Distributions | Normal.** Select **Inverse Cumulative probability.** Enter **.503** in the Mean edit box and **.004** in the Standard Deviation edit box. Enter **C2** in the input column edit box. Click the **OK** button. You will obtain the output displayed in the second panel of Figure 5.15 on page 194.

Using MINITAB to Obtain a Normal Probability Plot

In Section 5.5, we developed the normal probability plot to evaluate whether a given set of data was normally distributed. To obtain a normal probability plot in MINITAB for the male Dover sole data, open the file titled **FISH.MTW.** To separate the lengths for male from those for female Dover sole, select **Manip | Stack/Unstack | Unstack One Column.** In the Unstack One Column dialog box, enter **'Length' or C1** in the Unstack data in edit box. Enter **C7 C8** in the Store the unstacked data in edit box. Enter **'Gender' or C5** in the using Subscripts in edit box. Click the **OK** button. Enter the labels **Length-F** and **Length-M** in columns C7 and C8. Select **Graph | Probability Plot.** In the Distribution drop-down list box, select **Normal.** In the Variables: edit box, enter **'Length-M'** or C8 (the variable name for the length of male Dover sole). Click the **OK** button. Note that MINITAB provides a plot in which the variable is plotted on the X axis and the cumulative percentage is plotted on the Y-axis on a special scale, so that if the variable is normally distributed the data will plot along a straight line.

Using MINITAB for the Lognormal Distribution

Rather than using Equation (5.17) to compute probabilities from the lognormal distribution, we can use MINITAB. Consider the example in Section 5.6 in which the number of particles follows a lognormal distribution with a mean of 4 and a standard deviation of 1.5. To obtain the probability of obtaining a value of less than or equal to 100, enter **100** in row 1 of column C1. Select **Calc | Probability Distributions | Lognormal.** In the Lognormal dialog box, select the **Cumulative probability** option button. Enter **4.0** in the Location edit box, **1.5** in the Scale edit box, and **C1** in the Input column edit box. Click the **OK** button. You will obtain the output displayed in Figure 5.27 on page 208.

Using MINITAB to Obtain Exponential Probabilities

Rather than using Equation (5.21) on page 210 to model the length of time between arrivals and to compute probabilities from the exponential distribution, we can use MINITAB.

Suppose we return to the ATM customer-arrival application. In that example, we have $\lambda = 20$ and $X = 0.1$. To obtain this result using MINITAB, enter **.1** in column C1. Select **Calc | Probability Distributions | Exponential.** Select the **Cumulative probability** option button. In the Mean edit box, we enter $1/\lambda = 1/20 = 0.05$. Enter **C1** in the Input column edit box. Click the **OK** button. You will obtain the output displayed in Figure 5.29 on page 211.

Using MINITAB to Obtain Weibull Probabilities

Rather than using Equation (5.23) on page 212 to model the time necessary for smoothing a silicon wafer and compute probabilities from the Weibull distribution, we can use MINITAB. In that silicon wafer example, we have $\alpha = 2$ and $\beta = 50$. To obtain the Weibull probability by using MINITAB, enter **10** in column C1. Select **Calc | Probability Distributions | Weibull.** Select the **Cumulative probability** option button. In the Shape parameter: edit box, enter **2**. In the Scale parameter: edit box, enter **50.** Enter **C1** in the Input column edit box. Click the **OK** button. You will obtain the output displayed in Figure 5.31 on page 212.

Using MINITAB for Sampling Distributions

To illustrate the use of the Random Number Generator tool for simulating sampling distributions, we will develop sampling distributions of the mean based on a uniform population and a normal population.

To develop a simulation of the sampling distribution of the mean from a uniformly distributed population with 100 samples of $n = 30$, select **Calc | Random Data | Uniform.** Enter **100** in the Generate edit box. Enter **C1–C30** in the Store in column(s): edit box. Enter **0.0** in the Lower endpoint edit box and **1.0** in the Upper endpoint edit box. Click the **OK** button. You will observe that 100 rows of values are entered in columns **C1–C30.**

To calculate row statistics for each of the 100 samples, select **Calc | Row Statistics.** Select the **Mean** option button. Enter **C1–C30** in the Input variables edit box. Enter **C31** in the Store result in: edit box. Click the **OK** button. The mean for each of the 100 samples is stored in column C31. To compute statistics for the set of 100 sample means, select **Basic Statistics | Display Descriptive Statistics.** Enter **C31** in the Variables edit box. Click the **OK** button.

To obtain a histogram of the 100 sample means, select **Graph | Histogram.** Enter **C31** in row 1 of the Graph Variables edit box. Click the **Options** button. Click **Density** for type of histogram. Click the **OK** button to return to the Histogram dialog box. Click the **OK** button again.

To obtain a simulation of the sampling distribution of the mean for a normal population, select **Calc | Random Data | Normal.** Enter a value for μ in the Mean edit box and for σ in the Standard Deviation edit box. Follow the remainder of the instructions given for the Uniform population.

6 Statistical Process Control Charts I: Basic Concepts and Attributes Charts

---

"We do not what we ought;
What we ought not, we do;
And lean upon the thought
That chance will bring us through."

MATTHEW ARNOLD

USING STATISTICS

A medical supply company produces gauze sponges for use in surgical applications. There are numerous ways that defects can occur in each sponge. The company is interested in developing a quality improvement program to determine the current ability to produce sponges that do not contain defects and to improve the process of producing gauze sponges so as to reduce the number of sponges that contain defects.

6.1 INTRODUCTION TO CONTROL CHARTS AND THEIR APPLICATIONS

All systems and processes and their outputs exhibit variability. Variability is inherent to all processes, objects, and events. No two things are exactly the same. Things may appear to be very similar—even exactly the same—but, if they are examined closely enough, differences will be detected. If we are interested in quality, we must be able to understand the sources of variability that affect a process and its output. In this chapter, we will learn techniques for monitoring the variability of a process and for distinguishing common causes of variability from special causes of variability. Control charts can be used to

1. assess process stability;
2. assess process capability;
3. aid in process improvement.

Sources of variability can be broken down into two main categories. Shewhart called these categories *chance* and *assignable causes*. Deming called them *common* and *special causes* of variability.

Chance or Common Causes of Variability

At any time, numerous factors affect a system or process, causing variability. Most of these are not readily identifiable and yet have very small to moderate effects that, individually and in interaction with each other, cause detectable variability in the process and its output. These numerous small causes operate randomly or by chance. This is why Shewhart called them *chance causes*. Individually these causes operate in a random fashion, and at any moment an individual cause may or may not be operating. Because they are numerous, some subset of them will most likely be active at any given time. They are, therefore, inherent or common to the system, and so Deming refers to them as *common causes*.

Chance causes or **common causes** are numerous small causes of variability that are inherent to a system or process and operate randomly or by chance.

Shewhart realized that the system of chance causes that operates on a process is stable and constantly present. This stable system of chance causes produces patterns of variability that follow known statistical distributions. If a set of data is analyzed and the pattern of variation of the data is shown to conform to statistical patterns that are characteristic of those produced by chance, we can assume that only chance or common causes are operating on the system. In such situations, the process is said to be under control or in a **state of statistical control.** A process that is in a state of statistical control is considered to be **stable.**

A **stable process** is in a **state of statistical control** and has only chance or common causes of variability operating on it.

Because a system that is in a state of statistical control is considered to be stable, we can predict the status of output of the process for the near future.

Assignable or Special Causes of Variability

Assignable or special causes of variability usually have relatively large effects on the process and its output and occur occasionally or sporadically. They can be recognized and assigned or attributed to specific special circumstances or factors. Examples of special causes are

- differences between machinery;
- differences in a machine over time—for example, slippage since it was last calibrated or wear of parts could cause machinery to perform differently;
- a change in raw materials—for example, a change in supplier or grade;
- differences between workers;
- differences in an individual worker over time—for example, a worker could be more tired or more hungry at the end of the day or could become inattentive or ill;
- differences in the relationships among production equipment, materials, and workers;
- a change in manufacturing conditions.

Assignable or special causes of variability have relatively large effects on the process and are not inherent to it. The circumstances or factors that cause this kind of variability can be identified.

Special causes are not inherent to the process, so they are considered to be outside the system. When patterns of variability do not conform to the patterns we would expect if only chance or common causes are operating, we know that one or more special causes are operating on the system. If special causes are operating, the system is considered to be out of statistical control, and intervention is required to eliminate the special causes and reduce process variability.

A process is said to be **out of statistical control** if one or more special causes are operating on it.

Statistical control charts, introduced by Shewhart in 1924, allow us to monitor the variability of a process and determine the presence of special causes. They help us to detect the *signal* of variability due to a special cause against the *background noise* of variability due to common causes. If special causes are detected, they can be identified and eliminated, to reduce the variability of the process. Workers at all levels can use these charts to monitor their work and to identify and eliminate special causes that are under their control.

If the process is found to be in a state of statistical control, only common causes are operating. In such situations, the capability and future behavior of the process are known. The best efforts of workers can do nothing to reduce variability due to common causes. Any attempt to make adjustments and treat common causes as special causes will tend to increase overall variability, not reduce it. Treating common causes as special causes can result in over-adjustment or **tampering** with the process. In these situations, it is management's responsibility to change the process and to begin to reduce common causes of variability and improve quality. Managers and engineers can use design of experiments (as in Chapters 10 and 11) to identify the common causes that are acting on the system and to determine how these factors should be controlled or manipulated to reduce variability. The knowledge gained can then be used to redesign the process.

Control charts can also be used to assess **process capability.** If a control chart indicates that a process is stable, the output or performance of the process is predictable and we can meaningfully estimate such parameters of the process as the proportion of nonconforming items, or the mean, and the standard deviation of the output. We can then use this information to determine the average value of a quality characteristic of interest or to estimate the fraction or proportion of process output that we can expect to be nonconforming. Methods for assessing process capability are presented in Section 7.7.

Monitoring of a process with a control chart can also aid in process improvement. Charts can be used to identify and eliminate special causes of variability, thereby reducing the overall variability of the process and achieving stability. If process parameters such as the average or inherent variability are found to be unacceptable, further techniques, such as brainstorming, process flow diagrams, cause-and-effect diagrams (shown in Chapter 2), and designed experiments (as in Chapters 10 and 11), can be used to move the process average to a more desirable level or to further reduce variability. Continuous charting of the process provides the information necessary for us to make sound decisions to take action or to leave the process alone.

Types of Control Charts

Control charts can be divided into two categories that are determined by the type of measurements used to monitor a process. These two broad categories are called **attribute control charts** and **variables control charts.**

In Chapter 1, we defined attribute measures as discrete variables (such as counts or frequencies) and variables measures as continuous variables. If, in monitoring a process, we sample output and evaluate each member of the sample to see whether individual items or events are conforming or nonconforming, the frequency or proportion of nonconforming items in the sample represent an attribute measure. Attribute control charts are used to evaluate such attribute data. If our quality characteristic is measured on a continuous scale such as height, weight, temperature, or time, we employ a variables control chart.

The **attribute control charts** we will cover in this chapter are the following:

1. *Counts of Nonconforming Items* charts:
   (a) pieces or number nonconforming charts (*np* Charts);
   (b) fraction or proportion nonconforming charts (*p* Charts);
2. *Area of Opportunity* Charts:
   (a) number of nonconformities charts (*c* charts);
   (b) nonconformities per unit charts (*u* charts).

Variables control charts, which are presented in Chapter 7, contain more information than attribute charts and are generally used in pairs. One member of the pair monitors process variability while the other monitors central tendency or the average quality level of the output of the process. The major types of variables control charts include the following:

1. charts based on means of samples:
   (a) mean and range charts ($\overline{X}$ & R charts);
   (b) mean and standard deviation charts ($\overline{X}$ & s charts);
   (c) exponentially weighted moving average charts (EWMA charts);
   (d) cumulative sum charts (CUSUM charts).
2. charts based on individual measurements (*X* charts):
   (a) individual measurements using the range;
   (b) individual measurements using the standard deviation.

Figure 6.17 on page 268 is a process flow diagram that can help in deciding which type of chart is most appropriate for monitoring a given process.

6.2 INTRODUCTION TO THE THEORY OF CONTROL CHARTS

Stable systems are in a state of statistical control and exhibit only variability due to common causes. Control charts are based on the fact that chance variation follows known patterns. These patterns are the statistical reference distributions, such as the normal distribution, introduced in Section 5.3, and the binomial and Poisson distributions, presented in Sections 4.4 and 4.7. We can use these statistical reference distributions to estimate the probability of obtaining individual measurements or

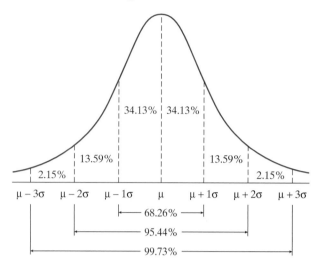

Figure 6.1   The normal distribution and the proportion of the area falling within various multiples of the standard deviation from the mean

sample statistics by chance alone. If the probability of obtaining the measurement by chance alone is high, it is likely that only common causes of variability are operating. If, on the other hand, the individual value or statistic is unlikely to have occurred by chance alone, something else must be happening, and one or more special causes might be operating on the process.

Figure 6.1 presents the normal distribution and the proportion of area that falls into segments defined by one, two and three standard deviations from the mean. As can be seen in Figure 6.1, 99.73 percent of the area under a normal curve falls between plus and minus 3 standard deviations ($\pm 3\sigma$) from the mean (μ). This means that only 0.0027 or 0.27 percent of the area lies beyond $\pm 3\sigma$ from the mean. If only chance or common causes are operating, we would expect that 0.9973 or 99.73 percent of our individual measurements or sample statistics will be within the range of $\pm 3\sigma$. The probability that a measurement falls beyond the $\pm 3\sigma$ range is only 0.0027. This is considered to be a sufficiently small probability for us to suspect that something other than chance is operating and that a special cause may be present.

Figure 6.2 shows a normal distribution paired with a simple control chart. Notice that the control chart has a **center line** (CL), which corresponds to the mean of the distribution, and upper and lower control limits. The **upper control limit** (UCL) is placed $+3\sigma$ above the mean, the **lower control limit** (LCL) is placed -3σ below the mean. Constructing a control chart requires the estimation of a measure of central tendency, such as the mean, and a measure of variability, such as the standard deviation or standard error of a statistic. Once these values are determined, trial control limits can be computed, the center line and trial control limits can be placed on the chart, and we can proceed to plot the individual measurements or sample statistics in time order from left to right. One or more points plotted above the UCL or below the LCL indicate that the system is out of control. Should this occur, the process is interrupted, and efforts to identify the special cause that resulted in the signal are undertaken. Special causes that increase overall variability

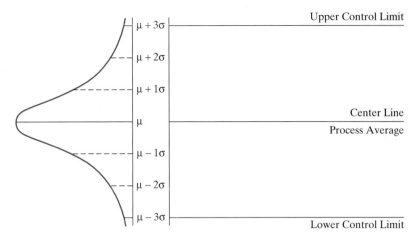

Figure 6.2   The normal distribution and the control chart

and move the process average in an undesirable direction can thus be identified and eliminated. The process is then restarted, and monitoring of the process continues.

The probability that a point falls above the UCL if only common causes are operating is approximately 0.00135, and the probability that one falls below the LCL is approximately 0.00135, so it is unlikely (but possible) to have measures fall beyond the control limits when no special cause is operating. Such **false alarms** are possible, but the placement of the control limits $\pm 3\sigma$ from the process average is thought to control the number of false alarms adequately in most situations. Figure 6.3 demonstrates the two types of errors that we can make when deciding whether a process is in control.

Actual State of Process

		Only Common Causes	Special Causes
Control Chart Indicates	Out of Control	A False Alarm	B Correct Decision
	Control	C Correct Decision	D Failure to Detect

Figure 6.3   Types of errors that can occur when using control charts

In situation C, the process has only common causes operating and we make the correct decision about its status. We are also correct in situation B, because the chart gives us a signal that a special cause is operating and we can take appropriate action. Situations A and D represent errors. In situation A, an error is made, because the signal given by the chart is a false alarm. False alarms occur whenever we decide that the process is out of control and it actually is not. The second type of error is represented by situation D and occurs whenever we fail to detect that a process is out of control.

We can reduce our risk of false alarms by increasing the distance of the UCL and LCL from the process average. If we place the control limits at $\pm 3\sigma$, the probability of a false alarm will be approximately 0.0027. Wider limits such as $\pm 3.29\sigma$ decrease our risk of this type of error to 0.001, but they have the unfortunate effect of increasing the probability of failing to detect the presence of special causes. The convention of placing the limits $\pm 3\sigma$ from the center line originated with Shewhart. Experience has shown that this adequately balances the risk of a false alarm against that of failing to detect that a process is out of control, when the statistical reference distribution underlying a chart adequately represents the process. We can further reduce our risk of failing to detect special causes by more frequent sampling of the process or by increasing the size of our samples.

One way to study the probability of a false alarm is through the run length. A **run** is a series of consecutive points which all increase in value or all decrease in value. Another kind of run occurs when a consecutive series of points all fall above the center line or all fall below the center line.

Run length is the number of chart points that occur after a shift in a parameter takes place before a signal is given by the chart that the shift has occurred.

The **average run length (ARL)** is the average number of points that must be plotted before a point indicates that the process is out-of-control or a shift has occurred.

Out of Control Signals and Patterns

The simplest rule for detecting the presence of a special cause is one or more points that fall beyond the $\pm 3\sigma$ limits of the chart. We can make the chart more sensitive and effective in detecting out-of-control states if we consider other signals and patterns that are unlikely to occur by chance alone.

If only common causes are operating, we would expect the points plotted to follow the statistical reference distribution employed. Figure 6.4 presents a control chart in which the area between the upper and lower control limits is subdivided into bands, each of which is 1 standard deviation wide. These additional limits or **zone boundaries** can be useful in detecting other unlikely patterns of data points.

Exhibit 6.1 provides rules for deciding when a process is out of control.

If only common causes are operating, each of these events is statistically unlikely to occur. For example, the probability of obtaining eight consecutive points on a given side of the center line by chance alone is $(0.5)^8 = 0.0039$. [This calculation is based on the binomial distribution—see Section 4.4.] The presence of one or more of these events indicates that one or more special causes *might* be operating, causing a process that is out of a state of statistical control. Rules 2 to 5 are designed to make the chart more sensitive to shifts in process level or to other special causes. They are optional, however, and should be used cautiously; in some situations, they can increase the false alarm rate. (See Reference 11.)

In addition to the five unlikely events that are based on plotting of individual points or sets of points, there are also overall patterns that are nonrandom and indicate an out-of-control process. Figures 6.5 to 6.9 on pages 237 and 238 present some of the patterns we should be alert to.

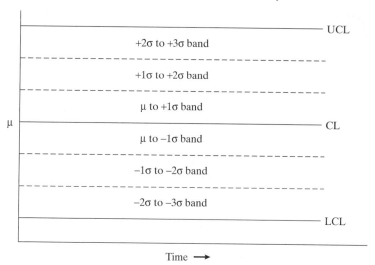

Figure 6.4   A control chart showing bands, each of which is one standard deviation wide

EXHIBIT 6.1   Rules for deciding when a process is out of control

We can conclude that the process is out of control if any of the following events occur.

1. A point falls above the upper control limit or below the lower control limit.

2. Two out of three *consecutive points* fall above the $+2\sigma$ limits or two out of three *consecutive points* fall below the -2σ limits.

3. Four out of five *consecutive points* fall above the $+1\sigma$ limit or four out of five *consecutive points* fall below the -1σ limit.

4. Eight or more *consecutive points* lie above the center line or eight or more *consecutive points* lie below the center line.

5. Eight or more *consecutive points* move upward in value or eight or more *consecutive points* move downward in value.

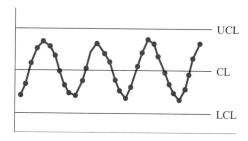

Figure 6.5   The cyclic pattern

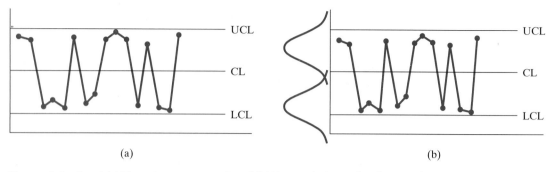

(a)   (b)

Figure 6.6   Panel (a) The mixture pattern; Panel (b) Two underlying distributions that create a mixture pattern

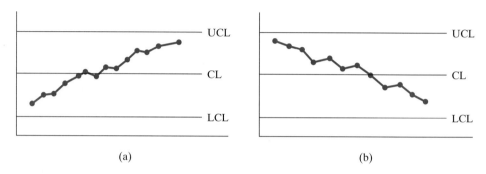

(a)   (b)

Figure 6.7   Panel (a) An upward trend; Panel (b) A downward trend

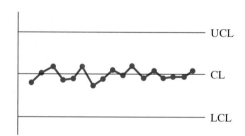

Figure 6.8   The stratification pattern

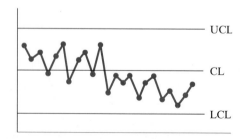

Figure 6.9   A shift in process level

The **cyclic pattern,** illustrated by Figure 6.5, is characterized by a wave-like design in which points systematically increase for a period, after which they decrease, and then later still increase again. Such repeating or cyclic patterns are nonrandom and are usually the result of special causes such as systematic environmental changes operating over a time period (shift, day, week, or season). Rotation of equipment or personnel, maintenance schedules, employee fatigue, and electrical fluctuations can also result in cyclic patterns.

Figure 6.6, Panel (a), represents a **mixture pattern,** which is characterized by alternately high and low values, with too few points plotted near the center line. It is referred to as a mixture pattern because it is often the result of the mixing of two underlying populations, such as two streams of raw materials, or the output of two machines or employees, some time before sampling took place. Figure 6.6, Panel (b), shows how the mixing of two populations can create the wide swings characteristic of the mixture pattern and how larger differences between the populations will result in greater fluctuations in the points plotted. This pattern will also result if operators over-control or tamper with a process in an attempt to improve it, instead of acting only when an out-of-control signal is obtained.

In Figure 6.7, Panel (a) and Panel (b) demonstrate trends in the data and are characterized by overall movement of points in one direction. Figure 6.7, Panel (a), represents a run up; Figure 6.7, Panel (b), represents a run down. The special causes underlying these patterns include fatigue of personnel or equipment, systematic environmental changes, build-up of waste products, or settling or separation in a chemical process.

The **stratification pattern,** illustrated by Figure 6.8, is characterized by too many points plotted close to the center line. When using the normal distribution as our reference distribution, we would expect about 68 percent of the points to fall within $\pm 1\sigma$ of the center line and about 32 percent to fall beyond these limits. Although it would seem that this is a desirable low-variability condition, too few points outside these limits is a nonrandom event and indicates that action should be taken. Stratification patterns are often the result of incorrect calculation of the control chart limits or of continued use of obsolete limits. For example, the limits could be considered obsolete if the variability of the process decreased over time, indicating improved process capability. The control limits should be checked and recalculated.

Figure 6.9 illustrates a **shift in process level,** indicating that something about the process has changed. Examples of such changes include the introduction of new personnel, methods, equipment, or sources of supply. If the shift is in a desirable direction, so that the average value of the characteristic being monitored represents higher quality, the cause of the shift should be identified and made a permanent part of the process. If, on the other hand, the shift indicates a lower quality level, corrective action should be taken.

6.3 INTRODUCTION TO ATTRIBUTES CONTROL CHARTS

Attributes control charts are used whenever samples or subgroups of process output are evaluated and the number of nonconforming items in a sample are counted or the number of nonconformities per item are counted. Because they are often considered to be easier to calculate than variables charts, attribute charts are frequently used in the initial stages of statistical process control or when a variables measure of the quality characteristic of interest is not readily available or is not feasible to obtain because of cost factors. It is often easier to evaluate items as conforming or nonconforming to specifications than to evaluate them on a variables measure; however, attribute measures contain less information than variables measures. The items or events evaluated can be service units or product units, but, in either case, it is essential that nonconformity be operationally defined and that everyone involved in the process be aware of what is being counted and of how to evaluate whether items are nonconforming.

6.4 *np* AND *p* CHARTS

The **number nonconforming chart** is based on the number of items in a sample or subgroup that are judged to be nonconforming under an operational definition. The number of nonconforming items in a sample is expected to be the proportion of nonconforming items, p, times the size of the sample, n, so these charts are often called ***np* charts**. These charts are based on the binomial distribution and, therefore, require that the process under study have the characteristics listed in Exhibit 6.2.

EXHIBIT 6.2 Assumptions for use of the *np* chart

1. There are only two possible outcomes for an event: An item must be found to be either conforming or nonconforming. No intermediate values are possible.

2. The probability, p, of a nonconforming item is constant.

3. The quality of successive items are independent.

4. All samples contain the same number of items, n.

The first three assumptions are required by the binomial probability model on which the charts are based. In practice, it is sometimes difficult to satisfy the third assumption, independence, because successive items or events are often related. Experience has shown that minor violations of this assumption will not usually invalidate the results obtained from these charts; if, however, the status of an individual item seems to be highly dependent on the status of the item before or after it in sequence, the chart can be misleading or of little use. The fourth assumption, equal sample size, is required for computation of the control limits. In cases where unequal sample sizes are employed, the *proportion nonconforming* (p) *chart* is more appropriate. If the number of conforming or acceptable items is counted instead of the number nonconforming, the chart is referred to as a **yield chart.**

Calculating Control Limits for *np* Charts

Before we can calculate trial control limits for the *np* chart, we must estimate the probability, p, that the process will produce a nonconforming item. To obtain a good estimate, we need to evaluate *at least* 20 to 25 samples or subgroups and count the number of nonconforming items in each. It is sometimes tempting to try to construct trial limits for a control chart with fewer samples, so that we can benefit from the information a chart provides as soon as possible.[1] This shortcut is not generally

[1]For cases in which production runs are too short to collect 25 samples or in which it is necessary or desirable to begin charting before data on 25 samples are available, Q charts designed for short runs can be used. (See References 6 and 7.)

advisable, because fewer samples will not provide sufficiently accurate estimates of process parameters such as *p*. Our best *estimate* of *p* will be $\bar{p}$, the average proportion of items nonconforming.

$$\bar{p} = \frac{\text{Total number of nonconforming items in all subgroups}}{\text{Total number of items in all subgroups}} \qquad (6.1a)$$

Or, using summation notation,

$$\bar{p} = \frac{\sum\limits_{i=1}^{k} X_i}{\sum\limits_{i=1}^{k} n_i} \qquad (6.1b)$$

where

X_i = number of nonconforming items in subgroup *i*

n_i = subgroup size

k = number of subgroups

The center line on a control chart represents the process average, which in this case is $n\bar{p}$. The average number of nonconforming units in a sample or subgroup serves as the value at which the center line is placed and is equal to

$$\text{Center Line} = n\bar{p} \qquad (6.2)$$

where

n = the common subgroup size

If we have not calculated the value of $\bar{p}$, we can calculate $n\bar{p}$ by

$$n\bar{p} = \frac{\text{Total number of nonconforming items in all subgroups}}{\text{Number of subgroups}} \qquad (6.3a)$$

or, using summation notation,

$$n\bar{p} = \frac{\sum\limits_{i=1}^{k} X_i}{k} \qquad (6.3b)$$

where

X_i = number of nonconforming items in subgroup *i*

k = number of subgroups

The upper control limit will then be placed at a value $+3\sigma$ above the center line and the lower control limit will be placed -3σ below the center line. To obtain these values, we need to estimate σ. For the standard deviation of a binomial distribution, see Section 4.4:

$$\sigma = \sqrt{np(1-p)} \tag{6.4}$$

Using $\bar{p}$ as our estimate of p, we can estimate σ by s, as follows:

$$s = \sqrt{n\bar{p}(1-\bar{p})} \tag{6.5}$$

The upper control limit is then calculated as

$$\text{UCL} = n\bar{p} + 3\sqrt{n\bar{p}(1-\bar{p})} \tag{6.6a}$$

and the lower control limit is calculated as

$$\text{LCL} = n\bar{p} - 3\sqrt{n\bar{p}(1-\bar{p})} \tag{6.6b}$$

To demonstrate the use of the np chart, we return to the *Using Statistics* example on page 230, which concerns the manufacture of gauze sponges. Suppose that, each day, 600 sponges are sampled and inspected and that the number of defective sponges (nonconforming items) is recorded. The data presented in Table 6.1 represent 32 samples of $n = 600$ sponges, along with the number of nonconforming sponges in each sample.

Computation of Center Line and Control Limits

If we sum the number of nonconforming sponges in the 32 subgroups, we find a total of 685 nonconforming sponges. There were 600 sponges in each of the 32 subgroups, so the total number of sponges under consideration is $nk = 600(32) = 19,200$. We can calculate the value at which the center line should be placed by first calculating $\bar{p}$. From Equation (6.1a),

$$\bar{p} = \frac{\text{Total number of nonconforming items in all subgroups}}{\text{Total number of items in all subgroups}}$$

and, therefore,

$$\bar{p} = \frac{685}{32 \times 600} = 0.0357$$

Then, using Equation (6.2), we have

$$\text{Center Line} = n\bar{p}$$
$$= 600(0.0357)$$
$$= 21.406$$

TABLE 6.1

NUMBER OF NONCONFORMING GAUZE SPONGES IN 32 SAMPLES OF SIZE *n* = 600

Day	Number of Nonconforming Items (X_i)	*n*	Proportion Nonconforming $p_i = X_i/n_i$
1	21	600	0.035
2	22	600	0.037
3	20	600	0.033
4	21	600	0.035
5	23	600	0.038
6	39	600	0.065
7	18	600	0.030
8	24	600	0.040
9	20	600	0.033
10	22	600	0.037
11	19	600	0.032
12	23	600	0.038
13	22	600	0.037
14	29	600	0.048
15	17	600	0.028
16	16	600	0.027
17	20	600	0.033
18	16	600	0.027
19	11	600	0.018
20	24	600	0.040
21	25	600	0.042
22	21	600	0.035
23	23	600	0.038
24	20	600	0.033
25	24	600	0.040
26	28	600	0.047
27	21	600	0.035
28	19	600	0.032
29	15	600	0.025
30	22	600	0.037
31	24	600	0.040
32	16	600	0.027 **SPONGE**

[2]Any difference in the calculation of control limits within the chapter and limits obtained from computer software are due to rounding error.

The upper control limit is then calculated by using Equation (6.6a)[2]:

$$UCL = n\bar{p} + 3\sqrt{n\bar{p}(1 - \bar{p})}$$

$$UCL = 21.406 + 3\sqrt{21.406(1 - 0.036)}$$

$$UCL = 21.406 + 13.628$$

$$UCL = 35.034$$

The Lower Control Limit can be calculated by using Equation(6.6b):

$$LCL = n\bar{p} - 3\sqrt{n\bar{p}(1 - \bar{p})}$$
$$LCL = 21.406 - 3\sqrt{21.406(1 - 0.036)}$$
$$LCL = 21.406 - 13.628$$
$$LCL = 7.778$$

Calculation of the Optional 1σ and 2σ Boundaries

If we choose to use the 1σ and 2σ limits, we estimate σ by s, where s is calculated by using Equation (6.5):

$$s = \sqrt{n\bar{p}(1 - \bar{p})}$$

Therefore,

$$s = \sqrt{21.406(1 - 0.036)}$$
$$s = 4.543$$

We then calculate the $+2\sigma$ boundary as

$$+2\sigma \text{ boundary} = n\bar{p} + 2s \tag{6.7a}$$

$$= 21.406 + 2(4.543) = 30.492$$

and the -2σ boundary as

$$-2\sigma \text{ boundary} = n\bar{p} - 2s \tag{6.7b}$$

$$= 21.406 - 2(4.543) = 12.320$$

The $+1\sigma$ and -1σ boundaries are, respectively,

$$+1\sigma \text{ boundary} = n\bar{p} + 1s \tag{6.8a}$$

$$= 21.406 + 1(4.543) = 25.949$$

and

$$-1\sigma \text{ boundary} = n\bar{p} - 1s \tag{6.8b}$$

$$= 21.406 - 1(4.543) = 16.863$$

The center line, upper and lower control limits, and optional 1σ and 2σ boundary limits are drawn on the chart, and the number of nonconforming sponges in each sample is plotted on the chart in the order in which samples were collected. Figure 6.10 presents the *np* chart obtained from MINITAB for the gauze sponges data. The chart can now be examined to see whether any out-of-control signals are present. Examination of the chart shows that the point representing sample

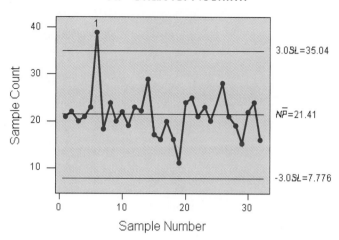

Figure 6.10   *np* chart obtained from MINITAB for the gauze sponge data

number 6 falls above the upper control limit. No violations of rules 2 to 5 (see Exhibit 6.1 on page 237) or other nonrandom patterns are apparent. (MINITAB does not plot zones on the chart, but instead lists any points that violate zone rules.)

In this example, the value obtained on day 6 was investigated, and it was determined that on that day there was an employee from another unit assigned to a work station because several regular employees were out ill. A group brainstormed ways of avoiding the problem in the future and recommended that a team of people from other units receive training on using the equipment. Members of this team could then cover one or more stations in emergencies by rotating in one-hour or two-hour shifts. Only because the cause of the out-of-control point could be *identified* and *eliminated* from the process was it appropriate to remove the data represented by point 6 from the analysis and recalculate the trial control limits.

Thus, for the gauze sponge data, with point 6 removed, we have 31 subgroups with a total of 646 nonconforming items in all subgroups. There are 600 items in each subgroup, so there are $nk = 600(31) = 18,600$ items under consideration. From Equations (6.1a) and (6.3), we have

$$\bar{p} = \frac{\text{Total number of nonconforming items in all subgroups}}{\text{Total number of items in all subgroups}}$$

$$\bar{p} = \frac{646}{31 \times 600} = 0.035$$

and

$$\bar{np} = \frac{\text{Total number of nonconforming items in all subgroups}}{\text{Number of subgroups}}$$

$$\bar{np} = \frac{646}{31} = 20.839$$

The upper and lower control limits are calculated by using Equations (6.6a) and (6.6b), respectively.

$$\text{UCL} = n\bar{p} + 3\sqrt{n\bar{p}(1 - \bar{p})}$$
$$\text{UCL} = 20.839 + 3\sqrt{20.839(1 - 0.035)}$$
$$\text{UCL} = 20.839 + 13.453$$
$$\text{UCL} = 34.292$$

$$\text{LCL} = n\bar{p} - 3\sqrt{n\bar{p}(1 - \bar{p})}$$
$$\text{LCL} = 20.839 - 3\sqrt{20.839(1 - 0.035)}$$
$$\text{LCL} = 20.839 - 13.453$$
$$\text{LCL} = 7.386$$

Figure 6.11 presents the revised *np* control chart obtained from MINITAB for the gauze sponge data.

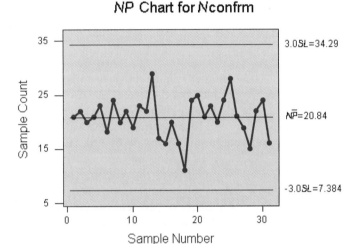

Figure 6.11   Revised *np* chart obtained from MINITAB for the gauze sponge data

There are no points outside the revised control limits, so these trial limits can be extended into the future, and new samples can continue to be drawn, evaluated, and plotted on the revised chart. These limits can be used until a change in the process occurs, either by design or as indicated by a shift in process level. Whenever such a change occurs, the current control chart limits should be considered obsolete, and new trial limits should be calculated. As long as the chart indicates that the process is in a state of statistical control, we assume that day-to-day differences are due only to chance or common causes of variation. If the average output of the process or the variability of process output is unacceptable in terms of quality, it is management's responsibility to *change the process* and move the process to a higher quality level. Management should be committed to continuous improvement of the quality of both the process and its output. The Shewhart-Deming Plan-Do-Study-Act cycle can serve as a model for continuous improvement efforts. Techniques that we studied in Chapter 2, such as process flow, cause-and-effect, and Pareto diagrams can be used to identify and understand the root causes of unacceptable quality.

p Charts for Equal Subgroup Sizes

Fraction or **proportion nonconforming charts,** referred to as **p charts,** differ from *np* charts in that they employ the *proportion* of nonconforming items in samples *instead of* the *number* nonconforming. Like *np* charts, they are based on the binomial distribution and therefore require that the first three assumptions listed under the *np* chart be met. Unlike the *np* chart, *p* charts can be used with either *equal or unequal* sample sizes. The center line on a *p* chart is determined by $\bar{p}$, the average proportion nonconforming, which can be calculated using Equation (6.1).

The upper and lower control limits are placed $+3\sigma$ and -3σ, respectively, from the center line, so we need to estimate σ_p, the standard error of a proportion. Using s_p to estimate σ_p, we have

$$s_p = \sqrt{\frac{\bar{p}(1-\bar{p})}{n}} \tag{6.9}$$

We obtain the upper control limit for a *p* chart from

$$\text{UCL} = \bar{p} + 3\sqrt{\frac{\bar{p}(1-\bar{p})}{n}} \tag{6.10a}$$

and the lower control limit from

$$\text{LCL} = \bar{p} - 3\sqrt{\frac{\bar{p}(1-\bar{p})}{n}} \tag{6.10b}$$

For our gauze sponge data presented in Table 6.1 on page 243, we calculate $\bar{p}$ from using Equation (6.1), as follows:

$$\bar{p} = \frac{685}{32 \times 600} = 0.036$$

The upper and lower control limits are then calculated by using Equations (6.10a) and (6.10b).

$$\text{UCL} = \bar{p} + 3\sqrt{\frac{\bar{p}(1-\bar{p})}{n}}$$

$$\text{UCL} = 0.036 + 3\sqrt{\frac{0.036(1-0.036)}{600}}$$

$$\text{UCL} = 0.036 + 3(0.0076) = 0.036 + 0.023$$

$$\text{UCL} = 0.059$$

$$\text{LCL} = \bar{p} - 3\sqrt{\frac{\bar{p}(1-\bar{p})}{n}}$$

$$\text{LCL} = 0.036 - 3\sqrt{\frac{0.036(1-0.036)}{600}}$$

$$\text{LCL} = 0.036 - 3(0.0076) = 0.036 - 0.023$$

$$\text{LCL} = 0.013$$

p Chart for Gauze Sponges

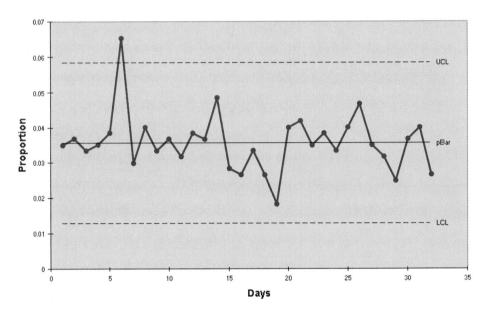

Figure 6.12   *p* chart obtained from the PHStat add-in for Microsoft Excel for the gauze sponge data

Figure 6.12 presents the *p* chart obtained from the PHStat add-in for Microsoft Excel for the gauze sponge data.

Notice that it is similar to the *np* chart presented in Figure 6.10, but the points plotted represent the proportion nonconforming in the samples and *not* the number nonconforming. The point representing day 6 is above the upper control limit, as it was in the *np* chart for these data. The special cause that resulted in this out of control point was identified and eliminated, so it would be appropriate to eliminate the data represented by point 6 and recalculate the center line and upper and lower control limits, as we did when we used the *np* chart.

p Charts for Unequal Subgroup Sizes

It is sometimes necessary to use samples or subgroups that are unequal in size. In such cases, the *np* chart is inappropriate, but the *p* chart can be used. As shown in Equation (6.9), the standard error of the proportion nonconforming, s_p, is based on *n*, the subgroup size. Therefore, each time *n* varies, the control limits will vary. In general, the standard error of a proportion for a subgroup will be:

$$s_{p_i} = \sqrt{\frac{\bar{p}(1 - \bar{p})}{n_i}} \qquad (6.11)$$

where

n_i = the number of observations in subgroup *i*

This problem can be handled in one of the following two ways:

1. *Use different limits for each subgroup.* This method is the most sensitive statistically, but it requires recalculation of the upper and lower control limits for each sample. Although computationally complex, this approach is used by statistical software packages such as MINITAB.

2. *Use $\bar{n}$, the average value of n, to compute the upper and lower control limits.* This method is computationally simpler than calculating individual control limits for each sample size, but it is not as sensitive. Using average sample size may result in erroneously accepting or rejecting the hypothesis that the process is in control. It should be used only if sample sizes are no more than ± 20 percent different from each other.

Calculating Control Limits Using Average Subgroup Size

To calculate the control limits for the *p* chart when sample sizes are not equal, we begin by calculating the average sample size $\bar{n}$.

$$\bar{n} = \frac{\text{Total number of items under consideration}}{\text{Total number of subgroups}} \qquad (6.12a)$$

or, in summation notation,

$$\bar{n} = \frac{\sum_{i=1}^{k} n_i}{k} \qquad (6.12b)$$

where

n_i = size of subgroup *i*

k = number of subgroups

We then substitute $\bar{n}$ for *n* in Equations (6.10a) and (6.10b) to obtain revised equations for the upper and lower control limits, so that

$$\text{UCL} = \bar{p} + 3\sqrt{\frac{\bar{p}(1 - \bar{p})}{\bar{n}}} \qquad (6.13a)$$

and

$$\text{LCL} = \bar{p} - 3\sqrt{\frac{\bar{p}(1 - \bar{p})}{\bar{n}}} \qquad (6.13b)$$

To illustrate the case of unequal sample sizes, suppose that a waste-recycling facility monitors the weights of trucks that enter the facility before they are permitted to tip and unload. Suppose that the management of the service wishes to reduce the number of trucks that are overweight. They begin by recording the number of overweight trucks over a four-week time period (for a Monday

TABLE 6.2

NUMBER OF TRUCKS ENTERING RECYCLING FACILITY AND NUMBER AND PROPORTION OVERWEIGHT ON EACH OF 20 CONSECUTIVE BUSINESS DAYS

Day	Number of Trucks	Number Overweight	Proportion Overweight
1	136	4	0.029
2	153	6	0.039
3	127	2	0.016
4	157	7	0.045
5	144	5	0.035
6	122	5	0.041
7	154	6	0.039
8	132	3	0.023
9	160	8	0.050
10	142	7	0.049
11	157	6	0.038
12	150	9	0.060
13	142	8	0.056
14	137	10	0.073
15	147	8	0.054
16	132	7	0.053
17	136	6	0.044
18	137	7	0.051
19	153	11	0.072
20	141	7	0.050 **TRUCKS**

through Friday workweek). The total number of trucks entering the facility daily and the number of overweight trucks are recorded, with the results presented in Table 6.2.

Computation of Center Line and Control Limits

A truck is considered nonconforming if it is overweight, so there are a total of 132 nonconforming items in the 20-day period selected for consideration in calculating trial control limits. There were a total of 2,859 trucks that used the facility during the 20 days, and the data for each day represents a subgroup; from Equations (6.12a) and (6.1),

$$\bar{n} = \frac{\text{Total number of items under consideration}}{\text{Total number of subgroups}}$$

$$\bar{n} = \frac{2{,}859}{20} = 142.95$$

and

$$\bar{p} = \frac{132}{2{,}859} = 0.046$$

From Equation (6.13a), the upper control limit for the chart is

$$UCL = \bar{p} + 3\sqrt{\frac{\bar{p}(1 - \bar{p})}{\bar{n}}}$$

$$UCL = 0.046 + 3\sqrt{\frac{0.046(1 - 0.046)}{142.95}}$$

$$UCL = 0.046 + 0.053$$

$$UCL = 0.099$$

and from Equation (6.13b), the lower control limit is

$$LCL = \bar{p} - 3\sqrt{\frac{\bar{p}(1 - \bar{p})}{\bar{n}}}$$

$$LCL = 0.046 - 3\sqrt{\frac{0.046(1 - 0.046)}{142.95}}$$

$$LCL = 0.046 - 0.053$$

$$LCL = -0.007.$$

We obtained a negative value for LCL, so the LCL either is considered not to exist or is set at 0.0. Figure 6.13 presents the *p* chart obtained from the PHStat add-in for Microsoft Excel for the waste-recycling data presented in Table 6.2.

p Chart for Overweight Trucks

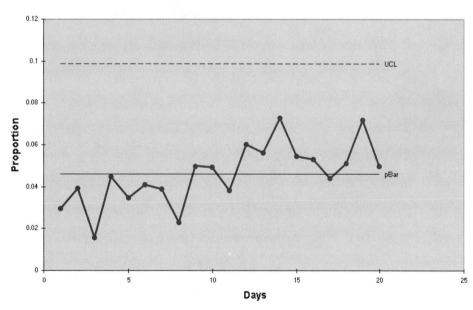

Figure 6.13   *p* chart obtained from the PHStat add-in for Microsoft Excel for the overweight trucks data by using average subgroup size

Using our rules for determining out-of-control points, we observe that there are no points either above the UCL or below the LCL; however, the first eight points all fall below the center line, thereby violating rule 4. There seems to be an upward shift in the data. The proportion of overweight trucks increased in the second half of the time period studied. This would indicate a need for the management of the facility to investigate and determine the reasons.

Calculating Control Limits Using Different Limits for Each Subgroup

The calculation of individual limits for each subgroup size can be tedious, so statistical software is often used to develop these charts. Figure 6.14 presents a *p* chart obtained from MINITAB by using individual limits for each sample in the waste-recycling example. Notice that the UCL is not represented by a straight line but varies according to the size of the samples. Thus, for example, we observe wider limits on days represented by smaller subgroup sizes (such as days 1 and 3) than on days with larger subgroup sizes (such as day 2 and days 4 and 5).

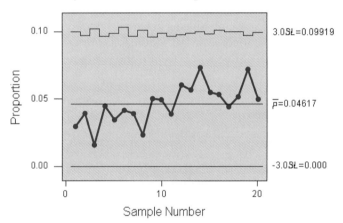

Figure 6.14   *p* chart obtained from MINITAB for the overweight trucks data by using actual subgroup size

Sample Sizes for *p* Charts and *np* Charts

Attribute measures are less sensitive than variables measures, so attribute charts generally require larger sample or subgroup sizes. Sample sizes should be large enough to pick up some nonconforming units, and some general rules have been developed to help determine the sizes of samples necessary to construct *np* and *p* charts. Rice (in Reference 8) recommended that samples should be large enough to have a 90 percent chance of detecting at least one nonconforming unit in a sample. Another guideline suggests that subgroups should be large enough so that the average number of nonconformities in a set of subgroups is at least 2.0. Alternatives to the *p* and *np* charts are discussed in references 3 and 13.

When attribute charts are used to monitor a process with a very low proportion of nonconforming items, or when the proportion nonconforming decreases as a result of quality-improvement efforts, the proportion nonconforming will tend to approach 0.0, and larger and larger sample sizes will be needed. In the extreme case of probabilities close to 0.0, we may end up requiring 100 percent inspection. In such situations, variables measures and variables charts should be used.

PROBLEMS

6.1 The director of telecommunications for an automotive parts supplier is concerned about the number of abandoned calls from a toll-free 800 line. Each day, a random sample of 50 calls is selected, and the number of abandoned calls in the sample is determined. The following table presents the number of abandoned calls in each of 30 samples of size 50.

Sample	Number of Abandoned Calls	Sample	Number of Abandoned Calls
1	3	16	4
2	1	17	5
3	2	18	6
4	6	19	3
5	1	20	7
6	0	21	5
7	2	22	1
8	5	23	3
9	8	24	2
10	4	25	3
11	2	26	5
12	5	27	3
13	1	28	2
14	2	29	0
15	2	30	3

ABANDON

(a) Construct an *np* control chart for these data.
(b) Is the process in a state of statistical control? Why?
(c) If the process is not in a state of control, eliminate out-of-control points, and recalculate the trial control limits.
(d) Construct a *p* chart for these data.
(e) Is the process in a state of statistical control? Why?
(f) If the process is not in a state of control, eliminate out-of-control points, and recalculate the trial control limits.
(g) Compare your results in (e) to the results you obtained in (b). Explain any similarities and differences.

6.2 A manufacturer of specialty machine tools performs final inspection on finished pieces for such nonconformities as burring, rough finish, improper sizing, and incorrect threading. The finished pieces are inspected in lots of 100. The following table presents the number of defective pieces found in 40 consecutive lots of tools.

Lot Number	Number Nonconforming	Lot Number	Number Nonconforming
1	17	21	20
2	12	22	3
3	8	23	11
4	12	24	18
5	9	25	13
6	14	26	12
7	6	27	12
8	15	28	21
9	13	29	17
10	8	30	16
11	10	31	12
12	13	32	12
13	14	33	12
14	10	34	17
15	16	35	10
16	12	36	10
17	11	37	13
18	15	38	13
19	13	39	12
20	13	40	13

TOOLS

(a) Construct an *np* control chart for these data.
(b) Is the process in a state of statistical control? Why?
(c) If the process is not in a state of control, eliminate out-of-control points, and recalculate the trial control limits.
(d) Construct a *p* chart for these data.
(e) Is the process in a state of statistical control? Why?
(f) If the process is not in a state of control, eliminate out-of-control points and recalculate the trial control limits.
(g) Compare your results in (e) to the results you obtained in (b). Explain any similarities and differences.

6.3 A manufacturer of specialty ceramic tiles for use in high-temperature furnaces subjects tiles to several quality checks. Tiles found to have surface deformities or failing to meet size specifications after firing are considered nonconforming. The table below presents the number of nonconforming tiles in 40 consecutive lots of size 100.

Lot Number	Number Nonconforming	Lot Number	Number Nonconforming
1	8	21	6
2	6	22	2
3	4	23	5
4	4	24	7
5	3	25	6
6	7	26	4
7	3	27	6
8	6	28	10
9	9	29	5
10	5	30	5
11	7	31	7
12	2	32	9
13	6	33	3
14	11	34	8
15	4	35	5
16	6	36	3
17	7	37	12
18	4	38	6
19	9	39	4
20	6	40	5

CERAMIC

(a) Construct an *np* control chart for these data.
(b) Is the process in a state of statistical control? Why?
(c) If the process is not in a state of control, eliminate out-of-control points, and recalculate the trial control limits.
(d) Construct a *p* chart for these data.
(e) Is the process in a state of statistical control? Why?
(f) If the process is not in a state of control, eliminate out-of-control points, and recalculate the trial control limits.
(g) Compare your results in (e) to the results you obtained in (b). Explain any similarities and differences.

6.4 Motor end shields are tested before being used in final motor assembly. The table at the top of the next column presents the number of nonconforming motor end shields in 34 consecutive lots of 100.

Lot Number	Number Nonconforming	Lot Number	Number Nonconforming
1	4	18	8
2	6	19	3
3	4	20	5
4	5	21	2
5	9	22	5
6	7	23	4
7	3	24	6
8	2	25	4
9	4	26	6
10	5	27	7
11	4	28	5
12	7	29	6
13	8	30	3
14	5	31	4
15	4	32	5
16	3	33	3
17	7	34	6

MOTOR

(a) Construct an *np* control chart for these data.
(b) Is the process in a state of statistical control? Why?
(c) If the process is not in a state of control, eliminate out-of-control points, and recalculate the trial control limits.
(d) Construct a *p* chart for these data.
(e) Is the process in a state of statistical control? Why?
(f) If the process is not in a state of control, eliminate out-of-control points, and recalculate the trial control limits.
(g) Compare your results in (e) to the results you obtained in (b). Explain any similarities and differences.

6.5 A company manufactures circuit-board components for electronic equipment. Each component is tested at the end of the process, and data is recorded on a weekly basis. The following table presents the number of components produced and the number nonconforming for a 40-week period.

Week	Number Made	Number Nonconforming
1	823	4
2	809	4
3	811	5
4	833	4
5	949	6
6	934	10

(*Continued*)

Week	Number Made	Number Nonconforming
7	948	8
8	930	13
9	957	8
10	949	7
11	940	7
12	955	9
13	944	5
14	935	6
15	932	6
16	932	5
17	913	5
18	905	3
19	958	5
20	953	5
21	830	3
22	889	4
23	845	3
24	915	7
25	922	8
26	944	8
27	935	9
28	945	11
29	950	7
30	944	5
31	957	6
32	942	7
33	939	6
34	940	7
35	863	5
36	929	5
37	897	3
38	881	4
39	958	6
40	914	5

CIRCUIT

(a) Construct a *p* control chart for these data.
(b) Is the process in a state of statistical control? Why?
(c) If the process is not in a state of control, eliminate out-of-control points, and recalculate the trial control limits.

6.6 A firm manufactures high-voltage capacitor film for the electronics industry. They are concerned with the yield on a slitter process that produces reels of film. Reels that are nonconforming must be scrapped. Reels were sampled and inspected each week for 30 weeks. The number of reels of film in each sample,

number of scrap reels, and proportion of scrap reels are presented as follows:

Week	Number of Total Reels	Number of Scrap Reels	Proportion of Scrap Reels
1	1,145	142	0.1240
2	1,013	55	0.0543
3	1,275	125	0.0980
4	686	57	0.0831
5	984	58	0.0589
6	717	37	0.0516
7	1,408	57	0.0405
8	1,254	38	0.0303
9	890	60	0.0674
10	1,155	99	0.0857
11	969	121	0.1249
12	858	69	0.0804
13	832	100	0.1202
14	839	101	0.1204
15	1,230	123	0.1000
16	843	49	0.0581
17	1,102	99	0.0898
18	1,039	111	0.1068
19	1,385	125	0.0903
20	1,352	142	0.1050
21	903	43	0.0476
22	976	64	0.0656
23	695	81	0.1165
24	1,123	82	0.0730
25	1,252	102	0.0815
26	857	113	0.1319
27	1,277	74	0.0579
28	1,182	97	0.0821
29	440	41	0.0932
30	916	123	0.1343

REELS

(a) Construct a control chart for these data.
(b) Is the process in a state of statistical control? Why?
(c) Can you make any recommendations on how to monitor the process in the future?

6.7 A water-testing laboratory tests samples for the presence of bacteria by culturing. It is important to report the results for samples on a timely basis, and the lab decided that five days should be adequate for culturing and for the writing of a final report on a sample. The total number of samples received in a day and the number and proportion of samples that are pending or not processed within five days are presented next.

Day	Pending	Total	Proportion
1	3	38	0.079
2	2	39	0.051
3	1	31	0.032
4	0	53	0.000
5	3	41	0.073
6	1	37	0.027
7	1	33	0.030
8	2	38	0.053
9	2	35	0.057
10	3	36	0.083
11	3	32	0.094
12	2	39	0.051
13	2	30	0.067
14	1	38	0.026
15	1	42	0.024
16	1	29	0.034
17	2	46	0.044
18	6	39	0.154
19	10	51	0.196
20	9	48	0.188
21	1	33	0.030
22	0	46	0.000
23	1	50	0.020
24	3	42	0.071
25	6	41	0.146
26	5	36	0.139
27	9	36	0.250
28	3	52	0.058
29	2	42	0.048
30	3	45	0.067

BACTERIA

(a) Construct a control chart for these data.
(b) Is the process in a state of statistical control? Why?
(c) What recommendations would you make for improving this process?

6.8 Electronic subassemblies are built by a subcontractor under a contract that requires 100-percent inspection for mechanical and electrical defects. The table in the next column presents the daily output of the assembly process and the number of subassemblies failing final electrical testing.

Day	Number Inspected	Number Nonconforming
1	201	5
2	205	3
3	292	6
4	224	5
5	300	7
6	293	8
7	203	5
8	356	9
9	290	6
10	359	5
11	343	6
12	232	6
13	290	4
14	312	5
15	284	5
16	350	7
17	249	6
18	185	3
19	203	4
20	386	10
21	269	7
22	271	6
23	374	8
24	263	5
25	315	6
26	349	5
27	292	8
28	273	6
29	314	7
30	328	5

ASSEMBLY

(a) Construct a p chart for these data.
(b) Is the process in a state of statistical control? Why?
(c) If the process is not in a state of control, eliminate out-of-control points, and recalculate the trial control limits.

6.5 AREA OF OPPORTUNITY CHARTS (c CHARTS AND u CHARTS)

Area of opportunity charts monitor the number of times a characteristic of interest occurs in an area of opportunity. If we refer to the aspect of interest or nonconformity as an event, we can define an **area of opportunity** as a unit in which one or more events can occur. Areas of opportunity can be individual product or service units or subgroups based on units of time, space, or area. Examples of counts of events in an area of opportunity are the number of incoming calls per hour on a telephone network, the number of vehicles passing an intersection per hour, the number of M&Ms in an 16-ounce bag, the number of equipment maintenance work orders per week, the number of errors in a computer program, the number of insects per square meter of lawn, the number of defective welds in a length of pipe, and the number of fleas on a dog. In a given application, events can be all of one type or can include different types of nonconformities. For example, surface nonconformities in sheets of plastic could be all of one type, such as pitting, or could include pitting, scratches, and pinholes. In the latter case, the occurrence of any one of these nonconformities would count as one event each time it occurred.

When areas of opportunity are the same size, a **c chart** is used; areas of opportunity of varying sizes require a **u chart.** To help clarify the difference between situations requiring the use of np or p charts versus c or u charts, consider the unpleasant example concerning fleas on dogs. If we are interested in the *number of dogs with fleas* in samples of dogs, we should use the np or p chart when there is the same number of dogs in each group and the p chart when the number of dogs in a group varies. If, however, we are interested in the *number of fleas on dogs,* we would use the c or u chart. If the dogs we are studying are all the same size, the c chart would be the more appropriate. Groups of dogs of different sizes, such as toy poodles mixed with Labrador retrievers and Great Danes, would require use of the u chart. The c chart and u chart are based on the Poisson probability distribution discussed in Section 4.7. Poisson distributions have a mean, λ, and a standard deviation equal to the square root of the average, $\sqrt{\lambda}$.

The c Chart for the Number of Nonconformities When Areas of Opportunity Are the Same Size

To construct a c chart, we estimate the process average, λ, with $\bar{c}$, and the process standard deviation, $\sqrt{\lambda}$, with $\sqrt{\bar{c}}$. The center line is represented by our estimate of the process average, $\bar{c}$, and can be calculated as follows:

$$\text{Centerline} = \bar{c} = \frac{\text{Total number of events of interest}}{\text{Number of areas of opportunity}} \qquad (6.14a)$$

or, in summation notation,

$$\bar{c} = \frac{\displaystyle\sum_{i=1}^{k} c_i}{k} \qquad (6.14b)$$

where

c_i = the number of events or nonconformities associated with unit i

k = the number of areas of opportunity

The standard deviation of a Poisson process, $\sqrt{\lambda}$, is estimated by $\sqrt{\bar{c}}$, so the upper control limit for the c chart is

$$\text{UCL} = \bar{c} + 3\sqrt{\bar{c}} \qquad (6.15a)$$

and the lower control limit is

$$\text{LCL} = \bar{c} - 3\sqrt{\bar{c}} \qquad (6.15b)$$

Once the control chart is constructed using trial limits, it is examined for out-of-control signals or patterns. All five rules for detecting out-of-control signals and patterns presented in Section 6.2.2 can be used. Because the Poisson distribution is nonsymmetrical or skewed, the risk of false alarms is not evenly distributed above the upper control limit and below the lower control limit. This asymmetry will not generally cause a problem when $\bar{c}$ is equal to or greater than 20, because in that case the Poisson distribution can be approximated well by the normal distribution. In cases where the average count is less than 20, we should interpret charts cautiously (and not use rules 2 to 4 regarding the 1σ and 2σ limits in looking for out-of-control signals).

To illustrate an application of the c chart, we consider data collected by a supervising engineer. The data are presented in Table 6.3 and represent the number of design changes necessary in designs submitted by 20 engineers that work in her division. In this example, the events being counted are the design changes requested by the supervising engineer before she would accept the designs submit-

TABLE 6.3

NUMBER OF ERRORS MADE BY DESIGN ENGINEERS IN A ONE-YEAR PERIOD

Engineer	Number of Design Changes
Alice	4
Basher	7
Darryl	10
Fayad	7
Gina	12
Guillermo	8
Juanita	6
Kathy	4
Linda	2
Mark	6
Marla	5
Mitchell	6
Nora	3
Paul	5
Sharyn	3
Susan	4
Thomas	7
Vera	5
Walter	10
Whitney	6

 DESIGN

ted, over a one-year period. The area of opportunity is the same for all engineers being evaluated (assuming that during the year each engineer had the same opportunity to make errors, i.e., worked the same number of days and handled approximately the same number of designs), so the c chart can be used to evaluate the group. The supervising engineer's data are presented in Table 6.3.

In this example, the total number of errors made by the engineers is 120, and there are 20 areas of opportunity. From Equation (6.14b), the center line is

$$\bar{c} = \frac{\sum\limits_{i=1}^{k} c_i}{k}$$

$$\text{Center line} = \bar{c} = \frac{120}{20} = 6.0$$

The upper control limit is calculated by using Equation (6.15a) as

$$\text{UCL} = \bar{c} + 3\sqrt{\bar{c}}$$
$$\text{UCL} = 6.0 + 3\sqrt{6.0}$$
$$\text{UCL} = 6.0 + 7.35$$
$$\text{UCL} = 13.35$$

The lower control limit is calculated by using Equation (6.15b) as

$$\text{LCL} = \bar{c} - 3\sqrt{\bar{c}}$$
$$\text{LCL} = 6.0 - 3\sqrt{6.0}$$
$$\text{LCL} = 6.0 - 7.35 = -1.35$$
$$\text{LCL} = 0.0$$

A negative value was obtained for the LCL, so a value of 0.0 can be used for the lower control limit, or the lower control limit can be considered not to exist.

This is an example of a control chart in which a longitudinal time factor *cannot* be considered, because the data represent a cross-sectional study of people evaluated over the same time period. Review of the control chart for these data, presented in Figure 6.15, shows no evidence to indicate a special cause of variation

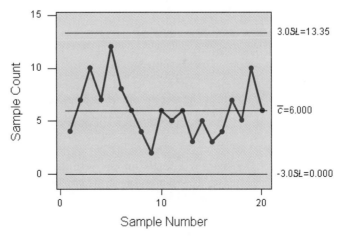

Figure 6.15 c chart obtained from MINITAB for errors by engineers

operating on the system. Without the control chart, it would seem that Gina, having made 12 errors, is not doing as well as Linda, who made only two errors. The control chart allows us to make meaningful comparisons of engineering performance and indicates that all engineers are operating within the system. We have *no evidence* that differences in their performance (as measured by the number of errors made) is due to anything other than common causes or chance. If personnel decisions to be made are based on these data alone, all engineers should be treated the same. If the performance of the group is not acceptable, it is up to management to change the system to obtain improvements.

u Chart for the Number of Nonconformities When Areas of Opportunity Vary in Size

In some situations, the areas of opportunity vary in size from subgroup to subgroup. In such situations, the *u* chart should be used. The statistic that is computed for each group is u_i, the ratio of the number of events of interest, such as the number of nonconformities, to the size of the area of opportunity in which the events occur. Therefore, for inspection unit i,

$$u_i = \frac{c_i}{n_i} \tag{6.16}$$

where

c_i = number of events observed in inspection unit i

n_i = the size of the area of opportunity, inspection unit, or subgroup of items i

The average number of events per area of opportunity, $\bar{u}$, can then be calculated as

$$\bar{u} = \frac{\sum\limits_{i=1}^{k} c_i}{\sum\limits_{i=1}^{k} n_i} \tag{6.17}$$

where

c_i = number of events observed in inspection unit i

n_i = the size of the ith area of opportunity, inspection unit, or subgroup

k = number of areas of opportunity

The size of the area of opportunity or subgroup varies from subgroup to subgroup, so the calculation of the control limits will vary from subgroup to subgroup. There is an inverse relationship between the size of the area of opportunity and the distance between the upper and lower control limits. Large subgroups or areas of opportunity will result in narrow limits; small subgroups or areas of opportunity will result in more widely spaced limits. One method to deal with this phenomenon is to calculate exact limits for each subgroup size. This method is the most desirable from the standpoint of statistical sensitivity, but it can be computationally complex. The increasing availability of statistical software, however, makes this method more feasible and easier to employ than it has been in the past. When this method is used, the upper control limit for inspection unit i is calculated as

$$UCL = \bar{u} + 3\sqrt{\frac{\bar{u}}{n_i}} \qquad (6.18a)$$

and the lower control limit is calculated as

$$LCL = \bar{u} - 3\sqrt{\frac{\bar{u}}{n_i}} \qquad (6.18b)$$

Once the control limits and data points are plotted, the chart is examined to see whether any out-of-control signals are present. Any points plotting above the upper control limit or below the lower control limit indicate that a special cause might be operating. Because the control limits are different for each observation, obtaining zones is computationally complex and is not generally recommended. When considering other out-of-control patterns, the variable control limits should be kept in mind and determinations should be made cautiously.

As an example, consider the director of operations for a large airline who was interested in improving the process of baggage handling at a particular airport. Records were available that reported the number of claims for lost baggage that were processed each day for a period of one month. The airline's traffic varied over the month; the number of daily flights was also recorded. Unfortunately, the exact number of bags carried per flight was not available. Therefore, the number of flights per day was considered as the area of opportunity. Table 6.4 on page 262 presents these data.

The center line is calculated from Equation (6.17) as

$$\text{Center line} = \bar{u} = \frac{\sum_{i=1}^{k} c_i}{\sum_{i=1}^{k} n_i}$$

$$\bar{u} = \frac{806}{5,379} = 0.1498$$

The upper and lower control limits for each day can then be calculated, by using Equations (6.18a) and (6.18b), as

$$UCL = \bar{u} + 3\sqrt{\frac{\bar{u}}{n_i}}$$

$$= 0.1498 + 3\sqrt{\frac{0.1498}{n_i}}$$

TABLE 6.4

NUMBER OF AIRLINE FLIGHTS PER DAY AND BAGGAGE CLAIMS FOR A 30-DAY PERIOD

Day	Area of Opportunity Number of Flights (n_i)	Number of Claims c_i	Claims per Flight u_i
1	172	14	0.0814
2	181	23	0.1271
3	168	17	0.1012
4	188	25	0.1330
5	157	27	0.1720
6	203	42	0.2069
7	191	35	0.1832
8	169	29	0.1716
9	180	30	0.1667
10	165	23	0.1394
11	185	15	0.0811
12	162	27	0.1667
13	200	41	0.2050
14	196	50	0.2551
15	172	23	0.1337
16	179	28	0.1564
17	164	20	0.1220
18	186	13	0.0699
19	160	2	0.1625
20	198	42	0.2121
21	195	38	0.1949
22	170	23	0.1353
23	175	28	0.1600
24	166	19	0.1145
25	185	26	0.1405
26	162	14	0.0864
27	195	30	0.1538
28	206	37	0.1796
29	175	17	0.0971
30	174	24	0.1379
Total	5,379	$\sum_{i=1}^{k} c_i = 806$	

BAGGAGE

and

$$\text{LCL} = \bar{u} - 3\sqrt{\frac{\bar{u}}{n_i}}$$

$$= 0.1498 - 3\sqrt{\frac{0.1498}{n_i}}$$

The control limits are different for each subgroup, because the size of the area of opportunity n_i differs for each subgroup. The daily values of n_i, u_i, and the upper and lower control limits associated with each are presented in Table 6.5, and the control chart obtained from MINITAB is presented in Figure 6.16.

TABLE 6.5

VALUES OF n_i, u_i, AND THE UPPER AND LOWER CONTROL LIMITS FOR THE BAGGAGE-CLAIM DATA

Day	n_i	u_i	LCL	UCL
1	172	0.0814	0.0613	0.2383
2	181	0.1271	0.0635	0.2361
3	168	0.1012	0.0602	0.2394
4	188	0.1330	0.0651	0.2345
5	157	0.1720	0.0571	0.2425
6	203	0.2069	0.0683	0.2313
7	191	0.1832	0.0658	0.2338
8	169	0.1716	0.0605	0.2391
9	180	0.1667	0.0633	0.2363
10	165	0.1394	0.0594	0.2402
11	185	0.0811	0.0644	0.2352
12	162	0.1667	0.0586	0.2410
13	200	0.2050	0.0677	0.2319
14	196	0.2551	0.0669	0.2327
15	172	0.1337	0.0613	0.2383
16	179	0.1564	0.0630	0.2366
17	164	0.1220	0.0585	0.2411
18	186	0.0699	0.0693	0.2303
19	160	0.1625	0.0580	0.2416
20	198	0.2121	0.0673	0.2323
21	195	0.1949	0.0667	0.2329
22	170	0.1353	0.0607	0.2389
23	175	0.1600	0.0620	0.2376
24	166	0.1145	0.0597	0.2399
25	185	0.1405	0.0644	0.2352
26	162	0.0864	0.0586	0.2410
27	195	0.1538	0.0667	0.2329
28	206	0.1796	0.0689	0.2307
29	175	0.0971	0.0620	0.2376
30	174	0.1379	0.0617	0.2379

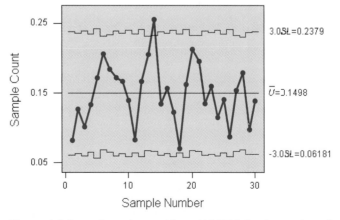

Figure 6.16   *u* chart obtained from MINITAB for the number of baggage claims

Examining Figure 6.16, and using our rules for determining out-of-control signals, we observe that rule 1, concerning points plotting outside the upper and lower control limits, is violated. Point 14 falls above the UCL. When an investigation was conducted into a possible special cause for point 14, it was determined that this day represented the end of a holiday weekend, in which flights were packed to capacity, and that a severe rainstorm was encountered at the airport on that day. Management decided that, in the future, extra baggage-handling personnel would be assigned to busy airports in such situations. Because the special cause could be eliminated, new trial control chart limits should be calculated without the data represented by point 14, to determine whether the system is stable in the absence of this single special cause. If evidence of special causes is not apparent on the revised chart, the control limits are extended, and new data are plotted on the chart as the process continues to be monitored.

PROBLEMS

6.9 Rolls of foil sheeting to be used in solar-collector assemblies are examined after their calendering, and the number of surface imperfections, such as pinholes and imbedded particulate matter, in 100-square-meter samples are counted. The following table presents the number of surface imperfections in 40 consecutive 100-square-meter samples of foil.

(a) Construct a *c* chart for these data.
(b) Is the process in a state of statistical control? Why?
(c) If the process is not in a state of control, eliminate out-of-control points, and recalculate the trial control limits.

6.10 Numerous quality checks are performed on subway cars as part of a final inspection. One check is on the number of rivets that are missing (nonconforming) in the body of the car. The following table presents the number of missing rivets found in 50 consecutively manufactured cars.

Sample Number	Number Imperfections	Sample Number	Number Imperfections
1	1	21	4
2	3	22	0
3	2	23	5
4	7	24	2
5	8	25	4
6	9	26	4
7	6	27	7
8	6	28	12
9	3	29	6
10	3	30	5
11	6	31	4
12	4	32	2
13	7	33	3
14	4	34	2
15	3	35	4
16	6	36	5
17	5	37	7
18	3	38	4
19	4	39	3
20	3	40	1

SURFACE

Car Number	Number of Missing Rivets	Car Number	Number of Missing Rivets
1	12	26	10
2	9	27	17
3	19	28	11
4	11	29	6
5	10	30	12
6	7	31	10
7	13	32	14
8	10	33	8
9	15	34	13
10	9	35	11
11	14	36	9
12	12	37	16
13	7	38	5
14	14	39	11
15	11	40	15
16	17	41	10

(Continued)

Car Number	Number of Missing Rivets	Car Number	Number of Missing Rivets
17	8	42	12
18	14	43	16
19	12	44	8
20	25	45	13
21	6	46	9
22	13	47	7
23	13	48	14
24	11	49	12
25	16	50	15

SUBWAY

(a) Construct a *c* chart for these data.
(b) Is the process in a state of statistical control? Why?
(c) If the process is not in a state of control, eliminate out-of-control points, and recalculate the trial control limits.

6.11 A utility company that provides electric, gas, and steam services maintains 700 service vehicles. The vehicle count has remained constant over several years. The company monitors the number of vehicle accidents each month. The following table presents the number of accidents each month for the years 1990 to 1995.

YEAR

Month	1990	1991	1992	1993	1994	1995
January	11	12	8	6	4	6
February	6	8	5	4	8	2
March	7	8	11	5	4	8
April	8	7	3	4	2	6
May	4	9	11	7	8	7
June	7	7	12	6	3	7
July	3	7	9	6	8	6
August	9	8	4	10	5	7
September	8	10	2	2	2	6
October	5	3	6	4	1	6
November	6	12	5	6	2	3
December	12	5	6	7	11	4

ACCIDENT

(a) Use the first 30 months of data to calculate trial limits and construct a *c* chart for these data. (For this problem, assume that all months have equal number of work days.)
(b) Is the process in a state of statistical control? Why?
(c) If the process is not in a state of statistical control, eliminate out-of-control points, and recalculate the trial control limits.

(d) Extend the trial control limits and plot the additional data. Is the process in a state of statistical control?
(e) The utility instituted a "safe driver" program in July, 1992. An eight-hour defensive-driving course was offered free of charge during company hours, at company locations. Any employee who wished could enroll in the course and be paid for it. Employees and their family members are allowed to take the course every two years. Does this information help to explain the results you obtained in (d)? Why?
(f) What advice would you give about future monitoring of the number of accidents?
(g) Use the first 30 months of data to calculate trial limits, and construct a *u chart* for these data. (For this problem, consider that all months do not have the same number of work days.)
(h) Compare your *c* chart and *u* chart. Does the type of chart used affect the conclusions you draw from the data? Why?

6.12 Developers of a new web site are interested in monitoring the number of hits on the site. They recorded the number of hits on the site during the first 50 days the site was operating. Their data are as follows.

Day	Number Hits	Day	Number Hits
1	20	26	19
2	15	27	17
3	19	28	21
4	24	29	20
5	11	30	15
6	20	31	12
7	32	32	17
8	22	33	22
9	14	34	14
10	23	35	18
11	17	36	20
12	16	37	22
13	27	38	15
14	18	39	24
15	13	40	19
16	19	41	20
17	21	42	16
18	18	43	19
19	20	44	21
20	30	45	23
21	17	46	18
22	19	47	20
23	22	48	24
24	18	49	21
25	23	50	28

WWWSITE

(a) Construct a c chart for these data.
(b) Is the process in a state of statistical control? Why?
(c) If the process is not in a state of control, eliminate out-of-control points, and recalculate the trial control limits.

6.13 A software development firm monitors the number of code errors in subroutines and programs under development. Programmers monitor their own work and record the number of lines of code and the number of errors in the initial version of each subroutine and program that they write. The table below presents the number of lines of code and the number of errors reported by the team of programmers.

Number Lines	Number of Code Errors	Number Lines	Number of Code Errors
881	31	398	17
277	14	977	33
966	75	203	5
512	26	314	15
214	2	761	20
217	24	728	22
521	21	152	9
61	1	54	3
264	25	129	8
235	5	541	28
243	18	995	84
289	18	100	7
270	25	69	5
962	33	548	33
165	9	615	21
43	3	227	6
917	41	428	14
51	5	636	15
224	9	287	11
486	21	134	3

ERRORCDE

(a) Construct a u chart for these data.
(b) Is the process in a state of statistical control? Why?
(c) If the process is not in a state of control, eliminate out-of-control points, and recalculate the trial control limits.

6.14 Final inspection of specialty wood paneling checks for flaws in surface finishing caused by uneven application of the final coat of finishing material or by the presence of inclusions of particulate and other foreign matter. Sheets of plywood paneling are manufactured in four sizes: 4 ft $\times$ 8 ft (32 square

feet), 4 ft $\times$ 4 ft (16 square feet), 2 ft $\times$ 10 ft (20 square feet), and 4 ft $\times$ 10 ft (40 square feet). The following table presents the panel size and the number of imperfections in the final finish found at inspection for 50 sheets of paneling.

Panel	Size (square feet)	Number of Flaws	Panel	Size (square feet)	Number of Flaws
1	32	0	26	16	1
2	32	1	27	16	0
3	32	4	28	16	2
4	20	0	29	40	0
5	16	0	30	20	0
6	16	0	31	20	0
7	20	0	32	40	1
8	32	3	33	40	2
9	16	1	34	40	2
10	32	2	35	32	0
11	32	0	36	32	1
12	20	1	37	20	2
13	16	0	38	32	1
14	16	3	39	32	3
15	16	1	40	16	2
16	40	1	41	32	2
17	32	0	42	16	0
18	32	2	43	16	1
19	20	1	44	32	1
20	32	0	45	20	0
21	40	6	46	40	0
22	40	0	47	32	0
23	20	3	48	40	1
24	16	0	49	40	5
25	16	0	50	40	4

FLAWS

(a) Construct a u chart for these data.
(b) Is the process in a state of statistical control? Why?
(c) If the process is not in a state of control, eliminate out-of-control points, and recalculate the trial control limits.

6.15 A computer systems team was concerned about a data-management system. Each day, decisions needed to be made that related to the way in which records and data files were to be maintained. Some information was required to be maintained for one day, some for seven days, some for thirty days, some for a year, and some forever. Data that was to be maintained for more than seven days had to be stored remotely on disk cartridges off the production site. The data cartridges used for the remote off-site storage involved both an acquisition expense and a cost for maintaining and managing the remote storage system. In an effort to study the stability of the process, weekly reports for the past six months were obtained. The numbers of data cartridges sent for remote storage each week during this period are presented in the following table.

Week	Data Cartridges Sent
1	123
2	116
3	115
4	116
5	115
6	120
7	140
8	137
9	141
10	142
11	164
12	148
13	160

(*Continued*)

Week	Data Cartridges Sent
14	134
15	162
16	174
17	174
18	176
19	193
20	173
21	147
22	159
23	147
24	147

CARTS

(a) Construct a control chart for these data.
(b) Is the process in a state of statistical control? Why?
(c) If the process is not in a state of control, eliminate out-of-control points, and recalculate the trial control limits.

6.6 SUMMARY

In this chapter, we have presented a variety of attribute control charts. Figure 6.17 is a flow diagram useful in deciding which type of chart is most appropriate for monitoring a given process.

KEY TERMS

area of opportunity   256
attribute control charts   233
average run length   236
c chart   257
center line   234
common causes   231
cyclic pattern   239
false alarm   234
fraction nonconforming chart   247
lower control limit   234
mixture pattern   239
np chart   240
number conforming chart   240
out of statistical control   232
p chart   247

process capability   232
proportion nonconforming chart   247
run   236
run length   236
shift in process level   239
special causes   231
stable process   231
statistical control   231
stratification pattern   239
tampering   232
u chart   257
upper control limit   234
variables control charts   233
yield chart   240
zone boundaries   236

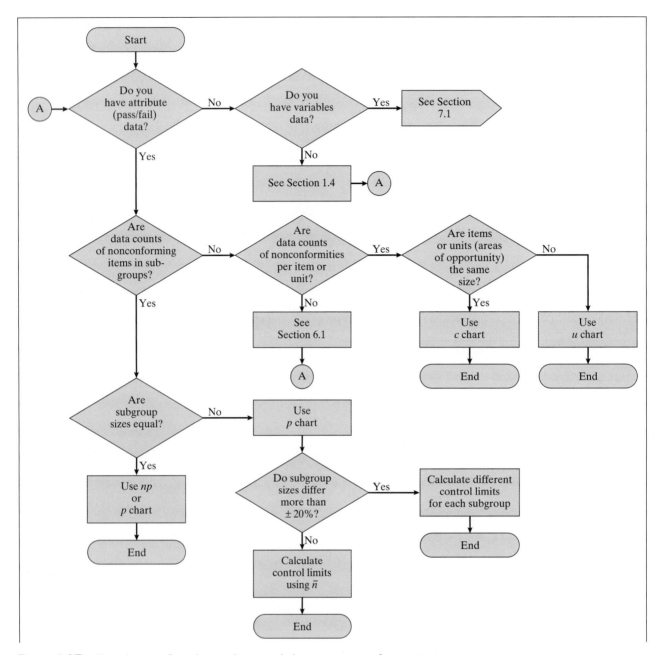

Figure 6.17   Flow diagram for selecting the control chart appropriate for monitoring a given process

CHAPTER REVIEW   *Checking Your Understanding*

6.16 What are the differences between common causes and special causes of variability?

6.17 When is a process considered stable?

6.18 When is a process in a state of statistical control?

6.19 How can statistical process control charts be used to increase quality?

6.20 What kinds of errors can be made when using a control chart?

6.21 How are the upper control limit and the lower control limit used to determine whether special causes are acting on the process?

6.22 What patterns would cause one to determine that a process is out of statistical control?

6.23 On which statistical distribution are *np* and *p* charts based?

6.24 On which statistical distribution are *c* and *u* charts based?

6.25 What are the assumptions for use of *np* and *p* charts?

6.26 What is a yield chart?

6.27 Where are the UCL and LCL usually placed on control charts in the United States?

6.28 Which charts are referred to as area of opportunity charts?

Chapter Review Problems

6.29 A medical transcription service enters medical data on patient files for hospitals. The service studied ways to improve the turnaround time (defined as the time between receiving data and time the client receives completed files). After studying the process, it was determined that turnaround time was increased by transmission errors. A transmission error was defined as data transmitted that did not go through as planned and needed to be re-transmitted. Each day, a sample of 125 record transmissions was randomly selected and evaluated for errors. The table below presents the number and proportion of transmissions with errors in samples of 125 records transmitted.

Date	Number of Errors	Proportion of Errors	Date	Number of Errors	Proportion of Errors
August:			*September:*		
1	6	0.048	3	14	0.112
2	3	0.024	4	6	0.048
5	4	0.032	5	7	0.056
6	4	0.032	6	3	0.024
7	9	0.072	9	10	0.080
8	0	0.000	10	7	0.056
9	0	0.000	11	5	0.040
12	8	0.064	12	0	0.000
13	4	0.032	13	3	0.024
14	3	0.024			
15	4	0.032			**TRANSMIT**
16	1	0.008			
19	10	0.080			
20	9	0.072			
21	3	0.024			
22	1	0.008			
23	4	0.032			
26	6	0.048			
27	3	0.024			
28	5	0.040			
29	1	0.008			
30	3	0.024			

(a) Construct an *np* control chart.

(b) Is the process in a state of statistical control? Why?

(c) Construct a *p* chart.

(d) Compare the results from the *np* chart with the results obtained from the *p* chart, and explain any similarities or differences.

6.30 The following data represent the findings from a study conducted at a factory that manufactures film canisters. Each day, 500 film canisters were sampled and inspected. The numbers of defective film canisters (nonconforming items) in each sample for a 32-day period were recorded as follows:

Day	# Non-Conforming	Day	# Non-Conforming
1	26	17	23
2	25	18	19
3	23	19	18
4	24	20	27
5	26	21	28
6	20	22	24
7	21	23	26
8	27	24	23
9	23	25	27
10	25	26	28
11	22	27	24
12	26	28	22
13	25	29	20
14	29	30	25
15	20	31	27
16	19	32	19 **CANISTER**

(a) Construct an *np* control chart using the first 25 data points, to calculate trial limits.
(b) Is the process in a state of statistical control? Why?
(c) If the process is in control, extend the limits, and record data for days 26 through 32.
(d) Construct a *p* chart using the first 25 data points, to calculate trial limits.
(e) Compare the results from the *np* chart with the results obtained from the *p* chart, and explain any similarities or differences.

6.31 The information systems department of a hospital was concerned with the time it took for patients' medical records to be processed after discharge. They determined that all records should be processed within five days. Any record not processed within five days of discharge was considered nonconforming. The number of patients discharged and the number and proportion of records not processed within the five-day standard were recorded and are as follows:

Day	Number of Discharges	Number of Medical Records Not Processed within 5 Days	Proportion of Non-Conforming Items
1	54	13	0.241
2	63	23	0.365
3	110	38	0.345
4	105	35	0.333
5	131	40	0.305
6	137	44	0.321
7	80	16	0.200
8	63	21	0.333
9	75	18	0.240
10	92	24	0.261
11	105	27	0.257
12	112	43	0.384

(*Continued*)

Day	Number of Discharges	Number of Medical Records Not Processed within 5 Days	Proportion of Non-Conforming Items
13	120	25	0.208
14	95	21	0.221
15	72	11	0.153
16	128	24	0.188
17	126	33	0.262
18	106	38	0.358
19	129	39	0.302
20	136	74	0.544
21	94	31	0.330
22	74	15	0.203
23	107	45	0.421
24	135	53	0.393
25	124	57	0.460
26	113	28	0.248
27	140	38	0.271
28	83	21	0.253
29	62	10	0.161
30	106	45	0.425 **MEDREC**

(a) Construct a control chart for these data.
(b) Is the process in a state of statistical control? Why?
(c) If the process is not in a state of statistical control, eliminate out-of-control points, and recalculate the trial control limits.

6.32 An automobile manufacturer subjects vehicles to a comprehensive testing process for all mechanical functions before vehicles leave the plant. Ideally, it hopes to achieve a first-time pass on every vehicle tested. The following data were collected on 26 days during the period from September 27 to October 31, to check on whether the process is in control.

Day	Number of Vehicles Tested	Number of Conforming Vehicles 1st-Time Pass
September:		
27	350	294
30	345	286
October:		
1	335	285
2	318	273
3	293	234
4	331	278
7	318	267
8	353	282
9	308	268
10	331	295
11	331	281
12	341	283
14	329	270

(*Continued*)

Day	Number of Vehicles Tested	Number of Conforming Vehicles 1st-Time Pass
October:		
15	238	200
16	320	266
17	332	276
20	319	274
21	327	275
22	312	250
23	341	297
24	334	281
27	307	255
28	311	267
29	334	291
30	343	281
31	295	248 **VEHICLE**

(a) Construct a control chart for these data.

(b) Is the process in a state of statistical control? Why?

6.33 A company filled bulk orders for electronic telephones and was concerned about the number of units returned. As part of their investigation of the problem, they sampled orders and recorded order size and the number of telephones returned.

Order	Order Size	Number Returned	Fraction Returned
1	350	12	0.034
2	420	29	0.069
3	384	23	0.060
4	840	33	0.039
5	405	20	0.049
6	752	40	0.053
7	409	13	0.032
8	385	28	0.073
9	780	24	0.031
10	820	46	0.056
11	392	25	0.064
12	818	24	0.029
13	399	23	0.058
14	355	21	0.059
15	414	22	0.053
16	754	44	0.058
17	366	24	0.066
18	839	34	0.041
19	411	28	0.068
20	387	26	0.067
21	353	18	0.051
22	415	28	0.068
23	390	17	0.044
24	358	28	0.078
25	411	22	0.053 **PHONES**

(a) Construct a control chart for these data.

(b) Is the process in a state of statistical control? Why?

(c) If the process is not in a state of control, eliminate points falling beyond the UCL and LCL, and recalculate the trial control limits.

6.34 A large metropolitan hospital provides laboratory services to physicians in the community. A physician who submits a specimen for analysis must fill out a form requesting services, stating the types of analyses requested and billing information. These lab slips also contain demographic information on the patient. Incomplete slips must be returned and resubmitted. This process is costly and can increase the time required to complete analyses. In an effort to establish whether the process was in a state of statistical control, data were collected for a 30-day period. The number of lab slips, the number of slips missing demographic information, and the fraction of incomplete slips are as follows.

Date	Number of Lab Slips Received	Number of Lab Slips Missing Demographics	Fraction Incomplete Lab Slips
September:			
16	187	11	0.0588
17	216	15	0.0694
18	144	9	0.0625
19	166	7	0.0422
20	192	16	0.0833
23	158	10	0.0633
24	146	9	0.0616
25	199	7	0.0352
26	221	10	0.0452
27	159	4	0.0252
30	222	6	0.0270
October:			
1	230	16	0.0696
2	214	15	0.0701
3	198	8	0.0404
4	147	8	0.0544
7	159	7	0.0440
8	145	4	0.0276
9	202	8	0.0396
10	217	11	0.0507
11	204	16	0.0784
14	229	13	0.0568
15	219	8	0.0365
16	211	5	0.0237
17	154	9	0.0584
18	188	13	0.0691
21	146	7	0.0479
22	172	12	0.0698
23	158	7	0.0443
24	148	6	0.0405
25	190	8	0.0421

LABSLIP

(a) Construct a control chart for these data.
(b) Is the process in a state of statistical control? Why?
(c) If the process is not in a state of control, eliminate out-of-control points, and recalculate the trial control limits.

6.35 A jewelry-manufacturing company has a data-processing department with 115 terminals in various locations in its building. A technician is responsible for investigating and correcting problems with the terminals. She was concerned with the rate at which terminals developed problems and collected the following data to see whether the system was in a state of statistical control.

Day	Number With Problems	Proportion With Problems	Day	Number With Problems	Proportion With Problems
1	2	0.0174	16	3	0.0261
2	5	0.0435	17	4	0.0348
3	3	0.0261	18	8	0.0696
4	13	0.1130	19	4	0.0348
5	8	0.0696	20	2	0.0174
6	6	0.0522	21	2	0.0174
7	12	0.1043	22	4	0.0348
8	1	0.0087	23	7	0.0609
9	1	0.0087	24	10	0.0870
10	5	0.0435	25	6	0.0522
11	7	0.0609	26	5	0.0435
12	10	0.0870	27	5	0.0435
13	5	0.0435	28	9	0.0783
14	6	0.0522	29	1	0.0087
15	9	0.0783	30	4	0.0348

JEWELRY

(a) Construct a control chart for these data.
(b) Is the process in a state of statistical control? Why?
(c) If the process is not in a state of control, eliminate out-of-control points, and recalculate the control limits.

6.36 A commuter railroad in a large northeastern city runs 122 trains from suburban areas into the city each weekday. A survey of rider satisfaction indicated that commuters were very concerned that trains arrive on time. Before making changes to the system to increase the proportion of on-time arrivals, the railroad wanted to know whether the proportion of on-time arrivals was in a state of statistical control. The number of late trains for 30 weekdays is as follows:

Day	Number Late	Day	Number Late
1	3	8	3
2	1	9	4
3	1	10	5
4	4	11	6
5	5	12	1
6	4	13	7
7	6	14	4

(*Continued*)

Day	Number Late	Day	Number Late
15	4	23	2
16	7	24	4
17	3	25	4
18	4	26	5
19	7	27	4
20	5	28	6
21	2	29	1
22	6	30	2 **RRLATE**

(a) Construct an np control chart for these data.
(b) Is the process in a state of statistical control? Why?
(c) If the process is not in a state of control, eliminate out-of-control points, and recalculate the trial control limits.
(d) Construct a p control chart based on proportion of on-time arrivals.
(e) Is the process in a state of statistical control? Why?
(f) If the process is not in a state of control, eliminate out-of-control points, and recalculate the trial control limits.
(g) Compare the np and p charts. How are they different and how are they similar?

6.37 A telephone company monitors customer satisfaction with its directory assistance by sampling customers. Up to 70 customer interviews are done monthly. If a customer expresses dissatisfaction with the service, the company considers it an alert and further investigates the problem. The number of customers interviewed each month and the number of alerts per month are presented for a 30-month period.

Month	Interviews	Alerts	Month	Interviews	Alerts
1	67	8	16	69	5
2	68	6	17	69	2
3	70	3	18	69	8
4	65	5	19	70	9
5	69	9	20	56	1
6	70	2	21	69	5
7	67	4	22	70	4
8	69	7	23	70	11
9	69	3	24	68	4
10	68	8	25	69	6
11	69	5	26	68	4
12	70	5	27	70	7
13	67	6	28	70	4
14	70	4	29	68	3
15	69	11	30	67	2 **ALERT**

(a) Construct a control chart for these data.
(b) Is the process in a state of statistical control? Why?
(c) If the process is not in a state of control, eliminate out-of-control points, and recalculate the trial control limits.

6.38 The management of a city rapid-transit system is concerned about the number of accidents reported and would like to know whether the number of accidents is in a state of statistical control before instituting changes in procedure. The numbers of accidents reported each week for a 52-week period are as follows.

Month	Week	Number of Accidents	Month	Week	Number of Accidents
January	1	175	July	26	134
	2	111		27	141
	3	77		28	98
	4	106		29	55
February	5	116		30	85
	6	57	August	31	101
	7	119		32	67
	8	109		33	98
March	9	106		34	96
	10	128	September	35	94
	11	104		36	82
	12	107		37	135
April	13	113		38	95
	14	99	October	39	86
	15	119		40	73
	16	99		41	101
May	17	112		42	113
	18	99		43	124
	19	76	November	44	110
	20	88		45	124
	21	76		46	108
June	22	98		47	81
	23	109	December	48	93
	24	100		49	111
	25	85		50	123
				51	103
				52	169

ACCIDENTS

(a) Construct a control chart for these data.

(b) Is the process in a state of statistical control? Why?

(c) If the process is not in a state of control, can you identify a special cause that may have operated on the system?

6.39 A retail chain maintains a centralized warehouse facility and is interested in reviewing the staff allocation at the warehouse. The staff required for warehouse functions is known to be dependent on the number of deliveries to the warehouse. The number of incoming deliveries each day for 32 days is as follows:

Day	Deliveries	Day	Deliveries
1	37	9	32
2	17	10	33
3	22	11	36
4	19	12	24
5	21	13	23
6	20	14	36
7	32	15	22
8	36	16	26

(*Continued*)

Day	Deliveries	Day	Deliveries
17	33	25	28
18	19	26	33
19	18	27	30
20	45	28	37
21	26	29	16
22	15	30	24
23	41	31	28
24	13	32	16 **WAREHSE**

(a) Construct a control chart for these data, using the first 25 data points to calculate trial limits.
(b) Is the process in a state of statistical control? Why?
(c) If the process is not in a state of control, eliminate out-of-control points, and recalculate the control limits.
(d) If the system is in control, extend the control limits and plot points 26 through 32.
(e) Can management forecast the number of deliveries and the number of people needed? Why?

6.40 A director of telecommunications systems is concerned with complaints of static and other electronic interference on telephone lines. He institutes a procedure whereby randomly selected calls are recorded and electronically analyzed for the presence of interference. Because call duration varies, he also records the length of each call in seconds. His data for length of calls and the number of incidents of interference for the first 25 calls sampled are as follows.

Call Number	Call Length	Number of Incidents	Call Number	Call Length	Number of Incidents
1	30	1	14	65	5
2	35	8	15	50	9
3	25	2	16	46	4
4	30	5	17	38	4
5	30	4	18	35	7
6	40	7	19	40	4
7	60	8	20	50	3
8	60	6	21	50	4
9	55	3	22	30	2
10	25	3	23	35	4
11	40	5	24	50	6
12	45	7	25	20	1
13	50	5			**STATIC**

(a) Construct a control chart for these data.
(b) Is the system that is causing the interference in a state of statistical control? Why?
(c) If the process is not in a state of control, eliminate out-of-control points, and recalculate the trial control limits.

6.41 A wallpaper manufacturer performs checks on the quality of the print on rolls of wallpaper by sampling rolls and examining them for such printing flaws as discoloration, spots, lines, creases, and imperfect color matching. Rolls are all 56 feet long but come in different widths. Presented on page 278 are the sizes of rolls in square feet and the numbers of imperfections found for each of 25 rolls sampled.

Roll Number	Size	Number of Imperfections	Roll Number	Size	Number of Imperfections
1	100	7	14	100	5
2	112	9	15	126	16
3	100	14	16	126	10
4	112	8	17	112	13
5	100	9	18	100	4
6	126	33	19	126	11
7	100	9	20	112	8
8	126	15	21	112	10
9	112	14	22	112	23
10	100	6	23	126	7
11	100	11	24	112	29
12	112	17	25	126	17
13	126	12			**WALLPAPR**

(a) Construct a control chart for these data.
(b) Is the printing process in a state of statistical control? Why?
(c) If the process is not in a state of control, eliminate out-of-control points, and recalculate the trial control limits.

6.42 The manager of a regional office of a telephone company has the responsibility of processing requests for additions, changes, or deletions of telephone service. A service-improvement team studies such orders in terms of central office equipment and facilities required to process orders. They find that errors requiring correction should be reduced. Before suggesting changes in the process, they decide to monitor the number of errors and determine whether the system is stable. Their data collected over a 30-day period are as follows.

Day	Number of Orders	Number Corrections	Day	Number of Orders	Number Corrections
1	690	80	16	831	91
2	676	88	17	816	80
3	896	74	18	701	96
4	707	94	19	761	78
5	694	70	20	851	85
6	765	95	21	678	65
7	788	73	22	915	74
8	794	103	23	698	68
9	694	100	24	821	72
10	784	103	25	750	101
11	812	70	26	600	91
12	759	83	27	744	64
13	781	64	28	698	67
14	682	64	29	820	105
15	802	72	30	732	112 **CORRECT**

(a) Construct a control chart for these data.
(b) Is the request process in a state of statistical control? Why?
(c) If the process is not in a state of control, eliminate out-of-control points, and recalculate the trial control limits.

6.43 Collect your own data on a simulated process by using a standard 52-card deck of playing cards. For purposes of this simulation, face or picture cards (king, queen and jack) will be considered nonconforming. Shuffle the deck of cards well and deal a five-card hand. Count and record the number of face cards and replace the cards in the deck. Continue shuffling the deck and dealing hands until you have recorded data for 25 samples of size $n = 5$.

    (a) Construct a control chart for these data.

    (b) Is the simulated process in a state of statistical control? Why?

    (c) If the process is not in a state of control, can you identify any special cause or causes operating on your process?

    (d) Repeat (a), (b), and (c) using data collected on 25 samples of size $n = 10$ (that is, 10-card hands). Compare the results obtained with those for samples of size $n = 5$. Discuss.

6.44 Collect your own data on a simulated process. To do this, you will need a set of colored poker chips and a brown paper bag. Select 40 white chips and 10 red chips, and place them in the bag. Shake the bag well to ensure that the chips are well mixed. Select samples of size $n = 5$ chips from the bag. Do not look into the bag while selecting your sample. After selecting your sample, count and record the number of red chips it contains. Return the chips to the bag, and shake it to mix well. Repeat sampling 5 chips, counting and recording the number of red chips until you have obtained data on 25 samples. Remember to replace sampled chips and shake the bag after drawing each sample.

    (a) Construct a control chart for this process.

    (b) Is the simulated process in a state of statistical control? Why?

    (c) If the process is not in a state of control, can you identify any special cause or causes operating on your process?

    (d) If the process is not in a state of control, eliminate points falling above the UCL or below the LCL, and recalculate the control limits.

    (e) Once the chart indicates that the process is in control, extend the trial control limits, place an additional 5 red chips in the bag, and draw an additional 10 samples of size $n = 5$. Count the number of red chips in each sample after it is drawn, and record the results on the chart. According to your control chart, is the process still in a state of control? Why?

WHITNEY GOURMET CAT FOOD COMPANY CASE

As the team studying ways of reducing the nonconformance in the canned cat food began to investigate the current process, they found out that, in some instances, production failed to meet the requirements requested by the market forecasting group without undergoing expensive overtime costs. The team also realized that, although data had been collected concerning the level of production and the rate of nonconformance for an entire day, no data were available about the stability and magnitude of the rate of nonconformance and the production volume throughout the day. Their previous study of the process indicated that output could be nonconforming for a variety of reasons. The reasons broke down into two categories, those quality characteristics due to the can, and those characteristics concerning the fill weight of the container. Because these nonconformities stem from different sets of underlying causes, they decided to study them separately. The group assigned to study and reduce the nonconformities due to the can decided that, at fifteen-minute intervals during each shift, a subgroup of 100 cans would be selected and the number of non-conforming cans would be determined. In addition, a count would be made of the number of cans produced dur-

ing this time period. The results for a single day's production of kidney cat food and a single day's production of shrimp cat food are provided in Table WG6.1 on pages 280 and 281.

Exercises

WG6.1 (a) Construct all appropriate control charts for these data.

    (b) Is the process in terms of nonconforming cans in a state of statistical control? Explain.

    (c) What should the team recommend as the next step to be taken to study and improve the process?

    (d) What reasons relating to the canning process can you think of that might explain any lack of control that was been found?

    (e) Does there appear to be any relationship between the number of nonconforming cans and the production volume? What might explain this?

    (f) What graph might be useful to plot these two variables?

TABLE WG6.1

NUMBER OF NONCONFORMING CANS OBTAINED FROM SUBGROUPS OF 100 CANS OF KIDNEY AND SHRIMP CAT FOOD AND PRODUCTION VOLUME FOR FIFTEEN-MINUTE TIME PERIODS

Shift 1—Kidney

Time Interval	Number of Nonconforming Cans	Production Volume	Time Interval	Number of Nonconforming Cans	Production Volume
1	4	852	16	12	724
2	3	826	17	11	716
3	6	828	18	11	736
4	5	838	19	13	718
5	6	844	20	13	714
6	7	804	21	14	698
7	6	830	22	12	720
8	8	782	23	13	714
9	8	774	24	15	688
10	7	796	25	14	690
11	9	768	26	17	672
12	10	744	27	16	680
13	10	750	28	15	700
14	11	732	29	15	706
15	9	766	30	14	698

Shift 2—Kidney

Time Interval	Number of Nonconforming Cans	Production Volume	Time Interval	Number of Nonconforming Cans	Production Volume
1	6	830	16	15	684
2	6	836	17	14	696
3	8	794	18	13	716
4	6	820	19	16	678
5	9	776	20	16	674
6	10	758	21	18	662
7	9	774	22	15	680
8	11	742	23	16	684
9	12	732	24	17	668
10	11	746	25	17	660
11	11	728	26	19	652
12	13	714	27	18	650
13	14	700	28	17	650
14	13	702	29	16	676
15	12	726	30	15	678

Shift 1—Shrimp

Time Interval	Number of Nonconforming Cans	Production Volume	Time Interval	Number of Nonconforming Cans	Production Volume
1	4	882	6	7	824
2	3	900	7	6	830
3	6	848	8	8	782
4	5	868	9	6	834
5	6	844	10	7	816

(Continued)

TABLE WG6.1 (*Continued*)

Shift 1—Shrimp

Time Interval	Number of Nonconforming Cans	Production Volume	Time Interval	Number of Nonconforming Cans	Production Volume
11	6	818	21	6	798
12	5	844	22	4	840
13	6	810	23	3	854
14	4	862	24	6	788
15	7	806	25	5	790
16	8	784	26	7	792
17	6	816	27	7	780
18	7	796	28	6	820
19	7	818	29	5	826
20	5	834	30	5	828

Shift 2—Shrimp

Time Interval	Number of Nonconforming Cans	Production Volume	Time Interval	Number of Nonconforming Cans	Production Volume
1	6	820	16	8	774
2	5	846	17	6	816
3	7	808	18	7	776
4	8	798	19	8	758
5	9	794	20	10	714
6	9	804	21	9	758
7	7	790	22	8	770
8	10	742	23	8	764
9	9	774	24	10	708
10	10	756	25	9	750
11	8	778	26	6	822
12	7	794	27	8	780
13	7	790	28	9	760
14	8	762	29	7	786
15	6	826	30	10	748

WHITNEY2

MARIPHIL FARMS DAIRY CASE

Phase 1

The Mariphil Farms dairy provides a variety of milk, milk byproducts, juices, and other drinks for sale in a large metropolitan region. The dairy receives quantities of raw ingredients of these products from suppliers and processes these raw materials into finished products that are then packaged for sale to supermarkets and other retail outlets in the region. In the food industry, quality control has traditionally been critical not only to a company's image but also to its long-term survival. Any company involved in the processing of milk products must be concerned with the fact that bacteria growth can shorten the shelf life of a product and can even result in serious health hazards. Thus, industry-wide efforts have focused on cleanliness in processing and on careful monitoring of incoming material and finished packaged products.

A management committee formed to undertake quality improvements at the dairy meets to come to consensus concerning which area of operations should have the highest priority. After several brainstorming sessions, the group agrees that the first project to be undertaken should involve the bottling process for 1-gallon containers of milk.

One test of quality used in the dairy industry is a standard plate count. This consists of a laboratory test in which 1 milliliter of milk is plated on a specified agar (or culture medium) and bacteria growth is monitored over a given time period. Milk is processed in a batch and is typically uniform throughout the batch, so that a single sample is considered to be representative of the entire batch. This standard plate count can be taken from the incoming raw supply, from storage areas, postpasteurization storage areas, and after packaging. From the perspective of the consumer, the most important aspect of the standard plate count refers to the quality of the finished product, so the consumer would be most interested in the plate counts of the packaged product.

After discussion by the entire group, Frank Connelly, the plant manager, has been provided with an agreed-upon operational definition for measuring the quality of the milk in a batch. First, a single 1-gallon container of whole milk (3.25 percent butterfat) is selected from those packaged on each day. A standard plate count is used to determine bacteria growth. The quality measurement is represented by the number of colonies of bacteria present per milliliter of processed whole milk after holding the sample for two days under refrigeration at 45° Fahrenheit. The results for samples cultured during a six-week period (36 workdays) are presented in Table MP6.1.

TABLE MP6.1

COLONIES/ML OF WHOLE MILK FOR SAMPLES REPRESENTING 36 DAYS AT THE MARIPHIL FARMS DAIRY

Day	Colonies/ml	Day	Colonies/ml
1	290	19	240
2	260	20	310
3	270	21	270
4	230	22	260
5	300	23	270
6	310	24	310
7	300	25	280
8	280	26	260
9	230	27	300
10	300	28	290
11	260	29	270
12	300	30	270
13	270	31	250
14	230	32	240
15	290	33	280
16	310	34	260
17	260	35	250
18	270	36	280

MP1

Exercises

MP.6.1 (a) Is the process in a state of statistical control? Why?

(b) What recommendations should be made about improving the process?

STOP

Do Not Continue Until the Phase-1 Exercises Have Been Completed

Phase 2

Frank Connelly, the plant manager, although glad that there were no special-cause points above the upper control limit, was not satisfied with the level of bacteria counts. A team of individuals involved in various aspects of the whole-milk bottling process was convened to investigate alternative approaches for reducing the bacteria counts. After several brainstorming sessions, and after the posting of a preliminary fishbone diagram, a

MARIPHIL FARMS DAIRY CASE (*Continued*)

more complete fishbone diagram was developed. (See Figure MP6.1.) The team noted that the issue of cleanliness was listed on each of the five branches of the diagram. It was not possible to determine which colonies were due to which causes, so the team decided to begin by enhancing the training methods provided to all workers involved in the milk-bottling process. After the training had been completed and the workers were familiar with the new sanitation procedures, data were collected for a time period of six additional weeks. The results for this time period are presented in Table MP6.2.

Exercises

MP.2 **(a)** Plot the data for the first ten days shown in Table MP6.2 on the control chart constructed by using the data provided in Table MP6.1. Does the additional training show up as a special cause on this chart? Explain.

(b) Construct the appropriate control chart using only the data of Table MP6.2.

(b) Is the process in a state of statistical control? Why?

(c) What recommendations should be made about improving the process?

STOP

Do Not Continue Until the Phase-2 Exercises Have Been Completed

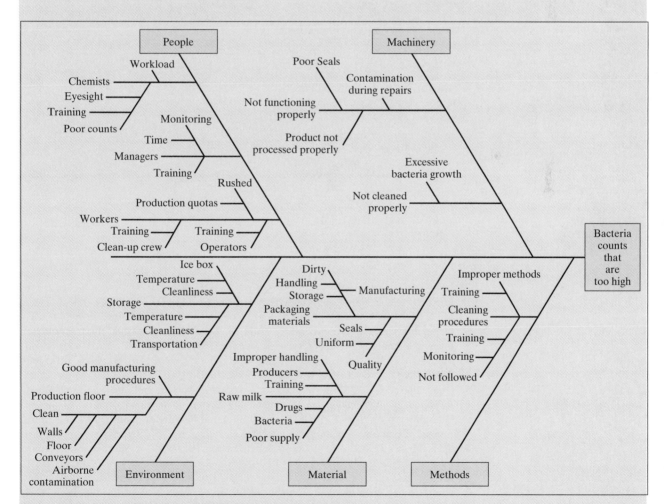

Figure MP6.1   Fishbone diagram for the milk-packaging process

MARIPHIL FARMS DAIRY CASE (*Concluded*)

TABLE MP6.2

COLONIES/ML OF WHOLE MILK FOR 36 DAYS AT THE MARIPHIL FARMS DAIRY AFTER THE NEW TRAINING METHODS WERE INSTITUTED

Day	Colonies/ml	Day	Colonies/ml
1	245	19	300
2	210	20	265
3	215	21	215
4	175	22	210
5	255	23	220
6	265	24	255
7	240	25	235
8	225	26	240
9	185	27	200
10	255	28	235
11	205	29	210
12	260	30	195
13	220	31	220
14	190	32	190
15	230	33	240
16	260	34	230
17	210	35	210
18	200	36	200

MP2

Phase 3

Frank examined the chart developed from the data of Table MP6.2. He discovered that the bacteria count for day 19 was above the upper control limit. He decided to speak with Helen Chan, the supervisor in the milk-bottling area, to see whether there was an explanation for this data points' being so high. Helen said that she needed to determine which people had been working in the bottling process that day. After some detailed study, she told Frank that, on this day, there were two relatively new workers assigned to the bottling process who had not received the new training. It is possible that their lack of familiarity with the methods caused the bacteria count to revert to the level experienced before the change in training. Frank and Helen made a note to themselves that in the future all workers must receive the new training prior to working in the milk-bottling process.

Exercises

MP.6.3 What should Frank do now concerning the data of Table MP6.2?

MP.6.4 Explain how the actions of Frank and Helen to avoid this particular problem in the future have resulted in quality improvement.

REFERENCES

1. *Microsoft Excel 2000;* Redmond, WA: Microsoft Corp, 1999
2. *MINITAB For Windows Version 12;* State College, PA: MINITAB, Inc., 1996
3. McCool, J. I. and T. Joyner-Motley; "Control charts applicable when the fraction conforming is small," *Journal of Quality Technology*, 30, 1998, 240–247
4. Montgomery, D. C; *Introduction to Statistical Quality Control,* 3rd ed.; New York: John Wiley, 1996
5. Quesenberry, C. P.; "SPC Q Charts for Start-Up Processes and Short or Long Runs," *Journal of Quality Technology,* 23 (1991), 213–224
6. Quesenberry, C. P.; "SPC Q Charts for a Binomial Parameter p: Short or Long Runs," *Journal of Quality Technology,* 23 (1991), 239–246
7. Quesenberry, C. P.; "SPC Q Charts for a Poisson Parameter λ: Short or Long Runs," *Journal of Quality Technology,* 23 (1991), 296–303
8. Rice, W. B.; *Control Charts in Factory Management;* New York: John Wiley, 1947
9. Shewhart, W. A.; *Economic Control of Quality of Manufactured Product;* New York: Van Nostrand-Reinhard, 1931, reprinted by the American Society for Quality Control, Milwaukee, 1980

10. Shewhart, W. A. and W. E. Deming; *Statistical Methods from the Viewpoint of Quality Control;* Washington, DC: Graduate School, Dept. of Agriculture, 1939, Dover Press, 1986

11. Walker, E., J. W. Philpot, and J. Clement; "False Signal Rates for the Shewhart Control Chart with Supplementary Runs Tests," *Journal of Quality Technology,* 23 (1991), 247–252

12. Western Electric; *Statistical Quality Control Handbook;* Indianapolis, IN: Western Electric Corporation, 1956

13. Woodall, W. H.; "Control charts based on attribute data: Bibliography and review," *Journal of Quality Technology,* 29 (1997), 172–183

APPENDIX 6.1   *Using Microsoft Excel for Attribute Control Charts*

Obtaining a *p* Chart by Using Microsoft Excel

To generate a *p* chart, use the **Control Charts | p Chart** choice of the PHStat add-in. As an example, consider the gauze sponges problem of section 6.4. To generate a *p* chart for the data of Table 6.1, open the **SPONGE.XLS** workbook, and click the **Data** sheet tab. Verify that the data of Table 6.1 on page 243 have been entered into columns A through D. Select **PHStat | Control Charts | p Chart**. In the *p* Chart dialog box, enter **B1:B33** in the Nonconformances Cell Range: edit box, and select the **First cell contains label** check box for this range. Select the **Size varies** option button. Enter **C1:C33** in the Sample/Subgroup Size Cell Range: edit box, and select the **First cell contains label** check box for this range. Enter *p* **Chart for Gauze Sponges** in the Output Title: edit box. Click the **OK** button. The add-in inserts two worksheets containing the data and calculations for the *p* chart and a chart sheet containing a *p* chart similar to the one shown in Figure 6.12 on page 248.

Using Microsoft Excel for *c* Charts

In section 6.5, we studied the *c* chart for the number of nonconforming items in an area of opportunity. Referring to equation (6.14) on page 257, we see that, in order to obtain the control limits for the *c* chart, we need to compute the average number of occurrences. For the data of Table 6.3 on page 258, the Data sheet is set up in the **DESIGN.XLS** workbook with the engineer number in column A and the number of errors in column B. The control limits and the center line can be computed on a Calculations sheet after selecting **Insert Worksheet.** To develop this Calculations sheet, enter appropriate labels in column A, in rows 3–6 for *c*bar, LCL, Center Line, and UCL. Then compute the average number of nonconforming items in cell B3 by using the formula **=SUM(Data!B:B)/COUNT(Data!B:B).** The lower control limit is obtained in cell B4 from the formula **=B3 −3 * SQRT(B3),** the center line in cell B5 is the contents of cell B3, and the upper control limit in cell B6 is obtained from the formula **=B3 + 3 * SQRT(B3).**

Now that the control limits and center line have been computed, we copy their values to columns C, D, and E of the Data sheet. After entering labels for LCL, Center, and UCL in cells C1 through E1, enter **=Calculations!$B$4** in C2, **=Calculations!$B$5** in D2, and **=Calculations!$B$6** in E2. Then, in order to plot a line for each of these variables across the days, copy the LCL value from C2 to C3 through C21, the center line value from D2 to D3 through D21, and the UCL value from E2 to E3 through E21.

We now use the Chart Wizard (see appendix 2.1) to obtain the control chart for the proportion. With the Data sheet active, select **Insert | Chart**.

In the Step 1 Dialog box, select the **Standard types** tab, and then select **XY (Scatter)** from the Chart type: list box. Select the first choice of the third row of chart Sub-types, the choice designated as "Scatter with data points connected by lines." Click the **Next** button.

In the Step 2 Dialog box, select the **Data Range** tab and enter **Data!A1:E21** in the Data range: edit box. Select the **Columns** option button in the Series in: group. Select the **Series** tab. Enter **=Data!A1:A21** in the Value (X) Axis edit box. Click the **Next** button.

In the Step 3 Dialog box, select the Titles tab. Enter "*c* Chart for Engineering Errors" in the Chart title: edit box, enter **Engineer** in the Category (X) axis: edit box, and enter **Number of Design Changes** in the Value (Y) axis: edit box. Select the **Gridlines** tab. Deselect all check boxes. Click the **Next** button.

In the Step 4 Dialog box, select the As new sheet: option button, and enter *c* chart in the edit box to the right of the option button. Click the **Finish** button.

APPENDIX 6.2 *Using MINITAB for Attribute Control Charts*

Using MINITAB for the *np* Chart

We illustrate the *p* chart by referring to the sponge data of Table 6.2 on page 250. Open the **SPONGE.MTW** file. Then select **Stat | Control Charts | np.** In the Variable edit box, enter **C2** or **'Nconfrm.'** Select the "Subgroups in" option button, and enter **C3** or **'Total'** in this edit box. Click the **OK** button. Note that the upper control limit, 35.04, is denoted by 3.0*SL*, the center line is labeled *Np*, and the lower control limit, 7.776, is called −3.0*SL*.

Using MINITAB for the *p* Chart

We illustrate the *p* chart by referring to the overweight truck data of Table 6.2 on page 250. Open the **TRUCKS. MTW** file, then select **Stat | Control Charts | P**. In the Variable edit box, enter **C2** or **'Overwgt'**. In the subgroups edit box area, there are two choices. If the subgroup sizes are equal, as they were in Table 6.1 on page 243, we can select the "Subgroup size" option button and enter the subgroup sample size in the edit box. If, however, the subgroup sizes are different (as they were in the overweight-truck data of Table 6.2), then select the Subgroups option button and enter **C2** or **'Trucks'** in this edit box. Click the **OK** button.

Note that the upper control limit, 0.09919, is denoted by 3.0*SL*, the center line is labeled *p*, and the lower control limit, 0.000, is called −3.0*SL*. Observe that the upper and lower control limit lines appear jagged. This is because MINITAB is computing different control limits for each day, ones based on the sample size on that day rather than on the average sample size.

Using MINITAB for the *c* Chart

For the data of Table 6.3 on page 258, open the **DESIGN.MTW** file. Select **Stat | Control Charts | C**. Enter **C2** or **'Design Changes'** in the Variable edit box. Click the **OK** button.

Using MINITAB for the *u* Chart

For the data of Table 6.4 on page 262, open the **BAGGAGE.MTW** file. Select **Stat | Control Charts | u**. Enter **C3** or **'Claims'** in the Variable edit box. Select the "Subgroups in" option button, and enter **C2** or **'Flights'** in its edit box. Click the **OK** button.

chapter
7
Statistical Process Control Charts II: Variables Control Charts

"We may dare to change things only when things be steady under our hands."

ARISTOTLE

USING STATISTICS

The quality of the water supplied by a municipal water company is of critical importance to members of the community. The water supplied must be tested on an ongoing basis for a variety of characteristics. Any changes that may occur to the water supply, particularly those that may have a negative impact on health, need to be ascertained as quickly as possible, so that improvements can be made to prevent similar problems.

7.1 INTRODUCTION TO VARIABLES CONTROL CHARTS

Whenever a quality characteristic is measured on a continuous variable, **variables control charts** can be used to monitor a process. Variables charts have an advantage over attribute charts, because variables measures contain more information than attributes measures. This fact makes variables charts more sensitive statistically and, therefore, more effective in detecting out-of-control states. When several special causes operate on a process, they can mask the effects of one another. This masking of effects is less likely to be a problem when variables charts are employed than when attribute charts are used.

Variables charts are usually used in pairs. One member of the pair monitors the inherent random variation of a process, while the second monitors variability in measures of process central tendency. When one is using variables charts, the chart that monitors inherent variability must be examined first. If this chart indicates that the process is not stable, interpretation of the chart for central tendency will be misleading. Both the variability and central tendency charts can be useful in detecting special causes and eliminating their effects, thereby reducing overall variability of process output.

287

7.2 RATIONAL SUBGROUPS AND SAMPLING DECISIONS

We begin construction of a variables chart by selecting samples or subgroups of process output for evaluation on a variables measure of a quality characteristic of interest. A measure of central tendency, such as the mean, and a measure of variability, such as the range or standard deviation, are then calculated for each subgroup, and these statistics are used to construct trial control limits. However, before we can begin to sample, several decisions must be made. We must decide sample size, frequency of sampling, whether we should sample consecutive units of output, and when in our process monitoring would be most effective.

Sample Size

Traditionally, as originally suggested by Shewhart, subgroup sizes of four or five have been used. In general, larger samples yield more powerful results than smaller samples and will permit detection of smaller shifts in process average. In Section 5.9, we noted that the standard deviation of a distribution of sample means $\sigma_{\bar{X}}$ (also referred to as the standard error of the mean) was equal to the standard deviation of the population of individual values divided by the square root of the sample size:

$$\sigma_{\bar{X}} = \frac{\sigma_X}{\sqrt{n}}$$

Therefore, larger sample sizes will result in smaller values of $\sigma_{\bar{X}}$.

Before we can decide on the best sample size to use, we must understand the size of the shift that we are interested in detecting and balance the cost of sampling against the risk of failing to detect a shift. Because large shifts will be detected even by very small samples, subgroups as small as $n = 2$ or $n = 3$ can be used when the cost of sampling is high and the cost of failing to detect a small shift is low. As we saw in Chapter 6, when we discussed attribute control charts, sample size is related inversely to the distance between the upper and lower control limits. The larger the sample size, the smaller the $\pm 3\sigma$ (or 6σ) spread will be.

Rational Subgroups

As pointed out in Section 7.1, subgroup data allows us to monitor two types of variability; inherent random variability of the process, and variability in process average. Inherent random variability is estimated by the **variability within subgroups** and is monitored by the variability portion of the chart. Differences between subgroup measures of central tendency, referred to as **between-group variability,** reflect process change and are monitored by the central-tendency portion of the chart. If a process is in a state of statistical control, variability between subgroups will reflect only the inherent variability of the process and will, therefore, be equal to the within-group variation.

There are two basic strategies that can be employed to select subgroups.

1. *Select units produced as closely together in time as possible.* For example, if our sample size was $n = 5$, we could select five consecutive units of process output every hour on the hour. This method of sampling will minimize

variation within subgroups and increase our chances of detecting between-group variability indicative of process shifts.

2. *Randomly sample continuously throughout production or the sampling interval.* For example, instead of selecting five consecutive units of output, we would select one unit of output every 12 minutes. If this method is used, the sample will be representative of all units produced during the interval in which the sample was selected. This method is appropriate whenever sample data are used to make decisions about the acceptability of all units of production in an interval. Unfortunately, this method maximizes within-sample variation and is not as effective when it is important to detect shifts in process average.

Frequency of Sampling

The frequency with which samples are drawn is directly related to the control chart's ability to detect the presence of special causes or process shifts and inversely related to the time it takes to detect a shift once it occurs. In other words, the more frequently samples are drawn, the more sensitive the chart will be to the presence of special causes and the more quickly a shift in process average will be detected. We could increase the probability of detecting shifts quickly by using large sample sizes and sampling frequently. However, the practical constraints of most situations require us to balance sample size and frequency of sampling against budgetary requirements, time, and the costs of failing to detect a shift in the process. Although all processes will have different constraints and risks, the guidelines listed in Exhibit 7.1 can be helpful in deciding how frequently to sample.

EXHIBIT 7.1   Guidelines for Sample Selection

1. In deciding between large infrequent samples and small frequent samples, small frequent samples will usually be more effective than large infrequent samples.

2. Use small frequent samples whenever the process is a high-volume one and units of output are produced rapidly. In such situations, it is important to detect shifts as soon as possible after they occur. The longer the interval between samples, the greater the risk that a large number of output units will be unacceptable in terms of quality. For example, selecting five subgroups of $n = 5$ during a production period would be a more effective allocation of sampling efforts than selecting one large sample of $n = 25$. Although subgroups of $n = 25$ would reduce the risk of failing to detect that the process is out of control (see Section 6.2), the longer time between samples could allow process shifts that occur in the intervals between samples to go undetected.

3. Use small frequent samples whenever many special causes are possible.

4. Increase the frequency of sampling whenever a special cause is suspected, either subjectively or by having points plot near the upper or lower control limits.

Stages in a Process Where Monitoring Should Take Place

Although, under certain conditions, it would be ideal to sample and monitor at every step or stage of a process, this is not always desirable or possible. The guidelines listed in Exhibit 7.2 will help to identify the process steps at which sampling and monitoring will provide the greatest payoff in terms of reducing overall process variability and the costs of variability.

EXHIBIT 7.2 Guidelines for Monitoring a Process

1. Small problems and minor variations at the beginning of a process tend to become magnified as the process progresses, so monitoring toward the beginning of a process will generally be of greater benefit than waiting to monitor at the end. The well-known saying "A stitch in time saves nine" illustrates this principle and should be kept in mind when selecting where to sample.

2. Sample at points where the likelihood that a problem will occur is greatest or where you feel that special causes are more likely to occur.

3. Sample where the potential for cost reduction is greatest should a special cause occur. Most processes have certain stages that are more critical than others. These are the points at which sampling and charting are crucial.

4. Sample where it is feasible to do so. No matter how critical a process stage is, if it is not feasible to sample at that stage (because of inadequate technology or prohibitive cost), do not allocate all resources to an attempt to sample at that stage. A better strategy is to sample as soon after that point as possible, thereby making resources available for sampling and monitoring at as many other points in the process as resources will allow.

7.3 CONTROL CHARTS FOR CENTRAL TENDENCY ($\bar{X}$ CHART) AND VARIATION (R AND s CHARTS)

One of the most commonly employed pair of charts is the $\bar{X}$ **chart** used in conjunction with the **R chart.** When these charts are used, the subgroup range, R, is plotted on the R chart, which monitors process variability, while the subgroup average, $\bar{X}$, is plotted on the $\bar{X}$ chart, which monitors the central tendency of the process. To construct the R chart, we need to estimate the average subgroup range, $\bar{R}$, which serves as the centerline. We also need to estimate the variability of the sample ranges, σ_R, which in this case represents the standard error of R. Construction of the $\bar{X}$ chart requires calculation of the grand mean of all samples, $\bar{\bar{X}}$, as an estimate of μ, the process average, and requires an estimate of the standard error of the mean, $\sigma_{\bar{X}}$.

To construct trial limits for these charts, we need to select and evaluate at least 20 to 25 samples of size n. A smaller number of samples can result in estimates of process parameters that are not sufficiently accurate for meaningful interpretation of the charts. Once a sample has been selected, each member of the sample is evaluated on the quality variable, and the results are recorded. When all members of a sample have been evaluated, the mean, $\overline{X}$, and range, R, for the sample are calculated.

Collection and recording of sample data can be facilitated if forms designed for the purpose are used. Such forms (for example, see Appendix B, Form B.3) should include space for data collectors to record the individual measurements, sample statistics, and notes on any unusual events or conditions that occurred near the time a sample was selected. These notes can prove to be very useful in identifying a special cause that resulted in an out-of-control signal.

Only when the control chart that measures within-group variability indicates that inherent process variability is stable can we meaningfully interpret the central tendency portion of a pair of charts. Therefore, we begin with the construction of the R chart.

Calculation of the Center Line and Control Limits for the Range Chart

The center line of the range chart represents the average of the sample ranges and is computed by

$$\text{Center Line} = \overline{R} = \frac{\sum_{i=1}^{k} R_i}{k} \tag{7.1}$$

where

R_i = individual sample or subgroup range for subgroup i

k = number of samples or subgroups

The value of σ used to obtain the $\pm 3\sigma$ control limits for the range chart can be estimated by using the average subgroup range $\overline{R}$ calculated from Equation (7.1).

The ratio of the range of a sample from a normal distribution to the standard deviation of the distribution is called the **relative range.**

The relative range is a random variable whose mean and standard deviation are a function of the size of the sample used. Using this relationship, we can estimate σ_R by s_R, as follows:

$$s_R = \frac{d_3 \overline{R}}{d_2} \tag{7.2}$$

where

d_2 is a control chart factor (see Appendix A, Table A.3) that represents the relationship between the range and the standard deviation for varying subgroup sizes; and

d_3 (see Appendix A, Table A.3) is a control chart factor that represents the relationship between the standard deviation of the range, σ_R, and the process standard deviation, σ, for varying subgroup sizes.

We want to place the upper control limit 3σ above the center line and the lower control limit 3σ below the center line. Therefore, we have

$$UCL(R) = \overline{R} + 3\sigma_R \qquad (7.3a)$$

and

$$LCL(R) = \overline{R} - 3\sigma_R \qquad (7.3b)$$

Because σ_R is unknown, we estimate its value by s_R. [See Equation (7.2).] Thus, the control limits are estimated by using

$$UCL(R) = \overline{R} + 3\frac{d_3\overline{R}}{d_2} \qquad (7.4a)$$

and

$$LCL(R) = \overline{R} - 3\frac{d_3\overline{R}}{d_2} \qquad (7.4b)$$

The values of d_2 and d_3 are a function of sample size n and will be constant for a given value of n, so the value of $3\dfrac{d_3}{d_2}$ will be a constant for a given subgroup size.

To simplify the calculation of control limits, values of $\left(1 + 3\dfrac{d_3}{d_2}\right)$, called D_4, and of $\left(1 - 3\dfrac{d_3}{d_2}\right)$, called D_3, are presented in Appendix A, Table A.3 Table of Control Chart Factors.

DERIVATION 7.1 (OPTIONAL) Derivation of D_4 and D_3 Factors

$$UCL = \overline{R} + 3\frac{d_3\overline{R}}{d_2},$$

and so we have

$\overline{R}\left(1 + \dfrac{3d_3}{d_2}\right)$, where $\left(1 + \dfrac{3d_3}{d_2}\right)$ is represented by the control chart factor D_4.

Similarly,

$$LCL = \overline{R} - 3\frac{d_3\overline{R}}{d_2},$$

and so we have

$\overline{R}\left(1 - \dfrac{3d_3}{d_2}\right)$, where $\left(1 - \dfrac{3d_3}{d_2}\right)$ is represented by the control chart factor D_3.

Using values of D_4 and D_3, the formulas for the upper and lower control limits can be simplified to

$$\text{UCL}(R) = D_4 \overline{R} \qquad (7.5a)$$

and

$$\text{LCL}(R) = D_3 \overline{R} \qquad (7.5b)$$

Calculation of the Center Line and Control Limits for the Means Chart

The center line for the $\overline{X}$ chart represents the process average, μ, which can be estimated by the grand mean of the sample means, $\overline{\overline{X}}$. The centerline is calculated as:

$$\text{Center Line} = \overline{\overline{X}} = \frac{\sum_{i=1}^{k} \overline{X}_i}{k} \qquad (7.6)$$

where

$\overline{X}_i$ is the sample mean for subgroup i

k is the number of samples or subgroups used

To construct the $\pm 3\sigma$ control limits for the $\overline{X}$ chart, we will need to obtain the standard error of the mean, $\sigma_{\overline{X}}$, which is equal to $\frac{\sigma_X}{\sqrt{n}}$. Now, d_2 is a control chart factor that represents the relationship between the range and the standard deviation, where $\sigma_X = \overline{R}/d_2$, so $\sigma_{\overline{X}}$ can be estimated by $s_{\overline{x}}$ as follows:

$$s_{\overline{x}} = \frac{\overline{R}}{d_2 \sqrt{n}} \qquad (7.7)$$

Thus, the value of the upper control limit is calculated as

$$\text{UCL}(\overline{X}) = \overline{\overline{X}} + 3\frac{\overline{R}}{d_2 \sqrt{n}} \qquad (7.8a)$$

and the value of the lower control limit is calculated as

$$\text{LCL}(\overline{X}) = \overline{\overline{X}} - 3\frac{\overline{R}}{d_2 \sqrt{n}} \qquad (7.8b)$$

Because $\dfrac{3}{d_2 \sqrt{n}}$ is a constant term for a given sample size, Equations (7.8a) and (7.8b) can be simplified by using tabled values of this term, called A_2. Using tabled values of A_2 (see Appendix A, Table A.3), simplified formulas for the upper and lower control limits for the $\overline{X}$ chart are

$$\mathrm{UCL}(\overline{X}) = \overline{\overline{X}} + A_2\overline{R} \qquad (7.9a)$$

and

$$\mathrm{LCL}(\overline{X}) = \overline{\overline{X}} - A_2\overline{R} \qquad (7.9b)$$

To illustrate the use of the $\overline{X}$ and R charts, we return to the *Using Statistics* example concerning the importance of monitoring the quality of water for a municipal water company. Suppose that data was obtained from a regional water supply company that supplies water to several large towns in New Jersey. The company routinely monitors the lead content of water supplied to customers by sampling in five randomly selected locations in each area served by the system. The lead content in parts per billion for each location sampled in one geographic area over a 30-day period is presented in Table 7.1.

TABLE 7.1

LEAD CONTENT IN PARTS PER BILLION OF FIVE WATER SAMPLES DRAWN EACH DAY IN A 30-DAY PERIOD

Day	Water Sample 1	2	3	4	5	$\overline{X}_i$	R_i
1	13	8	2	5	8	7.2	11
2	0	6	1	9	15	6.2	15
3	4	2	4	3	4	3.4	2
4	3	15	8	3	5	6.8	12
5	5	10	5	4	0	4.8	10
6	9	5	13	7	7	8.2	8
7	0	4	4	3	9	4.0	9
8	9	3	0	6	0	3.6	9
9	14	0	0	5	3	4.4	14
10	3	9	5	0	2	3.8	9
11	5	8	0	7	8	5.6	8
12	3	2	2	7	4	3.6	5
13	5	11	14	8	3	8.2	11
14	13	5	5	12	7	8.4	8
15	7	0	1	0	6	2.8	7
16	12	7	10	4	13	9.2	9
17	9	4	4	8	9	6.8	5
18	6	1	1	3	13	4.8	12
19	7	0	5	7	2	4.2	7
20	10	0	10	12	7	7.8	12
21	3	7	5	10	12	7.4	9
22	3	0	10	5	4	4.4	10
23	3	3	0	6	9	4.2	9
24	0	2	3	6	7	3.6	7
25	2	3	5	4	10	4.8	8
26	3	1	4	2	4	2.8	3
27	2	4	5	13	4	5.6	11
28	0	16	7	2	11	7.2	16
29	3	5	9	8	6	6.2	6
30	9	7	10	13	0	7.8	13 **LEAD**

Using Equation (7.1), we calculate the center line for the R chart as

$$\text{Center Line} = \overline{R} = \frac{\sum_{i=1}^{k} R_i}{k}$$

$$\overline{R} = \frac{275}{30} = 9.167$$

We can obtain the values of d_2 and d_3 by referring to Table A.3. Table 7.2 presents a replica of Table A.3. To obtain the appropriate value of d_2 from Table 7.2, we read the value from the row corresponding to sample size $n = 5$ and the column headed by d_2, and we find $d_2 = 2.326$. The appropriate value of d_3 is found in the column headed by d_3 and is 0.864.

TABLE 7.2

OBTAINING A CONTROL CHART FACTOR FROM TABLE A.3

	For Estimating Sigma			For R Charts		For $\overline{X}$ Charts		For s Charts		For X Charts
n	c_4	d_2	d_3	D_3	D_4	A_2	A_3	B_3	B_4	E_2
2	0.7979	1.128	0.853	0	3.267	1.880	2.659	0	3.267	2.659
3	0.8862	1.693	0.888	0	2.575	1.023	1.954	0	2.568	1.772
4	0.9213	2.059	0.880	0	2.282	0.729	1.628	0	2.266	1.457
5	0.9400	2.326	0.864	0	2.114	0.577	1.427	0	2.089	1.290
6	0.9515	2.534	0.848	0	2.004	0.483	1.287	0.030	1.970	1.184
7	0.9594	2.704	0.833	0.076	1.924	0.419	1.182	0.118	1.882	1.109
8	0.9650	2.847	0.820	0.136	1.864	0.373	1.099	0.185	1.815	1.054
9	0.9693	2.970	0.808	0.184	1.816	0.337	1.032	0.239	1.761	1.010
10	0.9727	3.078	0.797	0.223	1.777	0.308	0.975	0.284	1.716	0.975
⋮	⋮	⋮	⋮	⋮	⋮	⋮	⋮	⋮	⋮	⋮
25	0.9896	3.931	0.708	0.459	1.541	0.135	0.606	0.565	1.435	0.763

Calculating the upper control limit and the lower control limit using Equations (7.4a) and (7.4b), respectively, we obtain

$$\text{UCL}(R) = \overline{R} + 3\frac{d_3\overline{R}}{d_2}$$

$$\text{UCL}(R) = 9.167 + 3\frac{0.864(9.167)}{2.326}$$

$$\text{UCL}(R) = 9.167 + 3(3.405)$$

$$\text{UCL}(R) = 9.167 + 10.215$$

$$\text{UCL}(R) = 19.382$$

and

$$\text{LCL}(R) = \overline{R} - 3\frac{d_3\overline{R}}{d_2}$$

$$\text{LCL}(R) = 9.167 - 3\frac{0.864(9.167)}{2.326}$$

$$\text{LCL}(R) = 9.167 - 3(3.405)$$

$$\text{LCL}(R) = 9.167 - 10.215$$
$$\text{LCL}(R) = -1.048$$
$$\text{LCL}(R) = 0.0$$

The value calculated for the LCL is a negative number, and negative values for ranges do not exist, so a value of 0.0 can be used for the lower control limit, or the lower control limit can be considered not to exist.

If we use the simplified Equations (7.5a) and (7.5b) to calculate values for the upper and lower control limits, we obtain values for D_4 and D_3 for sample size $n = 5$ from Table A.3, which indicates that when $n = 5$, $D_4 = 2.114$ and $D_3 = 0.0$. We can then substitute these values in Equations (7.5a) and (7.5b) and obtain:

$$\text{UCL}(R) = D_4\overline{R}$$
$$\text{UCL}(R) = (2.114)(9.167)$$
$$\text{UCL}(R) = 19.38$$

and

$$\text{LCL}(R) = D_3\overline{R}$$
$$\text{LCL}(R) = (0.0)(9.167)$$
$$\text{LCL}(R) = 0.0$$

Figure 7.1 presents the R chart for the "lead content of water" example.

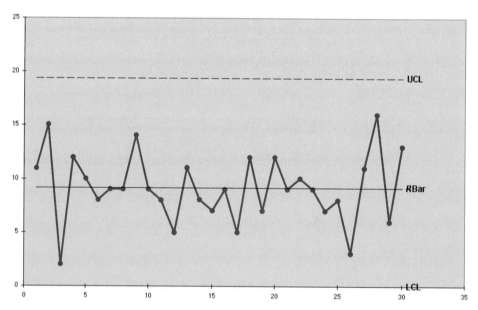

Figure 7.1   The range (R) control chart obtained from the PHStat add-in for Microsoft Excel for the "lead levels of water" data presented in Table 7.1

Examining Figure 7.1, and using our rules for determining out-of-control points (see Section 6.2), we observe that there are no points above the UCL or below the LCL.

Calculating the Optional 1σ and 2σ Limits

If we choose to use the optional 1σ and 2σ limits, the limits can be obtained using Equation (7.2) for the standard error of the range, s_R, to estimate σ_R.

$$s_R = \frac{d_3\overline{R}}{d_2}$$

$$s_R = \frac{0.864(9.167)}{2.326} = 3.405$$

The $\pm 2\sigma$ boundaries can be calculated as

$$+2\sigma \text{ boundary} = \overline{R} + 2s_R \tag{7.10a}$$

$$+2\sigma \text{ boundary} = 9.167 + 2(3.405) = 15.98$$

and

$$-2\sigma \text{ boundary} = \overline{R} - 2s_R \tag{7.10b}$$

$$-2\sigma \text{ boundary} = 9.167 - 2(3.405) = 2.36$$

The $\pm 1\sigma$ boundaries can be calculated from

$$+1\sigma \text{ boundary} = \overline{R} + 1s_R \tag{7.11a}$$

$$+1\sigma \text{ boundary} = 9.167 + 1(3.405) = 12.57$$

and

$$-1\sigma \text{ boundary} = \overline{R} - 1s_R \tag{7.11b}$$

$$-1\sigma \text{ boundary} = 9.167 - 1(3.405) = 5.76$$

If these boundaries were superimposed on Figure 7.1[1], from rules 2 and 3, concerning violations of 1σ and 2σ limits, there is no evidence of an out-of-control state. In addition, there does not seem to be any other evidence of an out-of-control state.

[1]The MINITAB software package lists points that violate zone rules instead of placing zone boundaries on the control chart.

Because the R chart shows no evidence of out-of-control patterns, we can proceed to construct and evaluate the $\overline{X}$ portion of the chart.

Constructing the $\overline{X}$ Chart

The center line for the $\overline{X}$ chart is calculated from Equation (7.6) as follows:

$$\text{Center Line} = \overline{\overline{X}} = \frac{\sum_{i=1}^{k}\overline{X}_i}{k}$$

$$\overline{\overline{X}} = \frac{167.8}{30} = 5.59$$

By using Equations (7.8a) and (7.8b), the upper and lower control limits are calculated as

$$UCL(\bar{X}) = \bar{\bar{X}} + 3\frac{\bar{R}}{d_2\sqrt{n}}$$

$$UCL(\bar{X}) = 5.59 + 3\frac{9.17}{2.326\sqrt{5}}$$

$$UCL(\bar{X}) = 5.59 + 5.29$$

$$UCL(\bar{X}) = 10.88$$

and

$$LCL(\bar{X}) = \bar{\bar{X}} - 3\frac{\bar{R}}{d_2\sqrt{n}}$$

$$LCL(\bar{X}) = 5.59 - 3\frac{9.17}{2.326\sqrt{5}}$$

$$LCL(\bar{X}) = 5.59 - 5.29$$

$$LCL(\bar{X}) = 0.30$$

If the simplified Equations (7.9a) and (7.9b) are used, we find from Table A.3 that, for subgroups of size $n = 5$, $A_2 = 0.577$. The values of the upper and lower control limits are then calculated as

$$UCL(\bar{X}) = \bar{\bar{X}} + A_2\bar{R}$$

$$UCL(\bar{X}) = 5.59 + 5.77(9.17)$$

$$UCL(\bar{X}) = 10.88$$

and

$$LCL(\bar{X}) = \bar{\bar{X}} - A_2\bar{R}$$

$$LCL(\bar{X}) = 5.59 - 0.577(9.17)$$

$$LCL(\bar{X}) = 0.30$$

Figure 7.2 presents the $\bar{X}$ control chart for the "lead content of water" data obtained from the PHStat add-in for Microsoft Excel.

Examining Figure 7.2, and using our rules for determining out-of-control points, we observe that there are no points above the UCL or below the LCL. If we choose to employ the optional 1σ and 2σ limits, we can use the standard error of the mean, $s_{\bar{X}}$, to estimate $\sigma_{\bar{X}}$. Using Equation (7.7), we have

$$s_{\bar{X}} = \frac{\bar{R}}{d_2\sqrt{n}}$$

so that

$$s_{\bar{X}} = \frac{9.17}{2.326\sqrt{5}} = 1.76$$

The $\pm 2\sigma$ boundaries are then calculated as

$$+2\sigma \text{ boundary} = \bar{\bar{X}} + 2s_{\bar{X}} \qquad (7.12a)$$

$$+2\sigma \text{ boundary} = 5.59 + 2(1.76) = 9.11$$

Chart for Lead Content

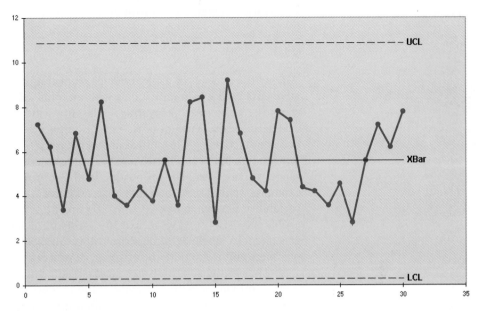

Figure 7.2   The means ($\overline{X}$) control chart obtained from the PHStat add-in for Microsoft Excel for the "lead levels of water" data

and

$$-2\sigma \text{ boundary} = \overline{\overline{X}} - 2_{S_{\bar{x}}} \qquad (7.12b)$$

$$-2\sigma \text{ boundary} = 5.59 - 2(1.76) = 2.07$$

The $\pm 1\sigma$ boundaries then become

$$+1\sigma \text{ boundary} = \overline{\overline{X}} + 1_{S_{\bar{X}}} \qquad (7.13a)$$

$$+1\sigma \text{ boundary} = 5.59 + 1(1.76) = 7.35$$

and

$$-1\sigma \text{ boundary} = \overline{\overline{X}} - 1_{S_{\bar{x}}} \qquad (7.13b)$$

$$-1\sigma \text{ boundary} = 5.59 - 1(1.76) = 3.83$$

Examination of the control chart for $\overline{X}$ shows no evidence of an out-of-control signal or pattern in the data. Whenever a process is found to be stable, but either the process average is not at an optimal level or the inherent variability of the process is too large, further measures to improve the process should be taken. Tools such as brainstorming, process flow, cause and effect, and Pareto diagrams (as in Chapter 2) can be used in conjunction with designed experiments (see Chapters 10 and 11).

$\overline{X}$ And s Charts

Among the benefits of using the $\overline{X}$ chart in conjunction with the R chart is the relative ease with which individuals with minimal knowledge of statistics can understand the concept of measuring variability with the range, and the simplicity of calculating sample values of R. As the sample size, n, increases, however, the range becomes increasingly less efficient as a measure of variability. The range ignores all information between the two most extreme values, so the sample size increases, the range will use a smaller proportion of the information available in a sample. For example, when $n = 4$, the range uses 50 percent of the available data to measure variability, but, when $n = 20$, only 10 percent of the data is used. In addition, the probability of observing an extreme or atypical score in a sample increases as n gets larger. A single extreme score will result in an unduly large value for the sample range and will inflate the estimate of process variability.

Thus, as the subgroup size increases, the individual subgroup standard deviations, s_i, provide a better estimate of the process standard deviation than does the range. The variability within each subgroup or sample is estimated by using s, the within-subgroup standard deviation.

As can be seen from Equation (3.10), on page 114, all scores in a sample contribute to the value of the sample standard deviation. Thus, the standard deviation makes use of all information available and reduces the effect of a single atypical or extreme score on the estimate of process variability.

As a general rule, for subgroup sizes $n < 10$, the range provides a reasonable estimate with greater simplicity and sometimes greater efficiency than the standard deviation. For samples of size $n = 10$ or more, the $\overline{X}$ and s charts should be used.

Construction of the $\overline{X}$ and s charts parallels that of the $\overline{X}$ and R charts, in that it begins with an examination of the chart that deals with the variability of the process, in this case, the s chart. To construct an **s chart**, the standard deviation must be calculated for each subgroup. Then the average standard deviation can be calculated as follows:

$$\overline{s} = \frac{\sum_{i=1}^{k} s_i}{k} \tag{7.14}$$

where

s_i is the sample standard deviation for sample or subgroup i

k is the number of subgroups

We can use $\overline{s}$ as the value for the center line of the s chart and to calculate an estimate of the process standard deviation, σ, which is necessary to calculate the $\pm 3\sigma$ control limits. The upper control limit for the s chart is found by

$$\text{UCL}(s) = \overline{s} + 3\overline{s}\frac{\sqrt{1 - c_4^2}}{c_4} \tag{7.15a}$$

and the value of the lower control limit by

$$\mathrm{LCL}(s) = \bar{s} - 3\bar{s}\frac{\sqrt{1 - c_4^2}}{c_4} \tag{7.15b}$$

where c_4 is a control chart factor (see Appendix A, Table A.3) that represents the relationship between the sample standard deviations and the process standard deviation for varying subgroup sizes.

The central tendency of the distribution of $\bar{s}$ does not equal the population parameter σ. The constant c_4 is used to adjust for this discrepancy, so that the central tendency of $\bar{s}/c_4$ provides a better estimate of σ. Because c_4 is constant for a given sample size, the term $\left(1 + \dfrac{3\sqrt{1 - c_4^2}}{c_4}\right)$ can be replaced by tabled values of control chart factor B_4, and the term $\left(1 - \dfrac{3\sqrt{1 - c_4^2}}{c_4}\right)$ can be replaced by control chart factor B_3 (see Table A.3). The factors B_4 and B_3 can be used to simplify Equations (7.15a) and (7.15b), respectively. Simplified versions of the equations for calculating the upper and lower control limits for the s chart are

$$\mathrm{UCL}(s) = B_4\bar{s} \tag{7.16a}$$

and

$$\mathrm{LCL}(s) = B_3\bar{s} \tag{7.16b}$$

where values of B_3 and B_4 are obtained from Table A.3.

As in the case of the $\bar{X}$ chart used in conjunction with the R chart, when the s chart is used, the center line for the $\bar{X}$ chart is represented by the grand mean, $\bar{\bar{X}}$, of the sample means and is calculated by using Equation (7.6).

$$\text{Center Line} = \bar{\bar{X}} = \frac{\sum\limits_{i=1}^{k}\bar{X}_i}{k}$$

The upper and lower control limits are then calculated by using

$$\mathrm{UCL}(\bar{X}) = \bar{\bar{X}} + 3\frac{\bar{s}}{c_4\sqrt{n}} \tag{7.17a}$$

and

$$\mathrm{LCL}(\bar{X}) = \bar{\bar{X}} - 3\frac{\bar{s}}{c_4\sqrt{n}} \tag{7.17b}$$

where c_4 is a control chart factor that represents the relationship between subgroup standard deviations and the process standard deviation for varying subgroup sizes, and n is the subgroup size.

Because $\dfrac{3}{c_4\sqrt{n}}$ is a constant term for a given subgroup size, the equations for the upper and lower control limits can be simplified by using tabled values of $\dfrac{3}{c_4\sqrt{n}}$, called A_3. The simplified formulas are

$$UCL(\bar{X}) = \bar{\bar{X}} + A_3\bar{s} \tag{7.18a}$$

and

$$LCL(\bar{X}) = \bar{\bar{X}} - A_3\bar{s} \tag{7.18b}$$

where the value of A_3 for a given sample size, n, is obtained from Table A.3.

The lead-content data can also be used to demonstrate the use of the $\bar{X}$ and s charts. Table 7.3 presents these data and includes the sample mean, $\bar{X}_i$, and the sample standard deviation, s_i, for each subgroup of $n = 5$ water samples.

To obtain the center line and control limits for the s chart, we begin by calculating $\bar{s}$. Using Equation (7.14), we obtain

$$\bar{s} = \dfrac{\sum\limits_{i=1}^{k} s_i}{k}$$

$$\bar{s} = \dfrac{111.42}{30} = 3.714$$

Because the value of $\bar{s}$ represents the center line of the s chart, we have

$$\text{Center Line} = \bar{s} = 3.714$$

The value of the upper control limit is then calculated by using Equation (7.15a). The value of $c_4 = .94$ when $n = 5$ (see Table 7.2 on page 296 or Table A.3), so the upper control limit is calculated as

$$UCL(s) = \bar{s} + 3\bar{s}\dfrac{\sqrt{1 - c_4^2}}{c_4}$$

$$UCL(s) = 3.714 + 3(3.714)\dfrac{\sqrt{1 - (0.94)^2}}{0.94}$$

$$UCL(s) = 3.714 + 4.044$$

$$UCL(s) = 7.76$$

Using Equation (7.15b) to calculate the value of the lower control limit, we obtain

$$LCL(s) = \bar{s} - 3\bar{s}\dfrac{\sqrt{1 - c_4^2}}{c_4}$$

$$LCL(s) = 3.714 - 3(3.714)\dfrac{\sqrt{1 - (0.94)^2}}{0.94}$$

$$LCL(s) = 3.714 - 4.044 = -0.33$$

$$LCL(s) = 0.0$$

TABLE 7.3

LEAD CONTENT IN PARTS PER BILLION OF FIVE WATER SAMPLES DRAWN EACH DAY IN A 30-DAY PERIOD

| | Water Sample | | | | | | |
Day	1	2	3	4	5	$\overline{X}_i$	s_i
1	13	8	2	5	8	7.2	4.09
2	0	6	1	9	15	6.2	6.14
3	4	2	4	3	4	3.4	0.89
4	3	15	8	3	5	6.8	5.02
5	5	10	5	4	0	4.8	3.56
6	9	5	13	7	7	8.2	3.03
7	0	4	4	3	9	4.0	3.24
8	9	3	0	6	0	3.6	3.91
9	14	0	0	5	3	4.4	5.77
10	3	9	5	0	2	3.8	3.42
11	5	8	0	7	8	5.6	3.36
12	3	2	2	7	4	3.6	2.07
13	5	11	14	8	3	8.2	4.44
14	13	5	5	12	7	8.4	3.85
15	7	0	1	0	6	2.8	3.42
16	12	7	10	4	13	9.2	3.70
17	9	4	4	8	9	6.8	2.59
18	6	1	1	3	13	4.8	5.02
19	7	0	5	7	2	4.2	3.11
20	10	0	10	12	7	7.8	4.71
21	3	7	5	10	12	7.4	3.65
22	3	0	10	5	4	4.4	3.65
23	3	3	0	6	9	4.2	3.42
24	0	2	3	6	7	3.6	2.88
25	2	3	5	4	10	4.8	3.11
26	3	1	4	2	4	2.8	1.30
27	2	4	5	13	4	5.6	4.28
28	0	16	7	2	11	7.2	6.53
29	3	5	9	8	6	6.2	2.39
30	9	7	10	13	0	7.8	4.87

 LEAD

Because the value obtained for the lower control limit is a negative number, and negative values of standard deviations do not exist, we can use 0.0 to represent LCL(s) or consider that the LCL(s) does not exist.

Alternately, we can use the simplified Equations (7.16a) and (7.16b) to calculate the upper and lower control limits. When $n = 5$, the tabled value of B_4 is 2.089 (see Table 7.2 on page 296 or Table A.3) and the value of B_3 is 0.0. (Note that for all values of $n = 5$ or fewer, the value of $B_3 = 0.0$.) Calculating the control limits by using the simplified formulas, we have

$$\text{UCL}(s) = B_4 \overline{s}$$

$$\text{UCL}(s) = 2.089(3.714)$$

$$\text{UCL}(s) = 7.76$$

and

$$LCL(s) = B_3 \bar{s}$$

$$LCL(s) = 0.0(3.714)$$

$$LCL(s) = 0.0$$

Figure 7.3 presents the s chart obtained from MINITAB for the "lead content of water" data.

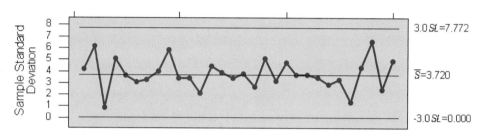

Figure 7.3   The standard deviation (s) chart obtained from MINITAB for the "lead levels of water" data presented in Table 7.3

Examination of the s chart presented in Figure 7.3 shows no evidence of out-of-control signals or patterns, so we can construct and meaningfully interpret the $\bar{X}$ chart.

Constructing the $\bar{X}$ Chart

To construct the $\bar{X}$ chart, the grand mean of the 30 sample means is calculated by using Equation (7.6):

$$\text{Center Line} = \bar{\bar{X}} = \frac{\sum_{i=1}^{k} \bar{X}_i}{k}$$

$$\bar{\bar{X}} = \frac{167.8}{30} = 5.593$$

From Equations (7.17a) and (7.17b), the upper and lower control limits are calculated as

$$UCL(\bar{X}) = \bar{X} + 3\frac{\bar{s}}{c_4\sqrt{n}}$$

$$UCL(\bar{X}) = 5.593 + 3\frac{3.714}{0.94\sqrt{5}}$$

$$UCL(\bar{X}) = 5.593 + 5.301$$

$$UCL(\bar{X}) = 10.894$$

and

$$\text{LCL}(\overline{X}) = \overline{\overline{X}} - 3\frac{\overline{s}}{c_4\sqrt{n}}$$

$$\text{LCL}(\overline{X}) = 5.593 - 3\frac{3.714}{.94\sqrt{5}}$$

$$\text{LCL}(\overline{X}) = 5.593 - 5.301$$

$$\text{LCL}(\overline{X}) = 0.292$$

From Table 7.2, on page 296, or Table A.3, if the simplified Equations (7.18a) and (7.18b), which use the control chart factor A_3, are employed we find that, when $n = 5$, $A_3 = 1.427$. The upper and lower control limits are then calculated as

$$\text{UCL}(\overline{X}) = \overline{\overline{X}} + A_3\overline{s}$$

$$\text{UCL}(\overline{X}) = 5.593 + 1.427(3.714)$$

$$\text{UCL}(\overline{X}) = 5.593 + 5.30$$

$$\text{UCL}(\overline{X}) = 10.893$$

and

$$\text{LCL}(\overline{X}) = \overline{\overline{X}} - A_3\overline{s}$$

$$\text{LCL}(\overline{X}) = 5.59 - 1.427(3.714)$$

$$\text{LCL}(\overline{X}) = 5.593 - 5.30$$

$$\text{LCL}(\overline{X}) = 0.293$$

Examination of Figure 7.4, which presents the $\overline{X}$ chart obtained from MINITAB for the lead-content data, indicates no evidence that the process is out of control. If one or more points had fallen above the upper control limit or below the lower control limit, efforts would have been made to identify the special cause or causes that resulted in such out-of-control signals. If the special causes could be eliminated from the process, we could eliminate those points and recalculate trial control limits with the remaining data. Because the process at this time appears to be stable, we can extend the trial control limits and continue to sample and record the means of our samples on the control chart.

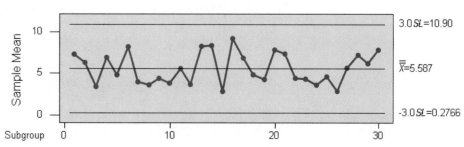

Figure 7.4   Means ($\overline{X}$) chart used with the standard deviation (s) chart obtained from MINITAB to monitor the "lead levels of water" data

PROBLEMS

7.1 The telecommunications department for a county general services agency is responsible for the repair of equipment used in radio communications by police, fire, and emergency medical services in the county. The timely repair of these radios is critically important for the efficient operation of these public service units. The following table presents the repair times in minutes for a daily sample of five radios taken over a 30-day period.

RADIO

Day	1	2	3	4	5	$\bar{X}_i$	R_i
1	114	499	106	342	55	223.2	444
2	219	319	162	44	87	166.2	275
3	64	302	38	83	93	116.0	264
4	258	110	98	78	154	139.6	180
5	127	140	298	518	275	271.6	391
6	151	176	188	268	77	172.0	191
7	24	183	202	81	104	118.8	178
8	41	249	342	338	69	207.8	301
9	93	189	209	444	151	217.2	351
10	111	207	143	318	129	181.6	207
11	205	281	250	468	79	256.6	389
12	121	261	183	606	287	291.6	485
13	225	83	198	223	180	181.8	142
14	235	439	102	330	190	259.2	337
15	91	32	190	70	150	106.6	158
16	181	191	182	444	124	224.4	320
17	52	190	310	245	156	190.6	258
18	90	538	277	308	171	276.8	448
19	78	587	147	172	299	256.6	509
20	45	265	126	137	151	144.8	220
21	410	227	179	298	342	291.2	231
22	68	375	195	67	72	155.4	308
23	140	266	157	92	140	159.0	174
24	145	170	231	60	191	159.4	171
25	129	74	148	119	139	121.8	74
26	143	384	263	147	131	213.6	253
27	86	229	474	181	40	202.0	434
28	164	313	295	297	280	269.8	149
29	257	310	217	152	351	157.4	199
30	106	134	175	153	69	127.4	106

RADIO

(a) Construct an R chart for these data.

(b) Does the R chart indicate that the process is in a state of statistical control? Why? If the R chart indicates the process is not in control, remove out-of-control points, and re-construct the chart with the remaining data.

(c) Construct a $\bar{X}$ chart based on the range for these data. Does the $\bar{X}$ chart indicate that the process is in a state of statistical control? Why?

(d) What conclusions can you draw about this process?

(e) Construct an s chart for these data.

(f) Does the s chart indicate that the process is in a state of statistical control? Why? If the s chart indicates the process is not in control, remove out-of-control points, and re-construct the chart with the remaining data.

(g) Construct a $\bar{X}$ chart based on the standard deviation for these data. Does the $\bar{X}$ chart indicate that the process is in a state of statistical control? Why?

(h) Compare your results in (e)–(g) with the results you obtained in (a)–(d).

(i) From (e)–(g), what conclusions can you draw about this process?

7.2 A coffee manufacturer imports green coffee beans from several countries and suppliers. Beans are usually shipped by sea in large containers. Each freighter is met at the dock as it is unloaded, and before containers of beans are accepted, samples from each container are drawn and tested. One of the quality characteristics monitored is moisture content. High moisture content can be evidence of water seepage into the container during shipment, which can result in beans that are contaminated, are fermented, or have unacceptable levels of mold. The target value for moisture is 11.5 percent, and the maximum acceptable value is 13.0 percent. Shipments with moisture readings above the maximum are rejected. The following data represent moisture content for four samples drawn from each of 35 containers from one supplier.

SAMPLE

Container	1	2	3	4
1	10.7	10.4	10.2	10.9
2	10.9	10.3	10.3	10.6
3	10.9	10.8	10.3	10.5
4	11.1	10.7	10.7	10.8
5	10.9	10.6	10.7	10.3
6	10.2	10.7	10.7	9.7
7	11.1	10.4	10.9	10.4
8	10.2	10.7	10.9	10.1
9	10.3	9.9	11.1	10.3
10	10.0	10.1	9.9	10.3
11	11.2	9.9	9.9	9.8
12	10.9	10.0	10.2	10.0
13	10.2	10.4	10.4	10.8

(Continued)

Container	1	2	3	4
14	10.4	10.3	10.3	10.0
15	10.1	10.1	10.0	10.5
16	11.4	11.8	11.9	11.7
17	11.3	11.0	11.6	11.4
18	10.7	10.8	11.1	10.9
19	10.9	10.3	10.9	10.7
20	11.0	11.4	11.5	10.9
21	11.5	11.6	11.6	11.4
22	11.1	11.1	11.3	11.2
23	11.3	10.9	10.9	11.4
24	10.8	11.0	11.5	10.9
25	10.6	10.5	10.8	11.2
26	11.2	11.3	11.4	11.7
27	10.9	10.7	11.3	10.8
29	11.3	11.1	11.4	11.3
30	11.0	11.7	10.9	11.4
31	10.4	10.3	10.6	10.4
32	9.9	10.0	10.3	10.4
33	10.2	10.6	10.2	10.3
34	10.7	10.9	10.4	10.3
35	9.6	10.0	9.8	9.8

COFFEE

(a) Construct an R chart for these data.
(b) Does the R chart indicate that the process is in a state of statistical control? Why? If the R chart indicates the process is not in control, remove out-of-control points, and re-construct the chart with the remaining data.
(c) Construct a $\overline{X}$ chart based on the range for these data. Does the $\overline{X}$ chart indicate that the process is in a state of statistical control? Why?
(d) What conclusions can you draw about this process?
(e) Construct an s chart for these data.
(f) Does the s chart indicate that the process is in a state of statistical control? Why? If the s chart indicates the process is not in control, remove out-of-control points, and re-construct the chart with the remaining data.
(g) Construct a $\overline{X}$ chart based on the standard deviation for these data. Does the $\overline{X}$ chart indicate that the process is in a state of statistical control? Why?
(h) Compare your results in (e)–(g) with the results you obtained in (a)–(d).
(i) From (e)–(g), what conclusions can you draw about this process?

7.3 The pressure-drop readings in a sewage-sludge incinerator exhaust stack are related to its combustion efficiency. Pressure-drop readings are monitored over time. If the pressure drop in the stack remains relatively stable, the sludge incinerator is operating efficiently. Unstable swings in the pressure-drop readings can indicate that some process changes are required. Monthly data consisting of six pressure-drop readings, in units of millimeters of mercury (mmHg), were collected for a 24-month period and are presented next.

SAMPLE

Month	1	2	3	4	5	6
1	42	36	33	29	35	44
2	44	41	42	43	36	33
3	28	35	30	30	31	28
4	43	42	41	40	39	28
5	42	43	49	47	42	45
6	46	47	48	47	46	44
7	28	32	41	40	40	42
8	55	48	49	53	54	47
9	43	46	47	36	28	42
10	42	41	42	43	36	27
11	40	35	28	27	33	44
12	43	43	42	40	33	32
13	41	40	39	41	48	50
14	40	45	46	45	51	54
15	50	43	45	45	41	47
16	52	39	43	48	42	49
17	37	43	45	31	42	43
18	53	53	51	47	45	43
19	47	41	41	43	40	37
20	31	26	28	29	32	40
21	30	34	31	46	35	43
22	40	39	38	34	28	26
23	45	29	40	32	33	32
24	54	50	43	54	48	46

SLUDGE

(a) Construct an R chart for these data.
(b) Does the R chart indicate that the process is in a state of statistical control? Why? If the R chart indicates the process is not in control, remove out-of-control points, and re-construct the chart with the remaining data.
(c) Construct a $\overline{X}$ chart based on the range for these data. Does the $\overline{X}$ chart indicate that the process is in a state of statistical control? Why?
(d) What conclusions can you draw about this process?
(e) Construct an s chart for these data.
(f) Does the s chart indicate that the process is in a state of statistical control? Why? If the s chart indicates the process is not in control, remove out-of-control points, and re-construct the chart with the remaining data.
(g) Construct a $\overline{X}$ chart based on the standard deviation for these data. Does the $\overline{X}$ chart indicate that the process is in a state of statistical control? Why?
(h) Compare your results in (e)–(g) with the results you obtained in (a)–(d).
(i) From (e)–(g), what conclusions can you draw about this process?

7.4 The inflow-infiltration of rain water into sanitary sewer systems can strain the capacity of sewage-treatment facilities. Municipalities have instituted measures to monitor and eliminate inflow-infiltration in sewage systems. One way to monitor inflow-infiltration is to install a flow meter in a sewer manhole. Should an increase in sewer flow be detected, it could serve as a signal for further investigation to determine the source of infiltration. Westchester County, New York performed a Sewer System Evaluation Determination Study that monitored infiltration in thousands of sewer man-holes throughout the county. The table below presents data collected at one location over a 30-day period in a recent year. Flows were recorded each hour over a 24-hour period each day. For each day, the table presents the mean of the 24 hourly observations, the range, the standard deviation, and the amount of rainfall recorded in the 24-hour period.

Day	Mean Flow (mD)	Range	Standard Deviation	Rainfall (inches)
1	0.0647	0.085	0.0228	0.042
2	0.0588	0.024	0.0058	0.000
3	0.0528	0.035	0.0078	0.000
4	0.0515	0.027	0.0066	0.000
5	0.0543	0.030	0.0071	0.010
6	0.0525	0.023	0.0066	0.000
7	0.0528	0.031	0.0084	0.000
8	0.0521	0.031	0.0062	0.000
9	0.0464	0.028	0.0079	0.000
10	0.0445	0.034	0.0081	0.020
11	0.0444	0.034	0.0080	0.000
12	0.0448	0.026	0.0062	0.000
13	0.0470	0.035	0.0080	0.000
14	0.0441	0.030	0.0081	0.000
15	0.0413	0.029	0.0065	0.000
16	0.0383	0.030	0.0081	0.000
17	0.0379	0.036	0.0081	0.000
18	0.0377	0.041	0.0089	0.000
19	0.0378	0.032	0.0080	0.000
20	0.0366	0.031	0.0084	0.000
21	0.0360	0.028	0.0082	0.000
22	0.0407	0.093	0.0216	0.380
23	0.0415	0.028	0.0066	0.050
24	0.0378	0.034	0.0081	0.000
25	0.0389	0.031	0.0077	0.000
26	0.0443	0.120	0.0237	0.000
27	0.0420	0.027	0.0074	0.000
28	0.0402	0.032	0.0092	0.000
29	0.0411	0.095	0.0176	0.430
30	0.0451	0.042	0.0101	0.090

SEWAGE

(a) Construct an R chart for these data.
(b) Does the R chart indicate that the process is in a state of statistical control? Why? If the R chart indicates the process is not in control, remove out-of-control points, and re-construct the chart with the remaining data.
(c) Construct a $\overline{X}$ chart based on the range for these data. Does the $\overline{X}$ chart indicate that the process is in a state of statistical control? Why?
(d) What conclusions can you draw about this process?
(e) Construct an s chart for these data.
(f) Does the s chart indicate that the process is in a state of statistical control? Why? If the s chart indicates the process is not in control, remove out-of-control points, and re-construct the chart with the remaining data.
(g) Construct a $\overline{X}$ chart based on the standard deviation for these data. Does the $\overline{X}$ chart indicate that the process is in a state of statistical control? Why?
(h) Compare your results in (e)–(g) with the results you obtained in (a)–(d).
(i) From (e)–(g), what conclusions can you draw about this process?

7.5 An investigation of the backwash operations in a water-treatment plant concentrated on the frequency with which filters were backwashed. Ideally, each filter should be backwashed once every 24 hours. The table below presents data obtained from the daily filter logs for the 31 days in the month of October. The data include the average time between backwash for samples of $n = 4$ filters, the range, the standard deviation, and any notable occurrences each day.

Day	Mean Time (hours)	Range	Standard Deviation	Notes
1	23.3	3	1.30	High turbidity in raw water
2	21.8	3	1.30	High turbidity in raw water
3	23.0	4	1.73	Manual mode of operation
4	24.5	1	0.50	
5	24.3	3	1.09	
6	23.4	5	1.85	Inadequate float removal
7	24.3	3	1.09	
8	24.3	2	0.83	
9	24.0	7	2.55	
10	24.0	2	0.71	
11	24.8	2	0.83	
12	25.5	4	1.66	
13	24.5	1	0.05	
14	24.7	1	0.47	

(Continued)

Day	Mean Time (hours)	Range	Standard Deviation	Notes
15	25.5	1	0.50	
16	25.3	1	0.47	
17	21.0	14	6.68	Experimentation with turbidimeter
18	24.0	0	0.00	
19	24.3	1	0.43	
20	23.8	1	0.43	
21	24.0	0	0.00	
22	24.8	1	0.43	
23	26.0	4	1.58	Inadequate float removal
24	24.8	1	0.43	
25	24.0	0	0.00	
26	24.5	1	0.50	
27	28.0	0	0.00	Training new filter operators
28	28.0	0	0.00	Training new filter operators
29	27.5	4	1.50	Training new filter operators
30	28.0	0	0.00	Training new filter operators
31	27.0	3	1.22	Training new filter operators

BACKWASH

(a) Construct an R chart for these data.

(b) Does the R chart indicate that the process is in a state of statistical control? Why? If the R chart indicates the process is not in control, remove out-of-control points, and re-construct the chart with the remaining data.

(c) Construct a $\overline{X}$ chart based on the range for these data. Does the $\overline{X}$ chart indicate that the process is in a state of statistical control? Why?

(d) What conclusions can you draw about this process?

(e) Construct an s chart for these data.

(f) Does the s chart indicate that the process is in a state of statistical control? Why? If the s chart indicates the process is not in control, remove out-of-control points, and re-construct the chart with the remaining data.

(g) Construct a $\overline{X}$ chart based on the standard deviation for these data. Does the $\overline{X}$ chart indicate that the process is in a state of statistical control? Why?

(h) Compare your results in (e)–(g) with the results you obtained in (a)–(d).

(i) From (e)–(g), what conclusions can you draw about this process?

7.6 The quality engineer in charge of a coffee-filter-pack production line was concerned about the weight of the filter packs being produced. The quality team sampled 5 packs every 20 minutes throughout the production day. The table below presents the weight in grams of each pack sampled, for 50 samples of $n = 5$.

WEIGHT (GRAMS)

Sample	1	2	3	4	5
1	19.8	20.1	19.9	19.4	19.8
2	19.3	19.3	19.2	20.3	20.1
3	19.8	20.1	20.5	20.3	19.2
4	20.7	21.0	20.4	20.7	20.5
5	20.4	19.2	19.7	19.3	19.1
6	19.4	19.2	19.6	20.0	19.5
7	20.5	19.8	20.2	19.8	19.8
8	20.0	20.3	20.1	20.1	20.0
9	20.3	20.3	20.4	20.0	20.4
10	20.4	21.0	20.8	20.9	20.4
11	20.7	20.5	20.7	20.8	20.4
12	20.4	20.9	20.6	20.1	20.7
13	20.2	20.4	20.3	20.4	20.6
14	20.9	20.6	20.6	20.3	20.5
15	20.6	20.5	20.2	20.7	20.7
16	20.4	20.9	20.4	20.2	20.6
17	20.2	19.9	20.2	19.9	20.2
18	20.4	20.0	20.2	20.3	20.3
19	20.7	20.3	20.4	19.9	20.3
20	20.4	20.3	20.1	20.5	20.1
21	20.4	20.2	20.1	19.9	20.5
22	19.9	19.7	20.5	19.6	20.4
23	20.1	20.3	20.3	20.2	20.6
24	20.3	20.6	20.0	19.2	19.8
25	20.6	20.5	20.1	20.2	20.3
26	20.2	20.5	19.8	20.5	20.3
27	20.2	20.2	20.5	20.2	20.3
28	20.4	20.4	20.6	20.1	20.0
29	20.4	20.5	20.8	20.4	20.2
30	20.2	20.4	20.4	20.6	20.4
31	20.5	20.1	20.6	20.5	20.0
32	20.3	20.8	20.2	20.1	20.3
33	19.8	20.2	20.0	20.5	20.1
34	20.7	20.3	20.2	20.4	20.0
35	20.5	20.9	20.5	20.4	20.7
36	19.9	20.2	20.1	20.1	20.0
37	20.2	19.8	20.5	20.2	19.9
38	20.7	20.2	20.6	20.2	20.4
39	20.3	20.4	20.7	20.4	20.2
40	20.8	19.9	20.0	19.7	19.3
41	20.3	20.1	20.4	20.3	20.5
42	20.4	20.4	20.8	20.2	21.0
43	20.3	20.5	20.3	20.6	21.2
44	20.8	19.6	20.4	21.3	20.4
45	20.9	20.7	21.1	20.9	21.1
46	21.0	20.8	21.0	20.7	20.8
47	20.9	20.6	21.1	21.1	20.7
48	20.5	20.6	20.3	20.0	20.5
49	20.7	20.3	20.8	20.5	20.1
50	20.6	20.8	20.2	20.6	20.4

FILTER

(a) Construct an R chart for these data.
(b) Does the R chart indicate that the process is in a state of statistical control? Why? If the R chart indicates the process is not in control, remove out-of-control points, and re-construct the chart with the remaining data.
(c) Construct a $\overline{X}$ chart based on the range for these data. Does the $\overline{X}$ chart indicate that the process is in a state of statistical control? Why?
(d) What conclusions can you draw about this process?
(e) Construct an s chart for these data.
(f) Does the s chart indicate that the process is in a state of statistical control? Why? If the s chart indicates the process is not in control, remove out-of-control points, and re-construct the chart with the remaining data.
(g) Construct a $\overline{X}$ chart based on the standard deviation for these data. Does the $\overline{X}$ chart indicate that the process is in a state of statistical control? Why?
(h) Compare your results in (e)–(g) with the results you obtained in (a)–(d).
(i) From (e)–(g), what conclusions can you draw about this process?

7.7 A pharmaceutical company produces reagents for diagnostic testing. Among the quality tests performed are medical decision pools that are run to monitor recovery at analyte values that are of medical significance (e.g., the borderline between normal and abnormal). Poor precision at this level could cause a misdiagnosis in assaying a patient's sample. The table below presents the medical decision pool results for the reagent for thyroid hormone T4. Samples of $n = 4$ replicates were tested each day for 30 days.

REPLICATES (UG/DL)

Day	1	2	3	4
1	4.10	4.12	4.15	4.13
2	4.09	4.13	4.11	4.11
3	4.14	4.13	4.12	4.10
4	4.08	4.06	4.08	4.10
5	4.08	4.07	4.12	4.09
6	4.12	4.13	4.13	4.10
7	4.13	4.11	4.11	4.10
8	4.10	4.12	4.13	4.12
9	4.12	4.12	4.10	4.14
10	4.12	4.14	4.10	4.13
11	4.21	4.18	4.18	4.12
12	4.15	4.13	4.15	4.14
13	4.15	4.14	4.12	4.13
14	4.14	4.13	4.12	4.11
15	4.12	4.12	4.13	4.16

(Continued)

Day	1	2	3	4
16	4.13	4.12	4.12	4.12
17	4.11	4.13	4.10	4.12
18	4.16	4.18	4.19	4.20
19	4.19	4.17	4.15	4.13
20	4.12	4.11	4.17	4.11
21	4.13	4.16	4.08	4.10
22	4.11	4.12	4.11	4.13
23	4.12	4.11	4.13	4.13
24	4.10	4.15	4.11	4.12
25	4.18	4.12	4.12	4.13
26	4.13	4.13	4.11	4.12
27	4.17	4.19	4.12	4.13
28	4.14	4.15	4.11	4.12
29	4.14	4.16	4.12	4.11
30	4.17	4.18	4.12	4.15

REAGENT

(a) Construct an R chart for these data.
(b) Does the R chart indicate that the process is in a state of statistical control? Why? If the R chart indicates the process is not in control, remove out-of-control points, and re-construct the chart with the remaining data.
(c) Construct a $\overline{X}$ chart based on the range for these data. Does the $\overline{X}$ chart indicate that the process is in a state of statistical control? Why?
(d) What conclusions can you draw about this process?
(e) Construct an s chart for these data.
(f) Does the s chart indicate that the process is in a state of statistical control? Why? If the s chart indicates the process is not in control, remove out-of-control points, and re-construct the chart with the remaining data.
(g) Construct a $\overline{X}$ chart based on the standard deviation for these data. Does the $\overline{X}$ chart indicate that the process is in a state of statistical control? Why?
(h) Compare your results in (e)–(g) with the results you obtained in (a)–(d).
(i) From (e)–(g), what conclusions can you draw about this process?

7.8 The weight of transdermal therapeutic systems or skin patches for delivery of medications through the skin and into the bloodstream must be carefully controlled to insure accurate patient doses. As part of the quality-control program, a weight check is performed every 30 minutes while the equipment producing the patches is in operation. To set up trial control limits, 12 weight checks were recorded each production day. The table below presents the mean and the standard deviation for each sample of $n = 12$ collected over a 27-day period. Measurements are in milligrams.

Day	Mean	Standard Deviation	Notes
1	1,894.67	31.33	
2	1,924.67	27.60	
3	1,894.00	34.98	
4	1,902.67	25.38	
5	1,912.67	34.86	
6	1,896.00	39.12	
7	1,908.00	21.57	
8	1,912.67	22.49	
9	1,937.92	33.09	End of batch
10	1,917.33	27.89	New batch
11	1,889.33	20.84	
12	1,910.00	18.09	
13	1,909.33	21.26	
14	1,900.00	26.20	
15	1,915.33	31.16	
16	1,911.33	32.62	
17	1,912.67	22.75	
18	1,901.33	17.67	
19	1,892.00	31.82	
20	1,888.67	38.06	

(*Continued*)

Day	Mean	Standard Deviation	Notes
21	1,918.67	31.14	
22	1,904.67	39.26	
23	1,909.33	22.59	
24	1,904.00	24.48	
25	1,912.00	32.27	
26	1,896.67	18.20	
27	1,923.33	38.21	

PATCH

(a) Construct an *s* chart for these data.
(b) Does the *s* chart indicate that the process is in a state of statistical control? Why? If the *s* chart indicates the process is not in control, remove out-of-control points, and re-construct the chart with the remaining data.
(c) Construct a $\overline{X}$ chart for these data. Does the $\overline{X}$ chart indicate that the process is in a state of statistical control? Why?
(d) What conclusions or recommendations can you make about this process?

7.4 CONTROL CHARTS FOR INDIVIDUAL VALUES (*X* CHARTS)

In some situations, it is not practical or possible to collect data on subgroups. For example, in low-volume operations, where there is a lengthy interval between output units, or where a single measurement represents work output for an entire time period, such as a shift or a day, the use of subgroups is impractical. When batches of product such as chemical mixtures are produced, obtaining more than one sample from the batch is not useful, because any variability in the results obtained may be due to measurement error (provided the batch was well mixed and had not settled). In other situations, automated equipment might routinely evaluate every unit of output. In situations in which evaluation of the quality characteristic requires destruction of the item or unit, testing samples greater than $n = 1$ might be prohibitively expensive. Situations such as these require **individual values charts** or ***X* charts.** (Sometimes the terminology *I chart* is used instead of *X* chart.) Although not as sensitive statistically as charts based on sample statistics like the $\overline{X}$ chart, charts for individual measurements can be useful in certain circumstances.

When only individual measurements are available, we can consider each individual observation as a "subgroup" of size $n = 1$. With larger subgroups, we could estimate process variability by using sample ranges or sample standard deviations and base our estimates of process variability on *within-sample* variability. When there is only one observation in each subgroup, there will be no variation within the subgroups. In such cases, we must estimate process variability another way. Two approaches are available. The first involves a statistic called the *moving range,* and the other employs the standard deviation of the entire set of individual values to estimate process variability.

The Individual Value (*X*) Chart with the Moving Range

The moving range method estimates process variability by considering the differences between consecutive observations or observations adjacent in time. The **moving range** (MR_i) is calculated by

$$MR_i = |X_{i+1} - X_i| \qquad (7.19)$$

where

        k is the number of samples or subgroups

    | | represents the absolute value

    X_{i+1} is the value for observation $i + 1$

      X_i is the value for observation *i*

Each value of MR_i requires two successive observations for its calculation, so for any set of *k* observations there will be only $k - 1$ values of the moving range. For example, the first moving range value is $MR_1 = |X_2 - X_1|$, the second moving-range value is $MR_2 = |X_3 - X_2|$, and the last moving range value is $MR_{k-1} = |X_k - X_{k-1}|$.

Once the individual moving-range values have been calculated, we estimate process variability by calculating the average value of the moving range, $\overline{MR}$.

$$\overline{MR} = \frac{\sum_{i=1}^{k-1} MR_i}{k - 1} \qquad (7.20)$$

where *k* is the number of observations.

$\overline{MR}$ is used as the center line of the moving range chart in a manner similar to the way the average of sample ranges, $\overline{R}$, represented the center line on the *R* chart.

Calculating Control Limits for the Moving Range Chart

To estimate the $\pm 3\sigma$ control limits for the **moving range chart** (*MR* chart) we use the average moving range, $\overline{MR}$, calculated from Equation (7.20) and control chart factors D_4 and D_3 (see Section 7.3). Using D_4 to calculate the upper control limit, we have

$$\text{UCL}(MR) = D_4 \overline{MR} \qquad (7.21a)$$

and, using D_3 to calculate the lower control limit, we have

$$\text{LCL}(MR) = D_3 \overline{MR} \qquad (7.21b)$$

where D_4 and D_3 are control chart factors from Table A.3.

Because each moving-range value is based on two consecutive observations, the "subgroup size" for each moving range is 2. As can be seen from Table A.3, in cases where $n = 2$, the value of D_4 is 3.267, and the value of D_3 is 0.00. Therefore, whenever we calculate moving ranges from two consecutive observations, Equations (7.21a) and (7.21b) become

$$\text{UCL}(MR) = 3.267\,\overline{MR} \qquad\qquad (7.22\text{a})$$

and

$$\text{LCL}(MR) = 0.00\,\overline{MR} \qquad\qquad (7.22\text{b})$$

As can be seen from Equation (7.22b), the value of the lower control limit will be 0.00 whenever moving ranges are calculated from two consecutive observations.

It should be noted that the values of the upper control limit and lower control limit for the moving range chart calculated by Equations (7.21) or (7.22), which use control chart factors D_4 and D_3, are estimates, because the tabled values for these factors are based on the assumption that the ranges used in calculating control limits are independent. This assumption will be satisfied when range values are based on independent samples. When moving ranges are used, however, this assumption is violated, because each observation contributes to two moving range values. (See References 11, 12, and 16.)

Once the trial limits for the moving range chart are established, we can proceed to construct the chart by plotting the individual values MR_i. Each value of MR_i is based on two observations adjacent in time, so some statisticians prefer to plot moving range values in the interval (on the X-axis or horizontal axis) between the two time periods used to calculate the value of the moving range. If the moving range chart indicates that the process is out of statistical control, we should investigate any out-of-control points and eliminate the data for any points that represent special causes that can be identified. If the moving range chart using trial limits indicates that the process is in a state of statistical control, we can be confident that $\overline{MR}$ will provide a sufficiently good estimate of σ to proceed with construction of trial limits for the individual values or X chart.

Calculating the Center Line and Trial Control Limits for the Individual Values Chart

The center line for the individual values or X chart represents the process average, μ, which can be estimated by the mean of the individual values, $\overline{X}$, where

$$\text{Center Line}(X) = \text{CL}(X) = \overline{X} = \frac{\displaystyle\sum_{i=1}^{k} X_i}{k} \qquad\qquad (7.23)$$

where

X_i is the ith individual value

k is the number of individual values available for calculating trial limits

To obtain the $\pm 3\sigma$ control limits for the individual values or X chart, we estimate the value of s by $\overline{MR}/d_2$. The value of the upper control limit can then be calculated as

$$\text{UCL}(X) = \overline{X} + 3\frac{\overline{MR}}{d_2} \tag{7.24a}$$

and the value of the lower control limit can be calculated as

$$\text{LCL}(X) = \overline{X} - 3\frac{\overline{MR}}{d_2} \tag{7.24b}$$

Because $3/d_2$ is a constant for a given subgroup size, the control chart factor E_2 presented in Appendix A, Table A.3 is used to simplify Equations (7.24a) and (7.24b), so that

$$\text{UCL}(X) = \overline{X} + E_2\,\overline{MR} \tag{7.25a}$$

and

$$\text{LCL}(X) = \overline{X} - E_2\,\overline{MR} \tag{7.25b}$$

Each of the moving ranges used to calculate $\overline{MR}$ is calculated from two consecutive observations, so we can consider subgroup size to be two. Whenever $n = 2$, the value of $E_2 = 2.66$. Therefore, Equations (7.25a) and (7.25b) become

$$\text{UCL}(X) = \overline{X} + 2.66\,\overline{MR} \tag{7.26a}$$

and

$$\text{LCL}(X) = \overline{X} - 2.66\,\overline{MR} \tag{7.26b}$$

To illustrate the use of the MR and X charts, let us consider quality-control data collected at an automobile assembly plant that produces minivans. Consumer research has shown that one of the variables affecting a customer's perception of quality in an automobile is the flushness of the top flange of a car door with the side surround of the body. Improper fit or flushness can result in airflow noise, squeaks, difficulty in opening and closing doors, and water leakage. Specifications call for a flushness measurement of 0, with an upper specified tolerance level of $+1.5$ mm and a lower specified tolerance level of -1.5 mm. The data presented in Table 7.4 represent flushness ratings in millimeters on 25 consecutively produced minivans.

To compute the center line for the moving-range chart, we must first calculate individual moving range values. Table 7.5 presents the flushness data and the $(k - 1) = 24$ moving range values calculated by using Equation (7.19). We can then

TABLE 7.4

FLUSHNESS OF TOP FLANGE OF DOORS ON 25 CONSECUTIVELY PRODUCED MINIVANS

Vehicle	Flushness	Vehicle	Flushness
1	2.63	14	1.71
2	1.93	15	2.23
3	3.36	16	2.13
4	1.88	17	1.05
5	3.56	18	2.98
6	1.04	19	1.85
7	1.83	20	0.90
8	1.32	21	3.93
9	4.83	22	3.81
10	2.32	23	3.95
11	2.81	24	0.74
12	1.40	25	0.50
13	2.31		**MINIVAN1**

TABLE 7.5

FLUSHNESS DATA AND MOVING RANGES FOR 25 CONSECUTIVELY PRODUCED MINIVANS

Vehicle	Flushness	Moving Range	Vehicle	Flushness	Moving Range
1	2.63		15	2.23	
		0.70			0.10
2	1.93		16	2.13	
		1.43			1.08
3	3.36		17	1.05	
		1.48			1.93
4	1.88		18	2.98	
		1.68			1.13
5	3.56		19	1.85	
		2.52			0.95
6	1.04		20	0.90	
		0.79			3.03
7	1.83		21	3.93	
		0.51			0.12
8	1.32		22	3.81	
		3.51			0.14
9	4.83		23	3.95	
		2.51			3.21
10	2.32		24	0.74	
		0.49			0.24
11	2.81		25	0.50	
		1.41			
12	1.40		$\sum_{i=1}^{k} X_i = 57.00$		$\sum_{i=1}^{k-1} MR_i = 30.99$
		0.91			
13	2.31				
		0.60			
14	1.71				
		0.52			

calculate $\overline{MR}$ by using Equation (7.20) as follows:

$$\overline{MR} = \frac{\sum_{i=1}^{k-1} MR_i}{k-1}$$

$$\overline{MR} = \frac{30.99}{25-1}$$

$$\overline{MR} = \frac{30.99}{24}$$

$$\overline{MR} = 1.291$$

Using Equation (7.21a), we calculate the value of the upper control limit as

$$\text{UCL}(MR) = D_4\,\overline{MR}$$
$$\text{UCL}(MR) = (3.267)(1.291)$$
$$\text{UCL}(MR) = 4.218$$

and, using Equation (7.21b), we calculate the value of the lower control limit as

$$\text{LCL}(MR) = D_3\,\overline{MR}$$
$$\text{LCL}(MR) = (0.0)(1.291)$$
$$\text{LCL}(MR) = 0.0$$

Figure 7.5 presents the moving range chart obtained from MINITAB for the flushness data presented in Table 7.4.

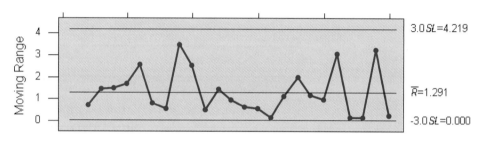

Figure 7.5   Moving-range (MR) chart obtained from MINITAB for flushness data presented in Table 7.4

Examination of Figure 7.5 shows that there are no points that fall above the UCL or below the LCL. Because the moving range appears to be in control, we can use $\overline{MR}$ to construct the control limits for the individual measurements chart.
We begin by calculating the sum of the individual observations as

$$\sum_{i=1}^{25} X_i = 57.00$$

The center line for the X chart is then obtained by using Equation (7.23) as follows:

$$\overline{X} = \frac{\sum_{i=1}^{k} X_i}{k}$$
$$\overline{X} = \frac{57.00}{25}$$
$$\overline{X} = 2.28$$

From Equations (7.26a), the upper control limit is calculated as

$$\text{UCL}(X) = \overline{X} + (2.66)\overline{MR}$$
$$\text{UCL}(X) = 2.28 + 2.66(1.291)$$
$$\text{UCL}(X) = 5.714$$

and the lower control limit is calculated from Equation (7.26b) as

$$\text{LCL}(X) = \bar{X} - (2.66)\overline{MR}$$
$$\text{LCL}(X) = 2.28 - 2.66(1.291)$$
$$\text{LCL}(X) = -1.154$$

Measures of flushness can be either positive or negative values, so, in this example, a negative control limit is valid. Figure 7.6 presents the individual values chart obtained from MINITAB for these data. Examination of the chart indicates that the process seems to be in a state of statistical control, so we can extend the trial limits and continue to record flushness measurements on the chart.

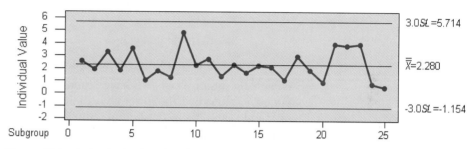

Figure 7.6   Individual values (*X*) chart using moving-range method obtained from MINITAB for the flushness data presented in Table 7.4

COMMENT: THE MOVING RANGE AND STANDARD DEVIATION METHODS FOR INDIVIDUAL OBSERVATIONS

It should be noted that, when one is estimating σ by the moving range method, variation between observations adjacent in time will be emphasized, while the standard deviation method emphasizes overall variability among the individual values. If trends are present in the data, the moving-range method can seriously underestimate σ and result in control limits that are *too narrow*. This will result in an increase in false alarms (see Reference 16).

The Individual Value (*X*) Chart with the Standard Deviation

The moving range method of estimating σ is frequently used in the early or initial stages of monitoring a process. This use can result in the early detection and elimination of special causes; however, the moving range method can result in an unacceptable number of false alarms. After a process has been monitored for some time and is considered to be stable, or after sufficient additional data have been collected, it is preferable to use the standard deviation of the set of available individual measurements to estimate σ. Recent research has shown that the moving range approach is statistically inefficient in comparison to the standard deviation approach, and, in the case of observations that are correlated over time, the moving range method can result in misleading control limits. (See References 4 and 16.)

Although a smaller number of observations can be used, to construct trial limits for individual values charts by using the standard deviation of the individual values to estimate the process standard deviation, σ, we should begin by collecting data on *at least* 50 individual units.

As shown previously, the center line of an individual values chart is represented by the mean of the individual values, which can be calculated using Equation (7.23):

$$\text{Center Line}(X) = \text{CL}(X) = \overline{X} = \frac{\sum_{i=1}^{k} X_i}{k}$$

where

X_i = the ith individual value

k = the number of individual values available for calculating trial limits

As with the other charts we have studied, the upper control limit is placed 3σ above the center line, the lower control limit 3σ below the center line. Because s is not a good estimate of σ when the number of observations used to calculate s is small, the correction factor c_4 can be used to improve our estimate of σ.

We can obtain an estimate of σ by:

$$\sigma = \frac{s}{c_4} \qquad (7.27)$$

where c_4 is a control chart factor that can be found in Table A.3 for sets of individual values up to size $n = 25$.

As n, the number of observations, increases, the value of c_4 approaches 1.0. In situations when 25 to 50 individual observations are used, the value of c_4 is approximately 0.99. In the case of n greater than 50, an uncorrected value of s is a sufficient estimate of σ, and $c_4 = 1.0$.

The upper and lower control limits are then calculated by using the following equations:

$$\text{UCL}(X) = \overline{X} + 3\frac{s}{c_4} \qquad (7.28a)$$

and

$$\text{UCL}(X) = \overline{X} - 3\frac{s}{c_4} \qquad (7.28b)$$

To illustrate the use of the X chart, we will consider the data presented in Table 7.6, which presents the flushness measurements of 50 consecutively produced minivans. The first 25 measurements presented in Table 7.6 were presented in Table 7.4 and were used to illustrate the moving range chart.

TABLE 7.6

FLUSHNESS RATINGS IN MILLIMETERS ON 50 CONSECUTIVELY PRODUCED MINIVANS

Vehicle	Flushness	Vehicle	Flushness
1	2.63	26	2.60
2	1.93	27	1.09
3	3.36	28	−0.81
4	1.88	29	1.32
5	3.56	30	1.43
6	1.04	31	−1.63
7	1.83	32	3.07
8	1.32	33	2.44
9	4.83	34	3.45
10	2.32	35	2.46
11	2.81	36	0.97
12	1.40	37	0.88
13	2.31	38	1.83
14	1.71	39	1.53
15	2.23	40	0.64
16	2.13	41	1.08
17	1.05	42	−0.04
18	2.98	43	3.93
19	1.85	44	3.36
20	0.90	45	2.14
21	3.93	46	1.64
22	3.81	47	2.80
23	3.95	48	2.81
24	0.74	49	2.87
25	0.50	50	−0.77 **MINIVAN2**

Calculating the Center Line and Control Limits for the Individual Values Chart

To calculate the value of the center line, we use Equation (7.23) to obtain the mean flushness measurement for the 50 minivans presented in Table 7.6.

$$\text{Center Line}(X) = \text{CL}(X) = \bar{X} = \frac{\sum\limits_{i=1}^{k} X_i}{k}$$

Thus,

$$\text{Center Line}(X) = \bar{X} = \frac{98.09}{50} = 1.962$$

We then can calculate s by using Equation (3.10). For these data, $s = 1.315$. Because the number of individual measurements is 50, the value of the correction factor c_4 is 0.99.

Thus, using Equations (7.28a) and (7.28b) for this data set, we have

$$\text{UCL}(X) = \overline{X} + 3\frac{s}{c_4}$$

$$\text{UCL}(X) = 1.962 + 3\left(\frac{1.315}{0.99}\right)$$

$$\text{UCL}(X) = 1.962 + 3(1.328)$$

$$\text{UCL}(X) = 1.962 + 3.985$$

$$\text{UCL}(X) = 5.947$$

and

$$\text{UCL}(X) = \overline{X} - 3\frac{s}{c_4}$$

$$\text{LCL}(X) = 1.962 - 3\left(\frac{1.315}{0.99}\right)$$

$$\text{LCL}(X) = 1.962 - 3(1.328)$$

$$\text{LCL}(X) = 1.962 - 3.985$$

$$\text{LCL}(X) = -2.023$$

Because our measures of flushness can be either positive or negative values in this example, a negative control limit is valid.

Figure 7.7 presents the individual values chart for the flushness data presented in Table 7.6. As in the moving-range example, which used the first 25 flushness measurements, there are no points outside the control limits or other out-of-control patterns. Therefore, the trial limits can be extended, and we can continue to plot flushness measurements as each minivan on the line is evaluated.

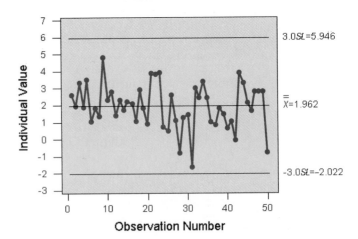

Figure 7.7 Individual values (X) chart using the standard-deviation method obtained from MINITAB for the flushness data presented in Table 7.6

Although this process is in a state of statistical control, the design specifications call for a flushness target value of 0.0 and specified tolerance limits of ±1.5 mm. The process average is 1.96 mm, therefore, the process mean is not centered on the target. This is an example of a process that is stable but unable to meet design specifications. Because it is stable, we can expect it to continue to produce output that is nonconforming unless some action is taken. Problem 7.9 presents the action taken by the design team and the data they collected after changes were made.

PROBLEMS

7.9 Although the control chart for individual values presented as an example on page 320 showed the process was stable, the flushness of the minivan doors was not within the tolerance limits specified in the design. The design team and assembly workers working on door installation brainstormed solutions to the flushness problem and decided that installation of a plastic or rubber piece on the lower inside flange would help reduce problems with flushness of the upper flange. This suggestion was implemented, and additional data were collected. The following data represent flushness measures in millimeters for the first 50 minivans produced after the design change was implemented.

Vehicle	Flushness	Vehicle	Flushness
1	−1.53	26	2.31
2	0.57	27	−0.39
3	−0.26	28	1.04
4	1.50	29	0.10
5	−0.98	30	0.16
6	−1.64	31	−1.17
7	0.20	32	1.92
8	0.48	33	0.58
9	2.52	34	−0.38
10	1.26	35	−0.43
11	0.91	36	0.04
12	0.33	37	1.60
13	1.00	38	−0.17
14	−0.71	39	1.54
15	2.31	40	1.59
16	−0.32	41	−1.33
17	0.95	42	0.35
18	1.18	43	1.56
19	−1.22	44	−0.73
20	0.98	45	−1.06
21	1.29	46	0.94
22	−0.62	47	−0.05
23	1.59	48	0.67
24	1.33	49	0.52
25	0.29	50	3.14

MINIVAN3

(a) Extend the trial control limits established in the flushness example in Table 7.6, and plot the first 25 measurements collected after the design change on that chart.

(b) Does the chart indicate that the process is in a state of statistical control? Why?

(c) Construct an *X* chart using only the data collected after the design change was implemented to calculate control limits using the standard deviation method.

(d) Does the *X* chart constructed in (c) indicate that the process is in a state of statistical control? Why?

(e) Specifications call for a flushness measurement of 0, with an upper specified tolerance level of +1.5 mm and a lower specified tolerance level of −1.5 mm. Compare the results you obtained with the data collected after the design change to the target value and tolerance limits specified in the design. Has the design change improved the process? Discuss your findings and conclusions.

7.10 A small independent public water utility in the San Francisco area monitored daily usage of water (1 unit = 748,000 gallons) for a period of ten weeks (Monday to Friday only) during September, October, and November in a recent year. The following table presents the daily water usage for 50 weekdays. Records show that on day 5, a water main broke, and a major leak occurred. No other anomalies were recorded.

Day	Water Usage	Day	Water Usage
1	2.50	10	2.63
2	2.67	11	2.47
3	2.73	12	2.59
4	2.64	13	3.20
5	4.45	14	3.02
6	2.74	15	2.31
7	3.31	16	2.30
8	2.49	17	2.50
9	2.76	18	3.31

(*Continued*)

Day	Water Usage	Day	Water Usage
19	2.48	35	3.22
20	2.22	36	2.33
21	2.61	37	2.27
22	2.64	38	2.30
23	2.92	39	2.29
24	2.10	40	2.20
25	3.18	41	3.31
26	2.39	42	3.45
27	3.51	43	3.23
28	2.23	44	2.29
29	2.55	45	2.33
30	2.64	46	2.34
31	2.58	47	3.31
32	2.98	48	2.31
33	2.43	49	2.64
34	2.39	50	2.24

WATER2

(a) Construct a moving range chart for these data. Does the moving range chart indicate that the process is in a state of statistical control? Why?

(b) If the moving range chart indicates the process is not in a state of statistical control, remove any out-of-control points, and calculate new limits for the chart. Does the revised chart indicate the process is in a state of statistical control?

(c) Construct an X chart for these data using the moving range method. Does the X chart indicate that the process is in a state of statistical control? Why?

(d) Construct an X chart for these data using the standard deviation method.

(e) Does the X chart using the standard deviation to estimate process variability indicate that the process is in a state of statistical control? Why? If the chart indicates the process is not in a state of statistical control, remove any out-of-control points, and calculate new limits for the chart. Does the revised chart indicate the process is in a state of statistical control?

(f) Compare the results you obtained in parts (a), (b), and (c) with the results you obtained in parts (d) and (e). Explain any similarities and differences.

7.11 Environmental regulations require monitoring of particulate-matter emissions from combustion sources. Particulate-matter emissions are related to the efficiency of many combustion sources. Regulations require that particulate-matter emissions not exceed 280 parts per million (ppm). Emissions should be relatively stable, to ensure steady-state operations of an engine generator operating at a wastewater-treatment facility. Continuous monitoring of particulate-matter emissions from the engine generator is performed. The following data represent the level of emissions observed each hour in a 50-hour period.

PM Emissions		PM Emissions	
Hour	(ppm)	Hour	(ppm)
1	260	26	254
2	257	27	254
3	252	28	257
4	254	29	260
5	256	30	259
6	259	31	258
7	254	32	257
8	258	33	255
9	256	34	256
10	255	35	258
11	253	36	254
12	251	37	255
13	252	38	256
14	253	39	258
15	252	40	257
16	254	41	255
17	256	42	253
18	254	43	256
19	255	44	260
20	257	45	257
21	259	46	260
22	256	47	257
23	256	48	255
24	252	49	253
25	254	50	252

EMISSION2

(a) Construct a moving range chart for these data. Does the moving range chart indicate that the process is in a state of statistical control? Why?

(b) If the moving range chart indicates the process is not in a state of statistical control, remove any out-of-control points, and calculate new limits for the chart. Does the revised chart indicate the process is in a state of statistical control?

(c) Construct an X chart for these data using the moving range method. Does the X chart indicate that the process is in a state of statistical control? Why?

(d) Construct an X chart for these data using the standard deviation method.

(e) Does the X chart using the standard deviation to estimate process variability indicate that the process is in a state of statistical control? Why? If the chart indicates the process is not in a state of statistical control, remove any out-of-control points, and calculate new limits for the chart. Does the revised chart indicate the process is in a state of statistical control?

(f) Compare the results you obtained in parts (a), (b), and (c) with the results you obtained in parts (d) and (e). Explain any similarities and differences.

7.12 The quality-control department of a sugar packager monitors the percent moisture in 10-gram samples of sugar drawn from bags it has packaged. Bags are randomly selected from warehouse stocks and subjected to a number of tests. Among the tests performed on each sample are a measure of moisture content and a measure of the percent of the sample that is pure sugar. The following table presents the moisture content measured in percent and the percent of the sample that is pure sugar for 50 bags of sugar.

Bag	Moisture	Purity	Bag	Moisture	Purity
1	1.81	93.76	26	1.79	94.12
2	1.89	94.32	27	1.89	94.22
3	1.09	97.72	28	2.10	93.40
4	2.80	88.66	29	2.49	91.72
5	2.40	92.40	30	1.31	95.12
6	1.49	92.53	31	1.99	93.92
7	1.21	90.52	32	1.97	92.90
8	2.21	93.28	33	2.50	92.56
9	1.79	93.90	34	2.61	93.32
10	1.80	93.34	35	2.41	93.76
11	2.10	95.00	36	2.50	92.56
12	2.00	93.58	37	1.99	92.04
13	1.61	91.50	38	2.35	93.46
14	2.20	94.94	39	2.70	91.06
15	2.70	91.98	40	2.80	88.16
16	2.47	92.45	41	2.57	92.08
17	1.91	92.00	42	2.73	92.86
18	1.90	94.80	43	2.50	92.97
19	1.70	94.22	44	2.41	93.70
20	1.70	94.36	45	2.70	91.49
21	1.61	94.68	46	2.20	95.44
22	2.24	93.7	47	3.00	94.48
23	2.61	93.90	48	2.40	95.93
24	2.10	93.72	49	1.99	92.38
25	2.70	90.86	50	2.41	91.46

SUGAR

(a) Construct a moving range chart for the moisture data. Does the moving range chart indicate that the process is in a state of statistical control? Why?

(b) If the moving range chart indicates the process is not in a state of statistical control, remove any out-of-control points, and calculate new limits for the chart. Does the revised chart indicate the process is in a state of statistical control?

(c) Construct an X chart for the moisture data using the moving range method. Does the X chart indicate that the process is in a state of statistical control? Why?

(d) Construct an X chart for the moisture data using the standard deviation method.

(e) Does the X chart using the standard deviation to estimate process variability indicate that the process is in a state of statistical control? Why? If the chart indicates the process is not in a state of statistical control, remove any out-of-control points, and calculate new limits for the chart. Does the revised chart indicate the process is in a state of statistical control?

(f) Compare the results you obtained in parts (a), (b), and (c) with the results you obtained in parts (d) and (e). Explain any similarities and differences.

7.13 Refer to the table in Problem 7.12 that presents quality characteristics of sugar and construct the following charts using the percent-purity data.

(a) Construct a moving range chart for the sugar-purity data. Does the moving range chart indicate that the process is in a state of statistical control? Why?

(b) If the moving range chart indicates the process in not is a state of statistical control, remove any out-of-control points, and calculate new limits for the chart. Does the revised chart indicate the process is in a state of statistical control?

(c) Construct an X chart for the purity data using the moving range method. Does the X chart indicate that the process is in a state of statistical control? Why?

(d) Construct an X chart for the purity data using the standard deviation method.

(e) Does the X chart using the standard deviation to estimate process variability indicate that the process is in a state of statistical control? Why? If the chart indicates the process is not in a state of statistical control, remove any out-of-control points, and calculate new limits for the chart. Does the revised chart indicate the process is in a state of statistical control?

(f) Compare the results you obtained in parts (a), (b), and (c) with the results you obtained in parts (d) and (e). Explain any similarities and differences.

7.14 An environmental engineer monitored sound level in a building every 15 seconds, to determine whether noise levels were within EPA standards and whether the sound levels were in a state of statistical control. The following table presents the noise levels recorded in dBA units for 60 15-second intervals.

Interval	dBA	Interval	dBA	Interval	dBA	Interval	dBA
1	66	16	66	31	85	46	70
2	56	17	70	32	70	47	74
3	70	18	72	33	76	48	70
4	72	19	72	34	70	49	72
5	67	20	65	35	74	50	69
6	68	21	70	36	72	51	70
7	70	22	70	37	70	52	70
8	71	23	72	38	70	53	68
9	74	24	64	39	75	54	72
10	69	25	68	40	70	55	71
11	72	26	71	41	70	56	69
12	70	27	70	42	68	57	72
13	70	28	70	43	70	58	70
14	70	29	78	44	69	59	68
15	72	30	86	45	73	60	72

SOUND

(a) Use the first 30 observations to construct a moving range chart for these data. Does the moving range chart indicate that the process is in a state of statistical control? Why?

(b) If the moving range chart indicates the process is not in a state of statistical control, remove any out-of-control points, and calculate new limits for the chart. Does the revised chart indicate the process is in a state of statistical control?

(c) Construct an X chart for these data using the moving range method. Does the X chart indicate that the process is in a state of statistical control? Why?

(d) Use all 60 observations to construct an X chart for these data using the standard deviation method.

(e) Does the X chart using the standard deviation to estimate process variability indicate that the process is in a state of statistical control? Why? If the chart indicates the process is not in a state of statistical control, remove any out-of-control points, and calculate new limits for the chart. Does the revised chart indicate the process is in a state of statistical control?

(f) Compare the results you obtained in parts (a), (b), and (c) with the results you obtained in parts (d) and (e). Explain any similarities and differences.

7.15 Silicon wafers are polished by a chemical-mechanical polisher. As part of a quality-control evaluation, each wafer is measured at several locations. The following table presents post polishing measurements taken at the center of the wafer for 60 wafers. Measurements are in angstrom units.

Wafer	Width	Wafer	Width
1	11678	31	11063
2	11742	32	12283
3	11674	33	12188
4	11804	34	12378
5	12110	35	12408
6	11933	36	12320
7	11955	37	12575
8	12091	38	12389
9	11230	39	12487
10	12241	40	12541
11	12171	41	12566
12	12173	42	12401
13	11096	43	12488
14	11207	44	12308
15	12307	45	12274
16	11266	46	12341
17	11185	47	12392
18	12200	48	12177
19	12143	49	12170
20	12451	50	12519
21	10941	51	12534
22	11324	52	12448
23	12088	53	12424
24	11149	54	12486
25	12299	55	12542
26	11310	56	12590
27	12244	57	11552
28	11239	58	12569
29	12174	59	11703
30	11262	60	12530

WAFER

(a) Use the first 30 observations to construct a moving range chart for these data. Does the moving range chart indicate that the process is in a state of statistical control? Why?

(b) If the moving range chart indicates the process is not in a state of statistical control, remove any out-of-control points, and calculate new limits for the chart. Does the revised chart indicate the process is in a state of statistical control?

(c) Construct an X chart for these data using the moving range method. Does the X chart indicate that the process is in a state of statistical control? Why?

(d) Use all 60 observations to construct an X chart for these data by using the standard deviation method.

(e) Does the X chart using the standard deviation to estimate process variability indicate that the process is in a state of statistical control? Why? If the chart indicates the process is not in a state of statistical control, remove any out-of-control points, and calculate new limits for the chart. Does the revised chart indicate the process is in a state of statistical control?

(f) Compare the results you obtained in parts (a), (b), and (c) with the results you obtained in parts (d) and (e). Explain any similarities and differences.

7.5 SPECIAL CONSIDERATIONS WITH VARIABLES CHARTS

All of the variables charts discussed in this chapter require that the underlying distribution of the data be normal. In the case of an $\overline{X}$ chart used either with the R chart or s chart, violation of this assumption will not seriously affect the usefulness of the charts or the accuracy of our decisions. In these situations, our calculations are based on sample means, and it is sample means that are plotted. Whenever we use sample means in this way, the *Central Limit Theorem* (see Section 5.9) will protect us from the consequences of violating the normality assumption underlying the use of these control charts. In the case of individual values charts, we do not have the Central Limit Theorem to protect us, and for this control chart, the normality assumption is more important. If the data are not normally distributed, individual values charts can be misleading and can lead to erroneous decisions about a process. Therefore, it is important to test for normality before constructing an individual values chart. This can be done using normal probability plots (see Section 5.5) or by testing for departures from normality (see Reference 14).

Shewhart's basic rule that the process should be declared out of a state of statistical control if one or more points plot above the upper control limit or below the lower control limit will generally limit the probability of false alarms to approximately 0.0027. Although using the other rules and patterns presented in Section 6.2 to determine the presence of special causes can enhance the ability of the charts to detect small shifts or special causes, they should be used cautiously. Recent research (see Reference 20) indicates that employing these rules may substantially increase the risk of false alarms. The risk of false alarms can be substantial when the normality assumption has been violated. False alarms can lead to tampering with the process and, as such, can increase variability and costs. In situations in which false alarms are costly or need to be minimized for other reasons, the supplementary optional rules should not be used. The $\pm 2\sigma$ limits can be used as warning limits to indicate that more frequent sampling is necessary. For example, if two out of three consecutive points fall above the $+2\sigma$ limits, we might suspect that a special cause is operating and increase sampling or monitor the process more closely.

Shifts in process average will usually be detected by the chart that monitors between-group variability, such as the $\overline{X}$ chart. However, if a shift in process average occurs in the interval in which a subgroup is being selected for evaluation, the shift is more likely to increase estimates of within-group variability and cause an out-of-control signal on the chart monitoring within-group variability (i.e., R or s chart) than on the $\overline{X}$ chart, which monitors between-group variability.

7.6 THE CUMULATIVE SUM (CUSUM) AND EXPONENTIALLY WEIGHTED MOVING AVERAGE (EWMA) CHARTS

The control charts presented thus far in this chapter and in Chapter 6 are called Shewhart control charts, because they are based on control chart principles developed by Walter Shewhart. One characteristic of these charts is that information concerning a single point is used, rather than information relating to an entire sequence of points. This feature reduces the ability of the Shewhart charts to detect small shifts of less than 1.5 standard deviations in the process. Two alternative charts that are more sensitive to smaller shifts in the process will be discussed in this section, the **cumulative sum (CUSUM) control charts** (see References 8 and 10) and the **exponentially weighted moving average (EWMA) chart** (see References 5 and 8). CUSUM charts differ from the Shewhart charts we have studied in that they plot cumulative sums of sample statistics or cumulative sums of deviations of the sample statistic from some target value. EWMA charts are based on a geometric moving average. An advantage of EWMA charts is that they can readily be used to forecast average process level for the next time period. (See References 8, 10, and 19.)

CUSUM Charts

CUSUM charts directly incorporate cumulative information from an entire series of points in developing both the center line and the control limits. In this section, we will study a cumulative sum chart that involves the process mean. The CUSUM chart is developed in two steps. First each $\overline{X}_i$ is expressed in deviations from $\overline{\overline{X}}$ in standard deviation (Z) units as shown in Equation (7.29)

$$Z_i = \frac{\overline{X}_i - \overline{\overline{X}}}{\dfrac{\bar{s}}{c_4\sqrt{n}}} \tag{7.29}$$

Then, the Z_i values are cumulated so that S_{H_i} and S_{L_i} are obtained from each subgroup from

$$S_{H_i} = \max[0, (Z_i - k) + S_{H_{i-1}}] \tag{7.30a}$$

$$S_{L_i} = \max[0, (-Z_i - k) + S_{L_{i-1}}] \tag{7.30b}$$

where k is selected to be one-half the average shift in the process mean to be detected (expressed in Z units).

If one wishes to detect a shift of one standard deviation, as is often the case, k is set at 0.5. It has been suggested by Montgomery (see Reference 8) that, with $k = 0.5$, a decision rule that detects a special cause when S_{H_i} or S_{L_i} is greater than 4 provides good average run length (see page 296) properties against a shift of up to one standard deviation in either direction.

To illustrate the CUSUM chart, we return to the example concerning the lead content of water supplied to customers by a public water utility that was studied by using the $\overline{X}$ chart in Section 7.3. Using Equations (7.29) and (7.30) for time period $i = 1$, we have

$$Z_i = \frac{7.2 - 5.587}{\dfrac{3.714}{0.94\sqrt{5}}} = 0.913$$

so that

$$S_{H_i} = \max[0, (0.913 - 0.5) + 0] = 0.413$$

and

$$S_{L_i} = \max[0, (-0.913 - 0.5) + 0] = 0$$

For time period $i = 2$,

$$Z_i = \frac{6.20 - 5.587}{\dfrac{3.714}{0.94\sqrt{5}}} = 0.347$$

and

$$S_{H_i} = \max[0, (0.347 - 0.5) + 0.413] = 0.260$$

and

$$S_{L_i} = \max[0, (-0.347 - 0.5) + 0.0] = 0$$

For time period $i = 3$,

$$Z_i = \frac{3.40 - 5.587}{\dfrac{3.714}{0.94\sqrt{5}}} = -1.238$$

so that

$$S_{H_i} = \max[0, (-1.238 - 0.5) + 0.260] = 0$$

and

$$S_{L_i} = \max[0, (-(-1.238) - 0.5) + 0.0] = 0.738$$

The entire set of S_{H_i} and S_{L_i} values is summarized in Table 7.7 on page 328.

We observe from Table 7.7 that none of the S_{H_i} and S_{L_i} values is above 4, so we conclude that there is no evidence that the process is out of control. This is the same conclusion arrived at previously by using the $\overline{X}$ chart.

EWMA Chart

Exponentially weighted moving average (EWMA) charts are based on a statistic that is a weighted average of the current data point and all the previous data points. The statistic used in the exponentially weighted moving average chart is based on the weighted average w_i expressed as follows:

$$w_i = r\overline{X}_i + (1 - r)w_{i-1} \tag{7.31}$$

TABLE 7.7

SUMMARY STATISTICS OBTAINED FROM MICROSOFT
EXCEL FOR THE CUSUM CHART FOR THE LEAD
CONTENT IN THE MUNICIPAL WATER SUPPLY DATA

	A	B	C	D	E
1	Day	Average	Z_i	SH_i	SL_i
2	1	7.2	0.913	0.413	0.000
3	2	6.2	0.347	0.260	0.000
4	3	3.4	-1.238	0.000	0.738
5	4	6.8	0.687	0.187	0.000
6	5	4.8	-0.445	0.000	0.000
7	6	8.2	1.479	0.979	0.000
8	7	4	-0.898	0.000	0.398
9	8	3.6	-1.124	0.000	1.022
10	9	4.4	-0.672	0.000	1.194
11	10	3.8	-1.011	0.000	1.705
12	11	5.6	0.008	0.000	1.197
13	12	3.6	-1.124	0.000	1.822
14	13	8.2	1.479	0.979	0.000
15	14	8.4	1.592	2.071	0.000
16	15	2.8	-1.577	0.000	1.077
17	16	9.2	2.045	1.545	0.000
18	17	6.8	0.687	1.732	0.000
19	18	4.8	-0.445	0.786	0.000
20	19	4.2	-0.785	0.000	0.285
21	20	7.8	1.253	0.753	0.000
22	21	7.4	1.026	1.279	0.000
23	22	4.4	-0.672	0.107	0.172
24	23	4.2	-0.785	0.000	0.456
25	24	3.6	-1.124	0.000	1.081
26	25	4.6	-0.558	0.000	1.139
27	26	2.8	-1.577	0.000	2.216
28	27	5.6	0.008	0.000	1.709
29	28	7.2	0.913	0.413	0.296
30	29	6.2	0.347	0.260	0.000
31	30	7.8	1.253	1.013	0.000
32	overall mean	5.587			
33	Sbar	3.714			
34	c4	0.94			
35	n	5			
36	k	0.5			

where

r = the weight given to the current observation

i = the time period

$w_0 = \overline{\overline{X}}$

Usually, r is set at 0.25 to detect shifts in the process mean of 1 standard deviation. Control limits for w_i are obtained from

$$\text{UCL}(w_i) = \overline{\overline{X}} + 3\frac{\overline{s}}{c_4\sqrt{n}}\sqrt{\frac{r}{2-r}[1-(1-r)^{2i}]} \qquad (7.32a)$$

and

$$\text{LCL}(w_i) = \bar{X} - 3\frac{\bar{s}}{c_4\sqrt{n}}\sqrt{\frac{r}{2-r}[1-(1-r)^{2i}]} \qquad (7.32b)$$

For $i \geq 5$,

$$\text{UCL}(w_i) = \bar{X} + 3\frac{\bar{s}}{c_4\sqrt{n}}\sqrt{\frac{r}{2-r}} \qquad (7.33a)$$

and

$$\text{LCL}(w_i) = \bar{X} - 3\frac{\bar{s}}{c_4\sqrt{n}}\sqrt{\frac{r}{2-r}} \qquad (7.33b)$$

To illustrate the EWMA chart, we return to the example concerning the lead content of water supplied to customers by a public water utility that was studied by using the $\bar{X}$ chart in Section 7.3 and the CUSUM chart in this section. Using Equations (7.31) and (7.32) for time period $i = 1$, we have

$$w_i = r\bar{X}_i + (1-r)w_{i-1}$$
$$w_1 = 0.25(7.2) + 0.75(5.587) = 5.99$$

and

$$\text{UCL}(w_1) = 5.587 + 3\frac{3.714}{0.94\sqrt{5}}\sqrt{\frac{0.25}{2-0.25}[1-(1-0.25)^{2(1)}]}$$
$$= 5.587 + 1.325$$
$$= 6.912$$

$$\text{LCL}(w_1) = 5.587 - 3\frac{3.714}{0.94\sqrt{5}}\sqrt{\frac{0.25}{2-0.25}[1-(1-0.25)^{2(1)}]}$$
$$= 5.587 - 1.325$$
$$= 4.262$$

For time period $i = 2$, we have

$$w_2 = 0.25(6.2) + 0.75(5.99) = 6.0425$$

and

$$\text{UCL}(w_2) = 5.587 + 3\frac{3.714}{0.94\sqrt{5}}\sqrt{\frac{0.25}{2-0.25}[1-(1-0.25)^{2(2)}]}$$
$$= 5.587 + 1.656$$
$$= 7.243$$

$$\text{LCL}(w_{2_1}) = 5.587 - 3\frac{3.714}{0.94\sqrt{5}}\sqrt{\frac{0.25}{2-0.25}[1-(1-0.25)^{2(2)}]}$$
$$= 5.587 - 1.656$$
$$= 3.930$$

For time period $i = 5$, we have

$$w_5 = 0.25(4.8) + 0.75(5.736) = 5.502$$

$$\text{UCL}(w_5) = 5.587 + 3\frac{3.714}{0.94\sqrt{5}}\sqrt{\frac{0.25}{2 - 0.25}}$$

$$= 5.587 + 2.003$$

$$= 7.590$$

$$\text{LCL}(w_{5_1}) = 5.587 - 3\frac{3.714}{0.94\sqrt{5}}\sqrt{\frac{0.25}{2 - 0.25}}$$

$$= 5.587 - 2.003$$

$$= 3.584$$

TABLE 7.8

SUMMARY STATISTICS OBTAINED FROM MICROSOFT
EXCEL FOR THE EWMA CHART FOR THE LEAD
CONTENT IN THE MUNICIPAL WATER SUPPLY DATA

	A	B	C	D	E
1	Day	Average	Wi	LCL	UCL
2	1	7.2	5.990	4.261	6.912
3	2	6.2	6.043	3.930	7.243
4	3	3.4	5.382	3.770	7.403
5	4	6.8	5.736	3.686	7.487
6	5	4.8	5.502	3.583	7.590
7	6	8.2	6.177	3.583	7.590
8	7	4	5.633	3.583	7.590
9	8	3.6	5.124	3.583	7.590
10	9	4.4	4.943	3.583	7.590
11	10	3.8	4.657	3.583	7.590
12	11	5.6	4.893	3.583	7.590
13	12	3.6	4.570	3.583	7.590
14	13	8.2	5.477	3.583	7.590
15	14	8.4	6.208	3.583	7.590
16	15	2.8	5.356	3.583	7.590
17	16	9.2	6.317	3.583	7.590
18	17	6.8	6.438	3.583	7.590
19	18	4.8	6.028	3.583	7.590
20	19	4.2	5.571	3.583	7.590
21	20	7.8	6.128	3.583	7.590
22	21	7.4	6.446	3.583	7.590
23	22	4.4	5.935	3.583	7.590
24	23	4.2	5.501	3.583	7.590
25	24	3.6	5.026	3.583	7.590
26	25	4.6	4.919	3.583	7.590
27	26	2.8	4.390	3.583	7.590
28	27	5.6	4.692	3.583	7.590
29	28	7.2	5.319	3.583	7.590
30	29	6.2	5.539	3.583	7.590
31	30	7.8	6.104	3.583	7.590
32	overall mean	5.587			
33	Sbar	3.714			
34	c4	0.94			
35	n	5			
36	r	0.25			

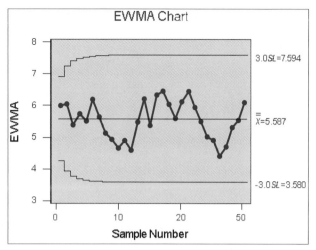

Figure 7.8   EWMA Chart obtained from MINITAB for the Lead Content in the Municipal Water Supply data

The entire set of w_i, UCL, and LCL values is summarized in Table 7.8.

We observe from Table 7.8 that none of the w_i values is above the UCL or below the LCL, so we conclude that there is no evidence that the process is out of control. This is the same conclusion arrived at previously by using the $\overline{X}$ chart and the CUSUM chart. Figure 7.8 illustrates the EWMA chart for these data obtained from MINITAB.

PROBLEMS

7.16 Refer to Problem 7.1 on page 306, concerning the repair time of radios.

RADIO

   (a) Construct a CUSUM chart for the average that is designed to detect a shift in the process mean of one standard deviation.

   (b) Construct an EWMA chart for the average that is designed to detect a shift in the process mean of one standard deviation.

   (c) Compare the results of (a) and (b) to those of Problem 7.1 (c) and (g).

7.17 Refer to Problem 7.2 on page 306, concerning the moisture content of coffee containers.

COFFEE

   (a) Construct a CUSUM chart for the average that is designed to detect a shift in the process mean of one standard deviation.

   (b) Construct an EWMA chart for the average that is designed to detect a shift in the process mean of one standard deviation.

   (c) Compare the results of (a) and (b) to those of Problem 7.2 (c) and (g).

7.18 Refer to Problem 7.3 on page 307, concerning the pressure drop readings in a sewage sludge incinerator.

SLUDGE

   (a) Construct a CUSUM chart for the average that is designed to detect a shift in the process mean of one standard deviation.

   (b) Construct an EWMA chart for the average that is designed to detect a shift in the process mean of one standard deviation.

   (c) Compare the results of (a) and (b) to those of Problem 7.3 (c) and (g).

7.19 Refer to Problem 7.4 on page 308, concerning the inflow infiltration of rainwater.

SEWAGE

(a) Construct a CUSUM chart for the average that is designed to detect a shift in the process mean of one standard deviation.

(b) Construct an EWMA chart for the average that is designed to detect a shift in the process mean of one standard deviation.

(c) Compare the results of (a) and (b) to those of Problem 7.4 (c) and (g).

7.20 Refer to Problem 7.5 on page 308, concerning back-wash operations in a water-treatment plant.

BACKWASH

(a) Construct a CUSUM chart for the average that is designed to detect a shift in the process mean of one standard deviation.

(b) Construct an EWMA chart for the average that is designed to detect a shift in the process mean of one standard deviation.

(c) Compare the results of (a) and (b) to those of Problem 7.5 (c) and (g).

7.21 Refer to Problem 7.6 on page 309, concerning the weight of coffee-filter packs.

FILTER

(a) Construct a CUSUM chart for the average that is designed to detect a shift in the process mean of one standard deviation.

(b) Construct an EWMA chart for the average that is designed to detect a shift in the process mean of one standard deviation.

(c) Compare the results of (a) and (b) to those of Problem 7.6 (c) and (g).

7.22 Refer to Problem 7.7 on page 310, concerning reagents for diagnostic medical testing.

REAGENT

(a) Construct a CUSUM chart for the average that is designed to detect a shift in the process mean of one standard deviation.

(b) Construct an EWMA chart for the average that is designed to detect a shift in the process mean of one standard deviation.

(c) Compare the results of (a) and (b) to those of Problem 7.7 (c) and (g).

7.23 Refer to Problem 7.8 on page 310, concerning the weight of transdermal therapeutic systems or skin patches for delivery of medications.

PATCH

(a) Construct a CUSUM chart for the average that is designed to detect a shift in the process mean of one standard deviation.

(b) Construct an EWMA chart for the average that is designed to detect a shift in the process mean of one standard deviation.

(c) Compare the results of (a) and (b) to those of Problem 7.8 (c) and (g).

7.7 PROCESS CAPABILITY

Process capability refers to the ability of a process to produce output that meets or exceeds the requirements set forth in design specifications. **Design specifications** are determined by an engineer or designer and usually include a target value, an upper specification limit, and a lower specification limit. The **target value,** which is sometimes referred to as the **nominal value,** represents the ideal value of a characteristic of a unit of output. The **upper specification limit,** also referred to as the **upper tolerance limit,** is the value above which the unit will not perform properly or at all; the **lower specification limit** or **lower tolerance limit** is the value below which the unit will not function properly. In other words, units above the upper specification limit or below the lower specification limit are considered nonconforming and should be reworked or scrapped. Nonconforming items that are supplied to consumers or are used to assemble composite products can fail in use and result in a dissatisfied customer or liability for damages caused by the product's failure. Because rework or scrap can add considerably to costs of production, it is important to monitor the ability of a process to produce output that is within specification or tolerance limits.

Assessing Process Capability

Once a process has been demonstrated by use of control charts to be stable, we can estimate the capability of the process to produce units that conform to the requirements called for in the design of the product or service.

If a process is stable, the quality characteristic is a variables measure, and the output is approximately normally distributed, we can estimate the proportion of items that will be beyond the specification limits as follows:

1. Estimate the process average by $\overline{\overline{X}}$ if using an $\overline{X}$ chart or by $\overline{X}$ if using an X chart.
2. Estimate the process standard deviation, σ, by using either R/d_2 or s/c_4.
3. Given lower specification limit (LSL) and upper specification limit (USL), find the distance between the process average and each of these limits in standardized units by calculating a standard normal score or Z score for the LSL and the USL by using Equations (7.34a) and (7.34b).

The Z value for the Lower Specification Limit is

$$Z_{LSL} = \frac{LSL - \overline{\overline{X}}}{\sigma} \tag{7.34a}$$

and Z value for Upper Specification Limit is

$$Z_{USL} = \frac{USL - \overline{\overline{X}}}{\sigma} \tag{7.34b}$$

4. Determine the proportion of the output that will fall outside the specification limits by referring to the table of areas under the standard normal curve (Table A.2).

To illustrate the use of Z values to estimate the proportion of output expected to be above the upper specification limit or below the lower specification limit, we consider an example of automobile tires that are designed to have an average diameter of 575 mm, with a lower specification limit of 565 mm and an upper specification limit of 585 mm. The production process is found to be stable with a process average of 575.2 mm and a process standard deviation of 4 mm.

To determine the proportion beyond the LSL or "too small" by using Equation (7.34a), we calculate

$$Z_{LSL} = \frac{LSL - \overline{\overline{X}}}{\sigma}$$

$$Z_{LSL} = \frac{565 - 575.2}{4} = -2.55$$

From Table A.2, we find the proportion of the area in a normal distribution below a Z value of -2.55 is

$$0.5000 - 0.4946 = 0.0054.$$

To determine the proportion above the USL or "too big," we can use Equation (7.34b) to calculate

$$Z_{USL} = \frac{USL - \overline{\overline{X}}}{\sigma}$$

$$Z_{USL} = \frac{585 - 575.2}{4} = 2.45$$

From Table A.2 we find the proportion of the area in a normal distribution above a Z value of 2.45 is

$$.5000 - .4929 = .0071.$$

Therefore, the total area or probability of being outside the specification limits is

Proportion Too Small + Proportion Too Large

or

$$.0054 + .0071 = .0125.$$

This means that 1.25 percent of the tires can be expected to fail to meet design specifications.

In some situations, we have one-sided specification limits. This will occur when only one specification limit is crucial or one specification is more important than the other. For example, if waiting time is our quality characteristic of interest, we will usually be concerned only with waiting too long.

We can illustrate the use of a one-sided specification limit by considering the case of a fast-food chain that is concerned with speed of service. Their procedures call for an upper limit of customer waiting time of 4 minutes. If the average serving time is 2.0 minutes and the standard deviation is 1.5, we can determine the proportion of customers who can be expected to wait more than 4 minutes. From Equation (7.34b),

$$Z_{USL} = \frac{USL - \overline{\overline{X}}}{\sigma}$$

$$Z_{USL} = \frac{4 - 2}{1.5} = 1.33$$

From Table A.2, we find the proportion of the area in a normal distribution above a Z value of 1.33 is 0.0918. Therefore, 9.18 percent of customers can be expected to be inconvenienced by waiting too long.

Process Capability Ratios

In addition to estimating the proportion of process output that can be expected to fall beyond specification limits, it is useful to express process capability by a standard measure or index. These indices are based on the ratio of the distance between the upper specification limit and the lower specification limit and the natural tolerance limits of the process. The **natural tolerance limits** of a process are empirically determined and are equal to the 6σ spread represented by the upper control limit (UCL) and the lower control limit (LCL) of the process used in the construction of the control chart.

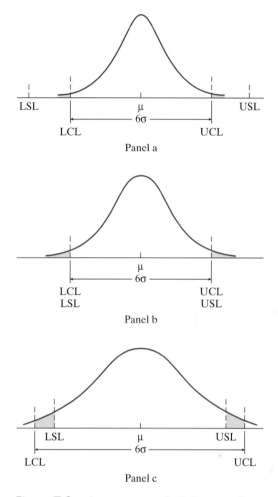

Figure 7.9   Three ways in which the natural tolerance limits and the specified tolerance limits can be related to each other

Figure 7.9 illustrates three ways in which the natural tolerance limits and the specified tolerance limits can be related to each other. Panel (a) depicts the situation in which the natural tolerance limits (6σ spread) represented by the empirically determined upper and lower control limits fall inside the lower and upper specification limits. In such situations, it is unlikely that the process will produce nonconforming units of output. We can be confident that virtually all units produced will be within the specification limits set forth in the design.

Panel (b) illustrates the case in which the natural tolerance limits and the specification limits are equal. That is, the upper control limit is equal to the upper specification limit and the lower control limit is equal to the lower specification limit. In this situation, the proportion of process output that can be expected to be nonconforming is approximately 0.0027, the area under the normal curve that falls beyond $\pm 3\sigma$ from the mean.

Panel (c) depicts the case in which the natural tolerance limits (6σ spread) is wider than the distance between the upper and lower specification limits. In such situations we can expect a substantial proportion of process output to be nonconforming.

Whenever the process mean is centered between the upper specification limit and the lower specification limit or equal to (USL + LSL)/2, we can estimate process capability to meet two-sided specification limits by the C_p **index.**

$$C_p = \frac{\text{USL} - \text{LSL}}{6\sigma} \tag{7.35}$$

where

$$6\sigma = \text{UCL} - \text{LCL}$$

Whenever the natural tolerance limits of the process are the same as the specification limits, as in Figure 7.9 panel (b), $C_p = 1.0$, and the process can be expected to produce 27/10,000 units beyond the specification limits. This may seem to be relatively few nonconforming items; however, if we have a high-volume process producing millions of units, we will be producing a considerable number of nonconforming or defective items.

If the natural tolerance limits of the process are narrower than the specification limits, as in Figure 7.9 panel (a), then $C_p > 1.0$, and the process is unlikely to produce nonconforming units.

If the natural tolerance limits of the process are wider than the specification limits, as in Figure 7.9 panel (c), then $C_p < 1.0$, and the process can be expected to produce many nonconforming units.

To illustrate the use of the C_p index, we can consider the case of a process that produces steel shafts. Design specifications call for each shaft to be milled to a thickness of 5.00 mm with a specified tolerance of ±0.025 mm. The process mean is found to be 5.0001 mm and the process standard deviation is determined to be 0.006. From Equation (7.35), we obtain

$$C_p = \frac{\text{USL} - \text{LSL}}{6\sigma}$$

$$C_p = \frac{5.025 - 4.975}{6(0.006)} = 1.38$$

C_p is greater than 1.0, so we can expect very few nonconforming steel rods.

The C_p index assumes that the process average, $\overline{\overline{X}}$ (or $\overline{X}$ if individual values are used), is centered between the USL and LSL and is equal to the target value or specified nominal value, m. Figure 7.10 illustrates an example in which a process is capable in terms of variability because the natural tolerance limits are narrower

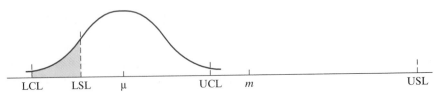

Figure 7.10   An example of a process that is capable yet produces a substantial proportion of nonconforming items

than the specified tolerance limits. However, the shaded portion of the figure indicates that a substantial proportion of process output is nonconforming, because the process average is not centered on the target value m.

In these situations, the C_p index will not accurately represent the capability of the process.

When specification limits are not equidistant from the mean, another index, called the **C_{pk} index,** should be used. C_{pk} can be calculated as

$$C_{pk} = \left| \frac{Z_{\min}}{3} \right| \qquad (7.36)$$

where

$Z_{\min} = Z_{LSL}$ or Z_{USL}, whichever is smaller. (See Equations 7.34a and 7.34b.)

Z_{LSL} is the distance in standard deviation units between the lower specification limit and the process mean, Z_{USL} is the distance in standard deviation units between the upper specification limit and the process mean, and $Z_{\min}$ is the number of standard deviation units between the mean and the closest specification limit. Whenever the specification limits are equidistant from the mean, $C_{pk} = C_p$.

To illustrate the C_{pk} index, we can consider the case of molded plastic O-rings that are designed to have an inner diameter of 2.0 cm. Because the plastic material is somewhat flexible and will stretch to fit if slightly too small, the LSL is 1.70 cm. The USL is only +2.15 cm, because rings that are too large will not provide a snug enough fit and will tend to slip out of position during installation or not center properly in use. The process mean is found to be on target, and the process standard deviation, σ, is estimated by $s = 0.03$. Because the USL is closer to the mean than is the LSL, Z_{USL} will be smaller than Z_{LSL}. We can calculate Z_{USL} by Equation (7.34b) as follows:

$$Z_{USL} = \frac{USL - \overline{X}}{\sigma}$$

$$Z_{USL} = \frac{2.15 - 2.0}{0.03} = 5.00$$

C_{pk} can be calculated from Equation 7.36 as

$$C_{pk} = \left| \frac{Z_{\min}}{3} \right|$$

$$C_{pk} = \left| \frac{5.00}{3} \right| = 1.67$$

As long as the process mean is at the target value, m, these indices can be of help in evaluating the quality of process output by demonstrating the ability of a process to produce items that meet specifications. In the United States and in Japan, the minimum acceptable value for C_{pk} is considered to be 1.33. To satisfy the requirement that $C_p = 1.33$, the specified tolerance (USL–LSL) must be equal to $\pm 4\sigma$. In other words, the process standard deviation would have to be maintained at 1/8th of the specified tolerance.

This is a minimum standard, and purchasers often demand higher values from their suppliers.

In general, the larger the C_p or C_{pk} index values, the greater the capability of a process. There are two ways to increase C_p and C_{pk}.

1. Reduce process variability
2. Make specification tolerance limits wider.

Both of these alternatives relate to quality. Reducing process variability is consistent with a Total Quality Philosophy, because reducing variability will result in an increase in quality of conformance. Making specification limits wider is related to quality of design. There may be some situations in which specified tolerance limits can be relaxed without compromising quality of design, but this is clearly not the preferred method of increasing measures of process capability.

PROBLEMS

7.24 An electrical circuit is designed to have an output voltage of 100v, and the specified tolerance limits are ± 3v. Monitoring of the process indicates that the process is stable with a mean of 100.003 v, and $s = 0.85$. The UCL and LCL are 102.553 and 97.453 respectively.
  (a) What is the value of C_p and C_{pk}?
  (b) Assuming that the output is normally distributed, what proportion of circuits can be expected to be nonconforming?
  (c) If the process average shifted to 101.00v, what proportion of circuits could we expect to be nonconforming?

7.25 A spray nozzle used to deliver specialty coatings has design specifications calling for a useful life of 200 ± 10 hours. Nozzles are periodically selected and tested to failure. The quality characteristic, time to failure, is monitored on a control chart which indicates the process is stable with a mean of 200 hours, a UCL of 220 hours, and an LCL of 180 hours.
  (a) What is the value of C_p and C_{pk}?
  (b) Assuming that the output is normally distributed, what proportion of nozzles can be expected to be nonconforming?
  (c) If the process standard deviation was reduced to 3.0, what proportion of nozzles could we expect to be nonconforming?
  (d) If the customer requires a C_{pk} value of 1.33, what must be done to meet this requirement?

7.26 The design specification of a pressed tablet calls for a target weight of 65.5 mg, with a tolerance of ± 1.25 mg. The process is stable with a mean of 65.6 mg, and the UCL and LCL are 66.86 and 64.34, respectively.
  (a) What is the value of C_p and C_{pk}?

  (b) Assuming that the output is normally distributed, what proportion of tablets can be expected to be nonconforming?
  (c) If the specifications were changed to 65.5 mg ± 2 percent of target weight, what would be the values of C_p and C_{pk}?
  (d) What proportion of tablets could be expected to be nonconforming?
  (e) If the customer requires a C_{pk} value of 1.33, what must be done to meet this requirement?

7.27 The design specifications for steel shafts to be used in an assembly with a bearing require a target value of 0.5 inches with an upper specification limit of 0.55 inches and a lower specification limit of 0.4 inches. The control chart for the process indicates that the process is stable with a mean of 0.5 inches and a standard deviation of 0.05.
  (a) What is the value of C_p and C_{pk}?
  (b) Assuming that the output is normally distributed, what proportion of shafts can be expected to be nonconforming?
  (c) If the customer requires a C_{pk} value of 1.33, what must be done to meet this requirement?

7.28 The design specifications of HDPE containers call for resistance to crushing of the empty container of 5 kilograms of pressure with a lower tolerance limit of 4.5 kp. The process is stable with a mean of 5.3 kp and a standard deviation of 0.12.
  (a) What is the value of C_p and C_{pk}?
  (b) Assuming that the output is normally distributed, what proportion of containers can be expected to be nonconforming?
  (c) If the customer requires a C_{pk} value of 1.33, what must be done to meet this requirement?

SUMMARY

In this chapter, we have studied numerous control charts for variables. As a road map for this chapter, Figure 7.11 on page 340 presents a flow diagram useful in selecting the control chart appropriate for monitoring your process when variables measures are used to evaluate the quality characteristic of interest.

KEY TERMS

between-groups variability   339
C_p 336
C_{pk} 337
CUSUM charts   326
design specifications   332
EWMA charts   326
individual values (X) chart   311
lower specification limit   332
lower tolerance limit   332
moving range   312
moving range (MR) chart   312
natural tolerance limits   334

nominal value   334
process capability   332
range (R) charts   290
relative range   291
standard deviation (s) chart   300
target value   332
upper specification limit   332
upper tolerance limit   332
variability within-subgroups   288
variables control chart   287
$\overline{X}$ chart   290

CHAPTER REVIEW *Checking Your Understanding*

7.29 Why are the $\overline{X}$ and R charts used together?

7.30 When is it more appropriate to use an s chart instead of an R chart?

7.31 How does the $\overline{X}$ chart differ from CUSUM and EWMA charts?

7.32 When should we sample units produced as closely in time as possible?

7.33 When should we sample continuously throughout a production interval?

7.34 Why is it important to monitor near the beginning of a process?

7.35 When are we justified in removing out-of-control points from our calculations of trial control limits?

7.36 How can a process be in a state of statistical control and yet produce a large number of nonconforming or defective items?

7.37 Why is the assumption of normality less important when using $\overline{X}$ charts than when using X charts?

7.38 What is process capability?

7.39 What is the difference between specified tolerance limits and natural tolerance limits?

Chapter Review Problems

7.40 The director of radiology at a large metropolitan hospital is concerned about scheduling of the radiology facilities. An average of 250 patients are transported each day from their hospital rooms to the radiology department for treatment or diagnostic procedures. If patients do not reach the radiology unit at their scheduled time, backups will occur, and other patients will experience delays. The time it takes to transport patients to the radiology unit was operationally defined as the time between when the transporter was assigned to the patient and the time the patient arrived at the radiology unit. A sample of size $n = 4$ patients was selected each day for 30 days, and the

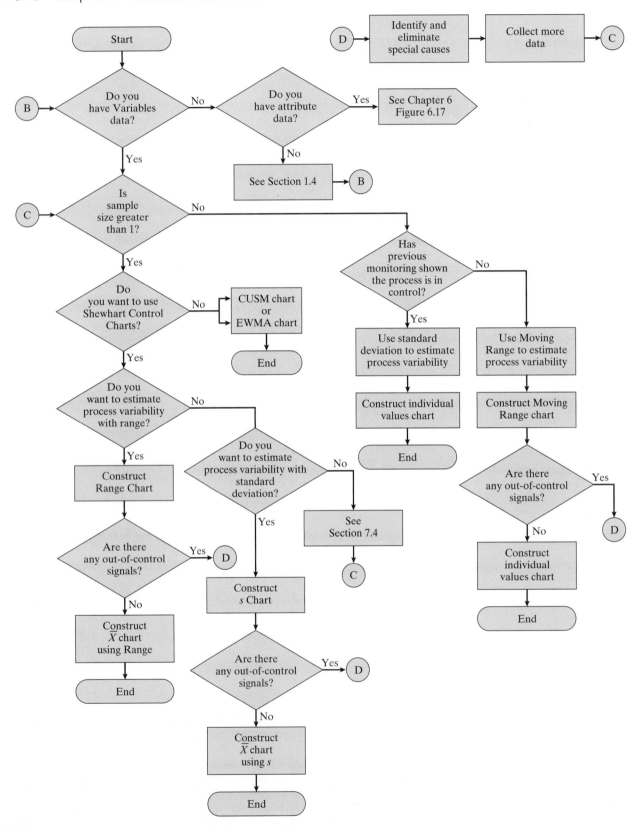

Figure 7.11 Flow diagram for selecting the control chart appropriate for monitoring a process

time to transport each patient (in minutes) was determined. The mean and range for each of the 30 samples are presented in the following table:

Day	Mean	Range
1	17.80	2.4
2	24.43	11.6
3	11.86	4.3
4	21.86	6.8
5	12.73	3.2
6	19.10	8.1
7	20.90	16.9
8	15.73	11.6
9	12.53	4.9
10	17.86	9.3
11	19.20	7.5
12	19.50	15.7
13	24.40	11.6
14	16.40	4.6
15	26.76	8.0
16	10.76	2.5
17	22.80	9.5
18	16.90	18.1
19	20.66	6.5
20	13.90	6.2
21	20.10	5.6
22	14.90	7.3
23	22.80	6.8
24	28.43	6.5
25	13.16	8.7
26	23.60	12.8
27	11.36	6.4
28	19.80	8.8
29	18.80	9.1
30	17.63	14.2 **PATRANS**

(a) Construct an R chart and an $\overline{X}$ chart.
(b) Does the R chart indicate that the process is in a state of statistical control? Why?
(c) Does the $\overline{X}$ chart indicate that the process is in a state of statistical control? Why?
(d) Construct a CUSUM chart to detect a shift in the process mean of one standard deviation.
(e) Construct an EWMA chart to detect a shift in the process mean of one standard deviation.
(f) Compare the results of (a), (d), and (e).
(g) Suggest another way in which timeliness of arrival at the radiology department could be monitored.

7.41 One of the responsibilities of the assistant supervisor in the engineering department of a large hospital is to oversee the correct operation of air-handling equipment that services 40 operating rooms, seven intensive-care units, and 250 patient rooms. Three intensive-care units and 24 operating rooms are served by eight fans that take in outside air. Depending on the season, the air is either heated or cooled to the desired temperature of 55 degrees. Ideally, temperatures should be within two degrees of the 55-degree setpoint, but any reading within five degrees is considered acceptable. To monitor the performance of the airflow system, the air temperature at a sample of four locations is measured each day. The temperature readings for each sample of $n = 4$ in a 35 day period are presented in the following table:

Sample	Observation			
	1	2	3	4
1	54	57	57	59
2	57	57	58	58
3	57	62	60	60
4	62	60	60	59
5	57	59	59	59
6	62	59	60	56
7	57	58	59	59
8	61	58	59	58
9	53	53	53	54
10	55	53	55	57
11	51	50	51	50
12	51	53	50	57
13	56	57	56	57
14	59	57	56	57
15	56	58	58	56
16	53	55	55	56
17	57	56	55	56
18	53	56	55	56
19	58	56	56	57
20	53	57	55	56
21	58	56	56	53
22	53	56	56	57
23	58	57	57	55
24	58	57	55	58
25	55	56	55	56
26	56	59	58	59
27	52	53	56	57
28	57	56	56	55
29	55	58	57	60
30	59	57	55	57
31	50	54	56	53
32	54	52	53	57
33	59	59	56	57
34	52	52	55	54
35	58	59	55	57 **AIRFLOW2**

(a) Construct an R chart and an $\bar{X}$ chart for these data.
(b) Does the R chart indicate that the process is in a state of statistical control? Why?
(c) Does the $\bar{X}$ chart indicate that the process is in a state of statistical control? Why?
(d) Construct an s chart and an $\bar{X}$ chart for these data.
(e) Does the s chart indicate that the process is in a state of statistical control? Why?
(f) Does the $\bar{X}$ chart constructed in conjunction with the s chart indicate that the process is in a state of statistical control? Why?
(g) Compare the results you obtained in parts (a), (b), and (c) with the results you obtained in parts (d), (e), and (f). Explain any similarities and differences.
(h) Construct a CUSUM chart to detect a shift in the process mean of one standard deviation.
(i) Construct an EWMA chart to detect a shift in the process mean of one standard deviation.

(j) Compare the results of (a), (d), (h) and (i).

(k) If the process is stable, compute the capability index for this process.

7.42 A company produces plastic sheeting to be used to manufacture credit cards. The nominal gauge value for thickness is 0.055 mm ±.005 mm. Gauge consistency is evaluated by randomly selecting sample rolls of sheeting from skids. The gauge values for 25 samples of size $n = 6$ follow.

Sample	\multicolumn{6}{c}{Observation}					
	1	2	3	4	5	6
1	0.0574	0.0570	0.0565	0.0558	0.0540	0.0556
2	0.0543	0.0585	0.0556	0.0551	0.0562	0.0563
3	0.0554	0.0550	0.0555	0.0551	0.0558	0.0544
4	0.0576	0.0580	0.0570	0.0580	0.0580	0.0569
5	0.0568	0.0570	0.0560	0.0570	0.0570	0.0560
6	0.0572	0.0580	0.0590	0.0580	0.0570	0.0570
7	0.0576	0.0560	0.0570	0.0580	0.0570	0.0550
8	0.0554	0.0560	0.0580	0.0580	0.0560	0.0550
9	0.0555	0.0570	0.0560	0.0550	0.0536	0.0544
10	0.0570	0.0566	0.0558	0.0550	0.0554	0.0556
11	0.0551	0.0552	0.0556	0.0547	0.0540	0.0544
12	0.0550	0.0552	0.0545	0.0551	0.0553	0.0548
13	0.0556	0.0548	0.0545	0.0550	0.0551	0.0550
14	0.0559	0.0550	0.0540	0.0538	0.0556	0.0546
15	0.0557	0.0554	0.0548	0.0556	0.0538	0.0545
16	0.0530	0.0535	0.0525	0.0546	0.0555	0.0538
17	0.0542	0.0550	0.0560	0.0543	0.0538	0.0570
18	0.0554	0.0560	0.0550	0.0570	0.0560	0.0570
19	0.0565	0.0560	0.0550	0.0560	0.0560	0.0570
20	0.0566	0.0560	0.0570	0.0560	0.0560	0.0550
21	0.0555	0.0560	0.0570	0.0570	0.0560	0.0560
22	0.0570	0.0580	0.0556	0.0559	0.0571	0.0576
23	0.0573	0.0565	0.0566	0.0576	0.0581	0.0554
24	0.0554	0.0573	0.0581	0.0570	0.0560	0.0580
25	0.0561	0.0569	0.0587	0.0575	0.0580	0.0568 **GAUGE**

(a) Construct an R chart and an $\overline{X}$ chart for these data.

(b) Does the R chart indicate that the process is in a state of statistical control? Why?

(c) Does the $\overline{X}$ chart indicate that the process is in a state of statistical control? Why?

(d) Construct an s chart and an $\overline{X}$ chart for these data.

(e) Does the s chart indicate that the process is in a state of statistical control? Why?

(f) Does the $\overline{X}$ chart constructed in conjunction with the s chart indicate that the process is in a state of statistical control? Why?

(g) Compare the results you obtained in parts (a), (b), and (c) with the results you obtained in parts (d), (e), and (f). Explain any similarities and differences.

(h) Construct a CUSUM chart to detect a shift in the process mean of one standard deviation.

(i) Construct an EWMA chart to detect a shift in the process mean of one standard deviation.

(j) Compare the results of (a), (d), (h), and (i).

(k) If the process is stable, compute the capability index for this process.

(l) What proportion of process output can we expect to be nonconforming?

(m) Is there anything about this data set that would lead you to believe that more than one technician made and recorded these measurements?

7.43 An automotive service center guarantees that customers can have their car's oil and oil filters changed, chassis lubricated, and air filters, wiper blades, and tire pressure checked in under an hour. The manager monitors the time it takes to complete each of the various servicing steps as well as preservice and postservice waiting times by sampling three cars each hour. The total time (in minutes) to complete an oil change for each automobile in 25 samples of $n = 3$ follows.

	Observation		
Sample	1	2	3
1	30	32	35
2	34	35	30
3	34	33	30
4	32	36	33
5	32	49	35
6	36	38	32
7	38	32	37
8	42	31	38
9	55	30	39
10	33	36	33
11	51	32	34
12	35	39	30
13	35	36	44
14	25	38	42
15	35	37	29
16	37	46	33
17	30	38	27
18	34	38	37
19	50	38	36
20	36	40	32
21	37	41	30
22	28	37	31
23	34	41	33
24	47	32	30
25	36	30	35

 OILCHANG

(a) Construct an R chart and an $\overline{X}$ chart for these data.

(b) Does the R chart indicate that the process is in a state of statistical control? Why?

(c) Does the $\overline{X}$ chart indicate that the process is in a state of statistical control? Why?

(d) Construct an s chart and an $\overline{X}$ chart for these data.

(e) Does the s chart indicate that the process is in a state of statistical control? Why?

(f) Does the $\overline{X}$ chart constructed in conjunction with the s chart indicate that the process is in a state of statistical control? Why?

(g) Compare the results you obtained in parts (a), (b), and (c) with the results you obtained in parts (d), (e), and (f). Explain any similarities and differences.

(h) Construct a CUSUM chart to detect a shift in the process mean of one standard deviation.

(i) Construct an EWMA chart to detect a shift in the process mean of one standard deviation.

(j) Compare the results of (a), (d), (h), and (i).

7.44 One of the important quality characteristics of paste ink used in lithographic printing presses is viscosity. For ink to flow properly through the press and be applied to the paper, it must be within a limited range of viscosity. If viscosity is too high, the ink will not flow through the press fast enough, while too low a viscosity value will result in too much ink flowing through the press. Either of these conditions will affect the quality of the printed material. A viscosity measure is taken at the end of production of each batch of ink. Viscosity measures for 50 consecutive batches follow.

Sample	Viscosity	Sample	Viscosity
1	305	26	291
2	274	27	301
3	290	28	290
4	314	29	290
5	291	30	308
6	315	31	306
7	301	32	292
8	298	33	279
9	306	34	276
10	305	35	285
11	270	36	296
12	296	37	275
13	307	38	299
14	284	39	301
15	280	40	294
16	264	41	312
17	299	42	289
18	270	43	278
19	275	44	288
20	276	45	299
21	294	46	270
22	313	47	308
23	304	48	298
24	310	49	294
25	271	50	306 **PASTEINK**

(a) Construct an X chart for these data using the moving-range method.
(b) Does the moving range chart indicate that the process is in a state of statistical control? Why?
(c) Does the X chart indicate that the process is in a state of statistical control? Why?
(d) Construct an X chart for these data using the standard deviation method.
(e) Does the X chart using the standard deviation to estimate process variability indicate that the process is in a state of statistical control? Why?
(f) Compare the results you obtained in parts (a), (b), and (c) with the results you obtained in parts (d) and (e). Explain any similarities and differences.

7.45 The telephone company repair bureau receives calls concerning customer problems with telephone service. Once a call is received, appropriate personnel are dispatched to isolate and correct the customer's problem. Many reported problems have their source in switching equipment within the company's central office. Once the source of a problem is identified as being within the central office, the repair bureau dispatches a "trouble ticket" to the central office control center, and problems are corrected. The company's objective is to clear problems within two hours of receipt of trouble tickets. The data at the top of page 346 represent the time (in hours) it took to correct problems and restore full service to customers after receipt of trouble tickets by the central office.

Customer	Time	Customer	Time
1	1.12	26	1.47
2	1.48	27	0.40
3	2.62	28	3.30
4	1.95	29	0.70
5	2.13	30	1.00
6	1.75	31	1.55
7	0.80	32	2.10
8	3.75	33	3.20
9	1.15	34	0.95
10	0.78	35	1.48
11	1.58	36	1.88
12	0.10	37	0.58
13	2.58	38	1.28
14	3.97	39	0.85
15	2.58	40	3.10
16	1.17	41	1.80
17	1.10	42	1.40
18	1.03	43	1.48
19	0.80	44	1.02
20	0.52	45	0.92
21	1.62	46	2.68
22	0.60	47	0.72
23	0.52	48	0.53
24	1.68	49	1.73
25	0.65	50	0.65 **PHONETME**

(a) Construct an X chart for these data using the moving-range method.

(b) Does the moving range chart indicate that the process is in a state of statistical control? Why?

(c) Does the X chart indicate that the process is in a state of statistical control? Why?

(d) Construct an X chart for these data using the standard deviation method.

(e) Does the X chart using the standard deviation to estimate process variability indicate that the process is in a state of statistical control? Why?

(f) Compare the results you obtained in parts (a), (b), and (c) with the results you obtained in parts (d) and (e). Explain any similarities and differences.

7.46 The production department of a newspaper has embarked upon a quality-improvement effort. After several brainstorming sessions, the team has chosen as its first project an issue that relates to the blackness of the print of the newspaper. Each day a determination needs to be made concerning how "black" the newspaper print is. This is measured on a densimometer that records the results on a standard scale. Each day, five spots on the first newspaper printed are chosen, and the blackness of each spot is measured. The results for 20 consecutive weekdays are presented in the table below.

Day	Spot				
	1	2	3	4	5
1	0.96	1.01	1.12	1.07	0.97
2	1.06	1.00	1.02	1.16	0.96
3	1.00	0.90	0.98	1.18	0.96
4	0.92	0.89	1.01	1.16	0.90
5	1.02	1.16	1.03	0.89	1.00

(*Continued*)

			Spot		
Day	1	2	3	4	5
6	0.88	0.92	1.03	1.16	0.91
7	1.05	1.13	1.01	0.93	1.03
8	0.95	0.86	1.14	0.90	0.95
9	0.99	0.89	1.00	1.15	0.92
10	0.89	1.18	1.03	0.96	1.04
11	0.97	1.13	0.95	0.86	1.06
12	1.00	0.87	1.02	0.98	1.13
13	0.96	0.79	1.17	0.97	0.95
14	1.03	0.89	1.03	1.12	1.03
15	0.96	1.12	0.95	0.88	0.99
16	1.01	0.87	0.99	1.04	1.16
17	0.98	0.85	0.99	1.04	1.16
18	1.03	0.82	1.21	0.98	1.08
19	1.02	0.84	1.15	0.94	1.08
20	0.90	1.02	1.10	1.04	1.08 **BLACK**

(a) Construct the appropriate control charts for these data.

(b) Is the process in a state of statistical control? Why?

7.47 The following data represent the amount of soft drink filled in a subgroup of 50 consecutive two-liter bottles. The nominal fill amount is 2.0 liters ± 0.11 liters. The results, listed horizontally in the order of being filled, were as follows:

2.109	2.086	2.066	2.075	2.065
2.057	2.052	2.044	2.036	2.038
2.031	2.029	2.025	2.029	2.023
2.020	2.015	2.014	2.013	2.014
2.012	2.012	2.012	2.010	2.005
2.003	1.999	1.996	1.997	1.992
1.994	1.986	1.984	1.981	1.973
1.975	1.971	1.969	1.966	1.967
1.963	1.957	1.951	1.951	1.947
1.941	1.941	1.938	1.908	1.894 **DRINK**

(a) Construct an X chart for these data using the moving-range method.

(b) Does the moving range chart indicate that the process is in a state of statistical control? Why?

(c) Does the X chart indicate that the process is in a state of statistical control? Why?

(d) Construct an X chart for these data using the standard deviation method.

(e) Does the X chart using the standard deviation to estimate process variability indicate that the process is in a state of statistical control? Why?

(f) Compare the results you obtained in parts (a), (b), and (c) with the results you obtained in parts (d) and (e). Explain any similarities and differences.

(g) Do you have any concerns about constructing an individual values control chart for these data? Explain.

(h) If the process is stable, compute the capability index for this process.

(i) What proportion of process output can we expect to be nonconforming?

7.48 A pharmaceutical company produces tablets that have a specified target tablet weight of 62.5 mg and tolerance limits of ± 2.0 percent of specified weight. Every 15 minutes, 5 tablets are selected for testing. The table at the top of page 348 presents the weights of tablets obtained for 33 samples of $n = 5$.

Sample	Observation				
	1	2	3	4	5
1	62.9	63.0	62.8	62.6	62.7
2	62.6	62.5	62.4	63.0	62.9
3	62.8	62.9	62.4	62.4	62.4
4	62.5	62.4	62.2	62.6	62.4
5	62.6	62.6	62.6	62.9	61.7
6	62.1	62.5	62.6	62.4	62.5
7	62.7	62.6	62.5	62.4	62.1
8	62.7	62.4	62.7	62.6	62.5
9	62.4	63.1	62.6	62.7	62.6
10	62.8	62.7	62.8	62.8	63.1
11	63.1	62.6	62.7	62.4	62.4
12	62.7	61.9	62.3	62.6	62.5
13	62.7	62.7	62.6	62.8	63.1
14	62.8	62.9	62.8	62.8	62.9
15	62.6	62.7	62.1	62.8	61.8
16	62.2	62.7	62.5	62.9	62.3
17	62.7	62.7	62.4	62.2	62.6
18	62.7	62.6	62.9	62.3	62.5
19	62.5	62.4	62.7	62.3	62.3
20	62.3	62.5	62.4	62.8	62.5
21	62.6	62.4	62.6	62.9	62.7
22	63.1	62.7	62.9	62.6	62.5
23	63.1	62.6	63.1	63.0	63.0
24	63.0	62.9	62.4	62.1	62.8
25	62.7	62.9	62.2	62.3	62.0
26	61.6	61.6	62.4	62.0	61.2
27	61.9	62.0	62.2	62.1	62.3
28	62.0	62.3	62.3	62.8	62.7
29	62.8	62.5	62.7	62.9	62.8
30	63.0	62.7	62.8	63.1	63.0
31	62.8	62.7	62.9	62.7	62.9
32	62.7	63.0	62.7	62.7	62.8
33	62.7	63.0	62.2	62.2	62.6

 TABLET 1

(a) Construct an R chart and an $\overline{X}$ chart for these data.

(b) Does the R chart indicate that the process is in a state of statistical control? Why?

(c) Does the $\overline{X}$ chart indicate that the process is in a state of statistical control? Why?

(d) Construct an s chart and an $\overline{X}$ chart for these data.

(e) Does the s chart indicate that the process is in a state of statistical control? Why?

(f) Does the $\overline{X}$ chart constructed in conjunction with the s chart indicate that the process is in a state of statistical control? Why?

(g) Compare the results you obtained in parts (a), (b), and (c) with the results you obtained in parts (d), (e), and (f). Explain any similarities and differences.

(h) Construct a CUSUM chart to detect a shift in the process mean of one standard deviation.

(i) Construct an EWMA chart to detect a shift in the process mean of one standard deviation.

(j) Compare the results of (a), (d), (h), and (i).

(k) If the process is stable, compute the capability index for this process.

(l) What proportion of process output can we expect to be nonconforming?

7.49 In addition to monitoring the weight of tablets described in Problem 7.48, the quality engineer randomly selects one tablet from each sample to be checked for hardness and thickness. Thickness is measured in inches, hardness in kilograms of pressure (kp) required to break the tablet. Specifications for hardness call for tablets to be within the range of 2.5 kp to 4.5 kp and for thickness to be within the range of 0.105 inches to 0.135 inches. There is no target value specified for hardness or for thickness. The table below presents the hardness and thickness measures obtained for 60 tablets.

Tablet	Hardness	Thickness	Tablet	Hardness	Thickness
1	3.8	0.112	31	3.6	0.112
2	3.8	0.112	32	3.8	0.112
3	3.6	0.112	33	4.0	0.111
4	4.1	0.112	34	3.8	0.110
5	3.9	0.112	35	3.2	0.111
6	3.6	0.112	36	4.3	0.113
7	3.8	0.113	37	3.6	0.113
8	3.8	0.113	38	3.8	0.112
9	3.3	0.113	39	3.6	0.110
10	3.6	0.111	40	4.4	0.112
11	4.1	0.112	41	3.6	0.113
12	3.3	0.112	42	4.0	0.112
13	4.2	0.110	43	3.6	0.115
14	3.8	0.110	44	3.8	0.113
15	4.3	0.111	45	3.8	0.111
16	3.8	0.112	46	3.8	0.113
17	3.9	0.110	47	3.8	0.112
18	3.8	0.111	48	4.1	0.112
19	3.8	0.113	49	3.8	0.113
20	3.9	0.112	50	3.9	0.111
21	3.6	0.113	51	3.8	0.112
22	4.1	0.110	52	3.9	0.111
23	3.8	0.111	53	3.6	0.113
24	4.0	0.111	54	3.8	0.115
25	4.1	0.113	55	3.8	0.111
26	3.8	0.112	56	3.6	0.117
27	3.5	0.112	57	3.3	0.112
28	3.8	0.112	58	4.0	0.112
29	3.8	0.114	59	3.6	0.111
30	4.3	0.112	60	3.8	0.114 **TABLET2**

For each of the variables (hardness and thickness), do the following:

(a) Construct a control chart for the variable.

(b) Is the process stable? Why?

(c) If the process is stable, compute the capability index for this process.

7.50 Specifications for toothpaste call for the amount of active ingredient in each sample to be 7.20 mg ±0.08 mg. Ten samples are drawn each day, and the amount of active ingredient in each sample is determined. The table below presents the mean amount in samples of $n = 10$, and the standard deviation for 30 days.

Day	Mean	Standard Deviation	Day	Mean	Standard Deviation
1	7.14	0.163	7	7.13	0.074
2	7.14	0.117	8	7.20	0.067
3	7.21	0.057	9	7.26	0.052
4	7.18	0.162	10	7.20	0.082
5	7.14	0.117	11	7.25	0.053
6	7.22	0.092	12	7.17	0.134

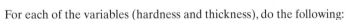

(Continued)

Day	Mean	Standard Deviation	Day	Mean	Standard Deviation
13	7.25	0.071	22	7.15	0.127
14	7.24	0.084	23	7.19	0.159
15	7.19	0.099	24	7.13	0.082
16	7.16	0.126	25	7.25	0.097
17	7.21	0.089	26	7.18	0.103
18	7.24	0.097	27	7.24	0.084
19	7.17	0.142	28	7.19	0.088
20	7.16	0.143	29	7.24	0.097
21	7.25	0.071	30	7.26	0.107 **TOOTH**

(a) Construct an s chart and an $\overline{X}$ chart for these data.

(b) Does the s chart indicate that the process is in a state of statistical control? Why?

(c) Does the $\overline{X}$ chart constructed in conjunction with the s chart indicate that the process is in a state of statistical control? Why?

(d) Construct a CUSUM chart to detect a shift in the process mean of one standard deviation.

(e) Construct an EWMA chart to detect a shift in the process mean of one standard deviation.

(f) Compare the results of (a), (d), and (e).

(g) If the process is stable, compute the capability index for this process.

7.51 Collect your own data on a simulated process by using a standard deck of 52 playing cards. For purposes of this simulation, picture cards (king, queen, and jack) will not be used and should be removed from the deck. The four aces remaining in the deck will have a value of 1 each and all other cards will be valued by their face amount (that is a two counts as 2, a three counts as 3 and so on). Shuffle the deck of cards well, and deal a five-card hand. The hand will represent a sample, of size $n = 5$. Record the value of each card in the sample, and return the cards to the deck. Continue shuffling the deck, dealing hands, and recording data until you have recorded data for 25 samples of size $n = 5$.

(a) Construct a control chart for the data you have collected.

(b) Is the process in a state of statistical control? Why?

(c) What are the true population mean and standard deviation of the process?

(d) Compare the mean and standard deviation values you estimated in (a) with the true population mean and standard deviation. How good do you think your estimate was?

(e) Combine your data with the data collected by other members of the class and estimate the process mean and standard deviation based on the combined data. Are the estimates based on a greater number of samples more or less accurate than your original estimates? Why?

7.52 Introduce a change in the process simulation of Problem 7.51 by changing the value of the four aces in the deck from a value of 1 to a value of 10, and repeat the sampling procedure used in Problem 7.51. Collect data on at least ten additional samples.

(a) Extend the control limits calculated in Problem 7.51 and plot these new data on the chart.

(b) Is the process in a state of statistical control? How many samples were required before you found evidence of a process shift?

(c) How could you have reduced the number of samples it took to produce an out-of-control signal?

(d) Verify your answer to (c) by collecting data and plotting it on the chart.

(e) What are the true population mean and standard deviation of the process now?

(f) Construct control charts for the new process.

(g) Is the process in a state of statistical control? Why?

(h) Compare your results to those obtained by other members of the class. How do you explain similarities and differences?

7.53 Collect your own data on a simulated process. To do this, you will need at least 100 pennies and a brown paper bag. Place the pennies in the bag, and shake it to make sure the pennies are well mixed. (When shaking the bag make sure to do it gently. Experience has shown that shaking with excessive vigor will result in dispersion of the pennies, resulting in an entirely different exercise.) Select samples of size $n = 4$ from the bag. Do not look into the bag while selecting your sample. After selecting your sample, record the last two digits of the date each penny was minted. Return the pennies to the bag and shake to mix well. Repeat, sampling four pennies and recording the last two digits of their dates, until you have at least 25 samples. Remember to replace sampled pennies and shake the bag after each drawing.

(a) Construct control charts for this process.

(b) Is the process in a state of statistical control? Why?

(c) If the process is not in a state of statistical control, can you identify any special causes operating on your process?

(d) What is your best estimate of the process mean and standard deviation?

(e) Compare the results obtained in (d) to those obtained by other members of the class. How do you explain any similarities or differences?

WHITNEY GOURMET CAT FOOD COMPANY CASE

Phase 1

Once the team analyzed the number of nonconforming cans that occurred in subgroups of 100 cans selected at 15-minute intervals (see Table WG6.1 on page 280), the group realized that the pattern of the production volume also needed to be studied.

Exercises

WG7.1 (a) Construct all appropriate control charts for the data on production volume.

(b) Is the process in a state of statistical control in terms of production volume? Explain.

(c) What should the team recommend as the next step to be taken to study and improve the process?

(d) What reasons relating to the canning process can you think of that might explain any lack of control that might have been found?

(e) Does there appear to be any relationship between the number of nonconforming cans and the production volume? What might explain this?

(f) What graph might be useful to plot these two variables?

STOP

Do Not Continue Until the Phase 1 Exercises Have Been Completed.

Phase 2

The production team investigating nonconformities due to the weight of the cans determined that, as was the case with the group studying nonconformance due to the cans, data had been collected over a daily and weekly time period, but no data were available about the stability of the canned weight throughout a specific time period, such as a day. After a thorough discussion, the group determined that, at 15-minute intervals during each shift, a subgroup of five cans would be selected, and the weight of each can would be measured. The results for a single day's production of kidney cat food and a single day's production of shrimp cat food are provided in Table WG7.1 on pages 352–353.

WG71

Exercises

WG7.2 (a) Construct the appropriate control charts for these data.

(b) Is the process in a state of statistical control? Why?

(c) What should the team recommend as the next step to be taken to study and improve the process?

(d) What reasons relating to the canning process can you think of that might explain any lack of control that might have been found?

TABLE WG7.1

WEIGHT OF CANNED CAT FOOD OBTAINED FROM A SUBGROUP OF 5 CANS OF KIDNEY AND SHRIMP CAT FOOD SELECTED AT CONSECUTIVE 15-MINUTE INTERVALS

Shift 1—Kidney

Time	Weight					Time	Weight				
1	3.0469	3.0555	3.0627	3.0412	3.0473	16	3.0753	3.0023	3.0193	3.0680	3.0674
2	2.9739	3.0609	3.0023	2.9813	3.0430	17	3.0113	3.0469	3.0592	3.0604	3.0258
3	3.0467	3.0465	3.0296	3.0701	2.9850	18	3.0646	3.0459	3.0532	3.0347	2.9950
4	3.0135	3.0308	2.9942	2.9724	3.0398	19	3.0322	3.0289	3.0165	3.0494	3.0399
5	3.0532	3.0098	2.9927	3.0323	2.9549	20	3.0240	3.0216	3.0480	3.0590	3.0135
6	3.0109	3.0142	3.0069	3.0436	3.0196	21	3.0469	3.0558	3.0627	3.0412	3.0473
7	3.0232	3.0334	3.0352	3.0476	3.0140	22	3.0545	3.0627	3.0231	3.0503	3.0498
8	3.0077	2.9686	3.0354	2.9890	3.0119	23	3.0844	3.0368	3.0512	3.0263	3.0687
9	3.0370	3.0111	3.0316	3.0774	3.0161	24	3.0726	3.0919	3.0237	3.0381	3.0495
10	3.0188	3.0339	2.9885	3.0423	3.0182	25	3.0423	3.0515	3.0548	3.0437	3.0890
11	3.0234	3.0749	3.0451	3.0165	3.0283	26	3.0562	3.0544	3.0579	3.0127	3.0768
12	3.0432	3.0652	3.0331	3.0412	3.0218	27	3.0162	3.0411	3.0971	3.0682	3.0555
13	3.0568	3.0373	3.0580	3.0918	3.0156	28	3.0327	3.0430	3.0372	3.0701	3.0371
14	3.0572	3.0795	3.0104	2.9942	3.0604	29	3.0497	3.0746	3.0541	3.0664	3.0781
15	3.0703	3.0506	3.0102	3.0335	3.0248	30	3.0881	3.0459	3.0524	3.0143	3.0713

Shift 2—Kidney

Time	Weight					Time	Weight				
1	3.0375	2.9948	3.0579	3.0681	3.0066	16	3.0525	3.0772	3.0880	3.0404	3.0547
2	3.0171	3.0543	3.0276	3.0407	3.0658	17	3.0278	3.1090	3.0493	2.9609	3.0592
3	3.0396	3.0166	3.0494	3.0223	3.0599	18	3.0443	3.0117	3.0575	3.0198	3.0799
4	3.0382	3.0553	3.0537	3.0464	3.0257	19	3.0711	3.1070	3.0213	3.0457	3.0626
5	3.0133	3.0105	3.0284	3.0313	3.0434	20	3.0778	3.0573	3.0861	3.0738	3.0611
6	2.9633	3.0168	3.0251	3.0299	3.0163	21	3.0494	2.9637	3.0941	3.0877	3.0800
7	3.0307	3.0535	3.0420	3.0626	3.0681	22	2.9855	3.0611	3.0227	3.0981	3.0479
8	3.0121	2.9772	3.0587	3.0332	2.9906	23	3.0908	3.0716	3.1603	3.0862	3.1155
9	3.0064	3.0190	3.0049	3.0744	3.0433	24	3.0090	3.1295	3.1638	3.0875	3.0243
10	3.0095	2.9479	3.0197	3.0117	3.0388	25	3.1273	3.1491	2.9957	3.0528	2.9669
11	3.0323	3.1076	3.0630	3.0472	3.0545	26	3.0800	3.0920	3.0297	3.1517	3.0362
12	3.0666	3.0303	3.0239	2.9633	3.0056	27	3.0091	3.0089	3.0452	3.1076	2.9953
13	3.0286	3.0994	3.0471	3.0256	3.1019	28	3.1298	3.0405	3.1641	3.0937	3.0430
14	2.9962	3.0417	3.0570	3.0883	3.0763	29	3.0209	3.0163	3.0362	3.0524	3.0794
15	2.9988	3.0273	3.0319	3.0853	3.0871	30	3.1185	3.0889	3.1126	3.0671	3.0249

Shift 1—Shrimp

Time	Weight					Time	Weight				
1	2.9878	3.0296	3.0113	3.0207	3.0112	9	2.9757	3.0162	3.0066	2.9963	2.9894
2	3.0199	3.0242	3.0238	3.0032	3.0573	10	3.0246	2.9813	3.0061	3.0145	3.0023
3	2.9754	3.0407	2.9537	2.9664	2.9834	11	3.0448	2.9462	3.0230	3.0219	2.9974
4	2.9952	2.9972	3.0407	3.0277	3.0082	12	2.9951	3.0144	3.0259	2.9543	2.9777
5	3.0543	3.0307	2.9892	2.9997	3.0231	13	3.0193	3.0429	3.0016	3.0927	3.0185
6	3.0680	2.9925	3.0420	2.9838	3.0567	14	2.9809	2.9886	2.9869	3.0047	3.0296
7	2.9901	3.0162	3.0126	3.0115	2.9716	15	3.0546	3.0202	2.9776	3.0399	2.9801
8	2.9917	2.9687	3.0240	3.0046	3.0267	16	3.0273	3.0342	2.9936	3.0402	3.0017

(Continued)

TABLE WG7.1 (Continued)

Shift 1—Shrimp

Time	Weight					Time	Weight				
17	3.0385	3.0144	3.0171	3.0089	3.0021	24	2.9712	2.9818	2.9967	2.9791	2.9870
18	2.9975	3.0550	2.9953	2.9857	3.0092	25	3.0345	2.9846	3.0298	3.0160	3.0485
19	3.0317	3.0368	3.0033	3.0347	3.0228	26	3.0536	3.0497	2.9997	3.0583	3.0445
20	3.0455	3.0035	3.0139	2.9934	3.0000	27	3.0193	3.0102	3.0338	3.1054	3.0382
21	3.0081	2.9607	3.0578	3.0015	3.0489	28	2.9675	3.0002	3.0000	3.0267	2.9990
22	2.9984	3.0017	3.0224	2.9441	3.0002	29	3.0516	2.9836	3.0057	3.0442	2.9892
23	3.0418	2.9935	2.9875	3.0376	3.0186	30	3.0014	3.0425	3.0371	3.0441	3.0013

Shift 2—Shrimp

Time	Weight					Time	Weight				
1	3.0252	2.9964	3.0046	3.0341	3.0118	16	2.9884	3.0071	2.9732	3.0670	3.1069
2	3.0276	3.0486	3.0267	3.0241	3.0485	17	3.0564	3.0531	2.9720	3.0179	3.0326
3	3.0426	3.0110	2.9867	2.9866	2.9962	18	3.0332	3.0263	3.0088	3.0557	3.0382
4	3.0478	2.9996	3.0388	3.0619	3.0524	19	3.0341	3.0200	3.0298	3.0987	3.0345
5	3.0337	3.0199	2.9919	3.0126	3.0528	20	2.9899	3.0843	2.9976	2.0585	2.9181
6	3.0242	3.0858	3.0236	3.0545	3.0466	21	2.9312	3.0082	3.0182	3.0032	3.0255
7	3.0062	2.9936	3.0508	3.0502	3.0160	22	3.1153	3.0723	3.0131	3.0920	3.0504
8	3.0125	3.0367	3.0086	3.0227	3.0531	23	2.0386	3.0153	3.0902	3.0176	3.0525
9	3.0307	3.0621	3.0114	3.0181	3.0080	24	3.0354	2.9645	2.9756	3.0379	3.0894
10	3.0199	3.0273	3.0194	3.0080	2.9785	25	3.0532	2.9473	3.0441	2.9786	3.0337
11	3.0837	3.0074	2.9401	3.0058	3.0568	26	3.0047	2.9941	3.0733	3.0473	3.0246
12	2.9749	3.0086	3.0347	3.0316	3.0769	27	3.0559	3.0066	2.9601	3.0739	3.0229
13	3.0136	3.0319	3.0238	2.9691	3.0530	28	2.0304	3.0612	3.0354	3.0476	3.0576
14	3.0313	2.9979	3.0482	3.0168	3.0081	29	2.9958	3.0052	2.9911	3.0737	2.9849
15	2.9661	3.0583	3.0020	3.0580	3.0127	30	3.0605	3.0391	2.9679	2.9848	3.0836

WHITNEY

HARNSWELL SEWING MACHINE COMPANY CASE

Phase 1

The Harnswell Sewing Machine Company is a manufacturer of industrial sewing machines that has been in business for almost 50 years. The company specializes in automated machines called pattern tackers that sew repetitive patterns on such mass production products as shoes, garments, and seat belts. Aside from the sales of machines, the company sells machine parts. The company's reputation in the industry is good, and it has been able to command a price premium because of this reputation.

Recently, Natalie York, the production manager of the company, purchased several books relating to quality at a local bookstore. After reading them, she began to wonder about the feasibility of beginning some type of quality program at the company. At the current time, the company has no formal quality program. Parts are 100 percent inspected at the time of shipping to a customer or installation in a machine, yet Natalie has always wondered why inventory of certain parts (in particular the half-inch cam roller) invariably falls short before a full year lapses, even though 7,000 pieces have been produced for a demand of 5,000 pieces per year.

After a great deal of reflection, and with some apprehension, Natalie has decided that she will approach John Harnswell, the owner of the company, about the possibility of beginning a program to improve quality in the company, starting with a trial project in the machine-parts area. As she is walking to Mr. Harnswell's

(Continued)

HARNSWELL SEWING MACHINE COMPANY CASE (*Continued*)

office for the meeting, she has second thoughts about whether this is such a good idea. After all, it was just last month that Mr. Harnswell told her, "Why do you need to go to graduate school for your masters degree in business? That is a waste of your time and will do the Harnswell Company no good. All those professors are just up in their ivory towers and don't know a thing about running a business like I do."

As she enters his office, Mr. Harnswell, ever courteous to her, invites Natalie to sit down across from him. "Well, what do you have on your mind this morning?" Mr. Harnswell asks her in an inquisitive tone. She begins by starting to talk about the books that she has just completed reading and about how she has some interesting ideas for making production even better than it is now and improving profits. Before she can finish, Mr. Harnswell has started to answer. "Look, my dear young lady," he says, "Everything has been fine since I started this company in 1948. I have built this company up from nothing to one that employs more than 20 people. Why do you want to make waves? Remember, if it ain't broke, don't fix it." With that he ushers her from his office with the admonishment of, "What am I going to do with you if you keep coming up with these ridiculous ideas?"

Exercises

HS7.1   Based upon what you have read, which of the themes of quality management are most lacking in the Harnswell Sewing Machine Company? Explain.

HS7.2   What changes if any, do think that Natalie York might be able to institute in the company? Explain.

STOP

Do Not Continue Until the Phase 1 Exercises Have Been Completed.

Phase 2

Natalie slowly walked down the hall after leaving Mr. Harnwell's office, feeling rather downcast. He just won't listen to anyone, she thought. As she walked, Jim Murante, the shop foreman, came up beside her. "So," he said, "Did you really think that the old man would just listen to you? I've been here more than 25 years. The only way he listens is if he is shown something that worked after it has already been done. Let's see what we can plan out together."

Natalie and Jim decide to begin by investigating the production of the cam rollers that are a precision ground

part. The last part of the production process involves the grinding of the outer diameter. After grinding, the part mates with the cam groove of the particular sewing pattern. The half-inch rollers technically have an engineering specification for the outer diameter of the roller of 0.5075 inch (the specifications are actually metric, but in factory floor jargon they are referred to as half-inch) plus a tolerable error of 0.0003 inch on the lower side. Thus, the outer diameter is allowed to be between 0.5072 and 0.5075 inch. Anything larger means that the roller has to be reclassified into a different and less costly category, while anything smaller means that the roller cannot be used for anything other than scrap.

The grinding of the cam roller is done on a single machine with a single tool setup and no change in the grinding wheel after initial setup. The operation is done by Dave Martin, the head machinist, who has 30 years of experience in the trade and specific experience producing the cam roller part. Production occurs in batches, so Natalie and Jim sample five parts produced from each batch. Data collected over 30 batches are presented in Table HS7.1.

Exercises

HS7.3   (a)   Is the process in a state of statistical control? Why?

(b)   What recommendations should be made about improving the process?

STOP

Do Not Continue Until the Phase 2 Exercises Have Been Completed.

Phase 3

Natalie examined the $\overline{X}$ and R charts developed from the data presented in Table HS7.1. The R chart indicated that the process was in a state of statistical control, but the $\overline{X}$ chart revealed that the average for day 17 was outside the lower control limit. This immediately gave her cause for concern because low values for the roller diameter could mean parts that had to be scrapped. Natalie went down to see Jim Murante, the shop foreman, to try to find out what had happened to batch 17. Jim looked up the production records to determine when this batch was produced. "Aha, "he exclaimed, " I think I've got the answer! This batch was produced on that really cold morning we had last month. I've been after Mr. Harnswell for a long time to let us put an automatic thermostat in the shop so that the place doesn't feel so cold when we get here in the morning. All he ever

HARNSWELL SEWING MACHINE COMPANY CASE (*Continued*)

TABLE HS7.1

DIAMETER OF CAM ROLLERS (INCH)

Batch	Cam Roller				
	1	2	3	4	5
1	0.5076	0.5076	0.5075	0.5077	0.5075
2	0.5075	0.5077	0.5076	0.5076	0.5075
3	0.5075	0.5075	0.5075	0.5075	0.5076
4	0.5075	0.5076	0.5074	0.5076	0.5073
5	0.5075	0.5074	0.5076	0.5073	0.5076
6	0.5076	0.5075	0.5076	0.5075	0.5075
7	0.5076	0.5076	0.5076	0.5075	0.5075
8	0.5075	0.5076	0.5076	0.5075	0.5074
9	0.5074	0.5076	0.5075	0.5075	0.5076
10	0.5076	0.5077	0.5075	0.5075	0.5075
11	0.5075	0.5075	0.5075	0.5076	0.5075
12	0.5075	0.5076	0.5075	0.5077	0.5075
13	0.5076	0.5076	0.5073	0.5076	0.5074
14	0.5075	0.5076	0.5074	0.5076	0.5075
15	0.5075	0.5075	0.5076	0.5074	0.5073
16	0.5075	0.5074	0.5076	0.5075	0.5075
17	0.5075	0.5074	0.5075	0.5074	0.5072
18	0.5075	0.5075	0.5076	0.5075	0.5076
19	0.5076	0.5076	0.5075	0.5075	0.5076
20	0.5075	0.5074	0.5077	0.5076	0.5074
21	0.5075	0.5074	0.5075	0.5075	0.5075
22	0.5076	0.5076	0.5075	0.5076	0.5074
23	0.5076	0.5076	0.5075	0.5075	0.5076
24	0.5075	0.5076	0.5075	0.5076	0.5075
25	0.5075	0.5075	0.5075	0.5075	0.5074
26	0.5077	0.5076	0.5076	0.5074	0.5075
27	0.5075	0.5075	0.5074	0.5076	0.5075
28	0.5077	0.5076	0.5075	0.5075	0.5076
29	0.5075	0.5075	0.5074	0.5075	0.5075
30	0.5076	0.5075	0.5075	0.5076	0.5075

HS1

tells me is that people aren't as tough as they used to be and if I want to see real cold I should have been back in that foxhole during the winter of 1944."

Natalie stood there almost in shock. What she realized had happened is that, rather than standing idle until the environment and the equipment warmed to acceptable temperatures, the machinist had opted to manufacture parts that might have to be scrapped. In fact, Natalie recalled that a major problem had occurred on that same day when several other expensive parts had to be scrapped. Natalie said to Jim, "We just have to do something. We can't let this go on now that we know what problems it is potentially causing." Natalie and Jim decided that enough money could be taken out of petty cash and other accounts to get the thermostat without having to obtain a requisition that required Mr. Harnswell's signature. They installed the thermostat and set the heating control so that the heat would turn on one half-hour before the shop opened each morning.

Exercises

HS7.4 What should Natalie now do concerning the data of Table HS7.1? Explain.

HS7.5 Explain how the action of Natalie and Jim to avoid this particular problem in the future has resulted in quality improvement.

STOP

Do Not Continue Until the Phase 3 Exercises Have Been Completed.

Phase 4

Once the data for day 17 were removed from the chart since local corrective action had been taken to eliminate the special cause, the control charts for the remaining days indicated a stable system with only common causes of variation operating on the system. Thus, Natalie and Jim sat down with Dave Martin and several other machinists to try to determine all the possible causes for the existence of oversized and scrapped rollers. A fishbone diagram of the process was developed and is presented in Figure HS7.1 on page 356.

Natalie was still troubled by the data that had been collected. After all, she wondered, what I really want to find out is whether or not the process is giving us oversizes (which are downgraded) and undersizes (which are scrapped). She thought about which tables and charts would really be helpful.

Exercises

HS7.6 **(a)** Set up a frequency distribution or a stem-and-leaf display of the cam roller diameters presented in Table HS7.1. Explain why you chose the tabular presentation that you used.

   (b) Based on your results in (a), set up all appropriate graphs of the cam roller diameters.

(Continued)

HARNSWELL SEWING MACHINE COMPANY CASE (*Concluded*)

(c) Write a report expressing your conclusions concerning the cam roller diameters. Be sure to discuss the diameters as they relate to the specifications.

STOP

Do Not Continue Until the Phase 4 Exercises Have Been Completed.

Phase 5

Natalie noticed immediately that the overall average diameter with day 17 eliminated was 0.507527, which was higher than the specification value. This meant that, on average, the rollers being produced were of a diameter that was so high that they would be downgraded in value. In fact, 55 of the 150 rollers sampled (36.67 percent) were above the specification value. This meant that if this percentage was extrapolated to the full year's production, 36.67 percent of the 7,000 pieces manufactured or 2567 could not be sold as half-inch rollers, leaving only 4433 available for sale. "No wonder we often seemed to have shortages that required costly emergency runs," she thought. She also noted that not one

diameter was below the lower tolerance of 0.5072, so not one of the rollers had to be scrapped.

Natalie realized that there had to be a reason for all this. Along with Jim Murante, she decided to show the results to Dave Martin, the head machinist. Dave said that the results didn't surprise him that much. "You know," he said "there is only 0.0003 inch in diameter that I'm allowed in variation. If I aim for exactly halfway between 0.5072 and 0.5075, I'm afraid that I'll make a lot of short pieces that will have to be scrapped. I know from way back when I first started here that Mr. Harnswell and everybody else will come down on my head if they start seeing too many of those scraps. I figure that if I aim at 0.5075, the worst thing that will happen will be a bunch of downgrades, but I won't make any pieces that have to be scrapped."

Exercises

HS7.7 What approach do you think the machinist should take in terms of the diameter of the roller that should be aimed for? Explain.

HS7.8 What do think that Natalie should do next? Explain.

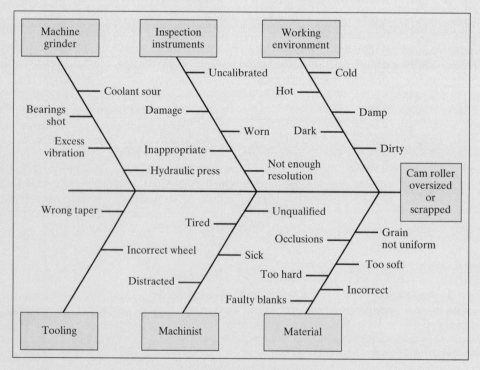

Figure HS7.1   Fishbone Diagram for cam Roller process

ANTELOPE PASS MINING COMPANY CASE

Phase 1

The Antelope Pass Mining Company operates a large heap leach gold mine in the western United States. The gold mined at this location consists of ore that is very low grade having about 0.0032 of an ounce of gold in a ton of ore. The process of heap leaching involves the mining, crushing, stacking, and leaching of millions of tons of gold ore per year. In the process, ore is placed in a large heap on an impermeable pad. A weak chemical solution is sprinkled over the heap and is collected at the bottom after percolating through the ore. As the solution percolates through the ore, the gold is dissolved and is later recovered from the solution. This technology, which has been used for almost 20 years, has made the operation profitable. Due to the tremendous quantity of ore that is handled, the owners are continually exploring ways of making the process more efficient. As part of a multimillion-dollar expansion completed several years ago, the stacking process for the leach pad was automated with the construction of a multimillion-dollar computer controlled stacker. The computer controlled stacker was designed to load 35,000 tons of ore per day at a cost that was less than that achieved with the former method of stacking that involved manually operated trucks and bulldozers. The goal was to replace a fleet of these manually operated trucks and bulldozers. Since its installation, although the costs of the computer-controlled stacker have been lower, the stacker has not been consistently able to achieve its designed capacity of 35,000 tons per day. Trucks and bulldozers must make up any shortfall, which decreases the benefit of the stacker's lower operating costs.

A team has been formed to investigate the problem of downtime (time in which the stacker is not operating) and make recommendations for future improvements. This committee decides to begin by examining available data relating to the daily tonnage stacked from the most recent five-week period. The relevant data are presented in Table AP7.1.

TABLE AP7.1

DAILY AMOUNT STACKED (TONS) FOR A FIVE-WEEK PERIOD

Day	Amount Stacked (tons)	Day	Amount Stacked (tons)
1	9,612	19	12,889
2	15,417	20	25,637
3	30,259	21	21,390
4	36,345	22	32,006
5	21,553	23	33,449
6	35,658	24	23,392
7	37,047	25	25,842
8	28,222	26	20,192
9	28,698	27	14,907
10	29,049	28	19,587
11	9,105	29	20,237
12	4,448	30	11,222
13	12,660	31	10,053
14	17,157	32	9,158
15	31,563	33	18,298
16	30,801	34	20,003
17	18,710	35	31,762
18	36,568		

AP1

Exercises

AP.1 Based on the data of Table AP7.1, do you think that the stacker process can achieve a tonnage of 35,000 per day? Explain.

AP.2 (a) Construct the appropriate control chart for these data.

(b) Is the process in a state of statistical control? Why?

(c) What recommendations should be made about improving the process?

REFERENCES

1. Albin, S., L. l. Kang, and G. Shea, "An X and EWMA chart for individual observations," *Journal of Quality Technology*, 29, (1997), 41–48
2. Amin, R. W. and R. A. Etheridge, "A note on individual and moving range control charts," *Journal of Quality Technology,* 30, (1998), 70–74
3. Bothe, D. R. *Measuring Process Capability* (New York: McGraw-Hill, 1997)

4. Cryer, J. D., and T. P. Ryan, "The estimation of sigma for an X chart: $\overline{MR}/d_2$ or s/c_4?" *Journal of Quality Technology*, 22, (1990), 187–192

5. Hunter, J. S., "The exponentially weighted moving average," *Journal of Quality Technology,* 18 (1986), 203–210

6. *Microsoft Excel 2000.* Redmond, WA: Microsoft Corp., (1999)

7. *MINITAB for Windows Version 12.* State College, PA: MINITAB, Inc., 1998

8. Montgomery, D. C. *Introduction to Statistical Quality Control* 3rd ed., New York: John Wiley, 1996

9. Montgomery, D. C. and C. M. Mastrongelo, " Some statistical process control methods for autocorrelated data," *Journal of Quality Technology* 23, (1991), 179–193

10. Montgomery, D. C. and W. H. Woodall, A discussion on statistically-based process monitoring and control, "*Journal of Quality Technology* 23, (1997), 121–157

11. Nelson, L. S., "Control charts for individual measurements," *Journal of Quality Technology,* 14 (1982), 179–173

12. Nelson, L. S., "The deceptiveness of moving averages," *Journal of Quality Technology*, 15 (1983), 99–100

13. Quesenberry, C. P., "SPC Q charts for start-up processes and short or long runs," *Journal of Quality Technology,* 23 (1991), 213–224

14. Ramsey, P. P., and P. H. Ramsey, "Simple tests of normality in small samples," *Journal of Quality Technology,* 22 (1990), 299–309

15. Roberts, S. W., "Control chart tests based on geometric moving averages," *Technometrics*, 1 (1959), 239–250

16. Roes, K. C. B., R. J. M. M. Does, and Y. Schurink, "Shewhart-type control charts for individual observations," *Journal of Quality Technology*, 25 (1993), 188–198

17. Shewhart, W. A., *Economic Control of Quality of Manufactured Product.* New York: Van Nostrand-Reinhard, 1931, reprinted by the American Society for Quality Control, Milwaukee, 1980

18. Shewhart, W. A., and W. E. Deming, *Statistical Methods from the Viewpoint of Quality Control.* Washington, D.C.: Graduate School, Dept. of Agriculture, 1939, Dover Press, 1986.

19. Sullivan, J. H. and W. H. Woodall, "A control chart for preliminary analysis of individual observations," *Journal of Quality Technology,* 28 (1996), 265–278

20. Walker, E., J. W. Philpot, and J. Clement, "False signal rates for the Shewhart control chart with supplementary runs tests," *Journal of Quality Technology,* 23 (1991), 247–252

21. Western Electric, *Statistical Quality Control Handbook.* Indianapolis, In: Western Electric Corporation, 1956

APPENDIX 7.1   *Using Microsoft Excel for Variables Control Charts*

Obtaining Control Charts for the Range and Mean using Microsoft Excel

To generate R and $\overline{X}$ charts, use the **Control Charts | R and XBar Charts** choice of the PHStat add-in. As an example, consider the lead content of water example of Section 7.3. To generate R and charts based on the lead content of water data of Table 7.1 on page 294, open the **LEAD.XLS** workbook and click the **Data** sheet tab. Verify that the data of Table 7.1 have been entered into columns A through F.

   You first need to compute the average and range for each day. Enter the label Average in cell G2. Enter the formula **=AVERAGE(B3:F3)** in cell G3, and copy this formula down the column through cell G32. Enter the label Range in cell H2. Enter the formula **=MAX(B3:F3) − MIN(B3:F3)** in cell H3 and copy the formula down the column through cell H32.

   Select **PHStat | Control Charts | R and XBar Charts.** In the R and XBar Charts dialog box, enter **5** in the Subgroup/Sample Size: edit box. Enter **H2:H32** in the Subgroup Ranges Cell Range: edit box and select the **First cell contains label** check box for this range. Select the **R and XBar Charts** option button. Enter **G2:G32** in the Subgroup Means Cell Range:

edit box and select the **First cell contains label** check box for this range. Enter **Control Charts for Lead Content** in the Output Title: edit box. Click the **OK** button. The add-in inserts two worksheets containing the data and calculations for the control charts and two chart sheets containing R and charts that are similar to the ones shown in Figures 7.1 and 7.2 on pages 296 and 299.

Obtaining Control Charts for the Standard Deviation and Mean using Microsoft Excel

To generate S and $\bar{X}$ charts, you need to use Equations (7.18a) and (7.18b) on page 302. As an example, consider the lead content of water example of Section 7.3. To generate S and $\bar{X}$ charts based on the lead content data of Table 7.1 on page 294, open the **LEAD.XLS** workbook and click the **Data** sheet tab. Verify that the data of Table 7.1 have been entered into columns A through F.

You first need to compute the average and standard deviation for each day. Enter the label Average in cell G2. Enter the formula **=AVERAGE(B3:F3)** in cell G3, and copy this formula down the column through cell G32. Enter the label Std. Dev. in cell H2. Enter the formula **=STDEV(B3:F3)** in cell H3 and copy the formula down the column through cell H32.

Once these have been entered on the Data sheet, select **Insert | Worksheet** and rename the sheet Calculations. Enter appropriate labels in column A, starting in row 3 for S chart, S Bar, B_3 factor, B_4 factor, LCL, Center Line, and UCL. Then obtain the control limits and the center line for the S chart on the Calculations sheet by using the formula **=AVERAGE(Data!H:H)** in B4. The values for the B_3 and B_4 factors are then entered in cells B5 and B6. The lower control limit is obtained in cell B7 from the formula **=B5*B4,** the center line in cell B8 is obtained from the formula **=B4,** and the upper control limit in cell B9 is obtained from the formula **=B6*B4.**

Now that the control limits and center line have been computed, we copy their values to columns I, J, and K of the Data sheet. After entering labels for LCL, Center, and UCL in cells I2 through K2, enter **=Calculations!$B$7** in I3, **=Calculations!$B$8** in J3, and **=Calculations!$B$9** in K3. Then, in order to be able to plot a line for each of these variables across the days, copy the LCL value from I3 to I4 through I32, the center line value from J3 to J4 through J32, and the UCL value from K3 to K4 through K32.

We now use the Chart Wizard (see Appendix 2.1) to obtain the control chart for the standard deviation. With the Data sheet active, select **Insert | Chart.**

In the Step 1 Dialog box, select the **Standard types** tab and then select **XY (Scatter)** from the Chart type: list box. Select the first choice of the third row of chart Sub-types, the choice designated as "Scatter with data points connected by lines." Click the **Next** button.

In the Step 2 Dialog box, select the **Data Range** tab and enter **Data!A2:A32, Data!H2:K32** in the Data range: edit box. (Be sure to include the comma as part of your entry.) Select the **Columns option** button in the Series in: group. Select the **Series** tab. Enter **=Data!A2:A32** in the Value (X) Axis edit box. Click the **Next** button.

In the Step 3 Dialog box, select the Titles tab. Enter **S Chart for Lead Content** in the Chart title edit box, enter **Days** in the Category (X) axis: edit box, and enter **Standard Deviation** in the Value (Y) axis: edit box. Select the **Gridlines** tab. Deselect all check boxes. Click the **Next** button.

In the Step 4 Dialog box, select the **As new sheet: option** button and enter S chart in the edit box to the right of the option button. Click the **Finish** button.

Now that we have obtained the S chart, we are ready to obtain the $\bar{X}$ chart. Using Equation (7.18) on page 302, we need to compute $\bar{\bar{X}}$, the average of all the sample averages. With the Calculations sheet active, enter labels starting in cell A10 for XBAR chart, AVERAGE XBAR, A_3 Factor, LCL, Center Line, and UCL. Compute $\bar{\bar{X}}$ in cell B11 using the formula **=AVERAGE(Data!G:G).** Enter the A_3 factor in cell B12. The lower control limit in cell B13 is obtained from the formula **=B11 − B12*B4,** the center line in cell B14 is obtained from the equation **=B11** and the upper control limit in cell B15 is obtained from the formula **=B11 + B12 * B4.**

Now that the control limits and center line for the $\overline{X}$ chart have been computed, we need to copy their values to columns L, M, and N of the Data sheet. After entering labels for LCL, Center, and UCL in cells L2 through N2, we enter **=Calculations!$B$13** in L3, **=Calculations!$B$14** in M3, and **=Calculations!$B$15** in N3. Then, in order to be able to plot a line for each of these variables across the days, copy the LCL value from L3 to L4 through L32, the center line value from M3 to M4 through M32, and the UCL value from N3 to N4 through N32.

We now use the Chart Wizard (see Appendix 2.1) to obtain the control chart for the mean. With the Data sheet active, select **Insert | Chart.**

In the Step 1 Dialog box, select the **Standard types** tab and then select **XY (Scatter)** from the Chart type: list box. Select the first choice of the third row of chart Sub-types, the choice designated as "Scatter with data points connected by lines." Click the **Next** button.

In the Step 2 Dialog box, select the **Data Range** tab and enter **Data!A2:A32, Data!G2:G32,Data!L2:N32** in the Data range: edit box. (Be sure to include the commas as part of your entry.) Select the **Columns option** button in the Series in: group. Select the **Series** tab. Enter **=Data!A3:A32** in the Value (X) Axis edit box. Click the **Next** button.

In the Step 3 Dialog box, select the **Titles** tab. Enter **X Bar Chart for Lead Content** in the Chart title edit box, enter **Days** in the Category (X) axis: edit box, and enter **XBar** in the Value (Y) axis: edit box. Select the **Gridlines** tab. Deselect all check boxes. Click the **Next** button.

In the Step 4 Dialog box, select the **As new sheet: option** button and enter X Bar chart in the edit box to the right of the option button. Click the **Finish** button.

Obtaining Control Charts for the Moving Range and Individual Value using Microsoft Excel

To generate a moving range value chart, you need to use Equations (7.21a) and (7.21b) on page 312. As an example, consider the flushness example of Section 7.4. To generate moving range and individual value charts based on the flushness data of Table 7.4 on page 315, open the **MINIVAN1.XLS** workbook and click the **Data** sheet tab. Verify that the data of Table 7.4 have been entered into columns A and B.

You first need to compute the moving range for each day. Enter the label Moving Range in cell C2. Enter the formula **=ABS(B2-B3)** in cell C2, and copy this formula down the column through cell C25.

Once these have been entered on the Data sheet, select **Insert | Worksheet** and rename the sheet Calculations. Enter appropriate labels in column A, starting in row 3 for Moving Range chart, MR Bar, D_3 factor, D_4 factor, LCL, Center Line, and UCL. Then obtain the center line for the Moving Range chart on the Calculations sheet by using the formula **=AVERAGE(Data!C2:C25)** in B4. The values for the D_3 and D_4 factors are then entered in cells B5 and B6. The lower control limit is obtained in cell B7 from the formula **=B5*B4,** the center line in cell B8 is obtained from the formula **=B4,** and the upper control limit in cell B9 is obtained from the formula **=B6*B4.**

Now that the control limits and center line have been computed, we copy their values to columns D, E, and F of the Data sheet. After entering labels for LCL, Center, and UCL in cells D1 through F1, enter **=Calculations!$B$7** in D2, **=Calculations!$B$8** in E2, and **=Calculations!$B$9** in F2. Then, in order to be able to plot a line for each of these variables across the days, copy the LCL value from D2 to D3 through D25, the center line value from E2 to E3 through E25, and the UCL value from F2 to F3 through F25.

We now use the Chart Wizard (see Appendix 2.1) to obtain the control chart for the standard deviation. With the Data sheet active, select **Insert | Chart**.

In the Step 1 Dialog box, select the **Standard types** tab and then select **XY (Scatter)** from the Chart type: list box. Select the first choice of the third row of chart Sub-types, the choice designated as "Scatter with data points connected by lines." Click the **Next** button.

In the Step 2 Dialog box, select the **Data Range** tab and enter **Data!A1:A25,C1:F25** in the Data range: edit box. (Be sure to include the commas as part of your entry.) Select the

Columns option button in the Series in: group. Select the **Series** tab. Enter **=Data!A2:A25** in the Value (X) Axis edit box. Click the **Next** button.

In the Step 3 Dialog box, select the **Titles** tab. Enter **Moving Range Chart for Flushness** in the Chart title edit box, enter **Days** in the Category (X) axis: edit box, and enter **Moving Range** in the Value (Y) axis: edit box. Select the **Gridlines** tab. Deselect all check boxes. Click the **Next** button.

In the Step 4 Dialog box, select the **As new sheet: option** button and enter Moving Range chart in the edit box to the right of the option button. Click the **Finish** button.

Now that we have obtained the Moving Range chart, we are ready to obtain the Individual Value chart. Using Equation (7.26) on page 326, we need to compute the average value. With the Calculations sheet active, enter labels starting in cell A10 for Individual Value chart, XBAR, E2 Factor, LCL, Center Line, and UCL. Compute $\bar{X}$ in cell B11 using the formula **=AVERAGE(Data!B:B).** Enter the E_2 factor in cell B12. The lower control limit in cell B13 is obtained from the formula **=B11 − B12 * B4,** the center line in cell B14 is obtained from the formula **=B11,** and the upper control limit in cell B15 is obtained from the formula **=B11 + B12 * B4.**

Now that the control limits and center line for the individual value chart have been computed, we need to copy their values to columns G, H, and I of the Data sheet. After entering labels for LCL, Center, and UCL in cells G1 through I1, we enter **=Calculations!$B$13** in G2, **=Calculations!$B$14** in H2, and **=Calculations!$B$15** in 13. Then, in order to be able to plot a line for each of these variables across the days, copy the LCL value from G2 to G3 through G26, the center line value from H2 to H3 through H26, and the UCL value from I2 to I3 through I26.

We now use the Chart Wizard (see Appendix 2.1) to obtain the control chart for the individual value. With the Data sheet active, select **Insert | Chart.**

In the Step 1 Dialog box, select the **Standard types** tab and then select **XY (Scatter)** from the Chart type: list box. Select the first choice of the third row of chart Sub-types, the choice designated as "Scatter with data points connected by lines." Click the **Next** button.

In the Step 2 Dialog box, select the **Data Range** tab and enter **Data!A1:B26, Data!G1:I26** in the Data range: edit box. (Be sure to include the commas as part of your entry.) Select the **Columns option** button in the Series in: group. Select the **Series** tab. Enter **=Data!A2:A26** in the Value (X) Axis edit box. Click the **Next** button.

In the Step 3 Dialog box, select the **Titles** tab. Enter **Individual Value Chart for Flushness** in the Chart title edit box, enter **Days** in the Category (X) axis: edit box, and enter **Flushness** in the Value (Y) axis: edit box. Select the **Gridlines** tab. Deselect all check boxes. Click the **Next** button.

In the Step 4 Dialog box, select the **As new sheet: option** button and enter Individual Value chart in the edit box to the right of the option button. Click the **Finish** button.

Obtaining a Control Chart for the Individual Value (with the Standard Deviation) by using Microsoft Excel

To generate an individual value chart, you need to use Equations (7.28a) and (7.28b) on page 318. As an example, consider the flushness example of Section 7.4. To generate an individual value chart based on the flushness data of Table 7.6 on page 319, open the **MINI-VAN2.XLS** workbook and click the **Data** sheet tab. Verify that the data of Table 7.6 have been entered into columns A and B.

Select **Insert | Worksheet** and rename the sheet Calculations. Enter appropriate labels in column A, starting in row 3 for Individual Value chart, XBar, S, c_4 factor, LCL, Center Line, and UCL. Then compute $\bar{X}$ and s on the Calculations sheet by using the formula **=AVERAGE(Data!B:B)** in B4 and **STDEV(Data!B:B)** in cell B5. The values for the E_2 factor is then entered in cell B6. The lower control limit is obtained in cell B7 from the formula **=B4 − 3 *(B5/B6),** the center line in cell B8 is obtained from the formula **=B4,** and the upper control limit in cell B9 is obtained from the formula **=B4 + 3 *(B5/B6).**

Now that the control limits and center line have been computed, we copy their values to columns, C, D, and E of the Data sheet. After entering labels for LCL, Center, and UCL in cells C1 through E1, enter **=Calculations!$B$7** in C2, **=Calculations!$B$8** in D2, and **=Calculations!$B$9** in E2. Then, in order to be able to plot a line for each of these variables across the days, copy the LCL value from C2 to C3 through C51, the center line value from D2 to D3 through D51, and the UCL value from E2 to E3 through E51.

We now use the Chart Wizard (see Appendix 2.1) to obtain the control chart for the standard deviation. With the Data sheet active, select **Insert | Chart.**

In the Step 1 Dialog box, select the **Standard types** tab and then select *XY* **(Scatter)** from the Chart type: list box. Select the first choice of the third row of chart Sub-types, the choice designated as "Scatter with data points connected by lines." Click the **Next** button.

In the Step 2 Dialog box, select the **Data Range** tab and enter **Data!A1:E51** in the Data range: edit box. Select the **Columns option** button in the Series in: group. Select the **Series** tab. Enter **=Data!A2:A51** in the Value (X) Axis: edit box. Click the **Next** button.

In the Step 3 Dialog box, select the **Titles** tab. Enter **Individual Values Chart for Flushness** in the Chart title edit box, enter **Days** in the Category (X) axis: edit box, and enter **Flushness** in the Value (Y) axis: edit box. Select the **Gridlines** tab. Deselect all check boxes. Click the **Next** button.

In the Step 4 Dialog box, select the **As new sheet: option** button and enter Individual Values chart in the edit box to the right of the option button. Click the **Finish** button.

Obtaining a CUSUM Chart by using Microsoft Excel

To generate a CUSUM chart, you need to use Equations (7.29) and (7.30) on page 326. As an example, consider the lead content of water example of Section 7.5. To generate a CUSUM chart based on the lead content data of Table 7.1 on page 294, open the **LEAD.XLS** workbook and click the **Data** sheet tab. Verify that the data of Table 7.1 have been entered into columns A through F.

Select **Insert | Worksheet** and rename the sheet **CUSUM.** Copy the days and the label from column A of the data sheet to cells A1 through A31. Enter the label Average in cell B1. Compute the average for day 1 in cell B2 by using the formula **=AVERAGE(Data!B3:F3).** Copy this formula down the column from cell B2 to cell B3 through B31. Enter the label Standard Deviation in cell C1. Compute the standard deviation for day 1 in cell C2 by using the formula **=STDEV(Data!B3:F3).** Copy this formula down the column from cell C2 to cell C3 through C31.

Enter the label overall mean in cell A32. Compute the overall mean in cell B32 using the formula **=AVERAGE(B2:B31).** Enter the label SBar in cell A33. Compute the average standard deviation in cell B33 using the formula **=AVERAGE(C2:C31).** Enter the label C4 in cell A34 and enter the value for c_4 in cell B34. Enter the label for the subgroup size n in cell A35 and enter the subgroup size in cell B35. Enter the label k in cell A36, and the value for k in cell B36.

To compute the Z values, enter the label Z_i in cell D1, and then enter the formula **=(B2-$B$32)/($B$33/($B$34*SQRT($B$35)))** in cell D2 and then copy the formula down the column to cells D3 through D31. Enter the label SH_i in cell E1, and then enter the formula **=MAX(0,(C2-$B$36))** in cell E2. Enter the formula **=MAX(0,(C3-$B$36)+E2)** in cell E3, and then copy the formula down the column to cells E4 through E31. Enter the label SL_i in cell F1, and then enter the formula **=MAX(0,(-C2-$B$36))** in cell F2. Enter the formula **=MAX(0,(−C3−$B$36)+F2)** in cell F3, and then copy the formula down the column to cells F4 through F31. The results obtained will be similar to those displayed in Table 7.7 on page 328.

Obtaining an EWMA Chart by using Microsoft Excel

To generate an EWMA chart, you need to use Equations (7.31), (7.32), and (7.33) on pages 327, 328, and 329. As an example, consider the lead content of water example of Section 7.5. To generate an EWMA chart based on the lead content data of Table 7.1 on page 294, open the **LEAD.XLS** workbook and click the **Data** sheet tab. Verify that the data of Table 7.1 have been entered into columns A through F.

Select **Insert | Worksheet** and rename the sheet EWMA. Copy the days and the label from column A of the data sheet to cells A1 through A31. Enter the label average in cell B1. Compute the average for day 1 in cell B2 by using the formula =**AVERAGE(Data!B3:F3).** Copy this formula down the column from cell B2 to cell B3 through B31. Enter the label standard deviation in cell C1. Compute the standard deviation for day 1 in cell C2 by using the formula =**STDEV(Data!D3:F3).** Copy this formula down the column from cell C2 to cell C3 through C31.

Enter the label overall mean in cell A32. Compute the overall mean in cell B32 using the formula =**AVERAGE(B2:B31).** Enter the label SBar in cell A33. Compute the average standard deviation in cell B33 using the formula =**AVERAGE(C2:C31).** Enter the label C4 in cell A34 and enter the value for c_4 in cell B34. Enter the label for the subgroup size n in cell A35 and enter the subgroup size in cell B35. Enter the label r in cell A36, and the value for r in cell B36.

To compute the W values, enter the label W_i in cell D1, and then enter the formula =**\$B\$36*B2+(1-\$B\$36)*\$B\$32** in cell D2. Enter the formula =**\$B\$36*B3+(1-\$B\$36)*D2** in cell D3 and then copy the formula down the column to cells D4 through D31. Enter the label LCL in cell E1, and then enter the formula =**\$B\$32-3*(\$B\$33/(\$B\$34*SQRT (\$B\$35))*SQRT((\$B\$36)/(2-\$B\$36)*(1-(1-\$B\$36)^(2*A2))))** in cell E2 and copy this formula through cell E5. Enter the formula =**\$B\$32-3*(\$B\$33/(\$B\$34*SQRT(\$B\$35))*SQRT ((\$B\$36)/(2-\$B\$36)))** in cell E6 and copy this formula through cell E31. Enter the label UCL in cell F1, and then enter the formula =**\$B\$32+3*(\$B\$33/(\$B\$34*SQRT(\$B\$35)) *SQRT((\$B\$36)/(2-\$B\$36)*(1-(1-\$B\$36)^(2*A2))))** in cell F2 and copy this formula through cell F5. Enter the formula =**\$B\$32+3*(\$B\$33/(\$B\$34*SQRT(\$B\$35))*SQRT ((\$B\$36)/(2-\$B\$36)))** in cell F6 and copy this formula through cell F31. The results obtained will be similar to those displayed in Table 7.8 on page 330.

We now use the Chart Wizard (see Appendix 2.1) to obtain the control chart for the standard deviation. With the EWMA sheet active, select **Insert | Chart.**

In the Step 1 dialog box, select the **Standard types** tab and then select *XY* **(Scatter)** from the Chart type: list box. Select the first choice of the third row of chart Sub-types, the choice designated as "Scatter with data points connected by lines." Click the **Next** button.

In the Step 2 Dialog box, select the **Data Range** tab and enter **EWMA!A2:A231, EWMA!D1:F31** in the Data range: edit box. Select the **Columns option** button in the Series in: group. Select the **Series** tab. Enter =**EWMA!A2:A31** in the Value (*X*) Axis: edit box. Click the **Next** button.

In the Step 3 Dialog box, select the **Titles** tab. Enter **EWMA Chart for Lead Content** in the Chart title edit box, enter **Days** in the Category (*X*) axis: edit box, and enter **W** in the Value (*Y*) axis: edit box. Select the **Gridlines** tab. Deselect all check boxes. Click the **Next** button.

In the Step 4 Dialog box, select the **As new sheet: option** button and enter EWMA chart in the edit box to the right of the option button. Click the **Finish** button. The results obtained will be similar to those displayed in Table 7.7 on page 328.

APPENDIX 7.2   *Using MINITAB for Variables Control Charts*

Using MINITAB for R and $\overline{X}$ Charts

R and $\overline{X}$ charts can be obtained from MINITAB by selecting **Stat | Control Charts | Xbar-R** from the menu bar. Once data are either entered or imported into a worksheet, in the Xbar-R chart dialog box enter the variable name. The format for entering the name is different, depending on whether the data are stacked down a single column or unstacked across a set of columns with the data for each time period in a single row. If the data for the variable of interest are stacked down a single column, select the Single Column option button and enter the variable name in the Single Column edit box and the subgroup size in the Subgroup size edit box (this assumes equal sample sizes in each subgroup). If the subgroups are unstacked with each row representing the data for a single time period, the Subgroups across rows option button must be selected and the columns that contain the samples entered.

As an example, consider the lead content of water example of Section 7.3. To generate R and $\bar{X}$ charts based on the lead content of water data of Table 7.1 on page 294, open the **LEAD.MTW** worksheet. Select **Stat | Control Charts | Xbar-R.** In the Xbar-R dialog box, select the **Data are arranged as Subgroups across rows of** option button and enter **C2 – C6.** Click the **OK** button.

Using MINITAB for S and $\bar{X}$ Charts

As an example, consider the lead content of water example of Section 7.3. To generate S and $\bar{X}$ charts based on the lead content of water data of Table 7.1 on page 294, open the **LEAD. MTW** worksheet. Select **Stat | Control Charts | Xbar-S.** In the Xbar-S dialog box, select the **Data are arranged as Subgroups across rows of** option button and enter **C2 – C6.** If tests using zone rules are to be done, select the **Tests** button and select the approximate check boxes before clicking the **OK** button to return to the Xbar-S dialog box. Click the **OK** button. The results obtained will be similar to those of Figures 7.3 and 7.4 on pages 304 and 305.

Using MINITAB for the Moving Range and Individual Value Control Charts

As an example, consider the flushness data of Section 7.4. To generate moving range and individual value charts based on the flushness data of Table 7.4 on page 315, open the **MINIVAN1.MTW** worksheet. Select **Stat | Control Charts | I-MR Chart.** In the I-MR chart dialog box, enter **C2** or **'Flushnss'.** in the Variable edit box. Click the **OK** button. The results obtained will be similar to those of Figures 7.5 and 7.6 on pages 316 and 317.

Using MINITAB for the Individual Value (with the Standard Deviation) Control Chart

As an example, consider the flushness data of Section 7.4. To generate moving range and individual value charts based on the flushness data of Table 7.6 on page 319, open the **MINIVAN2.MTW** worksheet. Compute the standard deviation of the flushness data in C2 and divide by the c_4 factor. Select **Stat | Control Charts | Individuals Chart.** In the Individuals chart dialog box, enter **C2** or **'Flushnss'.** in the Variable edit box. Enter **1.328** in the Historical Sigma edit box. Click the **OK** button. The results obtained will be similar to those of Figure 7.7 on page 320.

Using MINITAB for the CUSUM and EWMA Charts

The CUSUM chart discussed in Section 7.7 uses a tabular approach that does not contain actual control limits. The CUSUM charts that are included in MINITAB use more advanced approaches discussed in References 7 and 8.

To develop an EWMA Chart, consider the lead content of water example of Section 7.3. To generate an EWMA chart based on the lead content of water data of Table 7.1 on page 294, open the **LEAD.MTW** worksheet. Select **Stat | Control Charts | EWMA.** In the EWMA dialog box, select the **Data are arranged as Subgroups across rows of** option button and enter **C2–C6.** Enter **.25** in the Weight for EWMA edit box. Select the **Estimate** button. Select the **sbar** option button in Methods for estimating sigma. Click the **OK** button to return the EWMA dialog box, Click the **OK** button. The results obtained will be similar to those of Figure 7.8 on page 331.

chapter

8

Estimation Procedures

"The more numerous the number of observations and the less they vary among themselves, the more the results approach the truth."

MARQUIS DE LAPLACE (1820)

USING STATISTICS: TENSILE STRENGTH OF COMPOSITE MATERIAL
IN AIRCRAFT DESIGN

Allowable stress for a material is the maximum stress at which one can be reasonably certain that failure will not occur. In aircraft design, weight is an important consideration, so composite materials are being used with increasing frequency. These materials can provide the strength and stiffness of metallic components with less weight. An important issue in determining allowable strength is to estimate not only the average tensile strength of the material but also the likelihood that the tensile strength will be below a specific amount.

8.1 INTRODUCTION

Statistical inference is the process of using sample results to draw conclusions about the characteristics of a population. In this chapter, we examine statistical procedures that will enable us to *estimate* various population parameters, including the mean, variance, and proportion. To accomplish this, we develop an **interval estimate** of the population parameter by taking into account the sampling distribution of the statistic. The interval that we construct will have a specified confidence or probability of correctly estimating the population parameter.

8.2 PROPERTIES OF ESTIMATORS

In Section 1.1, we defined inferential statistics as methods that allow one to make inferences and estimates about population parameters on the basis of sample statistics. In Sections 5.9 and 5.10, we studied the sampling distribution of the mean and the proportion, two statistics that we will return to in making inferences in this

365

chapter. In using point estimators such as the sample mean, there are several properties that are particularly useful. Three important properties of point estimators are listed in Exhibit 8.1.

EXHIBIT 8.1 Properties of Point Estimators

1. Unbiasedness

2. Efficiency

3. Consistency

The first property, **unbiasedness,** means that the average of all possible sample statistics (of a given sample size n) will be equal to the population parameter. This can be expressed in the following definition.

A sample statistic is an unbiased estimator of the population parameter if the expected value of the statistic is equal to the population parameter.

In Section 3.2, we discussed two estimators that are unbiased, the sample mean and the sample variance. The sample mean is an unbiased estimator of the population mean, because the average of all the sample means is equal to the population mean. In addition, recall that $n - 1$, rather than n, was used in the denominator of the sample variance s^2. This was done to provide s^2 with the property of unbiasedness. The proof that the sample variance is an unbiased estimator of the population variance is shown in optional derivation 8.1.

DERIVATION 8.1 Proving That s^2 Is an Unbiased Estimator of σ^2

$$s^2 = \frac{1}{n-1} \sum_{i=1}^{n} (X_i - \bar{X})^2$$

$$s^2 = \frac{1}{n-1} \left[\sum_{i=1}^{n} X_i^2 - \frac{\left(\sum_{i=1}^{n} X_i \right)^2}{n} \right]$$

$$s^2 = \frac{1}{n-1} \left[\sum_{i=1}^{n} X_i^2 - n\bar{X}^2 \right]$$

Taking the expectation of both sides:

$$E(s^2) = \frac{1}{n-1} E\left[\sum_{i=1}^{n} X_i^2 - n\bar{X}^2 \right]$$

$$E(s^2) = \frac{1}{n-1} \left\{ E\left[\sum_{i=1}^{n} X_i^2 \right] - E[n\bar{X}^2] \right\}$$

$$E(s^2) = \frac{1}{n-1} \left\{ \left[E \sum_{i=1}^{n} X_i^2 \right] - nE[\bar{X}^2] \right\}$$

Since $\sigma^2 = E(X_i^2) - \mu^2, E(X_i^2) = \sigma^2 + \mu^2$

and therefore $\sigma_{\bar{X}}^2 = E(\bar{X}^2) - \mu^2 = \dfrac{\sigma^2}{n}$

$$E(s^2) = \frac{1}{n-1}\left\{ \sum_{i=1}^{n}(\sigma^2 + \mu^2) - n\left(\frac{\sigma^2}{n} + \mu^2\right)\right\}$$

$$E(s^2) = \frac{1}{n-1}\left[(n\sigma^2 + n\mu^2) - \sigma^2 - n\mu^2\right]$$

$$E(s^2) = \frac{1}{n-1}\left[n\sigma^2 - \sigma^2\right]$$

$$E(s^2) = \left(\frac{n-1}{n-1}\right)\sigma^2 = \sigma^2$$

The second property, **efficiency,** refers to the precision of a sample statistic as an estimator of the population parameter. For distributions such as the normal, the arithmetic mean is considered more stable from sample to sample than are other measures of central tendency. For a sample of size n, the sample mean will be closer, on average, to the population mean than any other unbiased estimator will be to its population parameter.

The third property, **consistency,** refers to the effect of the sample size on the usefulness of the estimator. For a statistic to be consistent as the sample size increases, the variation of the sample statistic from the population parameter becomes smaller, so that the sample statistic (such as the arithmetic mean) becomes a better estimator of the population parameter.

8.3 CONFIDENCE INTERVAL ESTIMATION OF THE MEAN

In Section 5.9 we observed that, from the Central Limit Theorem or knowledge of the population distribution, we could determine the percentage of sample means that fell within certain distances of the population mean. For instance, in Section 5.9 (see page 213), in the example concerning the diameter of ball bearings, we observed that 95% of all sample means fell between 0.501432 and 0.504568 inch. This statement is based on deductive reasoning; however, it is exactly opposite to the type of reasoning that is needed here, namely inductive reasoning. Inductive reasoning is needed because, in statistical inference, we must take the results of a single sample and draw conclusions about the population, not vice versa. In practice, the population mean is the unknown quantity that is to be estimated.

Suppose that, in the ball-bearing example, the population mean μ is unknown but the population standard deviation σ is known to be 0.004 inch. Thus, rather than taking $\mu \pm (1.96)(\sigma/\sqrt{n})$ to find the upper and lower limits around μ as in Section 5.9, we determine the consequences of substituting the sample mean $\bar{X}$ for the unknown μ. We can use $\bar{X} \pm (1.96)(\sigma/\sqrt{n})$ as an interval within which we estimate the unknown μ. Although in practice a single sample of size n is selected and the mean $\bar{X}$ is computed, we need to obtain a hypothetical set of all possible samples, each of size n, in order to understand the full meaning of the interval estimate to be obtained.

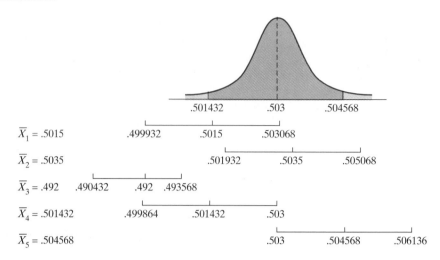

Figure 8.1   Confidence interval estimates for five different samples of $n = 25$ taken from a population where $\mu = 0.503$ and $\sigma = 0.004$

Suppose, for example, that our sample of size $n = 25$ ball bearings has a mean of 0.5015 inch. The interval developed to estimate μ is $0.5015 \pm (1.96)(0.004)/\sqrt{25}$ or 0.5015 ± 0.001568. That is, the estimate of μ is

$$0.499932 \leq \mu \leq 0.503068$$

The population mean μ (equal to 0.503) is included within the interval, so this sample has led to a correct statement about μ (see Figure 8.1).

To continue our hypothetical example, suppose that, for a different sample of $n=25$ ball bearings, the mean is 0.5035. The interval developed from this sample is $0.5035 \pm (1.96)(0.004)/(\sqrt{25})$ or 0.5035 ± 0.001568. That is, the estimate is

$$0.501932 \leq \mu \leq 0.505068$$

The population mean μ (equal to 0.503) is included within this interval, so we conclude that this statement about μ is correct as well.

Now, before we begin to think that we will *always* make correct statements about μ by developing a confidence interval estimate from the sample $\overline{X}$, suppose we draw a third hypothetical sample of size $n = 25$ ball bearings in which the sample mean is equal to 0.492 inch. The interval developed here is $0.492 \pm (1.96)(0.004)/(\sqrt{25})$ or 0.492 ± 0.001568. In this case, the estimate of μ is

$$0.490432 \leq \mu \leq 0.493568$$

Observe that this estimate is *not* a correct statement, because the population mean μ (equal to 0.503) is not included in the interval developed from this sample (see Figure 8.1). Thus, we are faced with a dilemma. For some samples, the interval estimate of μ will be correct, but for others it will be incorrect. In addition, we must realize that, in practice, we select only one sample, and, because we do not know the population mean, we cannot determine whether our particular statement is correct. What can we do to resolve this dilemma? We can determine the proportion of samples producing intervals that result in correct statements about the population mean μ. To do this, we need to examine two other hypothetical samples: the case in which $\overline{X} = 0.501432$ inch and the case in which

$\overline{X}$ = 0.504568 inch. If $\overline{X}$ = 0.501432, the interval is 0.501432 ± (1.96)(0.004)/($\sqrt{25}$) or 0.501432 ± 0.001568. That is,

$$0.499864 \le \mu \le 0.503$$

The population mean of 0.503 is at the upper limit of the interval, so the statement is a correct one (see Figure 8.1).

Finally, if $\overline{X}$ = 0.504568, the interval is 0.504568 ± (1.96)(0.004)/$\sqrt{25}$ or 0.504568 ± 0.001568. That is,

$$0.503 \le \mu \le 0.506136$$

In this case, the population mean of 0.503 is included at the lower limit of the interval, so the statement is also a correct one.

Thus, from these examples (see Figure 8.1), we can determine that, if the sample mean based on a sample of n = 25 ball bearings falls anywhere between 0.501432 and 0.504568 inch, the population mean is included *somewhere* within the interval. However, we know from our discussion of the sampling distribution in Section 5.9 that 95% of the sample means fall between 0.501432 and 0.504568 inch. Therefore, 95% of all sample means include the population mean within the interval developed.

In general, a 95% **confidence interval estimate** is interpreted to mean that if all possible samples of the same size n are taken, 95% of them include the true population mean somewhere within the interval around their sample means, and only 5% of them do not.

Because only one sample is selected in practice and μ is unknown, we never know for sure whether the specific interval obtained includes the population mean. However, we can state that we have 95% confidence that we have selected a sample whose interval does include the actual population mean.

In some situations, we might desire a higher degree of assurance (such as 99%) of including the population mean within the interval. In other cases, we might be willing to accept less assurance (such as 90%) of correctly estimating the population mean.

In general, the **level of confidence** is symbolized by $(1 - \alpha) \times 100\%$, where α is the proportion in the tails of the distribution that is outside the confidence interval. The proportion in the upper tail of the distribution is $\alpha/2$, and the proportion in the lower tail of the distribution that is outside the confidence interval is also $\alpha/2$. Therefore, to obtain the $(1 - \alpha) \times 100\%$ confidence interval estimate of the mean with σ known, we have

---

CONFIDENCE INTERVAL FOR A MEAN (σ KNOWN)

$$\overline{X} \pm Z\frac{\sigma}{\sqrt{n}}$$

or

$$\overline{X} - Z\frac{\sigma}{\sqrt{n}} \le \mu \le \overline{X} + Z\frac{\sigma}{\sqrt{n}} \qquad (8.1)$$

where Z = the value corresponding to an area of $(1 - \alpha)/2$ from the center of a standard normal distribution.

To construct a 95% confidence interval estimate of the mean, we select $\alpha = 0.05$. The Z value corresponding to an area of $0.95/2 = 0.4750$ from the center of the standard normal distribution is 1.96. The value of Z selected for constructing such a confidence interval is called the **critical value** for the distribution.

There is a different critical value for each *level of confidence*, $1 - \alpha$. As we have seen, a level of confidence of 95% leads to a Z value of ± 1.96 (see Figure 8.2). If a level of confidence of 99% is desired, the area of 0.99 is divided in half, leaving 0.495 between each limit and μ (see Figure 8.3). The Z value corresponding to an area of 0.495 from the center of the normal curve is approximately 2.58.

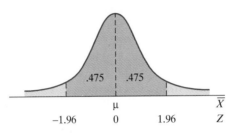

Figure 8.2   Normal curve for determining the Z value needed for 95% confidence

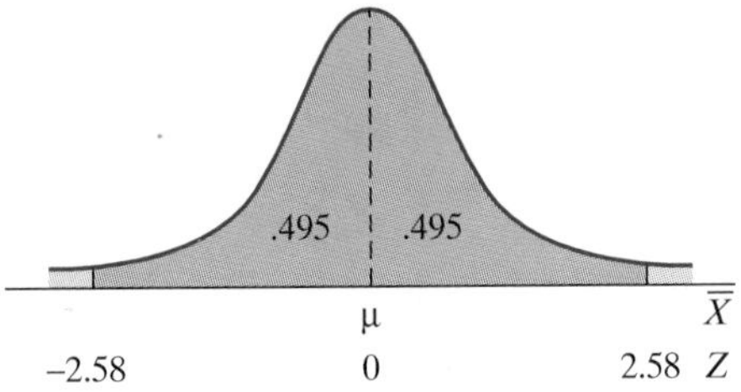

Figure 8.3   Normal curve for determining the Z value needed for 99% confidence

Now that we have considered various levels of confidence, why would we not want to make the confidence level as close to 100% as possible? Because any increase in the level of confidence is achieved only by simultaneously widening (and making less precise and less useful) the confidence interval obtained.

Just as the mean of the population μ is usually not known, the actual standard deviation of the population σ is also usually unknown. Therefore, we need to obtain a confidence interval estimate of μ by using only the sample statistics of $\overline{X}$ and s. To achieve this, we turn to the work of William S. Gosset.

Student's *t* Distribution

At the turn of the last century, a statistician named William S. Gosset, an employee of Guinness Breweries in Ireland (see Reference 3), was interested in making inferences about the mean when σ was unknown. Because Guinness employees were not permitted to publish research work under their own names, Gosset adopted the pseudonym A. Student. The distribution that he developed has come to be known as **Student's *t* distribution.**

If the random variable X is normally distributed, then the statistic

$$\frac{\overline{X} - \mu}{\dfrac{s}{\sqrt{n}}}$$

has a t distribution with $n - 1$ *degrees of freedom*. Notice that this expression has the same form as Equation (5.24) on page 216, except that s is used to estimate σ, which is presumed to be unknown in this case.

Properties of the t Distribution

In appearance, the t distribution is very similar to the normal distribution. Both distributions are bell-shaped and symmetrical. However, the t distribution has

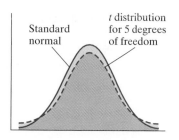

Figure 8.4   Standard normal distribution and t distribution for 5 degrees of freedom

more area in the tails and less in the center than does the normal distribution (see Figure 8.4). This is because σ is unknown, and we are using s to estimate it. We are uncertain of the value σ, so the values of t that we observe will be more variable than those of Z.

However, as the number of degrees of freedom increases, the t distribution gradually approaches the normal distribution until the two are virtually identical. This happens because, as the sample size gets larger, s becomes a better estimate of σ. With a sample size of about 120 or more, s estimates σ precisely enough that there is little difference between the t and Z distributions. For this reason, most statisticians use Z instead of t when the sample size is over 120.

COMMENT: CHECKING THE ASSUMPTIONS

Recall that the t distribution assumes that the random variable X being studied is normally distributed. In practice, however, as long as the sample size is large enough and the population is not very skewed, the t distribution can be used to estimate the population mean when σ is unknown. We should be concerned about the validity of the confidence interval primarily when we are dealing with a small sample size and a skewed population distribution. However, we can evaluate the shape of the data by using a histogram, stem-and-leaf display, box-and-whisker plot, or normal probability plot (see Sections 2.4, 3.3, and 5.5).

The critical values of t for the appropriate degrees of freedom can be obtained from the table of the t distribution (see Table A.4). The top of each column of the table indicates the area in the right tail of the t distribution. (Positive entries for t are supplied, so the values for t are for the upper tail.) Each row represents the particular t value for each specific degree of freedom. For example, with 24 degrees of freedom, if 95% confidence is desired, the appropriate value of t is found in the manner shown in Table 8.1. The 95% confidence level means that 2.5% of the values (an area of 0.025) are in each tail of the distribution. Looking in the column for an upper-tail area of 0.025 and in the row corresponding to 24 degrees of freedom results in a critical value for t of 2.0639. Because t is a symmetrical distribution, with a mean of 0, if the upper-tail value is +2.0639, the value for the lower-tail area (lower 0.025) will be −2.0639. A t value of 2.0639 means that the probability that t exceeds +2.0639 is 0.025 or 2.5% (see Figure 8.5).

TABLE 8.1

DETERMINING THE CRITICAL VALUE FROM THE t TABLE FOR AN AREA
OF 0.025 IN EACH TAIL WITH 24 DEGREES OF FREEDOM

	Upper-Tail Areas					
Degrees of Freedom	.25	.10	.05	.025	.01	.005
1	1.0000	3.0777	6.3138	12.7062	31.8207	63.6574
2	0.8165	1.8856	2.9200	4.3027	6.9646	9.9248
3	0.7649	1.6377	2.3534	3.1824	4.5407	5.8409
4	0.7407	1.5332	2.1318	2.7764	3.7469	4.6041
5	0.7267	1.4759	2.0150	2.5706	3.3649	4.0322
.	.	.	.	.	.	.
.	.	.	.	.	.	.
24	0.6848	1.3178	1.7109	2.0639	2.4922	2.7969
25	0.6844	1.3163	1.7081	2.0595	2.4851	2.7874

Source: Extracted from Table A.4.

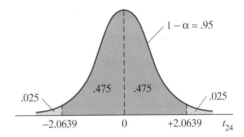

Figure 8.5 t distribution with 24 degrees of freedom

The Concept of Degrees of Freedom

Recall from Chapter 3 that the sample variance s^2 requires the computation of

$$\sum_{i=1}^{n} (X_i - \overline{X})^2$$

Thus, in order to compute s^2, we first need to know $\overline{X}$. Therefore, we can say that only $n - 1$ of the sample values are free to vary. That is, there are $n - 1$ **degrees of freedom.**

This concept is illustrated as follows. Suppose we have a sample of five values that have a mean of 20. How many distinct values do we need to know before we can obtain the remainder? The fact that $n = 5$ and $\overline{X} = 20$ also tells us that $\sum_{i=1}^{n} X_i = 100$, because $\sum_{i=1}^{n} X_i/n = \overline{X}$.

Thus, once we know four of the values, the fifth one will *not* be free to vary, because the sum must add to 100. For example, if four of the values are 18, 24, 19, and 16, the fifth value can only be 23 to make the sum equal to 100.

The Confidence Interval Statement

The $(1 - \alpha) \times 100\%$ confidence interval estimate for the mean of a normal population with σ unknown is expressed as follows.

CONFIDENCE INTERVAL FOR A MEAN (σ UNKNOWN)

$$\overline{X} \pm t_{n-1}\frac{s}{\sqrt{n}}$$

or

$$\overline{X} - t_{n-1}\frac{s}{\sqrt{n}} \leq \mu \leq \overline{X} + t_{n-1}\frac{s}{\sqrt{n}} \qquad (8.2)$$

where t_{n-1} is the critical value of the t distribution with $n-1$ degrees of freedom for an area of $\alpha/2$ in the upper tail.

To illustrate the application of the confidence interval estimate for the mean when the standard deviation σ is unknown, let us return to the *Using Statistics* example presented on page 365, concerning the tensile strength of composite material used in aircraft design. A sample of 25 specimens of composite material was selected. The results are presented in Table 8.2.

TABLE 8.2

TENSILE STRENGTH OF 25 SPECIMENS OF
COMPOSITE MATERIAL IN 1,000 PSI

203.41	209.58	213.35	218.56	242.76
185.97	190.67	207.88	210.80	231.46
184.41	200.73	206.51	209.84	212.15
160.44	180.95	201.95	204.60	219.51
174.63	185.34	205.59	212.00	225.25 **TENSILE**

Source: M. G. Vangel, "New methods for one-sided tolerance limits for a one-way balanced random-effects ANOVA model," *Technometrics,* 34, 1992, 176–185.

Using the PHStat add-in for Microsoft Excel (see Figure 8.6 on page 374) we compute $\overline{X} = 203.93$ and $s = 18.3204$. Because $n = 25$, we obtain the critical value from the t distribution as shown in Table 8.1. For 95% confidence, the critical value of t is 2.0639. Using Equation (8.2), we have

$$\overline{X} \pm t_{n-1}\frac{s}{\sqrt{n}}$$

$$= 203.93 \pm (2.0639)\frac{18.3204}{\sqrt{25}}$$

$$= 203.93 \pm 7.56$$

$$196.37 \leq \mu \leq 211.50$$

Thus, we conclude with 95% confidence that the average tensile strength of the composite material is between 196.37 and 211.50 thousands of pounds per square inch. The 95% confidence interval states that we are 95% sure that the

	A	B
1	**Tensile Strength of Composite Material**	
2		
3	**Sample Standard Deviation**	18.32042892
4	**Sample Mean**	203.9336
5	**Sample Size**	25
6	**Confidence Level**	95%
7	Standard Error of the Mean	3.664085783
8	Degrees of Freedom	24
9	*t* Value	2.063898137
10	Interval Half Width	7.562299821
11	**Interval Lower Limit**	196.37
12	**Interval Upper Limit**	211.50

Figure 8.6   Confidence interval estimate obtained from the PHStat add-in for Microsoft Excel of the tensile strength of composite material used in aircraft design

sample we have selected is one in which the population mean μ is located within the interval. This 95% confidence means that, if all possible samples of size 25 were selected (something that would never be done in practice), 95% of the intervals developed would include the population mean somewhere within the interval. The validity of this confidence interval estimate depends on the assumption of normality of the tensile strengths. With a sample of 25, as we noted on page 371, the use of the *t* distribution is likely to be appropriate.

PROBLEMS

8.1 If $\bar{X} = 85, \sigma = 8$, and $n = 64$, set up a 95% confidence interval estimate of the population mean μ.

8.2 Determine the critical value of *t* in each of the following circumstances.
 (a) $1 - \alpha = 0.95, n = 10$
 (b) $1 - \alpha = 0.99, n = 10$
 (c) $1 - \alpha = 0.95, n = 32$
 (d) $1 - \alpha = 0.95, n = 65$
 (e) $1 - \alpha = 0.90, n = 16$

8.3 If $\bar{X} = 75, s = 24$, and $n = 36$, assume that the population is normally distributed, and set up a 95% confidence interval estimate of the population mean μ.

8.4 The director of quality at a light-bulb factory needs to estimate the average life of a large shipment of light bulbs. The process standard deviation is known to be 100 hours. A random sample of 64 light bulbs indicated a sample average life of 350 hours.
 (a) Set up a 95% confidence interval estimate of the true average life of light bulbs in this shipment.

 (b) Do you think that the manufacturer has the right to state that the light bulbs last an average of 400 hours? Explain.
 (c) Does the population of light-bulb life have to be normally distributed here for the interval to be valid? Explain.
 (d) Explain why an observed value of 320 hours is not unusual, even though it is outside the confidence interval you calculated.
 (e) Suppose that the process is improved so that the standard deviation is reduced to 80 hours. What would be your answers in (a) and (b)?

8.5 The inspection division of the Lee County Weights and Measures Department is interested in estimating the actual amount of soft drink that is placed in 2-liter bottles at the local bottling plant of a large nationally known soft-drink company. The bottling plant has informed the inspection division that the standard deviation for 2-liter bottles is 0.05 liter. A random sample of 100 2-liter bottles obtained from this bottling plant indicates a sample average of 1.99 liters.

(a) Set up a 95% confidence interval estimate of the true average amount of soft drink in each bottle.

(b) Does the population of soft-drink fill have to be normally distributed here? Explain.

(c) Explain why an observed value of 2.02 liters is not unusual, even though it is outside the confidence interval you calculated.

(d) Suppose that the sample average had been 1.97 liters. What would be your answer to (a)?

8.6 The United States Department of Transportation requires tire manufacturers to provide tire performance information on the sidewall of the tire, so that a prospective customer can be better informed when making a purchasing decision. One very important measure of tire performance is the tread-wear index, which indicates the tire's resistance to tread wear compared to a tire grade with a base of 100. This means that a tire with a grade of 200 should last twice as long, on average, as a tire with a grade of 100. Suppose that a consumer organization wishes to estimate the actual tread-wear index of a brand name of tires graded 200 that are produced by a certain manufacturer. A random sample of 18 of these tires indicates a sample average tread-wear index of 195.3 and a sample standard deviation of 21.4.

(a) Set up a 95% confidence interval estimate of the population average tread-wear index for tires produced by this manufacturer under this brand name.

(b) Do you think that the consumer organization should accuse the manufacturer of producing tires that do not meet the performance information provided on the sidewall of the tire? Explain.

(c) Tell why an observed tread-wear index of 210 for a particular tire of a brand graded 200 is not unusual, even though it is outside the confidence interval developed in (a).

8.7 The Environmental Protection Agency was interested in studying the longevity of incandescent lamp bulbs. A random sample of 35 lamps was selected, and each bulb was tested until failure. The following data represent the times (in hours) that the incandescent lamp bulbs functioned:

1,011.4	978.3	1,307.8	1,039.4	1,181.7	1,092.7	968.4
839.0	1,178.3	1,351.9	785.6	1,075.3	893.7	1,067.6
961.3	1,224.5	800.2	1,352.2	1,116.1	1,038.7	985.9
1,282.8	744.6	885.5	1,528.7	1,140.7	1,265.1	1,089.2
1,660.3	1,021.2	900.9	1,263.5	1,054.7	816.8	530.7

LAMP

(a) Set up a 95% confidence interval estimate of the average life (in hours) of all such incandescent lamps.

(b) What assumption must be made in (a)? On the basis of these data, do you think that this assumption is valid? Explain.

8.8 An engineering consulting firm wanted to evaluate the diameter of rivet heads. The following data represent the diameters (in hundredths of an inch) for a random sample of 25 rivet heads:

6.81	6.79	6.69	6.59	6.65	6.60	6.74	6.70	6.76
6.84	6.81	6.71	6.66	6.76	6.76	6.77	6.72	6.68
6.71	6.79	6.72	6.72	6.72	6.79	6.83		

RIVET

(a) Set up a 95% confidence interval estimate of the average diameter of rivet heads (in hundredths of an inch).

(b) What assumption must be made in (a)? On the basis of these data, do you think that this assumption is valid? Explain.

8.9 The quality engineer of a multinational company involved in manufacturing synthetic rubber wants to examine the hardness of the rubber. In the rubber industry, hardness is measured in degrees Shore. A random sample of 50 pieces of rubber was evaluated, with the following results:

62.4	66.0	67.6	63.2	66.3	61.8	61.8	67.5	61.3	65.0
64.6	61.3	64.7	63.5	66.4	60.0	65.8	64.3	62.3	61.4
63.6	69.5	64.9	62.2	67.7	67.7	66.6	64.5	64.0	61.6
68.5	65.2	66.9	66.5	68.3	64.3	63.3	63.6	65.8	60.1
62.6	66.4	67.2	62.5	63.6	63.4	63.1	62.5	68.7	62.2

RUBBER2

(a) Set up a 95% confidence interval estimate of the average hardness (in degrees Shore) for all pieces of rubber of this type.

(b) What assumption must be made in (a)? On the basis of these data, do you think that this assumption is valid? Explain.

8.10 A manufacturer of plastics wishes to evaluate the hardness of rectangularly molded plastic blocks to be used in furniture. In the plastics industry, hardness is measured in Brinell units. The following data represent hardness measurements (in Brinell units) for a random sample of 40 plastic blocks:

294.8	272.7	268.2	291.8	281.0	244.0	257.7	290.7
263.0	324.3	258.3	226.9	291.8	286.4	296.4	293.9
252.0	285.4	229.9	284.3	235.6	218.1	307.8	272.6
251.7	248.2	239.1	280.5	262.9	274.6	247.5	288.4
330.1	271.8	282.3	279.8	270.5	286.4	300.9	281.1

PLASTIC2

(a) Set up a 95% confidence interval estimate of the average hardness (in Brinell units) for all plastic blocks of this type.

(b) What assumption must be made in (a)? On the basis of these data, do you think that this assumption is valid? Explain.

8.11 A consumer protection agency wants to investigate potential flammability in material to be used in children's clothing. A random sample of 36 strips of material is selected from batches of material. Each strip is subjected to a Vertical Semirestrained test that chars the material. The following data indicate the length of charred material (in

centimeters) for each of the 36 strips:

9.06	8.30	9.95	8.21	10.35	9.35	9.43	10.76	9.17
8.90	8.73	8.42	9.29	10.03	9.84	8.75	6.95	7.25
9.38	9.86	8.89	8.36	8.90	9.06	9.82	7.94	9.22
7.93	9.54	8.64	9.80	9.50	9.44	9.56	9.64	8.66

CHARRED

(a) Set up a 95% confidence interval estimate of the average length (in centimeters) of charred material for all strips of this type.

(b) What assumption must be made in (a)? Given these data, do you think this assumption valid? Explain.

8.4 CONFIDENCE INTERVAL ESTIMATION FOR THE VARIANCE

In analyzing numerical data, it is often important to estimate the population variance of a set of data, as well as the population average. In attempting to draw conclusions about the variability in the population, we first must determine what distribution the variability in the sample data follows. If the variable is assumed to be normally distributed, then the χ^2 distribution can be used to develop a confidence interval estimate of the population variance (or the population standard deviation). The $(1 - \alpha)\%$ confidence interval for the variance is expressed as follows.

CONFIDENCE INTERVAL ESTIMATE FOR THE VARIANCE

$$\frac{(n-1)s^2}{\chi_U^2} \leq \sigma^2 \leq \frac{(n-1)s^2}{\chi_L^2} \tag{8.3}$$

Where

   n = sample size

   s^2 = sample variance

   χ_L^2 = lower critical value of χ^2

   χ_U^2 = upper critical value of χ^2

For a given sample size n, the test statistic χ^2 follows a chi-square distribution with $n - 1$ degrees of freedom. A chi-square distribution is a skewed distribution whose shape depends on its number of degrees of freedom. As the number of degrees of freedom increases, a chi-square distribution becomes more nearly symmetrical. Table A.6 contains various upper-tail areas for chi-square distributions pertaining to different degrees of freedom. A portion of this table is displayed as Table 8.3.

   The value at the top of each column indicates the area in the upper portion (or right side) of a particular chi-square distribution. Some examples: with 24 degrees of freedom, the critical value of the χ^2 test statistic corresponding to an upper-tail area of 0.025 is 39.364, and the critical value corresponding to an

TABLE 8.3

OBTAINING THE CRITICAL VALUES FROM THE CHI-SQUARE DISTRIBUTION WITH 24 DEGREES OF FREEDOM

Degrees of Freedom	Upper-Tail Area									
	.995	.99	.975	.95	.90 ...	.10	.05	.025	.01	.005
1	...	...	0.001	0.004	0.016	2.706	3.841	5.024	6.635	7.879
2	0.010	0.020	0.051	0.103	0.211	4.605	5.991	7.378	9.210	10.597
3	0.072	0.115	0.216	0.352	0.584	6.251	7.815	9.348	11.345	12.838
.	.	.	.	.	.	.	.	.	.	.
.	.	.	.	.	.	.	.	.	.	.
23	9.260	10.196	11.689	13.091	14.848	32.007	35.172	38.076	41.638	44.181
24	9.886	10.856	12.401	13.848	15.659	33.196	36.415	39.364	42.980	45.559
25	10.520	11.524	13.120	14.611	16.973	34.382	37.652	40.646	44.314	46.928

Source: Extracted from Table A.6.

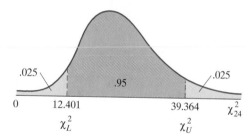

Figure 8.7　Determining the lower and upper critical values of a chi-square distribution with 24 degrees of freedom corresponding to a 0.95 level of confidence for a population variance or standard deviation

upper-tail area of 0.975 (that is, a lower-tail area of 0.025) is 12.401. These are seen in Figure 8.7. This means that, for 24 degrees of freedom, the probability of equaling or exceeding the critical value of 12.401 is 0.975, while the probability of equaling or exceeding the critical value of 39.364 is 0.025. By subtraction, the probability that a χ^2 test statistic falls between the critical values of 12.401 and 39.364 is 0.95. Therefore, once we determine the level of significance and the degrees of freedom, any critical value of the χ^2 test statistic can be found for a particular chi-square distribution.

To apply the confidence interval for the variance, let us return to the data concerning the tensile strength of composite material for aircraft design, which was used to develop a confidence interval estimate for the population average tensile strength. To develop a 95% confidence interval estimate for the population variance, with $n = 25$ and $s = 18.3204$, from Equation (8.3), the area in the lower tail of the distribution is $0.05/2 = 0.025$, and the area in the upper tail is also $0.05/2 = 0.025$, With $25 - 1 = 24$ degrees of freedom, from Figure 8.7, the lower critical value is 12.401, and the upper critical value is 39.304. Thus, we have the following:

$$\frac{(25-1)(18.3204)^2}{39.364} \leq \sigma^2 \leq \frac{(25-1)(18.3204)^2}{12.401}$$

$$204.64 \leq \sigma^2 \leq 649.56$$

$$14.3 \leq \sigma \leq 25.49$$

We are 95% confident that the population variance of the tensile strength is between 204.64 and 649.56. This means that we are 95% confident that the standard deviation of the tensile strength is between 14.31 and 25.49 thousands of pounds per inch.

COMMENT: CHECKING THE ASSUMPTIONS OF THE CONFIDENCE INTERVAL FOR THE VARIANCE OR STANDARD DEVIATION

In setting up a confidence interval estimate for a population variance or standard deviation, we assume that the data in the population are normally distributed. Unfortunately, the χ^2 distribution is quite sensitive to departures from this assumption; if the population is not normally distributed, particularly for small sample sizes, the accuracy of the confidence interval can be seriously affected (see Reference 7).

PROBLEMS

8.12 Determine the lower and upper critical values of χ^2 in each of the following circumstances.
  (a) 90% confidence level, $n = 16$
  (b) 95% confidence level, $n = 11$
  (c) 99% confidence level, $n = 8$

8.13 A manufacturer of candy must monitor the temperature at which the candies are baked. Too much variation will cause inconsistency in the taste of the candy. A random sample of 30 batches of candy is selected, and the sample standard deviation of the temperature is 2.1°F.
  (a) Set up a 95% confidence interval estimate of the population standard deviation.
  (b) What assumptions need to be made in (a)?

8.14 A manufacturer of doorknobs has a production process that is designed to provide a doorknob with a target diameter of 2.5 inches. In the past, the standard deviation of the diameter has been 0.035 inch. In an effort to reduce the variation in the process, various studies have been conducted that have led to a redesigned process. A sample of 25 doorknobs produced under the new process indicates a sample standard deviation of 0.025 inch.
  (a) Set up a 99% confidence interval estimate of the population standard deviation.
  (b) What assumptions need to be made in (a)?
  (c) Given the results of (a), do you think the redesigned process has resulted in a reduced variation? Explain.

8.15 In Problem 8.6 on page 375, the tread-wear index of a random sample of 18 tires indicated a sample average tread-wear index of 195.3 and a sample standard deviation of 21.4. Set up a 95% confidence interval estimate of the population standard deviation of the tread-wear index for tires produced by this manufacturer under this brand name.

8.16 In Problem 8.8 on page 375, an engineering consulting firm evaluated the diameter of rivet heads.

RIVET

(a) Set up a 95% confidence interval estimate of the standard deviation of the diameter of rivet heads (in hundredths of an inch).

(b) What assumption must be made in (a)? Given these data, do you think this assumption is valid? Explain.

8.17 A machine used for packaging seedless golden raisins is set so that the standard deviation of the weight of raisins packaged per box is 0.25 ounce. The quality-control engineer wishes to test the machine setting and selects a sample of 30 consecutive raisin packages filled during the production process. Their weights are recorded as follows:

```
15.2  15.3  15.1  15.7  15.3  15.0  15.1  14.3  14.6  14.5
15.0  15.2  15.4  15.6  15.7  15.4  15.3  14.9  14.8  14.6
14.3  14.4  15.5  15.4  15.2  15.5  15.6  15.1  15.3  15.1
```

RAISINS

(a) Set up a 95% confidence interval estimate of the population standard deviation.

(b) What assumptions are made in (a)? Given these data, do you think this assumption is valid? Explain.

(c) Based on the results of (a), do you think that the standard deviation is no longer 0.25 ounce? Explain.

8.18 A manufacturer claims that the standard deviation of a measure of capacity of a certain type of battery that the company produces is 2.5 ampere-hours. An independent consumer-protection agency wishes to test the credibility of the manufacturer's claim and measures the capacity of a random sample of 20 batteries from a recently produced batch. The results, in ampere-hours, are as follows:

137.4	140.0	138.8	139.1	144.4	139.2	141.8
137.3	133.5	138.2	141.1	139.7	136.7	136.3
135.6	138.0	140.9	140.6	136.7	134.1	

AMPHRS

(a) Set up a 95% confidence interval estimate of the population standard deviation battery capacity.

(b) What assumptions are made in (a)? Given these data, do you think this assumption valid? Explain.

(c) Based on the results of (a), do you think that the standard deviation is no longer 2.5 ampere-hours? Explain.

8.5 PREDICTION INTERVAL ESTIMATE FOR A FUTURE INDIVIDUAL VALUE

In addition to the need to obtain a confidence interval estimate for the population mean, it is often important to be able to predict the outcome of a future individual value (see Reference 2). Although the form of the prediction interval is similar to the confidence interval estimate of Equation (8.2), we must be careful to note that the **prediction interval** is estimating an observable future individual value X_f, not an unknown parameter μ. The prediction interval is provided in Equation (8.4).

$$\bar{X} \pm t_{n-1} s \sqrt{1 + \frac{1}{n}}$$

$$\bar{X} - t_{n-1} s \sqrt{1 + \frac{1}{n}} \leq X_f \leq \bar{X} + t_{n-1} s \sqrt{1 + \frac{1}{n}} \tag{8.4}$$

If we return to the *Using Statistics* example concerning the tensile strength of composite material for aircraft design, which we have discussed in Sections 8.3 and 8.4, suppose we wanted to obtain a 95% prediction interval estimate of the future tensile strength of an individual specimen of composite material. Using Equation (8.4), we have the following:

$$\overline{X} \pm t_{n-1} s \sqrt{1 + \frac{1}{n}}$$

$$= 203.93 \pm (2.0639)(18.3204)\sqrt{1 + \frac{1}{25}}$$

$$= 203.93 \pm 38.56$$

$$165.37 \le X_f \le 242.49$$

Observe that this result differs markedly from the one obtained when we developed a confidence interval estimate of the population mean. This interval is substantially wider, because we are estimating a *future individual value*, not the population mean.

PROBLEMS

8.19 In Problem 8.6 on page 375, the tread-wear index of a random sample of 18 tires indicated a sample average tread-wear index of 195.3 and a sample standard deviation of 21.4.
   (a) Set up a 95% prediction interval estimate for a future individual tire produced by this manufacturer under this brand name.
   (b) Compare the results of (a) with the confidence interval estimate of the population average tread-wear index obtained in Problem 8.6 (a), and explain the difference.

8.20 In Problem 8.7 on page 375, a random sample of 35 lamps was selected and each bulb was tested until failure.

LAMP

   (a) Set up a 95% prediction interval estimate of the life of a future individual bulb.
   (b) Compare the results of (a) with the confidence interval estimate of the population average life obtained in Problem 8.7 (a), and explain the difference.

8.21 In Problem 8.8 on page 375, an engineering consulting firm evaluated the diameter of rivet heads.

RIVET

   (a) Set up a 95% prediction interval estimate of the diameter of a future rivet head.
   (b) Compare the results of (a) with the confidence interval estimate of the population average

diameter of rivet heads obtained in Problem 8.8 (a), and explain the difference.

8.22 In Problem 8.9 on page 375, the quality engineer of a multinational company involved in manufacturing synthetic rubber examined the hardness of the rubber.

RUBBER2

   (a) Set up a 95% prediction interval estimate of the hardness (in degrees Shore) of a future piece of rubber of this type.
   (b) Compare the results of (a) with the confidence interval estimate of the population average hardness of pieces of rubber obtained in Problem 8.9 (a), and explain the difference.

8.23 In Problem 8.10 on page 375, the hardness of rectangularly molded plastic blocks to be used in furniture was studied.

PLASTIC2

   (a) Set up a 95% prediction interval estimate of the hardness (in Brinell units) of a future individual plastic block of this type.
   (b) Compare the results of (a) with the confidence interval estimate of the population average hardness of rectangularly molded plastic blocks obtained in Problem 8.10 (a), and explain the difference.

8.24 In Problem 8.11 on page 376, the potential flammability in material to be used in children's clothing was studied by subjecting strips of cloth to a Vertical Semirestrained test that chars the material.

CHARRED

(a) Set up a 95% prediction interval estimate of the length (in centimeters) of charred

material for a future individual strip of this type.

(b) Compare the results of (a) with the confidence interval estimate of the population average length (in centimeters) of charred material obtained in Problem 8.11 (a), and explain the difference.

8.6 TOLERANCE INTERVALS

In our discussion of estimation in Sections 8.1–8.5, we have focused on a population parameter, such as the mean or the variance, or on a single individual future value. However, in many practical engineering applications, interest is focused not on estimating a single value or the average value, but on the likelihood that a certain percentage of observations will be below or above a specific value. In the context of the example we have been considering in this chapter, the aircraft designer may be more interested in an interval estimate that at least a specific proportion of composite material specimens is below or above a specific value.

An interval that includes at least a certain proportion of measurements with a stated confidence is called a **tolerance interval.**

When the population mean, μ, and population standard deviation σ are known, and the variable is assumed to be normally distributed, a tolerance interval can be developed that gives approximately 100% confidence based on normal probabilities covered in Section 5.3. However, since these population parameters are rarely known, sample estimates must be used to develop a tolerance interval with a specified level of confidence. A two-sided tolerance interval in a normal population is developed as follows.

A $100(1 - \alpha)\%$ confidence interval for $100p\%$ of the measurements is given by

$$\overline{X} \pm K_2 s \tag{8.5}$$

where

$\overline{X}$ = sample mean

s = sample standard deviation

K_2 = value found in Table A.5a based on the values of the confidence coefficient $(1 - \alpha)$, p, and the sample size n

To illustrate this two-sided tolerance interval, suppose that we wanted to develop a 95% tolerance interval estimate for 90% of the tensile strengths of the composite material specimens. Because $p = 0.90$, $n = 25$, and the level of confidence is 95%, the value of K_2 from Table A. 5a is 2.215. Using Equation (8.5), we have the following:

$$\bar{X} \pm K_2 s = 203.93 \pm (2.215)(18.3204)$$
$$= 203.93 \pm 40.58$$
$$\text{or } 163.35 \text{ to } 244.51$$

Thus, we have 95% confidence that at least 90% of the specimens of composite material will have tensile strengths between 163.35 and 244.51 thousands of pounds per inch.

Now that we have discussed a two-sided tolerance interval, we turn to the development of a one-sided tolerance interval. In many circumstances, it is important to estimate only the lower bound or only the upper bound of the tolerance interval. For example, if the concern was with the strength of materials, as it is in aircraft design, it would be important to obtain a tolerance interval estimate of the lower tail of the population of strengths. A one-sided tolerance interval in a normal population is presented as follows.

One-Sided Tolerance Interval for Lower Bound

$$\bar{X} - K_1 s$$

One-Sided Tolerance Interval for Upper Bound

$$\bar{X} + K_1 s \tag{8.6}$$

where

$\bar{X}$ = sample mean

s = sample standard deviation

K_1 = value from Table A.5b for given level of confidence, given percentage of values in lower or upper bound, and sample size n

---

To illustrate this one-sided tolerance interval, suppose that we wanted to obtain a 95% lower tolerance interval for 10% of the tensile strengths of the composite material specimens. Because $p = 0.10$, $n = 25$, and the level of confidence is 95%, the value of K_1 from Table A.5b is 1.838. Using Equation (8.6), we have the following:

$$\bar{X} - K_1 s = 203.93 - (1.838)(18.3204)$$
$$= 203.93 - 33.67$$
$$= 170.26$$

Thus, we have 95% confidence that no more than 10% of the specimens of composite material will have a tensile strength below 170.26 thousands of pounds per inch. From another perspective, we can also state that we have 95% confidence that at least 90% of the specimens of composite material will have a tensile strength above 170.26 thousands of pounds per inch.

PROBLEMS

8.25 In Problem 8.6 on page 375, the tread-wear index of a random sample of 18 tires indicated a sample average tread-wear index of 195.3 and a sample standard deviation of 21.4.

(a) Set up a 95% tolerance estimate for the tread-wear index that will include at least 90% of the tires produced by this manufacturer under this brand name.

(b) Set up a 95% tolerance estimate for the tread-wear index that no more than 10% of the tires will be less than.

(c) Compare the results of (a) to the confidence interval estimate of the population average tread-wear index obtained in Problem 8.6 (a) and to the prediction interval for a single individual future value in Problem 8.19 (a), and explain the differences.

8.26 In Problem 8.7 on page 375, a random sample of 35 lamps was selected and each bulb was tested until failure.

LAMP

(a) Set up a 95% tolerance estimate for the life that will include at least 90% of the bulbs manufactured.

(b) Set up a 95% tolerance estimate for the life that no more than 10% of the bulbs exceed.

(c) Compare the results of (a) to the confidence interval estimate of the population average life obtained in Problem 8.7 (a) and to the prediction interval for a single individual future value in Problem 8.20 (a), and explain the differences.

8.27 In Problem 8.8 on page 375, an engineering consulting firm evaluated the diameter of rivet heads.

RIVET

(a) Set up a 99% tolerance estimate for the diameter that will include at least 95% of the bulbs manufactured.

(b) Compare the results of (a) to the confidence interval estimate of the population average diameter obtained in Problem 8.8 (a) and to the prediction interval for a single individual future value in Problem 8.21 (a), and explain the differences.

8.28 In Problem 8.9 on page 375, the quality engineer of a multinational company involved in manufacturing synthetic rubber examined the hardness of the rubber.

RUBBER2

(a) Set up a 95% tolerance estimate for the hardness that will include at least 95% of the rubber manufactured.

(b) Set up a 95% tolerance estimate for the hardness that will be exceeded by at least 99% of the rubber.

(c) Compare the results of (a) to the confidence interval estimate of the population average hardness obtained in Problem 8.9 (a) and to the prediction interval for a single individual future value in Problem 8.22 (a), and explain the differences.

8.29 In Problem 8.10 on page 375, the hardness of rectangularly molded plastic blocks to be used in furniture was studied.

PLASTIC2

(a) Set up a 99% tolerance estimate for the hardness that will include at least 90% of the rectangularly molded plastic blocks.

(b) Set up a 95% tolerance estimate for the hardness that will be exceeded by no more than 5% of the rectangularly molded plastic blocks.

(c) Compare the results of (a) to the confidence interval estimate of the population average hardness obtained in Problem 8.10 (a) and to the prediction interval for a single individual future value in Problem 8.23 (a) and explain the differences.

8.30 In Problem 8.11 on page 376, the potential flammability in material to be used in children's clothing was studied by subjecting strips of cloth to a Vertical Semirestrained test that chars the material.

CHARRED

(a) Set up a 95% tolerance estimate for the length of charred material that will include at least 99% of the strips of cloth.

(b) Set up a 99% tolerance estimate for the length of charred material that will be exceeded by at least 99% of the strips of cloth.

(c) Compare the results of (a) to the confidence interval estimate of the population average length obtained in Problem 8.11 (a) and to the prediction interval for a single individual future value in Problem 8.24 (a), and explain the differences.

8.7 CONFIDENCE INTERVAL ESTIMATION FOR THE PROPORTION

In this section, we extend the concept of the confidence interval to categorical data, to estimate the population proportion π from the sample proportion $p = X/n$. Recall from Section 5.10 that, in many circumstances, the binomial distribution can be approximated by the normal distribution. In such cases, we can set up the following $(1 - \alpha) \times 100\%$ confidence interval estimate for the population proportion π.

CONFIDENCE INTERVAL ESTIMATE FOR THE PROPORTION

$$p \pm Z\sqrt{\frac{p(1 - p)}{n}}$$

or

$$p - Z\sqrt{\frac{p(1 - p)}{n}} \leq \pi \leq p + Z\sqrt{\frac{p(1 - p)}{n}} \qquad (8.7)$$

where

$p = X/n$ = sample proportion

π = population proportion

Z = critical value from the normal distribution

n = sample size

To demonstrate an application of the confidence interval estimate of the proportion, we can examine the situation faced by the quality engineer for a large city newspaper. In the production of a newspaper, an important quality characteristic relates to the proportion of newspapers that are printed even though a nonconforming attribute, such as excessive ruboff, improper page set-up, missing pages, or duplicate pages is present. Since it is impractical (and would be extremely time consuming and expensive) to examine every newspaper printed, a random sample of 200 newspapers is selected for analysis. Suppose that, of this sample of 200, 35 contain some type of nonconformance. If 95% confidence was specified, for these data we would have

$$p = 35/200 = 0.175, \text{ with a 95\% level of confidence } Z = 1.96$$

Using Equation (8.7), we have the following:

$$p \pm Z\sqrt{\frac{p(1 - P)}{n}}$$

$$= 0.175 \pm (1.96)\sqrt{\frac{(0.175)(0.825)}{200}}$$

$$= 0.175 \pm (1.96)(0.0269)$$

$$= 0.175 \pm 0.053$$

$$0.122 \leq \pi \leq 0.228$$

Therefore, with 95% confidence we estimate that between 12.2% and 22.8% of the newspapers printed on that day have some type of nonconformance.

COMMENT: CHECKING THE ASSUMPTIONS

In the example concerning newspaper nonconformance, the number of successes and failures is sufficiently large that the normal distribution provides an excellent approximation to the binomial distribution. As a general rule, for a 95% confidence interval, the normal distribution will adequately approximate the binomial distribution as long as $np(1 - p)$ is at least 10. For a 99% confidence interval, $np(1 - p)$ should be at least 35 (Reference 6). The exact confidence intervals for various sample sizes and proportions of successes have been tabulated by Fisher and Yates (Reference 1).

For a given sample size, confidence intervals for proportions often seem to be wider than those for continuous variables. With continuous variables, the measurement on each item contributes more information than it does for a categorical variable. In other words, a categorical variable with only two possible values is a very crude measure compared with a continuous variable, so each observation contributes only a little information about the parameter we are estimating.

PROBLEMS

8.31 An article in *Environmental Progress* (1995), concerning companies' use of solvents for lithographic printing, discussed whether a company safely used solvents in different situations. In a sample of 63 evaluations, 40 of the companies were found to use the solvents safely. Set up a 95% confidence interval for the proportion of times in which the population of all such companies use the solvents safely.

8.32 A study (Hall, S. W., "Analysis of Defectivity of Semiconductor Wafers by Contingency Table." *Proceedings, Institute of Environmental Sciences*, Vol. 1, (1994), 177–183), done as part of a yield improvement effort at a semiconductor manufacturing facility, provided defect data for a sample of 450 wafers. 116 wafers were judged to be of bad quality. For 36 of the 116 bad wafers, a particle was found on the die that produced the wafer.
(a) Set up a 95% confidence interval for the proportion of wafers that were of bad quality.
(b) Set up a 95% confidence interval for the proportion of bad wafers for which a particle is on the die that produced the wafer.

8.33 A quality study was performed on the manufacture of Application Specific Integrated Circuits (ASIC). A sample of 1,126 units revealed 114 nonconforming units. Set up a 99% confidence interval for the proportion of nonconforming units.

8.34 The skulls of most mammals are symmetrical, but there are exceptions, such as odontocete whales. This is part of the normal growth pattern found throughout the taxa. Sea otters also have been noted to have naturally occurring asymmetrical skulls, with one side of the skull larger than the other. A study of a group of sea otters reported the results from measuring cranial asymmetry in 387 sea otter skulls. Each sea otter skull was categorized by age: pup, juvenile, or adult. The results were as follows.

	Saggital crest deflects to the			
Age Class	Left Side	Right Side	Sides Equal	Total
Pups	11	3	1	15
Juveniles	61	14	21	96
Adults	86	82	108	276

(a) Set up a 95% confidence interval for the population proportion of adults whose saggital crest deflects to the left side.
(b) Combining pups and juveniles, form a 95% confidence interval for the population proportion of nonadults whose saggital crest deflects to the left side.

8.35 In a computer system at a university with many new users constantly being introduced to the system, there will be many instances of a person locking up or freezing their account. Additionally, more experienced users trying to bypass system limitations or restrictions can also freeze their own accounts. A sample of 2,142 computer freezes of a system revealed the following:

- 115 of the freezes were severe;
- 722 of the freezes were caused by College of Engineering students;

- 588 of the freezes were considered standard.

(a) Set up a 95% confidence interval for the proportion of computer freezes caused by students from the College of Engineering.

(b) Set up a 90% confidence interval for the proportion of computer freezes that are severe.

(c) Set up a 99% confidence interval for the proportion of computer freezes that are standard.

SUMMARY

In this chapter we have developed several methods for estimating characteristics of a population. In the next chapter we turn to a hypothesis-testing approach in which we make decisions about population parameters.

KEY TERMS

confidence interval estimate 369
consistency 366
critical value 370
degrees of freedom 372
efficiency 366
interval estimate 365

level of confidence 369
prediction interval 379
Student's *t* distribution 370
tolerance interval 381
unbiasedness 366

CHAPTER REVIEW *Checking Your Understanding*

8.36 Why is it that we can never really have 100% confidence of correctly estimating the population characteristic of interest?

8.37 When is the *t* distribution used in developing the confidence interval estimate for the mean?

8.38 Why is it true that for a given sample size *n*, an increase in confidence is achieved by widening (and so making less precise) the confidence interval obtained?

8.39 What is the difference between a confidence interval estimate for a population mean and a prediction interval estimate for an individual value?

8.40 What is the difference between a confidence interval estimate for a population mean and a tolerance interval estimate?

8.41 When would a one-sided tolerance interval be more appropriate than a two-sided tolerance interval estimate?

Chapter Review Problems

8.42 The director of quality of a company manufacturing heavy fabrics is interested in studying the warpwise breaking strength of fabric. The following data represent the warpwise fabric breaking strengths (in pounds per square inch) for a random sample of 25 pieces:

196.5	198.1	192.1	200.1	203.2	202.9	207.3	201.7	207.5
207.7	195.5	198.4	192.3	189.9	196.1	197.9	202.4	189.9
198.1	204.7	205.3	189.5	202.1	210.2	196.9	**WARPFAB**	

(a) Set up a 95 percent confidence interval estimate of the population average breaking strength (in pounds per square inch) for all such fabric pieces.

(b) Set up a 95 percent confidence interval estimate of the population standard deviation of the breaking strength (in pounds per square inch) for all such fabric pieces.

(c) What assumption must be made in (a) and (b)? Given these data, do you think this assumption valid? Explain.

(d) Set up a 95 percent prediction interval estimate of the breaking strength (in pounds per square inch) for a future individual fabric piece.

(e) Set up a 95% tolerance estimate for the breaking strength that will include 99% of the pieces of fabric.

(f) Set up a 95% tolerance estimate for the breaking strength that will be exceeded by 99% of the pieces of fabric.

(g) Compare the results of (a), (d), and (e), and explain the differences.

8.43 A sample of 36 observations was collected that used a standard UNIX program called "ping" to measure the time (ms) taken to reach, and receive a reply from, another computer on the Internet.

1450	310	222	680	299	157
202	525	568	447	129	253
406	331	644	822	461	292
204	396	684	517	322	536
343	259	526	288	330	262
205	294	496	1043	366	511 **CONNECT**

(a) Set up a 95 percent confidence interval estimate of the population average time (ms) taken to reach, and receive a reply from, another computer on the Internet.

(b) Set up a 95 percent confidence interval estimate of the population standard deviation of the time (ms) taken to reach, and receive a reply from, another computer on the Internet.

(c) What assumption must be made in (a) and (b)? Given these data, do you think this assumption valid? Explain.

(d) Set up a 95 percent prediction interval estimate of the time (ms) taken to reach, and receive a reply from, another computer on the Internet.

(e) Set up a 95% tolerance estimate for the time (ms) taken to reach, and receive a reply from, another computer on the Internet that will include 99% of the connections.

(f) Compare the results of (a), (d), and (e), and explain the differences.

8.44 A sample of 52 observations gave the following results on the longitudinal compressive strength (Mpa) of the 1/4 in. MMFG series 500/525 plate material of 20 mm specimens.

255	256	259	260	260	261	261	261	262
263	264	266	266	267	267	267	268	268
268	269	269	269	270	270	271	272	273
274	274	275	276	277	279	279	279	279
280	280	280	281	282	282	283	283	283
284	287	287	287	289	290	296	**COMPRESS**	

(a) Set up a 95 percent confidence interval estimate of the population average longitudinal compressive strength (Mpa).

(b) Set up a 95 percent confidence interval estimate of the population standard deviation of longitudinal compressive strength (Mpa).

(c) What assumption must be made in (a) and (b)? Given these data, do you think this assumption valid? Explain.

(d) Set up a 95 percent prediction interval estimate of longitudinal compressive strength (Mpa).

(e) Set up a 95% tolerance estimate for longitudinal compressive strength (Mpa) that will include 90% of the specimens.

(f) Set up a 95% tolerance estimate for the longitudinal compressive strength (Mpa) that will be exceeded by 99% of the specimens.

(g) Compare the results of (a), (d), and (e), and explain the differences.

8.45 The following data represents the height (feet), diameter at breast height or dbh (inches), and bark thickness (inches) from a sample of 21 *Sequoia sempervirens* (coast redwoods).

Height	dbh	Bark	Height	dbh	Bark
122.00	20	1.1	164.00	40	2.3
193.50	36	2.8	203.25	52	2.0
166.50	18	2.0	174.00	30	2.5
82.00	10	1.2	159.00	22	3.0
133.50	21	2.0	205.00	42	2.6
156.00	29	1.4	223.50	45	4.3
172.50	51	1.8	195.00	54	4.0
81.00	11	1.1	232.50	39	2.2
148.00	26	2.5	190.50	36	3.5
113.00	12	1.5	100.00	8	1.4
84.00	13	1.4			**REDWOOD**

For each of the three variables [height (feet), diameter at breast height or dbh (inches), and bark thickness (inches)], do the following.

(a) Set up a 95 percent confidence interval estimate of the population average for each variable.

(b) Set up a 95 percent confidence interval estimate of the population standard deviation for each variable.

(c) What assumption must be made in (a) and (b)? Given these data, do you think this assumption valid? Explain.

(d) Set up a 95 percent prediction interval estimate for an individual redwood tree for each variable.

(e) Set up a 95% tolerance estimate for each variable that will include 99% of the redwood trees.

(f) Compare the results of (a), (d), and (e), and explain the differences.

WHITNEY GOURMET CAT FOOD COMPANY CASE

The team that was involved in selecting the weekly samples of kidney and shrimp cans (see Exercise WG3.1 on page 133) now determined that, in addition to descriptive statistics relating to the weights of the cans, various interval estimates should be obtained to make any report provided more useful.

Exercises

WG8.1 For each shift, set up separate estimates of the population average, population standard deviation, and a future individual weight of cans of kidney and shrimp cat food.

WG8.2 For each shift, for each of the kidney and shrimp varieties, develop a 95% tolerance interval estimate of the weight that will include 99% of the cans.

WG8.3 From the results of Exercises WG8.1 and WG8.2, what conclusions can you add to those made in Exercise WG3.1b on page 133?

REFERENCES

1. Fisher, R. A. and F. Yates; *Statistical Tables for Biological, Agricultural and Medical Research,* 5th ed.; Edinburgh: Oliver & Boyd, 1957
2. Hahn, G. J. and W. Nelson; "A survey of prediction intervals and their applications," *Journal of Quality Technology,* 5, 1973, pp. 178–188
3. Kirk, R. E., ed.; *Statistical Issues: A Reader for the Behavioral Sciences;* Belmont, CA: Wadsworth, 1972
4. Microsoft Excel 2000; Redmond, WA: Microsoft Corporation, 1999
5. *MINITAB for Windows Version 12;* State College, PA: MINITAB, Inc., 1998
6. Ramsey, P. H. and P. P. Ramsey; "Evaluating the normal approximation to the binomial test," *Journal of Educational Statistics,* 13, 1988, pp. 173–182
7. Solomon, H. and M. A. Stephens; "Sample variance," in *Encyclopedia of Statistical Sciences,* Vol. 9; Edited by Kotz, S. and N. L. Johnson; New York: Wiley, 1988, pp. 477–480

APPENDIX 8.1   *Using Microsoft Excel for Confidence Interval Estimation*

Obtaining Confidence Interval Estimates for the Mean Using the PHStat Add-In for Microsoft Excel

To calculate the confidence interval estimate for the mean (σ known), use the **Confidence Intervals | Estimate for the Mean, sigma known,** choice of the PHStat add-in. To calculate the confidence interval estimate for the mean, if the PHStat add-in has not been previously loaded, load the add-in using the instructions of Appendix 1.2. Select **File | New** to open a new workbook (or open the existing workbook into which the confidence interval estimate worksheet is to be inserted). Select **PHStat | Confidence Intervals | Estimate for the Mean, sigma known.** In the Estimate for the Mean, sigma known, dialog box, enter the population standard deviation in the Population Standard Deviation: edit box. Enter **95** in the Confidence Level: edit box for 95% confidence. Select the **Sample Statistics Known** option button, and enter the sample size in the Sample Size: edit box and the sample mean in the Sample Mean: edit box. Enter a title in the Output Title: edit box. Click the **OK** button.

The add-in inserts a worksheet containing calculations for the confidence interval estimate for the mean. (*Note:* For other problems in which the sample mean is not known, select the Sample Statistics Unknown option button instead of the Sample Statistics Known button and enter the cell range of the sample data in the Sample Cell Range: edit box.)

To calculate a confidence interval estimate for the mean (σ unknown), use the **Confidence Intervals | Estimate for the Mean, sigma unknown**, choice of the PHStat add-in. As an example, consider the tensile strengths of the composite material of Section 8.3. To calculate the confidence interval estimate for the average tensile strength for these data, if the PHStat add-in has not been previously loaded, load the add-in using the instructions of Appendix 1.2. Open the **TENSILE.XLS** workbook. **Select PHStat | Confidence Intervals | Estimate for the Mean, sigma unknown.** In the Estimate for the Mean, sigma unknown, dialog box, enter **95** in the Confidence Level: edit box. Select the **Sample Statistics Unknown** option button, and enter **A1:A26** in the Sample Cell Range: edit box. Select the **First cell contains label** check box. Enter **Confidence Interval Estimate for Tensile Strength** in the Output Title: edit box. Click the **OK** button.

The add-in inserts a worksheet containing calculations for a confidence interval estimate of the mean. (*Note:* For other problems in which the sample mean and sample standard deviation are known, select the Sample Statistics Known option button instead of the Sample Statistics Unknown button, and enter the sample size, sample mean, and sample standard deviation in their respective edit boxes.)

Obtaining a Confidence Interval Estimate for the Variance Using Microsoft Excel

To calculate the confidence interval estimate of the population variance for the tensile strength data of Section 8.4, we can use the CHIINV worksheet function, the format of which is

CHIINV(level of significance, degrees of freedom)

to return the critical value of χ^2 needed to compute the confidence interval. To obtain the confidence interval estimate for the variance, select **File | New** to open a new workbook (or open the existing workbook into which the confidence interval estimate worksheet is to be inserted).

Rename the new worksheet Confidence. Enter a title and labels in cell A1, and enter the labels Sample Standard Deviation in cell A3, Sample Size in A4, Confidence Level in A5, Degrees of Freedom in A6, Sum of Squares in A7, Lower Chi-Square Value in A8, Upper Chi-Square Value in A9, Interval Lower Limit for Variance in A10, Interval Upper Limit for Variance in A11, Interval Lower Limit for Standard Deviation in A12, and Interval Upper Limit for Standard Deviation in A13.

Enter the sample standard deviation, sample size, and confidence level in the cell range B3:B5. Enter **18.3204** in cell B3, **25** in cell B4, and **0.95** in cell B5. Select cell B5 and click the **Percent** style button on the formatting toolbar to format the decimal value 0.95 as 95%. Enter **=B4-1** in cell B6, **=B6*B3^2** in cell B7, **=CHIINV((1-(1-B5)/2),B6)** in cell B8, **=CHIINV((1 - B5)/2,B6)** in cell B9, **=B7/B9** in cell B10, **=B7/B8** in cell B11, **=SQRT(B10)** in cell B12, and **=SQRT(B11)** in cell B13. Had the sample standard deviation been unknown, we could have entered a formula using the STDEV function in cell B3 to compute the standard deviation from the cell range containing the data.

Obtaining a Confidence Interval Estimate for the Proportion Using the PHStat Add-In for Microsoft Excel

To calculate a confidence interval estimate for the proportion, use **the Confidence Intervals | Estimate for the Proportion** choice of the PHStat add-in. As an example, consider the newspaper example of Section 8.7. To calculate the confidence interval estimate for the proportion of nonconforming newspapers, if the PHStat add-in has not been previously loaded, load the add-in using the instructions of Appendix 1.2. Select **File | New** to open a new workbook (or open the existing workbook into which the confidence interval estimate worksheet is to be inserted). Select **PHStat | Confidence Intervals | Estimate for the Proportion.** In the Estimate for the Proportion dialog box, enter **200** in the Sample Size: edit box. Enter **35** in the Number of Successes: edit box. Enter **95** in the Confidence Level: edit box. Enter **Confidence Interval Estimation for the Proportion of Nonconforming Newspapers** in the Output Title: edit box. Click the **OK** button. The add-in inserts a worksheet containing calculations for a confidence interval estimate for the proportion.

APPENDIX 8.2 *Using MINITAB for Confidence Interval Estimation*

MINITAB can be used to obtain a confidence interval estimate for the mean when σ is known by selecting **Stat | Basic Statistics | 1-Sample Z** from the Menu bar. Enter the name of the variable in the Variables edit box. Select the **Confidence Interval** button, and enter the level of confidence in the Level edit box. Enter the value for σ in the Sigma: edit box. Click the **OK** button.

MINITAB can be used to obtain a confidence interval estimate for the mean when σ is unknown by selecting Stat | Basic Statistics | 1-Sample t from the Menu bar. As an example, consider the tensile strengths of the composite material of Section 8.3. To calculate the confidence interval estimate for the average tensile strength for these data, open the

TENSILE.MTW worksheet. Select **Stat | Basic Statistics | 1-Sample t,** and enter **C1** or **'Strength'** in the Variables edit box. Select the **Confidence Interval** button, and enter **95.0** in the Level edit box. Click the **OK** button.

MINITAB can be used to obtain a confidence interval estimate for the proportion by selecting Stat | Basic Statistics | 1-Sample Proportion from the Menu bar. As an example, consider the "proportion of newspapers with nonconforming attributes" example of Section 8.7. To calculate the confidence interval estimate for the proportion of nonconformances for these data, select **Stat | Basic Statistics | 1-Sample Proportion.** Select the **Summarized data** option button. Enter **200** in the Number of trials: edit box. Enter **35** in the Number of successes: edit box. Click the **Options** button. Enter **95** in the Confidence level edit box. Select the **Use test and interval based on the normal distribution** check box. Click the **OK** button to return to the 1-Sample proportion dialog box. Click the **OK** button.

9

Introduction to Hypothesis Testing

*"When it is not in our power to determine what is true, we ought
to follow what is most probable."*

DESCARTES

USING STATISTICS

Nondestructive evaluation (NDE) is a method that is used to discover the properties of a component or a unit of material without causing any permanent physical change to the unit. It includes the determination of properties of materials and the classification of flaws by size, shape, type, and location. Eddy-current nondestructive evaluation methods use a probe with alternating current-carrying coils to detect discontinuities in materials. These methods are most effective for detecting surface and near-surface flaws and for characterizing surface properties of electrically conductive materials. Recently, data was collected in a fluorescent–penetrant inspection system that classified each component as to whether it had a flaw (by manual inspection and operator judgment) and also measured the size of the crack in the material. The question to be determined is whether the components classified as flaws had (on average) a greater crack size than the components classified as unflawed.

9.1 INTRODUCTION

In Chapter 5, we began our discussion of statistical inference by developing the concept of a sampling distribution. In Chapter 8, we considered studies in which a statistic (such as the sample mean or sample proportion) obtained from a random sample is used to *estimate* its corresponding population parameter.

In this chapter, we focus on hypothesis testing, another phase of statistical inference that is also based on sample information. Here, we develop a step-by-step methodology that enables us to make inferences about a population parameter by analyzing differences between the results we observe (our sample statistic) and the results we expect to obtain if some underlying hypothesis is actually true. First, the fundamental and conceptual underpinnings of hypothesis-testing methodology are developed. Then, in this and the two chapters that follow, we present various hypothesis-testing procedures that are frequently employed in the analysis of data obtained from studies and experiments designed under a variety of conditions.

9.2 BASIC CONCEPTS OF HYPOTHESIS-TESTING

The Null and Alternative Hypotheses

Hypothesis testing typically begins with some theory, claim, or assertion about a particular parameter of a population. Let us return to the *Using Statistics* example discussed in Chapter 5 (see page 180), concerning the diameter of ball bearings for an industrial sewing machine operation. Recall that the diameter of the ball bearings has a population average of 0.503 inch and a population standard deviation of 0.004 inch. If we are interested in determining whether the population average value has changed from this value, we can select a sample of ball bearings and calculate the sample mean. For the purpose of statistical analysis, our hypothesis is that the average diameter has not changed, meaning that the average diameter is still 0.503 inch.

The hypothesis that the population parameter is equal to the claimed value is referred to as the **null hypothesis.** A null hypothesis is always one of *no difference.* We commonly identify the null hypothesis by the symbol H_0. The fact that the average diameter has been 0.503 inch leads to a null hypothesis that is stated as

$$H_0: \mu = 0.503$$

Note that, even though information is obtained only from a sample, the null hypothesis is written in terms of the population parameter. This is because we are interested in the entire population of all ball bearings being manufactured. The sample statistics will be used to make inferences about the entire population. If the null hypothesis is judged false, something else must be true. To anticipate this possibility, whenever we specify a null hypothesis, we must also specify an **alternative hypothesis:** one that must be true if the null hypothesis is found to be false. The alternative hypothesis (H_1) is the opposite of the null hypothesis (H_0). For the ball bearing diameters, this is stated as

$$H_1: \mu \neq 0.503$$

The alternative hypothesis represents the conclusion reached by rejecting the null hypothesis if there were sufficient evidence from sample information to decide that the null hypothesis is unlikely to be true. In our example, if the diameters of the sampled ball bearings are sufficiently above or below the expected 0.503 inch average, the null hypothesis is rejected in favor of the alternative hypothesis that the average diameter is different from 0.503 inch. The process may be further investigated at that point to determine why the average diameter is now closer to the target of 0.50 (or further away) than it has been in the past.

Hypothesis-testing methodology is designed so that our rejection of the null hypothesis is based on evidence from the sample that our alternative hypothesis is far more likely to be true. However, failure to reject the null hypothesis is not proof that it is true. If we fail to reject the null hypothesis, we can only conclude that there is insufficient evidence to warrant its rejection. A summary of the null and alternative hypotheses is presented in Exhibit 9.1.

EXHIBIT 9.1 The Null and Alternative Hypotheses

The following two key points summarize the null and alternative hypotheses:

1. The null hypothesis (H_0) is the hypothesis that is always tested.

2. The alternative hypothesis (H_1) is set up as the opposite of the null hypothesis and represents the conclusion supported if the null hypothesis is rejected.

In what is known as *classical* hypothesis-testing methodology, we have the following three key points:

1. The null hypothesis (H_0) always refers to a specified value of the *population parameter* (such as μ), not to a *sample statistic* (such as $\overline{X}$).

2. The statement of the null hypothesis *always* contains an equal sign regarding the specified value of the parameter (for example, $H_0: \mu = 0.503$ inch).

3. The statement of the alternative hypothesis *never* contains an equal sign regarding the specified value of the parameter (for example, $H_1: \mu \neq 0.503$ inch).

The Critical Value of the Test Statistic

We can develop the logic behind the hypothesis-testing methodology by considering how we can use only sample information to determine the plausibility of the null hypothesis.

The null hypothesis for the ball bearings is that in the population, the average diameter is 0.503 inch. Suppose that a sample of ball bearings is then obtained from the manufacturing process. The diameter of each ball bearing is measured, and the sample mean is computed. We realize that a statistic from a sample is an estimate of the corresponding parameter from the population from which the sample is drawn. Even if the null hypothesis is true, this statistic will likely differ from the actual parameter value, because of chance or sampling error. Nevertheless, when H_0 is true we expect the sample statistic to be close to the hypothesized population parameter. When this occurs, there is insufficient evidence to reject the null hypothesis. If, for example, the sample mean is 0.5029, our instinct is to conclude that the population mean has not changed (that is, $\mu = 0.503$), because a sample mean of 0.5029 is very close to the hypothesized value of 0.503. Intuitively, we might think that it is likely that we could obtain a sample mean of 0.5029 from a population whose mean is 0.503.

On the other hand, if there is a large discrepancy between the value of the statistic and its corresponding hypothesized parameter, our instinct is to conclude that the null hypothesis is unlikely to be true. For example, if the sample mean is 0.480, our instinct is to conclude that the population mean is not 0.503 (that is, $\mu \neq 0.503$), because the sample mean is not close to the hypothesized value of 0.503. In such a case, we reason that it is very unlikely that the sample mean of 0.480 can be obtained if the population mean is really 0.503 and, therefore, it is more reasonable to conclude that the population mean is not equal to 0.503. Here we reject the null hypothesis. In either case, our decision is reached because of our belief that randomly selected samples are truly representative of the underlying populations from which they are drawn.

Unfortunately, the decision-making process is not always so clear-cut, and cannot be left to an individual's subjective judgment as to the meaning of "very close" or "very different." Determining what is very close and what is very different is arbitrary without operational definitions. Hypothesis-testing methodology provides operational definitions for evaluating such differences and enables us to quantify the decision-making process, so that the probability of obtaining a given sample result can be found on the premise that the null hypothesis is true. This is achieved by first determining the sampling distribution for the sample statistic of interest (i.e., the sample mean) and then computing the particular *test statistic* based on the given sample result. The sampling distribution for the test statistic often follows a well-known statistical distribution, such as the normal or *t* distribution, and so we can use these distributions to determine the likelihood that a null hypothesis is true.

Regions of Rejection and Nonrejection

The sampling distribution of the test statistic is divided into two regions, a **region of rejection** (sometimes called the **critical region**) and a **region of nonrejection.** (See Figure 9.1.) If the test statistic falls into the region of nonrejection, the null hypothesis is not rejected. In the first ball-bearing example, a result falling into the region of nonrejection would lead us to conclude that the average diameter has not changed. If the test statistic falls into the rejection region, the null hypothesis is rejected. Here we would conclude that the population mean is not 0.503 inch.

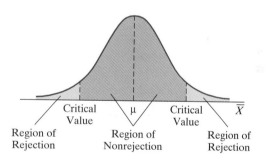

Figure 9.1   Regions of rejection and nonrejection in hypothesis testing

The region of rejection may be thought of as consisting of the values of the test statistic that are unlikely to occur if the null hypothesis is true. On the other hand, these values are not so unlikely to occur if the null hypothesis is false. Therefore, if we observe a value of the test statistic that falls into this *rejection region,* we reject the null hypothesis, because that value is unlikely if the null hypothesis is true.

To make a decision concerning the null hypothesis, we first determine the **critical value** of the test statistic. The critical value divides the nonrejection region from the rejection region. The determination of this critical value is directly related to the risks involved in using only sample evidence to make decisions about a population parameter, as we will see in Section 9.3.

Risks in Decision-Making Using Hypothesis-Testing Methodology

When we are using a sample statistic to make decisions about a population parameter, there is a risk that an incorrect conclusion will be reached. Indeed, two different types of errors can occur when applying hypothesis-testing methodology. These are referred to as Type I and Type II errors.

A **Type I error** occurs if the null hypothesis H_0 is rejected when in fact it is true and should not be rejected. The probability that a Type I error occurs is α.

A **Type II error** occurs if the null hypothesis H_0 is not rejected when in fact it is false and should be rejected. The probability that a Type II error occurs is β.

In our ball-bearing example, a Type I error occurs if we conclude (from sample information) that the average population diameter is *not* 0.503 when in fact it *is* 0.503. By contrast, a Type II error occurs if we conclude (from sample information) that the average population diameter *is* 0.503 when in fact it is *not* 0.503.

The Level of Significance

The probability of committing a Type I error, denoted by α, is referred to as the **level of significance** of the statistical test. Traditionally, one controls the Type I error rate by deciding the risk level α that it is appropriate to tolerate in terms of rejecting the null hypothesis when it is in fact true. The level of significance is specified before the hypothesis test is performed, so the risk of committing a Type I error, α, is directly under the control of the individual performing the test. Researchers traditionally select α levels of 0.05 or smaller. The choice of a particular risk level for making a Type I error is dependent on the cost of making a Type I error. Once the value for α is specified, the rejection region is known, because α is the probability of rejection of a true null hypothesis. Once an α level is selected, the critical value or values that divide the rejection from the nonrejection region(s) are determined.

The Confidence Coefficient

The complement $(1 - \alpha)$ of the probability of a Type I error is called the confidence coefficient. When multiplied by 100%, it yields the confidence level that we studied in Section 8.3.

The **confidence coefficient,** denoted by $1 - \alpha$, is the conditional probability that the null hypothesis H_0 is not rejected when it is true and should not be rejected.

In terms of hypothesis-testing methodology, this coefficient represents the probability of concluding that the specified value of the parameter being tested under the null hypothesis *is* plausible when, in fact, it *is* plausible. In our ball-bearing example, the confidence coefficient measures the probability of *concluding* that the average diameter is 0.503 inch when *in fact it is* 0.503 inch.

The β Risk

The probability of committing a Type II error, denoted by β, is often referred to as the *consumer's risk* level. Unlike the Type I error, which we control by our selection of α, the probability of making a Type II error is dependent on the difference between the hypothesized and the actual value of the population parameter. Large differences are easier to find, so, if the difference between the hypothesized value and the corresponding population parameter is large, β, the probability of committing a Type II error, will likely be small. For example, if the true population average (which is unknown to us) is 0.480 inch, there is a small chance (β) of concluding that the average has not changed from 0.503 inch. On the other hand, if the difference between the hypothesized value and the corresponding parameter value is small, the probability of committing a Type II error is large. Thus, if the true population average is really 0.5029 inch, there is a high probability of concluding that the population average diameter has not changed from the specified 0.503 inch (and we are making a Type II error).

The Power of a Test

The complement ($1 - \beta$) of the probability of a Type II error is called the power of a statistical test.

> The **power of a** statistical **test,** denoted by $1 - \beta$, is the conditional probability of rejecting the null hypothesis when it is false and should be rejected.

In our ball-bearing example, the power of the test is the probability of *concluding* that the average diameter is not 0.503 inch when in fact it *actually is not* 0.503 inch.

Risks in Decision-Making: A Delicate Balance

Table 9.1 illustrates the results of the two possible decisions (do not reject H_0, reject H_0) that can occur in any hypothesis test. Depending on the specific decision, either (a) one of two types of errors can occur or (b) one of two types of correct conclusions can be reached.

TABLE 9.1

HYPOTHESIS TESTING AND DECISION MAKING

Statistical Decision	Actual Situation	
	H_0 True	H_0 False
Do not reject H_0	Correct Decision Confidence = $1 - \alpha$	Type II error $P(\text{Type II error}) = \beta$
Reject H_0	Type I error $P(\text{Type I error}) = \alpha$	Correct Decision Power = $1 - \beta$

One way in which we can control the probability of making a Type II error in a study is to increase the size of the sample. Larger sample sizes generally permit us to detect even very small differences between sample statistics and true population parameters. For a given level of α, increasing the sample size will decrease β and therefore increase the power of the test to detect that the null hypothesis H_0 is false. Of course, however, there is always a limit to our resources. Thus, for a given sample size we must consider the trade-off between the two possible types of errors. Because we can directly control our risk of Type I error, we can reduce our risk by selecting a lower level for α. For example, if the negative consequences associated with making a Type I error are substantial, we can select α to be 0.01 instead of 0.05. When α is decreased, however, β will be increased, so a reduction in the risk of Type I error will result in an increase in the risk of Type II error. If, on the other hand, we wish to reduce β, our risk of Type II error, we could select a larger value for α. Therefore, if it is important to try to avoid a Type II error, we can select α to be 0.05 instead of 0.01.

In our ball-bearing example, the risk of a Type I error involves concluding that the average diameter has changed from the hypothesized 0.503 inch when in fact it has not changed. The risk of a Type II error involves concluding that the average diameter has not changed from the hypothesized 0.503 inch when in truth it has changed. The choice of reasonable values for α and β depends on the costs consequent upon each type of error. For example, if it were very costly to change the ball-bearing manufacturing process, then we would want to be very sure that a change would be beneficial, so the risk of a Type I error might be most important and would be kept very low. On the other hand, if we wanted to be very certain of detecting changes from a mean of 0.503 inch, the risk of a Type II error would be most important, and we might choose a higher level of α. It is important to note that an α level greater than 0.05 is not acceptable in scientific research. Tests using an α level as large as 0.10 may sometimes be used in preliminary investigations or pilot studies, but are never acceptable as final results.

9.3 ONE-SAMPLE TESTS FOR THE MEAN

Now that we have described the hypothesis-testing methodology, let us return to the question concerning the manufacture of ball bearings: whether the average diameter has remained at 0.503 inch. To study this, we can take a random sample of 25 ball bearings, measure the diameter of each one, and then evaluate the difference between the sample statistic and hypothesized population parameter by comparing the mean diameter in inches from the sample to the expected mean of 0.503 inch. For this example, the null and alternative hypotheses are

$$H_0: \mu = 0.503$$
$$H_1: \mu \neq 0.503$$

If we assume that the standard deviation σ is known, for large samples (or for samples from a normal population), the sampling distribution of the mean follows the normal distribution, resulting in the following test statistic.

Z TEST OF HYPOTHESIS FOR THE MEAN (σ KNOWN)

$$Z = \frac{\overline{X} - \mu}{\dfrac{\sigma}{\sqrt{n}}} \qquad (9.1)$$

In this equation, the numerator measures how far (in an absolute sense) the observed sample mean $\overline{X}$ is from the hypothesized mean μ. The denominator is the standard error of the mean, so Z represents how many standard errors $\overline{X}$ is from μ.

The Critical-Value Approach to Hypothesis Testing

If a level of significance of 0.05 is selected, the proportion of the area in the rejection region is 0.05, and the critical values of the normal distribution can be determined. These critical values can be expressed as standard normal or Z values. The rejection region is divided into the two tails of the distribution (this is called a **two-tailed test**), so the 0.05 is divided into two equal parts of 0.025 each. A rejection region of 0.025 in each tail of the normal distribution results in a cumulative area of 0.025 below the lower critical value and a cumulative area of 0.025 above the upper critical value. Looking up these areas in the normal distribution table (Table A.2), we find that the critical values that divide the rejection from the nonrejection regions are -1.96 and $+1.96$. Figure 9.2 illustrates this case; it shows that if the mean is actually 0.503 inch, as H_0 claims, then the values of the test statistic Z have a standard normal distribution centered at $\mu = 0.503$ (which corresponds to a Z value of 0). Observed values of Z greater than 1.96 or less than -1.96 indicate that $\overline{X}$ is so far from the hypothesized $\mu = 0.503$ that it is unlikely that such a value would occur if H_0 were true.

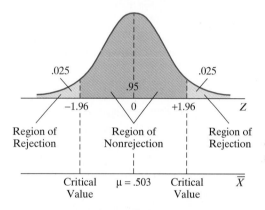

Figure 9.2   Testing a hypothesis about the mean (σ known) at the 0.05 level of significance

Therefore, the decision rule is

$$\text{Reject } H_0 \text{ if } Z > +1.96$$
$$\text{or if } Z < -1.96;$$
$$\text{otherwise do not reject } H_0.$$

Suppose that the sample of 25 ball bearings indicates a sample mean ($\overline{X}$) of 0.5018 inch and that the population standard deviation (σ) is assumed to remain at 0.004 inch. Using Equation (9.1), we have

$$Z = \frac{\overline{X} - \mu}{\dfrac{\sigma}{\sqrt{n}}} = \frac{0.5018 - 0.503}{\dfrac{0.004}{\sqrt{25}}} = -1.50$$

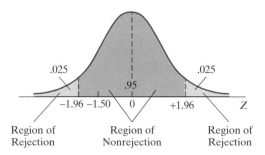

Figure 9.3   Testing a hypothesis about the mean (σ known) at the 0.05 level of significance

Because $Z = -1.50$, we see that $-1.96 < -1.50 < +1.96$. Thus, as seen in Figure 9.3, our decision is not to reject H_0. We would conclude that the average diameter is 0.503 inch. Alternatively, to take into account the possibility of a Type II error, we phrase the conclusion as "there is insufficient evidence to conclude that the average diameter is different from 0.503 inch."

Now that we have used hypothesis-testing methodology to draw a conclusion about the population mean in situations where the population standard deviation is known, we summarize the steps involved in Exhibit 9.2.

EXHIBIT 9.2 The Steps in Hypothesis Testing

1. State the null hypothesis, H_0. The null hypothesis must be stated in statistical terms. In testing whether the average diameter is 0.503 inch, the null hypothesis thesis states that μ equals 0.503.

2. State the alternative hypothesis, H_1. The alternative hypothesis must be stated in statistical terms. In testing whether the average diameter is 0.503 inch, the alternative hypothesis states that μ is not equal to 0.503 inch.

3. Choose the level of significance, α. The level of significance is specified according to the relative importance of the risks of committing Type I and Type II errors in the problem. We chose $\alpha = 0.05$.

4. Choose the sample size, n. The sample size is determined after taking into account the specified risks of committing Type I and Type II errors (i.e., selected levels of α and β) and considering budget constraints in carrying out the study. Here 25 ball bearings were randomly selected.

5. Determine the appropriate statistical technique and corresponding test statistic to use. Because σ is known from information about the manufacturing process, a Z test was selected.

6. Set up the critical values that divide the rejection from the nonrejection region(s). Once we specify the null and alternative hypotheses and we determine the level of significance and the sample size, the critical values for the appropriate statistical distribution can be found so that the rejection and nonrejection regions can be indicated. Here the values $+1.96$ and -1.96 were used to define these regions, because the Z-test statistic refers to the standard normal distribution.

7. Collect the data, and compute the sample value of the appropriate test statistic. Here, $\bar{X} = 0.5018$ inch, so $Z = -1.50$.

8. Determine whether the test statistic has fallen into the rejection or the non-rejection region. The computed value of the test statistic is compared with the critical values for the appropriate sampling distribution to determine whether it falls into the rejection or nonrejection region. Here, $Z = -1.50$ was in the region of nonrejection, because $-1.96 < Z = -1.50 < +1.96$.

9. Make the statistical decision. If the test statistic falls into the nonrejection region, the null hypothesis H_0 cannot be rejected. If the test statistic falls into the rejection region, the null hypothesis is rejected. Here, H_0 was not rejected.

10. Express the statistical decision in terms of the problem. In our ball-bearing manufacturing example, we concluded that there was insufficient evidence to conclude that the average length was different from 0.503 inch.

The *p*-Value Approach to Hypothesis Testing

In recent years, with the advent of widely available statistical and spreadsheet software, the concept of the *p*-value is an approach to hypothesis testing that has increasingly gained acceptance.

The **p-value** is the probability of obtaining a test statistic equal to or more extreme than the result obtained from the sample data, given that the null hypothesis H_0 is really true.

The *p*-value is often referred to as the *observed level of significance*, which is the smallest level at which H_0 can be rejected for a given set of data. The decision rule for rejecting H_0 in the *p*-value approach is as follows:

- If the *p*-value is greater than or equal to α, the null hypothesis is not rejected.
- If the *p*-value is smaller than α, the null hypothesis is rejected.

To understand the *p*-value approach, we again consider the ball-bearing example, in which we tested whether the average diameter was equal to 0.503 inch. We obtained a Z value of -1.50 and did not reject the null hypothesis, because -1.50 was greater than the lower critical value of -1.96 but less than the upper critical value of $+1.96$.

Now we use the *p*-value approach. For our *two-tailed test,* we wish to find the probability of obtaining a test statistic Z that is *more extreme* than 1.50 standard deviation units from the center of a standard normal distribution. This means that we need to compute the probability of obtaining a Z value greater than $+1.50$ along with the probability of obtaining a Z value less than -1.50. From Table A.2, the probability of obtaining a Z value below -1.50 is 0.0668. The probability of obtaining a value above $+1.50$ is 0.0668. Thus, the *p*-value for this two-tailed test is $0.0668 + 0.0668 = 0.1336$ (as in Figure 9.4 on page 402). This result may be interpreted to mean that the probability of obtaining a result equal to or more extreme than the one observed is 0.1336. This probability is greater than $\alpha = 0.05$, so the null hypothesis is not rejected.

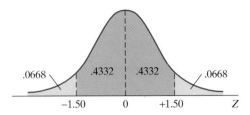

Figure 9.4 Finding the *p*-value for a two-tailed test

Unless we are dealing with a test statistic that follows the normal distribution, the computation of the *p*-value can be very difficult. Thus, it is fortunate that software such as Microsoft Excel (and the PHStat add-in) or MINITAB (see References 4 and 5) routinely present the *p*-value as part of the output for hypothesis-testing procedures. Figure 9.5 displays PHStat output for the ball-bearing example discussed in this section. Note that the PHStat output indicates both the computed *Z* value of -1.50 and the *p*-value of 0.1336.

	A	B
1	**Z Test of Hypothesis for the Mean**	
2		
3	**Null Hypothesis** $\mu=$	0.503
4	**Level of Significance**	0.05
5	**Population Standard Deviation**	0.004
6	**Sample Size**	25
7	**Sample Mean**	0.5018
8	Standard Error of the Mean	0.0008
9	Z Test Statistic	-1.5
10		
11	**Two-Tailed Test**	
12	**Lower Critical Value**	-1.959961082
13	**Upper Critical Value**	1.959961082
14	***p*-Value**	0.133614458
15	**Do not reject the null hypothesis**	

Figure 9.5 PHStat add-in for Microsoft Excel *Z* test output for the ball-bearing example

A summary of the *p*-value approach for hypothesis testing is displayed in Exhibit 9.3.

A Connection between Confidence Interval Estimation and Hypothesis Testing

Both in this chapter and in Chapter 8, we examined the two major components of statistical inference—confidence interval estimation, and hypothesis testing. Although they are based on the same set of concepts, we used them for different purposes. In Chapter 8, we used confidence intervals to estimate parameters; thus far in this chapter, we have used hypothesis testing for making decisions about specified values of population parameters.

EXHIBIT 9.3 Steps in Determining the p-value

1. State the null hypothesis, H_0.

2. State the alternative hypothesis, H_1.

3. Choose the level of significance, α.

4. Choose the sample size, n.

5. Determine the appropriate statistical technique and corresponding test statistic to use.

6. Collect the data and compute the sample value of the appropriate test statistic.

7. Calculate the p-value based on the test statistic. This involves
   (a) sketching the distribution under the null hypothesis H_0,
   (b) placing the test statistic on the horizontal axis, and
   (c) shading in the appropriate area under the curve, based on the alternative hypothesis H_1.

8. Compare the p-value to α.

9. Make the statistical decision. If the p-value is greater than or equal to α, the null hypothesis is not rejected. If the p-value is smaller than α, the null hypothesis is rejected.

10. Express the statistical decision in terms of the problem.

For example, we tested whether the population average diameter was different from 0.503 inch by using Equation (9.1).

$$Z = \frac{\bar{X} - \mu}{\dfrac{\sigma}{\sqrt{n}}}$$

Instead of testing the null hypothesis that $\mu = 0.503$ inch, we can also solve the problem by obtaining a confidence interval estimate of μ. If the hypothesized value of $\mu = 0.503$ falls into the interval, the null hypothesis is not rejected, and the value 0.503 would not be considered unusual for the data observed. On the other hand, if the hypothesized value does not lie in the interval, the null hypothesis is rejected, because 0.503 inch is then considered an unusual value. From Equation (8.1), the confidence interval estimate is set up from the following data:

$$n = 25, \quad \bar{X} = 0.5018, \quad \sigma = 0.004$$

For a confidence level of 95% (corresponding to $\alpha = 0.05$ level of significance), we have

$$\bar{X} \pm Z\frac{\sigma}{\sqrt{n}}$$

$$0.5018 \pm (1.96)\frac{0.004}{\sqrt{25}}$$

$$0.5018 \pm 0.001568$$

so that

$$0.500232 \leq \mu \leq 0.503368$$

Because the interval includes the hypothesized value of 0.503 inch, we do not reject the null hypothesis. There is insufficient evidence to conclude that the mean diameter is not 0.503 inch. This is the same decision we reached by using hypothesis-testing methodology.

One-Tailed Tests

So far we have used hypothesis-testing methodology to examine the question of whether the population average diameter of ball bearings is 0.503 inch. The alternative hypothesis ($H_1:\mu \neq 0.503$) contains two possibilities: Either the average is less than 0.503 inch, or the average is more than 0.503 inch. For this reason, the rejection region is divided into the two tails of the sampling distribution of the mean. As we have just observed in the previous section, because a confidence interval estimate of the mean contains both a lower and an upper limit, corresponding respectively to the left- and right-tail critical values from the sampling distribution of the mean, we are able to use the confidence interval to do a test of the null hypothesis that the average diameter is 0.503 inch.

In some situations, however, the alternative hypothesis focuses on a *particular direction*. One such situation occurs in the following application. Suppose that a company that makes processed cheese is interested in determining whether some suppliers who provide milk for the processing operation are adding water to their milk to increase the amount supplied to the processing operation. It is known that excess water reduces the freezing point of the milk. The freezing point of natural milk is normally distributed, with a mean of $-0.545°$ Celsius (C). The standard deviation of the freezing temperature of the milk is known to have been $0.008°$ C in the past. Because the cheese company is interested only in determining whether the freezing point of the milk is less than that which would be expected from natural milk, the entire rejection region is located in the lower tail of the distribution.

For this example, the null and alternative hypotheses are stated as follows:

$$H_0: \mu \geq -0.545°$$
$$H_1: \mu < -0.545°$$

The rejection region here is entirely contained in the lower tail of the sampling distribution of the mean, because we want to reject H_0 only when the sample mean is significantly below $-0.545°$. When the entire rejection region is contained in one tail of the sampling distribution of the test statistic, it marks a **one-tailed** or **directional test.** If we again choose a level of significance, α, of 0.05, the critical value on the Z distribution can be determined. As seen from Table 9.2 and Figure 9.6, the entire rejection region is in the lower tail of the standard normal distribution and contains an area of 0.05, so the area below the critical value must be 0.05; thus, the critical value of the Z test statistic is $+1.645$, the average of $+1.64$ and $+1.65$. (Note that some statisticians *round off* to two decimal places and select $+1.64$ as the critical value, while others *round up* to $+1.65$. We prefer to interpolate between the areas 0.0495 and 0.0505, so as to select the critical value with lower-tail area as close to 0.05 as possible. Thus, we take the average of $+1.64$ and $+1.65$.)

TABLE 9.2

OBTAINING THE CRITICAL VALUE OF THE Z TEST STATISTIC FROM THE STANDARD NORMAL DISTRIBUTION FOR A ONE-TAILED TEST WITH $\alpha = .05$

Z	.00	.01	.02	.03	.04	.05	.06	.07	.08	.09
⋮	⋮	⋮	⋮	⋮	⋮	⋮	⋮	⋮	⋮	⋮
1.3	.4032	.4049	.4066	.4082	.4099	.4115	.4131	.4147	.4162	.4177
1.4	.4192	.4207	.4222	.4236	.4251	.4265	.4279	.4292	.4306	.4319
1.5	.4332	.4345	.4357	.4370	.4382	.4394	.4406	.4418	.4429	.4441
1.6	.4452	.4463	.4474	.4484	.4495	.4505	.4515	.4525	.4535	.4545

Source: Extracted from Table A.2.

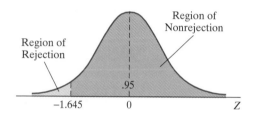

Figure 9.6   One-tailed test of hypothesis for a mean (σ known) at the 0.05 level of significance

The decision rule is

$$\text{Reject } H_0 \text{ if } Z < -1.645;$$

$$\text{otherwise do not reject } H_0.$$

If a sample of 25 containers of milk is selected, and the sample average freezing point is determined to be $-0.550°$, then, using the Z test given by Equation (9.1), we have

$$n = 25, \quad \overline{X} = -0.550°, \quad \sigma = 0.008°$$

and so we have

$$Z = \frac{\overline{X} - \mu}{\dfrac{\sigma}{\sqrt{n}}} = \frac{-0.550 - (-0.545)}{\dfrac{0.008}{\sqrt{25}}} = -3.125$$

Because $Z = -3.125 < -1.645$, our decision is to reject H_0, and we conclude that there is evidence that the average freezing is below $-0.545°C$. This means that the company should pursue an investigation of the milk supplier: the freezing point is significantly below what could be expected to occur by chance if water has not been added to the milk.

To obtain the p-value, because the alternative hypothesis indicates a rejection region entirely in the *lower* tail of the sampling distribution of the Z test statistic, we need to find the probability of obtaining a Z value *below* the test statistic of -3.125. From Table A.2, the probability of obtaining a Z value below -3.125 is 0.0009 (as in Figure 9.7). This p-value is less than the selected level of significance ($\alpha = 0.05$), so the null hypothesis is rejected. Figure 9.8 displays output from the PHStat add-in for this example.

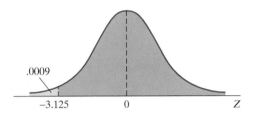

.0009

-3.125 0 Z

Figure 9.7   Determining the p-value for a one-tailed test

A	B
Z Test of Hypothesis for the Mean	
Null Hypothesis $\mu=$	**-0.545**
Level of Significance	**0.05**
Population Standard Deviation	**0.008**
Sample Size	**25**
Sample Mean	**-0.55**
Standard Error of the Mean	0.0016
Z Test Statistic	-3.125
Lower-Tail Test	
Lower Critical Value	-1.644853
***p*-Value**	0.000889093
Reject the null hypothesis	

Figure 9.8   PHStat add-in for Microsoft Excel Z test output for the milk production example

To perform one-tailed tests of hypothesis, we must properly formulate H_0 and H_1. A summary of the null and alternative hypotheses for one-tailed tests is presented in Exhibit 9.4.

t Test of Hypothesis for the Mean (σ Unknown)

In most hypothesis-testing situations dealing with numerical data, the standard deviation σ of the population is unknown; however, the standard deviation of the population can be estimated by computing s, the standard deviation of the sample. If the population is assumed to be normally distributed, we recall from Section 8.3 that the sampling distribution of the mean will follow a t distribution with $n - 1$ degrees of freedom. The test statistic t for determining the difference between the sample mean $\overline{X}$ and the population mean μ when the sample

EXHIBIT 9.4   The Null and Alternative Hypotheses in One-Tailed Tests

We summarize some key points about the null and the alternative hypothesis in one-tailed tests:

1. The null hypothesis (H_0) is the hypothesis that is always tested.

2. The alternative hypothesis (H_1) is set up as the opposite of the null hypothesis and represents the conclusion supported if the null hypothesis is rejected.

3. The null hypothesis (H_0) always refers to a specified value of the *population parameter* (such as μ), not a *sample statistic* (such as $\overline{X}$).

4. The statement of the null hypothesis *always* contains an equal sign regarding the specified value of the parameter (for example, $H_0 : \mu \geq -0.545°C$).

5. The statement of the alternative hypothesis *always* contains a less than or greater than sign regarding the specified value of the parameter (for example, $H_1: \mu < -0.545°C$).

standard deviation s is used is given by the following:

---

t TEST OF HYPOTHESIS FOR THE MEAN (σ UNKNOWN)

$$t = \frac{\overline{X} - \mu}{\dfrac{s}{\sqrt{n}}} \tag{9.2}$$

where the test statistic t follows a t distribution having $n - 1$ degrees of freedom.

To illustrate the use of this t test, we turn to an example that involves capacitors. The nominal value of the capacitors, as determined by the manufacturer, is 0.33 μF; however, it is known that, even if they are manufactured in the same way, electrical and electronic devices will vary in quality. Suppose that a sample of 30 capacitors is tested by using a Wavetech multimeter that tests the capacitance in μF or 1×10^{-6} Farads. The results are as follows.

0.342	0.309	0.335	0.333	0.327	0.346
0.321	0.346	0.334	0.322	0.322	0.326
0.334	0.341	0.321	0.343	0.315	0.341
0.345	0.314	0.348	0.337	0.311	0.352
0.329	0.337	0.324	0.339	0.331	0.313 **CAPACITOR**

The manufacturer is interested in whether there is evidence of a change in the average capacitance from the nominal value of 0.33, so the test is two-tailed, and the following null and alternative hypotheses are established:

$$H_0: \mu = 0.33$$
$$H_1: \mu \neq 0.33$$

For a given sample size n, the test statistic t follows a t distribution with $n - 1$ degrees of freedom. If a level of significance of $\alpha = 0.05$ is selected, the critical values of the t distribution with $30 - 1 = 29$ degrees of freedom can be obtained from Table A.4, as illustrated in Figure 9.9 and Table 9.3. Because the alternative hypothesis H_1 that $\mu \neq 0.33$ is *nondirectional,* the area in the rejection region of the t distribution's left (lower) tail is 0.025, and the area in the rejection region of the t distribution's right (upper) tail is also 0.025.

From the t table as given in Table A.4, a replica of which is shown in Table 9.3, the critical values are ± 2.0452. The decision rule is as follows:

Reject H_0 if $t < t_{29} = -2.0452$ or if $t > t_{29} = +2.0452$;

otherwise do not reject H_0.

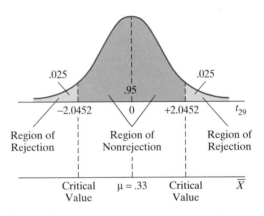

Figure 9.9   Testing a hypothesis about the mean (σ unknown) at the 0.05 level of significance, with 29 degrees of freedom

TABLE 9.3

DETERMINING THE CRITICAL VALUE FROM THE t TABLE FOR AN AREA OF .025 IN EACH TAIL WITH 29 DEGREES OF FREEDOM

Degrees of Freedom	Upper-Tail Areas					
	.25	.10	.05	.025	.01	.005
1	1.0000	3.0777	6.3138	12.7062	31.8207	63.6574
2	0.8165	1.8856	2.9200	4.3027	6.9646	9.9248
3	0.7649	1.6377	2.3534	3.1824	4.5407	5.8409
4	0.7407	1.5332	2.1318	2.7764	3.7469	4.6041
5	0.7267	1.4759	2.0150	2.5706	3.3649	4.0322
⋮	⋮	⋮	⋮	⋮	⋮	⋮
28	0.6834	1.3125	1.7011	2.0484	2.4671	2.7633
29	0.6830	1.3114	1.6991	2.0452	2.4620	2.7564
30	0.6828	1.3104	1.6973	2.0423	2.4573	2.7500

Source: Extracted from Table A.4.

For the sample of $n = 30$ capacitors, using the PHStat add-in for Microsoft Excel as illustrated in Figure 9.10 or MINITAB as shown in Figure 9.11, we observe that $\overline{X} = 0.33127$ and $s = 0.012$.

From Equation (9.2), we have

$$t = \frac{\overline{X} - \mu}{\frac{s}{\sqrt{n}}} = \frac{0.33127 - 0.33}{\frac{0.012}{\sqrt{30}}} = 0.575$$

	A	B
1	T Test for Capacitance	
2		
3	Null Hypothesis $\mu=$	0.33
4	Level of Significance	0.05
5	Sample Size	30
6	Sample Mean	0.331266667
7	Sample Standard Deviation	0.01206572
8	Standard Error of the Mean	0.002202889
9	Degrees of Freedom	29
10	t Test Statistic	0.575002472
11		
12	Two-Tailed Test	
13	Lower Critical Value	-2.045230758
14	Upper Critical Value	2.045230758
15	p-Value	0.569724244
16	Do not reject the null hypothesis	

Figure 9.10   PHStat add-in for Microsoft Excel t test output for the sample of capacitors

t-Test of the Mean

```
Test of mu = 0.33000 vs mu not = 0.33000

Variable         N       Mean     StDev     SE Mean        T          P
Capacitance      31    0.33127   0.01207    0.00217      0.58       0.56
```

Figure 9.11   MINITAB t test output for the sample of capacitors

Because $t = 0.575$ falls within the nonrejection region between the critical values of $t_{29} = \pm 2.0452$, we cannot reject H_0. There is insufficient evidence to believe that the average capacitance is different from 0.33 μF. Our observed difference is nonsignificant and likely due to chance. From either Figure 9.10 or 9.11, we observe that the two-tailed p-value is approximately 0.57. Because $0.57 > \alpha = 0.05$, we don't reject H_0.

The one-sample t test can be either a two-tailed test or a one-tailed test, depending on whether the alternative hypothesis is *nondirectional* or *directional,* respectively. If the alternative hypothesis is nondirectional, as in our capacitor example, we attempt to reject the null hypothesis that the value of the parameter is a specified amount such as $\mu = 0.33 \mu F$. In this two-tailed test, we reject H_0 if there is evidence from the sample that the value of the parameter being tested is likely to be either significantly more or significantly less than this hypothesized amount. In a one-tailed test, the alternative hypothesis is directional. We reject H_0 only if there is evidence from the sample that the value of the parameter being tested is too small or too large, depending on the direction specified in the alternative hypothesis. The regions of rejection and nonrejection for these one-sample t tests are depicted in Figure 9.12.

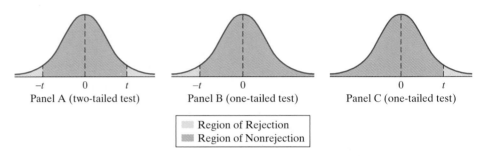

| Panel A (two-tailed test) | Panel B (one-tailed test) | Panel C (one-tailed test) |

Region of Rejection
Region of Nonrejection

Figure 9.12   Regions of rejection and nonrejection for the one-sample t test

The one-sample t test is considered a classical **parametric** procedure—one that makes a variety of stringent assumptions that must hold if we are to be assured that the results we obtain from employing the test are valid. Assumptions of the one-sample t test are presented in the accompanying Comment box.

COMMENT: ASSUMPTIONS OF THE ONE-SAMPLE t TEST

To use the one-sample t test, it is assumed that the data are independently drawn and represent a random sample from a population that is normally distributed. In practice, it has been found that, as long as the sample size is not very small and the population is not very skewed, the t distribution gives a good approximation to the sampling distribution of the mean when σ is unknown.

Software such as Microsoft Excel and MINITAB enables us to evaluate the assumptions necessary for using the t test on the capacitance data. As we learned in Section 5.5, the normality assumption can be checked in several ways. A determination of how closely the actual data match the normal distribution's theoretical properties can be made by a descriptive analysis of the obtained statistics along with a graphical analysis (using a histogram, a stem-and-leaf display, a box-and-whisker plot, or a normal probability plot), to provide a visual interpretation.

Using the capacitance data, Figure 9.13 presents a box-and-whisker plot obtained from MINITAB, while Figure 9.14 presents a normal probability plot obtained from the PHStat add-in for Microsoft Excel. For the capacitance data, the points on the normal probability plot appear to be increasing in an approximate straight line, and the box-and-whisker plot resembles one from a normal distribution. (See Figure 3.9 on page 123.) Thus, there is little reason to believe that the assumption of underlying population normality of the capacitance data is violated to any great degree, and we conclude that the results of the t test are valid.

Boxplot of Capacitance
(with Ho and 95% *t*-confidence interval for the mean)

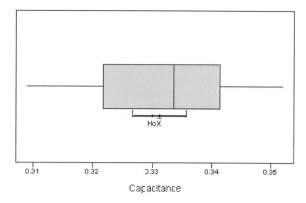

Figure 9.13   Box-and-whisker plot obtained from MINITAB for the capacitance data

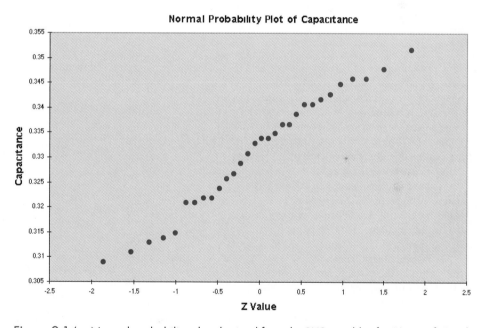

Figure 9.14   Normal probability plot obtained from the PHStat add-in for Microsoft Excel for the capacitance data

The *t* test is a **robust** test. That is, it does not lose much power if the shape of the population from which the sample is drawn departs somewhat from a normal distribution, particularly when the sample size is large enough to enable the test statistic *t* to be influenced by the central limit theorem (per Section 5.9). However, erroneous conclusions may be drawn and statistical power can be lost if the *t* test is incorrectly used. If the sample size *n* is small (i.e., less than 30), and we cannot easily make the assumption that the underlying population from which the sample was drawn is normally distributed, other, *nonparametric* testing procedures may be more appropriate. (See References 1 and 2.)

PROBLEMS

9.1 Suppose that the director of manufacturing at a clothing factory needs to determine whether a new machine is producing a particular type of cloth according to the manufacturer's specifications, which indicate that the cloth should have a mean breaking strength of 70 pounds and a standard deviation of 3.5 pounds. A sample of 49 pieces reveals a sample mean of 69.1 pounds.
  (a) State the null and alternative hypotheses.
  (b) Is there evidence that the machine is not meeting the manufacturer's specifications in terms of the average breaking strength? (Use a 0.05 level of significance.)
  (c) Compute the *p*-value and interpret its meaning.
  (d) What will your answer be in (b) if the standard deviation is 1.75 pounds?
  (e) What will your answer be in (b) if the sample mean is 69 pounds?

9.2 A manufacturer of salad dressings uses machines to dispense liquid ingredients into bottles that move along a filling line. The machine that dispenses dressings is working properly when 8 ounces are dispensed. The standard deviation of the process is 0.15 ounce. Periodically, a sample of 50 bottles is randomly selected, and the filling line is stopped if there is evidence that the average amount dispensed is different from 8 ounces. Suppose that the average amount dispensed in a particular sample of 50 bottles is 7.983 ounces.
  (a) State the null and alternative hypotheses.
  (b) Is there evidence that the population average amount is different from 8 ounces? (Use a 0.05 level of significance.)
  (c) Compute the *p*-value and interpret its meaning.
  (d) What will your answer be in (b) if the standard deviation is 0.05 ounce?
  (e) What will your answer be in (b) if the sample mean is 7.952 ounces?

9.3 The quality-control manager at a light-bulb factory wants to know if the average life of a large shipment of light bulbs is equal to 375 hours. The process standard deviation is known to be 100 hours. A random sample of 50 light bulbs indicates a sample average life of 350 hours.
  (a) State the null and alternative hypotheses.
  (b) At the 0.05 level of significance, is there evidence that the average life is different from 375 hours?
  (c) Compare the conclusions reached in (b) with those from Problem 8.4 on page 374. Are the conclusions the same? Why?

9.4 The inspection division of the Lee County Weights and Measures Department is interested in evaluating the actual amount of soft drink that is placed in 2-liter bottles at the local bottling plant of a large nationally known soft-drink company. The bottling plant has informed the inspection division that the standard deviation for 2-liter bottles is 0.05 liter. A random sample of 100 2-liter bottles obtained from this bottling plant indicates a sample average of 1.99 liters.
  (a) State the null and alternative hypotheses.
  (b) At the 0.05 level of significance, is there evidence that the average amount in the bottles is different from 2.0 liters?
  (c) Compare the conclusions reached in (b) with those from Problem 8.5 on page 374. Are the conclusions the same? Why?

9.5 A consumers' advocate group would like to evaluate the average energy efficiency rating (EER) of window-mounted, large-capacity (i.e., in excess of 7,000 Btu) air-conditioning units. A random sample of 36 such air-conditioning units is selected and tested for a fixed period of time. Their EER records are as follows:

8.9	9.1	9.2	9.1	8.4	9.5	9.0	9.6	9.3
9.3	8.9	9.7	8.7	9.4	8.5	8.9	8.4	9.5
9.3	9.3	8.8	9.4	8.9	9.3	9.0	9.2	9.1
9.8	9.6	9.3	9.2	9.1	9.6	9.8	9.5	10.0

EER

  (a) Using the 0.05 level of significance, is there evidence that the average EER is different from 9.0?
  (b) What assumptions are made to perform this test?
  (c) If you are using Microsoft Excel or MINITAB, find the *p*-value and interpret its meaning.
  (d) What will your answer in (a) be if the last data value is 8.0 instead of 10.0?

9.6 A manufacturer of plastics wants to evaluate the durability of rectangularly molded plastic blocks that are to be used in furniture. A random sample of 50 such plastic blocks is examined, and their hardness is measured (in Brinell units). The measurements are recorded as follows:

283.6	273.3	278.8	238.7	334.9	302.6	239.9	254.6
281.9	270.4	269.1	250.1	301.6	289.2	240.8	267.5
279.3	228.4	265.2	285.9	279.3	252.3	271.7	235.0
313.2	277.8	243.8	295.5	249.3	228.7	255.3	267.2
255.3	281.0	302.1	256.3	233.0	194.4	291.9	263.7
273.6	267.7	283.1	260.9	274.8	277.4	276.9	259.5
262.0	263.5						

PLASTIC3

(a) Using the 0.05 level of significance, is there evidence that the average hardness of the plastic blocks exceeds 260 (in Brinell units)?

(b) What assumptions are made to perform this test?

(c) If you are using Microsoft Excel or MINITAB, find the *p*-value and interpret its meaning.

(d) What will be your answer in (a) if the first data value is 233.6 instead of 283.6?

9.7 A machine being used for packaging seedless golden raisins has been set so that, on average, 15 ounces of raisins will be packaged per box. The quality-control engineer wishes to test the machine setting and selects a sample of 30 consecutive raisin packages filled during the production process. Their weights are recorded as follows.

15.2	15.3	15.1	15.7	15.3	15.0
15.1	14.3	14.6	14.5	15.0	15.2
15.4	15.6	15.7	15.4	15.3	14.9
14.8	14.6	14.3	14.4	15.5	15.4
15.2	15.5	15.6	15.1	15.3	15.1

RAISINS

(a) Is there evidence that the mean weight per box is different from 15 ounces? (Use $\alpha = 0.05$.)

(b) To perform the test in part (a), we assume that the observed sequence in which the data were collected is random. What other assumptions must be made to perform the test? Discuss.

(c) What is your answer in (a) if the weights for the last two packages are 16.3 and 16.1 instead of 15.3 and 15.1?

9.8 A manufacturer claims that the average capacity of a certain type of battery that the company produces is at least 140 ampere-hours.

An independent consumer-protection agency wishes to test the credibility of the manufacturer's claim and measures the capacity of a random sample of 20 batteries from a recently produced batch. The results, in ampere-hours, are as follows.

137.4	140.0	138.8	139.1	144.4	139.2	141.8
137.3	133.5	138.2	141.1	139.7	136.7	136.3
135.6	138.0	140.9	140.6	136.7	134.1	

AMPHRS

(a) At the 0.05 level of significance, is there evidence that the average capacity is less than 140 ampere-hours?

(b) What assumption must hold in order to perform the test in part (a)?

(c) Evaluate this assumption through a graphical approach. Discuss.

(d) What is your answer in (a) if the last two values are 146.7 and 144.1 instead of 136.7 and 134.1?

9.9 The manufacturer claims the mean bursting pressure for a certain type and size of PVC irrigation pipe to be at least 350 psi. A sample of 10 such pipes were experimentally determined to have the following bursting pressures:

401	359	383	427	414
415	389	463	394	428

BURST

(a) At the 0.05 level of significance, is there evidence that the average bursting pressure is less than 350 psi?

(b) What assumption must hold in order to validate the test in part (a)?

9.4 *t* TEST FOR THE DIFFERENCE BETWEEN THE MEANS OF TWO INDEPENDENT GROUPS

Suppose that we have two independent populations, each with a mean and standard deviation, symbolically represented as follows:

Population 1	Population 2
μ_1, σ_1	μ_2, σ_2

Let us also suppose that a random sample of size n_1 is taken from the first population, a random sample of size n_2 is drawn from the second population, and the data collected in each sample pertain to some continuous random variable of interest.

The test statistic used to determine the difference between the population means is based on the difference between the sample means $(\overline{X}_1 - \overline{X}_2)$. Because of the central limit theorem discussed in Section 5.9, this test statistic follows the standard normal distribution (for large enough sample sizes). The Z test for the difference between two means is as follows:

Z TEST FOR DIFFERENCE BETWEEN TWO MEANS

$$Z = \frac{(\overline{X}_1 - \overline{X}_2) - (\mu_1 - \mu_2)}{\sqrt{\dfrac{\sigma_1^2}{n_1} + \dfrac{\sigma_2^2}{n_2}}} \tag{9.3}$$

where

$\overline{X}_1 = $ mean of the sample taken from population 1

$\mu_1 = $ mean of population 1

$\sigma_1^2 = $ variance of population 1

$n_1 = $ size of the sample taken from population 1

$\overline{X}_2 = $ mean of the sample taken from population 2

$\mu_2 = $ mean of population 2

$\sigma_2^2 = $ variance of population 2

$n_2 = $ size of the sample taken from population 2

The test statistic Z follows a standard normal distribution.

In most cases, we do not know the actual variance or standard deviation of either of the two populations. The only information usually obtainable is the sample means ($\overline{X}_1$ and $\overline{X}_2$), the sample variances (s_1^2 and s_2^2), and the sample standard deviations (s_1 and s_2). If the assumptions are made that the samples are randomly and independently drawn from respective populations that are normally distributed and that the population variances are equal (that is, $\sigma_1^2 = \sigma_2^2$), a **pooled-variance t test** can be used to determine whether there is a significant difference between the means of the two populations.

To test the null hypothesis of no difference between the means of two independent populations,

$$H_0: \mu_1 = \mu_2 \quad \text{or} \quad \mu_1 - \mu_2 = 0$$

against the alternative that the means are not the same,

$$H_1: \mu_1 \neq \mu_2 \quad \text{or} \quad \mu_1 - \mu_2 \neq 0$$

we use the pooled-variance t-test statistic (also called the independent groups t test) for testing the difference between two means.

POOLED-VARIANCE *t* TEST FOR THE DIFFERENCE BETWEEN TWO MEANS

$$t = \frac{(\bar{X}_1 - \bar{X}_2) - (\mu_1 - \mu_2)}{\sqrt{s_p^2\left(\dfrac{1}{n_1} + \dfrac{1}{n_2}\right)}} \tag{9.4}$$

where

$$s_p^2 = \frac{(n_1 - 1)s_1^2 + (n_2 - 1)s_2^2}{(n_1 - 1) + (n_2 - 1)}$$

and

s_p^2 = pooled variance

$\bar{X}_1$ = mean of the sample taken from population 1

s_1^2 = variance of the sample taken from population 1

n_1 = size of the sample taken from population 1

$\bar{X}_2$ = mean of the sample taken from population 2

s_2^2 = variance of the sample taken from population 2

n_2 = size of the sample taken from population 2

The test statistic *t* follows a *t* distribution with $n_1 + n_2 - 2$ degrees of freedom.

From Equation (9.4) we observe that the pooled-variance *t* test gets its name because the test statistic requires that we pool or combine the two sample variances s_1^2 and s_2^2 to obtain s_p^2, the best estimate of the variance common to both populations under the assumption that the two population variances are equal.[1]

The pooled-variance *t*-test statistic follows a *t* distribution with $n_1 + n_2 - 2$ degrees of freedom. For a given level of significance, α, in a two-tailed test, we reject the null hypothesis if the computed *t*-test statistic exceeds the upper-tailed critical value from the *t* distribution or if the computed test statistic falls below the lower-tailed critical value from the *t* distribution. In a directional or one-tailed test in which the rejection region is in the lower tail, we reject the null hypothesis if the computed test statistic falls below the lower-tailed critical value from the *t* distribution. In a directional or one-tailed test in which the rejection region is in the upper tail, we reject the null hypothesis if the computed test statistic exceeds the upper-tailed critical value from the *t* distribution.

To demonstrate the use of the pooled-variance *t* test, let us return to our *Using Statistics* application presented on page 392. The question to be determined is whether the components classified as unflawed had (on average) a smaller crack size than the components classified as flawed. The results, in terms of crack size (in inches), are shown in Table 9.4 on page 416.

To answer this, the null and alternative hypotheses are as follows:

$$H_0: \mu_1 \geq \mu_2$$
$$H_1: \mu_1 < \mu_2$$

When we take samples from underlying normal populations having equal variances, the pooled-variance *t* test can be used. If the test were conducted at the $\alpha = 0.05$ level of significance, the *t*-test statistic follows a *t* distribution with

[1] We should note that when the two sample sizes are equal (that is, $n_1 = n_2$), the formula for the pooled variance can be simplified to

$$s_p^2 = \frac{s_1^2 + s_2^2}{2}$$

TABLE 9.4

CRACK SIZES OF FLAWED AND UNFLAWED SPECIMENS

Unflawed										
0.003	0.004	0.012	0.014	0.021	0.023	0.024	0.030	0.034	0.041	0.041
0.042	0.043	0.045	0.057	0.063	0.074	0.076				

Flawed									
0.022	0.026	0.026	0.030	0.031	0.034	0.042	0.043	0.044	0.046
0.046	0.052	0.055	0.058	0.060	0.060	0.070	0.071	0.073	0.073
0.078	0.079	0.079	0.083	0.090	0.095	0.095	0.096	0.100	0.102
0.103	0.105	0.114	0.119	0.120	0.130	0.160	0.306	0.328	0.440 **CRACK**

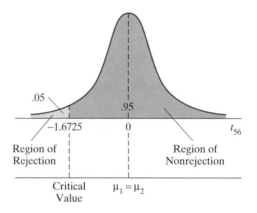

Figure 9.15 One-tailed test of hypothesis for the difference between two means at the 0.05 level of significance with 56 degrees of freedom

$18 + 40 - 2 = 56$ degrees of freedom. From Table A.4, the critical value for this one-tailed test is -1.6725. As depicted in Figure 9.15, the decision rule is as follows:

$$\text{Reject } H_0 \text{ if } t < t_{56} = -1.6725$$

otherwise do not reject H_0.

Using the data in Table 9.4, Figure 9.16 presents output from Microsoft Excel, while Figure 9.17 presents output from MINITAB.

A set of summary statistics is displayed in Table 9.5.

TABLE 9.5

SUMMARY STATISTICS ON CRACK SIZE (INCHES)

No Flaw	Flawed
$n_1 = 18$	$n_2 = 40$
$\overline{X}_1 = 0.0359$	$\overline{X}_2 = 0.0946$
$s_1^2 = 0.000481$	$s_2^2 = 0.007059$
$s_1 = 0.0218$	$s_2 = 0.0840$

	A	B	C
1	t-Test: Two-Sample Assuming Equal Variances		
2			
3		*No Flaw*	*Flaw*
4	Mean	0.035944	0.0946
5	Variance	0.000481	0.007059
6	Observations	18	40
7	Pooled Variance	0.005062	
8	Hypothesized Mean Difference	0	
9	df	56	
10	t Stat	-2.90467	
11	P(T<=t) one-tail	0.002627	
12	t Critical one-tail	1.672522	
13	P(T<=t) two-tail	0.005254	
14	t Critical two-tail	2.003239	

Figure 9.16   Microsoft Excel *t*-test output for the Flawed Crack data

```
Two-sample T for Crack Size

Flaw         N      Mean     StDev    SE Mean
No          18    0.0359    0.0219     0.0052
Yes         40    0.0946    0.0840     0.013

95% CI for mu (No ) - mu (Yes): ( -0.0991,  -0.018)
T-Test mu (No ) = mu (Yes) (vs <): T = -2.90   P = 0.0026   DF = 56
Both use Pooled StDev = 0.0711.
```

Figure 9.17   MINITAB *t*-test output for the Flawed Crack data

For our data, we have

$$t = \frac{(\bar{X}_1 - \bar{X}_2) - (\mu_1 - \mu_2)}{\sqrt{S_p^2\left(\dfrac{1}{n_1} + \dfrac{1}{n_2}\right)}}$$

where

$$s_p^2 = \frac{(n_1 - 1)s_1^2 + (n_2 - 1)s_2^2}{(n_1 - 1) + (n_2 - 1)}$$

$$= \frac{17(0.000481) + 39(0.007059)}{17 + 39} = 0.005062$$

Therefore,

$$t = \frac{0.0359 - 0.0946}{\sqrt{0.005062\left(\dfrac{1}{18} + \dfrac{1}{40}\right)}} = \frac{-0.0587}{\sqrt{0.004076}} = -2.90$$

At a 0.05 level of significance, the null hypothesis (H_0) is rejected because $t = -2.90 < t_{56} = -1.6725$. The *p*-value is 0.0026 (as obtained from Microsoft Excel or MINITAB). Because the *p*-value is less than α, we have sufficient evidence that the null hypothesis is not true, and we reject it. We conclude that the average crack size is lower for specimens that are classified as without flaw as compared to specimens that are classified as flawed. This makes intuitive sense: we would expect that those specimens judged to be without flaw should have cracks that are smaller than specimens that are judged to be flawed.

COMMENT: CHECKING THE ASSUMPTIONS

In testing for the difference between two means, we assume that we are sampling from normally distributed populations having equal variances. For situations in which we cannot or do not wish to make the assumption that the two populations having equal variances are actually normally distributed, the pooled-variance t test is robust (that is, not sensitive) to moderate departures from the assumption of normality, provided that the sample sizes are large. In such situations, the pooled-variance t test can be used without serious effect on its power.

On the other hand, if we cannot or do not wish to assume that the data in each group are taken from normally distributed populations, two choices exist:

1. We can make some *normalizing transformation* (see Reference 9) on each of the outcomes and then use the pooled-variance t test; or
2. Some *nonparametric* procedure such as the *Wilcoxon rank sum test* (to be covered in Section 9.9), that does not depend on the assumption of normality for the two populations, can be performed.

In our discussion of testing for the difference between the means of two independent populations, we pooled the sample variances together into a common estimate S_p^2 because we assumed that the population variances were equal. However, if either we are unwilling to assume that the two normally distributed populations have equal variances or we have evidence that the variances are not equal, then the pooled-variance t test is inappropriate. As a result, the **separate-variance t test** developed by Satterthwaite (see Reference 6) is used. In the Satterthwaite approximation procedure, the two separate sample variances are included in the computation of the t-test statistic—hence the name separate-variance t test. Although the computations for the separate-variance t test are complicated, either Microsoft Excel or MINITAB can be used to perform them. From Figure 9.16 or 9.17, as well as from Table 9.5, we observe that the variance for the specimens without flaws is much smaller than the variance for the specimens with flaws. Thus, pending a test of hypothesis for the difference between the two variances (to be discussed in Section 9.5), it would seem that a separate-variance t test might be appropriate. Figure 9.18 presents the output of this separate-variance t test obtained from Microsoft Excel for these specimens.

From Figure 9.18, we see that the test statistic for $t = -4.11 < -1.6766$, and that the p-value is 7.4E-05 or 0.000074, which is less than 0.05. Thus, the results for the separate-variance t test are consistent with those of the pooled-variance t test.

Note that we made the same decisions and drew the same conclusions from the two different t tests that we conducted. The assumption or equality of population variances had no real effect on our analysis. Sometimes, however, the results from the pooled- and separate-variance t tests conflict, because the assumptions of one of them are violated. This is why it is so important to evaluate the assumptions and use those results to guide the appropriate selection of a test procedure. Resolving such a dilemma is part of good data analysis. In Section 9.5 we develop

	A	B	C
1	t-Test: Two-Sample Assuming Unequal Variances		
2			
3		*No Flaw*	*Flaw*
4	Mean	0.035944	0.0946
5	Variance	0.000481	0.007059
6	Observations	18	40
7	Hypothesized Mean Difference	0	
8	df	49	
9	t Stat	-4.11472	
10	P(T<=t) one-tail	7.4E-05	
11	t Critical one-tail	1.676551	
12	P(T<=t) two-tail	0.000148	
13	t Critical two-tail	2.009574	

Figure 9.18   Microsoft Excel output of the separate-variance *t* test for the Flawed Crack data

the *F test* to determine whether there is evidence of a difference between the two population variances. Given the results of that test, we can be guided as to which of our previous tests is more appropriate to use.

If our exploratory data analysis reveals that the assumption of underlying normality in the two populations is questionable, it could lead us to conclude that neither test is appropriate. In such a situation, either a *data transformation* (see Reference 9) would be made (and then the assumptions rechecked to determine whether one of the *t* tests is more appropriate) or a *nonparametric procedure* which does not make these stringent assumptions would be employed. One such procedure, the *Wilcoxon rank sum test,* is presented in Section 9.9. A box-and-whisker plot obtained from the PHStat add-in for Microsoft Excel is displayed in Figure 9.19.

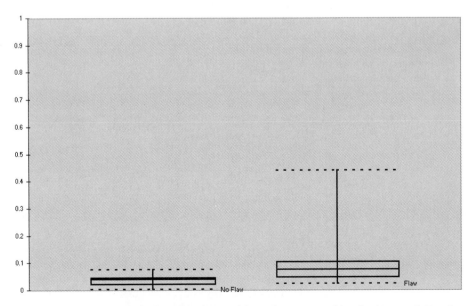

Figure 9.19   Box-and-whisker plot obtained from the PHStat add-in for Microsoft Excel for the Flawed Crack data

From Figure 9.19, we observe a long tail for the specimens with flaws, caused by several very large cracks. Thus, given the differences in the variances and this skewness in the distribution of the flawed specimens, there is some reason to believe that neither t test may be appropriate for these data.

www.prenhall.com

PROBLEMS

9.10 In intaglio printing, a design or figure is carved beneath the surface of hard metal or stone. Suppose that an experiment is undertaken to compare differences in average surface hardness is of steel plates used in intaglio printing (measured in indentation numbers), possibly caused by two different surface conditions— untreated, versus treated by light polishing with emery paper. From past experience, it is believed that the standard deviation in surface hardness (in indentation numbers) is 10.2 for untreated surfaces and 6.4 for lightly polished surfaces. In the experiment, 40 steel plates are randomly assigned, 20 that are untreated and 20 that are lightly polished. The sample mean for the untreated plates is 163.4, and the sample mean for the polished plates is 156.9. Use the 0.05 level of significance to determine whether there is evidence of a significant difference in average surface hardness between the untreated and the polished steel plates.

9.11 A manufacturer is developing a nickel–metal hydride battery that is to be used in cellular telephones in lieu of nickel–cadmium batteries. The director of quality control decides to evaluate the newly developed battery against the widely used nickel–cadmium battery with respect to performance. A random sample of 25 nickel–cadmium batteries and a random sample of 25 of the newly developed nickel–metal hydride batteries are placed in cellular telephones of the same brand and model. The performance measure of interest is the talking time (in minutes) prior to recharging. The results are as follows:

Nickel–Cadmium Battery			Nickel–Metal Hydride Battery		
54.5	71.0	67.0	78.3	103.0	79.8
67.8	41.7	56.7	95.4	81.3	91.1
64.5	69.7	86.8	69.4	46.4	82.8
70.4	40.8	74.9	87.3	82.3	71.8
72.5	75.4	76.9	62.5	83.2	77.5
64.9	81.0	104.4	85.0	85.3	74.3
83.3	90.4	82.0	85.3	85.5	86.1
72.8	71.8	58.7	72.1	112.3	74.1
68.8			41.1		

NICKELBAT

(a) Assuming that the population variances are equal, is there evidence of a difference between the two types of batteries with respect to average talking time (in minutes) prior to recharging? (Use $\alpha = 0.05$.)

(b) What other assumptions must be made in (a) of this problem?

(c) Find the p-value in part (a) and interpret its meaning.

(d) Assuming that the population variances are not equal, is there evidence of a difference between the two types of batteries with respect to average talking time (in minutes) prior to recharging? (Use $\alpha = 0.05$.)

(e) What other assumptions must be made in (d) of this problem?

(f) Find the p-value in (d) and interpret its meaning.

(g) Compare the results obtained in (a) with those in (d).

9.12 An experiment was conducted to assess the effect of using magnets at the filler point in the manufacture of coffee filter packs. The table below presents the weights of filter packs in grams. Thirty packs produced with magnets are to be compared against 45 packs produced without magnets.

With Magnets					
20.1	20.1	19.6	19.5	19.4	20.4
19.6	13.5	19.7	20.6	20.2	20.4
19.9	20.4	20.1	19.7	19.2	19.3
19.5	19.1	20.4	20.6	20.6	20.1
20.2	20.0	19.8	20.8	19.6	19.3

Without Magnets					
21.4	20.5	20.2	20.6	21.4	20.1
19.9	19.7	21.2	20.7	20.9	20.2
20.1	20.7	20.4	21.0	20.5	20.0
20.6	20.8	19.5	19.7	20.0	20.4
20.2	20.5	20.4	21.3	20.4	20.2
20.5	20.7	19.8	20.7	20.2	20.0
20.5	20.6	20.6	19.9	20.0	20.2
20.6	19.9	20.4			

MAGNETS

(a) Assuming that the population variances are equal, is there evidence of a difference between the average weights of filter packs made with and without magnets? (Use $\alpha = 0.05$.)

(b) What other assumptions must be made in (a) of this problem?

(c) Find the *p*-value in (a) and interpret its meaning.

9.13 An airflow experiment compared two different terminal devices that are used to diffuse air throughout a space, thereby providing heating and/or cooling. Fifty diffusers of each type were randomly selected in a building that contained 1100 diffusers per floor. The table below presents the airflow measurements (in cubic feet per minute) obtained in this experiment.

Carnes 3-Way Diffusers								
245	230	180	200	180	255	195	220	195
200	225	240	300	240	285	250	295	295
270	285	225	255	190	275	280	205	215
270	265	290	310	250	215	270	295	210
235	160	235	280	250	240	295	285	190
250	310	290	250	300				

Krueger 4-Way Diffusers								
275	225	230	240	205	225	265	225	190
275	240	205	250	265	230	300	275	240
245	250	200	270	245	230	225	285	275
250	200	255	265	230	250	195	240	225
230	290	230	250	225	275	205	245	250
300	275	260	255	230				

AIRFLOW

(a) Assuming that the population variances are equal, is there evidence of a difference between the two types of diffusers with respect to average airflow measurements? (Use $\alpha = 0.05$.)

(b) What other assumptions must be made in (a) of this problem?

(c) Find the *p*-value in part (a) and interpret its meaning.

9.14 A problem with a telephone line that prevents a customer from receiving or making calls is disconcerting both to the customer and to the telephone company. These problems can be of two types: those that are located inside a central office, and those located on lines between the central office and the customer's equipment. The following data represent samples of 20 problems reported to two different offices of a telephone company and the time to clear these problems (in minutes) from the customers' lines:

Central Office I Time to Clear Problems (minutes)									
1.48	1.75	0.78	2.85	0.52	1.60	4.15	3.97	1.48	3.10
1.02	0.53	0.93	1.60	0.80	1.05	6.32	3.93	5.45	0.97

Central Office II Time to Clear Problems (minutes)									
7.55	3.75	0.10	1.10	0.60	0.52	3.30	2.10	0.58	4.02
3.75	0.65	1.92	0.60	1.53	4.23	0.08	1.48	1.65	0.72

PHONE

(a) Assuming that the population variances are equal, is there evidence of a difference between the two central offices with respect to average time to clear these problems (in minutes)? (Use $\alpha = 0.05$.)

(b) What other assumptions must be made in (a) of this problem?

(c) Use a side-by-side box-and-whisker plot to evaluate the assumptions in (b).

(d) Find the *p*-value in part (a) and interpret its meaning.

9.15 In many manufacturing processes, there is a term called *work in process* (often abbreviated as WIP). In a book-manufacturing plant, this represents time it takes for sheets from a press to be folded, gathered, sewn, tipped on endsheets, and bound. The following data represents samples of 20 books at each of two production plants and the processing time (operationally defined as the time in days from when the books came off the press to when they were packed in cartons) for these jobs.

Plant A						
5.62	5.29	16.25	10.92	11.46	21.62	8.45
8.58	5.41	11.42	11.62	7.29	7.50	7.96
4.42	10.50	7.58	9.29	7.54	8.92	

Plant B						
9.54	11.46	16.62	12.62	25.75	15.41	14.29
13.13	13.71	10.04	5.75	12.46	9.17	13.21
6.00	2.33	14.25	5.37	6.25	9.71	

WIP

(a) Assuming that the population variances are equal, is there evidence of a difference between the two plants with respect to average processing time (in days)? (Use $\alpha = 0.05$.)

(b) What other assumptions must be made in (a) of this problem?

(c) Use a side-by-side box-and-whisker plot to evaluate the assumptions in (b).

(d) Find the p-value in (a) and interpret its meaning.

9.16 Shipments of meat, meat byproducts, and other ingredients are mixed together in several filling lines at a pet-food canning factory. Management suspects that, although the average amount filled in the can of pet food is usually the same, the variability of the cans filled on line A is much greater than that on line B. The following sample data are obtained (from filling eight-ounce cans):

	Line A	Line B
$\overline{X}$	8.005	7.997
s	0.012	0.005
n	11	16

Assuming that the population variances are not equal, at the .05 level of significance, is there evidence of a difference between the average weight of cans filled on the two lines?

9.5 TESTING FOR THE DIFFERENCE BETWEEN TWO VARIANCES

Often, we want to test whether two independent populations have the same variability. We may be interested in studying the variances of two populations in order to test the assumption of equal variances so that we can determine whether to use the pooled-variance t test or the separate-variance t test, or we may just be interested in comparing the variances of two populations.

We use a statistical test based on the ratio of the two sample variances to test for the equality of the variances of two independent populations. If the data from each population are assumed to be normally distributed, then the ratio s_1^2/s_2^2 follows a distribution called the **F distribution** (see Table A.7), named after the famous statistician R. A. Fisher. From Table A.7, we see that the critical values of the F distribution depend on two measures of degrees of freedom. The degrees of freedom in the numerator of the ratio pertain to the first sample and the degrees of freedom in the denominator of the ratio pertain to the second sample. The F-test statistic for testing the equality between two variances is found as follows.

F STATISTIC FOR TESTING THE EQUALITY OF TWO VARIANCES

The F test statistic is equal to the variance of sample one divided by the variance of sample two.

$$F = \frac{s_1^2}{s_2^2} \tag{9.5}$$

where

$s_1^2 =$ variance of sample 1

$s_2^2 =$ variance of sample 2

For a given level of significance, α, to test the null hypothesis of equality of variances

$$H_0: \sigma_1^2 = \sigma_2^2$$

against the alternative hypothesis that the two population variances are not equal

$$H_1: \sigma_1^2 \neq \sigma_2^2$$

we reject the null hypothesis if the computed F test statistic exceeds the upper-tailed critical value F_U from the F distribution with $n_1 - 1$ degrees of freedom from sample 1 in the numerator and $n_2 - 1$ degrees of freedom from sample 2 in the denominator, or if the computed F test statistic falls below the lower-tailed critical value F_L from the F distribution with $n_1 - 1$ and $n_2 - 1$ degrees of freedom in the numerator and denominator. Thus, the decision rule is

$$\text{Reject } H_0 \text{ if } F > F_U \text{ or if } F < F_L;$$

$$\text{otherwise do not reject } H_0.$$

This decision rule and rejection region are displayed in Figure 9.20.

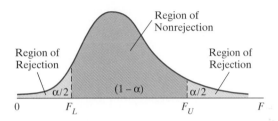

Figure 9.20   Regions of rejection and nonrejection for a two-tailed F test

To demonstrate how we can use the F test for the equality of two variances, we return to our *Using Statistics* application. We wanted to determine whether there is evidence of a significant difference in average crack size between specimens classified as unflawed and flawed. These data are shown in Table 9.4 on page 416 and the summary measures for the two samples are presented in Table 9.5 on page 417.

To determine whether the pooled-variance t test or the separate-variance t test is more appropriate for analysis of the collected data, we test for the equality of the two population variances. We have the following null and alternative hypotheses:

$$H_0: \sigma_1^2 = \sigma_2^2$$
$$H_1: \sigma_1^2 \neq \sigma_2^2$$

Because this is a nondirectional or two-tailed test, the rejection region is split into the lower and upper tails of the F distribution. If a level of significance of $\alpha = 0.05$ is selected, each rejection region contains 0.025 of the distribution.

F_U, the upper-tail critical value of the F distribution with 17 and 39 degrees of freedom, can be obtained directly from Table A.7. Because there are 17 degrees of freedom in the numerator and 39 degrees of freedom in the denominator, the approximate value for the upper-tail critical value F_U is found by looking in the column labeled "15" and the row labeled "40", which pertain to an upper-tail area of 0.025. Thus, the upper-tail critical value of this F distribution is approximately 2.18.

F_L, a lower-tail critical value on the F distribution with the desired $n_1 - 1$ degrees of freedom from sample 1 in the numerator and $n_2 - 1$ degrees of freedom from sample 2 in the denominator, is computed by taking the reciprocal of F_U, an upper-tail critical value on the F distribution with degrees of freedom "switched" (that is, $n_2 - 1$ degrees of freedom in the numerator and $n_1 - 1$ degrees of freedom in the denominator). This gives us Equation (9.6)

> ### OBTAINING LOWER-TAIL CRITICAL VALUES FROM THE *F* DISTRIBUTION
>
> $$F_L = \frac{1}{F_U} \qquad\qquad (9.6)$$

In our example concerning the flawed specimens, the degrees of freedom are 17 for the unflawed group and 39 for the flawed group. Therefore, to compute our desired lower-tail 0.025 critical value, we need to switch the degrees of freedom that we used to obtain the upper-tail value. The upper-tail 0.025 critical value of *F* with 39 degrees of freedom in the numerator and 17 degrees of freedom in the denominator, from Table A.7 is approximately 2.44. From Equation (9.6)

$$F_L = \frac{1}{F_U} = \frac{1}{2.44} = 0.41$$

As depicted in Figure 9.21, the decision rule is

Reject H_0 if $F > F_U = 2.18$ or if $F < F_L = 0.41$;

otherwise do not reject H_0.

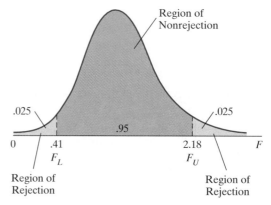

Figure 9.21 Regions of rejection and nonrejection for a two-tailed *F* test for the equality of two variances at the 0.05 level of significance with 17 and 39 degrees of freedom

Using Equation (9.5) for the flawed specimen data (see Table 9.5 on page 417), we compute the following *F*-test statistic:

$$F = \frac{s_1^2}{s_2^2}$$

$$= \frac{0.000481}{0.007059} = 0.068$$

Therefore, since $F = 0.068 < F_L = 0.41$, we reject H_0. There is evidence of a difference in the variability of the crack size between unflawed and flawed specimens. Alternatively, to use the *p*-value approach, *F* test output could be obtained

	A	B	C
1	F-Test: Two-Sample Variances		
2			
3		No Flaw	Flaw
4	Mean	0.035944	0.0946
5	Variance	0.000481	0.007059
6	Observations	18	40
7	df	17	39
8	F	0.068174	
9	P(F<=t) one-tail	1.66E-07	
10	F Critical one-tail	0.474513	

Figure 9.22   Microsoft Excel F test output for the flawed specimen data

from Microsoft Excel or MINITAB. Figure 9.22 represents output for the flawed specimen data obtained from Microsoft Excel.

Because there is evidence that the population variances differ significantly, if we assume that the two populations are normally distributed, the separate-variance t test would be more appropriate than the pooled-variance t test for comparing differences in the crack size.

COMMENT: CHECKING THE ASSUMPTIONS

In testing for the equality of two population variances, be aware that the test assumes that each of the two populations is normally distributed. That is, if the assumption of normality for each population is met, the F-test statistic follows an F distribution with $n_1 - 1$ degrees of freedom from sample 1 in the numerator and $n_2 - 1$ degrees of freedom from sample 2 in the denominator. Unfortunately, this F-test statistic is not *robust* to departures from the normality assumption (Reference 2), particularly when the sample sizes in the two groups are not equal. Therefore, if the populations are not at least approximately normally distributed, the accuracy of the procedure can be seriously affected. (References 2, 7, and 9 present other procedures for testing the equality of two variances.)

PROBLEMS

9.17 Determine F_L and F_u, the upper- and lower-tail critical values of F, in each of the following two-tailed tests:
(a) $\alpha = 0.10, n_1 = 16, n_2 = 21$.
(b) $\alpha = 0.05, n_1 = 16, n_2 = 21$.
(c) $\alpha = 0.02, n_1 = 16, n_2 = 21$.
(d) $\alpha = 0.01, n_1 = 16, n_2 = 21$.

9.18 Scientists have attempted to construct computer models to predict climate and weather. Two computer models tried to predict surface temperature under various environmental conditions. A sample of errors made by two of the models (°K) follow:

Model 1					
0.53	0.22	−0.09	−0.39	−0.69	−0.97
−1.26	−1.53	−1.80	−2.06	−2.32	−2.58

Model 2					
1.51	0.78	0.06	−0.64	−1.31	−1.96
−2.60	−3.22	−3.82	−4.42	−4.99	−5.56

CLIMATE

Assuming that these errors are normally distributed, test the hypothesis at the 0.05 level that the two computer models have the same population variances.

9.19 The California Dept. of Water Resources is currently building the California Coastal Aqueduct, which has three pumping plants along its route. When concrete is placed at such construction sites, sample cylinders are filled with some of the concrete and, after it cures, it is tested for compressive strength (psi). Sample data from two of the pumping plants, Polonio Pass and Devil's Den, follow.

Polonio Pass						
3520	4670	3780	3880	3470	3770	3420
3690	4090	3950	4030	5210	4380	3600
4020	4380	4210	3660	4600	5200	

Devil's Den						
4700	3550	4750	3600	4610	4010	4100
4030	4470	3940	3550	5330	4915	4090
3830	5460	4900	3960	3950	3760	

PUMPPSI

Assume that the populations of compressive strengths are normally distributed. Test the hypothesis at the 0.05 level that the two pumping plants have the same population variances.

9.20 Contamination of silicon wafer surfaces with particles and surface chemical oxidation have been shown to degrade device yield. In *A Portable Nitrogen Purged Microenvironment: Design Specification and Preliminary Field Test Data* (PROCEEDINGS—Institute of Environmental Sciences, 1995), C.W. Draper et. al. describe a nitrogen-purged portable microenvironment. Ten wafers receiving a standard clean in a cleanroom were compared to 5 wafers receiving a megasonics clean and transported through a non-clean environment in the microenvironment. Defects were measured on 2 vernier patterns/wafer:

Standard									
53	193	113	640	800	140	85	658	140	140

Megasonic				
26	90	546	90	120

MEGASONIC

(a) Test the hypothesis at the 0.01 level that the two methods have the same population variances.
(b) What assumption is necessary for this test to be valid?

9.21 In Problem 9.10 on page 420, concerning intaglio printing, a random sample of 25 nickel–cadmium batteries and a random sample of 25 of the newly developed nickel–metal hydride batteries are placed in cellular telephones of the same brand and model. The performance measure of interest is the talking time (in minutes) prior to recharging.
(a) Using a 0.05 level of significance, is there evidence of a difference between the variances in talking time (in minutes) prior to recharging for the two types of batteries?
(b) Based on the results obtained in (a), which test should be selected to compare the means of the two groups—the pooled-variance *t* test or the separate-variance *t* test? Discuss.

9.22 In Problem 9.13 on page 421, an airflow experiment compared two different terminal devices that are used to diffuse air throughout a space thereby providing heating and/or cooling.
(a) Using a 0.05 level of significance, is there evidence of a difference between the variances in airflow measurements for the two types of diffusers?
(b) Given the results obtained in (a), which test should be selected to compare the means of the two groups—the pooled-variance *t* test or the separate-variance *t* test? Discuss.

9.23 Shipments of meat, meat byproducts, and other ingredients are mixed together in several filling lines at a pet-food canning factory. The operation manager suspects that, although the average amount filled in the can of pet food is usually the same, the variability of the cans filled in line A is greater than that in line B. The following sample data are obtained (from filling eight-ounce cans):

	Line A	Line B
$\overline{X}$	8.005	7.997
s	0.012	0.005
n	11	16

Assuming that the population amounts are normally distributed, at the 0.05 level of significance, is there evidence that the variance in Line A is greater than the variance in Line B?

9.6 THE REPEATED MEASURES OR PAIRED *t* TEST

The hypothesis-testing procedures examined thus far enable us to make comparisons and examine differences between two *independent* populations based on samples containing numerical data. In this section, we develop a procedure for analyzing the difference between the means of two groups when the sample data are obtained from populations that are **related,** when results of the first group are *not* independent of the second group. This "dependency" characteristic of the two groups occurs either because the items or individuals are **paired** or **matched** according to some characteristic or because **repeated measurements** are obtained from the same set of items or individuals. In either case, the variable of interest becomes the *difference between the values* of the observations rather than the *values* of the observations themselves.

The first approach to the related-samples problem involves the matching or pairing of items or individuals according to some characteristic of interest. For example, in testing whether a new drug improves a physical measurement of interest, a sample of identical twins can be used. Since they are genetically identical, we can consider them matched pairs who will be similar on a variety of variables. By controlling these variables, we are better able to measure the effects due to the new drug.

The second approach to the related-samples problem involves taking repeated measurements on the same items or individuals. Under the theory that the same items or individuals will behave alike if treated alike, the objective of the analysis is to show that any differences between two measurements of the same items or individuals are due to different treatment conditions. For example, when performing an experiment on the hardness of concrete after one week and four weeks, each batch can be used as its own control so that *repeated measurements* on the same batch are obtained.

Regardless of whether matched (paired) samples or repeated measurements are utilized, the objective is to study the difference between two measurements by reducing the effect of the variability due to the items or individuals themselves. In this section we develop an important test procedure to accomplish this—the *t test for the mean difference in related samples.*

To determine whether any difference exists between two related groups, the differences in the individual values in each group are obtained as shown in Table 9.6.

TABLE 9.6

DETERMINING THE DIFFERENCE BETWEEN TWO RELATED GROUPS

Observation	Group 1	Group 2	Difference
1	X_{11}	X_{21}	$D_1 = X_{11} - X_{21}$
2	X_{12}	X_{22}	$D_2 = X_{12} - X_{22}$
.	.	.	.
.	.	.	.
.	.	.	.
i	X_{1i}	X_{2i}	$D_i = X_{1i} - X_{2i}$
.	.	.	.
.	.	.	.
.	.	.	.
n	X_{1n}	X_{2n}	$D_n = X_{1n} - X_{2n}$

To read this table, let $X_{11}, X_{12}, \ldots, X_{1n}$ represent the n observations from a sample. Now let $X_{21}, X_{22}, \ldots, X_{2n}$ represent either the corresponding n matched observations from a second sample or the corresponding n repeated measurements from the initial sample. Then, $D_1, D_2, \ldots, D_n$ will represent the corresponding set of n *difference scores,* such that $D_1 = X_{11} - X_{21}, D_2 = X_{12} - X_{22}$ and $D_n = X_{1n} - X_{2n}$.

From the central limit theorem, the average difference $\overline{D}$ follows a normal distribution when the population standard deviation of the difference σ_D is known and the sample size is large enough. The Z-test statistic is computed as follows.

Z TEST FOR THE MEAN DIFFERENCE

$$Z = \frac{\overline{D} - \mu_D}{\dfrac{\sigma_D}{\sqrt{n}}} \tag{9.7}$$

where

$$\overline{D} = \frac{\displaystyle\sum_{i=1}^{n} D_i}{n}$$

μ_D = hypothesized mean difference

σ_D = population standard deviation of the difference scores

n = sample size

and the test statistic Z follows a standard normal distribution.

As mentioned previously, in most cases we do not know the actual standard deviation of a population. The only information usually obtainable is the summary statistics, such as the sample mean, the sample variance, and sample standard deviation.

If we assume that the sample of difference scores is randomly and independently drawn from a population that is normally distributed, a t test can be used to determine whether there is a significant population mean difference. Thus, as in the (one-sample) t test developed in Section 9.3 [see Equation (9.2)], the t-test statistic developed here follows the t distribution with $n - 1$ degrees of freedom.

COMMENT

Although the population is assumed to be normally distributed, in practice it has been found that as long as the sample size is not very small and the population is not very skewed, the t distribution gives a good approximation to the sampling distribution of the average difference $\overline{D}$.

To test the null hypothesis of no difference between the means of two related populations (i.e., the population mean difference μ_D is 0)

$$H_0: \mu_D = 0 \text{ (where } \mu_D = \mu_1 - \mu_2)$$

against the alternative that the means are not the same (i.e., the population mean difference μ_D is not 0)

$$H_1: \mu_D \neq 0$$

the following t-test statistic is computed.

---

t TEST FOR THE MEAN DIFFERENCE

$$t = \frac{\overline{D} - \mu_D}{\dfrac{s_D}{\sqrt{n}}} \tag{9.8}$$

where

$$\overline{D} = \frac{\displaystyle\sum_{i=1}^{n} D_i}{n}$$

and

$$s_D = \sqrt{\frac{\displaystyle\sum_{i=1}^{n} (D_i - \overline{D})^2}{n - 1}}$$

and the test statistic t follows a t distribution with $n - 1$ degrees of freedom.

For a given level of significance, α, we reject the null hypothesis if the computed t-test statistic exceeds the upper-tailed critical value t_{n-1} from the t distribution or if the computed test statistic falls below the lower-tailed critical value $-t_{n-1}$ from the t distribution. That is, the decision rule is

$$\text{Reject } H_0 \text{ if } t > t_{n-1}$$
$$\text{or if } t < -t_{n-1};$$
$$\text{otherwise do not reject } H_0.$$

To illustrate the use of the t test for the mean difference, we will use a data set in which two different observers measured the cardiac output of 23 patients by using Doppler echocardiography. By using the same set of patients for both observers, each patient is his or her own control. If the observers agree on a patient, the difference between their measured outputs will be zero. Therefore, we can evaluate differences in the measured output by comparing the average differences between observers to 0.0. Here, however, we note that obtaining the two measurements (one for the observer A and one for observer B) for each patient serves to reduce the variability in the measurements compared with what would occur if two independent sets of patients were used. It enables us to focus on the differences between the two measurements for each patient.

The results displayed in Table 9.7 on page 430 are for a sample of $n = 23$ patients used in the experiment.

The question that must be answered is whether there is evidence of a difference in measured cardiac output between the two observers. Thus, we have the following null and alternative hypotheses:

$$H_0: \mu_D = 0$$
$$H_1: \mu_D \neq 0$$

TABLE 9.7

REPEATED MEASUREMENTS OF CARDIAC OUTPUT FOR 23 PATIENTS BY TWO DIFFERENT OBSERVERS

	Observer				Observer	
Patient	A	B	Patient	A	B
1	4.8	5.8	13	7.7	8.5
2	5.6	6.1	14	7.7	9.5
3	6.0	7.7	15	8.2	9.1
4	6.4	7.8	16	8.2	10.0
5	6.5	7.6	17	8.3	9.1
6	6.6	8.1	18	8.5	10.8
7	6.8	8.0	19	9.3	11.5
8	7.0	8.1	20	10.2	11.5
9	7.0	6.6	21	10.4	11.2
10	7.2	8.1	22	10.6	11.5
11	7.4	9.5	23	11.4	12.0
12	7.6	9.6			**CARDIAC**

Source: Ernst, M. L. R. Guerra, and W. R. Schucany, "Scatterplots for unordered pairs," *The American Statistician,* 1996, 50, 260–265.

Choosing a level of significance, α, of 0.05, and assuming the differences are normally distributed, we use the paired-sample t test [Equation (9.8)] to test the null hypothesis that there is no difference in measurements between the two observers. For a sample of $n = 23$ patients, using Table A.4, the decision rule is as follows:

$$\text{Reject } H_0 \text{ if } t < -t_{22} = -2.0739 \text{ or if } t > t_{22} = +2.0739;$$

$$\text{otherwise do not reject } H_0.$$

For the data set pertaining to the random sample of $n = 23$ differences, we compute the sample mean difference either by using Microsoft Excel, as illustrated in Figure 9.23, or by using MINITAB, as shown in Figure 9.24. We observe that $\overline{D} = -1.23$ and $s_D = 0.638$.

	A	B	C
1	t-Test: Paired Two Sample for Means		
2			
3		Observer A	Observer B
4	Mean	7.8	9.03043478
5	Variance	2.802727273	3.22130435
6	Observations	23	23
7	Pearson Correlation	0.934585253	
8	Hypothesized Mean Difference	0	
9	df	22	
10	t Stat	-9.24206917	
11	P(T<=t) one-tail	2.48242E-09	
12	t Critical one-tail	1.717144187	
13	P(T<=t) two-tail	4.96485E-09	
14	t Critical two-tail	2.073875294	

Figure 9.23   Microsoft Excel paired t test output for the sample of patients

```
Paired T-Test and Confidence Interval

Paired T for A - B

                 N        Mean      StDev     SE Mean
A               23       7.800      1.674       0.349
B               23       9.030      1.795       0.374
Difference      23      -1.230      0.638       0.133

95% CI for mean difference: (-1.507, -0.954)
T-Test of mean difference = 0 (vs not = 0): T-Value = -9.24   P-Value = 0.000
```

Figure 9.24   MINITAB paired *t* test output for the sample of patients

From Equation (9.8), we then obtain

$$t = \frac{\overline{D} - \mu_D}{\frac{s_D}{\sqrt{n}}} = \frac{-1.23 - 0}{\frac{0.638}{\sqrt{23}}} = -9.24$$

Because $t = -9.24 < -2.0739$, or because the *p*-value = 4.965E-09 (or 0.000000004965) $< \alpha = 0.05$, we reject the null hypothesis H_0 (see Figure 9.25). There is evidence of a difference in measured cardiac output between the two observers.

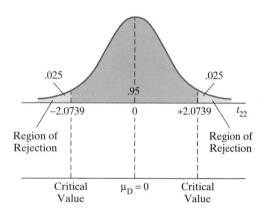

Figure 9.25   Region of rejection for a two-tailed *t*-test for the mean difference at the 0.05 level of significance with 22 degrees of freedom

COMMENT: TEST SELECTION

If our exploratory data analysis reveals that the assumption of underlying normality in the sampled population is questionable, it might lead us to conclude that the *t*-test is inappropriate. In such a situation, either a *data transformation* (see Reference 9) is made and then the assumptions rechecked to determine whether the *t*-test should be used, or a *nonparametric* procedure which does not make the stringent assumption of underlying normality could be employed. (See References 1 and 2.)

PROBLEMS

9.24 In hydraulic engineering, it is important to be able to take accurate measurements on flow or discharge. Discharge data was collected using two different methods. One type of measuring device used in closed conduits is a Rotameter, a device placed inside a pipe. The second method is known as the Weigh Tank method and involves timing how long it takes to fill a container of known volume. Sample data was collected on ten pairs of flow rates (mm^3/sec).

Container	Rotameter	Weigh Tank
1	0.2920	0.2940
2	0.2330	0.2340
3	0.1830	0.1840
4	0.1420	0.1430
5	0.1170	0.1120
6	0.0917	0.0951
7	0.2670	0.2590
8	0.2500	0.2730
9	0.2170	0.1980
10	0.1670	0.1660

ROTAMETER

(a) At the 0.05 level of significance, is there evidence of a difference in the average flow rate between the two measurements?
(b) What assumption is necessary to perform this test?
(c) Find the p-value in (a) and interpret its meaning.

9.25 The following data concern the thickness of nonmagnetic coatings of zinc. Two measurements are made on the same specimen, the first using a nondestructive method, the second a destructive method. The data are as follows (in mm.)

Specimen	Nondestructive method	Destructive method
1	105	116
2	120	132
3	85	104
4	181	139
5	115	114
6	127	129
7	630	720
8	155	174
9	250	312
10	310	338
11	443	465

THICKNESS

(a) At the 0.05 level of significance, is there evidence of a difference in the average measurement of thickness between the two methods?
(b) What assumption is necessary to perform this test?
(c) Find the p-value in (a) and interpret its meaning.
(d) Test for the difference in the average thickness between the two methods by using the t test for two independent samples.
(e) Explain the difference between the results in (a) and (d).
(f) Is it valid to use either method? Explain.

9.26 The following data represent the compressive strength, in pounds per square inch (psi), of 40 samples of concrete taken two and seven days after pouring.

Sample	Two days	Seven days
1	2.830	3.505
2	3.295	3.430
3	2.710	3.670
4	2.855	3.355
5	2.980	3.985
6	3.065	3.630
7	3.765	4.570
8	3.265	3.700
9	3.170	3.660
10	2.895	3.250
11	2.630	2.850
12	2.830	3.340
13	2.935	3.630
14	3.115	3.675
15	2.985	3.475
16	3.135	3.605
17	2.750	3.250
18	3.205	3.540
19	3.000	4.005
20	3.035	3.595
21	1.635	2.275
22	2.270	3.910
23	2.895	2.915
24	2.845	4.530
25	2.205	2.280
26	3.590	3.915
27	3.080	3.140
28	3.335	3.580
29	3.800	4.070
30	2.680	3.805
31	3.760	4.130

(*Continued*)

Sample	Two days	Seven days
32	3.605	3.720
33	2.005	2.690
34	2.495	3.230
35	3.205	3.590
36	2.060	2.945
37	3.425	4.030
38	3.315	3.685
39	3.825	4.175
40	3.160	3.430

CONCRETE1

Source: O. Carrillo-Gamboa and R. F. Gunst, "Measurement-error-model collinearities," *Technometrics,* 34, 1992, pp. 454–464.

(a) At the 0.01 level of significance, is there evidence that the average strength is less at two days than at seven days?
(b) What assumption is necessary to perform this test?
(c) Find the p-value in (a) and interpret its meaning.

9.27 In computer programming, it is often necessary to sort through a set of numbers and put them in ascending order. The efficiency of two methods is to be compared: Insertion Sort and Selection Sort. Forty different sets of data were sorted by using these two methods, with the results (in terms of time to sort in seconds) stored in the file **SORTING.**

(a) At the 0.05 level of significance, is there evidence of a difference in the average time for the two sorting methods?
(b) What assumption is necessary to perform this test?
(c) Find the p-value in (a) and interpret its meaning.

9.28 Suppose that a shoe company wants to test material for the soles of shoes. A sample of ten pairs of shoes is randomly selected for the experiment. For each pair of shoes, the new material is placed on one shoe and the old material is placed on the other shoe. After a given period of wear testing and mechanical abrasion, the wear is measured on a ten-point scale (higher is better) with the following results.

	Pair Number									
Material	I	II	III	IV	V	VI	VII	VIII	IX	X
New	2	4	5	7	7	5	9	8	8	7
Old	4	5	3	8	9	4	7	8	5	6
Differences	−2	−1	+2	−1	−2	+1	+2	0	+3	+1

SHOESOLE

(a) At the 0.05 level of significance, is there evidence that the average wear for the new material is lower than for the old material?
(b) What assumption is necessary to perform this test?
(c) Find the p-value in (a) and interpret its meaning.

9.29 A group of engineering students decided to see whether cars that supposedly do not need high-octane gasoline get more miles per gallon using regular or high-octane gas. They test several cars (under similar road surface, weather, and other driving conditions), using both types of gas in each car at different times. The mileage for each gas type for each car is as follows.

	Car									
Gas Type	#1	#2	#3	#4	#5	#6	#7	#8	#9	#10
Regular	15	23	21	35	42	28	19	32	31	24
High-octane	18	21	25	34	47	30	19	27	34	20

GASMILE

(a) Is there any evidence of a difference in the average gasoline mileage between regular and high-octane gas? (Use $\alpha = 0.05$.)
(b) What assumption is necessary to perform this test?
(c) Find the p-value in (a) and interpret its meaning.

9.7 CHI-SQUARE TEST FOR THE DIFFERENCES AMONG PROPORTIONS IN TWO OR MORE GROUPS

In the previous three sections, we compared differences between two groups involving continuous variables. When two categorical variables are studied, a two-way table of cross-classifications can be developed (see Section 2.8) to display the frequency of occurrence for each level of each variable. The layout for such a table is also called a **contingency table.** In this section, we develop methodology for analyzing data presented in such contingency tables.

The contingency table displayed in Table 9.8 has two rows and two columns and is called a 2 × 2 table. The cells in the table indicate the frequency for each row and column combination.

TABLE 9.8

LAYOUT OF A 2 × 2 CONTINGENCY TABLE

Row Variable	Column Variable (Group)		Totals
	1	2	
Successes	X_1	X_2	X
Failures	$n_1 - X_1$	$n_2 - X_2$	$n - X$
Totals	n_1	n_2	n

Where

X_1 is the number of successes in group 1

X_2 is the number of successes in group 2

$n_1 - X_1$ is the number of failures in group 1

$n_2 - X_2$ is the number of failures in group 2

$X = X_1 + X_2$ is the total number of successes

$n - X = (n_1 - X_1) + (n_2 - X_2)$ is the total number of failures

n_1 is the sample size in group 1

n_2 is the sample size in group 2

$n = n_1 + n_2$ is the total sample size

The overall proportion of successes is obtained by dividing the total number of successes by the total sample size. A methodology known as the chi-square test for equality of proportions can then be employed to compare the proportions for the two methods. When the proportions are different, the category an observation falls into on one variable depends on or is related to the category into which an observation falls on the other variable. If the proportions are not different, the likelihood of falling into a given category on one variable is independent of or not related to the category into which the observation falls on the other variable. Therefore, the test can be considered a test of the independence of the two variables that define the rows and columns of the table.

To test the null hypothesis of no differences between the two population proportions

$$H_0: \pi_1 = \pi_2$$

against the alternative that the two population proportions are different

$$H_1: \pi_1 \neq \pi_2$$

we obtain the chi-square test statistic as follows.

χ^2 TEST FOR THE DIFFERENCE BETWEEN TWO PROPORTIONS

The χ^2 test statistic is equal to the squared difference between the observed and expected frequencies, divided by the expected frequency in each cell of the table, summed over all cells of the table.

$$\chi^2 = \sum_{\text{all cells}} \frac{(f_0 - f_e)^2}{f_e} \tag{9.9}$$

where

f_0 = **observed frequency** or actual tally in a particular cell of a 2×2 contingency table

f_e = **theoretical or expected frequency** we would expect to find in a particular cell if the null hypothesis is true

---

To compute the expected frequency, f_e, in any cell requires an understanding of its conceptual foundation. If the null hypothesis were true, so that the proportion of successes was equal for each population, then the sample proportions computed from each of the two groups would differ from each other only by chance and would each provide an estimate of the common population parameter π. In such a situation, a statistic that would pool or combine these two separate estimates together into one overall or average estimate of the population parameter π provides more information than either one of the two separate estimates could provide by itself. This statistic, given by the symbol $\bar{p}$, represents the overall or average proportion of successes for the two groups combined (that is, the total number of successes divided by the total sample size). Using the notation presented in Table 9.8 on page 434, this can be stated as:

$$\bar{p} = \frac{X_1 + X_2}{n_1 + n_2} = \frac{X}{n} \tag{9.10}$$

---

and its complement, $1 - \bar{p}$, represents the overall or average proportion of failures in the two groups.

To obtain the expected frequency, f_e, for each cell pertaining to successes (that is, the cells in the first row in the contingency table), we multiply the sample size (or column total) for a group by $\bar{p}$. To obtain the expected frequency, f_e, for each cell pertaining to failure (that is, the cells in the second row in the contingency table), we multiply the sample size (or column total) for a group by $(1 - \bar{p})$.

The test statistic shown in Equation (9.9) approximately follows a chi-square (χ^2) distribution with degrees of freedom equal to the *number of rows in the contingency table, minus* 1 times *the number of columns in the table, minus 1:*

$$\text{Degrees of freedom} = (r - 1)(c - 1)$$

where

r = number of rows in the table

c = number of columns in the table

For our 2×2 contingency table, there is 1 degree of freedom; that is,

$$\text{Degrees of freedom} = (2 - 1)(2 - 1) = 1$$

For a level of significance α the null hypothesis is rejected in favor of the alternative if the computed χ^2 test statistic exceeds the upper-tailed critical value from the χ^2 distribution having 1 degree of freedom. That is, the decision rule is to reject H_0 if

$$\chi^2 > \chi_1^2$$

This is illustrated in Figure 9.26.

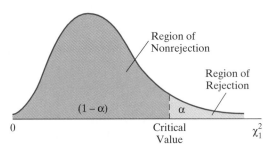

Figure 9.26   Regions of rejection and nonrejection when using the chi-square test for equality of proportions with level of significance α

If the null hypothesis were true, the computed χ^2 statistic should be close to zero, because the squared difference between what we actually observe in each cell, f_o, and what we theoretically expect, f_e, would be small. On the other hand, if H_0 is false, and there are real differences between the population proportions, we should expect the computed χ^2 statistic to be large. This is because the discrepancy between what we actually observe in each cell and what we theoretically expect will be magnified when we square the differences. Note that what constitutes a large difference in a cell is relative: The same actual difference between f_o and f_e contributes more to the χ^2 test statistic from a cell in which only a few observations are expected than from a cell where there are many observations expected.

To illustrate the use of the chi-square test for equality of two proportions, we turn our attention to the results of a major health study that has received much publicity. Hennekens investigated the effectiveness of aspirin in the reduction of the incidence of heart attacks, in a study begun in 1982 and completed in 1987. A total of 22,071 male physicians in the United States participated in the experiment. The physicians were randomly assigned to one of two groups. One group of 11,037 physicians took one 325-mg buffered aspirin tablet every other day. Of this group, 104 suffered heart attacks during the five-year period of the study. An additional 11,034 physicians were assigned to a group that took a placebo (that is, a pill that, unknown to the participants in the study, contained no active ingredients) every other day. In this group, 189 participants suffered heart attacks during the five-year period of the study. The results are displayed in Table 9.9.

The null hypothesis ($H_0: \pi_1 = \pi_2$) states that, when we are comparing the two groups, there is no difference between the proportions of participants who suffered a heart attack. Using Equation (9.10) on page 435, we can estimate the common

TABLE 9.9

CROSS-CLASSIFICATION OF OBSERVED HEART-ATTACK INCIDENCE BY STUDY GROUP

Results	Study Group		
	Aspirin	Placebo	Totals
Heart attack	104	189	293
No heart attack	10,933	10,845	21,778
Totals	11,037	11,034	22,071

Source: C. Hennekens, steering committee chair, "Preliminary Report: Findings from the Aspirin Component of the Ongoing Physician's Health Study," *New England Journal of Medicine,* 318, January 28, 1988, 262–264.

parameter π, the true proportion of male physicians in the United States who will suffer a heart attack in a five-year period. The overall or average proportion of male physicians who had a heart attack taken over both study groups is computed as follows:

$$\bar{p} = \frac{X_1 + X_2}{n_1 + n_2} = \frac{X}{n}$$

$$= \frac{(104 + 189)}{(11,037 + 11,034)} = \frac{293}{22,071}$$

$$= 0.0133$$

The estimated proportion of male physicians who will not suffer a heart attack in a five-year period is the complement, $(1 - \bar{p})$ or 0.9867. Multiplying these two proportions by the sample size used for each study group gives the number of physicians expected to have a heart attack and the number not expected to have a heart attack for each of the experimental groups when the null hypothesis is true. These expected frequencies are presented in Table 9.10.

TABLE 9.10

CROSS-CLASSIFICATION OF EXPECTED HEART-ATTACK INCIDENCE BY STUDY GROUP

Results	Study Group		
	Aspirin	Placebo	Totals
Heart attack	146.52	146.48	293
No heart attack	10,890.48	10,887.52	21,778
Totals	11,037.00	11,034.00	22,071

To test the null hypothesis of equality of proportions

$$H_0: \pi_1 = \pi_2$$

against the alternative that the true population proportions are not equal

$$H_1: \pi_1 \neq \pi_2$$

we use the observed and expected frequencies from Tables 9.9 and 9.10 to compute the chi-square test statistic given by Equation (9.9). The calculations are presented in Table 9.11.

If a 0.05 level of significance is chosen, the critical value of the χ^2 statistic is obtained from Table A.6, a portion of which is presented as Table 9.12.

TABLE 9.11

COMPUTATION OF THE CHI-SQUARE TEST STATISTIC FOR HEART-ATTACK INCIDENCE DATA

f_o	f_e	$(f_o - f_e)$	$(f_o - f_e)^2$	$(f_o - f_e)^2/f_e$
104	146.52	−42.52	1,807.9504	12.3393
189	146.48	42.52	1,807.9504	12.3426
10,933	10,890.48	42.52	1,807.9504	0.1660
10,845	10,887.52	−42.52	1,807.9504	0.1661
				$\chi^2 = 25.0140$

TABLE 9.12

DETERMINING THE CRITICAL VALUE FROM THE χ^2 TABLE FOR $\alpha = .05$ AND 1 DEGREE OF FREEDOM

Degrees of Freedom	Upper Tail Areas (α)								
	.995	.99	.975	...	.10	.05	.025	.01	.005
1			0.001	...	2.706	3.841	5.024	6.635	7.879
2	0.010	0.020	0.051	...	4.605	5.991	7.378	9.210	10.597
3	0.072	0.115	0.216	...	6.251	7.815	9.348	11.345	12.838
4	0.207	0.297	0.484	...	7.779	9.488	11.143	13.277	14.860
5	0.412	0.554	0.831	...	9.236	11.071	12.833	15.086	16.750

Source: Extracted from Table A.6.

The values in the body of this table refer to selected upper-tailed areas of the χ^2 distribution. Because a χ^2 test statistic for a 2×2 table has 1 degree of freedom, and because we test at the $\alpha = 0.05$ level of significance, the critical value of the χ^2 statistic is 3.841. Our computed test statistic χ^2 of 25.0140 exceeds this critical value, so the null hypothesis is rejected. At the 0.05 level of significance, there is sufficient evidence to conclude that the two study groups are different with respect to the proportion of male physicians in the United States who developed heart attacks. Since the proportion of physicians who had heart attacks in the aspirin group was significantly less than the proportion who had heart attacks in the placebo group we can conclude that aspirin is effective in decreasing the incidence of heart attacks in males.

Figures 9.27 illustrates output obtained from the PHStat add-in for Microsoft Excel for these data, while Figure 9.28 illustrates MINITAB output. The outputs present the observed and expected frequencies, the computed χ^2 test statistic, and the p-value. Because the p-value = 0.000000569 (or 5.69E-07), is less than $\alpha = 0.05$, the null hypothesis is rejected. There is evidence of a difference between the two proportions. The study group taking aspirin had a significantly lower incidence of heart attacks over the five-year study period.

	A	B	C	D	E	F
1	Heart Attack Incidence Study					
2						
3	Observed Frequencies:			Study Group		
4			Results	Aspirin	Placebo	Total
5			Heart Attack	104	189	293
6			No heart attack	10933	10845	21778
7			Total	11037	11034	22071
8						
9	Expected Frequencies:			Study Group		
10			Results	Aspirin	Placebo	Total
11			Heart Attack	146.519913	146.480087	293
12			No heart attack	10890.48009	10887.5199	21778
13			Total	11037	11034	22071
14						
15						
16	Level of Significance	0.05				
17	Number of Rows	2				
18	Number of Columns	2				
19	Degrees of Freedom	1				
20	Critical Value	3.841455				
21	Chi-Square Test Statistic	24.36638				
22	p-Value	5.69E-07				
23	Reject the null hypothesis					

Figure 9.27   PHStat add-in for Microsoft Excel output for the physician's health study

```
Expected counts are printed below observed counts

            C1        C2      Total
     1      104       189       293
          146.52    146.48


     2    10933     10845     21778
        10890.48  10887.52


Total    11037     11034     22071


Chi-Sq = 12.339 + 12.343 +
          0.166 +  0.166 = 25.014


DF = 1, P-Value = 0.000
```

Figure 9.28   MINITAB output for the physician's health study

CHECKING THE ASSUMPTIONS

For the χ^2 test to give accurate results, for a 2×2 table it is assumed that each expected frequency is at least 5. If this assumption is not satisfied, other procedures, such as Fisher's exact test (see Reference 2), can be used.

The Chi-Square Test for Differences in Proportions When Comparing More Than Two Groups

The chi-square method of testing for the difference between two proportions can be extended to the general case in which there are c independent populations to be compared. In such cases, the contingency table has two rows and c columns. To test the null hypothesis of no differences between the proportions among the c populations

$$H_0: \pi_1 = \pi_2 = \cdots = \pi_c$$

against the alternative that not all the c population proportions are equal

$$H_1: \text{Not all } \pi_j \text{ are equal (where } j = 1, 2, \ldots, c).$$

we use Equation (9.9) and compute the test statistic

$$\chi^2 = \sum_{\text{all cells}} \frac{(f_0 - f_e)^2}{f_e}$$

where

f_0 = observed frequency in a particular cell of a $2 \times c$ contingency table

f_e = theoretical or expected frequency in a particular cell if the null hypothesis is true

To compute the expected frequency, f_e, in any cell, we need to realize that, if the null hypothesis were true and the proportions were equal across all c populations, then the c sample proportions should differ from each other only by chance, because they would each be providing estimates of the common population parameter π. In such a situation, a statistic that pools or combines these c separate estimates together into one overall or average estimate of the population parameter π provides more information than any one of the c separate estimates alone. Expanding on Equation (9.10) on page 435, the statistic $\bar{p}$ represents the overall or average proportion for all c groups combined:

$$\bar{p} = \frac{X_1 + X_2 + \cdots + X_c}{n_1 + n_2 + \cdots + n_c} = \frac{X}{n} \tag{9.11}$$

To obtain the expected frequency, f_e, for each cell in the first row in the contingency table, we multiply each sample size (or column total) by $\bar{p}$. To obtain the expected frequency, f_e, for each cell in the second row in the contingency table, we multiply each sample size (or column total) by $(1 - \bar{p})$.

The test statistic shown in Equation (9.9) approximately follows a chi-square (χ^2) distribution with degrees of freedom equal to the number of rows in the contingency table minus 1 times the number of columns in the table minus 1. For a $2 \times c$ contingency table, there are $c - 1$ degrees of freedom; that is,

$$\text{degrees of freedom} = (2 - 1)(c - 1) = c - 1$$

For a level of significance α, the null hypothesis is rejected in favor of the alternative if the computed χ^2 test statistic exceeds the upper-tailed critical value from the χ^2 distribution having $c - 1$ degrees of freedom. That is, the decision rule is to reject H_0 if

$$\chi^2 > \chi^2_{\alpha, c-1}$$

This is depicted in Figure 9.29.

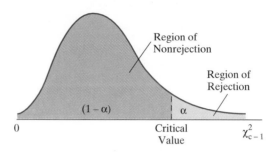

Figure 9.29   Regions of rejection and nonrejection when using the chi-square test for the equality of c proportions with level of significance α

CHECKING THE ASSUMPTIONS

For the χ^2 test to give accurate results when dealing with $2 \times c$ contingency tables, all expected frequencies must be large. For such situations, there has been much debate among statisticians as to the definition of "large." Some statistical researchers (see Reference 3) have found that the test gives accurate results as long as all expected frequencies equal or exceed 0.5. Other statisticians, more conservative in their approach, require that no more than 20% of the cells contain expected frequencies less than 5 and no cells have expected frequencies less than 1. We suggest that a reasonable compromise between these points of view is to make sure that all expected frequencies are at least 1. To accomplish this, it may be necessary to collapse two or more low-frequency categories into one category in the contingency table prior to performing the test. Such merging of categories usually results in expected frequencies sufficiently large to conduct the χ^2 test accurately. If the combining or pooling of categories is undesirable, alternative procedures are available (see References 1 and 2).

To illustrate the chi-square test for equality of proportions when there are more than two groups, let us suppose that a food processing plant funnels its baked cookies to sealing machines used for product packaging. In monitoring the process, the product manager finds that the quality of the seals as defined by the proportion of defective seals is stable, but at an unacceptably high level. The manager feels that the temperature setting on the sealing machine may affect the quality of the seals. Therefore, an experiment is designed in which five different temperature settings are evaluated. At each temperature setting, 500 boxes are sealed and evaluated for their seal quality. Table 9.13 presents the number of boxes with defective and nondefective package seals at each of the five temperature settings.

Under the null hypothesis of no differences between the proportions of defective or nonconforming seals obtained at the five temperature levels, we can

TABLE 9.13

CROSS-CLASSIFICATION OF OBSERVED FREQUENCIES FROM SEALING MACHINE TEMPERATURE-SETTING EXPERIMENT

| Packaging Result | Sealing Machine Temperature Setting | | | | | |
	A	B	C	D	E	Totals
Defective seals	22	20	34	23	41	140
Nondefective seals	478	480	466	477	459	2,360
Totals	500	500	500	500	500	2,500

use Equation (9.11) to calculate an estimate of the common parameter π, the population proportion of defective seals. That is, $\bar{p}$, the overall or average proportion of defective seals taken over all five temperature levels, is computed as follows:

$$\bar{p} = \frac{X_1 + X_2 + \cdots + X_c}{n_1 + n_2 + \cdots + n_c} = \frac{X}{n}$$

$$= \frac{(22 + 20 + 34 + 23 + 41)}{(500 + 500 + 500 + 500 + 500)} = \frac{140}{2,500}$$

$$= 0.056$$

The estimated proportion of nondefective or conforming seals in the population is the complement, $(1 - \bar{p})$ or .944. Multiplying each of these two proportions by the sample size used for each temperature setting results in the expected frequencies of defective and nondefective seals presented in Table 9.14.

TABLE 9.14

CROSS-CLASSIFICATION OF EXPECTED FREQUENCIES FROM SEALING MACHINE TEMPERATURE-SETTING EXPERIMENT

| Packaging Result | Sealing Machine Temperature Setting | | | | | |
	A	B	C	D	E	Totals
Defective Seals	28	28	28	28	28	140
Nondefective seals	472	472	472	472	472	2,360
Totals	500	500	500	500	500	2,500

To test the null hypothesis of homogeneity or equality of proportions

$$H_0: \pi_1 = \pi_2 = \pi_3 = \pi_4 = \pi_5$$

against the alternative that not all the five proportions are equal

$$H_1: \text{Not all } \pi_j \text{ are equal (where } j = 1, 2, \ldots, 5)$$

we use the observed and expected data from Tables 9.13 and 9.14 to compute the chi-square test statistic given by Equation (9.9). The calculations are presented in Table 9.15 on page 443.

TABLE 9.15

COMPUTATION OF THE CHI-SQUARE TEST STATISTIC FOR SEALING MACHINE TEMPERATURE-SETTING EXPERIMENT

f_o	f_e	$(f_o - f_e)$	$(f_o - f_e)^2$	$(f_o - f_e)^2/f_e$
22	28	−6	36	1.2857
20	28	−8	64	2.2857
34	28	6	36	1.2857
23	28	−5	25	0.8929
41	28	13	169	6.0357
478	472	6	36	0.0763
480	472	8	64	0.1356
466	472	−6	36	0.0763
477	472	5	25	0.0530
459	472	−13	169	0.3581
				$\chi^2 = \overline{12.4850}$

TABLE 9.16

DETERMINING THE CRITICAL VALUE FROM THE χ^2 TABLE FOR $\alpha = .05$ AND 4 DEGREES OF FREEDOM

Degrees of Freedom	Upper Tail Areas (α)								
	.995	.99	.975	...	.10	.05	.025	.01	.005
1			0.001	...	2.706	3.841	5.024	6.635	7.879
2	0.010	0.020	0.051	...	4.605	5.991	7.378	9.210	10.597
3	0.072	0.115	0.216	...	6.251	7.815	9.348	11.345	12.838
4	0.207	0.297	0.484	...	7.779	9.488	11.143	13.277	14.860
5	0.412	0.554	0.831	...	9.236	11.071	12.833	15.086	16.750

Source: Extracted from Table A.6

If a 0.05 level of significance is chosen, the critical value of the χ^2 statistic is obtained from Table A.6, a portion of which is presented as Table 9.16.
The values in the body of this table refer to selected upper-tailed areas of the χ^2 distribution. In our sealing-temperature experiment, there are five temperature levels being evaluated, so there are $(5 - 1) = 4$ degrees of freedom. The critical value of χ^2 with 4 degrees of freedom at the $\alpha = 0.05$ level of significance is 9.488. Our computed test statistic $\chi^2 = 12.4850$ exceeds this critical value, so the null hypothesis is rejected. (See Figure 9.30 on page 444.) We can state that, at the 0.05

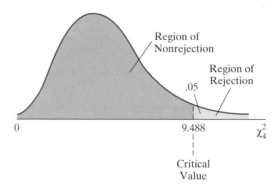

Figure 9.30 Testing for the equality of five proportions at the 0.05 level of significance with 4 degrees of freedom

level of significance, there is sufficient evidence to conclude that at least one of the five sealing temperatures is different with respect to the proportion of defective boxes produced.

Figures 9.31 illustrates output obtained from the PHStat add-in for Microsoft Excel for these data, while Figure 9.32 illustrates MINITAB output. The outputs present the observed and expected frequencies, the computed χ^2 test statistic, and the p-value. Because the p-value $= 0.014$ is less than $\alpha = 0.05$, the null hypothesis is rejected. There is evidence to conclude that at least one of the five sealing temperatures is different with respect to the proportion of defective boxes produced.

	A	B	C	D	E	F	G	H	I
1	Sealing Machine Temperature Study								
2									
3	Observed Frequencies:					Temperature Setting			
4			Result	A	B	C	D	E	Total
5			Defective seal	22	20	34	23	41	140
6			Nondefective seal	478	480	466	477	459	2360
7			Total	500	500	500	500	500	2500
8									
9	Expected Frequencies:					Temperature Setting			
10			Result	A	B	C	D	E	Total
11			Defective seal	28	28	28	28	28	140
12			Nondefective seal	472	472	472	472	472	2360
13			Total	500	500	500	500	500	2500
14									
15									
16	Level of Significance	0.05							
17	Number of Rows	2							
18	Number of Columns	5							
19	Degrees of Freedom	4							
20	Critical Value	9.487728							
21	Chi-Square Test Statistic	12.48485							
22	p-Value	0.014087							
23	Reject the null hypothesis								

Figure 9.31 PHStat add-in for Microsoft Excel output for the Sealing Machine Temperature-Setting Experiment

```
Expected counts are printed below observed counts

            C1        C2        C3        C4        C5      Total
   1        22        20        34        23        41        140
          28.00     28.00     28.00     28.00     28.00

   2       478       480       466       477       459       2360
         472.00    472.00    472.00    472.00    472.00

Total      500       500       500       500       500       2500

Chi-Sq =   1.286 +   2.286 +   1.286 +   0.893 +   6.036 +
           0.076 +   0.136 +   0.076 +   0.053 +   0.358 = 12.485
DF = 4, P-Value = 0.014
```

Figure 9.32   MINITAB output for the Sealing Machine Temperature-Setting Experiment

PROBLEMS

9.30 The following data represent the bivariate responses to two questions asked in a survey of 40 college students majoring in engineering—Gender (Male = M; Female = F) and Major (Computer Science = C; Electrical = E; Other = O).

Gender: M M M F M F F M F M F M M M M F F M
F F M M M M F M F F M M F M M M M F
M F M M

Major: E C C O E C E E C C E E E O C O E E E
C C C E E O O C E E E C C E E E E C C
E C

(a) Tally the data into a 2 × 3 contingency table where the two rows represent the gender categories and the three columns represent the student major categories.

(b) At the 0.05 level of significance, determine whether there is a relationship between gender and major.

(c) Determine the p-value in (b) and interpret its meaning.

9.31 As part of a study of lifestyle and women's health, it was found that, out of 32 women who smoked, 22 showed signs of osteoporosis, while 10 did not. Out of a sample of 44 women who did not smoke, 16 showed signs of osteoporosis, while 28 did not.

(a) At the 0.05 level of significance, determine whether there is a relationship between lifestyle and osteoporosis.

(b) Determine the p-value in (a) and interpret its meaning.

9.32 The results of a study made as part of a yield improvement effort at a semiconductor manufacturing facility provided defect data for a sample of 450 wafers. The following table presents a summary of the responses to two questions: "Was a particle found on the die that produced the wafer?" and "Is the wafer good or bad?"

CROSS-CLASSIFICATION OF CONDITION OF DIE AND WAFER QUALITY

Quality of Wafer	Condition of Die		
	No Particles	Particles	Totals
Good	320	14	334
Bad	80	36	116
Totals	400	50	450

Source: Hall, S. W., Analysis of Defectivity of Semiconductor Wafers by Contingency Table. *Proceedings Institute of Environmental Sciences,* Vol. 1, (1994), 177–183.

(a) At the 0.05 level of significance, determine whether there is a relationship between the condition of the die and the quality of the wafer.

(b) Determine the *p*-value in (a) and interpret its meaning.

(c) What conclusions do you draw from this analysis?

9.33 A computer engineer studied the differences between an unoptimized and an optimized program and found that of the 319 references in the unoptimized program, 186 were register references, 45 were immediate references, and 88 were indirect references. For the optimized program, there were 164 references, of which 88 were register references, 29 were immediate references, and 47 were indirect references.

(a) At the 0.05 level of significance, determine whether there is a relationship between the type of program and the type of references.

(b) Determine the *p*-value in (a) and interpret its meaning.

9.34 Each day, at a large hospital, several hundred laboratory tests are performed. The rate at which these tests are improperly done for a variety of reasons (and thereby need to be redone) seems steady at about 4 percent. In an effort to get at the root cause of these nonconformances (tests that need to be redone), the director of the lab decides to keep records for a period of one week of the nonconformances, subdivided by the shift of workers who performed the lab tests. The results were as follows:

	Shift		
Lab Tests Performed	Day	Evening	Totals
Nonconforming	16	24	40
Conforming	654	306	960
Totals	670	330	1000

(a) At the 0.05 level of significance, determine whether there is a difference between the proportions of nonconforming lab tests performed between the two shifts.

(b) Determine the *p*-value in (a) and interpret its meaning.

9.35 Dr. Lawrence K. Altman reported the results of a clinical trial (*The New York Times*, May 1, 1993, p. 7) comparing the effectiveness of four drug regimens randomly assigned for treatment of patients following the onset of a heart attack. A total of 40,845 patients were studied. Each was given one of the four drug regimens. The outcome measure compared was the proportion of severe adverse events (i.e., death or disabling stroke) reported within 30 days of treatment. His data are presented here:

	Drug Regimen				
Result	A	B	C	D	Totals
Severe	714	785	754	820	3,073
Not severe	9,630	9,543	9,042	9,557	37,772
Totals	10,344	10,328	9,796	10,377	40,845

where

A = accelerated TPA with intravenous heparin

B = combined TPA and streptokinase, with intravenous heparin

C = streptokinase with subcutaneous heparin

D = streptokinase with intravenous heparin

(a) At the $\alpha = 0.05$ level of significance, determine whether there is evidence of a significant difference among the four drug regimens with respect to the proportion of patients suffering severe adverse events (i.e., death or disabling stroke) within 30 days following treatment for heart attack.

(b) Discuss the impact that your findings may have on the community of health care administrators and policymakers if a dose of TPA costs $2,400 per patient, while a dose of streptokinase costs $240 per patient.

9.36 The quality-control manager of an automobile parts factory would like to know whether there is a difference between the proportions of defective parts produced on different days of the work week. Random samples of 100 parts produced on each day of the week were selected, with the following results:

Result	Mon.	Tues.	Wed.	Thurs.	Fri.
Number of defective parts	12	7	7	10	14
Number of acceptable parts	88	93	93	90	86
Totals	100	100	100	100	100

(a) At the 0.05 level of significance, is there evidence of a significant difference in the proportion of defective parts produced on the various days of the week?

(b) What would be your answer to (a) and (b) if 24 of the 100 parts produced on Friday were defective?

9.8 χ^2 TEST OF HYPOTHESIS FOR THE VARIANCE OR STANDARD DEVIATION (*OPTIONAL TOPIC*)

When analyzing numerical data, it is sometimes important to draw conclusions about the variability as well as the average of a characteristic of interest. For example, recall that, in the study of the diameter of ball bearings (described in Section 9.3), we assumed that the standard deviation σ is equal to 0.004 inch. Suppose, however, we are now interested in determining whether there is evidence that the standard deviation has changed from the previously specified level of 0.004 inch. In such a situation, we are interested in drawing conclusions about the population standard deviation σ.

In attempting to draw conclusions about the variability in the population, we first must determine what test statistic can be used to represent the distribution of the variability in the sample data. If the variable is assumed to be normally distributed, then the χ^2-test statistic for testing whether the population variance or standard deviation is equal to a specified value is computed as follows.

χ^2 TEST FOR THE VARIANCE OR STANDARD DEVIATION

$$\chi^2 = \frac{(n-1)s^2}{\sigma^2} \tag{9.12}$$

where

    n = sample size

    s^2 = sample variance

    σ^2 = hypothesized population variance

For a given sample size, n, the test statistic χ^2 follows a chi-square distribution with $n-1$ degrees of freedom. As we have seen in Sections 8.4 and 9.7, a chi-square distribution is a skewed distribution, whose shape depends solely on its number of degrees of freedom. Table A.6 contains various upper-tail areas for chi-square distributions pertaining to different degrees of freedom. A portion of this table is displayed as Table 9.17 on page 448.

The value at the top of each column indicates the area in the upper portion (or right side) of a particular chi-square distribution. As examples, with 24 degrees of freedom, the critical value of the χ^2 test statistic corresponding to an upper-tail area of 0.025 is 39.364, while the critical value corresponding to an upper-tail area of 0.975 (that is, a lower-tail area of 0.025) is 12.401. These are seen in Figure 9.33 on page 448. This means that, for 24 degrees of freedom, the probability of equaling or exceeding the critical value of 12.401 is 0.975, while the probability of equaling or exceeding the critical value of 39.364 is 0.025. By subtraction, the probability that a χ^2 test statistic falls between the critical values of 12.401 and 39.364 is 0.95. Therefore, once we determine the level of significance and the degrees of freedom, any critical value of the χ^2 test statistic can be found for a particular chi-square distribution.

To apply the test of hypothesis, let us again return to the ball-bearing example. We are interested in determining whether there is evidence that the standard deviation has changed from the previously specified level of 0.004 inch. Thus, we

TABLE 9.17

OBTAINING THE CRITICAL VALUES FROM THE CHI-SQUARE DISTRIBUTION WITH 24 DEGREES OF FREEDOM

Degrees of Freedom	Upper-Tail Area									
	.995	.99	.975	.95	.90	.75	.25	.10	.05	.025
1	...	...	0.001	0.004	0.016	0.102	1.323	2.706	3.841	5.024
2	0.010	0.020	0.051	0.103	0.211	0.575	2.773	4.605	5.991	7.378
3	0.072	0.115	0.216	0.352	0.584	1.213	4.108	6.251	7.815	9.348
⋮	⋮	⋮	⋮	⋮	⋮	⋮	⋮	⋮	⋮	⋮
23	9.260	10.196	11.689	13.091	14.848	18.137	27.141	32.007	35.172	38.076
24	9.886	10.856	12.401	13.848	15.659	19.037	28.241	33.196	36.415	39.364
25	10.520	11.524	13.120	14.611	16.473	19.939	29.339	34.382	37.652	40.646

Source: Extracted from Table A.6

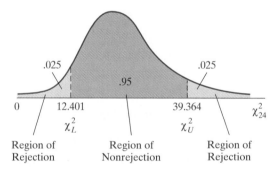

Figure 9.33   Determining the lower and upper critical values of a chi-square distribution with 24 degrees of freedom corresponding to a 0.95 level of confidence or a 0.05 level of significance for a two-tailed test of hypothesis about a population variance or standard deviation

have a two-tailed test in which the null and alternative hypotheses can be stated as follows:

$$H_0: \sigma = 0.004 \text{ inch. (or } \sigma^2 = 0.000016 \text{ "inches squared")}$$

$$H_1: \sigma \neq 0.004 \text{ inch. (or } \sigma^2 \neq 0.000016 \text{ "inches squared")}$$

If a sample of 25 ball bearings is selected, the null hypothesis is rejected if the χ^2 test statistic falls into either the lower or upper tail of a chi-square distribution with $25 - 1 = 24$ degrees of freedom, as shown in Figure 9.33. From Equation (9.12), the χ^2 test statistic falls into the lower tail of the chi-square distribution if the sample standard deviation (s) is sufficiently smaller than the hypothesized σ of 0.004 inch; it falls into the upper tail if s is sufficiently larger than 0.004 inch. From Table 9.17 (a replica of Table A.6, the table of the chi-square distribution) and from Figure 9.33, we observe that, if a level of significance of 0.05 is selected, the lower

(χ_L^2) and upper (χ_U^2) critical values are 12.401 and 39.364, respectively. Therefore, the decision rule is as follows:

$$\text{Reject } H_0 \text{ if } \chi^2 > \chi_U^2 = 39.364 \text{ or}$$
$$\text{if } \chi^2 < \chi_L^2 = 12.401$$

otherwise do not reject H_0.

Suppose that from the sample of 25 ball bearings, the standard deviation (s) is computed to be 0.0042 inch. To test the null hypothesis at the 0.05 level of significance by using Equation (9.12), we write

$$\chi^2 = \frac{(n-1)s^2}{\sigma^2} = \frac{(25-1)(0.0042^2)}{0.004^2} = 26.40$$

Note that 26.40, the computed value of the χ^2 test statistic, falls between the lower- and upper-tailed critical values of 12.401 and 39.364. Because $\chi_L^2 = 12.401 < \chi^2 = 26.40 < \chi_U^2 = 39.364$, we do not reject H_0. We conclude that there is little evidence that the actual process (that is, population) standard deviation is different from 0.004 inch.

The χ^2 test for the variance or standard deviation is considered a *classical parametric* procedure, one that makes assumptions, that must hold if we are to be assured that the results we obtain from employing the test are valid. Assumptions for the χ^2 test for the variance or standard deviation are presented in the following Comment box.

COMMENT: CHECKING THE ASSUMPTIONS OF THE χ^2 TEST FOR THE VARIANCE OR STANDARD DEVIATION

In testing a hypothesis about a population variance or a standard deviation, we assume that the data in the population are normally distributed. Unfortunately, this χ^2 test statistic is quite sensitive to departures from this assumption (i.e., it is not a *robust* test), and so, if the population is not normally distributed, particularly for small sample sizes, the accuracy of the test can be seriously affected. (See Reference 8.)

www.prenhall.com

PROBLEMS

9.37 Determine the lower- and upper-tail critical values of χ^2 for each of the following two-tailed tests:
(a) $\alpha = 0.01, n = 26$
(b) $\alpha = 0.05, n = 17$
(b) $\alpha = 0.10, n = 14$

9.38 A manufacturer of candy must monitor the temperature at which the candies are cooked. Too much variation will cause inconsistency in the taste of the candy. Past records show that the standard deviation of the temperature has been 1.2 degrees F. A random sample of 30 batches of candy is selected and the sample standard deviation of the temperature is 2.1 degrees F.

(a) At the 0.05 level of significance, is there evidence that the population standard deviation has increased above 1.2 degrees F?
(b) What assumptions are being made in order to perform this test?
(c) Compute the p-value in (a) and interpret its meaning.

9.39 A manufacturer of doorknobs has a production process that is designed to provide a doorknob with a target diameter of 2.5 inches. In the past, the standard deviation of the diameter has been 0.035 inch. In an effort to reduce the variation in the process, various studies have taken place that have resulted in a redesigned process. A sample of 25 doorknobs produced under the new process indicates a sample standard deviation of 0.025 inch.

(a) At the 0.05 level of significance, is there evidence that the population standard deviation is less than 0.035 inch in the new process?

(b) What assumptions are made in order to perform this test?

(c) Compute the p-value in (a) and interpret its meaning.

9.40 In construction, it is necessary to use materials with reliable, known strengths. Joist and plank size, grade No. 1, Hem-Fir wood is commonly used in agricultural structures, and agricultural engineers who use such wood believe that it has yield strength which is normally distributed with $\mu = 7,000$ psi and $\sigma = 875$ psi. Suppose it is reasonable to assume that the population of such strengths is normally distributed. To examine the yield strength of such Hem-Fir, six pieces were subjected to a compression machine until failure, with the following results (in psi).

7512	7620	6982	7256	6766	7145

HEM-FIR

Even if the mean is large enough for construction purposes, the standard deviation should also be small. Otherwise, while there would be pieces of wood much stronger than necessary, there would also be pieces too weak for construction. Using a level of significance of 0.05, is there evidence that σ is more than 875 psi?

9.41 Milk obtained from cows has an average fat composition of 4.0%. In *Causes Of Milk-Fat Test Variation* at *DHIA* (Extension Circular #340, College of Agricultural Sciences, Pennsylvania State University), Heald, Scibilia, & Barnard reported on the results of a DHIA (Dairy Herd Improvement Association) analysis on raw milk to determine the percent fat composition. Thirty-one days of data on the differences in the percent of fat from the monthly average follow.

DIFFERENCE IN MILK FAT

0.152	−0.048	0.152	−0.048	−0.548
0.052	0.652	−0.048	0.352	0.352
0.052	0.152	0.248	−0.348	0.052
−0.448	0.352	−0.048	−0.248	0.052
−0.248	−0.048	−0.048	−0.348	−0.148
0.352	−0.048	0.252	0.052	−0.148
0.052				

MILKFAT

Assuming that these represent a sample from a normally distributed population, is there evidence, at the 0.01 level of significance, that the population standard deviation of these differences exceeds 0.100?

9.42 Scientists interested in the natural environment have attempted to construct computer models of the Earth that are able to predict climate and weather. A study was carried out of the errors made by computer models trying to predict surface temperature under various environmental conditions. The errors (°K) made by a sample of one of the models (°K) follow:

−1.99	−1.37	−0.80	−0.25	0.27	0.76
1.24	1.69	2.13	2.56	2.97	3.42

CLIMATE2

Assuming that the population is normally distributed, is there evidence at the 0.05 level that the standard deviation is greater than 1.00°K?

9.43 Data were collected on the amount of free memory during peak usage times of the AIX system on a university campus. The unit used was a real memory page (4096 bytes), and the results from a sample of $n = 12$ were as follows:

1493	1319	1253	1651	1812	1682
1737	1193	1893	1532	1717	1842

MEMORY

Suppose the free memory is normally distributed. Using a significance level of 0.05, is there evidence that the standard deviation in the population of free memory during peak usage times is different from 100?

9.9 WILCOXON RANK SUM TEST FOR THE DIFFERENCE BETWEEN TWO MEDIANS (*OPTIONAL TOPIC*)

In Section 9.4, we evaluated the difference between the means of samples taken from two independent populations. If sample sizes are small, and if we cannot make the assumption that the data in each group are taken from normally distributed populations, two choices exist. We can use either the pooled-variance t test or separate-variance t test following some *normalizing transformation* on the data (see Reference 9), or we can employ some nonparametric procedure that does not depend on the assumption of normality for the two populations.

In this section, we introduce the Wilcoxon rank sum test, a widely used, very simple, and powerful nonparametric procedure for testing for differences between the medians of two populations (M_1 and M_2). The Wilcoxon rank sum test has proven to be almost as powerful as the pooled- and separate-variance t tests under conditions appropriate to these tests and is likely to be more powerful when the stringent assumptions of those tests are not met. In addition, the Wilcoxon rank sum test is a procedure to choose when only ordinal-scale data can be obtained. The t tests are not used in such situations, because these procedures require that the obtained data be measured on at least an interval scale.

To perform the Wilcoxon rank sum test, we replace the observations in the two samples of size n_1 and n_2 by their combined ranks (unless the obtained data contained the ranks initially). Let $n = n_1 + n_2$ be the total number of observations in both samples. The ranks are assigned in such a manner that rank 1 is given to the smallest of the $n = n_1 + n_2$ combined observations, rank 2 is given to the second smallest, and so on, until rank n is given to the largest. If several values are tied, we assign each the average of the ranks that would otherwise have been assigned had there been no ties.

For convenience, whenever the two sample sizes are unequal, we let n_1 represent the smaller-sized sample and n_2 the larger-sized sample. The Wilcoxon rank sum test statistic T_1 is chosen as the sum of the ranks assigned to the n_1 observations in the smaller sample. (For equal-sized samples, either group can be selected for determining T_1.)

For any integer value n, the sum of the first n consecutive integers is calculated as $n(n + 1)/2$. The test statistic T_1 plus the sum of the ranks assigned to the n_2 items in the second sample, T_2, must therefore be equal to this value, as illustrated in Equation (9.13).

CHECKING THE RANKINGS

$$T_1 + T_2 = \frac{n(n + 1)}{2} \tag{9.13}$$

When the sizes of the samples, n_1 and n_2, are both less than or equal to 10, we can use Table A.8 to obtain the critical values of the test statistic T_1 for both one- and two-tailed tests at various levels of significance. For a two-tailed test and for a particular level of significance, α, if the computed value of T_1 equals or exceeds the upper critical value or is less than or equal to the lower critical value, the null hypothesis is rejected. For one-tailed tests having the alternative H_1: $M_1 < M_2$, the decision rule is to reject the null hypothesis if the observed value of T_1 is less than or equal to the lower critical value. For one-tailed tests having the alternative H_1: $M_1 > M_2$, the decision rule is to reject the null hypothesis if the observed value of T_1 equals or exceeds the upper critical value.

For large sample sizes, the test statistic T_1 is approximately normally distributed with mean μ_{T_1} and standard deviation σ_{T_1}. The mean value of the test statistic T_1, μ_{T_1}, is computed as

$$\mu_{T_1} = \frac{n_1(n + 1)}{2}$$

and σ_{T_1}, the standard deviation of T_1, is calculated as

$$\sigma_{T_1} = \sqrt{\frac{n_1 n_2 (n + 1)}{12}}$$

Therefore, the standardized Z test statistic is defined in Equation (9.14) as follows.

"LARGE SAMPLE" WILCOXON RANK SUM TEST STATISTIC

$$Z = \frac{T_1 - \mu_{T_1}}{\sigma_{T_1}} \tag{9.14}$$

This large-sample approximation formula is used for testing the null hypothesis when sample sizes are outside the range of Table A.8.

For any α, the level of significance selected, the null hypothesis is rejected if the computed Z value falls in the appropriate region of rejection, depending on whether a two-tailed or a one-tailed test is used.

To demonstrate the use of the Wilcoxon rank sum test, suppose that a soft drink distributor is interested in obtaining more uniform fill heights in bottles filled during the bottling process. Available machinery fills each bottle; however, there is variation around the specified target height of the soft drink filled. One variable that must be controlled in the filling process is the operating pressure. Two dial settings, 25 and 30 psi, are to be studied during an experiment in filling performance with 10 bottles filled at each of these two operating pressure levels. One question that needs to be answered is whether there is evidence of a significant difference in the deviation from the specified target for bottles filled under settings that permit either 25 or 30 psi of operating pressure. If we do not wish to make the stringent assumption that the samples were taken from populations that are normally distributed, the Wilcoxon rank sum test can be used for evaluating possible differences in the median deviation in the specified target amount of soda fill. The data for this are shown in Table 9.18.

TABLE 9.18

COMPARING SOFT DRINK BOTTLE FILLS BASED ON TWO DIFFERENT PRESSURE SETTINGS

Pressure Settings									
25 psi									
−2.8	−1.6	0.2	1.2	−2.0	−1.0	1.4	3.4	0.6	0.9
30 psi									
0.2	2.1	2.6	0.4	1.7	3.3	1.6	4.0	2.7	3.4

Note: A "negative deviation" from target indicates the amount a bottle is underfilled in millimeters and a "positive deviation" shows the amount a bottle is overfilled in millimeters.

We do not specify which of the dial settings is likely to possess a greater median deviation from the specified target, so the test is two-tailed, and the following null and alternative hypotheses are established:

H_0: $M_1 = M_2$ (the median deviations from target are equal)

H_1: $M_1 \neq M_2$ (the median deviations from target are different)

TABLE 9.19

FORMING THE COMBINED RANKS

Pressure Settings			
25 psi ($n_1 = 10$)	Combined Rank	30 psi ($n_2 = 10$)	Combined Rank
−2.8	1	0.2	5.5
−1.6	3	2.1	14
0.2	5.5	2.6	15
1.2	10	0.4	7
−2.0	2	1.7	13
−1.0	4	3.3	17
1.4	11	1.6	12
3.4	18.5	4.0	20
0.6	8	2.7	16
0.9	9	3.4	18.5

Source: Data are taken from Table 9.18.

To perform the Wilcoxon rank sum test, we form the combined ranking of the deviations from the specified target obtained from the $n_1 = 10$ bottles filled under an operating pressure level of 25 psi and the $n_2 = 10$ bottles filled under an operating pressure level of 30 psi. The combined ranking of the deviations is displayed in Table 9.19.

We then obtain the test statistic T_1, the sum of the ranks assigned to the *smaller* sample. When the sample sizes are equal, as in our case, we select either sample as the group from which to obtain the test statistic T_1. Here, we arbitrarily choose the dial setting with an operating pressure level of 25 psi as our first sample. Therefore,

$$T_1 = 1 + 3 + 5.5 + 10 + 2 + 4 + 11 + 18.5 + 8 + 9 = 72$$

As a check on the ranking procedure, we also obtain T_2

$$T_2 = 5.5 + 14 + 15 + 7 + 13 + 17 + 12 + 20 + 16 + 18.5 = 138$$

We then use Equation (9.13) to show that the sum of the first $n = 20$ integers in the combined ranking is equal to $T_1 + T_2$:

$$T_1 + T_2 = \frac{n(n + 1)}{2}$$

$$72 + 138 = \frac{20(21)}{2} = 210$$

To test the null hypothesis of no difference between the median deviations from specified target fill in the two populations, we use Table A.8 to determine the lower- and upper-tail critical values for the test statistic T_1 in our two-tailed test. From Table 9.20, a replica of Table A.8, we note that, for a level of significance of 0.05, the critical values are 78 and 132. The decision rule is therefore

Reject H_0 if $T_1 \leq 78$ or if $T_1 \geq 132$;

otherwise do not reject H_0.

TABLE 9.20

OBTAINING THE LOWER- AND UPPER-TAIL CRITICAL VALUES
FOR THE WILCOXON RANK SUM TEST STATISTIC T_1 WHERE
$n_1 = 10$, $n_2 = 10$, AND $\alpha = .05$

			n_1						
	α		4	5	6	7	8	9	10
n_2	One-Tailed	Two-Tailed				(Lower, Upper)			
9	0.05	0.10	16,40	24,51	33,63	43,76	54,90	66,105	
	0.025	0.05	14,42	22,53	31,65	40,79	51,93	62,109	
	0.01	0.02	13,43	20,55	28,68	37,82	47,97	59,112	
	0.005	0.01	11,45	18,57	26,70	35,84	45,99	56,115	
10	0.05	0.10	17,43	26,54	35,67	45,81	56,96	69,111	82,128
	0.025	0.05	15,45	23,57	32,70	42,84	53,99	65,115	78,132
	0.01	0.02	13,47	21,59	29,73	39,87	49,103	61,119	74,136
	0.005	0.01	12,48	19,61	27,75	37,89	47,105	58,122	71,139

Source: Extracted from Table A.8

Because the test statistic $T_1 = 72 < 78$, we reject H_0. There is evidence of significant difference between the median deviations from the specified target fill level. The operating pressure level dial setting of 25 psi is superior to the setting of 30 psi, because the sample median deviation (0.40 mm) obtained from 25 psi dial setting is closer to the specified target than is the sample median deviation (2.35) obtained from the 30 psi dial setting. From the MINITAB output in Figure 9.34, we observe that the p-value is 0.014, which is less than $\alpha = 0.05$.

```
Mann-Whitney Confidence Interval and Test

25PSI        N =   10      Median =        0.400
30PSI        N =   10      Median =        2.350
Point estimate for ETA1-ETA2 is       -2.150
95.5 Percent CI for ETA1-ETA2 is (-3.701,-0.600)
W = 72.0
Test of ETA1 = ETA2   vs   ETA1 not = ETA2 is significant at 0.0140
The test is significant at 0.0139 (adjusted for ties)
```

Figure 9.34   Wilcoxon Rank Sum test output for the soft drink fill example obtained from MINITAB

We note that MINITAB provides output for the *Mann-Whitney U test*, which is numerically equivalent to our Wilcoxon rank sum test. (See References 1 and 2.) From Figure 9.34, we note that ETA1 and ETA2 refer to our hypothesized population medians M_1 and M_2. Also, the test statistic $W = 72$ is our test statistic T_1. The actual p-value for this two-tailed hypothesis test is 0.0139, adjusted for ties in the rankings. Although we should use these adjusted p-values in making our statistical decisions, a discussion of such adjustments is beyond the scope of this text. (See References 1 and 2.)

We note that Table A.8 (lower and upper critical values of the Wilcoxon rank sum test statistic T_1) provides critical values only for situations involving small samples, that is, where both n_1 and n_2 are less than or equal to 10. If either one or both of the sample sizes exceeds 10, the large-sample Z approximation formula (Equation 9.14) must be used to perform the test of hypothesis. Nevertheless, to demonstrate the effectiveness of the large-sample Z approximation formula, even for small sample sizes, we use it for the bottle-filling data. We use the large-sample Z approximation formula given by Equation (9.14):

$$Z = \frac{T_1 - \mu_{T_1}}{\sigma_{T_1}}$$

and compute the Z test statistic:

$$Z = \frac{T_1 - \mu_{T_1}}{\sigma_{T_1}}$$

where

$$\mu_{T_1} = \frac{n_1(n+1)}{2} = \frac{10(21)}{2} = 105$$

$$\sigma_{T_1} = \sqrt{\frac{n_1 n_2 (n+1)}{12}} = \sqrt{\frac{10(10)(21)}{12}} = 13.23$$

and

$$Z = \frac{72 - 105}{13.23} = -2.49$$

Because $Z = -2.49 < -1.96$, the critical value of Z at the 0.05 level of significance, the decision is to reject H_0. The null hypothesis is rejected because the test statistic Z has fallen into the region of rejection. The p-value, obtained from the PHStat add-in for Microsoft Excel (as displayed in Figure 9.35), is 0.013, which is less than $\alpha = 0.05$.

	A	B	C	D	E	F	G
1	Wilcoxon rank Sum Test for Differences in Bottle Fills						
2							
3	Level of Significance	0.05					
4	Population 1 Sample						
5	Sample Size	10					
6	Sum of Ranks	72					
7	Population 2 Sample						
8	Sample Size	10					
9	Sum of Ranks	138					
10	Warning: Large-scale approximation formula not designed for small sample sizes.						
11	Total Sample Size n	20					
12	T1 Test Statistic	72					
13	T1 Mean	105					
14	Standard Error of T1	13.22876					
15	Z Test Statistic	-2.49457					
16							
17	Two-Tailed Test						
18	Lower Critical Value	-1.95996					
19	Upper Critical Value	1.959961					
20	p-value	0.012611					
21	Reject the null hypothesis						

Figure 9.35   Wilcoxon Rank Sum test for the soft-drink fill example obtained from PHStat add-in for Microsoft Excel

PROBLEMS

9.44 The contamination of silicon wafer surfaces with particles and surface chemical oxidation have been shown to degrade device yield. In *A Portable Nitrogen Purged Microenvironment: Design Specification and Preliminary Field Test Data* (*Data* PROCEEDINGS—Institute of Environmental Sciences, 1995), C.W. Draper et. al. describe a nitrogen-purged portable microenvironment. Ten wafers receiving a standard clean in a cleanroom were compared to 5 wafers receiving a megasonics clean and transported through a non-clean environment in the microenvironment. Defects were measured on 2 vernier patterns/wafer.

Standard									
53	193	113	640	800	140	85	658	140	140

Megasonic				
26	90	546	90	120

MEGASONIC

   (a) Test the hypothesis at the 0.05 level that the two methods have the same population median.
   (b) What assumption is necessary for this test to be valid?

9.45 An experiment was conducted to compare the performances of electronic and magnetic ballasts used in fluorescent lighting. The variables compared included ballast efficiency factor (footcandles/watt), light output (Footcandles), total harmonic distortion (%), power factor (Watts), and the temperature (Celsius) of the lamp and ballasts themselves.

Type	BEF	LO	THD	PF	Lamp	Blst
Mag	0.480	43	12.6	0.991	37.8	33.0
Mag	0.490	42	15.6	0.988	40.4	33.2
Mag	0.483	43	11.5	0.975	34.7	37.0
Mag	0.482	42	16.1	0.987	38.8	35.3
Elec	0.583	40	26.6	0.959	30.6	27.5
Elec	0.571	41	16.0	0.988	32.2	28.8
Elec	0.564	41	23.4	0.966	30.6	27.2
Elec	0.576	40	9.8	0.958	37.5	28.9
Elec	0.548	39	14.9	0.951	29.7	30.7
Elec	0.588	41	32.0	0.952	35.9	20.4

BALLAST

Assume that the populations involved cannot be assumed to be normally distributed. For each of the six variables, test the hypothesis at the .05 level that the population medians for electronic and magnetic ballasts used in fluorescent lighting are equal.

9.46 In Problem 9.11 on page 420, the talking times of nickel–metal hydride batteries were compared to those of nickel–cadmium batteries. For these data, do the following.
   (a) At the 0.05 level of significance, is there evidence of a difference in the median talking time between nickel–metal hydride and nickel–cadmium batteries.
   (b) Determine the *p*-value in (a).
   (c) Compare the results of (a) to those of Problem 9.11 (a).

9.47 In Problem 9.12 on page 420, data were collected from an experiment that was conducted to assess the effect of using magnets at the filler point in the manufacture of coffee filter packs. For these data, do the following.
   (a) At the 0.05 level of significance, is there evidence of a difference between the median weights of filter packs with and without magnets.
   (b) Determine the *p*-value in (a).
   (c) Compare the results of (a) to those of Problem 9.12 (a).

9.48 In Problem 9.14 on page 421, data were collected from two central offices on the time to clear problems. For these data, do the following.
   (a) At the 0.05 level of significance, is there any evidence of a difference in the median time to clear problems between the two central offices?
   (b) Determine the *p*-value in (a).
   (c) Compare the results of (a) to those of Problem 9.14 (a).

9.49 In Problem 9.15 on page 421, data were collected from two plants on the processing time of work in process. For these data, do the following.
   (a) At the 0.05 level of significance, is there evidence of a difference in the median processing time between the two plants?
   (b) Determine the *p*-value in (a).
   (c) Compare the results of (a) to those of Problem 9.15 (a).

9.10 SUMMARY

In this chapter, we introduced statistical test procedures that are commonly employed when analyzing possible differences between the parameters of two or more independent populations. In addition, we developed test procedures that are frequently used when analyzing possible differences between the parameters of two related populations based on samples containing numerical data. Again, part of a good data analysis is to understand the assumptions underlying each of the hypothesis test procedures and, by using this as well as other criteria, to select the one most appropriate for a given set of conditions.

   To review, one major distinction for comparing two groups containing continuous data is based on whether the populations from which the samples were drawn are independent or related. We should not use test procedures designed for independent populations when dealing with paired data, and we should not use test procedures designed for related populations when dealing with independent samples. After focusing on an appropriate grouping of similar test procedures, we need to look carefully at the assumptions and other criteria prior to selecting a particular procedure. Another distinction relates to whether the variable to be analyzed is continuous or categorical. Procedures such as the test for the mean, the variance, differences between means, differences between variances, and differences between medians were based on continuous response variables of interest; the chi-square test for the difference between proportions was based on categorical data of interest.

KEY TERMS

$2 \times c$ contingency table 434
α (level of significance) 396
alternative hypothesis (H_1) 393
β risk 396
χ^2 test for a population variance or standard deviation 447
χ^2 test for differences among c proportions 440
χ^2 test for difference between two proportions 435
confidence coefficient ($1 - \alpha$) 396
contingency table 433
critical region 395
critical value 395
cross-classification table 433
difference score D_i 427
expected frequencies (f_e) 435
F distribution 422
F test for difference between two variances 422
hypothesis-testing 393
level of significance (α) 396
null hypothesis (H_0) 393

observed frequencies (f_o) 435
one-tailed or directional test 404
p-value 401
paired or matched items 427
parametric test 410
pooled estimate ($\overline{p}$) of common population proportion 435
pooled-variance t test for difference between two means 414
power of a test ($1 - \beta$) 397
probability of a Type II error (β) 396
region of nonrejection 395
region of rejection 395
related 427
repeated measurements 427
robust 411
separate-variance t test for difference between two means 418
t test for the mean difference 429
t test for a population mean 407
theoretical or expected frequencies 435
two-tailed or nondirectional test 399
Type I error 396

CHAPTER REVIEW *Checking Your Understanding*

9.50 What is the difference between a null hypothesis (H_0) and an alternative hypothesis (H_1)?

9.51 What is the difference between a Type I and Type II error?

9.52 What is meant by the power of a test?

9.53 What is the difference between a one-tailed and a two-tailed test?

9.54 What is meant by a *p*-value?

9.55 How can a confidence interval estimate for the population mean provide conclusions to the corresponding hypothesis test for the population mean?

9.56 What are some of the criteria used in the selection of a particular hypothesis-testing procedure?

9.57 Under what conditions should the pooled-variance *t* test be selected to examine a possible difference between the means of two independent populations?

9.58 Under what conditions should the separate-variance *t* test be selected to examine a possible difference between the means of two independent populations?

9.59 Under what conditions should the Wilcoxon rank sum test be selected to examine a possible difference between the medians of two independent populations?

9.60 Under what conditions should the *F* test be selected to examine a possible difference between the variances of two independent populations?

9.61 What is the difference between two independent and two related populations?

9.62 What is the distinction between repeated measurements and matched or paired items?

9.63 Under what conditions should the *t* test for the mean difference in two related populations be selected?

9.64 Under what conditions should the χ^2 test be used to examine possible differences among the proportions of *c* independent populations?

9.65 How can we determine which groups are different in the proportion of successes?

Chapter Review Problems

9.66 A computer professor is interested in studying the amount of time it would take students enrolled in the Introduction to Computers course to write and run a program in Visual Basic. The professor hires you to analyze the following results (in minutes) from a random sample of nine students:

| 10 | 13 | 9 | 15 | 12 | 13 | 11 | 13 | 12 | **VB** |

(a) At the 0.05 level of significance, is there evidence that the population average time is greater than 10 minutes? What will you tell the professor?

(b) Suppose that, when checking her results, the computer professor realizes that the fourth student needed 51 minutes rather than the recorded 15 minutes to write and run the Visual Basic program. At the 0.05 level of significance, reanalyze the revised data in part (a). What will you tell the professor now?

(c) The professor is perplexed by these paradoxical results and requests an explanation from you regarding the justification for the difference in your findings between (a) and (b). Discuss.

(d) A few days later, the professor calls to tell you that the dilemma is completely resolved. The original number 15 [shown in (a)] was correct, and therefore your findings in (a) are being used in the article she is writing for a computer magazine. Now she wants to hire you to compare the results from that group of Introduction to Computers students against those from a sample of 11 computer science majors, in order to determine whether there is evidence that computer science majors can write a Visual Basic program (on average) in less time than can introductory students. The sample mean for the computer science majors is 8.5 minutes, and the sample standard deviation is 2.0 minutes. At the 0.05 level of significance, completely analyze these data. What will you tell the professor?

(e) A few days later, the professor calls again to tell you that a reviewer of her article wants her to include the p-value for the "correct" result in (a). In addition, the professor inquires about the *unequal variances* problem, which the reviewer wants her to discuss in her article. In your own words, discuss the concept of p-value, and describe the unequal variances problem. Give the p-value in (a), and discuss whether the unequal variances problem had any meaning in the professor's study.

9.67 In Problem 2.13 on page 66, the lengths of life (in hours) of a sample of forty 100-watt light bulbs produced by Manufacturer A and a sample of forty 100-watt light bulbs produced by Manufacturer B were studied. Completely analyze the differences between the lengths of life for the two manufacturers, and write a summary of your findings.

9.68 In Problem 2.17 on page 68, data from an experiment to compare the effect of water-flow rate on a process designed to remove trichloroethylene (TCE) from waste water was studied for two groups of samples of treated water, one tested at a flow rate of $7.83m^3/h$ and the second tested at a flow rate of $4.09m^3/h$. Completely analyze the differences in the TCE concentrations between the two flow rates, and write a summary of your findings.

9.69 In Chapter 3, and in Problem 3.26 on page 126, the pH, Conductivity (μSiemens/cm), Total Aerobic Microbial Population (TAMP), and Total Organic Carbon (TOC) of Ultra-Pure and Deionizing systems were studied. Completely analyze the differences in each of these variables between the two water systems, and write a summary of your findings.

9.70 In the field of computers, one area of growing importance is *down time*. Data were collected from a sample of a company's computer systems or networks. The time in hours that they were down because of problems such as hardware malfunction, in a year, was as follows.

56.00	32.25	49.00	10.00	123.00	76.50	59.75	32.83
57.50	14.20	100.60	48.75	37.50	23.90	41.23	78.33
39.75	28.17	51.70	47.20	93.80	22.71	46.20	15.20
223.00	1.00	150.20	59.34	44.62	51.80	32.70	44.63
62.38	50.90	40.80	45.00	86.30	51.50	54.10	33.70
58.20	28.17	23.78					**DOWNTIME**

(a) Assuming that the computer systems of this company represent a sample of all such systems, is there evidence that the mean down time of this population is more than 50 hours per year? Use a level of significance of 0.05.

(b) For a level of significance of 0.01, is there evidence that the standard deviation of the population is different from 25 hours per year?

(c) What assumption needs to be made in (a) and (b)?

(d) Do you think that the assumption made in (c) is valid for these data?

9.71 McIntyre et. al., in "Dexamethasone as Adjunctive Therapy in Bacterial Meningitis" (*Journal of the American Medical Association,* 1997), looked at a number of studies that evaluated the use of dexamethasone as protection against hearing loss in childhood *Haemophilus influenza* type B (Hib) meningitis.

(a) Part of the paper reported that, in Canada, 57 of 101 cases of meningitis were caused by Hib, while in the United States, 83 of 143 were caused by Hib. At the 0.05 level of significance, is there evidence of a difference in the population percentages of cases of meningitis caused by Hib between Canada and the United States?

(b) The paper also reported that, in 260 cases of meningitis treated with dexamethasone, 8 patients suffered severe hearing loss. In 233 cases of meningitis not treated with dexamethasone, 27 patients suffered severe hearing loss. At the 0.01 level of significance, is there evidence of a difference in the population percentages of severe hearing loss, for people with meningitis, between those treated with dexamethasone and those not treated with dexamethasone?

(c) The paper also reported that, in 390 cases of meningitis treated with dexamethasone, 25 patients suffered neurological deficits other than hearing loss. In 367 cases of meningitis not treated with dexamethasone, 38 patients suffered neurological deficits other than hearing loss. At the 0.01 level of significance, is there evidence of a difference in the population percentages of neurological deficits other than hearing loss, for people with meningitis, between those treated with dexamethasone and those not treated with dexamethasone?

9.72 A brewery operates wastewater plants that treat municipal and brewery wastewater. An analysis of this wastewater included assaying the discharge for mercury, silver, cadmium, lead, and copper (all in micrograms/liter). The brewery staff suspected that some labs were using improper techniques, causing inconsistent results and false positives for dangerous amounts of these elements in the water. To check, two labs were sent similar samples of water to analyze, with the results stored in the file **BREWERY.** Completely analyze the differences in each of these variables between the two labs, and write a summary of your findings.

9.73 A typical cement facility uses a synthetic polymer to filter out dust particles that might be airborne from coking and cement processes. In order to achieve acceptable ambient air conditions, it is necessary to direct the exhaust from the various cement processes to a baghouse (think of it as a large vacuum cleaner element). Because the filters in the baghouse undergo harsh conditions, they do not last long. The following data compare the lifetimes (in days) of polymer filters to those of Nomex-type filters.

Polymer					Nomex				
35	25	28	26	31	33	32	30	30	33
34	31	29	33	33	32	32	31	31	29
31	27	31	33	28	29	30	33	27	27
28	30	33	29	31	32	32	28	27	30
26	29	35	32	30	26	30	34	31	26
33	30	29	33		28	28	28	28	

BAGHOUSE

Completely analyze the differences in the lifetime between the Polymer and Nomex filters, and write a summary of your findings.

9.74 In "Impaired Vasopressin Suppression and Enhanced Atrial Natriuretic Hormone Release Following an Acute Water Load in Primary Aldosteronism" by Kimura et. al. (*European Journal of Endocrinology*, 1997), a study was carried out involving 12 patients with aldosterone-producing adenomas before and after adrenalectomy. All patients had high blood pressure, took antihypertensive drugs, and showed a tendency toward hypernatraemia. Profiles of these patients with primary aldosteronism were taken at admission and two months after the operation. Some of the variables reported in the study include systolic blood pressure (SBP in mmHg), diastolic blood pressure (DBP in mmHg), serum Na concentration (SNa in mmol/l), serum K concentration (SK in mmol/l), and plasma aldosterone concentration (PAC in pmol/l).

	Admission						After Removal of Adrenal Tumor(s)				
Patient	SBP	DBP	SNa	SK	PAC	Patient	SBP	DBP	SNa	SK	PAC
1	160	90	149	2.7	560	1	108	88	144	5.4	70
2	164	104	147	3.0	720	2	130	80	142	5.5	170
3	152	88	145	4.0	680	3	130	82	144	4.8	90
4	150	86	144	3.7	1020	4	140	88	145	4.3	50
5	136	76	144	4.0	1450	5	152	90	140	5.0	100
6	140	80	146	2.7	4290	6	140	70	144	3.3	740
7	122	80	140	3.9	720	7	130	80	140	4.4	210
8	154	80	144	3.3	400	8	146	90	141	4.3	100
9	192	110	143	4.1	760	9	126	70	141	4.7	70
10	188	98	144	3.0	940	10	162	90	142	3.7	80
11	148	98	142	4.1	550	11	110	70	139	4.8	110
12	152	96	144	2.1	2240	12	140	88	141	4.1	120

ALDCONC

Assume all the populations involved are normally distributed. For each of the five variables, at the 0.05 level of significance, is there evidence of a difference in the population means before and after the operation?

WHITNEY GOURMET CAT FOOD COMPANY CASE

The team involved in the study of the weight of the canned kidney cat food was very concerned about the effect of the size of the pieces of food on the can weight. The opinion of the group clearly indicated that any change in the formulation of the food had to be considered very carefully, because the chunkier formulation might be one of the reasons that the cats liked the food. The group decided that, before any final decision was made concerning the formulation, an experiment should be conducted. A local animal shelter agreed to participate in the study. A random sample sample of 20 cats from the population at the shelter was selected. Ten cats were randomly assigned to each of the two size formulations (fine and chunky) of kidney cat food being tested. Each of the cats was then presented with 3 ounces of the selected formulation in its dish at feeding time. The response variable of interest was operationally defined as the amount of food (in ounces) that the cat consumed within a 10-minute time interval that began when the filled dish was presented. This definition was selected in an attempt to distinguish between what the cat seemed to really be attracted to and what would be eaten because nothing else was available. The results for this experiment are presented in Table WG9.1.

TABLE WG 9.1

OUNCES OF FOOD EATEN FOR TWO FORMULATIONS OF KIDNEY CAT FOOD

Fine									
2.31	2.01	2.07	1.75	1.45	2.11	1.93	2.27	2.04	2.38

Chunky									
2.76	2.22	2.32	1.88	1.98	2.09	1.64	2.65	2.54	2.51

WG91

Exercises

WG9.1 Analyze the results of the experiment. Write a report to the team that includes a recommendation for which formulation of kidney cat food should be used. Be prepared to discuss the limitations and assumptions of the experiment.

WG9.2 Provide a different operational definition for the amount of food eaten. What effect do you think the change of the operational definition might have on the results of the experiment?

REFERENCES

1. Conover, W. J.; *Practical Nonparametric Statistics,* 2d ed.; New York: Wiley, 1980
2. Daniel, W.; *Applied Nonparametric Statistics,* 2d ed.; Boston, MA: Houghton Mifflin, 1990
3. Lewontin, R. C. and J. Felsenstein; "Robustness of Homogeneity Tests in $2 \times n$ Tables," *Biometrics,* March 1965, Vol. 21, pp. 19–33
4. *Microsoft Excel 2000;* Redmond, WA: Microsoft Corporation, 1999
5. *MINITAB for Windows Version 12;* State College, PA: MINITAB, Inc., 1998
6. Satterthwaite, F. E.; "An Approximate Distribution of Estimates of Variance Components," *Biometrics Bulletin,* 1946, Vol. 2, pp. 110–114
7. Snedecor, G. W. and W. G. Cochran; *Statistical Methods,* 7th ed.; Ames, IA: Iowa State University Press, 1980
8. Solomon, H. and M. A. Stephens; "Sample Variance," *Encyclopedia of Statistical Sciences,* Vol. 9, Edited by Kotz, S. and N. L. Johnson; New York: Wiley, 1988, pp. 477–480
9. Winer, B. J.; *Statistical Principles in Experimental Design,* 2d ed.; New York: McGraw-Hill, 1971

APPENDIX 9.1 *Using Microsoft Excel for Hypothesis Testing*

Using Microsoft Excel for the Z Test of Hypothesis for the Mean (σ known)

To perform a Z test of hypothesis for the mean (σ known), use the One-Sample Tests | Z Test for the Mean, sigma known, choice of the PHStat add-in. As an example, consider the ball-bearing example of Section 9.3. To test the hypothesis that the diameter of the ball bearings remains at 0.503 inch, if the PHStat add-in has not been previously loaded, load the add-in using the instructions of Appendix 1.2. Select **File | New** to open a new workbook (or open the existing workbook into which the Hypothesis Testing worksheet is to be inserted). Select **PHStat | One-Sample Tests | Z Test for the Mean, sigma known.** In the Z Test for the Mean, sigma known, dialog box, enter **.503** in the Null Hypothesis: edit box. Enter **0.05** in the Level of Significance: edit box. Enter **.004** in the Population Standard Deviation: edit box. Select the **Sample Statistics Known** option button, and enter **25** in the Sample Size: edit box and **.5018** in the Sample Mean: edit box. Select the **Two-Tailed Test** option button. Enter **Z Test of the Hypothesis for the Mean Diameter of Ball Bearings** in the Output Title: edit box. Click the **OK** button.

The add-in inserts a worksheet containing calculations for the Z test of the hypothesis for the mean. (*Note:* For other problems in which the sample mean is not known and needs to be calculated, select the Sample Statistics Unknown option button instead of the Sample Statistics Known option button, and enter the cell range of the sample data in the Sample Cell Range: edit box.) To perform a one-tailed test, select the Upper-Tail Test or the Lower-Tail Test option button.

Using Microsoft Excel for the t Test of Hypothesis for the Mean (σ Unknown)

To perform a t test of the hypothesis for the mean (σ unknown), use the One-Sample Tests | t Test for the Mean, sigma unknown, choice of the PHStat add-in. As an example, consider the capacitor data of section 9.3. To test the hypothesis whether there is evidence that the average is $0.33\mu F$, if the PHStat add-in has not been previously loaded, load the add-in using the instructions of Appendix 1.2. Select **File | New** to open a new workbook (or open the existing workbook into which the hypothesis testing worksheet is to be inserted). Open the CAPACITOR workbook (**CAPACITOR.XLS**), and click the Data sheet tab. Verify that the capacitor values appear in column A. Select **PHStat | One-Sample Tests | t Test for the Mean, sigma unknown.** In the t Test for the Mean, sigma unknown dialog box, enter **.33** in the Null Hypothesis: edit box. Enter **0.05** in the Level of Significance: edit box. Select the **Sample Statistics Unknown** option button, enter **A1:A31** in the Sample Cell Range: edit box, and select the **First cell contains label** check box. Select the **Two-Tailed Test** option button. Enter **t Test for the Hypothesis of the Mean Capacitance** in the Output Title: edit box. Click the **OK** button.

The add-in inserts a worksheet containing calculations for the t test of the hypothesis for the mean similar to the one shown in Figure 9.10 on page 409. (*Note:* For other problems in which the sample size, sample mean, and sample standard deviation are previously known, select the Sample Statistics Known option button instead of the Sample Statistics Unknown option button, and enter these values in the appropriate edit boxes.) To perform a one-tailed test, select the Upper-Tail Test or the Lower-Tail Test option button.

Using Microsoft Excel for the Pooled-Variance *t* test

To perform the pooled-variance t test for a difference between two means when using sample data, use the Data Analysis t-Test: Two-Sample Assuming Equal Variances tool. As an example, consider the flawed specimens example of Section 9.4. To determine whether there is evidence of a significant difference in the average crack size between unflawed and flawed specimens, open the **CRACK.XLS** workbook. Click the **Data** sheet tab. Verify that the data of Table 9.4 on page 416 have been entered into columns A (type of specimen with 0 = unflawed and 1 = flawed) and B (crack size), respectively. Select **Tools | Data Analysis.** Select **t-Test: Two-Sample Assuming Equal Variances** from the Analysis Tools list box in the Data Analysis dialog box. Click the **OK** button. In the t-Test: Two-Sample Assuming Equal Variances dialog box, enter **B2:B19** in the Variable 1 Range: edit box. Enter **B20:B59** in the Variable 2 Range: edit box. Enter **0** (zero) in the Hypothesized Mean Difference: edit box. Enter **0.05** in the Alpha: edit box. Select the **New Worksheet Ply:** option button, and enter **Data Analysis t Test** as the name of the new sheet. Click the **OK** button. The Data Analysis tool add-in inserts a worksheet containing a t test similar to the one shown in Figure 9.16 on page 417. This worksheet is *not* dynamically changeable, so any changes made to the underlying data would require using the Data Analysis tool a second time in order to produce updated test results.

The Data Analysis t-test tool requires that the data for each group be contiguous, an arrangement known as unstacked data. Some data sets are "stacked": the data for both groups appear in a single column, identified by a grouping variable in another column. To use such stacked data with the Data Analysis t-test tool, select PHStat | Data Preparation | Unstack Data to unstack the data prior to using the Data Analysis t-test tool.

To perform the pooled-variance t test for difference between two means when using summary data, use the Two-Sample Tests | t Test for Differences in Two Means choice of the PHStat add-in.

Using Microsoft Excel for the *F* test for Difference between Two Variances

To perform the F test for difference between the variances of two populations when using sample data, use the Data Analysis F Test Two-Sample for Variances tool. As an example, consider the crack size example of Section 9.5. To determine whether there is evidence of a significant difference in variability in the crack size between unflawed and flawed specimens, open the **CRACK.XLS** workbook. Click the **Data** sheet tab. Verify that the unflawed and the flawed data of Table 9.4 on page 416 have been entered into columns A (type of specimen with 0 = unflawed and 1 = flawed) and B (crack size), respectively. Select **Tools | Data Analysis.** Select **F-Test Two-Sample for Variances** from the Analysis Tools list box in the Data Analysis dialog box. Click the **OK** button. In the F-Test Two-Sample for Variances dialog box, enter **B2:B19** in the Variable 1 Range: edit box. Enter **B20:B59** in the Variable 2 Range: edit box. Enter **0.05** in the Alpha: edit box. Select the **New Worksheet Ply:** option button, and enter **Data Analysis F Test** as the name of the new sheet. Click the **OK** button. The Data Analysis tool add-in inserts a worksheet containing an F test similar to the one shown in Figure 9.22 on page 425. This worksheet is *not* dynamically changeable, so any changes made to the underlying data would require using the Data Analysis tool a second time in order to produce updated test results.

The Data Analysis F test tool requires that the data for each group be contiguous, an arrangement known as unstacked data. Some data sets are "stacked": the data for both groups appear in a single column, identified by a grouping variable in another column. To use such stacked data with the Data Analysis F test tool, select PHStat | Data Preparation | Unstack Data to unstack the data prior to using the Data Analysis F test tool.

To perform the F test for difference between the variances of two populations when using summary data, use the Two-Sample Tests | F Test for Differences in Two Variances choice of the PHStat add-in.

Using Microsoft Excel for the Paired *t* Test

To perform the paired t test, use the Data Analysis t-Test: Paired Two Sample for Means tool. As an example, consider the cardiac output measurement example of Section 9.6. To determine whether there is evidence of a significant difference between the average measurements for the two observers, open the **CARDIAC.XLS** workbook. Click the **Data** sheet tab. Verify that the measurements for observers A and B of Table 9.7 on page 430 have been entered in columns B and C, respectively. Select **Tools | Data Analysis.** Select **t-Test: Paired Two Sample for Means** from the Analysis Tools list box in the Data Analysis dialog box. Click the **OK** button. In the t-Test: Paired Two Sample for Means dialog box, enter **B1:B24** in the Variable 1 Range: edit box. Enter **C1:C24** in the Variable 2 Range: edit box. Enter **0** (zero) in the Hypothesized Mean Difference: edit box. Select the **Labels** check box. Enter **0.05** in the Alpha: edit box. Select the **New Worksheet Ply:** option button, and enter **Data Analysis t Test** as the name of the new sheet. Click the **OK** button. The Data Analysis tool add-in inserts a worksheet containing the t test similar to the one shown in Figure 9.23 on page 430. This worksheet is *not* dynamically changeable, so any changes made to the underlying data would require using the Data Analysis tool a second time in order to produce updated test results.

The Data Analysis t-test: Paired Samples for Means tool requires that the data for each group be in separate columns, an arrangement known as unstacked data. Some data sets are "stacked": the data for both groups appear in a single column, identified by a grouping variable in another column. To use such stacked data with the Data Analysis t-test tool, select PHStat | Data Preparation | Unstack Data to unstack the data prior to using the Data Analysis: Paired Samples for Means tool.

Using the PHStat Add-In for Microsoft Excel for the Chi-Square Test for the Difference between Two Proportions

To perform the χ^2 test for difference between two proportions, use the Two-Sample Tests | Chi-Square Test for Differences in Two Proportions choice of the PHStat add-in. As an example, consider the heart-attack incidence example of Section 9.7. To determine whether there is evidence of a significant difference in the proportion of heart attacks between the study and placebo groups, if the PHStat add-in has not been previously loaded, load the add-in using the instructions of Appendix 1.2. Select **File | New** to open a new workbook (or open the existing workbook into which the worksheet is to be inserted). Select **PHStat | Two-Sample Tests | Chi-Square Test for Differences in Two Proportions.** In the Chi-Square Test for Differences in Two Proportions dialog box, enter **0.05** in the Level of Significance: edit box. Enter **Chi-Square Test for Difference between Two Proportions for Heart-Attack Incidence** in the Output Title: edit box. Click the **OK** button.

The add-in inserts a worksheet that contains tables for observed and expected frequencies and an area for test statistics. Because there are no observed frequencies, many cells display the message #DIV/0! at this point in the procedure. This is not an error. In the newly inserted worksheet, enter replacement labels for the row and column variables. Enter **Results** in cell C4 and **Study Group** in cell D3. Enter replacement labels for the row and column categories. Enter **Heart Attack** in cell C5 and **No heart attack** in cell C6. Enter **Aspirin** in cell D4 and **Placebo** in cell E4. Enter the values from Table 9.9 (see page 437) for the frequencies for the two groups in the cell range D5:E6. Enter **104** in cell D5, **10933** in cell D6, **189** in cell E5, and **10845** in cell E6. The completed worksheet will be similar to the one shown in Figure 9.27 on page 439.

Using the PHStat Add-In for Microsoft Excel for the Chi-Square Test for the Differences among c Proportions

To perform the χ^2 test for differences among c proportions, use the c-Sample Tests | Chi-Square Test choice of the PHStat add-in. As an example, consider the sealing-machine example of Section 9.7. To determine whether there is evidence of a significant difference in the proportions, if the PHStat add-in has not been previously loaded, load the add-in using the instructions of appendix 1.2. Select **File | New** to open a new workbook (or open the existing workbook into which the worksheet is to be inserted). Select **PHStat | c-Sample Tests | Chi-Square Test.** In the Chi-Square Test dialog box, enter **0.05** in the Level of Significance: edit box. Enter **2** in the Number of Rows: edit box. Enter **5** in the Number of Columns: edit box. Enter **Chi-Square Test for Differences in** c **Proportions for Sealing Temperatures** in the Output Title: edit box. Click the **OK** button.

The add-in inserts a worksheet that contains tables for observed and expected frequencies and an area for test statistics. Because there are no observed frequencies, many cells display the message #DIV/0! at this point in the procedure. This is not an error. In the newly inserted worksheet, enter replacement labels for the row and column variables. Enter **Packaging Result** in cell C4 and **Temperature Setting** in cell D3. Enter replacement labels for the row and column categories. Enter **Defective Seals** in cell C5 and **Nondefective seals** in cell C6. Enter **A** in cell D4, **B** in cell E4, and **C** in cell F4, **D** in G4, and **E** in H4. Enter the values from Table 9.13 (see page 442) for the frequencies in the cell range D5:H6. Enter **22** in cell D5, **478** in cell D6, **20** in cell E5, **480** in cell E6, **34** in cell F5, **466** in cell F6, **23** in cell G5, **477** in cell G6, **41** in cell H5, and **459** in cell H6.

The completed worksheet will be similar to the one shown in Figure 9.31 on page 444. Because of a fault in the Microsoft Excel worksheet function used to generate the chi-square test statistic, the message #NUM!—not the value of the statistic—might appear in cell B21. This fault appears only when the p-value approaches zero and does not affect the decision displayed in row 23.

Using Microsoft Excel for the Test for a Variance

To test a population variance for the ball-bearing data of Section 9.8, we can use the **CHIINV** worksheet function, the format of which is

CHIINV (level of significance, degrees of freedom)

to return the critical value of χ^2 needed to compute the test of hypothesis. To obtain the test for the variance, select **File | New** to open a new workbook (or open the existing workbook into which the confidence interval estimate worksheet is to be inserted). Enter the following labels and formulas as shown in Table 9.21 on page 466.

Enter the null hypothesis value, the level of significance, the sample size, and the sample standard deviation in the cell range B3:B6. Enter **0.000016** in cell B3, **0.05** in cell B4, **25** in cell B5, and **0.0042** in cell B6. Enter the formulas for cells B7, B8, B11, and B12. Had the sample standard deviation been unknown, we could have entered a formula using the STDEV function in cell B6 to compute the standard deviation from the cell range containing the data.

Using the PHStat Add-In for Microsoft Excel for the Wilcoxon Rank Sum Test

To perform the Wilcoxon rank sum test for difference between two medians, use the Two-Sample Tests | Wilcoxon Rank Sum Test choice of the PHStat add-in. As an example, consider the soft-drink bottling problem of Section 9.9. To determine whether there is evidence

TABLE 9.21

WORKSHEET DESIGN FOR THE χ^2 TEST OF THE HYPOTHESIS FOR THE VARIANCE

	A	B
1	Chi-Square Test of Hypothesis for the Variance	
2		
3	Null Hypothesis $\sigma^{\wedge}2=$	xxx
4	Level of Significance	xxx
5	Sample Size	xxx
6	Sample Standard Deviation	xxx
7	Degrees of Freedom	=B5-1
8	Chi-Square Test Statistic	=B7*B6^2/B3
9		
10	Lower-Tail Test	
11	Lower Critical Value	=CHIINV(1-B4,B7)
12	p-Value	=1-CHIDIST(B8,B7)
13	=IF(B12<B4,"Reject the null hypothesis," "Do not reject the null hypothesis")	
14		
15	Upper-Tail Test	
16	Upper Critical Value	=CHIINV(B4,B7)
17	p-Value	=CHIDIST(B8,B7)
18	=IF(B17<B4,"Reject the null hypothesis," "Do not reject the null hypothesis")	
19		
20	Two-Tailed Test	
21	Lower Critical Value	=CHIINV((1-B4/2),B7)
22	Upper Critical Value	=CHIINV(B4/2,B7)
23	p-Value	=IF(B8-B21,1-CHIDIST(B8,B7), CHIDIST(B8,B7))
24	=IF(B23<B4/2,"Reject the null hypothesis," "Do not reject the null hypothesis")	

of a significant difference between the median deviations from the specific target for bottles filled under two different operating pressures, if the PHStat add-in has not been previously loaded, load the add-in using the instructions of Appendix 1.2. Open the PRESSURE workbook **(PRESSURE.XLS),** and click the **Data** sheet tab. Verify that the 25 psi and the 30 psi fill data of Table 9.18 on page 452 have been entered into columns A (deviation from target) and B (pressure setting), respectively. **Select PHStat | Two-Sample Tests | Wilcoxon Rank Sum Test.** In the Wilcoxon Rank Sum Test dialog box, enter **0.05** in the Level of Significance: edit box. Enter **A2:A11** in the Population 1 Sample Cell Range: edit box. Enter **A12:A21** in the Population 2 Sample Cell Range: edit box. Select the **Two-Tailed Test** option button. Enter **Wilcoxon Rank Sum Test for Differences for Bottle Fills** in the Output Title: edit box. Click the **OK** button. The Data Analysis tool add-in inserts a worksheet containing calculations for the Wilcoxon test similar to the one shown in Figure 9.35 on page 455.

The PHStat Wilcoxon choice requires that the data for each group be contiguous, an arrangement known as unstacked data. Some data sets are "stacked": the data for both groups appear in a single column, identified by a grouping variable in another column. To use such stacked data with the PHStat Wilcoxon choice, select the **Data Preparation | Unstack Data** choice of the PHStat add-in to unstack the data before using the PHStat Wilcoxon choice.

APPENDIX 9.2　*Using MINITAB for Hypothesis Testing*

Using MINITAB for the *t* Test of Hypothesis for the Mean (σ unknown)

MINITAB can be used for a test of the mean when σ is unknown by using Stat | Basic Statistics | 1-Sample *t* from the Menu bar.

　We illustrate the test of hypothesis for the mean when σ is unknown by returning to the 30 capacitors discussed in section 9.3. Open the **CAPACITOR.MTW** file, and select **Stat | Basic Statistics | 1-Sample t.** Enter C1 or 'Capacitance' in the Variables edit box. Select the **Test Mean** option button, and enter .33 in the Test Mean: edit box. In the Alternative drop-down list box, select *less than* or *greater than* for one-tailed tests, or *not equal* for a two-tailed test. Click the **OK** button. The results obtained will be similar to those of Figure 9.11 on page 409.

Using MINITAB for the *t* Test of the Difference between Two Means

To illustrate the use of MINITAB for the *t* test of the difference between two means, open the **CRACK.MTW** worksheet. Select **Stat | Basic Statistics | 2-Sample t.** If the data are stacked with the values in one column and the categories in a second column, as they are in this worksheet, select the **Samples in one column** option button. (If the samples are in different columns, select the Samples in different Columns option button, and enter the column numbers or names.) In the Samples: edit box, enter C1 or 'Crack size'. In the Subscripts: edit box, enter C2 or 'Type'. If you wish to assume equal variances, select the Assume equal variances check box. In the Alternative drop-down list box, select *less than* or *greater than* for a one-tailed test, or *not equal* for a two-tailed test. Click on the **Graphs** options button, and select the **Boxplots of data** check box. Click the **OK** button to return to the 2-Sample t dialog box. Click the **OK** button. The output obtained will be similar to that of Figure 9.17 on page 417.

Using MINITAB for the Paired *t* Test

To illustrate the use of MINITAB for the paired *t* test, open the **CARDIAC.MTW** worksheet. Select **Stat | Basic Statistics | Paired t.** In the First Sample: edit box, enter C2 or 'A'. In the Second Sample: edit box, enter C3 or 'B'. Click the **Options** button. In the Alternative: drop-down list box, select *less than* or *greater than* for one-tailed test, or *not equal* for a two-tailed test. Click the **OK** button to return to the Paired t dialog box. Click the **Graphs** button, and select the **Boxplot of Differences** check box. Click the **OK** button to return to the Paired t dialog box. Click the **OK** button. The output obtained will be similar to that of Figure 9.24 on page 431.

Using MINITAB for Two-Sample and *c*-Sample Tests for Categorical data

To obtain a two-way contingency table from raw data, open the MINITAB worksheet of interest. Select **Stat | Tables | Cross Tabulation.** In the Classification variables edit box, enter the two variables to be cross-classified. Select the **Counts, Row percents, Column percents,** and **Total percents** check boxes. Select the **Chi-Square analysis** check box. Select the **Above** and **expected count** option button. Click the **OK** button.

If the cell frequencies are available, as in the heart-attack incidence example, enter them in columns in a new MINITAB worksheet. For the heart-attack incidence 2×2 table, enter **104** and **10933** in column C1 and **189** and **10845** in column C2. Select **Stat | Tables | Chi-Square Test.** In the Columns containing the table: edit box, enter **C1** and **C2.** Click the **OK** button.

Using MINITAB for the Wilcoxon Rank Sum Test

To illustrate the use of MINITAB for the Wilcoxon rank sum test, open the **PRESSURE.MTW** worksheet. If the data are stacked with the values in one column and the categories in a second column as they are in this worksheet, to unstack the data select **Manip | Stack/Unstack | Unstack One Column.** In the Unstack data edit box, enter **C1** or **'Deviation from target'.** In the Store the unstacked data in edit box, enter **C3 C4.** In the Using Subscripts edit box, enter **C2** or **'Setting'.** Click the **OK** button. Enter **25 PSI** as the label for C3 and **30PSI** as the label for C4.

Select **Stat | Nonparametrics | Mann-Whitney.** In the First sample edit **box,** enter **C3** or **'25 PSI'.** In the Second sample edit box, enter **C4** or **'30 PSI'.** Click the **OK** button. The output obtained will be similar to that of Figure 9.34 on page 454.

10

The Design of Experiments: One Factor and Randomized Block Experiments

"Figures don't lie, but liars figure."

DISRAELI

USING STATISTICS

Philips Semiconductors is a leading European manufacturer of integrated circuits. Integrated circuits are produced on silicon wafers, which are ground to target thickness early in the production process. The wafers are positioned in various locations on a grinder and kept in place through vacuum decompression. One of the goals of process improvement is to reduce the variability in the thickness of the wafers in different positions and in different wafers.

10.1 INTRODUCTION AND RATIONALE

In our first nine chapters, we have presented a variety of statistical tools widely used in many areas of engineering and the sciences. As we learned in Section 1.10, when we discussed quality management, the Shewhart-Deming cycle of Plan—Do—Study—Act represents a key element of the scientific approach for obtaining process improvement. Many tools that we have studied have been useful for understanding a process (fishbone and process flow diagrams), for determining whether a process contains special causes of variation (control charts), and for evaluating data obtained from the study of a process (Pareto diagrams, descriptive statistics, histograms, stem-and-leaf displays, box-and-whisker plots, confidence intervals, and hypothesis testing).

However, statistical process control (as discussed in Chapters 6 and 7) represented a passive intervention in a process: Any actions taken were the result of signals given by the process itself. In contrast to statistical process control, the concepts of experimental design considered in this and the next chapter represent purposeful active interventions in a process, because they consist of planned experimentation on the process. These interventions represent a formal scientific approach for assessing potential improvements to the process. Perhaps the distinction between passive and active intervention can best be illustrated with an analogy such as the one presented in Figure 10.1.

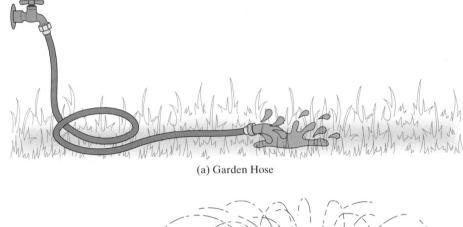

(a) Garden Hose

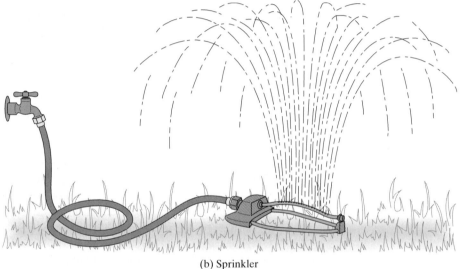

(b) Sprinkler

Figure 10.1   The garden hose and the sprinkler

Panel (a) represents a garden hose, in which the water that enters the hose when the spigot is turned on is allowed merely to trickle away into the ground. Any collection of the water at this stage is a passive activity: We are taking water (i.e., our data) that would otherwise just seep into the ground. On the other hand, panel (b) represents a situation in which an oscillating sprinkler has been attached to the end of the garden hose. In this instance, we have actively intervened in the process. Instead of allowing the water (our data) to seep into the ground in an uncontrolled manner, we have actively forced nature to provide us with a distribution of the water different from the one that otherwise would have happened. By actively intervening in the process, we can study the effects of various factors on the distribution of the water and specify the conditions under which water distribution can be optimized or can be made to serve our purposes best.

 10.2 HISTORICAL BACKGROUND

The ideas involved in the design of experiments are not new; they were originally developed by R. A. Fisher in England more than 70 years ago. (See References 1, 2, 3, 6, 13.) His original work was carried out to improve agricultural experimentation at the famous Rothamsted experimental station. Fisher's contributions to experimental design stem from several basic principles. First and foremost, Fisher conceptualized and developed an experimental strategy that explicitly designed experiments to study several factors of interest simultaneously. This approach was in marked contrast to the scientific method as practiced in the nineteenth century (and still practiced by many engineers and scientists in the United States and Europe) of varying only one factor at a time. Second, he developed the concept of randomization (to be discussed in Section 10.3) that allows for the control of variation resulting from extraneous factors or from factors that cannot be foreseen. Third, to control for the variation in factors that could be foreseen (such as the effect of the location of agricultural plots), Fisher developed the strategy of **blocking,** which allowed a more refined study of the effect of the treatment variable or factor of interest. When blocking is used, the sample is divided into relatively homogeneous blocks. This approach can result in a more precise understanding of the effects of the factors studied, because the variability between blocks can be removed from the estimates of the error variability.

The work of Fisher became widely disseminated across Europe and the United States in the years between World War I and World War II. Agricultural stations with statistical laboratories, modeled after those in England, were soon established at various universities throughout the United States. The years after World War II saw rapid expansion in the application of experimental design methods, not only in agriculture, but also in biological, medical, and pharmaceutical research and in psychology and education. Indeed, it is reasonable to say that because of the widespread application of these methods, no drug can be marketed today without extensive testing based on many designed experiments.

While experimental design methods were being widely applied in these fields, their use was not as prevalent in industrial applications in the United States. In contrast to this limited use by American industry, beginning in the 1980s, an entire philosophy concerning process improvement based upon experimental design principles developed by the Japanese engineer Genichi Taguchi (see Section 11.4) has been used in Japan. Over the past decade, many American companies, in their renewed quest for process improvement, have begun to rediscover experimental design principles that ironically have been available in the United States for more than a half-century.

10.3 THE CONCEPT OF RANDOMIZATION

One of Fisher's principal contributions to the design of experiments was his development of the concept of randomization. Fisher realized that, in doing an agricultural experiment in the world outside the laboratory, not all factors could be controlled or even foreseen. For such realistic situations, Fisher developed the idea of **randomization.** With this approach, in agriculture, for example, the particular levels of a factor received by the plots of land are determined by a method of random assignment. Thus, any differences between different plots that received the same treatment could be ascribed to random variation or experimental error. This approach of random assignment to treatment conditions became the basis upon which the inferential aspects of experimental design rest.

The concept of randomization can be illustrated in the context of an example that will be used throughout much of this and the next chapter. Suppose that an appliance manufacturer is interested in determining whether the brand of laundry detergent used affects the amount of dirt removed from standard household laundry loads. In particular, the manufacturer wants to compare four different brands of detergent (labeled A, B, C, and D). The main question involved in carrying out the experiment relates to the issue of how laundry loads should be assigned to the detergent brands. Even if a concerted effort is made to ensure that the loads are equal in measurable aspects, such as weight and type of fabric, it is impossible to control all factors other than detergent that might affect the amount of dirt removed. The random assignment of laundry loads to the various brands of detergent will ensure that all loads with a particular unforeseen characteristic would not be assigned to the same brand of detergent. The main idea here is that any difference between treatments (i.e., the detergent brands) would not be mixed up or *confounded* with any other factor of interest, such as the type of laundry load.

10.4 THE ONE-WAY ANALYSIS OF VARIANCE (ANOVA)

In Chapter 9, we used hypothesis-testing methodology to draw conclusions about possible differences between the parameters of two groups. Frequently, however, it is necessary to evaluate differences among the parameters of several groups. We might want to compare alternative materials, methods, or treatments according to some predetermined criteria.

In industrial applications, it has all too often been the case that experiments have been done in which only one factor of interest has been considered. We shall see that this experimental approach, although useful in some circumstances, can be both inefficient and shortsighted.

When the outcome measurements across the groups are continuous variables and certain assumptions are met, a methodology known as **analysis of variance (or ANOVA)** is used to compare the means of the groups. In a sense, the term "analysis of variance" appears to be a misnomer, because the objective is to analyze differences among the group means. However, through an analysis of the variation in the data, both among and within the c groups, we are able to draw conclusions about possible differences in group means. In ANOVA, we subdivide the total variation in the outcome measurements into that which is attributable to differences *among* the c groups and that which is due to chance or attributable to inherent variation *within* the c groups. (See Figure 10.2.) "Within group" variation is considered **experimental error,** while "among group" variation is attributable to treatment effects.

Under the assumptions that the c groups or levels of the factor being studied represent populations whose outcome measurements are randomly and

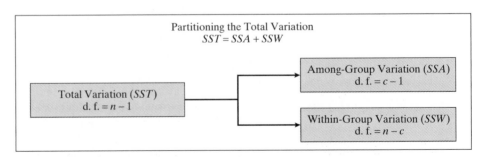

Figure 10.2 Partitioning the total variation in a one-way ANOVA model

independently drawn, follow a normal distribution, and have equal variances, the null hypothesis of no differences in the population means

$$H_0: \mu_1 = \mu_2 = \cdots = \mu_c$$

is tested against the alternative that the c means are not the same

$$H_1: \text{Not all } \mu_j \text{ are equal (where } j = 1, 2, \ldots, c)$$

Figure 10.3 displays what a true null hypothesis looks like when five groups are compared and the assumptions of normality and equality of variances hold. The five populations representing the different levels of the factor are identical and therefore superimpose on one another. The properties of central tendency, variation, and shape are identical for each.

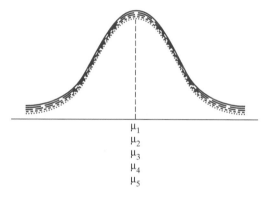

Figure 10.3   All five populations have the same mean: $\mu_1 = \mu_2 = \mu_3 = \mu_4 = \mu_5$

On the other hand, suppose that the null hypothesis is really false, with level 4 having the largest mean, level 1 having the second largest mean, and no differences between the other population means. (See Figure 10.4.) Note that, except for differences in central tendency (that is, $\mu_4 > \mu_1 > \mu_2 = \mu_3 = \mu_5$), the five populations are the same in appearance.

To perform an ANOVA test of equality of population means, we subdivide the total variation in the outcome measurements into two parts, that which is attributable to differences among the groups and that which is due to inherent

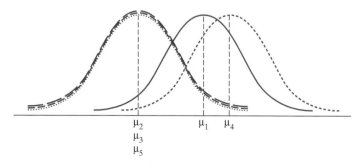

Figure 10.4   A treatment effect is present: $\mu_4 > \mu_1 > \mu_2 = \mu_3 = \mu_5$

variation within the groups. The **total variation** is usually represented by the **sum of squares total** (or **SST**). Under the null hypothesis, the population means of the c groups are presumed equal, so a measure of the total variation among all the observations is obtained by summing the squared differences between each individual observation and the **overall** or **grand mean** $\overline{\overline{X}}$ that is based on all the observations in all the groups combined. The total variation is computed as in Equation (10.1).

TOTAL VARIATION

$$\text{SST} = \sum_{j=1}^{c} \sum_{i=1}^{n_j} (X_{ij} - \overline{\overline{X}})^2 \tag{10.1}$$

where

$$\overline{\overline{X}} = \frac{\sum_{j=1}^{c} \sum_{i=1}^{n_j} X_{ij}}{n}$$ is called the overall or grand mean

X_{ij} = the ith observation in group or level j

n_j = the number of observations in group j

n = the total number of observations in all groups combined
(that is, $n = n_1 + n_2 + \cdots + n_c$)

c = the number of groups or levels of the factor of interest

The **among-group variation,** usually called the **sum of squares among groups** (or **SSA**), is measured by the sum of the squared differences between the sample mean of each group $\overline{X}_j$ and the overall or grand mean $\overline{\overline{X}}$, weighted by the sample size n_j in each group. The among-group variation is computed as in Equation (10.2).

AMONG-GROUP VARIATION

$$\text{SSA} = \sum_{j=1}^{c} n_j (\overline{X}_j - \overline{\overline{X}})^2 \tag{10.2}$$

where

c = the number of groups or levels being compared

n_j = the number of observations in group or level j

$\overline{X}_j$ = the sample mean of group j

$\overline{\overline{X}}$ = the overall or grand mean

The **within-group variation,** usually called the **sum of squares within groups** (or **SSW**), measures the difference between each observation and the mean of its own group and cumulates the squares of these differences over all groups. The within-group variation is computed as in Equation (10.3).

WITHIN-GROUP VARIATION

$$\text{SSW} = \sum_{j=1}^{c} \sum_{i=1}^{n_j} (X_{ij} - \overline{X}_j)^2 \qquad (10.3)$$

where

X_{ij} = the ith observation in group or level j

$\overline{X}_j$ = the sample mean of group j

Because c levels of the factor are being compared, there are $c - 1$ degrees of freedom associated with the sum of squares among groups. Because each of the c levels contributes $n_j - 1$ degrees of freedom, there are $n - c$ degrees of freedom associated with the sum of squares within groups:

$$\sum_{j=1}^{c} (n_j - 1) = n - c$$

In addition, there are $n - 1$ degrees of freedom associated with the sum of squares total, because each observation X_{ij} is being compared to the overall or grand mean $\overline{\overline{X}}$ based on all n observations.

DERIVATION 10.1 (OPTIONAL) The Sum of Squares for the One-Way ANOVA

X_{ij}, the ith observation for group j, can be represented by the model

$$X_{ij} = \mu + \beta_j + \varepsilon_{ij}$$

where

μ = overall response or mean common to all the observations

μ_j = population mean of the jth group

$\beta_j = \mu_j - \mu$, a treatment effect peculiar to the jth level of the factor $(j = 1, 2, \ldots, c)$

$\varepsilon_{ij} = X_{ij} - \mu_j$, random variation associated with the ith observation in group j $(i = 1, 2, \ldots, n_j$ and $j = 1, 2, \ldots, c)$

The population parameters μ, β_j, and ε_{ij} can be estimated by

$$\hat{\mu} = \overline{\overline{X}}$$
$$\hat{\beta}_j = \overline{X}_j - \overline{\overline{X}}$$
$$\hat{\varepsilon}_{ij} = X_{ij} - \overline{X}_j$$

and

$$\overline{\overline{X}} = \frac{\sum_{j=1}^{c} \sum_{i=1}^{n_j} X_{ij}}{n}$$

$$\overline{X}_j = \frac{\sum_{i=1}^{n_j} X_{ij}}{n_j}$$

Thus, from the model, we note that

$$X_{ij} = \hat{\mu} + \hat{\beta}_j + \hat{\varepsilon}_{ij}$$

and

$$X_{ij} = \bar{\bar{X}} + (\bar{X}_j - \bar{\bar{X}}) + (X_{ij} - \bar{X}_j)$$

If $\bar{\bar{X}}$ is subtracted from both sides, we get

$$X_{ij} - \bar{\bar{X}} = (\bar{X}_j - \bar{\bar{X}}) + (X_{ij} - \bar{X}_j)$$

Furthermore, if each side is squared and then summed over both i and j, we obtain

$$\sum_{j=1}^{c} \sum_{i=1}^{n_j} (X_{ij} - \bar{\bar{X}})^2 = \sum_{j=1}^{c} \sum_{i=1}^{n_j} (\bar{X}_j - \bar{\bar{X}})^2 + \sum_{j=1}^{c} \sum_{i=1}^{n_j} (X_{ij} - \bar{X}_j)^2$$

$$+ 2\sum_{j=1}^{c} \sum_{i=1}^{n_j} (\bar{X}_j - \bar{\bar{X}})(X_{ij} - \bar{X}_j)$$

However, from the above, $2\sum_{j=1}^{c} \sum_{i=1}^{n_j} (\bar{X}_j - \bar{\bar{X}})(X_{ij} - \bar{X}_j)$ equals zero, and so the following important identity is obtained:

$$\sum_{j=1}^{c} \sum_{i=1}^{n_j} (X_{ij} - \bar{\bar{X}})^2 = \sum_{j=1}^{c} \sum_{i=1}^{n_j} (\bar{X}_j - \bar{\bar{X}})^2 + \sum_{j=1}^{c} \sum_{i=1}^{n_j} (X_{ij} - \bar{X}_j)^2$$

Hence, SST = SSA + SSW

If each of these sums of squares is divided by its associated degrees of freedom, we obtain three variances or **mean square** terms—**MSA, MSW,** and **MST.** Because a variance is computed by dividing the sum of squared differences by its appropriate degrees of freedom, the mean square terms are all variances.

OBTAINING THE MEAN SQUARES

$$\text{MSA} = \frac{\text{SSA}}{c - 1} \tag{10.4a}$$

$$\text{MSW} = \frac{\text{SSW}}{n - c} \tag{10.4b}$$

$$\text{MST} = \frac{\text{SST}}{n - 1} \tag{10.4c}$$

Although our primary interest is in comparing the means of the c groups or levels of a factor to determine whether a treatment effect exists among them, the ANOVA procedure derives its name from the fact that this is achieved by analyzing variances. If the null hypothesis is true and there are no real differences among the c group means, all three mean square terms—MSA, MSW, and MST—which themselves are *variances,* provide estimates of the variance σ^2 inherent in the data. To test the null hypothesis

$$H_0\colon \mu_1 = \mu_2 = \cdots = \mu_c$$

against the alternative

$$H_1: \text{Not all } \mu_j \text{ are equal (where } j = 1, 2, \ldots, c)$$

we compute the test statistic, F, as the ratio of two of the variances, MSA to MSW, as in Equation (10.5).

THE ONE-WAY ANOVA F TEST STATISTIC

$$F = \frac{\text{MSA}}{\text{MSW}} \qquad (10.5)$$

The F-test statistic follows an F distribution with $c - 1$ degrees of freedom corresponding to MSA in the numerator and $n - c$ degrees of freedom corresponding to MSW in the denominator. For a given level of significance, α, we reject the null hypothesis if the computed F test statistic exceeds the upper-tailed critical value F_u from the F distribution having $c - 1$ degrees of freedom in the numerator and $n - c$ degrees of freedom in the denominator (see Table A.7). That is, as shown in Figure 10.5, our decision rule is

$$\text{Reject } H_0 \text{ if } F > F_u;$$

$$\text{otherwise don't reject } H_0$$

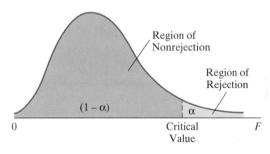

Figure 10.5   Regions of rejection and nonrejection when using ANOVA to test H_0

If the null hypothesis were true, we expect the computed F statistic to be approximately equal to 1, because both the numerator and the denominator mean square terms are estimating the true variance, σ^2, inherent in the data. On the other hand, if H_0 is false (and there are real differences among the means), we expect the computed F statistic to be substantially larger than 1, because the numerator, MSA, is estimating the treatment effect or differences among groups in addition to the inherent variability in the data, whereas the denominator, MSW, is measuring only the inherent variability. Hence the ANOVA procedure yields an F test in which the null hypothesis is rejected at a selected α level of significance only if the computed F statistic exceeds F_u, the upper-tail critical value of the F distribution having $c - 1$ and $n - c$ degrees of freedom, as illustrated in Figure 10.5.

The results of an analysis of variance are usually displayed in an **ANOVA summary** table, the format for which is presented in Table 10.1. The entries in this table include the sources of variation (i.e., among-group, within-group, and total),

TABLE 10.1

ANALYSIS-OF-VARIANCE SUMMARY TABLE

Source	Degrees of Freedom	Sums of Squares	Mean Square (Variance)	F
Among groups	$c - 1$	SSA	$MSA = \dfrac{SSA}{c - 1}$	$F = \dfrac{MSA}{MSW}$
Within groups	$n - c$	SSW	$MSW = \dfrac{SSW}{n - c}$	
Total	$n - 1$	SST		

the degrees of freedom, the sums of squares, the mean squares (i.e., the variances), and the calculated F statistic. In addition, the p value (i.e., the probability of obtaining an F statistic as large as or larger than the one obtained, given that the null hypothesis is true) is included in the ANOVA table of spreadsheet and statistical software packages. This presentation allows us to make direct conclusions about the null hypothesis without referring to a table of critical values of the F distribution. If the p value is less than the chosen level of significance, α, then the null hypothesis is rejected.

To illustrate the one-factor design, let us return to the laundry-detergent example introduced in Section 10.3, in which the single factor of interest is the brand of detergent. Suppose that, after a random assignment of ten loads to each brand, the amount of dirt removed (measured in milligrams) was determined, with the results summarized in Table 10.2.

We note from Table 10.2 that there are differences among the sample means for the four detergents. Detergent A has an average amount of dirt removed of 13.9 milligrams; detergents B, C, and D have 17.2, 18.3, and 14.9, respectively. The question that must be answered is whether these sample means are sufficiently different to decide that the *population* means are not all equal.

TABLE 10.2

AMOUNT OF DIRT (MG) REMOVED BY FOUR DETERGENT BRANDS

	Brand			
	A	B	C	D
	11	12	18	11
	13	14	16	12
	17	17	18	16
	17	19	20	15
	15	21	22	14
	16	18	15	17
	14	19	17	13
	10	18	21	16
	12	16	16	17
	14	18	20	18
MEAN	$\bar{X}_1 = 13.9$	$\bar{X}_2 = 17.2$	$\bar{X}_3 = 18.3$	$\bar{X}_4 = 14.9$

 LAUNDRY

The null hypothesis states that there is no difference among the four detergents in mean amount of dirt removed.

$$H_0: \mu_1 = \mu_2 = \mu_3 = \mu_4$$

The alternative hypothesis states that there is a **treatment effect;** that is, at least one of the detergents differs with respect to the average amount of dirt removed.

$$H_1: \text{Not all the means are equal}$$

To establish the ANOVA summary table, we first compute the sample mean in each group. (See Table 10.2 on page 478.) We then compute the overall or grand mean by summing all 40 observations in Table 10.2, and dividing by 40, the number of observations in the experiment.

$$\overline{\overline{X}} = \frac{\sum_{j=1}^{c} \sum_{i=1}^{n_j} X_{ij}}{n} = \frac{643}{40} = 16.075$$

and finally we compute the sums of squares, as follows:

$$
\begin{aligned}
\text{SSA} &= \sum_{j=1}^{c} n_j (\overline{X}_j - \overline{\overline{X}})^2 \\
&= (10)(13.9 - 16.075)^2 + (10)(17.2 - 16.075)^2 + (10)(18.3 - 16.075)^2 \\
&\quad + (10)(14.9 - 16.075)^2 \\
&= 123.275
\end{aligned}
$$

$$
\begin{aligned}
\text{SSW} &= \sum_{j=1}^{c} \sum_{i=1}^{n_j} (X_{ij} - \overline{X}_j)^2 \\
&= (11 - 13.9)^2 + \cdots + (14 - 13.9)^2 + (12 - 17.2)^2 + \cdots + (18 - 17.2)^2 \\
&\quad + (18 - 18.3)^2 + \cdots + (20 - 18.3)^2 + (11 - 14.9)^2 + \cdots + (18 - 14.9)^2 \\
&= 213.500
\end{aligned}
$$

$$
\begin{aligned}
\text{SST} &= \sum_{j=1}^{c} \sum_{i=1}^{n_j} (X_{ij} - \overline{\overline{X}})^2 \\
&= (11 - 16.075)^2 + (13 - 16.075)^2 + \cdots + (18 - 16.075)^2 \\
&= 336.775
\end{aligned}
$$

The respective mean square terms are obtained by dividing these sums of squares by their corresponding degrees of freedom. Because $c = 4$ and $n = 40$, we have

$$\text{MSA} = \frac{\text{SSA}}{c - 1} = \frac{123.275}{4 - 1} = 41.0917$$

$$\text{MSW} = \frac{\text{SSW}}{n - c} = \frac{213.5}{40 - 4} = 5.9306$$

so that, using Equation (10.5) to test H_0, we obtain

$$F = \frac{\text{MSA}}{\text{MSW}} = \frac{41.0917}{5.9306} = 6.93$$

TABLE 10.3

OBTAINING THE CRITICAL VALUE OF F WITH 3 AND 36 DEGREES OF FREEDOM AT THE 0.05 LEVEL OF SIGNIFICANCE

Denominator, df_2	Numerator, df_1										
	1	2	3	4	5	6	7	8	9	10	12
30	4.17	3.32	2.92	2.69	2.53	2.42	2.33	2.27	2.21	2.16	2.09
40	4.08	3.23	2.84	2.61	2.45	2.34	2.25	2.18	2.12	2.08	2.00

Source: Extracted from Table A.7

For a selected α level of significance, F_u, the upper-tail critical value from the F distribution is obtained from Table A.7, from which Table 10.3 has been extracted. In our detergent example, there are 3 degrees of freedom in the numerator of the F ratio and 36 degrees of freedom in the denominator, so F_u, the upper-tail critical value at the 0.05 level of significance, is approximately 2.87 (an interpolation between 30 and 40 degrees of freedom). Because our computed test statistic $F = 6.93$ exceeds $F_u = 2.87$, the null hypothesis is rejected. (See Figure 10.6.) We conclude that there is evidence of a significant difference in the average amount of dirt removed between the four detergents.

The corresponding ANOVA summary table is presented in Table 10.4 and contains the exact p-value obtained from Microsoft Excel or MINITAB (see

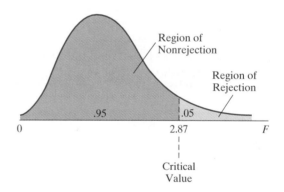

Figure 10.6   Regions of rejection and nonrejection for the analysis of variance at the 0.05 level of significance with 3 and 36 degrees of freedom

TABLE 10.4

ANALYSIS-OF-VARIANCE SUMMARY TABLE FOR THE DETERGENT STUDY

Source	Degrees of Freedom	Sums of Squares	Mean Square (Variance)	F	p-Value
Among groups	$4 - 1 = 3$	123.275	41.0917	6.93	0.001
Within groups	$40 - 4 = 36$	213.500	5.9306		
Total	$40 - 1 = 39$	336.775			

	A	B	C	D	E	F	G
1	**Anova: Single Factor**						
2							
3	**SUMMARY**						
4	*Groups*	*Count*	*Sum*	*Average*	*Variance*		
5	A	10	139	13.9	5.877778		
6	B	10	172	17.2	6.844444		
7	C	10	183	18.3	5.566667		
8	D	10	149	14.9	5.433333		
9							
10							
11	**ANOVA**						
12	*Source of Variation*	*SS*	*df*	*MS*	*F*	*P-value*	*F crit*
13	Between Groups	123.275	3	41.09167	6.928806	0.000844	2.866265
14	Within Groups	213.5	36	5.930556			
15							
16	Total	336.775	39				

Figure 10.7   Microsoft Excel output for one-way analysis of variance for the laundry-detergent data

```
One-way Analysis of Variance

Analysis of Variance
Source     DF        SS        MS        F         P
Factor      3     123.28     41.09      6.93      0.001
Error      36     213.50      5.93
Total      39     336.77
                                      Individual 95% CIs For Mean
                                      Based on Pooled StDev
Level      N       Mean      StDev   -+---------+---------+---------+-----
A          10     13.900     2.424   (------*-----)
B          10     17.200     2.616                    (-----*-----)
C          10     18.300     2.359                          (-----*-----)
D          10     14.900     2.331           (------*-----)
                                      -+---------+---------+---------+-----
Pooled StDev =     2.435             12.5      15.0      17.5      20.0
```

Figure 10.8   MINITAB output for one-way analysis of variance for the laundry-detergent data

Figures 10.7 or 10.8). Note that the p-value or probability of obtaining an F statistic of 6.93 or larger when the null hypothesis is true is approximately 0.001. Because this p-value is less than the specified α of 0.05, the null hypothesis is rejected.

Multiple Comparisons: The Tukey–Kramer Procedure

In the laundry-detergent example discussed thus far in this chapter, the one-way ANOVA F test was used to determine whether there was a difference among the detergents. Once a difference among the means of the groups or levels is found, it is important that we determine which particular groups or levels are different.

Although many procedures are available (see References 8 and 12), we now focus on the Tukey–Kramer procedure to determine which of the c means are significantly different from each other. This method is an example of a *post hoc* comparison procedure, because the hypotheses of interest are formulated *after* the data have been inspected.

The Tukey–Kramer procedure enables us to examine comparisons between all pairs of groups simultaneously. The first step involved is to compute the differences $\overline{X}_j - \overline{X}_{j'}$ (where $j \neq j'$) among all $c(c-1)/2$ pairs of means. The **critical range** for the Tukey–Kramer procedure is then obtained from the quantity given in Equation (10.6).

OBTAINING THE CRITICAL RANGE

$$\text{critical range} = q_u \sqrt{\frac{\text{MSW}}{2}\left(\frac{1}{n_j} + \frac{1}{n_{j'}}\right)} \tag{10.6}$$

where q_u = the upper-tail critical value from a *Studentized range* distribution having c degrees of freedom in the numerator and $n - c$ degrees of freedom in the denominator.

If the sample sizes differ, a critical range is computed for each pairwise comparison of sample means. The final step is to compare each of the $c(c-1)/2$ differences against its corresponding critical range. A specific pair is declared significantly different if the absolute difference between the sample means $|\overline{X}_j - \overline{X}_{j'}|$ exceeds the critical range.

To apply the Tukey–Kramer procedure, we return to the laundry-detergent example. Using the ANOVA procedure, we concluded that there was evidence of a significant treatment effect. The amount of dirt removed differs among the detergents. Because there are four levels, there are $4(4-1)/2$ possible pairwise comparisons to be made. From Table 10.2 on page 478, the absolute mean differences are calculated as follows.

1. $|\overline{X}_1 - \overline{X}_2| = |13.9 - 17.2| = 3.30$
2. $|\overline{X}_1 - \overline{X}_2| = |13.9 - 18.3| = 4.40$
3. $|\overline{X}_1 - \overline{X}_2| = |13.9 - 14.9| = 1.00$
4. $|\overline{X}_1 - \overline{X}_2| = |17.2 - 18.3| = 1.10$
5. $|\overline{X}_1 - \overline{X}_2| = |17.2 - 14.9| = 2.30$
6. $|\overline{X}_1 - \overline{X}_2| = |18.3 - 14.9| = 3.40$

Only one critical range needs to be obtained here, because the four groups had equal-sized samples. To determine the critical range from our ANOVA summary table (Table 10.4 on page 480), we have MSW = 5.9306 and also $n_j = 10$. From Table A.9, for $\alpha = 0.05$, $c = 4$, and $n - c = 40 - 4 = 36$, we find that q_u, the upper-tailed critical value of the test statistic with 4 degrees of freedom in the numerator and 36 degrees of freedom in the denominator, is 3.81. (See Table 10.5.) From Equation (10.6), we have

$$\text{critical range} = 3.81\sqrt{\left(\frac{5.9306}{2}\right)\left(\frac{1}{10} + \frac{1}{10}\right)} = 2.934$$

TABLE 10.5

OBTAINING THE STUDENTIZED RANGE q STATISTIC FOR $\alpha = 0.05$ WITH 4 AND 36 DEGREES OF FREEDOM

Denominator Degrees of Freedom	Numerator Degrees of Freedom									
	2	3	4	5	6	7	8	9	.	.
.	.	.	.	.	.	.	.	.	.	.
30	2.89	3.49	3.84	4.10	4.30	4.46	4.60	4.72		
40	2.86	3.44	3.79	4.04	4.23	4.39	4.52	4.63		

Source: Extracted from Table A.9

Because 3.30, 4.40, and 3.40 > 2.934, we conclude that there is a significant difference between the means of groups one and two, one and three, and three and four. All other pairwise differences are due to chance. We can conclude that detergent 1 is removing less than detergent 2 or detergent 3, and detergent 3 is removing more than detergent 4.

ANOVA Assumptions

In our laundry-detergent example, we have not yet thoroughly evaluated the assumptions underlying the one-way F test. How can we know whether the one-way F test was an appropriate procedure for analyzing these experimental data?

In Chapter 9, we mentioned the assumptions made in the application of each hypothesis-testing procedure and the consequences of departures from these assumptions. To employ the one-way ANOVA F test, we must again make certain assumptions about the data being investigated. These three major assumptions are randomness and independence, normality, and homogeneity of variance.

The first assumption, **randomness and independence,** always must be met, because the validity of any experiment depends on random sampling and/or the randomization process. To avoid biases in the outcomes, it is essential that either the obtained samples of data be considered as randomly and independently drawn from the c populations or that the items or subjects in a study be randomly assigned to the c levels of the factor of interest (i.e., the *treatment groups*). Departures from this assumption can seriously affect inferences from the analysis of variance. These problems are discussed more thoroughly in Reference 8.

The second assumption, normality, states that the values in each sampled group are drawn from normally distributed populations. Just as in the case of the t test, the one-way ANOVA F test is fairly robust against departures from the normal distribution. As long as the distributions are not extremely different from a normal distribution, the level of significance of the ANOVA F test is usually not greatly affected by lack of normality, particularly for large samples. When the normality assumption is seriously violated, *nonparametric* alternatives to the one-way ANOVA F test are available. (See Section 10.6.)

The third assumption, **homogeneity of variance,** states that the variance within each population should be equal for all populations (that is, $\sigma_1^2 = \sigma_2^2 = \cdots = \sigma_c^2$). This assumption is needed in order to combine or pool the variances within the groups into a single within-group source of variation SSW. If there are equal sample sizes in each group, inferences based on the F distribution might not be seriously affected by unequal variances. If, however, there are unequal sample sizes in different groups, unequal variances from group to group can have serious effects on any inferences developed from the ANOVA procedures. Thus, when possible, there should be equal sample sizes in all groups.

When only the homogeneity-of-variance assumption is violated, procedures similar to those used in the separate-variance t test of Section 9.4 are available. (See Reference 5.) However, if both the normality and homogeneity-of-variance assumptions have been violated, an appropriate *data transformation* can be used that will both normalize the data and reduce the differences in variances (see Reference 12) or, alternatively, a more general *nonparametric procedure* can be employed (see References 4 and 5).

Limitations of the One-Factor Design

This approach of studying only one treatment factor of interest at a time, although useful in some circumstances, is among the least efficient ways of conducting an experiment. The reasons for this statement are two-fold. First, if we now wished to study the effect of other factors (as we will in Section 11.1), such as the washing temperature or the type of detergent (powder versus liquid), we would need to conduct additional experiments, thereby making the approach of examining only one factor both time consuming and more costly. Second, and perhaps more important, varying only one factor at a time does not allow us to study how two or more factors interact in their effect on a response variable of interest. For example, it is possible that detergent brand A is the most efficient at removing dirt at a warm temperature, while detergent brand B is the most efficient at a hot temperature. In other words, temperature and detergent may interact and affect the amount of dirt removed. Whenever interactions between variables exist, analyzing the effects of a single variable can be misleading. Without varying several factors simultaneously, it is impossible to determine whether such an interaction exists. Experimental designs that enable us to study interactions will be discussed in Chapter 11.

PROBLEMS

10.1 For a class project, five students prepared popcorn in a similar fashion, using the same amount of popcorn and three different oils. Afterwards, they counted the number of popped kernels, with the results as follows.

Vegetable	Canola	Safflower
336	544	381
453	577	404
468	498	504
516	631	428

POPCORN

(a) At the 0.05 level, is there a significant difference in the average number of popped kernels between the three oils?

(b) If appropriate, at the 0.05 level of significance, determine which oils differ in the average number of popped kernels.

(c) Based on the results of (a) and (b), if you were making popcorn, if you wanted to maximize the number of popped kernels, which oil would you use? Explain.

10.2 A sporting-goods manufacturing company wanted to compare the distance traveled by golf balls produced by each of four different design molds. Ten balls were manufactured with each design and were brought to the local golf course for testing by the club professional. The order in which the balls were hit from the first tee with a driver was randomized, so that the pro did not know which design was being hit. All 40 balls were hit during a short period of time in which the environmental conditions were essentially the same. The results (distance traveled in yards) for the four designs were as follows:

	Designs		
1	2	3	4
206.32	203.81	217.08	213.90
226.77	223.85	230.55	231.10
207.94	206.75	221.43	221.28
224.79	223.97	227.95	221.53
206.19	205.68	218.04	229.43
229.75	234.30	231.84	235.45
204.45	204.49	224.13	213.54
228.51	219.50	224.87	228.35
209.65	210.86	211.82	214.51
221.44	233.00	229.49	225.09

GOLFBALL

(a) At the 0.05 level of significance, is there evidence of a difference between the average distances traveled by the golf balls differing in design?
(b) If the results you obtained in (a) indicate it is appropriate, use the Tukey–Kramer procedure to determine which groups differ in average distance.
(c) What assumptions are necessary in (a)? Do you think these assumptions are valid for these data? Explain.
(d) What golf ball design should the manufacturing manager choose if he wishes to maximize distance traveled? Explain.

10.3 Manufactured gas plants are used to produce gas for lighting, heating, and feedstock for the chemical industry. This process creates wastes that include toxic hydrogen sulfide. The following data represent the amount of sulfides (meg/g) for three independent runs produced by a gas plant.

Run 1	Run 2	Run 3
0.50	0.67	0.56
0.75	0.78	0.67
0.80	0.56	0.49
0.60	0.55	0.68
0.40	0.57	0.97

(Continued)

Run 1	Run 2	Run 3
0.80	0.68	0.68
0.60	0.88	0.59
0.76	0.98	0.99
0.54	1.20	0.57
0.87	0.65	0.66

SULFIDES

(a) At the 0.05 level of significance, is there evidence of a difference in the average amount of sulfides for the three runs?
(b) If the results you obtained in (a) indicate it is appropriate, use the Tukey–Kramer procedure to determine which runs differ in average sulfides.
(c) What assumptions are necessary in (a)? Do you think these assumptions are valid for these data? Explain.

10.4 The compressive strengths of five different concrete mixes were compared in an experiment. The first mix was a standard concrete mix designed for a compressive strength of 38 Mpa (1 Mpa = 145.04 psi). The second and third mixes have the same mix ratio but 25% and 35%, respectively, of the fine aggregate (sand) was replaced with discarded (dirty) foundry sand. The fourth and fifth mixes are similar to the second and third mixes except they use new (clean) foundry sand. The 28-day compressive strength data for hardened concrete (15 cm × 30 cm cylinder) are as follows.

Normal	25% Dirty	35% Dirty	25% Clean	35% Clean
43.0	32.3	30.2	44.4	43.0
44.5	32.3	30.7	41.5	44.6
44.0	36.2	31.1	44.9	42.6

MIXES

(a) At the 0.05 level of significance, is there evidence of a difference in the average compressive strength for the different mixes?
(b) If the results you obtained in (a) indicate it is appropriate, use the Tukey–Kramer procedure to determine which mixes differ in average compressive strength.
(c) Which concrete mix would you recommend? Why?

10.5 A sputtering machine is used for metalization on wafers in the semiconductor industry. The reflectance of different sputtering machines (larger numbers are better) was compared, with the following results.

Sputtering Machine		
A	B	C
88.80	90.20	94.80
90.20	91.70	93.50
91.30	90.00	90.90
89.50	90.90	94.20
90.30	92.50	94.10

SPUTTER

(a) At the 0.05 level of significance, is there evidence of a difference in the average reflectance for the different machines?
(b) If the results you obtained in (a) indicate it is appropriate, use the Tukey–Kramer procedure to determine which machines differ in average reflectance.
(c) Which machine would you recommend? Why?

10.6 An experiment was conducted to explore the effects of various amounts of fly ash in high-strength concrete. Data was collected that indicated the compressive strength of 28-day-old samples of 4000-psi specified-strength concrete using from 0 to 60% high calcium fly ash, with the following results.

Percent Fly Ash					
0	20	30	40	50	60
4779	5189	5110	5995	5746	4895
4706	5140	5685	5628	5719	5030
4350	4976	5618	5897	5782	4648

FLYASH

(a) At the .05 level of significance, is there evidence of a difference in the average compressive strength using different percentages of fly ash?
(b) If the results you obtained in (a) indicate it is appropriate, use the Tukey–Kramer procedure to determine which levels of fly ash differ in average compressive strength.
(c) Which percentage of fly ash would you recommend? Why?

10.7 Samples of a plastic product were selected from a given lot of material, and the tensile strength in pounds was measured over six time periods, with the following results.

Time Period					
1	2	3	4	5	6
606	683	514	608	551	578
601	603	539	544	578	572
384	604	592	283	483	326
701	477	502	492	607	652
463	438	393	570	474	337
293	371	473	440	250	410
549	237	443	533	320	438
520	480	467	588	413	283

PLASTIC

(a) At the 0.05 level of significance, is there evidence of a difference in the average tensile strength for the different time periods?
(b) If the results you obtained in (a) indicate it is appropriate, use the Tukey–Kramer procedure to determine which time periods differ in average tensile strength.
(c) Obtain a side-by-side box-and-whisker plot of the tensile strength for the different time periods.
(d) Given the results of (a)–(c), is there a difference in the tensile strength over the six time periods?

10.5 THE RANDOMIZED BLOCK MODEL

In Section 10.4, we developed the one-way ANOVA *F* test to evaluate differences among the means of *c* groups. The one-way ANOVA *F* test is employed in experimental situations in which *n* items or individuals (i.e., *experimental units* or *subjects*) are randomly assigned to the *c* levels of a factor of interest (i.e., the *treatment groups*). Such designed one-factor experiments are referred to as *one-way* or *completely randomized design models*.

In Section 9.6, we used the *t* test for the mean difference in situations involving repeated measurements or matched samples, in order to evaluate differences between two treatment conditions. Suppose, now, that we wish to extend this approach to situations in which there are more than two treatment groups or levels of a factor of interest. In such cases, the items or individuals that have been matched on one or more variables (or on whom repeated measurements have been taken) are called **blocks.**[1] Data are then obtained for the response or outcome of each treatment group and block combination. Thus, in designing experiments of this type, there are two things to consider: treatments and blocks; however, with respect to tests of hypotheses, we focus on the differences among the *c* levels of the factor of interest (i.e., the treatment groups).

Experimental situations such as this are referred to as **randomized block** or **repeated measures models.** The purpose of blocking is to remove as much block or subject variability as possible, so that the focus is on differences among the *c* treatment conditions. Thus, when appropriate, the reason for selecting a randomized block design model instead of a completely randomized design model is to provide a more efficient analysis by reducing the experimental error and thereby obtaining more precise results. (See References 7, 8, 12.)

[1] When dealing with repeated measures where the same subject is evaluated under different treatment conditions, the block represents a subject.

Tests for the Treatment and Block Effects

Recall from Figure 10.2 on page 472 that, in the completely randomized model, the total variation in the outcome measurements (SST) is subdivided into variation due to differences *among* the *c* groups (SSA) and chance variation *within* the *c* groups (SSW). Within-group variation is considered experimental error, and among-group variation is attributable to treatment effects.

To filter out the effects of the blocking for the randomized block design model, we need to further subdivide the within-group variation (SSW) into variation due to differences among the blocks (SSBL) and variation due to random error (SSE). Therefore, as presented in Figure 10.9, in a randomized block design model the total variation in the outcome measurements is the summation of three components—among-group variation (SSA), among-block variation (SSBL), and inherent random error (SSE).

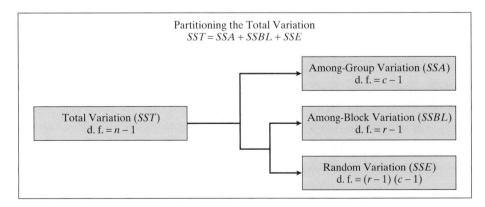

Figure 10.9   Partitioning the total variation in a randomized block-design model

To develop the ANOVA procedure for the randomized block-design model we need to define the following terms:

$$r = \text{the number of blocks}$$

$$c = \text{the number of groups or treatment levels}$$

$$n = \text{the total number of observations (where } n = rc)$$

$$X_{ij} = \text{the value in the } i\text{th block for the } j\text{th treatment level}$$

$$\overline{X}_{i.} = \text{the mean of all the values in block } i$$

$$\overline{X}_{.j} = \text{the mean of all the values for treatment level } j$$

$$\sum_{j=1}^{c} \sum_{i=1}^{r} X_{ij} = \text{the grand total—i.e., the summation of the values over all blocks and all treatment levels}$$

The total variation, also called **sum of squares total (SST)**, is a measure of the variation among all the observations. It can be obtained by summing the squared differences between each individual observation and the overall or grand mean $\overline{\overline{X}}$, which is based on all n observations. SST is computed as in Equation (10.7).

TOTAL VARIATION

$$SST = \sum_{j=1}^{c} \sum_{i=1}^{r} (X_{ij} - \overline{\overline{X}})^2 \tag{10.7}$$

where $\overline{\overline{X}} = \dfrac{\sum_{j=1}^{c} \sum_{i=1}^{r} X_{ij}}{rc}$ (i.e., the overall or grand mean)

The among-group variation, also called the **sum of squares among groups (SSA)**, is measured by the sum of the squared differences between the sample mean of each group, $\overline{X}_{.j}$, and the overall or grand mean $\overline{\overline{X}}$, weighted by the number of blocks r. The among-group variation is computed as in Equation (10.8).

AMONG-GROUP VARIATION

$$SSA = r \sum_{j=1}^{c} (\overline{X}_{.j} - \overline{\overline{X}})^2 \tag{10.8}$$

where $\overline{X}_{.j} = \dfrac{\sum_{i=1}^{c} X_{ij}}{r}$ (i.e., the treatment-group means)

The among-block variation, also called the **sum of squares among blocks (SSBL)**, is measured by the sum of the squared differences between the mean of each block $\overline{X}_{i.}$ and the overall or grand mean $\overline{\overline{X}}$, weighted by the number of groups c. The among-block variation is computed from Equation (10.9).

AMONG-BLOCK VARIATION

$$\text{SSBL} = c \sum_{i=1}^{r} (\overline{X}_{i.} - \overline{\overline{X}})^2 \tag{10.9}$$

where $\overline{X}_{i.} = \dfrac{\displaystyle\sum_{j=1}^{c} X_{ij}}{c}$ (i.e., the block means)

The inherent random variation or error, also called the **sum of squares error (SSE)**, is measured by the sum of the squared differences among all the observations after the effect of the particular treatments and blocks have been accounted for. SSE is computed from Equation (10.10).

RANDOM ERROR

$$\text{SSE} = \sum_{j=1}^{c} \sum_{i=1}^{r} (X_{ij} - \overline{X}_{.j} - \overline{X}_{i.} + \overline{\overline{X}})^2 \tag{10.10}$$

There are c treatment levels of the factor being compared, so there are $c - 1$ degrees of freedom associated with the sum of squares among groups (SSA). Similarly, because there are r blocks, there are $r - 1$ degrees of freedom associated with the sum of squares among blocks (SSBL). In addition, there are $n - 1$ degrees of freedom associated with the sum of squares total (SST), because each observation X_{ij} is being compared to the overall or grand mean $\overline{\overline{X}}$, which is based on all n observations. Therefore, because the degrees of freedom for each of the sources of variation must add to the degrees of freedom for the total variation, we obtain the degrees of freedom for the sum of squares error (SSE) component by subtraction and algebraic manipulation. The degrees of freedom is given by $(r - 1)(c - 1)$.

If each of the component sums of squares is divided by its associated degrees of freedom, we obtain the three *variances* or mean square terms (**MSA, MSBL, and MSE**), needed for ANOVA, depicted in Equation (10.11a–c).

OBTAINING THE MEAN SQUARES

$$\text{MSA} = \frac{\text{SSA}}{c - 1} \tag{10.11a}$$

$$\text{MSBL} = \frac{\text{SSBL}}{r - 1} \tag{10.11b}$$

$$\text{MSE} = \frac{\text{SSE}}{(r - 1)(c - 1)} \tag{10.11c}$$

If the assumptions pertaining to the analysis of variance are met, the null hypothesis of no differences among the c population means (i.e., no treatment effects)

$$H_0: \mu_{.1} = \mu_{.2} = \cdots = \mu_{.c}$$

is tested against the alternative that not all the c population means are equal

$$H_1: \text{Not all } \mu_{.j} \text{ are equal (where } j = 1, 2, \ldots, c)$$

by computing the test statistic F as in Equation (10.12).

THE RANDOMIZED BLOCK F-TEST STATISTIC FOR DIFFERENCES AMONG c MEANS

$$F = \frac{MSA}{MSE} \qquad (10.12)$$

The F-test statistic follows an F distribution with $c - 1$ degrees of freedom for the MSA term and $(r - 1)(c - 1)$ degrees of freedom for the MSE term. For a given level of significance, α, we reject the null hypothesis if the computed F test statistic exceeds the upper-tailed critical value F_u from the F distribution with $c - 1$ and $(r - 1)(c - 1)$ degrees of freedom, respectively, in the numerator and denominator. (See Table A.7.) That is, we have the following decision rule:

Reject H_0 if $F > F_u$;

otherwise, don't reject H_0.

To examine whether it is advantageous to block, some researchers suggest that the test of the null hypothesis of no block effects be performed. Thus, we test

$$H_0: \mu_{1.} = \mu_{2.} = \cdots = \mu_{r.}$$

against the alternative

$$H_1: \text{Not all } \mu_{i.} \text{ are equal (where } j = 1, 2, \ldots, r)$$

We form the F statistic depicted in Equation (10.13).

THE F TEST STATISTIC FOR BLOCK EFFECTS

$$F = \frac{MSBL}{MSE} \qquad (10.13)$$

The null hypothesis is therefore rejected at the α level of significance if the F test statistic exceeds the upper-tailed critical value F_u from the F distribution with $r - 1$ and $(r - 1)(c - 1)$ degrees of freedom, respectively, in the numerator and denominator. (See Table A.7.) That is, we have the following decision rule:

Reject H_0 if $F > F_u$;

otherwise, don't reject H_0.

It could be argued that this extra test is unnecessary, because the sole purpose of establishing the blocks was to provide a more efficient means of testing for treatment effects by reducing the experimental error.

As in Section 10.4, the results of an analysis-of-variance procedure are usually displayed in an ANOVA summary table, the format for which is presented in Table 10.6.

TABLE 10.6

ANALYSIS-OF-VARIANCE TABLE FOR THE RANDOMIZED BLOCK DESIGN

Source	Degrees of Freedom	Sums of Squares	Mean Square (Variance)	F
Among treatments	$c - 1$	SSA	$MSA = \dfrac{SSA}{c-1}$	$F = \dfrac{MSA}{MSE}$
Among blocks	$r - 1$	SSBL	$MSBL = \dfrac{SSBL}{r-1}$	$F = \dfrac{MSBL}{MSE}$
Error	$(r-1)(c-1)$	SSE	$MSE = \dfrac{SSE}{(r-1)(c-1)}$	
Total	$rc - 1$	SST		

To illustrate the randomized block F test, we return to the *Using Statistics* example on page 469. Data were collected from a sample of 30 wafers. For each wafer, the thickness of the wafers on positions 1 and 2 (outer circle), 18 and 19 (middle circle), and 28 (inner circle) was measured. The results are shown in Table 10.7.

TABLE 10.7

THICKNESS OF WAFERS IN AN INTEGRATED-CIRCUIT MANUFACTURING PROCESS

Wafer	Position 1	2	18	19	28	Wafer	Position 1	2	18	19	28
1	240	243	250	253	248	16	237	239	242	247	245
2	238	242	245	251	247	17	242	244	246	251	248
3	239	242	246	250	248	18	243	245	247	252	249
4	235	237	246	249	246	19	243	245	248	251	250
5	240	241	246	247	249	20	244	246	246	250	246
6	240	243	244	248	245	21	241	239	244	250	246
7	240	243	244	249	246	22	242	245	248	251	249
8	245	250	250	247	248	23	242	245	248	243	246
9	238	240	245	248	246	24	241	244	245	249	247
10	240	242	246	249	248	25	236	239	241	246	242
11	240	243	246	250	248	26	243	246	247	252	247
12	241	245	243	247	245	27	241	243	245	248	246
13	247	245	255	250	249	28	239	240	242	243	244
14	237	239	243	247	246	29	239	240	250	252	250
15	242	244	245	248	245	30	241	243	249	255	253

CIRCUITS

Source: K. C. B. Roes and R. J. M. M. Does, "Shewhart-Type Charts in Nonstandard Situations," *Technometrics,* 37, 1995, 15–24

To determine the results of a randomized block-design experiment, we access Microsoft Excel or MINITAB for our integrated circuit data. Figure 10.10 represents Microsoft Excel output, and Figure 10.11 represents MINITAB output.

When using the 0.05 level of significance to test for differences among the positions, the decision rule is to reject the null hypothesis ($H_0: \mu_{.1} = \mu_{.2} = \mu_{.3} = \mu_{.4} = \mu_{.5}$) if the calculated F value exceeds 2.45, the upper-tailed critical value from the F

34	SUMMARY	Count	Sum	Average	Variance
35	Position 1	30	7216	240.5333	6.878161
36	Position 2	30	7282	242.7333	7.788506
37	Position 18	30	7382	246.0667	8.409195
38	Position 19	30	7473	249.1	7.058621
39	Position 28	30	7412	247.0667	4.616092
40					
41					
42	ANOVA				

Wafers

43	Source of Variation	SS	df	MS	F	P-value	F crit
44	Rows	601.5	29	20.74138	5.922219	1.93E-12	1.565322
45	Columns	1417.733	4	354.4333	101.2002	6.84E-37	2.44988
46	Error	406.2667	116	3.502299			
47							
48	Total	2425.5	149				

Positions

Figure 10.10 Microsoft Excel output for a randomized block design for the integrated circuit data

Two-way Analysis of Variance

```
Analysis of Variance for Thicknes
Source      DF        SS        MS        F        P
Wafer       29      601.50     20.74     5.92    0.000
Position     4     1417.73    354.43   101.20    0.000
Error      116      406.27      3.50
Total      149     2425.50

                         Individual 95% CI
Position      Mean    -+---------+---------+---------+---------+
1           240.53    (--*--)
2           242.73           (--*--)
3           246.07                       (-*--)
4           249.10                                    (-*--)
5           247.07                         (-*--)
                      -+---------+---------+---------+---------+
                    240.00    242.50    245.00    247.50    250.00
```

Figure 10.11 MINITAB output for a randomized block design for the integrated circuit data

distribution with 4 and 116 degrees of freedom in the numerator and denominator, respectively. (See Figure 10.12.) Because $F = 101.20 > F_u = 2.45$, we reject H_0 and conclude that there is evidence of a difference in the average thickness for the different positions. Using Microsoft Excel or MINITAB (see Figures 10.10 or 10.11), we obtain a p-value of 0.0000 for the positions. Because $0.0000 < 0.05$, we reject H_0.

As a check on the effectiveness of blocking, we can test for differences among the wafers. The decision rule, using the 0.05 level of significance, is to reject the null hypothesis ($H_0: \mu_{1.} = \mu_{2.} = \cdots \mu_{30.}$) if the calculated F value exceeds 1.57, the upper-tailed critical value from the F distribution with 29 and 116 degrees of

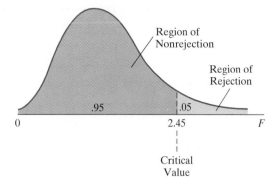

Figure 10.12 Regions of rejection and nonrejection for the integrated-circuits study at the 0.05 level of significance with 4 and 116 degrees of freedom

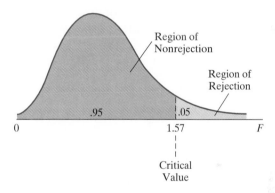

Figure 10.13 Regions of rejection and nonrejection for the integrated-circuits study at the 0.05 level of significance with 29 and 116 degrees of freedom

freedom in the numerator and denominator, respectively. (See Figure 10.13.) Because $F = 5.922 > F_u = 1.57$, or because the p-value $= 0.0000 < 0.05$, we reject H_0 and conclude that there is evidence of difference among the wafers. Thus we conclude that blocking has been advantageous in reducing the experimental error.

In addition to the assumptions of the one-way analysis of variance previously mentioned in Section 10.4, we need to assume that there is no *interaction effect* between the treatments and the blocks. That is, we need to assume that any differences between the treatments (the positions) are consistent across the entire set of blocks (the wafers). The concept of *interaction* will be discussed in Section 11.1.

Now that we have developed the randomized block model and have used it in the integrated-circuits study, the question arises as to what effect the blocking had on the analysis. Did the blocking result in an increase in precision in comparing the different treatment groups? To answer this, we compute the **estimated relative efficiency (RE)** in Equation (10.14) of the randomized block design as compared with the completely randomized design.

ESTIMATED RELATIVE EFFICIENCY

$$RE = \frac{(r-1)\text{MSBL} + r(c-1)\text{MSE}}{(rc-1)\text{MSE}} \qquad (10.14)$$

Thus, using Figure 10.10 or 10.11 on page 492, we have

$$RE = \frac{(29)(20.7418) + (30)(4)(3.5023)}{(149)(3.5023)} = 1.96$$

This means that 1.96 times as many observations in each treatment group would be needed in a one-way ANOVA design to obtain the same precision for comparison of treatment group means as would be needed for our randomized block design.

Multiple Comparisons: The Tukey Procedure

As in the case of the completely randomized design model, once the null hypothesis of no differences between the treatment groups has been rejected, we need to determine which of these treatment groups are significantly different from the others. For the randomized block design model, the sample sizes for each treatment group are equal, so we can use a procedure developed by John Tukey. (See References 12 and 14.) The critical range for the Tukey procedure is given by Equation (10.15).

OBTAINING THE CRITICAL RANGE

$$\text{critical range} = q_u \sqrt{\frac{\text{MSE}}{r}} \qquad (10.15)$$

where the statistic q_u = the upper-tail critical value from a *Studentized range* distribution having c degrees of freedom in the numerator and $(r-1)(c-1)$ degrees of freedom in the denominator.

Each of the $c(c-1)/2$ pairs of means is compared against the one critical range. A specific pair, (group j versus group j') is declared significantly different if the absolute difference in the sample means $|\bar{X}_j - \bar{X}_{j'}|$ exceeds this critical range.

To apply the Tukey procedure, we return to our integrated-circuits study. There are five positions, so there are $5(5-1)/2 = 10$ possible pairwise comparisons to be made. From Figure 10.10 on page 492, the absolute mean differences are as follows.

1. $|\bar{X}_{.1} - \bar{X}_{.2}| = |240.533 - 242.733| = 2.200$

2. $|\bar{X}_{.1} - \bar{X}_{.3}| = |240.533 - 246.067| = 5.534$

3. $|\bar{X}_{.1} - \bar{X}_{.4}| = |240.533 - 249.100| = 8.567$

4. $|\bar{X}_{.1} - \bar{X}_{.5}| = |240.533 - 247.067| = 6.634$

5. $|\bar{X}_{.2} - \bar{X}_{.3}| = |242.733 - 246.067| = 2.666$

6. $|\overline{X}_{.2} - \overline{X}_{.4}| = |242.733 - 249.100| = 6.367$

7. $|\overline{X}_{.2} - \overline{X}_{.5}| = |242.733 - 247.067| = 4.334$

8. $|\overline{X}_{.3} - \overline{X}_{.4}| = |246.067 - 249.100| = 3.033$

9. $|\overline{X}_{.3} - \overline{X}_{.5}| = |246.067 - 247.067| = 1.000$

10. $|\overline{X}_{.4} - \overline{X}_{.5}| = |249.100 - 247.067| = 2.033$

To determine the critical range, we use Figure 10. 10 or 10.11 on page 492, to obtain MSE = 3.503 and r = 30. From Table A.9 [for α = 0.05, c = 5, and $(r - 1)(c - 1)$ = 116], q_u, the upper-tailed critical value of the test statistic with 5 degrees of freedom in the numerator and 116 degrees of freedom in the denominator, is approximately 3.92. From Equation (10.15),

$$\text{critical range} = 3.92\sqrt{\frac{3.50}{30}} = 1.34$$

Note that all pairwise comparisons except $|\overline{X}_{.3} - \overline{X}_{.5}|$ are greater than the critical range. Therefore, we conclude that there is evidence of a significant difference in the average thickness between all pairs of positions except for positions 18 and 28.

PROBLEMS

10.8 A researcher in a pharmaceutical company wishes to perform an experiment to determine whether the choice of treatment substance affects the clotting time of plasma (in minutes). Five different clotting-enhancement substances (i.e., treatments) are to be compared, and seven female patients, all of whom are in their first term of pregnancy, are to be studied. For each patient, five vials of blood are drawn and one vial each is randomly assigned to one of the five treatments. The clotting-time data are shown below.

Patient	Treatment Substance				
	1	2	3	4	5
1	8.4	8.1	8.5	8.6	8.5
2	10.3	10.0	9.9	10.6	10.2
3	12.4	11.8	12.3	12.5	12.2
4	9.7	9.8	9.9	10.4	10.4
5	8.6	8.4	9.7	9.9	9.5
6	9.3	9.6	10.3	10.5	10.2
7	11.1	10.6	11.6	10.9	11.4

CLOTTING

(a) Construct an appropriate graph, plot, or chart of the data and describe any trends or relationships that might be apparent among the treatment groups and among the blocks.

(b) At the 0.05 level of significance, is there evidence of a difference in the average plasma clotting time among the five treatment substances?

(c) If appropriate, use the Tukey procedure to determine the treatment substances that differ in average clotting time. (Use α = 0.05.)

(d) What should the researcher conclude about the treatment substances?

(e) Determine the relative efficiency of the randomized block design as compared with that of the one-way ANOVA (completely randomized) design.

(f) Based on the results of (e), why do you think that a randomized block design is preferable to a completely randomized design for these data?

10.9 The following data represent the compressive strength in thousands of pounds per square inch (psi) of 40 samples of concrete taken two, seven, and 28 days after pouring.

Sample	Two days	Seven days	28 days
1	2.830	3.505	4.470
2	3.295	3.430	4.740
3	2.710	3.670	5.115
4	2.855	3.355	4.880
5	2.980	3.985	4.445
6	3.065	3.630	4.080
7	3.765	4.570	5.390
8	3.265	3.700	4.045
9	3.170	3.660	4.370
10	2.895	3.250	4.955
11	2.630	2.850	3.835
12	2.830	3.340	4.290
13	2.935	3.630	4.600
14	3.115	3.675	4.605
15	2.985	3.475	4.690
16	3.135	3.605	4.880
17	2.750	3.250	3.425
18	3.205	3.540	4.265
19	3.000	4.005	4.485
20	3.035	3.595	5.220
21	1.635	2.275	3.330
22	2.270	3.910	4.065
23	2.895	2.915	4.715
24	2.845	4.530	4.735
25	2.205	2.280	3.605
26	3.590	3.915	4.670
27	3.080	3.140	4.720
28	3.335	3.580	4.650
29	3.800	4.070	4.680
30	2.680	3.805	5.165
31	3.760	4.130	5.075
32	3.605	3.720	4.710
33	2.005	2.690	4.200
34	2.495	3.230	4.645
35	3.205	3.590	4.725
36	2.060	2.945	4.695
37	3.425	4.030	5.470
38	3.315	3.685	4.330
39	3.825	4.175	4.950
40	3.160	3.430	4.460

CONCRETE2

Source: O. Carrillo-Gamboa and R. F. Gunst, "Measurement-Error-Model Collinearities," *Technometrics,* 34, 1992, p. 454–464

(a) At the 0.05 level of significance, is there evidence of a difference in the average compressive strength after two, seven, and 28 days?
(b) If appropriate, use the Tukey procedure to determine the days that differ in average compressive strength. (Use $\alpha = 0.05$.)

(c) Determine the relative efficiency of the randomized block design as compared with the one-way ANOVA (completely randomized) design.
(d) Obtain a side-by-side box-and-whisker plot of the compressive strength for the different time periods.
(e) In the results of (a), (b), and (d), is there a pattern in the compressive strength over the three time periods?

10.10 A taste-testing experiment has been designed so that four brands of Colombian coffee are to be rated by nine experts. To avoid any carryover effects, the tasting sequence for the four brews is randomly determined for each of the nine expert tasters until a rating on a 7-point scale (1 = extremely unpleasing, 7 = extremely pleasing) is given for each of four characteristics: taste, aroma, richness, and acidity. The following table displays the summated ratings—accumulated over all four characteristics.

Expert	Brand			
	A	B	C	D
C.C.	24	26	25	22
S.E.	27	27	26	24
E.G.	19	22	20	16
B.L.	24	27	25	23
C.M.	22	25	22	21
C.N.	26	27	24	24
G.N.	27	26	22	23
R.M.	25	27	24	21
P.V.	22	23	20	19

COFFEE2

(a) Construct an appropriate graph of the data and describe any differences that might be apparent among the treatment groups and among the blocks.
(b) At the 0.01 level of significance, completely analyze the data to determine whether there is evidence of difference among the mean summated ratings of the four brands of Colombian coffee and, if so, which of the brands is rated highest (i.e., best). What can you conclude?

10.11 In an experiment concerning physiological effects under hypnosis, the skin potential (adjusted for initial level) in millivolts was measured for each of eight subjects under the emotions of fear, happiness, depression, and calmness, with the following results.

Subject	Fear	Happiness	Depression	Calmness
1	23.1	22.7	22.5	22.6
2	57.6	53.2	53.7	53.1
3	10.5	9.7	10.8	8.3
4	23.6	19.6	21.1	21.6
5	11.9	13.8	13.7	13.3
6	54.6	47.1	39.2	37.0
7	21.0	13.6	13.7	14.8
8	20.3	23.6	16.3	14.8

HYPNOSIS

(a) At the 0.05 level of significance, is there evidence of a difference in the average measured skin potential between the emotions?

(b) If appropriate, use the Tukey procedure to determine the emotions that differ in average measured skin potential. (Use $\alpha = 0.05$.)

(c) Determine the relative efficiency of the randomized block design as compared with the one-way ANOVA (completely randomized) design.

(d) Based on the results of (a) and (b), do you think emotion has an effect on measured skin potential? Explain.

10.12 An experiment was conducted by a professional baseball team to determine the fastest approach for a runner trying to reach second base. Three methods for rounding first base were to be evaluated; round out, narrow angle, and wide angle. Time trials were conducted for six players for each of the three methods, with the following results (in seconds).

Player	Round Out	Narrow Angle	Wide Angle
1	5.65	5.60	5.40
2	5.90	5.85	5.70
3	5.25	5.15	5.00
4	5.85	5.80	5.70
5	5.55	5.55	5.35
6	5.40	5.50	5.55

RUNNINGBB

(a) At the 0.05 level of significance, is there evidence of a difference in the time to run to second base between the methods?

(b) If appropriate, use the Tukey procedure to determine the methods that differ in average running time. (Use $\alpha = 0.05$.)

(c) Determine the relative efficiency of the randomized block design as compared with the completely randomized design.

(d) Given the results of (a) and (b), what method do you think the players should use to run to second base? Explain.

(e) Why do you think the randomized block design is better than the one-way ANOVA (completely randomized) design?

10.6 KRUSKAL–WALLIS RANK TEST FOR DIFFERENCES IN *c* MEDIANS (*OPTIONAL TOPIC*)

The Kruskal–Wallis rank test for differences among *c* medians (where $c > 2$) is an extension of the Wilcoxon rank-sum test for two independent samples, discussed in Section 9.9. Thus, the Kruskal–Wallis test enjoys the same power properties relative to the one-way ANOVA *F* test as does the Wilcoxon rank-sum test relative to the pooled-variance *t* test for two independent samples. That is, the Kruskal–Wallis procedure has proven to be almost as powerful as the *F* test under conditions appropriate to the latter and even more powerful than the *F* test when certain assumptions of the Analysis of Variance (see Section 10.4) are violated.

The **Kruskal–Wallis rank test** is most often used to test whether *c* independent sample groups have been drawn from populations possessing equal medians. That is, we test

$$H_0: M_1 = M_2 = \cdots = M_c$$

against the alternative that the *c* medians are not the same

$$H_1: \text{Not all } M_j \text{ are equal (where } j = 1, 2, \ldots, c)$$

For such situations, it is only necessary to assume that the measurements are ordinal over all sample groups and that the c populations from which the samples are drawn have the same *variability* and *shape*.

To perform the Kruskal–Wallis rank test, we first (if necessary) replace the observations in the c combined samples with their overall ranks, in such a way that rank 1 is given to the smallest of the combined observations and rank n to the largest of the combined observations (where $n = n_1 + n_2 + \cdots n_c$). If any values are tied, each is assigned the average of the ranks they would otherwise have been assigned if ties had not been present in the data.

The Kruskal–Wallis test was developed as an alternative to the one-way ANOVA F test. As such, the Kruskal–Wallis test statistic H is similar conceptually to SSA, the *among group variation* term [see Equation (10.2) on page 474] which is part of the test statistic F [see Equation (10.5) on page 477]. Instead of comparing each of the c group means $\overline{X}_j$ against the overall or grand mean $\overline{\overline{X}}$, we now compare the average of the ranks in each of the c groups against the overall average rank based on all n combined observations. If there exists a significant treatment effect among the c groups, the average of the ranks assigned in some or all of the groups will differ considerably from each other and from the overall average rank. In the process of squaring these differences, as we did when developing SSA, the test statistic H becomes large. On the other hand, if there is no treatment effect present, the test statistic H theoretically will have a value of 0. In practice, owing to random variation, the H test statistic will be small because the average of the ranks assigned in each group should be very similar to each other and to the overall average rank.

The Kruskal–Wallis test statistic H is obtained as in Equation (10.16).

KRUSKAL–WALLIS RANK TEST FOR DIFFERENCES AMONG c MEDIANS

$$H = \left[\frac{12}{n(n+1)} \sum_{j=1}^{c} \frac{T_j^2}{n_j} \right] - 3(n+1) \qquad (10.16)$$

where

n is the total number of observations over the combined samples

n_j = the number of observations in the jth sample; $j = 1, 2, \ldots, c$

T_j is the sum of the ranks assigned to the jth sample

T_j^2 is the square of the sum of the ranks assigned to the jth sample

---

As the sample sizes in each group get large (greater than 5), the test statistic H can be approximated by the chi-square distribution with $c - 1$ degrees of freedom. Thus, for any selected level of significance α, the decision rule is to reject the null hypothesis if the computed value of H exceeds χ_U^2, the upper-tail critical value, and not to reject the null hypothesis if H is less than or equal to χ_U^2. (See Figure 10.14.)

$$\text{Reject } H_0 \text{ if } H > \chi_U^2;$$

otherwise, don't reject H_0.

The critical values from the chi-square distribution are given in Table A.6.

To illustrate the Kruskal–Wallis rank test for differences among c medians, we return to the laundry-detergent example of Section 10.4. If we do not wish to

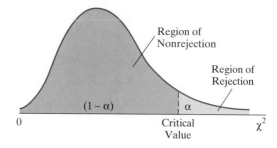

Figure 10.14   Determining the rejection region

make the assumption that the amount of dirt (in mgs) is normally distributed across the underlying populations, the nonparametric Kruskal–Wallis rank test for differences among the four population medians can be used.

The null hypothesis to be tested is that the median amounts of dirt removed for the four detergents are equal; the alternative is that at least one of the detergents differs from the others.

$$H_0: M_1 = M_2 = M_3 = M_4$$

$$H_1: \text{Not all } M_j \text{ are equal (where } j = 1, 2, \ldots, c)$$

The results of this experiment (in terms of amount of dirt removed in milligrams) are again displayed in Table 10.8, along with the corresponding ranks.

In converting the 40 amounts to ranks, as in Table 10.8, we note that, in the combined ranking, the eighth laundry load for detergent *A* had the lowest amount of dirt removed, with a value of 10. It was given a rank of 1. The first value for detergent *A* and the first value for detergent *D* each had the next lowest values, eleven. Because they were tied for ranks two and three, each was assigned the

TABLE 10.8

DATA ON AMOUNT OF DIRT (MG) REMOVED AND CONVERTED RANKS BY FOUR DETERGENT BRANDS

				Brand			
A		*B*		*C*		*D*	
Amount	Rank	Amount	Rank	Amount	Rank	Amount	Rank
11	2.5	12	5.0	18	30.5	11	2.5
13	7.5	14	10.5	16	18.5	12	5.0
17	24.5	17	24.5	18	30.5	16	18.5
17	24.5	19	34.5	20	36.5	15	14.0
15	14.0	21	38.5	22	40.0	14	10.5
16	18.5	18	30.5	15	14.0	17	24.5
14	10.5	19	34.5	17	24.5	13	7.5
10	1.0	18	30.5	21	38.5	16	18.5
12	5.0	16	18.5	16	18.5	17	24.5
14	10.5	18	30.5	20	36.5	18	30.5

LAUNDRY

average of these ranks, 2.5. Finally, we note that a rank of 40 is assigned to the fifth value for detergent C, because this value, 22, was the largest value.

After all the ranks are assigned, we obtain the following sum of the ranks for each group:

Rank sums:

$$T_1 = 118.5$$

$$T_2 = 257.5$$

$$T_3 = 288$$

$$T_4 = 156$$

As a check on the rankings, we have

$$T_1 + T_2 + T_3 + T_4 = \frac{n(n+1)}{2}$$

$$118.5 + 257.5 + 288 + 156 = \frac{(40)(41)}{2}$$

$$820 = 820$$

We choose a 0.05 level of significance and use Equation (10.16) to test the null hypothesis of equal population medians.

$$H = \left[\frac{12}{n(n+1)} \sum_{j=1}^{c} \frac{T_j^2}{n_j} \right] - 3(n+1)$$

$$= \left\{ \frac{12}{(40)(41)} \left[\frac{(118.5)^2}{10} + \frac{(257.5)^2}{10} + \frac{(288)^2}{10} + \frac{(156)^2}{10} \right] \right\} - 3(41)$$

$$= \left(\frac{12}{1640} \right) [18,762.85] - 123 = 14.289$$

This statistic H has a chi-square distribution with $c - 1$ degrees of freedom. Thus for any selected level of significance α, the decision rule is to reject the null hypothesis if the computed value of H exceeds χ_U^2, the upper-tail critical value, and not to reject the null hypothesis if H is less than or equal to χ_U^2.

Reject H_0 if $H > \chi_U^2$;

otherwise don't reject H_0.

Using a 0.05 level of significance from Table A.6, we see that χ_U^2, the upper-tail critical value of the chi-square distribution with $c - 1 = 3$ degrees of freedom, is 7.815. The computed value of the test statistic $H = 14.289$ exceeds the critical value, so we reject the null hypothesis and conclude that not all the detergents are the same with respect to median amount of dirt removed. Using the p-value approach, from Figure 10.15 or 10.16, the p-value is $0.003 < 0.05$. In addition to the p-value, MINITAB provides the sample size (N), the sample median for each detergent, the average assigned rank (AVE. RANK), and the Z VALUE for each detergent. The average assigned ranks are obtained by dividing the rank sums by the respective sample sizes. The overall average rank for all 40 observations is also shown. The Z values indicate how different, in standardized units, each average rank is from the overall average rank.

	A	B
Kruskal-Wallis Test for Laundry Detergents		
Level of Significance		0.05
	Group 1	
Sum of Ranks		118.5
Sample Size		10
	Group 2	
Sum of Ranks		257.5
Sample Size		10
	Group 3	
Sum of Ranks		288
Sample Size		10
	Group 4	
Sum of Ranks		156
Sample Size		10
Sum of Squared Ranks/Sample Size		18762.85
Sum of Sample Sizes		40
Number of groups		4
H Test Statistic		14.28915
Critical Value		7.814725
***p*-Value**		0.002537
Reject the null hypothesis		

Figure 10.15   PHStat add-in for Microsoft Excel output of Kruskal–Wallis rank test for differences among *c* medians in laundry-detergent study

```
Kruskal-Wallis Test on Amount of Dirt Removed

Detergent    N      Median    Ave Rank         Z
1            10     14.00       11.9        -2.70
2            10     18.00       25.7         1.64
3            10     18.00       28.8         2.59
4            10     15.50       15.6        -1.53
Overall      40                 20.5

H = 14.29   DF = 3   P = 0.003
H = 14.46   DF = 3   P = 0.002  (adjusted for ties)
```

Figure 10.16   MINITAB output of Kruskal–Wallis rank test for differences among *c* medians in laundry-detergent study

At the bottom of the MINITAB printout appear the test statistic *H*, the degrees of freedom (d.f.), and the *p*-value. If there are ties in the rankings, as is the case in our laundry-detergent example, MINITAB provides an adjustment to the test statistic *H* along with an adjusted *p*-value. We suggest that the adjusted *H* statistic be used for interpreting results. In this study, this adjustment has a minimal impact on our results. Note that these conclusions are the same that were reached using the one-way ANOVA *F* test in Section 10.4.

Because we have rejected the null hypothesis and concluded that there was evidence of a significant difference among the detergents with respect to the median amount of dirt removed, the next step is a simultaneous comparison of all possible pairs of detergents, to determine which ones differ from the others. As a follow-up to the Kruskal–Wallis rank test, a multiple comparison procedure proposed by O. J. Dunn (see References 4 and 5) can be used.

To use the Kruskal–Wallis rank test for differences among c medians, we make the assumptions, presented in Exhibit 10.1.

EXHIBIT 10.1 Assumptions of the Kruskal–Wallis Test

1. The c samples are randomly and independently drawn from their respective populations.

2. The underlying random phenomenon of interest is *continuous* (to avoid ties).

3. The observed data constitute at least an ordinal scale of measurement, both within and among the c samples.

4. The c populations have the same variability.

5. The c populations have the same shape.

Interestingly, the Kruskal–Wallis procedure still makes less stringent assumptions than does the F test. To employ the Kruskal–Wallis procedure, the measurements need only be ordinal over all sample groups, and the common population distributions need only be continuous—their common shapes are irrelevant. In fact, if we ignore the last two assumptions, the Kruskal–Wallis rank test still can be used to test the null hypothesis of no differences in the c populations against the general alternative that at least one of the populations differs from at least one of the other populations in some characteristic—be it central tendency, variation, or shape. On the other hand, to use the F test, the level of measurement must be interval or ratio scaled, and we must assume that the c samples are coming from underlying normal populations having equal variances.

For situations involving completely randomized designs, when the more stringent assumptions of the F test hold, we should select it over the Kruskal–Wallis test because it is slightly more powerful in its ability to detect significant treatment effects. On the other hand, if the more stringent assumptions cannot be met, the Kruskal–Wallis test likely is more powerful than the F test, and we should choose this procedure.

PROBLEMS

10.13 The quality engineer in a plant manufacturing stereo equipment wants to study the effect of temperature on the failure time of a particular electronic component. She designs an experiment wherein 24 of these components, all from the same batch, are randomly assigned to one of three levels of temperature and then simultaneously activated. The rank order of their times to failure (i.e., a rank of 1 is given to the first component to burn out) are as follows:

TEMPERATURE

150°F	200°F	250°F
4	2	1
7	8	3
10	11	5
13	12	6
18	17	9
21	19	14
22	20	15
24	23	16

COMPFAIL

(a) At the 0.05 level of significance, is there evidence of a significant temperature effect on the median life of this type of electronic component?

(b) Do you think that temperature has an effect on failure time? Explain.

10.14 Recent research has indicated that exposure of humans to heavy metals can be harmful even at low concentrations, because of their tendency to accumulate within body tissue. The study here focused specifically on lead concentrations in household drinking water and examined differences between untreated household drinking water, household drinking water treated magnetically, and household drinking water treated with softener. The results are summarized as follows.

Untreated	Magnetic	Softener
20.0	11.0	24.0
200.0	64.0	408.0
17.0	16.0	26.0
220.0	93.0	198.0
8.0	2.5	11.0

(*Continued*)

Untreated	Magnetic	Softener
200.0	54.0	126.0
3.0	17.0	25.0
55.0	76.0	200.0

LEAD2

(a) At the 0.05 level of significance, is there evidence of a difference in the median lead concentration between untreated household drinking water, household drinking water treated magnetically, and household drinking water treated with softener?

(b) Why might the Kruskal–Wallis test be more appropriate for these data than the one-way ANOVA *F* test?

10.15 Refer to Problem 10.2 on page 484, concerning the design of golf balls.
(a) At the 0.05 level of significance, is there evidence of difference among the median distances traveled by the golf balls differing in design?
(b) Are there any differences between the results in (a) and those of Problem 10.2 on page 484? Discuss.

10.16 Refer to Problem 10.3 on page 485, concerning the production of waste at a gas plant.
(a) At the 0.05 level of significance, is there evidence of difference in the median amount of sulfides between the three different runs?
(b) Are there any differences between the results in (a) and those of Problem 10.3 on page 485? Discuss.

10.17 Refer to Problem 10.7 on page 486, concerning the tensile strength of plastic.
(a) At the 0.05 level of significance, is there evidence of difference in the median tensile strength between the six time periods?
(b) Are there any differences between the results in (a) and those of Problem 10.7 on page 486? Discuss.

KEY TERMS

CHAPTER REVIEW   *Checking Your Understanding*

10.18 What is the difference between the among-groups variance, MSA, and the within-groups variance, MSW?

10.19 How can graphical methods be used to evaluate the validity of the assumptions of the analysis of variance?

10.20 What is the difference between the randomized block-design model and the (one-way) completely randomized design model?

10.21 What are the major assumptions of ANOVA?

10.22 Under what conditions should the one-way ANOVA *F* test to examine possible differences among the means of *c* independent populations be selected?

10.23 Under what conditions should the Kruskal–Wallis rank test to examine possible differences among the medians of *c* independent populations be selected?

10.24 When and how should multiple-comparison procedures for evaluating pairwise combinations of the group means be used?

10.25 Under what conditions should the randomized block *F* test to examine possible differences in the means of *c* related populations be selected?

Chapter Review Problems

10.26 A snack-products company that supplies stores in a metropolitan area with "healthy" snack products was interested in improving the shelf life of its potato chip product. Six batches (each batch containing 1 pound) of the product were made under each of four different formulations. The batches were then kept under the same conditions of storage. Product condition was checked each day for freshness. The shelf life, in days until the product was deemed to be lacking in freshness, was as follows:

	Formulation Method		
A	B	C	D
94	88	76	82
100	89	69	80
90	88	76	82
97	83	79	78
101	79	80	89
90	82	72	80

POTCHIP

(a) At the .05 level of significance, completely analyze the data to determine whether there is evidence of difference in the shelf life among the formulations.
(b) If appropriate, determine which groups differ in average shelf life.
(c) What conclusions about the shelf life of the formulations can the director of operations of the snack-foods company reach? Explain.

10.27 The use of polymers in medicine, especially in the area of drug delivery, is one of the fastest-growing areas of polymer chemistry. An experiment was conducted in which four different formulations were used in a passive plus delivery device. The data collected was the first total drug reading (mg) on each sample.

0.0 cc	0.5 cc	1.0 cc	2.0 cc
703	573	529	603
735	602	682	534
731	589	565	542
638	688	590	591
673	604	524	610
621	661	492	489
598	503	534	516
581	493	515	570
659	647	548	596
580	537	650	654 **POLYMER**

(a) At the 0.05 level of significance, completely analyze the data to determine whether there is evidence of difference among the drug readings that is based on the formulations.
(b) If appropriate, determine which groups differ in average drug reading.
(c) Construct a side-by-side box-and-whisker plot of the drug readings for the different formulations.
(d) Based on the results of (a)–(c), is there a pattern in the drug readings over the four formulations?

10.28 An experiment was concerned with the tensile strength of yarn spun for textile usage. Suppose that, in a replication of part of that experiment, a researcher wishes to examine the effect of air-jet pressure (in psi) on breaking strength. Three different levels of air-jet pressure are to be considered: 30 psi, 40 psi, and 50 psi. A random sample of 18 homogenous/similar filling yarns was selected from the same batch and they were randomly assigned, six each, to the three levels of air-jet pressure. The breaking strength scores are as follows.

AIR-JET PRESSURE

30psi	40psi	50psi
25.5	24.8	23.2
24.9	23.7	23.7
26.1	24.4	22.7
24.7	23.6	22.6
24.2	23.3	22.8
23.6	21.4	24.9 **YARN**

(a) At the 0.05 level of significance, is there evidence of a difference in mean breaking strengths for the three air-jet pressures?
(b) If appropriate, use the Tukey–Kramer procedure to determine which air-jet pressures significantly differ with respect to mean breaking strength. (Use $\alpha = 0.05$.)

(c) At the 0.05 level of significance, is there evidence of a difference in median breaking strengths for the three air-jet pressures?

(d) What will the researcher conclude?

Suppose that, when setting up his experiment, the researcher had access to only six samples of yarn, but was able to divide each yarn sample into three parts and randomly assign them, one each, to the three air-jet pressure levels. Thus, instead of the one-factor completely randomized design model in (a)–(d), he can set up a randomized block design model, the six yarn samples being the blocks and one yarn part each assigned to the three pressure treatments. The breaking strength scores are as follows:

AIR-JET PRESSURE

Yarn	30psi	40psi	50psi
1	25.5	24.8	23.2
2	24.9	23.7	23.7
3	26.1	24.4	22.7
4	24.7	23.6	22.6
5	24.2	23.3	22.8
6	23.6	21.4	24.9 **YARN**

(e) At the 0.05 level of significance, is there evidence of a difference in the mean breaking strengths for the three air-jet pressures?

(f) If appropriate, use the Tukey procedure to determine the air-jet pressures that differ in mean breaking strength. (Use $\alpha = 0.05$.)

(g) At the 0.05 level of significance, is there evidence of a blocking effect?

(h) Determine the relative efficiency of the randomized block design as compared with the completely randomized design.

(i) Compare your results from parts (b) and (e). Given your results in parts (g) and (h), what do you think happened here? What can you conclude about the "impact of blocking" when the blocks themselves are not different from each other?

10.29 From the *Los Osos Landfill Water Quality Monitoring Program, 1996*, Carmen Fojo, County Solid Waste Engineer, generously supplied voluminous amounts of data on the possible effects of a landfill on surface and groundwater chemistry. Part of the data included observations on characteristics of well water for several wells.

CONDUCTIVITY (μhos/cm)

MW-6	MW-7	MW-8	MW-9	MW-10	MW-11
1220	1680	1325	1810	970	1350
1130	1900	1150	1700	1150	1350
1400	1700	1300	1725	1100	1250
1400	1600	1400	1500	1010	1250
1625	1580	1360	1725	880	1300
1670	1620	1340	1700	975	1230
2100	1700	1250	2000	1300	1250
1070	1840	1360	1900	1050	1130
1622	1772	1417	2040	1116	1300 **LANDFILL1**

HARDNESS (mg/L)

MW-7	MW-8	MW-9	MW-10	MW-11	
908	692	1170	245	334	
1180	706	1120	242	327	
930	789	1110	252	326	
833	742	885	256	306	
960	780	1130	254	294	
871	776	840	270	290	
913	739	1320	256	291	
1040	782	1130	268	268	
918	736	1080	246	294	**LANDFILL2**

CHLORIDE ($\mu\gamma$/L)

MW-6	MW-7	MW-8	MW-9	MW-10	MW-11	
310	192	99	169	215	164	
323	202	98	162	215	146	
338	150	98	154	215	137	
323	130	95	115	214	133	
396	148	106	178	225	134	
407	136	98	119	218	130	
410	182	103	223	218	127	
374	170	103	163	211	120	
279	149	96	165	258	118	**LANDFILL3**

(a) For each of the three characteristics (conductivity, hardness, and chloride), analyze the data at the 0.05 level of significance to determine whether there is a difference between the wells.

(b) From the results in (a), what conclusions can you reach concerning the wells?

10.30 A recent wine tasting was held by the J. S. Wine Club, in which eight wines were rated by club members. Information concerning the country of origin and the price were not known to the club members until after the tasting took place. The wines rated (and the prices paid for them) were as follows:

(1) French white $8.59
(2) Italian white $6.50
(3) Italian red $6.50
(4) French burgundy (red) $8.69
(5) French burgundy (red) $9.75
(6) California Beaujolais (red) $8.50
(7) French white $7.75
(8) California white $11.59

The summated ratings over several characteristics for the 12 club members were as follows.

WINE

Respondent	1	2	3	4	5	6	7	8
A	10	17	15	9	12	6	15	9
B	9	14	11	5	16	2	15	7
C	10	18	10	5	18	5	10	10
D	9	11	13	10	17	11	14	9

(*Continued*)

Respondent	1	2	3	4	5	6	7	8	
E	10	16	12	8	18	8	10	10	
F	6	16	3	8	4	2	2	5	
G	9	12	14	9	9	6	6	5	
H	7	12	11	8	15	9	12	8	
I	10	18	12	12	16	10	10	16	
J	16	9	10	13	18	11	15	14	
K	14	16	13	12	15	15	17	11	
L	15	17	10	13	15	16	16	13	**WINE**

(a) At the 0.01 level of significance, is there evidence of difference in the average rating scores between the wines?

(b) What assumptions are necessary in order to do (a) of this problem? Comment on the validity of these assumptions.

(c) If appropriate, use the Tukey procedure to determine the wines that differ in average rating. (Use $\alpha = 0.01$.).

(d) Answer the following based upon your results in (c):
   (1) Do you think that country of origin has had an effect on the ratings?
   (2) Do you think that the type of wine (red versus white) has had an effect on the ratings?
   (3) Do you think that price has had an effect on the ratings? Discuss fully.

(e) Determine the relative efficiency of the randomized block design as compared with the completely randomized design.

(f) Ignore the blocking variable and "erroneously" reanalyze the data as a one-factor completely randomized design model where the one factor (brands of wines) has eight levels and each level contains a sample of 12 independent observations.

(g) Compare the SSBL and SSE terms in (a) to the SSW term in (f). Discuss.

(h) Using the results in (a), (f), and (g) as a basis, describe the problems that can arise when analyzing data if the wrong procedures are applied.

WHITNEY GOURMET CAT FOOD COMPANY CASE

The Whitney Gourmet Cat Food Company was interested in exploring ways of expanding its market share by offering new cat food products in addition to the existing kidney and shrimp foods. Experimental formulations were developed for two new products, one based on chicken livers and the other based on salmon. The team agreed that an experiment should be conducted to compare the two new foods against the two existing products and, in addition, against a supermarket brand of a beef-based product. A local animal shelter agreed to participate in the study. A random sample of 50 cats from the population at the shelter was selected. Ten cats were randomly assigned to each of the five products being tested. Each of the cats was then presented with 3 ounces of the selected food in a dish at feeding time. The response variable of interest was operationally defined as the amount of food (in ounces) that the cat consumed within a 10-minute time interval that began when the filled dish was presented. This definition was selected in an attempt to distinguish between what the cat seemed to really be attracted to and what would be eaten because nothing else was available. The results for this experiment are presented in Table WG10.1.

TABLE WG10.1

OUNCES EATEN FOR FIVE CAT-FOOD PRODUCTS

Kidney	Shrimp	Chicken Liver	Salmon	Beef
2.37	2.26	2.29	1.79	2.09
2.62	2.69	2.23	2.33	1.87
2.31	2.25	2.41	1.96	1.67
2.47	2.45	2.68	2.05	1.64
2.59	2.34	2.25	2.26	2.16
2.62	2.37	2.17	2.24	1.75
2.34	2.22	2.37	1.96	1.18
2.47	2.56	2.26	1.58	1.92
2.45	2.36	2.45	2.18	1.32
2.32	2.59	2.57	1.93	1.94

WG10

Exercises

WG10.1 (a) What are the advantages and disadvantages of conducting the experiment at the animal shelter?

(b) Can you think of any factors that might bias or confound the results of this experiment?

(c) Suggest an alternative approach for conducting the experiment. What would be the advantages and disadvantages of conducting the experiment under this alternative approach?

WG10.2 Analyze the results of the experiment concerning the different types of cat food. Write a report that discusses the implication of the results of the experiment for the Whitney Gourmet Cat Food Company.

REFERENCES

1. Bisgaard, S.; "Industrial Use of Statistically Designed Experiments: Case Study References and Some Historical Anecdotes," *Quality Engineering,* 4, (1992), 547–562
2. Box, J. F.; "R. A. Fisher and the Design of Experiments," *American Statistician,* 34, (1980), 1–10
3. Box, J. F.; *R. A. Fisher: The Life of a Scientist;* New York: John Wiley, 1978
4. Conover, W. J.; *Practical Nonparametric Statistics,* 2d ed.; New York: Wiley, 1980
5. Daniel, W. W.; *Applied Nonparametric Statistic,* 2d ed.; Boston, MA: PWS Kent, 1990
6. Fisher, R. A.; *Statistical Methods, Experimental Design, and Statistical Inference: A Re-Issue of Statistical Methods for Research Workers, The Design of Experiments, and Statistical Methods and Scientific Inference;* New York: Oxford University Press, 1990
7. Hicks, C. R. and K. V. Turner; *Fundamental Concepts in the Design of Experiments,* 5th ed.; New York: Oxford University Press, 1999
8. Kirk, R. E.; *Experimental Design,* 2d ed.; Belmont, CA: Brooks-Cole, 1982
9. *Microsoft Excel 2000;* Redmond, WA: Microsoft Corporation, 1999
10. Miller, R. G.; *Simultaneous Statistical Inference,* 2d ed.; New York: Springer-Verlag, 1980
11. *MINITAB for Windows Version 12;* State College, PA: MINITAB, Inc., 1998
12. Neter, J., M. H. Kutner, C. Nachtsheim, and W. Wasserman; *Applied Linear Statistical Models,* 4th ed.; Homewood, IL: Richard D. Irwin, 1996
13. Port, O. and J. Carney; "Quality: A Field with Roots That Go Back to the Farm," *Business Week,* Special 1991 Bonus Issue, October 25, 1991, 15
14. Tukey, J. W.; "Comparing Individual Means in the Analysis of Variance," *Biometrics,* 1949, Vol. 5, pp. 99–114

APPENDIX 10.1   *Using Microsoft Excel for the Analysis of Variance*

Using Microsoft Excel for the One-Way ANOVA

To perform the one-factor analysis of variance, use the Data Analysis Anova: Single Factor tool. As an example, consider the laundry-detergent example of Section 10.4. To determine whether there is evidence of a significant difference in the average amount of dirt removed for four different detergents, open the **LAUNDRY.XLS** workbook. Click the **Data** sheet tab. Verify that the amount of dirt removed for the four detergents of Table 10.2 on page 478 have been entered into columns A through D. Select **Tools | Data Analysis.** Select **Anova: Single Factor** from the Analysis Tools list box in the Data Analysis dialog box. Click the **OK** button. In the Anova: Single Factor dialog box, enter **A1:D11** in the Input Range: edit box. Select the **Columns** option button. Select the **Labels in First Row** check box. Enter **0.05** in the Alpha: edit box. Select the **New Worksheet Ply:** option button, and enter **One-Factor ANOVA** as the name of the new sheet. Click the **OK** button. The Data Analysis tool add-in inserts a worksheet containing the analysis of variance for the laundry-detergent example of Section 10.4, similar to the one shown in Figure 10.7 on page 481. This worksheet is *not* dynamically changeable, so any changes made to the underlying detergent data would require using the Data Analysis tool a second time to produce updated test results.

The Data Analysis Anova tool requires that the data for each group be contiguous, an arrangement known as unstacked data. Some data sets are "stacked": the data for all groups appear in a single column, identified by a grouping variable in another column. To use such stacked data with the Data Analysis Anova: Single Factor tool, select **PHStat | Data Preparation | Unstack Data** to unstack the data prior to using the Data Analysis Anova: Single Factor tool.

Using the PHStat Add-In for Microsoft Excel for the Tukey–Kramer Procedure

To perform the Tukey–Kramer procedure for making multiple comparisons among all possible pairs of c means, first obtain the necessary statistics for the procedure. As an example, consider the laundry-detergent example of Section 10.4. To generate multiple comparisons among all possible pairs of means of the amount of dirt removed for the four detergents, generate a worksheet containing analysis-of-variance statistics using the Data Analysis Anova: Single Factor tool. From the worksheet generated by the Data Analysis tool, obtain the sample sizes and means from the Count and Average columns, respectively, of the SUMMARY table that begins in row 4. Obtain the degrees of freedom within groups from the cell in the "df" column and "Within Groups" row of the ANOVA table. Obtain the *MSW* value from the cell in the "MS" column and "Within Groups" row of the ANOVA table. Obtain the Studentized range Q statistic from Table A.9 for the level of significance $\alpha = 0.05$ by using the appropriate degrees of freedom value.

Having obtained the sample means, the sample sizes, the degrees of freedom within groups, the *MSW* value, and the appropriate Studentized range Q statistic, continue by selecting **File | New** to open a new workbook (or open the existing workbook into which the Tukey–Kramer procedure worksheet is to be inserted). Select **PHStat | c-Sample Tests | Tukey-Kramer Procedure.** In the Tukey-Kramer Procedure dialog box, enter **4** in the Number of Groups: edit box. Enter **Tukey-Kramer Procedure for Laundry Detergents** in the Output Title: edit box. Click the **OK** button. The PHStat add-in inserts a worksheet containing calculations for the Tukey–Kramer procedure. At this point, the worksheet will display 0 or #DIV/0! in the cells used for each pairwise comparison. Continue entering the sample means and sample sizes in the shaded cells in column B. Enter the group 1 sample mean, 13.9, and sample size, 10, the group 2 sample mean, 17.2, and sample size, 10, the group 3 sample mean, 18.3, and sample size, 10, and the group 4 sample mean, 14.9, and sample size, 10. Enter the *MSW* value, 5.9306, and the Studentized range Q statistic, 3.81, to complete the entries needed.

Using Microsoft Excel for the Randomized Block Design

To illustrate the use of Microsoft Excel for the randomized block design, open the **CIRCUITS.XLS** workbook that contains the data for the integrated-circuits example of Table 10.7 on page 491. On the Data sheet, note that the data have been set up in a format that is similar to Table 10.7, except that column A provides a label for each block, and cell A1 is blank.

To obtain the results similar to those of Figure 10.10 on page 492, select **Tools | Data Analysis.** Select **Anova: Two Factors without Replication** from the Analysis tools list box. Click the **OK** button. In the Anova: Two Factors without Replication dialog box, which appears, enter **A1:F31** in the Input Range edit box, select the **Labels** check box, and enter the level of significance in the Alpha edit box. (0.05 is the default value.) Select the **New Worksheet Ply** option button and enter a name, such as **Randomized Block.** Click the **OK** button. In addition to the ANOVA table, Excel provides the sample size, sum, arithmetic mean, and variance for each row and column in the randomized block design.

Using the PHStat Add-In for Microsoft Excel for the Kruskal–Wallis Test

To perform the Kruskal–Wallis rank test for differences among c medians, use the c-Sample Tests | Kruskal-Wallis Rank Sum Test choice of the PHStat add-in. As an example, consider the laundry-detergent example of Section 10.6. To determine whether there is evidence of a significant difference in the median amount of dirt removed by the four different detergents, open the **LAUNDRY.XLS** workbook. Select **PHStat | c-Sample Tests | Kruskal-Wallis Rank Test.** In the Kruskal-Wallis Rank Test dialog box, enter **0.05** in the Level of Significance: edit box. Enter **A1:D11** in the Sample Data Cell Range: edit box. Select the **First cells contain label** check box. Enter **Kruskal-Wallis Test for Differences among Laundry Detergents** in the Output Title: edit box. Click the **OK** button. The Data Analysis tool add-in inserts a worksheet containing calculations for the Kruskal–Wallis test similar to the one shown in Figure 10.15 on page 501.

The PHStat Kruskal–Wallis choice requires that the data for each group be in separate columns, an arrangement known as unstacked data. Some data sets are "stacked": the data for all groups appear in a single column, identified by a grouping variable in another column. To use such stacked data with the PHStat Kruskal–Wallis choice, select the **Data Preparation | Unstack Data** choice of the PHStat add-in to unstack the data.

APPENDIX 10.2 *Using MINITAB for the Analysis of Variance*

Using MINITAB for the One-Way ANOVA

To illustrate the use of MINITAB for the one-factor ANOVA, open the **LAUNDRY.MTW** worksheet. Note that the data have been stored in an unstacked format, with each level in a separate column. Select **Stat | ANOVA | One-way(Unstacked).** In the Responses (in separate columns): edit box, enter **C1 C2 C3 C4.** Click the **Graphs** option button and select the **Boxplot of data** check box. Click the **OK** button to return to the One-Way Analysis of Variance dialog box. Click the **OK** button.

If the data are stored in a stacked format, select **Stat | ANOVA | One-way.** Enter the column in which the response variable is stored in the Response edit box and the column in which the factor is stored in the Factor edit box. You will obtain the output displayed in Figure 10.8 on page 481.

Using MINITAB for the Randomized Block Designs

The procedure for using MINITAB for the randomized block design requires that the data be in a stacked format. To illustrate the use of MINITAB for the randomized block design, open the **CIRCUITS.MTW** worksheet. Note that the data need to be stacked, because the positions are located in columns C2 to C6. Select **Manip | Stack/Unstack | Stack columns.** In the Stack dialog box, enter **C2–C6** in the Stack the data in edit box. Enter **C7** in the Store the stacked data in edit box and C8 in the Store subscripts edit box. Copy the batch numbers from rows 1–30 in C1 to rows 1–30, 31–60, 61–90, 91–120, and 121–150 in C9. Enter the labels Amount in C7, Positions in C8, and Batches in C9. Select **Stat | ANOVA | Two-Way.** In the Two-Way dialog box, enter **C7** or **'Amount'** in the Response edit box, **C9** or **'Batches'** in the Row factor edit box, and **C8** or **'Positions'** in the Column factor edit box. Select the **Display Means** check box for the row and column factors. Click the **OK** button. You will obtain the output displayed in Figure 10.11 on page 492.

Using MINITAB for the Kruskal-Wallis Test

To illustrate the use of MINITAB for the Kruskal–Wallis test, open the **LAUNDRY.MTW** worksheet. Note that the data have been stored in an unstacked format, with each level in a separate column. In order to perform the Kruskal–Wallis test, we need to stack the data. Select **Manip | Stack/Unstack | Stack Columns.** Enter **C1–C4** in the Stack the following Columns edit box, **C5** in the Store the Stacked data in: edit box, and **C6** in the Store the Subscripts in: edit box. Click the **OK** button. Enter labels for **Amount** in C5 and **Detergents** in C6.

Select **Stat | Nonparametrics | Kruskal-Wallis.** Enter **C5** or **'Amount'** in the Response edit box and **C6** or **'Detergents'** in the Factor: edit box. Click the **OK** button. You will obtain the output displayed in Figure 10.16 on page 501.

11 The Design of Experiments: Factorial Designs

"If we could begin by just getting engineers to run a simple design this will usually whet their appetite for more. For there are hundreds of thousands of engineers in this country, and even if the 2^3 was the only design they ever used, and even if the only method of analysis that was employed was to eyeball the data, this alone could have an enormous impact on the experimental efficiency, the rate of innovation, and the competitive position of this country."

GEORGE E. P. BOX

USING STATISTICS

Each year, millions of cake mixes are sold by food-processing companies. A cake mix consists of a packet containing flour, shortening, and egg powder that will provide a good-tasting cake. One issue in determining the amount of these ingredients to include in the packet in order to maximize the tastiness of the cake relates to the fact that consumers might not precisely follow the recommended oven temperature and baking time. An experiment is conducted in which each factor is tested at a higher level than called for in the instructions and at a lower level than called for in the instructions. The goal of the experiment is to determine which factors have an effect on the taste rating of the cake, and the levels of the factors that will provide the cake with the highest taste rating.

11.1 TWO-FACTOR FACTORIAL DESIGNS

In this section, we begin the study of experimental designs in which more than one factor is studied simultaneously. These experimental designs have been classified under the name of **factorial designs,** because they evaluate the effects of two or more factors simultaneously. We will begin our discussion in this section with the simplest factorial design, the two-factor design. In addition, although any number of levels of a factor can be included in a design, we will, for pedagogical simplicity, consider only the special circumstance in which there are two levels for each factor of interest. Designs that contain more than two levels of a factor are logical extensions of the two-level case. In addition, we will be concerned only with situations in which there are equal numbers of **replicates** (that is, sample sizes n') for each combination of the levels of factor A with those of factor B.

Owing to the complexity of the calculations involved, particularly as the number of levels of each factor increases and the number of *replications* in each cell increases, we assume that, in practice, a statistical software or spreadsheet package will be used when analyzing data obtained from factorial design models. Nevertheless, for purposes of illustration, we present the conceptual approach for the decomposition of the total variation for the two-factor factorial design model with equal replication. To do so, we need to define the following terms:

r = the number of levels of factor A

c = the number of levels of factor B

n' = the number of values (replications) for each cell

n = the total number of observations in the experiment (where $n = rcn'$)

X_{ijk} = the value of the kth observation for level i of factor A and level j of factor B

$$\overline{\overline{X}} = \frac{\sum_{i=1}^{r} \sum_{j=1}^{c} \sum_{k=1}^{n'} X_{ijk}}{rcn'} \text{ is the overall or grand mean}$$

$$\overline{X}_{i..} = \frac{\sum_{j=1}^{c} \sum_{k=1}^{n'} X_{ijk}}{cn'}, \text{ which is the mean of the } i\text{th level of factor } A \text{ (where } i = 1, 2, \ldots, r)$$

$$\overline{X}_{.j.} = \frac{\sum_{i=1}^{r} \sum_{k=1}^{n'} X_{ijk}}{rn'}, \text{ which is the mean of the } j\text{th level of factor } B \text{ (where } j = 1, 2, \ldots, c)$$

$$\overline{X}_{ij.} = \sum_{k=1}^{n'} \frac{X_{ijk}}{n'}, \text{ which is the mean of the cell } ij, \text{ the combination of the } i\text{th level of factor } A \text{ and the } j\text{th level of factor } B$$

Recall from Figure 10.1 (page 470) that, in the completely randomized design model, the sum of squares total (or SST) is subdivided into sum of squares among groups (or SSA) and sum of squares within groups (or SSW). Also, from Figure 10.9 (page 487), in the randomized block design model, the total variation (SST) is subdivided into sum of squares among treatment groups (SSA), sum of squares among blocks (SSBL), and sum of squares error (SSE). For the two-factor factorial design model with equal replication in each cell, the total variation (SST) is subdivided into sum of squares due to factor A (or SSA), sum of squares due to factor B (or SSB), sum of squares due to the effect of the interaction of A and B (or SSAB), and sum of squares due to inherent random error (or SSE). This decomposition of the total variation (SST) is displayed in Figure 11.1.

The **sum of squares total** (or **SST**) represents the total variation among all the observations around the grand mean. SST is computed as presented in Equation (11.1).

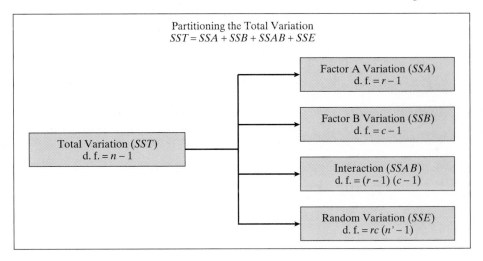

Figure 11.1   Partitioning the total variation in a two-factor factorial design model

---

TOTAL VARIATION

$$\text{SST} = \sum_{i=1}^{r} \sum_{j=1}^{c} \sum_{k=1}^{n'} (X_{ijk} - \overline{\overline{X}})^2 \qquad (11.1)$$

The **sum of squares** due to **factor A** (or **SSA**) represents the differences between the various levels of factor A and the grand mean. SSA is computed as in Equation (11.2).

FACTOR A VARIATION

$$\text{SSA} = cn' \sum_{i=1}^{r} (\overline{X}_{i..} - \overline{\overline{X}})^2 \qquad (11.2)$$

The **sum of squares** due to **factor B** (or **SSB**) represents the differences between the various levels of factor B and the grand mean. SSB is computed as in Equation (11.3).

FACTOR B VARIATION

$$\text{SSB} = rn' \sum_{j=1}^{c} (\overline{X}_{.j.} - \overline{\overline{X}})^2 \qquad (11.3)$$

The **sum of squares** due to the effect of the interaction between A and B (or **SSAB**) represents the effect of the combinations of levels of factor A and factor B. SSAB is computed as in Equation (11.4).

VARIATION DUE TO INTERACTION

$$\text{SSAB} = n' \sum_{i=1}^{r} \sum_{j=1}^{c} (\overline{X}_{ij.} - \overline{X}_{i..} - \overline{X}_{.j.} + \overline{\overline{X}})^2 \tag{11.4}$$

The **sum of squares error** (or **SSE**) represents the differences among the observations within each cell and the corresponding cell mean. SSE is computed as in Equation (11.5).

RANDOM ERROR

$$\text{SSE} = \sum_{i=1}^{r} \sum_{j=1}^{c} \sum_{k=1}^{n'} (X_{ijk} - \overline{X}_{ij})^2 \tag{11.5}$$

There are r levels of factor A, so there are $r - 1$ degrees of freedom associated with SSA. Similarly, there are c levels of factor B, so there are $c - 1$ degrees of freedom associated with SSB. Moreover, because there are n' replications in each of the rc cells, there are $rc(n' - 1)$ degrees of freedom associated with the inherent random error term. Carrying this further, there are $n - 1$ degrees of freedom associated with the sum of squares total (SST), because each observation X_{ijk} is being compared to the overall or grand mean $\overline{\overline{X}}$ based on all n observations. Therefore, because the degrees of freedom for each of the sources of variation must add to the degrees of freedom for the total variation (SST), we obtain the degrees of freedom for the interaction component (SSAB) by subtraction. Its degrees of freedom are given by $(r - 1)(c - 1)$.

If each of the sums of squares is divided by its associated degrees of freedom, we obtain the four variances or mean square terms (MSA, MSB, MSAB, and MSE) in Equation (11.6 a–d) needed for ANOVA:

OBTAINING THE MEAN SQUARES

$$\text{MSA} = \frac{\text{SSA}}{r - 1} \tag{11.6a}$$

$$\text{MSB} = \frac{\text{SSB}}{c - 1} \tag{11.6b}$$

$$\text{MSAB} = \frac{\text{SSAB}}{(r - 1)(c - 1)} \tag{11.6c}$$

$$\text{MSE} = \frac{\text{SSE}}{rc(n' - 1)} \tag{11.6d}$$

In the two-factor ANOVA model, there are three distinct tests that are performed. If we assume that the levels of factor A and factor B have been *specifically selected* for analysis (rather than being *randomly selected* from a population of possible levels), we have the following three tests of hypotheses.

1. To test the hypothesis of no difference due to factor A

$$H_0: \mu_{1..} = \mu_{2..} = \cdots = \mu_{r..}$$

against the alternative

$$H_1: \text{Not all } \mu_{i..} \text{ are equal}$$

we form the F statistic in Equation (11.7).

F TEST FOR FACTOR A EFFECT

$$F = \frac{\text{MSA}}{\text{MSE}} \qquad (11.7)$$

The null hypothesis is rejected at the α level of significance if

$$F = \frac{\text{MSA}}{\text{MSE}} > F_u$$

the upper-tail critical value from an F distribution with $r - 1$ degrees of freedom in the numerator and $rc(n' - 1)$ degrees of freedom in the denominator.

2. To test the hypothesis of no difference due to factor B

$$H_0: \mu_{.1.} = \mu_{.2.} = \cdots = \mu_{.c.}$$

against the alternative

$$H_1: \text{Not all } \mu_{.j.} \text{ are equal}$$

we form the F statistic in Equation (11.8).

F TEST FOR FACTOR B EFFECT

$$F = \frac{\text{MSB}}{\text{MSE}} \qquad (11.8)$$

The null hypothesis is rejected at the α level of significance if

$$F = \frac{\text{MSB}}{\text{MSE}} > F_u$$

the upper-tail critical value from an F distribution with $c - 1$ degrees of freedom in the numerator and $rc(n' - 1)$ degrees of freedom in the denominator.

3. To test the hypothesis of no interaction of factors A and B

$$H_0: \text{The interaction of } A \text{ and } B = 0$$

against the alternative

$$H_1: \text{The interaction of } A \text{ and } B \neq 0$$

we form the F statistic in Equation (11.9).

F TEST FOR INTERACTION EFFECT

$$F = \frac{\text{MSAB}}{\text{MSE}} \qquad (11.9)$$

The null hypothesis is rejected at the α level of significance if

$$F = \frac{\text{MSAB}}{\text{MSE}} > F_u$$

the upper-tail critical value from an F distribution with $(r-1)(c-1)$ degrees of freedom in the numerator and $rc(n'-1)$ degrees of freedom in the denominator.

The entire set of steps is summarized in the analysis-of-variance (ANOVA) table of Table 11.1.

TABLE 11.1

ANALYSIS-OF-VARIANCE TABLE FOR THE TWO-FACTOR MODEL WITH REPLICATION

Source	Degrees of Freedom	Sum of Squares	Mean Square (Variance)	F
A	$r-1$	SSA	$\text{MSA} = \dfrac{\text{SSA}}{r-1}$	$F = \dfrac{\text{MSA}}{\text{MSE}}$
B	$c-1$	SSB	$\text{MSB} = \dfrac{\text{SSB}}{c-1}$	$F = \dfrac{\text{MSB}}{\text{MSE}}$
AB	$(r-1)(c-1)$	SSAB	$\text{MSAB} = \dfrac{\text{SSAB}}{(r-1)(c-1)}$	$F = \dfrac{\text{MSAB}}{\text{MSE}}$
Error	$rc(n'-1)$	SSE	$\text{MSE} = \dfrac{\text{SSE}}{rc(n'-1)}$	
Total	$n-1$	SST		

To illustrate these procedures, let us return to the laundry example of Sections 10.4 and 10.6. Suppose that we want to consider the factor of water temperature (warm versus hot) as well as detergent brand (in this example, limited to only two brands—X and Y) on the amount of dirt removed from standard household laundry loads. This design is sometimes called a 2^2 or 2×2 (read as, "2 by 2") design. When the "2×2" terminology is used, the first number refers to the number of levels of the first factor, while the second number refers to the number of levels of the second factor. Suppose further that five different loads were randomly assigned to each of the $2^2 = 4$ treatment combinations of detergent brand and water temperature.[1] The results in terms of milligrams removed are presented in Table 11.2.

From this table, we have

$$r = 2, \quad c = 2, \quad n' = 5, \quad n = 20$$

Figure 11.2 depicts the Microsoft Excel output and Figure 11.3 on page 520 illustrates the MINITAB output of the ANOVA summary table for the laundry example.

From Figure 11.2, we note that summary tables provide the sample size, sum, arithmetic mean, and variance for each combination of detergent brand and temperature. The total column in the first two tables provides these statistics for each detergent brand, while the third table provides them for each temperature. In addition, we see in the ANOVA table that df is degrees of freedom, SS is sum of squares, MS is mean squares, and F is the computed F-test statistic. The MINITAB output in Figure 11.3 provides the ANOVA table and the arithmetic mean for each brand and each temperature.

[1] In the 2^2 design, the first 2 refers to the fact that there are two levels of each factor, while the exponent (in this case also 2) represents the number of factors.

TABLE 11.2

AMOUNT OF DIRT (MG) REMOVED FOR THE 2^2 FACTORIAL DESIGN
INVESTIGATING DETERGENT BRAND AND WATER TEMPERATURE

	Temperature		
Detergent Brand	Warm	Hot	Totals
X	14	18	
	16	19	
	15	17	167
	12	19	
	17	20	
Y	17	21	
	19	20	
	20	18	199
	17	22	
	22	23	
Totals	169	197	366

LAUNDRY2

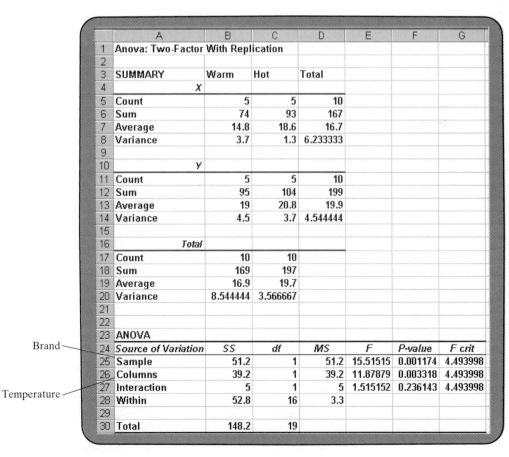

	A	B	C	D	E	F	G
1	Anova: Two-Factor With Replication						
2							
3	SUMMARY	Warm	Hot	Total			
4	X						
5	Count	5	5	10			
6	Sum	74	93	167			
7	Average	14.8	18.6	16.7			
8	Variance	3.7	1.3	6.233333			
9							
10	Y						
11	Count	5	5	10			
12	Sum	95	104	199			
13	Average	19	20.8	19.9			
14	Variance	4.5	3.7	4.544444			
15							
16	Total						
17	Count	10	10				
18	Sum	169	197				
19	Average	16.9	19.7				
20	Variance	8.544444	3.566667				
21							
22							
23	ANOVA						
24	Source of Variation	SS	df	MS	F	P-value	F crit
25	Sample	51.2	1	51.2	15.51515	0.001174	4.493998
26	Columns	39.2	1	39.2	11.87879	0.003318	4.493998
27	Interaction	5	1	5	1.515152	0.236143	4.493998
28	Within	52.8	16	3.3			
29							
30	Total	148.2	19				

Brand — (points to row 25, Sample)

Temperature — (points to row 27, Interaction / 26 Columns)

Figure 11.2   Microsoft Excel output for the laundry example

```
Two-way Analysis of Variance


Analysis of Variance for Amount
Source          DF        SS          MS          F          P
Brand            1      51.20       51.20       15.52      0.001
Temperat         1      39.20       39.20       11.88      0.003
Interaction      1       5.00        5.00        1.52      0.236
Error           16      52.80        3.30
Total           19     148.20


                            Individual 95% CI
Brand           Mean      -------+---------+---------+---------+-----+----
X              16.70      (-------*-------)
Y              19.90                                  (-------*-------)
                          -------+---------+---------+---------+-----+----
                              16.50      18.00      19.50      21.00


                            Individual 95% CI
Temperat        Mean      ------+---------+---------+---------+-----+----
Hot            19.70                                (-------*-------)
Warm           16.90      (-------*-------)
```

Figure 11.3   MINITAB output for the laundry example

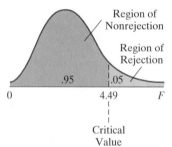

Figure 11.4   Regions of rejection and nonrejection at the 0.05 level of significance with 1 and 16 degrees of freedom

To interpret the results, we start by testing whether there is an interaction effect between factor A (brand) and factor B (temperature). If the interaction effect is significant, one must be cautious in the interpretation of any significant main effects. On the other hand, if the interaction effect is not significant, we focus on the main effects—potential differences in brand (factor A) and potential differences in temperature (factor B).

At the 0.05 level of significance to determine whether there is evidence of an interaction, the decision rule is to reject the null hypothesis of no interaction between brand and temperature if the calculated F value exceeds 4.49, the upper-tail critical value from the F distribution with 1 degree of freedom in the numerator and 16 degrees of freedom in the denominator. (See Figure 11.4.) Because $F = 1.515 < F_u = 4.49$, or, from Figure 11.2 or 11.3, because the p-value $= 0.236 > 0.05$, we do not reject H_0, and we conclude that there is insufficient evidence of an interaction between detergent brand and temperature. Our focus is now on the main effects.

In testing at the 0.05 level of significance for a difference between the two detergent brands (factor A), the decision rule is to reject the null hypothesis if the calculated F value exceeds 4.49, the upper-tail critical value from the F distribution with 1 degree of freedom in the numerator and 16 degrees of freedom in the denominator. (See Figure 11.4.) Because $F = 15.515 > F_u = 4.49$, or, from Figures 11.2 or 11.3, because the p-value $= 0.001 < 0.05$, we reject H_0, and we conclude that there is evidence of a difference between the two detergent brands in terms of the average amount of dirt removed. Brand Y is removing more dirt (an average of 19.9 mgs.) than Brand X (an average of 16.7 mgs.)

In testing at the 0.05 level of significance for a difference between the temperatures (factor B), the decision rule is to reject the null hypothesis of no difference if the calculated F value exceeds 4.49, the upper-tail critical value from the F distribution with 1 degree of freedom in the numerator and 16 degrees of freedom in the denominator. (See Figure 11.4.) Because $F = 11.879 > F_u = 4.49$, or, from Figure 11.2 or 11.3, because the p-value $= 0.003 < 0.05$, we reject H_0, and we conclude that there is evidence of a difference between the two temperatures in terms of the average amount of dirt removed. More dirt is being removed at a hot temperature (an average of 19.7 mgs.) than at a warm temperature (an average of 16.9 mgs.)

Interpreting Interaction Effects

Once the tests for the significance of factor A, factor B, and their interaction have been performed, we need to get a better understanding of the interpretation of the concept of interaction. What exactly do we mean by the term interaction? This interaction concept can first be approached by considering what would be meant by the absence of interaction.

> If there is no interaction between two factors (A and B), then any difference in the dependent or response variable between the two levels of factor A would be the same at each level of factor B.

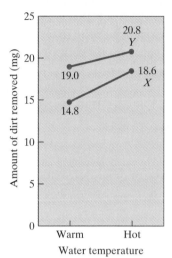

Figure 11.5 Average amount of dirt removed by each detergent for each water temperature

In terms of the factors in this example, if there were no interaction between detergent brand and water temperature, any difference between brand Y and brand X would be the same under conditions of hot water as it is under conditions of warm water. In the data of Table 11.2, we observe that, for hot water, brand Y is 2.2 mg. above brand X (20.8 compared to 18.6); for warm water, brand Y is 4.2 mg above brand X (19.0 compared to 14.8). Looking at this result another way, we can state that the average difference between brands when using hot water (2.2 mg) is 1.0 mg less than the average difference between brands for both water temperatures (3.2 mg).

The concept of interaction can be illustrated graphically by plotting the average values for each detergent brand for each water temperature obtained from Figure 11.2 on page 519. From Figure 11.5, we note that the difference between brands X and Y is larger for a warm-water temperature than for a hot-water temperature. In our analysis, we found the test for the interaction to be nonsignificant. Therefore the difference between the brands at each water temperature is considered to be a sample effect or due to chance. In the population, the lines would be parallel. This would have occurred if the average amount of dirt removed by detergent Y at a hot temperature was 22.8 mg instead of 20.8 mg. Such a situation is depicted in Figure 11.6.

We can contrast the parallel lines of Figure 11.6 with a different case in which there is a strong interaction. Suppose that, under the condition of hot water, the dirt removed was 19.7 mg for brands X and Y, whereas for a warm temperature the dirt removed was 13.7 mg for brand X and 20.1 mg for brand Y. The interaction graph for such a set of results is plotted in Figure 11.7 on page 522.

The results depicted in Figure 11.7 represent a pronounced interaction between the two factors: Clearly, any difference between the brands is different for the two water temperatures.

The concept of interaction can be carried even further by supposing that the average amount of dirt removed by brand Y at a hot temperature was 14.8 mg instead of 20.8 mg. The interaction graph for this situation is illustrated in

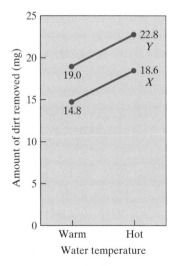

Figure 11.6 Hypothetical plot of detergent brand and water temperature to illustrate lack of interaction

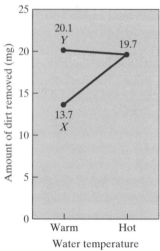

Figure 11.7 Hypothetical plot of detergent brand and water temperature to illustrate an interaction effect

Figure 11.8. Here we observe a crossing pattern in the lines for the two brands of detergent. What has happened in this situation is that brand X is better at a hot temperature and brand Y is better at a warm temperature.

Multiple Comparisons

As in the case of the one-way and randomized block models, when there are more than two levels of a factor, we can determine the particular levels that are significantly different from each other. A procedure developed by John Tukey (see Reference 13) can be used.

For factor A, we have the following:

OBTAINING THE CRITICAL RANGE FOR FACTOR A

$$\text{critical range} = q_u\sqrt{\frac{\text{MSE}}{rn'}} \qquad (11.10)$$

where q_u = the upper-tail critical value from a *Studentized range* distribution having r degrees of freedom in the numerator and $rc(n' - 1)$-degrees of freedom in the denominator.

For factor B, we have

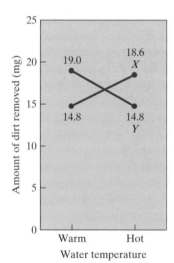

OBTAINING THE CRITICAL RANGE FOR FACTOR B

$$\text{critical range} = q_u\sqrt{\frac{\text{MSE}}{rn'}} \qquad (11.11)$$

where q_u = the upper-tail critical value from a *Studentized range* distribution having c degrees of freedom in the numerator and $rc(n' - 1)$ degrees of freedom in the denominator.

Figure 11.8 Hypothetical plot of detergent brand and water temperature to illustrate a strong interaction resulting in a crossing effect

Fixed, Random, and Mixed Models

In our discussion of analysis-of-variance models, we have not focused on the way in which the levels of a factor have been selected. From this perspective, there are three alternative models:

1. Fixed-Effects Model (Model I)
2. Random-Effects Model (Model II)
3. Mixed-Effects Model (Model III)

The **fixed-effects model** (the one used in the laundry example) assumes that the levels of a factor have been specifically selected for analysis. This means that inferences cannot be made about any levels other than the ones used in the experiment. The **random-effects model** contains factors in which the levels have been randomly selected from a population. In the laundry detergent experiment, for example, the water temperature could have been randomly selected. The objective with this model is not only to examine differences between levels but also to esti-

TABLE 11.3

F TESTS FOR TWO-FACTOR ANOVA MODELS

Null Hypothesis	Fixed Effects (A & B Fixed)	Random Effects (A & B Random)	Mixed Effects (A Fixed, B Random)	Mixed Effects (A Random, B Fixed)
$\mu_{i..} = 0$	$F = \dfrac{MSA}{MSE}$	$F = \dfrac{MSA}{MSAB}$	$F = \dfrac{MSA}{MSAB}$	$F = \dfrac{MSA}{MSE}$
$\mu_{.j.} = 0$	$F = \dfrac{MSB}{MSE}$	$F = \dfrac{MSB}{MSAB}$	$F = \dfrac{MSB}{MSE}$	$F = \dfrac{MSB}{MSAB}$
Interaction = 0	$F = \dfrac{MSAB}{MSE}$	$F = \dfrac{MSAB}{MSE}$	$F = \dfrac{MSAB}{MSE}$	$F = \dfrac{MSAB}{MSE}$

mate the variability due to each factor. The **mixed-effects model** contains some fixed and some random effects.

Our focus here concerns the differences in the tests for the significance of factors A and B between fixed-effects, random effects, and mixed-effects models. The appropriate F tests for the two-way ANOVA are summarized in Table 11.3.

As we observe in Table 11.3, the tests for the main effects differ with the type of model used. For the fixed-effects model, the F tests consist of the ratio of MSA or MSB to MSE. For the random-effects model, the F tests consist of the ratio of MSA or MSB to MSAB. For the mixed-effects model with factor A fixed and factor B random, the F test for factor A consists of the ratio of MSA to MSAB and the test for factor B consists of the ratio of MSB to MSE. For the mixed-effects model with factor A random and factor B fixed, the F test for factor A consists of the ratio of MSA to MSE and the test for factor B consists of the ratio of MSB to MSAB.

PROBLEMS

11.1 The quality-control director for a clothing manufacturer wants to study the effect of operators and machines on the breaking strength (in pounds) of wool serge material. A batch of the material is cut into square-yard pieces and these are randomly assigned, three each, to all 12 combinations of four operators and three machines chosen specifically for the experiment. The results are as follows:

Operator	Machine		
	I	II	III
A	115	111	109
	115	108	110
	119	114	107
B	117	105	110
	114	102	113
	114	106	114

(*Continued*)

Operator	I	II	III
C	109	100	103
	110	103	102
	106	101	105
D	112	105	108
	115	107	111
	111	107	110

BREAKSTW

For the .05 level of significance, answer the following questions:

(a) Is there an effect due to operator?

(b) Is there an effect due to machine?

(c) Is there an interaction due to operator and machine?

(d) Plot a graph of average breaking strength for each operator for each machine.

(e) If appropriate, use the Tukey procedure to determine which operators and which machines differ in their effect on average breaking strength. (Use $\alpha = 0.05$.)

(f) What can you conclude about the effect of operators and machines on breaking strength?

(g) How would your results differ if the operators were randomly selected from a population of operators?

11.2 An experiment is designed to study the effect of two factors on the amplification of a stereo recording. The factors are type of receiver (two brands) and type of amplifier (four brands). For each combination of factor levels, three tests are performed in which decibel output is measured. A higher decibel output means a better result. The coded results are as follows:

Receiver	Amplifiers			
	A	B	C	D
R_1	9	8	8	10
	4	11	7	15
	12	16	1	9
R_2	7	5	0	6
	1	9	1	7
	4	6	7	5

AMPLIFY

For the 0.01 level of significance, answer the following questions:

(a) Is there an effect due to receivers?

(b) Is there an effect due to amplifiers?

(c) Is there an interaction between receivers and amplifiers?

(d) Plot a graph of average decibel output for each receiver for each amplifier.

(e) If appropriate, use the Tukey procedure to determine which amplifiers differ in average decibel output. (Use $\alpha = 0.01$.)

(f) From the results, what conclusions can you reach concerning average decibel output?

11.3 An experiment was designed to study the effect of two factors on the fire-retardant treatment of fabrics. Factor A is the type of fabric (cotton versus polyester), and factor B corresponds to two different fire-retardant treatments (X and Y). The results from four replications of each combination of the two factors (expressed in terms of the number of inches of a fabric burned after a flame test, with a smaller value indicating a better result) were as follows:

Fabric	Treatment		Fabric	Treatment	
	X	Y		X	Y
Cotton	39	28	Polyester	46	29
	36	31		50	25
	42	31		45	32
	45	30		48	35

FIRE

For the 0.05 level of significance, answer the following questions:

(a) Is there an effect due to fabric?

(b) Is there an effect due to fire-retardant treatment?

(c) Is there an interaction due to fabric and fire-retardant treatment?

(d) Plot a graph of average fabric burned for each fabric for each fire-retardant treatment.

(e) What can you conclude about the effect of fabric and fire-retardant treatment on the amount of fabric burned?

11.4 The effects of developer strength (factor A) and development time (factor B) on the density of photographic plate film were being studied. Two strengths and two development times were used, and four replicates for each treatment combination were run. The results (larger is better) were as follows:

Developer Strength	Development Time (minutes)		Developer Strength	Development Time (minutes)	
	10	14		10	14
1	0	1	2	4	6
	5	4		7	7
	2	3		6	8
	4	2		5	7

PHOTO

For the 0.05 level of significance, answer the following questions:

(a) Is there an effect due to developer strength?

(b) Is there an effect due to development time?

(c) Is there an interaction due to developer strength and development time?

(d) Plot a graph of average density of each developer strength for each development time.

(e) What can you conclude about the effect of developer strength and development time on density?

11.5 Polyvinyl chloride (PVC) is a polymer that is used in numerous applications in industry. PVC is produced by polymerizing vinyl chloride monomer (VCM) in a batch chemical reactor. The VCM, dispersants, and initiators are added to water and reacted at a controlled temperature to produce resin of the desired molecular-weight. A study was conducted to measure the effect of operators and resin railcars on the particle size of the resin. The operators and the railcars were randomly selected from their populations, because the primary objective of the study was to measure the variation due to operators and due to railcars. Two resin samples were selected for each operator–railcar combination. The results were as follows:

Operator	Resin Railcar	Samples	
1	1	36.2	36.3
1	2	35.3	35.0
1	3	30.8	30.6
1	4	29.8	29.6
1	5	32.0	31.7
1	6	30.7	29.7
1	7	33.4	32.4
1	8	37.1	36.5
2	1	35.8	35.0
2	2	35.6	35.1
2	3	30.4	28.9
2	4	30.2	29.9
2	5	31.1	31.7
2	6	30.9	30.4

(*Continued*)

Operator	Resin Railcar	Samples	
2	7	32.9	32.1
2	8	36.7	36.2
3	1	36.0	34.6
3	2	33.0	33.7
3	3	31.3	27.1
3	4	30.0	27.3
3	5	28.7	29.9
3	6	30.8	28.7
3	7	35.4	30.1
3	8	32.6	33.7

PVC

Source: Morris, R. A. and E. F. Watson; "A comparison of the techniques used to evaluate the measurement process," *Quality Engineering*, 11, 1998. 213–219

For the 0.05 level of significance, answer the following questions:
(a) Is there an effect due to operator?
(b) Is there an effect due to resin railcar?
(c) Is there an interaction due to operator and resin railcar?
(d) Plot a graph of average particle size for each operator for each resin railcar.
(e) What can you conclude about the effect of operators and machines on particle size?
(f) How would your results differ if the operators were not randomly selected from a population of operators?

11.2 FACTORIAL DESIGNS INVOLVING THREE OR MORE FACTORS

The two-factor factorial design is the most elementary of all factorial designs. In this section, we extend the concepts developed for the two-factor 2^2 design in Section 11.1 to the more general factorial design that has three or more factors. For a three-factor fixed-effects model in which each factor has two levels (a 2^3 design), the ANOVA table is summarized in Table 11.4.

To illustrate the 2^3 design, suppose that, in addition to detergent brand and water temperature, we wanted to evaluate the effect of a third factor, the type of detergent (powder versus liquid), on the dependent or response variable, the amount of dirt removed. With this design, there are now $2^3 = 2 \times 2 \times 2 = 8$ treatment combinations. If two standard laundry loads were used for each of these treatment combinations, we would have $8 \times 2 = 16$ observations. The results from this experiment are presented in Table 11.5.

Note from Table 11.5 that a shorthand notation is used to identify the levels of the factors in the design by assigning a letter such as a, b, or c. One level of each factor is designated as the low level and the other level is designated as the high

TABLE 11.4

ANALYSIS-OF-VARIANCE TABLE FOR THE THREE-FACTOR (FIXED-EFFECTS) MODEL WITH REPLICATION

Source	Degrees of Freedom	Sum of Squares	Mean Square (Variance)	F
A	$i - 1$	SSA	$MSA = \dfrac{SSA}{i - 1}$	$F = \dfrac{MSA}{MSE}$
B	$j - 1$	SSB	$MSB = \dfrac{SSB}{j - 1}$	$F = \dfrac{MSB}{MSE}$
C	$k - 1$	SSC	$MSC = \dfrac{SSC}{k - 1}$	$F = \dfrac{MSC}{MSE}$
AB	$(i - 1)(j - 1)$	SSAB	$MSAB = \dfrac{SSAB}{(i - 1)(j - 1)}$	$F = \dfrac{MSAB}{MSE}$
AC	$(i - 1)(k - 1)$	SSAC	$MSAC = \dfrac{SSAC}{(i - 1)(k - 1)}$	$F = \dfrac{MSAC}{MSE}$
BC	$(j - 1)(k - 1)$	SSBC	$MSBC = \dfrac{SSBC}{(j - 1)(k - 1)}$	$F = \dfrac{MSBC}{MSE}$
ABC	$(i - 1)(j - 1)(k - 1)$	SSABC	$MSABC = \dfrac{SSABC}{(i - 1)(j - 1)(k - 1)}$	$F = \dfrac{MSABC}{MSE}$
Error	$ijk(n' - 1)$	SSE	$MSE = \dfrac{SSE}{ijk(n' - 1)}$	
Total	$n - 1$	SST		

where

i = number of levels of factor A

j = number of levels of factor B

k = number of levels of factor C

n' = number of replications for each combination of factors A, B, and C

TABLE 11.5

RESULTS FOR A 2^3 DESIGN INVOLVING LAUNDRY DETERGENTS

Treatment Combinations	Notation	Observed Responses		Total Responses	Average Response
Brand X, warm, powder	*(1)*	14.8	15.0	29.8	14.9
Brand Y, warm, powder	*a*	18.4	18.8	37.2	18.6
Brand X, hot, powder	*b*	17.8	18.2	36.0	18.0
Brand X, warm, liquid	*c*	19.9	20.3	40.2	20.1
Brand Y, hot, powder	*ab*	20.7	21.1	41.8	20.9
Brand Y, warm, liquid	*ac*	21.7	21.9	43.6	21.8
Brand X, hot, liquid	*bc*	22.6	23.2	45.8	22.9
Brand Y, hot, liquid	*abc*	23.4	24.6	48.0	24.0 **LAUNDRY3**

level. Which level is named as low and which is designated as high is arbitrary. For some factors, there will be a natural ordering of the levels. For other factors, no natural ordering is available, so the assignment is at the discretion of the experimenter. In Table 11.5, each treatment combination is listed, row by row, and is assigned a shorthand notation that shows which high levels of the factors are present. For example, if the only high level present is the one for factor *A*, the treatment combination is written as *a*. If the high levels for factors *A* and *B* are present, the treatment combination is written as *ab*. If the low level of all factors is present, the treatment combination is written as *(1)*.

The eight treatment combinations (and their average response) are presented geometrically in Figure 11.9.

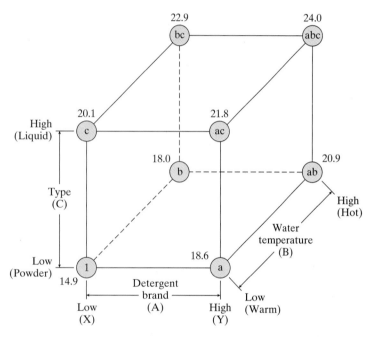

Figure 11.9 Geometric representation of the 2^3 design for the laundry detergent data of Table 11.5

Figure 11.10 on page 528 illustrates the MINITAB output of the ANOVA summary table for the laundry data of Table 11.5.

To interpret the results, we start by testing whether there are any interactions between factors *A* (brand), *B* (temperature), and *C* (type). If the interaction effects are significant, further analysis will pertain only to this aspect. On the other hand, if the interaction effects are not significant, we focus on the main effects—potential differences due to brand (factor *A*), temperature (factor *B*), and type (factor *C*).

When one is using the 0.05 level of significance to determine whether there is evidence of an interaction, the decision rule is to reject the null hypothesis of no difference between brands if the calculated *F* value exceeds 5.32, the upper-tail critical value from the *F* distribution with 1 degree of freedom in the numerator and 8 degrees of freedom in the denominator. From Figure 11.10, we observe that the *F* statistic for the temperature-brand-type interaction (*ABC*) is 0.06 < 5.32 (or

```
Analysis of Variance (Balanced Designs)


Factor       Type Levels Values
Brand        fixed    2    X      Y
Temperat     fixed    2    Hot  Warm
Type         fixed    2 Liquid Powder


Analysis of Variance for Amount

Source                   DF        SS        MS        F       P
Brand                     1    22.090    22.090   140.25   0.000
Temperature               1    27.040    27.040   171.68   0.000
Type                      1    67.240    67.240   426.92   0.000
Brand*Temperature         1     0.490     0.490     3.11   0.116
Brand*Type                1     3.610     3.610    22.92   0.001
Temperature*Type          1     0.040     0.040     0.25   0.628
Brand*Temperature*Type    1     0.010     0.010     0.06   0.807
Error                     8     1.260     0.157
Total                    15   121.780
```

Figure 11.10   MINITAB output for the laundry data of Table 11.5

that the p-value $= 0.807 > 0.05$). Thus, we do not reject H_0, and we conclude that there is no evidence of an interaction between brand, temperature, and type. We see that the F statistic for the brand-temperature interaction (AB) is $3.11 < 5.32$ (or that the p-value $= 0.116 > 0.05$). Thus, we do not reject H_0, and we conclude that there is insufficient evidence of an interaction between detergent brand and temperature. We also see from Figure 11.10 that the F statistic for the brand-type interaction (AC) is $22.92 > 5.32$ (or that the p-value $= 0.001 < 0.05$). Thus, we reject H_0, and we conclude that there is evidence of an interaction between detergent brand and type of detergent. Also, from Figure 11.10, we observe that the F statistic for the temperature-type interaction (BC) is $0.25 < 5.32$ (or that the p-value $= 0.628 > 0.05$). Thus, we do not reject H_0, and we conclude that there is insufficient evidence of an interaction between temperature and type. The interaction graphs obtained from MINITAB are presented in Figure 11.11.

Figure 11.11 displays the two-way interaction plots of Brand–Temperature, Brand–Type, and Temperature–Type. The interaction plot of brand and temperature is shown in the second column of the first row. This interaction is not significant. We observe that the differences between Brands X and Y are consistent for each of the temperatures. The interaction plot of brand and type is shown in third column of the first row. This interaction is significant. We observe that, for liquid detergent, the average amount of dirt removed is slightly higher for brand Y, but for powder detergent it is much higher. As was the case with the interaction of brand and temperature, we can see, in the third column of row 2, that differences in temperature are consistent for liquid and powder detergent.

Now we can turn our attention to the main effects. There is a significant interaction between brand and type, so any difference due to brand is not consistent across the types of detergent. Because none of the interactions involving factor B

Interaction Plot – Data Means for Amount

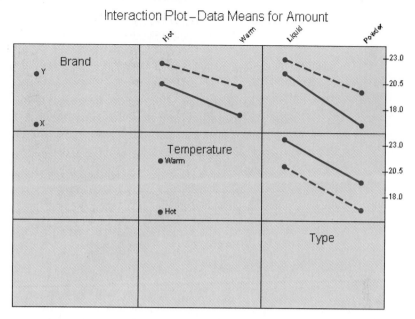

Figure 11.11   Interaction plots obtained from MINITAB for the laundry data of Table 11.4

(temperature) were significant, we can test this main effect. In testing at the 0.05 level of significance for a difference between the two temperatures (factor B), the decision rule is to reject the null hypothesis if the calculated F value exceeds 5.32, the upper-tail critical value from the F distribution with 1 degree of freedom in the numerator and 8 degrees of freedom in the denominator. Because $F = 171.68 > F_u = 5.32$, or because the p-value $= 0.000 < 0.05$, we reject H_0, and we conclude that there is evidence of a difference between the two temperatures in terms of the average amount of dirt removed. From Figure 11.12, which is a plot of

Main Effects Plot – Data Means for Amount

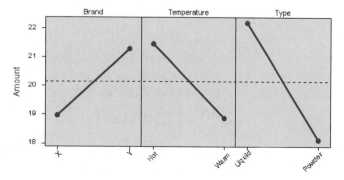

Figure 11.12   Main-effect plots obtained from MINITAB for the laundry data of Table 11.5

the main effects, we observe that the amount of dirt removed is higher for a hot temperature than for a warm temperature.

Contrasts, Effects, and Sum of Squares

The magnitude of the main effects and interactions can be measured by using the shorthand notation presented in Table 11.5. For each of the main effects, the estimated effect consists of the average at the high level of the factor minus the average at the low level of the factor. Thus, for factors A, B, and C, we calculate as follows:

$$A = \frac{1}{4n'}[a + ab + ac + abc - (1) - b - c - bc] \quad (11.12a)$$

$$B = \frac{1}{4n'}[b + ab + bc + abc - (1) - a - c - ac] \quad (11.12b)$$

$$C = \frac{1}{4n'}[c + ac + bc + abc - (1) - a - b - ab] \quad (11.12c)$$

The two-way interactions are measured as one-half the difference in the average of one effect at the two levels of the other effect. Thus, for the interactions AB, AC, and BC, we have the following

$$AB = \frac{1}{4n'}[abc - bc + ab - b - ac + c - a + (1)] \quad (11.13a)$$

$$AC = \frac{1}{4n'}[(1) - a + b - ab - c + ac - bc + abc] \quad (11.13b)$$

$$BC = \frac{1}{4n'}[(1) + a - b - ab - c - ac + bc + abc] \quad (11.13c)$$

The ABC interaction is defined as the average difference in the AB interaction for the two levels of factor C. Thus,

$$ABC = \frac{1}{4n'}[abc - bc - ac + c - ab + b + a - (1)] \quad (11.14)$$

The values in the brackets of each effect are referred to as the **contrasts.** A table of the signs for calculating the contrasts is shown in Table 11.6. The contrast is obtained by multiplying the total of all replicates for a treatment combination by the sign for the particular contrast and summing over all treatment combinations in a particular column.

For the laundry detergent example with three factors each with two replicates, using equations (11.12)–(11.14), we calculate as follows:

$$A = \frac{-29.8 + 37.2 - 36.0 - 40.2 + 41.8 + 43.6 - 45.8 + 48.0}{(4)(2)}$$

TABLE 11.6

OBTAINING CONTRASTS FOR FACTORS A, B, AND C, FOR INTERACTIONS AB, AC, AND BC, AND FOR ABC IN THE 2^3 DESIGN

Notation	Contrast						
	A	B	C	AB	AC	BC	ABC
(1)	−	−	−	+	+	+	−
a	+	−	−	−	−	+	+
b	−	+	−	−	+	−	+
c	−	−	+	+	−	−	+
ab	+	+	−	+	−	−	−
ac	+	−	+	−	+	−	−
bc	−	+	+	−	−	+	−
abc	+	+	+	+	+	+	+

$$A = \frac{18.8}{8} = 2.35$$

$$B = \frac{-29.8 - 37.2 + 36.0 - 40.2 + 41.8 - 43.6 + 45.8 + 48.0}{(4)(2)}$$

$$B = \frac{20.8}{8} = 2.60$$

$$C = \frac{-29.8 - 37.2 - 36.0 + 40.2 - 41.8 + 43.6 + 45.8 + 48.0}{(4)(2)}$$

$$C = \frac{32.8}{8} = 4.10$$

$$AB = \frac{29.8 - 37.2 - 36.0 + 40.2 + 41.8 - 43.6 - 45.8 + 48.0}{(4)(2)}$$

$$AB = \frac{-2.8}{8} = -0.35$$

$$AC = \frac{29.8 - 37.2 + 36.0 - 40.2 - 41.8 + 43.6 - 45.8 + 48.0}{(4)(2)}$$

$$AC = \frac{-7.6}{8} = -0.95$$

$$BC = \frac{29.8 + 37.2 - 36.0 - 40.2 - 41.8 - 43.6 + 45.8 + 48.0}{(4)(2)}$$

$$BC = \frac{-0.8}{8} = -0.10$$

$$ABC = \frac{-29.8 + 37.2 + 36.0 + 40.2 - 41.8 - 43.6 - 45.8 + 48.0}{(4)(2)}$$

$$ABC = \frac{-0.4}{8} = 0.05$$

From these results, we determine the following for these sample data:

1. The average amount of dirt removed is 2.35 mg higher for brand Y than for brand X.
2. The average amount of dirt removed is 2.60 mg higher for hot water than for warm water.
3. The average amount of dirt removed is 4.10 mg higher for liquid detergent than for powder detergent.
4. The interactions range in size from -0.95 for AC to $+0.05$ for ABC. The average effect of -0.95 for AC can be interpreted to mean that the effect of combining the high levels of factors A and C (brand Y and liquid detergent) is, on average, 0.95 mg less than the average difference between the brands over both types of detergent (powder and liquid).

In general, for any 2^k factorial design, the effect can be computed as in equation (11.15).

$$\text{Effect} = \frac{\text{Contrast}}{n'2^{k-1}} \tag{11.15}$$

where

k = the number of factors

n' = the number of replicates for each treatment combination

The Sum of Squares (SS) for any effect is

$$\text{SS} = \frac{(\text{Contrast})^2}{n'2^k} \tag{11.16}$$

Returning to the MINITAB output of Figure 11.10 for the three-factor factorial design, we observe that SSA = 22.09. By using equation (11.16), SSA can be computed from

$$\text{SSA} = \frac{(18.8)^2}{(2)(2^3)}$$

$$\text{SSA} = \frac{353.44}{16} = 22.09$$

The other sum of squares can be obtained from the contrasts in a similar manner.

Using a Normal Probability Plot to Assist in the Evaluation of the Factors and Interactions

In this laundry example, there were two replicates for each treatment combination. In many situations, especially as the number of factors becomes large, it is difficult or costly to obtain more than one replication for each treatment combination. One approach used when there is only one replication is based on the normal probability plot of Section 5.5. Instead of plotting the individual data points as in Section 5.5, the estimated effects are plotted in rank order on normal probability paper. For a factorial design with k factors, the cumulative percentage for an effect is obtained as follows.

$$p_i = \frac{R_i - 0.5}{2^k - 1} \tag{11.17}$$

where

R_i is the ordered rank of effect i

p_i is the cumulative percentage for ordered effect i

k is the number of factors

In Section 5.5, we used the normal probability plot to determine whether all the values fall close enough to a straight line to indicate a normal distribution. Now we use the normal probability plot to try to determine whether the entire set of factors and interaction effects is due to chance (and, thus, shows no effects significantly different from zero) or whether some factors and/or interactions have any effect. Any factors or interactions whose observed effects are due to chance are expected to be randomly distributed around zero, with some being slightly below zero and others being slightly above zero. These effects will tend to fall along a straight line. The effects that might be significant have average values different from zero and are located a substantial distance away from the line that represents no effect.

With only one replication per treatment combination, we are unable to obtain a separate estimate of the error variance (MSE). As a preliminary screening step, we use the normal probability plot to screen out interactions that do not appear to have any effect, and we combine them into a substitute measure of random error. The ANOVA table is then developed with these interaction terms combined and used as an estimate of the random error.

To study a situation in which only one replication could be obtained for each treatment combination, we return to the *Using Statistics* example presented at the beginning of this chapter, which concerned a food processing company that was manufacturing cake mixes. Five factors were to be considered; flour, shortening, egg powder, oven temperature, and baking time. In the experiment, each factor is tested at a higher level than recommended in the instructions and at a lower level than recommended in the instructions. Only one replication for each of the $2^5 = 32$ treatment combinations was obtained. The taste rating for each treatment combination is presented in Table 11.7 on page 534.

The estimated effects can be obtained either by extending equations (11.12)–(11.14) to the 2^5 factorial design or by using equations (11.15) and (11.16) as follows:

$$\text{Effect} = \sqrt{\frac{\text{sum of squares}}{n'2^{k-2}}} \tag{11.18}$$

TABLE 11.7

TASTE RATING FOR CAKE MIX COMBINATIONS

Treatment Combination	Design Parameters			Noise Factors		Rating Score
	Flour (F)	Shortening (S)	Egg Powder (E)	Oven Temperature (T)	Baking Time (B)	
(1)	−	−	−	−	−	1.1
(1)	−	−	−	+	−	5.7
(1)	−	−	−	−	+	6.4
(1)	−	−	−	+	+	1.3
a	+	−	−	−	−	3.8
a	+	−	−	+	−	4.9
a	+	−	−	−	+	4.3
a	+	−	−	+	+	2.1
b	−	+	−	−	−	3.7
b	−	+	−	+	−	5.1
b	−	+	−	−	+	6.7
b	−	+	−	+	+	2.9
c	−	−	+	−	−	4.2
c	−	−	+	+	−	6.8
c	−	−	+	−	+	6.5
c	−	−	+	+	+	3.5
ab	+	+	−	−	−	4.5
ab	+	+	−	+	−	6.4
ab	+	+	−	−	+	5.8
ab	+	+	−	+	+	5.2
ac	+	−	+	−	−	5.2
ac	+	−	+	+	−	6.0
ac	+	−	+	−	+	5.9
ac	+	−	+	+	+	5.7
bc	−	+	+	−	−	3.1
bc	−	+	+	+	−	6.3
bc	−	+	+	−	+	6.4
bc	−	+	+	+	+	3.0
abc	+	+	+	−	−	3.9
abc	+	+	+	+	−	5.5
abc	+	+	+	−	+	5.0
abc	+	+	+	+	+	5.4

CAKE

Source: Box, G.E.P., S. Bisgaard, and C. Fung; "An Explanation and Critique of Taguchi's Contributions to Quality Engineering," *Quality and Reliability Engineering International,* 4 (1988), 123–131

After using MINITAB to obtain the sum of squares for each effect, we then use equation (11.18) to obtain the following estimated effects.

$A = 0.431$; $B = 0.344$; $C = 0.781$; $D = 0.044$; $E = 0.006$; $AB = 0.131$; $AC = 0.081$; $AD = 0.394$; $AE = 0.094$; $BC = 0.994$; $BD = 0.131$; $BE = 0.244$; $CD = 0.294$; $CE = 0.056$; $DE = 2.194$; $ABC = 0.231$; $ABD = 0.344$; $ABE = 0.131$; $ACD = 0.006$; $ACE = 0.394$; $ADE = 1.194$; $BCD = 0.069$; $BCE = 0.044$; $BDE = 0.256$; $CDE = 0.394$; $ABCD = 0.194$; $ABCE = 0.181$; $ABDE = 0.181$; $ACDE = 0.056$; $BCDE = 0.406$; and $ABCDE = 0.281$.

Figure 11.13 is a normal probability plot of the estimated effects obtained from MINITAB.

Normal Probability Plot of Effects in Cake Experiment

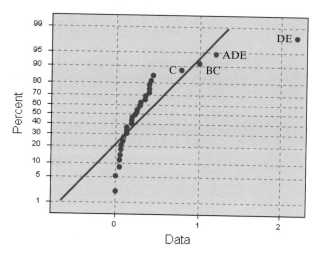

Figure 11.13   Normal probability plot obtained from MINITAB of the estimated effects for the cake-mix example

[2] The diagonal line appearing in the MINITAB output is not relevant to this analysis and should be ignored.

If there are no significant effects, all points will plot at or near an approximately straight vertical line position near a value of $X = 0$. From Figure 11.13, we observe that only effects C, BC, DE, and ADE plot far away from a straight line that is approximately zero on the X axis.[2] Thus, a reasonable approach is to consider all third-order interactions (except ADE), all fourth-order interactions, and the single fifth-order interaction ($ABCDE$) as consisting only of random error. These effects can be eliminated from the ANOVA model and combined together to estimate an error term. The ANOVA model obtained from MINITAB with these effects combined into an error term is displayed in Figure 11.14.

```
Analysis of Variance for Rating

Source                      DF       SS        MS       F       P
Flour                        1    1.4878    1.4878    3.03    0.102
Shortening                   1    0.9453    0.9453    1.92    0.186
Egg Powder                   1    4.8828    4.8828    9.93    0.007
ovenTemp                     1    0.0153    0.0153    0.03    0.862
BakeTime                     1    0.0003    0.0003    0.00    0.980
Flour*Shortening             1    0.1378    0.1378    0.28    0.604
Flour*Egg Powder             1    0.0528    0.0528    0.11    0.748
Flour*ovenTemp               1    1.2403    1.2403    2.52    0.133
Flour*BakeTime               1    0.0703    0.0703    0.14    0.711
Shortening*Egg Powd          1    7.9003    7.9003   16.07    0.001
Shortening*ovenTemp          1    0.1378    0.1378    0.28    0.604
Shortening*BakeTime          1    0.4753    0.4753    0.97    0.341
Egg Powder*ovenTemp          1    0.6903    0.6903    1.40    0.254
Egg Powder*BakeTime          1    0.0253    0.0253    0.05    0.824
ovenTemp*BakeTime            1   38.5003   38.5003   78.31    0.000
Flour*ovenTemp*BakeTime      1   11.4003   11.4003   23.19    0.000
Error                       15    7.3747    0.4916
Total                       31   75.3372
```

Figure 11.14   ANOVA model obtained from MINITAB for the cake-mix example

From Figure 11.14, using the 0.05 level of significance, we can see that factor C (egg powder), having a p-value of 0.007, the BC (shortening–egg powder) interaction (p-value $= 0.001$), the DE (oven temperature–baking time) interaction (p-value $= 0.000$), and the ADE (flour–oven temperature–baking time) interaction (p-value $= 0.000$) are all significant. The significance of these interactions complicates any interpretation of the main effects. Although egg powder significantly affects taste rating (with high amount providing a better rating than low amount), the significance of the shortening–egg powder interaction means that the difference in egg powder is not the same for the two levels of shortening. Because neither effect D nor effect E was significant, the significance of the DE (oven temperature–baking time) interaction indicates a crossing effect, as originally illustrated in Figure 11.8 on page 522. The significance of the ADE (flour–oven temperature–baking time) interaction means that the interaction of oven temperature and baking time is not the same for low and high amounts of flour.

To further our understanding of these results, we can examine the interaction plots in Figure 11.15, along with Tables 11.8, 11.9, 11.10, and 11.11, which provide

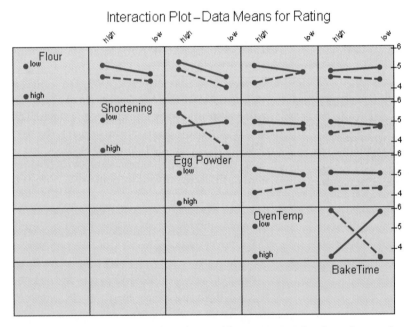

Figure 11.15   Interaction plots obtained from MINITAB for the cake-mix data

TABLE 11.8

AVERAGE RATING FOR EACH LEVEL OF SHORTENING AND EGG POWDER

Shortening	Egg Powder	
	Low	High
Low	3.7000	5.475
High	5.0375	4.825

TABLE 11.9

AVERAGE RATING FOR EACH LEVEL OF OVEN TEMPERATURE AND BAKING TIME

Oven Temperature	Baking Time	
	Low	High
Low	3.6875	5.8750
High	5.8375	3.6375

TABLE 11.10

AVERAGE RATING FOR EACH LEVEL OF OVEN TEMPERATURE AND BAKING TIME FOR THE LOW LEVEL OF FLOUR

Oven Temperature	Baking Time	
	Low	High
Low	3.025	6.500
High	5.975	2.675

TABLE 11.11

AVERAGE RATING FOR EACH LEVEL OF OVEN TEMPERATURE AND BAKING TIME FOR THE HIGH LEVEL OF FLOUR

Oven Temperature	Baking Time	
	Low	High
Low	4.35	5.25
High	5.70	4.60

the average values for combinations of shortening and egg powder, oven temperature and baking time, and oven temperature and baking time for each level of flour.

From Figure 11.15 and Table 11.8, we see that, for low levels of shortening, the rating is much better for the high level of egg powder (5.475) than for the low level of egg powder (3.70). For a high level of shortening, the results are quite different. The rating is slightly better for low egg powder (5.0375) than for high egg powder (4.825).

Turning to the interaction of oven temperature and baking time, we observe from Figure 11.15 and Table 11.9 that the average rating is best for low oven temperature and high baking time (5.875) or high oven temperature and low baking time (5.8375). The rating is worse when there is both low oven temperature and low baking time (3.6875) or high oven temperature and high baking time (3.6375). However, the interaction of oven temperature and baking time is different for each of the two levels of flour. From Tables 11.10 and 11.11, the interaction seen in Table 11.9 is much more pronounced for the low level of flour than for the high level of flour.

Thus, how can we choose the level of flour, shortening, and egg powder that will result in the highest rating? Given our results, we probably should choose high flour, low shortening, and high egg powder. The rationale for this is as follows.

1. From Tables 11.10 and 11.11, using a high level of flour will improve the rating and reduce the effect of oven temperature and baking time.
2. From Table 11.8, using a low level of shortening and a high level of egg powder provides the best rating.

In addition, we should warn the consumer not to use oven temperature and baking time that are either both too low or both too high.

PROBLEMS

11.6 A soft-drink bottler was interested in obtaining more uniform fill heights in the bottles filled in the bottling process. Theoretically, the filling machine fills each bottle to the correct fill level, but, in practice, there is variation around this target. Three variables can be controlled in the filling process: the percent carbonation (at 10 percent and 12 percent), the pressure (at 25 psi and 30 psi), and two levels for line speed (200 bottles per minute and 300 bottles per minute). The bottler decides to run five replicates for each of the 8 combinations of levels of these factors. The results in terms of deviation from target were as follows:

Percent Carbonation	Operating Pressure	Line Speed	Deviation from Target (mm)				
10	25 psi	200	−4.8	−3.7	−1.9	−0.8	−4.8
12	25 psi	200	0.2	2.1	2.6	0.4	1.7
10	30 psi	200	−3.0	−0.7	2.3	−1.5	−1.1
10	25 psi	300	−2.5	−0.9	−1.1	1.6	−0.1
12	30 psi	200	3.3	1.6	4.0	2.7	3.4
12	25 psi	300	3.0	1.7	5.3	4.0	1.5
10	30 psi	300	1.3	1.2	1.5	1.0	1.5
12	30 psi	300	6.8	5.4	4.3	7.2	7.3

SFTDRINK

For the 0.05 level of significance, answer the following questions:

(a) Is there a significant effect on the deviation from the target due to percent carbonation?

(b) Is there a significant effect on the deviation from the target due to operating pressure?

(c) Is there a significant effect on the deviation from the target due to line speed?

(d) Are any of the interactions of the factors significant?

(e) Obtain a plot of the main effects.

(f) Obtain a plot of the interactions.

(g) Compute the average effect for each main effect (factor) and interaction.

(h) On the basis of (g), set up a normal probability plot of the main effects and interactions.

(i) What conclusions can you draw from the results of (h)?

(j) Compare the results of (a)–(d) with those of (h). Explain any differences.

(k) What levels of percent carbonation, operating pressure, and line speed should be used to reduce the deviation from the target? Explain your reasons for selecting these levels.

11.7 An experiment was conducted to determine which paper airplane would fly for the longest distance as measured in inches from the takeoff point to the landing point. Three factors were considered: design (simple versus complex), weight (light versus heavy), and size (small versus large). Four trials were conducted for each treatment combination, with the following results:

Design	Weight	Size	Distance Flown in Inches			
Simple	Light	Small	230	241	244	255
Complex	Light	Small	156	177	155	147
Simple	Heavy	Small	233	165	200	278
Simple	Light	Large	180	216	206	204
Complex	Heavy	Small	108	127	147	137
Complex	Light	Large	226	259	231	246
Simple	Heavy	Large	278	264	206	194
Complex	Heavy	Large	229	222	258	266

PAPERAIR

For the 0.05 level of significance, answer the following questions:

(a) Is there a significant effect on the distance traveled due to design?

(b) Is there a significant effect on the distance traveled due to weight?

(c) Is there a significant effect on the distance traveled due to size?

(d) Are any of the interactions of the factors significant?

(e) Obtain a plot of the main effects.

(f) Obtain a plot of the interactions.

(g) Compute the average effect for each main effect (factor) and interaction.

(h) On the basis of (g), set up a normal probability plot of the main effects and interactions.

(i) What conclusions can you draw from the results of (h)?

(j) Compare the results of (a)–(d) with those of (i). Explain any differences.

(k) What levels of design, weight, and size should be used to maximize the distance traveled? Explain your reasons for selecting these levels.

11.8 It is widely believed, among one-tenth scale electric remote-control model-car racing enthusiasts, that spending more money on high-quality batteries and gold-plate connectors and storing batteries at low temperatures will improve battery-life performance. An experiment was conducted that used these three factors to determine the battery life as measured by the time to discharge (in minutes). The results were as follows:

Battery	Connector design	Temperature	Time
Low	Standard	Ambient	93
High	Standard	Ambient	489
Low	Gold-plated	Ambient	94
High	Gold-plated	Ambient	493
Low	Standard	Cold	72
High	Standard	Cold	612
Low	Gold-plated	Cold	75
High	Gold-plated	Cold	490

MODELCAR

Source: Wasiloff, E. and C. Hargitt; "Using DOE to Determine AA Battery Life," *Quality Progress,* March 1999, 67–71

(a) Compute the average effect for each main effect (factor) and interaction.

(b) Obtain a plot of the main effects.

(c) Obtain a plot of the interactions.

(d) On the basis of (a), set up a normal probability plot of the main effects and interactions.

(e) What conclusions can you draw from the results of (d)?

(f) Given the results of (d) and (e), combine all appropriate interactions into a measure of random error, and use the level significance 0.05 to determine which factors are significant.

(g) What conclusions can you reach from the results of (f)?

11.9 The following experiment concerned the manufacture of rolling bearings. Three factors were studied, each at a low and high setting. They were outer ring osculation (factor A), cage design (factor B), and heat treatment (factor C). The results in terms of the lengths of lives of the bearings follow:

Ring Osculation	Cage Design	Heat Treatment	Relative Life
Low	Low	Low	17
High	Low	Low	25
Low	High	Low	19
Low	Low	High	26
High	High	Low	21
High	Low	High	85
Low	High	High	16
High	High	High	128

BEARINGS

Source: Box, G.E.P.; "Do Interactions Matter?" *Quality Engineering,* 2, (1990), 365–369 and Hellestrand, C.; "The Necessity of Modern Quality Improvement and Some Experience with Its Implementation in the Manufacture of Rolling Bearings," *Philosophical Transactions of the Royal Society,* London, A327, (1989), 529–537.

(a) Compute the average effect for each main effect (factor) and interaction.

(b) Obtain a plot of the main effects.

(c) Obtain a plot of the interactions.

(d) On the basis of (a), set up a normal probability plot of the main effects and interactions.

(e) What conclusions can you draw from the results of (d)?

(f) Given the results of (d) and (e), combine all appropriate interactions into a measure of random error, and, using the level of significance 0.05, determine which factors are significant.

(g) What conclusions can you reach from the results of (f)?

11.10 The following experiment concerning the tensile strength of a metal rod was reported by Heinrich (1989). Three factors were considered: temperature of the molten metal at the start of the process

(300°F versus 400°F), pressure put on the molten metal to force it through a die (40 psi versus 70 psi), and the amount of a catalyst (20 rpm versus 30 rpm). The results were as follows:

Temperature (°F)	Pressure (psi)	Catalyst (rpm)	Tensile Strength
300	40	20	30
400	40	20	20
300	70	20	20
300	40	30	10
400	70	20	30
400	40	30	60
300	70	30	10
400	70	30	10

METALROD

Source: Reprinted from Heinrich, M.; "Experimental Design: Applications to System Testing," *Quality Engineering,* 1, (1989), 199–216

(a) Compute the average effect for each main effect (factor) and interaction.
(b) Obtain a plot of the main effects.
(c) Obtain a plot of the interactions.
(d) On the basis of (a), set up a normal probability plot of the main effects and interactions.
(e) What conclusions can you draw from the results of (d)?
(f) Given the results of (d) and (e), combine all appropriate interactions into a measure of random error, and, using the level of significance 0.05, determine which factors are significant.
(g) What conclusions can you reach from the results of (f)?

11.11 An experiment was performed to determine the importance of four factors on the efficiency of a distillation column that is used to separate two chemical compounds. The four factors were the relative volatility (expresses a chemical relationship between two items), bottom composition (indicates the ratio of compound A to the total volume of the two components at the bottom of the distillation column), top composition (indicates the ratio of compound A to the total volume of the two components at the top of the distillation column), and feed composition (the ratio of the two components where they enter the system). The results follow:

Relative Volatility	Bottom Composition	Top Composition	Feed Composition	Measured Efficiency
1.1	0.005	0.70	0.30	88
2.0	0.005	0.70	0.30	11
1.1	0.200	0.70	0.30	31
1.1	0.005	0.99	0.30	138
1.1	0.005	0.70	0.60	84
2.0	0.200	0.70	0.30	4
2.0	0.005	0.99	0.30	18
2.0	0.005	0.70	0.60	12
1.1	0.200	0.99	0.30	80
1.1	0.200	0.70	0.60	31
1.1	0.005	0.99	0.60	138
2.0	0.200	0.99	0.30	11
2.0	0.200	0.70	0.60	4
2.0	0.005	0.99	0.60	19
1.1	0.200	0.99	0.60	85
2.0	0.200	0.99	0.60	11

DISTILL

(a) Compute the average effect for each main effect (factor) and interaction.
(b) Obtain a plot of the main effects.
(c) Obtain a plot of the interactions.
(d) On the basis of (a), set up a normal probability plot of the main effects and interactions.
(e) What conclusions can you draw from the results of (d)?
(f) Given the results of (d) and (e), combine all appropriate interactions into a measure of random error, and, using the level of significance 0.05, determine which factors are significant.
(g) What conclusions can you reach from the results of (f)?

11.12 An experiment was conducted to determine the effect of four factors on the speed (measured in seconds) with which a stomach relief tablet dissolved in liquid. The four factors were brand of tablet (brand A versus brand B), type of liquid (water versus orange juice), whether the liquid was stirred (no versus yes), and the temperature of the liquid (cold versus hot). The results follow:

Brand	Liquid	Stirring	Temperature	Time (seconds)
A	Water	No	Cold	119
B	Water	No	Cold	153
A	Orange juice	No	Cold	201
A	Water	Yes	Cold	125

(Continued)

Brand	Liquid	Stirring	Temperature	Time (seconds)
A	Water	No	Hot	12
B	Orange juice	No	Cold	237
B	Water	Yes	Cold	157
B	Water	No	Hot	22
A	Orange juice	Yes	Cold	177
A	Orange juice	No	Hot	76
A	Water	Yes	Hot	20
B	Orange juice	Yes	Cold	235
B	Orange juice	No	Hot	122
B	Water	Yes	Hot	50
A	Orange juice	Yes	Hot	89
B	Orange juice	Yes	Hot	132

DISSOLVE

(a) Compute the average effect for each main effect (factor) and interaction.
(b) Obtain a plot of the main effects.
(c) Obtain a plot of the interactions.
(d) On the basis of (a), set up a normal probability plot of the main effects and interactions.
(e) What conclusions can you draw from the results of (d)?
(f) Given the results of (d) and (e), combine all appropriate interactions into a measure of random error, and, using the level of significance 0.05, determine which factors are significant.
(g) What conclusions can you reach from the results of (f)?

11.3 THE FRACTIONAL FACTORIAL DESIGN

When four or more factors are to be considered, often it becomes costly or impossible to simultaneously run all possible treatment combinations. For example, four factors, each having two levels, involve 16 treatment combinations; five factors, each having two levels, involve 32 treatment combinations; seven factors, each having two levels, involve 128 treatment combinations. Thus, as the number of factors in our experiment increases, we need to have a rational way of choosing a subset of the treatment combinations so that we can still conduct the experiment and obtain meaningful results. One way that this is accomplished is through the use of a fractional factorial design.

In a **fractional factorial design,** only a subset of all possible treatment combinations is used. Thus, we need to determine which subset or fraction of the treatment combinations will be chosen. For example, in the 2^4 design, there are many ways to choose eight treatment combinations out of the 16 available. In fact, there are 12,870 ways in which we could pick the treatments.[3]

One approach is to choose the treatment combinations so that each main effect can be independently estimated without being confused or **confounded** with any estimate of the two-factor interactions. When main effects or interactions are confounded, we cannot isolate the main effect of a factor from the main effect of another factor or an interaction. Designs in which main effects are confounded with two-way interactions (such as A being confounded with BC) are called **Resolution III designs.** Designs in which main effects are not confounded with two-way interactions are called **Resolution IV designs.** In Resolution IV designs, a two-way interaction such as AB is confounded with another two-way interaction such as CD. Designs in which each main effect and each two-factor interaction can be independently estimated without being confounded with any other main effects or interactions are called **Resolution V designs,** In these designs, main effects or two-way interactions are confounded with three-way or higher-order interactions (such as ABC or $ABCD$).

[3] The result is obtained using the rule of combinations (see Section 4.4), with $n = 16$ and $X = 8$.

Choosing the Treatment Combinations

We begin our discussion of how to choose a subset of the treatment combinations by referring to the 2^4 design. Table 11.12 presents all the possible treatment combinations for this full factorial design, along with the pattern of pluses and minuses for the main effects (the columns headed by A, B, C, and D) and the $ABCD$ interaction.

TABLE 11.12

TREATMENT COMBINATIONS FOR THE 2^4 DESIGN

Notation	A	B	C	D	$ABCD$
(1)	−	−	−	−	+
a	+	−	−	−	−
b	−	+	−	−	−
c	−	−	+	−	−
d	−	−	−	+	−
ab	+	+	−	−	+
ac	+	−	+	−	+
ad	+	−	−	+	+
bc	−	+	+	−	+
bd	−	+	−	+	+
cd	−	−	+	+	+
abc	+	+	+	−	−
abd	+	+	−	+	−
acd	+	−	+	+	−
bcd	−	+	+	+	−
abcd	+	+	+	+	+

In a fractional factorial design in which half the treatment combinations are chosen, only eight treatment combinations are available from the possible 16 combinations of a 2^4 design. With only eight treatment combinations, we cannot obtain as much information as we could from the full factorial 2^4 design, in which there are 16 combinations. If we are willing to assume that the four-way interaction, $ABCD$, is not significant, our fraction or subset of eight treatment combinations (called a half-replicate) out of the possible 16 could be selected either so that

1. the eight treatment combinations all have a plus sign in the column headed by $ABCD$; or so that
2. the eight treatment combinations all have a minus sign in the column headed by $ABCD$.

If such a design were used, the $ABCD$ interaction would be considered as the **defining contrast,** from which we could determine which factors and interactions were confounded with each other.

We begin our determination of the treatment combinations to be selected by focusing first on factor A. With $ABCD$ as the defining contrast, factor A is confounded with interaction BCD, because A and $ABCD$ differ only by BCD.[4] We could alternatively state that BCD is an **alias** of A, because the effects of BCD and A cannot be separated in this fractional factorial design. In essence, the A main effect is equivalent to the BCD interaction. If we are willing to assume that the

[4] We can view this from the perspective of binary (base 2) arithmetic, in which $A(ABCD) = A^2BCD = BCD$.

BCD interaction is negligible, then, when we evaluate the average main effect of A, we state that this is the effect of factor A (even though it could have been the effect of the BCD interaction).[5] In a similar manner, B is confounded with ACD; C is confounded with ABD; D is confounded with ABC; AB is confounded with CD; AC is confounded with BD, and AD is confounded with BC.

From this pattern of confounded effects, we observe that the penalty we pay for using this design (which is called a 2^{4-1} fractional factorial design) is that the two-factor or two-way interaction terms are confounded with each other. Thus, we cannot separate AB from CD, AC from BD, or AD from BC. If any of these interaction terms is found to be important, we will not be able to know whether the effect is due to one term or the other.

As a first example of a fractional factorial design, we will examine a 2^{4-1} design in which eight treatments have been chosen from the total of 16 possible combinations and the defining contrast is $ABCD$. The particular experiment is one that any of us can repeat (see Problem 11.41 on page 562). It involves four factors that could affect the time (in seconds) that it takes to boil 16 ounces of water. The factors to be considered are the following:

1. A, type of pot (aluminum versus stainless steel);
2. B, type of water (tap versus bottled);
3. C, size of pot (small (one quart) versus large (four quarts));
4. D, position of lid (off versus on).

The results of the experiment and the pattern of the pluses and minuses of the factors are summarized in Table 11.13.

[5] If the half replicate chosen has a plus sign in column $ABCD$, then A is confounded with BCD. If the half-replicate chosen has a minus sign in column $ABCD$; then A is confounded with $-BCD$.

TABLE 11.13

BOILING TIMES (SECONDS) FOR EIGHT TREATMENT COMBINATIONS IN THE 2^{4-1} EXPERIMENT

Notation	Boiling Time (seconds)	A	B	C	D	$AB+$ CD	$AC+$ BD	$AD+$ BC
(1)	195	−	−	−	−	+	+	+
ab	204	+	+	−	−	+	−	−
ac	216	+	−	+	−	−	+	−
ad	193	+	−	−	+	−	−	+
bc	167	−	+	+	−	−	−	+
bd	142	−	+	−	+	−	+	−
cd	158	−	−	+	+	+	−	−
$abcd$	153	+	+	+	+	+	+	+

 BOILING

From the results presented in Table 11.13 for this 2^{4-1} design, there are $2^{4-1} - 1 = 7$ effects that can be evaluated (A, B, C, D, AB, AC, and AD). Using a version of Equations (11.12)–(11.15) for the average effects of the factors that we have just calculated, we obtain the cumulative proportions for the effects ranked in ascending order. Table 11.14 presents the average effects, ranks, and cumulative proportions for this water-boiling experiment.

TABLE 11.14

AVERAGE EFFECTS, RANKS, AND CUMULATIVE PROPORTIONS FOR THE WATER-BOILING EXPERIMENT

Effect	Average Value	Rank (R_i)	Cumulative Proportion (p_i)
$D = ABC$	-34	1	0.071
$B = ACD$	-24	2	0.214
$C = ABD$	-10	3	0.357
$AC = BD$	-4	4	0.500
$AD = BC$	-3	5	0.643
$AB = CD$	-2	6	0.786
$A = BCD$	26	7	0.929

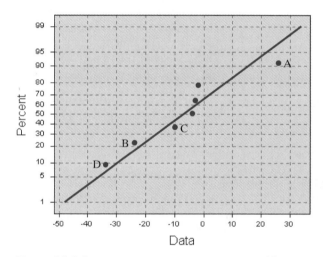

Figure 11.16   Normal probability plot for the 2^{4-1} design for the water-boiling experiment

These average effects are depicted in Figure 11.16 in a normal probability plot of the effects.

From Figure 11.16, we observe that the interactions and possibly factor C plot relatively close to a hypothetical straight vertical line near $X = 0$ representing no effect, while factors A, B, and D appear to plot away from this line. Thus, if we are willing to assume that the three-factor interactions (ABC, ABD, ACD, and BCD) and the four-factor interaction, $ABCD$, are unimportant, we reach the following conclusions:

1. We estimate that boiling time is, on average, 26 seconds longer in a stainless steel pot as compared to that in an aluminum pot.
2. We estimate that bottled water takes an average of 24 seconds less to boil than tap water.
3. We estimate that the time it takes to boil water in a large pot is, on average, 10 seconds less than in a small pot.

4.   We estimate that the time it takes to boil water when the lid is on is an average of 34 seconds shorter than that when the lid is off.
5.   There is no reason to believe that the two-factor interaction effects in this example are important.

Now that we have introduced the topic of fractional factorial designs by studying the 2^{4-1} design, we can expand our coverage by referring to an example of a 2^{5-1} design. Suppose that we wanted to study factors that affect the transmission of documents via Fax equipment. The response variable of interest was operationally defined as the amount of time it took to send a one-page document from the moment the Start button was pressed (the phone number had already been dialed) to the moment the Fax was completely received (the machine beeped), recorded in seconds. The five factors to be studied (with the low level shown first) are the following:

1. A, type of paper (bond versus regular);
2. B, type of spacing (single versus double);
3. C, type of print (from laser printer versus from copying machine);
4. D, fax machine (new versus old);
5. E, method of paper entry (bottom first versus top first);

Because of limitations of time, a half-replicate of a 2^5 factorial design was used. The results of the experiment are presented in Table 11.15.

TABLE 11.15

DATA FOR THE FAX EXPERIMENT

Treatment Combinations	Notation	Time (seconds)	Treatment Combinations	Notation	Time (seconds)
Regular, single, laser, new, bottom	a	61.42	Regular, single, copier, old, bottom	acd	48.79
Bond, double, laser, new, bottom	b	61.63	Regular, single, copier, new, top	ace	61.22
Bond, single, copier, new, bottom	c	60.27	Regular, single, laser, old, top	ade	49.13
Bond, single, laser, old, bottom	d	49.12	Bond, double, copier, old, bottom	bcd	47.44
Bond, single, laser, new, top	e	62.21	Bond, double, copier, new, top	bce	60.59
Regular, double, copier, new, bottom	abc	61.20	Bond, double, laser, old, top	bde	47.67
Regular, double, laser, old, bottom	abd	47.76	Bond, single, copier, old, top	cde	48.86
Regular, double, laser, new, top	abe	62.03	Regular, double, copier, old, top	$abcde$	47.47

FAX

The subset or fraction of 16 treatment combinations used in Table 11.15 is based on the five-factor interaction $ABCDE$ as the defining contrast. This produces a Resolution V design in which all main effects and two-factor interactions can be estimated independently of each other. Each main effect is confounded with a four-factor interaction, while each two-factor interaction is confounded with a three-factor interaction. For this design, the set of confounded effects is summarized in Table 11.16.

The results shown in Table 11.15 are organized in Table 11.17 so as to obtain estimates of the average effects for the factors and interactions.

Using a version of Equations (11.12)–(11.15) for the average effects for the factors that we have just calculated, we obtain the cumulative proportions for the

TABLE 11.16

CONFOUNDED EFFECTS FOR THE 2^{5-1} DESIGN WITH ABCDE AS THE DEFINING CONTRAST

Effect	Confounded With	Effect	Confounded With
A	BCDE	AE	BCD
B	ACDE	BC	ADE
C	ABDE	BD	ACE
D	ABCE	BE	ACD
E	ABCD	CD	ABE
AB	CDE	CE	ABD
AC	BDE	DE	ABC
AD	BCE		

TABLE 11.17

OBTAINING AVERAGE EFFECTS FOR THE 2^{5-1} FAX EXAMPLE

Notation	Response	A	B	C	D	E	AB	AC	AD	AE	BC	BD	BE	CD	CE	DE
a	61.42	+	−	−	−	−	−	−	−	−	+	+	+	+	+	+
b	61.63	−	+	−	−	−	−	+	+	+	−	−	−	+	+	+
c	60.27	−	−	+	−	−	+	−	+	+	−	+	+	−	−	+
d	49.12	−	−	−	+	−	+	+	−	+	+	−	+	−	+	−
e	62.21	−	−	−	−	+	+	+	+	−	+	+	−	+	−	−
abc	61.20	+	+	+	−	−	+	+	−	−	+	−	−	−	−	+
abd	47.76	+	+	−	+	−	+	−	+	−	−	+	−	+	−	−
abe	62.03	+	+	−	−	+	+	−	−	+	−	−	+	+	−	−
acd	48.79	+	−	+	+	−	−	+	+	−	−	+	+	−	−	−
ace	61.22	+	−	+	−	+	−	+	−	+	−	+	−	−	+	−
ade	49.13	+	−	−	+	+	−	−	+	+	+	−	−	−	−	+
bcd	47.44	−	+	+	+	−	−	−	−	+	+	+	−	+	−	−
bce	60.59	−	+	+	−	+	−	−	+	−	+	−	+	−	+	−
bde	47.67	−	+	−	+	+	−	+	−	−	−	+	+	−	−	+
cde	48.86	−	−	+	+	+	+	−	−	−	−	−	−	+	+	+
abcde	47.47	+	+	+	+	+	+	+	+	+	+	+	+	+	+	+

effects ranked in ascending order. Table 11.18 represents the average effects, ranks, and cumulative proportions for this Fax experiment.

These average effects and their cumulative probabilities are plotted in Figure 11.17, a normal probability plot of the effects.

If we are willing to assume that all three-way and higher-order interactions are negligible, we can observe from Figure 11.17 that all the two-way interactions and main effects, except for that of factor D (new versus old FAX machine), are distributed in an approximately straight vertical line close to a hypothetical vertical line plotted at a value of $X = 0$. Factor D is very far removed from our hypothetical plotted line. Thus, we conclude that only the effect of factor D seems important. From Table 11.18, we conclude that the average response time is 13.04 seconds less for the old machine than for the new machine. This finding may come as a surprise to the manufacturer of the new Fax machine.

TABLE 11.18

AVERAGE EFFECTS, RANKS, AND CUMULATIVE PROPORTIONS FOR THE FAX EXPERIMENT

Effect	Average Value	Rank (R_i)	Cumulative Proportion (p_i)
$D = ABCE$	−13.04125	1	0.033
$BD = ACE$	−0.73625	2	0.100
$B = ACDE$	−0.65375	3	0.167
$C = ABDE$	−0.64125	4	0.233
$BE = ACD$	−0.26125	5	0.300
$DE = ABC$	−0.18875	6	0.367
$AD = BCE$	−0.13875	7	0.433
$CE = ABD$	−0.08375	8	0.500
$AE = BCD$	−0.02375	9	0.567
$BC = ADE$	+0.04375	10	0.633
$AB = CDE$	+0.12875	11	0.700
$A = BCDE$	+0.15375	12	0.767
$E = ABCD$	+0.19375	13	0.833
$AC = BDE$	+0.22625	14	0.900
$CD = ABC$	+0.36125	15	0.967

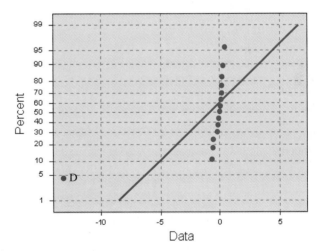

Figure 11.17   Normal probability plot of the 2^{5-1} design for the Fax experiment

In this section, we have discussed two examples of fractional factorial designs that are used when it is not feasible to evaluate all possible treatment combinations. These two designs are only a small subset of the variety of fractional factorial designs that are available for selection. The 2^{4-1} and 2^{5-1} designs are examples of designs that involve the selection of a half-replicate (8 out of 16, or 16 out of 32 treatment combinations) of a full factorial design. Other designs might involve a quarter-replicate (such as a 2^{5-2} and 2^{6-2} design) or even smaller portions of a factorial design in which only main effects can be estimated (for instance, a 2^{15-11} design). It is also possible to study designs in which there are more than two levels for a factor. Discussion of such designs are beyond the scope of this text. (For further information, see References 5 and 10.)

PROBLEMS

11.13 Problem 11.9 on page 539 concerned a study of ball bearings reported by Box (1989). In addition to the experimental design used in Problem 11.9, Box (1992) reported another experiment in which four factors were used to study the average life of bearings produced. The four factors were the manufacturing process for the balls (standard or modified), the cage design (standard or modified), the type of grease (standard or modified), and the amount of grease (normal or large). A half-replicate of a full factorial design was used. The results are summarized in the following table.

Type of Balls	Cage Design	Type of Grease	Amount of Grease	Average Life
Standard	Standard	Standard	Normal	0.31
Modified	Modified	Standard	Normal	2.17
Modified	Standard	Modified	Normal	1.37
Modified	Standard	Standard	Large	1.38
Standard	Modified	Modified	Normal	0.92
Standard	Modified	Standard	Large	0.73
Standard	Standard	Modified	Large	0.95
Modified	Modified	Modified	Large	2.57

BEARINGS2

Source: Reprinted from Box, G.E.P.; "What Can You Find Out From Eight Experimental Runs," *Quality Engineering*, 4, (1992), 619–627

(a) Compute the average effect for each of the four main effects and the interaction effects.
(b) Set up a normal probability plot of the average effects.
(c) From (b), which effects appear to be important?
(d) Set up all appropriate interaction graphs.
(e) What conclusions can you reach concerning the importance of each of the main effects and interactions on the average life of ball bearings?

11.14 An experiment was conducted to study the time (in minutes) it takes to cook rice in a cooker that has an inner water area and an outer water area. Four factors were considered: amount of rice (1 cup versus 2 cups); amount of inner water (2 cups versus 3 cups); amount of outer water (0.5 cup versus 1 cup); and type of rice (short grain versus long grain). A half-replicate of a full factorial design was used. The results follow:

Rice (cups)	Inner Water (cups)	Outside Water	Type of Rice	Cooking Time (minutes)
1	2	0.5	short	26.4
2	3	0.5	short	28.9
2	2	1.0	short	28.4
2	2	0.5	long	27.1
1	3	1.0	short	30.1
1	3	0.5	long	28.6
1	2	1.0	long	27.9
2	3	1.0	long	31.5

RICE

(a) Compute the average effect for each of the four main effects and the interaction effects.
(b) Set up a normal probability plot of the average effects.
(c) In (b), which effects appear to be important?
(d) Set up all appropriate interaction graphs.
(e) What conclusions can you reach concerning the importance of each of the main effects and interactions on the average cooking time of rice?

11.15 An experiment was conducted to study the effect of four factors on scores in the game of American darts. The four factors were amount of room lighting (75 watts versus 100 watts), practice prior to playing (none versus 5 minutes), consumption of beer (none versus two cans), and whether a radio was playing in the background (no versus yes). A half-replicate of a full factorial design was used. The scores of an experienced dart player in the experiment follow:

Lighting (watts)	Warm-up	Beer (cans)	Radio	Score
75	None	0	No	89
100	5 minutes	0	No	87
100	None	2	No	71
100	None	0	Yes	76
75	5 minutes	2	No	68
75	5 minutes	0	Yes	76
75	None	2	Yes	68
100	5 minutes	2	Yes	67

DARTS

(a) Compute the average effect for each of the four main effects and the interaction effects.
(b) Set up a normal probability plot of the average effects.
(c) In (b), which effects appear to be important?
(d) Set up all appropriate interaction graphs.
(e) What conclusions can you reach concerning the importance of each of the main effects and interactions on score?

11.16 The following experiment, reported by Kilgo (1989), was conducted to study the process of using carbon dioxide to extract oil from peanuts in a production process. The response variable was the amount of oil that could dissolve in the carbon dioxide (the solubility). Five factors were to be studied. They are labeled as follows: A = carbon dioxide pressure, B = carbon dioxide temperature, C = peanut moisture, D = carbon dioxide flow rate, E = peanut particle size. Two levels of each factor (a low and a high) were chosen. A half-replicate of a 2^5 design was selected. The results were as follows:

Treatment Combination	Response	Treatment Combination	Response
(1)	29.2	de	22.4
ae	23.0	ad	37.2
be	37.0	bd	31.3
ab	139.7	abde	48.6
ce	23.3	cd	22.9
ac	38.3	acde	36.2
bc	42.6	bcde	33.6
abce	141.4	abcd	172.6

PEANUT

Source: Reprinted from Kilgo, M.; "An Application of Fractional Factorial Experimental Designs," *Quality Engineering,* 1 (1989), 45–54

(a) Compute the average effect for each of the five main effects and the interaction effects.
(b) Set up a normal probability plot of the average effects.
(c) In (b), which effects appear to be important?
(d) Set up all appropriate interaction graphs.
(e) What conclusions can you reach concerning the importance of each of the main effects and interactions on solubility?
(f) Suppose that the response for treatment combination *abde* was incorrectly reported as 48.6 and, in fact, was actually 148.6. Revise the results you obtained in (a) through (e) in the light of this correction.
(g) Compare the conclusions reached in (e) and (f).
(h) In analyzing the original data, in retrospect, what might have made you realize that the result for treatment combination *abde* was incorrect?

11.17 Refer to the experiment discussed in Problem 11.16. In addition to a response measure of solubility, the total yield of oil per batch of peanuts was obtained. The results follow:

Treatment Combination	Response	Treatment Combination	Response
(1)	63	de	23
ae	21	ad	74
be	36	bd	80
ab	99	abde	33
ce	24	cd	63
ac	66	acde	21
bc	71	bcde	44
abce	54	abcd	96

PEANUT2

Source: Reprinted from Kilgo, M.; "An Application of Fractional Factorial Experimental Designs," *Quality Engineering,* 1 (1989), 45–54

(a) Compute the average effect for each of the five main effects and the interaction effects.
(b) Set up a normal probability plot of the average effects.
(c) In (b), which effects appear to be important?
(d) Set up all appropriate interaction graphs.
(e) What conclusions can you reach concerning the importance of each of the main effects and interactions on the yield?

11.4 THE TAGUCHI APPROACH

At the beginning of Chapter 10, we chronicled the historical development of design of experiments. We noted that, until recently, these methods were not widely used for process and quality improvement by American and European companies. In contrast to this lack of widespread use by Western industry, these methods were enthusiastically embraced by Japanese engineers in the post-World War II period. The Japanese not only used such quality-improvement methods as statistical process control in an ongoing on-line approach but also used tools such as design of experiments from the very initial stages of product and process design. Using these tools in the design stage is often called **off-line process control.** Perhaps the person who has made the greatest contribution to this approach is the Japanese engineer Genichi Taguchi. (See References 1 and 7.) In this section, we will provide an introduction to Taguchi's contributions to quality improvement.

Taguchi's Contributions to Design of Experiments

Among the many contributions of Taguchi are those that relate to what is usually referred to as **parameter design.** This approach uses fractional factorial and other designs to focus on the following:

1.   minimizing the squared error around a target value;
2.   making products robust against variation in environmental conditions;
3.   making products less sensitive to unit-to-unit variation.

The first of these contributions relates to the concept of variation from a target value (for example, the inner diameter of an automobile tire). Traditionally, the focus was on just meeting specifications. With such an approach, any difference from a target was considered inconsequential as long as the result was within the design or engineering specifications indicated for the product use. In contrast, Taguchi's approach postulates a **quadratic loss function** expressed as:

$$\text{Loss} = k(Y_i - T)^2 \tag{11.19}$$

where

k is a non-negative constant

Y_i is the value for a particular observation i

T is the target value

Such a loss function is depicted in Figure 11.18.

With this approach, the expected loss in quality (or cost of poor quality) increases dramatically as the result moves away from the target, even if the result is within design specifications.

The second part of Taguchi's approach relates to the attempt to make products robust against or insensitive to variation in environmental conditions. Thus, experimental designs are developed that divide factors into two types; **design parameters** and **noise factors.** The design parameters are controllable factors, on which we need to focus in the process improvement study. Such factors are called **inner array** factors. The noise factors are environmental and represent conditions

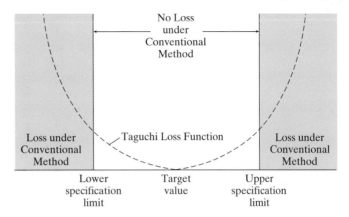

Figure 11.18   Taguchi loss function

under which the product is expected to perform. These are called **outer array** factors. By subjecting the design parameters to a variety of environmental conditions, one hopes to determine the levels of the controllable factors of interest that result in an output that is as insensitive as possible to a variety of environmental conditions.

The third part of the Taguchi approach relates to the attempt to make products less sensitive to unit-to-unit variation. With this approach, the decision criteria take into account not only the average value for a particular treatment combination but also its standard deviation. This is done by using **signal-to-noise ratios** to evaluate treatment combinations. These ratios are of three types: SN_T, SN_S, and SN_L.

If the goal is to meet a specific target value, the signal-to-noise ratio (called SN_T) can be expressed as

$$SN_T = -10 \log_{10} \frac{\sum_{i=1}^{n} (Y_i - T)^2}{n} \tag{11.20}$$

where

   Y_i is the ith value for a particular treatment combination

   n is the number of values for a particular treatment combination

   T is the target value

or, under an alternative approach (see Reference 3), as

$$SN_T = 10 \log_{10} \frac{\overline{Y}^2}{s^2} \tag{11.21}$$

where

   $\overline{Y}$ is the average for a particular treatment combination

   s^2 is the variance for a particular treatment combination

If the quality characteristic being evaluated is such that a lower value indicates higher quality, the goal would be to minimize the response, and the signal-to-noise ratio (SN_S) is:

$$SN_s = -10 \log_{10} \frac{\sum_{i=1}^{n} Y_i^2}{n} \tag{11.22}$$

where

Y_i is the ith value for a particular treatment combination

n is the number of values for a particular treatment combination

If the quality characteristic being evaluated is such that a higher value indicates higher quality, the aim would be to maximize the response, and the signal-to-noise ratio (SN_L) is:

$$SN_L = -10 \log_{10} \frac{\sum_{i=1}^{n} \left(\frac{1}{Y_i}\right)^2}{n} \tag{11.23}$$

We can illustrate Taguchi's approach to experimental design with the *Using Statistics* example already discussed in Section 11.2, concerning a food processing company. In addition to the treatment combinations listed in Table 11.7 on page 534, the cake is also baked by using the recommended levels (shown by a zero in Table 11.19) of flour, shortening, egg powder, oven temperature, and baking time.

With a 2^3 design in the inner array factors of flour, shortening, and egg powder, plus an additional treatment combination for the recommended amounts of these three factors, there are $2^3 + 1 = 9$ treatment combinations. Each of these appears for each combination of noise factors (oven temperature and baking time). Thus, with two environmental factors in the outer array plus a treatment combination that represents the recommended temperature and baking time, there are $2^2 + 1 = 5$ replications for each treatment combination of design factors. The results in terms of $9 \times 5 = 45$ taste-testing scores are summarized in Table 11.19 on page 553.

There are three design factors, so, following the geometric approach used in Figure 11.9, we present the treatment combinations for the data in Table 11.19 in Figure 11.19 on page 554. We note that this figure also depicts a two-dimensional square of environmental factors for each treatment combination. In addition, we observe that the combinations representing the recommended amounts in the instructions have been displayed at the center of the complete cube and at the center of each appropriate square.

For each treatment combination, we compute the average rating and the variance of the ratings, and Equation (11.21) is used to obtain the signal-to-noise ratio (SN_T) for the data in Table 11.19. This information is summarized in Table 11.20 on page 554.

From Table 11.19, we observe that the standard recipe baked at a temperature and time suggested on the instructions (treatment combination 0 0 0 0 0)

TABLE 11.19

TASTE RATING FOR CAKE MIX COMBINATIONS

Treatment Combination	Design Parameters			Noise Factors		Rating Score
	Flour (F)	Shortening (S)	Egg Powder (E)	Oven Temperature (T)	Baking Time (B)	
0	0	0	0	0	0	6.7
0	0	0	0	−	−	3.4
0	0	0	0	+	−	5.4
0	0	0	0	−	+	4.1
0	0	0	0	+	+	3.8
(1)	−	−	−	0	0	3.1
(1)	−	−	−	−	−	1.1
(1)	−	−	−	+	−	5.7
(1)	−	−	−	−	+	6.4
(1)	−	−	−	+	+	1.3
a	+	−	−	0	0	3.2
a	+	−	−	−	−	3.8
a	+	−	−	+	−	4.9
a	+	−	−	−	+	4.3
a	+	−	−	+	+	2.1
b	−	+	−	0	0	5.3
b	−	+	−	−	−	3.7
b	−	+	−	+	−	5.1
b	−	+	−	−	+	6.7
b	−	+	−	+	+	2.9
c	−	−	+	0	0	6.3
c	−	−	+	−	−	4.2
c	−	−	+	+	−	6.8
c	−	−	+	−	+	6.5
c	−	−	+	+	+	3.5
ab	+	+	−	0	0	4.1
ab	+	+	−	−	−	4.5
ab	+	+	−	+	−	6.4
ab	+	+	−	−	+	5.8
ab	+	+	−	+	+	5.2
ac	+	−	+	0	0	6.1
ac	+	−	+	−	−	5.2
ac	+	−	+	+	−	6.0
ac	+	−	+	−	+	5.9
ac	+	−	+	+	+	5.7
bc	−	+	+	0	0	3.0
bc	−	+	+	−	−	3.1
bc	−	+	+	+	−	6.3
bc	−	+	+	−	+	6.4
bc	−	+	+	+	+	3.0
abc	+	+	+	0	0	4.5
abc	+	+	+	−	−	3.9
abc	+	+	+	+	−	5.5
abc	+	+	+	−	+	5.0
abc	+	+	+	+	+	5.4

Source: Box, G.E.P., S. Bisgaard, and C. Fung; "An Explanation and Critique of Taguchi's Contributions to Quality Engineering," *Quality and Reliability Engineering International,* 4, (1988), 123–131.

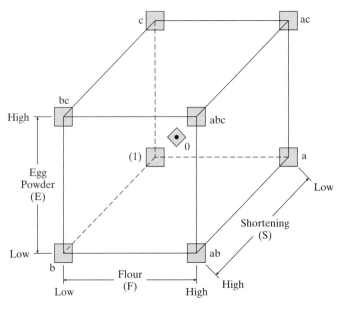

Figure 11.19   Geometric interpretation of the inner and outer arrays for the cake-mix example
Source: Table 11.19 on page 553

TABLE 11.20

AVERAGE RATING SCORE, VARIANCE, AND SIGNAL-TO-NOISE
RATIO FOR EACH TREATMENT COMBINATION

Treatment Combinations	Average Y	Variance s^2	Signal-to-Noise Ratio (SN_T)
0	4.68	1.84	10.757
(1)	3.52	6.00	3.149
a	3.66	1.15	10.663
b	4.74	2.19	10.111
c	5.46	2.12	11.480
ab	5.20	0.88	14.875
ac	5.78	0.47	18.518
bc	4.36	3.30	7.605
abc	4.86	0.49	16.831 **CAKESN**

produced a very high taste rating score, 6.7. However, we also note that, when the environmental conditions are changed, the taste rating for this treatment combination declines markedly. We also note that six of the eight other treatment combinations [*(1)*, *b*, *c*, *ab*, *ac*, and *bc*] also produce a high taste rating score under certain environmental conditions.

The signal-to-noise ratios shown in Table 11.20 can now be used, instead of the raw data, to analyze the inner-array factors: flour, shortening, and egg powder. The estimated effects can be obtained by first using MINITAB to obtain the sum

Normal Probability Plot of Estimated Effects using SN ratio

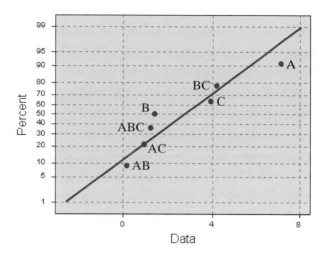

Figure 11.20   Normal probability plot obtained from MINITAB of the effects for the cake-mix example estimated by using the signal-to-noise ratio

of squares for each effect (with the ABC term substituted for the error term in the model) and then using Equation (11.18) on page 533. The estimated effects based on the signal-to-noise ratio are

$$A = 7.136, B = 1.403, C = 3.909, AB = 0.140,$$
$$AC = 0.996, BC = 4.184, ABC = 1.235$$

Figure 11.20 is a normal probability plot of the estimated effects obtained from MINITAB.

From Figure 11.20, we observe that the only effect that plots close to a hypothetical vertical line at $X = 0$ is the AC interaction. Thus, it is not advisable to pool interactions together to form an error term. From the interaction plot obtained from MINITAB in Figure 11.21 on page 556, there appears to be a strong interaction effect between shortening and egg powder, similar to that seen in the factorial experiment of Section 11.2.

From Table 11.20 and Figure 11.21, it appears that treatment combination ac (high levels of flour and egg powder, low level of shortening) produces cakes that are robust against changes in environmental conditions: The taste rating score is relatively high, the variance is low, and SN_T is high. Therefore, increasing the levels of flour and egg powder and lowering the level of shortening would lead to a more nearly "fail-safe" product.

The Controversy Concerning the Taguchi Approach

Since the introduction of Taguchi's approach in the United States in the past decade, a great deal of discussion has been generated about the appropriateness of Taguchi's methods. (See References 1, 3, 4, 7, and 12.) Perhaps it is best to consider two aspects

Interactions for Cake–Mix Experiment using SN Ratio

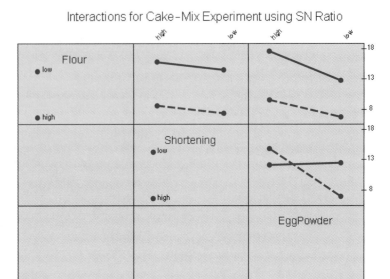

Figure 11.21   Interaction plots obtained from MINITAB for the
cake-mix data by using the signal-to-noise ratio

of Taguchi's contributions: those that relate to quality engineering, and those that relate to experimental design. There appears to be a consensus concerning Taguchi's contributions to quality engineering, specifically the loss function expressed in Equation (11.19) on page 550, and the desirability of products that are robust against environmental variation. These ideas are clearly consistent with the themes of quality management discussed in Chapter 1.

It is Taguchi's approach to experimental design that has engendered the most controversy. Two major points of controversy are (1) the appropriateness of the fractional factorial designs that Taguchi advocates and (2) the validity of the use of signal-to-noise ratios.

The criticism of the experimental designs seems to center on the types of fractional factorial designs used with the Taguchi approach. Often, these designs are Resolution III designs that contain a complicated confounding structure in which main effects are confounded with simple two-factor interactions. Such designs are appropriate in circumstances where there is a great deal known about the process, so that one can be confident in assuming that it is safe to ignore certain interaction effects; however, fractional factorial designs can provide misleading results in circumstances where there is a lack of extensive experience with the process or when these designs are used without sufficient awareness of the design assumptions and limitations.

The criticism of the signal-to-noise ratios seem to pertain to several issues. One primary difficulty relates to the ability of the signal-to-noise ratio to separate location and dispersion effects. As such, the signal-to-noise ratio is equivalent to the analysis of the standard deviation of the logarithm of the data. The criticism of the validity relates to the method's implication that this separation of location and dispersion effects can always be accomplished merely by using a log transformation. The argument is made (as in Reference 4) that situations may exist in which a different transformation (or no transformation) is needed to obtain this separation. Further criticisms of the signal-to-noise ratio concern its complexity and inefficiency. (See References 1 and 12.)

PROBLEMS

11.18 What are the similarities and differences between the analysis of the cake-mix data using the Taguchi approach of this section and that using the factorial design approach in Section 11.2.

11.19 Refer to Problem 11.2 on page 524, concerning the amplification of a stereo recording.
 (a) Compute the signal-to-noise ratio for each treatment combination, under the response criterion "the larger, the better."
 (b) Given the results of (a), which treatment combination would you choose?
 (c) Compare the conclusion reached in (b) to that of Problem 11.2 (f).

11.20 Refer to Problem 11.3 on page 524, concerning the fire-retardant treatment of fabrics.
 (a) Compute the signal-to-noise ratio for each treatment combination, under the response criterion "the smaller, the better."
 (b) Given the results of (a), which treatment combination would you choose?
 (c) Compare the conclusion reached in (b) to that of Problem 11.3 (e).

11.21 Refer to Problem 11.4 on page 524, concerning the density of photographic plate-film.
 (a) Compute the signal-to-noise ratio for each treatment combination, under the response criterion "the larger, the better."
 (b) Given the results of (a), which treatment combination would you choose?
 (c) Compare the conclusion reached in (b) to that of Problem 11.4 (e).

11.22 Refer to Problem 11.6 on page 538, concerning the deviation from the target fill heights of soft drinks.
 (a) Compute the signal-to-noise ratio for each treatment combination, under the response criterion "the smaller the deviation, the better."
 (b) Reanalyze the treatment combinations by using the signal-to-noise ratio.
 (c) Given the results of (a) and (b), which treatment combination would you choose?
 (d) Compare the conclusion reached in (c) to that of Problem 11.6 (k).

11.23 Refer to Problem 11.7 on page 538, concerning the distance traveled by a paper airplane.
 (a) Compute the signal-to-noise ratio for each treatment combination, under the response criterion "the larger, the better."
 (b) Reanalyze the treatment combinations by using the signal-to-noise ratio.
 (c) Given the results of (a) and (b), which treatment combination would you choose?
 (d) Compare the conclusion reached in (c) to that of Problem 11.7 (k).

11.5 SUMMARY AND OVERVIEW

In this chapter, we have shown how the factorial design, by allowing for the measurement of the size of interaction effects, offers a substantial benefit as compared to the one-factor design approach. In addition, we have considered the fractional factorial design for situations in which many factors need to be evaluated simultaneously. Finally, we have provided a brief introduction to the Taguchi approach to design of experiments.

Although an extensive set of issues was discussed, we should be aware that we have barely "scratched the surface" of the subject of the design of experiments. Many designs have not been considered. For information about these aspects of design of experiments, see References 5, 6, and 10.

KEY TERMS

alias   542
confounded   541
contrast   541
defining contrast   542
design parameters   550
F test for interaction effect   517
factorial design model   513
fixed-effects model   522
fractional factorial design   541
inner array   550
interaction   514
mixed-effects model   523
noise factors   550
off line process control   550
outer array   551
parameter design   550

quadratic loss function   550
random-effects model   552
replicates   514
Resolution III designs   541
Resolution IV designs   541
Resolution V designs   541
Signal-to-noise ratio   551
Sum of Squares due to factor
   A (SSA)   515
Sum of Squares due to factor
   B (SSB)   515
Sum of Squares due to interaction
   (SSAB)   515
Sum of Squares Error (SSE)   516
Sum of Squares Total (SST)   514
Taguchi approach   550

CHAPTER REVIEW   *Checking Your Understanding*

11.24 What is the difference between the one-factor and two-factor ANOVA models?

11.25 What is the difference between the randomized block-design model and the two-factor factorial design model?

11.26 What do we mean by the concept of interaction in a factorial design?

11.27 How can we use the two-way ANOVA F test to examine possible interactions among the levels of the factors in a factorial design?

11.28 Discuss the purpose, limitations, and assumptions of the fractional factorial design.

11.29 Explain the differences between the one-way design, the factorial design, and the fractional factorial design, and indicate the circumstances in which each would be used.

11.30 Discuss the differences between Resolution III, IV, and V fractional factorial designs.

11.31 Explain what is meant by the alias structure of a fractional factorial design, and provide an example.

11.32 Explain the Taguchi philosophy for quality engineering in terms of experimental-design considerations.

11.33 Explain the difference between the inner and outer arrays (also known as controllable and noise factors) in the Taguchi approach to experimental design.

11.34 Explain the signal-to-noise ratios and their potential advantages and disadvantages.

11.35 Compare the classical approach to fractional factorial designs against the Taguchi approach. Indicate potential advantages and disadvantages.

Chapter Review Problems

11.36 A chef in a restaurant that specializes in pasta dishes has experienced difficulty in getting brands of pasta to be *al dente,* that is, cooked just enough, so as to feel not starchy or hard but still firm when bitten into. She decides to conduct an experiment in which two brands of pasta, one American and one Italian, are cooked for either 4 or 8 minutes. The response variable measured is weight of the pasta, because the cooking of the pasta enables it to absorb water. A pasta with a faster rate of water absorption might provide a shorter interval during which the pasta is *al dente,* thereby increasing the chance that it might become overcooked. The experiment was conducted by using 150 grams of uncooked pasta. Each trial began by taking a pot containing 6 quarts of cold unsalted water and bringing it to a moderate boil. The 150 grams of uncooked pasta was added; then, after a given period of time, it was weighed by lifting it from the pot by means of a built-in strainer. The results (in terms of weight in grams) for two replications of each combination of pasta and cooking time were as follows:

	Cooking Time (minutes)			Cooking Time (minutes)	
Type of Pasta	4	8	Type of Pasta	4	8
American	265	310	Italian	250	300
	270	320		245	305

PASTA

For the 0.05 level of significance, answer these questions:
(a) Is there an effect due to type of pasta?
(b) Is there an effect due to cooking time?
(c) Is there an interaction due to type of pasta and cooking time?
(d) Plot a graph of average cooking time for each type of pasta for each cooking time.
(e) What conclusions can you reach concerning the importance of each of these two factors on the weight of the pasta?
(f) If you were to conduct this experiment, what other factors might you include? Why?
(g) Perform this experiment, using these two factors (type of pasta and cooking time) and any other factors you included in (f).
(h) How do the conclusions you reached in (e) differ, if at all, from those of (g)? Explain.

11.37 Spherical tipped locators and clamps are used for the restraint of castings during manufacturing. Workpiece displacement is influenced by workpiece bending, contact region deformation, and micro-slippage. An experiment was carried out to measure the effect of clamp actuation intensity and the location of fixture elements on the maximum displacement. Three samples were obtained for each actuation intensity and location combination. The results were as follows:

Clamp Actuation Intensity	Location		
	1	2	3
890	0.1085 0.1292 0.1501	0.3436 0.3167 0.3569	0.114 0.1222 0.1275
1041	0.1245 0.1417 0.1613	0.3546 0.3292 0.3690	0.1270 0.1405 0.1455
1246	0.1488 0.1654 0.1781	0.3703 0.3292 0.3863	0.1516 0.1600 0.1702

DISPLACE

Source: DeMeter, E. C.; "The Min-Max Load Criteria as a Measure of Machining Fixture Performance," *Journal of Engineering for Industry,* 1994, 116, 500–507

For the 0.05 level of significance, answer these questions:
(a) Is there an effect due to clamp actuation intensity?
(b) Is there an effect due to location?
(c) Is there an interaction due to clamp actuation intensity and location?
(d) Plot a graph of average maximum displacement for each clamp actuation intensity for each location.
(e) What conclusions can you reach concerning the importance of each of these two factors on the maximum displacement?

11.38 A manufacturer of telephones was experiencing difficulties with the ability of the shell of the telephone to resist fading of its color. A manufacturing engineer determined that three factors could be studied to determine their effect on color fading, as measured with a photoelectric spectrometer. (The lower the reading, the higher the stability of the color.) The three factors were color (red versus pink), temperature (100°F versus 300°F), and amount of light (obscure versus bright). The results were as summarized in the following table:

Color	Temperature (°F)	Light	Spectrometer Reading
Red	100	Obscure	212
Pink	100	Obscure	215
Red	300	Obscure	983
Red	100	Bright	920
Pink	300	Obscure	1,090
Pink	100	Bright	945
Red	300	Bright	1,253
Pink	300	Bright	1,375 **FADE**

(a) Compute the average effect for each main effect (factor) and interaction.
(b) Obtain a plot of the main effects.
(c) Obtain a plot of the interactions.
(d) Using (a), set up a normal probability plot of the main effects and interactions.
(e) What conclusions can you draw from the results of (d)?
(f) Using the results of (d) and (e), combine all appropriate interactions into a measure of random error, and, using the level of significance 0.05, determine which factors are significant.
(g) What conclusions can you reach from the results of (f)?
(h) Ignore the factor of color, and reanalyze the data as a two-factor ANOVA with the factors of temperature and light, using the level of significance 0.05.
(i) Compare the results of (e), (g), and (h).

11.39 Considerable effort has been made to develop and utilize Polycrystalline Diamond Compact (PDC) cutters in oil and mining applications. An experiment was conducted to evaluate the effect of rake angle (in degrees), thrust (in pounds), and speed (in rpm). Two performance variables, the penetration rate (inches/minute) and the torque (inch–pounds) were considered. A high penetration rate and a low torque were considered desirable performance attributes. Two samples were obtained for each combination of rake angle, thrust, and speed. The results were as follows:

Rake Angle	Thrust	Speed	Penetration	Rate	Torque	
7	100	500	4.00	1.09	13	12
7	100	750	12.54	5.00	20	3
7	200	500	6.75	8.18	62	45
7	200	750	6.25	20.00	25	65
15	100	500	5.25	5.57	7	20
15	100	750	9.27	7.03	13	10
15	200	500	13.50	16.92	75	55
15	200	750	24.60	20.57	45	37 **PDCBIT**

Source: Hough, C. J.; "The Effect of Back Rake Angle on the Performance of Small-Diameter Polycrystalline Diamond Rock Bits: ANOVA Tests," *Journal of Energy Resources Technology,* 1986, pp. 305–309

For each of the performance variables of penetration rate and torque, at the 0.05 level of significance, answer these questions:

(a) Is there a significant effect due to rake angle?
(b) Is there a significant effect due to thrust?
(c) Is there a significant effect due to speed?
(d) Are any of the interactions of the factors significant?
(e) Obtain a plot of the main effects.
(f) Obtain a plot of the interactions.
(g) Compute the average effect for each main effect (factor) and interaction.
(h) Using (g), set up a normal probability plot of the main effects and interactions.
(i) What conclusions can you draw from the results of (h)?
(j) Compare the results of (a)–(d) with those of (i). Explain any differences.
(k) What levels of rake angle, thrust, and speed should be used to improve performance? Explain your reasons for selecting these levels.
(l) Compute the appropriate signal-to-noise ratio for each treatment combination.
(m) Reanalyze the treatment combinations by using the signal-to-noise ratio.
(n) Given the results of (l) and (m), which treatment combination would you choose?
(o) Compare the conclusion reached in (n) to that of (k).

11.40 The following experiment, reported by Johnson, Clapp, and Baqai (1989), concerned the tensile strength of yarn spun for textile usage. Four factors were considered in measuring the tenacity or breaking strength in the filling yarn. They were side-to-side aspects of the fabric (nozzle versus opposite), yarn type (air spun versus ring spun), pick density (represents the number of yarns across a fabric (35 versus 50)), and air-jet pressure (30 psi versus 45 psi). The results are summarized in the following table:

Side to Side	Yarn Type	Pick Density	Air Pressure	Tenacity
Nozzle	Air spun	35	30	24.50
Opposite	Air spun	35	30	23.55
Nozzle	Ring spun	35	30	25.98
Nozzle	Air spun	50	30	24.63
Nozzle	Air spun	35	45	23.73
Opposite	Ring spun	35	30	25.00
Opposite	Air spun	50	30	24.51
Opposite	Air spun	35	45	22.05
Nozzle	Ring spun	50	30	24.68
Nozzle	Ring spun	35	45	24.52
Nozzle	Air spun	50	45	25.68
Opposite	Ring spun	50	30	23.93
Opposite	Ring spun	35	45	23.64
Opposite	Air spun	50	45	25.78
Nozzle	Ring spun	50	45	24.10
Opposite	Ring spun	50	45	24.23 **YARN2**

Source: Johnson, R., T. Clapp, and N. Baqai; "Understanding the Effect of Confounding in Design of Experiments: A Case Study in High Speed Weaving," *Quality Engineering,* 1989, 1, 501–508

(a) Compute the average effect for each main effect (factor) and interaction.
(b) Obtain a plot of the main effects.
(c) Obtain a plot of the interactions.
(d) Using (a), set up a normal probability plot of the main effects and interactions.
(e) What conclusions can you draw from the results of (b)?
(f) Using the results of (d) and (e), combine all appropriate interactions into a measure of random error, and, at the level of significance 0.05, determine which factors are significant.
(g) What conclusions can you reach from the results of (f)?

Suppose that only the following fractional factorial design could be used in the experiment:

Side to Side	Yarn Type	Pick Density	Air Pressure	Tenacity	
Nozzle	Air spun	35	30	24.50	
Opposite	Ring spun	35	30	25.00	
Opposite	Air spun	50	30	24.51	
Opposite	Air spun	35	45	22.05	
Nozzle	Ring spun	50	30	24.68	
Nozzle	Ring spun	35	45	24.52	
Nozzle	Air spun	50	45	25.68	
Opposite	Ring spun	50	45	24.23	**YARN3**

(h) Using this design, reanalyze the data, following steps (a) through (f).

(i) Compare the conclusions reached in (g) and (h). What conclusions can you reach about the limitations of using fractional factorial designs under certain circumstances?

11.41 (Individual or Class Project) Suppose that we wanted to study the factors that affect the time it takes to boil 1 quart of water on a stove. Among the factors that could be studied are the following:

(1) A, type of water (tap, bottled, or distilled could be considered)
(2) B, use of a cover for the pot (no or yes)
(3) C, size of pot (small (1 quart) or large (4 quarts))
(4) D, two tablespoons of salt added to water (no or yes)
(5) E, type of pot (aluminum or stainless steel)

(a) Provide an operational definition for the time it takes to boil 1 quart of water on a stove.

(b) Compare the operational definitions of others that have performed the same experiment. Are there any differences among them? Explain.

Once the factors have been chosen, use either a fractional factorial design or a full factorial design to obtain the boiling time for each treatment combination. With the results obtained, answer these questions:

(c) Completely analyze the data to determine the factors and interactions that affect the boiling time.

(d) Which treatment combinations will result in the lowest boiling time? Explain.

(e) If a full factorial design was used, take a half-replicate of that design to conduct the experiment. Compare the results and explain.

11.42 (Individual or Class Project) Suppose that we wanted to study the factors that affect the time (and distance) that a paper airplane is able to fly. Among the factors that could be studied are the following:

(1) A, type of paper (construction versus bond)
(2) B, weight of the plane, that is, paper clips on bottom of the plane (no versus yes)
(3) C, front width
(4) D, front diameter
(5) E, rear width
(6) F, rear diameter

(a) Provide an operational definition for flying time and distance.

(b) Compare the operational definitions of others that have performed the same experiment. Are there any differences among them? Explain.

Once the factors have been chosen, use either a fractional factorial design or a full factorial design to obtain the flying time and distance traveled for each treatment combination. With the results obtained:

(c) Completely analyze the data to determine the factors and interactions that affect the flying time and distance.

(d) Which treatment combinations will result in the longest flying time and longest distance? Explain.

(e) If a full factorial design was used, take a half-replicate of that design to conduct the experiment. Compare the results and explain.

11.43 (Individual or Class Project) Box (1992) has described an experiment that involves the construction of a paper helicopter. The objective is to design a paper helicopter that has maximum flying time when dropped from a particular height (such as 12 feet). Among the factors described by Box (1992) are the following:

(1) A, paper type (regular versus bond)
(2) B, wing length (3.00 in. versus 4.75 in.)
(3) C, body length (3.00 in. versus 4.75 in.)
(4) D, body width (1.25 in. versus 2.00 in.)
(5) E, paper clip (no versus yes)
(6) F, fold (no versus yes)
(7) G, taped body (no versus yes)
(8) H, taped wing (no versus yes)

Source: Reprinted from Box, G. E. P.; "Teaching Engineers Experimental Design with a Paper Helicopter," *Quality Engineering,* 4, (1992), 453–459

(a) Provide an operational definition for flying time.
(b) Compare the operational definitions of others that have performed the same experiment. Are there any differences between them? Explain.

Once the factors have been chosen, use either a fractional factorial design or a full factorial design to obtain the flying time for each treatment combination. With the results obtained, answer these questions:

(c) Completely analyze the data to determine the factors and interactions that affect the flying time.
(d) Which treatment combinations will result in the longest flying time? Explain.
(e) If a full factorial design was used, take a half-replicate of that design to conduct the experiment. Compare the results and explain.

WHITNEY GOURMET CAT FOOD COMPANY CASE

Phase 1

When the team studying the canned weight of the cat food and production volume examined the results of a single day's production, the group realized that the weights of the cans of kidney were higher than those of shrimp. After several brainstorming sessions, the team determined that four factors needed to be studied to determine their effect on the weight of the cans:

1. the size of the pieces of meat that were contained in the can. The team wondered whether the current larger chunk size produced higher can weight and more variability, so a finer cutting size was studied along with the current size.
2. the speed of the filling machine. The speed was varied from the current 60 cans per minute to a slower 50 cans per minute, to determine the effect on can weight.
3. the pressure of the filling machine. The pressure was reduced from the current level to determine the effect on can weight.
4. can fill height. The target for the sensing mechanism that determines the fill height was lowered slightly to determine the effect on can weight.

The team decided that a preliminary experiment would be undertaken, but it would be unable to produce cans at all 16 combinations of the four factors. Only eight combinations of the four factors could be used. Four cans were filled for each of these combinations, with the results summarized in Table WG11.1 on page 564.

Exercise

WG11.1 Analyze these data, and write a report, for presentation to the team, that indicates the importance of each of the four factors for the weight of the canned cat food. Be sure to include in the report (1) a recommendation for the level of each factor that will come closest to meeting the target weight and (2) the limitations of this experiment, along with recommendations for future experiments that might be undertaken.

Do Not Continue Until the Phase 1 Exercises Have Been Completed.

(Continued)

WHITNEY GOURMET CAT FOOD COMPANY CASE (*Continued*)

TABLE WG11.1

CODED WEIGHT (BELOW OR ABOVE 3 OUNCES LISTED WEIGHT) IN HUNDREDTHS OF AN OUNCE, FOR THE 2^{4-1} FACTORIAL DESIGN

Piece Size	Speed	Pressure	Fill Height	Coded Weight			
Fine	50	Low	Low	0.01	−0.06	−0.10	−0.05
Current	60	Low	Low	2.15	2.25	2.28	2.22
Current	50	Current	Low	2.75	2.82	2.65	2.78
Current	50	Low	Current	3.02	2.97	3.05	2.96
Fine	60	Current	Low	0.21	0.16	0.22	0.21
Fine	60	Low	Current	1.51	1.40	1.47	1.48
Fine	50	Current	Current	1.49	1.53	1.60	1.58
Current	60	Current	Current	3.87	4.07	3.92	4.14

WG11-1

Phase 2

When the team evaluated the results of the experiment, it became clear that additional experimentation would be desirable, because of the possible interactions between the factors that could not be separated because of the nature of the fractional factorial design. There appeared to be little effect of the speed of the filling machine on weight, so this factor was dropped from the experiment. For each of the eight combinations of the remaining three factors (piece size, pressure, and fill height), ten cans were filled. The results are presented in Table WG11.2.

TABLE WG11.2

CODED WEIGHT (BELOW OR ABOVE 3 OUNCES LISTED WEIGHT) IN HUNDREDTHS OF AN OUNCE, FOR THE 2^3 FACTORIAL DESIGN

Piece Size	Pressure	Fill Height	Coded Weight				
Fine	Low	Low	−0.10	+0.06	+0.13	+0.05	−0.04
			+0.20	+0.08	+0.10	+0.02	−0.10
Current	Low	Low	+1.90	+2.13	+2.22	+1.96	+1.87
			+2.17	+2.05	+2.11	+2.19	+2.03
Fine	Current	Low	+0.32	+0.21	+0.17	+0.28	+0.26
			+0.22	+0.26	+0.19	+0.16	+0.24
Fine	Low	Current	+1.12	+1.06	+0.94	+1.11	+1.08
			+1.02	+1.04	+0.98	+1.10	+1.05
Current	Current	Low	+2.81	+2.90	+2.69	+2.72	+2.80
			+2.71	+2.76	+2.83	+2.68	+2.77
Current	Low	Current	+3.05	+2.94	+2.98	+3.10	+3.09
			+3.02	+2.97	+3.11	+3.06	+3.04
Fine	Current	Current	+1.57	+1.48	+1.63	+1.59	+1.60
			+1.51	+1.60	+1.62	+1.58	+1.53
Current	Current	Current	+3.96	+3.89	+4.07	+4.02	+4.06
			+3.95	+4.07	+4.11	+3.92	+3.95

WG11-2

Exercises

WG11.2 Analyze these data, and write a report, for presentation to the team, that indicates the importance of each of the three factors for the weight of the canned cat food. Be sure to include in the report (1) a recommendation for the level of each factor that will come closest to meeting the target weight and (2) the limitations of this experiment, along with recommendations for future experiments that might be undertaken.

WG11.3 Are there any considerations that might cause you to recommend a level for any of the factors that you did not choose in Exercise WG11.2? Explain.

REFERENCES

1. Barker, T. B.; "Quality Engineering by Design: Taguchi's Philosophy," *Quality Progress,* December 1986, 32–42
2. Box, G.E.P.; "Signal-to-Noise Ratios, Performance Criteria and Transformations," *Technometrics,* 30, 1988, 1–40, with discussion
3. Box, G.E.P., S. Bisgaard, and C. Fung; "An Explanation and Critique of Taguchi's Contributions to Quality Engineering," *Quality and Reliability Engineering International,* 4, 1988, 123–131
4. Daniel, W. W.; *Applied Nonparametric Statistics,* 2d ed.; Boston, MA: PWS Kent, 1990
5. Hicks, C. R. and K. V. Tarner; *Fundamental Concepts in the Design of Experiments,* 5th ed.; New York: Oxford University Press, 1999
6. Kirk, R. E.; *Experimental Design,* 2d ed.; Belmont, CA: Brooks-Cole, 1982
7. Lochner, R. H.; "Pros and Cons of Taguchi," *Quality Engineering,* 3, 1991, 537–549
8. *Microsoft Excel 2000;* Redmond, WA: Microsoft Corporation, 1999
9. *MINITAB for Windows Version 12;* State College, PA: MINITAB, Inc., 1998
10. Montgomery, D. C.; *Design and Analysis of Experiments,* 3d ed.; New York: John Wiley, 1991
11. Neter, J., M. H. Kutner, C. Nachtsheim, and W. Wasserman; *Applied Linear Statistical Models,* 4th ed.; Homewood, IL: Richard D. Irwin, 1996
12. Tribus, M. and G. Szonyi; "An Alternative View of the Taguchi Approach," *Quality Progress,* May 1989, 46–52
13. Tukey, J. W.; "Comparing Individual Means in the Analysis of Variance," *Biometrics,* 1949, Vol. 5, pp. 99–114

APPENDIX 11.1   *Using Microsoft Excel for the Two-Factor Factorial Design*

To illustrate the use of Microsoft Excel for the two-factor ANOVA, **open** the **LAUNDRY2.XLS** workbook that contains the data for the laundry-detergent example of Table 11.2 on page 519. On the Data sheet, note that the data have been set up in a format that is similar to Table 11.2, except that (1) column A provides a label corresponding to each level of factor A and (2) cell A1 is blank.

To obtain the results of Figure 11.2 on page 519, select **Tools | Data Analysis.** Select **Anova: Two Factors with Replication** from the Analysis tools list box. Click the **OK** button. In the Anova: Two Factors with Replication dialog box which appears, enter **A1 : C11** in the **Input Range** edit box, enter **5** in the Rows per Sample edit box, and enter the level of significance in the Alpha edit box. (.05 is the default value.) Select the **New Worksheet Ply** option button, and enter a name such as **TwoWayANOVA.** Click the **OK** button. In addition to the ANOVA table, Excel provides the sample size, sum, arithmetic mean, and variance for each row, each column, and each cell in the two-factor design.

APPENDIX 11.2 *Using MINITAB for the Factorial Designs*

Using MINITAB for the Two-Factor Design

The procedure for using MINITAB is similar for the randomized block design and the two-factor design. To illustrate the use of MINITAB for the two-factor design, open the **LAUNDRY2.MTW** worksheet. Note that amount of dirt removed is in C1, brand is in C2, and temperature is in C3. Select **Stat | ANOVA | Two-Way.** In the Two-Way dialog box, enter **C1** or **'Amount'** in the **Response** edit box, **C2** or **'Brand'** in the **Row factor** edit box, and **C3** or **'Temperature'** in the **Column factor** edit box. Select the **Display Means** check box for the row and column factors. Click the **OK** button. The results obtained will be similar to that of Figure 11.3 on page 520.

Using MINITAB for the General Factorial Design

To use MINITAB for the 2^k factorial design, we select Stat | ANOVA | Balanced ANOVA. To illustrate the use of MINITAB for the 2^k design, open the **LAUNDRY3.MTW** worksheet. Note that Brand is stored in C1, Temperature in C2, Type of detergent in C3, and amount of dirt removed in C4. Select **Stat | ANOVA | Balanced ANOVA.** In the Balanced ANOVA dialog box, enter **C4** or **'Amount'** in the **Response** edit box. In the Model edit box, enter the terms to be included in the model. For the 2^3 design, enter **C1 C2 C3 C1*C2 C1*C3 C2*C3 C1*C2*C3.** Click the **OK** button. The results obtained will be similar to that of Figure 11.10 on page 528.

To obtain an interaction plot, select **Stat | ANOVA | Interactions Plot.** In the Interactions Plot dialog box, enter **C4** or **'Amount'** in the **Response** edit box. In the Factors edit box, enter **C1 C2 C3.** Click the **OK** button. To obtain a Main Effects plot, select **Stat | ANOVA | Main Effects Plot.** In the Main Effects Plot dialog box, enter **C4** or **'Amount'** in the **Response** edit box. In the Factors edit box, enter **C1 C2 C3.** Click the **OK** button. The results obtained will be similar to that of Figures 11.11 and 11.12 on page 529.

chapter

12

Simple Linear Regression and Correlation

"...And now remains that we find out the cause of the effect. Or rather say the cause of this defect. For this effect, defective comes by cause."

HAMLET, ACT II, SCENE II

USING STATISTICS

In mining engineering, holes are often drilled through rock by using drill bits. As the drill hole gets deeper, additional rods are added to the drill bit to enable still deeper drilling to take place. It is expected that drilling time will increase with depth. This effect could be caused by several factors, including the mass of the drill rods that are strung together. A key question relates to whether drilling is faster in dry drilling holes or in wet drilling holes. Dry drilling holes involve forcing compressed air down the drill rods to flush the cuttings and drive the hammer. Wet drilling holes involve forcing water rather than air down the hole.

12.1 INTRODUCTION

In previous chapters, we focused primarily on a single response variable, such as the length of Dover sole, the pH of water, and the thickness of a silicon wafer. We studied various measures of statistical description (see Chapter 3) and applied different techniques of statistical inference to make estimates and draw conclusions about a response variable. (See Chapters 8–11.) In this and the following chapter, we will concern ourselves with situations involving two or more continuous variables as a means of viewing the relationships that exist between them. Two techniques will be discussed: regression and correlation.

Regression analysis is used primarily for the purpose of prediction. The goal in regression analysis is the development of a statistical model that can be used to predict the values of a **dependent** or **response variable** from the values of at least one **explanatory** or **independent variable.** In this chapter, we focus on a **simple linear regression** model—one that utilizes a *single* independent variable X to predict the dependent variable Y. In Chapter 13, we will develop *multiple-regression*

[1]Regression models in which the dependent variable is categorical involve the use of logistic regression. (See Reference 3.)

models, which utilize *several* explanatory variables $(X_1, X_2, \ldots, X_k)$ to predict a dependent variable Y.[1]

Correlation analysis, in contrast to regression, is used to measure the strength of the association between variables. For example: In Section 12.11, we will determine the correlation between two measures of cardiac output. In this instance, the objective is not to use one variable to predict another, but rather to measure the strength of the association or covariation that exists between two continuous variables.

12.2 TYPES OF REGRESSION MODELS

In Chapter 2, when the length of Dover sole was studied, various graphs were used for data presentation. In regression analysis, a **scatter diagram** is used to plot an independent variable on the horizontal X axis and a dependent variable on the vertical Y axis. The nature of the relationship between two variables can take many forms, ranging from simple ones to extremely complicated mathematical functions. The simplest relationship consists of a straight-line or **linear relationship.** An example of this relationship is shown in Figure 12.1.

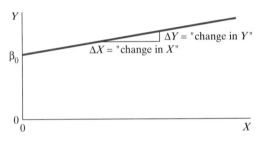

Figure 12.1 A positive straight-line relationship

The straight-line (linear) model can be represented as follows:

SIMPLE LINEAR REGRESSION MODEL

$$Y_i = \beta_0 + \beta_1 X_i + \varepsilon_i \qquad (12.1)$$

where

$\beta_0 = Y$-intercept for the population

$\beta_1 = $ slope for the population

$\varepsilon_i = $ random error in Y for observation i

In this model, the **slope** of the line, β_1, represents the expected change in Y per unit change in X. It represents the average amount that Y changes (either positively or negatively) for a particular unit change in X. The **Y-intercept,** β_0, represents the average value of Y when X equals 0. The last component of the model, ε_i, represents the random error in Y for each observation i that occurs.

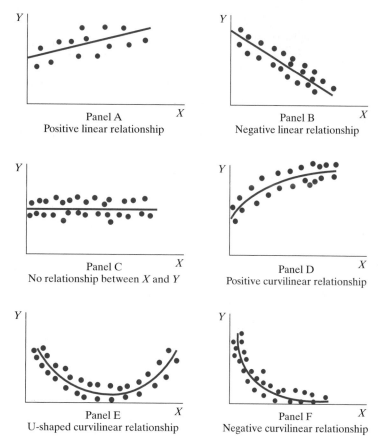

Figure 12.2   Examples of types of relationships found in scatter diagrams

The selection of the proper mathematical model is influenced by the distribution of the X and Y values on the scatter diagram. This can be seen readily from an examination of Panels A–F in Figure 12.2.

In Panel A, we observe that the values of Y are generally increasing linearly as X increases. This panel is similar to Figure 12.3 on page 571, which illustrates the positive relationship between (1) the drilling depth and (2) the time to drill an additional five feet.

Panel B is an example of a *negative* linear relationship. As X increases, we note that the values of Y are decreasing. Panel C shows a set of data in which there is very little or no relationship between X and Y. High and low values of Y appear at each value of X.

The data in Panel D show a positive curvilinear relationship between X and Y. The values of Y are increasing as X increases, but this increase tapers off beyond certain values of X. An example of this positive curvilinear relationship might be the productivity of a machine operator and his or her years of experience. As an operator gains experience, his or her productivity may rise rapidly at first but then levels off beyond a certain number of years.

Panel E shows a parabolic or U-shaped relationship between X and Y. As X increases, at first Y decreases; but as X continues to increase, Y not only stops decreasing but actually increases above its minimum value. An example of this type of relationship could be that between the number of errors per hour at a task and the number of hours worked. The number of errors per hour may decrease as the individual becomes more proficient at the task, but then it could increase beyond a certain point because of factors such as fatigue and boredom.

Finally, Panel F indicates a decaying exponential negative curvilinear relationship between X and Y. In this case, Y decreases very rapidly while X increases, but then it decreases much less rapidly as X increases further. An example of this exponential relationship could be that between the resale value of a particular type of automobile and its age. In the first year, the resale value drops drastically from its original price; however, the resale value then decreases much less rapidly in subsequent years.

In this section, we have briefly examined a variety of different models that could be used to represent the relationship between two variables. Although scatter diagrams can be extremely helpful in determining the mathematical form of the relationship, more sophisticated statistical procedures are available to determine the most appropriate model for a set of variables. In subsequent sections of this chapter, we will primarily focus on building statistical models for fitting linear relationships between variables.

12.3 DETERMINING THE SIMPLE LINEAR REGRESSION EQUATION

In the *Using Statistics* example introduced earlier, we stated that a mining engineer wanted to study the relationship between drilling depth and the time it took to drill an additional five feet for dry holes and wet holes. Suppose that we decide to focus first on the dry holes. For a particular hole drilled, measurements were obtained for each five feet of depth down to 250 feet. The results are summarized in Table 12.1.

TABLE 12.1

DRILLING DEPTH AND TIME TO DRILL EACH ADDITIONAL
FIVE FEET (IN MINUTES)

Depth (feet)	Time (minutes)	Depth (feet)	Time (minutes)	Depth (feet)	Time (minutes)
5	4.90	90	6.23	175	7.75
10	5.07	95	6.60	180	7.11
15	6.77	100	5.84	185	7.07
20	6.65	105	5.17	190	7.17
25	6.99	110	6.03	195	6.91
30	7.41	115	6.84	200	6.15
35	6.07	120	6.58	205	6.19
40	7.04	125	7.03	210	6.29
45	5.49	130	6.89	215	5.58
50	6.03	135	7.27	220	7.22
55	6.19	140	6.92	225	7.62
60	6.43	145	7.15	230	8.28
65	6.27	150	7.25	235	7.59
70	6.03	155	7.05	240	6.42
75	6.34	160	6.95	245	7.12
80	5.57	165	6.76	250	6.62
85	5.70	170	5.97		**DRILL**

Source: Penner, R. and D. G. Watts, "Mining Information," *The American Statistician*, 45, 1991, 4–9

Scatter Diagram

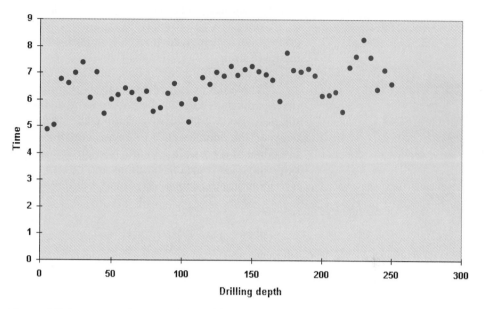

Figure 12.3   Scatter diagram obtained from Microsoft Excel for the drilling data

The scatter diagram for the data in Table 12.1 is shown in Figure 12.3.

An examination of Figure 12.3 indicates an increasing relationship between depth (X) and drilling time (Y). As the depth of the hole increases, the time it takes to drill an additional five feet increase linearly, approximately as a straight line.

If we assume that a straight line provides a useful mathematical model of this relationship, we can use regression analysis to determine the particular straight-line model that is the best fit for these data.

The Least-Squares Method

In the preceding section, we hypothesized a statistical model to represent the relationship between two variables, drilling depth and drilling time. As shown in Table 12.1, we have obtained data from only a sample of the dry holes that *could* have been drilled. If certain assumptions are valid (see Section 12.5), the sample Y-intercept (b_0) and the sample slope (b_1) can be used as estimates of the respective population parameters (β_0 and β_1). Thus, the sample regression equation representing the straight-line regression model is as follows:

SAMPLE LINEAR REGRESSION MODEL

The predicted value of Y equals the Y-intercept, plus the slope times the X value.

$$\hat{Y}_i = b_0 + b_1 X_i \tag{12.2}$$

where

    $\hat{Y}_i$ = predicted value of Y for observation i

    X_i = value of X for observation i

This equation requires the determination of two regression coefficients—b_0 (the Y-intercept) and b_1 (the slope)—in order to predict values of Y. Once b_0 and b_1 are obtained, the straight line is known and can be plotted on the scatter diagram; then, we can make a visual comparison of how well our particular statistical model (a straight line) fits the original data by observing whether the original data lie close to the fitted line or deviate greatly from the fitted line.

Simple linear regression analysis is concerned with finding the straight line that fits the data best. The *best fit* could be defined in a variety of ways. Perhaps the simplest way would involve finding the straight line for which the differences between the actual values (Y_i) and the values that would be predicted from the fitted line of regression ($\hat{Y}_i$) are as small as possible. Because these differences will be positive for some observations and negative for other observations, one choice is to *minimize* the sum of the squared differences:

$$\sum_{i=1}^{n} (Y_i - \hat{Y}_i)^2$$

where

Y_i = actual value of Y for observation i

$\hat{Y}_i$ = predicted value of Y for observation i

Because $\hat{Y}_i = b_0 + b_1 X_i$, we are minimizing

$$\sum_{i=1}^{n} [Y_i - (b_0 + b_1 X_i)]^2$$

which has two unknowns, b_0 and b_1.

A mathematical technique that determines the values of b_0 and b_1 that minimizes this sum of squares is known as the **least-squares method.** Any values for b_0 and b_1 other than those determined by the least-squares method result in a greater sum of squared differences between the actual values of Y and the predicted values of Y.

In using the least-squares method, we take partial derivatives with respect to b_0 and b_1, set them equal to 0, and obtain the following two normal equations:

SIMPLE LINEAR REGRESSION NORMAL EQUATIONS

$$\sum_{i=1}^{n} Y_i = nb_0 + b_1 \sum_{i=1}^{n} X_i \qquad (12.3a)$$

$$\sum_{i=1}^{n} X_i Y_i = b_0 \sum_{i=1}^{n} X_i + b_1 \sum_{i=1}^{n} X_i^2 \qquad (12.3b)$$

From these two equations, we must solve for b_1 and b_0 the **regression coefficients.** In this text, we take the view that, in solving regression equations, the Microsoft Excel spreadsheet software or the MINITAB statistical software will be used to perform the calculations; however, to understand how the results displayed in the output of this software have been computed for the case of simple linear regression, in Section 12.10 we illustrate many of the computations involved.

Figure 12.4 represents output from Microsoft Excel for the data of Table 12.1, while Figure 12.5 represents MINITAB output.

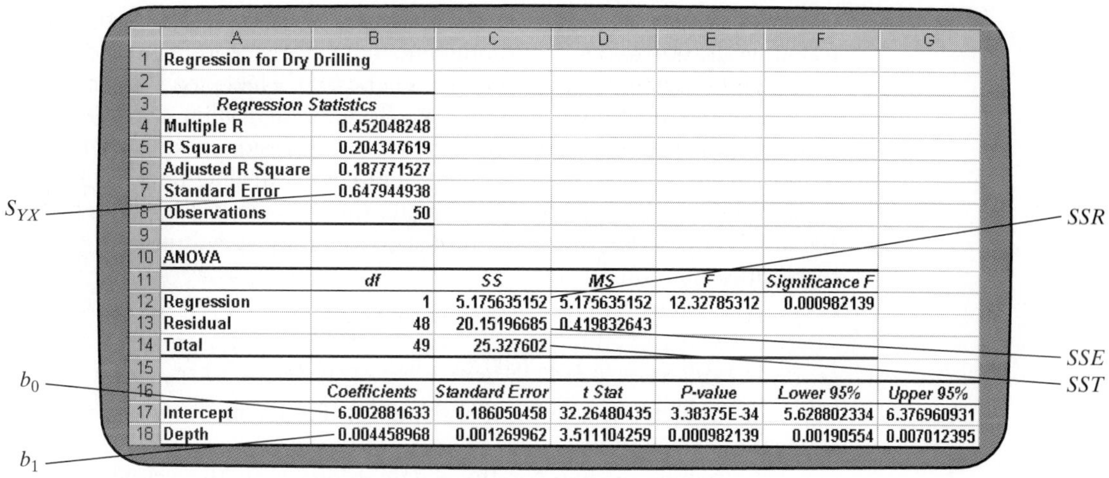

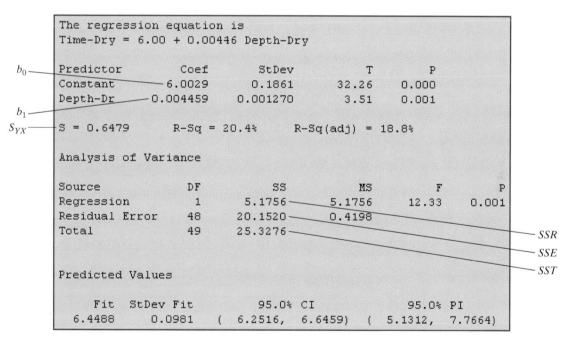

Figure 12.4   Microsoft Excel output for the drilling problem

Figure 12.5.   MINITAB output for the drilling problem

From either Figure 12.4 or Figure 12.5, we observe that $b_1 = 0.00446$ and $b_0 = 6.0029$. Thus, the equation for the best fit straight line for these data is

$$\hat{Y}_i = 6.0029 + 0.00446X_i$$

The slope, b_1, was computed as 0.00446. This means that, for each increase of one unit in X, the value of Y is estimated to increase by an average of 0.00446 units. In other words, for each increase of one foot in the drilling depth, the fitted model estimates that the expected drilling time increases by 0.00446 minutes (or 0.446

minutes for every 100 additional feet in depth). Thus, the slope can be viewed as representing the portion of the drilling time that varies according to the drilling depth.

The Y-intercept, b_0, was computed to be 6.0029 feet. The Y-intercept represents the average value of Y when X equals 0. Because the drilling depth cannot be 0, this Y-intercept has no direct interpretation. The regression model that has been fitted to the drilling data can now be used to predict the drilling time for a given drilling depth. Suppose that we want to estimate the average drilling time for a depth of 100 feet. We can determine the predicted value by substituting $X = 100$ into our regression equation.

$$\hat{Y}_i = 6.0029 + 0.00446X_i$$
$$\hat{Y}_i = 6.0029 + 0.00446(100) = 6.449$$

Thus, the predicted average drilling time for the five feet that end with a depth of 100 feet is 6.449 minutes.

The regression line for these data, along with the actual observations, is shown in Figure 12.6.

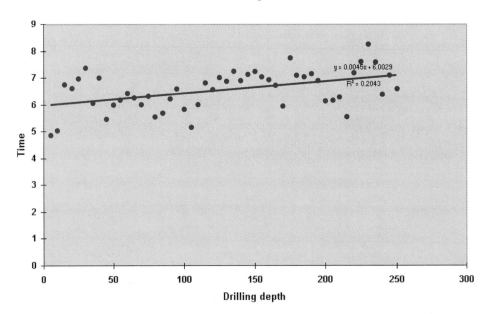

Figure 12.6   Scatter diagram and line of regression obtained from Microsoft Excel for the drilling problem

Predictions in Regression Analysis: Interpolation Versus Extrapolation

When we are using a regression model for prediction purposes, it is important that we consider only the **relevant range** of the independent variable in making our predictions. This relevant range encompasses all values from the smallest to the largest X used in developing the regression model. Hence, when predicting Y for a given value of X, we can *interpolate* within this relevant range of the X values, but we should not *extrapolate* beyond the range of X values. For example, when we use the drilling depth to predict drilling time, we note from Table 12.1 that the drilling depth varies from 5 to 250 feet. Therefore, predictions of drilling time should be made only for depths that are between 5 to 250 feet. Any prediction of drilling time for depths outside this range presumes that the fitted relationship holds outside the 5 to 250 feet range, and such might not be the case.

PROBLEMS

Note: Use Microsoft Excel or MINITAB to solve Problems 12.3–12.7.

12.1 Fitting a straight line to a set of data yields the following regression equation:

$$\hat{Y}_i = 2 + 5X_i$$

(a) Interpret the meaning of the Y-intercept, b_0.
(b) Interpret the meaning of the slope, b_1.
(c) Predict the average value of Y for $X = 3$.
(d) If the values of X range from 2 to 25, should you use this model to predict the average value of Y when X equals
  (1) 3?   (2) −3?   (3) 0?   (4) 24?   (5) 26?

12.2 Fitting a straight line to a set of data yields the following regression equation:

$$\hat{Y}_i = 16 - 0.5X_i$$

(a) Interpret the meaning of the Y-intercept, b_0.
(b) Interpret the meaning of the slope, b_1.
(c) Predict the average value of Y for $X = 6$.

12.3 A study was done on the thickness (in angstroms) of SiO_2 film grown on silicon wafers during a high-temperature oxidation in dry oxygen. Also reported was the distance (in inches) that each wafer was positioned from the end of the furnace. The results were as follows.

Distance (in)	Thickness (Angstrom)	Distance (in)	Thickness (Angstrom)
10	625	27	1400
13	900	29	1350
15	1150	31	1550
17	1125	33	1500
19	1250	35	1475
21	1300	37	1400
23	1400	39	1200
25	1400		

FILM

Suppose that we wanted to use the position of the wafer to predict the thickness of the film.
(a) Set up a scatter diagram.
(b) Assuming a linear relationship, use the least-squares method to find the regression coefficients b_0 and b_1.
(c) Interpret the meaning of the slope, b_1, in this problem.
(d) Predict the average thickness (in angstroms) of wafers that are positioned 20 inches from the end of the furnace.
(e) Suppose that the last wafer has a thickness of 2,200 angstroms. Do parts (b)–(d) with this value, and compare the results.

12.4 Suppose an experiment was done to study the accuracy of a wave-function generator. The experiment was carried out by comparing the dial frequency to the frequency actually generated. The goal of the experiment was to see how well the dial setting predicted the actual frequency. The results were as follows.

FREQUENCY (Hz)

Dial	Actual	Dial	Actual
100	112	2000	2031
200	210	3000	3042
300	318	4000	4072
400	421	5000	5069
500	516	6000	6077
600	630	7000	7130
700	728	8000	8210
800	827	9000	9218
900	945	10000	12021
1000	1060		

GENERATOR

(a) Set up a scatter diagram.
(b) Assuming a linear relationship, use the least-squares method to find the regression coefficients b_0 and b_1.

(c) Interpret the meaning of the slope, b_1, in this problem.

(d) Predict the average actual frequency (in Hz) for a dial frequency of 5,000.

(e) How does an actual frequency of 5,069 for a dial frequency of 5,000 compare to the predicted value in (d)? How can you explain the difference?

12.5 The following data provide measurements on the hardness and tensile strength of 35 specimens of die-cast aluminum.

Tensile Strength (Thousands of pounds per square inch)	Hardness (Rockwell E units)	Tensile Strength (Thousands of pounds per square inch)	Hardness (Rockwell E units)
53.0	29.31	77.8	28.67
70.2	34.86	52.4	24.64
84.3	36.82	69.1	25.77
55.3	30.12	53.5	23.69
78.5	34.02	64.3	28.65
63.5	30.82	82.7	32.38
71.4	35.40	55.7	23.21
53.4	31.26	70.5	34.00
82.5	32.18	87.5	34.47
67.3	33.42	50.7	29.25
69.5	37.69	72.3	28.71
73.0	34.88	59.5	29.83
55.7	24.66	71.3	29.25
85.8	34.76	52.7	27.99
95.4	38.02	76.5	31.85
51.1	25.68	63.7	27.65
74.4	25.81	69.2	31.70
54.1	26.46		

HARDNESS

Suppose that we want to use the hardness to predict the tensile strength.

(a) Set up a scatter diagram.

(b) Assuming a linear relationship, use the least-squares method to find the regression coefficients b_0 and b_1.

(c) Interpret the meaning of the slope, b_1, in this problem.

(d) Predict the average tensile strength for die-cast aluminum that has a hardness of 30 Rockwell E units.

12.6 A large mail-order house believes that there is an association between the weight of the mail it receives and the number of orders to be filled. It would like to investigate the relationship, in order to be able to predict the number of orders based on the weight of

the mail. From an operational perspective, knowledge of the number of orders will help in the planning of the order-fulfillment process. A sample of 25 mail shipments is selected within a range of 200 to 700 pounds. The results were as follows.

Weight of Mail (pounds)	Orders (thousands)	Weight of Mail (pounds)	Orders (thousands)
216	6.1	432	13.6
283	9.1	409	12.8
237	7.2	553	16.5
203	7.5	572	17.1
259	6.9	506	15.0
374	11.5	528	16.2
342	10.3	501	15.8
301	9.5	628	19.0
365	9.2	677	19.4
384	10.6	602	19.1
404	12.5	630	18.0
426	12.9	652	20.2
482	14.5		

MAIL

(a) Set up a scatter diagram.

(b) Assuming a linear relationship, use the least-squares method to find the regression coefficients b_0 and b_1.

(c) Interpret the meaning of the slope, b_1, in this problem.

(d) Predict the average number of orders when the weight of the mail is 500 pounds.

12.7 During the fall-harvest season in the United States, pumpkins are sold in large quantities at farm stands. Often, instead of weighing the pumpkins prior to sale, the farm stand operator will just place the pumpkin in the appropriate circular cutout on the counter. When asked why this was done, one farmer replied "I can tell the weight of the pumpkin from its circumference." To determine whether this was really true, a sample of 22 pumpkins was measured for their circumference and weighed, with the following results.

Circumference (cms.)	Weight (grams)	Circumference (cms.)	Weight (grams)
50	1200	57	2000
55	2000	66	2500
54	1500	82	4600
52	1700	83	4600
37	500	70	3100

(Continued)

Circumference (cms.)	Weight (grams)	Circumference (cms.)	Weight (grams)
52	1000	34	600
53	1500	51	1500
47	1400	50	1500
51	1500	49	1600
63	2500	60	2300
33	500	59	2100
43	1000		

PUMPKIN

(a) Set up a scatter diagram.
(b) Assuming a linear relationship, use the least-squares method to find the regression coefficients b_0 and b_1.
(c) Interpret the meaning of the slope, b_1, in this problem.
(d) Predict the average weight for a pumpkin that is 60 centimeters in circumference.
(e) Do you think it is a good idea for the farmer to sell pumpkins by circumference instead of weight? Explain.

12.4 MEASURES OF VARIATION IN REGRESSION AND CORRELATION

Obtaining the Sum of Squares

To examine how well the independent variable predicts the dependent variable in our statistical model, we need to develop several measures of variation. The first measure, the **total sum of squares** (SST), is a measure of variation of the Y_i values around their mean $\overline{Y}$. In a regression analysis, the total sum of squares can be sub-divided into **explained variation** or **regression sum of squares** (SSR), that which is attributable to the relationship between X and Y, and **unexplained variation** or **error sum of squares** (SSE), that which is attributable to factors other than the relationship between X and Y. These different measures of variation can be seen in Figure 12.7.

The regression sum of squares (SSR) represents the sum of the squared differences between $\overline{Y}$ (the average value of Y) and $\hat{Y}_i$ (the value of Y that is predicted from the regression relationship). The error sum of squares (SSE) represents

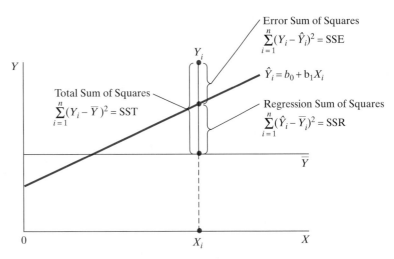

Figure 12.7   Measures of variation in regression

that part of the variation in Y that is not explained by the regression. It is based on the difference between Y_i and $\hat{Y}_i$.

These measures of variation can be represented as follows:

MEASURES OF VARIATION IN REGRESSION

Total sum of squares = regression sum of squares + error sum of squares

$$SST = SSR + SSE \qquad (12.4)$$

TOTAL SUM OF SQUARES (SST)

The total sum of squares (SST) is equal to the sum of the squared differences between each observed Y value and $\overline{Y}$, the mean of Y.

$$SST = \text{total sum of squares} = \sum_{i=1}^{n}(Y_i - \overline{Y})^2 \qquad (12.5)$$

REGRESSION SUM OF SQUARES (SSR)

The regression sum of squares (SSR) is equal to the sum of the squared differences between the predicted value of Y and the mean of Y.

$$SSR = \text{explained variation or regression sum of squares}$$

$$= \sum_{i=1}^{n}(\hat{Y}_i - \overline{Y})^2 \qquad (12.6a)$$

or

$$= SST - SSE \qquad (12.6b)$$

ERROR SUM OF SQUARES (SSE)

The error sum of squares (SSE) is equal to the sum of the squared differences between the observed value of Y and the predicted value of Y.

$$SSE = \text{unexplained variation or error sum of squares} \qquad (12.7)$$

$$= \sum_{i=1}^{n}(Y_i - \hat{Y}_i)^2$$

Examining either Figure 12.4 or Figure 12.5 on page 573, we observe that SSR = 5.176, SSE = 20.152, and SST = 25.328.

We note also, from Equation (12.4), that

$$SST = SSR + SSE$$

$$25.328 = 5.176 + 20.152$$

The total sum of squared differences around the average value of Y is equal to 25.328. This amount is subdivided into the sum of squares that is explained by the regression (SSR), equal to 5.176, and the sum of squares that is unexplained by the regression (the error sum of squares), equal to 20.152.

The Coefficient of Determination

Individually, SSR, SSE, and SST provide little that can be directly interpreted; however, a simple ratio of the regression sum of squares (SSR) to the total sum of squares (SST) provides a measure of the usefulness of the regression equation. This ratio is called the **coefficient of determination, r^2**, and is defined as follows:

COEFFICIENT OF DETERMINATION

The coefficient of determination is equal to the regression sum of squares divided by the total sum of squares.

$$r^2 = \frac{\text{regression sum of squares}}{\text{total sum of squares}} = \frac{\text{SSR}}{\text{SST}} \qquad (12.8)$$

This coefficient of determination measures the proportion of variation in the dependent variable Y, that is shared with or explained by the independent variable, X, in the regression model. For the drilling example, with SSR = 5.176, SSE = 20.152, and SST = 25.328,

$$r^2 = \frac{5.176}{25.328} = 0.204$$

Therefore, 20.4% of the variation in drilling time can be explained by the variability in the drilling depth. This is an example where there is a weak positive linear relationship between two variables. The use of a regression model has reduced the error variability in predicting drilling time by only 20.4%. In this situation, it is imperative that other factors be considered to provide a model that will be more useful in predicting drilling time. Several such models will be developed in Chapter 13.

Standard Error of the Estimate

Although the least-squares method results in the line that fits the data with the minimum amount of squared variation, we have seen in the computation of the error sum of squares (SSE) that, unless all the observed data points fall on the regression line, the regression equation is not a perfect predictor. Just as we do not expect all data values to be exactly equal to their arithmetic mean, neither can we expect all data points to fall exactly on the regression line. Therefore, we need to develop a statistic that measures the variability of the actual Y values from the predicted Y values, in the same way that we developed the standard deviation in Chapter 3 as a measure of the variation of each observation from its mean. This standard deviation of the line of regression is called the **standard error of the estimate.**

The variability around the line of regression for the drilling data was illustrated in Figure 12.6 on page 574. We can see from Figure 12.6 that, although many of the actual values of Y fall near the predicted line of regression, there are numerous values above the line of regression as well as below the line of regression.

The standard error of the estimate, given by the symbol s_{YX} is defined as follows:

STANDARD ERROR OF THE ESTIMATE

$$s_{YX} = \sqrt{\frac{SSE}{n-2}} = \sqrt{\frac{\sum_{i=1}^{n}(Y_i - \hat{Y}_i)^2}{n-2}} \qquad (12.9)$$

where

Y_i = actual value of Y for a given X_i

$\hat{Y}_i$ = predicted value of Y for a given X_i

SSE = error sum of squares

From Equation (12.9), with SSE = 20.152, we have

$$s_{YX} = \sqrt{\frac{20.152}{50-2}}$$

$$s_{YX} = 0.648$$

This standard error of the estimate, equal to 0.648 minutes, is labeled on the Microsoft Excel output of Figure 12.4 as Standard Error and is labeled on the MINITAB output of Figure 12.5 as S. The standard error of the estimate represents a measure of the variation around the fitted line of regression. It is measured in units of the dependent variable Y. The interpretation of the standard error of the estimate is similar to that of the standard deviation. Just as the standard deviation measures variation around the arithmetic mean, the standard error of the estimate measures variation around the fitted line of regression. As we shall see in Sections 12.7 and 12.8, the standard error of the estimate can be used to determine whether a statistically significant relationship exists between the two variables and to make inferences about a predicted value of Y.

PROBLEMS

12.8 Assume that SSR = 36 and SSE = 4.
  (a) Compute SST.
  (b) Compute the coefficient of determination, r^2, and interpret its meaning.

12.9 If SSR = 120, why is it impossible for SST to equal 110?

12.10 In Problem 12.3 on page 575, the position of the wafer was used to predict the thickness of the film. Using the computer output you obtained to solve that problem:
  (a) Determine the coefficient of determination, r^2, and interpret its meaning.
  (b) Find the standard error of the estimate.
  (c) How useful do you think this regression model is for predicting the thickness of the film?

12.11 In Problem 12.4 on page 575, the dial frequency was used to predict the actual frequency of a generator. Using the computer output you obtained to solve that problem:
  (a) Determine the coefficient of determination, r^2, and interpret its meaning.
  (b) Find the standard error of the estimate.
  (c) How useful do you think this regression model is for predicting the actual frequency of the generator?

12.12 In Problem 12.5 on page 576, the hardness was used to predict the tensile strength of die-cast aluminum. Using the computer output you obtained to solve that problem:

(a) Determine the coefficient of determination, r^2, and interpret its meaning.

(b) Find the standard error of the estimate.

(c) How useful do you think this regression model is for predicting the tensile strength of die-cast aluminum?

12.13 In Problem 12.6 on page 576, the weight of mail was used to predict the number of orders received. Using the computer output you obtained to solve that problem:

(a) Determine the coefficient of determination, r^2, and interpret its meaning.

(b) Find the standard error of the estimate.

(c) How useful do you think this regression model is for predicting the number of orders received?

12.14 In Problem 12.7 on page 576, the circumference was used to predict the weight of a pumpkin. Using the computer output you obtained to solve that problem:

(a) Determine the coefficient of determination, r^2, and interpret its meaning.

(b) Find the standard error of the estimate.

(c) How useful do you think this regression model is for predicting the weight of a pumpkin?

12.5 ASSUMPTIONS OF REGRESSION AND CORRELATION

In our study of hypothesis testing and the analysis of variance, we stated that the appropriateness of the application of a particular statistical procedure is dependent on how well a set of assumptions for that procedure are met. The assumptions necessary for regression and correlation analysis are similar to those for the analysis of variance, because they fall under the general heading of *linear models* (Reference 6). Although there are some differences between the assumptions made by the regression model and by correlation (see Reference 6), such a topic is beyond the scope of this text, and we will consider only the former.

The three major **assumptions of regression** are listed in Exhibit 12.1.

The first assumption, normality, requires that errors around the line of regression be normally distributed at each value of X. (See Figure 12.8.) Like the t test

---

EXHIBIT 12.1 Assumptions of Regression

1. Normality of error

2. Homoscedasticity

3. Independence of errors

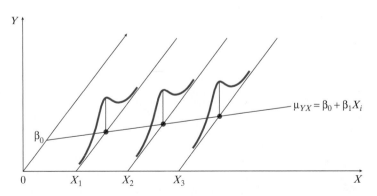

Figure 12.8   Assumptions of regression

and the ANOVA F test, regression analysis is fairly robust against departures from the normality assumption. As long as the distribution of the errors around the line of regression at each level of X is not extremely different from a normal distribution, inferences about the line of regression and the regression coefficients will not be seriously affected.

The second assumption, **homoscedasticity**, requires that the variation around the line of regression be constant for all values of X. This means that the errors vary by the same amount when X is a low value as when X is a high value. (See Figure 12.8.) The homoscedasticity assumption is important for using the least-squares method of determining the regression coefficients. If there are serious departures from this assumption, either data transformations (see Section 13.8) or weighted least-squares methods (Reference 6) can be applied.

The third assumption, **independence of errors**, requires that the errors should be independent for each value of X. This assumption is particularly important when data are collected over a period of time. In such situations, the errors for a particular time period are often correlated with those of the previous time period. If this occurs, alternatives to least-squares regression analysis need to be considered (see Reference 6).

12.6 RESIDUAL ANALYSIS

In the preceding discussion of the drilling data, we have relied on a simple linear regression model in which the dependent variable is predicted by a straight-line relationship with a single independent variable. In this section, we use a graphical approach called **residual analysis** to evaluate the aptness of the regression model that has been fitted to the data. In addition, this approach also allows us to study potential violations in the assumptions of our regression model.

Evaluating the Aptness of the Fitted Model

The **residuals**, or estimated error values, (e_i), are defined as the differences between the observed (Y_i) and predicted $(\hat{Y}_i)$ values of the dependent variable, for given values of X_i. Thus, the following definition applies:

THE RESIDUAL

The residual equals the difference between the observed value of Y and the predicted value of Y.

$$e_i = Y_i - \hat{Y}_i \tag{12.10}$$

We evaluate the aptness of the fitted regression model by plotting the residuals on the vertical axis against the corresponding X_i values of the independent variable on the horizontal axis. If the fitted model is appropriate for the data, there will be no apparent pattern in this plot of the residuals versus X_i. If the fitted model is not appropriate, there will be a relationship between the X_i values and the residuals e_i. Such a pattern can be observed in Figure 12.9.

Panel (a) depicts a situation in which, although there is an increasing trend in Y as X increases, the relationship seems curvilinear: The upward trend decreases for increasing values of X. Thus, a curvilinear relationship between the two variables seems more appropriate than a simple linear regression model. This curvi-

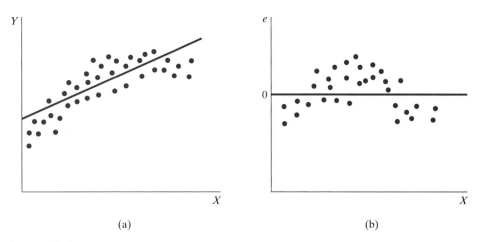

Figure 12.9   Studying the appropriateness of the simple linear regression model

linear effect is highlighted in Panel (b). Here, there is a clear curvilinear effect between X_i and e_i. By plotting the residuals, we have filtered out or removed the linear trend of X with Y, thereby exposing the lack of fit in the simple linear model. Thus, we conclude that the curvilinear model is a better fit and should be evaluated in place of the simple linear model. (See Section 13.6 for further discussion of fitting curvilinear quadratic models.)

Having considered Figure 12.9, let us return to the evaluation of the drilling data. Figure 12.10 provides the residuals plotted against the independent variable (drilling depth).

From Figure 12.10, we observe that, although there is widespread scatter in the residual plot, there is no apparent pattern or relationship between the residuals

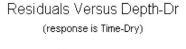

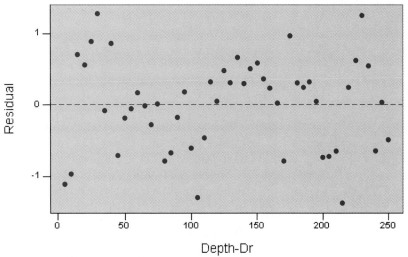

Figure 12.10   Residual plot obtained from MINITAB of the residuals against the drilling depth

and X_i. The residuals appear to be evenly spread above and below 0 for the differing values of X. This result leads us to conclude that the fitted straight-line model is appropriate for the drilling data.

Evaluating the Assumptions

Homoscedasticity

The assumption of homoscedasticity can also be evaluated from a plot of the residuals with X_i. For the drilling data of Figure 12.10, there do not appear to be major differences in the variability of the residuals for different X_i values, as is the case in Figure 12.11. Thus, we can conclude that, for our fitted model, there is no apparent violation of the assumption of equal variance at each level of X.

If we wish to observe a case in which the homoscedasticity assumption is violated, we should examine the *hypothetical* plot of the residuals with X_i in Figure 12.11. In this hypothetical plot, there appears to be a *fanning* effect, in which the variability of the residuals increases as X increases, demonstrating the lack of homogeneity in the variances of Y_i at each level of X.

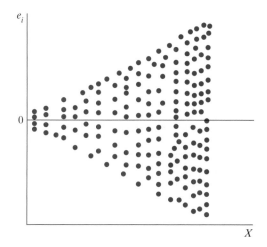

Figure 12.11   Violation of homoscedasticity

Normality

The assumption of normality in the errors around the line of regression can be evaluated from a residual analysis by plotting the results in a histogram (see Chapter 2) or a normal probability plot (see Section 5.5).

For the drilling data, Figure 12.12 is a histogram of the residuals obtained from MINITAB, and Figure 12.13 is a normal probability plot of the residuals obtained from the PHStat add-in for Microsoft Excel.

We can see from Figures 12.12 and 12.13 that the data do not appear to differ substantially from a normal distribution, so we should not be concerned about any serious consequences of departures from the normality assumption.

Independence

The assumption of the independence of the errors can be evaluated by plotting the residuals in the order or sequence in which the observed data were obtained. Data collected over periods of time sometimes exhibit an *autocorrelation* effect among

Histogram of the Residuals

(response is Time-Dry)

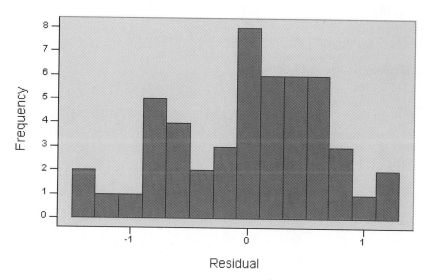

Figure 12.12   Histogram obtained from MINITAB of the residuals for the drilling data

Normal Probability Plot of Residuals

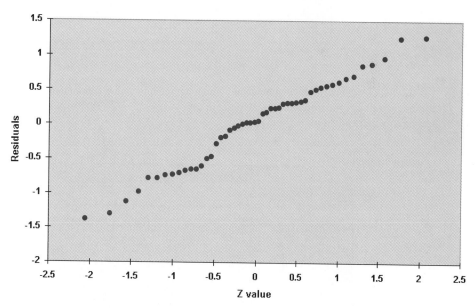

Figure 12.13   Normal probability plot (obtained from the PHStat add-in for Microsoft Excel) of the residuals for the drilling data

successive observations. In these instances, there exists a relationship between consecutive residuals. Such a relationship, which violates the assumption of independence, is readily apparent in the plot of the residuals versus the time at which they were collected. This effect is measured by the Durbin–Watson statistic. (See Reference 6.)

PROBLEMS

12.15 The following represents the residuals and X values obtained from a regression analysis, along with the accompanying residual plot.

Is there any evidence of a pattern in the residuals? Explain.

	A	B	C	D	E	F	G
1	X	Residuals					
2	1	0.7					
3	2	-0.78					
4	3	1.03					
5	4	0.33					
6	5	2.39					
7	6	-0.67					
8	7	-0.16					
9	8	1.65					
10	9	-1.19					
11	10	0.84					
12	11	0.29					
13	12	-1.28					
14	13	1.21					
15	14	-0.37					
16	15	1.02					
17	16	-0.16					
18	17	1.42					
19	18	-0.71					
20	19	-0.63					
21	20	0.67					

Residual Plot

12.16 The following represents the residuals and X values obtained from a regression analysis, along with the accompanying residual plot.

Is there any evidence of a pattern in the residuals? Explain.

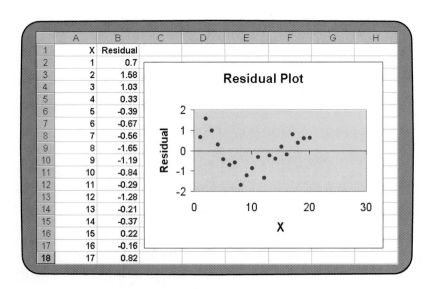

	A	B	C	D	E	F	G	H
1	X	Residual						
2	1	0.7						
3	2	1.58						
4	3	1.03						
5	4	0.33						
6	5	-0.39						
7	6	-0.67						
8	7	-0.56						
9	8	-1.65						
10	9	-1.19						
11	10	-0.84						
12	11	-0.29						
13	12	-1.28						
14	13	-0.21						
15	14	-0.37						
16	15	0.22						
17	16	-0.16						
18	17	0.82						

Residual Plot

12.17 In Problem 12.3 on page 575, the position of the wafer was used to predict the thickness of the film. Using the computer output you obtained to solve that problem, perform a residual analysis for these data, and then do the following:
- **(a)** Determine the aptness of the fit of the model.
- **(b)** Evaluate whether the assumptions of regression have been seriously violated.

12.18 In Problem 12.4 on page 575, the dial frequency was used to predict the actual frequency of a generator. Using the computer output you obtained to solve that problem, perform a residual analysis for these data, and then do the following:
- **(a)** Determine the aptness of the fit of the model.
- **(b)** Evaluate whether the assumptions of regression have been seriously violated.

12.19 In Problem 12.5 on page 576, the hardness was used to predict the tensile strength of die-cast aluminum. Using the computer output you obtained to solve that problem, perform a

residual analysis for these data, and then do the following:
- **(a)** Determine the aptness of the fit of the model.
- **(b)** Evaluate whether the assumptions of regression have been seriously violated.

12.20 In Problem 12.6 on page 576, the weight of mail was used to predict the number of orders received. Using the computer output you obtained to solve that problem, perform a residual analysis for these data, and then do the following:
- **(a)** Determine the aptness of the fit of the model.
- **(b)** Evaluate whether the assumptions of regression have been seriously violated.

12.21 In Problem 12.7 on page 576, the circumference was used to predict the weight of a pumpkin. Using the computer output you obtained to solve that problem, perform a residual analysis for these data, and then do the following:
- **(a)** Determine the aptness of the fit of the model.
- **(b)** Evaluate whether the assumptions of regression have been seriously violated.

12.7 INFERENCES ABOUT THE SLOPE

In Sections 12.1–12.4, we were concerned with the use of regression solely for the purpose of description. The least-squares method was used to determine the regression coefficients and to predict the value of Y from a given value of X. In addition, the standard error of the estimate was discussed along with the coefficient of determination.

Now that we have used residual analysis in Section 12.6 to assure ourselves that the assumptions of the least-squares regression model have not been seriously violated and that the straight-line model is appropriate, we concern ourselves with making inferences about the linear relationship between the variables in a population based on our sample results.

t Test for the Slope

We can determine whether a significant relationship between the X and Y variables exists by testing whether β_1 (the population slope) is equal to 0. If this hypothesis is rejected, one could conclude that there is evidence of a linear relationship. The null and alternative hypotheses are stated as follows:

$$H_0: \beta_1 = 0 \quad \text{(There is no linear relationship.)}$$

$$H_1: \beta_1 \neq 0 \quad \text{(There is a linear relationship.)}$$

The test statistic is given by the following:

TESTING A HYPOTHESIS FOR A POPULATION SLOPE, β_1, BY USING A t TEST

The t statistic equals the difference between the sample slope and the hypothesized population slope, divided by the standard error of the sample slope.

$$t = \frac{b_1 - \beta_1}{s_{b_1}} \tag{12.11}$$

where

$$s_{b_1} = \frac{s_{YX}}{\sqrt{SSX}}$$

$$SSX = \sum_{i=1}^{n} (X_i - \overline{X})^2$$

and the test statistic t follows a t distribution with $n - 2$ degrees of freedom.

Returning to our drilling example, now we will test whether there is a significant relationship between the drilling depth and the drilling time at the .05 level of significance. From the Microsoft Excel output of Figure 12.4 on page 573 or the MINITAB output of Figure 12.5 on page 573, we have[2]

[2]More detailed computations of the t test statistic are contained in Section 12.10.

$$b_1 = +0.004459 \qquad n = 50 \qquad s_{b_1} = 0.00127$$

Therefore, to test the existence of a relationship at the 0.05 level of significance, we have

$$t = \frac{b_1 - 0}{s_{b_1}} = \frac{b_1}{s_{b_1}}$$

$$= \frac{0.004459}{.00127} = 3.51$$

This t statistic is provided in the column titled t *Stat* by Microsoft Excel and T by MINITAB. Because $t = 3.51 > t_{48} = 2.0106$ (or because the p-value = $0.00098 < 0.05$), we reject H_0. Hence, we conclude that there is a significant linear relationship between drilling time and drilling depth. (See Figure 12.14.)

F Test for the Slope

An alternate approach to testing whether the slope in simple linear regression is statistically significant is to use an F test, as shown in Table 12.2 on page 590.

Recall, from Section 9.5, that the F test is used to test the ratio between two variances. When testing for the significance of the slope, the measure of random error is the error variance (the error sum of squares divided by its degrees of freedom), so the F test is the ratio of the variance due to the regression (the regression sum of squares divided by the number of independent variables k) divided by the

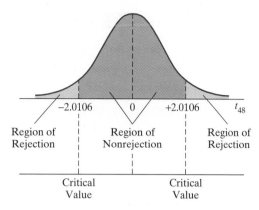

Figure 12.14   Testing a hypothesis about the population slope at the 0.05 level of significance with 48 degrees of freedom

error variance, as shown in Equation (12.12):

TESTING A HYPOTHESIS FOR A POPULATION SLOPE, β_1, BY USING THE F TEST

The F statistic is equal to the regression mean square (MSR) divided by the error mean square (MSE).

$$F = \frac{\text{MSR}}{\text{MSE}} \tag{12.12}$$

where

$$\text{MSR} = \frac{\text{SSR}}{k}$$

$$\text{MSE} = \frac{\text{SSE}}{n - k - 1}$$

k = number of independent or explanatory variables in the regression model

F = test statistic from an F distribution with k and $n - k - 1$ degrees of freedom

The decision rule is as follows:

Reject H_0 at the α level of significance if $F > F_{U(k, n - k - 1)}$;

otherwise do not reject H_0.

The complete set of results is organized into an Analysis of Variance (ANOVA) table, as illustrated in Table 12.2 on page 590.

The completed ANOVA table is available as part of the output from Microsoft Excel (see Figure 12.4) or MINITAB (see Figure 12.5). We observe, from either figure, that the computed F statistic is 12.33 and the p-value is 0.00098.

TABLE 12.2

ANOVA TABLE FOR TESTING THE SIGNIFICANCE OF A REGRESSION COEFFICIENT

Source	df	Sums of Squares	Mean Square (Variance)	F
Regression	k	SSR	$MSR = \dfrac{SSR}{k}$	$F = \dfrac{MSR}{MSE}$
Error	$n - k - 1$	SSE	$MSE = \dfrac{SSE}{n - k - 1}$	
Total	$n - 1$	SST		

If a level of significance equal to 0.05 is chosen, we can determine from Table A.7 that the critical value on the F distribution (with 1 and 48 degrees of freedom) is approximately 4.04, as depicted in Figure 12.15. From Equation (12.12), because $F = 12.33 > 4.04$ (or because the p-value $= 0.00098 < 0.05$), we reject H_0 and conclude that the drilling time is significantly related to drilling depth.

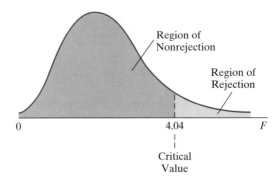

Figure 12.15   Testing for the significance of the slope at the 0.05 level of significance with 1 and 48 degrees of freedom

Confidence Interval Estimate of the Slope (β_1)

An alternative to testing the existence of a linear relationship between the variables is to set up a confidence interval estimate of β_1 and to determine whether the hypothesized value ($\beta_1 = 0$) is included in the interval. The confidence interval estimate of β_1 is obtained by the following calculation:

CONFIDENCE INTERVAL ESTIMATE OF THE SLOPE

$$b_1 \pm t_{n-2} s_{b_1} \tag{12.13}$$

From the Microsoft Excel output of Figure 12.4 on page 573, or from the MINITAB output of Figure 12.5 on page 573, we have

$$b_1 = +0.004459 \qquad n = 50 \qquad s_{b_1} = 0.00127$$

Thus,

$$b_1 \pm t_{n-2}\, s_{b_1} = +0.004459 \pm (2.0106)(0.00127)$$
$$= +0.004459 \pm 0.002553$$
$$= 0.0019 \le \beta_1 \le +0.0070$$

From Equation (12.13), the population slope is estimated with 95% confidence to be between +0.0019 and +0.0070 minutes. Both these values are above 0, so we can conclude that there is a significant linear relationship between drilling time and drilling depth.

PROBLEMS

12.22 In Problem 12.3 on page 575, the position of the wafer was used to predict the thickness of the film. Using the computer output you obtained to solve that problem, do the following:
- **(a)** At the .05 level of significance, is there evidence of a linear relationship between the position of the wafer and the thickness of the film?
- **(b)** Set up a 95% confidence interval estimate of the population slope, β_1.

12.23 In Problem 12.4 on page 575, the dial frequency was used to predict the actual frequency of a generator. Using the computer output you obtained to solve that problem, do the following:
- **(a)** At the .05 level of significance, is there evidence of a linear relationship between dial frequency and actual frequency?
- **(b)** Set up a 95% confidence interval estimate of the population slope, β_1.

12.24 In Problem 12.5 on page 576, the hardness was used to predict the tensile strength of die-cast aluminum. Using the computer output you obtained to solve that problem, do the following:

- **(a)** At the .05 level of significance, is there evidence of a linear relationship between hardness and tensile strength?
- **(b)** Set up a 95% confidence interval estimate of the population slope, β_1.

12.25 In Problem 12.6 on page 576, the weight of mail was used to predict the number of orders received. Using the computer output you obtained to solve that problem, do the following:
- **(a)** At the .05 level of significance, is there evidence of a linear relationship between the number of orders and the weight of mail received?
- **(b)** Set up a 95% confidence interval estimate of the population slope, β_1.

12.26 In Problem 12.7 on page 576, the circumference was used to predict the weight of a pumpkin. Using the computer output you obtained to solve that problem, do the following:
- **(a)** At the .05 level of significance, is there evidence of a linear relationship between the circumference and the weight of a pumpkin?
- **(b)** Set up a 95% confidence interval estimate of the population slope, β_1.

12.8 CONFIDENCE AND PREDICTION INTERVAL ESTIMATION

In this section, we will discuss methods of making inferences about the mean of Y and about an individual response value Y_I.

Obtaining the Confidence Interval Estimate

In Section 12.3 on page 574, the fitted regression equation was used to make predictions about the value of Y for a given X. In the drilling example, we predicted that the average drilling time for the five feet that end at a depth of 100 feet would be 6.449 minutes. This estimate, however, is just a *point estimate* of the population average value. In Chapter 8, we developed the concept of the confidence interval as an estimate of the population average. In a similar fashion, a **confidence interval estimate for the mean response** can now be developed to make inferences about the average value of Y for a given value of X.

CONFIDENCE INTERVAL ESTIMATE FOR THE MEAN OF Y ($\mu_{Y|X}$)

$$\hat{Y}_i \pm t_{n-2} s_{YX} \sqrt{h_i} \qquad (12.14)$$

where

$$h_i = \frac{1}{n} + \frac{(X_i - \overline{X})^2}{\displaystyle\sum_{i=1}^{n}(X_i - \overline{X})^2}$$

$\hat{Y}_i$ = predicted value of Y; $\hat{Y}_i = b_0 + b_1 X_i$

s_{YX} = standard error of the estimate

n = sample size

X_i = given value of X

An examination of Equation (12.14) indicates that the width of the confidence interval is dependent on several factors. For a given level of confidence, increased variation around the line of regression, as measured by the standard error of the estimate, results in a wider interval. As would be expected, however, increased sample size reduces the width of the interval. In addition, the width of the interval also varies at different values of X. For values of X close to $\overline{X}$, the interval is much narrower than it is for predictions at X values more distant from the mean. This effect can be seen from the square-root portion of Equation (12.14) and from Figure 12.16.

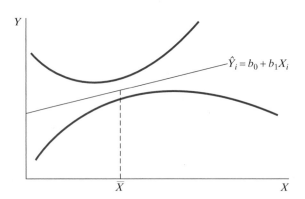

Figure 12.16   Interval estimates of $\mu_{Y|X}$ for different values of X

As displayed in Figure 12.16, the interval estimate of the true mean of Y varies as a function of the closeness of the given X to $\overline{X}$. This means that, when predictions are to be made for X values that are distant from $\overline{X}$, a much wider interval will occur.

Although the PHStat Add-in for Microsoft Excel (see Figure 12.17) or MINITAB (see Figure 12.5) can be used to obtain a confidence interval estimate for the mean response, we will illustrate the computations by using Equation (12.14) for the drilling example.

	A	B
1	**Confidence Interval Estimate**	
2		
3	**X Value**	**100**
4	**Confidence Level**	**95%**
5	Sample Size	50
6	Degrees of Freedom	48
7	t Value	2.01063358
8	Sample Mean	127.5
9	Sum of Squared Difference	260312.50
10	Standard Error of the Estimate	0.647944938
11	h Statistic	0.022905162
12	Average Predicted Y (YHat)	6.448778391
13		
14		
15	**For Average Predicted Y (YHat)**	
16	Interval Half Width	0.197168584
17	**Confidence Interval Lower Limit**	**6.251609807**
18	**Confidence Interval Upper Limit**	**6.645946975**
19		
20	**For Individual Response Y**	
21	Interval Half Width	1.317615569
22	**Prediction Interval Lower Limit**	**5.131162822**
23	**Prediction Interval Upper Limit**	**7.766393961**

Figure 12.17   Confidence and prediction interval estimates obtained from the PHStat Add-in for Microsoft Excel, for the drilling example

For a 95% confidence interval estimate of the population average drilling time for all dry holes for the five feet of depth that end at 100 feet, we use our simple linear regression equation. With $X_i = 100$, we obtain $\hat{Y}_i = 6.0029 + 0.004459(100) = 6.4488$ minutes.

Also, given the following:

$$\overline{X} = 127.50 \qquad s_{YX} = 0.6479 \qquad \sum_{i=1}^{n} (X_i - \overline{X})^2 = 260{,}312.50$$

and from Table A.4, $t_{48} = 2.0106$. Thus,

$$\hat{Y}_i \pm t_{n-2}\, s_{YX}\, \sqrt{h_i}$$

where

$$h_i = \frac{1}{n} + \frac{(X_i - \overline{X})^2}{\sum_{i=1}^{n} (X_i - \overline{X})^2}$$

so that we have

$$\hat{Y}_i \pm t_{n-2}\, s_{YX} \sqrt{\frac{1}{n} + \frac{(X_i - \overline{X})^2}{\sum_{i=1}^{n} (X_i - \overline{X})^2}}$$

and

$$6.4488 \pm (2.0106)(0.6479)\sqrt{\frac{1}{50} + \frac{(100 - 127.5)^2}{260{,}312.5}} = 6.4488 \pm 0.1972$$

As a final result, then,

$$6.2516 \le \mu_{Y|X} \le 6.6459$$

Therefore, our estimate is that the average drilling time is between 6.2516 and 6.6459 minutes when $X = 100$.

Obtaining the Prediction Interval Estimate

In addition to the need to obtain a confidence interval estimate for the average value, it is often important to be able to predict the response that would be obtained for an individual value. Although the form of the prediction interval estimate is similar to the confidence interval estimate of Equation (12.14), the prediction interval is estimating an individual value, not a parameter. This **prediction interval for an individual response** Y_I at a particular value X_i is provided in Equation (12.15).

PREDICTION INTERVAL ESTIMATE FOR AN
INDIVIDUAL RESPONSE Y_I

$$\hat{Y}_i \pm t_{n-2}\, s_{YX}\, \sqrt{1 + h_i} \qquad (12.15)$$

where $h_i, \hat{Y}_i, s_{YX}, n,$ and X_i are defined as for Equation (12.14) on page 592.

Although the PHStat Add-in for Microsoft Excel (see Figure 12.17) or MINITAB (see Figure 12.5 on page 573) can also be used to obtain a prediction interval estimate for the individual response, we will illustrate Equation (12.15) by the drilling example. In this example, we obtained the simple linear regression model

$$\hat{Y}_i = 6.0029 + 0.00446\, X_i$$

To set up a 95% prediction interval estimate of the drilling time for a dry hole at a depth that ends at 100 feet, for $X_i = 100$, we obtain $\hat{Y}_i = 6.0029 + 0.004459\,(100) = 6.4488$ minutes.
Also,

$$\overline{X} = 127.50 \qquad s_{YX} = 0.6479 \qquad \sum_{i=1}^{n} (X_i - \overline{X})^2 = 260,312.50$$

and, from Table A.4, $t_{48} = 2.0106$. Thus,

$$\hat{Y}_i \pm t_{n-2}\, s_{YX}\, \sqrt{1 + h_i}$$

where

$$h_i = \frac{1}{n} + \frac{(X_i - \overline{X})^2}{\sum_{i=1}^{n} (X_i - \overline{X})^2}$$

so that we have

$$\hat{Y}_i \pm t_{n-2}\, s_{YX}\, \sqrt{1 + \frac{1}{n} + \frac{(X_i - \overline{X})^2}{\sum_{i=1}^{n} (X_i - \overline{X})^2}}$$

and

$$6.4488 \pm (2.0106)(0.6479)\sqrt{1 + \frac{1}{50} + \frac{(100 - 127.5)^2}{260,312.5}} = 6.4488 \pm 1.3176$$

As a final result, then,

$$5.1312 \le Y_I \le 7.664$$

Therefore, our estimate is that the predicted drilling time for an individual dry hole at a depth that ends at 100 feet will fall between 5.1312 and 7.664 minutes. If we compare the results of the confidence interval and the prediction interval, we observe that the width of the prediction interval for an individual dry hole is wider than the width of the confidence interval estimate for the average dry hole. This is because there will be more variation in predicting an individual value than in predicting an average value.

PROBLEMS

12.27 From a sample of 20 observations, the least-squares method was used to obtain the following linear regression equation: $\hat{Y}_i = 5 + 3X_i$. In addition,

$$s_{YX} = 1.0, \bar{X} = 2, \text{ and } \sum_{i=1}^{n}(X_i - \bar{X})^2 = 20$$

(a) Set up a 95% confidence interval estimate of the population average response for $X = 2$.
(b) Set up a 95% prediction interval estimate of the individual response for $X = 2$.
(c) Set up a 95% confidence interval estimate of the population average response for $X = 4$.
(d) Set up a 95% prediction interval estimate of the individual response for $X = 4$.
(e) Compare the results of (c) and (d) with those of (a) and (b). Which interval is wider? Why?

12.28 In Problem 12.3 on page 575, the position of the wafer was used to predict the thickness of the film. Using the computer output you obtained to solve that problem, do the following:
(a) Set up a 95% confidence interval estimate of the population average thickness for wafers whose position is 20 inches from the end of the furnace.
(b) Set up a 95% prediction interval estimate of the thickness for an individual wafer whose position is 20 inches from the end of the furnace.
(c) Explain the difference between the results obtained in (a) and (b).

12.29 In Problem 12.4 on page 575, the dial frequency was used to predict the actual frequency of a generator. Using the computer output you obtained to solve that problem, do the following:
(a) Set up a 95% confidence interval estimate of the population average actual frequency for a dial frequency of 5,000.
(b) Set up a 95% prediction interval estimate of the actual frequency for an individual dial frequency of 5,000.
(c) Explain the difference between the results obtained in (a) and (b).

12.30 In Problem 12.5 on page 576, the hardness was used to predict the tensile strength of die-cast aluminum. Using the computer output you obtained to solve that problem, do the following:
(a) Set up a 95% confidence interval estimate of the population average tensile strength for a hardness of 30 Rockwell E units.
(b) Set up a 95% prediction interval of the tensile strength for an individual specimen that has a hardness of 30 Rockwell E units.
(c) Explain the difference between the results obtained in (a) and (b).

12.31 In Problem 12.6 on page 576, the weight of mail was used to predict the number of orders received. Using the computer output you obtained to solve that problem, do the following:
(a) Set up a 95% confidence interval estimate of the population average number of orders received for a weight of 500 pounds.
(b) Set up a 95% prediction interval estimate of the number of orders received for an individual mail delivery with a weight of 500 pounds.
(c) Explain the difference between the results obtained in (a) and (b).

12.32 In Problem 12.7 on page 576, the circumference was used to predict the weight of a pumpkin. Using the computer output you obtained to solve that problem, do the following:
(a) Set up a 95% confidence interval estimate of the population average weight for a pumpkin that has a circumference of 60 centimeters.
(b) Set up a 95% prediction interval estimate of the weight for an individual pumpkin that has a circumference of 60 centimeters.
(c) Explain the difference between the results obtained in (a) and (b).

12.9 PITFALLS IN REGRESSION AND ETHICAL ISSUES

Some of the difficulties involved in using regression analysis are summarized in Exhibit 12.2.

EXHIBIT 12.2 Difficulties in Using Regression Analysis

1. Lacking an awareness of the assumptions of least-squares regression

2. Not knowing how to evaluate the assumptions of least-squares regression

3. Not knowing what the alternatives to least-squares regression are if a particular assumption is violated

4. Using a regression model without knowledge of the subject matter

---

The widespread availability of spreadsheet and statistical software has removed the computational block that prevented many users from applying regression analysis to situations that required forecasting. With this positive development of enhanced technology comes the realization that, for many users, the access to powerful techniques has not been accompanied by an understanding of how to use regression analysis properly. How can a user be expected to know what the alternatives to least-squares regression are if a particular assumption is violated, when he or she in many instances is not even aware of the assumptions of regression, let alone how the assumptions can be evaluated?

The necessity of going beyond the basic number crunching—the computing of the Y-intercept, the slope, and r^2—can be illustrated by referring to Table 12.3, a classical pedagogical piece of statistical literature that deals with the importance of observation through scatter plots and residual analysis.

TABLE 12.3

FOUR SETS OF ARTIFICIAL DATA

Data Set A		Data Set B		Data Set C		Data Set D	
X_i	Y_i	X_i	Y_i	X_i	Y_i	X_i	Y_i
10	8.04	10	9.14	10	7.46	8	6.58
14	9.96	14	8.10	14	8.84	8	5.76
5	5.68	5	4.74	5	5.73	8	7.71
8	6.95	8	8.14	8	6.77	8	8.84
9	8.81	9	8.77	9	7.11	8	8.47
12	10.84	12	9.13	12	8.15	8	7.04
4	4.26	4	3.10	4	5.39	8	5.25
7	4.82	7	7.26	7	6.42	19	12.50
11	8.33	11	9.26	11	7.81	8	5.56
13	7.58	13	8.74	13	12.74	8	7.91
6	7.24	6	6.13	6	6.08	8	6.89

ANSCOMBE

Source: F. J. Anscombe; "Graphs in Statistical Analysis," *American Statistician,* Vol. 27 (1973), pp. 17–21

Anscombe (Reference 1) showed that, for the four data sets given in Table 12.3, the following results are obtained:

$$\hat{Y}_i = 3.0 + 0.5X_i$$

$$s_{YX} = 1.237$$

$$s_{b_1} = 0.118$$

$$r^2 = 0.667$$

$$SSR = \text{explained variation} = \sum_{i=1}^{n} (\hat{Y}_i - \bar{Y})^2 = 27.51$$

$$SSE = \text{unexplained variation} = \sum_{i=1}^{n} (Y_i - \hat{Y}_i)^2 = 13.76$$

$$SST = \text{total variation} = \sum_{i=1}^{n} (Y_i - \bar{Y})^2 = 41.27$$

Thus, with respect to these statistics associated with a simple linear regression, the four data sets are identical. Had we stopped our analysis at this point, valuable information in the data would be lost. This effect can be observed by examining Figure 12.18, which represents scatter diagrams for the four data sets, and Figure 12.19, which represents residual plots for the four data sets.

From the scatter diagrams of Figure 12.18 and the residual plots of Figure 12.19 on page 598, we see how different the data sets are. The only data set that seems to follow an approximate straight line is data set A. The residual plot for data set A does not show any obvious patterns or outlying residuals. This is certainly not

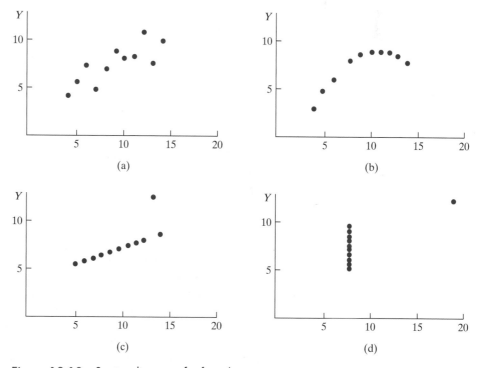

Figure 12.18 Scatter diagrams for four data sets

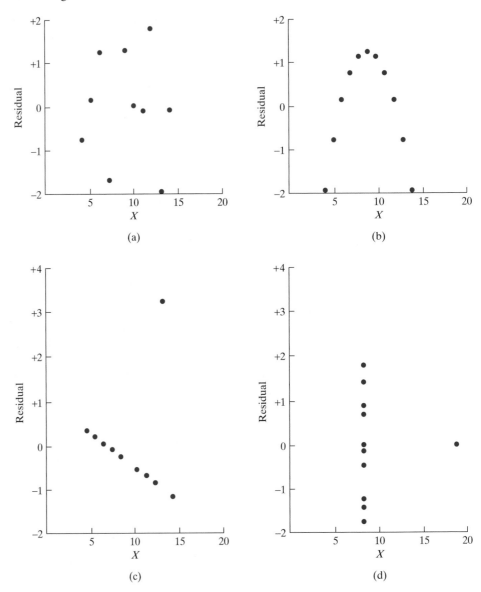

Figure 12.19   Residual plots for four data sets

the case for data sets B, C, and D. The scatter plot for data set B seems to indicate that a quadratic regression model (to be covered in Section 13.6) should be considered. This conclusion is reinforced by the clear parabolic form of the residual plot for B. The scatter diagram and the residual plot for data set C clearly depict what may very well be an outlying observation. If this is the case, we may want to remove the outlier and reestimate the basic model. Methodology that allows us to study whether the removal of observations is appropriate is called influence analysis. (See Reference 2.) The result of reestimating the model might be a relationship much different from the one originally conjectured. Similarly, the scatter diagram for data set D represents the unusual situation in which the fitted model is very heavily dependent on the outcome of a single response ($X_8 = 19$ and $Y_8 = 12.50$). Any regression model fit to the data should be evaluated cautiously, because its regression coefficients are heavily dependent on a single observation.

In summary, residual plots are of vital importance to a complete regression analysis. The information they provide is so basic to a credible analysis that these plots should always be included as part of a regression analysis. Thus, a strategy that can help avoid the first three pitfalls of regression listed can be summarized in Exhibit 12.3.

EXHIBIT 12.3   Strategy for Avoiding the Pitfalls of Regression

1. Always start with a scatter plot to observe the possible relationship between X and Y.

2. Check the assumptions of regression after the regression model has been fitted, before moving on to using the results of the model.

3. Plot the residuals versus the independent variable. This chart will enable you to determine whether the model fitted to the data is an appropriate one and will allow you to check visually for violations of the homoscedasticity assumption.

4. Use a histogram, stem-and-leaf display, box-and-whisker plot, or normal probability plot of the residuals to evaluate graphically whether the normality assumption has been seriously violated.

5. If the evaluation done in 3 and 4 indicates violations in the assumptions, use methods alternative to least-squares regression or alternative least-squares models (quadratic or multiple regression), depending on what the evaluation has indicated.

6. If the evaluation done in 3 and 4 does not indicate violations of the assumptions, then the inferential aspects of the regression analysis can be undertaken. Tests for the significance of the regression coefficients can be done, and confidence and prediction intervals can be developed.

12.10 COMPUTATIONS IN SIMPLE LINEAR REGRESSION

In our development of the simple linear regression model, we have focused primarily on using the output of software such as Microsoft Excel and MINITAB. In this section, we illustrate the computations that were involved in developing many of the statistics obtained for the simple linear regression model.

Computing the Y-Intercept, b_0, and the Slope, b_1

Equations (12.3a) and (12.3b) on page 572 represent the two equations that need to be solved simultaneously to obtain the regression coefficients b_1 and b_0. There are two equations with two unknowns, so we solve these equations simultaneously, as follows:

COMPUTATIONAL FORMULA FOR THE SLOPE, b_1

$$b_1 = \frac{SSXY}{SSX} \qquad (12.16)$$

where

$$SSXY = \sum_{i=1}^{n}(X_i - \overline{X})(Y_i - \overline{Y}) = \sum_{i=1}^{n} X_i Y_i - \frac{\left(\sum_{i=1}^{n} X_i\right)\left(\sum_{i=1}^{n} Y_i\right)}{n}$$

$$SSX = \sum_{i=1}^{n}(X_i - \overline{X})^2 = \sum_{i=1}^{n} X_i^2 - \frac{\left(\sum_{i=1}^{n} X_i\right)^2}{n}$$

---

and

COMPUTATIONAL FORMULA FOR THE Y-INTERCEPT, b_0

$$b_0 = \overline{Y} - b_1 \overline{X} \qquad (12.17)$$

where

$$\overline{Y} = \frac{\sum_{i=1}^{n} Y_i}{n} \qquad \text{and} \qquad \overline{X} = \frac{\sum_{i=1}^{n} X_i}{n}$$

Examining Equations (12.16) and (12.17), we see that there are five quantities that must be obtained to determine b_1 and b_0. These are n, the sample size; $\sum_{i=1}^{n} X_i$, the sum of the X values; $\sum_{i=1}^{n} Y_i$, the sum of the Y values; $\sum_{i=1}^{n} X_i^2$, the sum of the squared X values, and $\sum_{i=1}^{n} X_i Y_i$, the sum of the cross products of X and Y. For the data in Table 12.1, the drilling depth is used to predict the drilling time. The various sums needed [including $\sum_{i=1}^{n} Y_i^2$, the sum of the squared Y values, which will be used to compute the sum of squares total (SST)] are as follows:

$$\sum_{i=1}^{n} X_i = 6{,}375$$

$$\sum_{i=1}^{n} Y_i = 328.57$$

$$\sum_{i=1}^{n} X_i^2 = 1{,}073{,}125$$

$$\sum_{i=1}^{n} Y_i^2 = 2{,}184.493$$

$$\sum_{i=1}^{n} X_i Y_i = 43{,}053.4$$

Using Equations (12.16) and (12.17), we compute the values of b_0 and b_1:

$$b_1 = \frac{SSXY}{SSX}$$

$$SSXY = \sum_{i=1}^{n}(X_i - \bar{X})(Y_i - \bar{Y}) = \sum_{i=1}^{n}X_iY_i - \frac{\left(\sum_{i=1}^{n}X_i\right)\left(\sum_{i=1}^{n}Y_i\right)}{n}$$

$$SSXY = 43{,}053.4 - \frac{(6{,}375)(328.57)}{50}$$

$$= 1{,}160.726$$

$$SSX = \sum_{i=1}^{n}(X_i - \bar{X})^2 = \sum_{i=1}^{n}X_i^2 - \frac{\left(\sum_{i=1}^{n}X_i\right)^2}{n}$$

$$= 1{,}073{,}125 - \frac{(6{,}375)^2}{50}$$

$$= 260{,}312.5$$

Then, we calculate

$$b_1 = \frac{1{,}160.726}{260{,}312.5}$$

$$= 0.004459$$

and

$$b_0 = \bar{Y} - b_1\bar{X}$$

where

$$\bar{Y} = \frac{\sum_{i=1}^{n}Y_i}{n} = \frac{328.57}{50} = 6.5714$$

$$\bar{X} = \frac{\sum_{i=1}^{n}X_i}{n} = \frac{6{,}375}{50} = 127.5$$

so that:

$$b_0 = 6.5714 - (0.004459)(127.5)$$

$$= 6.0029$$

Computing the Measures of Variation

Computational formulas can be developed to compute SST, SSR, and SSE, which were defined in Equations (12.4), (12.5), and (12.6) on page 578.

COMPUTATIONAL FORMULA FOR THE TOTAL SUM OF SQUARES (SST)

$$SST = \text{total sum of squares} = \sum_{i=1}^{n}(Y_i - \bar{Y})^2 = \sum_{i=1}^{n}Y_i^2 - \frac{\left(\sum_{i=1}^{n}Y_i\right)^2}{n} \qquad (12.18)$$

COMPUTATIONAL FORMULA FOR THE REGRESSION SUM OF SQUARES (SSR)

SSR = explained variation or regression sum of squares

$$= \sum_{i=1}^{n} (\hat{Y}_i - \bar{Y})^2$$

$$= b_0 \sum_{i=1}^{n} Y_i + b_1 \sum_{i=1}^{n} X_i Y_i - \frac{\left(\sum_{i=1}^{n} Y_i\right)^2}{n} \tag{12.19}$$

COMPUTATIONAL FORMULA FOR THE ERROR SUM OF SQUARES (SSE)

SSE = unexplained variation or error sum of squares

$$= \sum_{i=1}^{n} (Y_i - \hat{Y}_i)^2 \tag{12.20}$$

$$= \sum_{i=1}^{n} Y_i^2 - b_0 \sum_{i=1}^{n} Y_i - b_1 \sum_{i=1}^{n} X_i Y_i$$

From the summary results from the computations for the slope and Y-intercept,

$$\text{SST} = \text{total sum of squares} = \sum_{i=1}^{n}(Y_i - \bar{Y})^2 = \sum_{i=1}^{n} Y_i^2 - \frac{\left(\sum_{i=1}^{n} Y_i\right)^2}{n}$$

$$= 2{,}184.493 - \frac{(328.57)^2}{50}$$

$$= 25.3276$$

SSR = explained variation or regression sum of squares

$$= \sum_{i=1}^{n} (\hat{Y}_i - \bar{Y})^2$$

$$= b_0 \sum_{i=1}^{n} Y_i + b_1 \sum_{i=1}^{n} X_i Y_i - \frac{\left(\sum_{i=1}^{n} Y_i\right)^2}{n}$$

$$= (6.0029)(328.57) + (0.004459)(43{,}053.4) - \frac{(328.57)^2}{50}$$

$$= 5.1756$$

SSE = unexplained variation or error sum of squares

$$= \sum_{i=1}^{n} (Y_i - \hat{Y}_i)^2$$

$$= \sum_{i=1}^{n} Y_i^2 - b_0 \sum_{i=1}^{n} Y_i - b_1 \sum_{i=1}^{n} X_i Y_i$$

$$= 2{,}184.493 - (6.0029)(328.57) - (0.004459)(43{,}053.4)$$

$$= 20.152$$

Computing the Standard Error of the Slope

In Section 12.7, the standard error of the slope was used to test the existence of a relationship between the X and Y variables. The computational formula can be developed as follows:

$$s_{b_1} = \frac{s_{YX}}{\sqrt{SSX}}$$

$$SSX = \sum_{i=1}^{n} (X_i - \bar{X})^2$$

$$= \sum_{i=1}^{n} X_i^2 - \frac{\left(\sum_{i=1}^{n} X_i\right)^2}{n}$$

$$= 1,073,125 - \frac{(6,375)^2}{50}$$

$$= 260,312.5$$

$$s_{b_1} = \frac{0.647945}{\sqrt{260,312.5}}$$

$$= 0.00127$$

12.11 CORRELATION—MEASURING THE STRENGTH OF THE ASSOCIATION

The Correlation Coefficient

In our discussion of regression analysis, we have been concerned with the prediction of the dependent variable Y from the independent variable X. In contrast to this, in a correlation analysis, our focus is on measuring the degree of association between two variables.

The strength of a relationship between two variables in a population is usually measured by the **coefficient of correlation**, ρ, whose values range from -1.0 for perfect negative correlation up to $+1.0$ for perfect positive correlation. Figure 12.20 illustrates three different types of association between variables.

In Panel A of Figure 12.20, there is a perfect negative linear relationship between X and Y. Y will decrease in a perfectly predictable manner as X increases.

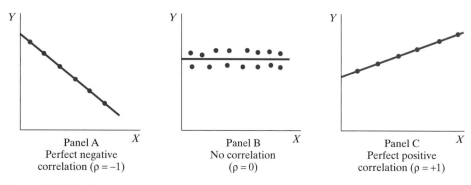

Figure 12.20   Types of association between variables

Panel B is an example in which there is no relationship between X and Y. As X increases, there is no systematic change in Y, so there is no association between the values of X and the values of Y. Panel C depicts a perfect positive correlation between X and Y. In this case, Y increases in a perfectly predictable manner as X increases.

For situations in which our primary interest is regression analysis, the sample coefficient of correlation (r) is obtained from the coefficient of determination, r^2, as follows:

$$r^2 = \frac{\text{regression sum of squares}}{\text{total sum of squares}} = \frac{\text{SSR}}{\text{SST}}$$

so that

THE COEFFICIENT OF CORRELATION

$$r = \sqrt{r^2} \qquad (12.21)$$

where r takes the sign of b_1.

In the drilling example, $r^2 = 0.204$, and the slope, b_1, is positive, so the coefficient of correlation is computed as $+0.452$.

We have now computed and interpreted the correlation coefficient from a regression perspective. As we mentioned at the beginning of this chapter, regression and correlation are two separate techniques. Regression is concerned with prediction, correlation with association. In many applications, we are concerned only with measuring association between variables, not with using one variable to predict another.

If we are specifically interested in measuring correlation, the sample correlation coefficient r can be computed directly by using the following formula.

THE COEFFICIENT OF CORRELATION

$$r = \frac{SSXY}{\sqrt{SSX}\sqrt{SSY}} \qquad (12.22)$$

where

$$SSXY = \sum_{i=1}^{n}(X_i - \bar{X})(Y_i - \bar{Y})$$

$$SSX = \sum_{i=1}^{n}(X_i - \bar{X})^2$$

$$SSY = \sum_{i=1}^{n}(Y_i - \bar{Y})^2$$

One application of the correlation coefficient occurs in using the paired t test. This test will be better than the two-sample test using independent samples only if there is positive correlation between the repeated or paired measurements. In Section 9.6, we studied the cardiac output of patients by using two different measurements.

	A	B	C	D	E	F	G	H
1	Patient	Observer A	Observer B	(X - XBAR)^2	(Y - YBAR)^2	(X - XBAR)(Y - YBAR)		
2	1	4.8	5.8	9	10.43570888	9.691304348	Summary	
3	2	5.6	6.1	4.84	8.587448015	6.446956522	Xbar	7.8
4	3	6	7.7	3.24	1.770056711	2.394782609	Ybar	9.030435
5	4	6.4	7.8	1.96	1.513969754	1.722608696	SSXY	61.78
6	5	6.5	7.6	1.69	2.046143667	1.859565217	SSX	61.66
7	6	6.6	8.1	1.44	0.865708885	1.116521739	SSY	70.8687
8	7	6.8	8	1	1.061795841	1.030434783	r	0.934585
9	8	7	8.1	0.64	0.865708885	0.744347826		
10	9	7	6.6	0.64	5.907013233	1.944347826		
11	10	7.2	8.1	0.36	0.865708885	0.55826087		
12	11	7.4	9.5	0.16	0.220491493	-0.187826087		
13	12	7.6	9.6	0.04	0.324404537	-0.113913043		
14	13	7.7	8.5	0.01	0.281361059	0.053043478		
15	14	7.7	9.5	0.01	0.220491493	-0.046956522		
16	15	8.2	9.1	0.16	0.004839319	0.027826087		
17	16	8.2	10	0.16	0.940056711	0.387826087		
18	17	8.3	9.1	0.25	0.004839319	0.034782609		
19	18	8.5	10.8	0.49	3.131361059	1.238695652		
20	19	9.3	11.5	2.25	6.098752363	3.704347826		
21	20	10.2	11.5	5.76	6.098752363	5.926956522		
22	21	10.4	11.2	6.76	4.707013233	5.640869565		
23	22	10.6	11.5	7.84	6.098752363	6.914782609		
24	23	11.4	12	12.96	8.81831758	10.69043478		

Figure 12.21   Summary computations obtained from Microsoft Excel for the correlation of two measurements of cardiac output

(See Table 9.7 on page 430.) For these data, we use Microsoft Excel to compute SSX, SSY, SSXY, and r, as displayed in Figure 12.21.

To obtain the correlation coefficient, r, we have

$$SSXY = \sum_{i=1}^{n} (X_i - \bar{X})(Y_i - \bar{Y}) = 61.78$$

$$SSX = \sum_{i=1}^{n} (X_i - \bar{X})^2 = 61.66$$

$$SSY = \sum_{i=1}^{n} (Y_i - \bar{Y})^2 = 70.8687$$

so that

$$r = \frac{SSXY}{\sqrt{SSX}\sqrt{SSY}} = \frac{61.78}{\sqrt{61.66}\sqrt{70.8687}}$$

$$= 0.9346$$

The coefficient of correlation, $r = +0.9346$, between the two measurements indicates a very strong positive association.

Now that we have computed the correlation coefficient, r, we can use the sample result to determine whether there is any evidence of a statistically significant association between these two measurements. The population correlation coefficient, ρ, is hypothesized as being equal to zero. Thus, the null and alternative hypotheses are as follows:

$H_0: \rho = 0$ (There is no correlation.)

$H_1: \rho \neq 0$ (There is correlation.)

The test statistic for determining the existence of a significant correlation is given by the following:

TESTING FOR THE EXISTENCE OF CORRELATION

$$t = \frac{r - \rho}{\sqrt{\dfrac{1 - r^2}{n - 2}}} \tag{12.23}$$

where the test statistic t follows a t distribution with $n - 2$ degrees of freedom.

For the cardiac-measurement data summarized in Figure 12.21, $r = +0.9346$ and $n = 23$, so, testing the null hypothesis, we have

$$t = \frac{r}{\sqrt{\dfrac{1 - r^2}{n - 2}}}$$

$$= \frac{0.9346}{\sqrt{\dfrac{1 - (0.9346)^2}{50 - 2}}} = 18.20$$

Using the .05 level of significance (because $t = 18.20 > t_{48} = 2.0796$), we reject H_0. We conclude that there is evidence of an association between the two cardiac measurements.

When inferences concerning the population slope were discussed, confidence intervals and tests of hypothesis were used interchangeably. The development of a confidence interval for the correlation coefficient is more complicated, because the shape of the sampling distribution of the statistic r varies for different values of the true correlation coefficient. Methods for developing a confidence interval estimate for the correlation coefficient are presented in Reference 6.

PROBLEMS

12.33 If $r^2 = 0.81$, and the slope of the fitted regression line is positive, find r.

12.34 If the coefficient of determination is 0.49, and the slope of the fitted regression line is -3, find the coefficient of correlation.

12.35 If SSR = SST, and the slope is a negative value, find r.

12.36 If SSE = 0, and the slope is a positive value, find r.

12.37 In Problem 3.27 on page 127, a hydrologic study of rainfall and water discharge through wadis in Saudi Arabia collected data on rainfall depth and runoff depth during and after storms.
  (a) Compute the correlation coefficient r.
  (b) At the 0.05 level of significance, is there a relationship between rainfall depth and runoff depth? Explain.

  (c) Would you expect there to be a positive relationship between rainfall depth and runoff depth? Explain.

12.38 In Problem 3.29 on page 129, data on dry-matter yield (DMY) and nitrogen concentration (NC) for sorghum grown on the Lincoln, Nebraska, municipal water bio-solids use site in 1990 and 1991 was studied.
  (a) Compute the correlation coefficient, r, between dry-matter yield (DMY) and nitrogen concentration (NC).
  (b) At the 0.05 level of significance, is there a relationship between dry-matter yield (DMY) and nitrogen concentration (NC)?

12.39 In Problem 9.25 on page 432, data was collected concerning the thickness of nonmagnetic coatings of zinc. Two measurements are made on the same specimen, first by using a nondestructive method, then by using a destructive method.

(a) Compute the correlation coefficient, r, between the thickness of nonmagnetic coatings of zinc measured by using a non-destructive method and those measured by using a destructive method.

(b) At the .05 level of significance, is there a relationship between the measurements of thickness of nonmagnetic coatings of zinc made by using a non-destructive method and those made by using a destructive method?

(c) From the results of (b), do you think that the paired t test used in Problem 9.25 was a better choice than a t test for independent samples? Explain.

12.40 In Problem 9.26 on page 432, data was collected on the compressive strength, in thousands of pounds per square inch (psi), of 40 samples of concrete taken two and seven days after pouring.

(a) Compute the correlation coefficient, r, between the compressive strength of concrete taken two and seven days after pouring.

(b) At the 0.05 level of significance, is there a relationship between the compressive strengths of concrete as taken at two and seven days after pouring?

(c) Given the results of (b), do you think that the paired t test used in Problem 9.26 was a better choice of method than a t test for independent samples? Explain.

12.41 In Problem 12.3 on page 575, the position of the wafer was used to predict the thickness of the film. Using the computer output you obtained to solve that problem, do the following:

(a) Determine the coefficient of correlation.

(b) Is there evidence of a significant correlation at the 0.05 level of significance?

(c) Compare the results of (b) to Problem 12.22(a). What conclusion do you reach about the two tests?

12.42 In Problem 12.4 on page 575, the dial frequency was used to predict the actual frequency of a generator. Using the computer output you obtained to solve that problem, do the following:

(a) Determine the coefficient of correlation.

(b) Is there evidence of a significant correlation at the 0.05 level of significance?

(c) Compare the results of (b) to Problem 12.23(a). What conclusion do you reach about the two tests?

12.43 In Problem 12.5 on page 576, the hardness was used to predict the tensile strength of die-cast aluminum. Using the computer output you obtained to solve that problem, do the following:

(a) Determine the coefficient of correlation.

(b) Is there evidence of a significant correlation at the 0.05 level of significance?

(c) Compare the results of (b) to Problem 12.24(a). What conclusion do you reach about the two tests?

12.44 In Problem 12.6 on page 576, the weight of mail was used to predict the number of orders received. Using the computer output you obtained to solve that problem, do the following:

(a) Determine the coefficient of correlation.

(b) Is there evidence of a significant correlation at the 0.05 level of significance?

(c) Compare the results of (b) to Problem 12.25(a). What conclusion do you reach about the two tests?

12.45 In Problem 12.7 on page 576, the circumference was used to predict the weight of a pumpkin. Using the computer output you obtained to solve that problem, do the following:

(a) Determine the coefficient of correlation.

(b) Is there evidence of a significant correlation at the 0.05 level of significance?

(c) Compare the results of (b) to Problem 12.26(a). What conclusion do you reach about the two tests?

KEY TERMS

residual analysis   582
response variable   567
scatter diagram   568
simple linear regression   567
slope   568

standard error of the estimate   579
total sum of squares (SST)   577
unexplained variation   577
Y-intercept   568

CHAPTER REVIEW *Checking Your Understanding*

12.46 What are the interpretations of the Y-intercept and the slope in a regression model?
12.47 What is the interpretation of the coefficient of determination?
12.48 When will the unexplained variation or error sum of squares be equal to 0?
12.49 When will the explained variation or sum of squares due to regression be equal to 0?
12.50 Why should a residual analysis always be done as part of the development of a regression model?
12.51 What are the assumptions of regression analysis, and how can they be evaluated?
12.52 What is the difference between a confidence interval estimate of the mean response μ_{YX} and a prediction interval estimate of Y_I?

Chapter Review Problems

12.53 On January 28, 1986, the space shuttle *Challenger* exploded, and seven astronauts were killed. Prior to the launch, when freezing weather was predicted for the launch site, engineers for Morton Thiokol (the manufacturer of the rocket motor) prepared charts to make the case that the launch should not take place, because of the cold. These arguments were rejected, and, tragically, the launch took place. During an investigation after the tragedy, experts agreed that the disaster occurred because of leaky rubber O-rings that did not seal properly in the cold temperature. Data indicating the atmospheric temperature at the time of 23 of the previous 24 launches and the value of the associated O-ring damage index are as follows:

Flight Number	Temperature (°F)	O-ring Damage Index	Flight Number	Temperature (°F)	O-ring Damage Index
1	66	0	51-A	67	0
2	70	4	51-B	75	0
3	69	0	51-C	53	11
5	68	0	51-D	67	0
6	67	0	51-F	81	0
7	72	0	51-G	70	0
8	73	0	51-I	67	0
9	70	0	51-J	79	0
41-B	57	4	61-A	75	4
41-C	63	2	61-B	76	0
41-D	70	4	61-C	58	4
41-G	78	0			**O-RING**

Note: Data from flight 4 is omitted because the O-ring condition is not known. "Zero" means "no damage."

Primary Sources: Report of the Presidential Commission on the Space Shuttle Challenger Accident, Washington, D. C., 1986, Vol. II (pp. H1–H3) and Volume IV (p. 664); *Post Challenger Evaluation of Space Shuttle Risk Assessment and Management,* Washington, D. C., 1988, pp. 135–136

Secondary Source: Tufte, E. R.; *Visual and Statistical Thinking: Displays of Evidence for Making Decisions,* Cheshire, Ct.: Graphics Press, 1997

(a) Set up a scatter diagram for the seven flights in which there was O-ring damage. What conclusions, if any, can you draw about the relationship between atmospheric temperature and O-ring damage?

(b) Set up a scatter diagram for all 23 flights.

(c) Explain any differences between the interpretation of the relationship between atmospheric temperature and O-ring damage in (a) and (b).

(d) Given the scatter diagram in (b), provide reasons for why a prediction should not be made for an atmospheric temperature of 31 °F, the temperature on the morning of the launch of the *Challenger*.

(e) Although the assumption of a linear relationship with atmospheric temperature may not be valid, fit a straight line to predict O-ring damage from atmospheric temperature.

(f) Plot the straight line fit in (e) on the scatter diagram developed in (b).

(g) Given the results of (f), do you think a straight line is an appropriate model for these data? Explain.

(h) Perform a residual analysis of the linear relationship fit in (f). What conclusions do you reach?

12.54 Over the past thirty years, public awareness and concern over air pollution have escalated dramatically. Venturi scrubbers have been used for the removal of submicron particulate matter found in dust, fogs, fumes, odors, or smoke from gas streams. An experiment was conducted to determine the effect of air flowrate on the performance of the scrubber, as measured by the number of transfer units. The results were as follows.

Air Flowrate (m^3/minute)	Number of Transfer Units (NTU)	Air Flowrate (m^3/minute)	Number of Transfer Units (NTU)
2.475	1.93	2.475	2.04
2.475	1.95	1.295	1.29
1.484	1.16	1.295	1.25
1.484	1.17	1.286	1.24
1.294	1.10	1.286	1.09
1.294	1.04	1.274	1.11
1.286	0.98	1.274	1.14
1.286	0.99	0.665	0.65
2.475	2.01	0.665	0.72 **SCRUBBER**

Source: Marshall, D. A., R. J. Sumner, and C. A. Shook; "Removal of SiO_2 Particles with an Ejector Venturi Scrubber," *Environmental Progress*, 14, 1995, 28–32

(a) Set up a scatter diagram.

(b) Use the least-squares method to find the regression coefficients b_0 and b_1.

(c) State the regression equation.

(d) Interpret the meaning of b_0 and b_1 in this problem.

(e) Predict the NTU for an air flowrate of 2.0.

(f) Would it be appropriate to use the model to predict the NTU for an air flowrate of 4.0? Why?

(g) Compute the coefficient of determination, r^2, and explain its meaning in this problem.

(h) Compute the coefficient of correlation.

(i) Compute the standard error of the estimate.

(j) Perform a residual analysis. Is there any evidence of a pattern in the residuals? Explain.

(k) At the 0.05 level of significance, is there evidence of a linear relationship between air flowrate and NTU?

(l) Set up a 95% confidence interval estimate of the average NTU for an air flowrate of 2.0.

(m) Set up a 95% prediction interval estimate of NTU for an air flowrate of 2.0.

(n) Set up a 95% confidence interval estimate of the population slope.

12.55 Measuring the height of a California redwood tree is a very difficult undertaking. It is understood that the height of a California redwood tree is related to other characteristics of the tree, including the diameter of the tree at the breast height (dbh) of a person. The following data represent the height and dbh for a sample of 21 California redwood trees.

Height (feet)	Diameter at Breast Height (inches)	Height (feet)	Diameter at Breast Height (inches)
122.00	20	164.00	40
193.50	36	203.25	52
166.50	18	174.00	30
82.00	10	159.00	22
133.50	21	205.00	42
156.00	29	223.50	45
172.50	51	195.00	54
81.00	11	232.50	39
148.00	26	190.50	36
113.00	12	100.00	8
84.00	13		**REDWOOD**

Suppose we want to develop a linear model to predict the height from the diameter at breast height.

(a) Set up a scatter diagram.

(b) Use the least-squares method to find the regression coefficients b_0 and b_1.

(c) State the regression equation.

(d) Interpret the meaning of b_0 and b_1 in this problem.

(e) Predict the height for a redwood tree that has a dbh of 30 inches.

(f) Would it be appropriate to use the model to predict the height for a redwood tree that has a dbh of 100 inches? Why?

(g) Compute the coefficient of determination, r^2, and explain its meaning in this problem.

(h) Compute the coefficient of correlation.

(i) Compute the standard error of the estimate.

(j) Perform a residual analysis. Is there any evidence of a pattern in the residuals? Explain.

(k) At the 0.05 level of significance, is there evidence of a linear relationship between the height of a redwood tree and the dbh?

(l) Set up a 95% confidence interval estimate of the average height for a redwood tree that has a dbh of 30 inches.

(m) Set up a 95% prediction interval estimate of the height for a redwood tree that has a dbh of 30 inches.

(n) Set up a 95% confidence interval estimate of the population slope.

(o) Do you have any concerns about either of the two variables involved in this analysis? Why or why not?

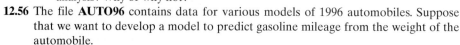

12.56 The file **AUTO96** contains data for various models of 1996 automobiles. Suppose that we want to develop a model to predict gasoline mileage from the weight of the automobile.

(a) Set up a scatter diagram.

(b) Use the least-squares method to find the regression coefficients b_0 and b_1.

(c) State the regression equation.

(d) Interpret the meaning of b_0 and b_1 in this problem.

(e) Predict the gasoline mileage for an automobile that weighs 2,500 pounds.

(f) Would it be appropriate to use the model to predict the gasoline mileage for an automobile that weighs 6,000 pounds? Why?

(g) Compute the coefficient of determination, r^2, and explain its meaning in this problem.

(h) Compute the coefficient of correlation.

(i) Compute the standard error of the estimate.

(j) Perform a residual analysis. Is there any evidence of a pattern in the residuals? Explain.

(k) At the 0.05 level of significance, is there evidence of a linear relationship between the weight of an automobile and the gasoline mileage?

(l) Set up a 95% confidence interval estimate of the average gasoline mileage for automobiles that weigh 2,500 pounds.

(m) Set up a 95% prediction interval estimate of the gasoline mileage for an automobile that weighs 2,500 pounds.

(n) Set up a 95% confidence interval estimate of the population slope.

12.57 A study was conducted on men with moderate hypercholesterolemia. Previous research indicates that increased calcium intake might reduce the serum cholesterol level. Data were collected for a sample of 13 men with moderate hypercholesterolemia. The results were as follows.

Serum Cholesterol mmol/L	Calcium Intake mg/d	Serum Cholesterol mmol/L	Calcium Intake mg/d
5.99	814	6.15	386
6.46	323	6.38	189
6.30	273	6.15	680
6.77	519	5.71	365
5.50	379	6.54	926
5.68	547	6.51	252
6.25	400		**CALCIUM**

Suppose that we want to develop a linear model to predict serum cholesterol from calcium intake.

(a) Set up a scatter diagram.

(b) Use the least-squares method to find the regression coefficients b_0 and b_1.

(c) State the regression equation.

(d) Interpret the meaning of b_0 and b_1 in this problem.

(e) Predict the serum cholesterol for a man who has a calcium intake of 500 mg/d.

(f) Would it be appropriate to use the model to predict the serum cholesterol for a man who has a calcium intake of 1,500 mg/d? Why?

(g) Compute the coefficient of determination, r^2, and explain its meaning in this problem.

(h) Compute the coefficient of correlation.

(i) Compute the standard error of the estimate.

(j) Perform a residual analysis. Is there any evidence of a pattern in the residuals? Explain.

(k) At the .05 level of significance, is there evidence of a linear relationship between the calcium intake and the serum cholesterol?

(l) Set up a 95% confidence interval estimate of the average serum cholesterol for men who have a calcium intake of 500 mg/d.

(m) Set up a 95% prediction interval of serum cholesterol for a man who has a calcium intake of 500 mg/d.

(n) Set up a 95% confidence interval estimate of the population slope.

12.58 In Problem 2.57 on page 89, fat and cholesterol information concerning popular protein foods (fresh red meats, poultry, and fish) was provided.
  (a) Determine the coefficient of correlation between fat and cholesterol for the protein foods.
  (b) At the 0.05 level of significance, determine which correlations are different from zero.

12.59 In Section 3.1 and Problem 3.26 on page 126, the pH values, conductivity, total aerobic microbial population, and total organic carbon of water samples were measured.
  (a) Determine the coefficient of correlation between each pair of variables.
  (b) At the 0.05 level of significance, determine which correlations are different from zero.

12.60 In Problem 3.28 on page 128, data were provided concerning emission of hydrocarbons, of carbon monoxide, and of nitrogen oxide from a sample of 46 automobiles.
  (a) Determine the coefficient of correlation between each pair of variables.
  (b) At the 0.05 level of significance, determine which correlations are different from zero.

WHITNEY GOURMET CAT FOOD COMPANY CASE

One of the concerns of the company is the ability to forecast product demand accurately over the next few months. The ability to forecast with a minimum amount of error directly affects the sales force of the company and its manufacturing goals. Underestimating sales will result in shortages of the Whitney product line on retailers' shelves, with the possibility of loss of consumer loyalty through brand switching and the need for costly overtime production to make up for these shortages. Overestimating sales can lead to high inventory levels, to the possibility that product in a distributor's warehouse will become outdated and lose quality, and to a negative effect on the cash flow of the company.

A team consisting of managers and sales associates was convened to try to develop a better mechanism for forecasting sales. Will Lacey, the department head, asked Allison

Abramski, who specialized in forecasting, to provide some ideas about how the forecasting methods used could be improved. Allison, who was recently hired by the company to provide special skills in quantitative forecasting methods, asked the team how sales forecasting had been done in the past. Caesar Penia, a member of the team, answered that what he usually did was to examine sales in the previous two months and the previous year's sales in the time period for which they were trying to predict. Because the company was growing, he then increased these figures by an "expansion factor" based on the growth rate. Caesar added that the forecasts were sometimes pretty accurate and sometimes off-base. The group discussed possible reasons for the inaccuracy of these forecasts. They suspected that it might have something to do with the fact that, in some months in

TABLE WG12.1

NUMBER OF SALES OUTLETS AND MONTHLY SALES VOLUME (IN CASES OF 24 CANS) OF WHITNEY CANNED CAT FOOD, FOR A TWO-YEAR TIME PERIOD

Time Period	Sales Outlets	Cases Sold	Time Period	Sales Outlets	Cases Sold	Time Period	Sales Outlets	Cases Sold
1	412	23,123	9	596	26,445	17	789	32,361
2	443	18,092	10	621	26,344	18	818	37,687
3	456	11,513	11	642	23,429	19	850	32,520
4	479	18,268	12	667	31,053	20	875	39,691
5	502	20,441	13	686	28,071	21	898	41,136
6	520	23,961	14	714	33,598	22	944	43,380
7	558	25,462	15	742	35,274	23	974	44,149
8	587	18,751	16	775	30,160	24	1,016	41,228

WG12

the last year, many new sales outlets were added, whereas in other months the channels of distribution were unchanged from the previous month. Allison suggested that data for the past two years be obtained from company records. She was particularly interested in obtaining data on the sales volume for each month. She recommended that sales to veterinarians be excluded from the analysis, because the amount of sales per month they represented was a very small proportion of total sales. Table WG12.1 indicates the sales for the month and the number of retail sales outlets for the Whitney product line.

Exercises

WG12.1 What criticism can you make concerning the method that Caesar has been using to make forecasts?

WG12.2 What factors other than number of sales outlets might be useful in predicting cases sold? Explain.

WG12.3 **(a)** Analyze the data presented in Table WG12.1, and develop a statistical model to predict the sales of cases of canned cat food from the number of sales outlets. Write a report giving detailed findings concerning the model that has been fitted to the data.

(b) If 1,050 sales outlets are expected in the coming month, predict the number of cases that you would expect to be sold. Indicate the assumptions upon which this prediction is based. Do you think these assumptions are valid? Explain.

(c) What would be the danger of predicting sales one year from now (when you expect that there will be 1,500 sales outlets)? Explain.

REFERENCES

1. Anscombe, F. J.; "Graphs in Statistical Analysis," *American Statistician,* 1973, Vol. 27, pp. 17–21
2. Hoaglin, D. C. and R. Welsch; "The Hat Matrix in Regression and ANOVA," *The American Statistician,* 1978, Vol. 32, pp. 17–22
3. Hosmer, D. and S. Lemeshow; *Applied Logistic Regression;* New York: John Wiley, 1989
4. Microsoft Excel 2000; Redmond, WA: Microsoft Corp., 1999
5. *MINITAB for Windows Version 12;* State College, PA: MINITAB, Inc., 1998
6. Neter, J., M. H. Kutner, C. J. Nachtsheim, and W. Wasserman; *Applied Linear Statistical Models,* 4th ed.; Homewood, IL: Richard D. Irwin, 1996

APPENDIX 12.1   *Using Microsoft Excel for Simple Linear Regression and Correlation*

Using Microsoft Excel to Obtain a Scatter Diagram

To generate a scatter diagram to plot the relationship between an X variable and a Y variable, use the XY (Scatter) choice of the Chart Wizard. As an example, consider the drilling problem of Section 12.3. To generate a scatter diagram that explores the relationship between the drilling depth and the drilling time, open the **DRILL.XLS** workbook, and click the **Data** sheet tab. Verify that the drilling data of Table 12.1 on page 570 have been entered into columns A and B.

Select **Insert | Chart.** In the Step 1 dialog box, select the **Standard Types** tab, and then select **XY (Scatter)** from the Chart type: list box. Select the first (top) choice from the Chart sub-types:, which is identified as "Scatter. Compares pairs of values" when selected. Click the **Next** button. In the Step 2 dialog box, select the **Data Range** tab. Enter **A1:B51** in the Data range: edit box. Select the **Columns** option button in the Series in: group. Click the **Next** button. In the Step 3 dialog box, select the **Titles** tab. Enter **Regression Analysis for Drilling** in the Chart title: edit box, **Depth** in the Value (X) Axis: edit box, and **Time** in the Value (Y) axis: edit box. Select the **Gridlines** tab, and deselect all the check boxes. Select the **Legend** tab. Deselect the Show legend check box. Click the **Next** button. In the Step 4 dialog box, select the **As new sheet:** option button, and enter **Trend** in the edit box to the right of the option button. Click the **Finish** button. The Chart Wizard inserts a chart sheet containing the scatter diagram for the data of Table 12.1, similar to the one shown in Figure 12.3 on page 571.

When generating scatter diagrams, the Chart Wizard always assumes that the first column (or row) of data of the data range entered in the Step 2 dialog box contains values for the X variable (as it does in the preceding example). Had the X variable data been located in the second column of the data range, it would have been necessary to select the Series tab of the Step 2 dialog box and change the cell ranges in the X Values: and Y Values: edit boxes. Furthermore, because of a quirk in this wizard, the revised cell ranges must be entered as formulas that include sheet names; for example, =Data!A2:B51. Using the simplified cell range form, for example, =A2:B51, would cause Microsoft Excel to display the misleading error message, "The formula you typed contains an error."

After the Chart Wizard generates a scatter diagram, we can modify the chart by adding a trend line, the regression equation, and the value of r^2. As an example, consider the chart produced in Figure 12.3 for the drilling problem of Section 12.3. To add a trend line to this scatter diagram, click the **Trend** sheet tab. Select **Chart | Add Trendline**. (*Note:* The Chart choice appears on the Microsoft Excel menu bar only when a chart or chart sheet is selected.) In the Add Trendline dialog box, select the **Type** tab, and select the **Linear** choice in the Trend/Regression type group. Select the **Options** tab, and select the **Automatic** option button and **the Display equation on chart and Display R-squared value on chart** check boxes. Click the **OK** button. Microsoft Excel modifies the scatter diagram by adding a line of regression, the regression equation, and the value of the r^2 to the scatter diagram. The modified scatter diagram will be similar to the one shown in Figure 12.6 on page 574.

Using Microsoft Excel for Simple Linear Regression

To calculate the coefficients of the simple linear regression equation, use the **Regression | Simple Linear Regression** choice of the PHStat add-in. This add-in modifies and extends the output generated by the Data Analysis Regression tool, which can also be used to calculate the regression coefficients. As an example, consider the drilling problem of Section 12.3. To calculate the coefficients of the simple linear regression equation that represents the relationship between the drilling depth and the drilling time, open the **DRILL.XLS** workbook, and click the **Data** sheet tab. Verify that the drilling depth and the drilling time from Table 12.1 on page 570 have been entered into columns A and B. Select **PHStat | Regression | Simple Linear Regression**. In the Simple Linear Regression dialog box, enter **B1:B51** in the Y Variable Cell Range: edit box. Enter **A1:A51** in the X Variable Cell Range: edit box. Select the **First cells in both ranges contain label** check box. Enter **95** in the Confidence lvl. for regression coefficients: edit box. Select the **Regression Statistics Table**, the **ANOVA and Coefficients Table**, the **Residual Table, and** the **Residual Plot** check boxes. Select the **Confidence and Prediction Interval for X =** check box, and enter **100** in its edit box. Enter 95 in the Confidence level for int. estimates: edit box. Enter **Regression Analysis for Drilling** in the Output Title: edit box. Click the **OK** button.

The add-in inserts a worksheet that contains the regression coefficients and other summary information for the simple linear regression for the Table 12.1 data. This worksheet is *not* dynamically changeable, so any changes made to the underlying drilling data would require using the PHStat add-in a second time to produce updated results.

Using Microsoft Excel to Obtain the Correlation Coefficient

We can use the CORREL worksheet function to calculate the correlation coefficient for two variables. The format of this function is:

CORREL(X variable cell range, Y variable cell range)

As an example, consider the cardiac output problem of Section 12.11. To implement the calculation for the correlation coefficient for this problem, open the **CARDIAC.XLS** workbook, and click the **Data** sheet tab. Verify that the patient, observer A, and observer B data of Table 9.7 on page 430 have been entered into columns A, B, and C, respectively. Enter the label Correlation Coefficient in cell E3. Enter the formula **=CORREL(B2:B24, C2:C24)** in cell F3.

APPENDIX 12.2   *Using MINITAB for Simple Linear Regression and Correlation*

MINITAB can be used for simple linear regression by using Stat | Regression | Regression. To illustrate the use of MINITAB for simple linear regression with the drilling example of this chapter, open the **DRILL.MTW** file. To analyze only the data for the dry drilling holes, select **Manip | Stack/Unstack | Unstack a Block of Columns.** Enter **C1** or **'Depth'** and **C2** or **'Time'** in the Unstack the following columns: edit box. Enter **C3** or **'Type'** in the Using subscripts in: edit box. In the Store unstacked data in blocks (one per subscript): edit box, enter **C4 C5** on the first line and **C6 C7** on the second line. Click the **OK** button. Enter the label **Depth-Dry** in C4 and the label **Time-Dry** in C5. Select **Stat | Regression | Regression.** Enter **C5** or **'Time-Dry'** in the Response edit box and **C4** or **'Depth-Dry'** in the Predictors edit box. Click the **Graphs** button. In the Graphs dialog box, for Residuals for Plots, select the **Regular** option button. For Residual Plots, select the **Histogram of residuals** check box. In the residuals versus the variables edit box, enter **C4** (or **'Depth-Dry'**). Click the **OK** button to return to the Regression dialog box. Click the **Results** button. In the Regression-Results dialog box, click the **Regression equation, table of coefficients, s, R-squared,** and **basic analysis of variance** option buttons. Click the **OK** button to return to the Regression dialog box. Click the **Options** button. In the Prediction interval for new observations: edit box, enter **100.** In the Confidence level edit box, enter **95.** Click the **OK** button to return to the Regression dialog box. Click the **OK** button. The results obtained will be similar to those of Figure 12.5 on page 573.

chapter

13 Multiple Regression

"I hear, I forget; I see, I remember; I do, I understand."

AN ANCIENT CHINESE PROVERB

USING STATISTICS

The Mountain States Potato Company is a potato-processing firm in eastern Idaho. A by-product of the production process, called a filter cake, is sold to area feedlots as cattle feed. Recently, the feedlot owners complained that the cattle are not gaining weight. They believe the problem may be the filter cake purchased from the Mountain States Potato Company.

Initially, all that is known of the filter-cake system is that historical records show that the solids had been running in the neighborhood of 11.5% in years past. Currently, the solids are running in the 8–9% range. Several additions have been made to the plant in recent years that significantly increased the water and solids volume and the clarifier temperature. What is actually affecting the solids is a mystery, but the plant needs to get rid of its solid waste, so something has to be done quickly. The only practical solution is to determine some way to get the solids content back up to the previous levels. Individuals involved in the process are asked to identify variables whose values could affect the solids content.

13.1 DEVELOPING THE MULTIPLE-REGRESSION MODEL

In our discussion of simple regression in Chapter 12, we focused on a model in which one independent or explanatory variable X was used to predict the value of a dependent or response variable Y. It is often the case that a better-fitting model can be developed if more than one explanatory variable is considered. Thus, in this chapter we extend our discussion to consider **multiple-regression** models, in which several explanatory variables can be used to predict the value of a dependent variable.

To study an application of multiple regression, we turn to the *Using Statistics* example above. We begin our analysis of the potato-processing data by examining two independent variables as predictors of the percent of solids in the filter cake: the pH (which is a measure of the acidity of the clarifier) and the pressure in the vacuum line below the fluid line on the rotating drum (the variable labeled as LOWER in the data file). Data from 54 observations were obtained by monitoring the process. These data are stored in the file named **POTATO.**

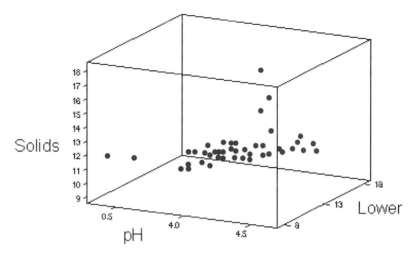

Figure 13.1 Scatter diagram obtained from MINITAB of pH (X_1), lower pressure (X_2), and percent of solids (Y)

With two explanatory variables in the multiple-regression model, a scatter diagram of the points can be plotted on a three-dimensional graph obtained from MINITAB, as shown in Figure 13.1.

Interpreting the Regression Coefficients

When there are several explanatory variables present, the simple linear regression model of Equation (12.1) on page 568 can be extended by assuming a linear relationship between each explanatory variable and the dependent variable. For example, with k explanatory variables, the multiple linear regression model is expressed as follows.

MULTIPLE-REGRESSION MODEL WITH k INDEPENDENT VARIABLES

$$Y_i = \beta_0 + \beta_1 X_{1i} + \beta_2 X_{2i} + \beta_3 X_{3i} + \cdots + \beta_k X_{ki} + \varepsilon_i \qquad (13.1)$$

where

$\beta_0 = Y$-intercept

$\beta_1 = $ slope of Y with variable X_1 when variables $X_2, X_3, \ldots, X_k$ are held constant

$\beta_2 = $ slope of Y with variable X_2 when variables $X_1, X_3, \ldots, X_k$ are held constant

$\beta_3 = $ slope of Y with variable X_3 when variables $X_1, X_2, X_4, \ldots, X_k$ are held constant

.
.
.

$\beta_k = $ slope of Y with variable X_k when variables $X_1, X_2, X_3, \ldots, X_{k-1}$ are held constant

$\varepsilon_i = $ random error in Y for observation i

For data with two explanatory variables, the multiple linear regression model is expressed as follows:

MULTIPLE REGRESSION MODEL WITH TWO INDEPENDENT VARIABLES

$$Y_i = \beta_0 + \beta_1 X_{1i} + \beta_2 X_{2i} + \varepsilon_i \tag{13.2}$$

where

$\beta_0 = Y$ intercept

$\beta_1 =$ slope of Y with variable X_1 when variable X_2 is held constant

$\beta_2 =$ slope of Y with variable X_2 when variable X_1 is held constant

$\varepsilon_i =$ random error in Y for observation i

This multiple linear regression model can be compared to the simple linear regression model [Equation (12.1)], expressed as follows:

$$Y_i = \beta_0 + \beta_1 X_i + \varepsilon_i$$

In the case of the simple linear regression model, we note that the slope β_1 represents the change in the mean of Y per unit change in X and does not take into account any variables other than the single independent variable included in the model. In the multiple linear regression model [Equation (13.2)], the slope β_1 represents the change in the mean of Y per unit change in X_1, taking into account the effect of X_2. It is referred to as a **net regression coefficient.**

As in the case of simple linear regression, the sample regression coefficients (b_0, b_1, and b_2) are used as estimates of the population parameters (β_0, β_1, and β_2). Thus, the regression equation for a multiple linear regression model with two explanatory variables is expressed as follows:

MULTIPLE LINEAR REGRESSION EQUATION WITH 2 INDEPENDENT VARIABLES

$$\hat{Y}_i = b_0 + b_1 X_{1i} + b_2 X_{2i} \tag{13.3}$$

By using the least squares method, the values of the three sample regression coefficients are obtained from Microsoft Excel (as in Appendix 13.1) and MINITAB (as in Appendix 13.2). Figure 13.2 presents partial output for the potato-processing data from Microsoft Excel and Figure 13.3 presents partial output from MINITAB.

From Figure 13.2 or 13.3, we observe that the computed values of the regression coefficients in this problem are as follows

$b_0 = 3.8162$

$b_1 = 2.8437$

$b_2 = -0.2805$

Therefore, the multiple-regression equation can be expressed as

$$\hat{Y}_i = 3.8162 + 2.8437 X_{1i} - 0.2805 X_{2i}$$

S_{YX}

	A	B	C	D	E	F	G
1	Multiple Regression for Potato Study						
2							
3	*Regression Statistics*						
4	Multiple R	0.64481978					
5	R Square	0.415792549					
6	Adjusted R Square	0.392882453					
7	Standard Error	1.070159691					
8	Observations	54					
9							
10	ANOVA						
11		*df*	*SS*	*MS*	*F*	*Significance F*	
12	Regression	2	41.56970707	20.78485354	18.14887842	1.11548E-06	
13	Residual	51	58.40732997	1.145241764			
14	Total	53	99.97703704				
15							
16		*Coefficients*	*Standard Error*	*t Stat*	*P-value*	*Lower 95%*	*Upper 95%*
17	Intercept	3.816249739	2.339343029	1.631333965	0.108980582	-0.880173744	8.512673221
18	PH	2.843701884	0.554451281	5.128857989	4.56187E-06	1.730595347	3.956808421
19	Lower Pressure	-0.280453647	0.074543486	-3.762282442	0.000435688	-0.430105823	-0.13080147

b_0

b_1

b_2

Figure 13.2   Partial output obtained from Microsoft Excel for the potato-processing data

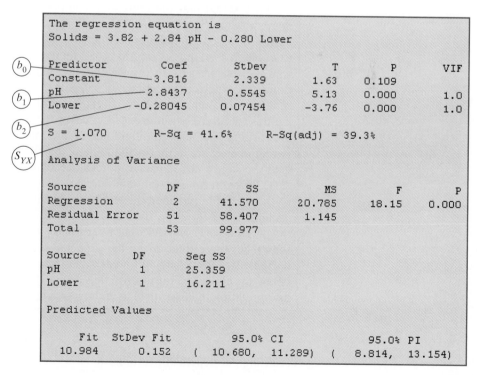

Figure 13.3   Partial output obtained from MINITAB for the potato-processing data

where

$\hat{Y}_i$ = predicted percentage of solids in the filter cake

X_{1i} = pH of the clarifier

X_{2i} = pressure in the vacuum line below the fluid line on the rotating drum

The Y intercept b_0, computed to be 3.8162, estimates the expected percentage of solids in the filter cake when the average pH of the clarifier is zero and the pressure in the vacuum line below the fluid line on the rotating drum is zero. As is sometimes the case, these values do not make sense in the context of the problem.

The slope of percentage of solids in the filter cake (b_1, computed to be 2.8437) with pH of the clarifier means that, for a filter cake with a given pressure in the vacuum line below the fluid line on the rotating drum, the expected percentage of solids is estimated to increase by 2.8437 percent for each 1-unit increase in the pH of the clarifier. The slope of the percentage of solids in the filter cake (b_2, computed to be -0.2805) with the pressure in the vacuum line below the fluid line on the rotating drum means that, for a given pH of the clarifier, the expected percentage of solids in the filter cake is estimated to decrease by 0.2805 percent for each additional unit of pressure in the vacuum line below the fluid line on the rotating drum.

COMMENT: INTERPRETING THE SLOPES IN MULTIPLE REGRESSION

We have stated that the regression coefficients in multiple regression are net regression coefficients that measure the change in Y per unit change in a particular X when one is holding constant the effects of the other X-variables. For example, in our study of potato processing, we have stated that, for a filter cake with a given pressure in the vacuum line below the fluid line on the rotating drum, the expected percentage of solids is estimated to increase by 2.8437 percent for each unit increase in the pH of the clarifier. Another way of interpreting this is to think of different filter cakes with an equal amount of pressure in the vacuum line below the fluid line on the rotating drum. For such filter cakes (with the pressure in the vacuum line below the fluid line on the rotating drum held the same), the expected percentage of solids is predicted to increase by 2.8437 percent for each one-unit increase in the pH of the clarifier.

In a similar manner, the slope of percentage of solids with pressure in the vacuum line below the fluid line on the rotating drum can be viewed from the perspective of two different filter cakes (with the pH of the clarifier held the same). For these filter cakes, the expected percentage of solids is estimated to decrease by 0.2805 percent for each unit increase in pressure in the vacuum line below the fluid line on the rotating drum. It is this conditional nature of the interpretation that is critical to understanding the magnitude of each slope.

Predicting the Dependent Variable Y

Now that the multiple-regression model has been fitted to these data, we can predict the percentage of solids and develop a confidence interval estimate and a prediction interval estimate by assuming that the regression model fitted is an appropriate one.

Suppose that we want to predict the percentage of solids for a filter cake that has a clarifier pH of 4 and a pressure of 15 in the vacuum line below the fluid line on the rotating drum. From our multiple regression equation,

$$\hat{Y}_i = 3.8162 + 2.8437X_{1i} - 0.2805X_{2i}$$

with $X_{1i} = 4$ and $X_{2i} = 15$, we have

$$\hat{Y}_i = 3.8162 + 2.8437(4) - 0.2805(15)$$

and thus

$$\hat{Y}_i = 10.984$$

Therefore, we estimate that the percentage of solids would average 10.984 for filter cakes with a pH of 4 and a pressure of 15 in the vacuum line below the fluid line on the rotating drum.

The prediction of $\hat{Y}_i$ has now been obtained; after we conduct a residual analysis (see Section 13.2), our next step involves the development of a desired confidence interval estimate of the mean response and a prediction interval for the individual response. In Section 12.9, methods for obtaining these estimates were examined for the simple linear regression model. The development of similar estimates for the multiple regression model is more complex computationally; however, confidence and prediction interval estimates obtained from MINITAB for the case of predicting the percentage of solids for filter cakes with a pH of 4 and a pressure of 15 in the vacuum line below the fluid line on the rotating drum are presented in Figure 13.3 on page 619. (See Appendix 13.1 for using the PHStat add-in for Microsoft Excel to obtain these estimates.) The 95% *confidence interval estimate* of the average percentage of solids under these circumstances is between 10.68 and 11.289 percent; the *prediction interval estimate* for an individual filter cake is between 8.814 and 13.154 percent. Once again we note that, because the prediction interval is for a single filter cake, it is much wider than the estimate for the average of all filter cakes.

Coefficients of Multiple Determination

Recall from Section 12.3 that, once a regression model has been developed, we can compute the coefficient of determination, r^2. In multiple regression, there are at least two explanatory variables, so the **coefficient of multiple determination** represents the proportion of the variation in Y that is explained by the set of explanatory variables selected. For data with two explanatory variables, the coefficient of multiple determination ($R^2_{Y.12}$) is given by the following calculation:

THE COEFFICIENT OF MULTIPLE DETERMINATION

The coefficient of multiple determination is equal to the regression sum of squares divided by the total sum of squares.

$$R^2_{Y.12} = \frac{\text{SSR}}{\text{SST}} \tag{13.4}$$

where

SSR = regression sum of squares

SST = total sum of squares

In the potato-processing example, from Figure 13.2 or 13.3 on page 619, SSR = 41.5697 and SST = 99.977 (rounded). Thus,

$$R^2_{Y.12} = \frac{SSR}{SST} = \frac{41.5697}{99.977} = .4158$$

This coefficient of multiple determination, computed to be 0.4158, means that 41.58% of the variation in the percentage of solids can be explained by the variation in the pH of the clarifier and the pressure in the vacuum line below the fluid line on the rotating drum. However, when dealing with multiple-regression models, some researchers suggest that an **adjusted R^2** be computed to reflect both the number of explanatory variables in the model and the sample size. This approach is especially necessary when we are comparing two or more regression models that predict the same dependent variable but have different numbers of explanatory or predictor variables. The adjusted R^2 is computed as follows:

ADJUSTED R^2

$$R^2_{adj} = 1 - \left[(1 - R^2_{Y.12...k}) \frac{n-1}{n-k-1} \right] \tag{13.5}$$

where k = number of explanatory variables in the regression equation.

Thus, for our potato-processing data, $R^2_{Y.12} = 0.4158$, $n = 54$, and $k = 2$, so

$$R^2_{adj} = 1 - \left[(1 - R^2_{Y.12}) \frac{(54-1)}{(54-2-1)} \right]$$

$$= 1 - \left[(1 - 0.4158) \frac{53}{51} \right]$$

$$= 1 - 0.6071$$

$$= 0.3929$$

Hence, 39.29% of the variation in the percentage of solids can be explained by our multiple regression model (adjusted for number of predictors and sample size).

PROBLEMS

13.1 Suppose that you have obtained the following multiple-regression model:

$$\hat{Y}_i = 10 + 5X_{1i} + 3X_{2i} \text{ and } R^2_{Y.12} = 0.60$$

(a) Interpret the meaning of the slopes.
(b) Interpret the meaning of the Y-intercept.
(c) Interpret the meaning of the coefficient of multiple determination $R^2_{Y.12}$.

13.2 A researcher for a major shoe manufacturer is considering the development of a new brand of running shoes. The researcher wishes to determine which variables can be used in predicting durability (or the effect of long-term impact). Two independent variables are to be considered, X_1 (FOREIMP), a measurement of the forefoot shock-absorbing capability, and X_2 (MIDSOLE), a measurement of the change in impact properties over time, along with the dependent variable Y (LTIMP), which is a measure of the long-term ability to absorb shock after a repeated impact test. A random sample of 15 types of running shoes currently manufactured was selected for testing. From Microsoft Excel, the following (partial) output is provided.

ANOVA	df	SS	MS	F	Significance F
Regression	2	12.61020	6.30510	97.69	0.0001
Residual	12	0.77453	0.06454		
Total	14	13.38473			

Variable	Coefficients	Standard Error	t Stat	p-value
INTERCEPT	−0.02686	0.06905	−0.39	
FOREIMP	0.79116	0.06295	12.57	0.0000
MIDSOLE	0.60484	0.07174	8.43	0.0000

(a) Assuming that each independent variable is linearly related to long-term impact, state the multiple-regression equation.
(b) Interpret the meaning of the slopes in this problem.
(c) Compute the coefficient of multiple determination $R^2_{Y.12}$, and interpret its meaning.
(d) Compute the adjusted R^2.

13.3 The file **AUTO96** contains data on 89 automobile models from the year 1996. Among the variables included are the gasoline mileage, the weight (in pounds), and the length (in inches) of each automobile. Suppose we wanted to develop a model to predict the gasoline mileage based on the weight and the length of each automobile.

(a) State the multiple regression equation.
(b) Interpret the meaning of the slopes in this equation.
(c) Predict the average gasoline mileage for an automobile that has a weight of 3,000 pounds and a length of 195 inches.
(d) Interpret the meaning of the coefficient of multiple determination $R^2_{Y.12}$ in this problem.

13.4 In Problem 12.55 on page 610, the diameter at breast height was used to develop a simple linear regression model to predict the height of redwood trees. Suppose we also wanted to use the bark thickness (inches) to predict the height of redwood trees. Use the **REDWOOD** file.

(a) State the multiple-regression equation.
(b) Interpret the meaning of the slopes in this equation.

(c) Predict the average height for a tree that has a breast diameter of 25 inches and a bark thickness of 2 inches.
(d) Interpret the meaning of the coefficient of multiple determination $R^2_{Y.12}$ in this problem.

13.5 An experiment was conducted in which the performances of ballasts used in fluorescent lighting were compared. The ballast efficiency factor (BEF) in foot-candles/watt was to be predicted based on light output (LO) in foot-candles and on the temperature of the lamp (Lamp) in degrees Celsius. The data were as follows.

BEF	LO	Lamp	BEF	LO	Lamp
0.480	43	37.8	0.571	41	32.2
0.490	42	40.4	0.564	41	30.6
0.483	43	34.7	0.576	40	37.5
0.482	42	38.8	0.548	39	29.7
0.583	40	30.6	0.588	41	35.9

BALLAST

(a) State the multiple-regression equation.
(b) Interpret the meaning of the slopes in this equation.
(c) Predict the average ballast efficiency factor for a ballast that has a light output of 40 foot-candles and a lamp temperature of 40° Celsius.
(d) Interpret the meaning of the coefficient of multiple determination $R^2_{Y.12}$ in this problem.

13.6 A flux chamber is a Plexiglas dome about two feet in diameter that is placed over soil, usually contaminated, for a period of time, to sample soil gases. A study was carried out at a suspected radon hot spot, to predict radon concentration (pCi/L) based on solar radiation (Ly/Day) and soil temperature (°F). The data is contained in the **RADON** file.

(a) State the multiple-regression equation.
(b) Interpret the meaning of the slopes in this equation.
(c) Predict the average radon concentration for a soil sample that has solar radiation of 100 (Ly/Day) and soil temperature of 71°F.
(d) Interpret the meaning of the coefficient of multiple determination $R^2_{Y.12}$ in this problem.

13.2 RESIDUAL ANALYSIS FOR THE MULTIPLE-REGRESSION MODEL

In Section 12.6, we utilized residual analysis to evaluate whether the simple linear regression model is appropriate for the set of data being studied. When examining a multiple linear regression model with two explanatory variables, the residual plots listed in Exhibit 13.1 are of particular interest.

EXHIBIT 13.1 Residual Plots used in Multiple Regression

1. Residuals versus X_{1i}
2. Residuals versus X_2
3. Residuals versus $\hat{Y}_i$
4. Residuals versus time.

The first residual plot examines the pattern of residuals for the predicted values of Y. If the residuals show a pattern for different values of the predicted value of Y, there is evidence of a possible curvilinear effect in at least one explanatory variable and/or the need to transform the Y variable. The second and third residual plots involve the explanatory variables. Patterns in the plot of the residuals versus an explanatory variable can indicate the existence of a curvilinear effect and, therefore, lead to the need to transform the explanatory variable. The fourth type of plot is used to investigate patterns in the residuals when the data have been collected in time order. From the residuals plot versus time, possible existence of positive autocorrelation among the residuals can be investigated. (See Reference 5.)

The residual plots are available as part of the output of virtually all statistical and spreadsheet software. Figure 13.4 displays the residual plots obtained from

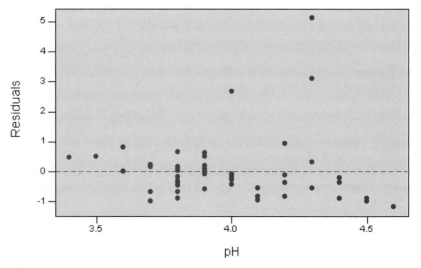

Figure 13.4 Residual plots for the potato-processing model obtained from MINITAB: Panel A; Panel B; Panel C

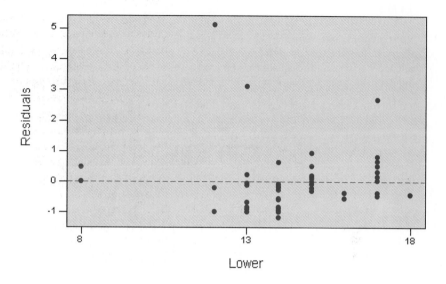

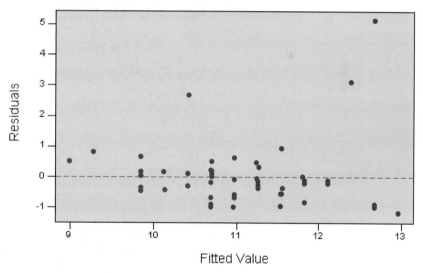

Figure 13.4   (*Continued*)

MINITAB for the potato-processing example. We can observe from Figure 13.4 that there appears to be very little or no pattern in the relationship between the residuals and either, the value of X_1 (pH), the value of X_2 (lower pressure), or the predicted value of Y. Thus, we conclude that the multiple linear regression model is appropriate for predicting the percentage of solids. We note that there is one very large residual (for observation 35) that might need investigation by those familiar with the process.

PROBLEMS

13.7 In Problem 13.3 on page 623, the weight and length of an automobile were used to predict gasoline mileage. Perform a residual analysis on your results and determine the adequacy of fit of the model.

13.8 In Problem 13.4 on page 623, the breast diameter and the bark thickness were used to predict the height of redwood trees. Perform a residual analysis on your results and determine the adequacy of fit of the model.

13.9 In Problem 13.5 on page 623, the light output and the temperature of the lamp were used to predict the ballast efficiency factor. Perform a residual analysis on your results and determine the adequacy of fit of the model.

13.10 In Problem 13.6 on page 623, the solar radiation and soil temperature were used to predict radon concentration. Perform a residual analysis on your results and determine the adequacy of fit of the model.

 ## 13.3 TESTING FOR THE SIGNIFICANCE OF THE MULTIPLE REGRESSION MODEL

Now that we have used residual analysis to assure ourselves that the multiple linear regression model is appropriate, we can determine whether there is a significant relationship between the dependent variable and the set of explanatory variables. Because there are two explanatory variables, the null and alternative hypothesis can be set up as follows.

$$H_0: \beta_1 = \beta_2 = 0$$

(There is no linear relationship between the dependent variable and the explanatory variables.)

$$H_1: \text{At least one } \beta_j \neq 0$$

(There is a linear relationship between the dependent variable and at least one of the explanatory variables.)

As was done in Section 12.7 for simple linear regression, this null hypothesis is tested with an F test, as summarized in Table 13.1.

TABLE 13.1

ANOVA TABLE FOR TESTING THE SIGNIFICANCE OF A SET OF REGRESSION COEFFICIENTS IN A MULTIPLE-REGRESSION MODEL WITH k EXPLANATORY VARIABLES

Source	df	Sums of Squares	Mean Square (Variance)	F
Regression	k	SSR	$MSR = \dfrac{SSR}{k}$	$F = \dfrac{MSR}{MSE}$
Error	$n-k-1$	SSE	$MSE = \dfrac{SSE}{n-k-1}$	
Total	$n-1$	SST		

F TEST FOR THE ENTIRE REGRESSION MODEL
IN MULTIPLE REGRESSION

$$F = \frac{MSR}{MSE}$$

(13.6)

where

k = number of explanatory variables in the regression model

F = test statistic from an F distribution with k and $n - k - 1$ degrees of freedom

The decision rule is

Reject H_0 at the α level of significance if $F > F_{u(k, n-k-1)}$;

otherwise do not reject H_0.

The complete set of computations for our potato-processing example is shown in Figure 13.2 and Figure 13.3 on page 619.

If the level of significance 0.05 is chosen, we can determine from Table A.7 that the critical value on the F distribution (with 2 and 51 degrees of freedom) is approximately 3.19, as depicted in Figure 13.5. By using Equation (13.6), the F statistic can be obtained from Figure 13.2 or Figure 13.3. Because $F = 18.15 > F_{u(2,51)} = 3.19$, or because the p-value $= 0.000001 < 0.05$, we can reject H_0 and conclude that at least one of the explanatory variables (pH and/or lower pressure) is related to the percentage of solids.

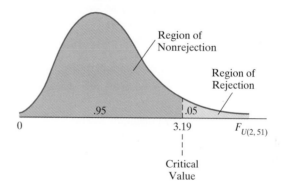

Figure 13.5 Testing for the significance of a set of regression coefficients at the 0.05 level of significance with 2 and 51 degrees of freedom

PROBLEMS

13.11 The following Analysis of Variance table was obtained from a multiple-regression model having two independent variables.

Source	Degrees of Freedom	Sum of Squares	Mean Square	F
Regression	2	60		
Error	18	120		
Total	20	180		

(a) Determine the Mean Square due to regression (MSR) and the Mean Square due to Error (MSE).
(b) Determine the computed F statistic.
(c) Determine whether there is a significant relationship between Y and the two explanatory variables at the 0.05 level of significance.

13.12 In Problem 13.2 on page 622, the durability of a running shoe was predicted from a measurement of the forefoot shock-absorbing capability and from a measurement of the change in impact properties over time. The following Analysis of Variance Table was obtained.

ANOVA	df	SS	MS	F	Significance F
Regression	2	12.61020	6.30510	97.69	0.0001
Residual	12	0.77453	0.06454		
Total	14	13.38473			

(a) Determine whether there is a significant relationship between long-term impact (durability) and at least one of the two explanatory variables at the 0.05 level of significance.
(b) Interpret the meaning of the p-value.
(c) Do the results in (a) and (b) imply that both of the independent variables are useful in predicting durability? Explain.

13.13 In Problem 13.3 on page 623, the weight and length of an automobile were used to predict gasoline mileage. Use the computer output that you obtained in solving that problem.
(a) Determine whether there is a significant relationship between gasoline mileage and at least one of the two explanatory variables (weight and length) at the 0.05 level of significance.
(b) Interpret the meaning of the p-value.
(c) Do the results in (a) and (b) imply that both of the independent variables are useful in predicting gasoline mileage? Explain.

13.14 In Problem 13.4 on page 623, breast diameter and the bark thickness were used to predict the height of redwood trees. Use the computer output that you obtained in solving that problem.
(a) Determine whether there is a significant relationship between height of redwood trees and at least one of the two explanatory variables (breast diameter and the bark thickness) at the 0.05 level of significance.
(b) Interpret the meaning of the p-value.
(c) Do the results in (a) and (b) imply that both of the independent variables are useful in predicting the height of redwood trees? Explain.

13.15 In Problem 13.5 on page 623, light output and the temperature of the lamp were used to predict the ballast efficiency factor. Use the computer output that you obtained in solving that problem.
(a) Determine whether there is a significant relationship between ballast efficiency factor and at least one of the two explanatory variables (light output and the temperature of the lamp) at the 0.05 level of significance.
(b) Interpret the meaning of the p-value.
(c) Do the results in (a) and (b) imply that both of the independent variables are useful in predicting the ballast efficiency factor? Explain.

13.16 In Problem 13.6 on page 623, solar radiation and soil temperature were used to predict radon concentration. Use the computer output that you obtained in solving that problem.
(a) Determine whether there is a significant relationship between radon concentration and the two explanatory variables (solar radiation and soil temperature) at the 0.05 level of significance.
(b) Interpret the meaning of the p-value.
(c) Do the results in (a) and (b) imply that both of the independent variables are useful in predicting radon concentration? Explain.

13.4 INFERENCES CONCERNING THE POPULATION REGRESSION COEFFICIENTS

In Section 12.7, a test of hypothesis was performed on the slope in a simple linear regression model to determine the significance of the relationship between X and Y. In addition, a confidence interval was used to estimate the population slope. In this section, these procedures will be extended to situations involving multiple regression.

Tests of Hypothesis

To test the hypothesis that the population slope β_1 was 0, we used Equation (12.11):

$$t = \frac{b_1}{s_{b_1}}$$

This equation can be generalized for multiple regression as follows:

TESTING FOR THE SLOPE IN MULTIPLE REGRESSION

$$t = \frac{b_j}{s_{b_j}} \tag{13.7}$$

where

k = number of explanatory variables in the regression equation

b_j = slope of variable j with Y when the effects of all other independent variables are held constant

s_{b_j} = standard error of the regression coefficient b_j

t = test statistic for variable j from a t distribution with $n - k - 1$ degrees of freedom

---

The results of this t test for each of the independent variables included in the regression model are provided as part of the output obtained in Figure 13.2 for Microsoft Excel and Figure 13.3 for MINITAB (see page 619).

Thus, if we wish to determine whether variable X_2 (lower pressure) has a significant effect on the percent of solids, taking into account the pH, the null and alternative hypotheses would be as follows:

H_0: $\beta_2 = 0$

H_1: $\beta_2 \neq 0$

From Equation (13.7), we have

$$t = \frac{b_2}{s_{b_2}}$$

and from the data of this example,

$$b_2 = -0.2805 \quad \text{and} \quad s_{b_2} = 0.0745$$

so

$$t = \frac{-0.2805}{0.0745} = -3.762$$

If the level of significance 0.05 is selected, from Table A.4 we find that, for 51 degrees of freedom, the critical values of t are -2.0076 and $+2.0076$. (See Figure 13.6.) From Figure 13.2 or 13.3 on page 619, we also observe that the p-value is 0.000436.

Because $t = -3.762 < t_{51} = -2.0076$, or because the p-value of $0.000436 < 0.05$, we reject H_0 and conclude that there is a significant relationship between variable X_2 (lower pressure) and the percentage of solids, taking into account the pH (X_1).

In a similar manner, we test for the significance of β_1, the slope of percentage of solids with the pH of the clarifier. From Figure 13.2 or 13.3 on page 619, $t = 5.129 > 2.0076$ (the critical value for t with 51 degrees of freedom for $\alpha = 0.05$) or the p-value $= 0.00000456 < 0.05$. Therefore, there is a significant relationship between pH (X_1) and the percentage of solids, taking into account the lower pressure (X_2).

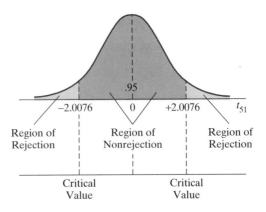

Figure 13.6   Testing for the significance of a regression coefficient at the 0.05 level of significance with 51 degrees of freedom

For each of these two X variables, the test of significance for a particular regression coefficient is actually a test for the significance of adding a particular variable into a regression model given that the other variables have already been included. Therefore, the t test for the regression coefficient is equivalent to testing for the contribution of each explanatory variable.

Confidence Interval Estimation

Instead of testing the significance of a regression coefficient, we might be more concerned with estimating the population value of a regression coefficient. In multiple-regression analysis, a confidence interval estimate for the slope can be obtained as follows:

CONFIDENCE INTERVAL ESTIMATE FOR THE SLOPE

$$b_j \pm t_{n-k-1} s_{b_j} \tag{13.8}$$

For example, if we wish to obtain a 95% confidence interval estimate of the population slope β_1 [the effect of pH (X_1) on the percentage of solids Y, holding constant the lower pressure (X_2)], from Equation (13.8) and Figure 13.2 we have

$$b_1 \pm t_{n-k-1} s_{b_1}$$

The critical value of t at the 95% confidence level with 51 degrees of freedom is 2.0076 (see Table A.4), so we have

$$2.8437 \pm (2.0076)(0.554445)$$
$$1.731 \leq \beta_1 \leq 3.957$$

Thus, taking into account the effect of lower pressure, we estimate that the effect of pH is to increase the average percentage of solids by between approximately 1.73 and 3.96 percent. From a hypothesis-testing viewpoint, because this confidence interval does not include 0, we conclude that the regression coefficient β_1 has a significant effect.

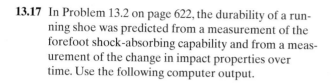

PROBLEMS

13.17 In Problem 13.2 on page 622, the durability of a running shoe was predicted from a measurement of the forefoot shock-absorbing capability and from a measurement of the change in impact properties over time. Use the following computer output.

Variable	Coefficients	Standard Error	t Stat	p-value
Intercept	−0.02686	0.06905	−0.39	
Foreimp	0.79116	0.06295	12.57	.0000
Midsole	0.60484	0.07174	8.43	.0000

(a) Set up a 95% confidence interval estimate of the population slope between long-term impact (durability) and forefoot impact.

(b) At the 0.05 level of significance, determine whether each explanatory variable makes a significant contribution to the regression model. On the basis of these results, indicate the independent variables that should be included in this model.

13.18 In Problem 13.3 on page 623, the weight and length of an automobile were used to predict gasoline mileage. Use the computer output that you obtained in solving that problem.

(a) Set up 95% confidence interval estimates of the population slopes between gasoline mileage and the weight of an automobile and between gasoline mileage and the length of an automobile.

(b) At the 0.05 level of significance, determine whether each explanatory variable makes a significant contribution to the regression model. On the basis of these results, indicate the independent variables that should be included in this model.

13.19 In Problem 13.4 on page 623, breast diameter and the bark thickness were used to predict the height of redwood trees. Use the computer output that you obtained in solving that problem.

(a) Set up 95% confidence interval estimates of the population slopes between the height of redwood trees and breast diameter and between the height of redwood trees and the bark thickness.

(b) At the 0.05 level of significance, determine whether each explanatory variable makes a significant contribution to the regression model. On the basis of these results, indicate the independent variables that should be included in this model.

13.20 In Problem 13.5 on page 623, light output and the temperature of the lamp were used to predict the ballast efficiency factor. Use the computer output that you obtained in solving that problem.

(a) Set up 95% confidence interval estimates of the population slopes between the ballast efficiency factor and light output and between the ballast efficiency factor and the temperature of the lamp.

(b) At the 0.05 level of significance, determine whether each explanatory variable makes a significant contribution to the regression model. On the basis of these results, indicate the independent variables that should be included in this model.

13.21 In Problem 13.6 on page 623, solar radiation and soil temperature were used to predict radon concentration. Use the computer output that you obtained in solving that problem.

(a) Set up 95% confidence interval estimates of the population slopes between radon concentration and solar radiation and between radon concentration and soil temperature.

(b) At the 0.05 level of significance, determine whether each explanatory variable makes a significant contribution to the regression model. On the basis of these results, indicate the independent variables that should be included in this model.

13.5 TESTING PORTIONS OF THE MULTIPLE-REGRESSION MODEL

In developing a multiple-regression model, the objective is to utilize only those explanatory variables that are useful in predicting the value of a dependent variable. If an explanatory variable is not helpful in making this prediction, it could be deleted from the multiple-regression model, and a model with fewer explanatory variables could be used instead.

An alternative method for determining the contribution of an explanatory variable is called the **partial *F*-test criterion.** It involves determining the contribution to the regression sum of squares made by each explanatory variable after all the other explanatory variables have been included in the model. The new explanatory variable is included only if it significantly improves the model.

To apply the partial *F*-test criterion in the potato-processing example, we need to evaluate the contribution of the variable lower pressure (X_2) after pH (X_1) has been included in the model. Conversely, we must also evaluate the contribution of the variable pH (X_1) after lower pressure (X_2) has been included in the model.

The contribution of each explanatory variable to be included in the model can be determined by taking into account the regression sum of squares of a model that includes all explanatory variables except the one of interest, SSR (all variables except *j*). Thus, in general, to determine the contribution of variable *j* given that all other variables are already included, we have the following:

DETERMINING THE CONTRIBUTION OF AN INDEPENDENT VARIABLE TO THE REGRESSION MODEL

$$\text{SSR } (X_j \mid \text{all variables } except \; j)$$
$$= \text{SSR (all variables } including \; j) - \text{SSR (all variables } except \; j) \qquad (13.9)$$

If, as in the potato-processing example, there are two explanatory variables, the contribution of each can be determined from Equations (13.10a) and (13.10b).

Contribution of Variable X_1, Given that X_2 Has Been Included:
$$\text{SSR } (X_1 \mid X_2) = \text{SSR } (X_1 \; and \; X_2) - \text{SSR } (X_2) \qquad (13.10a)$$

Contribution of Variable X_2, Given that X_1 Has Been Included:
$$\text{SSR } (X_2 \mid X_1) = \text{SSR } (X_1 \; and \; X_2) - \text{SSR } (X_1) \qquad (13.10b)$$

The terms SSR(X_2) and SSR(X_1), respectively, represent the sum of squares due to regression for a model that includes only the explanatory variable X_2 (lower pressure) and only the explanatory variable X_1 (pH). Output obtained from Microsoft Excel for these two models is presented in Figures 13.7 and 13.8.

We can observe from Figure 13.2 on page 619 and from Figure 13.7 that

$$\text{SSR } (X_2) = 11.4439$$

and, therefore, from Equation (13.10a),

$$\text{SSR } (X_1 \mid X_2) = \text{SSR } (X_1 \; and \; X_2) - \text{SSR } (X_2)$$

so we have

$$\text{SSR } (X_1 \mid X_2) = 41.5697 - 11.4439 = 30.1258$$

To determine whether X_1 significantly improves the model after X_2 has been included, we can now subdivide the regression sum of squares into two component parts, as shown in Table 13.2.

Figure 13.7 Partial output, obtained from Microsoft Excel, of simple linear regression model for the percentage of solids and lower pressure

Figure 13.8 Partial output, obtained from Microsoft Excel, of simple linear regression model for the percentage of solids and pH

TABLE 13.2

ANOVA TABLE DIVIDING THE REGRESSION SUM OF SQUARES INTO COMPONENTS TO DETERMINE THE CONTRIBUTION OF VARIABLE X_1

Source	df	Sums of Squares	Mean Square (Variance)	F
Regression	2	41.5697	20.7849	
$\left\{ \begin{array}{c} X_2 \\ X_1 \mid X_2 \end{array} \right.$	$\left\{ \begin{array}{c} 1 \\ 1 \end{array} \right\}$	$\left\{ \begin{array}{c} 11.4439 \\ 30.1258 \end{array} \right\}$	30.1258	26.31
Error	51	58.4073	1.1452	
Total	53	99.9770		

The null and alternative hypotheses to test for the contribution of X_1 to the model are as follows:

H_0: Variable X_1 does not significantly improve the model once variable X_2 has been included;

H_1: Variable X_1 significantly improves the model once variable X_2 has been included.

The partial F-test criterion is expressed as follows:

THE PARTIAL F-TEST CRITERION FOR DETERMINING THE CONTRIBUTION OF AN INDEPENDENT VARIABLE

$$F = \frac{\text{SSR}(X_j \mid \text{all variables } except\ j)}{\text{MSE}} \tag{13.11}$$

In Equation (13.11), F represents the F-test statistic that follows an F distribution with 1 and $n - k - 1$ degrees of freedom.

Thus, from Table 13.2, we have

$$F = \frac{30.1258}{1.1452} = 26.31$$

There are 1 and 51 degrees of freedom, respectively, so, if the level of significance 0.05 is selected, we observe from Table A.7 that the critical value for F is approximately 4.04. (See Figure 13.9.)

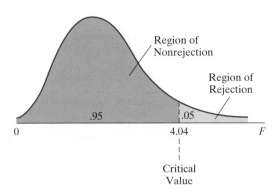

Figure 13.9   Testing for the contribution of a regression coefficient to a multiple-regression model at the 0.05 level of significance with 1 and 51 degrees of freedom

The computed F value exceeds this critical F value ($26.31 > 4.04$), so our decision is to reject H_0 and conclude that the addition of variable X_1 (pH) significantly improves a regression model that already contains variable X_2 (lower pressure).

To evaluate the contribution of variable X_2 (lower pressure) to a model in which variable X_1 has already been included, we need to use Equation (13.10b):

$$\text{SSR}\,(X_2 \mid X_1) = \text{SSR}\,(X_1 \ and \ X_2) - \text{SSR}\,(X_1)$$

From Figures 13.2 on page 619 and 13.8 on page 633, we determine that

$$\text{SSR}(X_1) = 25.3591$$

Therefore,

$$\text{SSR}(X_2 \mid X_1) = 41.5697 - 25.3591 = 16.2106$$

Thus, to determine whether X_2 significantly improves a model after X_1 has been included, the regression sum of squares can be subdivided into two component parts, as shown in Table 13.3. The null and alternative hypotheses to test for the contribution of X_2 to the model are as follows:

H_0: Variable X_2 does not significantly improve the model once variable X_1 has been included;

H_1: Variable X_2 significantly improves the model once variable X_1 has been included.

Using Equation (13.11), we obtain

$$F = \frac{16.2106}{1.1452} = 14.16$$

as indicated in Table 13.3.

TABLE 13.3

ANOVA TABLE DIVIDING THE REGRESSION SUM OF SQUARES
INTO COMPONENTS TO DETERMINE THE CONTRIBUTION
OF VARIABLE X_2

Source	df	Sums of Squares	Mean Square (Variance)	F
Regression	2	41.5697	20.78485	
$\left\{\begin{array}{c} X_1 \\ X_2 \mid X_1 \end{array}\right\}$	$\left\{\begin{array}{c} 1 \\ 1 \end{array}\right\}$	$\left\{\begin{array}{c} 25.3591 \\ 16.2106 \end{array}\right\}$	16.2106	14.16
Error	51	58.4073	1.1452	
Total	53	99.977		

There are 1 and 51 degrees of freedom, respectively, so, if a 0.05 level of significance is selected, we again observe from Figure 13.9 that the critical value of F is approximately 4.04. The computed F value exceeds this critical value ($14.16 > 4.04$), so our decision is to reject H_0 and conclude that the addition of variable X_2 (lower pressure) significantly improves the multiple regression model already containing X_1 (pH).

Thus, by testing for the contribution of each explanatory variable after the other had been included in the model, we determine that each of the two explanatory variables significantly improves the model. Therefore, our multiple regression model should include both pH (X_1) and the lower pressure (X_2) in predicting the percent of solids.

Focusing on the interpretation of these conclusions, we note that there is a relationship between the value of the t-test statistic obtained from Equation (13.7) and the partial F test statistic [Equation (13.11)] used to determine the contributions of X_1 and X_2 to the multiple-regression model. The t values were computed to be 5.129 and -3.762, and the corresponding values of F were 26.31 and 14.16. This points up the following relationship[1] between t and F.

THE RELATIONSHIP BETWEEN A t STATISTIC AND AN F STATISTIC

$$t_\nu^2 = F_{1,\nu} \qquad (13.12)$$

where ν = number of degrees of freedom.

Coefficient of Partial Determination

In Section 13.1, we discussed the coefficient of multiple determination ($R_{Y.12}^2$), which measured the proportion of the variation in Y that was explained by variation in the two explanatory variables. Now that we have examined ways in which the contribution of each explanatory variable to the multiple regression model can be evaluated, we can also compute the **coefficients of partial determination** ($R_{Y1.2}^2$ and $R_{Y2.1}^2$). The coefficients measure the proportion of the variation in the dependent variable that is explained by each explanatory variable while one is controlling for, or holding constant, the other explanatory variable(s). Thus, in a multiple-regression model with two explanatory variables, we have the following:

COEFFICIENTS OF PARTIAL DETERMINATION FOR A MODEL WITH TWO INDEPENDENT VARIABLES

$$R_{Y1.2}^2 = \frac{\text{SSR}(X_1 \mid X_2)}{\text{SST} - \text{SSR}(X_1 \text{ and } X_2) + \text{SSR}(X_1 \mid X_2)} \qquad (13.13a)$$

and

$$R_{Y2.1}^2 = \frac{\text{SSR}(X_2 \mid X_1)}{\text{SST} - \text{SSR}(X_1 \text{ and } X_2) + \text{SSR}(X_2 \mid X_1)} \qquad (13.13b)$$

where

$\text{SSR}(X_1 \mid X_2)$ = sum of squares of the contribution of variable X_1 to the regression model, given that variable X_2 has been included in the model

SST = total sum of squares for Y

$\text{SSR}(X_1 \text{ and } X_2)$ = regression sum of squares when variables X_1 and X_2 are both included in the multiple-regression model

$\text{SSR}(X_2 \mid X_1)$ = sum of squares of the contribution of variable X_2 to the regression model, given that variable X_1 has been included in the model

In a multiple-regression model containing several (k) explanatory variables, for the jth variable we have the following:

COEFFICIENTS OF PARTIAL DETERMINATION FOR A MULTIPLE-REGRESSION MODEL CONTAINING k INDEPENDENT VARIABLES

$$R^2_{Yj.\text{(all variables } except\, j)}$$

$$= \frac{\text{SSR}\,(X_j\,|\,\text{all variables } except\, j)}{\text{SST} - \text{SSR}\,(\text{all variables } including\, j) + \text{SSR}\,(X_j\,|\,\text{all variables } except\, j)}$$

$$(13.14)$$

For the potato-processing example, we can compute

$$R^2_{Y1.2} = \frac{30.1258}{99.977 - 41.5697 + 30.1258}$$

$$= 0.3403$$

and

$$R^2_{Y2.1} = \frac{16.2106}{99.977 - 41.5697 + 16.2106}$$

$$= 0.2172$$

The coefficient of partial determination of variable Y with X_1 while holding X_2 constant ($R^2_{Y1.2}$) means that, for a fixed (constant) lower pressure, 34.03% of the variation in solids can be explained by the variation in the pH. The coefficient of partial determination of variable Y with X_2 while holding X_1 constant ($R^2_{Y2.1}$) means that, for a given (constant) pH, 21.72% of the variation in the percent of solids can be explained by variation in the lower pressure. Figure 13.10 illustrates these coefficients obtained from the PHStat Add-In for Microsoft Excel.

	A	B	C	D
1	Multiple Regression for Potato Study			
2	Coefficients of Partial Determination			
3				
4	SSR(X1,X2)	41.56970707		
5	SST	99.97703704		
6	SSR(X2)	11.44391143	SSR(X1 | X2)	30.12579564
7	SSR(X1)	25.35907426	SSR(X2 | X1)	16.21063282
8				
9	r2 Y1.2	0.340277105		
10	r2 Y2.1	0.217248397		

Figure 13.10   Coefficients of partial determination obtained from the PHStat Add-In for Microsoft Excel for the potato processing example

PROBLEMS

13.22 The following Analysis of Variance table was obtained from a multiple-regression model having two independent variables.

Source	Degrees of Freedom	Sum of Squares	Mean Square	F
Regression	2	60		
Error	18	120		
Total	20	180		

$$SSR\ (X_1) = 45,\ SSR\ (X_2) = 25$$

(a) Determine whether there is a significant relationship between Y and the each of the explanatory variables at the 0.05 level of significance.

(b) Compute the coefficients of partial determination $R^2_{Y1.2}$ and $R^2_{Y2.1}$, and interpret their meaning.

13.23 In Problem 13.3 on page 623, the weight and length of an automobile were used to predict gasoline mileage.

(a) At the 0.05 level of significance, determine whether each explanatory variable makes a significant contribution to the regression model. On the basis of these results, indicate the regression model that should be utilized in the problem.

(b) Compute the coefficients of partial determination $R^2_{Y1.2}$ and $R^2_{Y2.1}$, and interpret their meaning.

13.24 In Problem 13.4 on page 623, breast diameter and the bark thickness were used to predict the height of redwood trees.

(a) At the 0.05 level of significance, determine whether each explanatory variable makes a significant contribution to the regression model. On the basis of these results, indicate the regression model that should be utilized in the problem.

(b) Compute the coefficients of partial determination $R^2_{Y1.2}$ and $R^2_{Y2.1}$, and interpret their meaning.

13.25 In Problem 13.5 on page 623, light output and the temperature of the lamp were used to predict the ballast efficiency factor.

(a) At the 0.05 level of significance, determine whether each explanatory variable makes a significant contribution to the regression model. On the basis of these results, indicate the regression model that should be utilized in the problem.

(b) Compute the coefficients of partial determination $R^2_{Y1.2}$ and $R^2_{Y2.1}$, and interpret their meaning.

13.26 In Problem 13.6 on page 623, solar radiation and soil temperature were used to predict radon concentration.

(a) At the 0.05 level of significance, determine whether each explanatory variable makes a significant contribution to the regression model. On the basis of these results, indicate the regression model that should be utilized in the problem.

(b) Compute the coefficients of partial determination $R^2_{Y1.2}$ and $R^2_{Y2.1}$, and interpret their meaning.

13.6 THE QUADRATIC CURVILINEAR REGRESSION MODEL

In our discussion of simple regression in Chapter 12 and of multiple regression so far in this chapter, we assumed that the relationship between Y and each explanatory variable is linear. However, in Section 12.1, several different types of relationships between variables were introduced. One of the more common nonlinear relationships illustrated was a quadratic curvilinear relationship between two variables (as in Figure 12.1 on page 568, Panels D–F) in which Y increases (or decreases) at a changing rate for various values of X. This model of such a relationship between X and Y can be expressed as follows:

QUADRATIC CURVILINEAR REGRESSION MODEL

$$Y_i = \beta_0 + \beta_1 X_{1i} + \beta_2 X_{1i}^2 + \varepsilon_i \qquad (13.15)$$

where

$\beta_0 = Y$ intercept

$\beta_1 =$ linear effect on Y

$\beta_2 =$ curvilinear effect on Y

$\varepsilon_i =$ random error in Y for observation i

This **quadratic curvilinear regression model** is similar to the multiple regression model with two explanatory variables [see Equation (13.1) on page 617], except that the second explanatory variable is the square of the first explanatory variable.

As in the case of multiple linear regression, the sample regression coefficients $(b_0, b_1, \text{ and } b_2)$ are used as estimates of the population parameters $(\beta_0, \beta_1, \text{ and } \beta_2)$. Thus, the regression equation for the quadratic curvilinear polynomial model with one explanatory variable (X_1) and a dependent variable (Y) is as follows:

QUADRATIC CURVILINEAR REGRESSION MODEL

$$\hat{Y}_i = b_0 + b_1 X_{1i} + b_2 X_{1i}^2 \qquad (13.16)$$

In this equation, the first regression coefficient, b_1, represents the linear effect, while the second regression coefficient b_2 represents the quadratic effect.

Finding the Regression Coefficients and Predicting Y

To illustrate the quadratic curvilinear regression model, suppose that an experiment was carried out to study the effect of various amounts of fly ash in high strength concrete. A sample of 18 specimens of 28-day-old 4,000-psi specified-strength concrete using from 0 to 60% fly ash is obtained. The data are presented in Table 13.4.

TABLE 13.4

FLY ASH % AND STRENGTH OF 18 SAMPLES OF 28-DAY-OLD CONCRETE

Fly Ash %	Strength (psi)	Fly Ash %	Strength (psi)
0	4779	40	5995
0	4706	40	5628
0	4350	40	5897
20	5189	50	5746
20	5140	50	5719
20	4976	50	5782
30	5110	60	4895
30	5685	60	5030
30	5618	60	4648

FLYASH

To help select the proper model for expressing the relationship between fly ash percentage and strength, a scatter diagram is plotted in Figure 13.11. An examination of Figure 13.11 indicates that the increase in strength as the percent of fly ash increases levels off for increasing percentages and actually drops after achieving maximum strength at about 40% fly ash. Strength for 50% fly ash is lightly below strength at 40%, but strength at 60% is substantially below strength at 40%. Therefore, it appears that a quadratic curvilinear model rather than a linear model may be the more appropriate choice to estimate strength based on percentage of fly ash.

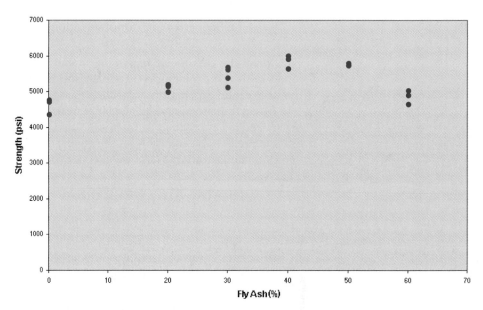

Figure 13.11   Scatter diagram, obtained from Microsoft Excel, of fly ash percent (X) and strength (Y)

As in the case of multiple regression, the values of the three sample regression coefficients (b_0, b_1, and b_2) are obtained from Microsoft Excel as illustrated in Figure 13.12.

From Figure 13.12, we observe that

$$b_0 = 4,486.361$$
$$b_1 = 63.005$$
$$b_2 = -0.876$$

Therefore, the quadratic curvilinear model can be expressed as

$$\hat{Y}_i = 4,486.361 + 63.005X_{1i} - 0.876X_{1i}^2$$

where

$\hat{Y}_i$ = predicted average strength for sample i

X_{1i} = percentage of fly ash for sample i

	A	B	C	D	E	F	G
1	SUMMARY OUTPUT						
2							
3	*Regression Statistics*						
4	Multiple R	0.80527402					
5	R Square	0.64846625					
6	Adjusted R Square	0.60159508					
7	Standard Error	312.112908					
8	Observations	18					
9							
10	ANOVA						
11		*df*	*SS*	*MS*	*F*	*Significance F*	
12	Regression	2	2695473.49	1347737	13.83508	0.000393326	
13	Residual	15	1461217.01	97414.47			
14	Total	17	4156690.5				
15							
16		*Coefficients*	*Standard Error*	*t Stat*	*P-value*	*Lower 95%*	*Upper 95%*
17	Intercept	4486.36111	174.753147	25.67256	8.25E-14	4113.883366	4858.83886
18	Flyash%	63.0052381	12.3725453	5.092342	0.000132	36.63376582	89.3767104
19	Flyash%^2	-0.87646825	0.196612651	-4.45784	0.00046	-1.295538458	-0.4573981

b_0

b_1

b_2

Figure 13.12   Partial output obtained from Microsoft Excel for the concrete strength data

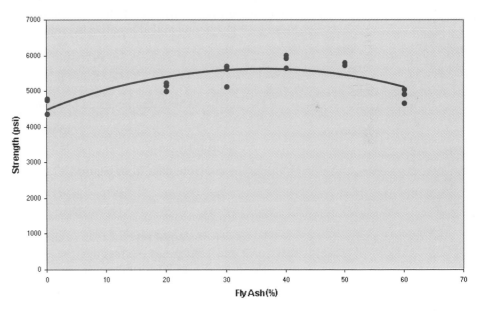

Figure 13.13   Scatter diagram, obtained from Microsoft Excel, expressing the quadratic curvilinear relationship between fly ash percentage and strength, for the concrete data

As depicted in Figure 13.13, this curvilinear regression equation is plotted on the scatter diagram to see how well the selected regression model fits the original data.

From our quadratic curvilinear regression equation, the Y intercept (b_0, computed to be 4,486.361) is the predicted average strength for 0% fly ash. To interpret the coefficients b_1 and b_2, we see from Figure 13.13 that, after an initial increase, strength decreases with fly ash percentage. This can be demonstrated by predicting average strength for fly ash percentages of 20, 40, and 60. Using our curvilinear regression equation,

$$\hat{Y}_i = 4{,}486.361 + 63.005X_{1i} - 0.876X_{1i}^2$$

for $X_{1i} = 20$, we have

$$\hat{Y}_i = 4{,}486.361 + 63.005(20) - 0.876(20) = 5{,}395.88$$

For $X_{1i} = 40$, we have

$$\hat{Y}_i = 4{,}486.361 + 63.005(40) - 0.876(40) = 5{,}604.22$$

For $X_{1i} = 60$, we have

$$\hat{Y}_i = 4{,}486.361 + 63.005(60) - 0.876(60) = 5{,}111.39$$

Thus, the strength for concrete that has 40% fly ash is expected to be 208.34 psi above the strength for 20% fly ash, but concrete that has 60% fly ash is expected to be 492.83 psi below the strength for 40% fly ash.

Testing for the Significance of the Quadratic Curvilinear Model

Now that the curvilinear model has been fitted to the data, we can determine whether one of the regression coefficients is a significant predictor of strength, Y, based on percent of fly ash, X. In a manner similar to multiple regression (see Section 13.1), the null and alternative hypotheses can be set up as follows:

$$H_0: \beta_1 = \beta_2 = 0$$

$$H_1: \beta_1 \text{ and/or } \beta_2 \neq 0$$

The null hypothesis can be tested by using Equation (13.6):

$$F = \frac{\text{MSR}}{\text{MSE}}$$

For the concrete data from Figure 13.12 on page 641, we have

$$F = \frac{\text{MSR}}{\text{MSE}} = \frac{1{,}347{,}737}{97{,}414.47} = 13.84$$

If a level of significance of 0.05 is chosen, we consult Table A.7 and find that, for 2 and 15 degrees of freedom, the critical value on the F distribution is 3.68. Because $F = 13.84 > 3.68$, or because, from Figure 13.12, the p-value $= 0.00039 < 0.05$, we reject the null hypothesis (H_0) and conclude that β_1 and/or β_2 is a significant predictor of strength based on the percentage of fly ash.

Obtaining the Coefficient of Multiple Determination

In the multiple-regression model, we computed the coefficient of multiple determination $R_{Y.12}^2$ (see Section 13.1) to represent the proportion of variation in Y that is explained by variation in the explanatory variables. In curvilinear regression analysis, this coefficient can be computed from Equation (13.4):

$$R_{Y.12}^2 = \frac{\text{SSR}}{\text{SST}}$$

From Figure 13.12,

$$SSR = 2,695,473.49$$
$$SST = 4,156,690.5$$

Thus,

$$R^2_{Y.12} = \frac{SSR}{SST} = \frac{2,695,473.49}{4,156,690.5} = 0.6485$$

This coefficient of multiple determination, computed to be 0.6485, means that 64.85% of the variation in strength can be explained by the curvilinear relationship between strength and the percentage of fly ash. An adjusted $R^2_{Y.12}$ can also be obtained that takes into account the number of explanatory variables and the degrees of freedom. In our curvilinear regression model, $k = 2$, because we have two explanatory variables, X_1, and its square, X^2_1. Thus, using Equation (13.5) for the fly ash data, we have

$$R^2_{adj} = 1 - \left[(1 - R^2_{Y.12}) \frac{(18 - 1)}{(18 - 2 - 1)} \right]$$

$$= 1 - \left[(1 - 0.6485) \frac{17}{15} \right]$$

$$= .6016$$

Testing the Curvilinear Effect

In using a regression model to examine a relationship between two variables, we would like to fit not only the most accurate model, but also the simplest model expressing that relationship. Therefore, it becomes important to examine whether there is a significant difference between the curvilinear model

$$Y_i = \beta_0 + \beta_1 X_{1i} + \beta_2 X^2_{1i} + \varepsilon_i$$

and the simple linear model

$$Y_i = \beta_0 + \beta_1 X_{1i} + \varepsilon_i$$

We can compare these two models by determining the regression effect of adding the curvilinear term, given that the linear term has already been included $[SSR(X^2_1 \mid X_1)]$.

You may recall that, in Section 13.4, we used the t test for the regression coefficient to determine whether each particular variable made a significant contribution to the regression model. Because the standard error of each regression coefficient and its corresponding t statistic is available as part of the Excel output (see Figure 13.12 on page 641), we test the significance of the contribution of the quadratic curvilinear effect with the following null and alternative hypotheses:

H_0: Including the quadratic curvilinear effect does not significantly improve the model ($\beta_2 = 0$).

H_1: Including the quadratic curvilinear effect significantly improves the model ($\beta_2 \neq 0$).

For our data,

$$t = \frac{b_2}{s_{b_2}}$$

so that

$$t = \frac{-0.8765}{0.1966} = -4.46$$

If the level of significance 0.05 is selected, we use Table A.4 and find that, with 15 degrees of freedom, the critical values for t are -2.1315 and $+2.1315$.

Because $t = -4.46 < t_{15} = -2.1315$, or because the p-value $= 0.00046 < .05$, we reject H_0 and conclude that the curvilinear model is significantly better than the linear model in representing the relationship between strength and the percentage of fly ash.

PROBLEMS

13.27 A researcher for a major oil company wishes to develop a model to predict miles per gallon based on highway speed. An experiment is designed in which a test car is driven during two trial periods at speeds ranging from 10 miles per hour to 75 miles per hour. The results are as follows:

Observation	Miles per Gallon	Speed (miles per hour)
1	4.8	10
2	5.7	10
3	8.6	15
4	7.3	15
5	9.8	20
6	11.2	20
7	13.7	25
8	12.4	25
9	18.2	30
10	16.8	30
11	19.9	35
12	19.0	35
13	22.4	40
14	23.5	40
15	21.3	45
16	22.0	45
17	20.5	50
18	19.7	50
19	18.6	55
20	19.3	55
21	14.4	60
22	13.7	60

(Continued)

Observation	Miles per Gallon	Speed (miles per hour)
23	12.1	65
24	13.0	65
25	10.1	70
26	9.4	70
27	8.4	75
28	7.6	75

SPEED

Assume a quadratic curvilinear relationship between speed and mileage, and use the results obtained from Excel or MINITAB.

(a) Set up a scatter diagram between speed and miles per gallon.

(b) State the equation for the quadratic curvilinear model.

(c) Predict the mileage obtained when the car is driven at 55 miles per hour.

(d) Determine whether there is a significant quadratic curvilinear relationship between mileage and speed at the 0.05 level of significance.

(e) Interpret the meaning of the coefficient of multiple determination $R^2_{Y.12}$.

(f) Compute the adjusted R^2.

(g) Perform a residual analysis on your results, and determine the adequacy of the fit of the model.

(h) At the 0.05 level of significance, determine whether the quadratic curvilinear model is a better fit than the linear regression model.

13.28 An industrial psychologist would like to develop a model to predict the number of typing errors based on the amount of alcohol consumption (in ounces). A random sample of 15 typists is selected, with the following results.

Typist	Alcoholic Consumption	Number of Errors
1	0	2
2	0	6
3	0	3
4	1	7
5	1	5
6	1	9
7	2	12
8	2	7
9	2	9
10	3	13
11	3	18
12	3	16
13	4	24
14	4	30
15	4	22

ALCOHOL

Assume a quadratic curvilinear relationship between alcohol consumption and the number of errors.
(a) Set up a scatter diagram between alcohol consumption, X, and number of errors, Y.
(b) State the equation for the quadratic curvilinear model.
(c) Predict the number of errors made by a typist who has consumed 2.5 ounces of alcohol.
(d) Determine whether there is a significant quadratic curvilinear relationship between alcohol consumption and the number of errors made at the 0.05 level of significance.
(e) Interpret the meaning of the coefficient of multiple determination $R^2_{Y.12}$.
(f) Compute the adjusted R^2.
(g) Perform a residual analysis on your results, and determine the adequacy of the fit of the model.
(h) At the 0.05 level of significance, determine whether the quadratic curvilinear model is a better fit than the linear regression model.

13.29 Suppose an agronomist wants to design a study in which a wide range of fertilizer levels (pounds per hundred square feet) is to be used to determine whether the relationship between the yield of tomatoes and amount of fertilizer can be fit by a quadratic curvilinear model. Six rates of

application are to be used: 0, 20, 40, 60, 80, and 100 pounds per hundred square feet. These rates are then randomly assigned to plots of land, with the following results.

Plot	Fertilizer Application	Rate Yield (pounds)
1	0	6
2	0	9
3	20	19
4	20	24
5	40	32
6	40	38
7	60	46
8	60	50
9	80	48
10	80	54
11	100	52
12	100	58

TOMATO

Assume a quadratic curvilinear relationship between the application rate and tomato yield, and use the results obtained from Microsoft Excel or MINITAB.
(a) Set up a scatter diagram between application rate and yield.
(b) State the regression equation for the quadratic curvilinear model.
(c) Predict the yield of tomatoes (in pounds) for a plot that has been fertilized with 70 pounds per hundred square feet of fertilizer.
(d) Determine whether there is a significant relationship between the application rate and tomato yield at the 0.05 level of significance.
(e) Compute the p-value in (d), and interpret its meaning.
(f) Compute the coefficient of multiple determination $R^2_{Y.12}$, and interpret its meaning.
(g) Compute the adjusted R^2.
(h) At the 0.05 level of significance, determine whether the quadratic curvilinear model is superior to the linear regression model.
(i) Compute the p-value in (h), and interpret its meaning.
(j) Perform a residual analysis on your results, and determine the adequacy of the fit of the model.

13.30 An auditor for a county government would like to develop a model to predict the county taxes from the age of single-family houses. A random sample of 19 single-family houses has been selected, with the following results.

County Taxes ($)	Age (Years)	County Taxes ($)	Age (Years)
925	1	480	20
870	2	486	22
809	4	462	25
720	4	441	25
694	5	426	30
630	8	368	35
626	10	350	40
562	10	348	50
546	12	322	50
523	15		

TAXES

Assuming a quadratic curvilinear relationship between the age and county taxes and using Microsoft Excel or MINITAB:

(a) Set up a scatter diagram between age and county taxes.
(b) State the regression equation for the quadratic curvilinear model.
(c) Predict the average county taxes for a house that is 20 years old.
(d) Perform a residual analysis on your results, and determine the adequacy of the fit of the model.
(e) Determine whether there is a significant overall relationship between age and county taxes at the 0.05 level of significance.
(f) What is the p-value in (e)? Interpret its meaning.
(g) At the 0.05 level of significance, determine whether the quadratic curvilinear model is superior to the linear regression model.
(h) What is the p-value in (g)? Interpret its meaning.
(i) Interpret the meaning of the coefficient of multiple determination $R^2_{Y.12}$.
(j) Compute the adjusted R^2.

13.7 DUMMY-VARIABLE MODELS

In our discussion of multiple regression models, we have assumed that each explanatory (or independent) variable is interval or ratio-scaled; however, there are many occasions in which categorical variables need to be included in the model-development process. For example, in Section 12.1, we used the drilling depth to predict the drilling time in mining engineering. In addition to this independent variable, one of the objectives of the analysis was to study the effect of the type of drilling hole (dry versus wet) on the drilling time.

The use of **dummy variables** is the mechanism that permits us to consider categorical explanatory variables as part of the regression model. If a given categorical explanatory variable has two categories, then only one dummy variable will be needed to represent the two categories. A particular dummy variable (X_d) is defined as

$X_d = 0$ if the observation is in category 1

$X_d = 1$ if the observation is in category 2

To illustrate the application of dummy variables in regression, we will examine a model for predicting the drilling time of a sample of 100 drilling holes based on the drilling depth and on whether the hole used forced air (dry hole) or water (wet hole). The data are included in the file **DRILL.**

A dummy variable for type of drilling hole (X_2) can be defined as

$X_2 = 0$ if the drilling hole is dry

$X_2 = 1$ if the drilling hole is wet

Assuming that the slope of drilling depth with drilling time is the same for dry and wet holes, the regression model fit is

$$Y_i = \beta_0 + \beta_1 X_{1i} + \beta_2 X_{2i} + \varepsilon_i$$

where

Y_i = drilling time in minutes

β_0 = Y intercept

β_1 = slope of drilling time with drilling depth when the type of hole is held constant

β_2 = incremental effect of the type of hole when the drilling depth is held constant

ε_i = random error in Y for hole i

Figure 13.14 illustrates the output for this model obtained from Microsoft Excel.

	A	B	C	D	E	F	G
1	Regression with Dummy Variable (Type)						
2							
3	*Regression Statistics*						
4	Multiple R	0.834345233					
5	R Square	0.696131968					
6	Adjusted R Square	0.689866647					
7	Standard Error	0.75008467					
8	Observations	100					
9							
10	ANOVA						
11		*df*	*SS*	*MS*	*F*	*Significance F*	
12	Regression	2	125.0255798	62.51278992	111.1087605	8.13248E-26	
13	Residual	97	54.57482016	0.562627012			
14	Total	99	179.6004				
15							
16		*Coefficients*	*Standard Error*	*t Stat*	*P-value*	*Lower 95%*	*Upper 95%*
17	Intercept	5.90484898	0.169765372	34.78241116	1.39913E-56	5.567911898	6.241786062
18	Depth	0.005227851	0.001039556	5.028928173	2.26014E-06	0.003164622	0.00729108
19	Type	2.1052	0.150016934	14.03308243	4.37575E-25	1.807458079	2.402941921

Figure 13.14   Microsoft Excel output for the regression model that includes drilling depth and type of hole

From this output, the regression model is stated as

$$\hat{Y}_i = 5.9048 + 0.0052\,X_{1i} + 2.1052\,X_{2i}$$

For dry drilling holes, the model reduces to

$$\hat{Y}_i = 5.9048 + 0.0052\,X_{1i} + 2.1052(0) = 5.9048 + 0.0052\,X_{1i}$$

For wet drilling holes, the model is

$$\hat{Y}_i = 5.9048 + 0.0052\,X_{1i} + 2.1052(1) = 8.01 + 0.0052\,X_{1i}$$

In addition, we can interpret the slopes as follows:

1. Holding constant the type of drilling hole, for each increase of one foot in drilling depth, we predict the average drilling time to increase by 0.0052 minutes.
2. Holding constant the drilling depth, we predict a wet drilling hole to increase the drilling time by an average of 2.1052 minutes.

We note from Figure 13.14 that the t statistic for the slope of drilling depth with drilling time is 5.029, and the p-value is 0.0000, while the t statistic for type of drilling hole is 14.033, and the p-value is 0.0000. Thus, each of the two variables is making a significant contribution to the model at a level of significance less than 0.01. In addition, 69.9% of the variation in drilling time is explained by variation in the drilling depth and the type of drilling hole. This compares to a coefficient of determination of only 20.4% for the regression model that included drilling depth, but not the type of drilling hole.

Before we can use this model, however, we need to assure ourselves that the slope of drilling depth with drilling time is the same for dry holes as it is for wet holes. A hypothesis of equal slopes of an X variable with Y can be evaluated by defining an **interaction term** that consists of the product of the X variable and the dummy variable, and then testing whether this variable makes a significant contribution to a regression model that contains the other X variables.

The Microsoft Excel output for the regression model that includes the drilling depth (X_1), the type of drilling hole (X_2), and the interaction of X_1 and X_2 (which we have defined as X_3) is provided in Figure 13.15.

	A	B	C	D	E	F	G
1	Regression Analysis						
2							
3	*Regression Statistics*						
4	Multiple R	0.835371584					
5	R Square	0.697845684					
6	Adjusted R Square	0.688403361					
7	Standard Error	0.75185213					
8	Observations	100					
9							
10	ANOVA						
11		*df*	*SS*	*MS*	*F*	*Significance F*	
12	Regression	3	125.3333639	41.77778798	73.90614885	7.43385E-25	
13	Residual	96	54.26703607	0.565281626			
14	Total	99	179.6004				
15							
16		*Coefficients*	*Standard Error*	*t Stat*	*P-value*	*Lower 95%*	*Upper 95%*
17	Intercept	6.002881633	0.215886297	27.8057557	1.01571E-47	5.574350392	6.431412873
18	Depth	0.004458968	0.001473618	3.025863916	0.003181974	0.001533857	0.007384078
19	Type	1.909134694	0.305309329	6.253116141	1.11163E-08	1.303100002	2.515169386
20	Depth*Type	0.001537767	0.002084011	0.737888337	0.46238222	-0.002598964	0.005674499

Figure 13.15   Microsoft Excel output for the regression model that includes drilling depth, type of drilling hole, and the interaction of drilling depth and type of drilling hole

To test the null hypothesis H_0: $\beta_3 = 0$ versus the alternative hypothesis H_1: $\beta_3 \neq 0$, from Figure 13.15 we observe that the t statistic for the interaction of drilling depth and type of drilling hole is 0.74. The p-value = 0.462 > 0.05, so the null hypothesis is not rejected. We conclude that the interaction term does not make a significant contribution to the model, given that drilling depth and type of drilling hole are already included.

PROBLEMS

13.31 The chair of the Computer Sciences department of a large public university wishes to develop a regression model to predict the grade-point average of computer science students who are graduating as computer science majors. The prediction is to be based on total SAT score for the student and on whether the student received a grade of B or higher in the introductory statistics course (0 = no and 1 = yes).

(a) Explain the steps involved in developing a regression model for these data. Be sure to indicate the particular models that need to be evaluated and compared.

(b) If the regression coefficient for the variable of whether the student received a grade of B or higher in the introductory statistics course was +0.30, how would this be interpreted?

13.32 In Problem 12.56 on page 610, the weight of an automobile was used to predict gasoline mileage. Suppose that we also wanted to consider whether the car used front wheel drive (code 1) or rear wheel drive (code 0). Use the results obtained from Microsoft Excel or MINITAB.

(a) State the multiple-regression equation.

(b) Interpret the meaning of the slopes in this problem.

(c) Predict the average gasoline mileage for a car that weighs 2,500 pounds and uses front wheel drive.

(d) Determine whether there is a significant relationship between the gasoline mileage and the two explanatory variables (weight and the dummy variable type of drive) at the 0.05 level of significance.

(e) Interpret the meaning of the coefficient of multiple determination $R^2_{Y.12}$.

(f) Compute the adjusted R^2.

(g) Perform a residual analysis of your results, and determine the adequacy of the model's fit.

(h) At the .05 level of significance, determine whether each explanatory variable makes a contribution to the regression model. On the basis of these results, indicate the regression model that should be used in this problem.

(i) Set up 95% confidence interval estimates of the population slope for the relationship between the gasoline mileage and weight and the gasoline mileage and type of drive.

(j) Compute and interpret the coefficients of partial determination.

(k) What assumption about the slope of gasoline mileage and weight must be made in this problem?

(l) Include an interaction term in the model, and, at the 0.05 level of significance, determine whether it makes a significant contribution to the model.

(m) Given the results of (h) and (l), what model is most appropriate? Explain.

13.33 In Problem 13.9 on page 626, light output and the temperature of the lamp were used to predict the ballast efficiency factor. The first four observations are on magnetic ballasts and the last six observations are on electronic ballasts. Use lamp temperature and the

type of ballast to develop a regression model. Use the results obtained from Microsoft Excel or MINITAB.

(a) State the multiple-regression equation.

(b) Interpret the meaning of the slopes in this problem.

(c) Predict the average ballast efficiency factor for a magnetic ballast that has a lamp temperature of 40° Celsius.

(d) Determine whether there is a significant relationship between the ballast efficiency factor and the two explanatory variables (lamp temperature and the dummy variable type of ballast) at the .05 level of significance.

(e) Interpret the meaning of the coefficient of multiple determination $R^2_{Y.12}$.

(f) Compute the adjusted R^2.

(g) Perform a residual analysis of your results, and determine the adequacy of the model's fit.

(h) At the 0.05 level of significance, determine whether each explanatory variable makes a contribution to the regression model. Using these results, indicate the regression model that should be used in this problem.

(i) Set up 95% confidence interval estimates of the population slope for the relationship between the ballast efficiency factor and the lamp temperature and the ballast efficiency factor and the type of ballast.

(j) Compute and interpret the coefficients of partial determination.

(k) What assumption about the slope of the ballast efficiency factor and lamp temperature must be made in this problem?

(l) Include an interaction term in the model, and, at the .05 level of significance, determine whether it makes a significant contribution to the model.

(m) Given the results of (h) and (l), what model is most appropriate? Explain.

13.34 The file **UNIV&COL** contains data on 80 colleges and universities. Among the variables included are the annual total cost (in thousands of dollars), the average total score on the Scholastic Aptitude Test (SAT), and whether the school is public or private (0 = public, 1 = private). Suppose we want to develop a model to predict the annual total cost from SAT score and from whether the school is public or private.

(a) State the multiple-regression equation.

(b) Interpret the meaning of the slopes in this problem.

(c) Predict the average total cost for a school with an average total SAT score of 1,000 that is a public institution.

(d) Perform a residual analysis on your results and determine the adequacy of the fit of the model.

(e) Determine whether there is a significant relationship between annual total cost and the two explanatory variables (total SAT score and whether the school is public or private) at the 0.05 level of significance.

(f) At the 0.05 level of significance, determine whether each explanatory variable makes a contribution to the regression model. On the basis of these results, indicate the regression model that should be used in this problem.

(g) Set up 95% confidence interval estimates of the population slope for the relationship between annual total cost and total SAT score and between annual total cost and whether the school is public or private.

(h) Interpret the meaning of the coefficient of multiple determination.

(i) Compute the adjusted R^2.

(j) Compute the coefficients of partial determination, and interpret their meaning.

(k) What assumption about the slope of annual total cost with total SAT score must be made in this problem?

(l) Include an interaction term in the model, and, at the 0.05 level of significance, determine whether it makes a significant contribution to the model.

(m) Given the results of (f) and (l), which model is more appropriate? Explain.

13.35 A study examined the relation between diastolic blood pressure and the heart recovery rate. Each person in the experiment exercised on a stationary bike until they reached 65% of their maximum heart rate. Then the time to recovery (in seconds) of their normal rate was observed. The objective is to develop a multiple-regression model relating the recovery time to the diastolic blood pressure and gender (where a 0 represents a female and a 1 represents male). The data are as follows.

Gender	Diastolic	Recovery
M	82	183
M	70	140
M	80	451
F	70	131
M	68	149
F	62	154
F	70	183
F	62	135
M	82	384

RECOVERY

Use the results obtained from Microsoft Excel or MINITAB.

(a) State the multiple-regression equation.

(b) Interpret the meaning of the slopes in this problem.

(c) Predict the average heart recovery rate for a female who has a diastolic blood pressure of 80.

(d) Determine whether there is a significant relationship between the heart recovery rate and the two explanatory variables (diastolic blood pressure and the dummy variable gender) at the 0.05 level of significance.

(e) Interpret the meaning of the coefficient of multiple determination $R^2_{Y.12}$.

(f) Compute the adjusted R^2.

(g) Perform a residual analysis of your results, and determine the adequacy of the model's fit.

(h) At the 0.05 level of significance, determine whether each explanatory variable makes a contribution to the regression model. On the basis of these results, indicate the regression model that should be used in this problem.

(i) Set up 95% confidence interval estimates of the population slope for the relationship between the heart recovery rate and each of the independent variables.

(j) Compute and interpret the coefficients of partial determination.

(k) What assumption about the slope of heart recovery rate and diastolic blood pressure must be made in this problem?

(l) Include an interaction term in the model, and, at the 0.05 level of significance, determine whether it makes a significant contribution to the model.

(m) From the results of (h) and (l), what model is most appropriate? Explain.

13.36 A construction company wanted to be able to predict monthly heating oil usage (in gallons) for single-family homes from atmospheric temperature (°F), the amount of attic insulation, and whether the house was a ranch-style house. A sample of 15 houses of similar size was selected during the month of January in various locations. The results are included in the file **HTNGOIL.** Use the results obtained from Microsoft Excel or MINITAB.

(a) State the multiple-regression equation.

(b) Interpret the meaning of the slopes in this problem.

(c) Predict the expected heating oil usage for a ranch-style house that had six inches of attic insulation during a month in which the atmospheric temperature averaged 30°F.

(d) Determine whether there is a significant relationship between the monthly heating oil usage and the explanatory variables at the 0.05 level of significance.

(e) Interpret the meaning of the coefficient of multiple determination $R^2_{Y.12}$.

(f) Compute the adjusted R^2.

(g) Perform a residual analysis of your results, and determine the adequacy of the model's fit.

(h) At the 0.05 level of significance, determine whether each explanatory variable makes a contribution to the regression model. Using these results, indicate the regression model that should be used in this problem.

(i) Set up 95% confidence interval estimates of the population slope for the relationship between the heating oil usage and each of the independent variables.

(j) Compute and interpret the coefficients of partial determination.

(k) What assumption about the slope of heating oil usage with atmospheric temperature and heating oil usage with attic insulation must be made in this problem?

(l) Include appropriate interaction terms in the model, and, at the 0.05 level of significance, determine whether it makes a significant contribution to the model.

(m) Given the results of (h) and (l), what model is most appropriate? Explain.

13.8 USING TRANSFORMATIONS IN REGRESSION MODELS

In our discussion of multiple-regression models, we have thus far examined the multiple linear regression model [Equations (13.1a and b)], the quadratic curvilinear model [Equation (13.15)], and the dummy-variable model. In this section, we discuss regression models in which the independent X variable, the Y variable, or both are transformed. Transformations can be used to either to overcome violations of the assumptions of regression analysis or to make a model linear in its transformation. Among the many transformations available (see Reference 5) are the square-root transformation and transformations involving the natural logarithm.[2]

[2]The natural logarithm, usually abbreviated as ln, is the logarithm to the base e, the mathematical constant approximately equal to 2.717128.

The Square-Root Transformation

The **square-root transformation** is often used to transform a model that is not linear into a linear model. If a square-root transformation were applied to the values of each of two explanatory variables, the multiple regression model would be as follows:

SQUARE-ROOT TRANSFORMATION

$$Y_i = \beta_0 + \beta_1 \sqrt{X_{1i}} + \beta_2 \sqrt{X_{2i}} + \varepsilon_i \qquad (13.17)$$

The use of a square-root transformation is illustrated for the data in Table 13.5 on page 652.

Figure 13.16 displays the scatter diagrams of X against Y and of the square root of X against Y. Note that the square-root transformation has taken a nonlinear relationship and created a linear relationship.

In some situations, the use of a transformation can change a model whose form is nonlinear into a linear model. For example, the multiplicative model

ORIGINAL MULTIPLICATIVE MODEL

$$Y_i = \beta_0 X_{1i}^{\beta_1} X_{2i}^{\beta_2} \varepsilon_i \qquad (13.18)$$

TABLE 13.5

HYPOTHETICAL VALUES FOR
X AND *Y* TO ILLUSTRATE
A SQUARE-ROOT
TRANSFORMATION

Y	*X*
42.7	1
50.4	1
69.1	2
79.8	2
90.0	3
100.4	3
104.7	4
112.3	4
113.6	5
123.9	5

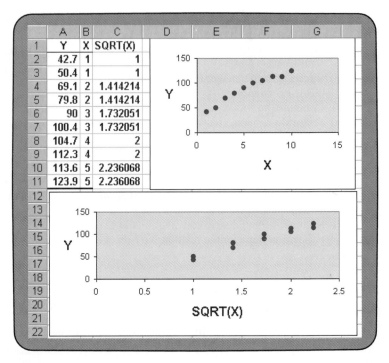

Figure 13.16   Scatter diagrams obtained from Microsoft Excel of
X against *Y* and of *Y* against the square root of *X*

can be transformed (by taking natural logarithms of both the dependent and explanatory variables) to the model

---

TRANSFORMED MULTIPLICATIVE MODEL

$$\ln Y_i = \ln \beta_0 + \beta_1 \ln X_{1i} + \beta_2 \ln X_{2i} + \ln \varepsilon_i \qquad (13.19)$$

Hence, Equation (13.19) is linear in the natural logarithms. In a similar fashion, the exponential model

---

ORIGINAL EXPONENTIAL MODEL

$$Y_i = e^{\beta_0 + \beta_1 X_{1i} + \beta_2 X_{2i}} \varepsilon_i \qquad (13.20)$$

---

can also be transformed to linear form (by taking natural logarithms of both the dependent and explanatory variables). The resulting model is

---

TRANSFORMED EXPONENTIAL MODEL

$$\ln Y_i = \beta_0 + \beta_1 X_{1i} + \beta_2 X_{2i} + \ln \varepsilon_i \qquad (13.21)$$

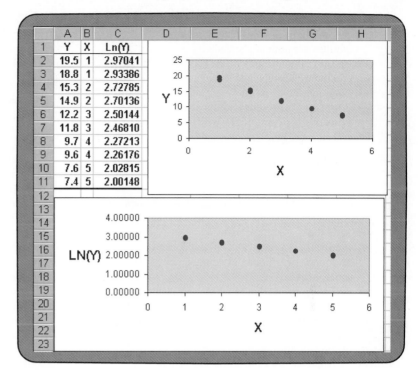

TABLE 13.6

HYPOTHETICAL VALUES FOR
X AND Y TO ILLUSTRATE
A NATURAL-LOG
TRANSFORMATION

Y	X
19.5	1
18.8	1
15.3	2
14.9	2
12.2	3
11.8	3
9.7	4
9.6	4
7.6	5
7.4	5

Figure 13.17   Scatter diagrams obtained from Microsoft Excel of X against Y and of X against the natural logarithm of Y

The use of a natural-logarithm transformation is illustrated for the data in Table 13.6. Figure 13.17 displays the scatter diagrams of X against Y and of X against the natural logarithm of Y. Note that the natural-log transformation has taken a non-linear relationship and created a linear relationship.

PROBLEMS

13.37 Referring to the data of Problem 13.27 on page 644 and using the file **SPEED,** perform a square-root transformation of the explanatory variable (speed).
  (a) State the regression equation.
  (b) Predict the average mileage obtained when the car is driven at 55 miles per hour.
  (c) Perform a residual analysis of your results, and determine the adequacy of the fit of the model.
  (d) At the 0.05 level of significance, is there a significant relationship between mileage and the square root of speed?
  (e) Interpret the meaning of the coefficient of determination R^2 in this problem.
  (f) Compute the adjusted R^2.

  (g) Compare your results with those obtained in Problem 13.27. Which model would you choose? Why?

13.38 Referring to the data of Problem 13.27 on page 644 and using the file **SPEED,** perform a natural-logarithmic transformation of the response variable miles per gallon, and reanalyze the data using this model. On the basis of your results,
  (a) State the regression equation.
  (b) Predict the average mileage obtained when the car is driven at 55 miles per hour.
  (c) Perform a residual analysis of your results, and determine the adequacy of the fit of the model.

(d) At the 0.05 level of significance, is there a significant relationship between the natural logarithm of miles per hour and speed?

(e) Interpret the meaning of the coefficient of determination R^2 in this problem.

(f) Compute the adjusted R^2.

(g) Compare your results with those obtained in Problems 13.27 and 13.37. Which model would you choose? Why?

13.39 Referring to the data of Problem 13.29 on page 645 and using the file **TOMATO**, perform a natural-logarithmic transformation of the response variable yield and reanalyze the data. On the basis of your results,

(a) State the regression equation.

(b) Predict the average yield obtained when 55 pounds of fertilizer are applied per 1,000 square feet.

(c) Perform a residual analysis of your results, and determine the adequacy of the fit of the model.

(d) At the 0.05 level of significance, is there a significant relationship between the natural logarithm of yield and the amount of fertilizer?

(e) Interpret the meaning of the coefficient of determination R^2 in this problem.

(f) Compute the adjusted R^2.

(g) Compare your results with those obtained in Problem 13.29. Which model would you choose? Why?

13.40 Referring to the data of Problem 13.29 on page 645 and using the file **TOMATO,** perform a square-root transformation of the explanatory variable amount of fertilizer, and reanalyze the data. On the basis of your results,

(a) State the regression equation.

(b) Predict the average yield obtained when 55 pounds of fertilizer are applied per 1,000 square feet.

(c) Perform a residual analysis of your results and determine the adequacy of the fit of the model.

(d) At the 0.05 level of significance, is there a significant relationship between yield and the square root of the amount of fertilizer?

(e) Interpret the meaning of the coefficient of determination R^2 in this problem.

(f) Compute the adjusted R^2.

(g) Compare your results with those obtained in Problems 13.29 and 13.39. Which model would you choose? Why?

13.9 COLLINEARITY

One important problem in the application of multiple-regression analysis involves the possible **collinearity** of the explanatory variables. This condition refers to situations in which some of the explanatory variables are highly correlated with each other. In such situations, collinear variables do not provide new information, and it becomes difficult to separate the effects of these variables on the dependent or response variable. In such cases, the values of the regression coefficients for the correlated variables can fluctuate drastically depending on which variables are included in the model.

One method of measuring collinearity uses the **variance inflationary factor** (VIF) for each explanatory variable. This VIF is defined as in Equation (13.22).

VARIANCE INFLATIONARY FACTOR

$$\text{VIF}_j = \frac{1}{1 - R_j^2} \qquad (13.22)$$

where R_j^2 = coefficient of multiple determination of explanatory variable X_j with all other X variables.

If there are only two explanatory variables, R_j^2 is just the coefficient of determination between X_1 and X_2. If, for example, there were three explanatory variables, then R_1^2 would be the coefficient of multiple determination of X_1 with X_2 and X_3.

If a set of explanatory variables is uncorrelated, then VIF_j will be equal to 1. If the set is highly intercorrelated, then VIF_j might even exceed 10. Marquardt (see Reference 2) suggests that, if VIF_j is greater than 10, there is too much correlation between variable X_j and the other explanatory variables. However, other researchers (see Reference 6) suggest a more conservative criterion, which would employ alternatives to least-squares regression if the maximum VIF_j exceeds 5.

If we reexamine the potato-processing data of Section 13.1, we compute the correlation between the two explanatory variables, pH and lower pressure equal to 0.121. Therefore, because there are only two explanatory variables in the model, from Equation (13.18) the VIF_j is

$$\text{VIF}_1 = \text{VIF}_2 = \frac{1}{1 - (0.121)^2}$$

$$\cong 1.014$$

Thus, we conclude that there is no reason to suspect any collinearity for the potato-processing data.

PROBLEMS

13.41 Refer to Problem 12.3 (automobiles) on page 575, and determine the VIF for each explanatory variable in the model. Is there reason to suspect the existence of collinearity?

13.42 Refer to Problem 12.4 (redwood trees) on page 575, and determine the VIF for each explanatory variable in the model. Is there reason to suspect the existence of collinearity?

13.43 Refer to Problem 12.5 (ballasts) on page 576, and determine the VIF for each explanatory variable in the model. Is there reason to suspect the existence of collinearity?

13.44 Refer to Problem 12.6 (radon) on page 576, and determine the VIF for each explanatory variable in the model. Is there reason to suspect the existence of collinearity?

13.10 MODEL-BUILDING

In this chapter, we have developed the multiple linear regression model and subsequently discussed the quadratic curvilinear model, models involving dummy variables, and models involving transformations of variables. In this section, we culminate our discussion of regression by studying a model-building approach that considers a set of explanatory variables. We begin by referring to the *Using Statistics* example at the beginning of this chapter, in which a regression model was developed to predict the percentage of solids in filter cakes from a potato-processing plant. At the beginning of the chapter, we considered two variables, the pH of the filter cake and the pressure in the vacuum line below the fluid line on the rotating drum. Now, we will consider four additional variables. These are pressure of the vacuum line above the fluid line on the rotating drum (UPPER), cake thickness measured on the drum (THICK), setting used to control the drum speed

(VARIDRIV), and the speed at which the drum was rotated when collecting filter cake (DRUMSPD). These data are contained in the **POTATO** file.

Before we begin to develop a model to predict the percent of solids, we should keep in mind that a widely used criterion of model-building is parsimony. This means that we wish to develop a regression model that includes the fewest number of explanatory variables that permits an adequate interpretation of the dependent variable of interest. Regression models with fewer explanatory variables are inherently easier to interpret, particularly because they are less likely to be affected by the problem of collinearity. (See Section 13.9.)

In addition, we should realize that the selection of an appropriate model, when many explanatory variables are to be considered, involves complexities that are not present for a model that contains only two explanatory variables. First, the evaluation of all possible regression models becomes more complex computationally. Second, although competing models can be quantitatively evaluated, there may not exist a uniquely best model but rather several equally appropriate models.

We begin our analysis of the potato-processing data by first measuring the amount of collinearity that exists between the explanatory variables through the use of the variance inflationary factor. [See Equation (13.22).] Figure 13.18 represents partial MINITAB output for a multiple linear regression model in which the percent of solids is predicted from the six explanatory variables.

```
The regression equation is
Solids = - 13.5 + 2.94 pH - 0.154 Lower - 0.106 Upper + 1.50 Thick
         + 1.80 Varidriv + 0.149 Drumspd

Predictor      Coef       StDev         T        P       VIF
Constant     -13.503       7.854     -1.72    0.092
pH            2.9442      0.6482      4.54    0.000     1.5
Lower        -0.1542      0.2101     -0.73    0.467     8.5
Upper        -0.1062      0.1964     -0.54    0.591     8.4
Thick         1.503       1.392       1.08    0.286     1.6
Varidriv      1.7955      0.8389      2.14    0.038     9.9
Drumspd       0.14897     0.07001     2.13    0.039     9.6
```

Figure 13.18   Regression model obtained from MINITAB to predict percent of solids from six explanatory variables

We observe that four of the VIFs are above 5.0, ranging from 9.9 for VARIDRIV to 8.4 for Upper. Thus, based on the criteria developed by Snee (see Reference 6), there is evidence of collinearity among at least some of the explanatory variables. A reasonable strategy is to remove the independent variable with the largest VIF above 5 and determine what effect this has on the VIF of the remaining independent variables. Figure 13.19 represents the regression model obtained from MINITAB with only the VARIDRIV variable removed from the model.

From Figure 13.19, we see that the VIF for the DRUMSPEED independent variable has been reduced from 9.6 to 1.1. This indicates that VARIDRIV and DRUMSPEED were very highly correlated with each other but uncorrelated with the other independent variables. We also observe that the VIF values for LOWER and UPPER are still above 5, being equal to 8.4 and 8.3 respectively. Using the criterion of removing the independent variable with the highest VIF above five, we

```
The regression equation is
Solids = 2.05 + 3.26 pH - 0.200 Lower - 0.137 Upper + 1.71 Thick
          + 0.0082 Drumspd

Predictor       Coef        StDev        T          P        VIF
Constant       2.054        3.086       0.67      0.509
pH             3.2564       0.6547      4.97      0.000       1.4
Lower         -0.1999       0.2167     -0.92      0.361       8.4
Upper         -0.1373       0.2030     -0.68      0.502       8.3
Thick          1.705        1.440       1.18      0.242       1.6
Drumspd        0.00819      0.02487     0.33      0.744       1.1
```

Figure 13.19   Regression model obtained from MINITAB to predict percent of solids from five explanatory variables (excluding the VARIDRIV independent variable)

```
The regression equation is
Solids = 2.31 + 3.18 pH - 0.308 Upper + 1.52 Thick + 0.0048 Drumspd

Predictor       Coef        StDev        T          P        VIF
Constant       2.311        3.069       0.75      0.455
pH             3.1778       0.6482      4.90      0.000       1.4
Upper         -0.30814      0.08296    -3.71      0.001       1.4
Thick          1.518        1.423       1.07      0.292       1.6
Drumspd        0.00483      0.02457     0.20      0.845       1.1

S = 1.080        R-Sq = 42.9%      R-Sq(adj) = 38.2%
```

Figure 13.20   Regression model obtained from MINITAB to predict percent of solids from four explanatory variables (excluding the LOWER and VARIDRIV independent variables)

can remove the independent variable LOWER from the model. Figure 13.20 represents MINITAB output for a model that has excluded the LOWER and VARIDRIV independent variables.

From Figure 13.20, we see that none of the remaining four independent variables has a VIF value above 1.6. The LOWER independent variable was undoubtedly highly correlated with the UPPER independent variable, and its removal left us with four relatively uncorrelated independent variables: pH, UPPER, THICK, and DRUMSPEED.

The Stepwise Regression Approach to Model-Building

We now continue our analysis of these data by attempting to determine the explanatory variables that might be deleted from the final model. We shall first utilize a widely used search procedure called **stepwise regression,** which attempts to find the "best" regression model without examining all possible regressions. Once a best model has been found, residual analysis is utilized to evaluate the aptness of the model.

Recall that, in Section 13.5, the partial F-test criterion was used to evaluate portions of a multiple-regression model. Stepwise regression extends this partial F-

test criterion to a model with any number of explanatory variables. An important feature of this stepwise process is that an explanatory variable that has entered into the model at an early stage can subsequently be removed, once other explanatory variables are considered. Variables are either added to or deleted from the regression model at each step of the model-building process. The stepwise procedure terminates with the selection of a best-fitting model, when no variables can be added to or deleted from the last model fitted.

Figure 13.21 represents a partial output obtained from the PHStat add-in for Microsoft Excel for the potato-processing data.

	A B	C	D	E	F	G	H
1	Stepwise Regression for Potato Processing						
2	Table of Results for General Stepwise						
3							
4	PH entered.						
5							
6		df	SS	MS	F	Significance F	
7	Regression	1	25.35907426	25.35907426	17.67231123	0.000103538	
8	Residual	52	74.61796278	1.434960823			
9	Total	53	99.97703704				
10							
11		Coefficients	Standard Error	t Stat	P-value	Lower 95%	Upper 95%
12	Intercept	0.782076396	2.45805091	0.318169324	0.751630817	-4.150360268	5.714513059
13	PH	2.589618022	0.616011802	4.203844815	0.000103538	1.353500744	3.825735299
14							
15							
16	Upper Pressure entered.						
17							
18		df	SS	MS	F	Significance F	
19	Regression	2	41.46414438	20.73207219	18.07013179	1.16804E-06	
20	Residual	51	58.51289266	1.147311621			
21	Total	53	99.97703704				
22							
23		Coefficients	Standard Error	t Stat	P-value	Lower 95%	Upper 95%
24	Intercept	3.839576804	2.344527788	1.637675963	0.107645513	-0.86725551	8.546409118
25	PH	2.834310878	0.554678372	5.109827637	4.87591E-06	1.720748436	3.947873319
26	Upper Pressure	-0.263257541	0.070265187	-3.74662834	0.00045751	-0.404320681	-0.1221944
27							
28							
29	No other variables could be entered into the model. Stepwise ends.						

Figure 13.21   Stepwise regression output obtained from the PHStat add-in for Microsoft Excel for the potato-processing data

For this example, a significance level of 0.05 was utilized either to enter a variable into the model or to delete a variable from the model. The first variable entered into the model is pH. The p value of 0.0001 is less than 0.05, so pH is included in the regression model.

The next step involves the evaluation of the second variable to be included in this model. The variable to be chosen is the one that will make the largest contribution to the model, given that the first explanatory variable has already been selected. For this model, the second variable is Upper pressure. The p-value of 0.00046 for Upper pressure is less than 0.05, so Upper pressure is included in the regression model.

Now that Upper pressure has been entered into the model, we determine whether pH is still an important contributing variable or whether it can be eliminated from the model. The p-value of 0.000004876 (4.87591E-06 in scientific notation) for pH is also less than 0.05, so pH should remain in the regression model.

The next step involves the determination of whether any of the remaining variables should be added to the model. None of the other variables meets the 0.05 criterion for entry into the model, so the stepwise procedure terminates with a model that includes pH and Upper pressure only.

This stepwise regression approach to model-building was originally developed more than thirty years ago, in an era in which regression analysis on mainframe computers involved the costly use of large amounts of processing time. Under such conditions, a search procedure such as stepwise regression, although providing a limited evaluation of alternative models, became widely used. In this current era of personal computers and extremely fast hardware, the evaluation of many different regression models can be done in very little time, at a very small cost. Thus, we turn to a more general way of evaluating alternative regression models, the *best subset* approach.

The *Best Subset* Approach to Model Building

The **best subset approach** evaluates either all possible regression models for a given set of independent variables or at least the best subset of models for a given number of independent variables. Figure 13.22 represents partial output obtained from the PHStat add-in for Microsoft Excel in which the all regression models for a given number of parameters were provided according to two widely used criteria, the adjusted R^2 and the C_p statistic.[3]

[3]The PHStat Add-In for Microsoft Excel uses p rather than k to indicate the number of independent variables.

	A	B	C	D	E	F	G
1	**Best Subsets for Potato Processing**						
2							
3	*R2T*	0.428728					
4	1 - *R2T*	0.571272					
5	n	54					
6	T	5					
7	n - T	49					
8							**Consider**
9		Cp	p+1	R Square	Adj. R Square	Std. Error	**This Model?**
10	X1	14.0171	2	0.253649	0.239296084	1.197899	No
11	X1X2	2.200053	3	0.414737	0.391785177	1.071126	Yes
12	X1X2X3	3.038685	4	0.428277	0.393973229	1.069198	Yes
13	X1X2X3X4	5	5	0.428728	0.382093161	1.079627	Yes
14	X1X2X4	4.136941	4	0.415472	0.380400828	1.081104	No
15	X1X3	15.01919	3	0.265283	0.236470785	1.200121	No
16	X1X3X4	16.79688	4	0.267875	0.223947575	1.209923	No
17	X1X4	15.80859	3	0.25608	0.226906562	1.207614	No
18	X2	25.90084	2	0.115101	0.098083637	1.304354	No
19	X2X3	25.97922	3	0.137504	0.103681097	1.3003	No
20	X2X3X4	27.03666	4	0.148493	0.097402952	1.304846	No
21	X2X4	26.46649	3	0.131823	0.097777342	1.304575	No
22	X3	28.92168	2	0.079882	0.062187562	1.330057	No
23	X3X4	30.54398	3	0.084286	0.048375212	1.339816	No
24	X4	34.92666	2	0.009872	-0.009168586	1.37973	No

Figure 13.22 Best subsets regression output obtained from the PHStat add-in for Microsoft Excel for the potato-processing data

The first criterion that is often used is the adjusted R^2, which adjusts the R^2 of each model to account for the number of independent variables in the model. (See Section 13.4.) Models with different numbers of independent variables are to be compared, so the adjusted R^2 is the appropriate criterion here rather than R^2.

Referring to Figure 13.22, we observe that the adjusted R^2 reaches a maximum value of 0.39397 for the model that includes the independent variables pH, UPPER, and THICK plus the intercept term (for a total of four terms). We note that the model selected by using stepwise regression, which includes only pH and UPPER, has an adjusted R^2 of 0.39179. Thus, the best-subset approach, unlike stepwise regression, has provided us with several alternative models to evaluate in greater depth by using other criteria, such as parsimony, interpretability, and departure from model assumptions (as evaluated by residual analysis).

A second criterion often used in the evaluation of competing models is a statistic developed by Mallows. (See References 1 and 5.) This statistic, which is called C_p, measures the differences of a fitted regression model from a true model, along with random error. The **C_p statistic** is defined as follows:

THE C_p STATISTIC

$$C_p = \frac{(1 - R_k^2)(n - T)}{1 - R_T^2} - (n - 2(k + 1)) \qquad (13.23)$$

where

k = number of independent variables included in a regression model

T = total number of parameters (including the intercept) to be considered for inclusion in the regression model

R_k^2 = coefficient of multiple determination for a regression model that has k independent variables

R_T^2 = coefficient of multiple determination for a regression model that contains all T parameters

---

Using Equation (13.23) to compute C_p for the model containing the three independent variables of pH, UPPER, and THICK, we have

$$n = 54, \quad k = 3, \quad T = 4 + 1 = 5, \quad R_k^2 = 0.428277, \quad R_T^2 = 0.428728$$

so that

$$C_p = \frac{(1 - 0.428277)(54 - 5)}{1 - 0.428728} - [54 - 2(3 + 1)]$$

$$C_p = 3.04$$

When a regression model with k independent variables contains only random differences from a true model, the average value of C_p is $k + 1$, the number of parameters. Thus, in evaluating many alternative regression models, our goal is to find models whose C_p is less than or equal to $k + 1$.

From Figure 13.22, we observe that there are three models that contains a C_p value equal to or below $k + 1$. These are the models with X_1 and X_2, with X_1, X_2, and X_3, and with X_1, X_2, X_3, and X_4. Because the models with X_1 and X_2 and with X_1, X_2, and X_3 have fewer variables and also have C_p less than $k + 1$, we will focus on these two models. One approach for choosing between models that meet the criteria that C_p be less than $k + 1$ is to determine whether the models contain a subset of variables that are common and then test whether the contribution of the additional variables is significant. In this case, that would mean testing whether variable X_3 made a significant contribution to the regression model, given that variables X_1 and X_2 were already included in the model. If the contribution were statistically significant, then variable X_3 would be included in the regression model. If variable X_3 did not make a statistically significant contribution, variable X_3 would not be included in the model. Figure 13.23 represents a regression model that includes variables X_1, X_2, and X_3 (pH, UPPER, and THICK).

```
The regression equation is
Solids = 2.63 + 3.15 pH - 0.309 Upper + 1.53 Thick

Predictor        Coef        StDev           T          P         VIF
Constant        2.626       2.593         1.01      0.316
pH              3.1481      0.6243         5.04      0.000        1.3
Upper          -0.30935     0.08193      -3.78      0.000        1.4
Thick           1.532       1.408         1.09      0.282        1.6

S = 1.069       R-Sq = 42.8%        R-Sq(adj) = 39.4%
```

Figure 13.23   Regression model obtained from MINITAB to predict percent of solids from three explanatory variables including the pH, UPPER, and THICK independent variables

From Figure 13.23, we observe that THICK (X_3) has a t value of 1.09 and a p-value of 0.282. Because the p-value of $0.282 > 0.05$, we can conclude that THICK (X_3) does not make a significant contribution to the regression model, given that pH (X_1) and Upper pressure (X_2) are included. Therefore, a reasonable approach is to eliminate THICK (X_3) from the model and to fit the regression model that includes pH (X_1) and Upper pressure (X_2). Figure 13.24 on page 662 represents MINITAB output for this model.

As would be expected since Lower pressure and Upper pressure were so highly correlated, the resulting model is very similar to the regression model that included pH and Lower pressure that was discussed in Sections 13.1–13.5. In addition, the residual plots were similar as well. Thus, we can conclude that either raising the pH and or reducing the Lower or Upper pressure should result in an increased percentage of solids.

Exhibit 13.2 summarizes the steps involved in model building, and Figure 13.25 on page 663 represents a road map of these steps in model-building.

```
Solids = 3.84 + 2.83 pH - 0.263 Upper

Predictor          Coef         StDev            T          P        VIF
Constant          3.840         2.345         1.64      0.108
pH               2.8343        0.5547         5.11      0.000        1.0
Upper          -0.26326       0.07027        -3.75      0.000        1.0

S = 1.071        R-Sq = 41.5%      R-Sq(adj) = 39.2%

Analysis of Variance

Source               DF            SS           MS          F          P
Regression            2        41.464       20.732      18.07      0.000
Residual Error       51        58.513        1.147
Total                53        99.977

Source         DF      Seq SS
pH              1      25.359
Upper           1      16.105
```

Figure 13.24   Regression model obtained from MINITAB to predict percent of solids from two explanatory variables (pH and Upper)

EXHIBIT 13.2 Steps Involved in Model-Building

1. Choose a set of independent variables to be considered for inclusion in the regression model.

2. Fit a full regression model that includes all the independent variables to be considered, so that the Variance Inflationary Factor (VIF) for each independent variable can be determined.

3. Determine whether any independent variables have a VIF > 5.

4. There are three possible results that can occur.
   (a) None of the independent variables has a VIF > 5. If this is the case, proceed to step 5.
   (b) One of the independent variables has a VIF > 5. If this is the case, eliminate that independent variable, and proceed to step 5.
   (c) More than one of the independent variables has a VIF > 5. If this is the case, eliminate the independent variable that has the highest VIF, and go back to step 2.

5. Perform a best-subset regression with the remaining independent variables to obtain the best models (in terms of C_p) for a given number of independent variables.

6. List all models that have $C_p \leq (k + 1)$.

7. Among those models listed in step 6, choose a best model.

8. Perform a complete analysis of the model chosen including residual analysis.

9. Given the results of the residual analysis, add curvilinear terms, transform variables, and reanalyze the data, as necessary.

10. Use the selected model for prediction.

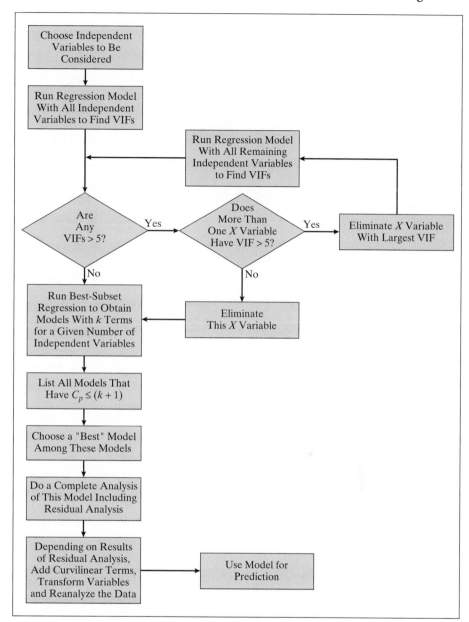

Figure 13.25   Road map for model-building

PROBLEMS

13.45 Suppose that four independent variables were to be considered for inclusion in a regression model. A sample of 50 observations is selected, with the following results:

The model that includes independent variables A and B has a C_p value equal to 4.6;

The model that includes independent variables A and C has a C_p value equal to 2.4;

The model that includes independent variables A, B, and C has a C_p value equal to 2.7.

(a) Given these results, which models meet the criterion for further consideration? Explain.

(b) How would you compare the model that contains independent variables *A*, *B*, and *C* to the model that contains independent variables *A* and *C*? Explain.

13.46 The file **AUTO96** contains data on 89 automobile models from the year 1996. Among the variables included are gasoline mileage, weight, width, length of each automobile, and whether the car has front wheel drive or rear wheel drive. Develop the most appropriate multiple regression model to predict gasoline mileage. Be sure to perform a thorough residual analysis. In addition, provide a detailed explanation of your results.

13.47 In Problem 13.35 on page 650, diastolic blood pressure and gender were used to predict heart recovery rate. Now consider the variables age, gender, systolic blood pressure, and diastolic blood pressure for inclusion in a multiple regression model to predict heart recovery rate (**RECOVERY** file). Be sure to perform a thorough residual analysis. In addition, provide a detailed explanation of your results.

13.48 As part of a landfill quality-monitoring project, data were collected on the possible effects of a landfill on surface and groundwater chemistry. Observations on characteristics of well water from one of the wells, relating total dissolved solids (TDS) to pH, conductivity, and chemical oxygen demand (COD), are contained in the data file **LANDFILL**. Develop the most appropriate multiple-regression model to predict total dissolved solids (TDS). Be sure to perform a thorough residual analysis. In addition, provide a detailed explanation of your results.

13.49 The file **UNIV&COL** contains data on 80 colleges and universities. Among the variables included are the annual total cost (in thousands of dollars), the average total score on the Scholastic Aptitude Test (SAT), the room and board expenses (in thousands of dollars), whether the institution is public or private, and whether the TOEFL criterion is at least 550. Develop the most appropriate multiple-regression model to predict annual total cost. Be sure to perform a thorough residual analysis. In addition, provide a detailed explanation of your results.

13.11 PITFALLS IN MULTIPLE REGRESSION

In Section 12.9, we discussed pitfalls in regression and ethical issues. Now that we have examined a variety of multiple-regression models, we need to concern ourselves with some additional pitfalls related to the use of regression analysis. These are displayed in Exhibit 13.3.

EXHIBIT 13.3 Additional Pitfalls in Multiple Regression

1. The need to understand that the regression coefficient for a particular independent variable is interpreted from a perspective in which the values of all other independent variables are held constant

2. The need to use residual plots for each independent variable

3. The need to evaluate interaction terms to determine whether the slope of other independent variables with the response variable is the same at each level of the dummy variable

4. The need to obtain the VIF for each independent variable before determining which independent variables should be included in the model

5. The need to examine several alternative models using best-subsets regression

6. The need to have a large enough sample size. It is recommended that the sample size should be at least ten times the number of explanatory variables in the model.

7. The need to have a sufficiently wide range in the values of the independent variable so that the relationship with the dependent variable is not underestimated.

8. The need to realize that a good fitting model does not necessarily mean that the model can truly be used for prediction. The researcher with knowledge of the subject matter would have to be convinced that the process that produced the data will remain stable in the future in order to use the model for predictive purposes.

KEY TERMS

Adjusted R^2 622
Best-subset approach 659
C_p statistic 660
coefficient of multiple
  determination 621
coefficient of partial
  determination 636
collinearity 654
dummy variables 646
exponential model 652

interaction term 648
logarithmic transformation 652
multiple regression 616
net regression coefficient 618
partial F-test criterion 632
quadratic curvilinear regression
  model 639
square-root transformation 651
stepwise regression 657
variance inflationary factor (VIF) 654

CHAPTER REVIEW *Checking Your Understanding*

13.50 How does the interpretation of the regression coefficients differ in multiple regression as compared to simple linear regression?

13.51 How does testing the significance of the entire regression model differ from testing the contribution of each independent variable in the multiple-regression model?

13.52 How do the coefficients of partial determination differ from the coefficient of multiple determination?

13.53 Why and how are dummy variables used?

13.54 How can we evaluate whether the slope of an independent variable with the response variable is the same for each level of the dummy variable?

13.55 What is the purpose of using transformations in multiple-regression analysis?

13.56 How do we evaluate whether independent variables are intercorrelated?

13.57 Under what circumstances would we want to include a dummy variable in a regression model?

13.58 What assumption concerning the slope between the response variable Y and the explanatory variable X must be made when a dummy variable is included in a regression model?

13.59 What is the difference between stepwise regression and best-subset regression?

13.60 How do we choose among models that have been selected according to the C_p statistic in best-subset regression?

Chapter Review Problems

13.61 A research and development plan was carried out to determine the effect of thickness and Brinell hardness on the ballistic limit of armor plate placed at an angle of 40° obliquity to the line of fire. (Ballistic limit is defined as the average of two velocities within 30 feet/second of each other: one is the lowest velocity of projectiles fired at the place that gives complete penetration; the other is the highest velocity of incomplete or partial penetrations.) In this study, armor-piercing bullets were fired against armor plate of the following thickness and Brinell hardness, (thousandths of an inch) with the resulting ballistic limits.

Ballistic Limit	Thickness	Hardness	Ballistic Limit	Thickness	Hardness
927	253	317	1393	253	407
978	258	321	1401	252	426
1028	259	341	1436	246	432
906	247	350	1327	250	469
1159	256	352	950	242	275
1055	246	363	998	243	302
1335	257	365	1144	239	331
1392	262	375	1080	242	355
1362	255	373	1276	244	385
1374	258	391	1062	234	426

ARMOR

Use Microsoft Excel or MINITAB to develop the regression model.
(a) State the multiple-regression equation.
(b) Interpret the meaning of the slopes in this equation.
(c) Predict the average ballistic limit for an armor plate that has a thickness of 0.275 inches and a hardness of 350 Brinell units.
(d) Perform a residual analysis on your results, and determine the adequacy of the fit of the model.
(e) Determine whether there is a significant relationship between ballistic limit and the two explanatory variables (thickness and hardness) at the 0.05 level of significance.
(f) Determine the p-value in (e), and interpret its meaning.
(g) Interpret the meaning of the coefficient of multiple determination in this problem.
(h) Determine the adjusted R^2.
(i) At the 0.05 level of significance, determine whether each explanatory variable makes a significant contribution to the regression model. Using these results, indicate the regression model that should be used in this problem.
(j) Determine the p-values in (i), and interpret their meaning.
(k) Set up a 95% confidence interval estimate of the population slope between ballistic limit and each of the independent variables.
(l) Compute the coefficients of partial determination and interpret their meaning.

13.62 The term hydroponics is used to describe the growing of plants without soil. This includes growing plants in media such as sand, gravel, vermiculite, and Styrofoam plastic. The effect of boron and calcium on the yield of tomato plants grown hydroponically was studied, with the following results.

Yield (grams)	Calcium (ppm)	Boron (ppm)	Yield (grams)	Calcium (ppm)	Boron (ppm)
897	500	5	809	500	10
690	500	5	952	500	10
780	500	5	765	500	10
1020	500	5	810	500	10
676	250	5	580	250	10
725	250	5	610	250	10
582	250	5	492	250	10
567	250	5	667	250	10	**TOMATOHYD**

Use Microsoft Excel or MINITAB to develop the regression model.
 (a) State the multiple-regression equation.
 (b) Interpret the meaning of the slopes in this equation.
 (c) Predict the average yield for a tomato plant that has 250 ppm of calcium and 10 ppm of boron.
 (d) Perform a residual analysis on your results, and determine the adequacy of the fit of the model.
 (e) Determine whether there is a significant relationship between yield and the two explanatory variables (calcium and boron) at the 0.05 level of significance.
 (f) Determine the p-value in (e), and interpret its meaning.
 (g) Interpret the meaning of the coefficient of multiple determination in this problem.
 (h) Determine the adjusted R^2.
 (i) At the 0.05 level of significance, determine whether each explanatory variable makes a significant contribution to the regression model. On the basis of these results, indicate the regression model that should be used in this problem.
 (j) Determine the p-values in (i), and interpret their meaning.
 (k) Set up a 95% confidence interval estimate of the population slope between yield and each of the independent variables.
 (l) Compute the coefficients of partial determination and interpret their meaning.

13.63 The acidification of lakes in North America and Europe is a problem of great concern. Data have been collected (Crawford, S. L., M. H. DeGroot, J. B. Kadane, and M. L. Small; Modeling lake chemistry distributions: Approximate Bayesian methods for estimating a finite-mixture model, *Technometrics,* 34, 1992, 441–453) on the acid neutralizing capacity (ANC), dissolved organic carbon, lake area, and type of lake. (See the **LAKE** data file.) Develop the most appropriate multiple-regression model to predict acid-neutralizing capacity. Be sure to perform a thorough residual analysis. In addition, provide a detailed explanation of your results.

13.64 In Problem 12.54 on page 609, an experiment was described (see datafile **SCRUBBER**) concerning the effect of air flowrate on the performance of the scrubber, as measured by the number of transfer units. In addition to the air flowrate, we would now like to consider the water flowrate (liters/minute), the recirculating water flowrate (liters/minute), and the orifice size (mm) in the air side of the pneumatic nozzle. Develop the most appropriate multiple-regression model to predict the number of transfer units. Be sure to perform a thorough residual analysis. In addition, provide a detailed explanation of your results.

13.65 In Problem 13.6 on page 623, solar radiation and soil temperature were used to predict radon concentration (see the **RADON** file). In addition to these variables, consider vapor pressure (mBars), wind speed (mph), relative humidity (%), dew point (°F), and ambient air temperature (°F). Develop the most appropriate multiple-regression model to predict radon concentration. Be sure to perform a thorough residual analysis. In addition, provide a detailed explanation of your results.

13.66 San Luis Obispo Creek is plagued by excess algal growth. A study measured a variety of attributes that its authors believed influence algal growth (% cover). These included water velocity (m/sec), volume rate flow (m^3/sec), rainfall (cm. 11 days before sampling), ammonia (NH_4-mg/L), nitrite (NO_2-mg/L), nitrate (NO_3-mg/L), phosphate (PO_4-mg/L), dissolved oxygen (ppm), saturation of oxygen (%), total dissolved solids (mg/L), leaves (% cover), roots (% cover), stems (% cover), and light (foot-candles). The data are contained in the **ALGAE** file. Develop the most appropriate multiple-regression model to predict algal growth. Be sure to perform a thorough residual analysis. In addition, provide a detailed explanation of your results.

13.67 The file **UNIV&COL** contains data on 80 colleges and universities. Among the variables included are the academic calendar type (1 = semester; 0 = other), annual total cost (in thousands of dollars), average total score on the Scholastic Aptitude Test (SAT), room and board expenses (in thousands of dollars), whether the institution is public or private, whether the TOEFL criterion is at least 550, and average indebtedness at graduation. Develop the most appropriate multiple-regression model to predict average indebtedness at graduation. Be sure to perform a thorough residual analysis. In addition, provide a detailed explanation of your results.

REFERENCES

1. Hocking, R. R.; "Developments in Linear Regression Methodology: 1959–1982," *Technometrics* 25, 1983: 219–250
2. Marquardt, D. W.; "You Should Standardize the Predictor Variables in Your Regression Models," discussion of "A Critique of Some Ridge Regression Methods," by G. Smith and F. Campbell, *Journal of the American Statistical Association* 75, 1980: 87–91
3. *Microsoft Excel 2000;* Redmond, WA: Microsoft Corp., 1999
4. *MINITAB for Windows Version 12;* State College, PA: MINITAB, Inc., 1998
5. Neter, J., M. Kutner, C. Nachtsheim, and W. Wasserman; *Applied Linear Statistical Models,* 4th ed.; Homewood, IL: Irwin, 1996
6. Snee, R. D.; "Some Aspects of Nonorthogonal Data Analysis, Part I. Developing Prediction Equations," *Journal of Quality Technology,* 5, 1973: 67–79

APPENDIX 13.1 *Using Microsoft Excel for Multiple-Regression Models*

In Chapter 12, we used the Data Analysis tool, its Regression option, and the PHStat add-in for Microsoft Excel for the simple linear regression model. In this chapter, we developed a variety of multiple-regression models whose computations can also be done with the Regression option of the Data Analysis tool or with the PHStat add-in for Microsoft Excel. In using the Regression option or PHStat for multiple regression models, it is important to remember that the *entire set of X variables* must be placed in *consecutive* columns, because the Regression tool will allow us to specify only a single contiguous range for the X variable.

To illustrate the use of PHStat and the Regression tool of Microsoft Excel for multiple regression, open the **POTATO.XLS** workbook, and click the **Data** sheet tab. Verify that Percentage of Solids is in column A, pH is in column B, and Lower is in column C. **Select PHStat | Regression | Multiple Regression.** In the Multiple Regression dialog box, enter **A1:A55** in the Y Variable Cell Range: edit box. Enter **B1:C55** in the X Variables Cell Range: edit box. Select the First cells in the Both ranges contain label check box. Enter **95** in the Confidence Level for regr. coefficients: edit box. Select the **Regression Statistics Table,** the **ANOVA and Coefficients Table,** the **Residuals Table,** and the **Residual Plots** check boxes. Enter **Regression Analysis for Potato Processing** in the Output Title: edit box. Select the **Coefficients of Partial Determination, Variance Inflationary Factor (VIF), and Confidence** and **Prediction Interval Estimates** check boxes. Enter **95** in the Confidence level for int. estimates: edit box. Click the **OK** button. To obtain confidence and prediction interval estimates for specific values of the X variables, click the **Intervals** sheet tab. For the potato-processing data, to obtain estimates for a pH of 4 and a Lower value of 15, enter **4** in cell B5 and **15** in cell B6.

Obtaining Quadratic Curvilinear Regression Models by Using Microsoft Excel

We can use simple formulas in the form $=A2^2$ to create the square of a first explanatory variable. As an example, consider the fly-ash data of Section 13.6. To implement the quadratic curvilinear model for these data, open the **FLYASH.XLS** workbook, and click the **Data** sheet tab. Verify that the fly-ash and strength data of Table 13.4 on page 639 have been entered into columns A and B, respectively. With the cursor in cell B1, select **Insert | Columns.** Enter the label flyash% in cell B1 (of the Data sheet). Enter the formula $=A2^2$ in cell B2, and copy it down through row 19. Select **PHStat | Regression | Multiple Regression.** In the Multiple Regression dialog box, enter **C1:C19** in the Y Variable Cell Range: edit box. Enter **A1:B19** in the X Variables Cell Range: edit box. Select the **First cells in both ranges contain label** check box. Enter **95** in the Confidence Level for regr. coefficients: edit box. Select the **Regression Statistics Table,** the **ANOVA and Coefficients Table,** the **Residuals Table,** and the **Residual plots** check boxes. Enter **Regression Analysis for Concrete Strength** in the Output Title: edit box. Click the **OK** button. The output will be similar to that shown in Figure 13.12 on page 641.

Obtaining Dummy Variable Regression Models Using Microsoft Excel

We can use the Excel *find and replace* feature to change a two-category categorical variable into a dummy variable with the values 0 and 1. As an example, consider the drilling-hole data of Section 13.7. To implement a regression model that includes a dummy variable for the type of drilling hole, open the **DRILL.XLS** workbook, and click the **Data** sheet tab. Verify that the drilling depth, drilling time, and type of drilling-hole data have been entered into columns A, B, and C, respectively. For later data verification, copy the contents of column C to column D. Select the range C2:C101, containing the categorical responses Dry and Wet, then select **Edit | Replace.** In the Replace dialog box, enter **Wet** in the Find what: edit box. Enter **1** in the Replace with: edit box. Click the **Replace All** button. With the cell range C2:C101 still selected, select **Edit | Replace** a second time. In the Replace dialog box, enter **Dry** in the Find what: edit box. Enter **0** in the Replace with: edit box. Click the **Replace All** button. Verify the changes by comparing the dummy-variable values in column C with their categorical equivalents in column D. Once verified, the contents of columns A, B, and C can be used in a dummy-variable regression analysis. The X variables need to be located in contiguous columns, so use the Insert Columns command to insert column C in column B so that the dummy variable is located next to the drilling-depth variable. To generate this regression analysis, select **PHStat | Regression | Multiple Regression.** In the Multiple Regression dialog box, enter **C1:C101** in the Y Variable Cell Range: edit box. Enter **A1:B101** in the X Variables Cell Range: edit box. Select the **First cells in both ranges contain label** check box. Enter **95** in the Confidence Level for regr. coefficients: edit box. Select the **Regression Statistics Table** and the **ANOVA and Coefficients Table, the Residual Tables,** and the **Residual Plots** check boxes. Enter **Regression Analysis for Drilling Holes** in the Output Title: edit box. Click the **OK** button. The output obtained will be similar to that obtained in Figure 13.14 on page 647.

Using Microsoft Excel for Transformations

Models involving transformations (see page 651) can also be developed by using an appropriate Excel function. To apply the square-root transformation of the model shown in Equation (13.17) on page 651, we can use the **SQRT** function. To apply transformations involving the natural logarithm (ln), we can use the **LN** function; we use the **LOG** function for transformations involving the common (base 10) logarithms.

Using the PHStat Add-In for Microsoft Excel for Model-Building

To perform the best-subset analysis, use the Regression | Best Subsets choice of the PHStat add-in. As an example, consider the potato-processing problem of Section 13.10. To perform the best-subset analysis for this problem, open the **POTATO.XLS** workbook, and click the **Data** sheet tab. Because the Lower and Varidriv variables have been eliminated from consideration (on account of collinearity), temporarily delete these variables, so that the remaining four independent variables are in contiguous columns B–E. Select **PHStat | Regression | Best Subsets.** In the Best Subsets dialog box, enter **A1:A55** in the Y Variable Cell Range: edit box. Enter **B1:E55** in the X Variables Cell Range: edit box. Select the **First cells in both ranges contain label** check box. Enter **95** in the Confidence Level for regr. coefficients: edit box. Enter **Best Subsets Analysis for Potato-Processing Models** in the Output Title: edit box. Click the **OK** button.

The add-in inserts multiple worksheets, including a worksheet, similar to one shown in Figure 13.22 on page 659 that contains the best-subset analysis summary. Because this worksheet is *not* dynamically changeable, any changes made to the underlying data would require using the PHStat add-in a second time to produce updated results. (*Note:* The Best Subsets procedure accepts up to seven X variables. On systems with slower processors or smaller main-memory sizes, this procedure may take many seconds or minutes to complete. When used with many X variables on systems with limited memory sizes, the procedure may cause Microsoft Excel to end with a fatal error.)

To perform stepwise regression, use the Regression | Stepwise choice of the PHStat add-in. As an example, consider the potato-processing problem of Section 13.10. To perform the stepwise regression analysis for this problem, open the **POTATO.XLS** workbook, and click the **Data** sheet tab. Because the Lower and Varidriv variables have been eliminated from consideration (on account of collinearity), temporarily delete these variables, so that the remaining four independent variables are in contiguous columns B–E. Select **PHStat | Regression | Stepwise Regression.** In the Stepwise dialog box, enter **A1:A55** in the Y Variable Cell Range: edit box. Enter **B1:E55** in the X Variables Cell Range: edit box. Select the **First cells in both ranges contain label** check box. Enter **95** in the Confidence Level for regr. coefficients: edit box. Under Stepwise Criteria, select *p* **values.** Under Stepwise options, select **General Stepwise.** In the p value to enter: edit box, enter **.05.** In the p value to remove: edit box, enter **.05.** Enter Stepwise Analysis for Potato Processing Models in the Output Title: edit box. Click the **OK** button. The results obtained will be similar to those of Figure 13.21 on page 658.

APPENDIX 13.2 *Using MINITAB for Multiple-Regression Models*

In Appendix 12.2, instructions were provided for using MINITAB for simple linear regression. The same set of instructions are valid in using MINITAB for multiple regression. To obtain a regression analysis for the potato-processing data, open the **POTATO.MTW** worksheet, and select **Stat | Regression | Regression.** Enter **C1** or **'Solids'** in the Response: edit box and **C2** or **'pH'** and **C3** (or **'Lower'**) in the Predictors: edit box. Click the **Graphs** button. In the Residuals for Plots: edit box, select the **Regular** option button. For Residual Plots, select the **Histogram of residuals** check box. In the Residuals versus the variables: edit box, select **C2** or **'pH'** and **C3** or **'Lower'.** Click the **OK** button to return to the Regression dialog box. Click the **Results** option button. In the Regression Results dialog box, click the **In addition, the full table of fits and residuals** option button. Click the **OK** button to return to the Regression dialog box. Click the **Options** button. Under Display, select the **Variance inflation factors** check box. In the Prediction interval for new observations: edit box, enter **4 15.** Enter **95** in the Confidence level: edit box. Click the **OK** button to return to the Regression dialog box. Click the **OK** button. The results obtained will be similar to those of Figures 13.3 and 13.4 on pages 619 and 624.

Using MINITAB for Quadratic Curvilinear Regression

To create a new X variable that is the square of another X variable, select **Calc | Calculator.** In the Store result in variable: edit box, enter the column number or name for the new variable. In the Expression: edit box, enter {name or column number of the X variable to be squared}**2. Click the **OK** button. A new X variable that is the square of another X variable has been entered in the specified column. Continue with the regression analysis as discussed previously.

Using MINITAB for Dummy Variables

In order to do regression analysis with dummy variables, the categories of the dummy variable must be coded as 0 and 1. If the dummy variable has not already been recoded as a 0–1 variable, MINITAB can recode the variable. As an illustration, open the **DRILL.MTW** worksheet. Note that the type variable in column C3 had been entered as Dry and Wet. To recode this variable by using MINITAB, select **Calc | Make Indicator Variables.** In the Indicator variables for: edit box, enter **C3** or **'Type'.** In the Store results in: edit box, enter **C4 C5,** because we need to specify a column for each possible definition of the dummy variable. Click the **OK** button.

Note that Dry has been coded as 1 in C4, and Wet has been coded as 1 in C5. To define an interaction term that is the product of drilling depth and the dummy variable type, select **Calc | Calculator.** In the Store result in variable: edit box, enter **C6.** In the Expression: edit box, enter the **'Depth * Type'** or **C1 * C5.** Click the **OK** button. A new X variable that is the product of these two variables has been entered in column C6.

Using MINITAB for Transforming Variables

To transform a variable, select **Calc | Calculator.** In the Store result in variable edit box, enter the column number or name for the new variable. Select the function to be used for the transformation (such as $\log_{10}$, natural log, or square root). In the Expression edit box, after the function has been selected, enter the name of the X variable to be transformed in the parentheses of the function. Click the **OK** button. Continue with the regression analysis as discussed previously.

Using MINITAB for Stepwise Regression and Best-Subset Regression

MINITAB can be used for model-building with either stepwise regression or best-subset regression. To illustrate model building with the potato-processing data, open the **POTATO.MTW** worksheet. To obtain a stepwise regression, select **Stat | Regression | Stepwise.** In the Response: edit box, enter **'Solids'** or **C1.** In the Predictors: edit box, enter **C2** or **'pH', C4** or **'Upper', C5** or **'Thick',** and **C7** or **'Drumspeed'.** Click the **Options** button. The entries for F to enter: and F to remove: should be **4.0.** Click the **OK** button to return to the stepwise regression dialog box. Click the **OK** button.

To obtain a best-subset regression, select **Stat | Regression | Best Subsets.** In the Response: edit box, enter **'Solids'** or **C1.** In the Predictors: edit box, enter **C2** or **'pH', C4** or **'Upper', C5** or **'Thick',** and **C7** or **'Drumspeed'.** Click the **Options** button. Enter **3** in the Models of each size to print: edit box. Click the **OK** button to return to the Best-subsets regression dialog box. Click the **OK** button.

Using MINITAB for a Three-Dimensional Plot

MINITAB can be used to obtain a three-dimensional plot, when there are two independent variables in the regression model. To illustrate the three-dimensional plot with the potato-processing data, open the **POTATO.MTW** worksheet. Select **Graph | 3D Plot.** In the 3D Plot dialog box, enter **C1** or **'Solids'** in the Z edit box, **C2** or **'pH'** in the Y edit box, and **C3** or 'Lower' in the X edit box. Click the **OK** button. The results obtained will be similar to those of Figure 13.1 on page 617.

Appendix A

TABLES

TABLE A.1

TABLE OF RANDOM NUMBERS

	Column							
ROM	00000 12345	00001 67890	11111 12345	11112 67890	22222 12345	22223 67890	33333 12345	33334 67890
1	49280	88924	35779	00283	81163	07275	89863	02348
2	61870	41657	07468	08612	98083	97349	20775	45091
3	43898	65923	25078	86129	78496	97653	91550	08078
4	62993	93912	30454	84598	56095	20664	12872	64647
5	33850	58555	51438	85507	71865	79488	76783	31708
6	97340	03364	88472	04334	63919	36394	11095	92470
7	70543	29776	10087	10072	55980	64688	68239	20461
8	89382	93809	00796	95945	34101	81277	66090	88872
9	37818	72142	67140	50785	22380	16703	53362	44940
10	60430	22834	14130	96593	23298	56203	92671	15925
11	82975	66158	84731	19436	55790	69229	28661	13675
12	39087	71938	40355	54324	08401	26299	49420	59208
13	55700	24586	93247	32596	11865	63397	44251	43189
14	14756	23997	78643	75912	83832	32768	18928	57070
15	32166	53251	70654	92827	63491	04233	33825	69662
16	23236	73751	31888	81718	06546	83246	47651	04877
17	45794	26926	15130	82455	78305	55058	52551	47182
18	09893	20505	14225	68514	46427	56788	96297	78822
19	54382	74598	91499	14523	68479	27686	46162	83554
20	94750	89923	37089	20048	80336	94598	26940	36858
21	70297	34135	53140	33340	42050	82341	44104	82949
22	85157	47954	32979	26575	57600	40881	12250	73742
23	11100	02340	12860	74697	96644	89439	28707	25815
24	36871	50775	30592	57143	17381	68856	25853	35041
25	23913	48357	63308	16090	51690	54607	72407	55538
26	79348	36085	27973	65157	07456	22255	25626	57054
27	92074	54641	53673	54421	18130	60103	69593	49464
28	06873	21440	75593	41373	49502	17972	82578	16364
29	12478	37622	99659	31065	83613	69889	58869	29571
30	57175	55564	65411	42547	70457	03426	72937	83792
31	91616	11075	80103	07831	59309	13276	26710	73000
32	78025	73539	14621	39044	47450	03197	12787	47709
33	27587	67228	80145	10175	12822	86687	65530	49325
34	16690	20427	04251	64477	73709	73945	92396	68263
35	70183	58065	65489	31833	82093	16747	10386	59293
36	90730	35385	15679	99742	50866	78028	75573	67257
37	10934	93242	13431	24590	02770	48582	00906	58595
38	82462	30166	79613	47416	13389	80268	05085	96666
39	27463	10433	07606	16285	93699	60912	94532	95632
40	02979	52997	09079	92709	90110	47506	53693	49892
41	46888	69929	75233	52507	32097	37594	10067	67327
42	53638	83161	08289	12639	08141	12640	28437	09268
43	82433	61427	17239	89160	19666	08814	37841	12847
44	35766	31672	50082	22795	66948	65581	84393	15890
45	10853	42581	08792	13257	61973	24450	52351	16602
46	20341	27398	72906	63955	17276	10646	74692	48438
47	54458	90542	77563	51839	52901	53355	83281	19177
48	26337	66530	16687	35179	46560	00123	44546	79896
49	34314	23729	85264	05575	96855	23820	11091	79821
50	28603	10708	68933	34189	92166	15181	66628	58599

(*Continued*)

			Column				
ROM	00000 12345	00001 67890	11111 12345	11112 67890	22222 12345	22223 67890	33333 12345	33334 67890
51	66194	28926	99547	16625	45515	67953	12108	57846
52	78240	43195	24837	32511	70880	22070	52622	61881
53	00833	88000	67299	68215	11274	55624	32991	17436
54	12111	86683	61270	58036	64192	90611	15145	01748
55	47189	99951	05755	03834	43782	90599	40282	51417
56	76396	72486	62423	27618	84184	78922	73561	52818
57	46409	17469	32483	09083	76175	19985	26309	91536
58	74626	22111	87286	46772	42243	68046	44250	42439
59	34450	81974	93723	49023	58432	67083	36876	93391
60	36327	72135	33005	28701	34710	49359	50693	89311
61	74185	77536	84825	09934	99103	09325	67389	45869
62	12296	41623	62873	37943	25584	09609	63360	47270
63	90822	60280	88925	99610	42772	60561	76873	04117
64	72121	79152	96591	90305	10189	79778	68016	13747
65	95268	41377	25684	08151	61816	58555	54305	86189
66	92603	09091	75884	93424	72586	88903	30061	14457
67	18813	90291	05275	01223	79607	95426	34900	09778
68	38840	26903	28624	67157	51986	42865	14508	49315
69	05959	33836	53758	16562	41081	38012	41230	20528
70	85141	21155	99212	32685	51403	31926	69813	58781
71	75047	59643	31074	38172	03718	32119	69506	67143
72	30752	95260	68032	62871	58781	34143	68790	69766
73	22986	82575	42187	62295	84295	30634	66562	31442
74	99439	86692	90348	66036	48399	73451	26698	39437
75	20389	93029	11881	71685	65452	89047	63669	02656
76	39249	05173	68256	36359	20250	68686	05947	09335
77	96777	33605	29481	20063	09398	01843	35139	61344
78	04860	32918	10798	50492	52655	33359	94713	28393
79	41613	42375	00403	03656	77580	87772	86877	57085
80	17930	00794	53836	53692	67135	98102	61912	11246
81	24649	31845	25736	75231	83808	98917	93829	99430
82	79899	34061	54308	59358	56462	58166	97302	86828
83	76801	49594	81002	30397	52728	15101	72070	33706
84	36239	63636	38140	65731	39788	06872	38971	53363
85	07392	64449	17886	63632	53995	17574	22247	62607
86	67133	04181	33874	98835	67453	59734	76381	63455
87	77759	31504	32832	70861	15152	29733	75371	39174
88	85992	72268	42920	20810	29361	51423	90306	73574
89	79553	75952	54116	65553	47139	60579	09165	85490
90	41101	17336	48951	53674	17880	45260	08575	49321
91	36191	17095	32123	91576	84221	78902	82010	30847
92	62329	63898	23268	74283	26091	68409	69704	82267
93	14751	13151	93115	01437	56945	89661	67680	79790
94	48462	59278	44185	29616	76537	19589	83139	28454
95	29435	88105	59651	44391	74588	55114	80834	85686
96	28340	29285	12965	14821	80425	16602	44653	70467
97	02167	58940	27149	80242	10587	79786	34959	75339
98	17864	00991	39557	54981	23588	81914	37609	13128
99	79675	80605	60059	35862	00254	36546	21545	78179
00	72335	82037	92003	34100	29879	46613	89720	13274

Source: Partial extract from The Rand Corporation; A Million Random Digits with 100,000 Normal Deviates; *Glencoe, IL: The Free Press, 1955*

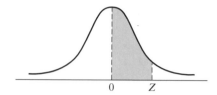

TABLE A.2

THE STANDARD NORMAL DISTRIBUTION

ENTRY REPRESENTS AREA UNDER THE STANDARD
NORMAL DISTRIBUTION FROM THE MEAN TO Z

Z	.00	.01	.02	.03	.04	.05	.06	.07	.08	.09
0.0	.0000	.0040	.0080	.0120	.0160	.0199	.0239	.0279	.0319	.0359
0.1	.0398	.0438	.0478	.0517	.0557	.0596	.0636	.0675	.0714	.0753
0.2	.0793	.0832	.0871	.0910	.0948	.0987	.1026	.1064	.1103	.1141
0.3	.1179	.1217	.1255	.1293	.1331	.1368	.1406	.1443	.1480	.1517
0.4	.1554	.1591	.1628	.1664	.1700	.1736	.1772	.1808	.1844	.1879
0.5	.1915	.1950	.1985	.2019	.2054	.2088	.2123	.2157	.2190	.2224
0.6	.2257	.2291	.2324	.2357	.2389	.2422	.2454	.2486	.2518	.2549
0.7	.2580	.2612	.2642	.2673	.2704	.2734	.2764	.2794	.2823	.2852
0.8	.2881	.2910	.2939	.2967	.2995	.3023	.3051	.3078	.3106	.3133
0.9	.3159	.3186	.3212	.3238	.3264	.3289	.3315	.3340	.3365	.3389
1.0	.3413	.3438	.3461	.3485	.3508	.3531	.3554	.3577	.3599	.3621
1.1	.3643	.3665	.3686	.3708	.3729	.3749	.3770	.3790	.3810	.3830
1.2	.3849	.3869	.3888	.3907	.3925	.3944	.3962	.3980	.3997	.4015
1.3	.4032	.4049	.4066	.4082	.4099	.4115	.4131	.4147	.4162	.4177
1.4	.4192	.4207	.4222	.4236	.4251	.4265	.4279	.4292	.4306	.4319
1.5	.4332	.4345	.4357	.4370	.4382	.4394	.4406	.4418	.4429	.4441
1.6	.4452	.4463	.4474	.4484	.4495	.4505	.4515	.4525	.4535	.4545
1.7	.4554	.4564	.4573	.4582	.4591	.4599	.4608	.4616	.4625	.4633
1.8	.4641	.4649	.4656	.4664	.4671	.4678	.4686	.4693	.4699	.4706
1.9	.4713	.4719	.4726	.4732	.4738	.4744	.4750	.4756	.4761	.4767
2.0	.4772	.4778	.4783	.4788	.4793	.4798	.4803	.4808	.4812	.4817
2.1	.4821	.4826	.4830	.4834	.4838	.4842	.4846	.4850	.4854	.4857
2.2	.4861	.4864	.4868	.4871	.4875	.4878	.4881	.4884	.4887	.4890
2.3	.4893	.4896	.4898	.4901	.4904	.4906	.4909	.4911	.4913	.4916
2.4	.4918	.4920	.4922	.4925	.4927	.4929	.4931	.4932	.4934	.4936
2.5	.4938	.4940	.4941	.4943	.4945	.4946	.4948	.4949	.4951	.4952
2.6	.4953	.4955	.4956	.4957	.4959	.4960	.4961	.4962	.4963	.4964
2.7	.4965	.4966	.4967	.4968	.4969	.4970	.4971	.4972	.4973	.4974
2.8	.4974	.4975	.4976	.4977	.4977	.4978	.4979	.4979	.4980	.4981
2.9	.4981	.4982	.4982	.4983	.4984	.4984	.4985	.4985	.4986	.4986
3.0	.49865	.49869	.49874	.49878	.49882	.49886	.49889	.49893	.49897	.49900
3.1	.49903	.49906	.49910	.49913	.49916	.49918	.49921	.49924	.49926	.49929
3.2	.49931	.49934	.49936	.49938	.49940	.49942	.49944	.49946	.49948	.49950
3.3	.49952	.49953	.49955	.49957	.49958	.49960	.49961	.49962	.49964	.49965
3.4	.49966	.49968	.49969	.49970	.49971	.49972	.49973	.49974	.49975	.49976
3.5	.49977	.49978	.49978	.49979	.49980	.49981	.49981	.49982	.49983	.49983
3.6	.49984	.49985	.49985	.49986	.49986	.49987	.49987	.49988	.49988	.49989
3.7	.49989	.49990	.49990	.49990	.49991	.49991	.49992	.49992	.49992	.49992
3.8	.49993	.49993	.49993	.49994	.49994	.49994	.49994	.49995	.49995	.49995
3.9	.49995	.49995	.49996	.49996	.49996	.49996	.49996	.49996	.49997	.49997

TABLE A.3

CONTROL CHART FACTORS

Number of Observations in Sample	d_2	d_3	D_3	D_4	A_2
2	1.128	0.853	0	3.267	1.880
3	1.693	0.888	0	2.575	1.023
4	2.059	0.880	0	2.282	0.729
5	2.326	0.864	0	2.114	0.577
6	2.534	0.848	0	2.004	0.483
7	2.704	0.833	0.076	1.924	0.419
8	2.847	0.820	0.136	1.864	0.373
9	2.970	0.808	0.184	1.816	0.337
10	3.078	0.797	0.223	1.777	0.308
11	3.173	0.787	0.256	1.744	0.285
12	3.258	0.778	0.283	1.717	0.266
13	3.336	0.770	0.307	1.693	0.249
14	3.407	0.763	0.328	1.672	0.235
15	3.472	0.756	0.347	1.653	0.223
16	3.532	0.750	0.363	1.637	0.212
17	3.588	0.744	0.378	1.622	0.203
18	3.640	0.739	0.391	1.609	0.194
19	3.689	0.733	0.404	1.596	0.187
20	3.735	0.729	0.415	1.585	0.180
21	3.778	0.724	0.425	1.575	0.173
22	3.819	0.720	0.435	1.565	0.167
23	3.858	0.716	0.443	1.557	0.162
24	3.895	0.712	0.452	1.548	0.157
25	3.931	0.708	0.459	1.541	0.153

Source: Reprinted from ASTM-STP 15D, by kind permission of the American Society for Testing and Materials.

TABLE A.4

CRITICAL VALUES OF t

For particular number of degrees of freedom,
entry represents the critical value of t
corresponding to a specified upper tail area (α)

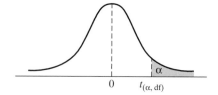

Degrees of Freedom	Upper Tail Areas					
	.25	.10	.05	.025	.01	.005
1	1.0000	3.0777	6.3138	12.7062	31.8207	63.6574
2	0.8165	1.8856	2.9200	4.3027	6.9646	9.9248
3	0.7649	1.6377	2.3534	3.1824	4.5407	5.8409
4	0.7407	1.5332	2.1318	2.7764	3.7469	4.6041
5	0.7267	1.4759	2.0150	2.5706	3.3649	4.0322
6	0.7176	1.4398	1.9432	2.4469	3.1427	3.7074
7	0.7111	1.4149	1.8946	2.3646	2.9980	3.4995
8	0.7064	1.3968	1.8595	2.3060	2.8965	3.3554
9	0.7027	1.3830	1.8331	2.2622	2.8214	3.2498
10	0.6998	1.3722	1.8125	2.2281	2.7638	3.1693
11	0.6974	1.3634	1.7959	2.2010	2.7181	3.1058
12	0.6955	1.3562	1.7823	2.1788	2.6810	3.0545
13	0.6938	1.3502	1.7709	2.1604	2.6503	3.0123
14	0.6924	1.3450	1.7613	2.1448	2.6245	2.9768
15	0.6912	1.3406	1.7531	2.1315	2.6025	2.9467
16	0.6901	1.3368	1.7459	2.1199	2.5835	2.9208
17	0.6892	1.3334	1.7396	2.1098	2.5669	2.8982
18	0.6884	1.3304	1.7341	2.1009	2.5524	2.8784
19	0.6876	1.3277	1.7291	2.0930	2.5395	2.8609
20	0.6870	1.3253	1.7247	2.0860	2.5280	2.8453
21	0.6864	1.3232	1.7207	2.0796	2.5177	2.8314
22	0.6858	1.3212	1.7171	2.0739	2.5083	2.8188
23	0.6853	1.3195	1.7139	2.0687	2.4999	2.8073
24	0.6848	1.3178	1.7109	2.0639	2.4922	2.7969
25	0.6844	1.3163	1.7081	2.0595	2.4851	2.7874
26	0.6840	1.3150	1.7056	2.0555	2.4786	2.7787
27	0.6837	1.3137	1.7033	2.0518	2.4727	2.7707
28	0.6834	1.3125	1.7011	2.0484	2.4671	2.7633
29	0.6830	1.3114	1.6991	2.0452	2.4620	2.7564
30	0.6828	1.3104	1.6973	2.0423	2.4573	2.7500
31	0.6825	1.3095	1.6955	2.0395	2.4528	2.7440
32	0.6822	1.3086	1.6939	2.0369	2.4487	2.7385
33	0.6820	1.3077	1.6924	2.0345	2.4448	2.7333
34	0.6818	1.3070	1.6909	2.0322	2.4411	2.7284
35	0.6816	1.3062	1.6896	2.0301	2.4377	2.7238
36	0.6814	1.3055	1.6883	2.0281	2.4345	2.7195
37	0.6812	1.3049	1.6871	2.0262	2.4314	2.7154
38	0.6810	1.3042	1.6860	2.0244	2.4286	2.7116
39	0.6808	1.3036	1.6849	2.0227	2.4258	2.7079
40	0.6807	1.3031	1.6839	2.0211	2.4233	2.7045
41	0.6805	1.3025	1.6829	2.0195	2.4208	2.7012
42	0.6804	1.3020	1.6820	2.0181	2.4185	2.6981
43	0.6802	1.3016	1.6811	2.0167	2.4163	2.6951
44	0.6801	1.3011	1.6802	2.0154	2.4141	2.6923
45	0.6800	1.3006	1.6794	2.0141	2.4121	2.6896
46	0.6799	1.3002	1.6787	2.0129	2.4102	2.6870
47	0.6797	1.2998	1.6779	2.0117	2.4083	2.6846
48	0.6796	1.2994	1.6772	2.0106	2.4066	2.6822
49	0.6795	1.2991	1.6766	2.0096	2.4049	2.6800
50	0.6794	1.2987	1.6759	2.0086	2.4033	2.6778

(Continued)

Degrees of Freedom	Upper Tail Areas					
	.25	.10	.05	.025	.01	.005
51	0.6793	1.2984	1.6753	2.0076	2.4017	2.6757
52	0.6792	1.2980	1.6747	2.0066	2.4002	2.6737
53	0.6791	1.2977	1.6741	2.0057	2.3988	2.6718
54	0.6791	1.2974	1.6736	2.0049	2.3974	2.6700
55	0.6790	1.2971	1.6730	2.0040	2.3961	2.6682
56	0.6789	1.2969	1.6725	2.0032	2.3948	2.6665
57	0.6788	1.2966	1.6720	2.0025	2.3936	2.6649
58	0.6787	1.2963	1.6716	2.0017	2.3924	2.6633
59	0.6787	1.2961	1.6711	2.0010	2.3912	2.6618
60	0.6786	1.2958	1.6706	2.0003	2.3901	2.6603
61	0.6785	1.2956	1.6702	1.9996	2.3890	2.6589
62	0.6785	1.2954	1.6698	1.9990	2.3880	2.6575
63	0.6784	1.2951	1.6694	1.9983	2.3870	2.6561
64	0.6783	1.2949	1.6690	1.9977	2.3860	2.6549
65	0.6783	1.2947	1.6686	1.9971	2.3851	2.6536
66	0.6782	1.2945	1.6683	1.9966	2.3842	2.6524
67	0.6782	1.2943	1.6679	1.9960	2.3833	2.6512
68	0.6781	1.2941	1.6676	1.9955	2.3824	2.6501
69	0.6781	1.2939	1.6672	1.9949	2.3816	2.6490
70	0.6780	1.2938	1.6669	1.9944	2.3808	2.6479
71	0.6780	1.2936	1.6666	1.9939	2.3800	2.6469
72	0.6779	1.2934	1.6663	1.9935	2.3793	2.6459
73	0.6779	1.2933	1.6660	1.9930	2.3785	2.6449
74	0.6778	1.4931	1.6657	1.9925	2.3778	2.6439
75	0.6778	1.2929	1.6654	1.9921	2.3771	2.6430
76	0.6777	1.2928	1.6652	1.9917	2.3764	2.6421
77	0.6777	1.2926	1.6649	1.9913	2.3758	2.6412
78	0.6776	1.2925	1.6646	1.9908	2.3751	2.6403
79	0.6776	1.2924	1.6644	1.9905	2.3745	2.6395
80	0.6776	1.2922	1.6641	1.9901	2.3739	2.6387
81	0.6775	1.2921	1.6639	1.9897	2.3733	2.6379
82	0.6775	1.2920	1.6636	1.9893	2.3727	2.6371
83	0.6775	1.2918	1.6634	1.9890	2.3721	2.6364
84	0.6774	1.2917	1.6632	1.9886	2.3716	2.6356
85	0.6774	1.2916	1.6630	1.9883	2.3710	2.6349
86	0.6774	1.2915	1.6628	1.9879	2.3705	2.6342
87	0.6773	1.2914	1.6626	1.9876	2.3700	2.6335
88	0.6773	1.2912	1.6624	1.9873	2.3695	2.6329
89	0.6773	1.2911	1.6622	1.9870	2.3690	2.6322
90	0.6772	1.2910	1.6620	1.9867	2.3685	2.6316
91	0.6772	1.2909	1.6618	1.9864	2.3680	2.6309
92	0.6772	1.2908	1.6616	1.9861	2.3676	2.6303
93	0.6771	1.2907	1.6614	1.9858	2.3671	2.6297
94	0.6771	1.2906	1.6612	1.9855	2.3667	2.6291
95	0.6771	1.2905	1.6611	1.9853	2.3662	2.6286
96	0.6771	1.2904	1.6609	1.9850	2.3658	2.6280
97	0.6770	1.2903	1.6607	1.9847	2.3654	2.6275
98	0.6770	1.2902	1.6606	1.9845	2.3650	2.6269
99	0.6770	1.2902	1.6604	1.9842	2.3646	2.6264
100	0.6770	1.2901	1.6602	1.9840	2.3642	2.6259
110	0.6767	1.2893	1.6588	1.9818	2.3607	2.6213
120	0.6765	1.2886	1.6577	1.9799	2.3578	2.6174
∞	0.6745	1.2816	1.6449	1.9600	2.3263	2.5758

TABLE A.5a

K_2 FACTORS FOR NORMAL DISTRIBUTIONS

	95% Confidence			99% Confidence		
n	$p = .90$	$p = .95$	$p =. 99$	$p = .90$	$p = .95$	$p = .99$
2	31.092	36.519	46.944	155.569	182.720	234.877
3	8.306	9.789	12.647	18.782	22.131	28.586
4	5.368	6.341	8.221	9.416	11.118	14.405
5	4.291	5.077	6.598	6.655	7.870	10.220
6	3.733	4.422	5.758	5.383	6.373	8.292
7	3.390	4.020	5.241	4.658	5.520	7.191
8	3.156	3.746	4.889	4.189	4.968	6.479
9	2.986	3.546	4.633	3.860	4.581	5.980
10	2.856	3.393	4.437	3.617	4.294	5.610
11	2.754	3.273	4.282	3.429	4.073	5.324
12	2.670	3.175	4.156	3.279	3.896	5.096
13	2.601	3.093	4.051	3.156	3.751	4.909
14	2.542	3.024	3.962	3.054	3.631	4.753
15	2.492	2.965	3.885	2.967	3.529	4.621
16	2.449	2.913	3.819	2.893	3.441	4.507
17	2.410	2.868	3.761	2.828	3.364	4.408
18	2.376	2.828	3.709	2.771	3.297	4.321
19	2.346	2.793	3.663	2.720	3.237	4.244
20	2.319	2.760	3.621	2.675	3.184	4.175
25	2.215	2.638	3.462	2.506	2.984	3.915
30	2.145	2.555	3.355	2.394	2.851	3.742
35	2.094	2.495	3.276	2.314	2.756	3.618
40	2.055	2.448	3.216	2.253	2.684	3.524
50	1.999	2.382	3.129	2.166	2.580	3.390
60	1.960	2.335	3.068	2.106	2.509	3.297
80	1.908	2.274	2.988	2.028	2.416	3.175
100	1.875	2.234	2.936	1.978	2.357	3.098
150	1.826	2.176	2.859	1.906	2.271	2.985
200	1.798	2.143	2.816	1.866	2.223	2.921
500	1.737	2.070	2.721	1.777	2.117	2.783
1000	1.709	2.036	2.676	1.736	2.068	2.718
∞	1.645	1.960	2.576	1.645	1.960	2.576

This table was adapted from *Tables for Normal Tolerance Limits, Sampling Plans and Screening* by R. E. Odeh and D. B. Owen. Reprinted by permission of Marcel Dekker Inc.

TABLE A.5b

K_1 FACTORS FOR ONE-SIDED TOLERANCE INTERVALS FOR NORMAL DISTRIBUTIONS

n Lower Upper	95% Confidence			99% Confidence		
	$p = .10$ $p = .90$	$p = .05$ $p = .95$	$p = .01$ $p = .99$	$p = .10$ $p = .90$	$p = .05$ $p = .95$	$p = .01$ $p = .99$
2	20.581	26.260	37.094	103.029	131.426	185.617
3	6.155	7.656	10.553	13.995	17.370	23.896
4	4.162	5.144	7.042	7.380	9.083	12.387
5	3.407	4.203	5.741	5.362	6.578	8.939
6	3.006	3.708	5.062	4.411	5.406	7.335
7	2.755	3.399	4.642	3.859	4.728	6.412
8	2.582	3.187	4.354	3.497	4.285	5.812
9	2.454	3.031	4.143	3.240	3.972	5.389
10	2.355	2.911	3.981	3.048	3.738	5.074
11	2.275	2.815	3.852	2.898	3.556	4.829
12	2.210	2.736	3.747	2.777	3.410	4.633
13	2.155	2.671	3.659	2.677	3.290	4.472
14	2.109	2.614	3.585	2.593	3.189	4.337
15	2.068	2.566	3.520	2.521	3.102	4.222
16	2.033	2.524	3.464	2.459	3.028	4.123
17	2.002	2.486	3.414	2.405	2.963	4.037
18	1.974	2.453	3.370	2.357	2.905	3.960
19	1.949	2.423	3.331	2.314	2.854	3.892
20	1.926	2.396	3.295	2.276	2.808	3.832
25	1.838	2.292	3.158	2.129	2.633	3.601
30	1.777	2.220	3.064	2.030	2.515	3.447
35	1.732	2.167	2.995	1.957	2.430	3.334
40	1.697	2.125	2.941	1.902	2.364	3.249
50	1.646	2.065	2.862	1.821	2.269	3.125
60	1.609	2.022	2.807	1.764	2.202	3.038
80	1.559	1.964	2.733	1.688	2.114	2.924
100	1.527	1.927	2.684	1.639	2.056	2.850
150	1.478	1.870	2.611	1.566	1.971	2.740
200	1.450	1.837	2.570	1.524	1.923	2.679
500	1.385	1.763	2.475	1.430	1.814	2.540
1000	1.354	1.727	2.430	1.385	1.762	2.475
∞	1.282	1.645	2.326	1.282	1.645	2.326

This table was adapted from *Tables for Normal Tolerance Limits, Sampling Plans and Screening* by R. E. Odeh and D. B. Owen. Reprinted by permission of Marcel Dekker Inc.

TABLE A.6

CRITICAL VALUES OF χ^2

For a particular number of degrees of freedom,
entry represents the critical value of χ^2
corresponding to a specified upper tail area (α)

Upper Tail Areas (α)

Degrees of Freedom	.995	.99	.975	.95	.90	.75	.25	.10	.05	.025	.01	.005
1			0.001	0.004	0.016	0.102	1.323	2.706	3.841	5.024	6.635	7.879
2	0.010	0.020	0.051	0.103	0.211	0.575	2.773	4.605	5.991	7.378	9.210	10.597
3	0.072	0.115	0.216	0.352	0.584	1.213	4.108	6.251	7.815	9.348	11.345	12.838
4	0.207	0.297	0.484	0.711	1.064	1.923	5.385	7.779	9.488	11.143	13.277	14.860
5	0.412	0.554	0.831	1.145	1.610	2.675	6.626	9.236	11.071	12.833	15.086	16.750
6	0.676	0.872	1.237	1.635	2.204	3.455	7.841	10.645	12.592	14.449	16.812	18.548
7	0.989	1.239	1.690	2.167	2.833	4.255	9.037	12.017	14.067	16.013	18.475	20.278
8	1.344	1.646	2.180	2.733	3.490	5.071	10.219	13.362	15.507	17.535	20.090	21.955
9	1.735	2.088	2.700	3.325	4.168	5.899	11.389	14.684	16.919	19.023	21.666	23.589
10	2.156	2.558	3.247	3.940	4.865	6.737	12.549	15.987	18.307	20.483	23.209	25.188
11	2.603	3.053	3.816	4.575	5.578	7.584	13.701	17.275	19.675	21.920	24.725	26.757
12	3.074	3.571	4.404	5.226	6.304	8.438	14.845	18.549	21.026	23.337	26.217	28.299
13	3.565	4.107	5.009	5.892	7.042	9.299	15.984	19.812	22.362	24.736	27.688	29.819
14	4.075	4.660	5.629	6.571	7.790	10.165	17.117	21.064	23.685	26.119	29.141	31.319
15	4.601	5.229	6.262	7.261	8.547	11.037	18.245	22.307	24.996	27.488	30.578	32.801
16	5.142	5.812	6.908	7.962	9.312	11.912	19.369	23.542	26.296	28.845	32.000	34.267
17	5.697	6.408	7.564	8.672	10.085	12.792	20.489	24.769	27.587	30.191	33.409	35.718
18	6.265	7.015	8.231	9.390	10.865	13.675	21.605	25.989	28.869	31.526	34.805	37.156
19	6.844	7.633	8.907	10.117	11.651	14.562	22.718	27.204	30.144	32.852	36.191	38.582
20	7.434	8.260	9.591	10.851	12.443	15.452	23.828	28.412	31.410	34.170	37.566	39.997
21	8.034	8.897	10.283	11.591	13.240	16.344	24.935	29.615	32.671	35.479	38.932	41.401
22	8.643	9.542	10.982	12.338	14.042	17.240	26.039	30.813	33.924	36.781	40.289	42.796
23	9.260	10.196	11.689	13.091	14.848	18.137	27.141	32.007	35.172	38.076	41.638	44.181
24	9.886	10.856	12.401	13.848	15.659	19.037	28.241	33.196	36.415	39.364	42.980	45.559
25	10.520	11.524	13.120	14.611	16.473	19.939	29.339	34.382	37.652	40.646	44.314	46.928
26	11.160	12.198	13.844	15.379	17.292	20.843	30.435	35.563	38.885	41.923	45.642	48.290
27	11.808	12.879	14.573	16.151	18.114	21.749	31.528	36.741	40.113	43.194	46.963	49.645
28	12.461	13.565	15.308	16.928	18.939	22.657	32.620	37.916	41.337	44.461	48.278	50.993
29	13.121	14.257	16.047	17.708	19.768	23.567	33.711	39.087	42.557	45.722	49.588	52.336
30	13.787	14.954	16.791	18.493	20.599	24.478	34.800	40.256	43.773	46.979	50.892	53.672

For larger values of degrees of freedom (df), the expression $Z = \sqrt{2\chi^2} - \sqrt{2(df)} - 1$ can be used, and the resulting upper tail area can be obtained from the table of the standard normal distribution (Table A.2).

TABLE A.7

CRITICAL VALUES OF F

For a particular combination of numerator and denominator degrees of freedom, entry represents the critical values of F corresponding to a specified upper tail area (α)

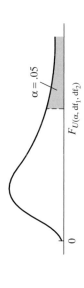

$\alpha = .05$

$F_{U(\alpha, df_1, df_2)}$

Denominator	Numerator, d.f.$_1$																		
d.f.$_2$	1	2	3	4	5	6	7	8	9	10	12	15	20	24	30	40	60	120	∞
1	161.4	199.5	215.7	224.6	230.2	234.0	236.8	238.9	240.5	241.9	243.9	245.9	248.0	249.1	250.1	251.1	252.2	253.3	254.3
2	18.51	19.00	19.16	19.25	19.30	19.33	19.35	19.37	19.38	19.40	19.41	19.43	19.45	19.45	19.46	19.47	19.48	19.49	19.50
3	10.13	9.55	9.28	9.12	9.01	8.94	8.89	8.85	8.81	8.79	8.74	8.70	8.66	8.64	8.62	8.59	8.57	8.55	8.53
4	7.71	6.94	6.59	6.39	6.26	6.16	6.09	6.04	6.00	5.96	5.91	5.86	5.80	5.77	5.75	5.72	5.69	5.66	5.63
5	6.61	5.79	5.41	5.19	5.05	4.95	4.88	4.82	4.77	4.74	4.68	4.62	4.56	4.53	4.50	4.46	4.43	4.40	4.36
6	5.99	5.14	4.76	4.53	4.39	4.28	4.21	4.15	4.10	4.06	4.00	3.94	3.87	3.84	3.81	3.77	3.74	3.70	3.67
7	5.59	4.74	4.35	4.12	3.97	3.87	3.79	3.73	3.68	3.64	3.57	3.51	3.44	3.41	3.38	3.34	3.30	3.27	3.23
8	5.32	4.46	4.07	3.84	3.69	3.58	3.50	3.44	3.39	3.35	3.28	3.22	3.15	3.12	3.08	3.04	3.01	2.97	2.93
9	5.12	4.26	3.86	3.63	3.48	3.37	3.29	3.23	3.18	3.14	3.07	3.01	2.94	2.90	2.86	2.83	2.79	2.75	2.71
10	4.96	4.10	3.71	3.48	3.33	3.22	3.14	3.07	3.02	2.98	2.91	2.85	2.77	2.74	2.70	2.66	2.62	2.58	2.54
11	4.84	3.98	3.59	3.36	3.20	3.09	3.01	2.95	2.90	2.85	2.79	2.72	2.65	2.61	2.57	2.53	2.49	2.45	2.40
12	4.75	3.89	3.49	3.26	3.11	3.00	2.91	2.85	2.80	2.75	2.69	2.62	2.54	2.51	2.47	2.43	2.38	2.34	2.30
13	4.67	3.81	3.41	3.18	3.03	2.92	2.83	2.77	2.71	2.67	2.60	2.53	2.46	2.42	2.38	2.34	2.30	2.25	2.21
14	4.60	3.74	3.34	3.11	2.96	2.85	2.76	2.70	2.65	2.60	2.53	2.46	2.39	2.35	2.31	2.27	2.22	2.18	2.13
15	4.54	3.68	3.29	3.06	2.90	2.79	2.71	2.64	2.59	2.54	2.48	2.40	2.33	2.29	2.25	2.20	2.16	2.11	2.07
16	4.49	3.63	3.24	3.01	2.85	2.74	2.66	2.59	2.54	2.49	2.42	2.35	2.28	2.24	2.19	2.15	2.11	2.06	2.01
17	4.45	3.59	3.20	2.96	2.81	2.70	2.61	2.55	2.49	2.45	2.38	2.31	2.23	2.19	2.15	2.10	2.06	2.01	1.96
18	4.41	3.55	3.16	2.93	2.77	2.66	2.58	2.51	2.46	2.41	2.34	2.27	2.19	2.15	2.11	2.06	2.02	1.97	1.92
19	4.38	3.52	3.13	2.90	2.74	2.63	2.54	2.48	2.42	2.38	2.31	2.23	2.16	2.11	2.07	2.03	1.98	1.93	1.88
20	4.35	3.49	3.10	2.87	2.71	2.60	2.51	2.45	2.39	2.35	2.28	2.20	2.12	2.08	2.04	1.99	1.95	1.90	1.84
21	4.32	3.47	3.07	2.84	2.68	2.57	2.49	2.42	2.37	2.32	2.25	2.18	2.10	2.05	2.01	1.96	1.92	1.87	1.81
22	4.30	3.44	3.05	2.82	2.66	2.55	2.46	2.40	2.34	2.30	2.23	2.15	2.07	2.03	1.98	1.94	1.89	1.84	1.78
23	4.28	3.42	3.03	2.80	2.64	2.53	2.44	2.37	2.32	2.27	2.20	2.13	2.05	2.01	1.96	1.91	1.86	1.81	1.76
24	4.26	3.40	3.01	2.78	2.62	2.51	2.42	2.36	2.30	2.25	2.18	2.11	2.03	1.98	1.94	1.89	1.84	1.79	1.73
25	4.24	3.39	2.99	2.76	2.60	2.49	2.40	2.34	2.28	2.24	2.16	2.09	2.01	1.96	1.92	1.87	1.82	1.77	1.71
26	4.23	3.37	2.98	2.74	2.59	2.47	2.39	2.32	2.27	2.22	2.15	2.07	1.99	1.95	1.90	1.85	1.80	1.75	1.69
27	4.21	3.35	2.96	2.73	2.57	2.46	2.37	2.31	2.25	2.20	2.13	2.06	1.97	1.93	1.88	1.84	1.79	1.73	1.67
28	4.20	3.34	2.95	2.71	2.56	2.45	2.36	2.29	2.24	2.19	2.12	2.04	1.96	1.91	1.87	1.82	1.77	1.71	1.65
29	4.18	3.33	2.93	2.70	2.55	2.43	2.35	2.28	2.22	2.18	2.10	2.03	1.94	1.90	1.85	1.81	1.75	1.70	1.64
30	4.17	3.32	2.92	2.69	2.53	2.42	2.33	2.27	2.21	2.16	2.09	2.01	1.93	1.89	1.84	1.79	1.74	1.68	1.62
40	4.08	3.23	2.84	2.61	2.45	2.34	2.25	2.18	2.12	2.08	2.00	1.92	1.84	1.79	1.74	1.69	1.64	1.58	1.51
60	4.00	3.15	2.76	2.53	2.37	2.25	2.17	2.10	2.04	1.99	1.92	1.84	1.75	1.70	1.65	1.59	1.53	1.47	1.39
120	3.92	3.07	2.68	2.45	2.29	2.17	2.09	2.02	1.96	1.91	1.83	1.75	1.66	1.61	1.55	1.50	1.43	1.35	1.25
∞	3.84	3.00	2.60	2.37	2.21	2.10	2.01	1.94	1.88	1.83	1.75	1.67	1.57	1.52	1.46	1.39	1.32	1.22	1.00

Source: Reprinted from Pearson, E. S. and H. O. Hartley, eds.; Biometrika Tables for Statisticians, 3d ed.; 1966; by permission of the Biometrika Trustees, London

TABLE A.7

CRITICAL VALUES OF F (CONTINUED)

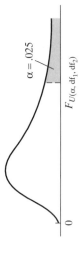

$\alpha = .025$

$F_{U(\alpha, df_1, df_2)}$

Numerator, d.f.$_1$

Denominator d.f.$_2$	1	2	3	4	5	6	7	8	9	10	12	15	20	24	30	40	60	120	∞
1	647.8	799.5	864.2	899.6	921.8	937.1	948.2	956.7	963.3	968.6	976.7	984.9	993.1	997.2	1001	1006	1010	1014	1018
2	38.51	39.00	39.17	39.25	39.30	39.33	39.36	39.37	39.39	39.40	39.41	39.43	39.45	39.46	39.46	39.47	39.48	39.49	39.50
3	17.44	16.04	15.44	15.10	14.88	14.73	14.62	14.54	14.47	14.42	14.34	14.25	14.17	14.12	14.08	14.04	13.99	13.95	13.90
4	12.22	10.65	9.98	9.60	9.36	9.20	9.07	8.98	8.90	8.84	8.75	8.66	8.56	8.51	8.46	8.41	8.36	8.31	8.26
5	10.01	8.43	7.76	7.39	7.15	6.98	6.85	6.76	6.68	6.62	6.52	6.43	6.33	6.28	6.23	6.18	6.12	6.07	6.02
6	8.81	7.26	6.60	6.23	5.99	5.82	5.70	5.60	5.52	5.46	5.37	5.27	5.17	5.12	5.07	5.01	4.96	4.90	4.85
7	8.07	6.54	5.89	5.52	5.29	5.12	4.99	4.90	4.82	4.76	4.67	4.57	4.47	4.42	4.36	4.31	4.25	4.20	4.14
8	7.57	6.06	5.42	5.05	4.82	4.65	4.53	4.43	4.36	4.30	4.20	4.10	4.00	3.95	3.89	3.84	3.78	3.73	3.67
9	7.21	5.71	5.08	4.72	4.48	4.32	4.20	4.10	4.03	3.96	3.87	3.77	3.67	3.61	3.56	3.51	3.45	3.39	3.33
10	6.94	5.46	4.83	4.47	4.24	4.07	3.95	3.85	3.78	3.72	3.62	3.52	3.42	3.37	3.31	3.26	3.20	3.14	3.08
11	6.72	5.26	4.63	4.28	4.04	3.88	3.76	3.66	3.59	3.53	3.43	3.33	3.23	3.17	3.12	3.06	3.00	2.94	2.88
12	6.55	5.10	4.47	4.12	3.89	3.73	3.61	3.51	3.44	3.37	3.28	3.18	3.07	3.02	2.96	2.91	2.85	2.79	2.72
13	6.41	4.97	4.35	4.00	3.77	3.60	3.48	3.39	3.31	3.25	3.15	3.05	2.95	2.89	2.84	2.78	2.72	2.66	2.60
14	6.30	4.86	4.24	3.89	3.66	3.50	3.38	3.29	3.21	3.15	3.05	2.95	2.84	2.79	2.73	2.67	2.61	2.55	2.49
15	6.20	4.77	4.15	3.80	3.58	3.41	3.29	3.20	3.12	3.06	2.96	2.86	2.76	2.70	2.64	2.59	2.52	2.46	2.40
16	6.12	4.69	4.08	3.73	3.50	3.34	3.22	3.12	3.05	2.99	2.89	2.79	2.68	2.63	2.57	2.51	2.45	2.38	2.32
17	6.04	4.62	4.01	3.66	3.44	3.28	3.16	3.06	2.98	2.92	2.82	2.72	2.62	2.56	2.50	2.44	2.38	2.32	2.25
18	5.98	4.56	3.95	3.61	3.38	3.22	3.10	3.01	2.93	2.87	2.77	2.67	2.56	2.50	2.44	2.38	2.32	2.26	2.19
19	5.92	4.51	3.90	3.56	3.33	3.17	3.05	2.96	2.88	2.82	2.72	2.62	2.51	2.45	2.39	2.33	2.27	2.20	2.13
20	5.87	4.46	3.86	3.51	3.29	3.13	3.01	2.91	2.84	2.77	2.68	2.57	2.46	2.41	2.35	2.29	2.22	2.16	2.09
21	5.83	4.42	3.82	3.48	3.25	3.09	2.97	2.87	2.80	2.73	2.64	2.53	2.42	2.37	2.31	2.25	2.18	2.11	2.04
22	5.79	4.38	3.78	3.44	3.22	3.05	2.93	2.84	2.76	2.70	2.60	2.50	2.39	2.33	2.27	2.21	2.14	2.08	2.00
23	5.75	4.35	3.75	3.41	3.18	3.02	2.90	2.81	2.73	2.67	2.57	2.47	2.36	2.30	2.24	2.18	2.11	2.04	1.97
24	5.72	4.32	3.72	3.38	3.15	2.99	2.87	2.78	2.70	2.64	2.54	2.44	2.33	2.27	2.21	2.15	2.08	2.01	1.94
25	5.69	4.29	3.69	3.35	3.13	2.97	2.85	2.75	2.68	2.61	2.51	2.41	2.30	2.24	2.18	2.12	2.05	1.98	1.91
26	5.66	4.27	3.67	3.33	3.10	2.94	2.82	2.73	2.65	2.59	2.49	2.39	2.28	2.22	2.16	2.09	2.03	1.95	1.88
27	5.63	4.24	3.65	3.31	3.08	2.92	2.80	2.71	2.63	2.57	2.47	2.36	2.25	2.19	2.13	2.07	2.00	1.93	1.85
28	5.61	4.22	3.63	3.29	3.06	2.90	2.78	2.69	2.61	2.55	2.45	2.34	2.23	2.17	2.11	2.05	1.98	1.91	1.83
29	5.59	4.20	3.61	3.27	3.04	2.88	2.76	2.67	2.59	2.53	2.43	2.32	2.21	2.15	2.09	2.03	1.96	1.89	1.81
30	5.57	4.18	3.59	3.25	3.03	2.87	2.75	2.65	2.57	2.51	2.41	2.31	2.20	2.14	2.07	2.01	1.94	1.87	1.79
40	5.42	4.05	3.46	3.13	2.90	2.74	2.62	2.53	2.45	2.39	2.29	2.18	2.07	2.01	1.94	1.88	1.80	1.72	1.64
60	5.29	3.93	3.34	3.01	2.79	2.63	2.51	2.41	2.33	2.27	2.17	2.06	1.94	1.88	1.82	1.74	1.67	1.58	1.48
120	5.15	3.80	3.23	2.89	2.67	2.52	2.39	2.30	2.22	2.16	2.05	1.94	1.82	1.76	1.69	1.61	1.53	1.43	1.31
∞	5.02	3.69	3.12	2.79	2.57	2.41	2.29	2.19	2.11	2.05	1.94	1.83	1.71	1.64	1.57	1.48	1.39	1.27	1.00

Source: Reprinted from Pearson, E. S. and H. O. Hartley, eds.; Biometrika Tables for Statisticians, 3d ed.; 1966; by permission of the Biometrika Trustees, London

TABLE A.7

CRITICAL VALUES OF F (CONTINUED)

$\alpha = .01$

$F_{U(\alpha,\, df_1,\, df_2)}$

Denominator d.f.$_2$	Numerator, d.f.$_1$																		
	1	2	3	4	5	6	7	8	9	10	12	15	20	24	30	40	60	120	∞
1	4052	4999.5	5403	5625	5764	5859	5928	5982	6022	6056	6106	6157	6209	6235	6261	6287	6313	6339	6366
2	98.50	99.00	99.17	99.25	99.30	99.33	99.36	99.37	99.39	99.40	99.42	99.43	99.45	99.46	99.47	99.47	99.48	99.49	99.50
3	34.12	30.82	29.46	28.71	28.24	27.91	27.67	27.49	27.35	27.23	27.05	26.87	26.69	26.60	26.50	26.41	26.32	26.22	26.13
4	21.20	18.00	16.69	15.98	15.52	15.21	14.98	14.80	14.66	14.55	14.37	14.20	14.02	13.93	13.84	13.75	13.65	13.56	13.46
5	16.26	13.27	12.06	11.39	10.97	10.67	10.46	10.29	10.16	10.05	9.89	9.72	9.55	9.47	9.38	9.29	9.20	9.11	9.02
6	13.75	10.92	9.78	9.15	8.75	8.47	8.26	8.10	7.98	7.87	7.72	7.56	7.40	7.31	7.23	7.14	7.06	6.97	6.88
7	12.25	9.55	8.45	7.85	7.46	7.19	6.99	6.84	6.72	6.62	6.47	6.31	6.16	6.07	5.99	5.91	5.82	5.74	5.65
8	11.26	8.65	7.59	7.01	6.63	6.37	6.18	6.03	5.91	5.81	5.67	5.52	5.36	5.28	5.20	5.12	5.03	4.95	4.86
9	10.56	8.02	6.99	6.42	6.06	5.80	5.61	5.47	5.35	5.26	5.11	4.96	4.81	4.73	4.65	4.57	4.48	4.40	4.31
10	10.04	7.56	6.55	5.99	5.64	5.39	5.20	5.06	4.94	4.85	4.71	4.56	4.41	4.33	4.25	4.17	4.08	4.00	3.91
11	9.65	7.21	6.22	5.67	5.32	5.07	4.89	4.74	4.63	4.54	4.40	4.25	4.10	4.02	3.94	3.86	3.78	3.69	3.60
12	9.33	6.93	5.95	5.41	5.06	4.82	4.64	4.50	4.39	4.30	4.16	4.01	3.86	3.78	3.70	3.62	3.54	3.45	3.36
13	9.07	6.70	5.74	5.21	4.86	4.62	4.44	4.30	4.19	4.10	3.96	3.82	3.66	3.59	3.51	3.43	3.34	3.25	3.17
14	8.86	6.51	5.56	5.04	4.69	4.46	4.28	4.14	4.03	3.94	3.80	3.66	3.51	3.43	3.35	3.27	3.18	3.09	3.00
15	8.68	6.36	5.42	4.89	4.56	4.32	4.14	4.00	3.89	3.80	3.67	3.52	3.37	3.29	3.21	3.13	3.05	2.96	2.87
16	8.53	6.23	5.29	4.77	4.44	4.20	4.03	3.89	3.78	3.69	3.55	3.41	3.26	3.18	3.10	3.02	2.93	2.84	2.75
17	8.40	6.11	5.18	4.67	4.34	4.10	3.93	3.79	3.68	3.59	3.46	3.31	3.16	3.08	3.00	2.92	2.83	2.75	2.65
18	8.29	6.01	5.09	4.58	4.25	4.01	3.84	3.71	3.60	3.51	3.37	3.23	3.08	3.00	2.92	2.84	2.75	2.66	2.57
19	8.18	5.93	5.01	4.50	4.17	3.94	3.77	3.63	3.52	3.43	3.30	3.15	3.00	2.92	2.84	2.76	2.67	2.58	2.49
20	8.10	5.85	4.94	4.43	4.10	3.87	3.70	3.56	3.46	3.37	3.23	3.09	2.94	2.86	2.78	2.69	2.61	2.52	2.42
21	8.02	5.78	4.87	4.37	4.04	3.81	3.64	3.51	3.40	3.31	3.17	3.03	2.88	2.80	2.72	2.64	2.55	2.46	2.36
22	7.95	5.72	4.82	4.31	3.99	3.76	3.59	3.45	3.35	3.26	3.12	2.98	2.83	2.75	2.67	2.58	2.50	2.40	2.31
23	7.88	5.66	4.76	4.26	3.94	3.71	3.54	3.41	3.30	3.21	3.07	2.93	2.78	2.70	2.62	2.54	2.45	2.35	2.26
24	7.82	5.61	4.72	4.22	3.90	3.67	3.50	3.36	3.26	3.17	3.03	2.89	2.74	2.66	2.58	2.49	2.40	2.31	2.21
25	7.77	5.57	4.68	4.18	3.85	3.63	3.46	3.32	3.22	3.13	2.99	2.85	2.70	2.62	2.54	2.45	2.36	2.27	2.17
26	7.72	5.53	4.64	4.14	3.82	3.59	3.42	3.29	3.18	3.09	2.96	2.81	2.66	2.58	2.50	2.42	2.33	2.23	2.13
27	7.68	5.49	4.60	4.11	3.78	3.56	3.39	3.26	3.15	3.06	2.93	2.78	2.63	2.55	2.47	2.38	2.29	2.20	2.10
28	7.64	5.45	4.57	4.07	3.75	3.53	3.36	3.23	3.12	3.03	2.90	2.75	2.60	2.52	2.44	2.35	2.26	2.17	2.06
29	7.60	5.42	4.54	4.04	3.73	3.50	3.33	3.20	3.09	3.00	2.87	2.73	2.57	2.49	2.41	2.33	2.23	2.14	2.03
30	7.56	5.39	4.51	4.02	3.70	3.47	3.30	3.17	3.07	2.98	2.84	2.70	2.55	2.47	2.39	2.30	2.21	2.11	2.01
40	7.31	5.18	4.31	3.83	3.51	3.29	3.12	2.99	2.89	2.80	2.66	2.52	2.37	2.29	2.20	2.11	2.02	1.92	1.80
60	7.08	4.98	4.13	3.65	3.34	3.12	2.95	2.82	2.72	2.63	2.50	2.35	2.20	2.12	2.03	1.94	1.84	1.73	1.60
120	6.85	4.79	3.95	3.48	3.17	2.96	2.79	2.66	2.56	2.47	2.34	2.19	2.03	1.95	1.86	1.76	1.66	1.53	1.38
∞	6.63	4.61	3.78	3.32	3.02	2.80	2.64	2.51	2.41	2.32	2.18	2.04	1.88	1.79	1.70	1.59	1.47	1.32	1.00

Source: Reprinted from Pearson, E. S. and H. O. Hartley, eds.; Biometrika Tables for Statisticians, 3d ed.; 1966; by permission of the Biometrika Trustees, London

TABLE A.7

CRITICAL VALUES OF F (CONTINUED)

$\alpha = .005$

$F_{U(\alpha,\ df_1,\ df_2)}$

Numerator, d.f.$_1$

Denominator d.f.$_2$	1	2	3	4	5	6	7	8	9	10	12	15	20	24	30	40	60	120	∞
1	16211	20000	21615	22500	23056	23437	23715	23925	24091	24224	24426	24630	24836	24940	25044	25148	25253	25359	25465
2	198.5	199.0	199.2	199.2	199.3	199.3	199.4	199.4	199.4	199.4	199.4	199.4	199.4	199.5	199.5	199.5	199.5	199.5	199.5
3	55.55	49.80	47.47	46.19	45.39	44.84	44.43	44.13	43.88	43.69	43.39	43.08	42.78	42.62	42.47	42.31	42.15	41.99	41.83
4	31.33	26.28	24.26	23.15	22.46	21.97	21.62	21.35	21.14	20.97	20.70	20.44	20.17	20.03	19.89	19.75	19.61	19.47	19.32
5	22.78	18.31	16.53	15.56	14.94	14.51	14.20	13.96	13.77	13.62	13.38	13.15	12.90	12.78	12.66	12.53	12.40	12.27	12.14
6	18.63	14.54	12.92	12.03	11.46	11.07	10.79	10.57	10.39	10.25	10.03	9.81	9.59	9.47	9.36	9.24	9.12	9.00	8.88
7	16.24	12.40	10.88	10.05	9.52	9.16	8.89	8.68	8.51	8.38	8.18	7.97	7.75	7.65	7.53	7.42	7.31	7.19	7.08
8	14.69	11.04	9.60	8.81	8.30	7.95	7.69	7.50	7.34	7.21	7.01	6.81	6.61	6.50	6.40	6.29	6.18	6.06	5.95
9	13.61	10.11	8.72	7.96	7.47	7.13	6.88	6.69	6.54	6.42	6.23	6.03	5.83	5.73	5.62	5.52	5.41	5.30	5.19
10	12.83	9.43	8.08	7.34	6.87	6.54	6.30	6.12	5.97	5.85	5.66	5.47	5.27	5.17	5.07	4.97	4.86	4.75	4.64
11	12.23	8.91	7.60	6.88	6.42	6.10	5.86	5.68	5.54	5.42	5.24	5.05	4.86	4.76	4.65	4.55	4.44	4.34	4.23
12	11.75	8.51	7.23	6.52	6.07	5.76	5.52	5.35	5.20	5.09	4.91	4.72	4.53	4.43	4.33	4.23	4.12	4.01	3.90
13	11.37	8.19	6.93	6.23	5.79	5.48	5.25	5.08	4.94	4.82	4.64	4.46	4.27	4.17	4.07	3.97	3.87	3.76	3.65
14	11.06	7.92	6.68	6.00	5.56	5.26	5.03	4.86	4.72	4.60	4.43	4.25	4.06	3.96	3.86	3.76	3.66	3.55	3.44
15	10.80	7.70	6.48	5.80	5.37	5.07	4.85	4.67	4.54	4.42	4.25	4.07	3.88	3.79	3.69	3.58	3.48	3.37	3.26
16	10.58	7.51	6.30	5.64	5.21	4.91	4.69	4.52	4.38	4.27	4.10	3.92	3.73	3.64	3.54	3.44	3.33	3.22	3.11
17	10.38	7.35	6.16	5.50	5.07	4.78	4.56	4.39	4.25	4.14	3.97	3.79	3.61	3.51	3.41	3.31	3.21	3.10	2.98
18	10.22	7.21	6.03	5.37	4.96	4.66	4.44	4.28	4.14	4.03	3.86	3.68	3.50	3.40	3.30	3.20	3.10	2.99	2.87
19	10.07	7.09	5.92	5.27	4.85	4.56	4.34	4.18	4.04	3.93	3.76	3.59	3.40	3.31	3.21	3.11	3.00	2.89	2.78
20	9.94	6.99	5.82	5.17	4.76	4.47	4.26	4.09	3.96	3.85	3.68	3.50	3.32	3.22	3.12	3.02	2.92	2.81	2.69
21	9.83	6.89	5.73	5.09	4.68	4.39	4.18	4.01	3.88	3.77	3.60	3.43	3.24	3.15	3.05	2.95	2.84	2.73	2.61
22	9.73	6.81	5.65	5.02	4.61	4.32	4.11	3.94	3.81	3.70	3.54	3.36	3.18	3.08	2.98	2.88	2.77	2.66	2.55
23	9.63	6.73	5.58	4.95	4.54	4.26	4.05	3.88	3.75	3.64	3.47	3.30	3.12	3.02	2.92	2.82	2.71	2.60	2.48
24	9.55	6.66	5.52	4.89	4.49	4.20	3.99	3.83	3.69	3.59	3.42	3.25	3.06	2.97	2.87	2.77	2.66	2.55	2.43
25	9.48	6.60	5.46	4.84	4.43	4.15	3.94	3.78	3.64	3.54	3.37	3.20	3.01	2.92	2.82	2.72	2.61	2.50	2.38
26	9.41	6.54	5.41	4.79	4.38	4.10	3.89	3.73	3.60	3.49	3.33	3.15	2.97	2.87	2.77	2.67	2.56	2.45	2.33
27	9.34	6.49	5.36	4.74	4.34	4.06	3.85	3.69	3.56	3.45	3.28	3.11	2.93	2.83	2.73	2.63	2.52	2.41	2.29
28	9.28	6.44	5.32	4.70	4.30	4.02	3.81	3.65	3.52	3.41	3.25	3.07	2.89	2.79	2.69	2.59	2.48	2.37	2.25
29	9.23	6.40	5.28	4.66	4.26	3.98	3.77	3.61	3.48	3.38	3.21	3.04	2.86	2.76	2.66	2.56	2.45	2.33	2.21
30	9.18	6.35	5.24	4.62	4.23	3.95	3.74	3.58	3.45	3.34	3.18	3.01	2.82	2.73	2.63	2.52	2.42	2.30	2.18
40	8.83	6.07	4.98	4.37	3.99	3.71	3.51	3.35	3.22	3.12	2.95	2.78	2.60	2.50	2.40	2.30	2.18	2.06	1.93
60	8.49	5.79	4.73	4.14	3.76	3.49	3.29	3.13	3.01	2.90	2.74	2.57	2.39	2.29	2.19	2.08	1.96	1.83	1.69
120	8.18	5.54	4.50	3.92	3.55	3.28	3.09	2.93	2.81	2.71	2.54	2.37	2.19	2.09	1.98	1.87	1.75	1.61	1.43
∞	7.88	5.30	4.28	3.72	3.35	3.09	2.90	2.74	2.62	2.52	2.36	2.19	2.00	1.90	1.79	1.67	1.53	1.36	1.00

Source: Reprinted from Pearson, E. S. and H. O. Hartley, eds.; Biometrika Tables for Statisticians, 3d ed.; 1966; by permission of the Biometrika Trustees, London

TABLE A.8

LOWER AND UPPER CRITICAL VALUES T_1 OF WILCOXON RANK SUM TEST

n_2	α One-Tailed	α Two-Tailed	n_1 4	5	6	7	8	9	10
4	.05	.10	11,25						
	.025	.05	10,26						
	.01	.02	—,—						
	.005	.01	—,—						
5	.05	.10	12,28	19,36					
	.025	.05	11,29	17.38					
	.01	.02	10,30	16,39					
	.005	.01	—,—	15,40					
6	.05	.10	13,31	20,40	28,50				
	.025	.05	12,32	18,42	26,52				
	.01	.02	11,33	17,43	24,54				
	.005	.01	10,34	16,44	23,55				
7	.05	.10	14,34	21,44	29,55	39,66			
	.025	.05	13,35	20,45	27,57	36,69			
	.01	.02	11,37	18,47	25,59	34,71			
	.005	.01	10,38	16,49	24,60	32,73			
8	.05	.10	15,37	23,47	31,59	41,71	51,85		
	.025	.05	14,38	21,49	29,61	38,74	49,87		
	.01	.02	12,40	19,51	27,63	35,77	45,91		
	.005	.01	11,41	17,53	25,65	34,78	43,93		
9	.05	.10	16,40	24,51	33,63	43,76	54,90	66,105	
	.025	.05	14,42	22,53	31,65	40,79	51,93	62,109	
	.01	.02	13,43	20,55	28,68	37,82	47,97	59,112	
	.005	.01	11,45	18,57	26,70	35,84	45,99	56,115	
10	.05	.10	17,43	26,54	35,67	45,81	56,96	69,111	82,128
	.025	.05	15,45	23,57	32,70	42,84	53,99	65,115	78,132
	.01	.02	13,47	21,59	29,73	39,87	49,103	61,119	74,136
	.005	.01	12,48	19,61	27,75	37,89	47,105	58,122	71,139

Source: Adapted from Table 1 of Wilcoxon, F. and R. A. Wilcox; Some Rapid Approximate Statistical Procedures; *Pearl River, NY:* © *Copyright Lederle Laboratories, 1964 and reprinted with permission of American Cyanamid Company*

TABLE A.9

CRITICAL VALUES[1] OF THE STUDENTIZED RANGE Q

Upper 5% Points ($\alpha = .05$)

v \ η	2	3	4	5	6	7	8	9	10	11	12	13	14	15	16	17	18	19	20
1	18.0	27.0	32.8	37.1	40.4	43.1	45.4	47.4	49.1	50.6	52.0	53.2	54.3	55.4	56.3	57.2	58.0	58.8	59.6
2	6.09	8.3	9.8	10.9	11.7	12.4	13.0	13.5	14.0	14.4	14.7	15.1	15.4	15.7	15.9	16.1	16.4	16.6	16.8
3	4.50	5.91	6.82	7.50	8.04	8.48	8.85	9.18	9.46	9.72	9.95	10.15	10.35	10.52	10.69	10.84	10.98	11.11	11.24
4	3.93	5.04	5.76	6.29	6.71	7.05	7.35	7.60	7.83	8.03	8.21	8.37	8.52	8.66	8.79	8.91	9.03	9.13	9.23
5	3.64	4.60	5.22	5.67	6.03	6.33	6.58	6.80	6.99	7.17	7.32	7.47	7.60	7.72	7.83	7.93	8.03	8.12	8.21
6	3.46	4.34	4.90	5.31	5.63	5.89	6.12	6.32	6.49	6.65	6.79	6.92	7.03	7.14	7.24	7.34	7.43	7.51	7.59
7	3.34	4.16	4.68	5.06	5.36	5.61	5.82	6.00	6.16	6.30	6.43	6.55	6.66	6.76	6.85	6.94	7.02	7.09	7.17
8	3.26	4.04	4.53	4.89	5.17	5.40	5.60	5.77	5.92	6.05	6.18	6.29	6.39	6.48	6.57	6.65	6.73	6.80	6.87
9	3.20	3.95	4.42	4.76	5.02	5.24	5.43	5.60	5.74	5.87	5.98	6.09	6.19	6.28	6.36	6.44	6.51	6.58	6.64
10	3.15	3.88	4.33	4.65	4.91	5.12	5.30	5.46	5.60	5.72	5.83	5.93	6.03	6.11	6.20	6.27	6.34	6.40	6.47
11	3.11	3.82	4.26	4.57	4.82	5.03	5.20	5.35	5.49	5.61	5.71	5.81	5.90	5.99	6.06	6.14	6.20	6.26	6.33
12	3.08	3.77	4.20	4.51	4.75	4.95	5.12	5.27	5.40	5.51	5.62	5.71	5.80	5.88	5.95	6.03	6.09	6.15	6.21
13	3.06	3.73	4.15	4.45	4.69	4.88	5.05	5.19	5.32	5.43	5.53	5.63	5.71	5.79	5.86	5.93	6.00	6.05	6.11
14	3.03	3.70	4.11	4.41	4.64	4.83	4.99	5.13	5.25	5.36	5.46	5.55	5.64	5.72	5.79	5.85	5.92	5.97	6.03
15	3.01	3.67	4.08	4.37	4.60	4.78	4.94	5.08	5.20	5.31	5.40	5.49	5.58	5.65	5.72	5.79	5.85	5.90	5.96
16	3.00	3.65	4.05	4.33	4.56	4.74	4.90	5.03	5.15	5.26	5.35	5.44	5.52	5.59	5.66	5.72	5.79	5.84	5.90
17	2.98	3.63	4.02	4.30	4.52	4.71	4.86	4.99	5.11	5.21	5.31	5.39	5.47	5.55	5.61	5.68	5.74	5.79	5.84
18	2.97	3.61	4.00	4.28	4.49	4.67	4.82	4.96	5.07	5.17	5.27	5.35	5.43	5.50	5.57	5.63	5.69	5.74	5.79
19	2.96	3.59	3.98	4.25	4.47	4.65	4.79	4.92	5.04	5.14	5.23	5.32	5.39	5.46	5.53	5.59	5.65	5.70	5.75
20	2.95	3.58	3.96	4.23	4.45	4.62	4.77	4.90	5.01	5.11	5.20	5.28	5.36	5.43	5.49	5.55	5.61	5.66	5.71
24	2.92	3.53	3.90	4.17	4.37	4.54	4.68	4.81	4.92	5.01	5.10	5.18	5.25	5.32	5.38	5.44	5.50	5.54	5.59
30	2.89	3.49	3.84	4.10	4.30	4.46	4.60	4.72	4.83	4.92	5.00	5.08	5.15	5.21	5.27	5.33	5.38	5.43	5.48
40	2.86	3.44	3.79	4.04	4.23	4.39	4.52	4.63	4.74	4.82	4.91	4.98	5.05	5.11	5.16	5.22	5.27	5.31	5.36
60	2.83	3.40	3.74	3.98	4.16	4.31	4.44	4.55	4.65	4.73	4.81	4.88	4.94	5.00	5.06	5.11	5.16	5.20	5.24
120	2.80	3.36	3.69	3.92	4.10	4.24	4.36	4.48	4.56	4.64	4.72	4.78	4.84	4.90	4.95	5.00	5.05	5.09	5.13
∞	2.77	3.31	3.63	3.86	4.03	4.17	4.29	4.39	4.47	4.55	4.62	4.68	4.74	4.80	4.85	4.89	4.93	4.97	5.01

[1]Range/$S \sim Q_{1-\alpha;\eta,\nu}$; η is the size of the sample from which the range is obtained, and ν is the number of degrees of freedom of S.

Source: Reprinted from Pearson, E. S. and H. O. Hartley, eds.; Table 29 of Biometrika Tables for Statisticians, Vol. 1, 3d ed.; 1966; by permission of the Biometrika Trustees, London

TABLE A.9

CRITICAL VALUES[1] OF THE STUDENTIZED RANGE Q (CONTINUED)

Upper 1% Points ($\alpha = .01$)

ν \ η	2	3	4	5	6	7	8	9	10	11	12	13	14	15	16	17	18	19	20
1	90.0	135	164	186	202	216	227	237	246	253	260	266	272	277	282	286	290	294	298
2	14.0	19.0	22.3	24.7	26.6	28.2	29.5	30.7	31.7	32.6	33.4	34.1	34.8	35.4	36.0	36.5	37.0	37.5	37.9
3	8.26	10.6	12.2	13.3	14.2	15.0	15.6	16.2	16.7	17.1	17.5	17.9	18.2	18.5	18.8	19.1	19.3	19.5	19.8
4	6.51	8.12	9.17	9.96	10.6	11.1	11.5	11.9	12.3	12.6	12.8	13.1	13.3	13.5	13.7	13.9	14.1	14.2	14.4
5	5.70	6.97	7.80	8.42	8.91	9.32	9.67	9.97	10.24	10.48	10.70	10.89	11.08	11.24	11.40	11.55	11.68	11.81	11.93
6	5.24	6.33	7.03	7.56	7.97	8.32	8.61	8.87	9.10	9.30	9.49	9.65	9.81	9.95	10.08	10.21	10.32	10.43	10.54
7	4.95	5.92	6.54	7.01	7.37	7.68	7.94	8.17	8.37	8.55	8.71	8.86	9.00	9.12	9.24	9.35	9.46	9.55	9.65
8	4.74	5.63	6.20	6.63	6.96	7.24	7.47	7.68	7.87	8.03	8.18	8.31	8.44	8.55	8.66	8.76	8.85	8.94	9.03
9	4.60	5.43	5.96	6.35	6.66	6.91	7.13	7.32	7.49	7.65	7.78	7.91	8.03	8.13	8.23	8.32	8.41	8.49	8.57
10	4.48	5.27	5.77	6.14	6.43	6.67	6.87	7.05	7.21	7.36	7.48	7.60	7.71	7.81	7.91	7.99	8.07	8.15	8.22
11	4.39	5.14	5.62	5.97	6.25	6.48	6.67	6.84	6.99	7.13	7.25	7.36	7.46	7.56	7.65	7.73	7.81	7.88	7.95
12	4.32	5.04	5.50	5.84	6.10	6.32	6.51	6.67	6.81	6.94	7.06	7.17	7.26	7.36	7.44	7.52	7.59	7.66	7.73
13	4.26	4.96	5.40	5.73	5.98	6.19	6.37	6.53	6.67	6.79	6.90	7.01	7.10	7.19	7.27	7.34	7.42	7.48	7.55
14	4.21	4.89	5.32	5.63	5.88	6.08	6.26	6.41	6.54	6.66	6.77	6.87	6.96	7.05	7.12	7.20	7.27	7.33	7.39
15	4.17	4.83	5.25	5.56	5.80	5.99	6.16	6.31	6.44	6.55	6.66	6.76	6.84	6.93	7.00	7.07	7.14	7.20	7.26
16	4.13	4.78	5.19	5.49	5.72	5.92	6.08	6.22	6.35	6.46	6.56	6.66	6.74	6.82	6.90	6.97	7.03	7.09	7.15
17	4.10	4.74	5.14	5.43	5.66	5.85	6.01	6.15	6.27	6.38	6.48	6.57	6.66	6.73	6.80	6.87	6.94	7.00	7.05
18	4.07	4.70	5.09	5.38	5.60	5.79	5.94	6.08	6.20	6.31	6.41	6.50	6.58	6.65	6.72	6.79	6.85	6.91	6.96
19	4.05	4.67	5.05	5.33	5.55	5.73	5.89	6.02	6.14	6.25	6.34	6.43	6.51	6.58	6.65	6.72	6.78	6.84	6.89
20	4.02	4.64	5.02	5.29	5.51	5.69	5.84	5.97	6.09	6.19	6.29	6.37	6.45	6.52	6.59	6.65	6.71	6.76	6.82
24	3.96	4.54	4.91	5.17	5.37	5.54	5.69	5.81	5.92	6.02	6.11	6.19	6.26	6.33	6.39	6.45	6.51	6.56	6.61
30	3.89	4.45	4.80	5.05	5.24	5.40	5.54	5.65	5.76	5.85	5.93	6.01	6.08	6.14	6.20	6.26	6.31	6.36	6.41
40	3.82	4.37	4.70	4.93	5.11	5.27	5.39	5.50	5.60	5.69	5.77	5.84	5.90	5.96	6.02	6.07	6.12	6.17	6.21
60	3.76	4.28	4.60	4.82	4.99	5.13	5.25	5.36	5.45	5.53	5.60	5.67	5.73	5.79	5.84	5.89	5.93	5.98	6.02
120	3.70	4.20	4.50	4.71	4.87	5.01	5.12	5.21	5.30	5.38	5.44	5.51	5.56	5.61	5.66	5.71	5.75	5.79	5.83
∞	3.64	4.12	4.40	4.60	4.76	4.88	4.99	5.08	5.16	5.23	5.29	5.35	5.40	5.45	5.49	5.54	5.57	5.61	5.65

[1]Range/$S \sim Q_{1-\alpha;\eta,\nu}$, η is the size of the sample from which the range is obtained, and ν is the number of degrees of freedom of S.

Source: Reprinted from Pearson, E. S. and H. O. Hartley, eds; Table 29 of Biometrika Tables for Statisticians, Vol. 1, 3d ed.; 1966; by permission of the Biometrika Trustees, London

Appendix B

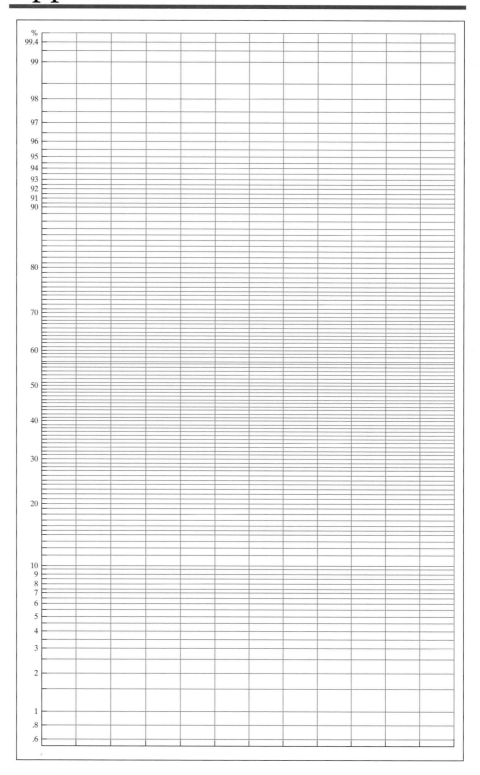

Figure B1   Normal probability paper

NUMBER/NAME	CHART TYPE (CIRCLE ONE)	DEPARTMENT
	p np c	
OPERATION	QUALITY/CHARACTERISTIC	

Avg. =   UCL. =   LCL. =   Avg. Sample size =   Frequency:

Sample (n)	
Number (np, c)	
Proportion (p, u)	
Date	

Sample/Date	Notes and Comments

Figure B2   Sample form for data collection and construction of attribute control charts

Appendix C

See the CD Rom on the inside back cover.

Appendix D

INSTALLING THE PHSTAT MICROSOFT EXCEL ADD-IN

Before the PHStat add-in can be used with this text, it must first be properly set up and installed on a computer system running Microsoft Excel 7.0 (also known as Excel 95) or Excel 97 or Excel 2000.

Files necessary to set up and install PHStat are located in the PHStat directory. To install PHStat, run the setup program (Setup.exe) in that directory. The setup program installs the files that are required by PHStat and creates Desktop and Start Menu icons that facilitate its use. Review the PHStat *readme* file (PhStat readme.doc) before running the setup program, to learn the latest information about the setup process and the technical requirements and limitations of PHStat. Further information and updates to the latest version of PHStat can be found at the following World Wide Web address: **http://www.prenhall.com/phstat**

CD-ROM Overview

In addition to the PHStat directory, the CD-ROM that accompanies this text contains all the software files used by this text. The CD-ROM includes several directories. The Excel directory contains Excel97/2000 workbook files (.XLS) for each of the data files used in the text. The MINITAB directory contains MINITAB worksheet files (.MTW) for each of the data files used in the text. The Text directory contains all of the data files in text format (.TXT). These files are indicated by an icon.

Although the Excel and text files can be used directly from the CD-ROM, you may want to copy them to a hard disk first. Certain methods of copying will leave these files marked as read-only on your hard disk. Should this occur, use the following procedure to eliminate their read-only status.

1. Open Windows Explorer.
2. Select the hard disk files that are read-only.
3. Select Files | Properties from the Explorer menu bar.
4. In the Properties dialog box that appears, deselect (leave unchecked) the read-only check box in the General tab, and click the OK button.

Appendix E

ANSWERS TO SELECTED ODD PROBLEMS

1.1 **(a)** continuous **(b)** discrete **(c)** continuous **(d)** discrete **(e)** discrete
(f) continuous

1.5 **(a)** Variables measure **(b)** Variables measure **(c)** Attribute measure
(d) Attribute measure **(e)** Variables measure **(f)** Attribute measure

1.9 **(a)** 39, 8, 77, 19, 38, 40, 35, 55, 43, and 24
(b) 39, 8, 77, 19, 38, 40, 35, 55, 43, and 24
(c) The results are the same, because, in this series of numbers, no two-digit numbers occurred more than once.

1.25 **(a)** Continuous and ratio scale. Time in minutes, measured from the time the student enters the bookstore until he or she passes through the exit door.
(b) Discrete and nominal scale. Gender is male or female, as self-reported by the student.
(c) Discrete and nominal scale. Freshman, Sophomore, Junior, or Senior, as defined in the school bulletin.
(d) Discrete and nominal scale. Academic major, as defined in the school bulletin.
(e) Continuous variable and interval scale. Grade-point average, as calculated by the registrar.
(f) Discrete and nominal scale. Payment; defined as currency, personal check, or credit card.
(g) Discrete variable count. Number of books, either paperback or hardcover, as defined by the bookstore.

2.11 STEM-AND-LEAF OF CALCULUS SCORES

5	34
6	9
7	4
8	0
9	38
	$n = 7$

2.13 (c) FREQUENCY

	Mfr. A	Mfr. B
650–699	2	0
700–749	1	0
750–799	1	0
800–849	4	2
850–899	9	2
900–949	11	6
950–999	5	6
1000–1049	4	10
1050–1099	3	5
1100–1149	0	4
1150–1199	0	4
1200–1249	0	1

(d)

	Mfr. A	Mfr. B
650–749	7.5%	0.0%
750–849	12.5	5.0
850–949	50.0	20.0
950–1049	22.5	40.0
1050–1149	7.5	22.5
1150–1249	0.0	12.5

(g)   FREQUENCY LESS THAN

	Mfr. A	Mfr. B
650–749	3	0
750–849	8	2
850–949	28	10
950–1049	37	26
1050–1149	40	35
1150–1249	40	40

(h)   LESS THAN

	Mfr. A	Mfr. B
650–749	7.5%	0.0%
750–849	20.0	5.0
850–949	70.0	25.0
950–1049	92.5	65.0
1050–1149	100.0	87.5
1150–1249	100.0	100.0

(j) Manufacturer B produces bulbs with longer lives than those from Manufacturer A. The cumulative percentage for Manufacturer B shows that 65% of their bulbs lasted 1049 hours or less, while 70% of Manufacturer A's bulbs lasted 949 hours or less. None of Manufacturer A's bulbs lasted more than 1149 hours, but 12.5% of Manufacturer B's bulbs lasted between 1150 and 1249 hours. At the same time, 7.5% of Manufacturer A's bulbs lasted less than 750 hours, while all of Manufacturer B's bulbs lasted at least 750 hours.

2.17 (a)

Number of Calls	Frequency	Percentage
2650–2850	1	3.33
2850–3050	1	3.33
3050–3250	16	53.33
3250–3450	9	30.00
3450–3650	2	6.67
3650–3850	1	3.33

(f) There is very little variation in the daily number of calls over the 30-day period sampled.

2.37 (d) The row percentages allow us to block the effect of disproportionate group size and show us that the pattern for day and evening tests among the nonconforming group is very different from the pattern for day and evening tests among the conforming group. While 40% of the nonconforming group was tested during the day, 68% of the conforming group was tested during the day.

(e) The director of the lab might be able to cut the number of nonconforming tests by reducing the number of tests run in the evening, when there is a higher percent of tests run improperly.

3.1 (a)

	Grade X	Grade Y
Mean	575	575.4
Median	575	575
Standard deviation	6.40	2.07

(b) If quality is measured by the average inner diameter, Grade X tires provide slightly better quality, because X's mean and median are both equal to the target value, 575 mm. If, however, quality is measured by consistency, Grade Y provides better quality because, even though Y's mean is slightly larger than the target value, Y's standard deviation is much smaller than X's. The range in values for Grade Y is 5 mm; the range in values for Grade X is 16 mm.

(c)

	Grade X	Grade Y, Altered
Mean	575	577.4
Median	575	575
Standard deviation	6.40	6.11

In the event the fifth Y tire measures 588 mm rather than 578 mm, Y's average inner diameter becomes 577.4 mm, which is much larger than X's average inner diameter, and Y's standard deviation swells from 2.07 mm to 6.11 mm. In this case, X's tires are providing better quality in terms of the average inner diameter with only slightly more variation among the tires than Y's.

3.7 (a)

	Plant A	Plant B
(1) Mean	9.382	11.354
(2) Median	8.515	11.96
(3) Midrange	13.02	14.04
(4) Q_1	7.29	6.25
(5) Q_3	11.42	14.25
(6) Midhinge	9.355	10.25
(7) Range	17.2	23.42
(8) Interquartile range	4.13	8.00
(9) Variance	15.981	26.277
(10) Standard deviation	3.998	5.126
(11) Coefficient of variation	42.61%	45.15%

(b) A: 4.42 7.29 8.515 11.42 21.62 B: 2.33 6.25 11.96 14.25 25.75

(c) The distribution of processing times for Plant A is right-skewed. The distribution of processing times for Plant B is left-skewed.

(d) Processing times for Plants A and B are quite different. Plant B has a greater range of processing times, much more dispersion among data values, a higher median, a higher value for the third quartile, and a greater extreme value than Plant A.

4.5 **(a)** 245 **(b)** .157 **(c)** .25, .154

4.9 **(a)** A: $E(X) = 1.50$ B: $E(X) = 1.40$

(b) A: $\sigma_x = 1.118$ B: $\sigma_x = 1.01$

(c) Distribution A has a higher expected value and a higher standard deviation.

4.15 **(a)** If $p = 0.25$ and $n = 5$,

(1) $P(X = 5) = 0.0010$

(2) $P(X \geq 4) = P(X = 4) + P(X = 5) = 0.0146 + 0.0010 = 0.0156$

(3) $P(X = 0) = 0.2373$

(4) $P(X \leq 2) = P(X = 0) + P(X = 1) + P(X = 2) = 0.2373 + 0.3955 + 0.2637 = 0.8965$

(b) Two assumptions:

(1) Independence of her answers.

(2) Only two outcomes—answer correct or answer incorrect.

(c) Mean: $\mu = 1.25$, Standard Deviation: $\sigma = 0.968$.

4.17 **(a)** (1) 0.735092   (2) 0.967226   (3) 0.264908

(b) That whether each appliance that is discharging is independent of whether any other appliances are discharging and that an appliance is either discharging or not discharging.

(c) $E(X) = 0.30$ $\sigma_x = 0.533854$

4.19 **(a)** (1) 0.6561   (2) 0.0001   (3) 0.9477   (4) 0.0037

(b) That whether each compact disk that passes is independent of whether any other compact disk passes and that a compact disk passes or does not pass.

(c) $E(X) = 3.60$ $\sigma_x = 0.60$

(d) **(a)** (1) 0.960596   (2) 0.00000001   (3) 0.999408   (4) 0.000592

4.25 **(a)**

	A	B	C
1	Defective Disks		
2			
3	Sample size	4	
4	No. of successes in population	5	
5	Population size	15	
6			
7	Hypergeometric Probabilities Table		
8		X	P(x)
9		0	0.153846
10		1	0.43956
11		2	0.32967
12		3	0.07326
13		4	0.003663

(b) $\mu = n \bullet p = 4 \bullet (0.333) = 1.33$

4.33 **(a)** (1) 0.216   (2) 0.20736   (3) 0.01274

(b) $E(X) = 5.00$ $\sigma_x = 1.826$

(c) (1) 0.096   (2) 0.01536   (3) 0.000157

(d) $E(X) = 1.667 \, \sigma_x = 1.054$

4.37 **(a)** 0.082085   **(b)** 0.256616   **(c)** 0.917915   **(d)** 0.087297

4.39 **(a)** 0.112599   **(b)** 0.237709   **(c)** 0.000045

5.1 **(a)** (1) .20 (2) .10 **(b)** 5.0 **(c)** 2.887

5.7 **(a)**

    (1) .4772

    (2) .8822

    (3) .9198

    (4) .0668

    (5) .9332

    (6) .2255

    (7) .0027

  (b) -1.28

  (c) 2.33

  (d) -2.58 and $+2.58$

5.9 **(a)**

    (1) .2734

    (2) .2038

    (3) .7333

    (4) .9599

    (5) .2266

  (b) 4.404

  (c) 4.042

5.33 **(a)** $P(\text{arrival time} \le 0.05) = 1 - e^{-(50)(0.05)} = 0.9179$

  (b) $P(\text{arrival time} \le 0.0167) = 1 - 0.4339 = 0.5661$

  (c) .02 minute

  (d) .02 minute

  (e) If $\lambda = 60$, $P(\text{arrival time} \le 0.05) = 0.9502$, $P(\text{arrival time} \le 0.0167) = 0.6329$

  (f) If $\lambda = 30$, $P(\text{arrival time} \le 0.05) = 0.7769$, $P(\text{arrival time} \le 0.0167) = 0.3941$

5.43 **(a)** .6915

  (b) 13.634 grams

  (c) That the distribution of the sample mean is normally distributed.

  (d) .7157 and 13.69225 grams

6.29 **(a)** Center Line = 4.71; $LCL = 0$ or does not exist; $UCL = 11.10$

  (b) No, because the point representing September 3 is above the UCL. This day is probably the day after Labor Day, a holiday in the United States.

  (c) Center Line = .0377; $LCL = 0$ or does not exist; $UCL = .0888$

  (d) The results are the same, because the charts differ only in scale.

6.31 **(a)** Under the average-sample-size method: center line = .3087; $LCL = .1719$; $UCL = .4456$

  (b) Out of statistical control, because points representing days 20 and 25 are above the UCL and points representing days 15 and 29 are below the LCL.

  (c) Revised chart using the average sample size method: center line = .2974; $LCL = .1624$; $UCL = .4324$

6.39 **(a)** Center Line = 26.96, $LCL = 11.3831$, $UCL = 42.5369$

  (b) No, because the point representing day 20 is above the UCL.

(c) Center Line = 26.21, LCL = 10.85, UCL = 41.5665

(d) All points are within the revised control limits.

(e) Yes, because the system is stable.

6.41 (a) Center Line = .1126; LCL and UCL vary with sample size. When n = 100, LCL = .0119 and UCL = .2133. When n = 112, LCL = .0175 and UCL = .2077. When n = 126, LCL = .0229 and UCL = .2023.

(b) No, because the points representing roll 6 and roll 24 are above the UCL.

(c) After the elimination of points 6 and 24, Center Line = .0989, and LCL and UCL vary with sample size. When n = 100, LCL = .0046 and UCL = .1932. When n = 112, LCL = .0098 and UCL = .1880. When n = 126, LCL = .0149 and UCL = .1829.

7.1 (a) $\bar{R}$ = 271.57, $UCL = D_4; \bar{R}$ = (2.114) (271.57) = 574.09, $LCL = D_3; \bar{R}$ = 0 (271.57) = 0, LCL does not exist.

(b) There are no points outside the control limits, and there is no evidence of a pattern in the range chart.

(c) $\bar{\bar{X}}$ = 198.67; $LCL = \bar{\bar{X}} - A_2; \bar{R}$ = 198.67 − (0.577)(271.57) = 41.97 $UCL = \bar{\bar{X}} + A_2; \bar{R}$ = 198.67 + (0.577) (271.57) = 355.36

(d) There are no points outside the control limits, and there is no evidence of a pattern in the $\bar{X}$ chart.

(e) Center Line (s) = 107.79; UCL = 225.16; LCL = 0

(f) There are no points outside the control limits, and there is no evidence of a pattern in the s chart.

(g) $\bar{\bar{X}}$ = 198.67; UCL = 352.82; LCL = 44.82
There are no points outside the control limits, and there is no evidence of a pattern in the $\bar{\bar{X}}$ chart.

7.9 (b) No, point 6 is below the LCL by the moving-range method but is within the limits by the standard deviation method.

(c) $\bar{X}$ = .4752, LCL(X) = −2.9298, UCL(X) = 3.8802

(d) Yes, because no points fall beyond the control limits.

(e) The flushness measurement has been reduced from 1.962 to .4752. In addition, the number of points outside the control limits has been reduced from 32 to 12. Further work needs to be done on the system to reduce the average value further and/or reduce the variability, so that more points will be between the specification limits.

8.1 $\bar{X} \pm Z \cdot \dfrac{\sigma}{\sqrt{n}} = 85 \pm 1.96 \cdot \dfrac{8}{\sqrt{64}}$

$83.04 \le \mu \le 86.96$

8.5 (a) $\bar{X} \pm Z \cdot \dfrac{\sigma}{\sqrt{n}} = 1.99 \pm 1.96 \cdot \dfrac{0.05}{\sqrt{100}}$

$1.9802 \le \mu \le 1.9998$

(b) No. because σ is known and n = 100, we can assume, from the central limit theorem, that the sampling distribution of $\bar{X}$ is approximately normal.

(c) An individual value of 2.02 is only 0.60 standard deviation above the sample mean of 1.99. The confidence interval represents bounds on the estimate of a sample of 100, not of an individual value.

(d) A shift of 0.02 units in the sample average shifts the confidence interval by the same distance without affecting the width of the resulting interval.

(e) $\bar{X} \pm Z \cdot \dfrac{\sigma}{\sqrt{n}} = 1.97 \pm 1.96 \cdot \dfrac{0.05}{\sqrt{100}}$

$$1.9602 \leq \mu \leq 1.9798$$

8.7 (a) $991.44 < \mu < 1{,}147.69$

(b) We assume that the life of the lamps is normally distributed. A normal probability plot of the life indicates only slight departure from a normal distribution.

8.9 (a) $63.80 < \mu < 65.17$

(b) We assume that the hardness is normally distributed. A normal probability plot of the hardness indicates only slight departure from a normal distribution.

8.13 $1.672 < \sigma^2 < 2.823$

8.31 $0.516 < \pi < .754$

8.33 $0.078 < \pi < 0.124$

9.1 (a) $H_0: \mu = 70$ pounds. The cloth has an average breaking strength of 70 pounds.

$H_1: \mu \neq 70$ pounds. The cloth has an average breaking strength that differs from 70 pounds.

(b) Decision rule: Reject H_0 if $Z < -1.96$ or $Z > +1.96$.

$$\text{Test statistic: } Z = \frac{\bar{X} - \mu}{\dfrac{\sigma}{\sqrt{n}}} = \frac{69.1 - 70}{\dfrac{3.5}{\sqrt{49}}} = -1.80$$

Decision: Because $Z_{\text{calc}} = -1.80$ is between the critical bounds, ± 1.96, do not reject H_0. There is not enough evidence to conclude that the cloth has an average breaking strength that differs from 70 pounds.

(c) Decision rule: Reject H_0 if $Z < -1.96$ or $Z > +1.96$.

$$\text{Test statistic: } Z = \frac{\bar{X} - \mu}{\dfrac{\sigma}{\sqrt{n}}} = \frac{69.1 - 70}{\dfrac{1.75}{\sqrt{49}}} = -3.60$$

Decision: Because $Z_{\text{calc}} = -3.60$ is less than the lower critical bound, -1.96, reject H_0. There is enough evidence to conclude that the cloth has an average breaking strength that differs from 70 pounds.

(d) Decision rule: Reject H_0 if $Z < -1.96$ or $Z > +1.96$.

$$\text{Test statistic: } Z = \frac{\bar{X} - \mu}{\dfrac{\sigma}{\sqrt{n}}} = \frac{69 - 70}{\dfrac{3.5}{\sqrt{49}}} = -2.00$$

Decision: Because $Z_{\text{calc}} = -2.00$ is less than the lower critical bound, -1.96, reject H_0. There is enough evidence to conclude that the cloth has an average breaking strength that differs from 70 pounds.

9.5 (a) $H_0: \mu = 9.0$ The average energy efficiency rating of window-mounted large-capacity air-conditioning units is equal to 9.0.

$H1: \mu \neq 9.0$ The average energy efficiency rating of window-mounted large-capacity air-conditioning units is not equal to 9.0.

Decision rule: $df = 35$. If $t > 2.0301$ or $t < -2.0301$, reject H_0.

$$\text{Test statistic: } t = \frac{\bar{X} - \mu}{\dfrac{S}{\sqrt{n}}} = \frac{9.2111 - 9.0}{\dfrac{0.3838}{\sqrt{36}}} = 3.3002$$

Decision: Because $t_{calc} = 3.3002$ is above the upper critical bound, 2.0301, reject H_0. There is enough evidence to conclude that the average energy efficiency rating of window-mounted large-capacity air-conditioning units is not equal to 9.0.

(b) To perform this test, you must assume (1) that the observed sequence in which the data were collected is random and (2) that the sample size is sufficiently large for the central limit theorem to apply, so that the sampling distribution of the mean is approximately normally distributed.

(c) p-value $= 0.0022$. The probability of obtaining a sample whose mean is further away from the hypothesized value of 9.0 than 9.2111 is 0.0022.

(d) $H_0: \mu = 9.0$. The average energy efficiency rating of window-mounted large-capacity air-conditioning units is equal to 9.0.
$H_1: \mu \neq 9.00$. The average energy efficiency rating of window-mounted large-capacity air-conditioning units is not equal to 9.0.

Decision rule: $df = 35$. If $t > 2.0301$ or $t < -2.0301$, reject H_0.

$$\text{Test statistic:} \; t = \frac{\overline{X} - \mu}{\dfrac{S}{\sqrt{n}}} = \frac{9.1556 - 9.0}{\dfrac{0.4102}{\sqrt{36}}} = 2.2754$$

Decision: Because $t_{calc} = 2.2754$ is above the critical bound, 2.0301, reject H_0. There is enough evidence to conclude that the average energy efficiency rating of window-mounted large-capacity air-conditioning units is not equal to 9.0.

9.7 (a) $H_0: \mu = 15$ ounces. The average weight of raisins is 15 ounces per box.
$H_1: \mu \neq 15$ ounces. The average weight of raisins is not equal to 15 ounces per box.

Decision rule: $df = 29$. If $t > 2.0452$ or $t < -2.0452$, reject H_0.

$$\text{Test statistic:} \; t = \frac{\overline{X} - \mu}{\dfrac{S}{\sqrt{n}}} = \frac{15.1133 - 15.0}{\dfrac{0.4058}{\sqrt{30}}} = 1.5298$$

Decision: Because $t_{calc} = 1.5298$ is between the critical bounds $t = \pm 2.0452$, do not reject H_0. There is not enough evidence to conclude that the average weight of raisins is not equal to 15 ounces per box.

(b) In addition to assuming that the observed sequence in which the data were collected is random, to perform this test, you must assume that the sample size is sufficiently large for the central limit theorem to apply, so that the sampling distribution of the mean is approximately normally distributed.

(c) $H_0: \mu = 15$ ounces. The average weight of raisins is 15 ounces per box.
$H_1: \mu \neq 15$ ounces. The average weight of raisins is not equal to 15 ounces per box.

Decision rule: $df = 29$. If $t > 2.0452$ or $t < -2.0452$, reject H_0.

$$\text{Test statistic:} \; t = \frac{\overline{X} - \mu}{\dfrac{S}{\sqrt{n}}} = \frac{15.18 - 15.0}{\dfrac{0.4909}{\sqrt{30}}} = 2.0084$$

Decision: Because $t_{calc} = 2.0084$ is between the critical bounds $t = \pm 2.0452$, do not reject H_0. There is not enough evidence to conclude that the average weight of raisins is not equal to 15 ounces per box.

9.11 (a)–(c) p-value $= 0.337 < .05$ or $t = -2.1862 - 2.0106$. There is evidence of a difference between the two types of batteries.

	A	B	C	D
1	t-Test: Two-Sample Assuming Equal Variances			
2				
3		Cadmium	Metal Hydride	
4	Mean	70.748	79.728	
5	Variance	195.7884	226.0296	
6	Observations	25	25	
7	Pooled Variance	210.909		
8	Hypothesized Mean	0		
9	df	48		
10	t Stat	-2.18617		
11	P(T<=t) one-tail	0.016856		
12	t Critical one-tail	1.677224		
13	P(T<=t) two-tail	0.033712		
14	t Critical two-tail	2.010634		

9.15 (a) $-2.0244 < t = -1.356 > +2.0244$ Do not reject H_o. There is no evidence of a difference in the average processing time between the two plants.

  (b) That the processing time in each plant is normally distributed and that the variances in the two plants are equal.

  (c) There is some skewness in each of the plants and there is some difference in the variances, but not enough to seriously affect the results.

  (d) p-value $= 0.183$ The probability of obtaining a result more significant than 1.356 randomly by chance if H_o is true is 0.183.

9.17

  (a) $F_U = 2.20, F_L = \dfrac{1}{2.33} = 0.429$

  (b) $F_U = 2.57, F_L = \dfrac{1}{2.76} = 0.362$

  (c) $F_U = 3.09, F_L = \dfrac{1}{3.37} = 0.297$

  (d) $F_U = 3.50, F_L = \dfrac{1}{3.88} = 0.258$

9.19 $F = 0.83$ p-value $= 0.688 > .05$. Do not reject H_o. There is no evidence of a difference in the variances of the compressive strength between the two plants.

9.23 $F = 5.76 > 2.544$ or p-value $= 0.001333 < .05$. Reject H_o. There is evidence that the variance in line A is greater than the variance in line B.

9.25 (a) $-2.2281 < t = -1.975 > +2.2281$. Do not reject H_o. There is no evidence of a difference in the average thickness between the two methods.

  (b) That the thickness in each method is normally distributed and that the variances in the two methods are equal.

  (c) p-value $= 0.0765$ The probability of obtaining a result more significant than 1.975 randomly by chance if H_o is true is 0.0765.

9.29 (a) $H_0: \mu_{\bar{D}} \neq 0$
There is no difference in the average gas mileage between regular and high-octane gas.

$H_1: \mu_{\bar{D}} \neq 0$

There is a difference in the average gas mileage between regular and high-octane gas.

Decision rule: $df = 9$. If $t < -2.2622$ or $t > 2.2622$, reject H_0.

$$\text{Test statistic: } t = \frac{\bar{D} - \mu_{\bar{D}}}{\dfrac{S_{\bar{D}}}{\sqrt{n}}} = \frac{-0.5 - 0}{\dfrac{3.44}{\sqrt{10}}} = -0.4596$$

Decision: Because $t_{calc} = -0.4596$ is between the critical bounds $t \pm 2.2622$, do not reject H_0. There is not enough evidence to conclude that there is a difference in the average gas mileage between regular and high-octane gas.

(b) One must assume that the distribution of the difference in the average gas mileage between regular and high-octane gas is approximately normal.

(c) From the t-table, p-value $> 2(0.25) = 0.50$. From Excel, p-value $= 0.6567$.

The probability of obtaining a mean difference that deviates from 0 by 0.4596 or more when the null hypothesis is true is 0.6567.

9.31 (a) $\chi^2 = 7.7728 > 3.841$ Reject H_0. There is evidence of a relationship between lifestyle and osteoporosis.

(b) p-value $= 0.0053$ The probability of obtaining a result more significant than 7.7728 randomly by chance if H_0 is true is 0.0053

9.35 (a) $H_0: p_A = p_B = p_C = p_D$

H_1: At least one proportion differs.

Decision rule: $df = (c - 1) = (4 - 1) = 3$. If $\chi^2 > 7.815$, reject H_0.

$$\text{Test statistic: } \chi^2 = 8.383$$

Decision: Because $\chi^2_{calc} = 8.383$ is above the upper critical bound, 7.815, reject H_0. There is adequate evidence to conclude that there is a difference across the four drug regimens in the proportion of patients suffering severe adverse events within 30 days following treatment for heart attack.

9.39 (a) $H_0: \sigma = 0.035$ inch. The standard deviation of the diameter of doorknobs is equal to 0.035 inch in the redesigned production process.

$H_1: \sigma < 0.035$ inch. The standard deviation of the diameter of doorknobs is less than 0.035 inch in the redesigned production process.

Decision rule: $df = 24$. If $\chi^2 < 13.848$, reject H_0.

$$\text{Test statistic: } \chi^2 = 12.245$$

Decision: The test statistic, $\chi^2 = 12.245$, is below the critical boundary of 13.848, so reject H_0. There is sufficient evidence to conclude that the standard deviation of the diameter of doorknobs is less than 0.035 inch in the redesigned production process.

(b) We must assume that the data in the population are normally distributed to be able to use the chi-square test of a population variance or standard deviation.

(c) p-value $= (1 - 0.9770) = 0.0230$. The p-value is the probability that a sample is obtained whose standard deviation is less then that of this sample when the null hypothesis is true, namely 0.0230.

9.49 **(a)** $-1.96 < t = -1.745 > +1.96$ Do not reject H_0. There is no evidence of a difference in the median processing time between the two plants.

(b) p-value $= 0.081$ The probability of obtaining a result more significant than 1.745 randomly by chance if H_0 is true is 0.081.

10.1 **(a)** $F = 5.443 > 4.256$ or p-value $= .028 < .05$ Reject H_0. There is evidence of a difference in the average number of popped kernels between the three oils.

(b) Critical range $= 123.97$ Canola oil has a significantly higher number of popped kernels than safflower oil.

(c) Based on the criteria of maximizing the number of popped kernels, I would use canola oil.

10.5 **(a)** $F = 11.144 > 3.885$ or p-value $= .00184 < .05$ Reject H_0. There is evidence of a difference in the average reflectance between the machines.

(b) Critical range $= 2.0173$ Machine 3 has a significantly higher reflectance than the other machines.

(c) Based on the criteria of maximizing the reflectance, I would recommend machine 3.

10.9 **(a)** **(a)** $F = 268.2556 > 3.114$ or p-value $= .00000 < .05$ Reject H_0. There is evidence of a difference in the average compressive strength after 2, 7, and twenty-eight days.

(b) Critical range $= 0.164$ The compressive strength is different after 2, 7, and 28 days.

(c) RE $= 2.122$

(e) Compressive strength increases as the number of days after pouring increases, within a range of two to twenty-eight days.

10.13 **(a)** $H_0: M_A = M_B = M_C$
H_1: At least one of the medians differs.
Decision rule: If $H > \chi_U^2 = 5.991$, reject H_0.

Test statistic: $H = 3.66$

Decision: Because $H_{calc} = 3.66$ is below the critical bound, 5.991, do not reject H_0. There is insufficient evidence to show any real difference in the median life of this type of electronic component across the three levels of temperature. The p-value is 0.161.

11.1 **(a)** $H_0: \mu_A = \mu_B = \mu_C = \mu_D$
H_1: At least one mean differs.
Decision rule: If $F > 3.01$, reject H_0.

Test statistic: $F = 26.55$

Decision: Because $F_{calc} = 26.55$ is above the critical bound $F = 3.01$, reject H_0. There is sufficient evidence to conclude that the breaking strengths of wool serge material differ with which operator ran the machine.

(b) $H_0: \mu_I = \mu_{II} = \mu_{III}$
H_1: At least one mean differs.
Decision rule: If $F > 3.40$, reject H_0.

Test statistic: $F = 43.57$

Decision: Because $F_{calc} = 43.57$ is above the critical bound of $F = 3.40$, reject H_0. There is adequate evidence to conclude that the breaking strengths of wool serge material differ among the three machines that were used to produce the material.

(c) H_0: There is no interaction between operator and machine.
H_1: There is an interaction between operator and machine.
Decision rule: If $F > 2.51$, reject H_0.

Test statistic: $F = 3.81$

Decision: Because $F_{calc} = 3.18$ is above the critical bound $F = 2.51$, reject H_0. There is enough evidence to conclude that there is an interaction between operator and machine.

(f) Operators create fabric of varying strengths depending on which machines individuals use. One suggestion is to use the 12 operator-machine combinations as the levels of a single factor and completely analyze the data by performing a one-way ANOVA.

11.13 (a) $A = 1.14$, $B = .60$, $C = .31$, $D = .22$, $AB + CD = .40$, $AC + BD = -.11$, $AD + BC = -.01$

(c) A and B.

(e) Modified balls have an average life that is 1.14 higher than that of standard balls. A modified cage design resulted in an average life that is .60 higher than the standard cage design. There is no reason to suspect important interaction effects.

11.15 (a) $A = 0$, $B = -1.5$, $C = -13.5$, $D = -7$, $AB + CD = 5$, $AC + BD = 1$, $AD + BC = -0.5$

(c) C, D and $AB + CD$

(e) Consumption of 2 cans of beer reduced the average score by 13.5. Playing the radio reduced the average score by 7. The interaction of lighting and practice time and/or beer consumption and radio playing seems important, but these two interactions cannot be separated by this fractional factorial design.

11.19 (a)

Treatments	Signal-to-noise ratio
(1)	15.644
a	4.425
b	20.491
ab	15.317

(b) Treatment combination b, consisting of cartridge X and amplifier 2, provides the highest signal-to-noise ratio.

12.1 (a) When $X = 0$, the expected value of Y is 2.

(b) For an increase in the value of X by 1 unit, we can expect an increase by 5 units in the value of Y.

(c) $\hat{Y} = 2 + 5X = 2 + 5(3) = 17$

(d) (1) yes, (2) no, (3) no, (4) yes, (5) no

12.3 (b) $b_0 = 770.4334$ $b_1 = 19.9692$

(c) For each increase of one inch in distance, average thickness is predicted to increase by 19.9692 angstrom.

(d) 1,169.8174

12.7 (b) $b_0 = 33.2929$ $b_1 = 0.01136$

(c) For each increase of one centimeter in circumference, average weight is predicted to increase by 0.01136 gram .

(d) 59.4312

(e) Since circumference is such a strong predictor of weight, for simplicity purposes, the farmer might want to use circumference as a substitute for weight.

12.17 The residual plot indicates a quadratic curvilinear pattern, so the linear model fit is not appropriate.

12.21 (a) There is no pattern in the plot of the residuals, so the model is appropriate.

(b) The residuals appear to be normally distributed and there is no evidence of serious violation of the homoscedasticity assumption.

12.27 (a) When $X = 2, \hat{Y} = 5 + 3X = 5 + 3(2) = 11$

$$h = \frac{1}{n} + \frac{(X_i - \bar{X})^2}{\sum_{i=1}^{n}(X_i - \bar{X})^2} = \frac{1}{20} + \frac{(2-2)^2}{20} = 0.05$$

95% confidence interval: $\hat{Y} \pm t_{18} s_{YX} \sqrt{h} = 11 \pm 2.1009 \cdot 1 \cdot \sqrt{0.05}$

$$10.53 \le \mu_{Y|X} \le 11.47$$

(b) 95% prediction interval: $\hat{Y} \pm t_{18} s_{YX} \sqrt{1 + h} = 11 \pm 2.1009 \cdot 1 \cdot \sqrt{1.05}$

$$8.847 \le Y_I \le 13.153$$

(c) When $X = 4, \hat{Y} = 5 + 3X = 5 + 3(4) = 17$

$$h = \frac{1}{n} + \frac{(X_i - \bar{X})^2}{\sum_{i=1}^{n}(X_i - \bar{X})^2} = \frac{1}{20} + \frac{(4-2)^2}{20} = 0.25$$

95% confidence interval: $\hat{Y} \pm t_{18} s_{YX} \sqrt{h} = 11 \pm 2.1009 \cdot 1 \cdot \sqrt{0.25}$

$$15.95 \le \mu_{Y|X} \le 18.05$$

(d) 95% prediction interval: $\hat{Y} \pm t_{18} s_{YX} \sqrt{1 + h} = 11 \pm 2.1009 \cdot 1 \cdot \sqrt{1.25}$

$$14.651 \le Y_I \le 19.349$$

(e) The intervals in this problem are wider, because the value of X is farther from $\bar{X}$.

12.55 (b) $b_0 = 78.7963\ b_1 = 2.6732$

(c) Predicted Height = 78.7963 + 2.6732 diameter at breast height

(d) For each increase of one inch in the diameter at breast height, average height is predicted to increase by 2.6732 feet.

(e) 158.9928 feet

(f) A breast diameter of 100 inches is outside the range of the X variable in the data.

(g) $r^2 = .7288$ 72.88% of the variation in tree height can be explained by the diameter at breast height.

(h) 0.8537

(i) 24.7486

(j) There is no evidence of any pattern in the residuals.

(k) $t = 6.45 > 2.093$ or p-value $= 0.00000086 < .05$ Reject H_o. There is evidence of a linear relationship between tree height and diameter at breast height.

(l) $147.6754 < \mu_{y|x} < 170.3102$

(m) $105.9713 < Y_1 < 212.014$

(n) $1.890 < B_1 < 3.456$

(o) The definition diameter at breast height is vague, since the breast height will vary depending on who is doing the measurement. A better definition would be diameter five feet above ground.

13.1 (a) When one is holding constant the effect of X_2, for each additional unit of X_1, the response variable Y is expected to increase on average by 5 units. When one is holding constant the effect of X_1, for each additional unit of X_2, the response variable Y is expected to increase on average by 3 units.

(b) The Y-intercept, 10, represents the portion of the measurement of Y that is not affected by the factors measured by X_1 and X_2.

(c) 60% of the variation in Y can be explained or accounted for by the variation in X_1 and the variation in X_2.

13.5 (a) BEF $= 1.5901 - 0.0237$ Light Output -0.0022 Lamp temperature

(b) Holding constant the lamp temperature, for each increase of light output by one footcandle, the average ballast efficiency factor is predicted to decrease by 0.0237 footcandle. Holding constant the light output, for each increase in lamp temperature of one degree Celsius, the average ballast efficiency factor is predicted to decrease by 0.0022 footcandle.

(c) 0.5533 footcandle

(d) 62.54% of the variation in the ballast efficiency factor can be explained by variation in the light output and variation in the lamp temperature.

13.9 There is no evidence of any pattern in the residuals.

13.11 (a) $MSR = SSR/k = 60/2 = 30$

$$MSE = SSE/(n - k - 1) = 120/18 = 6.67$$

(b) $F = MSR/MSE = 30/6.67 = 4.5$

(c) $F = 4.5 > F_{U(2,21-2-1)} = 3.555$. Reject H_0. There is evidence of a significant linear relationship.

13.15 (a) $F = 5.843 > 4.74$ or p-value $= 0.0322 < .05$. Reject H_o. There is evidence of a significant relationship between the ballast efficiency factor and at least one of the independent variables.

(b) The probability of obtaining an F value greater than 5.843 if H_o is true is 0.0322.

13.17 (a) 95% confidence interval on
β_1: $b_1 \pm t_{n-p-1}s_{b_1}, 0.79116 \pm 2.1788 \cdot 0.06295$

$$0.65400 \le \beta_1 \le 0.92832$$

(b) For X_1: $t = b_1/s_{b_1} = 0.79116/0.06295 = 12.57 > t_{12} = 2.1788$ with 12 degrees of freedom, for $\alpha = 0.05$. Reject H_0. There is evidence that the variable X_1 contributes to a model already containing X_2.

For X_2: $t = b_2/s_{b_2} = 0.60484/0.07174 = 8.43 > t_{12} = 2.1788$ with 12 degrees of freedom, for $\alpha = 0.05$. Reject H_0. There is evidence that the variable X_2 contributes to a model already containing X_1.

Both variables, X_1 and X_2, should be included in the model.

13.25 (a) $-2.3646 < t = -2.32 < 2.3646$ or p-value $= 0.053$. Do not reject H_o and $-2.3646 < t = -0.64 < 2.3646$ or p-value $= 0.542$. Do not reject H_o. neither independent variable is significant given that the other is included in the model. A simple linear regression model including only one independent variable should be investigated.

(b) Holding constant the effect of lamp temperature, 43.48% of the variation in the ballast efficiency factor can be explained by variation in light output. Holding constant the light output, 5.54% of the variation in the ballast efficiency factor can be explained by variation in lamp temperature.

13.27 (b) $\hat{Y} = -7.556 + 1.2717X - 0.0145X^2$

(c) $\hat{Y} = -7.556 + 1.2717(55) - 0.0145(55^2) = 18.52$

(d) The residuals analysis shows patterns in the residuals vs. highway speed, vs. the curvilinear variable (speed squared), and vs. the fitted values.

(e) $F = 141.46 > F_{2,25} = 3.39$. Reject H_0. The overall model is significant. The p-value < 0.001.

(f) $t = -16.63 < -t_{25} = -2.0595$. Reject H_0. The curvilinear effect is significant. The p-value < 0.001.

(g) $r^2_{Y.12} = 0.919$. 91.9% of the variation in miles per gallon can be explained by the curvilinear relationship between miles per gallon and highway speed.

(h) $r^2_{adj} = 0.912$

13.31 (a) First, develop a multiple-regression model using X_1 as the variable for the SAT score and X_2 a dummy variable (with $X_2 = 1$ if a student had a grade of B or better in the introductory statistics course). If the dummy variable coefficient is significantly different from zero, you need to develop a model with the interaction term $X_1 X_2$ to make sure that the coefficient of X_1 is not significantly different between $X_2 = 0$ and $X_2 = 1$.

(b) If a student received a grade of B or better in the introductory statistics course, the student would be expected to have a grade-point average in computer science that is 0.30 higher than that of a student who had the same SAT score but did not get a grade of B or better in the introductory statistics course.

13.35 (a) Recovery $= -575.3503 + 10.9522$ diastolic blood pressure $+ 3.2532$ gender

(b) For a given gender of the individual, for each increase of one unit in diastolic blood pressure, average recovery time is predicted to increase by 10.9522 seconds. Holding constant the diastolic blood pressure, the average recovery time is predicted to be 3.2532 seconds higher in females than in males.

(c) 304.08 seconds

(d) $F = 3.0688 < 5.14$ or p-value $= 0.1208 > .05$ Do not reject H_0. There is no evidence of a relationship between recovery time and the two independent variables. Note: If gender is deleted from the model, the relationship of diastolic blood pressure and recovery time is significant.

(e) 50.57% of the variation in recovery time can be explained by diastolic blood pressure and gender.

(f) Adjusted $R^2 = 0.3409$

(g) There is no evidence of any pattern in the residuals.

(h) $-2.4469 < t = 1.7959 < 2.4469$ p-value = 0.1226 > .05 and $-2.4469 <$ $t = 0.0359 < 2.4469$ p-value = 0.9726 > .05. Neither independent variable makes a significant contribution given that the other variable is included in the model.: If gender is deleted from the model, the relationship of diastolic blood pressure and recovery time is significant ($t = 2.6753$ p-value = .0318.)

(i) $-3.9701 < \beta_1 < 25.8746$ and $-218.6838 < \beta_2 < 225.1902$

(j) For an individual of a given gender, 34.96% of the variation in recovery time can be explained by variation in diastolic blood pressure. Holding constant the diastolic blood pressure, 0.02% of the variation in recovery time can be explained by varition in gender.

(k) That the slope of diastolic blood pressure and recovery time is the same for each gender.

(l) $-2.5706 < t = -0.8837 < 2.5706$ or p-value = 0.4173 > .05 Do not reject H_o. There is no evidence of an interaction effect between diastolic blood pressure and gender.

(m) Since the interaction term is not significant, and gender does not have any effect, a model that includes only diastolic blood pressure in predicting recovery time should be investigated.

13.37 (a) $\hat{Y} = 9.04 + 0.852\sqrt{X_1}$

(b) $\hat{Y} = 9.04 + 0.852\sqrt{55} = 15.36$ miles per gallon

(c) The residual analysis indicates a clear curvilinear pattern. The model does not adequately fit the data.

(d) $t = 1.35 < t_{26} = 2.0555$. Do not reject H_0. The model does not provide a significant relationship.

(e) $r_{Y.12}^2 = 0.066$. Only 6.6% of the variation in miles per gallon can be explained by variation in the square root of highway speed.

(f) $r_{adj}^2 = 0.030$

(g) The curvilinear model in Problem 13.27 is far superior to the inadequate model here. The square root of highway speed did virtually nothing to enhance the fit.

13.43 VIF = 1.54

13.45 (a) For the model that includes independent variables A and B, the value of C_p exceeds 3, the number of parameters, so this model does not meet the criterion for future consideration.

For the model that includes independent variables A and C, the value of C_p is less than or equal to 3, the number of parameters, so this model does meet the criterion for future consideration.

For the model that includes independent variables A, B, and C, the value of C_p is less than or equal to 4, the number of parameters, so this model does meet the criterion for future consideration.

(b) The inclusion of variable C in the model appears to improve the model's ability to explain variation in the dependent variable sufficiently to justify the inclusion of variable C in a model that contains only variables A and B.

13.67 Let Y = annual total cost, X_1 = average SAT, X_2 = Room and board expense, X_3 = whether house was public or private (0 = public, 1 = private), and X_4 = TOEFL criterion is at least 550.

Based on a full regression model involving all of the variables, all of the VIF values (1.5, 1.9, 2.2, and 1.2, respectively) are less than 5. There is no reason to suspect the existence of collinearity.

Based on a best subsets regression and examination of the resulting C_p values, the best model easily appears be the full regression model.

A residual analysis shows no strong patterns.

The resulting model: $\hat{Y} = -7.786 + 0.013629X_1 + 1.1338 \, X_2 + 6.096 \, X_3 + 2.5191X_4 \, r^2_{Y.1234} = 0.854, r^2_{adj} = 0.846$

Overall significance of the model: $F = 109.53, p < 0.001$

Each independent variable is significant at the 0.05 level.

Index